A T·E·X·T·B·O·O·K O·F

Social Psychology

J.E. Alcock
GLENDON COLLEGE, YORK UNIVERSITY

D.W. Carment
McMASTER UNIVERSITY

S.W. Sadava
BROCK UNIVERSITY

Prentice-Hall Canada Inc., Scarborough, Ontario

Canadian Cataloguing in Publication Data

Alcock, James E.
 A textbook of social psychology

Bibliography: p.
Includes index.
ISBN 0-13-912874-3

1. Social psychology. I. Carment, D.W.
II. Sadava, S. W. III. Title.

HM251.A55 1987   302   C87-094939-X

1988 Prentice-Hall Canada Inc., Scarborough, Ontario

Prentice-Hall, Inc., Englewood Cliffs, New Jersey
Prentice-Hall International, Inc., London
Prentice-Hall of Australia, Pty., Ltd., Sydney
Prentice-Hall of India Pvt., Ltd., New Delhi
Prentice-Hall of Japan, Inc., Tokyo
Prentice-Hall of Southest Asia (Pte.) Ltd., Singapore
Editora Prentice-Hall do Brasil Ltda., Rio de Janeiro
Prentice-Hall Hispanoamericana, S.A., Mexico

ISBN 0-13-912874-3

Production Editor: Jessica Pegis
Book design: Robert Garbutt
Drawings: Suzanne Boehler
Production Coordinator: Matt Lumsdon
Typesetting: Compeer Typographic Services Limited
Cover painting by Sandra Calderaro
Cover photography: John Fornasier

1 2 3 4 5   JD   92 91 90 89 88

Printed and bound in Canada by John Deyell Company

For   *Johanna*
               Eleanor
               Maria Jesús

C·O·N·T·E·N·T·S

CHAPTER 10   *Altruism*   320

xiii

P·R·E·F·A·C·E

We had several goals in writing the first textbook of social psychology intended especially for Canadian students. First, we sought to provide readers with a current, comprehensive introduction to social psychological theory and research. Second, we wanted readers to re-examine generally shared assumptions about their lives and their society.

The initial incentive to write this book came from many directions, particularly from our colleagues in this country who wanted a textbook which spoke of the Canadian experience. Social psychology has been primarily a U.S. enterprise, but Canadian and other researchers have made important contributions. We have tried to offer the student the best research available, whether from the United States, Canada, Europe, or elsewhere. We integrate this research with examples drawn largely from the Canadian milieu, and where relevant, we bring social psychology to bear on the analysis of social problems which are especially pertinent to the Canadian experience.

Our goal is also to show that social psychology is a discipline with both a history and a contemporary vitality, and that it is relevant to Canadians. Therefore, we have placed classical studies side by side with contemporary research, and we have covered topics found in other social psychology texts as well as those which are rarely discussed in textbooks. For example, we have included a chapter on language and communication (including bilingualism), a topic of great importance to Canadians, and we have restored to its traditional place in social psychology the topic of collective behaviour. We also have provided coverage of contemporary social issues such as those relating to law, innovation, the environment, health, and the nuclear threat.

This book is the product of a genuine collaborative effort; the order of the authors' names is alphabetical. We owe a great debt to many people who have had faith in us and who helped us along the way. First, we wish to remember the late Frank Hintenberger who, as Prentice-Hall Canada's college editor, agreed with us that the book was worth doing, and signed us to the contract that committed us to writing it. Between the signing of that contract and the appearance of the finished book, there have been many delays and moments of doubt along the way.

We are deeply indebted to Senior Project Editor Marta Tomins, who kept us from giving in to either doubt or frustration. It is she who kept us moving along the track when we thought the engine was out of steam or the switches were closed. Somehow she always managed to keep the engine chugging away; we are grateful that she was able to coax and hector us all the way into the station. We also thank Patrick Ferrier and Jerry Smith and others at Prentice-Hall Canada for their encouragement and support.

Above all, the style and quality of this book reflect in significant measure the astuteness, dedication, and professionalism of Jessica Pegis, former Associate Editor at Prentice-Hall Canada, now a dedicated *freelance* editor! We were very grateful for her continued involvement in this project, and we found our collaboration with her to be a delightful and rewarding experience.

We would like to thank everyone who assisted in the enormous task of producing this text, especially designer Bob Garbutt of Robert Garbutt Productions; Sandra Calderaro, whose cover painting we admire greatly; all the photographers, newspapers and associations who loaned us photographs illustrating various aspects of Canadian life; Marina Santin and Melissa McClellan, who set up shots especially for *A Textbook of Social Psychology*; Denyse O'Leary, our proofreader and proper name indexer, and finally, P-H editor Katherine Mototsune, who provided some last minute editorial work on the bibliography.

We would like to thank those who reviewed the manuscript in its early stages: Michael L. Atkinson, University of Western Ontario; T. Edward Hannah, Memorial University; Chok C. Hiew, University of New Brunswick; W. David Pierce, University of Alberta; Alan Pomfret, University of Western Ontario; and J.D.T. Roth, Ryerson Polytechnical Institute.

A special thank you also goes to some of our colleagues for their helpful and constructive comments: Richard Bourhis, John Lavery, Jeff Pfeiffer, Beverly McLeod, Pat McCoy, Cheryl McCormick and Lila Krishnan. Typists Joyce Litster, Wendy Selbie and Beverly Bardy-Platt deserve a round of applause as well.

Social psychology is dynamic, exciting, and challenging. We hope that the readers enjoy the textbook and come to share our excitement about our discipline. We invite you to write to us with your comments and suggestions, which will aid us in planning the next edition.

Anyway, not bad for a couple of guys from Saskatchewan and a renegade from the Ottawa valley, *eh*?

JIM ALCOCK
BILL CARMENT
STAN SADAVA

December, 1987
Toronto

A T·E·X·T·B·O·O·K O·F

Social Psychology

Introducing Social Psychology

Esau asked, "What was the meaning
of all the company that I have met?"

"ABSENCE MAKES THE heart grow fonder"; "Out of sight, out of mind"; Dress for success"; Power corrupts — absolute power corrupts absolutely"; "First impressions last"; "Opposites attract"; "Actions speak louder than words."

All of these familiar expressions contain common sense ideas about social behaviour, our "naive psychology" which has grown out of generations of experience. Think how all these aphorisms could easily be translated into hypotheses, predictions which we could test experimentally. If we could somehow cause lovers to be apart for varying periods of time, would attraction or love really increase? If we were to control for other factors, would people who dress in a certain way really meet with measurably greater success? Can we demonstrate historically, or could we demonstrate in group experiments, that leaders who have greater personal power tend to act in a "corrupt" way? Social psychology begins with the "stuff" of common experience and applies the methods of science to build valid and verifiable explanations or theories of social behaviour (see Box 1-1).

B·O·X 1-1

FROM COMMON SENSE TO RESEARCH HYPOTHESIS

Consider another old saying: Familiarity breeds contempt. That is, the more familiar we become with people or things, the less attractive they become to us. Even when two people are familiar enough to marry, we know that the honeymoon will eventually end and that it will be difficult, if not impossible, to recapture the magic of that early stage.

The saying also seems to hold true of objects and places: we often feel bored, with an "itch to travel" or for a "change of scenery."

And yet, there are many events in our experience which do *not* demonstrate that "familiarity breeds contempt." Consider the following:

(1) Students tend to feel rather uncomfortable in class in the first days of the new school year, particularly if they don't know many other students. As the course goes on, they feel more and more comfortable and positive about the experience, even though they may not have interacted with many classmates. The people, the professors, the lecture room all seem familiar now. The same experience often occurs with people who commute daily to work by bus or train, immersed in their newspapers or daydreams but comfortable with the "familiar strangers" beside them, as Stanley Milgram has called them.

(2) The Eiffel Tower is one of the best-known and loved physical landmarks. When it was first built in 1889 for a World Fair, it was almost universally detested by the citizens of Paris who felt that France had lost its position as a cultural leader in the world (Harrison, 1977). Similar reactions first greeted the construction of Toronto's distinctive City Hall. Eventually, residents of both cities developed strong

Toronto City Hall

pride in these monuments as symbols of their civic identity.

(3) In recent years, many radio stations have switched from a Top Twenty format, in which new music is aired, to a format in which *only* familiar and popular music from the present and recent past is played.

(4) Another familiar common-sense expression assures us that "there's no place like home." Certainly no place is as familiar as home.

How can we subject the principle that "familiarity breeds contempt" to experimental test? Zajonc (1968a) conducted a series of controlled experiments in which he varied the number of times different groups of subjects were exposed to certain stimuli. In one such experiment, subjects were shown a series of photographs from a university yearbook. Some of the faces were repeatedly shown, as often as 25 times, while others were shown only once or twice. Here are the results:

Frequency of exposure to photograph	Average favourability rating (scale of 1–4)
once	2.8
twice	2.9
five times	3.0
ten times	3.6
twenty-five times	3.7

As you can see, subjects were considerably more favourable to the faces seen more frequently. In other experiments by Zajonc, the same was found to be true for other stimuli, including Chinese alphabet characters, foreign words, and the frequency with which names of cities, flowers, trees and vegetables occur naturally in speech.

In later chapters, consideration will be given to more of the research on this "mere exposure effect," when and why it occurs, what it means, and what other factors influence our like or dislike of someone or something.

WHAT SOCIAL PSYCHOLOGY IS AND IS NOT

Social psychology is the discipline which sets out to understand how the thoughts, feelings and behaviours of individuals are influenced by the actual, imagined or implied presence of others (Allport, 1935). What does this definition tell us about social psychology? First, social psychologists study not only actual, observable behaviour but also what can be inferred about the inner lives of people: how they feel, their attitudes, opinions and ideologies, how they form impressions and try to make sense of their world. Second, human experience is understood in terms of the influence of other people. Obviously, social influence is not the only kind — we may be affected by our physical state of health, physical aspects of weather, what we have learned, our brain and nervous system processes, psychotic and drug states, hormones, or what we have eaten. However, social psychologists focus on the vital role of social influences and relationships. Finally, the definition tells us that people are influenced by other people even if they are not immediately present. We are aware of belonging to certain family, occupational and cultural groups and we are aware of liking, loving, or feeling responsible to certain people in our lives. We are profoundly influenced by these groups and individuals in our thoughts and actions.

To appreciate better the range of phenomena studied by social psychologists, let us consider the following examples:

(1) Concern is often expressed about the level of violence in hockey, from the "pee-

Social psychologists study not only actual, observable behaviour but also what can be inferred about the inner lives of people: how they feel, their attitudes, opinions and ideologies.

wee" league to the National Hockey League. Human *aggression* is an area of substantial research in social psychology.

(2) In a highly competitive economic situation, a job interview can be decisive. Social psychologists have studied how *first impressions are formed* and how people act to influence or *"manage" the impression* that others have of them.

(3) Amnesty International has documented the physical torture used routinely in many countries. For the most part, those who practice torture are not unusually sadistic by nature but simply *obedient* to the instructions of authority. A series of important experiments has been conducted on *obedience to authority*.

(4) A large proportion of all marriages in North America will eventually end in divorce. *Social attraction* and the evolution of *intimate relationships* are areas of current, intensive research.

(5) While Québécois entrepreneurs move into the North American, English-speaking business milieu, English Canadian parents in unprecedented numbers enroll their children in French immersion programs. There has been extensive research on the social aspects of *bilingualism*.

(6) In 1984, John Turner lost his lead in the polls and eventually lost power as prime minister in a crushing electoral defeat. *Persuasion* and *attitude change*, phenomena studied by social psychologists, had much to do with that historical event.

(7) Society has become more concerned with the protection and rehabilitation of the victims of sexual and other crimes. Research on *social cognition* has shed light on their experience and how they might best be helped.

(8) Recently, attention has been focused on strikes by physicians in Ontario and by meat packers in Alberta. These events represent the outcome of *conflict* and failure in the *negotiation* process, which have been researched extensively by social psychologists.

(9) Many trials are decided by the credibility of a key witness. Social psychologists have studied *eyewitness testimony* and other aspects of the legal system.

(10) *Prejudice*, a continuing problem in human societies, has also endured as a topic of research in social psychology.

As you can see, social psychologists study a wide range of social phenomena. Some of their concerns involve practical problems: Why don't patients do what their physicians recommend? What kinds of decisions do groups make and can they be improved? Why do people persist in stereotyping males, females, professors, students, and ethnic groups, regardless of the realities? Other equally important questions are more theoretical in nature: What consistencies and inconsistencies are there between people's attitudes and their behaviour? What biases operate in the perception of cause and effect in interpersonal situations? How can we explain aggression in terms of social learning?

To clarify what social psychology is about, let us compare it with other areas of psychology and other related disciplines. Social psychology shares with other areas of psychology a focus on the individual. In particular, there is considerable overlap in the interests of social psychology and the study of personality. However, the study of personality takes into account individual differences in the way people think, feel or act, and emphasizes above all factors operating within individuals. Social psychology, by contrast, looks at the situational factors which cause people in general to behave in certain ways. Thus, for example, personality psychologists study the characteristics of those people who tend to behave aggressively; social psychologists also investigate situations in which people are likely to behave aggressively. Of course, behaviour is determined by both person and environment, and students of social psychology must understand both types of variables.

Social psychology also shares many areas of interest with other social sciences, especially sociology (the study of society and social institutions) and anthropology (the study of human culture). Perhaps the major differences are found in each discipline's basic *unit of analysis* and *level of explanation*. The usual focus of study in these other social sciences is the large group, institution, or custom (e.g., the school, the family, social norms, social class structure). The *rate* or typical pattern of behaviour in a population is also of concern. By contrast, social psychology focuses on the individual or, at most, a small group. Sociologists and anthropologists explain phenomena in terms of external characteristics such as social class mobility, customs of parental discipline, and the distribution of power in a society. Social psychologists generally explain the behaviour of individuals in terms of specific situations as well as psychological processes such as attitudes, emotional states, or perception of cause and effect.

Both psychology and sociology have subdisciplines called "social psychology" which have subject areas in common but differ in research methods, theories, and theoretical orientation. Psychological social psychologists frequently do laboratory experiments, while sociological social psychologists often rely on participant observation, in which the researcher actually joins the institution or group and describes it from the inside. And while most social psychologists in sociology work within the framework of "symbolic interactionism" (how people come to attach meaning to experience through interaction with other persons), within the field of psychology, social psychologists study the cognitive processes within individuals by which they come to make sense of the world.

SOCIAL PSYCHOLOGY YESTERDAY AND TODAY

While social psychology is relatively young as a discipline, its roots run deeply through the history of Western thought. Like all of psychology, social psychology emerged from the work of philosophers. Aristotle thought and wrote about the nature of such phenomena as friendship in social life, while Plato was deeply concerned with the nature of leadership and the most desirable form of government. English empiricist philosophers such as John Stuart Mill and Thomas Hobbes attributed all social behaviour to the search for pleasure and avoidance of pain (hedonism) or to the need for

TABLE 1–1

Historical highlights in social psychology the 1980s

Triplett: experiment (1898)	**1900**	
MacDougall: textbook (1908)		
	1910	World War I (1914–1918)
		Russian Revolution (1917)
F. Allport: textbook (1924)	**1920**	automobile and radio become part of life (1920s)
Thurstone: attitude measurement (1929)		beginning of Great Depression (1929)
LaPiere: attitudes and actions (1934)	**1930**	Hitler takes power (1932)
Sherif: norms and perception (1935)		
Dollard: frustration and aggression (1939)		
Lewin: leadership and groups (1939)		World War II begins (1939)
Research on leadership, morale, propaganda	**1940**	the Holocaust
		Hiroshima (1945)
		Israel independence (1948)
		Chinese revolution (1949)
authoritarian personality (1950)	**1950**	Korean War (1950-52)
Asch: conformity experiments (1956)		Cold War/McCarthyism (1952–58)
Festinger: cognitive dissonance (1957)		TV age begins (1950s)
Heider: attributions (1958)		
Lambert: bilingualism (1960s)	**1960**	Cuban revolution
Newcomb: attraction (1961)		
Milgram: obedience (1963)		President Kennedy's assassination (1963)
		U.S. — Vietnam war, (1965–1974)
		youth counterculture (1966–1973)
Kelley: attribution (1967)		
Latané and Darley: bystander intervention (1967)		
		Trudeau elected (1968)
	1970	Québec October crisis (1970)
		Watergate (1974)
social cognition	**1980**	conflict in Central America
applied social psychology		Reagan elected (1980)
research in Europe and Third World		Mulroney elected (1984)

power. The nineteenth century French philosopher, Gabriel Tarde, wrote that "society is imitation." In other words, people have an innate tendency to imitate, which causes them to conform in order to live together. While all these themes continue to be of interest to social psychologists, the "simple and sovereign theories" which explain social behaviour in terms of a single variable such as power, pleasure, or imitation have been abandoned and replaced by more complex explanations.

Social psychology did not emerge dramatically through the declaration of a doctrine, a scientific breakthrough, or the influence of a personality such as Sigmund Freud. Rather, it evolved over several decades, marked by several key events (see Table 1-1). One was the first laboratory experiment in social psychology, performed by Norman Triplett (1897). Observing that cyclists went much faster when riding with other cyclists than when riding alone, he set out to investigate whether performance in general might be affected in a consistent way by the presence of other people. While the experiment was flawed, it was an excellent beginning, demonstrating that questions about social behaviour could be studied through scientific experiments.

In 1908 the first two textbooks of social psychology appeared. In the absence of a significant body of research, both were largely speculative in nature. E.A. Ross, a sociologist, based his discussion on instinctive forms of imitation and suggestion, while William MacDougall, a psychologist, postulated a variety of biologically-based instincts. It was not until 1924 that Floyd Allport published the first textbook based on empirical research. This highly influential book presented social psychology as a science of how behaviour is influenced by the presence and reactions of other people, and discussed such topics as conformity and how people recognize emotional states in other persons.

Research through the decades

There have been several broad trends in the history of social psychology from then to now. In the '20s and '30s, a dominant concern was the measurement and study of attitudes and related concepts such as stereotypes. Later, work began on group-related phenomena — the influence of social norms on perception and action (Sherif), the effects of styles of leadership on group functioning (Lewin), and the effects of frustration on aggression (Dollard, Doob, and Miller). The Second World War generated research on topics relating to politics and combat — group morale, leadership and propaganda. By the '50s, there was a renewed interest in attitudes, evident in research on persuasion by Carl Hovland and colleagues, and on prejudice and personality (Adorno, Frenkel-Brunswick, Levinson, and Sanford, 1950). Others studied the relationship between social behaviour and individual differences in need for achievement and social approval, and persuasibility.

The '50s also marked the appearance of two seminal books which are still influential. Leon Festinger (1957) published his theory of cognitive dissonance, which explains how people deal with inconsistencies among attitudes and behaviours. In the following year, Fritz Heider (1958) outlined a psychology of interpersonal relations based on how we infer what causes people to act as they do. In the same decade, the laboratory experiment became the predominant method of research (Adair, 1980).

In the '60s, social psychology expanded dramatically in scope. Social psychologists directed their attention to new areas of research — why we sometimes display excessive obedience to authority, how we make judgments about other people's behaviour,

How do people attract and make friends? Social psychologists began studying this issue in the '60s.

how we negotiate and resolve conflicts, how we attract and make friends, and why bystanders often fail to help in emergencies. In Canada, Wallace Lambert, Robert Gardner and others launched ground-breaking research into the social and psychological aspects of bilingualism. Elsewhere, in that highly-politicized decade, research continued in areas of social concern, including aggression, prejudice, and attitude change.

In the social psychology of the '70s and '80s several new directions are evident. One is an interest in social cognition (the study of how we "make sense" of our social world), which has been influenced by fundamental research on cognitive processes such as memory, attention, and problem-solving. A second trend is a growing interest in applying social psychology to areas of daily living. Social psychologists may now be found working in the fields of medicine, law, organizational management, the environment, or counselling. Moreover, a social psychology which has been dominated by research and theory in the United States is becoming increasingly internationalized with research and new journals emerging in Europe, Asia and Latin America. In the long run, these trends can only enrich social psychology and extend the validity of its theories and findings.

In summary, social psychology is a dynamic field, continually evolving as new ideas, methods, research findings, and theories emerge and affect each other: a theory can generate innovative research and controversy; research findings and new ideas can lead to an evolution in the theory; new areas of research can open up as a result of random events (for example, a widely-publicized incident of a murder in the presence of bystanders who failed to intervene stimulated research and theory on the problem). Some areas of research become "hot topics" almost overnight, generating ideas on the "cutting edge," while interest in other topics may be slow to build or wane for awhile. A textbook can only provide a picture of the discipline at the time of writing — with some idea of where we have been and where we are going.

A NOTE ON THE TEXT

In the final analysis, the best way to understand what social psychology is about is to get involved in it. This begins in the next chapter, which introduces the fundamental principles of how research is conducted in social psychology. Then, a series of chapters explores the basic aspects of social cognition — how we perceive and understand other people and events, how we form values and attitudes, how attitudes change — and provides a detailed examination of prejudice as an important attitude problem. The next set of chapters deals with interpersonal relations — how social influences lead us to conform, comply with and obey other people, how people become attracted to others and form relationships, how people communicate through language and non-verbal means. The causes of altruistic and aggressive behaviour are discussed and consideration is given to how conflict develops and can be resolved. Then, the individual within groups and larger collectivities is discussed. Finally, some contemporary areas of practical concern are considered, including the law, the environment, the threat of nuclear war, and human health.

Sources of Information

At the end of each chapter, important, recent publications are listed which provide further information on topics discussed in that chapter. The following list of basic reference works will serve as an introduction to most research areas in the field.

Some Basic Reference Works

BERKOWITZ, L. (Ed.) *Advances in Experimental Social Psychology* (an annual series). New York: Academic Press.

BICKMAN, L. (Ed.) *Applied Social Psychology Annual* (an annual series). Beverly Hills: Sage.

LINDZEY, G. and ARONSON, E. (Eds.) (1985). *The handbook of social psychology*. Third edition (Vols. 1–2). New York: Random House.

ROSENZWEIG, M.R. AND PORTER, L.W. (Eds.) *Annual Review of Psychology* (an annual series). Palo Alto, CA: Annual Reviews, Inc.

SHAW, M.E. and COSTANZO, P.R. (1980). *Theories of social psychology*. New York: McGraw-Hill.

TRIANDIS, H.C. (Ed.) (1979/1980). *Handbook of cross-cultural psychology*, Vols. 1–5. Boston: Allyn and Bacon.

WEST, S.G. and WICKLUND, R.A. (1980). *A primer of social psychological theories*. Monterey, CA: Brooks/Cole.

Journals

To keep abreast of the latest research and findings in the field of social psychology, it is also necessary to refer to journal articles. A literature search through the *Psycho-*

logical Abstracts or library data base will provide specific references. For papers and research of general interest, the following journals are most useful:

Psychological Bulletin (literature and methodological reviews in all areas of psychology)
Psychological Review (theory in all areas of psychology)
Journal of Personality and Social Psychology
Journal of Social Issues
Canadian Journal of Behavioural Science
European Journal of Social Psychology
British Journal of Social Psychology
Journal of Applied Social Psychology
Journal of Experimental Social Psychology
Journal of Social Psychology
Personality and Social Psychology Bulletin

There are also journals which feature research in one particular area of social psychology:

Journal of Clinical and Social Psychology
Journal of Studies on Alcohol
Aggression and Behaviour
Journal of Conflict Resolution
Health Psychology
Environment and Behavior
Journal of Cross-Cultural Psychology.

C·H·A·P·T·E·R T·W·O

Research and Research Methods

I pass with relief from the tossing sea of
Cause and Theory to the firm ground of
Result and Fact.
Winston Churchill

FOR REFLECTION

- Can social psychology be a "science"?
- Can we measure prejudice, our first impressions of people, aggression, intimacy?
- What is a good experiment?
- Is it ethical to deceive subjects during an experiment or cause them distress?

ALTHOUGH IT IS difficult to say whether or not human beings have made much progress over the centuries in ethics, religion, or politics, science is one field in which progress is apparent (Harris, 1970). We live in an age where "scientific research" is generally taken to be the most dependable route to knowledge. Even commercial advertising reflects this assumption. Who has not heard of toothpaste that has been "scientifically proven" to fight cavities, or over-the-counter medications "scientifically proven" to reduce wrinkles, shrink hemorrhoids or absorb more than 40 times their weight in stomach acids?

What is "science"? Science is a *method of studying nature*. And it is the method, and not the people who do science or the equipment used or the facts proclaimed which differentiates science from other approaches to knowledge. Indeed, as we shall see, the scientific approach is as valuable a tool for the study of human social behaviour as it is for research into chemical reactions and biological processes.

THE RISE OF MODERN SCIENCE

Until the scientific revolution of the sixteenth and seventeenth centuries, Western thought was dominated by appeal to authority: the biblical scriptures and the pronouncements of the ancient Greek philosophers were taken to be the wellsprings of truth and knowledge. The works of Aristotle, the greatest philosopher of antiquity, provided the foundation for medieval scholastic thought, and great importance was attached to the belief that pure reason could validate and illuminate what was already accepted on religious faith. Reason which contradicted dogma was presumed to be in error.

To understand the importance of the scientific approach to the study of behaviour, it is useful to understand how the scientific method evolved and gradually replaced the appeal to pure reason and dogma. The shift began with the rise of astronomy, an interesting event in itself because astronomers do not fit the usual image of the scientist: they are observers, not experimenters.

For many centuries, Western scholars accepted without question that the sun revolved around the earth — a reasonable supposition, for it was in keeping with the experience of everyday life. It also complemented the prevailing Judeo-Christian viewpoint that Homo Sapiens had a special place in the order of things. Moreover, no less an authority than Aristotle himself had declared that the earth is stationary and at the centre of the universe and, until the time of Copernicus in the sixteenth century, no astronomer seriously challenged this assumption, despite the fact that observations of planetary movement were not entirely consistent with it. Thus, when Copernicus proclaimed in *De Revolutionibus Orbium Caelestium* (1543) that not only was the earth *not* the centre of the universe, but that it revolved around the sun, he was not believed. Even though astronomers quickly adopted his improved techniques for computing planetary positions, they ignored and even ridiculed his views about the movement of the earth. (This is not as irrational as it may seem: evidence supporting Copernicus' theory was weak, and counter-evidence at that time was strong (Kuhn, 1959)). Galileo, who later promoted Copernicus' theory, encountered harsh opposition from scholars and Church alike, and was prosecuted by the Roman Catholic Church and forced to recant his "heretical" views.

Ultimately, however, Copernican ideas won out because they accorded better with what astronomers observed in the heavens. In the end, accordance with observation triumphed over accordance with scripture. The scientific revolution was born.

While it is not clear just why modern science began to develop at that time, its remarkable development was due to the importance given on the one hand to curiosity, which led people to develop theories about how nature works, and on the other, to the emphasis put upon testing expectation against experience (Boulding, 1980). Whether in astronomy, physics, or psychology, generating theory and testing it against observation is fundamental. Theory is essential to guide research, to organize research results into a coherent structure, and to provide ideas for testing, for without theory there is nothing to test. (And, without testing, there is no way to evaluate the accuracy of theory.)

THE SCIENTIFIC METHOD

The methodology of science has evolved over several centuries into a series of procedural steps:

(1) *Observation*. First we must *observe*: we isolate the phenomenon to be studied and form generalizations about it. We may begin with *casual* observation. For example, suppose we notice that there seem to be more "one-hour" dry cleaning establishments in the poorer parts of our city. At this point, we should be aware that casual observation can be very misleading; we may not notice such establishments in the "better" parts of town because we are distracted by more fashionable stores. Or, having formed the idea, we may think about the one-hour shops only when passing

through the poorer parts of town. If this is the case, selective observation alone supports our notion. Therefore, we must turn to more *systematic* observation. For example, we could obtain records from city hall about average income levels in various districts of the city, and then go out and count how many dry cleaning establishments there are in each area, and how many of them advertise one-hour service.

(2) *Hypothesis generation.* Suppose that such systematic observation supports our initial observations that there are more one-hour dry cleaners in poorer districts. We do not know why, of course, and if no prior research has been done to suggest reasons for our observations, we may then speculate about why "one-hour" dry cleaning is associated more with poorer than with richer areas. Suppose we posit that poorer people are more likely to have only one set of clothes to wear to work; thus it is essential for them to obtain rapid dry cleaning. And that people who are better off may possess several different outfits, and so can easily leave one outfit at the cleaner's for a few days. Drawing from this speculation, combined with our earlier observations, we might deduce that more people in poorer areas than in wealthier areas should report owning only one work outfit.

(3) *Hypothesis-testing.* Our deduction can serve as a prediction, or *hypothesis*, which can be tested empirically. We could, for example, go from door to door in various districts of the city and ask people how many sets of work clothes they own. If more people in poorer areas than in richer areas report having only one work outfit, confidence in our own speculation will be increased. If the prediction is not supported, then we must modify or discard our assumption.

Indeed, the ability to falsify an hypothesis, to demonstrate empirically that it is incorrect, may be as important in the long run as finding evidence which supports (but cannot "prove" the correctness of) the hypothesis. For example, if we find in our survey that poorer people tend to have only one set of work clothes, we may be content to assume that since our hypothesis was supported, we have found the correct explanation for our observations. Even if our prediction is supported by our evidence, however, this by itself should not be taken as *proof* that our speculation is correct. It could be, for example, that some people in richer areas were unwilling to admit that they owned only one work outfit, while people in poorer areas were generally more honest. It is also possible that we made errors in our data collection, either in the original count of dry cleaning establishments or in the survey of residents. Perhaps the person who went door to door made errors in the recording of the data, or perhaps he or she even cheated and did not really collect data in some districts but sat in a pub and made up the data in order to be paid quickly. Moreover, we did not even inquire whether most of those people with only one set of work clothes did indeed take it to the dry cleaner's. When our hypothesis is shown to be wrong, we must do some more thinking and collect some more data; when our hypothesis is supported, we may be tempted prematurely to accept it as true.

Although not all philosophers of science agree with him, Popper (1959, 1972) argues that such *falsificationism* is the very basis for any scientific progress: if we cannot — at least in principle — prove a hypothesis to be false, then, according to this view, the hypothesis is not a scientific one. A religious person may argue that prayers are always answered, even when no answer is apparent. However, such a claim cannot be tested, since it cannot be disproved: "no answer" is also taken to be an answer.

(4) *Replication.* Methodological weaknesses and fraud are potential hazards in any area of research, but we can guard against these in the long run by insisting on *rep-*

B · O · X   2 - 1

N-RAYS: NOW YOU SEE THEM, NOW YOU DON'T

In 1903 Professor R. Blondot, head of the physics department at the University of Nancy in France, reported that he had discovered a new kind of ray that was very different from the recently discovered "X-rays" and radioactivity. He called these rays "N-rays," N referring to Nancy, his university. N-rays were said to be emitted by metal objects. It was claimed that a person could actually read a calendar on the wall in the dark by pointing a metal object at it.

Blondot built a spectroscope, using aluminum lenses and prisms, and reported that he had identified various wavelengths of the N-rays. In the next year, almost 100 scientific papers "confirming" the reality of N-rays were published by various researchers. It

was soon discovered that all materials, whether mineral, vegetable or animal, emitted N-rays, except for one substance — wood.

In 1904 an American scientist (ironically named Wood) who had been unable to find N-rays in his own research visited Blondot's laboratory. During Blondot's demonstration of N-ray spectral lines using the spectroscope, the researcher secretly removed the aluminum prism, an action which should have made the spectroscope inoperable. But Blondot continued to describe the lines in the N-ray spectrum as though the prism were still there! This spelled the end of N-rays. Blondot, an honest researcher, had fallen victim to his own suggestibility and pulled a number of fellow researchers along with him (Alcock, 1981).

lication as an essential step in the scientific method. In other words, before accepting something as true, we wait to see if other people, in other situations, can reproduce our results. If they can, confidence in our "theory" is strengthened; if not, confidence is weakened.

Error and self-correction in science

We should never take any theory, no matter how well-confirmed, to represent absolute truth; rather, a theory should be treated as the most reasonable explanation or description of the phenomenon in question available at a given time. The wisdom of one era is sometimes viewed as folly in the next (see Box 2-1). Scientists have often been mistaken. Over the years they have refused to believe in such ideas as the extraterrestrial origin of meteorites or continental drift, ideas which are now taken for granted. Although originally rejected, these ideas eventually won out because further observation supported them. The insistence upon testing theory against observation, upon replicability of observations and falsifiability of theory endows the scientific procedure with this advantage: it is self-correcting. Errors are inevitably made, but sooner or later, as better theories come along and as recourse to observation confirms their superiority, errors are weeded out.

A formal model of scientific method

A formal representation of how both theory and research combine to produce scientific knowledge is presented in Figure 2-1.

FIGURE 2–1
A formal model of the scientific method

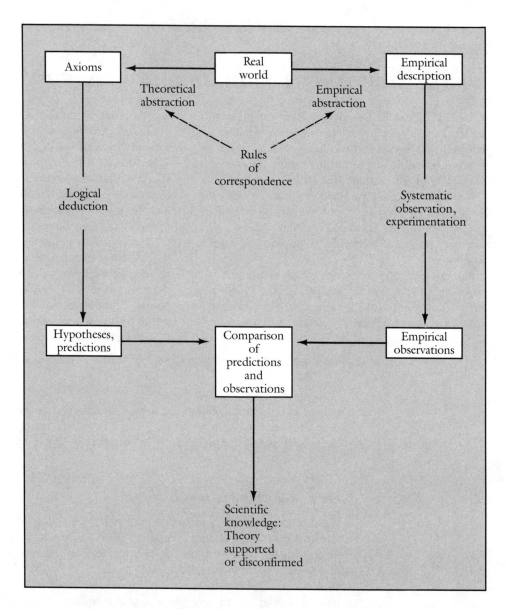

The theoretical process is shown on the left side of the figure, while the empirical process is shown on the right. Both are linked to each other, for both start out with reference to the real world, and both result in comparable end products. We begin with some curiosity about something in the real world. Suppose we wondered whether a steel needle would float on water. On the theoretical side, we would analyze this question by beginning with some statements about the real world which we already presume to be true (although we cannot be certain of their truth). Such assumptions are called *axioms*. In this case, our axioms might be, "Solid metal does not float on water" and "A needle is made of solid metal." These assumptions seem reasonable enough. Based on them, we can deduce that if they are both true, a needle will not float on water. This is our hypothesis.

On the empirical side, we also begin with the real world. *Empirical abstraction* would involve taking a needle and some water, and testing to see whether or not the needle would float. In doing so, we would decide what kind of situation to use — we could try floating a knitting needle on the open sea, or we could try floating a small sewing needle in a bowl of water. Before deciding what situation is most appropriate, we must be sure that the empirical terms we use correspond in a meaningful way to our theoretical terms. In other words, the terms "needle" and "water," as they are understood on the theoretical side, must correspond to the needle and water we use in testing our hypothesis. Does "water" mean salt water, distilled water, or tap water? Does "needle" mean knitting needle or sewing needle? Is there any ambiguity about the term "float"? The *rules of correspondence* provide the link between theoretical and empirical terms. In testing the theory, we may define "needle" as sewing needle of a certain length, for example. (However, our test results will be specific to that particular needle, and if the needle does not float, we can not be certain that other metal needles of different lengths will not float.)

The actual observation process involves taking the needle and some water and trying to see if the needle will float. Through *systematic observation* we would try a number of approaches to floating the needle. We might begin by placing it in the water in a vertical position; if it does not float, we might then vary the angle at which it is placed in the water. In fact, if we are careful enough, the needle will indeed float (as a result of surface tension)!

If we observe that the needle floats, we would then compare this observation with the prediction. In this case, they do not agree. This means that our logical deduction was wrong, which also means that one or more of our axioms was wrong. We must revise our "theory," that is, we must change one or more of our axioms. In this simple case, we would no doubt decide that the axiom that "metal does not float on water" is wrong.

Now, if we had not been careful enough in our observations, or patient enough in our attempts, we would have produced observations that were consistent with theory, even though the theory is not correct. Thus observations can support a theory even when the theory is wrong.

This formal model of the scientific method describes the process scientists typically adhere to, even if they do not always formally delineate the various steps in the process. However, the process is rarely as neat in practice as the model suggests (see Box 2-2). Now consider an example which we would be more likely to encounter in the field of social psychology. Suppose we were interested in an important social question, such as the possible influence of pornography on the incidence of violence against women. We would first generate some theoretical hypotheses by starting with a set of assumptions that seem reasonable to us. They might be: "The less a group is respected in a society, the more likely it is that anti-social elements will direct hostility towards it"; or "Pornography teaches disrespect for women"; or "Pornography arouses feelings which are difficult to control."

By simple logic, then, we reach the prediction that observation of pornography will generate violence toward women. If our basic assumptions are correct, the prediction should be borne out. If the prediction is not confirmed, then we must modify our basic assumptions.

The "rules of correspondence" in the centre of Figure 2-1 describe how theoretical terms are translated into terms that can be measured unambiguously. Setting up rules of correspondence is often very difficult in the social sciences. What do we really mean by terms such as "pornography" and "disrespect" and "hostility"? Before we

B · O · X   2 - 2

JUDGMENT CALLS IN DOING RESEARCH

A "judgment call" is a decision that must be made, often quickly, without the benefit of a fixed or "objective" rule. Baseball constantly requires such decisions: Was the pitch in the strike zone? Did the shortstop control the ball long enough (before he dropped it) for the runner to be called out? Has the pitcher lost his effectiveness and should he be replaced? Should the manager choose the flashy, light-hitting fielder or the error-prone slugger to play against a certain team? While experience is often helpful, we cannot always go "by the book." Decisions of this type are characterized by difficulty and ambiguity and yet, the eventual outcome may be determined by the cumulative results of many such decisions.

Decisions of this type also confront the researcher (McGrath, Martin and Kulka, 1982). This may seem surprising, for science is fundamentally a rational process. In its simplest form, the rational model consists of four steps: (1) the formulation of a theoretical problem which is then translated into testable hypotheses; (2) the selection of the appropriate research method, and the design and carrying out of the study; (3) the analysis and interpretation of the results; and (4) the use of the results to confirm, deny or modify the theory. What could be more rational?

Out in the real world where research is done, many decisions are required in which the "right" answer does not follow, neatly and inevitably, from the "objective" rules of theory and research. Let us compare the ideal of the rational model to the reality of doing research:

(1) The researcher should begin with the problem, then decide what methods should be used to investigate it. However, research often begins with an opportunity — then the problem and method are selected to take advantage of that opportunity. Researchers may decide to work in an area where funding is available. For example, the process of aging, and the social effects of technology have been identified recently as priority areas by the Social Sciences and Humanities Research Council of Canada. Researchers may take advantage of access to a population of interest, e.g., hospitalized patients or bilingual subjects located in Montreal. Other resources, such as laboratory facilities or the special-ized skills of the researchers, often determine the decisions about what to study and how to study it.

(2) How to research a problem should be determined by the nature of the problem. Those who want to study the movement of stars and galaxies will use different methods from those who want to study the movement of subatomic particles. However, sicence often begins with a method in search of

can do any empirical research, we must be specific about our terminology, in order that the behaviours and attitudes that we are measuring correspond to the concepts that are embodied in our theory.

Suppose we are able to define pornography and violence, at least for our purposes. At this point, we would gather data, perhaps by running an experiment. Suppose such an experiment produced evidence which, when statistically evaluated, was in line with our prediction. While this outcome would strengthen our belief that our initial generalizations are correct, it does not tell us how they might be modified and improved. On the other hand, if the data do not support the theoretical prediction, then confidence in our theory is reduced, and one or more of our initial generali-zations may be wrong.

Both theory-building and data collection combine to form the scientific method. Theories generate testable hypotheses, while observation serves to demonstrate which

problems and theories. For example, the increasingly sophisticated methodologies of survey research have been applied to the study of a wide range of new problems and to the generation of new theories. In the extreme case, this tendency becomes the "law of the instrument": give a child a hammer, and the child will find that everything needs pounding. Scientists may act similarly with an electron microscope, a questionnaire measure, an experimental technique, or a Skinner box.

Researchers must also use what is available rather than what is ideal. For example, a study of students may use grades as a less-than-perfect indicator of how involved and committed the students were. Some problems can only be studied in less-than-ideal ways. For example, aggression cannot be studied directly by observing violent acts, so researchers must devise construed situations in the laboratory or rely on crime statistics.

(3) Rationally, it can be stated that different methods, applied properly, should lead to the same conclusion. However, it is rare that different methods are applied to study the same theoretical problem. Cronbach (1957) has argued that, in effect, two parallel psychologies have developed. Experimental studies compare the average values of an attribute between different groups, usually in relation to changes in aspects of the situation, while correlational studies examine how different attributes covary, usually by studying patterns of individual differences in attributes. Some psychologists may investigate whether aggression levels are higher among subjects who have been provoked than among those who were not, while others may investigate whether habitually aggressive people tend to have certain personality characteristics.

(4) The rational model of research conceives of results as the end-point of the process. However, in many cases, the results may be unexpected, and the researcher can capitalize on serendipity. For example, a French surgeon once observed that chlorpromazine, a drug which had been used in combination with surgical anaesthetics, did not itself make the patients drowsy but seemed to make them unconcerned about their upcoming surgery. He reasoned that the drug might reduce emotionality in mental patients; when it was tested on some patients, it not only calmed them but also seemed to reduce the psychotic state. As evidence mounted that this drug was often effective in treating schizophrenia, research was conducted on where and how the drug acted on the brain. These results, in turn, influenced theories about schizophrenia itself.

As you can see, doing research involves many judgment calls about theories, methods and results, and these decisions often cannot be anticipated in advance. If you are considering research in your future, you will need liberal doses of theoretical thinking, practical skills, and imagination. You will also need to be able to cope with the joys and frustrations of the unexpected.

hypotheses best fit reality. The ultimate goal of science is to develop general theories which are supported by observation, for theories organize observations and make explanation possible. Replication is a critical part of the scientific method, for unless a researcher's results can be reproduced in other situations, we can have little confidence in those results.

SOCIAL PSYCHOLOGY AND SCIENTIFIC METHOD

For most people, "science" describes specific fields of study (physics, chemistry, geology, astronomy, biology), impressive laboratory technology, and precise measurement. It may seem surprising that a field such as social psychology can be "scientific." How can the study of violence, helping, leadership, bilingual communication, impression formation and attitudes be "scientific" in the sense that research into the mysteries of the human cell, the atom, and reactions of chemical elements and compounds is scientific? Yet the scientific method is arguably even more important in a field where it is difficult to quantify data because it is in such areas of study that the opportunity for fuzzy and erroneous thinking is greatest.

It is not nearly so straightforward to apply the scientific method to social behaviour as it is to the realm of inanimate objects or biological processes. Much of what we loosely refer to as "theory" in social psychology is not really theory in the sense the term is used in the natural sciences. Our theories are more like models, or descriptions, usually built upon a loosely related set of assumptions, and the logical deduction process is typically informal in nature.

Theory in social psychology

Because social psychology is a relatively young discipline, and because human social behaviour is so complex, no single, grand theory has yet emerged. As we will see in subsequent chapters, various mini-theories or models have been developed to account for specific phenomena, such as leadership, attitude change, or aggressive behaviour. While there is considerable variety among these theories, two major theoretical orientations have dominated: the behaviourist and the cognitive perspectives. Both have been adapted from the mainstream of psychological theory and research.

Behaviourism developed through the pioneering work of Ivan Pavlov on conditioned reflexes and of B.F. Skinner on operant conditioning. It is based on the premise that behaviour is governed by external reinforcement. So called "radical behaviourists" such as Skinner argue that reinforcement is all that we need to explain and predict behaviour. On the other hand, "neo-behaviourists" argue that inner psychological processes, such as beliefs, feelings, and motives, are influenced by external reinforcement and in turn influence behaviour. Most social psychologists prefer the latter approach, in which both external events and psychological states must be studied.

The behaviourist perspective has led social psychologists to search for environmental or situational factors which influence behaviour, and behaviourism forms the basis of a number of theories in social psychology, including the following:

(1) The *reinforcement-affect model of attraction* explains why we come to like someone by associating that person with some positive experience;

(2) Researchers have explained the influence of film and television on aggression in terms of *social modelling* theory, which states that we imitate what we see others do and learn by the consequences of what they do.

(3) *Social exchange theory* explains interactions and relationships in terms of the social reinforcements (e.g., affection, respect, power) which people provide for each other.

However, many theorists have felt that the behaviourists have exaggerated the degree to which we are passive recipients of external influences, arguing that we also act to interpret and change our environment. According to this view, it is also important to look within individuals, particularly at their *cognitive processes*, in order to understand behaviour. The cognitive perspective gained recognition with the early work on perception by the Gestalt psychologists, and was used early in the development of social psychology by Kurt Lewin (1951) in his *field theory*. Lewin argued that the "environment" which influences human actions is *not* a set of physical characteristics and events *per se*, but the "life space" of individuals — the environment in the context of what it means to them. People actively construct or make sense of the situations in which they find themselves. Lewin suggested an example from his own combat experience in World War I: A physical landscape might consist of hills and valleys, trees, bushes and open spaces. However, this landscape would be a very different environment to soldiers in combat than to friends on a picnic, and would influence their behaviour in different ways.

Many contemporary theories in social psychology have developed within the cognitive perspective:

(1) *Social comparison theory* is based on the premise that we have a need to evaluate ourselves. Since no one is grading us on our daily activities, we often compare our actions, beliefs or abilities with other people in order to see how well we are doing or if we are "right."

(2) The *theory of cognitive dissonance* is based on the assumption that we need to feel consistent in our attitudes and actions, and are often motivated to change in order to feel consistent.

(3) *Attribution theories* are concerned with how we explain why people act as they do, how we "make sense" of how people behave in everyday life.

While the behaviourist and cognitive perspectives are dominant in social psychology, there are other influences to be considered. *Biological theories* cannot be ignored in understanding human altruism, aggression, and intimacy. *Psychoanalytical concepts* have been applied in theories of prejudice and aggression. *Role theory* has influenced our understanding of social interaction and relationships, as well as what it means to be male or female, sick, or healthy.

Empirical research in social psychology

In discussing the forms of data collection used in the evaluation of hypotheses in social psychology, it is important to understand both what it means to *measure* something and how to *analyze* measurements that are made (see Box 2-3).

We usually take measurement for granted. We buy a litre of milk or a kilogram of beef, we drive for 100 kilometres, and we know that water boils at 100 degrees Celsius (at sea level). Yet, living in Canada, we are well aware of the arbitrariness of measurement units. For example, we use both pounds and kilograms in stores, and when we cross the border into the United States, we must buy gasoline in gallons instead of in litres and measure our speed in miles per hour instead of kilometres per hour. And before we switched to the metric system, anyone who drove from Canada to the United States suddenly found that the capacity of the automobile gas tank had "expanded," for the American gallon is only about 83 percent of the volume of the Imperial gallon, which was used in Canada at that time.

Measurement is as important in social psychology as it is in any other scientific research. However, no psychological attribute can ever be directly observed; it must be inferred on the basis of its presumed manifestation through behaviour. Sometimes

B·O·X   2-3

THE ARBITRARINESS OF MEASUREMENT UNITS

Before the rise of modern science, measurement was a matter of choosing an arbitrary unit as a standard to guide construction and trade. For example, the length of a monarch's foot might be chosen as a unit of measurement; provided that particular length were recorded in some way so that copies of a "foot ruler" could be made, all would go well. However, when arbitrary standards are used, a hodge-podge of units bearing little logical relationship to one another can result.

This is exactly what happened with the British system of measurements. Consider linear distance, for example. There are four inches to a hand (used principally in the measurement of the height of horses), 12 inches to a foot, three feet to a yard, six feet to a fathom (originally based on the length of someone's outstretched arms), 66 feet to a surveyor's chain, 100 feet to an engineer's chain, 220 yards to a furlong, 5280 feet to a "statute" mile, 6080 feet to a "nautical" mile, and 6076.1155 feet to an "international nautical mile."

Whatever the system, every unit of measurement must be physically recorded somewhere so that other measuring instruments can be calibrated against it. For instance, the basic unit of length in the metric system, the metre, was originally defined as 1/10 000 000 of the distance between the equator and the north or south poles. Because it was not possible to accurately measure that distance, the metre was eventually redefined. The best estimate of the theoretical length of the metre, described above, was marked off by two scratches on a bar of a platinum-iridium alloy kept safely in a Paris suburb. Everyone in the world could calibrate their metre sticks against this common international standard.

For many years, this bar provided the only definition of the metre. However, as science progressed, an even more precise definition of the metre was required, as it became necessary to measure microscopic distances. Therefore, by international convention, the metre is now defined as 1 650 763.73 wavelengths in vacuum of the orange-red line of krypton-86's spectrum.

this is easy; usually it is difficult. For example, if we are studying memory, it is easy enough to observe that of a list of 20 paired associates, a subject correctly recalled ten. Yet, it is not nearly so simple to "count" how much conformity there was, or how much aggression occurred, or how altruistically a subject responded. The fact of the matter is that social psychologists deal almost exclusively in *hypothetical constructs*, that is, in variables which are presumed to exist and which can be used to explain other behaviours or outcomes. Thus, if we observe that an individual eschews gambling, never buys lottery tickets, abhors alcohol, and does not smoke, we might start to presume that this person's attitude structure is of a specific kind; we might predict that he would also be opposed to extramarital sex. However, we are guessing that something called an attitude exists and accounts for the stability of his behaviour across a variety of situations.

If attitudes exist, how do we measure them? How can we measure altruism? Or aggression? In order to be able to define a hypothetical construct in a quantifiable way, we employ *operational definitions* (the "rules of correspondence" of the formal scientific model discussed earlier), that is, we define the construct in terms of the operation we use to measure it. Thus, in one experiment, aggression may be defined and measured in terms of how many electrical shocks one subject believes he or she is administering to another subject. In another experiment, aggression might be operationally defined in quite a different manner, for example, the number of kicks a child delivers to an inflated doll. There may or may not be much correspondence between the construct as it is operationally defined and the construct as we tend to view it ordinarily.

What is a good measure? Whenever we conduct empirical research, we must be concerned with the *reliability* and *validity* of the measuring instrument as well as with the instrument's effect on what is being measured (*reactivity*). Each of these will be addressed in turn.

(1) *Reliability*. Reliability refers to the degree to which a measuring instrument yields the same measurement when used more than once to measure some unchanging object or trait or behaviour. If we used a foot ruler made of elastic to measure the length of a table, and obtained three substantially different results on three different measurements, we would consider the ruler unreliable. Similarly, if we administered an attitude scale to the same subjects on two different occasions and found that the subjects' scores had changed considerably from the first testing to the second, even though we had reason to believe that the attitudes themselves had not changed, we would have no way of knowing which, if either, set of scores was more accurate, and we would again conclude that our measure is unreliable.

(2) *Validity*. While we can take for granted that a foot ruler measures distance, can we be equally sure that an attitude scale measures attitudes? If the questions on a questionnaire pertain to beliefs, how can we be sure that the subject's responses really reflect his or her underlying beliefs? To the extent that there is a correspondence between the scale scores and the supposed belief or trait of interest, we would say that the scale possesses validity. While it is usually straightforward to establish the reliability of a measuring instrument, it is much more difficult to establish validity. Yet, if our measuring instruments are lacking in validity, we measure in vain, only deceiving ourselves.

(3) *Reactivity*. Measurement can be either *reactive* or *non-reactive*. A reactive measure is one which may itself influence the behaviour that we are interested in studying. Administering a questionnaire is a reactive approach because the subject may answer differently to formal questioning than he or she would if the questions were asked

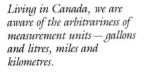

Living in Canada, we are aware of the arbitrariness of measurement units — gallons and litres, miles and kilometres.

UNOBTRUSIVE MEASURES

The greatest risk to validity in any psychological study arises from the subject's perception that he or she is being observed or assessed. Whether as a result of trying to be seen in the best possible light, or trying to "help" the experimenter, or simply as a result of self-consciousness, the subject's behaviour may be contrived, i.e., not what it would be under ordinary circumstances.

In some cases, *unobtrusive*, or *non-reactive*, measures can be used in social psychological research. Such measures are used without subjects being aware of them. Thus they will display no reaction to the measurement process itself. Archival research is obviously non-reactive since the subjects are never directly contacted, and may be long dead in some cases! By monitoring variations in the consumption of water in a city, and keeping track of when commercials appear on various television channels, it is possible (provided there are not too many channels) to estimate the proportion of the population that is watching a given program: this hypothesis is based on the assumption that people are more likely to go to the bathroom and flush the toilet and

use the sink during commercials. There are a number of other unobtrusive measures—some quite accurate—which can be used (Webb, Campbell, Schwartz and Sechrest, 1966), among which are the following:

(1) *Erosion measures*. An erosion measure is a measure of selective wear on some material. For example, by assessing the degree to which various library books have become worn, we could assess the interest shown in them by the community. Webb *et al.* (1966) give the example of how people at the Chicago Museum of Science and Industry assessed the popularity of various psychology exhibits by comparing how often the floor tiles around various displays had to be replaced. In this case, although erosion was the measure, the rate of erosion was obtained by checking the records of the museum's maintenance department.

(2) *Accretion measures*. In this case, the data come from some physical trace which reflects behaviour. Some studies using accretion measures have assessed the readership of advertisements by examining the number of different fingerprints on magazine pages.

by a friend over a beer. In other words, the questionnaire itself influences the behaviour (the subject's responses) that it is supposed to measure. A non-reactive measure, on the other hand, is one which cannot affect the behaviour under study (Webb, Campbell, Schwartz, Sechrest and Grove, 1981). Asking people how much alcohol they consume is a reactive procedure: they may be likely to be less than straightforward in their reply. Counting how many liquor bottles people throw away in their garbage is a non-reactive one, so long as they are unaware that we are spying on their garbage. The measure does not and cannot affect their behaviour (see Box 2-4).

Methods of empirical research

Social psychological research methods can be divided into two types: (1) *non-experimental* methods, and (2) *experimental* methods. If a *non-experimental method* is used, no effort is made to influence the conditions under which the subjects respond. Correlation (a statistical measure of the degree to which two variables "go together") is generally a central feature of data analysis in this type of research. For example, a researcher might wish to study the relationship between intelligence, as represented

Radio dial settings have been employed to assess audiences for various radio stations, using auto mechanics as the data gatherers (Webb *et al.*, 1966). A psychologist studying differences between obese and non-obese people in anxiety-arousing situations may provide measured amounts of snack foods to students who believe they are taking part in a study measuring the social acceptability of various commercial films. The amount of food left uneaten would provide a direct and unobtrusive measure of food consumed.

(3) *Petition-signing and volunteering.* Asking people to volunteer or to sign a petition can provide a useful measure of their attitudes without letting on that they are involved in a psychological study. Let's take as an example a study of prosocial behaviour in which students, after having been in an experiment in which they experienced either "success" or "failure," are approached shortly after leaving the laboratory and asked to participate in an emergency blood drive. The number of subjects who go and donate blood provides an unobtrusive measure of prosocial behaviour. If more of the subjects who experienced success in the experiment rather than failure give blood, such an outcome would support the hypothesis that a positive mood promotes prosocial behaviour.

Similarly, a researcher could randomly divide a class of students into two parts and show each part of the class one of two films, one which included scenes of sexual violence, and one with the scenes omitted. Subsequently, students could be asked to sign a petition calling for a return to capital punishment or a ban on wet T-shirt contests. By comparing the number of students from each of the two conditions who signed the petition, the researcher would have a measure of the effects of witnessing sexual aggression.

There are many other possible unobtrusive measures which are useful to psychologists. For example, Milgram (1969) assessed community attitudes towards various groups by means of his "lost letter" technique. He dropped stamped envelopes addressed to various groups, all bearing his address, and simply looked at the return rate as a function of the group name. Suppose we wished to examine attitudes toward immigrants at a university and in a factory. We might drop envelopes addressed to the "Committee to encourage immigration" and the "Committee against immigration" and compare the response rates as a function of location. Of course, we would have to be careful not to drop so many letters that it would become apparent that something unusual was occurring.

by an IQ score, and aggressiveness. By using some measure of aggressiveness and by obtaining an aggressiveness score and an IQ score for each of a collection of subjects, the researcher can determine whether people with high IQs tend to be more or less aggressive than people with low IQs. In other words, the researcher will assess the degree to which the two variables are correlated. However, such data will give no clue about whether or not one variable "causes" the other.

Using the *experimental method*, the researcher deliberately assigns subjects randomly to two (or more) groups and applies a treatment variable (*independent* variable) to one group and not the other. Then the researcher measures the effect of the treatment by comparing the two groups with regard to some behavioural variable of interest (*dependent* variable), while excluding other factors (*extraneous* variables) which might interfere with the outcome. For example, suppose the researcher is interested in the effects of sleep deprivation on aggression. Subjects in one group might be asked to go without sleep for 24 hours, while subjects in the other would be allowed their usual amount of sleep. In this case, amount of sleep is the *independent variable* manipulated by the researcher. Subsequently, the subjects could be assessed for the amount of aggression displayed — the *dependent variable*. If those who went without sleep were generally found to be more aggressive than those in the other group, the researcher could conclude that the lack of sleep caused the greater aggressiveness, since the two groups of subjects were otherwise treated the same. However, this conclusion would be invalidated if there were *extraneous variables* involved. These are influences (often referred to as "artifacts") which the researcher did not plan for, but which could be responsible for the observed difference in aggression between the two groups. Suppose, for example, that (unbeknownst to the researcher) the sleep-deprived subjects sat up all night watching violent films. In this case, it could be the effect of the movie viewing which produced the greater aggressiveness, rather than the lack of sleep.

Both non-experimental and experimental methods are characterized by several different approaches to data collection. These are now described.

Non-experimental methods

The social psychologist, like the ordinary layperson, obtains information about the world through direct observation. The difference between the two is that while the layperson depends on his or her direct experience, the social psychologist relies upon systematic observation under conditions allowing for the control of variables which might otherwise interfere with such observation. Following a standardized scoring system and using observers who are unaware of the researcher's hypotheses are only two of several ways that systematic observation can reduce the biases that plague casual observation.

Suppose, for instance, that a female high school student notices that the male students who "leer" the most (defined in terms of how often the student whistles at girls) in the hallway or yard also happen to be those whom she has observed keeping pin-ups inside their school lockers. She may conclude that it is the availability of such photographs that leads to a lessening of respect for women.

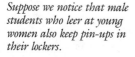

Suppose we notice that male students who leer at young women also keep pin-ups in their lockers.

The social psychologist would not accept such a conclusion out of hand. He or she would want to know: Do the males who do *not* leer also not read sex magazines? Perhaps all male students have sex magazines, but only a few clip out photos for their locker doors. Perhaps the observing student evaluates whether or not someone leers *after* she is aware of the pin-ups. Irritated by the pin-up, she perhaps judges the male to be leering even when he is not. Thus the social psychologist would want to collect data in a way that eliminates such biases. Moreover, it would be important to establish that such an effect, if observed, holds for more than that particular female student and for those particular males.

How might we go about studying this question?

The archival approach We might start by examining existing data to see if they support the hypothesis that sexually oriented magazines lead to antisocial behaviour towards women. We could compare, for example, rates of crime towards women in liberal countries with no censorship laws with those in conservative and censorial nations. Alternatively, we might examine data related to events which rarely occur and which could never be captured in the laboratory: for example, we might look at the rate of violence towards women for a period of time prior to and a period of time subsequent to changes in the law which led to wider availability of sexually oriented materials.

Such an approach, in which the data have been collected by someone other than the experimenter, for some purpose other than that of the experimenter, is referred to as an *archival* approach. While it provides the benefit of allowing the exploration of an hypothesis using data from many periods of history and many places, and while it also has the advantage of being non-reactive (the researcher cannot interfere with or influence the behaviour that was the basis for the data), it has some severe limitations. In this example, we would have no way of knowing whether or not the "liberal" countries differed in other crucial respects from the more conservative ones. We would have no way of knowing whether reporting of crimes was as diligent in the two countries. Furthermore, even if we could forget about such problems, and even if we did discover that the rate of violent sexual crime was higher in countries with liberal laws on pornography, we could not simply assume that pornography caused sexual violence. For one thing, we would be unlikely to suspect that every individual who consumed pornography was likely to become a criminal. For another, it may be that some third variable is responsible for both increased consumption of pornography and for increased sexual violence. If both are manifestations of the same process, taking away pornography would have no effect on the rate of sexual violence.

IN SUMMARY

Advantages of the archival approach:
- large populations over an expanse of time may be studied
- events which could not be studied by other means may be examined
- non-reactive

Disadvantages of the archival approach:
- researcher has no control over the dependent variable to be studied
- data may be missing or inconsistent in its presentation
- researcher cannot draw conclusions about whether or not there is a causal relationship between variables

Case studies   The case study is an in-depth investigation and analysis of a single instance of a phenomenon of interest. Such a study, which might focus on a single individual, group of people, or specific event, is often the only way of studying a phenomenon which is rare and which cannot be duplicated in the laboratory. For example, in an examination of the effects of sexual literature on behaviour towards women, the case study approach might involve in-depth interviews with incarcerated sexual offenders, examining in detail the role played by sexually oriented literature.

The advantage of the case study approach is that it allows for intensive investigation of a phenomenon in a specific instance and lets us follow the development of the phenomenon over time. Case studies are often excellent starting points for research in that they can generate research hypotheses which can then be explored in more detail by other means.

On the other hand, case studies have several drawbacks. First, the case we study is unlikely to be typical of *all* such cases, and we will have no way of knowing how much of the information we gather is idiosyncratic, that is, specific only to that particular instance and not to other similar instances.

Second, the respondent's accounts may be inaccurate or distorted, remembrances may be incomplete or biased, and the subject or subjects may deliberately try to put themselves in a good light. Their concern about being evaluated, known as *evaluation apprehension*, may lead them to give responses which they consider to be socially desirable. Third, it is difficult for the researcher to exclude totally his or her own biases, both in the collection and the interpretation of data. The very choice of questions asked may be enough to bias the data. Finally, it is not possible to draw causal inferences on the basis of case study data.

IN SUMMARY

Advantages of the case study:
• in-depth investigation of a specific instance of a phenomenon possible
• useful approach in generating hypotheses

Disadvantages of the case study:
• findings may not be applicable to other instances of the phenomenon
• researcher or subject bias a problem
• conclusions about cause and effect not possible

This method involves going out and asking questions about the phenomenon of interest. For example, in an attempt to gather more information about the relationship between the availability of pornography and antisocial behaviour towards women, we could *ask* people about pornography and violence, posing questions about pornographic consumption and attitudes to rape. (Such a survey was conducted by Rosenstein and Check in 1985 when they examined the relationship between the amount of time respondents spent watching rock videos and their beliefs and behavioural inclinations with respect to sexuality and violence.) After collecting the responses, we would then be in a position to see whether or not those who report frequent consumption of pornography are also more callous about sexual crimes.

There are a variety of survey techniques. One is the *structured interview*. Using a series of questions which have carefully been chosen and listed in a specific order, the interviewer poses each question to the respondent and records the answer. Another survey technique is the *questionnaire*, in which the respondent is asked to give written

"Has there ever been a poll to discover what percentage of people are liars?"

responses to a set of printed questions. If the research involves potentially embarrassing questions, respondents may be too embarrassed to reply orally but willing to give honest answers on a written questionnaire. On the other hand, in an oral interview, the researcher has more flexibility; there is always the opportunity to seek clarification when responses are ambiguous, or to seek greater depth, when appropriate. An advantage of the questionnaire, however, is that it does not require the time and effort that must go into interviews. A large amount of data can be gathered quickly and inexpensively.

Questionnaires can be either *open-ended*, in which case the respondent can provide as detailed an answer as he or she wishes, or *closed*, in which case the respondent must choose one of several answers available on the questionnaire itself. While closed questionnaires make scoring and analysis simpler, there is always the danger that the respondent may be forced to choose a response which does not really reflect his or her position, but is only the closest to it, since none of the alternatives really apply.

The survey method is especially useful for collecting data from a large number of people and is often the only way of obtaining data about thoughts, feelings, and private behaviour not open to direct observation. However, like other methods discussed in this section, it only provides information about interrelationships among variables of interest and cannot directly establish whether or not one variable *causes* another.

Survey methods are based on self-reporting, and self-reporting can be unreliable for a number of reasons:

(1) The questions can either "lead" or confuse the respondent. Consider the question, "Is it not true that capital punishment has no effect on the murder rate?" This is difficult to answer without trying to sort out the question. Some respondents may be confused by it. The effect of more straightforward questions can be even more subtle.

(2) The interviewer's bias can easily influence both the course of the interview and the coding or recording of the data. Let us say we are interviewing students in a dormitory about their use of sexual literature. If we notice that a student's room is covered with pin-ups, we might categorize the student mentally and then fail to explore certain issues with him or her as a result of this prejudgement. Even the interviewer's tone of voice may vary depending upon his or her response to the respondent and could also bias the interview. In this respect, the questionnaire approach has one advantage: the same questions are always presented in the same manner and in the same order, without any allowance for verbal cues.

(3) The respondents may not accurately report their feelings, thoughts, or behaviours. As with case study interviews, this approach is vulnerable both to faulty memory and to evaluation apprehension. After all, suppose you were stopped on the street-corner and asked: "How many times a week do you look at pornographic magazines?" Are you likely to answer with total candour, if indeed you read such magazines regularly?

Although the responses generated through the survey method are all "self-reports" about the phenomenon of interest, the researcher may disguise the purpose of the survey by asking questions that do not seem to bear directly on the respondent. Instead of asking about personal attitudes towards sexual crimes, for example, the researcher might ask the respondent to rank a number of crimes, including sexual offences, in order of the general public's view of their relative severity. In this way, no information about the respondent's own behaviour is directly elicited, and the problem of obtaining an accurate answer is minimized.

(4) People tend to respond to questions in "sets" or in a systematically biased manner: some people tend to give answers that are always "middle of the road" while others may lean towards extreme responses. Some even give "yes" responses or "no" responses all too frequently, regardless of the questions. (Such people have been referred to as "yea-sayers" and "nay-sayers" respectively). For example, if we asked such questions as "Are you in favour of greater restrictions on the availability of sexually oriented literature?" and "Are you opposed to any form of censorship?", the yea-sayer would answer "yes" to both, making the bias obvious. We can minimize this problem by careful design of the question series.

A critical step in using the survey method is choosing a sample. Who is going to answer our questionnaire or take part in our interview? If we are simply interested in the responses of a particular classroom of students, there is no problem. But if the goal is to generalize from our sample to a much larger population, then we must be very careful about how representative the sample is of the larger group. Suppose, for example, we were to have our questionnaire on pornography printed in a magazine with the request that readers fill it out and mail it to us. We might gather a great many responses this way, but would it allow us a reasonable basis for drawing conclusions? The answer is, definitely not. Depending on what magazine is used, we are likely to get a sample of society that is only representative of one group of people. The attitudes of the average *Playboy* reader may be very different from those of the average reader of *Maclean's*. Moreover, most magazine readers will not bother to fill out and return the questionnaire, which means that those who *do* might be in some way unrepresentative even of the readership of that magazine. They may be people who are particularly opposed to or particularly in favour of pornography. Thus, it is extremely important to take great care to select a sample which is likely to be representative of the population of interest.

IN SUMMARY

Advantages of the survey technique:
• data can be collected about a wide range of beliefs, thoughts, and behaviours which might be inaccessible through other methods
• data can be collected easily and cheaply

Disadvantages of the survey technique:
• many sources of potential bias, including the questionnaire itself, the researcher, the respondents, and the sampling technique
• conclusions about cause and effect not possible

Field study The field study involves direct observation of a group of people in a natural setting. Data may be recorded by means of audiotape or film, or by manually recording various behaviours by shorthand (and so "coding" behaviours of interest). A field study can take one of two forms: either the observer remains aloof and simply observes, or he or she becomes a *participant* observer, living with the group in as unobtrusive a way as possible. Participant observation is the traditional approach of the anthropologist who lives among the people he or she wishes to study, usually for periods of a year or more.

However, we are never sure just how typical is the situation we are studying. And it is difficult to remain unbiased, working in close proximity with the people of interest over a considerable period of time. We may come to sympathize with them and adopt their point of view, thus losing objectivity. Or the people under observation may change temporarily or permanently, either as a result of knowing they are under study, or as a result of the influence of the participant observer's ideas and personality. Another problem, of course, is that one cannot say very much about causality based on this type of experience. For example, if the researcher observes that people who smoke cigarettes are more nervous in some way, it is not possible to conclude either that smoking causes nervousness or vice versa.

IN SUMMARY

Advantage of the field study:
• spontaneously occurring behaviours may be observed in a natural environment

Disadvantages of the field study:
• generalizability to other situations may be poor
• researcher bias is a problem
• researcher's behaviour can itself influence the behaviours observed
• conclusions about cause and effect not possible

Non-experimental methods are particularly useful for gathering information about what goes on in real-life situations. However, such information, while extremely important for generating hypotheses to guide further research, can offer a distorted picture of reality, owing to the biases of both the researcher and the respondents. The most serious shortcoming of the non-experimental methods is their inability to demonstrate causal relationships among variables of interest.

Experimental methods

It was because of the need to draw causal inferences about how variables influence one another that experimental methods came into being. As we have discussed earlier, an experiment involves at least two groups of subjects typically chosen at random from a population of interest. One is referred to as the control group, while the other is referred to as the experimental group. The two groups are treated identically except with respect to the independent variable.

The comparison of an experimental condition with a control condition is a relatively recent development in the history of science, one which can be traced to John Stuart Mill's *A system of logic* (1973/1843). The notion of equating experimental and control groups by randomly assigning subjects to groups before applying the independent variable came about only in the twentieth century through the work of R.A. Fisher (Einhorn and Hogarth, 1978).

Thus, if the two groups are identical with respect to the measures of interest at the beginning of the experiment, and if nothing is done to subjects in one group, while the experimental treatment or manipulation is applied to the other, then we can infer that any differences between the two groups at the end of the experiment are due to the manipulation. Of course, it is essential to exclude any other influences ("extraneous variables" or "artifacts") which might lead to effects improperly attributed to the independent variable.

Using the example of "leering" discussed earlier, were it not for both practical and ethical considerations, we could begin with male high school students who had never seen a sex magazine, divide the students into two groups, make sex magazines avail-

B · O · X   2 - 5

THE IMPORTANCE OF CONTROLS

Control groups are essential to the evaluation of causal relationships, as this anecdote about the assessment of surgical procedures, recounted by a physician, makes clear: "One day when I was a junior medical student, a very important Boston surgeon visited the school and delivered a great treatise on a large number of patients who had undergone successful operations for vascular reconstruction. At the end of the lecture, a young student at the back of the room timidly asked, 'Do you have any controls?' Well, the great surgeon drew himself up to his full height, hit the desk, and said, 'Do you mean did I not operate on half of the patients?' The hall grew very quiet then. The voice at the back of the room very hesitantly replied, 'Yes, that's what I had in mind.' Then the visitor's fist really came down as he thundered, 'Of course not. That would have doomed half of them to their death.' God, it was quiet then, and one could scarcely hear the small voice ask, 'Which half?' "

able to the subjects in the experimental group, and withhold them from subjects in the control group. After a suitable period of time, we could administer our "leeringness" scale. If we found that the experimental group scored more highly than the control group, we could infer that the availability of the sex magazines was responsible, since the two groups were otherwise undifferentiated.

Three diffferent types of experimental methods are discussed in the pages that follow: laboratory experiments, field experiments, and quasi-experiments.

The laboratory experiment   Most social psychological experiments are conducted in a laboratory setting. Apart from the obvious convenience, there are compelling reasons to bring behaviour into the laboratory for careful scrutiny. First, it is very difficult to carry out experiments in a natural setting for it is not always possible to eliminate all extraneous variables, and sometimes it is difficult even to foresee what the potential sources of such variables might be. Second, since social behaviour is complex, it is usually necessary to reduce it to its component parts and study each of them in turn in order to understand the ways in which several variables interact to determine behaviour.

However, there are also a number of drawbacks to the laboratory experiment. Although the experiment seems straightforward enough, it is actually complex, for there are a number of important considerations which we must take into account (some of which apply not just to laboratory experiments but to experiments in general) to avoid being misled by the results:

(1) *Randomization.*   Experimental research, unlike survey research, is not usually concerned with judging the population on the basis of the sample. Rather, random sampling is used to generate two or more groups that are presumed to be the same with regard to the characteristic being measured so that later, we can arrive at a judgment about whether an independent variable led to changes in a dependent variable (Berkowitz and Donnerstein, 1982). Indeed, the notion that the various samples are undifferentiated prior to the treatment is crucial to the logic of the experiment. Therefore, when we form our groups, we want to be reasonably sure that there is no difference between them with respect to any important variable. If we had a great deal of time and a very large subject pool, we might evaluate each subject on a large number of potentially relevant variables and then assign subjects to groups in such a way that the groups are more or less the same with regard to these variables. This technique is called *matching* and is used only infrequently due to the time, effort, and difficulty involved. Most of the time, we assign our subjects at random, using some randomizing procedure such as random number tables or rolls of dice. Most of the time, this is a satisfactory method. The problem is that we are not always aware of those times when it is *not* satisfactory. If we have 20 subjects and we assign them randomly to two groups and find that one group is almost entirely female and the other almost entirely male, we may be unwilling to proceed if we think gender is a relevant variable. Suppose then that we reassign subjects in some manner such that half the men and half the women go into each group. Perhaps then we notice that most of one group is composed of arts students, while most of the other group is made up of science students. If this is also a relevant consideration, we would be unwilling to proceed because we know that if the two groups vary with regard to some variable at the end of the experiment, the difference could be due to this distinction.

B · O · X   2 - 6

THE HAWTHORNE EFFECT

The "Hawthorne effect" takes its name from the Western Electric Hawthorne plant in Cicero, Illinois, where a study examined the effects of fatigue and boredom on the productivity of assembly-line workers (Mayo, 1933). It was discovered that when workers were given coffee breaks, productivity increased; when lighting was improved, productivity increased; when the working hours were shortened, productivity increased. It seemed that any change, including a subsequent lengthening of the work day and a decrease in lighting also increased productivity.

A control group, which was not exposed to these changes, *also* increased its productivity. It was concluded that the simple fact of being subjects in a study led to the increases in productivity. This type of phenomenon is now known as the "Hawthorne effect."

Ironically, the original study was so poorly done that the observed results were likely due to artifact and confounding; the Hawthorne effect probably did not occur at Hawthorne! (Rice, 1982)

Though random assignment does not allow us to rule out such differences, it *minimizes* the likelihood of their occurrence. Furthermore, when we apply statistical analysis to our results, the techniques take into account the possibility that the differences we observed could have arisen by chance at the time of the assignment into groups.

(2) *Extraneous variables.* As we have noted earlier, sometimes the variation in the dependent variable, which *seems* to be due to the manipulation of the independent variable, may actually be due to some other extraneous variable which we have failed to exclude. When it seems impossible to discriminate between the effects of the independent variable and those of another variable, the independent variable and the other, extraneous, variable are said to be *confounded*, or that the results were due to an artifact. Some major sources of artifact are discussed in the sections that follow (see also Box 2-6).

(3) *Experimenter effects.* The experimenter, knowing the hypothesis under study, can unintentionally influence the subjects to act in a way that confirms his or her hypothesis (Rosenthal, 1966). Suppose, for example, we have randomly divided subjects into two groups. One group, the experimental group, is shown pornographic films, while the other is shown travel films. Suppose that our hypothesis is that watching pornographic films generates exploitative attitudes toward women and that we intend to measure these attitudes by rating the subject's behaviour toward a female confederate (i.e., a person who, unbeknownst to the subject, is the experimenter's assistant and who behaves in a predetermined manner toward the subject). In judging whether or not a certain "exploitative" behaviour has occurred, we may be more likely to judge in the affirmative when it is known that the subject in question saw the pornographic film. Or we may subtly and unintentionally give cues to the subjects in the experimental group indicating that we expect them to behave poorly towards women.

This is the reason for using *blind* and *double-blind* techniques. When the subjects are unaware which group they belong to (they are "blind"), they cannot act to sup-

Is it medication or placebo?

port the experimenter's hypothesis even if they know what it is. When the experimenter who interacts with the subjects is also unaware of the subjects' group (the "double-blind" situation), then he or she cannot distinguish between subjects based on whether they are in the experimental or control group.

A control group must always be treated in exactly the same manner as the experimental group except for the treatment itself — whether the experiment is being conducted by social psychologists or scientists in other fields. In drug efficacy studies, for instance, the control group receives an apparent dose of medication (actually a neutral substance with no pharmacological effect). A sugar pill believed to be medicine can lead to the alleviation of symptomatology, and researchers must be able to distinguish between such an effect and the actual pharmacological effect of the drug being tested.

Similarly, in our experiment on the effect of pornographic movies, we expose both the experimental and control groups to films. If we expose the treatment (experimental) group to seven hours of sexually explicit films and don't show the control group any films at all, then whatever effects we observe might in principle be due to the experimental subjects having watched *films*, rather than to the content of the films. They may feel more "important" or more "professional" than the other subjects since they are being allowed to view highly restricted films in a "scientific" experiment. Or perhaps they have become so frustrated by sitting in one spot for seven hours that they have become irritable, and this irritability has been translated into hostility by the time the dependent variable can be evaluated.

(4) *Subject effects.* There are two important ways that artifact can be introduced into an experiment by the subjects. The first of these concerns the ability of the subject to guess or infer the hypothesis being studied. The term "demand characteristics" was coined by Martin Orne (1962) to describe characteristics of the experimental situation that seem to cry out for, or "demand," a certain response. A demand characteristic is any cue which gives the subject an idea, correct or incorrect, about the hypothesis under investigation. Consequently, the helpful or compliant subject may well respond in a manner which supports the perceived hypothesis, rather than in a spontaneous manner (Adair, 1973).

A second potential source of artifact is one we first encountered in our earlier discussion of non-experimental methods, that of *evaluation apprehension and social desirability*. As subjects try to look good in the eyes of the experimenter, whom they may view as judging them, they may tailor their reactions to the experiment accordingly (Rosenberg, 1969).

It is important to recognize that behaviour in the laboratory is also "real" behaviour, for the psychological experiment is, of itself, a unique social psychological situation in which people assume the role of subjects being directed by an experimenter; these directions often generate suspicion since subjects cannot know for certain what is being studied or observed. More understanding of the subject's behaviour may be gained by viewing it as a natural reaction to the experimental situation rather than indicative of artifact-generating bias (Adair and Spinner, 1983).

Nonetheless, most research in social psychology regarding the very "social psychology" of experiments has been limited to the study of artifact, that is, the degree to which the subject acts not in a natural way but plays a role influenced by demand characteristics (Adair, 1973). Weber and Cook (1972) have suggested on the basis of their literature review that there is not just one subject role, but as many as four possible roles which a subject can assume. They have labelled these roles: *faithful* (the subject attempts to ignore his or her suspicions about the experiment); *cooperative* (the subject behaves in a manner that supports what he or she believes to be the experimenter's hypothesis); *negative* (the subject deliberately behaves in a manner which contradicts the perceived hypothesis); and *apprehensive* (the subject simply attempts to present him or herself in the best possible light). However, empirical support for the existence of these four roles has not emerged (Spinner, Adair, and Barnes, 1977) and, in any case, the apprehensive role would produce behaviour that is difficult to distinguish from that of the other three roles (Adair and Schachter, 1972; Spinner *et al.*, 1977).

The focus on roles has not really led to any improvement in our understanding of subject behaviour in the experiment. Perhaps it is time to abandon the idea that the subject plays a specific, unchanging, and unidimensional role upon entering the laboratory (Adair and Spinner, 1983).

(5) *Generalizability*. Much concern has been expressed over the narrowness and lack of realism of many social psychological experiments. Perhaps, the criticism goes, the behaviour observed in the laboratory has little or nothing to do with what occurs in the "real world." The debate about this issue has raged for some time now, and will no doubt continue. However, in defense of the laboratory experiment, we must be careful to distinguish between *mundane realism*, defined as the realism subjects encounter in a laboratory experiment set up to resemble some situation in the outside world, and *experimental realism*, defined as the extent to which the experimental situation "grabs" subjects and involves them so that they react naturally to the situation rather than as they might think appropriate to the laboratory situation (Aronson and Carlsmith, 1968).

While experimental realism is essential, mundane realism is less important than it might at first appear, for it in no way ensures that the subjects are really involved in the experimental situation (Carlsmith, Ellsworth, and Aronson, 1976). What is most important is the *meaning* of what is happening to the subjects and not the external appearances (Berkowitz and Donnerstein, 1982). Thus, in a study of aggressiveness, if a subject really believes that he or she is causing pain to another subject, then the results of such a study should generalize to other situations where subjects have a similar belief, quite apart from how contrived is the experimental situation.

Experimental and mundane realism are related in meaning to *external validity* and *internal validity* (Campbell and Stanley, 1963); these terms are in more general use than are the two types of realism throughout social psychology. External validity refers to the degree to which the behaviour observed in the laboratory corresponds to "real" behaviour in the outside world. Internal validity, on the other hand, refers to the degree to which changes in dependent variables have been brought about as a result of changes in independent variables rather than by some uncontrolled extraneous variable. If an experimenter compares the aggressiveness of subjects in each of two groups, one of which has viewed a violent film, the other, a nature documentary, then internal validity in this case would refer to the degree to which observed differences in aggressiveness are actually due to the effects of the independent variable (type of film). Suppose that all the subjects who viewed the nature film had a 20 minute nap while those who viewed the violent film were kept awake by the film. Although this is a somewhat silly example, it points out that differences in aggressiveness observed after the film could, in principle, be due to the fact that one group is more rested than the other. Such an extraneous influence, to the extent that it actually affected the observed variation in the dependent variable, would decrease internal validity. Obviously, then, before worrying about external validity, it is essential that internal validity be satisfactory; otherwise, we can have no confidence in the results of our research.

Even when external validity is high, and we can generalize from our laboratory situation to life outside the laboratory, it is important to remember that we cannot automatically assume that our research findings apply beyond the culture and subculture from which the subjects were drawn (see Box 2-7). *Cross-cultural research*, in which comparisons are made by running experiments with subjects from two or more different subcultures or societies, is important not only for isolating differences among cultures, but also for establishing the generality of human social behaviours.

IN SUMMARY

Advantages of the laboratory experiment:
- high degree of control over extraneous variables
- complex situations and behaviours can be broken down into smaller units
- cause and effect relationships among variables can be established

Disadvantages of the laboratory experiment:
- not all variables amenable to manipulation in the laboratory setting
- experimenter effects, evaluation apprehension, and demand characteristics (bias) a problem
- difficulty of generalizing results from laboratory to real world

B · O · X   2 - 7

CAN WE GENERALIZE ACROSS CULTURES?

Social psychology has been justifiably criticized for biased sampling in research. University students are the most available and, therefore, typical subjects in social psychological experiments. And because most social psychology research has been conducted in the United States, it follows that most experiments have been carried out on U.S. college students. Yet there is no particular reason to assume that such subjects are representative of people in general everywhere. The findings of any experiment are much more convincing if they can be replicated in diverse populations.

Thus the case can be made for cross-cultural research in which social psychological experiments are carried out in a number of different cultures (Triandis and Brislin, 1980). Such studies often involve close collaboration among social psychologists of many

nations. In some cases, social psychologists have repeated experiments which were originally designed and carried out elsewhere, usually in the United States (Rodrigues, 1983). While such research is not restricted by a narrow sample base, there are problems to consider (Berry, 1978).

Research methods may be difficult to adapt. Verbal instructions, interviews, or questionnaires must be translated into other languages, and the translations must be accurate and equivalent in the nuances of meaning. It may be troublesome or impossible to find equivalents in several languages of slang, idioms, or expressions such as "hassle," "once bitten, twice shy," or "on-line." References to famous personalities or events in one society may be meaningless or not equivalent to students of other societies. For example, a widely-used IQ test developed in the United States asks students to name the first president of the United States. In adapting this test for Canadians, we cannot assume that Canadians are equally familiar with George Washington, or even that Sir John A. Macdonald, the first prime minister, is equally familiar to Canadians as is Washington to Americans.

Situations may also have different meanings in different cultures, confounding the experimental results. To be a subject in a psychology experiment may, in itself, be a more profound or unusual experience to an Indian or African than to a North American student because discussion of human relationships has permeated the consciousness of North America more than it has some Eastern countries. Experimental manipulations may not represent the same processes in different cultures; for example, being confronted with a group opinion contrary to our own may be experienced as strong social pressure to conform in one culture but not in another. Similarly, our criteria for measuring some behavioural result may not make sense in another culture. For example, our criteria for measuring a leader (e.g., he or she who speaks the most, whose ideas are most acceptable, who is selected by a group vote) may not be applicable in an Asian culture.

Research problems may also be defined differently in different cultures. Sampson (1977) has described how much of contemporary psychology has been shaped by the highly individualistic values of U.S. society. Thus American social psychologists emphasize research on many problems concerning group influences against individual initiative: why people conform, why they obey authority, why they are persuaded, why people in groups are more likely to accept wrongdoing and less likely to help in an emergency than individuals. In cultures more oriented toward group welfare and communal values, social psychologists might be more interested in why people do not conform — perhaps defining the phenomenon as "anti-solidarity behaviour." In short, it is important to understand that the researchers who ask questions and define problems are inevitably influenced by their own culture.

In the final analysis, our objective is to arrive at an understanding of human behaviour which is universal — valid across time, groups, and societies. Berry (1978) suggests that there are two approaches toward this objective, the "emic" and the "etic." The first of these refers to intensive research carried out in a given society, using the concepts and world view which characterize that society. The etic approach, on the other hand, is to study behaviour by comparing different cultures, using concepts and ideas which are, ideally, valid in different cultures. For example, "family" is a concept which is universally meaningful and valid, although the details of family life vary considerably. On the other hand, a strong sense of identification with and pride in one's own group may be seen as "emic" in the sense that it may be valued and encouraged in some multicultural societies, but seen as equivalent to prejudice in another.

Certainly, cooperative "etic" research across cultures is valuable, particularly in showing us how far our theories can be generalized. Berry argues for the development of many emic or distinctive, local, social psychologies, each studying problems as defined by that particular culture. From cross-fertilization of these emic theories, we may begin to derive a truly universal social psychology, and learn more about human nature in the process.

The field experiment One way to increase external validity (as well as mundane realism) is through the *field experiment*, an experiment run not in the laboratory but in the "real world." As in a laboratory experiment, two or more groups of subjects are formed, one a control group, and the experimenter manipulates an independent variable. Subjects in field experiments have no idea that research is being conducted or that their behaviour is being monitored. Since subjects are not aware that they are subjects, the procedure is a non-reactive one, and demand characteristics and evaluation apprehension are ruled out. "Random assignment" occurs in an automatic way in field experiments: the subjects happen to be those who at a given moment are passing a street corner or lining up at an ice cream parlour. (In choosing the locale, however, the experimenter must be sensitive to the possibility that only certain types of people frequent the area chosen for the study. Thus the results may not be generally applicable. For example, if we carried out a study in the National Arts Centre, it is likely that the subjects would be above average in income and education. A similar study carried out in a pool hall would most likely involve people who are less well-educated).

An example of a field experiment is provided by Doob and Gross (1968). They wanted to test the notion that frustration leads to aggression (the so called "frustration-aggression hypothesis" which is discussed in Chapter 9) in a natural setting. It occurred to them that traffic jams are a natural source of frustration. However, it is difficult to create a traffic jam for an experiment! Instead they examined what happened when a driver (a confederate) stalled at a traffic light. They used horn honking as a measure of aggression, and then studied a factor which might influence such aggression — the social status of the driver as reflected by the status (high or low) of the stalled car. They found, as expected, that there was more honking (i.e., "aggression") towards the low-status driver.

Despite the advantages of the field experiment with regard to external validity, it has one important shortcoming: The field situation makes it more difficult to control or eliminate extraneous variables. Whether this "trade-off" — more extraneous variables for increased external validity — is worthwhile must be evaluated carefully in advance in each situation. What would have happened in the Doob study had a police car cruised by during one of the conditions? It is difficult to control such extraneous influences and, indeed, the experimenter may not even be aware of the presence of

In choosing a locale for a field study, the experimenter should be aware that only certain types of people may frequent the area chosen for the study.

them. It is also more difficult to obtain accurate measures of the dependent variable in such real-life situations. Horn-honking is easy enough to measure if only one car is honking, but what if several are honking? Should we record the overall decibel level? How would we differentiate between the level caused by honking and that of the background noise? It is not easy to count a number of horn honks occurring at the same time, or to measure their duration.

IN SUMMARY

Advantages of the field experiment:
- non-reactive
- high external validity
- behaviour that is difficult to bring into the laboratory can be studied

Disadvantages of the field experiment:
- lack of control over extraneous variables
- greater difficulty of measuring the dependent variable in some situations

Taking advantage of real life: **The quasi-experiment**   Sometimes events in the real world (outside the laboratory) provide the opportunity to study the effects of naturally occurring changes in some social psychological variable of interest to the researcher. The researcher has no control over the independent variable, but takes advantage of some spontaneously occurring event to produce the "treatment." This approach is referred to as a *quasi-experiment*. For example, we might choose subjects at random from each of two cities, one which had experienced a rash of sexual crimes, and the other which had not. We could then measure attitudes towards pornography in the two samples. Such a study is called a *control group post-test design* since there is a kind of control group, but both groups are only measured once, after the event of interest has taken place (in this case, sexual crimes). Of course, we have no way of knowing whether any observed differences are due to the sexual crimes or due to pre-existing differences between the two groups.

Another quasi-experimental design is the *single group pre-test/post-test* design. In this case, subjects are measured before and after some event which, although not under the researcher's control, is scheduled to occur. For example, as part of a research program carried out by Joy, Kimball, and Zabrack (1977) (discussed in detail in Chapter 9), the aggressiveness of children was measured before and two years after the introduction of television to a small, remote British Columbia logging town, one of the last towns in North America to obtain television. While the results of such a study are inherently interesting, it is difficult to know what has caused the results. Was the introduction of television responsible for any observed changes in aggressiveness? Or did aggressiveness change over the years between the times of measurement for reasons having nothing to do with television? The quasi-experiment provides no answer to these questions.

IN SUMMARY

Advantage of the quasi-experiment:
- effects of powerful manipulations (introduction of television, a crime wave) which the researcher cannot *produce* can be studied

Disadvantage of the quasi-experiment:
- conclusions about cause and effect not possible

The experimental versus the correlational approach

Given that the experimental approach provides so much more control over situations than the non-experimental approach and allows us to draw causal inferences, why would we ever choose to use the non-experimental or correlational approach to studying human behaviour? The fact is that both approaches have their strengths and weaknesses. While the experimental approach allows us to test causal hypotheses, it is tied to the rigid necessity of assigning subjects to groups, manipulating an independent variable, and keeping extraneous variables at bay. As a result, we may not be able to bend important variables to our control or provide a great enough range within the experiment to illuminate important social questions. By contrast, the correlational approach allows for the study of a large number of variables at the same time.

Although the strength of the experimental method for making causal inferences is emphasized in psychology, a caution is in order. Because we infer causal relationships in an experiment, it should not be assumed that the same relationships exist outside the laboratory. In the "real world" there are many other factors which will interact with and possibly change the effects of these variables. Moreover, the experiment by its very nature directs attention to the ways in which behaviour *changes* as a result of the influence of the independent variable, but overlooks the ways in which behaviour stays the same (behavioural *stabilities*). Such stabilities are more likely to be detected in correlational studies which are *longitudinal*, that is, studies in which two or more variables are measured on the same subjects at several different points in time (Bowers, 1973). Moreover, powerful statistical techniques are emerging for the analysis of longitudinal/correlational data which allow causal inferences to be drawn, though not with the clarity obtained in the experimental setting.

Empirical research: Statistics and data analysis

Almost all social psychological research depends upon the application of statistical analysis to the data. Before any such analysis can be undertaken, however, it is important for the researcher to know about the subjects who have participated in the experiment.

Prior to 1960, social psychological research was conducted with a wide range of subjects but, since that time, research has been done primarily with university undergraduates (Sears, 1986). This is not because of a preoccupation with the species *homo*

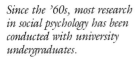

Since the '60s, most research in social psychology has been conducted with university undergraduates.

universitas. The choice of subject is a practical one: university students are available in large numbers and usually willing to participate. However, critics have often suggested that the reliance on these particular subjects jeopardizes the general applicability of our findings, for university students differ, on average, in many important ways from the general populace. It may even be that social psychology's view of human nature has been exaggerated or distorted as a result of this practice (Sears, 1986). If we want to study the general population, we should use subjects who are representative of that group.

The group of persons we wish to study is called a *population*. By studying these people or, more properly, a set of measurements of their characteristics, we can hope to discover laws of behaviour which allow us to understand and predict behaviour for our subjects and for the population as a whole. Sometimes our population is narrowly defined: we may be studying the behaviour of spouse beaters, for example. At other times, we would like to think we are studying all human beings everywhere.

Because it is not feasible to measure the effect of a variable of interest on our entire population, we must rely on *samples*, small groups of subjects assumed to be representative of the larger population of interest. How can we generate a representative sample? Suppose, for example, we wished to take a public opinion poll on some electoral question in order to predict how people would vote. There is no point, if the election is a national one, in only polling people in Val d'Or or St. John's. We need to make sure our sample includes people who are representative of people living in various regions all across the country. Thus we may wish to do *representative* sampling, so that our sample reflects in some proportionate way the various subgroups of interest. If 24 percent of the population we wish to study is employed on the farm, then about 24 percent of our sample should be made up of farm workers. If 50 percent of the population is male, then half of our sample should be male. As you can well imagine, gathering our sample may quickly become complicated!

In fact, we can best assure representativeness by using random sampling, that is, using a procedure that guarantees every member of the population an equal chance of being chosen for our sample. Yet, with very large populations, this is easier said than done. Perhaps we could choose names at random from telephone books? If there is a substantial number of people who do not own a telephone, however, (e.g., people in institutions), this would exclude them from the sample.

When certain variables are so important that we do not want to leave them to chance, it is wise to superimpose representativeness on our random sampling technique (e.g., where only sex of subject is a concern, choose women at random until they make up 50 percent of the sample).

Statistical inference Statistical analysis is a powerful research tool which helps us to make sense out of data; it is rare to see an empirical research report in psychology which does not have some recourse to it. Many undergraduate students are uncomfortable or even frightened by the prospect of having to be a "mathematician" in order to do psychological research or to understand psychological research reports. Fortunately, with a little knowledge of the purpose of statistical evaluation, we can feel comfortable interpreting statistics without thoroughly understanding their usage.

The following discussion is concerned with two kinds of statistical inference, or the testing of hypotheses by applying statistical analysis to data: inferences about whether or not two samples are different, e.g., an experimental group's scores are compared with those of a control group, and inferences about whether or not two variables vary in some systematic way with each other, e.g., aggressive behaviour in children is observed in relation to the amount of time they spend watching violence on television.

When we take random samples from a population, there is no way of knowing just how representative the sample is of that population. Suppose we were to gather together a group of one thousand people, measure their attitudes toward abortion on a ten-point scale, and obtain the *average* or *mean* attitude strength of the group (by adding together all the measures and dividing by one thousand). Now, suppose that we take, at random, samples of 20 of these measures and we calculate the average for each sample. In fact, most of these *sample means* will be pretty close to the population mean. However, a few of them will be quite different from the population mean if, by chance, we have obtained an overrepresentation of strongly pro-abortion or strongly anti-abortion people in our sample. Now, suppose that we take two samples of 20 measures, each selected at random, assuming that they are equal in terms of average attitude. Then, we give all these people something to read. Those in one group receive a treatise on the positive aspects of abortion, while those in the other group receive something of equal length to read, but on a neutral subject. Now, if we again measure the two groups' attitudes towards abortion, and find that the group reading pro-abortion material changed attitudes in a positive direction, can we infer that the reading material was responsible for the shift?

Unfortunately, we could never be sure that the two groups did not differ in the first place: The differences we observe might have been there all along. We cannot be sure whether the observed difference was due to the "treatment" or to chance.

The likelihood that the observed difference between the means of two groups occurred by chance can be calculated through statistical analysis. Although we can never eliminate entirely the possibility that the observed difference was due to chance, we can minimize the possibility of erroneous interpretation by applying a test of *statistical significance*, in other words, determining how likely it is that the observed difference between the two groups would occur *by chance alone*, 5 percent of the time or less. When we say that "$p < .05$," we mean the probability (p) that the observed results occurred by chance alone is less than .05, i.e., the results would be expected by chance less than five times out of one hundred. We then apply this test statistic to the results of our experiment. (Sometimes, a tougher criterion is applied; if we determine that $p < .01$, then we say the difference would occur by chance only once in a hundred times.)

We must always be aware of the difference between statistical significance and *psychological* significance. We can run an experiment and obtain "highly significant" results according to the criteria we have set, but the results might be meaningless psychologically if the actual difference that we observe is tiny. Unfortunately, we can often be blinded by the statistical significance. We must also take into account the *size* of the difference.

Correlation   At times, research is carried out under such conditions that it is impossible to divide subjects into two groups and compare their scores after exposing one group to a treatment variable. A researcher might wish, for example, to relate various behavioural measures to early childhood experience. In such cases, a *correlational* approach is often necessary.

As researchers of human social behaviour, we are interested in learning what factors determine behaviour. One way of gaining insight is to search for variables which seem to "go together." If we can determine that chubby people are usually jolly, we gain some insight into jolliness. If people with high IQs seem to be gregarious, we have a starting point for research into gregariousness: Why are people of lower IQ not so gregarious? Are the high-IQ people gregarious with everyone, or just with others of similar IQ? By noting that two variables go together, we can generate all sorts of possible explanations which can then be tested empirically.

The mathematical equivalent of the statement that two variables "go together" is to say they are "correlated." Suppose that we are studying the possible effects of sex magazines on behaviour, and we have obtained measures of each of two variables for each of 30 male high school students: (1) the number of occasions he looks at a sex magazine in a month ("frequency of reading"); and (2) on a scale from one to ten, the degree to which he believes women like men to whistle at them (a measure which we refer to as "leeringness"). Suppose that if we arrange the subjects' pairs of scores in increasing order with reference to frequency of reading, we find that the "leeringness" scores also increase in a more or less regular fashion. We would describe this situation by saying that these two variables are *positively correlated*. If, on the other hand, we found that as the frequency of reading increased, the "leeringness" scores tended to decrease, we would describe our results by saying that the two variables are *negatively correlated*.

Figure 2-2 illustrates that by plotting pairs of scores on a graph, it is easy to observe strong positive or negative correlations, for the data points fall in a pattern resembling a diagonal line. If, however, we cannot establish a relationship between the values of the two variables, then our data plot would show no tendency for the points to form a line (zero correlation).

If the correlation is not strong, it may be difficult to distinguish it on the graph from zero correlation. In order to describe more precisely the degree to which two variables covary, statisticians have developed the *correlation coefficient*, a number which can be of any value between -1.00 and $+1.00$. Rather than staring at a graph of data points, trying to "eyeball" or make an educated guess about the degree of rela-

FIGURE 2-2
Looking for correlation: Plots of pairs of scores

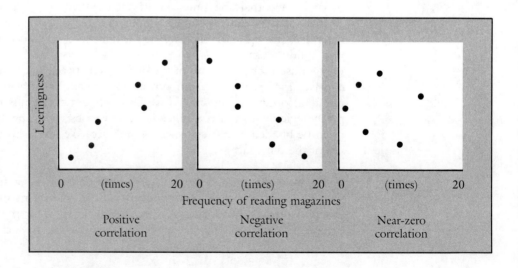

tionship between the variables, we can compute statistically this coefficient which will indicate for us both the direction and the strength of the relationship. If the coefficient has been calculated to be at or near + 1.00, we would know that as the values of one variable increase, so do the values of the other. On the other hand, a coefficient of − 1.00 would indicate that as the values of one variable increase, those of the other decrease. A coefficient of zero would indicate that there is no relationship at all between the two variables.

Statistical tests similar to those used to assess whether two means differ significantly are used to examine whether there really is a relationship between two variables when the correlation coefficient obtained on the basis of two samples is greater or less than zero. In other words, if we measure the IQs and gregariousness of a small number of people, it is unlikely that the correlation coefficient we calculate will be exactly equal to zero. In fact, it may sometimes be quite removed from zero in either direction, even when there is *no* relationship between the two variables in the population. By chance, we may have selected a number of people for whom there is a relationship between the variables, even though this relationship is not representative of the population as a whole.

Correlation and causality It is tempting to impute a causal relationship between variables that show a strong correlation. Using our original example, a strong positive correlation between frequency of reading sex magazines and "leeringness" is consistent with the hypothesis that the former causes the latter. However, it could also be that the latter causes the former: perhaps people who are high in "leeringness" are not only likely to whistle at women but also to seek out sex magazines! Or perhaps both factors are totally unrelated but covary because each is related independently to a third variable; it could be that socialization is the key and that "undersocialized" males tend to view women as objects and therefore both seek out sex magazines and show disrespect through whistling. We should not conclude, even on the basis of a strong correlation, that one of the variables is the cause of variation in the other.

ETHICAL CONSIDERATIONS IN RESEARCH

It is the researcher's responsibility to conduct research in an ethically responsible manner so that participants in the research do not suffer in any way as a result. Although every empirical approach is vulnerable to ethical compromise, the experiment, more so than the non-experimental methods, poses serious ethical problems, primarily because it uses *deception*. It is difficult to observe subjects' natural reactions in a situation when they are aware of being observed; one of the appeals of field experiments is that subjects act naturally since they do not know that they are subjects. However, if the experimenter is clever, it is often possible to disguise the real aim of the experiment to the degree that subjects react almost as though they were in a real-life situation (Elms, 1982). Between one half and three quarters of published social psychological research reports involve some element of deception (Rosnow, 1981; Gross and Fleming, 1982).

In recent years, concern has been expressed about the ethics of such deception. What if subjects approach an experiment believing that they are going to be involved in a memory study, and leave the experiment having learned that in the face of a contrived emergency they reacted with cowardice? We must ask ourselves if the experimenter has the right to foist this truth upon the unsuspecting individual who may otherwise never confront that cowardice.

Although the field experiment may appear to have fewer ethical problems, closer scrutiny proves otherwise for at least two reasons. The first reason concerns the *right to privacy*. What gives the experimenter the moral right to manipulate a person's environment and then observe and record his or her reaction? Even if anonymity is assured, is such deceit conscionable? Most of the time, such "eavesdropping" and manipulation is harmless, but how can we always know this is the case for every individual?

A second related concern in the field experiment is the possible physical consequences the experimental manipulation might have on the subject. Should the experimenter be concerned about how a confederate's behaviour in a field experiment might be imitated in the future (especially if the behaviour has been negative), perhaps to the detriment of the subject?

What if we were to conduct experiments without using deception? Kelman (1967) has advocated an approach in which subjects *role-play*. Instead of being deceived about the nature of the research, subjects are given a description of a situation by the experimenter and then asked to behave as they think other people would in such a situation. However, as you can imagine, role-playing studies have not proven very useful to psychologists, for all they tell us is how the subjects *think* that others would act in that situation; the researcher's intuition, informed by a thorough knowledge of the research literature, would in all likelihood provide a better guide.

A related and somewhat more useful technique is that of *simulation*. Again, no deception is employed and the subjects are informed of the situation in which they find themselves. In this case, however, the subjects act and react to each other and to the situation rather than simply playing a role corresponding to how they think others would act. Although simulations can evoke powerful emotional responses and therefore appear to have both greater experimental and mundane reality, they pose several problems. First, although outright deception is not involved, another serious ethical question is: if the researcher can foresee that the subjects may experience discomfort, is it ethical, even if they are forewarned in general terms, to expose them to such discomfort? Moreover, what use can be made of the results? Can we be certain that the observed outcome was truly an indication of how people in general would react in such situations or that it was not idiosyncratic? We may be able to generalize from our results less than we think, despite apparent mundane realism.

Returning to the issue of the laboratory experiment, in ruling out deception, we make social psychological research all but impossible. Do we stop our research? In so doing, may we not one day be judged guilty of a greater sin, that of failing to use the powerful methodology of science to understand human social behaviour so that we can learn how to reduce aggression, diminish prejudice, and enhance quality of life? Besides, *most* deception in social psychological experiments is so benign that few would fault it seriously, except on the general principle that we have no right to deceive. No one has yet shown any long-term negative consequences resulting from deception in a social psychological experiment (Elms, 1982).

The codes of ethics of both the Canadian Psychological Association and the American Psychological Association try to deal with the problem of deception. They specify that the experimenter must be careful to protect the welfare of subjects, and to weigh the importance of the research against the need to deceive subjects or invade their privacy. Furthermore, most universities and granting agencies require that experiments involving human subjects first be cleared by an ethics committee whose task it is to protect subjects from undue exploitation, unnecessary deception, or potential harm.

Obtaining *informed consent* is one way of safeguarding potential subjects: if subjects are informed to the maximum extent possible (without destroying the effectiveness of the experimental manipulation) about what will happen to them in the experiment, they may freely choose whether or not to participate. Such informed consent will also help curb resentment toward whatever deception is practiced, for if subjects are told that it is impossible to describe the experiment in full detail without influencing their behaviour in it, they are likely to accept the necessity for deception when they eventually learn they were deceived.

Another protection against any long-term harm fostered by deception is the practice of *debriefing*. Most social psychologists go to great lengths to debrief their subjects following an experiment. Debriefing involves both dehoaxing and desensitization (Holmes, 1976). Dehoaxing involves informing subjects that they have been deceived and explaining the purpose of the experiment. Desensitization is intended to help the subjects accept the new information they have about themselves and put it into context, and respond to any questions and anxieties which might arise.

However, when highly stressful situations are involved, debriefing may not always undo whatever damage has been done. Indeed, the debriefing session may even make matters *worse*. Subjects who follow orders in an experiment on obedience may not perceive their actions as "blind obedience" until so informed in the debriefing. Moreover, it may not be desirable for subjects to witness role models (university professors or their assistants) in the act of lying. The fact is that the major advantage of debriefing may be in reducing the experimenter's guilt rather than in helping the subject (Campbell, 1969a).

There is no general solution to the problem of deception, except to say that the experimenter must take all reasonable precautions to ensure that the negative consequences of the deception are likely to be minimal and that even this risk is justified by the importance of what might be learned from the experiment. Ethics committees, which evaluate the work of peers, are usually more objective in making judgments about ethical risks than individual researchers eager to verify some hypothesis.

SUMMARY

(1) Science is an effective method of gaining knowledge and understanding. It consists of formulating hypotheses, testing them through systematic observation, and building theories from these findings. Scientific research must meet the tests of replicability (i.e., others can repeat the same study) and falsifiability (i.e., a hypothesis must be capable of being proven false).

(2) Precise measurement is the basic tool of science. In social psychology it is often difficult to translate a hypothetical construct (a construct such as "attitude") into an operational definition, i.e., a measure. Measurement problems include: a) reliability — does the measure yield consistent readings?; b) validity — does it measure what it is intended to measure?; c) reactivity — does the measure affect the very thing that is

being measured?; and d) sampling — are the data obtained representative of a population of interest?

(3) In social psychology both experimental and non-experimental methods of research are used. All methods have both advantages and disadvantages.

(4) Non-experimental research involves studying the correlation among several characteristics, or variables. Non-experimental research methods include: a) archival method; b) case studies; c) survey interviews or questionnaires; and d) field studies, in which behaviour is observed systematically in a natural setting.

(5) In experimental research subjects are assigned randomly to experimental and control groups so that we assume they are identical before the experiment. Situational variables are then manipulated systematically to create an identical impact on both groups. Other confounding variables which may influence results are controlled. Experimental research methods include: a) laboratory experiments; b) field experiments; and c) quasi-experiments.

(6) Non-experimental and experimental research is subject to experimenter biases; the expectations and unintentional actions by experimenters may affect the results. Subjects may also bias results by acting as they believe they should act (demand characteristics) or by acting to create a "good" impression in reaction to evaluation apprehension.

(7) Generalizations drawn from experiments are limited by: a) the external validity, i.e., how comparable it is to a real-life situation; and b) internal validity, the extent to which the results were due to manipulation of the independent variable rather than to artifact.

(8) Statistical analysis lets us interpret the significance of our research findings. In particular, we can determine whether the scores of different groups are really different — or whether two variables are truly correlated — or whether our results occurred by chance alone.

(9) Ethical concerns in social psychological research include: the use of deception in experiments; the subjects' right to privacy; and the possibility of undue stress.

FURTHER READING

ADAIR, J.G. (1973). *The human subject*. Boston: Little, Brown.

AGNEW, N.M and PYKE, S.W. (1969). *The science game*. Englewood Cliffs, NJ: Prentice-Hall.

CRANO, W.D. and BREWER, M.B. (1973). *Principles of research in social psychology*. New York: McGraw-Hill.

SHAW, M.E. and COSTANZO, P.R. (1982). *Theories of social psychology*. Second Edition. New York: McGraw-Hill.

WEBB, E.T., CAMPBELL, D.T., SCHWARTZ, B.D., SECHREST, L. and GROVE, J.B. (1981). *Non-reactive measures in the social sciences*. Boston: Houghton-Mifflin.

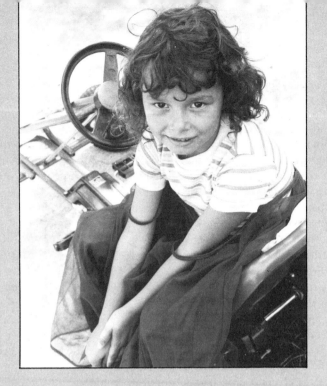

Social Perception and Cognition

Men seldom make passes at girls who wear
glasses.
Dorothy Parker

FOR REFLECTION

- How do we form first impressions of people? Are they accurate?
- How do we influence the image that others have of us?
- Can we tell whether someone is lying to us? How?
- Are there differences in how we make sense of our physical world and our
  social world?

THE JUROR WATCHES and listens attentively to the witness, trying to decide if she is telling the truth. The student attends the first lecture in social psychology to find out if the professor is interesting or boring, tough or demanding, concerned or distant. While a man and a woman converse, they may wonder: What is she or he like? Does she or he like me? Negotiators for labour and management sit down at the bargaining table and immediately begin to "size each other up." The personnel manager interviews the applicant to find out whether that person is suitable for the job. The journalist tries to find out what the politician is "really" like and what policies we can expect.

The perception of a person is a complex and subtle process. Think about the similarities and differences between perceiving a person and perceiving an inanimate object such as a chair. We may notice the size, shape, style, materials and colours of a chair to form an impression of it as ugly or attractive, comfortable or uncomfortable, durable or shoddy. Similarly we may look at surface characteristics of people to arrive at an impression of what they are like. However, unlike inanimate objects, we also assume that a person has an "interior life" of attitudes, beliefs, motives and emotions. These are hypothetical constructs, which we can never experience directly but only infer from what we observe of the person's behaviour. Thus, for example, good old Charlie greets you with a big smile, an embrace, and some nice words. You then *infer* that Charlie is a friendly person, a characteristic that extends back and forward in time from this one instance. You may also infer or guess that Charlie was motivated, that he intended to be friendly to you (unless Charlie is running for election or trying to sell you a used car at the time).

Sizing each other up: Canadian and German officials sit down to negotiate during the final days of WWII.

What is impressive is that, while we all agree that people are complicated, we tend to arrive at such decisions about them rather quickly and without much conscious thought. Indeed Fiske and Taylor (1984) describes us as "cognitive misers," expending as little effort as necessary to make judgments about people. Social psychologists have studied the processes of social perception and cognition, and have made some intriguing discoveries. In the present chapter, discussion is first directed to the formation of impressions of what a person is like. Then, discussion turns to the study of attributions, the processes by which we perceive causality in our social world. Finally, the more subtle processes of social cognition, by which we "construct" our own view of reality, are examined.

It is important to remember that much of this discussion is fundamental to social psychology. Whether we love or hate someone, whether we attempt to help or harm someone, how we interact and communicate — all these reactions depend on how we have interpreted the person, the situation, and the actions that we observe. Thus some of the concepts and findings discussed in this chapter also will be applied in later chapters.

FORMING IMPRESSIONS OF PEOPLE

You will have realized, through your own experience, that first impressions are important. The questions of how particular pieces of information (real or imagined) about another person are processed, the extent of the impact made, and the way in which various elements are combined, are of continuing interest to researchers.

One of the first experiments on this topic was conducted by Asch (1946). To one group of students he read a list of personal traits: "intelligent, skillful, industrious, warm, determined, practical, cautious." Another group was read an identical list, except that "cold" was substituted for "warm." All the subjects then wrote a brief paragraph describing the type of person to whom the traits applied. They also were given a new list of adjectives and asked to check those which applied to the person they had just described.

When the responses were examined, the descriptions of the stimulus person obtained from the two groups were found to be strikingly different. The trait "warm" as compared with "cold" generated impressions of a person who was more popular, wise, humorous, and imaginative. Asch also found by substituting "polite" and "blunt" for "warm" and "cold" that not all characteristics had this rather extensive effect. He called traits such as "warm" and "cold" *central traits* because they seemed to be implicitly correlated with the existence of a wide range of other traits, contrasted with *peripheral traits* such as "polite" and "blunt" which did not have such a broad impact.

Kelley (1950) was able to demonstrate that the effect wasn't confined to the laboratory when he had a "guest lecturer" give a talk to various psychology classes. In half of these classes, the introduction included the adjective "warm" and in the other half, the adjective "cold." The actual introduction went as follows: "Mr. _____ is a graduate student in the Department of Economics and Social Science at M.I.T. He has had three semesters of teaching experience in psychology at another college. This is his first semester teaching EC-70. He is 26 years old, a veteran and married.

People who know him consider him to be a rather cold (or "a very warm") person, industrious, critical, practical and determined." In all cases, the content and delivery of the lecture was the same. Afterwards, the students were asked to give their impressions of the lecturer. The results showed that the students given the "cold" cue rated the lecturer as more unsociable, self-centred, unpopular, formal, irritable, humourless and ruthless. These data clearly support those originally obtained by Asch. In addition, Kelley found that students in the "warm" condition were more likely to ask the speaker questions and to interact with him, indicating that behaviour, as well as perception, was affected.

Asch argued that these results indicated that impressions of others were "dynamic wholes," an overall, general impression, rather than the sum of a number of separate components. This view was subsequently challenged by Wishner (1960) who had a large number of students rate their introductory psychology teachers on the same traits used by Asch. Wishner demonstrated that whether a trait was central or peripheral depended on the context. In other words, a stimulus trait would be central if the characteristics to be subsequently judged were correlated with it, but it would be peripheral if they were uncorrelated. All these experiments serve to emphasize that impressions can be formed on the basis of subtle and minimal information.

Biases

Researchers have noted a couple of interesting biases in impression formation. First, a *positivity bias*, in which impressions of people are much more likely to be positive than negative, has been found. For example, students at one university rated 97 percent of their professors as "above average" (Sears, 1983), although most students have mixed experiences with professors, occasionally even negative ones. Matlin and Stang (1978) explain this bias as an example of the *Pollyanna principle*; like Voltaire's *Candide*, we like to believe that we live in the "best of all possible worlds," surrounded by nice people. However, Sears found that 74 percent of the time, the professor was rated more highly than impersonal aspects of the course such as examinations, books and content. Thus, while we tend to be markedly "Pollyanna-ish" in our impressions of specific people, we may be more critical of objects and situations.

On the other hand, there also is a *negativity effect*. This means that our impressions of people are more strongly influenced by negative than positive information about them (Fiske, 1980). We tend to be more confident of an impression formed on the basis of negative traits (Hamilton and Zanna, 1972) and we tend to form a very negative impression of a person with one negative trait, regardless of whether the person has other positive, ostensibly redeeming, characteristics (Anderson, 1965). For example, a politician who appears to be a "crook" is evaluated negatively, regardless of all the wonderful things that he or she may have done. Such an evaluation would illustrate the principle of *figure-ground* in perception — a strongly negative trait stands out because it is unusual and contrasts with the other, often positive, characteristics. We pay more attention to it, remember it and give it more weight in forming an impression.

Each of us also has our personal way of looking at the world which we bring to the situation. Kelly (1955) proposes that each person has his or her own set of *personal constructs*, a set of bipolar adjectives (e.g., honest-dishonest or friendly-unfriendly) which become our essential terms for characterizing people. Even within a common

CHANGING IMAGES OF SMOKING

The late movies are full of images of the glamour of smoking. Images always included Sherlock Holmes with his pipe, Groucho Marx with his cigar, Bogart with his cigarettes. Romantic scenes showed lovers gazing at each other through a haze of smoke, and when she asked for a "light," much more was implied. In a less romantic context, the condemned man was offered a cigarette, the professor puffed thoughtfully on his pipe, and the big cigar symbolized power and success. Politics was conducted in smoke-filled rooms and proud fathers passed out cigars to announce the great event. Perhaps above all, smoking represented the sexy sophistication to which we all aspire at some time in our lives.

Times and fashions change, and smoking is no longer in style. Indeed, the evidence now suggests that smoking reduces the level of perceived attractiveness of a person. In a series of experiments (Dermer and Jacobsen, 1986), subjects were shown photographs of people (male and female), some who held a lit cigarette and were seated near a pack of cigarettes on a table, and some who did not show any evidence of smoking. Subjects were asked to rate the target persons on a number of dimensions.

Except for cases in which the person was either extremely attractive or unattractive, a person was rated less positively by subjects who saw him or her smoking than by other subjects who saw that same person *not* smoking. Persons with cigarettes were

A less favourable image?

rated lower on scales labelled "considerate," "calm," "honest," "healthy," "well-mannered," and "happy." In some cases, the smoker was also rated as less self-controlled, imaginative, or mature, more likely to use illegal drugs, be an alcoholic, or be an inattentive driver.

The data showed somewhat less favourable images of smokers among older subjects; other studies have shown less unfavourable images of smokers among other smokers (Polivy, Hackett and Bycio, 1979). Perhaps feeding back such data to young people might further erode the image of smoking.

culture or subgroup, construct systems are unique to individuals. Thus, in the case of "good old Charlie," one person may interpret his behaviour as friendly-unfriendly, while another person may view it as sincere-insincere, warm-cold, or outgoing-shy. Our reactions to Charlie may be different because the fundamental constructs we use to interpret his behaviour differ.

Similarly, Bruner and Tagiuri (1954) suggest that we have our own *implicit personality theories*, a set of unstated assumptions about certain types of people or about people in general. For example, many people seem to assume that persons described as intelligent also tend to be friendly and not self-centred (Rosenberg and Sedlak, 1972).

These implicit personality theories may be described in terms of individual *philosophies of human nature* (Wrightsman, 1964). That is, we vary from each other in how we conceive of people along certain lines: (1) the extent to which we believe people are trustworthy or untrustworthy; (2) the extent to which we believe that people are rational and can control their destinies; (3) the extent to which people seem to be altruistic or selfish; (4) the extent to which people are seen as independent or conformist; (5) the extent to which we see different people as unique or similar to each other; and (6) the extent to which we believe that people are basically complicated and different or rather easy to understand.

While we generally are not aware of these assumptions, "theories," and "philosophies," they can profoundly influence how we form impressions and react to people (Schneider, 1973). Moreover, biases and assumptions tend to persist, even in the face of contradictory evidence (Anderson, Lepper and Ross, 1980). In one experiment, subjects were asked to write a paragraph describing a "working man" based on the following list of adjectives: works in a factory; reads a newspaper; goes to movies; average height; cracks jokes; strong; active. The same request was made to a second group except that the trait "intelligent" was inserted in the list. While those in the first group had no difficulty writing the paragraph, those in the second group showed a number of signs of disruption in their thinking. For instance, some denied the existence of the characteristic "intelligent," others modified it and some even promoted the man from worker to supervisor. It is apparent that some of these subjects had an "implicit" idea of what a working man is like, and that idea did not include "intelligent" (Haire and Grune, 1950).

The cognitive algebra of impression formation

Usually, when we meet another person or learn about someone from a third party, the information is acquired sequentially. That is, we may first notice that a person is attractive and then, during conversation, discover that this person also appears stupid and arrogant. How do we put these elements, and any others that may subsequently become evident, together to form an overall evaluation?

There are two points of view, or models, which explain how this occurs: the additive model and averaging model. Each model operates as the name implies. The additive model predicts that, as we learn more about a person, our overall impression accumulates, while the averaging model predicts that our overall impression is a "running average" of what we know about the person. In some circumstances, the two models would predict that we would form substantially different overall impressions of the same person.

Let us examine these models in more detail. First, in both cases, arithmetic values must be attached to the items of information. In other words, let us assume that each of us has a "mental rating scale" which we apply to the various things we learn about others. For the purposes of illustration, our evaluations can range between $+3$ (very positive) and -3 (very negative). Thus, for example, on the characteristic of sincerity we might rate the person as very sincere ($+3$), somewhat sincere ($+1$), rather inconsistent on this trait (0) or rather insincere (-2). Similarly, we may evaluate a person as extremely intelligent ($+3$), average in intelligence ($+1$ or 0) or utterly stupid (-3).

The additive model would predict that, if we evaluate a person as very intelligent

($+3$) and somewhat sincere ($+1$), our overall evaluation rises to $+4$, even more positive. By contrast, the averaging model would predict that our overall impression would be $+2$ (i.e., $3+1)/2$), a less positive result. Although inherently simple, the discrepancies between the two models are important. The additive model, for example, predicts that as additional, positive information is obtained — irrespective of the value — the impression of the person continues to be enhanced, while the averaging model predicts that an additional piece of positive information, if it is less positive than the current impression, would lead to a decrease in our estimation of the person. In other words, unless the new information is better than the average of what we already know, it is not going to improve our image of the person.

The controversy over which of these two approaches is correct has been going on for some time. So far, most of the evidence favours the averaging model. However, there were a sufficient number of instances in which the model didn't work that Anderson (1978) was led to propose a *weighted averaging model* which seems, in general, to be more satisfactory. Anderson argued that information should not only be *evaluated* but judged as to its *importance*. The importance, or weighting, could, for example, depend on the particular circumstances in which the evaluation was being made. Suppose you were introduced to a person who is a candidate in a federal election and you observed that she was intelligent, sincere and boring. Further, suppose that on your evaluation scale "intelligent" was $+3$, "sincere" $+2$, and "boring" -1. Now, if the person to whom you were being introduced was a potential friend, each of these characteristics would be of some importance and might be weighted as follows:

As a friend	Value Weight Total
intelligent	$+3 \times 2 = 6$
sincere	$+2 \times 3 = 6$
boring	$-1 \times 3 = -3$
	Total 9
	Average $+3$

But if she were introduced as a politician, the weights you assign might be different:

As a politician	Value Weight Total
intelligent	$+3 \times 3 = 9$
sincere	$+2 \times 2 = 4$
boring	$-1 \times 0 = 0$
	Total 13
	Average $+4.33$

If we compare the weights in each of these examples, we see that sincerity and boring-ness bear more weight than intelligence in the evaluation of a potential friend but that intelligence bears more weight in the evaluation of a politician — and that "boring-ness" has become unimportant! In this example, the result is that the stimulus person would create a better impression if introduced as a political candidate than as a possible friend. In another situation, judged by another person, the results might differ.

In general, research indicates that the weighted averaging principle best accounts for how we combine information to form an impression of a person (see Table 3-1).

TABLE 3–1
*Models for forming
impressions of people*

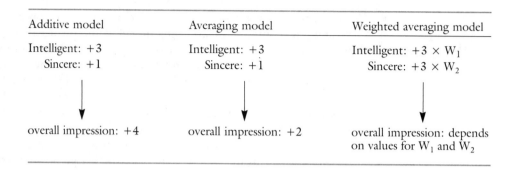

Additive model	Averaging model	Weighted averaging model
Intelligent: +3	Intelligent: +3	Intelligent: +3 × W₁
Sincere: +1	Sincere: +1	Sincere: +3 × W₂
↓	↓	↓
overall impression: +4	overall impression: +2	overall impression: depends on values for W₁ and W₂

Official press photos selected by two Canadian politicians: (top) Dennis Timbrell (PC) as a Member of the Ontario Legislative Assembly; (bottom) Sheila Copps (L), MP for Hamilton East. How likely is it that a man would choose the cheerful, outgoing pose or that a woman would choose the pensive, unsmiling pose?

However, it is certainly not the only principle at work. In addition to the importance of different traits to the perceiver, we must also take into consideration the *order* in which the elements of information are received. Does it make any difference, for example, if we learn that a person is a political radical before, rather than after, we discover that he also is an Albertan, a Rhodes Scholar, and supports the legalization of marijuana? The evidence indicates that it does, but whether *primacy* (what is learned first) or *recency* (what is learned last) dominates the impression formed depends on the time separating the acquisition of pieces of information. When the items are closely spaced, primacy plays the major role; if, however, there is a time gap between the first and last elements, recency usually becomes more important (see Chapter 5's discussion of persuasion).

Experimental research has clarified how these principles operate. For example, Asch (1946) asked a group of students to indicate their overall impression of a person who was "intelligent, industrious, impulsive, critical, stubborn and envious." The same request was made of another group of students but the traits were presented in reverse order. While the traits become increasingly negative in the first instance, they become increasingly positive in the second. The impressions gained by each group clearly supported the operation of a primacy effect. The first group perceived the person in much more positive terms than the second group. It would appear that as information is being processed, later information is discounted, watered down, or distorted in some way to remain compatible with the information first acquired. However, with the lapse of time, a loss of memory for the initial characteristics may allow new information to have more of an impact (Anderson and Hubert, 1963).

Thus far, our examination of how we form impressions of people reveals that we arrive at judgments rather quickly and often with minimal information. One problem with these models is that they assume human traits are what they seem without taking into account the fact that people don't necessarily present themselves as they really are. As an example, look at the photographs of the graduating students in your university's yearbook. You will probably notice that most of the women are smiling and most of the men have serious, no-nonsense expressions (Deaux, 1976). This situation has nothing to do with the inherent happiness of women or seriousness of men. Rather, women tend to be socialized to present themselves as warm, happy, and affable, and men as serious and "businesslike." We often try to influence the impression that others have of us, sometimes deliberately and often inadvertently. In the next section, we explore the topic of impression management.

IMPRESSION MANAGEMENT

Unless we are depressed or have very low self-esteem, we usually want to present ourselves to others in the best possible light, to put "our best foot forward." This wish may extend from dressing in the "correct" fashion to saying the "right" things — that is, what we think the other person wants to hear. While often there is nothing consciously deliberate about this process, at other times, we may use ingratiation, lying, and various other tactics to satisfy our own social needs.

One way of being liked, as we will see in Chapter 6, is to be a conformist, to adhere, as closely as possible, to the norms of the group without rocking the social boat — not particularly difficult for most people. Other techniques, such as "*playing hard-to-get*," do involve more deliberate and intricate scenarios. Does the person who adopts this posture have more success in attracting friends and lovers? Apparently not, at least not as much as is supposed. Walster and her co-workers (1976) found that the women to whom men were most attracted were those whom they perceived as being "hard-to-get" for others, but not for themselves. In adopting this tactic, then, we would need to avoid creating the impression that we are about to reject a person whom we want to attract.

In two studies of the "hard-to-get" tactic (Wilson and Contrada, 1983) subjects were presented with descriptions of an individual of the opposite sex in which that person was characterized as being very selective, moderately selective, or not at all selective about whom they would be willing to date. Both studies showed that subjects were not attracted to someone who would be willing to go out with almost anyone. However, people described as very selective, those who said they would go

"Try not to get carried away, Miss Greenblat — I assure you that back home I'm just an ordinary guy."

out only with "exceptional" people, were perceived as conceited, and subjects preferred the moderately selective person. It was also found that females tended to respond more negatively to an extremely selective male, than males to an extremely selective female. Evidently, the hard-to-get female is more socially acceptable than the hard-to-get male.

In order to appear likeable, people often use *ingratiation* tactics. As receivers of flattery, we must decide if it is sincere or whether it is a deliberate attempt to manipulate. Those who are attractive or in positions of power are especially likely to be the targets of ingratiation (Jones, Gergen and David, 1962), and it would not be surprising to find that these people are somewhat more suspicious than most of people's motives. It seems obvious that ingratiation strategies should be subtle because detection is likely to alienate the target person (Jones, Jones and Gergen, 1963), yet even given this risk, many people are willing to take a chance.

The manipulative personality

In fact, some individuals characteristically resort to social tactics in order to influence others. This syndrome, called *Machiavellianism*, has been most thoroughly measured and investigated by Christie and Geis (1968, 1970). It is typified by emotional detachment and an impersonal view that others can be manipulated. Christie and Geis stress, however, that high "Machs" are not hostile or vindictive but have a cool detachment which makes them less emotionally involved with other people or with sensitive issues, and less concerned with face-saving in embarrassing situations. For example, Exline and his colleagues (1970) induced high Machs and low Machs to cheat on a test. Subsequently, a confederate confronted each subject and accused him or her of cheating. One measure of the degree to which subjects were able to hide their guilt was the length of time they looked the confederate in the eye. The high Machs not only didn't avert their gaze but actually increased their eye contact as the interaction progressed, whereas low Machs behaved in precisely the opposite manner.

The specific interpersonal tactics employed by Machiavellians are of some interest and also reveal differences in the approaches used by males and females. Braginsky (1970), for example, selected fifth grade children who could be characterized as high and low Machs and then offered them 5 cents if they could convince another child to eat a cookie which had been flavoured with quinine (a bitter taste). The high Machs had a higher success rate than the low Machs but, in accomplishing the task, the girls used different techniques of persuasion than the boys. The high Mach girls manipulated primarily by means of subtle, evasive methods of impression management, using such strategies as the offering of a bribe to split the money. High Mach boys, on the other hand, manipulated by a direct, aggressive approach and appeared less concerned with future personal encounters than with their immediate success.

It has also been noted that, with ability held constant, high Mach male undergraduates achieve better grades than their low Mach counterparts. You will be interested to learn that Christie and Geis report " . . . it is not too surprising to find that graduate students in Social Psychology are more in tune with Machiavelli than any other aggregate of subjects yet tested" (1968, p. 965).

In general, we use various tactics, deliberately or otherwise, in order to create a desired impression of ourselves (see Box 3-2). At times, we may wish to create an impression which is not entirely honest or realistic, and our success will depend on

B · O · X   3 - 2

THE TRAVELLER AND THE CUSTOMS OFFICER: PERCEPTION AND DECEPTION

Consider the roles of traveller and customs inspector. Travellers want to avoid arousing suspicion if they are smuggling, a practice which is extremely widespread at a petty level. Even if they have been completely honest, travellers dislike the inconvenience of a search, particularly at the end of a long, exhausting trip. The customs official, of course, is assigned the duty of detecting smuggling, particularly on the large scale of contraband substances (e.g., illegal drugs). They also are responsible for running the system smoothly and not slowing down the process in order to search the innocent. Thus with very little time, a few questions, and a lot of visual and non-verbal cues, the officer must decide whom to search.

Kraut and Poe (1980) set out to investigate this complex and common real-life process. First, they recruited "stimulus persons" from people in airport waiting rooms. Each was asked to go through a mock customs inspection, conducted by an experienced officer. Some were assigned objects to smuggle (miniature cameras, even small packets of white powder), while others were the innocent travellers with nothing to declare. In all cases, the object of the game was to convince the inspector that there was no need to search the traveller or his or her luggage. Financial incentives for a successful performance were provided in order to make this a more realistic situation, i.e., the person had something to gain.

All of these performances were videotaped, and the videotapes were shown to judges who rated various behaviours. Some were verbal (such as hesitancy in responding to questions, slips of the "tongue" and other errors, evasive responses, whether the responses were long or short), while others were non-verbal, including smiling, posture or gestures indicating tension or nervousness, avoiding eye contact. Inter-rater reliabilities for various judgments ranged from .56 to .90, which indicates relatively good agreement between judges. Then the tapes were shown to two

groups of subjects, 39 real-life customs inspectors and 49 laypersons from the community. They were told that about 50 percent of the tapes were of people attempting to smuggle something, and that their task was to indicate in each case whether they would want to search that person.

The results are fascinating. They showed, first of all, that ordinary people in the role of smugglers are good liars; both the professional inspectors and the amateurs were *less* likely to say they would search the smuggler than the innocent person. Further, there were no differences between smugglers and innocents on any of the behaviours, verbal or non-verbal. It seems that smuggling by itself does not make people unusually ill-at-ease, and that everyone is uncomfortable in the situation of facing a customs officer, regardless of guilt or innocence. There was also no evidence that different behavioural cues were relied upon by the professionals or by those who were most successful at identifying the guilty.

What cues were most important to these real and would-be customs inspectors in this situation? Six variables had the greatest influence on their decision: the apparent nervousness of the person, hesitating before answering, giving one word or very brief responses to questions, shifting body posture, and avoiding eye contact. Subjects were more likely to recommend a search if the person was young, of lower class, and had been travelling for pleasure rather than business. Often, inspectors showed evidence of having hypotheses regarding certain types, perhaps from previous experience. For example, many would have wanted to search an apparently respectable old lady in an obviously expensive fur coat. Many also would have searched a young woman who made several "sassy remarks" to inspectors. Of course, travellers who had been in certain areas of the world were suspected of smuggling illegal drugs.

the perceiver's ability to detect our evasions, manipulations, and little white lies. Some interesting studies have explored whether people can detect deception when it is used.

Deception and its detection

Liars and manipulators always take the risk that their tactics will be exposed and that the target will feel "conned." Although research on deception has not yet explored all aspects of why lying can fail, there are some reasonably clear findings as well as some hints available. The questions which have been investigated concern whether some individuals are better "liars" than others, whether there are individual differences in skill at detecting deception, and whether there are any special detection techniques.

It has been found that, in general, people can distinguish lies from the truth at a level somewhat better than chance (Miller and Burgoon, 1982). However, there are several varieties of deception. Hiding how we *really* feel about another person may not be equivalent to saying something that is contrary to what we really believe. Eckman and Friesen (1969) have distinguished between *deception clues*, which are present when a person's behaviour suggests a lie, and *leakage*, in which the truth is mistakenly revealed. For example, patients who wring their hands while assuring the doctor that they feel fine would be providing a deception clue that they may feel ill, or may be angry at the doctor, or fearful about the future. A slip of the tongue or a non-verbal response to a specific question may provide leakage about the fact that they are feeling ill, angry or fearful. Research has not indicated whether people who are skillful at detecting one of these types of clues are also skillful in detecting the other.

In one complex study (DiPaulo and Rosenthal, 1979) male and female students were videotaped while they described several acquaintances whom they liked, felt ambivalent about, and disliked. They were then instructed to express feelings which were opposite to their real feelings, such as describing someone they liked as if that person were disliked. These descriptions were also videotaped. The subjects later were asked to judge those videotapes on which they did not appear. The results confirmed most previous studies, revealing that the judges were good at identifying the occurrence of deception but they were not very good at identifying the real underlying affect. It also was found that those subjects who were especially good at recognizing the leakage of positive affect (a favourable attitude not concealed by lying) were not necessarily good at recognizing the leakage of negative affect (an unfavourable attitude not concealed by lying). In a similar vein, the study pointed out that people who know when women are lying do not necessarily recognize dissimulation by men. In fact, there is some suggestion that women and men may behave in different ways when lying (Mehrabian, 1971; McClintock and Hunt, 1975).

It was also observed that some individuals were consistently good and others were consistently bad liars and that good liars were not necessarily good "detectors." In addition, it was found that while the Machiavellians were not any better than the others at detecting lies, they were effective liars, and most likely to "ham" when they lied. Of even more interest, however, was the finding that in spite of the exaggerated style hamming involved, it was a successful strategy.

In another study, it was found that subjects who attempted to hide certain facts were less successful when they thought the other person was an "expert" rather than a "non-expert" (Fugita, Hogrebe and Wexley, 1980). It was also observed that subjects were more confident of the likelihood of their success at deception than was actually the case.

Since deception can sometimes be detected, there must be valid cues which observers use to decide whether or not a person is being deceptive. Police can use "lie detectors" to monitor physiological changes and psychoanalysts have relied on dreams and other subtle behaviours such as slips of the tongue. However these techniques are not available to the majority of people and, in any case, there are serious doubts as to their reliability and validity. It appears, however, that there are some verbal and non-verbal indicators which are more likely to occur when a person is lying. In general, when people are lying, their speech has a higher pitch, they are more nervous and less fluent, and they give less plausible and shorter answers with longer hesitations prior to responding. The long pause seems to be particularly powerful in alerting observers to the possibility that deception is taking place (Kraut, 1978).

While individuals make some effort to control facial expression when trying to deceive someone, they are less aware of the "language" of the rest of the body (Ekman and Friesen, 1974). It has been reported that judges are more accurate in detecting deception when viewing the body rather than the face. However, this may only be true when emotional material is being disguised. When factual material is involved, judgments based on the face are more accurate (Littlepage and Pineault, 1979). As we will see in Chapter 11, non-verbal cues can be extremely informative.

ATTRIBUTIONS OF CAUSALITY

So far, we have been discussing visible cues which suggest deception. It is important to understand that we use these cues to draw an inference about what a person intends, and is trying to do. For instance, when we detect deception, we interpret what we see as being caused by the person's desire to deceive us. Such inferences, or interpretations of intent, are called *attributions*, a topic of great interest and importance in social psychology (see Box 3-3).

Consider the case in which someone says something that "hurts your feelings." It becomes very important to understand why, and there is a wide selection of possible explanations. Did the person mean it? If so, is it because that person has a grudge against you, or no longer loves you, or is just a nasty individual by nature? Perhaps the person was in a bad mood, under pressure at work, or not feeling well? Perhaps everyone had too much to drink and said things that should not have been said? Or perhaps you're just too sensitive and are hurt too easily. As you can imagine, your causal explanation or *attribution* will determine how you react emotionally, how you respond to the person and perhaps how you evaluate that person.

These are the concerns of Fritz Heider (1958), the pioneer in this area of research, who argued that attributions are fundamental to social relations. Remember that you do not have direct access to the mind of the person who uttered that hurtful remark. Rather, you pick up a few indirect cues and apply your own "naive psychology" to try to make sense of the situation.

How do we arrive at an attribution? To begin, let us examine the principles of discounting and covariation which have been substantiated over the past three decades of research. The *discounting principle* (Kelley, 1972a) states that we are less confident

B · O · X   3 - 3

PERCEIVING PEOPLE AND THINGS

As we all know, people are not things, and do not want to be treated as such. And yet, it is interesting to consider whether the same principles apply when we perceive people and objects. Indeed, much of the research on social perception and cognition has developed out of fundamental research on perceptual and cognitive processes. We may, for example, judge both a person and a chair as being attractive, useful, or reliable. Here are some differences:

(1) Objects remain relatively constant over time, other than the usual wear-and-tear or repairs. However, people change over time, and their characteristics often vary with different circumstances. Thus our perceptions of people may be overgeneralized or obsolete.

(2) When we perceive other people, they may also be perceiving us. Thus we are concerned both with forming impressions of others and creating impressions of ourselves.

(3) People do things for reasons, to achieve their own purposes; that is, people are causal agents— we are concerned with *why* people act as they do. While we may occasionally feel that the car is "being stubborn" when it "refuses" to start on a cold winter's morning, we know that objects do not act intentionally.

(4) One way in which people act intentionally is to change their appearance or actions when they are aware that others are watching them. Objects do not change when they are being observed.

(5) People are very complex and there is inevitably much about them that is private, hidden from view. Even among experts it is much easier for an auto mechanic to understand a car than a psychotherapist to understand a person.

Thus social cognitive psychology cannot be a "literal translation" of cognitive psychology (Fiske and Taylor, 1984).

of our attributions if more than one explanation seems plausible to us at that time. For example, if a used car salesperson is nice to us we may tend to discount the possibility that he likes us because he obviously wants to sell us a car. But if we tell him firmly that we're not buying, and he's still nice to us, we may accept the attribution that he really does like us (see Box 3-4).

The *principle of covariation* concerns the case in which two events are associated over a number of instances. If one event always occurs with another, and does not occur when the other is absent, then you infer that one "causes" the other. For example, suppose a person laughs uncontrollably during every Woody Allen movie (even the "serious" one) but rarely, if ever, laughs at other movies. You would be likely to attribute his laughing to Woody Allen movies, rather than to comedians in general, or to that person's inherent "jolliness."

Attribution theories

Building on these principles, several attribution theories have been proposed. All of them deal with a specific and limited subset of attribution phenomena. The following discussion focuses on the three which have proved most influential: Kelley's covariation model, Jones and Davis' model of correspondent inferences, and Weiner's model of achievement attributions.

THE OVERJUSTIFICATION EFFECT

During the past year, you have devoted almost all of your spare time both to working on environmental issues and working for the election of a mayoral candidate whose commitment to environment issues you value. The work has been immensely satisfying and becomes even more so when the candidate is elected. Now the newly-elected mayor offers you a well-paying job, working as you did before on environmental issues. Nothing could please you more, and you accept the offer.

And yet, research suggests that you will find your well-paying job less satisfying than your former position. When you were a volunteer, you attributed your behaviour to commitment, altruism, excitement — to the *intrinsic* aspects of the work. Now, you are likely to shift at least part of your attributions to an *extrinsic* factor: money. This is the *overjustification effect* which occurs when extrinsic rewards cause us to discount the importance of intrinsic factors and lose interest in the task itself (Deci, 1971; Lepper, Greene and Nisbett, 1973). This concept has been applied

productively in areas such as education and sports (Vallerand, 1986).

Does this mean, for example, that school systems based on extrinsic rewards (grades, praise, gold stars) and punishment (verbal castigation, detentions, failing grades) can cause students to lose interest in school? To a considerable extent, this is probably true. When teachers use reward to control classroom behaviour, students' intrinsic motivation is low (Deci, Nezlek and Sheinman, 1981). However, rewards can be used as *information*, to provide people with feedback on how well they are performing; they can be a signal of encouragement and an acknowledgment of competence. When this is the case, intrinsic motivation is not adversely affected (Deci and Ryan, 1985). Thus, in using rewards, it is important to avoid the competitive and controlling messages usually associated with them. In the end, we don't want students to discount their own interest in other studies.

Covariation model   Building on Fritz Heider's work, H.H. Kelley has developed an attributional model of covariation in which he analyzes how we explain multiple events which occur together, over time. He is particularly concerned with social interactions in which events may be caused by the *actor* (the person performing the behaviour), the *entity* (the person to whom the behaviour is directed), or the *situation* (the social context in which the action takes place). He argues that people behave as "naive scientists" in the sense that we sift through various events, past and present, attempting to eliminate alternative possible causes ("noise in the system") in order to arrive at a "best guess" or hypothesis about the "real cause."

Let's consider an example: Mike greets Anne very affectionately when she arrives. You may attribute his behaviour to the actor (Mike is an affectionate person), to the entity (Anne is very lovable), or to the situation (a reunion of close friends). The perceiver evaluates the available evidence:

(1) *Distinctiveness of the entity.* Does the actor respond "distinctively," that is, in a special way, to this entity? Does Mike show the same affection to everyone or only to Anne? If the latter is true (high distinctiveness), an entity attribution would be appropriate: otherwise, the attribution would be to the actor, that affectionate person called Mike.

Mike greets Anne affectionately when she arrives. How do we arrive at the "real cause" of his behaviour?

(2) *Consensus across actors.* Do others act in the same way toward the entity? If everyone is affectionate to Anne (high consensus), we would attribute Mike's behaviour to the entity (Anne) or situation, while if only Mike acted in this way (low consensus), an attribution to the actor is likely.

(3) *Consistency.* Does the actor behave in this way to the entity across situations? Is Mike always affectionate towards Anne? If consistency is high, we would attribute his behaviour to the actor or the entity, whereas low consistency would lead to a situational attribution.

Of course, wherever possible, we would use all three sources of information together. For example, knowing only that Mike's behaviour is consistent would tell us that it was caused by the actor or entity. But, knowing that consistency was high and that consensus and distinctiveness were also high (i.e., that Mike is always affectionate to Anne and only to Anne, and so is everyone else) would lead to a confident entity attribution: Anne really is lovable. However, if consistency is high but consensus and distinctiveness are low (i.e., if Mike is always affectionate to Anne but others are not, and Mike is also affectionate to Ruth, Angie, Dana, David and Mel), we would attribute the action to the actor: Mike is really a very affectionate person (see Figure 3-1 for a summary).

McArthur (1972) systematically tested this model. Participants were given information about a hypothetical person. This information was varied in terms of distinctiveness, consensus and consistency. For example, they were told that Maria laughed at the comedian, that she didn't laugh at anyone else (high distinctiveness), everyone else laughed too (high consensus) and she always laughs at him (high consistency). In this case, 61 percent attributed Maria's behaviour to the comedian. In another case, Connie laughed at the comedian, she always laughs at comedians (low distinctiveness), hardly anyone else laughed (low consensus) and she always laughs at

FIGURE 3–1
*How we attribute social
behaviour to internal or
external causes*

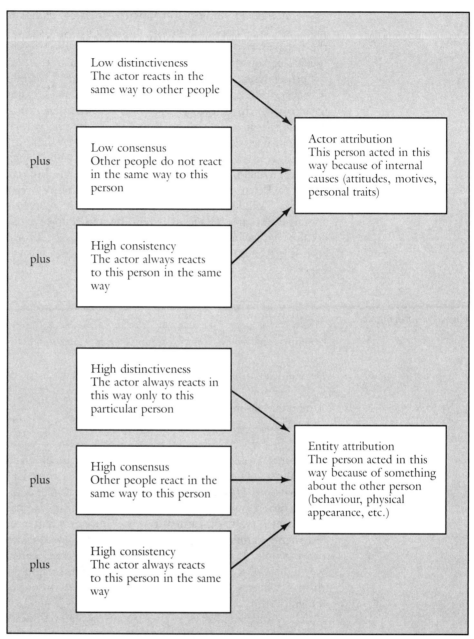

SOURCE: Kelly, 1972.

him (high consistency). As predicted, most subjects (86 percent) attributed the behaviour to the actress (Connie). A third person, Simon, laughed at this comedian when he didn't laugh at anyone else (high distinctiveness), almost everyone else laughed (high consensus) and he has not laughed, before or since, at this comedian (low consistency). As expected, most subjects (72 percent) attributed his behaviour to the situation.

An interesting finding corroborated in later studies (e.g., Nisbett and Borgida, 1975) is that we use consensus information less than expected. Information about the behaviour of others influences our attributions more when presented about a specific person than about "others" in general.

Further research has clarified the covariation principle in some interesting ways (Crocker, 1981). Consider that covariation implies evaluating positive and negative instances which confirm or disconfirm a particular explanation (see Table 3-2). For example, Kevin trips over Jill's feet while dancing with her. To attribute this event to Kevin as a "klutz," we might apply the covariation principle by searching for positive, confirmatory instances (Kevin trips while dancing), negative confirmatory instances (other men don't trip while dancing with Jill), and disconfirmatory instances in which Kevin stays on his dancing feet (positive) and Jill's other partners don't (negative). While it seems that, in practice, we tend to rely most on positive confirming events and, to a lesser extent, disconfirming events, we tend to ignore negative confirming events. That is, we wouldn't bother to watch while other men danced with Jill. We also seem to notice and remember events that confirm what we already expect.

TABLE 3–2
Matrix of covariation

	Positive	*Negative*
Confirmation	Kevin stumbles while dancing with others.	Nobody else stumbles while dancing with Jill.
Disconfirmation	Kevin doesn't stumble while dancing.	Someone else stumbles dancing with Jill.

Attribution: Kevin is a clumsy dancer.

Another problem lies in how we make judgments of "consistency" and "consensus." We would not likely regard jogging four times in five years as a consistent pattern of behaviour. However, if someone were to obtain four divorces in five years, we would probably see this as a steady habit. In short, we use our own expectations and those which we have learned in our culture as a frame of reference for making these judgments. Similarly, consensus judgments will be influenced by the identity of the other people. If we observe members of a political party cheering their own leader, we might well attribute this action to the self-interest or commitments of the cheering throng, whereas we might attribute cheering by other people to the charisma of the leader.

Kelley has provided us with a useful model of how we use information to make social attributions. However, it presupposes that we have sufficient consensus, consistency, and distinctiveness information, that is, that we know how a person has acted at other times and how others are acting in the same situation. Often, we do not have such information, and must make attributions after observing a single episode (Higgins and Bryant, 1982). In these cases, we tend to use certain cues to arrive at a decision, and then discount other possibilities, as the following discussion reveals.

Correspondent inferences (Jones and Davis, 1965) A politician promises to solve all your problems — but does she or he really mean it? The salesperson invites you to "have a good day" but does that person really care? The problem the perceiver often faces is the extent to which a *disposition* can be inferred from a single action. Can we use the behaviour of someone as a guide to what the person is really like, how that person is feeling, or what that person intends, particularly when we have only that one event to guide us? Again, remember that we cannot *know* the inner state of another person — we can only use what information is available to make a more or less reasonable guess or inference. At first glance, behaviour would seem to be a rich and reliable source of information. After all, "actions speak louder than words." However, at least two important factors complicate the picture. First, as we saw earlier, others may seek to mislead us about their true feelings or what they are like. The poker player with a straight flush, the salesperson who knows the real "bottom line" price of an automobile, the family member who assures us that "everything is fine" in order not to worry us, are all examples of people being deceptive. Second, actions often stem from external factors lying beyond the volition of the actor. Politicians are *expected* to make promises and the salesperson is *ordered* to gush cheerfully for each customer. Their behaviour is often explained by the situation, not by a disposition.

How, then, can we infer that an action corresponds to a disposition, that a friendly action corresponds to the characteristic of friendliness in a person? The theory of correspondent inferences (Jones and Davis, 1965; Jones and McGillis, 1976) concerns how we use certain cues which we may perceive in a given action.

FIGURE 3–2
How we decide on a correspondent inference

Cues	Attribution of a correspondent inference
1. The act was freely chosen.	
2. The act produced a non-common effect, not expected of other actions.	
3. The act was not considered socially desirable (non-conforming).	The act reflects some "true" characteristic of the actor (trait, motive, intention, attitude, etc.).
4. The act had a direct impact on us (hedonic relevance).	
5. The act seemed intended to affect us (personalism).	

First, the theory states that we focus upon behaviours which are *freely chosen* and ignore those which are coerced, i.e., performed under threat of punishment or withholding a reward. We can probably guess that the excessively sweet salesperson is following the orders of the corporation manager who pays that person — and we would be unlikely to make a correspondent inference. Second, we notice behaviours that produce *non-common effects*, those which seem unique to that behavioural choice. For example, Don may choose between two women, both of whom are bright, beautiful, witty, and drive expensive cars. His choice would not tell us much about what's important to Don. However, if we were also to discover that Mary Elizabeth is Roman Catholic (as is Don) while Sarah is Jewish, then Don's choice would tell us something about the importance of religious compatibility to Don. A third important feature of behaviour is *social desirability*. If a politician or salesperson speaks to us in a flattering way, the behaviour is "expected" from someone in that role and tells us nothing about that person (except, perhaps, that he or she tends to do what's expected). However, we would willingly make correspondent inferences about a politician who makes rude gestures or a salesperson who is entirely honest about the quality of the merchandise because such behaviour is unexpected and "out-of-role," and thus revealing.

All of these inferences seem to be rather logical "best guesses" when we don't have much information. There are also two non-logical biases which arise from our own reactions to an event. Jones and Davis suggest that we tend to make more confident correspondent inference attributions when the action has a strong consequence for us rather than someone else (*hedonic relevance*) and when we believe that the actor intended to benefit or harm us (*personalism*). For example, I am more likely to make a correspondent inference about you as a violent person if you hit, rather than miss my nose, if the nose you hit is my own and not someone else's, and if I feel that you really mean it.

A series of experiments has supported the model of correspondent inferences (Jones and Harris, 1967; Jones, Davis and Gergen, 1961). In several of these, subjects were asked to view or read speeches about controversial issues of the time, such as U.S. policy toward Fidel Castro. In some cases, the speeches represented socially popular positions (e.g., anti-Castro), while others argued unpopular positions. Some subjects were told that the speakers had been assigned to argue a particular position, while others were told that the speakers had been allowed to speak as they wished on the issue. As predicted by the model, subjects were more likely to attribute the speech to the "real attitude" of the speaker when they believed that the position had been freely chosen and when it was an unpopular position. However, there was a tendency to attribute the speech to the speaker's own disposition even when the speaker was only following instructions. This tendency represents the "fundamental error" in attributions, a bias toward making personal attributions.

In another study (Jones, Davis and Gergen, 1961) subjects listened to an interview with a job applicant. Half the subjects were led to believe that the person was applying to be a member of a submarine crew, a job described as requiring a friendly, outgoing and cooperative person. The other half were told that the person was applying to be an astronaut, requiring someone who was quiet, reserved, inner-directed. Half of each group heard an interview with a friendly, outer-directed person, and half with a reserved, inner-directed person. When asked later to make judgments about what the person was *really* like, those hearing in-role behaviour rated the person near the neutral point on the relevant personality dimensions. However, the inner-directed, would-be submariner was rated as very reserved and quiet, while the outer-directed astronaut was seen as very friendly and extroverted. In these cases, observers did not have available to them an alternative, plausible explanation. Since the candidates were not acting as "suitable" applicants would be expected to act, observers could confidently make correspondent inferences.

Attributions about achievement (Weiner, 1974, 1980)   We evaluate much of our social experience in terms of success and failure. In some cases, it is defined in concrete ways: passing an examination, getting a job or promotion, selling an insurance policy, publishing a paper, making a lot of money, winning that tennis match or election, being named to the Senate or the Order of Canada. Beyond these milestones, success and failure can be experienced in more subtle ways: being well-liked at a party, having a child who is admired, being "lucky at love." Many who experience divorce must deal with feelings of having failed in the relationship (Weiss, 1975), and attributions regarding success and failure are crucial in dealing with loneliness (Peplau and Perlman, 1982).

Weiner suggests that achievement attributions involve a two-step process. First, we decide whether the success or failure was caused by something about the actor (internal) or something about the situation (external). Then we must decide whether the internal or external cause was stable or unstable in nature. In the later (1980) version of the theory, Weiner added a third dimension — whether the occurrence was controllable by the actor. Thus we can choose among eight types of explanations for success or failure. In Figure 3-3, we outline one example, based on a student's final grade in social psychology.

FIGURE 3–3
Attributions about achievement: A final grade in social psychology

	Stable		Unstable	
	Internal	External	Internal	External
Controllable	typical effort	professor dislikes student	unusual effort	unusual disruption by other student
Not controllable	lack of ability	task difficulty	mood	luck

SOURCE: Weiner, 1979

Now the problem is to predict the attributional choice. How do we decide what determined this particular success or failure? In one experiment, Frieze and Weiner (1971) gave different subjects information about someone who had succeeded or failed in a task. They were told that the person had succeeded or failed at a similar task in the past, and that most other people had succeeded or failed at the same task. Thus the subjects received consistency and consensus data. Then, subjects were told that the person tried one more time at the task and either succeeded or failed.

The subjects were now asked to explain the success or failure of the person. They tended to attribute the outcome to internal causes when the performance was consistent with past performance by that person and different from the outcome of others. Thus, for example, when someone had succeeded as usual where others usually failed, that person's success was seen as due to great effort or outstanding ability. If the performance outcome reflected both high consistency for the person and high consensus with others, it was attributed to task difficulty. Thus, for example, if someone failed again, but others also had failed, the outcome was seen as due to a very difficult task. Where the outcome was inconsistent with past performance, effort and luck were seen as important in explaining that outcome.

Using this model, Deaux (1984) demonstrated the influence of sex roles on attributions about success and failure. In one study, male and female subjects viewed a man or woman ostensibly participating in a perception task, in which the object was to identify "hidden objects" in pictures. For half of each group, the objects were "female-typed" (e.g., household utensils) and in the other, "male-typed" (e.g., mechanical tools). The data showed a clear trend, with both males and females attributing male success to internal factors and female success (particularly in the "male task") to luck. Other studies show that in many tasks, success is expected of males but not of females; thus attributions tend to be internal/stable for male success, but unstable (luck or unusual effort) for females. As expected, stereotypes profoundly influence our interpretations of social reality.

Weiner's model has also been tested with data from the sports pages (Lau and Russell, 1980). Content analyses were performed with reports of games in which causal explanations for winning and losing were recorded. In general, unexpected outcomes ("upsets") generated a greater number of attributions — there seemed to be more to explain or justify. Also, a "self-serving bias" was evident. Winning was generally attributed to internal factors ("We all had a great day, everyone gave 150 percent), and losing to unstable/external factors ("It just wasn't our day"). Clichés such as these are often useful as attributions.

Self-attributions and exacerbation Sometimes thinking about things makes them worse. For example, people with insomnia go to bed with the expectation that they will have trouble getting to sleep. Hence, they experience restlessness, irritability, or anxiety, and perhaps, confusing thoughts and an accelerated heart rate. These symptoms of course, make it more difficult for them to fall asleep. While they began with the one problem — insomnia — they now face the additional problem of worrying about insomnia, which exacerbates the original problem.

Storms and Nisbett (1970) reasoned that the problem is attributional: "Something is wrong with me." They recruited subjects who reported having difficulty falling asleep. Two groups of them were given a placebo "medication" to take before bedtime while a control group received no pills. One medication group was told that the pills would reduce arousal, making them feel relaxed, while the others were told that they would increase arousal.

The results showed a "reverse placebo effect"; those who were told that the pills would decrease arousal fell asleep an average of 15 minutes later than before, while those who expected the pills to increase arousal fell asleep 12 minutes faster. These data are consistent with an attributional interpretation. Those subjects who believed that the pills caused their aroused state were no longer attributing this problem to "something wrong with me," and had broken the exacerbation cycle. Worrying about insomnia no longer kept them awake.

We might question the usefulness of this procedure. Ethically, such deception with patients is questionable, and practically, a patient who suffers from insomnia might wonder why a stimulant or arousing drug would be prescribed. Indeed, attempts to replicate the study have not been successful (Bootzin, Herman and Nicassio, 1976). Still, other approaches have been developed which assist people in making other truthful and non-exacerbating attributions about their problems. Indeed, another group of insomniacs was informed that the problem might be caused by a relatively high baseline level of physiological arousal. Not having to worry about some deep psychological problem which was keeping them awake, they had less difficulty in falling asleep (Lowery, Denney and Storms, 1979).

Attributional biases

Thus far, we have seen that these attribution theories are models of an essentially conscious and rational process. Indeed, Kelley uses the metaphor of the "naive scientist" who searches systematically for relevant information, and who then uses that information logically to explain behaviour. We have reviewed several experiments which show that, if you provide people with relevant information, they will use it in a rational way to explain behaviour and make sense of their world.

And yet, there is ample evidence to suggest that people may fall short of the idea of rationality implied by the "naive scientist" metaphor. Biases, as we will see, can have a pronounced effect on the process of attribution.

Fundamental attribution error (Ross, 1977) In explaining why people do what they do, we tend to use dispositional attributions and to underestimate the power of the situation. This tendency to exaggerate the importance of personal factors and to underestimate the influence of other people and other aspects of the situation is called the "fundamental error" because it is so widespread. For example, as we noted earlier, we tend to attribute what people write or say to their "true beliefs" even when we are told that the person was instructed to argue a certain position (Jones and Harris, 1967). If we meet someone who is abrupt and rude to us, we tend to attribute this to a personal characteristic of "rudeness," despite the fact that there may have been external causes, such as family problems, unreasonable professors, illness, or lateness for an important appointment.

The fundamental attribution error is so pervasive that readers of this textbook may find themselves surprised at the results of much research described. Studies will demonstrate the power of the situation in causing people to conform, to do what they have been told to do by authority, to help or harm someone, or to act in ways contrary to their own attitudes. These studies challenge our assumption that our actions flow from our own beliefs, values and moral character.

Actor vs. observer bias   People generally tend to attribute the actions of others to stable trait dispositions, but see their own behaviour as relatively more strongly influenced by situational factors. This does not contradict what we just described; both actors and observers tend to attribute behaviour to dispositions. However, in addition to the "fundamental error," we also are more likely to interpret *our own* behaviour rather than the behaviour of others to situational causes (Watson, 1982).

In one simple demonstration, male students were asked to write paragraphs explaining why *they* had chosen their girlfriends and university majors, and why *their best friends* had chosen their own girlfriends and majors. Responses were then coded for causal attributions. Subjects tended to attribute their own decisions to external reasons, e.g., "I decided to major in psychology because it is interesting," but their friend's decisions to dispositions, e.g., "He's going out with her because he's insecure" (Nisbett, Caputo, Legant and Marecek, 1973). In a medium security Canadian prison, inmates tended to attribute their actions to situational factors, while their social workers blamed the criminal, even though their training stressed the social causes of crime (Saulnier and Perlman, 1981).

Studies which compare smokers with non-smokers show that both groups believe that smoking has undesirable consequences (Loken, 1982). If we consider smokers as "actors" and non-smokers as "observers," we find some evidence of the bias: Smokers attribute their actions to situational factors (pleasure, difficulty of quitting, presence of others) and non-smokers to the dispositional weaknesses of smokers (Eiser, 1982). However, perhaps as a result of changes in social norms, more recent data show smokers to be unwilling to endorse any reason for smoking other than the strength of the habit (Sadava and Wiethe, 1985). Ex-smokers who have switched from actor to observer roles respond similarly to non-smokers.

Why do the attributions of actors and observers differ in this consistent manner? One reason is that they have *different perspectives* from which to view the same event. The actor's behaviour captures the attention of observers by engulfing their field of perception. By contrast, actors generally cannot directly observe themselves, and are more aware of the situation than they are of themselves. However when actors are shown a videotaped replay of themselves in a conversation, they tend to attribute their actions more in terms of their own characteristics (Storms, 1973). Also, actors and observers have access to *different information*. Actors know how they have acted in *different situations* (i.e., consistency and distinctiveness) and would be better able to judge how various situations influence their behaviour. Lacking this information, observers resort to a correspondent inference, that friendly people do friendly things.

This bias, however, is not an invariant law. When we can clearly identify external causes for a behaviour, we make external attributions as actors and observers alike (Monson and Hesley, 1982). For example, we would readily attribute the fear of people in a devastating earthquake to the situation. On the other hand, if we know someone well, and like or identify with that person, we tend to see the world more as they do, and even as observers, we use more situational attributions (Regan and

Totten, 1975). Moreover, one bias may overcome another. We often give ourselves the benefit of the doubt or take credit for what goes right (internal attributions). Let us now explore how attributions can help us to feel good.

Self-serving bias Protecting one's ego is an important need in the world of sports — there are ego-defensive tactics that occur after the goalie's save, the double-play or the heroic goal-line stand. Since success and failure have important implications for our self-esteem, we tend to attribute our own success to internal factors and failure to external factors. For example, students receiving examination grades of A or B attribute these to ability or effort, but, C, D or F grades are attributed to task difficulty or bad luck (Bernstein, Stephan and Davis, 1979). Incidentally, this bias does not seem to be limited to Western, achievement-oriented cultures. Subjects in Yugoslavia, Japan and several South American nations also are more likely to attribute success than failure to their own ability (Chandler, Shama, Wolf and Planchard, 1981).

The explanation may be more complicated than we might expect. An obvious hypothesis is that, because success and failure are so important to our self-esteem, internal attributions for failure would lower self-esteem and, thus, be very difficult to accept emotionally. A second, more subtle explanation is that self-serving attributions are self-presentations reflecting people's concern about their image to others. We want others to respect and admire us, to give us credit for success and to excuse our failures. Thus, in responding to someone or to a questionnaire, we will respond that our failures were externally caused, although we really may know differently. An interesting exception concerns divorced people, who often attribute the failure of their marriages to themselves, particularly when they are strongly attached to their ex-partners (Lussier and Alain, 1986).

Are self-serving attributions used to protect our self-image or the image we present to others? Riess, Rosenfeld, Melburg and Tedeschi (1981) tested these competing hypotheses in a rather ingenious way. Subjects were told that they had succeeded or failed in a test of word associations. They were asked to attribute their success or failure to ability, effort, task difficulty, or luck. To measure attributions, half of the subjects completed the usual paper-and-pencil questionnaire. The other half were hooked up to electrodes and told that this was a new, improved, extremely powerful lie detector which would indicate how they *really* felt. Then they were asked to respond to attributional questions in the way that they expected would be shown by the machine.

It was reasoned in this experiment that if self-serving attributions represented conscious impression-management tactics, then the success-internal/failure-external bias would be greatly reduced. Nobody wants to create an impression of being insincere. However, if the bias were an unconscious, defensive process, then the ruse would have no effect. The results showed that even where the subjects believed that the machine would reveal their true feelings, they responded in a self-serving manner, attributing success to themselves and failure to external factors. However, the self-serving bias was not as great in this situation as it was when questionnaires were administered.

Thus, both ego-defensive and self-presentation motives are involved in self-serving attributional biases. The relative importance of these two motives is dependent on a number of other factors. Failure in a task where competence is highly important to the person will arouse defensiveness; losing a tennis match will likely mean more to the self-esteem of a Boris Becker or Carling Bassett than to an average player. On the other hand, certain situations will tend to elicit subtle self-presentation needs. For example, after such a notable success as receiving an academy award, actors and actresses tend to give "gracious" acceptance speeches in which they attribute this achievement to their directors, producers, fellow performers, writers, cinematographers, spouses, parents, children, friends, and, of course, the adoring public. Thus, attributions are useful in creating the appropriate impression.

Defensive attributions Other attributions, in addition to those involving success and failure, are influenced by defensiveness, a need to protect our self-esteem and feelings of security. This influence is shown in an experiment by Walster (1966) in which subjects were given a report about an accident. The driver, Lennie, left his car parked at the top of the hill. The parking brake cable came loose, the car rolled down the hill and caused some damage. Subjects were asked to indicate the extent to which they attributed responsibility to Lennie for the accident. Interestingly, Lennie was held more responsible when severe damage happened or when someone was hurt than when the damage was minimal, even though there is no logic in making this distinction. Lennie was no more or less negligent in not having his brake checked, whether the consequences were severe, mild or non-existent. This effect, although rather small, has been found in many studies (Burger, 1981).

Why would severity of consequences affect the attribution of responsibility? Walster (1966) has suggested that we act in a defensive manner, avoiding the idea of a threatening event. We hold the victim more responsible for the action because to interpret it as an outcome of bad luck or an "act of God" would be to admit to the possibility that it could happen to us. Shaver (1970) has added two conditions which will arouse this defensiveness: (1) the situation described is one similar to our own; and (2) the protagonist is similar enough to us that we could imagine ourselves "in that person's shoes." Generally, experiments have supported this interpretation (Burger, 1981). For example, students attribute greater responsibility for a severe-consequences accident when the protagonist is described as a student than a middle-aged business executive (see Box 3-5).

An act of God? To whom might you attribute responsibility for this accident?

B · O · X   3   5

ATTRIBUTION OF RESPONSIBILITY AND THE LAW

Attribution of responsibility is fundamental to our legal system. Convicting someone of a crime implies not only that an action occurred but that the person intended to cause a consequence; the murderer shot with the purpose of killing the victim rather than in self-defense or accidentally confusing the victim with a nearby moose.

Similarly, a successful lawsuit for medical malpractice implies an attribution of responsibility to the physician in the sense of neglect or incompetence. The law also accepts the influence of consequences in judging an action. The only difference between murder and attempted murder might be inaccurate shooting, an absence of emergency medical care for the victim, or pure luck.

The law also accepts the attribution of diminished responsibility. In 1843 a young man named Daniel M'Naghten killed the private secretary to Sir Robert Peel while attempting to kill the British prime minister. His lawyer argued the novel defense that he could not be held legally responsible for his actions because he was under the "insane delusion" that he was being hounded by Peel and many other enemies. The historic judgment, known as the M'Naghten Rule, acquitted the defendant because "he did not know the nature and quality of the act he was doing, or if he did know it, that he did not know he was doing wrong."

With various modifications, this rule still applies in most jurisdictions. For example, in 1982 a man was not convicted of the attempted murder of President Ronald Reagan because he was acting under the obsession of winning the heart and mind of a movie star. The principle is still controversial, and many people believe that the defendant "got away with it" by using this defense. (On the other hand, diagnoses of impaired responsibility have been abused in some nations, e.g., the U.S.S.R., Uruguay, sometimes along with the use of neuroleptic drugs, to suppress political dissent (Stover and Nightingale, 1985).)

In a replication of Walster's accident-consequences study (Sadava, Angus and Forsyth, 1980) subjects were also provided with descriptions of persons behaving normally or in ways indicative of mental illness. When the protagonist was described as paranoid or highly anxious, less responsibility was attributed to the person for the accident. However, an alcoholic was assigned *more* blame, even though the alcoholic was also rated as highest in "mental illness." It appears that these subjects were still highly ambivalent about alcoholism as a sickness or a sin. For normal and anxious protagonists, the severity of consequences influenced the level of attributed responsibility as found in previous experiments.

The illusion of control   Let's follow this reasoning further — what, precisely, are we "defending" ourselves from in these cases? When we think about all the terrible things that can happen in life, we realize that much of it is beyond our control. Langer (1975) suggests that we cling to an *illusion of control*, an exaggerated belief in our own capacity to determine what happens to us in life. In one demonstration (Wortman, 1975), subjects were presented with two coloured marbles in a can, each representing a different prize. Some were told which marble represented the desirable prize, while others were not. Then subjects either chose a marble or were given one, without being allowed to see which was which. Consider that, in all cases, the subjects had absolutely no control over the outcome. However, they attributed more responsibility to themselves when they picked their marble without looking at it. Of course, those who run lotteries understand the illusion of control, often allowing people to select a ticket or select their "own combinations" of numbers.

The illusion of control can have more profound social implications. Lerner (1977) suggests that, to varying extents, people may have an illusory belief in a *just world*. This is a particular correspondent inference, in which good outcomes are believed to happen to good people and bad outcomes to bad people, and in which you get what you deserve and deserve what you get. For example, when you read about an automobile accident in which the driver was killed instantly, your anxiety level about driving may increase. However, when you find that the driver was not wearing a seatbelt, your anxiety decreases because you always wear one. Indirectly, you have blamed the victim in order to reduce your own anxiety. In several laboratory experiments, Lerner found that after seeing someone picked at random and ostensibly subjected to electric shocks, subjects who observed the event tended to denigrate the victims, to see them as somehow deserving of their predicament.

In this world view, victims do not exist — poverty, oppression, tragedy and injustice all happen because they're deserved. For example, in a recent comparative study of both children and university students, scores on a scale of just world beliefs were higher among white South Africans than white British subjects, even though the South Africans came from the relatively more liberal English-speaking population (Furnham, 1985). These beliefs may be useful to justify practices in an "unjust society." Two other examples provide further illustration: (1) Some have argued that the 6 million Jewish victims of the Holocaust were responsible for their fate because of their acquiescence, ignoring both the overwhelming and brutal force directed against them and the heroic revolts which did occur in ghettos and concentration camps (Davidowicz, 1975); (2) There is a persistent tendency, somewhat greater among men, including male police officers, to attribute responsibility for a rape to the victim, a belief that the victim was somehow "asking for it."

Victim blame may become self-blame when disaster or misfortune strikes. A major traumatic event such as a debilitating illness or injury, or being victimized by incest, rape, or other forms of violence, shatters the "illusion of control," the sense of living in a world which is meaningful, predictable, or just. In examining the research on people who have been victimized, Miller and Porter (1983) present the following, rather unexpected, findings: (1) Victims of such negative events often exaggerate their own responsibility for the event and its consequences; and (2) the degree of self-blame is often positively related to how successfully the person will cope. Self-blame may enable the person to maintain the "illusion of control" in life which can be channelled into constructive coping strategies. It also enables someone to believe in a just world, allowing for the possibility of deserving better in the future. Finally, self-blame is one way to impose meaning on an otherwise incomprehensible event.

Victor Frankl (1963) a psychoanalyst and survivor of the Holocaust, maintains that a search for meaning in life and experience is an essential component of human nature. The search for satisfactory attributions becomes particularly poignant and significant when suffering and grief are involved. For example, people who have emerged paralyzed from an accident struggle with the question, "Why me?"; their success in finding a philosophical answer enables them to cope more effectively with their circumstances (Bulman and Wortman, 1977). In some forms of victimization, the search for meaning is more difficult. Silver, Boon and Stones (1983) interviewed 77 adult women in Ontario who had been victimized in childhood by familial incest. Although an average of 20 years had elapsed since the last episode, over 80 percent were still searching for meaning. In contrast with the accident victims, most of the minority who felt they had made some sense of the event attributed it to specifics such as the psychopathology of the father or other perpetrator, or the troubled marriage of their parents, rather than viewing it in more abstract, philosophical terms. Finding an explanation did not end the search for meaning, however; it had not become a closed issue for these women.

An evaluation of attribution theories

In the years following the publication of Heider's (1958) seminal book, attributions have become a major focus of attention in social psychology. In addition to the theories about attributions described in this chapter, attribution-based theories and research have been published on such topics as aggressive behaviour, altruistic or helping behaviour, marital interaction, romantic love, loneliness, and attitude change. In the dialectical progression of any scientific discipline, an idea or trend tends to bring about its opposite idea or counter-trend. We will now examine several important evaluations of attribution theory.

Three critiques have been made: (1) that attribution theory is peculiar to a particular culture and does not describe human nature *per se*; (2) that attribution research is an artifact of what is asked of subjects in that people are not really aware of why they do what they do; and (3) that much of what people do is pretty "mindless" — they usually don't ask "why" of themselves or others. All of these criticisms have some validity.

The cultural critique begins with the premise that both the theorists and the subjects have come almost entirely from the U.S.A., a culture characterized by Sampson (1977) as being based upon the ideal of the self-contained individual. Attribution studies in other cultures reveal some different patterns. Relative to U.S. subjects, Hindu adults and children in India tend to stress external or situational attributions for both prosocial and deviant behaviour and do not seem to be prone to the "fundamental error" of overestimating dispositional attributions (Miller, 1984). Rodrigues (1981) reports that Brazilians tend to differ from U.S. subjects in their reactions to achievement-related attributions. Earlier research had provided subjects with various explanations for successes and failures of hypothetical persons; for example, Tom, the world's greatest tennis player, won without even trying. U.S. subjects (and West Germans) tended to reward those with low ability but high effort who succeeded, and to punish those with high ability and low effort who failed (Weiner and Kukla, 1970). However, Brazilians focused on those high in both ability and effort, rewarding them most for success and punishing them most for failure.

Certainly, cross-cultural research may alter or transform many of our hypotheses about attributions. Indeed, we may find completely different implications for attributions in less individualistic, more communally oriented cultures, in more fatalistic cultures less preoccupied with the "illusion of control," or in cultures less concerned with thinking in terms of linear cause-and-effect.

Even in Western cultures, can we assume that people generally are aware of causes, particularly of their own actions? Nisbett and Wilson (1977) reported a series of studies which challenge the model of human nature as thoughtful, insightful, deliberate, introspective. It seems that we are often unaware of that which influences our actions, unaware of how we respond in a given situation, often unaware and unconcerned that something is "causing" what we do. Some of the experiments are rather ingenious. In one, shoppers were asked to evaluate the quality of four totally identical nightgowns or nylon hose. Subjects showed a strong bias toward preferring the article on the right-hand side — although, in later questioning, the majority were unaware of this tendency and denied that they were influenced by it. In another experiment, subjects were asked to memorize a list of word pairs. Some pairs were designed to influence later responses by association. For example, those who had memorized the pair "ocean-moon" were twice as likely to name "Tide" when asked for a laundry detergent as were control subjects. However, rarely did subjects make this connection when asked to explain their choice. Rather, they responded with apparently "top of the head" remarks, attributing their response to the brand their mothers used. Nisbett and Wilson (1977) conclude that we often do not make attributions in our daily activities unless asked to do so, as happens in an experiment.

It also appears that much of what we do happens in a state of "mindlessness" in which we simply follow a well-learned "script." With repeated experience in certain social situations, we have "over-learned" the appropriate actions without demanding conscious attention. As one rather mundane example, we flush the toilet after using it without being aware of doing so, let alone thinking of why we do it. In an experiment, subjects were approached by an experimental stooge as they were about to use a photocopying machine. Some were asked to let the person use the machine before them, but were given no reason. Others were presented with a similar request along with a meaningful reason: "I'm in a rush." And others were given the same request with a meaningless, "placebo" reason: "May I use the machine first because I have to make some copies?" When the delay would be minimal to the subjects, they complied when presented with what sounded like a reason — even when it was no reason at all. They simply responded automatically according to a script: when someone asks a small favour and offers a reason or excuse for it, you comply. Obviously, no conscious thought was involved regarding the action or its causes (Langer, Blank and Chanowitz, 1978).

Are attributions really a normal part of our interior lives? Or do we usually only think "why" when someone asks us — for instance, in a social psychology experiment? To answer this question, we must turn to the experiments in which attributions are studied indirectly. Several methods have been employed. Some have used content analyses of written material, coding attributions in personal letters, newspapers, and personal journals. In others, subjects are asked to "think out loud" when engaged in a task. A third approach has observers indicate what questions they would like to ask an actor; these questions are later coded for causal content. These studies, most of which have concerned achievement-related situations, reveal considerable evidence that people often do think spontaneously about causal explanations for actions (Weiner, 1985).

Thus, the question now seems to be *when* attributional thinking occurs or what impells us to engage in an "attributional search." The evidence, some of which we have reviewed, suggests three types of situations in which we tend to ask "why": (1) when something unexpected happens, e.g., the underdog wins the game, the mark obtained on an examination is a pleasant or unpleasant surprise, the victim is not helped by bystanders; (2) when an event is personally very relevant, e.g., a major consequence affects you rather than someone else; and (3) when someone feels a desire to find some meaning in an important event, e.g., victims of major crime, illness or injury. A recent study by Holtsworth-Munroe and Jacobson (1985) of spontaneous attributional thinking in marriage found two points at which it occurs most frequently: in the early "honeymoon" stages of the relationship and during conflict.

B · O · X   3 - 6

THINKING ABOUT DRINKING: TIME OUT, SELF-HANDICAPPING, AND BLAMING THE BOTTLE

Some of our attributional searches involve alcohol. If we are aware of evidence that a person seems to have been under the influence, we tend to attribute responsibility to that fact (although in some situations, e.g., driving while intoxicated, we may then attribute responsibility to the person for being drunk).

In reviewing what is expected from alcohol in various cultures, MacAndrew and Egerton (1969) extracted a common theme of "time out": a widely-shared understanding that alcohol is a signal that normal social rules are suspended, and we can get away with behaviour that would otherwise be considered unacceptable. Careful experiments which vary both whether the subjects actually receive alcohol or a placebo, and whether they believe that they were drinking, reveal that this expectancy greatly accounts for the "disinhibiting" effects of alcohol (Marlatt and Rohsenow, 1980).

How do our attributions change when alcohol is involved? Based on a pilot study, certain behaviours were identified as being more likely to occur when a person is drunk (e.g., interrupting when someone else was talking, vandalism) or equally likely to occur when drunk or sober (e.g., eating too much, forgery). Short scenarios were then constructed for each behaviour, depicting a middle-class, middle-aged male who was presented as either a chronic alcoholic or a social drinker who was either drunk or sober at the time. For each story, subjects were then asked questions concerning attribution of responsibility or blame, and the severity of a recommended punishment.

In general, less responsibility and blame for the act were attributed to intoxicated actors, although

equally severe punishment was suggested. Whether the act was usually associated with drunkenness, and whether the person was identified as a chronic alcoholic had no significant effects on attributions. The influence of an intoxicated actor on attributions was much stronger in the cases of more serious or deviant acts such as robbery, assault, forgery, and embezzlement. It seems that, especially in more unusual criminal acts, we are impelled to search for a cause. Lacking other information, we tend to rely on a *causal schema* (Kelley, 1972), a general assumption about cause and effect built on a lifetime of personal experience and shared beliefs in our culture. One such belief is that alcohol diminishes personal responsibility; when alcohol is present, we will discount other possible explanations (Critchlow, 1985).

If we believe that alcohol diminishes personal responsibility in moral situations, then the same would be true in achievement situations — we are less responsible for failure when alcohol is involved. Indeed, alcohol can be seen as one of a set of self-handicapping devices which we may use to protect our self-esteem from the effects of failure. If students feel strongly threatened by the possibility of failing a course, they may handicap themselves in advance by not studying, losing important notes, not getting enough sleep, getting too involved in other activities, or by drinking too much. If, despite all odds, they succeed, they can attribute their success to impressive ability. If they should fail, as expected, they can then attribute responsibility to the handicap. In some cases, self-handicapping as a defensive attribution is linked to problem drinking (Berglas, 1987).

SOCIAL COGNITION

So far, we have been discussing how individuals try to understand and make sense of their social world. In assessing what is known about impression formation and attributional processes, two facts stand out. First, we tend to form impressions and make judgments about people quite rapidly. And, we do not simply absorb information and apply logic, but we are active in processing information, often in biased ways. Despite our tendencies to take "cognitive shortcuts," not waiting for all the evidence, we seem to carry on effectively in our daily lives. Thus the ways we deal with information may be described as rather subtle, rapid, and yet sufficiently accurate for us to function in our environment.

In the past decade, social psychologists have become increasingly interested in these processes, and have linked their work to basic research in cognitive psychology. We now examine how information about the social world is organized or "coded" in terms of meaningful categories. Then we will consider how these categories are used in interpreting people and events, using cognitive "rules of thumb" and certain biases.

Categorical thinking

Of course, we know that every person is unique, and that no two parties, classes, or hockey matches are exactly alike. And yet, we cannot ignore that there are also similarities among certain types of people or events. If we were to approach every person and event as totally unique, without having any expectations about what they will be like, we would be overwhelmed by the uncertainty and complexity of modern life. Thus, we tend to organize our view of the world in terms of categories. People are generally categorized in terms of easily observable characteristics. We can (usually) assign people to categories of sex, racial group, or age. We can use other observable cues such as type of clothing, speech characteristics or language, or place of work to assign people to ethnic group category, nationality, or occupation.

Prototypes   But the process is often much more complex. Cantor and Mischel (1979) suggest that we often use *prototypes*, representations or mental images of a typical example of that category. For example, you may picture a dog as a prototype of the category of mammals (four legs, fur, lives on land). If you were to see an unfamiliar animal in the zoo, you would decide whether it was a mammal by comparing it to a dog (which might give you trouble when it comes to whales). Similarly, you may have a prototype of the elderly, perhaps a grandparent, or the smiling, silver-haired, wrinkled, kindly person often shown on television or in elementary school books. The extent to which a particular person (or animal) resembles the prototype, and the extent to which you allow for variations, will determine how readily the person is identified with the category. For example, Brewer, Dull and Lui (1981) presented subjects with photos and verbal labels of people in certain categories, e.g., grandmother. Then they provided more information about the person. This information was processed more rapidly and included more frequently in the subject's impression of the person when it was consistent with the prototype (e.g., "kindly" for a grandmother) than when it was not consistent (e.g., "aggressive" for a grandmother).

Stereotypes   A *stereotype* refers to a particular kind of prototype for which "a consensus exists among members of a group regarding the attributes of another" (Taylor, 1981,

p. 155). Borrowing from the terminology of the printing industry (a stereotype is a plate taken from a mold of composed type), journalist Walter Lippmann (1922) originally described stereotypes as "pictures in the head" that we have about members of a group. Lippmann and others (e.g., Brigham, 1971) conceived of stereotypes as fundamentally negative, motivated by prejudice, and enabling us to assume that members of a disadvantaged out-group are "all the same." They are also seen as lacking external validity, and research points to numerous examples of stereotypes which exist without any basis in fact, e.g., Blacks as "inferior in intelligence," Jews as "mercenary."

Since stereotypes are intrinsic to prejudice, and fulfill needs related to this problem, a full discussion of them will be presented in that context (see Chapter 7). However, it is important to understand that stereotypes enable us to organize our thoughts about people, reducing complexity to manageable proportions where we might otherwise suffer from information overload. They help to guide our own behaviour and to interpret the behaviour of people from other groups. While the content of the stereotype may or may not be accurate, its existence aids our capacity to make sense of the social world.

Lay Epistemology   Evidence that stereotyping represents a fundamental cognitive process has been reported in some elegant research by Kruglanski (Kruglanski and Freund, 1983). Kruglanski is concerned with how people arrive at what they "know," the process of "lay epistemology." In particular, he is concerned with "freezing," in which the individual becomes unaware of other possible explanations, or of new evidence which is not consistent with the person's conclusion. (For instance, during the Watergate scandal of 1972–1974, a U.S. Senator expressed his unconditional support for President R.M. Nixon, adding, "Don't confuse me with the facts.") It was proposed that "freezing" occurs (i.e., that people become more closed-minded) under certain conditions. One of these is when we feel a high need for structure, a sense of certainty under pressure, such as "little time" — then we tend to want to reduce confusion and come to a decision quickly. Another condition related to "freezing" is a "fear of invalidity"; when we are concerned about being wrong, freezing may occur.

Kruglanski and Freund (1983) manipulated both need for structure and fear of invalidity in three experiments involving very different tasks. Evaluation apprehension was manipulated by informing some subjects that their performance would be judged and communicated to others, while other subjects were assured that only group data and norms were being looked at in the experiment. Some subjects were allowed only a very limited time to complete the task, while others were allowed more than enough time. In one experiment Israeli student teachers were asked to read and grade a composition ostensibly written by a child with an Ashkenasi or Sephardi name (note: these are the two major cultural groups of Jews in Israel, the former primarily of European background and the latter of Arab and North African backgrounds; Sephardic Jews tend to be relatively disadvantaged in contemporary Israeli society). The results of all three experiments showed a similar pattern. That is, "freezing" such as that which was elicited by stereotypes was greatest when there was no evaluation apprehension and when there was time pressure. In other words, stereotyping as a cognitive process is influenced in the same way by the same factors as other cognitive processes. It is not simply a socially learned "picture in the head" but one example of a way of making sense of our world.

Social Schemata   At a more complex level are cognitive *schemata* (derived from the Greek word for plan or structure). These are sets of interconnected beliefs, information and examples about social objects: all that we "know" about something. For example, we may have a schema of a "Yuppie" (young urban professional) who wears designer clothes, eats gourmet foods but never to excess, drinks Perrier water, fine wine or light alcohol beverages, is very conscious of health and physical appearance, is very ambitious and career-oriented, advances on the "fast track" by "networking" and distributing personal business cards. The schema may also include exclusionary features, cues which indicate that this is not a Yuppie: having a large family, eating beef stew, driving a truck, bowling, having a beer belly. As with prototypes and stereotypes, schemata help us to organize and simplify a lot of information that we have received, help us to interpret new information more rapidly and determine what will be encoded and remembered. Note that prototypes and stereotypes are relatively simple examples of schemata.

There are various types of schemata. *Person schemata* refer to specific people such as a famous star, a public figure, your parent, a professor. For example, we may have a schema of a prime minister as being honest, hard-working, decisive, concerned with people in distress, wanting to conciliate and resolve conflicts between people, groups and regions. What makes this a schema, rather than simply a collection of ideas or traits, is that we see all of these characteristics as logically fitting together, as aspects of a sincere, conscientious politician. If he or she were to appear on TV with an eloquent request that all of us work hard and sacrifice for the good of the nation, we would interpret this speech in terms of our schema. We also have schemata about types of persons, e.g., people who are "extroverts," "enthusiastic," "out-going," "self-assured," etc. Of course, we also have schemata about objects such as automobiles — what they look like, how they are used, what they can do for us in terms

Do you have a schema for this group of people?

of transportation, comfort, social status, and how they are different from boats, buses and burros.

One important person schema is the one people have of themselves. *Self-schemata* do not simply represent how we view or rate ourselves on various dimensions but, also which dimensions we consider to be the important ones. For example, Markus (1977) asked people to rate themselves along a dimension of independence-dependence, and to indicate how important the trait was to them. Regardless of how they rated themselves, those who had self-schemata which included independence-dependence (i.e., the dimension was self-rated at either extreme and the dimension itself was rated important) were compared with those who were "aschematic" on this dimension (self-rated around the middle, the dimension rated low importance). Several weeks later, subjects were shown slides containing various words and asked to push a button labelled "me" if it applied to them or "not me" if it didn't. Subjects with self-schemata which included independence-dependence made decisions more quickly about words related to that dimension (e.g., "conforming") but not about irrelevant words (e.g., "creative"). Thus, self-schemata helped them process information more rapidly. These same subjects were also able to think of personal examples of these traits more quickly (e.g., "conforming": "I had my ears pierced just because everyone else did.")

Another interesting type of schema refers to *events*. For example, we may have an *event schema* referring to a group of friends going to a hockey game. It begins with purchasing the ticket, presenting it to a ticket taker, finding our seats. Perhaps we might buy a program and begin to identify players as they warm up. We stand for the national anthem, then sit and shout encouragement during the opening face-off. Purchasing snacks and liquid refreshments between periods is usually part of the ritual. We have standard reactions to a goal by our team, to a goal by their team, we know when and how to express disapproval of actions by the referee or opposition (in much of Europe, they whistle rather than "boo"). All of these events "fit" as part of what happens to us when we go to a game. Think of other event schemata: writing a university examination, a date for the movies, supper in a Chinese restaurant, going to the beach, a day at work. Of course, we follow scripts, albeit more complex than the compliance script involving the photocopying machine, described earlier. We have learned the script through personal experience and social modelling, and so we experience the events as predictable, understandable and comfortable.

Finally, we have schemata about *social roles*, organized mental structures about people who belong to social categories. We may have role schemata about physicians, professors, students, friends, lovers, insurance salespeople, butchers, mothers, and bureaucrats. Note that while person schemata refer to a specific individual, role schemata refer to people in general from a certain category. Thus, we may have role schemata about politicians in general and perhaps about prime ministers in general, as well as a person schema about a specific prime minister.

Role schemata are generally restricted to role-relevant situations, although physicians may often find themselves seen and treated as physicians in a social situation. A role schema may be idealized and unrealistic: few people can live up to a schema of "lover" as being *always* devoted, understanding, supportive, affectionate, passionate — and never selfish, childish, or tired. Conflict often arises when people in different roles have different schemata of their own and other roles. A professor's schema about a student role may include constant interest and attention while the student feels that she or he must balance the student role with other roles, demands, and problems. The student's schema of professor may, in turn, consist entirely of teaching and showing concern for students, while the professor's own schema includes research and publishing, participation in department and university committees, and consulting in the community. Thus, the professor is exasperated when the student hasn't kept up with assigned reading, while the student is exasperated when the professor is not always available in the office.

There are several characteristics common to these types of schemata. First, schemata tend to be organized hierarchically, from the general to the more specific. For example, we may have a general schema for the concept "party" and more specific schemata for an informal, loud-music bash in someone's basement, children's birthday parties, wine and cheese parties at an art gallery, parties of the local business elite at the country club, parties in student residences, even faculty parties. Second, people or groups of people may differ in specific schemata. For example, university students think of intelligence primarily in relation to academic and intellectual matters, while people interviewed in supermarkets tend to see it in terms of being able to solve practical problems and not to "act stupidly" in social situations (Sternberg, Conway, Ketron and Bernstein, 1981). Finally, remember what all this is about: social reality is extremely complex and we make sense of it by simplifying it. While making our thinking more efficient, schemata may not make it more accurate. The following section evaluates social schemata.

Processing social information

In discussing social schemata, we have stressed the fact that social categorization is useful to us. Given that we are constantly exposed to an enormous amount of information, much of it complex and ambiguous, schemata enable us to process this information swiftly and efficiently. But what do we mean by "processing information"? We have already seen evidence that those who held a particular self-schema (e.g., independence-dependence) were able to make decisions more rapidly about whether a particular, related adjective described them (Markus, 1977). Schemata help us to interpret information and events, for example, to decide whether we agree with something. While we can rarely know everything about anything, schemata help to "fill in the gaps" by providing us with a "best guess" about what is likely to be true. They can help us to be prepared for the future by providing us with expectations. And they can help us to recall information by providing a structural framework. Indeed, the research which has accumulated in a relatively few years provides impressive evidence of how pervasive and fundamental are schemata in all social experience (Fiske and Taylor, 1984).

Attention Selective attention is one important effect of schematic thinking. In one experiment by Swann and Read (1981) subjects were asked to rate themselves on the traits of assertiveness and emotionality. On the basis of high or low ratings on these two characteristics, subjects could be divided into four groups. They were then told that as part of a "get acquainted" experiment, their self-ratings would be shown to someone else who would answer a series of questions about the subject. Subjects were then given the list of questions about themselves and asked to select which ones they would prefer be used. The questions were about assertiveness and emotionality and were phrased or slanted in such a way as to elicit an answer confirming the presence or absence of a trait. For example, "What makes you think that X would complain in a restaurant?" would be seen as eliciting an answer confirming assertiveness, while "Why do you think this person doesn't get angry, even when provoked?" would be perceived as asking for evidence that the person is not highly emotional.

Subjects showed preference for questions likely to confirm their self-schemata. For example, assertive subjects would tend to select the first question, while subjects who rated themselves as emotional would tend to avoid the second question. Note that ego-defensiveness is not the issue here; while people may prefer positive to negative feedback, they also prefer feedback consistent with their self-image, even where it is negative. Thus, people with a very poor self-concept tend to pay special attention to their failures and shortcomings, and to ignore strengths and successes or reinterpret them (e.g., "I was lucky").

Memory Schemata have important effects on memory. They can influence what is remembered and even distort our memory of past events. We may have difficulty in remembering information not related to a schema or inconsistent with it. Rothbart, Evans and Fulero (1979) told groups of subjects that they would receive information about a hypothetical group of men who tended to be "more friendly and sociable than average" or "more scholarly and oriented toward achievement than average." Thus, the two groups were given different schemata about these men. All subjects were then presented with a list of 50 behaviours, including 17 friendly behaviours (e.g., invited friends to a potluck supper) and 17 scholarly achievement behaviours (e.g., he was the class valedictorian). After seeing all 50 behaviours, they were asked to estimate how many were friendly, how many were intellectual achievements, and to recall as many of them as possible. The results show how schemata, even those which have been experimentally induced, influence remembering and forgetting. For example, those with the "friendly" schema estimated 14.4 friendly actors and recalled 4.7 of them (of a total of 17) but estimated only 11.6 intellectual behaviours. This particular effect of schemata is called *priming*, an effect which makes a subsequent cognitive process more efficient. We will see more of this effect later.

In another study concerning stereotypes, school teachers were provided with a detailed case description of a child, including a photograph. Subjects saw a photo of a young girl taken in front of an obviously middle class house or an obviously lower class house. They were then shown a videotape of the child taking an achievement test in which the child appeared either attentive and interested or bored and distracted. Then the teachers were asked to predict future academic performance and to support their prediction with what they had seen in the tapes. Those who saw a middle class child predicted better performance in school than those who saw a lower class child. More startling, they recalled instances of the middle class child acting like a "good student" — even on the "bored and distracted" tape — and instances of the lower class child acting like a "poor student," even when they had been shown the videotape of an attentive and interested child. Thus, the photo acted as a cue for social class stereotypes which served to bias the teachers' judgments and to prime the recall of consistent information (Darley and Gross, 1983).

Conway and Ross (1984) have demonstrated that our memory of past events can be influenced by a particular aspect of schemata — our expectation or "theory" of what should have happened. In this study subjects had enrolled in an extravagantly advertised study skills program. After an initial questionnaire in which they evaluated their own skills, subjects were assigned to the program or to a waiting list. After the

Typist at work: Automatic information processing takes over once schemata are well ingrained.

program was completed, all subjects were re-interviewed. A follow-up showed that the program had no significant effect on their grades. However, subjects *believed* that they had improved. When asked to recall how they had rated their skills previously, subjects who completed the program recalled "before" as worse than it had seemed to them at the time. These subjects applied a schema of self-improvement to distort their memory of the past in order to improve the present.

In another study subjects were exposed to persuasive messages about frequent bathing or toothbrushing which either stressed the benefits or dangers of the behaviour. Later, they were asked in a different situation to recall how often in the recent past they had done a number of things, including bathing and toothbrushing. These estimates were consistent with the persuasive message they had received. For example, subjects who had been persuaded that too much bathing could be dangerous later recalled that they had bathed less often than other subjects. Thus our memories of the past can be revised to be consistent with present thinking. For example, we may recall our high school years as happier than they were because we now have a "good old days" schema of that period of life (Ross, McFarland, Conway and Zanna, 1983).

Thus far, we have pursued a model in which schemata enable us to remember *consistent* information. However, inconsistency—the novel or unexpected—can sometimes demand attention. For example, Hastie and Kumar (1979) provided subjects with an initial description of a person, thus providing them with a person schema. Then they were given a list of behaviours which were consistent, inconsistent or irrelevant to the initial description. For example, if the schema provided to the subjects included "honesty," then the list might include returning a lost wallet (consistent), cheating on an examination (inconsistent) and going to the movies (irrelevant). Subjects later recalled the *inconsistent* information better, which seems inconsistent with the powerful directive function of schemata already discussed. Hastie suggests that we are attracted to inconsistent stimuli and pay attention to them — if we have time. When life is too busy or complex, however, and we don't have the time, we depend on schemata to direct our attention and influence our memory.

In these situations, or in situations where the schemata are well ingrained, automatic information processing takes over. The novice first learning to drive is aware of everything: the gas pedal, gears, brakes, steering, the on-coming car. With experience, we rarely think about what we are doing when we drive unless something unexpected attracts our attention. Although a lot of information is being processed (e.g., the appearance of the road, the sound of the motor, the feel of the steering wheel), the process is automatic.

The same process has been demonstrated in the area of social perception. (Bargh and Cerny, 1983). By asking subjects to "describe types of people," a group was identified who frequently used the category of "honesty." That is, they had an *available* schema about persons around this characteristic. This group and control groups were then presented with a list of behaviours of a person at a very rapid rate, allowing just enough time to read, but not think about, the list. Half of the subjects read a list including six honest acts and 12 dishonest acts while the other half read a list of 12 honest and six dishonest acts. Later, all subjects were asked to rate the target person on a ten-point scale.

Those who had an available schema for honesty were influenced by the proportion of honest to dishonest acts, rating the 12-honest person significantly more highly than the 12-dishonest person. However, the control subjects' ratings were not influenced by this information because they were unable to process it. There is no doubt that given more leisurely circumstances, these subjects would also be influenced by the honest or dishonesty of the person's behaviour. As we saw earlier, in the case of attributions, certain situations elicit schematic processing (e.g., rapid information flow, priming) and others do not.

Biases in social inferences

As we have warned, efficiency does not mean accuracy. Just as humans often fail to follow the rules of formal logic in making causal attributions, they often conserve cognitive energy in arriving at social inferences. These shortcuts tend to follow certain rules or regularities underlying the process. Recent research and analysis has uncovered some of these rules, or *heuristics* (see Table 3-3).

(1) *Ignoring baserates.* In judging people, we tend to fall prey to the "gambler's fallacy." Suppose you're betting on flips of a coin and "heads" comes up ten times in a row. Would you be willing, as most people would, to give 2:1 odds that tails

TABLE 3–3
Some strategies for making judgments in situations of uncertainty

Heuristic	Judgment	Example
1. Representativeness	Probability	Decide that Steve is a librarian because he looks and acts like your stereotype of librarians.
2. Availability	Frequency/probability	Decide that divorce is very common because you can quickly think of several couples who broke up recently.
3. Adjustment and anchoring	Position on a dimension	Decide how aggressive or shy someone is on the basis of how you rate yourself.
4. Simulation	How something will come out	Decide how someone is likely to react to failing the course based on how easily you can image various possibilities.

SOURCE: Tversky and Kahneman, 1974; Kahneman and Tversky, 1982

would come up next time? If so, you probably should abstain from gambling; there is a 50-50 chance (i.e., baserate) riding on each flip in an independent event.

Hamill, Wilson and Nisbett (1980) conducted a study which provided a rather dramatic social demonstration of this principle. Subjects saw a videotape in which a psychologist was ostensibly interviewing a prison guard. For half of the subjects, the guard expressed very negative, even brutal, attitudes toward prisoners (i.e., they're all "losers" who should be kept locked up). The other half saw a guard expressing more optimistic, humane attitudes toward prisoners and their rehabilitation. Some of each group were told that this guard was quite "typical" of prison guards, others that the guard was quite "atypical" (humane or inhumane) and others were given no baserate feedback about how typical or representative this person was of prison guards.

Subjects were then administered a questionnaire concerning their attitude toward prison guards in general. Those who had viewed an interview with a humane guard expressed significantly more positive attitudes toward this group, regardless of whether the person was represented as typical or atypical. That is, people tend to infer about a group from a particular example and to ignore baserate information. Needless to add, we frequently see this dynamic in instances of prejudice — one instance of being treated rudely can cause a tourist to condemn an entire nation. It can also lead to a false historical analogy; because of some superficial similarities, a situation in Central America may be perceived as representative of the European surrender to Hitler at Munich, ignoring all other relevant baserate data (see Chapter 13 on "deterrence" versus "conflict spiral" schemata).

(2) *The illusory correlation*. When two events covary or are correlated, they tend to occur together. As noted earlier, we tend to look for covarying events in our social world, and to draw inferences of cause and effect from them. However, when we expect such a linkage between events or characteristics, we tend to inflate the relationship well beyond its true value. This inflation is called the "illusory correlation" and can cause people to make unwarranted inferences or assumptions. For example, in an experiment, subjects were shown pairs of words. Although all word pairs were shown the same number of times, subjects tended to overestimate the frequency of word pairs which seemed to belong together, such as bacon-eggs, and tiger-lion (Chapman and Chapman, 1969).

Subjects in another study were shown photos of a stranger and later asked to recognize them among a larger group of photos. They were much more successful when the stranger was from their own race (Black or White) than from the other race (Barkowitz and Brigham, 1982). In a more realistic setting, two experimental accomplices, one Black and one White, visited a number of "convenience stores" in Florida. Each accomplice engaged in at least one activity designed to enhance his or her uniqueness, e.g., paying entirely in pennies for a purchase, asking for directions to the airport. About two hours later, the clerks were shown a set of photos of six Black or White persons and asked to indicate whether any had visited the store recently. While overall accuracy was only 48.6 percent (see discussion on eye witness testimony in Chapter 15), it was particularly low where the race of the customer differed from the race of the clerk. The illusory correlation becomes manifest as an expectation that people who are unlike ourselves are "all alike."

Contemporary research has challenged the notion that "masculinity" and "femininity" are opposite ends of one psychological dimension. Thus, associating "male" or "female" with many other traits can be considered an illusory correlation. Many individuals see themselves as having a mixture of characteristics typically considered "masculine" (e.g., competitiveness, independence, self-confidence) and typically seen as "feminine" (e.g., warmth, kindness, gentleness). That is, if we consider "masculinity" and "femininity" as separate scales, some score high in one and low in the other (i.e., masculine/feminine sex-typed), some score low in both (undifferentiated), and some score high in both. Bem (1974) suggests the label *psychological androgyny* to describe those who perceive themselves as having both masculine and feminine characteristics.

We can consider sex-role self-perception in terms of a particular self-schema: a high/low pattern of sex-role self-typing would be indicative of a schema, while androgynous and undifferentiated individuals would be called aschematic, that is, without sex-typed schemata. These two types of individuals were compared in an experiment (Frable and Bem, 1985) in which they listened individually to a taped conversation among six people while pictures (stills) were shown of the speakers as they spoke. For half of the subjects, the conversation group consisted of three males and three females. For the control subjects, the group consisted of three Whites and three Blacks, all the same sex as the subject. Then, subjects were presented with a list of 72 quotes from the conversation and asked to identify the speaker for each one.

What was important in the results was the *pattern of errors* made by each group of subjects. In the race-difference condition, no strong pattern was evident. But, with the sex-difference group, the sex-typed subjects made most of their errors by confusing who said what among the opposite-sex members. That is, a sex-typed self-schema caused subjects to see members of the opposite sex as, somehow, "all alike," a special case of the illusory correlation.

In another study, subjects were presented with a list of opinions about building a nuclear plant near a town. The statements were purported to be taken from two towns, one of which was larger than the other; thus one list contained more statements than the other. In both lists, two thirds of the statements took one side of the issue and one third took the other side (i.e., for or against building the nuclear plant). Later, subjects were asked to remember as many statements as possible from each town. Although the *proportion* of pro vs. anti opinions was the same for both towns, subjects consistently overestimated the extent of the minority opinion in the small town. They also tended to overestimate the proportion of attitudes similar to their own, particularly when it represented the minority opinion (Spears, van der Pligt and Eiser, 1985).

(3) *Overemphasizing extremity.* One bias in our reasoning processes which departs from logic is our tendency to be excessively influenced by extreme examples. This is illustrated by a study (Rothbart, Fulero, Jensen, Howard and Birrell, 1978), in which subjects read 50 statements about actions by hypothetical strangers. While 40 of them were innocuous, ten described crimes. For one group of subjects, the crimes were fairly mild and non-violent (e.g., petty vandalism, shoplifting), while for the other, ten were serious crimes such as murder and rape. When later asked to estimate the *frequency* of crime in that group, estimates were much higher among those who read about serious crimes, even though the real proportion was not greater in that group. Since extreme cases bias our inferences about the rate of an event, it is not surprising that television may distort our perception of reality by its focus on crime, scandal, violence, and other bad news.

(4) *The availability heuristic.* A heuristic is a "rule of thumb" in our minds which guides our inferences without our being aware that we are following a rule. One of

the most important heuristics discovered by Tversky and Kahneman (1974) is deceptively simple: if something comes readily to mind, we tend to assume that it is probably true and use it. For example, someone may ask you how (or whether) you're
enjoying this course in psychology. You may quickly recall an interesting lecture, a
fascinating tidbit of information, an interesting seminar discussion, and then use this
available information to answer the question. While there may have been less-than-
ideal moments in class, they don't come readily to mind.

Two simple experiments illustrate the phenomenon. During the 1976 presidential
election campaign in the U.S.A., subjects were first asked to imagine what it would
be like if either Jimmy Carter or Gerald Ford were to win the election. When asked
later to predict the winner, their prediction tended to be the same candidate they
had earlier been asked to imagine as the winner (Carroll, 1978). In another study,
subjects were presented with evidence concerning a trial for driving while intoxicated.
While the evidence was equally strong in both cases, one incident was described
differently to subjects. One group was told that the defendant had staggered and
fallen against a table at a party. The other group was told that when he fell against
a table, he knocked over a bowl of bright green guacamole onto a white shag carpet.
Forty-eight hours later, the subjects who had read the second description judged the
defendant as more probably guilty of drunk driving. Thus, availability was enhanced
by vividness of the information.

The evidence of an availability heuristic raises interesting questions about the interpretation of ambiguous social events. Are psychiatrists or psychologists more likely
to interpret an action as indicating mental illness because these are their working
concepts which are readily available? Similarly, do police officers perceive an escalating
crime wave? Do auto mechanics see problems which need repairing? Do physicians
see sickness behind every symptom? Do accountants see mostly financial ruin or tax
breaks? Of course, being an "expert" means having attained special skills and qualifications to make certain judgments. However, there may be an availability heuristic
bias that "goes with the territory" of being an expert.

(5) *Priming and availability*. Schemata are also subject to the availability heuristic.
Suppose, for example, we have just watched a particularly "tear-jerking" episode of
a soap opera involving a marriage conflict, infidelity, and all the other aspects of "day-
to-day life." Then we meet the new couple who moved in next door. Are we more
likely to notice or interpret signs of tension between them, or to interpret their tension as a marital problem (rather than the tensions and fatigue of moving)? Research
evidence suggests that this is often the case. A schema about marriage problems has
been activated for us which we may then use to interpret events. On the other hand,
if we had just seen a particularly passionate episode of the same soap opera (involving
a married couple) we might notice, interpret, and remember very different types of
information about our new neighbours.

As we saw earlier, the phenomenon involving the activation into availability of
certain categories or schemata is called *priming*. In an elaborate experiment (Srull and
Wyer, 1980) male and female subjects were instructed to construct sentences from
four word sets. Some of the word sets contained hostile content or suggestion (e.g.,
leg, break, arm, his), while others contained neutral content only (e.g., her, found,
know, I). For one group of subjects, 15 of the 50 sets suggested hostility, while for
the other, 35 of the sets had hostile connotations. The object was to prime a memory
category — in particular, hostility — in the subject group using 35 sets suggestive of
hostility.

Then, the effects of this priming were tested on the subjects' memory of a person. Subjects read a paragraph which described the behaviour of a stranger in neutral terms with respect to hostility. Then, subjects were asked to rate the stranger on a number of characteristics, one of which was hostility, the primed category. To further explore the effects of priming on person memory, time was also varied. The interval between priming and presentation to various subjects of the information about the person was 24 hours, one week, or no delay at all. The interval between receiving the information and rating the stranger was also varied for different subjects as no delay, 24 hours, or one week. Thus, for example, some subjects received the information immediately after priming and rated the person 24 hours later and some received the information 24 hours after priming and rated the stranger one week later.

The results confirmed two predictions and contained a surprise. As expected, the same stranger was perceived as more hostile after subjects were primed with 35 items rather than with 15, thus confirming the effect of priming on category availability. Also as expected, the priming effect was greater when the information was received immediately than when there was delay. However, here is the surprise: the effects of priming were *greatest* when there was a rather long interval between receiving information and making judgments about the stranger. That is, once the category of hostility had been primed and made available when subjects formed their initial impression of the person, the subjects later remembered that person as being even more hostile than he or she had appeared earlier.

Simulation heuristic   One example of availability is in how readily we can imagine or construct various scenarios to try to guess what to expect (Kahneman and Tversky, 1982). For example, imagine the case in which Mr. Crane and Mr. Tees were scheduled to leave the same airport at the same time but on different flights. Both are caught in the same traffic jam on the way to the airport, and both arrive 30 minutes after the scheduled departure of their flights. Mr. Crane is told that his flight left on time, while Mr. Tees is told that the flight had been delayed and left five minutes ago. Who is more upset?

Most people would respond that Mr. Tees is more upset. This is because we cannot imagine that Mr. Crane could have made his flight, while Mr. Tees might well have made it, were it not for that slow traffic light or the illegally parked car or the misunderstanding about which gate. The simulation heuristic enables us to imagine "if only" conditions, which explains much about our reactions to near misses, second-guessing, and other frustrations.

INDIVIDUAL DIFFERENCES IN SOCIAL COGNITION

In discussing the processes of social cognition, we have seen the general patterns and biases which characterize how people think. However, individuals also differ in their cognitive styles, or dispositions, and these individual distinctions lead to important differences in how people make sense of their social world. Two of these variables are the ability to self-monitor, and integrative complexity.

Snyder (1979) has described how individuals vary in *self-monitoring*, the extent to which individuals are sensitive to the subtle cues observed in others, and in trying to manage the impressions that others have of them. His scale measures people's concern with the appropriateness of their self-presentation, whether they look to others for cues as to how to act appropriately, whether people can use these cues to modify their behaviour. As we would expect, high self-monitors tend to be more friendly, conformist, adaptive, and less shy. That people who score high and low differ in how much effort they devote to such information suggests cognitive differences. That is, high self-monitors should have a particularly rich and complex set of social schemata and stereotypes, useful both in categorizing and judging new people or new contexts and in deciding how to respond to create the desired impression. On the other hand, low self-monitors may tend to spend more time and effort in organizing the information that they have about themselves. Thus they would have a more secure and more complex image of who they are and their self-schemata would be more available.

Another difference in cognitive style refers to the complexity of the individual's information processing. People who are high in *integrative complexity* tend to be open-ended, flexible, able to make free differentiations and multiple integrations; in other words, they have access to a rich and complex set of social schemata. On the other hand, individuals who are low in complexity tend to be rather rigid and closed-minded, making relatively crude differentiations, and are incapable of integrating different perspectives. For example, the high-complexity person would consider a person in terms of various characteristics and social roles, could see both the favourable and unfavourable characteristics in the same person, and could change his or her mind about that person. The low-complexity person would tend to see someone simply as good or bad, a friend or an enemy, and would stick to that conclusion. Thus, for the low-complexity group, a particular situation would cue one, rather simple, schema and the judgment would follow. Suedfeld has explored this dimension of information processing, using non-experimental evidence in intriguing ways. Suedfeld and Rank (1976) coded the writings of a number of revolutionary leaders, comparing them before and after the revolution. They reasoned that during a revolutionary struggle, the leader must be relatively categorical and single-minded, whereas after a successful revolution, the leader must be more complex in both understanding and communicating in order to govern successfully. Indeed, leaders who remained powerful after the revolution (e.g., Lenin, Stalin, Castro, Jefferson) showed this shift toward greater complexity, while those who lost their influence (e.g., Trotsky, Guevara, Hamilton) remained relatively simple in their writings.

In another study researchers coded the published correspondence of a number of eminent men and women over the last ten years of their lives (e.g., Lewis Carroll, D.H. Lawrence, Freud, Liszt, Proust, Queen Victoria, Mary W. Shelley). Those who died after a long illness or at a ripe old age showed a gradual decline in integrative complexity over their last four years. However, those who died suddenly and unexpectedly showed a relatively steep decline in integrative complexity in their last year. Suedfeld and Piedrahita (1984) suggest that a decline in integrative complexity, a simplification in schematic processing, may occur naturally over time, particularly as an "intimation of mortality" in the period preceding death. Of course, considerably more direct evidence would be needed to support this interpretation.

A FINAL NOTE

The rather extensive and complex material in this chapter reveals a paradox of social life. It is important for people to understand and make sense of their world — particularly the people in it. We all know in theory how best to understand anything: get as much information about it as possible and think about it, carefully and logically. The paradox is that we cannot do this. There is just too much information to process and too little time to do it. We must decide and act, and cannot take the time and effort to do what we logically must do in order to "understand."

In other words, it is not sufficient to assume that we take in information, and that information determines whatever sense that we can make of the world. Our minds are active and our cognitive processes influence what information we notice or ignore, remember or forget, believe or disbelieve, weigh carefully or not at all. In short, we construct our view of the world just as the world constructs our minds.

Thus we take "cognitive shortcuts." We quickly form an impression of someone, apply some quick "rules of thumb" to arrive at explanations for their actions, apply schemata to filter information and react. We are subject to an impressive array of biases: central trait; positivity, and negativity; the effect of primacy and recency; the assumptions of our "implicit personality theories"; the "fundamental attribution error" of overestimating dispositional attributions, the actor vs. observer bias; self-serving and defensive attributions; the "severity of consequences" bias, or attributions of responsibility; the illusion of control, and belief in a just world; schemata and scripts; ignoring baserates; the illusory correlation; the availability heuristic; epistemic freezing; and cognitive rigidity. We have travelled far from a model of human nature based on rational information-processing. And yet, we are correct enough — often enough — to function.

SUMMARY

(1) In forming overall impressions of people, we have a bias toward forming positive impressions, and to be influenced more by certain salient characteristics (central traits) and negative information. In addition, we have our own unconscious assumptions about "human nature" (implicit personality theory).

(2) In combining information about various traits, we may simply add them together or average them to form an overall impression. A weighted averaging model best accounts for most data.

(3) We use tactics of impression management to influence how others perceive us, e.g., "playing hard-to-get," ingratiation.

(4) We vary in the extent to which we can detect certain cues in others who are deceiving us by concealing information or by overt lying.

(5) Attributions are causal explanations. When more than one explanation seems possible at the time, we tend to be less confident of our attribution (discounting). If one event tends to be associated in time and place with another, we tend to perceive a cause-effect relation between them (covariation).

(6) Kelley suggests that we function as "naive scientists" in making social attributions. We focus on information about consensus among actors, consistency across situations, and distinctiveness of the entity.

(7) In making a correspondent inference that an action was caused by a corresponding disposition, we are influenced by whether the act was freely chosen, was not con-

sidered socially desirable, led to a non-common outcome, had a direct impact on us (hedonic relevance) and seemed intended to affect us rather than someone else (personalism).

(8) Weiner's achievement attribution model focuses on whether a result was caused by something internal or external, and stable or unstable.

(9) Attributions are influenced by certain biases: we overestimate dispositional causes (the "fundamental error"); attribute our own behaviour to situations and others' to dispositions (actor vs. observer bias); we use self-serving attributions and attribute greater personal responsibility after severe consequences.

(10) We tend to believe that we control our environment, and that the world is just, and to blame victims for their fate. Victims themselves undergo a "search for meaning" through attributions.

(11) Attribution theory has been criticized as being peculiar to an individualistic North American-type culture, an artifact, not representative of the "mindlessness" of much behaviour.

(12) Our thinking about our social environment is organized into categories including prototypes and stereotypes. Schemata represent complex integrations of information and examples within categories of people, events, social roles, and the self. Schemata influence us in what to attend to or ignore, what to remember and how to interpret information.

(13) We tend to follow certain rules (heuristics) as cognitive shortcuts. We tend to ignore information about baserates, exaggerate the relationships between events (illusory correlations), overemphasize extreme cases, believe and use what comes readily to mind (availability) or what has been primed by external cues.

(14) Social cognition is influenced by individual differences in self-monitoring and integrative complexity.

FURTHER READING

EKMAN, P. (1985). *Telling lies: Clues to deceit in the marketplace, politics and marriage.* New York: W.H. Norton.

FISKE, S.T. and TAYLOR, S.E. (1985). *Social cognition.* Reading: Addison-Wesley.

HARVEY, J.H. and WEARY, G. (1981). *Perspectives on attributional processes.* Dubuque: W.C. Brown.

HASTORF, A. and ISEN, A. (Eds.) (1981). *Cognitive social psychology.* New York: Elsevier-North Holland.

NISBETT, R. and ROSS, L. (1980). *Human inference: Strategies and shortcomings of social judgement.* Englewood Cliffs, NJ: Prentice-Hall.

SHAVER, K.G. (1984). *An introduction to attributive processes.* Hillsdale, NJ: Erlbaum.

SHAVER, K.G. (1985). *The attribution of blame: causality, responsibility and blame worthiness.* New York: Springer-Verlag.

SCHLENKER, B.R. (1980). *Impression management: The self-concept, social identity and interpersonal relations.* Belmont, CA: Brooks/Cole.

SCHNEIDER, D., HASTORF, A., and ELLSWORTH, P. (1979). *Person perception.* Second edition. Reading: Addison-Wesley.

Attitudes and Values

I have but one love, Canada. One
purpose, its greatness . . . one aim, unity
from the Atlantic to the Pacific.
John Diefenbaker

The world needs Canada. If Canada
wasn't here, the Chinese could sail right
across and invade Denmark.
Dave Broadfoot

FOR REFLECTION

- Why should we study attitudes and values?
- How are attitudes measured? Are these measures reliable and valid?
- Do political beliefs reflect values or self-interest?
- Do people usually act on the basis of what they believe to be true or right?
- What is the relationship between attitudes and behaviour?

VERY FEW EXAMPLES of human behaviour can be found which are not, in some way, influenced by attitudes and values. The effect of attitudes can extend from the mundane, such as food preferences (chow mein or pirogi, hamburgers, or sushi), to issues of war and peace and the sublime aspects of religious experience. The form of government we prefer, the candidate we vote for, the type of mate we seek, and even the breed of dog we choose all reflect underlying beliefs and feelings. It is not surprising that the study of attitudes has been at the core of social psychology almost since the beginning. Indeed, during the 1930s social psychology and attitude research were almost synonymous.

However, social psychologists have not devoted a great deal of attention to the study of values. There is no obvious reason for this neglect, for it certainly cannot be argued that values are any less important than attitudes. Robinson and Shaver (1973) suggest that psychologists may have neglected values because they have seemed so vague and imprecise that adequate measurement and experimentation would be impossible. Recently, however, there have been signs of a renewed interest in values and their relationship to attitudes.

The present chapter examines the nature of attitudes and values at both individual and social levels. We then ask why people have attitudes and how values are important in relation to them. Finally, we explore the relationship between attitudes and values and the puzzling problem of why our thoughts and words often do not match our actions.

THE NATURE OF ATTITUDES

In the 1930s Gordon Allport (1935), a major contributor to research on attitudes, defined an attitude as "a mental and neural state of readiness, organized through experience, exerting a directive or dynamic influence upon the individual's response to all objects and situations with which it is related." Although opinions differ regarding the adequacy of this definition, it does emphasize certain important characteristics of the construct of attitude. First, an attitude implies an internal state which, given the occurrence of certain stimulus events, will ultimately result in some sort of response or behaviour. The definition also implies that an attitude is learned and that our actions are consistent with it. This latter characteristic is important because it gives us the basis for deciding whether or not a given attitude exists, that is, whether a label can be attached to an individual, e.g., "conservative," "séparatiste," "socialist," with some degree of confidence. For example, you probably can identify some of your friends as being anti-abortion and others as pro-abortion. It is important to note that you have never observed the attitudes of these people. (Even if attitudes are stated, only behaviour is actually observed.) Attitudes are hypothetical constructs; you can only infer or guess the existence of an attitude from what people say or do. This, of course, holds true for the measurement of attitudes (see Boxes 4-1 and 4-2).

Two other features of attitudes are significant. Not only do we typically describe an attitude a person holds as "pro" or "con," we also estimate the *intensity* of the attitude, from "extremely positive" to "extremely negative." For example, it is one thing for an individual to state that "Government policies leave a lot to be desired," and quite another to claim that "Government policies make me sick!". Attitudes also vary in *centrality*, the degree to which the issue or object is important to the individual. To continue with the same example, a negative attitude toward govern-

SELF-REPORT MEASURES OF ATTITUDES

The most common way of measuring attitudes is observing how people respond when we ask their opinions. We could use an open-ended question: "What do you think about free trade between Canada and the U.S.A.?" However, in most cases, we use methods which require subjects to choose among alternative responses in order to gain greater reliability and precision of measurement. The following are most commonly used:

(1) *Likert summated ratings.* This is the method most widely used today. It is simple for subjects to understand and respond to, and lets researchers apply sophisticated statistical techniques in order to refine the measure. Subjects are presented with a list of statements about the attitudinal object. For each, they are instructed to respond along a scale, usually 5 or 7 points in length.

Example: Indicate the extent to which you agree or disagree with each of the following statements by circling the response:

a) War brings out the best qualities in people.

    strongly   agree   uncertain   disagree   strongly
    agree   disagree

b) Under some conditions, war is necessary in the interest of justice.

    strongly   agree   uncertain   disagree   strongly
    agree   disagree

c) I would rather be called a coward than go to war.

    strongly   agree   uncertain   disagree   strongly
    agree   disagree

Responses are scored from 1 (strongly disagree) to 5 (strongly agree), indicating the extent to which the subject is favourable toward war. However, on item (c), agreement indicates an unfavourable attitude toward war: thus the item is reverse-scored. Adding up the scores for all items would give a total score of attitudes toward war (i.e., *summated* ratings). This method allows for item analysis, enabling the researcher to see whether each item discriminates between those who are favourable and unfavourable (e.g., people in military and peace groups). Items can be dropped or reworded if they are found to be ambiguous or otherwise invalid.

(2) *Thurstone equal-appearing intervals.* This is the oldest of the more sophisticated methods. A group of subjects acting as judges are given a list of statements on a topic (e.g., war) and asked to *rate* each statement by sorting them into 11 categories from "most unfavourable" to "most favourable." Those statements which show a high level of agreement among judges are retained and combined in a scale. Each item has the scale value of how it was ranked, so that if a subject checks agreement with an item rated as "most favourable," a score of 11 is assigned. The investigator then determines the person's attitude by calculating the mean of the score values of those items checked by that person.

(3) *Semantic differential (Osgood, Suci and Tannenbaum, 1957).* Subjects are asked to rate a concept along a set of bipolar adjective scales.

Example: Rate the idea of *war* by circling one of the numbers for each scale below.

good	1	2	3	4	5	6	7	bad
attractive	1	2	3	4	5	6	7	unattractive
worthless	1	2	3	4	5	6	7	valuable
fair	1	2	3	4	5	6	7	unfair

By adding each response, reversing where the negative adjective is at the low end (that is, scoring "7" as "1" and "6" as "2," etc.), we can obtain an evaluation of the overall attitude. Through a factor analytic study, it is possible to determine the groups or sets of items to which people respond in a consistent way. In this way, we can determine what these items, taken together, are measuring. The underlying dimensions are:

(1) *evaluation*, e.g., good-bad, valuable-worthless

(2) *potency*, e.g., strong-weak, large-small

(3) *activity*, e.g., active-passive, fast-slow

We may find these three subscale scores useful to give us a more detailed picture of what war means to the person.

B·O·X   4-2

INDIRECT MEASURES OF ATTITUDES

As we have seen, self-report measures of attitudes are useful and widely used. However, they can be subject to biases, particularly the tendency to respond in socially desirable ways in order to create a favourable impression or to maintain a favourable self-concept. Thus, a number of approaches have been developed in which attitudes are inferred from other reactions. Here are several, most of them reviewed by Cook and Selltiz (1964):

(1) We can infer attitudes from behaviour toward the attitudinal object. For example, Cook and Selltiz (1968) had a confederate present himself as a representative of a publishing company and ask subjects whether they would be willing to pose for textbook photographs. If so, the subjects were shown a book of drawings on which the photos would be based, many of which involved Black people in equal, inferior, or superior role relationships with the subject-model. Those scenes which the subjects would allow themselves to be photographed in constituted a measure of attitudes toward Blacks.

(2) We can infer attitudes from people's performance on an apparently objective test. For example, subjects are presented with a series of multiple-choice questions about some issue that concerns "facts, not opinions." The "facts" might be unknown (e.g., how much soap is used by an average family from a given ethnic group) or have clearly erroneous, even absurd, response alternatives (e.g., since capital punishment was ended in Canada, the murder rate has increased (1000 times? 10 000 times?) Responses would, in fact, directly reflect attitudes, since no subject would have access to the correct information.

(3) We can infer attitudes from physiological reactions to tests which are more complex than the "lie detector." In several experiments, subjects were first classically conditioned to the word "good" by pairing presentation of that word with a mildly painful shock, and measuring arousal, such as heart rate, galvanic skin response (skin perspiration). Then, subjects are presented with a word or concept, e.g., capital punishment, and their physiological responses were measured. If they felt capital punishment was a "good" thing, their physiological reaction to that concept was strong, reflecting a generalization from the word "good." This is called conditioned semantic generalization.

(4) We can infer attitudes from non-reactive measures. For example people tend to read books which advocate the positions they favour.

(5) An interesting procedure is called the "bogus pipeline" (Jones and Sigall, 1971). Subjects are shown an elaborate electronic apparatus, and told that it provides an accurate reading of their "true feelings" toward some object. After being hooked up, they are instructed to give verbal reports of their attitudes, trying to "match the machine." Of course, the experimenter's description of the apparatus is false, and the pipeline is, indeed, bogus. However, subjects are less likely to be influenced by social desirability and motivated to provide authentic responses since they believe the machine will detect false ones (Sigall and Page, 1971). In another study, pregnant women were asked to sign consent forms for blood tests to check for alcohol and other drugs. Those who signed the consent were almost twice as likely as a control group to admit to alcohol use during their pregnancy. However, no significant differences were found in reports of tranquillizer or aspirin use (Lowe, Windsor, Adams, Morris and Reese, 1986).

ment policy would be highly central to members of opposition parties, somewhat less central to concerned citizens, and quite peripheral to people who feel apolitical and "turned off" by the political process. Of course, if a particular government policy directly affects these people, their attitudes may change rapidly from peripheral to central.

Tripartite model of attitudes

The traditional view has been that attitudes consist of a relatively enduring organization of three components: a cognitive component, an affective component, and a behavioural component (Oskamp, 1977) as illustrated in Figure 4-1. The *cognitive component* refers to the particular *beliefs* or ideas held about the object or situation, the *affective component* to the associated *emotions*, and the *behavioural component* to the associated *action* or actions. For instance, a person may believe that university students are arrogant (cognitive), may feel tense in the presence of a university student (affective), and may refuse to pick up a student who is hitch-hiking to classes (behavioural). It is important to add, however, that attitudes are not always directly expressed in action. This issue will be discussed in detail later.

The tripartite model of attitude suggests something basic about human nature. Many traditional theories and philosophies have grappled with the question of whether thinking (rationality) or emotions are the essence of being human. Indeed, some schools of psychotherapy seek to minimize thinking so that we can "get in touch" with our "real" feelings. A recent Canadian prime minister adopted as a family motto "Reason over Passion," suggesting the two competing sides of humanity. In contrast, attitude is a concept which implies that our thoughts, feelings and actions are integrated in some way, and that we usually think, feel *and* act rather than choose one behaviour by itself.

However, it *is* possible to distinguish among cognition, affect, and behaviour. Breckler (1984) was interested in the extent to which these three components gave similar estimates of the direction and strength of attitudes. He used a variety of measures of each component. For example, he monitored changes in heart rate and had subjects rate their mood in the presence of snakes (affective), measured their beliefs

FIGURE 4–1
The tripartite model of attitude structure

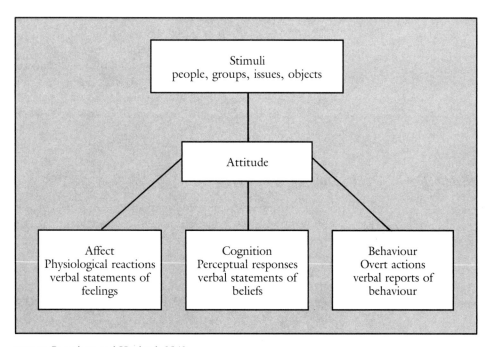

SOURCE: Rosenberg and Hovland, 1960

about the dangers and benefits of snakes and had them list their thoughts about them (cognitive), had people indicate how they would react to a snake, and observed how close they were actually willing to approach a snake (behavioural). His analyses showed clearly that beliefs, feelings, and behaviour were moderately but not highly inter-related, and that each provided distinctive contributions to the hypothetical construct called "attitude," particularly when measures in addition to verbal self-reports were included. Thus, we should not assess someone's attitudes by asking only about feelings or beliefs, or only by observing behaviour.

Attitude complexity

Some attitudes are rather simple and straightforward while others are complex. For instance, a person may be asked, "What do you think of the Social Credit Party?" and respond, "I think it's the best thing that has happened in British Columbia" but if pressed, be unable to present more detail. On the other hand, another person in response to the same query might reply, "I'm generally in favour of their basic orientation toward the economy, but they tend to attract some dubious characters as candidates." Whether an attitude is simple or complex may be a function of the characteristics of the person, or it may be a function of the particular topic. There are some issues which by their nature do not allow for much mental intricacy. Thus the attitudes of individuals concerning the brushing of teeth after meals would likely be considerably more simple than attitudes toward the question of economic or political union of Canada with the United States.

Attitudes also have more or less complex associations with other attitudes. For example, a person might believe that agricultural cooperatives are economically beneficial and should be fostered, but this attitude may exist in isolation and may not be related to other attitudes concerning, for instance, the NDP, Mennonite communities, or socialized medicine. In other cases, very complicated networks of interconnected attitudes may occur. Thus an individual's attitude toward immigration may be connected with many other attitudes concerning unemployment, multiculturalism, prejudice, and the nature of cities. All of these attitudes are based upon values, which are more fundamental orientations that people have about issues such as freedom, equality, or comfort and security.

PERSONAL AND SOCIAL VALUES

While attitudes are associated with specific objects, events or issues, values are global, abstract principles. They are a person's judgments as to what is "desirable," what "ought to be," and what is ideal or important in life to a person. For example, a person may hold attitudes against racial discrimination and be in favour of equal pay to men and women for work of equal value. Both of these may be reflections of a value for "equality" which is important to that person. Often, when we have intensely felt attitudes about controversial issues, we describe our attitude in terms of a value, such as the so called "pro-life" and "pro-choice" positions on abortion.

In describing our positions this way, we use the value to define, from our own perspective, what the issue is "really all about."

Some social psychologists have attempted to catalogue a set of basic values on which individuals differ. For instance, Allport and Vernon (1931), building on the writings of the German philosopher Spranger, developed a measure for six values: theoretical, economic, social, aesthetic, political and religious. Morris (1956) listed five general value dimensions: social restraint and self-control; enjoyment and progress in action; withdrawal and self-sufficiency; receptivity and sympathetic concern; self-indulgence and sensuous enjoyment. While it is probably futile to try to establish the exact number of values, it is clear that people have many attitudes and relatively few values.

In more recent research (Rokeach, 1968, 1979) a distinction is drawn between *terminal values* and *instrumental values*. Terminal values are preferences for certain end-states in life, such as "salvation," "a comfortable life," "freedom," "inner harmony,"

Slogans used by people on both sides of the abortion debate convey that each side knows what the issue is "really all about."

FIGURE 4–2
Rokeach terminal values

_____	a comfortable life	_____	inner harmony
_____	an exciting life	_____	mature love
_____	a sense of accomplishment	_____	national security
_____	a world at peace	_____	pleasure
_____	a world of beauty	_____	salvation
_____	equality	_____	self-respect
_____	family security	_____	social recognition
_____	freedom	_____	true friendship
_____	happiness	_____	wisdom

Instructions: Read this list of values carefully. Then rank them from #1 to #18 in order of importance to you, as guiding principles in your life.

A sample of Canadian students in 1975 ranked them as follows: 13, 11, 9, 12, 15, 10, 7, 1, 2, 6, 3, 17, 14, 18, 4, 16, 5, 8.

SOURCE: Rokeach, 1973

and "equality" (see Figure 4-2), while instrumental values describe people's preferred modes of conduct, such as being "ambitious," "obedient," "imaginative." Subjects are asked to rank the 18 terminal and 18 instrumental values in terms of their relative importance. In this way, the *value priorities* of an individual can be determined. For example, while almost everyone would feel that a "comfortable life" is a good thing, people would vary tremendously on the issue of its importance.

Using this method, researchers have reported some interesting findings (Rokeach, 1979). Not surprisingly, people who attach high importance to "salvation" as a value are more likely to attend church regularly, while those who value "a world of beauty" are likely to be concerned with environmental issues. Habitual cigarette smokers tend to rank the terminal values of an exciting life, freedom, happiness, mature love, and pleasure more highly than non-smokers, who value a sense of accomplishment, a world of beauty, family security, salvation and self-respect. Among the instrumental values, smokers feel it is important to be broadminded, capable, imaginative, and independent, while non-smokers prefer to be cheerful, obedient, helpful, polite and self-controlled (Weir, Getzlaf and Rokeach, 1984). People who take care of themselves by exercising regularly, using alcohol moderately, eating a balanced diet, and wearing a car seat belt, place a high value upon "pleasure," "an exciting life," and "happiness."

Health in itself can be considered a value. Rokeach (1973) felt that health would be so important a value to everybody that there would be no point in measuring it. However, Ware and Young (1979) included health in Rokeach's list of terminal values, and found that while the majority rated it first, about one third of the subjects did not include it among their five highest values. In general, those who value health highly tend to perform health-protective behaviours when they believe that such behaviours will, in fact, improve their own health (Lau, Hartman and Ware, 1986).

Value conflict and change

In certain cases, placing a high priority on one value may cause conflict with another value. For example, it may be difficult to reconcile the values of freedom and equality, when freedom implies the right to earn as much money as you want, while equality implies the duty of the state to tax some of your wealth and redistribute it to people with less wealth. In one study Rokeach (1968) analyzed the writings of well-known authors representing different political ideologies. He found that moderate liberals or social democrats valued both freedom and equality highly, conservatives valued freedom more highly than equality, communists valued equality more highly than freedom, and an extreme right-wing writer (Hitler) did not consider either freedom or equality to be important. Several other studies of the speeches of U.S. senators and British members of parliament show a similar pattern of values in relation to liberal or conservative ideology (Tetlock, 1986).

Rokeach (1968) also found that while those who were active in U.S. civil rights organizations ranked both freedom and equality quite highly, those who were uninvolved or unsympathetic to that cause ranked freedom as much more important than equality. Rokeach then devised a procedure, *value confrontation*, in which subjects were made aware of the discrepancies in their rankings of freedom and equality. It was suggested to them that people who consider freedom so much more important than equality may be concerned only with their own freedom, and not that of others. (In a control group, there was no such intervention.) Three months later, all of the subjects received a letter from a well-known U.S. civil rights organization, inviting them to join. Over twice as many subjects who had been prompted into self-awareness as control group subjects responded favourably by joining the organization. In another study (Conroy *et al.*, 1973) subjects at a smoking cessation clinic were administered a similar procedure with regard to the instrumental values, "broadminded" and "self-disciplined." Smokers rated the value "broadminded" higher than "self-disciplined" but those who had quit smoking ranked self-discipline as the most important value. After treatment, these subjects and a control group were contacted. During the 16 days of treatment, more self-awareness subjects than control subjects had quit smoking. The results held firm for two months, although after six months, both groups had returned to higher and equivalent rates of smoking.

To test this procedure with a mass audience, Ball-Rokeach and Rokeach (1984) produced a television show which featured two well-known stars (Edward Asner and Sandy Hill) talking about "freedom vs. equality" and a "world of beauty" as values. Follow-up studies showed that, in comparison with people in a control group who didn't watch the show, those who had were more likely to support or become involved in organizations concerned with sexism, racism and environmental pollution. These studies indicate that even though values are fundamental to humanity, they are susceptible to change through subtle manipulation.

Value pluralism

Tetlock (1986) has investigated how value conflicts are reflected in political attitudes. In one study, subjects were asked to indicate their attitudes about some controversial issues involving conflicting values, such as higher taxes to help the poor (equality vs. a comfortable life), whether the U.S. Central Intelligence Agency should be allowed to open the mail of citizens (national security vs. individual freedom), and whether physicians should be restrained from setting fees which some people could not afford (equality vs. freedom). Then they were asked to write their "thoughts" about each issue and to rank order the Rokeach values.

When an issue did not involve a value conflict, subjects responded as expected on the attitude scales. For example, those who ranked equality high and a "comfortable life" low were quite willing to pay more taxes to assist the poor. However, if both values were ranked high, the conflict in values was shown in their ambivalence about the issue. When subjects were faced with an issue which involved competing values (*value pluralism*), they thought more about the issue and their responses showed higher levels of integrative complexity. It was concluded that value pluralism stimulates "trade-off reasoning," a flexible way of thinking in which all sides of an issue must be considered.

Value pluralism has also been studied in relation to political ideologies (Tetlock, 1984). We have already seen that liberal/social democrats, conservatives, fascists, and communists differ in their value priorities for equality and freedom. It has also been found that people with liberal/social democratic political attitudes are higher in integrative complexity than others. Many political issues involve conflicts between freedom and equality, such as social programs, anti-discrimination laws, and governmental intervention in the economy. Because liberal/social democrats rank both values highly, they must be able to think flexibly and in more complex ways in order to resolve the conflicts. On the other hand, people whose political ideologies dictate a clear priority of one value over the other can resolve the issues more easily.

We must be cautious in our conclusions about these studies. It is not possible to infer cause and effect, whether liberals show more integrative complexity because of the equality-freedom conflict, or whether people who think in this way tend as a result to value freedom and equality highly and to adopt social democratic political attitudes. Another issue concerns the culture being studied: Tetlock's research has

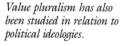

Value pluralism has also been studied in relation to political ideologies.

been conducted entirely in economically developed democracies where there is the wealth, political means, and human capacity to balance freedom and equality more readily. Arguably, the realities of poverty, dictatorships, and economic underdevelopment in the Third World would make such a "trade-off" more difficult, if not unrealistic, and could result in a different relationship between values and political ideology. The study of successful revolutionary leaders described in Chapter 3 suggests that more "extreme" political ideologies are not necessarily lacking in integrative complexity.

Comparing national values

Since values are so fundamental to individuals, perhaps we can describe and compare people of different nations by examining their aggregate values. A recent study of values by a Dutch psychologist (Hofstede, 1983) involved a monumental number of subjects (116 000) in 40 different countries. Through statistical analyses of these data, he identified four underlying value dimensions on which inhabitants of various nations could be compared. These value dimensions are: power distance, avoidance of uncertainty, individualism, and masculinity-femininity. Let us examine them, particularly as a way of studying "national character":

(1) The dimension of *power distance* refers to differences in the extent to which people can determine the behaviour of each other. In nations scoring high on this value (e.g., Mexico, India), individuals expect and accept autocratic leaders and employers, and parents expect obedient children. By contrast, in countries low in power distance (e.g., Canada, U.S.A.), children are trained to be independent, managers tend to consult with subordinates, and governments are pluralistic and based on majority votes.

(2) *Avoidance of uncertainty* refers to the feeling of being threatened by ambiguity and acting to avoid it. In cultures where this value is strong (e.g., Greece), it is reflected in a concern with security, low risk-taking, and written rules, and the presence of a dominant state religion.

(3) *Individualism-collectivism* refers to the extent to which people are supposed to look after themselves, rather than expecting certain groups or society to take care of them. Many of the Western nations score high on individualism (e.g., Canada, Australia, U.S.A.), while collectivist-oriented cultures included otherwise-capitalist nations such as Hong Kong, Taiwan, Singapore, Peru, Venezuela, and Chile. In collectivist cultures, there is less occupational mobility but greater group decision-making, while individualist cultures stress achievement, initiative, and employees who defend their own interests.

(4) The fourth value dimension is called *masculinity-femininity*. It refers to the extent to which members of a society value success (including, of course, money), as opposed to caring for others and for the quality of life. On this dimension, Japan scores highly "masculine" and Sweden highly "feminine." The "success-oriented" societies have more differentiation between sex roles and more stress and competition in schools and jobs.

Of course, we have described the extremes, or polarities — most nations and cultures fall somewhere in the middle of each continuum. In any case, it is clear that differences in values within a nation permeate virtually all aspects of life, from child-rearing to work, and even driving (Hofstede, 1983).

Mallette

FREE TRADE
OR
WHAT EH?

'. . . and like, we don't want our culture to get hosed . . . so take off, eh!!'

Many Canadians ask tourists or friends from the United States whether they have noticed any differences between the two countries. Many will also admit to being disappointed when the answer, as it frequently occurs, is no. This reply, however, is usually based on rather superficial resemblances between the two societies — the same goods in the shops, the same programs on television, similar styles in clothing and music, and similar fast-food outlets. (At this superficial level, many societies throughout the world are losing their unique features owing to the spread of the so called "Coca-Cola" culture.) Often the only distinctions which may be observed by a U.S. visitor in Canada are the feeling of being safer on the streets, the colours of our money, and the superior quality of the Canadian Broadcasting Corporation.

Nevertheless, differences in our "national characters" can be discerned and studied. In comparing the two societies, a political scientist (Lipset, 1968) described Canadians as being more conservative, less competitive and individualistic, less self-confident and innovative, and more prepared to accept government control, elitism, and inequalities. However, Rokeach (1973) obtained data on values from university students in Ontario and Michigan. He found that in his samples, Canadians valued equality, freedom, and independence *more* than the U.S. students, and self-control *less*, and both nations ranked obedience as lowest. Thus the data did not indicate that Canadians were less individualistic and more elitist than Americans. However, Canadians did rank several values as lower: a sense of accomplishment, being capable, logical, and ambitious. This information suggests that Canadians are somewhat less concerned with achievement and competition. While Lipset argues that this orientation stems from pessimism and a lack of faith in the future, Rokeach points out that Canadians have other important values, including mature love, inner harmony, a world of beauty, being loving and . . . being cheerful!

The Canadian approach to law and order is frequently singled out for comment. As Margaret Atwood (1972) has noted, we are the only country in the world to have a police officer as a national symbol! It has been argued (Fearn, 1973) that we have more respect for the police and, while we do have fewer police officers and lawyers per capita than the United States, we also have proportionally much less crime. Canada also has remarkably little military tradition and does not spend much money on its military forces. It is claimed that unlike the citizens of the United States, Canadians tend to prefer law and order to individual liberty. And while Americans were promised by their constitution "life, liberty, and the pursuit of happiness," Canadians were offered by the British North America Act "peace, order and good government."

On the other hand, it is not insignificant that Canadians have been willing to accept refugees — the United Empire Loyalists during the war of Independence in the 1700s, Sitting Bull and his warriors after the defeat of Custer in 1877, young American men refusing to serve in Vietnam in the '60s and, most recently, refugees from Latin America and India. However, our history is not untainted. We were considerably more reluctant to accept Jewish refugees escaping from Nazi terrorism prior to and during World War II. While Britain accepted 70 000 of them, the U.S.A. 200 000, Argentina 50 000, and Brazil 27 000, Canada accepted fewer than 5000, and 6 million were left to die (Abella and Troper, 1983).

B · O · X   4 - 3

CANADA AND U.S. VALUES: A HISTORICAL LESSON

Americans like to elect their law officers but we appoint ours. Thus the country sheriffs and town marshals of the American frontier gained their posts on the sufferance of the voters. . . .

In the ranching and mining states and territories of the Union, quarrels were also settled at the grass-roots level, by hastily sworn-in posses, by vigilante groups or by a single individual with a gun. In Canada, order was imposed from above by the Queen's constabulary. If California, during the gold rush of '49, came close to anarchy, the Canadian Yukon, during the gold rush of '98, came close to being a police state. The Mounties directed the great stampede like an army manoeuvre, often over the protests of Americans who always preferred to run

their own affairs through the democratic device of the miners' meeting. (In Alaska, men were often banished, lashed or hanged by majority vote — not by the courts).

American grass-roots democracy enshrined a whole series of individual liberties: the right to carry a gun (and use it), to buy liquor in an open saloon, or to gamble at faro, poker or roulette; all these helped contribute to the wildness of the American west. We Canadians preferred a more orderly frontier, albeit a less libertarian one. This country was not forged in the crucible of rebellion or civil war and when anarchy, violence or intemperance threaten us we tend to adopt Draconian measures (Berton, 1976).

Values can influence the economic behaviour of individuals, groups and societies. It has been suggested by a number of investigators that French Canadians are less interested than Anglophones in economic success, placing more emphasis on social and family concerns (Kanungo *et al.*, 1976; Tremblay, 1953; Jain, Normond and Kanungo, 1979). Historically, French-speaking Canadians have been underrepresented among managers, business executives, and entrepreneurs, even in Québec. It has been argued, with justification, that this discrepancy has reflected a bias in hiring and promotion. However, there also is evidence that French Canadian *fathers* and English Canadian *mothers* are more likely than their spouses to extend both comfort and discipline to their children (Lambert, Yackley and Hein, 1971), parenting styles which have been linked to later achievement-related and risk-taking behaviour among English Canadian males. Values have also been reflected in differences between the French and the English in education. In Québec the liberal arts and religion have been stressed, and commerce, science, and technology de-emphasized.

Research on cultural values can only be specific to time and place, and the Québecois culture has changed dramatically over the past generation. Two important manifestations are the marked decline in the influence of religious institutions, and a phenomenal increase in students enrolled in business programs. Baer and Curtis (1984) present evidence that the "two solitudes" have grown more similar in values. Comparing nation-wide samples of 2277 Anglophones and 896 Francophones, they report *no* differences on the values of "achievement," "prosperity," "independence," and "family security," contrary to the earlier impression of French-Canadians as uninterested in achievement and success. They conclude that French Canadian culture does not restrain Francophones from developing interests in economic achievement.

FUNCTIONS OF ATTITUDES

We have described values as the "global abstractions" on which we base our attitudes. In other words, values are considered to be generalities, or basic principles, and attitudes as the more specific instances of those principles. Do attitudes necessarily follow from values? Can we infer people's values from their attitudes toward certain objects or issues? Or can we predict people's attitudes toward capital punishment, the welfare state, or rock videos if we know their values? The answer is: yes, no, and sometimes. To understand this, we must turn to a more fundamental question: Why do we have attitudes?

In the next chapter, we will focus on how and why attitudes can change. We know that the skills of writing and speaking, and the industries of public relations and advertising are all devoted to changing attitudes. And yet, we know from experience that attitudes often are difficult to change and that people are not easily persuaded. In fact, there is an important reason why people hold their attitudes: attitudes are *functional* in the sense that they satisfy important needs. Several functions of attitudes have been identified and studied (Katz, 1960; Oskamp, 1977).

First, attitudes may serve a utilitarian or *instrumental* function, helping us to maximize rewards and minimize costs. In particular, holding specific attitudes may help us gain approval and acceptance from others. Indeed (see Chapter 8), people tend to be attracted to other people who apparently hold similar attitudes. Thus attitudes may enable people to adjust in their society and in their own groups.

Second, attitudes can serve a *knowledge* function, enabling us to make sense of our world and to feel that we do understand. That is, attitudes serve as schemata, helping us to avoid the uncomfortable feelings of uncertainty and ambiguity, guiding our reactions and interpretations of events. For example, acts of terrorism seem even more terrifying when they seem to be senseless, inexplicable, beyond understanding. Thus we may accept the explanations of politicians that some people are just evil or are agents of some insane leader or evil empire.

Research has shown how attitudes function as schemata, enabling us to avoid thinking. Fazio and his associates have investigated how quickly subjects respond to various objects by pushing buttons labelled "good" or "bad" (Fazio, Sanbonmatsu, Powell and Kardes, 1986). They demonstrate that some attitudes are activated spontaneously or automatically from memory and do not require thinking, e.g., "Cockroaches are disgusting," while other attitudes require more time and thought to be formed. Some attitudes are borne with strength and confidence, while others are held with uncertainty. It is argued that strong, automatically activated attitudes free people from the effort required for information processing and reflective thought and allow them simply to react.

Attitudes may also serve an *ego-defensive* function, protecting people from becoming aware of harsh, uncomfortable truths about themselves or their world. Here, the influence of Freud's psychoanalytic thought is evident. People often feel and act in ways which "defend" them from becoming aware of what may be threatening. As discussed in Chapter 7, prejudiced attitudes often serve ego-defensive functions. For instance, the bigot may hate members of some out-group in order to feel more important and powerful than he or she really is. If people feel bad about themselves, it is comforting and protective to believe that others are worse.

Finally, attitudes can serve a *value-expression function*. Value-expressive attitudes enable us to demonstrate our uniqueness, and what is important to us. They may take an apparently trivial form, as in the case of those who express positive opinions about certain styles in music, clothing, and cars which represent certain values. Similarly, members of a religion may adhere to certain salient attitudes which indicate their devotion to their faith.

Value-expressive attitudes allow us to express our individuality and may take a trivial form.

Research

The analysis of attitude function suggests why attitudes are important and why they often are resistant to change. However, until recently, little research has been done on the subject, primarily because it has been difficult to arrive at precise definitions and adequate measures of the various functions. However, several recent studies show that attitude functions can be researched.

In an early study, McClintock (1958) administered personality tests which assessed the need for conformity and ego defensiveness. Then subjects were presented with one of two persuasive messages about prejudice. One message contained information concerning different groups being different but equal, information which was expected to have more effect on subjects having a high need for conformity. The other message interpreted the psychodynamics of prejudice and was expected to provide insight and provoke attitude change among those subjects high in ego defensiveness. The results supported the hypothesis that high conformity subjects show more change after exposure to the informational message. However, it was those scoring in the mid-range in ego defensiveness who changed in response to the interpretational message. It was argued, *post hoc*, that the most defensive subjects would be too rigid to accept insight into themselves or contemplate significant attitude change.

McClintock reasoned that if subjects scored high on a measure of ego defensiveness, then any attitude would serve an ego-defensive function. But even if a person has an unusually high need for defense in some area, it is quite a leap of faith to assume that any of his or her actions are necessarily intended to satisfy that need. The problem is that the particular attitude or action may serve other important functions or needs.

Kristiansen and Zanna (1986) deal with this problem in a study of value-expressive attitudes. Subjects were asked for their terminal value priorities (Rokeach measure) and their attitudes toward two controversial issues: (1) the reinstatement of capital punishment in Canada for certain crimes; and (2) affirmative action in the workplace for women and disadvantaged minorities. On another occasion, these subjects were asked to rate how each of the issues helped or hindered them in achieving various goals in their lives, as represented by the 18 values. For example, the subjects were asked to rate how reinstating capital punishment would help or hinder them in achieving freedom, happiness, equality, and so on. It was found that attitudes were related to values when the issue was linked, in the subject's mind, to the attainment of these values. For example, if a subject believed that "reinstating capital punishment" would help them to achieve "freedom" (e.g., being free to walk the streets at night) and if freedom was a highly-ranked value, then subjects would favour reinstating capital punishment.

It is important to understand that we cannot infer attitudes from values, or values from attitudes. Indeed, people with different attitudes toward the same issue often relate their positions to entirely different values, rather than to differences in the importance of a particular value. For example, both people who favour extensive government involvement in health care and those who oppose it may place high importance on the values of freedom and equality. However, those in favour may base their position on the value of equality, and those opposed may refer to the value of freedom. A selective appeal to values can enable them to support and justify their attitudes (Eiser and van der Pligt, 1984).

This *value justification effect* has been demonstrated by Zanna and Kristiansen (1986).

Subjects in an experiment were asked to indicate their attitudes toward two controversial issues of the time, abortion on demand and the deployment of nuclear weapons in Canada. Then they were asked to rank the 18 Rokeach terminal values in terms of how relevant each was to the abortion and nuclear weapons issues. There were significant differences between proponents and opponents of each issue in terms of which values were ranked as most highly relevant. For example, pro-abortion subjects rated freedom, happiness, and a comfortable life as more relevant to the issue than anti-abortion subjects. Interestingly, both sides rated equality, self-respect and inner harmony as equally relevant. On the nuclear weapons issue, national security was more relevant to those in favour, and wisdom and salvation to those opposed. It starts to become apparent why people on opposite sides of some controversies cannot communicate. In terms of fundamental values, neither side understands or agrees with the other.

What can be concluded about the link between values and attitudes? Do people with different value structures arrive at distinctive attitudes which express these values? Or, do people with different attitudes relate their opinions to different values? Certainly, a functionalist theory assumes that we begin with a need to express more fundamental values, and then arrive at attitudes which fulfill that need. Yet, as we saw in Rokeach's work, values can change; it may be the kind of "self-confrontation" which occurs when people face intensely controversial issues that especially gives rise to such change.

THE RELATIONSHIP BETWEEN ATTITUDES AND BEHAVIOUR

One of the major reasons for measuring a particular psychological variable is to allow some reasonably precise statement to be made about how it affects behaviour. There is no question that attitudes have a powerful influence on how we act, yet attempts to demonstrate that behaviour can be attributed to the underlying attitude have frequently been unsuccessful. In one well-known "classic" study, LaPiere (1934) accompanied a young Chinese couple as they toured the United States. In over 250 hotels and restaurants which they visited during that journey, they were refused service only once. Later, when LaPiere wrote to the same establishments, asking whether they were willing to serve Chinese patrons, a startling 92 percent of those who responded said that they would refuse. The study has been criticized on several grounds; only 50 percent of the establishments responded, and there is no way to ascertain whether the person who responded to LaPiere's letter was the same person who had offered service.

A similar study conducted in the northern United States (Kutner, Wilkins and Yarrow, 1952) when segregation still existed revealed that although Blacks were served satisfactorily in a number of restaurants, the same restaurants would later refuse to make reservations for a social event including Blacks. As with the LaPiere study, different constraints were operating under different conditions. It is much more difficult to discriminate on a face-to-face basis than by letter or telephone and there was no guarantee that the person handling reservations was the same person who originally had served the Blacks. Similarly, Bickman (1972) reported that although 94 percent of 500 individuals questioned said that they felt personally responsible for the disposal of litter, only 2 percent actually picked up a piece of litter planted by the experimenter.

It has been argued that these and other such studies fail to show the expected

Single behaviours	r	Categories of behaviour	r	All behaviours	r
Sign petitions					
offshore oil	.41	Petitioning	.50		
nuclear power	.36				
auto exhaust	.39				
Circulate petitions	.27				
Pick up litter				Comprehensive index of environmental behaviours	.62
yourself	.34	Litter pick-up	.36		
recruit friend	.22				
Recycling program					
week 1	.34				
2	.57				
3	.34	Recycling participation	.39		
4	.33				
5	.12				
6	.20				
7	.20				
8	.34				

r = correlation coefficient

SOURCE: Weigel and Newman, 1976

TABLE 4–1
Correlations between environment attitudes and environment behaviours

relationships between attitude and behaviour because too much reliance is placed on a single behavioural act (Weigel and Newman, 1976). In an experiment, subjects first filled out a questionnaire which measured their concerns about the environment including various aspects of pollution and conservation. Then, at different times over the next few months, the subjects were contacted for 14 environment-relevant actions, such as circulating a petition, agreeing to pick up litter, recruiting a friend, and recycling bottles and paper. The researchers found that the correlations between attitudes and single behaviours were quite modest (average of .29). However, when all 14 behaviours were combined into one index, a strong correlation of .62 was obtained. Notice that in this study, attitudes were predicting observable behaviour in the real world rather than self-reported behaviour or behaviour in a laboratory. Thus there is some compelling evidence that attitudes are linked to actions. Now the problem is, when and why do attitudes predict behaviour?

Variables which influence the attitude-behaviour relationship

A review by Wicker (1969) of the attitude-behaviour problem had a strong influence on the direction of subsequent research. He reviewed extensive evidence which, in sum, challenged the notion that attitude leads inevitably to action. At the same time, he outlined a set of intervening variables which explain why many studies have been unable to demonstrate that they are related. Characteristics of both the person and the situation can determine whether people will act according to their attitudes.

A number of personal factors can be involved: (1) The person may hold other relevant attitudes. For example, people who are or are not willing to demonstrate against nuclear power will be influenced not only by their attitudes toward nuclear power as dangerous but also by their attitudes toward the possible economic benefits of nuclear power. (2) People may be motivated to satisfy other needs. For example, people may have attitudes about the negative environmental effects of extensive logging but also may fear losing their jobs in that industry. (3) If people do not see how an action would be relevant to a particular attitude, their actions may not follow from their attitudes. For example, voters who oppose a certain political party may not realize that this party stands for policies that they favour.

Situational factors may also intrude and prevent people from acting in accordance with their attitudes: (1) The real or implied presence of others may influence behaviours. For example, a person holding an unpopular attitude may feel too ashamed or pressured to act on it in public. (2) Social norms may conflict with certain attitudes. Thus the prejudiced hotel keeper may feel that it is inappropriate to turn away actual, paying customers of whatever race, creed or national origin. (3) People may act in a certain way, regardless of attitudes, because they have no acceptable alternatives. For example, they may subscribe to a mediocre newspaper with a repugnant editorial policy because it's the only one in town. (4) Unforeseen extraneous events can drastically change behaviour, regardless of attitudes. People who are opposed to welfare may suddenly become unemployed or disabled, and thus compelled to seek public assistance.

In short, behaviour is influenced by much more than one specific attitude. Clearly, it is affected by previous experience, habit, social norms, and the anticipated consequences in that situation. This has been shown in a study which took advantage of a referendum concerning a proposal to raise the minimum drinking age (Sivacek and Crano, 1982). It was found that there were no differences in the attitudes expressed by samples from various age groups. However, people with a "vested interest," who would have been most affected by the change in the law (those under the age of 21), were most willing to work actively to defeat the proposal.

Research has also shown that action is more likely to follow from attitudes which are activated automatically, i.e., when merely encountering the attitudinal object elicits a spontaneous reaction (Fazio et al., 1982). About four months prior to the 1984 presidential elections in the U.S.A., the attitudes of subjects to the incumbent were assessed. In addition, subjects were asked to press one of two keys, labelled "good" and "bad," when each of a series of names, including Ronald Reagan's, was flashed on the screen. In a follow-up study of how the subjects voted, attitudes predicted behaviour accurately only among those who had responded earlier by pressing a "good" or "bad" key very quickly. Their rapid reaction time indicated an easily-activated attitude.

It is evident that behaviour can be predicted to a greater extent when all possible influences are known. Thus, a junior executive who believes unions have some positive aspects but who would support his anti-union boss when the prevailing norm among his colleagues is anti-union would not surprise us: the consequences of stating his views are likely to be negative or may have been so in the past. Such a multiple-variable approach was followed by Shetz (1974) who was interested in predicting the intentions as well as the actual behaviour of consumers. He took into consideration habits, beliefs, emotions, the general social environment, the anticipated situation, and unexpected events. In the end, a multiple correlation of + .70 was obtained with the *intention* of a group of 954 housewives to purchase an instant breakfast product, and a correlation of + .50 was obtained with the *actual frequency* of purchases.

It is clear that Shetz was more successful in predicting intentions than actual purchases. The subject of intentions and the relationship of intentions to behaviour have dominated much recent research and theorizing about attitudes and the attitude-behaviour relationship.

Theory of reasoned action

Ajzen and Fishbein (1980) have tackled the attitude-behaviour problem directly (see Figure 4-3). They begin with the premise that people usually consider the implications of their actions, and then act consciously and deliberately. In short, we eventually do what we *intend* to do, and the best single predictor of a behaviour is an intention to act in that way. Of course, intentions vary in strength, and we may intend to do a number of different things. A student may intend to study tonight unless he or

FIGURE 4–3

The Ajzen and Fishbein model of reasoned action

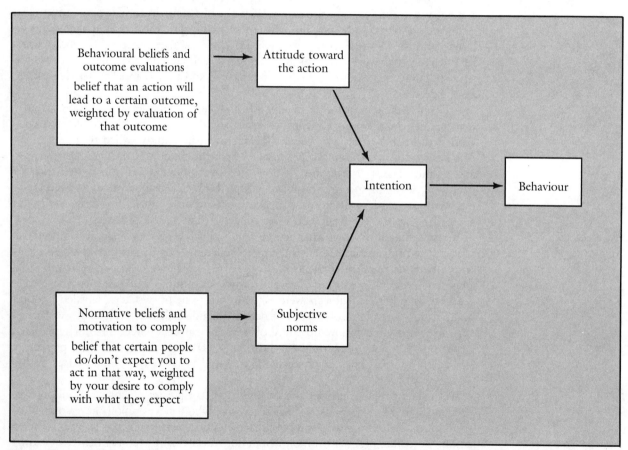

SOURCE: Ajzen and Fishbein, 1980

she is invited to a party — an invitation he or she intends to accept. Thus, we must specify what determines how strongly the student intends to study. According to Fishbein and Ajzen, the strength of an intention to act in a certain way is determined by two factors: attitudes toward that action, and subjective norms. That is, our intention to vote for candidate X is determined by our attitudes toward voting in that

Going to a movie: Intentions to behave in a certain way are determined by a combination of attitudes toward that action and subjective norms.

way (*not* attitudes toward the candidate) and our perception that the action is encouraged or approved by other people. Ajzen and Fishbein suggest that the two factors are not necessarily equal in importance, and that one may be weighted more than the other by different people, and in different situations. For example, while two people may be equally determined to vote for candidate X, one may be influenced primarily by feeling positive about voting in that way (attitudes) and the other by how family and friends intend to vote (subjective norms). (In one study of weight loss among women, the subjective norm component (close friends) far outweighed the attitude component in predicting eventual success (Fishbein and Ajzen, 1975).)

The Ajzen-Fishbein theory also specifies what determines attitudes and subjective norms. Attitudes toward a given action are: (1) determined by beliefs that the action will lead to certain outcomes; and (2) weighted by evaluations of these outcomes. For example, you will have a positive attitude toward voting for a certain candidate if you believe that this action will lead to relatively favourable outcomes (honest government, full employment, low inflation, a less hazardous environment) *and* you place a relatively high value on such outcomes. If you believe that voting in this way is unlikely to bring about such outcomes *or* you really don't care whether such outcomes occur, your attitude will be less positive. Subjective norms (i.e., perception of social pressure to act) consist of: (1) beliefs that certain people or groups expect the action of you; and (2) the strength of your motives to comply with these expectancies. Thus, you will feel encouraged or pressured to vote for candidate X if you believe that your friends want you to vote that way and if you want to do what they expect of you.

Putting it all together — behaviour can be predicted by intentions. Intentions to behave in a given way are determined by some combination of attitudes to act in that way, and the subjective norms surrounding the behaviour. Attitudes are determined by expected consequences and evaluations of those consequences, while subjective norms are determined by beliefs about what others expect, and the motives to comply with these expectations. Thus, if you expect to enjoy a certain movie and would really like to enjoy it, and if you perceive that your friends want you to go with them to the movie and you want to please them, you are likely to intend to go.

Research The Ajzen and Fishbein model has been supported in a series of studies of socially significant behaviours, such as family planning, consumer behaviour (buying particular brands), voting in U.S. and British elections, choice of occupation, changes in smoking and drinking, and losing weight (Ajzen and Fishbein, 1980). While much of the research on attitudes has been criticized for focusing on relatively insignificant, short-term, laboratory-generated attitudes, this model has been tested with real-life behaviours and attitudes. For example, in the Ajzen and Fishbein study, subjects were asked to indicate their intentions to perform various purchasing behaviours with regard to five brand names in each of three classes of products, e.g., intention to buy a Chevrolet/Volkswagen/Mercedes, intention to buy in the next two weeks each of five toothpaste brands, intention to buy various brands of beer to serve friends at a party. For each behaviour, attitudes were assessed by rating of bipolar adjectives, e.g., buying X beer for my own use in the next week would be wise/foolish, have good consequences/have bad consequences. Subjective norms were assessed by having subjects rate the extent to which they believed their families and friends thought that they should/should not buy X toothpaste, etc. When the attitudes and subjective norms corresponded exactly to the behaviour, these two factors were highly predictive of behavioural intention. In another study, attitudes and subjective norms of married women regarding the use of birth control pills (but not birth control in general) predicted their use of birth control pills two years later (Davidson and Morrison, 1983).

It was noted earlier in this chapter that attitudes vary in complexity. Yet the research which has been generated by the Ajzen and Fishbein model usually measures attitudes in terms of simple positive or negative evaluations. As people become more involved and more experienced in an activity, they develop a more complex set of expectancies about various consequences. This pattern has been shown in a study of marijuana use among high school students (Schlegel and DiTecco, 1981). Subjects were asked to complete a questionnaire concerning marijuana attitudes, including items about the morality of smoking marijuana, expected pleasant and unpleasant effects and consequences for physical and mental health, intellectual functioning, and the desire to achieve. The analyses compared subjects at various levels of use and involvement with marijuana (Sadava, 1972). Those who were non-users or who rarely used marijuana tended to respond in a consistent manner, indicating a generalized pro or anti-marijuana position. However, those who had extensive experience with marijuana tended to respond quite differently to items about different aspects of marijuana use, indicating much greater attitude complexity. Among these subjects, a *pattern* of scores concerning marijuana attitudes predicted the extent of their use to a much greater degree than did a single score, pro or anti-marijuana.

In addition to its apparent failure to measure attitude complexity, the theory of reasoned action has been criticized on several other grounds (Liska, 1984). First, according to the model our attitudes influence our intention to act in a certain way but do not influence our behaviour directly. However, it has been shown in several field studies using sophisticated statistical analyses that attitudes influence behaviour, even after accounting for intentions (Bentler and Speckart, 1981). In partially bypassing intentions, the theory of a direct attitude-behaviour link seems to challenge the logic of a sequence of reasoned actions: I am favourable toward doing it, so I decide to do it (intention), and then act.

Several other problems with the theory have been suggested. One is a confusion between normative beliefs and beliefs about behavioural outcomes. Normative beliefs refer to the expected reactions of others, which are the most significant outcomes of many of our actions. Another problem is that the theory neglects a number of other important variables, such as other relevant attitudes, which were discussed earlier. Finally, in this theory, attitudes are conceived as a cause, and behaviour as the ultimate effect. As the next chapter will show, behaviour is often a cause of subsequent attitude change, and thus cause and effect can be seen to flow in both directions between attitudes and behaviour.

In short, while the model has an elegant simplicity and has generated much research, it does not fully account for the complexities of the relationship between attitude and behaviour. Clearly, research will continue and new approaches will emerge which contribute to a better understanding of this fascinating and important problem.

A FINAL NOTE

From the beginning, the study of attitudes has been at the core of social psychology. Much of the early research was devoted to developing reliable and valid measures of attitudes, largely because it was believed that attitudes are accurate indicators of important social behaviour. However, as the evidence accumulated, indicating that attitudes are not as closely linked to behaviour as was expected, social psychologists began to wonder what the fuss was all about. Many turned to other problems and some even predicted that attitude research would soon be a thing of the past.

These prophecies were not fulfilled. Instead, attitude research has progressed through three distinct phases, or "generations," in which different problems have been explored. The first generation asked "is" questions, in particular, "Is attitude related to behaviour?" The second asked "when" attitudes are related to behaviour — this chapter has reviewed some of the "boundary conditions" which determine when attitudes become translated into action. The third generation of research concentrates on "how" attitudes influence behaviour and, indeed, "how" behaviour influences attitude. In this respect, attitude research has become integrated with work on social cognition.

In the next chapter, the influence of social cognition will be evident as the important issue of attitude change is explored. It will become clear that the concept of attitude is alive and well in social psychology.

SUMMARY

(1) An attitude is a predisposition to react in a certain way to an object or experience. It includes cognitive, affective, and behavioural components.

(2) A value is a higher-order abstraction of what is considered ideal or desirable by a person. Terminal values represent preferences for certain end-states in life, instrumental values, preferences for certain modes of conduct.

(3) Value conflicts can lead to changes in values, attitudes, and actions. The value pluralism model relates relative priorities of values such as "freedom" and "equality" to trade-off reasoning and political ideology.

(4) Citizens of various nations show considerable variations in values ("national character") related to their culture and history. One study compared nations along value dimensions of power distance, avoidance of uncertainty, individualism-collectivism, and masculinity-femininity (i.e., achievement vs. interpersonal relations).

(5) Attitudes serve a number of functions: instrumental or adaptive, knowledge, ego defensive, and expressive. Research has demonstrated the value justification effect, which is a selective appeal to values in order to bolster or "justify" attitudes.

(6) Attitudes are not strongly linked to behaviour. For accurate prediction, specific attitudes and multiple indices of behaviour must be assessed.

(7) A variety of personal and situational factors increase or decrease the predictability of behaviour on the basis of attitudes. These include: other relevant attitudes, other needs, relevance of the action, the presence of others, social norms, access to alternative behaviours, unforeseen events, and personal relevance of the object or issue. Attitudes which are immediately accessible to memory and awareness are more likely to lead to action.

(8) The most influential model of the attitude-behaviour relationship is Ajzen and Fishbein's theory of reasoned action: The most immediate determinant of an action is an intention, which is determined by attitudes toward the action (beliefs that it will lead to valued consequences) and perceived norms (beliefs about what others expect of us and our motives to comply).

FURTHER READING

AJZEN, I. and FISHBEIN, M. (1980). *Understanding attitudes and predicting social behavior*. Englewood Cliffs, NJ: Prentice-Hall.

OSKAMP, S. (1977). *Attitudes and opinions*. Englewood Cliffs, NJ: Prentice-Hall.

ROKEACH, M. (Ed.) (1979). *Understanding human values: Individual and social*. New York: Free Press.

Attitude Change

Loyalty to a petrified opinion never yet
broke a chain or freed a human soul.
Mark Twain

FOR REFLECTION

- How do people react when they think they are being inconsistent?
- What happens to us when we act in a way that is contrary to our beliefs?
- How can we become conditioned to hold certain attitudes?
- How does advertising persuade us? How do we resist persuasion?

119

EVERY DAY WE encounter attempts to change our attitudes. Aging hockey stars invite us to drink a particular brand of beer and toothpaste manufacturers assure us that their product will enhance our sexual allure. Other messages warn us of the terrible consequences of drinking and driving or neglecting to fasten our seatbelts. A friend tries to convince us that his or her opinion is correct, telling us of all the other people who agree. A professor urges us to keep up with assignments. A member of the government assures us that their policies will produce "jobs, jobs, jobs," while someone from the opposition warns of impending doom and gloom. Some of the messages in advertising, propaganda, and person-to-person situations are direct and designed to manipulate us for fun or profit. Others, such as those found in novels, plays, and movies, are more subtle.

Given the huge expenditure of time, money, and talent, the manipulation of human attitudes is a prolific enterprise. At the same time, many advertising campaigns fail and many politicians lose elections even though they use the same techniques and hire the same consultants. Thus, while a great deal has been learned about how attitudes change, attitude manipulation is neither foolproof technology nor black magic.

In studying how attitudes change, we examine two factors: "cognitive consistency" and external influences. For example, perhaps your attitude toward opera has changed: you used to hate it, but now you enjoy it. We might study what happened in your thinking that led to this change, or how external influences caused you to change. Cognitive theorists would examine how you came to like opera after spending $35 on an opera ticket. Other theorists would emphasize how advertisements and your best friend persuaded you of opera's value.

COGNITIVE PROCESSES IN ATTITUDE CHANGE

In analyzing the process of thinking by which attitudes change, many social psychologists have based theories on the principle of cognitive consistency. That is, it is theorized that people want to be consistent in their various beliefs, and actions which are related to those beliefs. While the precise definition of cognitive consistency varies from one theory to another, it states in general that people are motivated to maintain a state of psychological harmony, or equilibrium, within their system of attitudes because disharmony is a tension-producing, uncomfortable state. The discomfort which results from inconsistency of attitudes often leads to an attitude change which will restore a sense of harmony and reduce discomfort.

While a number of theories based on the principle of consistency have been developed, one has been pre-eminent in its scope and influence. Originally conceived by Leon Festinger in 1957 and subsequently modified and expanded (Brehm and Cohen, 1962; Aronson, 1968; Wicklund and Brehm, 1976), the *cognitive dissonance theory* has received considerable attention and criticism and continues to generate productive research. It is a disarmingly simple theory, yet provocative, especially since it has led to a number of interesting unexpected predictions.

In the following discussion the basics of the theory are outlined and some of the research generated by the theory is reviewed. The discussion then turns to a consideration of some criticisms of the original theory, and later developments are outlined.

Because it makes a particularly interesting case history in how theory develops in social psychology, the evolution of cognitive dissonance theory over the three decades since its inception is traced.

Basic principles

The theory of cognitive dissonance explains how "cognitive elements" — ideas, beliefs, preferences regarding behaviour — stand in relation to each other. These elements can have either *consonant, dissonant,* or *irrelevant* relationships with each other. Dissonance is said to exist when *one cognitive element is logically opposed to another cognitive element.* For example, if a person believes that "whales should be protected" and also believes that whales destroy cod traps in Newfoundland, thus jeopardizing the fishing industry, he or she could be in a state of dissonance. One example used by Festinger concerns the two cognitions, "I smoke" and "Smoking causes cancer"; another is "I like my new car" and "It has been recalled three times to correct various defects." In these examples, according to the theory:

(1) The dissonance aroused is psychologically uncomfortable and will motivate the person to try to reduce the dissonance. For example, he or she will avoid situations and information which would likely increase the dissonance.

(2) The dissonance will increase in magnitude as the importance or value of the elements increases. For instance, dissonance aroused in the smoking/cancer situation may become more intense if a family member is diagnosed as having the disease.

(3) As the magnitude of the dissonance increases, the pressure to reduce dissonance also increases.

Two factors determine the overall level of discomfort, or cognitive dissonance. The first is the ratio of the number of dissonant cognitions to the number of consonant cognitions. Thus, for example, while smoking may be dissonant with a belief that smoking is hazardous to health, the overall level of dissonance experienced may be reduced by consonance between smoking and a belief that smoking is pleasurable or provides relaxation. The second factor in determining dissonance is the relative importance of the various elements to the person involved. In other words, while smoking may be consonant with a smoker's various beliefs about pleasure and relaxation, the importance of the health risk to this smoker may outweigh the consonant element. In summary, the magnitude of dissonance can be expressed as the following ratio: the number of dissonant cognitions weighted by the importance of each of these cognitions, in relation to the number of consonant cognitions weighted by the importance of each of these cognitions to the person.

Reducing dissonance   What will a person do to reduce dissonance when it is aroused? Theoretically, there are a number of solutions although, depending on the person and the situation, one may be preferable to another (see summary in Figure 5-1):

(1) The person may change behaviour in order to make it consistent with attitudes. For example, the smoker may decide to give up smoking in order to achieve consonance with beliefs about the importance of health. Of course, the dissonance may not be strong enough to bring about this change in a true addict. As Mark Twain commented, "It's easy to stop smoking, I've done it many times."

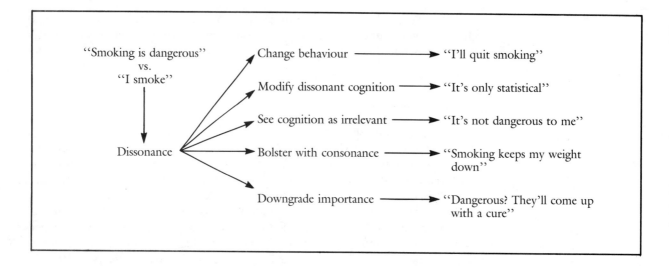

FIGURE 5-1
Reducing dissonance

(2) The person may modify a cognition so that it is now consonant with other cognitions. For example, the smoker may decide that smoking is not really harmful to health: "It's only statistical and, besides, my grandmother smoked and lived to a ripe old age."

(3) The person may rationalize that the two cognitions are not really relevant to each other. Thus, smokers may conclude that the health risks of smoking really do not apply to their own smoking.

(4) A person may bolster the case for smoking by adding new, consonant cognitions (e.g., "Smoking helps me to avoid overeating"). One variation of this solution is the "worse peril" ploy: the person reduces dissonance by comparing the risks of the behaviour in question with the risks of another common activity. For example, it is claimed that the most avid readers of automobile accident statistics are people who must fly a great deal. Because more people are killed by cars than by airplanes and because driving is almost a necessity of life, travelling by air becomes more attractive, and less dissonance is produced by the opposed cognitions, "I fly; flying is dangerous."

(5) The person may downgrade the importance of the dissonant cognition. For example, to a person of 16, the health risks of smoking exist in the future; by that time, "medicine will be able to cure anything."

Dissonance in action

We have seen how dissonance is created, what determines the intensity of dissonance, and how it can be reduced. Research in cognitive dissonance has concentrated on four areas: the discomfort often experienced after a difficult decision; reducing dissonance by avoiding exposure to new, dissonant information and seeking support from others; and the dissonance experienced after we act in ways contrary to our beliefs.

Post-decision dissonance It is important to understand the distinction between conflict and cognitive dissonance. Before we make a choice among a number of equally desirable alternatives, we are often in a state of conflict which produces discomfort. Festinger (1957) has argued that while conflict is resolved by making a choice, we may still experience discomfort because of *post-decision cognitive dissonance*. The magnitude of post-decision dissonance will depend on: (1) the importance of the decision; for example, choosing which magazine to buy would not be as important to most people as choosing which automobile to buy; (2) the extent to which the choices were equally desirable; for example, if you are a great admirer of both the Porsche and Mercedes automobiles, a choice between these two would arouse more dissonance in you than a choice between one of them and a less-desired car.

It has also been shown that we experience a "regret phase" (Walster, 1964) in which we *undervalue* the choice we have made and are very attracted to the rejected alternative. This phase occurs immediately after the decision and is short-lived. It is then followed by the dissonance-reducing *over-valuing* of our decision. For example, immediately after writing the cheque for the chosen car, we may have a transitory feeling of panic: "What have I done?!" Then, we reduce dissonance: "I purchased the best car on the market." In time, we can judge our decision more objectively.

There have been a number of laboratory tests in which predictions of post-decision dissonance have usually been supported (Festinger, 1964). Furthermore, the phenomenon has been demonstrated outside the laboratory. For instance, researchers went to a racetrack in British Columbia and asked bettors to estimate the chance of

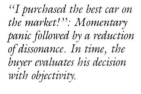

"I purchased the best car on the market!": Momentary panic followed by a reduction of dissonance. In time, the buyer evaluates his decision with objectivity.

their horse winning (Knox and Inkster, 1968). Some of these bettors were interviewed *before* they placed their bets, others *immediately after* they had placed their bets. Those in the second group showed significantly higher confidence that their horse would win the race. In short, placing the bet seemed to create post-decision dissonance which the bettors then reduced by increasing their confidence that the correct choice had, indeed, been made. These results were replicated in a similar study of wagering in a game of chance at the Canadian National Exhibition (Younger, Walker and Arrowood, 1977).

The effect of post-decision dissonance is not limited to people who frequent racetracks or bingo games, as the results of another study illustrate (Frenkel and Doob, 1976). Individuals in this case were interviewed either before or after they cast their vote in the 1971 Ontario provincial and the 1972 federal elections. In both cases voters just leaving the polling station were more inclined to think that their candidate was best and was most likely to win than voters entering the polling station.

Two other important factors have been shown to influence the arousal of post-decision dissonance. One is the individual's *commitment* to the decision; dissonance will not be experienced unless the individual feels committed to or bound by the decision (often by making the decision public) and responsible for its consequences (Kiesler, 1968). The other is *volition*, the person's ability to exercise free choice: if the person was instructed or compelled to make a particular decision, post-decision dissonance is unlikely (Linder, Cooper and Jones, 1967).

Selective exposure to information   Dissonance theory predicts that information which decreases dissonance will be sought, while that which increases dissonance will be avoided. For example, after purchasing a new car, the owner may read only those ads extolling the virtues of that car and avoid those depicting other cars which had been considered and rejected. If new, dissonance-arousing information cannot be avoided, then the individual might employ other strategies, such as discounting or misperceiving the message, denigrating the source, or actually changing his or her attitude.

While a few studies have found support for other strategies (e.g., Ehrlich et al., 1957), the effects often have appeared to be unreliable (see Zajonc, 1968b; Kiesler, 1971), casting doubt on this particular prediction. In a revised statement of cognitive dissonance theory, Festinger (1964) argued that dissonant information is not always avoided and may even be preferred in some circumstances. When we perceive that dissonant information can be easily refuted, we may actually seek out such information in order to bolster our confidence and reduce dissonance. Or, if we believe the information will help us make the right decisions, we may accept some dissonance today to avoid more dissonance tomorrow. Or, if we are in a state of post-decision dissonance and can still change our mind, we may not selectively avoid uncomfortable information. However, more recent research suggests that it is the seeking out of consonant information that is most important; the avoidance of dissonant information matters less (Frey, 1986).

Outside the laboratory researchers have studied how people respond to new information which disconfirms previously held beliefs (Silverman, 1971; MacDonald and Majunder, 1973; Bishop, 1975). The studies concerned changes in attitudes toward U.S. political figures following highly publicized events in which they were involved: the Chappaquidick incident in which Senator Ted Kennedy abandoned his female passenger (who drowned) and delayed informing the police; the resignation of Senator Eagleton as a nominee for vice president in 1972 after it became public knowledge that he had been treated for a serious mental disorder; and the resignation of President Richard Nixon when it became evident that he had lied and "covered up" about the break-in at the Watergate Hotel and his own role in the affair. As often happens when research is transferred from the laboratory to the real world, the data became more variable and less precise. In general, dissonance theory was supported in the studies, although a number of individuals were found who appeared tolerant of some incon-sistency in the context of public affairs issues.

Social Support Festinger also claimed that dissonance may be aroused by other indi-viduals voicing disagreement with us, especially if the topic is important to us, cannot be verified through reference to "facts," and our opponents are attractive and cred-ible. Again, there are a number of options available to reduce the dissonance created: we might change our minds, get the others to change their opinions, or undermine their credibility. If these solutions do not work, other people could be found to support our views or those who are not yet committed could be persuaded.

Festinger, Riecken and Schachter (1956) studied the role of social support among the members of a doomsday cult. The members of this cult believed they would escape a flood by being taken on a spaceship to a distant planet; subsequently, they realized that neither the flood nor their rescuers were coming. It was predicted that this hitherto secretive group, instead of giving up its beliefs, would now proselytize actively. This indeed happened, but subsequent attempts to replicate the outcome with other similar groups have been unsuccessful (see, for example, Hardyck and Braden, 1962). However, there are so many variables at work in field settings of this sort that it is unlikely the effect, if it exists, can be expected to appear consistently (Thompson and Oskamp, 1974).

Counter-attitudinal behaviour and insufficient justification Cognitive dissonance theory has also been applied to the relationship between attitude and behaviour, with significant results. One of the first experiments concerned with dissonance (Festinger and Carlsmith, 1959) showed that if people could be induced to behave in a manner opposed to their attitude, then their attitude would change to be compatible with the behaviour. This is an interesting and counter-intuitive outcome which suggests that we act *first* and *then* form an attitude. The theory and research which flowed from this study is extensive.

In the original experiment subjects were brought individually to a laboratory and seated in front of a board containing a large number of pegs. Their task was to turn each peg a ¼ turn in sequence and to continue turning for 20 minutes. The task was deliberately designed to be tedious and boring. At the end of the "experimental session" the experimenter informed the subjects that the experiment was designed to test the effect of a "preparatory set on motor performance." They also were told that they were in the "control group" and therefore had not been given any prior instructions. However, they were informed that the next subject was waiting and was to be told that the task was interesting and enjoyable; unfortunately, the assistant who was supposed to pass on this information had not yet shown up. Each subject then was asked whether he or she would agree to take the assistant's place. Half of the subjects were offered $1 for their help, the other half were offered $20. The

Yet another Montreal transit strike

majority of the subjects agreed to help whether they were in the $1 condition or in the $20 condition.

The subjects then proceeded to tell the waiting "subject" (actually a confederate of the experimenter) that the task, which they knew to be boring, was quite interesting. That is, they expressed a point of view which was contrary to their real attitude about the experiment. Then, during a post-experimental interview, subjects were asked to rate the extent to which they found the experimental task to be boring or interesting. The question was, would a counter-attitudinal behaviour (lying to the confederate) lead to an attitude change that represented a more positive evaluation of the task?

The key factor in this study was the magnitude of the incentive to lie. Incentive theory predicts that those paid more for their counter-attitudinal sales pitch would experience the situation in general as more rewarding, and would be more likely to adopt a more positive attitude to the boring task. Dissonance theory predicts that those paid only $1 to lie about the task would have *insufficient external justification* for their action. They would experience cognitive dissonance, which could be reduced by deciding that the task was "sort of interesting" and that they had not, in fact, lied. Subjects paid $20 could justify their actions by this payment, whereas few people would feel comfortable "selling out" for a paltry one dollar. Thus, the two theories predicted opposite results in the 1959 experiment.

The results supported dissonance theory; that is, attitude change was greater among those paid $1 than those paid $20. However, this experiment generated much debate, and was followed by a series of other investigations designed to deal with criticisms of the methods and of the interpretation of results. Rosenberg (1965), for example, argued that $20 was an unrealistic sum to be paid for such a small task and likely aroused *evaluation apprehension* in the subjects, making them suspicious that they were still under experimental observation. In order to show that they could not be "bought" and that they were still in control of their actions, they deliberately resisted changing their attitudes. Therefore, Rosenberg claimed that the experiment did not adequately test for the influence of incentives.

Rosenberg repeated the experiment and offered subjects $10, $5, $1, or 50¢ to write an essay which contradicted their own attitudes about their university football team. He also separated in time and place the measurement of attitudes from the procedure by which dissonance was created. In other words, as far as the subjects were concerned, they were participating in two independent studies — one about their attitudes toward a variety of issues (the football item was embedded among a number of other topics), and another in which they wrote an essay. He reasoned that these modifications would eliminate or substantially reduce evaluation apprehension, especially in the high-incentive condition. Rosenberg found, in accordance with *incentive theory*, that the more a subject had been paid the *more* his attitude would change. At about the same time, two other experiments were conducted (Elms and Janis, 1965; Janis and Gilmore, 1965) which supported Rosenberg's contention that when subjects' suspicions of the experimenter's motives are removed, dissonance effects disappear.

At this point it appeared that the weight of evidence had swung *against* the insufficient justification phenomenon and cognitive dissonance theory and *for* incentive theory. However, not long thereafter other experiments (Carlsmith, Collins and

FIGURE 5–2
*Attitude after public and
private discrepant behaviour*

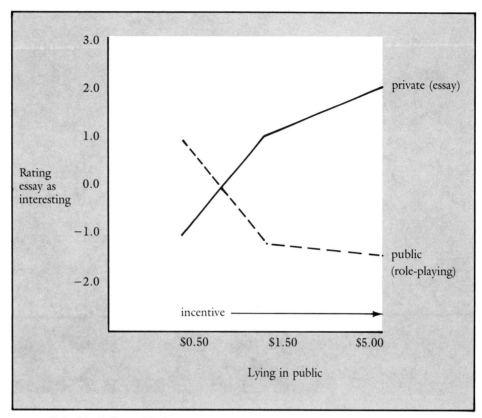

FIGURE 5–2
*Attitude after public and
private discrepant behaviour*

SOURCE: Carlsmith, Collins and Helmreich, 1966

Helmreich, 1966; Linder, Cooper and Jones, 1967) provided a solution to the debate. Both theories apply, depending on the experimental conditions.

It was pointed out that writing an anonymous essay differs from the face-to-face deception engaged in by the subjects in the Festinger and Carlsmith study (Carlsmith, Collins and Helmreich, 1966). Since *public commitment* was lacking in the counter-attitudinal essay writing task, it was hypothesized that this factor might be crucial for the occurrence of dissonance. An experiment was conducted in which some subjects wrote anonymous essays and others publicly lied for either 50¢, $1.50 or $5. As anticipated, the attitudes of those writing anonymously changed in the direction predicted by *incentive* theory, and those publicly committed changed in the direction predicted by *dissonance* theory (see Figure 5-2).

Another critical difference between the Rosenberg and the 1959 Festinger and Carlsmith research had concerned the point at which the subjects decided whether or not to participate. During the experiment, Festinger and Carlsmith asked the subjects to lie for either $1 or $20; the subjects then replied. By contrast, the subjects agreed to take part in Rosenberg's bogus experiment *before* being made aware of the conditions of pay. The point is that if we agree to do something first and subsequently find out how much the reward is, then the higher the reward, the more we will

Do we appreciate public transit more if we must endure a long wait?

appreciate what we are doing. On the other hand, insufficient justification only operates when the payment is an integral part of the decision process.

Insufficient justification also seems to offer a satisfactory explanation for the outcome of an experiment performed by Aronson and Mills (1959) which was concerned with the relationship between severity of "hazing" or initiation into a group and fondness for the group. In this study, female undergraduates were assigned to either a control, a mild initiation, or a severe initiation condition. The control subjects were simply asked by the male experimenter whether they could freely discuss sex. The mild initiation subjects were asked the same question and also required to read aloud five sex-connoted but ordinary words (e.g., "screw"). Those undergoing the severe initiation, in addition to being asked the question, were required to read aloud twelve obscene words (e.g., "fuck") and two passages containing explicit reference to sexual activity. (Keep in mind that this experiment took place in 1959; these conditions might not be considered severe today.) All the subjects then listened to a tape-recording of what appeared to be an earlier, rather tedious, discussion session of the group they were to join. The subjects then evaluated the discussion on a scale.

It was found that the most favourable evaluations were made by those who had experienced the severe initiation. In their case, the dissonance aroused by undergoing a severe initiation into a dull group could only be reduced by enhancing the evaluation of the group. In other words, the dull discussion was insufficient justification for the severe initiation, so the subjects made it interesting.

This process also has been related to the results of the "forbidden toy" experiments with children (Aronson and Carlsmith, 1963; Freedman, 1965; Lepper, Zanna and Abelson, 1970). Since it had been shown that an activity which is engaged in for insufficient justification is likely to become more attractive, it was reasoned that an activity *prohibited* by insufficient justification could become *less attractive*. In this study individual young children were at first allowed to play with any of five attractive toys. Then the experimenter noted the order of preference that each child expressed for the toys. He then placed the second most attractive toy on a table and distributed the remainder throughout the room. At this point the experimenter said that he had to leave for a few minutes but just before going out the door he told some of the children that he would be "annoyed" if they played with the toy on the table (mild threat condition); for others he substituted "angry" for "annoyed" and also threatened to take all the toys and leave if the child disobeyed (severe threat condition). Other children were assigned to a control condition in which the experimenter did not say anything but took the second ranked toy with him when he left.

The children were observed for ten minutes and it was noted that none of the children in either of the threat conditions played with the forbidden toy. The experimenter then returned, replaced the toy, and obtained a second ranking of the toys. It was found that the children in the mild threat condition now ranked the forbidden toy lower than they had previously while none of the other subjects decreased the rank of this toy. In fact, those in the severe threat condition actually now ranked it higher. Thus no dissonance was aroused in the control and severe threat treatments. On the other hand, those children who received the mild threat could not justify ignoring the toy for such a trivial admonition and therefore reduced the dissonance by devaluing the toy.

Another study showed that this devaluation can be a real and lasting change (Freedman, 1965). The toy in question was an irresistible battery-powered robot. The experimenter asked some children not to play with it, threatened severe or mild punishment, and then left. Several weeks later, a woman came to administer some paper-and-pencil tests in the same room, with the same toys scattered about. After she administered the tests to each child, she asked the child to wait while she scored the tests, and suggested in an off-hand manner that he or she could play with the toys. As in the previous study, the toy held more attraction for the children threatened with severe punishment. Even though they had been admonished weeks earlier, they played with the forbidden toy, while those who had been mildly threatened did not play with the toy. In this experiment, of course, none of the children were aware that the woman's presence had anything to do with Freedman or his threats. Think of the implications of these findings for child-rearing or education, and recall what usually happens when a teacher leaves the classroom.

In short, behaviour which is contrary to attitudes may arouse cognitive dissonance and lead to subsequent attitude change. This is particularly likely if the person is offered a small reward or threatened with a mild punishment, and is therefore unable to justify the act in terms of expected reward or punishment. For dissonance to occur, the individual must believe that the act was freely chosen, and that a public commitment has been made in which responsibility for the action has been expressed. Careful analysis and research has led to an understanding of the conditions in which cognitive dissonance occurs.

The problem of arousal in cognitive dissonance

Dissonance theory postulates that dissonance produces an unpleasant state of tension which the person is motivated to reduce or relieve through some cognitive adjustment. Does such a state of arousal actually arise or is the notion of tension merely a convenient "explanatory" device? The evidence has been reviewed by Kiesler and Pallak (1976) and they conclude that the manipulations used in dissonance experiments are arousing. Notice that they say that the *manipulations* are arousing, *not* that dissonance itself is arousing. They also point out that very few of the investigations reviewed offered *direct* evidence of arousal, and those that did employed measures of physiological changes. For example, Gerard (1967) created two states of dissonance, high and low, by offering to give some subjects one painting chosen from two which they had ranked third and fourth choices in a group of 12 paintings, and other subjects a choice between a highly desired (third choice) and less desired (eighth choice) painting. Presumably, the former subjects would experience more dissonance than the latter subjects. Gerard measured the amplitude of the finger pulse by means of a plethysmograph after a subject had made a choice. The post-decision amplitude of the pulse of the "high dissonance" subjects was reduced, an effect which usually accompanies stress or tension.

While we can be reasonably confident that arousal does occur under dissonant conditions is it *necessary* for attitude change to take place? Cooper, Zanna and Taves (1978) reported an experiment which throws some light on this question. They divided their subjects into three groups: those in group I were given a tranquilizer, those in group II a placebo, and those in group III an amphetamine. Then all subjects were asked to write a counter-attitudinal essay which, in this case, was to argue that the pardon of Richard Nixon by President Ford was justified. In addition, the groups were further subdivided so that half the subjects were presented with a high degree of choice in pursuing the task ("I will leave it entirely to you to decide if you would like to help the Research Institute by writing the essay") and half were not presented with an overt choice (no reference was made to a choice). Whether presented with a free choice or an instruction, almost all agreed to perform the task. According to dissonance theory, the first group should have experienced more dissonance than the second group. The results of the experiment indicated that those in the placebo condition show the attitude change effect usually obtained in this type of experiment. This effect was eliminated by the tranquilizer (which decreased arousal) and enhanced by the amphetamine (which increased arousal). Some critics might argue that this outcome was due to varying amounts of attention paid by the subjects to their tasks in the three conditions, but a test of recall revealed no differences among groups. Nor were there differences in the quality or length of the essays. Thus the state of cognitive dissonance which leads to attitude change is a state of arousal, not simply an intellectual awareness of inconsistency.

If dissonance arousal leads to attitude change, then reducing arousal should lead to no attitude change, even where inconsistency exists. In one study the effects of alcohol were investigated (Steele, Southwick and Critchlow, 1981). Subjects were asked to write a counter-attitudinal essay — then some subjects were induced to drink alcohol under the guise of rating the taste of various beverages, while others consumed coffee or water. When tested later, those who drank alcohol showed less attitude change. Presumably, the alcohol reduced arousal while the caffeine in the coffee increased it.

Reinterpreting cognitive dissonance

There are problems with the concept of cognitive dissonance. As discussed earlier, Festinger (1957) described it as the result of a logical inconsistency in our thinking: B does not follow from A. For example, he suggested that if we were to observe someone standing in the rain and not getting wet, these two cognitions would be dissonant. As a result of subsequent research, we would not consider this to be an example in which cognitive dissonance would be experienced. We might be amused, amazed, curious, or concerned about own own sanity, but we would not experience the psychological discomfort which leads to attitude change.

Bem (1970) argued that, for most people, most of the time, inconsistency is "our most enduring cognitive commonplace." Further, when our thinking is inconsistent, it "just sits there" and does not bother us. This is probably true because many or most of our cognitions are experienced as unrelated to each other. In fact, Abelson (1968) suggests that much of our thinking consists of isolated "opinion molecules," consisting of an attitude, a belief, and a perception of social support (i.e., a fact, a feeling, and a following). For example: "I really like the idea of French immersion programs in schools" (attitude). "I believe that it would help my child become bilingual and get ahead in this world" (a belief). "So do many other people, because most of these programs have waiting lists" (perception of social support). The alert reader will recognize in this triad elements of the Ajzen and Fishbein (1980) theory of reasoned action (Chapter 4). The point made by Bem and by Abelson is that we may not be concerned or even aware that those cognitions are consistent or inconsistent with other cognitions. The question now becomes: when and why do certain inconsistencies become uncomfortable to us?

Self-justification   Several investigators argue that inconsistency is uncomfortable and motivating only when it threatens our own self-concept (Greenwald and Ronis, 1978; Steele and Liu, 1983). Indeed, Aronson (1984), one of the early pioneers in disso-nance research, now argues that the dissonance effect is really one of *self-justification*. For example, cigarette smokers may be uncomfortable about their behaviour, not because it is inconsistent with their beliefs about smoking and cancer or about the discomfort of non-smokers, but because it is inconsistent with their own view of themselves as rational, thoughtful and considerate — in short, they feel stupid or guilty about it.

Several experiments which required subjects to give a speech which contradicted their own attitudes have shown that it is inconsistency of the self-image that is crucial. In one (Nel, Helmreich and Aronson, 1969) subjects were given high or low incen-tives to talk in favour of legalizing the use of marijuana. Different subjects were led to believe that their audience was in favour or against this policy or that they were a group of school children with no position on it. It was only in the non-committal audience condition that subjects given low incentives showed more attitude change. Evidently dissonance was aroused when they believed that they were addressing an impressionable audience of children who might be persuaded to use drugs. Another study (Cooper and Worchel, 1970) showed that the dissonance effect occurred when subjects were led to believe that they had actually persuaded someone that a boring task was interesting, but not if it seemed that the person was unconvinced. In a third experiment, the dissonance effect occurred after subjects were induced to lie to some-one they liked, but not when they lied to someone they disliked (Cooper, Zanna

I never did a thing
that made a smaller person
lose the way,
or try to follow blindly
for my love.
My freedom won't allow it.

A BROKEN CIGARETTE IS A LITTLE FREEDOM GAINED.

2/3 OF CANADIANS DON'T SMOKE.

Health and Welfare Canada   Santé et Bien-être social Canada

HERE COMES THE BREAKAWAY GENERATION!

Canadä

Feelings of personal responsibility for the outcome of a counter-attitudinal act.

and Goethals, 1974). In summary, the evidence points to the importance of feelings of personal responsibility for the outcome of a counter-attitudinal act.

How can we test the hypothesis that cognitive dissonance represents a state in which people feel uncomfortable about themselves? One way would be to arouse dissonance in the usual ways, and then manipulate the situation so that the self-esteem of some subjects is enhanced. If the attitude changes predicted by the theory are not found in these cases, then self-justification is a plausible interpretation of cognitive dissonance.

In one such study, ego enhancement was brought about by having some subjects express some strongly held personal values (Steele and Liu, 1983). In another study (Rodrigues, 1983) ego enhancement was induced by telling some subjects that psychological tests administered earlier showed them to be mature and well-adjusted individuals. In both studies, the dissonance effect was not observed among those whose egos had been enhanced, but did occur as predicted among those who had not received this treatment. Thus the self-concept plays a central role in cognitive dissonance.

Self-perception   Thus far, evidence has been reviewed suggesting that much of cognitive dissonance is tied to self-justification. A completely different position is advocated by Bem (1972) who argues that the effect of counter-attitudinal behaviour on attitudes is a result of self-perception. He contends that, in effect, we discover or arrive at our attitudes by observing what we do in what circumstances. For example, subjects in the Festinger and Carlsmith (1959) experiment were paid to tell a person that a boring task was really interesting. Those given $20 could easily explain their actions, and would still remember how utterly bored they had been. On the other hand, those paid $1 would not be able to explain their actions in terms of the money, and could therefore infer actual enjoyment in the task. In other words, Bem explains the effect of insufficient justification in terms of internal and external *attributions* about behaviour.

For several years, the debate has raged between dissonance and self-perception advocates. In fact, this debate is now viewed as a conflict over different models of human nature — people as irrational and driven by a need to feel consistent, or people as "naive scientists," rationally weighing alternative explanations of their own behaviour (Fiske and Taylor, 1984). The research has provided some support for each side and has failed to demolish either. Eventually, a consensus has emerged, allowing that both explanations have validity in different conditions.

Two such conditions can be specified. It seems that when the discrepancy between attitude and behaviour is large, people tend to reduce dissonance; however, people tend to infer attitudes from actions when the discrepancy is small (e.g., Fazio, Zanna and Cooper, 1977). Thus, if we must tell someone that the boring task was "absolutely thrilling," we will probably not change attitudes but look for external justification. But if we tell someone that the task was "not all *that* bad," we may, indeed, infer that we are really telling the truth. It also has been shown that self-perception is involved when individuals do not possess prior, clearly-defined attitudes (Chaiken and Baldwin, 1981). If we are uncertain whether a task we have performed was boring, but have subsequently told others it was interesting, we may interpret this action, i.e., telling others it was interesting, as stemming from a positive attitude towards the task.

A new integration

Cooper and Fazio (1984) have outlined a revised model of cognitive dissonance which accounts for the diverse research findings (see Figure 5-3). It pertains especially to the outcome of counter-attitudinal behaviour and has a strong attributional flavour. They reason that when we act contrary to our beliefs, we assess the consequences of our actions. If our act is perceived to have actual or potential negative consequences, we search for an explanation. If it is clear that we had a free choice to act and that the consequences could have been foreseen, we attribute responsibility to ourselves. At this point, dissonance is aroused. If we attribute this feeling of discomfort to our reaction to the action, rather than to an external source, e.g., a drug or the situation,

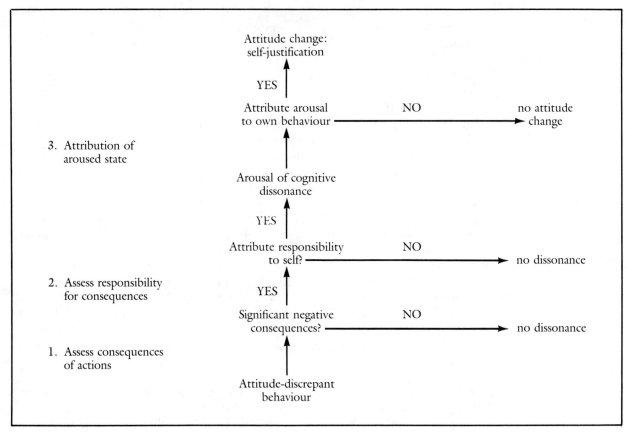

SOURCE: adapted from Cooper and Fazio, 1984

FIGURE 5–3
"New Look" model of
cognitive dissonance

then we are motivated to reduce dissonance. Now our attitude changes, and we come to believe that the boring task was really exciting.

Note the many exits from dissonance that are available along the way. We may decide that no harm was done by our little lie. We may decide that we really had no choice but to lie — the money was too good or the devil made us do it. If arousal is experienced, we may ignore or minimize it, or attribute it to the weather, indigestion, or nervousness in a psychology experiment. In short, the cognitive dissonance process involves both dissonance arousal and motivation to reduce dissonance, and both processes involve complex sets of attributions. The Cooper and Fazio model is useful in that it can predict *when* the induced compliance-insufficient justification effect will occur.

After three decades, the theory of cognitive dissonance remains influential. Rather than breaking new ground, much of the research today is concerned with clarifying concepts and establishing the "boundary conditions" under which dissonance takes place. Nonetheless, there are several major unresolved issues:

(1) The theory does not specify the *mode* of dissonance in a given situation. For example, after purchasing a new car, we may reduce dissonance by over-valuing our choice, devaluing the rejected alternative, bolstering our feelings of consonance, or

agreement, or deciding that our decision was irrelevant rather than dissonant with our evaluation of a number of cars.

(2) Individuals differ in their tolerance of dissonance. Some of us are quite comfortable acting spontaneously, regardless of attitudes, while others are quite acutely aware of and uncomfortable about inconsistencies.

(3) At times we may deliberately seek out cognitive dissonance. We may act unexpectedly or perversely or we may adopt a position which we know is inconsistent. For instance, people may decide to travel somewhere different, even though they had not previously been interested in that place. Perhaps too much consistency is boring — which is also an uncomfortable state.

So far, we have discussed attitude change from the perspective of internal cognitive processes. While dissonance often occurs in response to external events, it is the internal interpretation of these events that induces dissonance and generates change.

EXTERNAL PROCESSES IN ATTITUDE CHANGE

It is obvious that attitudes usually do not germinate spontaneously in the mind, but are acquired and modified as we live and act in our social environment. We will now discuss the role of external influences on attitude change. We begin by examining the acquisition and modification of attitudes through classical, or Pavlovian, conditioning. Then we turn to a more extensive exploration of how people can be persuaded to change their attitudes.

Classical conditioning

An important early development in the history of psychology was the work on learning by association. In the original research by Pavlov, a bell was sounded each time a hungry dog was presented with food. Eventually, the sound of the bell alone (conditioned stimulus) caused the dog to salivate, since it was associated with the food (unconditioned stimulus) and could evoke the same reaction. It is believed that our attitudes may be conditioned the same way.

A number of experiments have demonstrated that positive or negative attitudes can be conditioned to otherwise neutral words or names. In one series of studies (Staats and Staats, 1958), subjects were asked to learn two lists of words (e.g., names of nationalities, adjectives). One list was presented visually on a screen at the same time that the other was presented orally through audiophones. Each time certain nationalities were presented, a positive or negative adjective was presented at the same time. Although subjects were not aware of the associations, their subsequent ratings of a certain nationality were influenced by whether positive or negative adjectives had been coupled with it.

It appears that much prejudice is learned by children from parents in this way. While parents may not directly teach the child to despise or avoid members of a certain ethnic group, the group label may come to be associated in the child's mind with reactions by the parents, e.g., "bad" words, negative feelings, or discomfort (see further discussion in relation to prejudice in Chapter 7).

Studies involving classical conditioning have been criticized because subjects might have interpreted associations as cues as to what the experimenter was expecting. Why else would they experience an unpleasant noise or negative adjective every time a certain word came up? In one experiment, however, demand characteristics were controlled (Zanna, Kiesler and Pilkonis, 1970). The strategy adopted was to give subjects an alternative and convincing explanation for the association. They were told that, in order to test some new apparatus, they were to be given a series of electric shocks, interspersed with rest periods. They also were told that a word (e.g., "dark") would signal the onset of shock, and another word (e.g., "light") would signal when the shock would end and the rest period would begin. Thus, after a series of trials, both words should have become conditioned stimuli: one to the unpleasant emotional response to the onset of shock, the other to the pleasant feeling of relief when it ended.

After these trials ended, subjects went to another laboratory where they were invited by a different experimenter to take part in a different experiment. This one involved rating a series of key words, including, of course, the two conditioned stimuli, on a set of semantic differential scales. For instance:

good	1	2	3	4	5	6	7	bad
strong	1	2	3	4	5	6	7	weak

Because this was a different experiment, and because the previous experiment had simply involved being signalled and testing the shock apparatus, the subjects' responses should not have been influenced by demand characteristics. Indeed, subjects evaluated the word positively when it previously had been associated with the end of shock, and negatively when it had been associated with the onset of shock. In essence, an attitude had been formed through Pavlovian classical conditioning.

PERSUASION

Persuasion is the process of getting others to engage in a particular behaviour or to agree to an advocated position by means of a rational or emotional appeal. The foundations for research on persuasive communication were established in the 1950s by the Yale University Communications Research Program led by Carl Hovland and his colleagues (Hovland, Janis and Kelley, 1953). They concentrated on the stages people go through in order to be persuaded: attention, comprehension, acceptance or yielding, and retention of the message. First, the target or audience must pay attention to the message. (Television commercials exemplify some of the techniques used to capture attention: catchy musical jingles, flashy visual displays, humour, novel presentation and, of course, sex.) After attention has been secured, the message must be presented in such a way that it will be understood. Both the clarity of the presentation and the intellectual capacity of the audience are factors at this stage. The next stage is crucial — will the audience accept the message and yield to the persuasive powers of the persuader? Finally, the audience should retain or remember the message long enough to act on it.

The problem of *acceptance* has attracted the most research attention. In order to research the problem systematically, we can organize the variables around four questions: Who presents the message? (source) What is the message? (message) To whom is the message directed? (audience) How is it presented, and by what means is the message sent and received? (channel)

B · O · X   5 - 1

PERSUASION SCHEMATA: WHEN WE USE WHAT MESSAGE

What do we do when we want to persuade someone of something?

In fact, we usually begin with some idea of what we are going to do and, if our plan should fail, we often have another plan of attack ready. In other words, we approach the task of changing someone's attitude with a set of *persuasion schemata*, which are evoked and used almost automatically in a variety of situations.

In one study by Rule, Bisanz and Kohn (1986) subjects were asked whom they persuaded, who persuaded them, and how people tried to persuade their friends, enemies, fathers, and other people in general. Their data showed that most persuasion attempts occur in close relationships, and that attempts tend to be reciprocal, that is, both people attempt to persuade each other. A list of persuasion goals was also derived, the most common being *activity* (to go somewhere, do something, or acquire some object).

The study also showed that we tend to follow a sequence of methods in our attempts at persuasion. We tend first to ask for what we want, although it is certainly not always advisable to be direct! Then, we use "self-oriented methods," citing a personal reason ("I really need it") or personal expertise ("I have one and it's great"). Then, we invoke "dyadic" methods, referring to the ongoing relationship we have with this person ("Be a friend!") or we bargain ("If you do it for me, I'll take you out for supper"). Finally, we appeal to more abstract principles, such as social norms ("Everybody is doing it"), altruism ("Surely you don't want your child to imitate you and smoke") or morality ("We could pay that bribe but it would be wrong"). Two approaches stand out from the sequence of persuasion strategies observed in the study: we tend to use flattery or "buttering up" quite early, perhaps at the beginning, and we almost always use physical force as a last resort, if at all. If threats, deception and emotional appeals are to be used (guilt, sulking) they will also be used as last resorts.

Characteristics of the source

The major characteristic of the communicator or source which affects acceptance of the message is *credibility*. In turn, credibility has been shown to be mainly a function of perceived *expertness* and *trustworthiness*. Communicators are more effective if the audience assumes they know what they are talking about and are sincere. Trustworthiness is especially enhanced if the audience believes the communicator has nothing personal to gain from his or her efforts. It is no accident that toothpaste is promoted by individuals in lab coats (expertness) and that detergents are recommended by ordinary people who only want to pass on their experience to others. It also is true that the source's credibility will only have impact if the audience is aware of it *before* the message is presented rather than after (Mills and Harvey, 1972).

In most cases, the topic or item and the expertise of the source must be compatible. Ordinarily, it would not be very sensible to have a nuclear physicist talk about nutrition. However, "high-status" sources may be influential even outside their sphere of knowledge (Aronson and Golden, 1962). Nobel prize winners, for instance, often

Canadian citizens being persuaded by government during WWII: A credible source, a compatible message.

become accepted experts on an amazing variety of subjects. (But Linus Pauling, a Nobel laureate in chemistry and an eloquent contributor to the cause of peace, was considerably less credible expounding on the supposed benefits of taking megadoses of Vitamin C.)

One of the early, and intriguing, findings related to communicator variables (Hovland, Lumsdaine and Sheffield, 1949) was called the *sleeper effect*. In a pioneering experiment one group of soldiers viewed a propaganda film and another group did not. Attitudes towards the topic of the film were measured five days and then nine weeks later; it was found that the differences between the two groups was greater at nine weeks than at five days. The most popular explanation for this unexpected outcome was called the *discounting cue* hypothesis, which stated that the source of the film (message), i.e., the U.S. army, was perceived as untrustworthy. This led the soldiers to discount the message, thus reducing its immediate effect. But as time elapsed, the connection between the source and the message would be forgotten or weakened, and the message itself would appear more prominent.

It is still argued whether the sleeper effect is a real phenomenon. Attempts to replicate this finding have often been unsuccessful, leading some to conclude that "it's time to lay the sleeper effect to rest" (Gillig and Greenwald, 1974). However, others have pointed out that when the methodological and statistical problems in the earlier experiments are corrected, the effect can be demonstrated. They suggest that "laying the sleeper effect to rest at this time would constitute a premature burial" (Cook *et al.*, 1979).

Message factors

Suppose you have been nominated as a candidate for some elected office and you must now convince the electorate to vote for you, or suppose that you are a lawyer about to present your summation to the jury. In each case you have to "get your message across" in a way that increases your chances of winning the political contest or having your client declared innocent. There is some information available which could help you organize your message in the most effective way.

Hovland *et al.* (1957) conducted the initial studies on this topic. Among several findings was the discovery that — especially with intelligent audiences — it is best to present both the positive and negative sides of the argument, and then to refute the negative evidence. However, when it is evident that the audience has a firm position on an issue (e.g., in the case of delegates to a political convention), it would not be effective to present a two-sided argument. In addition, when it is probable that the audience will hear the other side from someone else, it is usually more effective to present both sides. Therefore, it is important to examine the situation in selecting a one-sided or two-sided communication strategy (Karlins and Abelson, 1970).

Primacy-Recency   One aspect of the message which has been thoroughly investigated turns on the issue of *primacy-recency*. If both sides of an argument are to be presented, which is likely to have the advantage, the side given first (primacy) or the side given last (recency)? Most of the early experiments (e.g., Lund, 1925; Asch, 1946) supported the operation of primacy. However, Hovland *et al.* (1957) and others (Luchins, 1957; Anderson, 1959) showed that under certain conditions, recency was likely to be dominant. The critical factor turned out to be the passage of time. If one set of arguments immediately follows the other, the first set is likely to have the most impact (primacy). However, as the time between the presentation of the sets is increased, recency is more likely to account for the results (Miller and Campbell, 1959; Insko, 1964; Wilson and Miller, 1968). These results imply, for example, that if two lawyers are to present their cases to the jury on the same day, the one who goes first is likely to have the advantage, but if it is late in the day and the case is adjourned and the other lawyer will be heard the next morning, the advantage will be reversed.

It is interesting to note that in our courts, the prosecution (Crown) presents its case, and its final argument to the jury, before the defense. This custom is presumably derived from the proposition that a defendant is innocent until proven guilty. However, it may also give the defense the opportunity to take advantage of recency. On the other hand, the case for the Crown is first to be presented, thus having the advantage of the primacy effect. We can only speculate about which side may have the overall advantage in persuading the jury — all other factors being equal.

B·O·X 5-2

ATTITUDES AS SOCIAL JUDGMENTS

How do we react to a persuasive message? We may dismiss it out of hand or reject it completely. We may respond positively because someone is telling us what we already believe. We may react with indifference, finding the message unconvincing but not entirely unreasonable. Or we may react with great interest, and may be convinced to change our own position. In short, we make a judgment about a message or argument, thus determining whether the message will influence us.

Muzafer Sherif and his colleagues developed a model by which we can understand such judgments (Sherif, Sherif and Nebergall, 1965). They argue that for any attitudinal object or issue, people have a continuum, or range, of possible positions. For example, some individuals may be strongly in favour of the death penalty for all acts of violence, while others are in favour of it only for certain acts, in favour only in exceptional circumstances, uncertain, mildly opposed, or strongly opposed without exception and committed to the abolition of capital punishment. This range of possible positions can be divided into three groupings, or *latitudes*: (1) the latitude of acceptance, which encompasses all positions or arguments that are convincing or acceptable, including of course, the individual's own position; (2) the latitude of non-commitment, which includes those positions that are neither acceptable nor unacceptable; and (3) the latitude of rejection, which is the range of those positions or arguments that are not acceptable, and to which the individual would be opposed.

Let us take, for example, attitudes toward the federal government currently in power. We can conceive of a range of positions along a 15-point scale (we are using such a scale only as a hypothetical example). Position 1 would be selected by a totally committed party member; 2 or 3 would be the position of party members who were less strongly committed; 4 or 5 might be selected by non-members who generally supported the party; 6 or 7

would be positions of less strongly identified supporters. A neutral or undecided position is presented by 8, and 9–15 represent the range of opposing positions including members of opposition parties (13–15). You can probably locate your own position along this continuum (see Figure 5-4).

Sherif argues that how people react to a particular message will depend on both their own position and the range of positions that would be acceptable to them. That is, individuals with the same specific attitude may vary in their latitudes of acceptance and rejection around that attitude. For example, consider three people, all of whom are relatively committed party members. Brian may consider acceptable only messages which advocate party memberships and would reject messages which offer lukewarm support to the party's policies, while John would accept any strong pro-party support, and Flora would accept any kind of supportive messages.

In general, a wide latitude of acceptance means that the person is more open to influence by a persuasive message (Eagly and Telaak, 1972). A message which is relatively far from, or discrepant with, the person's own position will produce the greatest amount of attitude change *if* that message still falls within the latitude of acceptance. Of course, the farther the message is from the target's own position, the more likely it is to be outside his or her latitude of acceptance. The trick is to find the message which falls as close as possible to the borderline of acceptable positions.

The structure of the latitudes has been shown to produce interesting distortions. Messages that barely fall within the latitude of acceptance tend to be perceived as closer or more supportive of the person's own position than they really are: this phenomenon is called *assimilation*. On the other hand, messages which just fall within the latitude of rejection seem to be less supportive or farther from the individual's position than they really are; this phenomenon is called *contrast*. In short, we perceive messages in a very simple way: for or against, pro or con. In our example, a number 6 message would strike Flora as relatively close to her own 3, but quite distant from Brian's 3.

A classic study by Hovland, Harvey and Sherif (1957) illustrates how these processes operate. Opinion within a community had been divided on the issue of the sale of alcoholic beverages. Some residents favoured the abolition of all restrictions ("wets"), some wanted to abolish all alcohol ("drys") and others favoured the regulated and controlled sale of alcohol ("moderates"). Subjects from this community listened to a 15-minute speech on the issue, and then rated it. Both the "wets" and "drys" judged the message as less positive than it actually was (contrast), since it did not fall within their latitude of acceptance. However, the moderates showed an assimilation effect, perceiving the message to be within their latitude of acceptance, and therefore being closer to their own position. This study, and the theory, also explain why advocates of opposite sides of emotionally loaded issues, such as abortion, tend to engage in parallel monologues, rather than in a genuine dialogue and debate. Deep commitment on both sides of an issue is associated with polarized positions, narrow latitudes of acceptance, strong contrast effects, and little communication.

FIGURE 5–4
Attitude structures for three party members

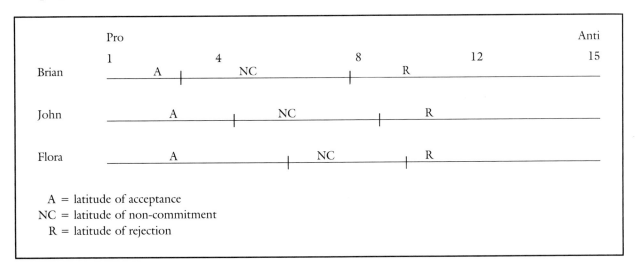

A = latitude of acceptance
NC = latitude of non-commitment
R = latitude of rejection

Arousal of Fear The content of the arguments presented has also been a subject of study, especially attempts to arouse *fear* in the audience. Suppose you are in charge of public relations for a provincial department of highways, and seatbelt legislation has recently been enacted. What would your best advertising strategy be to encourage citizens to obey this law? The Government of Ontario used a relatively mild approach on television a few years ago by showing what happens when unrestrained watermelons strike the road and by comparing loose and taped-down eggs being shaken in a box. In England, on the other hand, television ads have shown the actual fatal aftermaths of automobile accidents.

FIGURE 5–5
*Relationship between fear
arousal and persuasion*

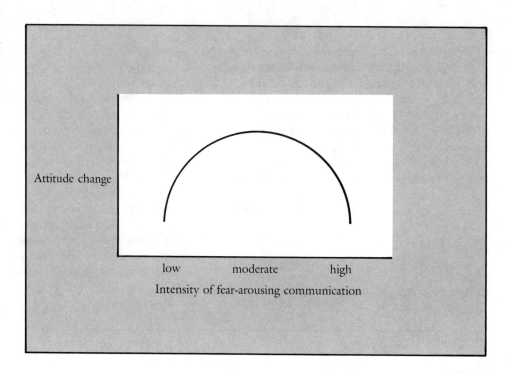

The research on fear messages began with an experiment by Janis and Feshbach (1953) who were interested in finding out how appeals which varied in the amount of fear they were intended to generate affected people's dental habits. The researchers created three levels of fear arousal. The most extreme employed colour pictures of diseased mouths, gums, and teeth, and the least extreme used only X-rays and showed pictures of healthy mouths. They found that the most threatening appeal had the least effect and that the most change followed the mild appeal. The results seemed to show that the instigation of high fear leads to avoidance. In addition, it is well known that high fear or anxiety interferes with learning; thus the subjects in the extreme message group may not have absorbed the hygiene techniques which were advocated. It is also possible, since the high fear condition was so unpleasant, that the association decreased the credibility of the source of the message and led to the message being discounted.

In contrast, many subsequent studies (e.g., Higbee, 1969; McGuire, 1969; Leventhal, 1970) have found that as fear increases, attitude change also increases. To explain these seemingly contradictory outcomes, McGuire (1968) has proposed a two-factor interpretation, pointing out that fear can act as both a cue and a drive. When fear is a drive, fear and attitude change increase in a positive direction. But if fear acts as a cue — in other words, regenerates the unpleasantness of the original experience — then the reverse would be true. However, if fear acts in both ways, the interaction of the two functions will result in a curvilinear inverted-U relationship (see Figure 5-5). This indicates that low to medium amounts of fear will be positively related to attitude change but beyond this point, as the fear increases, the relationship will become negative.

It must be remembered that the effects of fear are not independent of the type of issue under consideration. Using extreme fear in messages concerning oral hygiene was ineffective because it led people to avoid the issue altogether, and to neglect cleaning their teeth. Conceivably, avoidance may be desirable if, for example, the issue concerns AIDS or venereal disease. However, the drawback is that the audience may avoid thinking about precautions or hygienic practices, but not avoid sex itself.

Other studies have found that the use of fear affects the attitude and the intention to act but has little effect on actual behaviour. Leventhal (1970) reports that although he could get people to agree that tetanus inoculations were worthwhile and that they should have one, the only way he could get them to actually show up at the clinic was by explicitly indicating its location and how to get there, and by setting up an appointment at a specific time.

A practical example of the use of fear to modify attitudes and behaviour is found in the "scared straight" program conducted by the inmates of Kallway State Prison in New York State. Juveniles who have been apprehended for various misdemeanours are brought by the police to the prison. The prisoners then subject them to the treatment they could expect to receive if they ever found themselves incarcerated. It has been claimed in a report in the popular press that sixteen of the seventeen juveniles who were given this experience had had no further trouble with the law one year later.

Advertisers must consider certain factors about an audience — age, intelligence, socio-economic background.

Audience factors

As we have noted, it is often necessary to obtain some information about the characteristics of the audience when constructing a persuasive communication. For instance, intelligence and socio-economic background are important variables which advertisers must consider.

However, a more basic question, one in which Hovland was first interested, has been concerned with whether persuasibility is a general trait or is specific to certain topics and not to others (Hovland *et al.*, 1953; Janis and Hovland, 1959). Their findings indicate that individual differences in persuasibility, independent of the situation, do exist but that the effect is quite small and easily overwhelmed by other variables.

A natural extension of this line of investigation was the search for other personality traits which might make people more or less susceptible to persuasion. Initially, it was thought that traits such as introversion or authoritarianism would have consistent effects but, in general, experiments have not borne this out. Typically, a trait will interact with other variables or with the situation. For example, it might be expected that a person with an "authoritarian personality" (see Chapter 7) would be rigid and unyielding in the face of persuasive communication. Although this would probably be the case if the communicator were perceived as being of inferior status, it would not be so if the communicator were perceived as being of higher status. In the second situation the authoritarian person would likely be acquiescent. Similar complications arise with self-esteem, a personality trait which has been the focus of considerable study. It has been found that low self-esteem is associated with increased attitude change if the message is uncomplicated and the arguments are poorly supported; on the other hand, intricate, well-supported messages are most effective with individuals of high self-esteem (Nisbett and Gordon, 1967).

McGuire (1968) has proposed that the difficulty in demonstrating a direct relationship between personality traits and persuasion is that the traits affect both the probability of *reception* (attention and comprehension) and the probability of *yielding*. McGuire argues that any factor which is positively related to reception will be negatively related to yielding. As self-esteem increases, the likelihood that the individual will be receptive to the message also increases. At the same time, however, the likelihood of the individual succumbing to the persuasive arguments decreases so that, when the two functions are combined, the probability of opinion change increases as self-esteem increases up to a point — and then decreases.

The channel

Does it make any difference whether a persuasive message is presented face-to-face, via TV or radio, or in a written document? The data on this question are not consistent. Some studies indicate that messages presented live or via TV are more effective than audio-only messages which, in turn, are more effective than written messages (Williams, 1975) while other research has been unable to specify clearly any differences (Worchel, Andreoli and Eason, 1975). Chaiken and Eagly (1976) point out that one factor which may account for these inconsistent findings is message comprehensibility, which may have varied between investigations. There is evidence that messages are better *understood* when written than when presented by video or audiotape, especially when the content is complex (Eagly, 1974).

While it is also the case that there are more distracting influences associated with auditory and visual presentations, it is possible that these negative influences may be offset by the visual presentation, since the appearance of the communicator can be manipulated to enhance his or her credibility. An experiment which took all these factors into account provided subjects with two types of persuasive messages, easy or difficult to understand, either written, audiotaped or videotaped. The difficult messages were more effective when written, while the easy messages were most effective on videotape and least effective in writing. It is of interest that confronted with the difficult message, the subjects rated the written presentation as more pleasant (see Table 5-1). It was concluded that the effectiveness of the written message in this case could be attributed both to its positive tone and to the fact that more information

TABLE 5–1
Ratings of message pleasantness based on modality and difficulty

	Message difficulty	
	Easy	Difficult
Modality		
written	2.94	4.73
audiotape	3.75	2.32
videotape	4.78	3.02

SOURCE: Chaiken and Eagly, 1976

was retained. However, the study did not find any differences which could be attributed to the image projected by the communicator (Chaiken and Eagly, 1976).

How these factors combine

Of course, in real life, we cannot hold three of the four sets of variables constant while varying one of them. Source, message, audience, and channel effects interact, and we must consider them together in various combinations. Several experiments illustrate this problem.

In one experiment (Wiegman, 1985) two interviews were taped with each of two Dutch politicians who were confederates of the experimenter, and who represented the main political parties. The issue, whether an airport should be built in a particular location, was one on which neither political party had taken a position. In one interview, the politician advocated the proposal in a cool, sober, rational manner, while in the other, the same politician spoke in a strongly emotional, committed, dynamic manner. One of the four interviews was shown to delegates at meetings of the two parties. Therefore, the experiment varied the source of the message (same vs. other political party), the audience (political party) and the message (emotional vs. rational presentation). When attitudes were subsequently measured, the data indicated that the rational presentation resulted in a higher rating for the speaker but not in greater attitude change. Regardless of the content of the message, attitude change was greater when the source and the audience belonged to the same political party.

A second experiment shows how the medium (channel) affects perception of the message (Chaiken and Eagly, 1983). The likability of a speaker as perceived by students was varied by having the speaker praise or derogate the students, faculty, and general quality of their institution. Then, they were presented with either a video, audio, or written message from that speaker advocating change to a trimester system. It was found that attitude change was greater when subjects liked the speaker if the speaker was seen or heard, but that liking was not a factor in the written transcript condition. Evidently, the transfer of affect (positive or negative) from source to message occurs only when non-verbal cues are available. Indeed, other data have shown that subjects think more about the communication and less about the communicator when presented with a written argument. A third study shows how a message can be tailored to the audience (Snyder and DeBono, 1985). Subjects were presented with advertisements utilizing "hard sell" or "soft sell" techniques. "Hard sell" methods stressed the quality, value, and usefulness of the product, while "soft sell" techniques appealed to the image of the product (colour, texture) or of the consumer (smart, affluent, sexy, discriminating). It was reasoned that certain subjects would be more receptive or susceptible to each approach, and a measure of self-monitoring was administered for this purpose. Since high self-monitors tend to adapt their behaviour to fit the social situation, it was thought that they should be more concerned with how others perceive them, and would thus be more sensitive to the "soft sell" emphasis on images. On the other hand, since low self-monitors are guided more by inner feelings, dispositions and beliefs, they would be more receptive to messages directed toward their attitude about the product itself via the hard sell. In three studies, the data showed these combinations of message and audience characteristics to be most effective in increasing the willingness of subjects to try the product and how much they would be willing to pay for it.

WHAT IS PROPAGANDA?

Think about the following words: persuasion, advertising, selling, education, brainwashing, propaganda. What are their differences? When do education, persuasion, or advertising become "propaganda," a word that evokes the sinister image of people chanting mindless slogans? Can propaganda assume more subtle forms which are accepted in our relatively open and democratic societies? Consider the following examples:

(1) Some of the present-day religious cults indoctrinate their members under conditions of extreme stress, strong group pressure, endless repetition of messages, and deprivation of food or sleep. They may call it "re-education"; we may call it "brainwashing." However, somewhat similar techniques are used to initiate new recruits into some religious orders and into the military.

(2) Education is also concerned with attitude and behavioural changes, usually (or ideally) by providing information and training in intellectual skills and reasoning. Zimbardo, Ebbeson and Maslach (1977) point out that much of the teaching of arithmetic in schools involves problems of buying, renting, selling, and calculating interest. Are these simply practical, survival skills or do they serve a purpose of legitimizing ("propagating") the existing economic system?

(3) A study of the ubiquitous TV crime shows reveals a consistent pattern: the crime is solved by the police and the correct culprit is identified and arrested. Of course, this is far from an accurate picture of crime and punishment today in North America. Does this type of programming represent "wishful thinking" propaganda on behalf of the criminal justice system? (Haney and Manzolati, 1981)

(4) Propaganda may also be achieved by selective reporting — by omission rather than fabrication. Chomsky (1986) studied reports in the major U.S. dailies of elections held in the mid-1980s in Nicaragua and El Salvador, and found that the vast majority of stories concerning the elections in leftist Nicaragua contained references to irregularities, censorship, and human rights violations. However, violations which were at least equally serious in El Salvador, a country whose government has been strongly supported by the U.S. government, were rarely mentioned, even in the more "liberal" newspapers which purported to include all the news that's fit to print. The result, of course, was a distorted comparative picture of the state of democracy in Central America.

In his terrifying novel, *Nineteen eighty-four*, George Orwell described a "Ministry of Truth" which dispensed outright lies and propaganda. Truth and propaganda make strange bedfellows, but may often end up together. At times it is difficult to distinguish one from the other and, when propaganda is subtle, it may be even more effective.

Limits to persuasion

It is easy to be impressed by the extensive repertoire of persuasion techniques. Whether on a one-to-one basis or as members of a mass audience, we are subjected to an ever increasing barrage of persuasive messages. Yet, it is important to realize the limits of persuasion. Many products fail to win a market, many politicians lose elections, many used cars are not sold, and most of us remained unconvinced by a great deal of what we see and hear. It is an enlightening experience to observe the skeptical reactions of young children to many TV commercials so cynically directed at them. In the age of mass communications, people seem to have adapted rather well. It is important to consider how people resist persuasion, and whether genuine persuasion really occurs in most cases. This issue is discussed in more detail in the next section which looks at forewarning and inoculation effects, and then examines the nature of change produced by persuasive messages.

Forewarning   It is important to distinguish between two types of forewarning, although both result in a similar outcome. First, individuals may simply be warned ahead of time of *persuasive intent*, and second, they also may be informed of *message content*. In both instances the likelihood of persuasion will be reduced. In the second case it appears that individuals are stimulated by the warning to rehearse their own position and to generate anticipatory counter-arguments (McGuire and Papageorgis, 1962; Petty and Cacioppo, 1977). Petty and Cacioppo (1977) provide particularly strong evidence that forewarned subjects review their own arguments — they have been able to show that *unwarned* individuals who were asked to record their thoughts and ideas on a given topic were also resistant to a *subsequent* persuasive appeal.

It is the case, of course, that when intent only, not content, is anticipated, rehearsal and counter-argumentation cannot take place. The increased resistance observed under this condition is attributed to reactance (Hass and Grady, 1975). In other words, the individual is acting to protect his threatened freedom.

Inoculation   Usually, the more strongly people feel about an issue, the less likely they will be to change their minds about it. Paradoxically, however, certain attitudes are especially vulnerable to persuasion, even though a person initially is in strong agreement (McGuire and Papageorgis, 1961). These attitudes are called "cultural truisms" because a large majority of the population supports them or believes them to be true. Examples include: "We should brush our teeth after every meal if at all possible"; "Democracy is the best form of government"; and "The effects of penicillin have been, almost without exception, of great benefit to humankind." McGuire used a medical analogy to help explain what he thought accounted for this finding. He pointed out that an individual is susceptible to infection when the body's defenses are weak, and that in order to build up these defenses, inoculations are administered. These inoculations, or injections of the microbe in weakened form, lead the body to build up its defensive system and resist infection. Similarly, cultural truisms are vulnerable to persuasion because the individual has not developed any means of resisting an opposing, persuasive message. In other words, because the truism is so generally accepted, the individual has rarely, if ever, experienced an opposing point of view. He or she must, therefore, be "inoculated" by being confronted with persuasive arguments and refuting them. The person will then be able to utilize these counter-arguments to ward off any attempts at persuasion in the future. There is some disagreement about whether the refutation should be passive or active. McGuire felt that active refutation, e.g., writing a counter-attitudinal essay, would not be particularly effective because it would be distracting and because people are not very good at thinking up counter-arguments, especially when dealing with truisms. He preferred the passive strategy of having the person read a well-reasoned essay on the topic. His data support this contention.

IS ATTITUDE CHANGE REAL?

As you may have noticed, most estimates of attitude change depend on an individual's self-report. It is important, therefore, to consider first, whether these statements reflect actual changes in the underlying attitude structure and second, if we are confident that some persuasion has actually taken place, whether it is transient or lasts over time.

The first question emphasizes the need to distinguish between *compliance* and attitude change. Kelman (1958, 1961) defines compliance as publicly yielding to a persuasive communication without private acceptance. It usually occurs because the communicator is perceived as having the power to reward recipients for appropriate behaviour and punish them for inappropriate behaviour. In the absence of power figures (or their agent) the target person would likely revert to his or her original opinion. Kelman goes on to point out that more basic changes are likely if the recipient *identifies* with the communicator or is able to *internalize* the message. Identification enhances persuasion because the individual has a positive emotional attraction to the communicator and wishes to be similar to him or her. Internalization takes place when the new position is in line with the person's value system and is judged as being useful or valuable. While an attractive source would likely lead to identification, a credible source would more likely lead to internalization (Mills and Harvey, 1972). These characteristics of the communicator are not necessarily independent. For example, a parent is often a source who is simultaneously powerful, attractive and credible.

During laboratory investigations, attitude change is usually measured immediately after the administration of the persuasive message — often no additional estimates of attitude change at later times are obtained. Thus, whether the induced change has any "staying power" is not known. Certainly we would not be very impressed with a persuasive technique if individuals reverted to their original position an hour or even a day later.

Investigation into attitude change which have monitored subjects over an extended period of time have generally found (as have studies on forgetting) that most of the reversion occurs relatively quickly and then tapers off. For example, McGuire (1969), summarizing the results of a number of experiments, concludes that attitude change has a "half-life" of about six months. In other words, on the average, about 50 percent of the initial change is still present six months later. Remember, these data are based on a single administration of a persuasive message. Readministration of the communication will maintain any change which was originally induced.

Women and attitude change

For many years it was assumed in social psychology that women were more susceptible to influence, were more easily persuaded, and conformed more than men. The reasoning behind this assumption was that females in our society have been socialized to be passive and yielding (Middlebrook, 1974). Subsequently, Eagly (1978) thoroughly reviewed the literature dealing with sex differences in persuasibility and concluded that when all the available evidence is taken into consideration, there is little support for the contention that females are generally more persuasible than males. She noted, for example, that some of the reported differences between the sexes resulted from the researchers' use of experimental materials which were biased against the interests and abilities of women. She also suggests that women may indeed have a tendency to comply, but that the trait may indicate a concern with group harmony and a reluctance to disrupt positive group feelings. It is important to understand that compliance — doing what others expect of you — does not necessarily reflect a genuine attitude change. As we saw in Chapter 4, many factors, including social stereotypes and sex roles, may mediate the relationship between attitudes and actions.

PERSUASION AND COGNITION

When we think of our own experience, it becomes apparent that persuasion does not necessarily imply "changing" our minds. There are times when we are persuaded because we have been stimulated to think about the issue and are convinced by the argument presented to us. However, there are other situations in which attitude change and behaviour change occur without much thought. While one might say that people are "persuaded" to buy a certain brand of beer, it is unlikely that they are "convinced" or that they have reflected on the merits of various brands of beer.

Current research on persuasion, called *cognitive response analysis*, focuses on the role of cognition in persuasion (Petty, Ostrom and Brock, 1981). It concerns those instances which involve cognitive mediation, such as weighing the arguments for and against something, as opposed to those in which the person simply invokes a rule of thumb such as, "Believe an attractive person more than an unattractive person" (Eagly and Chaikin, 1984). Recall that Hovland's group analyzed persuasive communication in terms of such rules: an attractive source, expertise, the discrepancy between message and audience. Cognitive response analysis allows us to extend this analysis to include instances in which someone is really convinced, and to show that, in some cases but not others, attitude change occurs when the audience is induced to think about the message (Wu and Shaffer, 1987).

A fundamental premise is that cognitive mediation occurs when the audience is involved in the issue (see Figure 5-6). Consider, for example, the effects of source

FIGURE 5–6
Audience involvement, mediating effects of source and message characteristics on persuasion

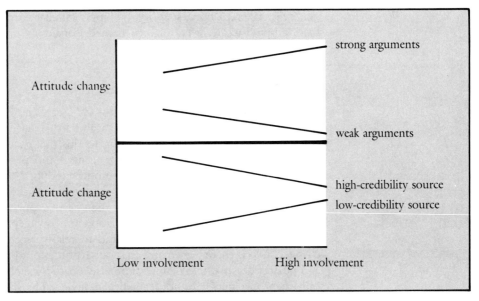

SOURCE: Petty and Cacioppo, 1986

credibility, which earlier research showed to increase persuasion. Now an interesting complication is introduced. Suppose that you, as a student, have rather little concern or involvement about government programs to assist small business. In this situation, a low-credibility source — an ordinary person on the street — who tried to convince you that this was a good idea might well provoke questions and counter-arguments in your mind, while you would likely accept the word of a high-credibility source, such as an economist. Thus, as expected, a high-credibility source would be more likely to persuade you, mostly because you would not bother to think about the issue in depth.

However, suppose that the issue is government assistance to universities, one in which students would be expected to feel more personally involved. In this case, you would tend to pay attention to the message itself. If the message came from a high-credibility source, you would likely consider it to be more important or influential, and you would likely examine it even more closely. Thinking about an issue means that you are more likely to come up with counter-arguments or to see flaws in the argument presented to you. Thus a high-credibility source, by eliciting a greater degree of cognitive mediation, may well lead to *less* attitude change than a low-credibility source.

The effects of message characteristics will also be mediated by cognitive activity. For example, a complex, difficult message will be more persuasive if the person is motivated to pay attention to it and to think about it. However, a non-involved person is unlikely to expend that effort, and may well ignore the details of the argument. If one has a strong case to present, then cognitive mediation is desirable, and it is advisable to provoke thought by presenting the arguments (although not too often) in a logical and comprehensive way, and to avoid distractions such as humour, novelty, or sexuality. However, in those many cases in which the arguments are not strong (e.g., which beer to buy), it is advisable to avoid having the audience think very much about it. In this case, a single exposure to the arguments, with lots of distractions, becomes more likely to succeed. Indeed, much of contemporary advertising dispenses entirely with persuasive arguments, and resorts to images which denote social status, sex, sociality, or simply familiar corporate symbols — a company logo, a brand name, even a clown named Ronald.

An integrated model

A theory called the *elaboration likelihood model* (Petty and Cacioppo, 1981, 1986) deals with the extent to which people will "elaborate," that is, examine and think about the arguments in a message. According to this theory, there are fundamentally two routes by which attitudes may change: central and peripheral. The *central route* of persuasion involves cognitive activity — understanding the message and thinking about the issue. The *peripheral route* to attitude change involves factors which are not relevant to the issue itself, such as the attractiveness of the source, flattery, distractions, e.g., novelty or humour in the communication, or a perception that others believe the message. Central processes tend to lead to relatively enduring and "real" attitude change. Indeed there is evidence that our attitudes tend to become more committed and polarized as we think more about the attitudinal object (Tesser, 1978). On the other hand, we may have not really been convinced by the argument when persuaded by peripheral factors. Thus, attitude change could persist only as long as the relevant cues are salient. (For example, we may believe in or accept certain policies only as long as the politician who represents them is popular or attractive to us.)

This model suggests that "real" attitude change by means of persuasion is difficult and uncommon. For "central route" persuasion to happen, the recipient must have both the ability and the motivation to process the information — and the argument must be logical or otherwise convincing. As we noted in Chapter 3, we often act as "cognitive misers," take cognitive shortcuts, and act in rather automatic and "mindless" ways. Thus it is not surprising that peripheral route persuasion is so common, particularly in our society of the 20-second commercial. Yet real change can result. Even superficial attitude change may lead to immediate behavioural change consistent with it, and bolstering cognitions may then be used to avoid cognitive dissonance. At this point, "peripheral" becomes "central," and the cognitive processes are set in motion, leading to enduring attitude change.

SUMMARY

(1) Attitude change can be viewed in terms of internal processes and external influences.

(2) The theory of cognitive dissonance states that when two related cognitions are not consistent or in harmony, the individual is motivated to reduce discomfort by changing or reducing the importance of a dissonant cognition or adding consonant cognitions (bolstering).

(3) Four important areas of study in cognitive dissonance theory are: post-decision dissonance (after making a difficult choice); social support; selective information seeking; and dissonance after attitude-discrepant behaviour.

(4) The magnitude of dissonance experienced after attitude-discrepant behaviour is a function of insufficient external justification for performing that action. This effect occurs when the action involves public commitment and free choice.

(5) Cognitive dissonance is a state of arousal which can be reduced when the arousal itself is reduced or when alternative attributions are made for the resulting uncomfortable state.

(6) Dissonance occurs, not in response to logical inconsistency, but in response to an inconsistency within the self-concept. Bem interprets this phenomenon as an attribution about an attitude.

(7) Cooper and Fazio have developed a "new look" attributional model which explains when cognitive dissonance occurs.

(8) An attitude, defined as an evaluation of some entity, can be classically conditioned through repeated association of the entity with negative or positive stimuli.

(9) Factors involved in persuasion include the source, audience, message, and the channel. Source credibility is generally determined by judging the source's trustworthiness and expertise.

(10) Message effectiveness is influenced by primacy or recency in presentation. Fear arousal up to a moderate level can increase persuasibility.

(11) Whether an audience will be receptive to a message can be determined by certain personality characteristics, such as self-esteem. A written communication tends to cause the audience to focus more on the argument than the source; in oral or visual presentations, the audience focuses more on the source.

(12) The effect of persuasion is reduced by forewarning the audience of an attempt to persuade, and by inoculation, confronting the audience with mild counter-arguments.

(13) In determining whether an individual has been persuaded, it is necessary to distinguish changes represented by behavioural compliance from changes associated with identification with the source, or internalization of the message.

(14) The elaboration likelihood model of persuasion differentiates between central routes (understanding the arguments, thinking about the issue) and peripheral routes (focusing on characteristics of the source or distractions in the message). While changes are more likely to occur through the peripheral route, they are less likely to persist in the absence of salient cues; central-route changes have more staying power.

FURTHER READING

CIALDINI, R. (1984). *Influence: Science and Practice*. New York: Morrow.

HOVLAND, C.I., Janis, I.L. and Kelley, H.H. (1955). *Communication and persuasion*. New Haven: Yale University Press.

PETTY, R.E., OSTROM, T.M. and BROCK, T.C. (Eds.). *Cognitive responses in persuasion*. Hillsdale: Erlbaum.

PETTY, R.E. and CACIOPPO, V.T. (1981). *Attitudes and persuasion: Classic and contemporary approaches*. Dubuque: W.C. Brown.

RAJECKI, D.W. (1982). *Attitudes: Themes and advances*. Sunderland, MA: Sinauer Associates.

WICKLUND, R.A. and BREHM, J.W. (1976). *Perspectives on cognitive dissonance*. Hillsdale: Erlbaum.

ZIMBARDO, P., EBBESEN, E.B. and MASLACH, C. (1977). *Influencing attitudes and changing behavior*. Reading: Addison-Wesley.

C·H·A·P·T·E·R S·I·X

Social Influence and Conformity

I want to be a non-conformist like everyone else.
Anonymous Vancouver teenager

HAMLET: Do you see that cloud, that's almost in shape like a camel?
POLONIUS: By the mass, and 'tis like a camel indeed.
HAMLET: Methinks, it is like a weasel.
POLONIUS: It is backed like a weasel.
HAMLET: Or, like a whale?
POLONIUS: Very like a whale.

Shakespeare

FOR REFLECTION

- What causes people to yield to the pressure to conform?
- When might a minority have influence on a majority?
- Are independence and innovation possible, given the pressure to conform?
- Why do people sometimes do what they are told even when they don't want to?

153

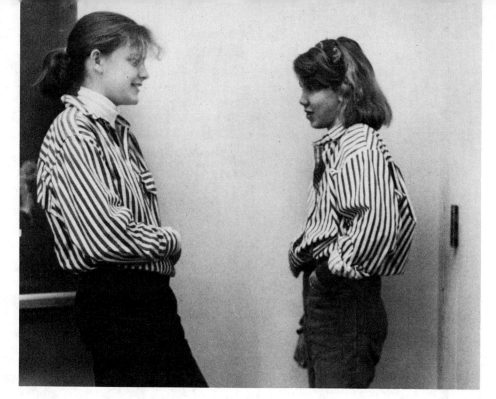

Wearing similar clothes: An accident?

CONSIDER THE NUMBER of times you have changed your opinion or modified your behaviour so that it becomes more similar to that of another person. It may have happened because in an argument you were convinced of the "correctness" of another point of view; at other times the change may have occurred simply because you became aware that you were deviating from common practice. We do not operate in a social vacuum. What others think and how they behave is important to us, and we consistently monitor our thoughts and actions in relation to those of other people in our social environment. These may be friends and classmates or even the "role-models" depicted in lifestyle advertising. It is no accident that people in a given segment of society wear similar clothes, vote for the same political party, extol the virtues of beaujolais nouveau and have similar ideas about how to raise children.

Of course, we do not always go along with the majority. Sometimes we "dig in our heels" and maintain our independence in spite of pressures to do otherwise. At other times, in spite of holding a minority view, we are able to swing others to our side.

In this chapter we examine how the presence of others affects our behaviour, and why people conform or are able to maintain their independence. Some of the negative aspects of excessive conformity are also discussed.

THE EFFECTS OF MERE PRESENCE

Social facilitation

Social facilitation, defined as any increment of individual activity resulting from the presence of another individual (Crawford, 1939), was the topic of an article by Triplett which appeared in *The American Journal of Psychology* in 1897 entitled "The Dynamogenic Factors in Pacemaking and Competition." It is considered to be the first published report of experimental research in social psychology. Triplett, who was apparently interested in bicycle racing, had noticed that bicyclists who were paced travelled faster than those who cycled alone (in 1954 the first four-minute mile was achieved by Roger Bannister while being paced by another runner.) This observation led Triplett to ask the question: How does the behaviour of a person who is alone change when another person is present? This problem dealt with social influence in its simplest form, in that there was no direct interaction or communication between the individuals involved, only the *presence of another person*.

Rather than pursue his research at the racetrack Triplett transferred it to the laboratory. Instead of observing professional bicyclists he used school children as subjects. The task he employed was winding fishing reels, a task which the children performed both alone and in the presence of a classmate. Triplett then compared the amount of line wound under each of these two conditions. He expected to find that the "together" amount would exceed the "solitary" amount. The results of his study showed that 20 subjects were "stimulated positively," ten subjects were "stimulated adversely" and ten subjects were unaffected. On the basis of his finding Triplett concluded that the most likely effect of the presence of another person was to facilitate behaviour. In his words "From the above facts regarding the laboratory races we infer that the bodily presence of another contestant participating simultaneously in the race served to liberate latent energy not ordinarily available" (p. 533). Triplett also noted that the female students were more likely than the males to be positively influenced by the other person.

Obviously many questions were not answered by Triplett's research, although it did set the stage for numerous subsequent studies. These branched in two separate directions — the study of *audience effects* resulting from the presence of one or more passive observers, and *coaction effects* resulting from participants working simultaneously, but independently, on the same task. Triplett's research also led to extensive research on coaction in species other than human beings, including ants, cockroaches, opossums and armadillos (see Zajonc, 1969; Cottrell, 1972).

Early studies of audience effects (e.g., Meumann, 1904; Travis, 1925) generally found that performance improved in the presence of observers. At about the same time an extensive experiment on coaction was carried out by Allport (1924). In this experiment subjects engaged in five different tasks. For each of the five tasks, subjects spent half of the time working alone and half of the time working in groups of four or five. For four of the five tasks, the results were similar to those obtained in the presence of an audience. The one exception was a task in which the subject read epigrams (e.g., "To err is human, to forgive is divine") and was then given five minutes to write as many refutations of the epigram as possible. Subjects did generate more refutations when coacting than when alone but, according to Allport, the refutations were of a lower quality in the coaction situation. He concluded that overt responses, such as writing, were facilitated in the presence of coworkers, while thinking was hampered.

A few years later Pessin (1933) reported that the presence of an audience impaired performance. Pessin had subjects learn two lists, each containing seven nonsense syllables. One list was learned while the subject was left alone in a cubicle and the other was learned while the subject was being observed. Pessin found that when the subject was alone, the list was learned with fewer repetitions than was the case when the subject was under observation.

As the research evidence accumulated it became increasingly clear that audience and coaction situations might either improve or impair individual behaviour (Dashiell,

1935). Those who attempted to reconcile these seemingly contradictory findings usually resorted to explanations in terms of personality traits of the participants or simply explained it as a relatively unreliable phenomenon. In any case, after the flurry of activity in the 1920s and early '30s interest in social facilitation waned until it was rekindled by Zajonc (rhymes with science) in 1965. Reviewing the research on this topic, he noticed that there was something quite consistent about the situations in which behaviour was enhanced compared with those situations in which it was affected adversely. Zajonc observed that responding was usually facilitated by the presence of others when the behaviour was simple or well-learned, in other words, when the subject was *performing* a task. By contrast, if the subject was required to *learn a new or novel response*, then the presence of others was likely to interfere with the rate of acquisition.

Arousal

Zajonc went on to postulate that a single underlying process, arousal, can *either* facilitate or interfere depending on the situation, and that the presence of another person increases the level of arousal. Arousal is defined as a heightened state of physiological activity which enhances the general reactivity of the individual. Zajonc pointed out that when a behaviour is being learned, not only is the correct response present in the person's repertoire but other, incorrect, responses are present as well. Ordinarily these incorrect responses disappear as learning progresses. However, according to Zajonc, the arousal induced by the presence of another person has two effects that influence this process. First, as arousal increases, the strength or vigour with which the correct response is emitted increases. Second, as arousal increases the strength with which incorrect responses are emitted also increases. This means that errors will take longer to decline in frequency and learning will be hampered. On the other hand, when only the correct response is available, that is, when the person is performing rather than learning, the increased arousal can only have the effect of facilitating the behaviour in question since there are no "wrong" responses remaining.

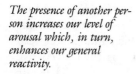

The presence of another person increases our level of arousal which, in turn, enhances our general reactivity.

Zajonc also proposed that this reaction to the physical presence of others was innate rather than acquired: this question became the focus of many subsequent investigations. Cottrell (1972), for example, argued that the reaction to the presence of others was a *learned drive* based on evaluation apprehension. In other words, in order for coaction or audience effects to occur, the subject had to feel that his performance was, in some way, being judged by the others present.

Evaluation apprehension

This challenge to the theoretical views of Zajonc was tested by Cottrell and his colleagues (1968) who had subjects perform either alone or in the presence of one of two different types of audiences. In one of these audience conditions, two spectators stood at a distance of six feet and watched the subject as he or she performed the task. In the other audience condition, two individuals were present but they were blindfolded, ostensibly to prepare for being in the dark for an experiment in which they were later to take part. Clearly, if Zajonc was correct in his contention that the "mere presence" of others was critical, then both types of audience should enhance performance equally. If Cottrell's hypothesis was correct, then only the observing audience would facilitate task performance since this was the only situation in which evaluation apprehension could play a role.

The results of the study showed that there is no difference between the "alone" and "mere presence" conditions. However, responding was considerably facilitated when the passive observers were present. The outcome of this and other studies (e.g., Paulus and Murdock, 1971) led Cottrell to postulate that the "drive-increasing property of the presence of others is created through social experience and is not, as is implied by the Zajonc hypothesis, a biological given. This information states that the presence of others is a *learned source of drive*" (Cottrell, 1972, p. 227). For Cottrell, the evaluation apprehension induced by the presence of others meant the anticipation of both rewards and punishments. However, a number of investigations (cf. Geen and Gange, 1977) suggest that it is only the anticipation of negative evaluations that increases arousal.

A considerable proportion of the research on social facilitation has been reviewed by Bond and Titus (1983). They examined 241 studies involving 24 000 subjects and on the basis of a statistical "meta-analysis" concluded that we can have reasonable confidence that: (1) the presence of others heightens an individual's physiological arousal only if the individual is performing a complex task; (2) the presence of others increases the speed of simple task performance and decreases the speed of complex task performance; (3) the presence of others impairs the quality of complex performance and slightly facilitates the quality of simple performance; and (4) social facilitation effects are unrelated to the performer's evaluation apprehension.

This should not be taken to mean that evaluation apprehension does not lead to increased arousal and to facilitation of dominant responses. The question is whether evaluation apprehension is *necessary* for social facilitation to occur. An experiment by Schmidt *et al.* (1986) strongly indicates that mere presence is *sufficient* to produce social facilitation. They recruited subjects who believed they were participating in an investigation of "sensory deprivation." When they arrived they were seated before a computer which asked them, *before* they proceeded to the experiment, to type in their name (an easy task), then to enter a code name by typing their names backward, interspersing each letter with ascending digits (a difficult task). The time to complete each task was recorded by the computer. The subjects had been assigned to three conditions. In the *alone* condition, the experimenter left the room before the subject answered the computer questions. In the *mere presence* condition a confederate remained in the room. He was wearing a blindfold and headphones and was turned away from the computer. Subjects were told that the confederate was being deprived of sensory stimulation for the sensory deprivation experiment. In the *evaluation apprehension* condition the experimenter stayed in the room and looked over the subject's shoulder during the session with the computer. Keep in mind that, as far as the subject was concerned, all this took place *before* the experiment started and the computer was being used only to obtain "background information." The results of the study, shown in Table 6-1, reveal that mere presence resulted in faster performance of the simple task and slower performance of the difficult task. Evaluation apprehension operated in similar manner but clearly, social facilitation can take place in the absence of evaluation apprehension.

TABLE 6–1

Mean time in seconds to complete the easy and difficult tasks

	Alone	Mere presence	Evaluation apprehension
Easy task	14.77	9.83	7.07
Difficult task	52.41	72.57	62.52

These data contradict the contention that evaluation apprehension is *necessary* for the effects to occur. But it also is evident that evaluation can heighten arousal and facilitate dominant response tendencies. Note that the subjects in the evaluation apprehension condition performed the simple task even more rapidly than those in the mere presence condition.

Arousal has achieved a firm place as the major contributor to the effects observed in these mere presence situations but the reasons for the aroused state continue to be questioned. For example, Baron and others (e.g., Sanders, 1983; Sanders, Baron and Moore, 1978) claim that the distraction engendered by an audience or coactors is the prime instigator of arousal. Their elaboration of this possibility is called *distraction-conflict theory*.

Distraction-conflict theory In the presence of others the subject not only pays attention to the task but to the audience or coactors as well. Distracted in this way, the subject is in a state of conflict. It is this conflict that leads to arousal which, in turn, facilitates dominant responses. Behaviour then will be enhanced or impaired, depending on the nature of the task. There has been some empirical support for this model (e.g., Baron, Moore, and Sanders, 1978; Sanders, 1983) but not without dissent (Berger *et al.*, 1982). More recently, R.S. Baron (1986) has suggested that it may not be conflicting attention that is the operative factor and that arousal may not be the key. He notes the presence of others could lead to "information overload." That is, subjects have more sensory input than they can handle efficiently. In order to bring things under control they concentrate harder on the task and shut out distracting cues. Increased attention improves simple task performance, but complex or novel tasks require less focused and intense concentration and suffer accordingly.

It is more difficult to demonstrate the effects of increased arousal in coaction than in audience situations because of the likelihood that feelings of competition or rivalry are also present when individuals are responding simultaneously. Although it is difficult, at least in North America, to remove rivalry from situations in which two people are performing the same task, these effects can be minimized. For example, Carment (1970) had subjects perform a simple motor task either alone or together. Half of the coacting subjects were told that two people were being run simultaneously merely to save time. The others were informed that their performance would be judged against that of the other subjects and a prize would be awarded to "the winner." The data (see Figure 6-1) showed that coaction enhanced performance and that competitive instructions increased it still further but that the competitive instructions had no effect on subjects performing alone. Thus it seems that competitive motivation cannot be ruled out as a factor which contributes to responding in coaction situations. Other studies (Klinger, 1964; Martens and Landers, 1972; Innes, 1972) have supplied some evidence that knowledge of results and eye contact between the coactors also may be important.

In addition, as is the case with many psychological phenomena, coaction effects — as well as competitive motivation — may be influenced by cultural factors. For example, Carment and Hodkin (1973) compared the performance of East Indian and Canadian university students and found that the East Indians were less sensitive than the Canadians to both competitive instructions and the presence of a coactor. It may be that the Indian subjects, most of whom lived in extended families under crowded conditions, had become used to these living conditions and no longer were "aroused" by the presence of others.

It is clear that many questions remain unanswered in spite of the long history of research on this topic.

FIGURE 6–1
Mean number of responses each minute as a function of competition and coaction

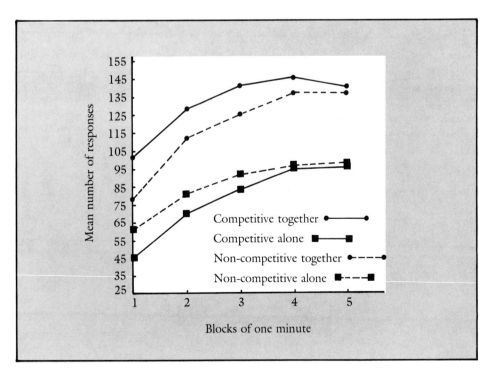

Social loafing — when more is less

We have seen that people tend to "work harder" in the presence of others than when they are alone. If we were to extend this principle to include people working together toward a common goal, the general principle might then become "Many hands make light the work." This saying implies that social coordination might actually reduce the effort of each individual involved. In other words, collective efforts may be less efficient than individual ones. This effect was first observed by Ringelmann (1913) who asked a number of people to pull on a rope and found that as group size increased, the effort of each group member declined (see Kravitz and Martin, 1986). However, as Latané *et al.* (1979) have observed, this tendency leads to a less than optimal outcome: if everyone were working at least as hard as they would if they were alone, the overall effect should be considerably more impressive. Latané *et al.* (1979) call this phenomenon "social loafing," which is defined as a decrease in individual effort due to the presence of other persons. As can be seen in Figure 6-2, Latané and his colleagues were able to replicate Ringelmann's findings for two tasks, clapping and cheering.

It is possible that these results might be due simply to inadequate coordination, a "too many cooks spoil the broth" problem (Steiner, 1972). This proposition was tested by Ingham *et al.* (1974) who blindfolded subjects and led each one to believe that others were present when they were actually alone. Even then, subjects who *thought* they were with one other person pulled at 90 percent of their solitary rate and decreased to 85 percent of this rate when they believed they were assisted by two to six others. Thus there does not seem to be any doubt that social loafing accounts for the reduced effort.

Although caution is advised when generalizing from rope-pulling or clapping to situations of substantial social significance. Latané nevertheless suggests that social loafing has implications for the efficiency of human organizations such as collective

FIGURE 6–2
Intensity of noise as a function of group size and response mode

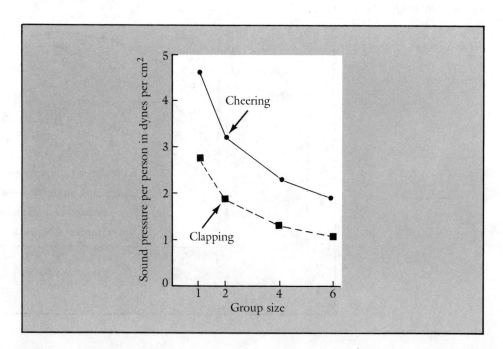

COOPERATION AND SOCIAL LOAFING AMONG THE BEATLES

Over a period of eight years, John Lennon and Paul McCartney collaborated on 162 songs which formed the creative heart of the Beatles. From the beginning, they agreed to put both their names on all songs, whether actually written collaboratively or by one of them (unlike many other song-writing teams, both were capable of writing lyrics and composing music). Later, they disclosed that, of the 162 songs, 47 were genuine collaborations, 70 had been written by Lennon, and 45 by McCartney. In the earlier years (1963–1967) they identified strongly with each other and with the group. However, in the later period (1967–1970), they had moved in different personal and artistic directions. In these years, few songs were co-written, and more were written individually.

Jackson and Padgett (1982) reasoned that, in the earlier period of identification, collaboration should have led to higher-quality work. And, during the later period of greater individuality and less identification with the group, the quality of collaborative work should have been expected to suffer as a result of social loafing.

Each of their 162 songs was coded as having been written jointly or individually, and in the earlier or later period. The songs were assessed for quality on the basis of whether they were released as a single — indicating a high rating by record company executives — record sales, and performance on the charts, representing sales and radio airplay.

The results showed a shift in success which

The Beatles in the early days.

matched the shift in their relationship. In the earlier years, the songs written collaboratively by Lennon and McCartney were more successful. However, the later collaborations were less successful (while the songs written individually started drawing acclaim).

Clearly, when partners identify with each other and with common goals, cooperation, enhanced creativity, and productivity all become possible. However, when this identification is lost, even the extrinsic goals of money and success cannot prevent social loafing and a loss of quality in work.

Perhaps recognizing this tendency, the Beatles decided to "let it be" and the group was disbanded.

---

farms in the U.S.S.R. and kibbutzim in Israel. The major question is why the U.S.S.R. collective farms seem to follow the social loafing principle (i.e., 1 percent of agricultural land is worked privately but accounts for 27 percent of total Soviet farm output), while the kibbutzim do not (i.e., 22 percent of the egg output is produced with 16 percent of the chickens). Among a number of possible explanations is that individuals usually have a choice about participating in a kibbutz, whereas choice *per se* is emphasized less in the Soviet Union. Closer to home, social loafing has even been implicated in the dissolution of the Beatles (see Box 6-1).

Social loafing should not be confused with the "free rider" problem (see Chapter 13). In the case of social loafing, everyone is working or participating to some extent.

The free rider, on the other hand, does not contribute to the group effort but does take advantage of the outcome.

CONFORMITY

So far, we have been concerned with a type of influence which has not involved direct communication between the participants, and the cues or stimuli which are present have not been easily identified. In other influence situations, although communication may be subtle, it is nevertheless more evident.

Imagine yourself in a completely dark room with a pinpoint of light at eye level some distance in front of you. Although the light actually remains stationary it will appear to move and, for some people, it will appear to traverse considerable distances. This phenomenon is the well-known *autokinetic effect*. Sherif (1936, 1937) placed groups of subjects in this situation and, for a number of trials, asked each subject to call out an estimate of how far the light moved. Although the subjects started out with quite different distance estimates, their estimates gradually became more and more similar until there was very little variability among them.

Sherif proposed this as a model of social conformity in which, without any direct pressure, individuals ultimately arrive at a common form of behaviour. This "standard" behaviour is called a *social norm* and subsequently exhibits very little variation. In other words, conformity is the outcome of interpersonal influence and is accompanied by a reduction in the variability of the behaviour in question. This process is illustrated in Figure 6-3 and is exemplified by output norms in industry and dress codes among students at university. It is not by chance that members of a work team each produce about the same number of items on their shift or that many students wear very similar jackets.

FIGURE 6–3
Conformity as the outcome of interpersonal influence

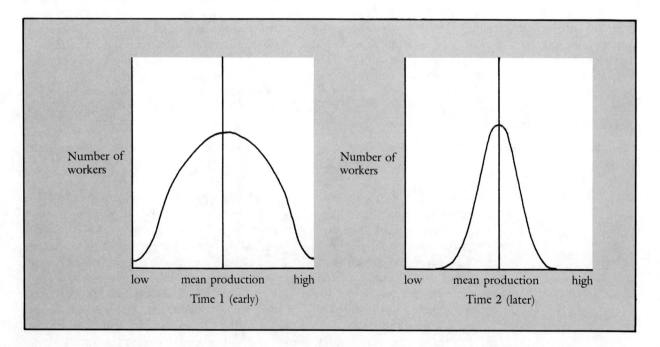

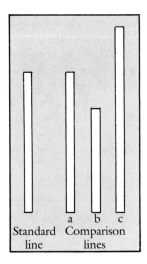

FIGURE 6–4
Typical comparison lines used in Asch's study of group effects on judgment

In the Sherif situation the participants were merely aware of the judgments of the others and the influence was mutual. In a sense, this outcome reflects what happens in the early stages of group formation in which the norms have not yet been clearly defined. However, individuals often join groups which have been in existence for some time and in which norms are already well established. An early experiment by Asch (1951) illustrates what might then happen, again without any direct pressure on the subject, to modify his or her behaviour. This study used one "real" subject along with a number of confederates of the experimenter. Their task was to match the length of a standard line with one of three other unequal lines. (A sample set of these lines can be seen in Figure 6-4.) Notice that the judgment required in this situation is not a particularly difficult one but, unknown to the real subject, each confederate had been instructed to make the same wrong choice on 12 of the 18 trials they experienced. In addition, the subject was seated so that he responded after all the confederates but one. What do you think you would do under these circumstances — trust your eyes or the judgments of the others? As it turned out, in a control group without any confederates 95 percent of the subjects were error-free, while in the presence of an incorrect majority, 76 percent of the subjects made at least one error by going along with the group.

It also is true that this type of pressure exists even though the other group members are not physically present. For example, Wiener, Carpenter and Carpenter (1957) first asked subjects to select names for some ambiguous designs after which they were shown fictitious percentages said to represent the choices of others in their group. On a retest, the design names given by the subjects shifted in the direction of the popular choices. The assumption that if everybody is doing it, it must be right, is sometimes referred to as the *"bandwagon effect."* In real-life the bandwagon effect can escalate rapidly: once a majority is seen, correctly or incorrectly, to be acting in a common manner, agreement with the majority continues to be enhanced as others join in.

The work of Asch was extended by Crutchfield (1955) who developed a procedure whereby he could study five subjects simultaneously, thus surpassing the need to recruit, organize, and pay a number of confederates. This technique also allowed any effects which might be due to individual differences in the behaviour of the confederates to be ruled out. In Crutchfield's procedure the subjects were isolated in booths, facing panels with lights used to represent the responses of the other subjects. Since there was no communication between the subjects, the experimenter was free to create any pattern of outcomes. In this way, Crutchfield was able to reproduce Asch's work in a different situation with a variety of other stimuli. For instance, he found that 79 percent of his subjects agreed with an erroneous "group judgment" regarding which was the larger of two identical circles.

In these and other Asch-type studies conducted up to the present time, only a few subjects totally succumb to group influence and there are some who resist it completely. However, it is clear that the effect is powerful and that most individuals are unable, at least to some degree, to maintain their independence. There is some question, however, as to whether people in other parts of the world would respond in the same way as Americans. For example, Perrin and Spencer (1981) noted that the Asch studies had not been replicated outside the United States. When they then placed British students in the same situation they found that in only one out of 396 critical trials did compliance occur. Asch had asked his American subjects why they went along with the majority; they reported they were afraid of "sticking out like a sore thumb," or "being thought that there was something wrong with them." On the other hand, the British students did not yield because they felt that to conform to an erroneous majority would make them look "weak, ridiculous, and stupid."

Once again, it is emphasized that the cultural and historical context in which research takes place should not be ignored. Asch, for instance, carried out his studies in the 1950s when the political and social climate of the United States encouraged conformity in an overt way. ("McCarthyism" — a term coined during the anti-communist crusade of Senator Joe McCarthy, which resulted in the blacklisting of left-wing politicians and media figures — was but one example of this overt pressure.) We do not know whether U.S. students would behave in the same way in an Asch-type study today. In fact, Larsen, 24 years later (1974) obtained a rate of conformity in the U.S. about one half of that reported by Asch.

As we noted in Chapter 5 (on attitude change), we must always be alert to the distinction between behaviour change and attitude change. Behaviour change does not necessarily imply acceptance. Thus, when Asch allowed his subjects to write rather than verbalize their decisions, the number of conforming responses was dramatically reduced. Nevertheless, Flament (1958) found that when he had subjects adjust a measuring device to match a standard line, although it was outside the view of the confederates, the majority opinion still had a marked effect on the accuracy of the subjects' adjustments.

Does the size of the group make a difference?

Asch conducted a number of variations on his basic theme, one of which was concerned with determining whether increasing the number of confederates would lead to more conformity. He formed groups of one, two, three, four, eight, and ten to 15 confederates and found that when only one other person voiced a discrepant judgment, no conformity effects were observed. The effects appeared with two and reached a maximum with three confederates. Majorities larger than three had no additional impact. Although other investigators have reported the optimum number of confederates to vary upward slightly (e.g., four or six), there is general agreement that the pressure to conform does not simply continue to accumulate as the size of the group increases. A mathematical model of this process has been described by Tanford and Penrod (1984).

Wilder (1977) pointed out that the effect of increases in group size may be limited because, beyond a certain number, the subject does not perceive the individuals as separate entities. That is, since all the members express identical judgments, the subject treats them as a single point of view. Thus information from four *individuals* would be treated as four separate pieces of information whereas information from a *group* of four would be treated as one piece of information. He demonstrated that the judgments of the members of two groups had more impact on subjects than the judgments of the members of one group, although the number of members was the same in each case. Wilder (1977) comments that this outcome implies that candidates for political office should try to get themselves endorsed by individuals with a variety of backgrounds (e.g., physicians, plumbers, professors, housewives etc.), who would be perceived individually by the voters, rather than by people with homogeneous backgrounds (e.g., only bus drivers), who would be treated as a single entity.

Direct influence

Keep in mind that in the foregoing types of groups no direct sanctions are applied to a person to conform. Real-life groups, on the other hand, may not be so benign. This was the question to which Schachter (1951) directed his research attention. He formed groups of university students to discuss the case of Johnny Rocco, an apparently incorrigible delinquent. After reading the case history each member of the group voiced his opinion as to how Johnny should be treated. Their opinions could range, on a five-point scale, from extreme kindness to extreme harshness. The case was then discussed. After the discussion each participant again publicly voiced an opinion regarding appropriate treatment. However, three members of the group, confederates of Schachter, had been coached to act in a very specific and systematic manner before and during the discussion. One, the "deviate," took an initial position opposed to the majority and maintained it throughout the session. Another, the "slider," began by acting like a deviate but, as the session progressed, gradually changed his opinion toward the majority view. A third confederate, the "mode," expressed the majority view from beginning to end. It is nearly always the case in this experiment that the initial opinion about Johnny Rocco's treatment by real subjects is in the lenient direction (i.e., 1, 2, or 3 on the five-point scale) so that the confederates could be reasonably certain beforehand what position they would have to support or oppose.

"Must be some sort of nut."

Schachter observed two processes which are of interest to us here. He noted: (1) the amount of communication directed to each type of confederate; and (2) how each confederate was treated at the end of the discussion session. Figure 6-5 illustrates the direction of communication. Notice that the "mode" received very few communications and that there was only a slight change as the discussion progressed. In other

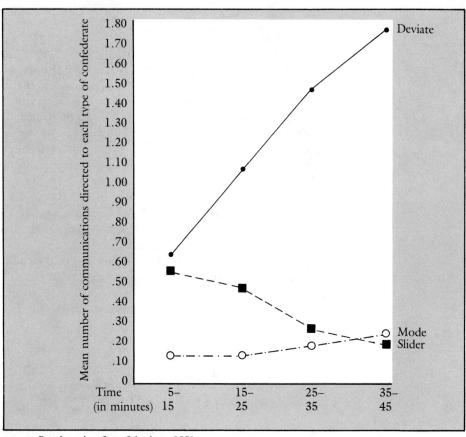

FIGURE 6–5

Subjects' communication to "the deviate," "the mode," and "the slider"

SOURCE: Based on data from Schachter, 1951

words, there is little merit in preaching to the converted. By contrast, the slider in the early stages of the discussion received almost as much attention as the deviate but, as it became clear that he was modifying his stand, the group diverted more attention to the unchanging deviate. The content of the communications directed to the deviate did not consist of social chit-chat but were attempts to modify the position being maintained.

At the conclusion of each discussion session Schachter administered two measures of interpersonal attraction. One required the participants to submit nominations for memberships in one of three committees, executive, steering or correspondence, which varied in degree of status or desirability. The deviates were invariably nominated for the least desirable (and least important) job — correspondence. In addition, a sociometric measure was obtained by asking the participants to rank the others in the order of their desirability as fellow group members. The instructions emphasized the importance of congeniality and compatibility. By now you will not be surprised to learn that the deviate was ranked as a much less desirable group member than were either the mode or the slider. Moreover, the slider's case illustrates that the group does not penalize an individual for being different initially as long as he or she ultimately comes to accept the group norm.

One final point arising from Schachter's research should be made. Schachter assigned his group members to three categories in terms of the extent to which they rejected the deviate at the conclusion of the discussion. Then he calculated the relationship between this degree of rejection and the pattern of communication to the deviate during the discussion. He found that the amount of communication to the deviate by those who rejected the deviate most at the conclusion of the discussion, compared with those who showed little or no rejection, increased as the session progressed. But when it became apparent that the deviate wasn't going to modify his opinion, communication rapidly declined. Not only did these individuals dislike the deviate — they eventually chose to ignore him. This sort of treatment, ostracism or, as it is called in England, being "sent to Coventry," is well-documented in industry where work groups pressure fellow workers to conform to "output norms." A "rate buster" who overproduces or a "chiseler" who underproduces will find himself or herself subjected not only to verbal pressure (or abuse) but often to some physical harassment. In extreme cases this treatment is also extended to their families.

For example, a student of one of the authors obtained a summer job in a factory manufacturing sewer pipes. After a few days, he was surprised and pained to find that the sewer pipes frequently fell onto his legs. At first he attributed these "accidents" to clumsiness and his own lack of skill because no one else seemed to suffer from the problem. But even after he had learned the necessary techniques, pipes still kept falling on him. After some time and numerous bruises, a co-worker casually suggested that it might help if he slowed down a bit. When he did, the pipes "magically" no longer fell on him. He had inadvertently been exceeding the output norm and, once he "got in line," the group pressure stopped.

Output norms in industry: Employees who "chisel" or overproduce may experience problems.

Obviously it's not easy to be a deviate. Given the pressures and sanctions the majority bring to bear on other people, it is little wonder that most people simply choose to conform. It should not, however, be implied that the deviate is completely without influence. Under some conditions which we consider next, a minority can affect a majority.

The adamant minority

Asch (1951) discovered that if one other person responded correctly to the task of judging the length of lines, it was sufficient to radically reduce and, in some cases, entirely remove conforming responses. This observation was later confirmed by Morris and Miller (1975) (see Figure 6-6) who also showed that a supporter (i.e., a person making a correct judgment) who precedes the majority reduces conformity to a greater extent than does one who responds after the majority. There is additional evidence that the quality of the support is not critical and that any support is better than none. For example, Allen and Levine (1971) provided some subjects being asked to make visual judgments with a supporter who wore glasses so thick as to raise serious doubts about his ability to see anything clearly. Other subjects had a supporter who had

FIGURE 6–6
The effect of social support on judgment in a conformity situation

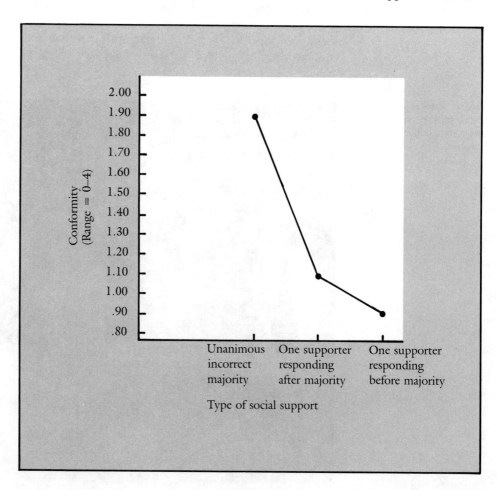

normal vision. They report that when there was a unanimous majority, subjects conformed 97 percent of the time. With the addition of a "competent" supporter, conformity declined to 36 percent but even when the supporter was "incompetent" conformity was reduced to 64 percent.

Given that conformity pressures can be resisted, Moscovici and his colleagues (1969, 1974) have examined how a persistent minority can affect the majority. In one of their experiments, groups of six women, two of whom were confederates of the experimenter, were asked to look at slides and report what colour they saw. Actually, all the slides were blue and varied only in terms of light intensity, but the two confederates consistently said they saw "green." Moscovici found that about 8 percent of the responses of the subjects also were "green" and that 32 percent of the subjects said "green" at least once. In a control group without confederates, only 0.25 percent of responses were "green," owing to one subject who said "green" twice. The impact of the minority became even more impressive when subjects were individually given sixteen discs ranging in colour from "very definitely blue" to "very definitely green" and were asked to label each disc as either green or blue on their own. (They were not allowed to make compromise judgments such as "blue-green.") Those subjects who had previously been in the experimental condition were much more likely to call a disc "green" than were those who had been in the control condition. In addition, the tendency to say "green" was even observed in those subjects who had not said "green" in the group situation. It would seem that all the subjects had been influenced by the minority even though some of them had not been willing to reveal it publicly.

Another experiment by Moscovici's group showed that it is critical that the minority be consistent in its view. When the confederates were coached to respond in a more variable and inconsistent manner, the effects outlined above almost entirely disappeared.

This research indicates that the outcome of majority pressure is usually confined to behaviour, while minorities can produce real change and conversion (Maass and Clark, 1984; Moscovici, 1980). This happens because considerably more "cognitive work" is stimulated by the minority view; by contrast, the majority view leads to relatively superficial thinking. Although the minority position is often quickly rejected, it can, stated with consistency and confidence, lead others to consider many alternative and unique viewpoints. This *divergent thinking* results in decision-making that is therefore more reasoned, complex, and stable (Nemeth, 1986).

Why conform?

The reasons why people conform have been advanced by various researchers. These reasons are not all mutually exclusive and they could operate simultaneously and in different combinations.

(1) *Reward and punishment*. We have seen that groups in general are intolerant of heresy in their midst and that any individual who chooses to behave in a manner which contradicts or ignores important norms may experience some unpleasant moments, including the threat of social ostracism. These pressures, by themselves, may be sufficient to move a person in a conforming direction. Anticipation of the consequences of deviation owing to similar past experiences may serve the same purpose. In addition, the group rewards the conformer with liking and social approval.

Therefore, it is easy to see why *cohesive groups* (i.e., groups in which there is a high degree of interpersonal liking and attachment) exert considerable control over the behaviour of the members. Because cohesive groups offer more liking and approval to members, the individual has more to lose by deviation than he or she would in less cohesive groups. A striking example of this phenomenon is drawn from recent history: During the Korean conflict (1950 to 1953) the United States government was disturbed to discover that one of three U.S. prisoners engaged in some form of collaboration with the enemy. In contrast, none of the Turkish and only a few of the British prisoners collaborated. As an explanation, it has been suggested that the American soldiers broke down because of a lack of group solidarity and morale. Unlike the Americans, who were individualistic, the Turks and the British behaved as a social unit with discipline and order of command remaining intact. As long as *the group* resisted, and supported the individual, pressures to deviate were ineffective (Brown, 1963).

Although deviation from group norms is not viewed lightly, it is true that high status group members are allowed more leeway to deviate than low status members. This occurs, it is claimed (Homans, 1974), because high status members have earned *idiosyncrasy credits* by contributing more than others to the effectiveness of the group. Each unit of such *good* behaviour is rewarded with an idiosyncrasy credit, reflecting the importance of the person to the well-being of the group. These credits can be accumulated and used to deviate beyond what would ordinarily be the permissible limit. However, once credits have been used in this way, more credits must be earned before further deviation will be allowed. Ostracism for deviant behaviour must, of course, remain the final threat. If the individual is able to tolerate this rejection once it has been carried out, the group will have lost control over that person.

(2) *Reality testing*. There are many aspects of our personal worlds, social and physical, that are not clearly defined and are ambiguous in some way or other. For example, the autokinetic effect arises from an ambiguous situation in which reality has to be almost totally imposed by the observer. Although Asch's situation is more structured than the autokinetic situation, substantial ambiguity still remains.

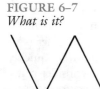

FIGURE 6–7
What is it?

Consider the drawing in Figure 6-7. What does it appear to be? Some might say "two X's," others may insist on a "W sitting on an M," or a "V superimposed on an inverted V." It may be difficult for others to deny that it is "a diamond with whiskers." The point is, although the design appears to be simple and straightforward, it can still generate considerable uncertainty. Everyone is similarly confronted on a day-to-day basis with events and situations which are undefined, ambiguous and amenable to a variety of interpretations. In these cases the group serves to structure, label, and identify the situations, thus reducing both the ambiguity and the anxiety or discomfort which often accompanies these situations.

Constructive reality is exemplified in an extreme form by the fundamentalist and "cult" religions — the Moonies, Hare Krishna, the Church of Scientology — which provide adherents with "solutions" to all of life's ills. These organizations often go so far as to dicate the complete daily routine of the members. It was under this sort of system that the ultimate example of conformity and compliance, the mass suicide and murder of nearly 1000 members of the Peoples' Church founded by Jim Jones, took place in Guyana in November, 1978 (see Chapter 14).

(3) *Social comparison*. Dissenters also face the difficulty of questioning their own competence. According to Festinger (1954) we have a basic drive to evaluate our

abilities and opinions. The obvious way of doing this is to make comparisons with other people — we want to know where we stand relative to our peers and colleagues. This drive is exemplified by the need of students to compare their marks on tests with those of their classmates and of employees to judge the adequacy of their salaries relatively rather than absolutely. In other words, although our salary may be quite adequate, considerable dissatisfaction will be aroused if we discover that a coworker with similar seniority and ability is receiving more money. (see Chapter 13).

It can be an uncomfortable experience to be wrong and, in many instances, being different is perceived as being wrong. We use what Festinger has termed *informational social influence* to determine whether our ideas are "correct." In most cases we do so when there is no demonstrably right answer. Thus, although we can determine whether a pound of feathers falls more slowly than a pound of lead or whether a container of canaries will weigh less when all the birds are flying than when they are all on their perches, most social questions are not amenable to empirical or objective verification. If we want answers to these questions we frequently must turn to the judgment of the majority. The result is increased conformity.

It is worth noting that any variable affecting a personality trait (e.g., decreasing an individual's self-confidence) will be associated with increased dependence on the judgment of others. Research on self-esteem makes this assertion quite clear. For instance, Stang (1972) placed individuals who had scored high or low on a test of self-esteem in a Crutchfield visual judgment situation and found that those estimated to have low self-esteem were considerably more likely to conform than those with high self-esteem. (Some sample items from a scale of self-esteem (Eagly, 1967) are in Table 6-2.) It is not difficult to understand why a person who would answer these and similar questions in the affirmative would also be unlikely to maintain an independent position in a conformity situation.

(4) *Conformity as a social tactic*. The positive relationship between liking and conformity may lead some individuals to use conforming behaviour deliberately as a means of impression management (see also Chapter 3). Jones, Gergen, Gumpert and

TABLE 6–2
Sample items from scale of self-esteem

1. How often do you have the feeling that there is *nothing* you can do well?

| very often | fairly often | sometimes | once in a great while | practically never |

2. How often do you worry about whether other people like to be with you?

| very often | fairly often | sometimes | once in a great while | practically never |

3. How often do you feel that you dislike yourself?

| very often | fairly often | sometimes | once in a great while | practically never |

4. Do you ever feel so discouraged with yourself that you wonder whether anything is worthwhile?

| very often | fairly often | sometimes | once in a great while | practically never |

SOURCE: Eagly, 1967

Thibaut (1965) conducted an experiment in which individuals of low status exchanged written messages with persons of higher status. These messages expressed opinions on various topics and were collected, but not delivered, by the experimenters who substituted statements of their own which they had previously prepared. Some of these prepared statements expressed deviant opinions. It was found that individuals of low status were likely to shift their opinions in the direction of opinions believed held by high status individuals. This was especially likely to occur when the low status subjects were told that the experiment was concerned with compatibility. These individuals deliberately conformed in order to increase the probability of being liked.

(5) *Conformity due to similar backgrounds and values.* Most groups do not draw their members from the population at random. Almost all groups are formed for some purpose, and the members have in common at least an interest in the group goal. However, the particular purpose of the group is also likely to be correlated with certain attitudes and values; therefore, the participants may show similarities in other dimensions. For instance, the members of a group formed to protect a heritage building from being torn down by developers will likely share other interests and have similar

B · O · X   6 - 2

CONFORMITY IN MEN AND WOMEN

For several decades social psychologists described women as more susceptible than men to social influences and pressures. This characterization, assumed to be factual and supported by early studies, was consistent with the stereotype of women as meek, submissive and easily swayed by emotion rather than reason. However, careful reviews of the literature and later studies punctured this myth (Eagly, 1978; Eagly and Wood, 1985).

The vast majority of persuasion studies, in which subjects are presented with a counter-argument and then asked to indicate their attitudes on a questionnaire (see Chapter 4), show no gender differences. Even conformity situations, in which discrepant positions (e.g., an obviously wrong answer) are advanced by a group of people, show no significant gender differences.

However, one third of the published studies show that females are likely to yield to group pressures. Let us consider why. One possible reason concerns possible biases in the actual studies. Typically, questions are asked for which there is a "right answer" — tests of perception (lengths of lines and geometric shapes) or questions in subject areas such as geography, politics, or science. It has been argued that men are more familiar with these topics, and would therefore be more likely to resist social pressure to conform. A study by Sistrunk and McDavid (1971) set out to correct for this bias. A panel of subjects judged questions as being "typically masculine" (sports cars, mathematics, politics), "typically feminine" (cosmetics, cooking, sewing), or neutral. The questionnaire was then administered to male and female subjects. In order to induce conformity pressures, subjects were told beside each question how a majority of students had supposedly responded. Results showed that women conformed more to "masculine" items, but that men conformed more than women to "feminine" items. Overall, there was no difference in conformity levels between men and women.

There is some evidence that greater female conformity is found when the experiment has been conducted by a male (Eagly and Carli, 1981). There is

political and social values. Thus many groups begin with a minimum of heterogeneity among the members and deviation is not likely to be a serious issue or threat.

Keep in mind that the group insists on people "toeing the line" only for those behaviours which are deemed relevant to the group's well-being and efficiency. It is unlikely, for instance, that the members of a work group whose major concerns are related to production would become agitated about variations in the dress of the members. On the other hand, standards of dress would be of major importance to a motorcycle gang.

COMPLIANCE

Obviously people have lives which extend beyond their memberships in groups. Frequently, we stand alone and, when we are alone, attempts may be made to influence our behaviour — to get us to buy some product, to vote for a certain politician, or to donate to a particular charity. Some of the techniques are sophisticated, employed

no reason to believe that male social psychologists are male chauvinists who deliberately set out to prove the female stereotype. However, they may unintentionally design conformity situations in which males feel more comfortable. On the other hand, female social psychologists, aware of the stereotype of female submissiveness, may design experiments in which females feel more comfortable and confident. In any case, the conflict reveals the sensitivity of research in social psychology to subtle influences.

It has been argued that women and men are socialized differently in how to respond to social pressures and influence. For example, many traditional tests of sex-role identification link "femininity" with such traits as nurturance, warmth, and expressiveness, and "masculinity" with dominance, mastery, and task-related competence. To the extent that the role-related difference may be a real one, it can be interpreted differently. That is, what may be labelled negatively as "submissive" and "passive" can also be seen as enhancing interdependence rather than independence (Greenglass, 1982) or the "communal concern" of women, a commitment to preserving social harmony and encouraging positive feelings within a group (Eagly and Wood, 1985). In

this sense, expressing agreement may be a way of showing concern and support for others, which may be more important in many situations than giving the "right answer." Another clue is that men resist conforming only when others are watching in order to convey an image as a non-conformist. Without surveillance there are no differences in conformity between males and females (Eagly, Wood and Fishbaugh, 1981).

In short, we cannot support a generalization that women are more easily influenced than men. The effect is small, inconsistent, and limited to certain situations. It also seems to be tied into another assumption, that women are usually in lower-status positions than men. Indeed, there is evidence that women are expected to conform more because of their low-status positions and that these expectations disappear when we perceive women in a higher-status role (Eagly and Wood, 1982). Stereotypes can become self-fulfilling prophecies and women may conform because of these expectations. As stereotypes change and better opportunities for women emerge in the workplace, even this small difference may disappear.

in a deliberate manner, successful, and undetectable by the individual involved. Five of these procedures are reviewed next.

We have already stated that attempts at persuasion are often not very subtle. We argue, cajole, wheedle, insist, or demand. However, there are procedures which effectively *increase* the likelihood of compliance without revealing to the target audience that it is *being manipulated*.

(1) *The foot-in-the-door technique.* One process, well-known to door-to-door sales representatives, is straightforward: An individual who agrees to carry out a small request is subsequently more likely to agree to carry out a larger request. This means that if we want someone to do something and we are not sure whether they will acquiesce, we should first make a request we are reasonably certain will be honoured. Freedman and Fraser (1966) carried out a study using housewives in which the "large" request was to allow a survey team of five or six men to enter their homes and itemize their household products. In some cases this was the only request made (one-contact condition); in others, it had been preceded nine days earlier by a telephone call and by a request to answer a few questions about their soap brand. Some of these subjects were actually asked the questions (performance condition) while only the agreement of other subjects to answer the questions was obtained (agreement condition). This allowed the investigators to determine whether acquiescence only was necessary or whether the act actually had to be carried out. In order to rule out the effects of the initial contact, a fourth control condition was used in which the housewife was told the nature of the survey but was not asked to agree to the product inventory and was not asked any questions (familiarization condition). The results of the study are shown in Table 6-3. It is clear from these data that prior compliance considerably increased the likelihood of the larger request being carried out (52.8 percent). As is obvious, merely agreeing helped a bit (33.3 percent) but the most effective inducement was having the person actually carry out the small request.

TABLE 6–3
Percentage of subjects complying with large request

Condition	%
Performance	52.8
Agree only	33.3
Familiarization	27.8
One contact	22.2

SOURCE: Freedman and Fraser, 1966

Freedman and Fraser (1966) carried out a second experiment which, among other things, showed that the person making the second, larger request does not need to be the same person who had made the smaller request. In this study the procedure was the same but the small request was for subjects either to put up a small sign on their lawn or to sign a petition concerning either safe driving or keeping California beautiful. In all cases the second request was for subjects to allow a large sign which said "Drive carefully" to be placed on their lawn. The persons who made the first and second request were always different. One result of this experiment can be found in Table 6-4. The baseline for comparison here is the one-contact group in which fewer than 20 percent agreed to the large request. Clearly, all the other treatments improved on this outcome, but the most marked improvement occurred when both the issue (safe driving) and the sign ("Drive carefully") were similar (76 percent).

TABLE 6–4
Percentage of subjects complying with large request

| | Task | |
Issue	Similar	Different
Similar	76.0	47.8
Different	47.6	47.4

One contact only: 16.7

SOURCE: Freedman and Fraser, 1966

While this experimental paradigm is clear-cut, the reasons behind the frequency with which acquiescence increases are not as apparent. Freedman and Fraser (1966) and Dejong (1979) have suggested that the "self-perception" of the subjects who agreed to the small request changed. These individuals observed that they had agreed and, from this evidence, came to the conclusion that they were cooperative and helpful people. Then they set out to maintain this image by also agreeing to the second request.

(2) *The door-in-the-face technique.* This is a variation of the foot-in-the-door procedure, one that many of us have either deliberately or inadvertently used at one time or another. In this case, the first request made is so extreme that the target is almost certain to refuse. Then the second request is made considerably smaller and more reasonable. Cialdini and a number of colleagues (1975) have shown this strategy to be an effective means of inducing compliance to the second request. For example, they accosted university students on the street and asked them if they would act as unpaid counselors for two hours a week for two years. Not unexpectedly, they were refused by everyone. The next request was whether they would accompany a group of juvenile delinquents on a trip to the zoo. Fifty percent of the students were then willing to help. Compare this figure with the 16.7 percent (from another group) who also agreed but of whom only the second request was made.

Two explanations have been offered for the effectiveness of this procedure. One is based on the concept of *reciprocal concessions*. When the person making the large request reduces it to a smaller one, the other person then feels obligated to make a matching concession. The second explanation involves *self-presentation*. Most people prefer to present themselves to others in a positive light. By acceding to the second request, the students demonstrated that they were not really as bad as might have originally been implied. For example, Pendleton and Batson (1979) observed that those who refused a moderate request thought that they would be perceived as "less helpful, less friendly, and less concerned" than if they had refused an extremely large request.

(3) *The low-ball technique.* This is frequently used by automobile sales people to enhance the likelihood of a sale and to maximize the selling price. Low-balling is based on the proposition that once an individual has agreed to carry out an act, he or she will still comply even though the act is made more costly. The process begins typically with the salesperson accepting an offer of an extremely good price on a car which interests the customer. The intent is to get the customer to make an *active decision* to purchase the automobile. Once this is done, and the necessary forms are filled out, the salesperson says that since the price is so low, she must check with her supervisor. She then leaves for a few minutes and returns to say that the boss would not allow it because they would be losing money on the deal. (In some cases, it is the generous offer on a trade-in that is negated by the manager.) In any case, the

purchase price goes up. However, anecdotal evidence indicates that the customer will still enter into the agreement. In spite of the increased cost, the initial decision persists.

Cialdini and his colleagues (1978) were interested in whether this tactic could be reproduced in the laboratory. They asked students to participate in an experiment scheduled at 7:00 in the morning. Those in the control condition were told about the study and the time. In the low-ball condition subjects were *first* asked whether they would participate and, if they agreed, were *then* told the experiment would take place at 7:00 a.m. Two measures of compliance were obtained — the percentage of subjects in each condition who agreed to participate, and the percentage who actually showed up at the scheduled time. The results of the study, shown in Table 6-5, indicate that a much higher percentage of the students who were "low-balled" agreed to participate and actually showed up for the appointment.

TABLE 6–5
Percentage of subjects making appointment and complying

	Condition	
	Control	Low ball
Made appointment	31	56
Actually appeared	24	53

SOURCE: Cialdini *et al.*, 1978

In another study Cialdini and colleagues (1979) demonstrated the effect under controlled conditions in the field and also showed that low-balling was more effective than the foot-in-the-door procedure. They argue for a *commitment* interpretation of the low-ball effect. Burger and Petty (1981), following the suggestion of Kiesler (1971), showed that once an individual is committed to a decision, the decision will be resistant to change. They also note that one means of creating commitment is to get the person to take action, for example, agree to sign an offer to purchase. In such cases we can obviously be our own worst enemy!

(4) *Improving the deal: The "that's-not-all-technique."* This procedure consists of offering a product to a person at a high price, preventing the person from responding for a few seconds, and then enhancing the deal either by adding another product or decreasing the price. For example, Burger (1986) had two experimenters sit at a table in various locations selling cupcakes and cookies. The cupcakes were visible but the cookies were not. Some of those who approached the table were told that the cupcakes were 75¢ each. Just then the second experimenter tapped the first experimenter on the shoulder. The first experimenter would ask the customer to "wait a second." After a brief exchange, the first experimenter turned to the customer and said that the price included two cookies. In the control group the subjects were told about the cookies as soon as they asked the price of the cupcakes. It was found that 73 percent of those in the "That's-not-all" condition bought the cupcakes (and cookies) whereas only 40 percent of those in the control condition made a purchase. Burger also showed that lowering the price had the same effect. Given that the technique seems to work, the question becomes, "Why?" Burger suggests two possible explanations: the norm of reciprocity and the effect of different anchoring points in attitudinal judgments.

The norm of reciprocity indicates that people feel under some obligation to reciprocate gifts, favours, and concessions. In the case of the "that's-not-all" procedure, the seller improves the offer and the buyer then feels obliged to purchase the product as a reciprocal action.

Attitudinal judgment in this situation would operate as follows: First, customers are likely to have only a vague notion regarding a reasonable price for a cupcake. The salesperson first establishes an anchor point of $1.00, allows this to firm up for a few seconds, and then reduces the price to 75¢. Against the anchor point of $1.00, the 75¢ price looks better than it would if introduced initially, and is more likely to fall within the person's latitude of acceptance (Chapter 5). Burger (1986) offers a number of studies which support these propositions. Moreover, he also presents data that suggest this technique is more effective than the door-in-the-face method of inducing compliance.

(5) *Guilt: "Thus conscience doth make cowards of us all."* Feelings of guilt have been shown to have powerful and pervasive influences on behaviour. Parents, for example, can be experts at creating feelings of guilt in their offspring when some particular action is desired. "After all I've done for you" is a typical remark. (The "difficult delivery" ploy also is very effective.) In laboratory investigations of guilt subjects are usually led to transgress in some way; then a request is made of them. For instance, Freedman, Wallington and Bless (1967) induced subjects to lie and then requested their volunteer participation in an additional study. The data for the "lie" experiment are reproduced in Table 6-6. In comparison with subjects in the "non-lie" control condition, almost twice as many subjects complied. Darlington and Macker (1966) used a similar procedure to increase the likelihood of individuals donating blood.

TABLE 6–6
Number of subjects complying in the "lie" and "non-lie" condition

	Condition	
	Lie	*Non-lie*
Comply	20	11
Not comply	11	20

SOURCE: Freedman, Wallington and Bliss, 1967

This effect is not confined to helping only those against whom the subject transgressed. Regan, Williams and Sparling (1972) had a male confederate ask female shoppers to take a picture with his camera. When they tried, the camera wouldn't work. Some of the subjects were made to feel that it was their fault, while others were assured they were not to blame. A second confederate then appeared carrying a bag of groceries which was torn so that the contents were falling out. Fifty-five percent of the subjects in the "guilt" condition and only 15 percent in the control condition informed the confederate of the problem. Although in this study there was no direct request for assistance, it does suggest that individuals who have been made to feel guilty are then motivated to expiate the guilt in some positive way, and that it does not necessarily have to be directed at the injured party. In fact, Freedman *et al.* (1967) found that those made to feel guilty were reluctant to directly contact the person who had been damaged and preferred to help a third individual who originally had not been involved. This means that the timing of the request is important. If it does not occur shortly after the guilt manipulation, something else may occur which could make the transgressor feel better. It would then be unnecessary for him to react to the request. Cialdini, Darby and Vincent (1973) refer to this process as *negative-state release* which could either be a voluntary altruistic act or accedence to a request.

These five procedures, though often applied deliberately and systematically, are rarely detected by the unsuspecting target person. On a day-to-day basis the most frequently encountered and relatively innocuous procedures for inducing compliance are simple requests such as "Please pick up a case of beer on your way home from work." It is important, however, to distinguish between requests and *demands*, which also are very direct and undisguised. In the case of demands, the option not to comply is considerably reduced. Parents demand obedience from their children, soldiers must obey their officers and students are required to obey their teachers. Why do people set aside their independence of action and do what someone else demands even when they find it distasteful? Obedience to authority is considered next.

OBEDIENCE

The attention of social psychologists was drawn to the study of obedience by the controversial research of Milgram (1963, 1965, 1974). Milgram's research arose from his reflections on the Holocaust during which, from 1933–1945, millions of innocent people, mostly Jews, were slaughtered by the Nazis. He quotes C.P. Snow, who wrote: "The German Officers' Corps were brought up in the most rigorous code of obedience . . . in the name of obedience they were party to, and assisted in, the most wicked large scale actions in the history of the world" (1961, p. 24). Was the obedience that led to this horrendous action unique to Germany or, given the appropriate circumstances, could it occur elsewhere? Of course, not all obedience has aggressive action as the outcome, but it was this type of "destructive obedience" that Milgram studied based on the premise that "the individual who is commanded by a legitimate authority ordinarily obeys."

His procedure was to record the amount of electric shock a subject would be willing to administer to another person. He devised a fake apparatus which subjects believed was a "shock machine" and which they would use to deliver shocks at a range of settings from "slight shock" to "Danger: Severe Shock." There were 30 settings in all, each defined in terms of volts which ranged from 15 to 450!

In each session, in addition to the experimenter, there was one subject and an accomplice of the experimenter who, in a rigged selection, were assigned the roles of learner and teacher. The subject was always designated as teacher and was informed he was to teach the learner a list of paired word associates and to administer a shock whenever the learner was unable to recall a correct word. The shock was to be increased one level on each additional trial. The "learner" had been coached to make many errors while other verbal responses, presented by means of a tape recorder, varied with shock level. For example, at 75 volts the learner would grunt and moan, at 150 he demanded to be released, at 180 he cried that he could no longer stand it and at 300 he refused to provide any more answers. The subject was then told to

FIGURE 6–8
*Predicted and obtained
behaviour in "learning
exercise"*

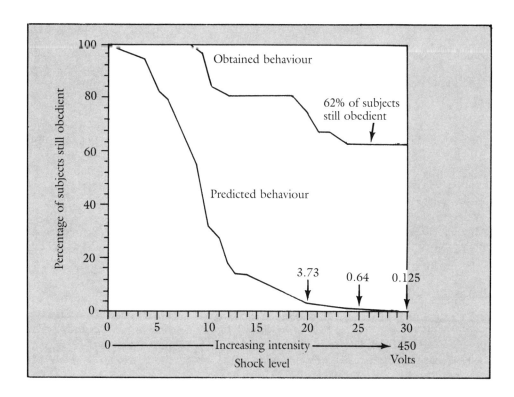

treat silence as a wrong answer. It should be noted that during the introduction the "learner" deliberately mentioned he had a heart condition.

How far would subjects go? Most of them became agitated and tense and frequently tried to break off the experiment. If a subject showed any sort of hesitation the experimenter (dressed in a white laboratory coat) told him to proceed and that the experimenter would accept the responsibility if anything happened to the "learner."

Forty psychiatrists predicted that most subjects would not go beyond the tenth shock level (150 volts), that not more than 4 percent would reach the twentieth level (300 volts) and that only about one tenth of one percent would administer the highest shock. However, Figure 6-8 reveals that 62 percent of the subjects completely obeyed the experimenter's commands!

Remember that in this study the victim was hidden from the subject, although they had been introduced at the beginning of the session. Other experiments by Milgram showed that as the victim and the subject became physically closer, the amount of obedience was reduced. For example, in the closest condition the subject was required to hold the victim's hand on the shock-plate. In this case, the number of subjects who administered the highest level of shock was reduced to 30 percent, still a substantial and disturbing proportion. Milgram also found that obedience decreased (to 45 percent) when the experimenter was physically absent from the laboratory and gave his orders by phone.

It should be noted that all Milgram's subjects were males and included university students, postal clerks, high school teachers, salesmen, engineers, and labourers. The extent to which women would obey under these conditions has not been thoroughly

B · O · X   6 - 3

CHARACTER VS. SITUATIONAL PRESSURE: WHAT SOME STUDENTS THINK

If asked, most people *underestimate* the extent to which the "teacher" will shock the "learner" in Milgram's obedience experiment, described in this chapter. However Safer (1980) discovered that students, after viewing a film of Milgram's research (Milgram, 1965) and learning about a control study Milgram carried out in which "teachers" could set their own shock levels without being coerced by the experimenter, *overestimated* how much shock would be delivered when subjects made their own decision. Safer postulated that these students felt that the obedience situation — even in the absence of the experimenter — released aggressive reactions that people harbour. In other words, they seemed to believe that people are inherently evil, ordinarily keeping it under control, but displaying it in

behaviour under the right circumstances.

Safer went on to test this hypothesis by asking students who had seen the film and others who had not how subjects would respond in the Milgram control situation. Students who had not seen the film predicted that when they had personal responsibility for setting the shock level, fewer subjects would choose the maximum shock level and predicted lower levels of average shock and maximum shock than students who had.

Safer points out that the students did not seem to understand how much of behaviour arises from situational pressures rather than the character of the individual. As "naive psychologists" they felt that most people, being "evil" rather than decent, would harm a stranger.

---

investigated. However, Hofling *et al.* (1966) reported that 95 percent of the nurses in their experiment were willing to issue an overdose of a certain medicine on the doctor's authority. This figure dropped to 11 percent when the nurses were familiar with the medicine and were given time to consult others (Rank and Jacobson, 1977). Nevertheless, in this setting even an 11 percent rate of obedience could have tragic consequences.

Milgram's research has been repeated many times in various locations of the United States and in other countries (Jordan, Spain, Germany, Italy, and Australia) with consistent results — between 50 and 85 percent of subjects used the highest shock level overall. Although much attention has been paid to violent aspects of Milgram's research, obedience is commonplace in many less dramatic situations as shown in an investigation by Meeus and Raaijmakers (1986). Their study involved a research worker at a university (the experimenter), male and female subjects, and a third person who was applying for a job (an accomplice). The "applicant" had been invited to the laboratory to take a selection test which, if passed, would guarantee a job. The subjects were directed to disturb the applicant while he was doing the test by making negative remarks about his test achievement and denigrating remarks about his personality. The remarks were to be made in spite of any objections by the applicant and were scripted to become increasingly strenuous as the time passed. If the subject proceeded, the applicant became unable to cope, failed the test, and forfeited the job. The subjects administered the test orally to the applicants whom they knew were currently unemployed. There were a maximum of 15 remarks that the subjects were told they could make and it was found that 91.7 percent of the subjects made all 15 remarks thereby ensuring that the applicant would not get the job. This outcome represents a considerably higher level of obedience than was observed by Milgram and others and suggests that this type of psychological harm is easier to perpetrate than physical violence.

These experiments clearly reveal that destructive obedience, either psychological or physical, is not restricted to any one social or cultural group. Individuals are willing to assign responsibility for their actions to authority figures and carry out their orders even when refusal is relatively easy. In the case of physical harm, obedience is reduced but not eliminated by the proximity of the victim and the proximity of the person in authority. The closer the victim and the more distant the authority, the smaller the obedience.

Many people find it difficult to accept that the *situation* can have such a profound effect on behaviour. After reading about Milgram's study or after seeing the movie *Obedience* (Milgram, 1965) they are likely to attribute evil to the subject rather than attribute the obedience to situational influences. Why this happens is suggested in Box 6-3.

There is nothing subtle about the manipulation of behaviour in these obedience investigations. However, during much of our day-to-day life we are subjected to influences that modify our actions and which are unintentional. These influences are considered next.

B · O · X 6 - 4

LEGITIMIZED AGGRESSION AND SOCIETY'S "PROTECTORS"

While people worry about more violence on the streets, society empowers some of its citizens, such as members of the police force and the armed services, to use violence in the course of their duties. Whether or not society sanctions an aggressive act is of crucial importance in determining the way we judge it. In war time, those who shoot down the most enemy airplanes or kill the most enemy soldiers are considered heroes. Yet sometimes, soldiers go too far in the eyes of the citizenry at home; atrocities carried out by American servicemen in Vietnam are examples of actions which "went too far" (Kelman, 1973; Opton, 1971).

From time to time, the public hears vague accusations of police brutality, but since the average person has little sympathy for criminals anyway, it is usually easier for them to believe that the victims are deserving, and that the charges are exaggerated or totally false. For instance, a number of years ago in an all-but-forgotten incident, when police raided the Landmark Hotel in Welland, Ontario, in 1974 and had patrons of the bar searched intimately (women were subjected to a vaginal exam) for hidden drugs, there was a flurry of moralizing against the action, but the subject quickly faded from the public's mind. It was probably easier to believe that the patrons of the bar were unscrupulous characters anyway, just as a large proportion of American males consider violence by the police against hoodlums and rioters to be fully justified (Blumenthal *et al.*, 1972).

Socially deviant groups can often be the victims of police discrimination because the police, like society, may hold a dislike for them. In the 1960s, during the heyday of the "hippies," a sociologist at the University of Montreal surveyed Québec police and found that they harboured more hostility toward hippies than toward criminals (Szabo, cited by Wrightsman (1972)). More Rimouski police (54 percent) expressed hostility toward hippies than toward criminals (28 percent). In Montreal, however, about 23 percent expressed hostility toward hippies and 23 percent expressed hostility toward criminals. Yet only 8 percent of Montreal police said that they had friendly feelings toward hippies. Such attitudes and values may lead individual police officers to justify the use of violent methods against socially deviant groups.

Why do society's "protectors" sometimes resort to unnecessary aggression? There are several possible influences:

(1) *The social environment.* Police often work in circumstances that are likely to elicit frustration or anger. Such circumstances include encounters with people who spit or swear as they are arrested or the risk of being shot at, stabbed, or hit by someone being arrested or questioned. As a result, a defensive, almost paranoid, attitude may begin to develop.

(2) *Selective attraction of aggressive individuals.* When an institution is legally permitted to use violence, it is likely to attract some people who seek or enjoy power and aggression. Police forces have a very difficult problem in trying to weed such people out. Many do not even try.

(3) *The influence of weapons.* If a person is given a choice of weapons, the presence of a very powerful weapon may make other weapons appear to be relatively mild in nature (Harrison and Pepitone, 1972). A British "bobby" who carries only a nightstick may only use it as a "last resort," when words fail to obtain the necessary action. However, if the bobby is also permitted to carry a gun, the gun is likely to be perceived as the instrument of last resort, and use of the nightstick may seem less serious.

In a laboratory analogy to this situation (Harrison and Pepitone, 1972), subjects were required to train a rat to press a bar using either "mild" or "slightly painful" shocks. Subjects who also had available a more painful shock, but were not allowed to use it, delivered significantly more mildly painful shocks than did subjects for whom "mildly painful" was the maximum punishment. The mild shock was reserved for use as a "last resort" when it was the maximum punishment available; its use was perceived as being less undesirable when there was another, more painful, punishment available.

(4) *Norms.* Another important factor which may encourage unnecessary use of force by police may be a "spreading apart" of competing normative systems (Goldstein *et al.*, 1975). A new recruit to the military or the police brings with him or her a set of "civilian" norms, and may initially be horrified by the violent actions of others. However, once he or she decides or is forced to act aggressively, it becomes easier to accept the group's set of norms, since they provide justification for the aggressive behaviour. The new norms not only are likely to justify violence under certain circumstances, but to derogate certain kinds of people against whom the violence is often directed (e.g., "The only thing that those punks understand is rough stuff; be nice to them and they won't have any respect for you").

The "role" of police officer carries its own set of expectations and values. Zimbardo *et al.* (1982) studied the behaviour of ordinary "normal" college students given the roles of either prison guard or prisoner in a realistic but mock prison. (See Chapter 14 for more detail.) The "guards" became so authoritarian, even sadistic, and the prisoners so abject and disturbed that the study had to be stopped prematurely. This suggests that the role associated with "prison guard" also defines the role of prisoners — they are undeserving of respect. Similar expectations may be operating with respect to police and society.

UNINTENTIONAL SOCIAL INFLUENCES

Social influence involves direct or indirect pressure exerted by people to encourage or discourage certain actions by others. We may use a wide variety of cues from explicit verbal messages to subtle non-verbal communication in order to get someone to conform, comply, or obey. However, it also is possible to observe other social influences which a person or group may not even be aware of exerting. *Reference group influences* and *social modelling* are two such processes.

Reference group influences

People often identify with certain groups whose values, attitudes, and interests are perceived as similar to their own. They would like to be accepted by the group, or be considered by others as "one of them." Often without being aware of it, they "refer" to the group as a source of their own thoughts and actions. For example, a hustling, up-and-coming person, ambitious for wealth and status, may identify with the "rich and famous" as a reference group. The person will thus dress in the "right" designer clothes, drive the "right" car, belong to the "right" organizations, volunteer for the "right" political party, and hold the "right" attitudes. Reference groups have even been observed to influence the choice of a partner in marriage.

Reference groups serve two functions for people. They serve a *normative* function, setting standards for beliefs and actions. For example, religious people will look to their own religious group for guidance in how to live. And, they serve a *comparison* function, allowing people to evaluate themselves. Indeed, the reference group also provides people with a means of evaluating others, influencing both prejudices and friendships.

The unintentional and unconscious influence of reference groups is shown in a classic study by Siegel and Siegel (1957). At the end of their first university year, female students were asked to indicate where they wished to live next year. As it happened, a group of residences called "Row Houses" was generally considered to be the desirable, high-status place to live on campus. As expected, the majority of these students listed the Row Houses as their first choice. In a random drawing, some were assigned to this first choice while other disappointed students were not. A third group of students, assigned to other housing, was quite content with the outcome. Thus some subjects became members of their reference group, others were excluded from membership in their reference group, and still others did not identify "Row Houses" as a reference group.

By means of survey data, it was determined that Row Houses residents tended to have relatively ethnocentric and authoritarian attitudes (see Chapter 7). As expected, those who identified with them as a reference group tended to score higher on measures of these attitudes than those who did not. At the end of the second year, attitudes were again measured in all subjects. Again as expected, those who had lived in the Row Houses showed the greatest amount of attitude change, presumably as a result of direct social influence and pressure. However, even those who did not actually live in the Row Houses changed their attitudes, becoming more similar to their reference group. Thus, even in the absence of interaction, pressure, or persuasion, reference groups can exert a powerful influence.

Social modelling

From the outset, social psychologists have recognized and been fascinated by imitation. Albert Bandura (1977) has developed a comprehensive analysis (social learning theory) of the process of observational learning which extends beyond the limits of child-like imitation.

In order for modelling to occur, the observer must *attend* to the model and what the model is doing. Factors such as the status or attractiveness of the model and the novelty of the behaviour will affect attention. Then the observer must *remember* what has been observed, as an image or in words. As we saw in Chapter 3, schemata can strongly influence both attention and memory. In order to duplicate the behaviour which has been observed, the person must be *able to perform* it, i.e., the behaviour itself — or a capacity to perform it must be in the observer's repertoire. Although Wayne Gretzky may be a compelling model for many young hockey players, few will possess his ability to perform.

Finally, if modelling is to occur, the observer must be *motivated* to learn and perform what is observed. To a considerable extent, the observer will be motivated by rewards and punishments already experienced and the expectations he or she has of the situation. Bandura points out that reinforcement need not be experienced directly. If we identify with a model on the basis of attractiveness, high status, or similarity to ourselves, and we observe the consequences of the behaviour to the model, then we may experience *vicarious reinforcement*. This experience of "feeling what they feel" may influence our future behaviour.

It is clear that this analysis encompasses more than simple imitation. In modelling, we observe what the person does, in what situation, and with what consequences. For example, in the case of television aggression, we see the aggressive act, but also observe the situation in which it occurs, the characteristics of the victim, and possibly the consequences to the aggressor (see Chapter 9). All these observations provide us with information about what is expected or appropriate in a situation, and what is likely to happen.

Modelling may involve the *observational learning of a new behaviour*. Most modelling influences tend to change the probability of a behaviour which already exists (or potentially exists — most of us could fire a gun even if we have never done so). Modelling may have *inhibiting or disinhibiting* effects on such behaviour as aggression, sexuality, assertiveness, and even suicide. Observing a model may actually reduce the probability of modelling if the model is unattractive or the action has undesirable consequences. On the other hand, modelling may also have *response facilitation* effects, eliciting a behaviour in a specific situation. This may occur because modelling provides information about what is expected or simply increases awareness and availability of the act.

THE DANGERS OF CONFORMITY — "GROUP THINK"

Few would deny that some conformity is necessary for the well-being of groups and society in general. Clearly, a "laissez-faire" system in which individuals could make up their own minds about whether to stop at intersections or pay income tax would be highly chaotic. At the same time, we must consider whether, under some conditions, conformity also might be counter-productive. Would Bethune have gone to

China, Riel mounted a rebellion or Banting and Best have discovered insulin if they had been strict conformists? Progress in many fields is charted by the names of those who are willing to take a stand against majority opinion. Among these was Freud, whose theory flew in the face of Victorian morality, and the early explorers who, according to common belief, were expected to fall off the edge of a flat world.

Janis (1972) and Janis and Mann (1977) have called the tendency for people to assume that the group invariably has the correct answer, "group think." Group think depends on the type of leadership and the cohesiveness of the group, and is especially evident in crisis situations. Janis (1972) developed his ideas about this phenomenon from an analysis of a number of important policy-making committees in the United States. The recommendations of these committees had crucial national implications but, as Janis noted, the members of these groups were more concerned with maintaining group solidarity than with voicing unpopular views which might be correct but were also disruptive. Examples of these decisions — described by Janis (1972) as "political fiascos" — are: to pursue the defeated North Korean Army beyond the 38th parallel, to launch the Bay of Pigs invasion of Cuba, and to escalate involvement in the war in Vietnam.

Flowers (1977) conducted an experiment to test the group think hypothesis in the laboratory. She had groups of college students deal with a crisis situation. Some of these groups had an *open leader* and others a *closed leader*. The open leader, in contrast with the closed leader (1) did not state his or her own solution until all the others had offered their preferred solutions; (2) asked for and encouraged discussion of each suggested course of action; (3) emphasized that it was important to air all possible viewpoints in order to reach a wise decision. In addition, some groups were composed of individuals who were strangers to one another (low cohesiveness) and others were made up of individuals who were friends (high cohesiveness).

The groups discussed a problem about a 62-year-old high school teacher who was becoming senile and unable to handle discipline in her classroom. The discussion continued until a solution agreeable to all members was reached. *More potential solutions* and *better use of information* took place under the open style than the closed style of leadership, although it did not make any difference whether group members were friends or not.

Tetlock (1979) has pointed out that there are problems with such simulations. For instance, the cohesiveness variable, which contrary to expectations was not significant, may not be the same among college students as it is among policy-makers, upon whom Janis based his analysis. Accordingly, Tetlock (1979) analyzed the content of the statements actually made by important U.S. decision-makers — Truman, Kennedy and Johnson — during the crisis originally examined by Janis. Tetlock's results strongly support Janis' predictions. Public statements by policy-makers during a crisis were more simplistic and were more oriented toward their own group. As Janis (1972) indicates, decision-makers believe that the group is invulnerable to external influence. The members of the group ignore or discount warnings about the validity of their common solution and they are unquestioning in their acceptance of the righteousness of the group's policies. Direct pressure is applied to elicit conformity, and self-appointed "mind guards" shield the group from outside counter-attitudinal pressures. "Mind guards" are individuals like Robert Kennedy who, during the Cuban Missile Crisis (when the U.S. demanded that the U.S.S.R. remove its missiles and blockaded Cuban ports), filtered information from outside so that the group learned little, if anything, about external, dissenting opinions. Clearly, conformity under these conditions is both intellectually stultifying and dangerous. There is no room for individualism or innovation. Yet without innovation (and its acceptance) our society would be considerably more primitive than it is. Indeed, Nemeth contends that "robust dissent is not only a manifestation of a democratic principle, but it is the mechanism by which better solutions are found and better decisions are made" (1986, p. 31).

NON-CONFORMITY AND INNOVATION

In 1934 the Chrysler Corporation developed a car which was mechanically and stylistically far ahead of its competitors. Yet the Chrysler Airflow did not sell well and production of it was soon stopped. Clearly, the Chrysler engineers and stylists had been willing to deviate markedly from the standards of the day but they misjudged the flexibility of the buying public. A similar error was made by brewers who put "diet beer" on the market in the '70s. It didn't sell. When it was reintroduced later as "light beer" it captured a substantial proportion of beer sales. In the interim, the public had become considerably more health conscious. There are many reasons why innovative ideas and products may have difficulty finding acceptance. The decision to resist innovation may be a political decision. Canada, for example, stopped both the production of the world's first commercial jetliner and the Avro Arrow, a jet fighter which would have been by far the best plane of its type in the world.

It is evident that innovation does not simply involve doing something different. Merton (1957), for instance, argues that innovators adhere to group goals while departing from approved means, typically through behaviours that are novel. An individual who invents something or improves on an existing device may not be truly innovative because there may be no real break with current practices or principles. Thus it could be questioned whether the Wright Brothers were true innovators since they simply improved upon knowledge and techniques which already were available. On the other hand, Henry Ford's contribution to modern industry, the assembly line, completely revolutionized the manufacturing process. This ability to break out

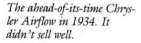

The ahead-of-its-time Chrysler Airflow in 1934. It didn't sell well.

of the "lock-step" pattern of conformity is critical. Barron (1969) reports a study in which scientists classified as either "original" or "less original" were placed in a Crutchfield conformity situation. It was found that members of the former group conformed in 10 percent of the trials, while the "less originals" conformed in 18 percent of the trials. In the same study it was observed that military officers conformed an average of 33 percent of the time.

Not only must innovators be able to resist normative pressures, they must also be willing to tolerate the risk of failure as well as potential public ridicule or scorn: recall how Galileo was forced to recant his outlandish view that the earth was not the centre of the solar system.

"*Brainstorming*" has been advocated as one way to foster innovative ideas. The major characteristic of this type of group situation is that the participants must feel no restrictions on the type of ideas they put forth. All notions, no matter how bizarre, are welcome. Under such conditions, as Gordon (1961) points out, the atmosphere maximizes the likelihood of "making the familiar strange" (p. 28) which, he argues, is the essence of innovation. (See Box 6-5 for an excerpt from Gordon's book on "synectics," the term he prefers.)

B · O · X   6 - 5

THE SES SYNECTICS SESSION

A group was trying to invent a dispenser which could be used with a variety of products and without a top which had to be removed and replaced.

A: *A clam sticks its neck out of its shell . . . brings the neck in and closes the shell again.*

B: *Yeah, but the clam's shell is an exoskeleton. The real part, the real anatomy of the clam is inside.*

C: *What difference does that make?*

A: *Well, the neck of the clam doesn't clean itself . . . it just drags itself back into the protection of the shell.*

D: *What other analogies are there to our problem?*

E: *How about the human mouth?*

B: *What does it dispense?*

E: *Spit . . . the mouth propels spit whenever it wants . . . on, oh. It isn't really self cleaning . . . you know, dribbling on the chin.*

A: *Couldn't there be a mouth which was trained so that it wouldn't dribble?*

E: *Maybe, but it would be contrived as hell . . . and if*

the human mouth can't keep itself clean with all the feedback in the human system. . . .

D: *When I was a kid I grew up on a farm. I used to drive a hay rack behind a pair of draft horses. When a horse would take a crap, first his outer . . . I guess you call it a kind of mouth, would open. Then the anal sphincter would dilate and a horse ball would come out. Afterwards, everything would close up again. The whole picture would be clean as a whistle.*

E: *What if the horse had diarrhea?*

D: *That happened when they got too much grain . . . but the horse would kind of wink a couple of times while the anal mouth was drawn back . . . the winking would squeeze out the liquid . . . then the outer mouth would cover the whole thing up again.*

B: *You're describing a plastic motion.*

D: *I guess so . . . could we simulate a horse's ass in plastic?*

In fact they could, and they did (Gordon, 1961, p. 41).

We should not be overly enthusiastic about group brainstorming. First, it is not necessarily the case that group "brainstorming" is better than individual "brainstorming" and second, many people are unable to break out of traditional, normative patterns of thought and behaviour. For instance, Lamm and Trommsdorff (1973) conclude from a review of the literature that group brainstorming sessions produce fewer ideas than subjects brainstorming individually. (Less clear evidence is available on measures of quality, uniqueness, and variety of these ideas.) Similarly, McGrath (1984) noted that individuals working separately generate many more and more creative ideas (as rated by judges) than do groups. Of course, it is the quality and uniqueness of the ideas expressed which are critical. If these characteristics are not enhanced by the brainstorming procedure, either group or individual, then quantity, in itself, is likely to be of little value.

It also is the case that some people, although intellectually competent, are unable to deviate from standard or expected modes of reasoning on account of certain personality traits. One such inhibiting trait is what Rokeach (1960) termed "close-mindedness." Among other things, close-minded individuals have difficulty dealing with problems in new ways. As Adams (1980) points out, they have difficulty because they interpret the problem too narrowly — they fail to consider a variety of viewpoints and don't use all the information that is available. For example, a "close-minded" individual would likely have difficulty with the following problem: Without lifting your pencil from the paper and using no more than four straight lines, connect the nine dots shown below.

FIGURE 6–9

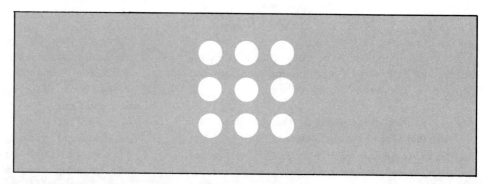

When most people see this problem for the first time, they assume they are not to go outside the boundaries set by the dots themselves — even though that is neither stated nor implied in the puzzle. Once they overcome that self-imposed constraint, there are a number of possible solutions, two of which are given below:

FIGURE 6–10

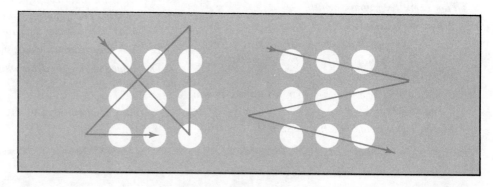

In the second solution, an additional assumed constraint has been broken. The puzzle said only "connect the dots"; most people assume that means the lines must go through the centre of each dot.

In one study by Rokeach (1960) subjects had to set aside three commonly accepted beliefs in order to solve a problem: (1) that organisms face food in order to eat it; (2) that organisms can move in whatever direction they wish; and (3) that they can change direction at will. Close-minded subjects took longer to solve the problem and were less able than open-minded individuals to give up an unworkable belief system. Rokeach comments: "[C]losed subjects remain loyal, that is, continue to believe that there is a solution. Conversely, open subjects more frequently find an ingenious creative solution" (1960, p. 256).

The diffusion and acceptance of innovation

Some innovations have no immediate or obvious practical use while others have not only arisen in response to real needs but have important implications for the continued or improved well-being of substantial segments of the human population. We should also remember that what may be commonplace in one society may be innovative when transferred to another society. This is especially so when advanced technologies are introduced into less developed countries, particularly in such fields as health, agriculture, and family planning. For example, the "Green Revolution" in India and other parts of Asia required farmers to accept a new type of wheat which had a considerably higher yield than traditional types and which earned a Nobel prize for its developer, Norman Borlaug. At the same time, this new wheat had a number of features which could reduce the probability of its acceptance. It did not tolerate drought as well as traditional wheat, which meant that some form of irrigation had to be available in the case of a failed or poor monsoon. Also, the new wheat had a shorter stem than the older varieties and provided less straw for other uses — feeding cattle, for instance. It did not respond well to organic fertilizers, so chemical fertilizers had to be used. Finally, people complained that the chapatties (a type of unleavened bread and a dietary staple throughout Northern India) made from the flour had an unpleasant flavour (Nossiter, 1970). Given these conditions, it is surprising that the hybrid variety did gain acceptance, with ultimately good results. It is claimed that India currently has enough grain in reserve to tolerate a failure of the monsoon in two consecutive years.

What happens when an individual is confronted with a new device, seed, or manufacturing process which is promoted as a great improvement over what has been used in the past? There has been a considerable amount of research devoted to this question, although Weiss (1971) expresses some concern that theory and methodology are often of dubious quality. Nevertheless we can discern some characteristics of the process and of the individuals involved which are worth noting.

You will no doubt have realized that the adoption of innovation involves risk, and that some individuals are more willing to tolerate risk than others. It has also been shown that adopters of innovation are better off financially, have had more past experience with other innovations and are better able to evaluate abstract and technical information than non-adapters (Weiss, 1971). Moulik and Lokhande (1969) also found that the more modern a farmer was in his or her outlook, especially towards science, the more likely he or she was to adopt farm innovations.

The rate and likelihood of the adoption of an innovation, according to Rogers and Shoemaker (1971), is a function of five factors: (1) the *relative advantage* of the innovation over the system it supersedes; (2) the *value compatibility* with the needs and experiences of the receivers; (3) *complexity*, the extent to which the innovation is perceived as difficult to understand or use; (4) *trialability*, the extent to which the innovation can be tested for effectiveness; and (5) *observability* of the outcome which affects the probability that others will adopt the innovation.

If a person can be persuaded to try an innovation which then proves successful, there is a strong chance that he or she will continue using it. Obviously this step is the most difficult — although it actually is the third step. First, the individual must be made aware of the innovation. Second, the individual must go through an evaluation process. It is at this point that a decision will be made about whether or not to try it out. The role of *opinion leaders* or *key communicators* is important during the preliminary steps in this sequence. Singh and Pareek (1970) observed that a person who was higher in socio-economic status, superior in social preference, and who had greater contact with agents of change was a better adopter and also could influence the decision of the other members of his or her community. Research suggests that *change agents* (e.g., agricultural extension workers, family planning consultants) are most important for inducing awareness while personal contacts — friends and neighbours — are of greatest importance at the evaluation, trial, and adoption stages (Sawhney, 1967). Similarly, Rogers (1969) points out that external sources provide technical information and local sources affect the attitude toward the use of the innovation. Clearly, if the majority of the members of a community are opposed to the introduction of an innovation, only those who are able to resist the pressures to conform will be willing to give the innovation a try. Among these persons may be those with higher levels of achievement motivation (McClelland, 1961), a motive that is associated with a greater flexibility in problem solving as well as with more independence of thought and action.

Successful innovations are mainly diffused through social networks of interpersonal contacts via a "two-step flow of communication" (Katz, 1957). Early adopters tend to be the higher-status members of the community (opinion-leaders) who have many contacts over greater geographical distances than do those of lower status (opinion-followers). The friends of opinion-leaders are usually at similar positions in the social hierarchy and they take the new ideas away to disseminate in their own social context. The evidence suggests that this process of communication, through group or private conversations, has more impact than the mass media (Hagerstrand, 1965).

SUMMARY

(1) The most primitive form of social influence arises from the mere presence of others. Mere presence of an audience or coactors facilitates the performance of simple tasks and impedes performance on complex or novel tasks.

(2) Zajonc has postulated that arousal induced by the presence of others is innate. Cottrell has argued that the presence of others leads to arousal due to evaluation apprehension which is learned.

(3) Distraction-conflict theory claims that the arousal is due to conflict which arises from the need to attend to both the others present and the task.

(4) Social loafing refers to the reduction in the effort of individuals in group situations. Conformity is the modification of behaviour or attitudes to be consistent with social norms. Compliance is behavioural change which arises in response to requests or demands of others without underlying attitude change. Obedience is a response to a demand or a command of someone who is perceived as having some form of authority.

(5) Most conformity and compliance arise in response to majorities but consistent and confident minorities can affect majorities.

(6) Tactics employed to enhance compliance include the following techniques: the foot-in-the-door; the door-in-the-face; low-balling; improving the offer; and guilt inducement.

(7) A negative aspect of conformity is group think.

(8) Innovation requires open-minded individuals to think in non-normative ways. Innovations are diffused mainly through social contact from opinion-leaders to opinion-followers.

FURTHER READING

CIALDINI, R. (1984). *Influence*. New York: Morrow.

JANIS, I.L. (1982). *Groupthink: Psychological studies of policy decisions and fiascos*. Second Edition. Boston: Houghton Mifflin.

MILGRAM, S. (1974). *Obedience to authority*. New York: Harper & Row.

MOSCOVICI, S. (1976). *Social influence and social change*. London: Academic.

NAYAK, P.R. and KETTERINGHAM, J.M. (1986). *Breakthroughs*. Don Mills: Collier Macmillan Canada.

C·H·A·P·T·E·R S·E·V·E·N

Prejudice, Discrimination, and Sexism

This has always been a man's world, and none of the reasons hitherto brought forward in explanation of this fact has seemed adequate.
Simone de Beauvoir

No Chinaman, Japanese or Indian shall have his name placed on the register of voters for any electoral district, or be entitled to vote in any election.
Provincial Elections Act of B.C. 1895–1949

FOR REFLECTION

- What is prejudice? Can anyone be free of prejudice?
- Are stereotypes of people based on prejudice or reality?
- Who is most prone to prejudice?
- Is contact between groups a solution to prejudice?
- How do people react when they are the victims of prejudice?

OVER A PERIOD of three years in the 1980s, Eckville, a town of about 800 persons in central Alberta, captured headlines across Canada and beyond. It was revealed that for more than a decade, high school teacher James Keegstra taught a view of history based upon medieval mythology and pure bigotry regarding Judaism and the Jewish people. Although students, other teachers, and members of the community were generally aware of his views, he continued to teach prejudice, even after complaints were received. Only when the pressure of a few horrified parents and the attention of the media became too intense was Keegstra fired and his teaching license revoked. Eventually, he was charged and convicted in court for the felony of "wilfully promoting hatred against any identifiable group." The entire affair has been ably described by Bercuson and Wertheimer (1985) (see Box 7-1).

Prejudice is defined as a positive or negative attitude based on information or knowledge which is either illogical, unrelated to reality, or is a distortion of fact, and which is unjustifiably generalized to all the members of a group. Although prejudice can be either favourable or unfavourable, psychologists use the term most frequently in the negative sense.

Prejudices about individuals or groups are usually developed on the basis of perceived differences of one or more characteristics or traits. These differences may be physical, sexual, racial, national, or religious, or pertain to such particulars as language, accent, social status, or age. In other words, any characteristic that in some way sets a person or persons apart from others is potentially the basis for categorization which may ultimately lead to prejudice. The cues individuals use to discriminate among people are often superficial and trivial and may also be more or less important according to culture. For example, Triandis (1967) observed that race is more important in the United States than in Europe or Japan, while social class is more important to Japanese and Europeans than to Americans. Skin colour is emphasized more in the United States than in Hong Kong (Morland, 1969), and in Wales, Belgium and Québec, language is of considerable importance (Giles and Powesland, 1975). Moreover, "normal" behaviour in one culture may be misinterpreted by the members of other cultures. For example, unlike Whites, Blacks in the U.S. look away when someone is speaking to them, an action which may be attributed incorrectly to lack of interest, or hostility. Interpersonal distance may also pose problems: Arabs, for instance, who prefer small interpersonal spaces, may be perceived as "pushy" by North Americans, while Arabs may see North Americans as cold and aloof.

Also important, as Tajfel and his associates (e.g., Tajfel and Turner, 1979) point out, is that once persons have identified themselves as belonging to one group (the *in-group*) and others as belonging to another group (the *out-group*), regardless of the original reasons for this *social categorization*, they will *expect* to find *inter*group differences and will go so far as to create them if necessary (Dion, 1973). Moreover, they will likely assume that there is greater *intra*group similarity than may actually exist (see Chapters 8 and 12).

Although prejudice is an attitude and subject to the principles outlined in Chapter 4, there are a number of reasons why a separate chapter is devoted to this topic. First, prejudice initiates behaviours and actions which have clear and serious implications, not only for our daily lives, but also for the well-being of our society. In addition, a substantial body of experimental and observational evidence has been derived from investigations which have had prejudice as their primary focus.

It is also true that Canada with its multiculturalism and regional diversity needs to be especially sensitive to the effects of prejudice. Although it is generally believed that

TEACHING PREJUDICE: THE KEEGSTRA CASE

We do not have social psychological data on the episode, and we cannot engage in a long-distance analysis of the mind of James Keegstra, a high school teacher from Eckville, Alberta. However, careful journalistic and historical accounts can reveal much about the nature of prejudice, the bigot, and the social environment in which prejudice can go unchallenged. It is important to understand what Keegstra was teaching, how he was able to do so for so long, and what the impact was upon his students.

Keegstra taught an elaborate, internally consistent ideology which explained everything — once the basic

Keegstra and his reading material.

premises were accepted. His view of the world was rigid and dualistic. On one side was truth, virtue and Christianity; on the other was the "false, evil doctrine" of Judaism. Keegstra believed that the fundamental fact of past and present history was a powerful Jewish-dominated conspiracy whose aims were to promote sexual perversion and other sins, to destroy Christianity, and to dominate the world. The Jews were seen not only as different, not only stereotyped as undesirable, but as the enemies of Christianity. He assigned books purporting to "prove" that the Talmud, a collection of commentaries by rabbinical scholars on the Old Testament, sanctioned these goals and instructed Jews to cheat and murder Christians.

Of course, this led to peculiar interpretations of history. The Jews, according to Keegstra, had somehow caused the French Revolution, the United States Civil War, the Bolshevik Revolution in Russia, and World War I. The Nazi Holocaust was said to be a hoax designed to gain support for Israel, while the Jews secretly cooperated with Hitler! Non-Jews who also were seen as "enemies of Christianity" — Hegel, Lenin, the Rockefellers — were defined as Jews. Altogether, Socialism, Communism, and certain capitalist organizations, such as the Trilateral Commission and the International Monetary Fund, were part of the conspiracy. Jesus was not Jewish, and even the Jews were not really Jewish, but descended from a Mongolian tribe, said Keegstra.

Keegstra was considered by students and colleagues to be an effective teacher. It was said that he encouraged and stimulated his students to search for the "truth," and was simply presenting his own version of it. However, the students clearly received a double message. Keegstra told his students that the Jewish conspiracy controlled universities, publishing houses, and the media, and had thus "censored" history to suit their purposes. Only the anti-Semitic books and pamphlets provided by Keegstra had escaped this censorship; library sources were not to be believed. One student noted that Keegstra "had in books" everything that he said about the Jews.

Did Keegstra influence his students to adopt prejudice? Certainly, some rejected his views completely, and many went along skeptically in order to pass the course. However, as we have seen, behaviour change can lead to subsequent attitude change and, years later, some former students expressed anti-Semitic views at his trial. After the story became public knowledge, the students at Eckville High School were shown a graphic National Film Board documentary about the Nazi concentration/extermination camps and many were unimpressed. It is important to understand that there were no Jews in Eckville. Thus the students had no opportunity for the kind of daily, informal contact with them, which would enable them to test the reality of their beliefs. In many of the students' essays, we find not only the ideology but the terminology of anti-Semitism — "money thugs," "gutter rats," and "so-called Jews." One chilling quote from an essay (awarded 75 percent by Keegstra) will suffice: "If people would have been listening [to Hitler] he could have rid the world of Jews forever. It's funny how people never want to hear the truth" (cited by Bercuson and Wertheimer, 1985).

While parents, principals, and colleagues are usually unaware of the views a teacher expresses in a classroom, Keegstra's particular teachings were no secret in this small community. How was he able to continue for so long? First, we note that the stereotype of a fanatic as a raving, Hitler-type character is not valid. Keegstra was generally well-liked and respected by students, colleagues, and the community. Indeed, he had been elected to the town council several times, and to the position of mayor in 1980. He was known as a devout Christian, espousing values which were considered important in his community.

He also lived in a time and place where anti-Semitism was widely tolerated, if not encouraged. Anti-Semitism had deep roots in rural Alberta, going back to the Social Credit movement of the 1930s. Even after the story became public knowledge, Keegstra received considerable sympathy for his "freedom of speech," and two members of the ruling provincial Progressive Conservative Party expressed views about the Holocaust-as-hoax-theory which supported Keegstra's interpretation. Finally, we must consider the dynamics of the small town in which people know each other and are unwilling to disturb the calm. Bercuson and Wertheimer write: "Apathy, complacency and conformist pressure prevents most from speaking out against what was occurring. Others sympathized with Keegstra's worldview or found him to be a 'likeable villain' " (1985, p. xi).

Two courageous mothers, also residents of Eckville, resisted the pressure to conform and forced the issue out into the open and onto the agenda of school board officials. Leaders in the Edmonton Jewish community reacted strongly, unwilling to be passive victims of prejudice. Finally, the media, especially the CBC and the *Edmonton Journal*, focused public attention on what had happened and the real issues involved. Thus non-conformity by a minority and non-passivity by the victimized group, amplified by national attention, removed one bigot from a position of influence and roused Canadians from complacency about our "tolerant society."

Canada is a tolerant society, Jackson, Kelly and Mitchell (1977) argue that until Confederation in 1867, Canada was a relatively disorderly nation and the stage for many conflicts — between Canadians and Americans, English and French, Whites and Indians, and agents of different fur trading companies. Religion and race were the recurring factors in the violence. The murderous feud between the infamous "Black Donnellys" and other local families in Southern Ontario was exacerbated — perhaps even caused — by religious antagonism between Catholics and Orangemen. The "Shiners' war" (1837–1845) and the Northwest rebellion led by Louis Riel (1884) were fueled by race related conflicts. Even political slogans such as "Vote Conservative or your barns burn" were commonplace in the early days of the nation (Jackson *et al.*, 1977).

Examples of individual groups of people suffering prejudice are numerous: the Beothuk Indians of Newfoundland, who were pursued by bounty hunters; the Hutterites of Alberta, who were restricted in their purchase of land by government legislation; Blacks, who have been discriminated against in Nova Scotia and Southern Ontario (the Northern end points of the underground railroad from the United States); the Japanese, who were interned by the Canadian government during World War II, and who were feared and suspected by many. (In 1941 *Time* even ran an article called "How to tell your friends from the Japs" which offered hints such as, "Japanese are hesitant, nervous in conversation, laugh loudly at the wrong time.") Nor should we forget the largest membership in the Ku Klux Klan outside the United States could be found in the '30s around Estevan in Southern Saskatchewan, and that until 1954, schools in Nova Scotia were segregated. There have been cases of physical abuse of East Indians in Toronto and, recently, considerable anti-immigration sentiment has become evident throughout the country.

Even the likelihood of being executed for murder in Canada has been affected by prejudice. Avio (1987) reviewed 440 capital murder cases (1926–1957) and has discovered that English Canadians were significantly less likely than Native Canadians, Ukrainians, and French Canadians to be executed. In other words, English Canadians were more likely than others to have had their sentence commuted by the federal Cabinet. Those at the greatest risk were Native Canadians who, according to Avio,

Notice of a citizens' meeting appearing in the Penticton Herald *in 1920: Examples of individual groups of people suffering prejudice in Canada are numerous.*

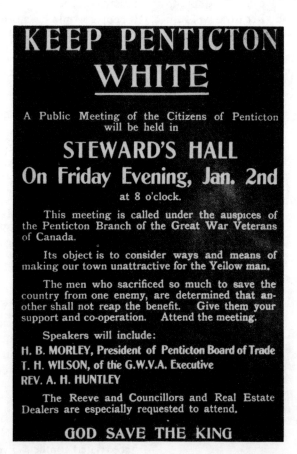

KEEP PENTICTON WHITE

A Public Meeting of the Citizens of Penticton will be held in

STEWARD'S HALL
On Friday Evening, Jan. 2nd
at 8 o'clock.

This meeting is called under the auspices of the Penticton Branch of the Great War Veterans of Canada.

Its object is to consider ways and means of making our town unattractive for the Yellow man.

The men who sacrificed so much to save the country from one enemy, are determined that another shall not reap the benefit. Give them your support and co-operation. Attend the meeting.

Speakers will include:

H. B. MORLEY, President of Penticton Board of Trade
T. H. WILSON, of the G.W.V.A. Executive
REV. A. H. HUNTLEY

The Reeve and Councillors and Real Estate Dealers are especially requested to attend.

GOD SAVE THE KING

were the subject of memoranda from the Ministry of Indian Affairs emphasizing that they needed "special deterrence." (It was also found that other things being equal, such as the type of crime committed, males were more likely to be executed than females.)

The discussion to follow will shed some light on the nature of prejudice, how it arises and is maintained, and will suggest some means by which it may be modified.

THE NATURE OF PREJUDICE

As with other attitudes, prejudice can be thought of as consisting of three components: cognitive, affective and behavioural.

The cognitive component

The beliefs which make up the cognitive component of prejudice are called *stereotypes* (see also Chapter 3). Stereotypes, a term coined by the journalist Walter Lippman (1922), are categories of cognitions concerning the members of a particular group. Lippman considered these cognitions usually to be simple, often to be over-generalized, and frequently to be inaccurate. However, more recent writers on the subject (e.g., Brigham, 1973) emphasized that stereotypes are not *necessarily* incorrect, illogical, or rigid and that they are not inherently different from other generalizations. In other words, generalizations about the attributes of *categories of people* — ethnic groups, women, immigrants and musicians — are called stereotypes, while generalizations about the attributes of other things — mammals, Canadian cities or the Great White North — remain generalizations.

Stereotypes may be *idiosyncratic* in that they are held only by a single person or they may be *general* and believed by many people (cultural stereotypes). No one can go through life without being aware of stereotypes and no one is completely free of them. In one sense, stereotypes serve a useful purpose in that they can help us deal more efficiently with our environment. For example, consider how complicated it would be if single trees had to be considered as seperate entities instead of being included in one general category. This process of categorization extends to our classification of people, so that just as we might say, "Trees are green" (which is not always true), we might say, "Jocks are not interested in art" (which is not always true). Stereotypes can refer to any characteristic of individuals including their appearance ("Homosexuals are effeminate"), their aptitudes ("Blacks are good dancers"), their personality ("Italians are gregarious"), and their attitudes ("The French are anti-semitic").

Stereotypes also help us distinguish among groups of people, a very useful thing to do. They also influence how we relate to people. For example, a series of experiments was carried out by Taylor and Gardner (1969) in which audio or video tape recordings of a French Canadian person were presented to Anglophone subjects. The French Canadian, speaking an accented English, described himself in ways consistent or inconsistent with the existing stereotype of that group. When asked later to form an impression of that person, subjects' impressions were influenced by the stereotype. Even when the French Canadian indicated that he was neither religious nor emotional, the stereotype prevented the subjects from fully accepting this information — although other information provided which was not relevant to the stereotype was taken at face value. Similarly, Grant (1978) presented Anglophone subjects with an Irish target person described as ambitious and scientific, two traits which are not usually part of the Irish stereotype. Subjects later rated the person as scientific and ambitious — as well as stereotypically happy-go-lucky, pleasure-loving, talkative. Thus stereotypes are not simply abstractions about group categories. They can act as "cognitive filters" through which we select what information to use, what to ignore, and how to interpret it.

There are three important questions concerning stereotypes: pervasiveness, persistence, and accuracy. Let us consider the question of pervasiveness first.

Pervasiveness   Do the residents of Newfoundland, Saskatchewan and British Columbia maintain similar beliefs about what the members of other groups are like? Unfor-

B · O · X   7 - 2

A PORTRAIT OF CANADIAN ETHNIC ATTITUDES

A detailed picture of Canadian ethnic attitudes is provided in an extensive survey published a decade ago (Berry, Kalin, and Taylor, 1977). Their study consisted of intensive interviews with a stratified sample of 2628 Canadians selected as representatives of different regions, ethnic groups, and socioeconomic levels. Events in the succeeding decade, such as a changing "mix" of immigrant groups, chronic unemployment problems, and controversies about refugee policies suggest that we must be cautious in interpreting these data. Nonetheless, they provide revealing and important documentation of attitudes in an evolving nation. Some highlights:

(1) Canadians were generally accepting of immigrants, including those from areas of the world toward which Canada had practiced discrimination. Acceptance was substantial toward immigrants with relatives in Canada (71 percent), those who were highly educated (79 percent) had skilled trades (79 percent), and those who were "coloured" (66 percent). However, the majority would not accept immigration "from communist countries" (32.5 percent — notwithstanding the Vietnamese "boat people") or "anyone who wants to immigrate" (24 percent). The majority disagreed with statements that immigration would cause English Canadians and French Canadians to lose their identity, that it would

affect the "purity of the Canadian race," or that it would cause there to be more criminals. However, considerable concern was shown about the effect of immigration on unemployment (53 percent) and its role in causing political problems (48 percent).

(2) Canadians generally showed tolerance toward the range of ethnic groups which constitute the Canadian population. However, preferences were evident. English Canadians and French Canadians were most favourable to each other and to Northern Europeans (Germans, Dutch, Scandanavians), less to Southern and Eastern Europeans (Italians, Greeks, Hungarians) and still less to East Indians, Chinese, Blacks, Spanish, and Portuguese.

(3) Attitudes toward multiculturalism (see Table 7-1) revealed more acceptance than rejection of the idea of ethnic diversity as a positive feature of Canadian society. However, there was considerable variation in these attitudes. For example, subjects were generally positive toward some kinds of multiculturalism, such as community centres and folk festivals, but not to others, such as radio and television programs in other languages, or the teaching of "heritage" languages in public schools.

tunately, there is little information on this question but it would be unwise to assume, for example, that stereotypes about Ukrainian Canadians in Manitoba, where they reside in large numbers, would be the same as the stereotypes in Cape Breton where many locals have probably never met a member of this group. A study conducted in the United States (Allport and Kramer, 1946) revealed that in spite of the almost total absence of Blacks and Jews in one part of South Dakota, attitudes towards these groups were more negative there than they were among a sample of individuals in one of the Eastern states. In Canada, an extensive investigation by Berry, Kalin and Taylor (1977), using a national sample, found regional differences in attitudes and stereotypes towards a number of different ethnic groups (see Box 7-2). They found substantial regional differences in how various ethnic groups were perceived. For example, respondents from the Prairies were more negative about Canadian Indians

(4) Greater prejudice and less acceptance of immigration and multicultural programs was found among older, less educated subjects, among French Canadians, and Canadians of Russian and Ukrainian backgrounds.

The authors conclude: "Respondents in our survey showed a reasonably high level of overt tolerance for ethnic diversity and a general acceptance for multiculturalism as a social fact. However, a certain level of covert concern and reluctance to accept ethnic diversity was also uncovered" (p. 248).

TABLE 7–1
Multicultural ideology in the total sample (n = 1835)

General items	% Disagree	% Neutral	% Agree
1. Canada would be a better place if members of ethnic groups would keep their own way of life alive.	36.0	17.4	46.7
2. If members of ethnic groups want to keep their own culture, they should keep it to themselves and not bother other people in the country.	38.0	13.1	48.9
3. There is a lot that Canadians can gain from friendly relations with immigrants.	8.6	10.5	81.0
4. Having lots of different cultural groups in Canada makes it difficult to solve problems.	45.3	18.9	35.8
5. It would be good to see all the ethnic groups in Canada retain their cultures.	18.7	16.9	64.4
6. It is best for Canada if all immigrants forget their cultural background as soon as possible.	61.6	12.3	26.1
7. People who come to Canada should change their behaviour to be more like us.	34.5	15.8	49.7
8. The unity of this country is weakened by ethnic groups sticking to their old ways.	47.0	16.8	35.7
9. A society which has a variety of ethnic groups is more able to tackle new problems as they occur.	23.1	24.4	52.5

SOURCE: Berry, Kalin and Taylor

than were those from other parts of Canada. Residents of the Atlantic Provinces were most unfavourable toward German Canadians and those in the West were most positive. Jewish Canadians received the most positive evaluations from respondents in Ontario and the least positive evaluations from the Maritimes. Regional differences also appeared for the other groups under consideration, Chinese, Ukrainians, and Italians.

Persistence How stable are stereotypes? Do they change readily or do they last over long periods of time? As with attitudes in general, stereotypes are often modified (see Ehrlech, 1973). Obvious examples can be found in the characterization of Japanese or Germans during World War II and today, Russians, depending on the state of the cold war, Arabs as the price of petroleum increases or decreases, or Iranians before and during the Khomeini era. As might be expected, stereotypes about the out-group become more negative in the face of overt conflict, such as war, but other, less aggressive forms of conflict — economic and social — can have similar effects. Thus, when the economic situation is favourable and jobs are plentiful, people tend to be considerably more tolerant than when jobs are scarce. For example, at the turn of the century there was a large influx into California of Chinese who were easily absorbed into the work force. At that time, local newspapers described them as "sober, inoffensive and law-abiding." However, over a very short period, economic conditions deteriorated and the Chinese began to compete for jobs with native Californians. The same Chinese were now described as "criminal, clannish and mentally and morally inferior." Not surprisingly, governments facing increasing unemployment usually curtail immigration. And, although Canadians generally are tolerant toward immigration, there are some indications that if economic conditions deteriorate and unemployment increases, attitudes toward immigration and immigrants may become more negative (Berry, Kalin and Taylor, 1977). In fact, in 1987 a national survey published in *The Globe and Mail* showed that in all regions of Canada, a majority of respondents agreed that there was too much immigration into Canada. Individuals with a university education and those with professional and administrative jobs did not support this position but 74 percent of skilled and semi-skilled workers, those most vulnerable to unemployment, preferred to have immigration curtailed. The complete data are found in Table 7-2.

TABLE 7–2
Public opinion on immigration into Canada

Do you agree strongly, agree somewhat, disagree somewhat or disagree strongly that overall, there is too much immigration into Canada?

	Total %	Atlantic %	Quebec %	Ontario %	West %	18-29 %	Over 60 %	University Educated %	Professionals Administrators %	Skilled Semi-Skilled Workers %
Agree strongly	39	40	41	35	42	37	43	13	15	49
Agree somewhat	26	24	26	25	29	30	27	22	22	25
Disagree somewhat	23	22	22	25	21	20	22	40	40	14
Disagree strongly	9	9	10	11	5	10	6	23	20	9
No opinion	3	5	1	3	3	3	3	3	3	3

SOURCE: Environics Research Group, 1987

Trait	Katz and Braly (1933)	Gilbert (1951)	Karlins, Coffman and Walters (1969)
Superstitious	84	41	13
Lazy	75	31	26
Happy-go-lucky	38	17	27
Ignorant	38	17	27
Musical	26	33	47

TABLE 7–3
Percentage of respondents assigning traits to Blacks

Three key studies in this area were conducted in the United States by Katz and Braly in 1933, by Gilbert in 1951, and by Karlins, Coffman and Walters in 1969. In all three investigations subjects were asked to select, from an extensive list of traits, those which best described the members of each of ten ethnic groups — Americans, Chinese, English, Germans, Irish, Italians, Japanese, Jews, Negroes and Turks. The traits most frequently assigned to Blacks by Katz and Braly's subjects in 1933 were "superstitious," "lazy," "happy-go-lucky," "ignorant," and "musical." The percentage of the subjects who assigned these traits can be compared (in Table 7-3) with the percentages obtained in the two later experiments. These results indicate a favourable shift away from two of the more negative traits, "superstitious" and "lazy." The percentage of subjects selecting "ignorant" declined as well, but not in such a systematic fashion. One trait which more and more people endorsed over the 36-year interval was "musical."

Is it reasonable to infer that stereotypes of Blacks in the United States have lost their impact? This is not necessarily the case. First, these data were obtained from university students, and do not necessarily represent the stereotypes held by the general population. Second, we may know that the application of certain negative characteristics has declined, but we do not know if equally derogatory characteristics have taken their place. Third, it is possible that a social desirability bias may have had some effect (see Chapter 2). In the two more recent studies, a substantial number of subjects complained that they could not make the generalizations requested of them. We do not know in how many instances the responses reflected the person's "true" feeling or whether, because the public has become more sensitized to this issue, they were responding "as expected," that is, in a socially desirable manner.

This possibility, that the stereotypes haven't changed — only that the willingness to verbalize them has — was tested by Sigall and Page (1971). They replicated the Karlins *et al.* study with an additional condition. They connected some of their subjects to a "bogus pipeline" (see Chapter 4). These subjects, who believed that if they lied, they would be detected, gave considerably more negative evaluations than the other subjects.

The accuracy of stereotypes   It has been argued that because stereotypes seem both persistent and pervasive they must, at least to some extent, be true (the *kernel of truth hypothesis*). However, there are a number of grounds on which this notion often can be refuted:

— the simultaneous existence of incompatible stereotypes concerning the same group of people, e.g., "Jews are pushy"; "Jews are seclusive";
— the labelling of the same behaviour in positive or negative terms depending

on which group exhibits it, e.g., "The Dutch are frugal and careful about their finances"; "Scots are miserly and penny-pinching";

— changes in the stereotype not accompanied by any change in the target group e.g., "Immigrants are energetic, reliable workers"; "Immigrants work excessively and take jobs away from Canadians";

— the application of the stereotype to all members of the group without consideration of individual differences. For example, the Welsh are stereotyped as being good singers. Yet, examination of the residents of Wales would reveal a distribution of singing competence and, no doubt, some mediocre singers.

Nevertheless, in some instances it seems possible to verify the accuracy of stereotypes. It is true, for example, that Indians often score below the national average on standard intelligence tests, that Jews often belong only to their own clubs, and that many Blacks excel at sports and music. However, this does not mean that Indians are innately unintelligent, that Jews are cliquish and that Blacks have a built-in sense of rhythm. What is usually ignored by the prejudiced person is the situational pressure which prejudice creates to make stereotypes come true.

For instance, if it is believed that Indians are genetically inferior, then little effort will be directed toward satisfying their educational needs and the attempts made may be thwarted by cultural bias. Moreover, the typical intelligence test, having been standardized on middle-class Whites, may yield little relevant information. All these and other types of treatment will guarantee that, at least by the dominant group's standards, Indians appear intellectually "below-normal."

Situational pressure may have also been operating in the past when Jews were refused admission to so many clubs that they formed their own associations. It was then argued that staying together was actually what they preferred. And sports and entertainment have been two occupational fields in which Blacks have had a reasonable opportunity for success. It is therefore a logical and rational step for them to enter these professions. (In spite of this inroad, Blacks continue to be under-represented as football quarterbacks and coaches. And compared with Whites, Black U.S. servicemen were over-represented in the war in Vietnam. Does this mean that they were innately more competent at this sort of activity?)

An additional factor which serves to validate stereotypes is the *self-fulfilling prophecy*. Members of minority, or out-groups, are frequently confronted with the stereotypes maintained by the majority, or in-group, about them. Ultimately, they may come to believe that the stereotypes are true, and behave accordingly. For example, because females are often stereotyped as inadequate at mathematics, the motivation of women to learn mathematics is likely to be reduced and they may avoid, whenever possible, academic courses and careers which require some sort of numerical background.

Measuring stereotypes Although stereotypes are the beliefs of individuals, the traditional methods of measurement result only in averages obtained from groups (Brigham, 1971). For example, the check list originally used by Katz and Braly and most other investigators asks the subjects to select the traits "most typical" of a given group. It would be possible, using this trait selection procedure, for half of a group of subjects to agree on three traits and for the other half to agree on three different traits. The social stereotype would then be composed of six traits but would not represent the stereotype of anyone in the group (Brigham, 1971). Brigham (1971) found that the traits identified as being most typical were also perceived as being present in less than half of the target group. In other words, it seems that people do not use "most typical" and "present in the majority" synonomously. Brigham (1971, 1973) suggested that stereotypes could be better measured by asking subjects to estimate the percentage of the members of a group who exhibit a given trait.

Extending Brigham's original idea, McCauley and Stitt (1978) developed a measure of stereotypes called the *diagnostic ratio*. Subjects in a study they conducted were asked, for example, to estimate both the percentage of Germans who are efficient and the percentage of all the world's people who are efficient. The diagnostic ratio in this instance was:

$$\frac{\text{the percentage of Germans who are efficient}}{\text{the percentage of all the world's people who are efficient}}$$

Whether the group was stereotyped on this or another trait would be indicated by a diagnostic ratio significantly larger or smaller than 1.0.

In this case it was found that the subjects estimated that 63.4 percent of Germans are efficient and that 49.8 percent of the world's people are efficient, resulting in a diagnostic ratio of 1.27. Similarly, the diagnostic ratio for "extremely nationalistic" was 1.59, while the diagnostic ratio for "superstitious" was .72. These results indicate that part of the German stereotype is that Germans are more efficient, more nationalistic and *less* superstitious than other people.

It is also possible to determine whether the *kernel of truth* hypothesis applies to any example of stereotyping. The kernel of truth hypothesis states that stereotypes may have some basis in reality but that perceptual processes are likely to exaggerate real differences between groups (Levine and Campbell, 1972). The hypothesis can be tested by calculating a *criterion ratio* in addition to the diagnostic ratio.

The criterion ratio is the estimated percentage of the group with the characteristic divided by the *actual* percentage of the group with the characteristic (obtained from empirical data). If the kernel of truth hypothesis applies, the actual percentage of the group with the characteristic should be higher than the estimate of the percentage of the population with the characteristic. Since the numerator in each ratio is the same, this means that the diagnostic ratio should be larger than the criterion ratio.

With this in mind, McCauley and Stitt investigated seven characteristics of Blacks: the percentage who completed high school; the percentage of illegitimate children; the percentage unemployed; the percentage who were victims of violent crimes; the percentage on welfare; the percentage of families with four or more children; and the percentage of families with a female head of household. It was found that the subjects were stereotyped for all these characteristics — but, when the diagnostic ratios were compared with the criterion ratios they were either not different or were significantly *less* extreme. In other words, Blacks were seen as more likely to have these characteristics than the general population, an observation which is supported by government statistics. However, the comparison of diagnostic and criterion ratios contradicted the kernel of truth hypothesis. The subjects, rather than having exaggerated ideas about the proportion of Blacks exhibiting the attributes, frequently *underestimated* the actual percentages. In no case did a diagnostic ratio exceed a criterion ratio.

Illusory correlation and stereotypes

It has been suggested (Hamilton and Gifford, 1976; Hamilton, 1979; Hamilton, 1981; Hamilton and Rose, 1980; Crocker, 1981) that many instances of stereotyping arise and are maintained through the operation of *illusory correlations*. An illusory correlation is an information-processing bias whereby the association between characteristics or events is overestimated (see also Chapter 3). For example, Hamilton and Gifford (1976) had subjects read short descriptive statements about the behaviour of members of two groups, A and B. There were twice as many Group A statements as Group B statements but, in both groups, for every four undesirable statements, there were nine desirable statements. In other words, the *proportion* of desirable to undesirable behaviours was the same for the two groups but the absolute frequency was different. This meant that the co-occurrence of undesirable acts such as, "Allan, a member of Group B, dented the fender of a parked car *and* didn't leave his name," was less frequent for Group B.

Evidently the subjects paid more attention to these relationships in Group B because they judged the members of Group B more negatively and attributed more undesirable behaviour to the "minority" group than was actually the case. In other words, the subjects in this study overestimated the number of co-occurrences of the negative behaviour in the minority group B. Once such an association has been made, subsequent information will be biased in the same direction. For instance, if the belief has been acquired that Francophones are more conservative risk-takers than Anglophones then, even if there is no actual difference between the two groups, this expectation will influence subsequent judgments about the extent of risk-taking in each group. It has been suggested that this is so because disconfirmations of the stereotype are learned more slowly and/or forgotten more quickly than neutral or confirming information (Hamilton and Rose, 1980).

To summarize this cognitive approach to stereotypes, once a stereotype has been established — often on the basis of an inaccurate estimation of the covariation of attributes or characteristics — it will be maintained, owing to biased processing of subsequent information. In other words, "Believing is seeing."

The affective component

Stereotypes do not exist in isolation. They are accompanied by *emotions* which are usually expressed in terms which can be distributed along a continuum ranging from the intensely negative, e.g., contempt, disgust, hate, to the very positive, e.g., admiration, liking, identification.

Feelings such as these may not be verbalized but there may be some arousal of the sympathetic nervous system and the increased physiological activity can be measured by the galvanic skin response (GSR). Such responses can be used, at least for research purposes, to determine whether there is an emotional reaction, even though the subject may be unable or unwilling to overtly express it. In this way, Porier and Lott (1967) were able to demonstrate that individuals who scored high on a scale of ethnocentrism (the extent to which people believe in the superiority of their own ethnic or cultural group) showed a greater GSR in the presence of Black, compared with White, research assistants, than did those who scored low on the scale.

Behaviour

It is not long ago that Black members of the Hamilton Tiger Cats (football team) were refused haircuts in a major hotel and Blacks in Dresden, Ontario, were refused service in local restaurants. Fortunately, the frequency of overt discrimination has decreased, in part, perhaps, because of safeguards such as the Canadian Bill of Rights and more active prosecution (see Box 7-3). No longer do signs appear in Halifax restaurants stating, as they did during World War II, "Sailors and dogs not admitted." In fact, recently, a Nova Scotia Human Rights board ordered that souvenir buttons

B · O · X   7 - 3

DO LAWS AGAINST INCITING HATE CAUSE MORE HATE?

In Canada there are penalties for inciting hatred against members of a minority group. Such laws are controversial, for some argue that they infringe upon free speech, while others counter that free speech does not give anyone the right to cry "Fire!" in a crowded room. One key issue is how the enforcement of these laws influences the level of prejudice in a society. Some have argued that prejudice should be reduced because society has clearly defined it as wrong and outlawed the bigot. Others are concerned that the bigots receive undue publicity and are granted a public forum for their views, which seems to make them a matter for legitimate debate.

In 1985, Ernst Zundel, a Toronto publisher, was tried and convicted of one count of transgressing section 177 of the Criminal Code of Canada: "Everyone who wilfully publishes a statement, tale, or news that is known to be false and that causes or is likely to cause injury or mischief to a public interest is guilty of an indictable offense and is liable to imprisonment for two years." Zundel's press churned out material which extolled Nazi ideology, portrayed Zionism as a racist and manipulative creed, and claimed that the Holocaust was a hoax perpetrated by Jews to extort money from West Germany and garner political support around the world. One passage spoke of "vicious, greedy and militant people who call themselves Jews . . . as God's Chosen People." Ironically, the trial of James Keegstra (see Box 7-1) began six weeks later.

At this time, a study of public opinion revealed some interesting shifts in public sentiment (Weimann and Winn, 1986). Only about half of Canadians knew why Zundel had been convicted, casting some doubt on the proposition that the trial was an effective publicity stunt for him. Moreover, those who were most sympathetic to his position were least aware of the trial. When asked whether their attitudes toward Jews had changed as a result of the trial, 24 percent said they had become more sympathetic, and only 2 percent said they were less sympathetic (the others were unchanged or uncertain). The vast majority of people continued to believe that 6 million Jews had died in the Nazi Holocaust and that the Jews were blameless. Thus the trial did not incite anti-Semitism, although the data reveal that such prejudice persists among a minority of Canadians.

And yet, a "climate of doubt" appeared. Respondents were asked whether they believed the trial affected the attitudes of other Canadians. Those who were aware of the trial were twice as likely as others to attribute doubt to Canadians as to the historical record of the Holocaust. That is, while the trial increased knowledge and sympathy for Jews and this terrible and tragic crime, it also led people to believe that their friends and neighbours had changed in the opposite direction. In the long run, such an outcome may create the impression that prejudice has considerable social support and could conceivably become its own self-fulfilling prophecy.

B·O·X 7-4

STORE REBUFFS INDIAN GIVEN CANADA AWARD

VANCOUVER (CP) — Dorothy Maquabeak Francis, 65, of New Westminster, B.C., was refused service at a jewelry store last week, the same week she was named to the Order of Canada.

Mrs. Francis, a Saulteaux Indian, said in an interview that the store proprietor told her he had never served "people like you" in his 11 years at the store.

She told the owner that her race had been in Canada for more than 1,000 years and "we've had to learn to serve to survive."

Mrs. Francis, a mother of eight, grandmother of 33, and great-grandmother of five, was given the award for her cultural native work in British Columbia and the Prairies.

She grew up on the Waywaseecappo reserve near Russell, Man., and her early married life was spent on a reserve just outside of Broadview, Sask.

"We had no rights, we couldn't do anything without a government permit — sell our cattle, buy farm equipment, go after more education for our children — so we struck out on our own," she said.

"We packed all our pots and pans, our bedding and clothes and the youngsters into a half-ton and moved to Regina. But nobody would rent a house to Indians with so many kids so we ended up pitching a tent on the outskirts of town."

She founded the first Friendship Centre there and later worked in Winnipeg as an arts and crafts manager and as a family counsellor.

Mrs. Francis said native people do not have the chance to grow up and mature on reserves and as wards of the government they do not learn to be independent.

She said she tells young Indians to keep their identity and not be talked into trying to turn white overnight. (*The Globe and Mail*, January 25, 1978)

proclaiming, "I'm a big mouth Cape Bretoner — so kiss me," be destroyed on the grounds that the message was offensive to a group of Maritimers (Hunter, 1987).

Does this mean that prejudice in Canada has declined, or is it simply that its outlets are more subtle and indirect? Certainly discrimination is difficult to eradicate (see Box 7-4). Most university housing bureaus are well aware of the difficulty many foreign students (especially the "visible minorities") have in locating accommodation even when there is no shortage of rooms or apartments.

Discrimination may occur at the level of interaction between individuals, as our previous examples have indicated, or it may be *institutionalized* and supported by either implicit or explicit regulations. For instance, apartheid as practiced in South Africa is a case of discrimination required by law. It has been argued that the language and educational laws enacted in Québec in the 1970s also are examples of legal support for discrimination (see Chapter 11). Of course, many of us have forgotten that the Manitoba government passed a law in 1890 which abolished French as an official language and prohibited education in that language, a law which has only recently been struck down by the Supreme Court of Canada.

Much more discrimination undoubtedly occurs through covert, subtle means. Thus an informal "rule" in a personnel office, although never made explicit, may effectively place a quota on the number of minority group members who are hired or promoted. To test this possibility, Henry and Ginzberg (1985) created four teams of job applicants with one White "applicant" and one Black "applicant" on each team. The members of each team were matched for age and sex so that there were two teams of men, one older and one younger team, and two teams of women, one older and one younger. Job openings were then selected from the classified ads in a major Toronto newspaper. The next day, both members of a team applied for a number of these jobs; in each case, the Black member went first. The applicants received 36 job offers of which 27 went to the White person only. In just nine instances was the Black person preferred.

In an extension of this study Henry and Ginzberg had "applicants" with West Indian, East Indian, and Canadian accents phone about the possibility of employment. They report that 52 percent of all the employers contacted discriminated against the members of racial minority groups who called, either by telling them the job was closed when it was still open to Whites, or by screening them but not screening White applicants.

Aside from the problems faced by its minorities, Canada faces another, more insidious, problem — discrimination against Canadians *by* Canadians who believe that Canada is second-rate. The problems that Canadians encountered in gaining access to jobs in their own universities eventually led the government to insist that applications from Canadians and permanent residents be given first priority. Now, only when it is demonstrated that no qualified Canadian candidates are available can foreign applications be entertained.

It has been suggested that a similar negative bias extends to the hiring of Canadians, especially quarterbacks, in the Canadian Football League. For example, in 1979, former University of Western Ontario quarterback Jamie Bone appealed to the Ontario Human Rights Commission that the Hamilton Tiger Cats had denied him a tryout *because he was a Canadian* (and therefore perhaps less competent). The Commission agreed with him and the Tiger Cats were compelled to give him a tryout to become a member of the team. Similarly, French Canadians, even though they are no less competent than other Canadians, are underrepresented in the National Hockey League (Lavoie, Grenier and Coulombe, 1986) (see Box 7-5).

Clearly discrimination can take many forms and can be disguised in many ways. The expulsion of the Japanese Canadians from the west coast during World War II is a case in point. Because they were considered a security risk, these citizens were rounded up on short notice, their homes and goods, including their fishing boats, were seized, and they were relocated in often-secluded areas of British Columbia, Alberta, and Ontario. The comments of one Japanese victim express the resentment which many must have felt:

> Don't think the authorities weren't waiting for us when Pearl Harbor came. Within two hours things began to happen. . . . I got a call from Navy Headquarters to report at 9 o'clock next morning. The Commander was very frank. He said, 'Mr. Suzubi, we were caught with our pants down,' and he said that all fishing vessels would have to be turned over to the authorities right then.
>
> To this day I don't know what they thought about those fishing boats . . . . They were small boats, made of wood. We had no radar, no radio, no echo sounder . . . . But try and convince these people that we were not spies, we were just ordinary fishermen. As far back as the late 1890's they had determined that one day they would kick the damn Japs off the river. There was one common statement you could hear along the river: 'There's only one damn good Jap and that's a dead Jap' (Broadfoot, 1978).

Yet there was not a single instance of breach of security on which to base this action. There was, however, a history in British Columbia of hostility towards Asians

IL LANCE ET COMPTE — BUT HE'D BETTER BE GOOD!

In the intensely competitive world of professional hockey, it is difficult to believe that teams would discriminate on the basis of ethnic or linguistic group. Names such as Dionne, Perrault, Savard, Trottier and Goulet attest to the French Canadian presence in the game. And yet, a recent study presents disturbing evidence of discrimination in the National Hockey League (NHL) itself (Lavoie, Grenier and Coulombe, 1986).

They compared English Canadians and French Canadians (as well as Europeans and the few U.S. citizens) on a number of measures of performance, including goals and points per game, shots on goal, and the plus-minus ratio (ratio of goals scored by the player's team compared with opponents while he was on the ice). On these indicators of excellence, and over two seasons, French Canadians consistently performed better than English Canadians. We have no reason to believe that French Canadians as a group are better equipped biologically to check, stickhandle, or shoot a puck. Hockey at the minor or junior levels is not more popular in Québec than in the rest of Canada. What accounts for this finding?

The important clue is that French Canadians make up only about 12 percent of the Canadian players in the NHL, although over twice that proportion of Canadians report French as their maternal language. Thus, while the French Canadian players as a group perform more effectively, they are significantly underrepresented in the league. Obviously, while the stars are accepted, the average or less-than-average English Canadian hockey player has a better chance than his French Canadian counterpart of making it in the NHL. The authors trace this situation back to the initial scouting and recruitment of players. Few of the scouts speak French, and most share a stereo-typed belief that French speaking players are too small, too light, and reluctant to fight. Therefore, proportionally fewer Francophone minor league players are recommended for major league tryouts than their Anglophone counterparts.

and it is of interest that the most active agitators for the removal of the Japanese citizens were rival Canadian fishermen to whom the government eventually sold the Japanese boats and equipment at give-away prices. The Japanese Canadians have never been fully compensated for the government's action (for detailed descriptions see Adachi, 1976; Broadfoot, 1977). Similar motives may have been behind the expulsion of Asians, who controlled a large portion of the economy, from Uganda when Idi Amin gained power and for some of the difficulties Chinese citizens are currently experiencing in Malaysia.

Too often, discrimination is based on the belief that certain races are genetically inferior to others — with disturbing consequences. The so-called "medical experi-ments" conducted by the Nazis were rationalized in this manner, and it is probably no accident that the first human trials of the contraceptive pill were carried out on women in Puerto Rico. More recently, an experiment has been brought to light in which the United States Public Health Service allowed 200 men to go untreated for syphilis in order to study the disease and its side effects. All the men were Black (see Box 7-6).

BLACKS DIED IN U.S. SYPHILIS EXPERIMENT

WASHINGTON (AP) — During a 40-year federal experiment, a group of syphilis victims was denied proper medical treatment for the disease. Some participants died as a result, but survivors are getting whatever aid is possible, the U.S. Public Health Service says.

The experiment, conducted by the PHS, was designed to determine through autopsies what damage untreated syphilis does to the human body.

Of about 600 Alabama black men who originally took part in the study, 200 or so were allowed to suffer the disease and its side effects without treatment, even after penicillin was discovered as a cure for syphilis. Treatment then probably could have saved or helped many of the experiment participants, PHS officals say.

They contend that survivors of the experiment are now too old to treat for syphilis, but add that PHS doctors are giving the men thorough physical examinations every two years and are treating them for whatever other ailments and diseases they have developed.

Members of Congress reacted with shock to disclosure yesterday by The Associated Press that the PHS experiment on human guinea pigs had taken place.

Senator William Proxmire, (D, Wis.), a member of the Senate appopriations subcommittee which oversees PHS budgets, called the study "a moral and ethical nightmare."

"It's incredible to me that such a thing could ever have happened," he said in a statement.

Senator Edward Kennedy, (D, Mass.), chairman of the Senate health subcommittee, said through a committee spokesman that he deplores the facts of the case and is concerned about whether any other such experiments exist.

The syphilis experiment, called the Tuskegee Study, began in 1932 in Tuskegee, Ala., an area which had the highest syphilis rate in the United States.

Treatment in the Nineteen Thirties consisted primarily of doses of arsenic and mercury.

Of the 600 original participants in the study, one third showed no signs of having syphilis; the others had the disease.

According to PHS data, half the men with syphilis were given the arsenic-mercury treatment.

Men were persuaded to participate by promises of free transportation to and from hospitals, free hot lunches, free medical treatment for ailments other than syphilis and free burial.

Seventy-four of the untreated syphilitics were still alive last January.

Syphilis is a highly contagious infection spread through sexual contact. If left untreated it can cause blindness, deafness, deterioration of bones, teeth and the central nervous system, insanity, heart disease and death.

In 1969, the PHS, Centre for Disease Control in Atlanta, which has been in charge of the Tuskegee Study, reviewed records of 276 men.

It found that seven men had died as a direct result of syphilis. Another 154 died of heart failure, but CDC officials say they cannot determine how many of those deaths were caused by syphilis or how many additional deaths may have been linked to the disease.

PHS officials responsible for initiating the Tuskegee Study have long since retired and current PHS officials say they do not know their identity.

"I think a definite moral problem existed when the study was undertaken, a more serious moral problem was overlooked in the postwar years when penicillin became available but was not given to these men, and a moral problem still exists," said Dr. J.D. Millar, chief of the venereal disease branch of CDC. (*The Globe and Mail*, July 26, 1972)

Reverse discrimination

As society becomes more sensitive to racial issues, many people will resist expressing prejudicial attitudes. In fact, some may go so far as to behave in a manner which implies that they are considerably more tolerant than they really are. This process, called *reverse discrimination*, has been demonstrated in a number of studies by Dutton and his colleagues (Dutton, 1971, 1973; Dutton and Lake, 1973; Dutton and Lennox, 1974). In the first experiment, either Black or White couples entered a restaurant in Vancouver or Toronto. In each case the man was wearing a turtleneck sweater in violation of the restaurant's dress code requiring ties for men. Only 30 percent of the White couples were seated in spite of the rule, while 75 percent of the Black couples were let in. It is evident that the persons in charge went out of their way to appear non-discriminatory. Accordingly, Dutton (1973) hypothesized that minority groups perceived by the public as being most discriminated against would experience the most reverse discrimination. A survey had indicated that middle-class Whites in Vancouver felt that Blacks and Native peoples were the focus of considerable discrimination but Asians were not. Dutton then asked Indians, Blacks and Asians to solicit donations for a charity and found, as hypothesized, that more money was given to the Indians and Blacks than to the Asians.

It should be noted that this effect appears to be most common among educated middle and upper-middle-class Whites who are especially concerned not to appear intolerant. Dutton and Lake (1973) selected 80 students who had been identified as having a low degree of anti-Black prejudice and who valued equality. In the laboratory, through means of false feedback, half of these students were made to feel that they might be prejudiced; the rest of the students acted as controls. After the laboratory session all the participants were approached by either a White or a Black panhandler. Those subjects who had been led to doubt their tolerance towards Blacks gave significantly more money to the Black panhandler. The experimental manipulation had no effect on the amounts given to the White panhandler.

The non-discriminatory behaviour described in these studies is relatively trivial. But once a person has demonstrated tolerance by such a *token* act, he or she may be less likely to exhibit reverse discrimination the next time. In a study which addressed this issue (Dutton and Lennox, 1974) three groups of students again were made to doubt their tolerance towards Blacks. Subsequently, one group was approached by a Black panhandler, the second by a White panhandler, while the third was not panhandled. The next day they all were asked to give some of their time for an "interracial brotherhood campaign." Those students who had been panhandled by the Black volunteered less of their time than those in the other two groups. These results suggest that reverse discrimination may be restricted to relatively unimportant behaviours and may have the counterproductive effect of discouraging real and long-lasting tolerance.

Ethnicity

Some of the findings obtained by Berry, Kalin and Taylor (1977) emphasize that in many instances, ethnicity interacts with other factors to determine the extent of discrimination. In particular, the status of the individual and the type of relationship which is entered into appear to be important to people. In their study, respondents were asked to indicate on a scale from 1 to 7 the extent to which they would be willing to interact with immigrants in both a business relationship and a friendship relationship. In addition, the immigrants were classified as representing four occupations, two of high status (dentist and teacher) and two of low status (shoemaker and plumber). Not surprisingly, the results indicated that in friendship relationships individuals of high status would be preferred over those of low status and that French and English Canadians would be preferred as friends over immigrants. However, the data concerning business relationships were more complicated. It was found that the respondents were willing to do business with English and French Canadians regardless of their status, but they expressed much greater willingness to seek the services of a low-status immigrant (shoemaker, plumber) than of high-status immigrant (teacher, dentist). This result implies that while Canadians are happy to admit well-educated, high-status immigrants into the country, they may be reluctant to use their professional services.

In a survey conducted in Toronto, Henry (1978) observed that not only did the ethnicity of the target relate to the extent of discrimination, but that the ethnicity of the source was also important. Among her respondents, individuals from Italy, Greece and Portugal were least likely to wish close relationships with the members of other groups. As Henry points out, these are people who are strongly committed to their own ethnic origins, suggesting that as in-group identity increases social distance from other groups also increases.

One factor that may contribute to in-group identity is the number of members of the group in a given location. Kalin and Berry (1979) observe that a very high concentration of a given group may be detrimental to national unity by leading to cultural encapsulation of that group and, therefore, to greater ethnocentrism. If this is so, increased ethnocentrism should challenge the multicultural philosophy of the Canadian social system. The *multiculturalism hypothesis* states that *positive* feelings towards members of other groups will be related to how secure and comfortable a person feels

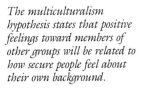

The multiculturalism hypothesis states that positive feelings toward members of other groups will be related to how secure people feel about their own background.

with his or her own cultural identity and background. This proposition was tested by Lambert, Mermigis and Taylor (1986), using Greek Canadians in Montreal as subjects. They measured attitudes toward their own group, other ethnic groups, cultural assimilation, and cultural maintenance. Data also were obtained on the degree of ethnocentrism, religiosity, and amount of formal education. It was found that the respondents took a strong stand on the need to maintain Greek culture and language and, compared with a number of other ethnic groups (English Canadians, French Canadians, Jewish Canadians, Black Canadians, Italian Canadians and Portugese Canadians), rated their own group most positively. In addition, social contacts with members of their own group were preferred over contacts with members of the other groups. The other groups were rated most favourably by those Greek Canadians who were the most culturally secure and who were the most ethnocentric. However, these same individuals were *less willing* to interact with members of those groups. The Greek Canadians who were least ethnocentric, and better educated, were most willing to associate with members of the other groups.

These results do not fully support the multiculturalism hypothesis. Cultural security and well-being, although correlated with a positive evaluation of other groups, was not associated with a willingness to socialize with them. Lambert *et al.* suggest that further research may reveal education as the critical factor in decreasing ethnocentrism while maintaining security and increasing the likelihood of social interaction between groups.

Relationships among the three components

As we have noted (Chapter 4), the various components that make up an attitude may be incongruent, or not in agreement. Prejudice is no exception. A crucial factor in prejudice appears to be the affective component; often it is the component that best predicts behaviour. Thus, while an individual may intellectually accept that Native people are not inherently less capable or lazier than Whites, he or she may nevertheless avoid them whenever possible. However, in the case of people who are racist or bigoted in the extreme sense, attitude components are more likely to be highly correlated. This type of person not only will have strong negative feelings but usually will have a rather extensive set of negative stereotypes, some of which may be quite bizarre. For instance, a person who was charged with assaulting a Sikh in Toronto expressed the view that "Pakis" worshipped a number of animal gods, and ritually slaughtered goats in their living room gardens during their religious festivals. Their living rooms, he claimed, were filled with earth and posed a danger to the structure of the buildings they lived in (Pittman, 1977).

ACQUISITION OF PREJUDICE

Innate or acquired

Hebb and Thompson (1968) have described incidents which suggested to them that the higher animals — chimpanzees and human beings — have an inherent fear of the unfamiliar and unusual. If Hebb is correct, though, as yet, there is no strong empirical support for his contention, it would be reasonable to argue that this tendency could form the basis for the development of prejudice, which is directed toward objects perceived as being in some way different. It is generally agreed that people are anxious or fearful in situations which they do not understand. Perhaps the negative emotions directed at the members of an out-group have their roots in the spontaneous arousal generated by a new or novel stimulus.

It has been shown that infants as young as three months of age are able to distinguish between the face of their mother and that of a stranger. Although at this age their reactions to the unfamiliar stimulus do not show signs of avoidance or fear, by about the age of nine months, aversive reactions often do appear, frequently to the mother's embarrassment when, for instance, the unfamiliar stimulus is the child's grandmother.

It also is possible that a finding first reported by Zajonc (1968a) can be used to support Hebb's view (see also Chapter 8). Zajonc demonstrated that there is a relationship between the frequency of occurrence of an event, or the number of times an individual is exposed to a stimulus, and the extent to which the stimulus is subsequently found to be attractive. This occurs in the absence of any additional information or interaction. Initially it was thought that this "mere exposure" effect happened regardless of whether a subject's initial attitude toward the stimulus was negative, positive, or neutral but later research (Perlman and Oskamp, 1971) indicates that only positive or neutral stimuli are enhanced. The evaluation of negative stimuli is not only unlikely to improve, but may deteriorate further.

Whether, in fact, there are inherent predispositions which could form the primitive rudiments of prejudice remains to be confirmed. There is, however, little doubt concerning the importance of *learning* in the development of prejudice. The first setting in which this learning takes place is the home.

Learning

Role of the parents   Parents have a powerful influence, not only because they play a role in what the child learns from day to day, but because this learning forms the foundation for all subsequent experience, both familial and extra-familial. In order for prejudicial attitudes to be acquired, children must first become "racially aware." That is, they must be able to distinguish themselves from others who are, in some way, different. Racial awareness has been shown to be present in children as young as three years of age and, in one study, it was found that 25 percent of the four-year-old children observed were already expressing strong race-related values (Goodman, 1964).

It appears that the child passes through eight stages in the acquisition of prejudicial attitudes (Katz, 1976). These are:

(1) *Early observation of racial cues*. In order for the process to begin, the child must be able to identify cues, such as skin colour or facial features, associated with another race or group.

(2) *Formation of rudimentary concepts*. Once the child expresses an awareness of these cues they can be labelled (e.g., "Oh yes, that colour of person is Chinese") and learning can begin (e.g., "I don't want you to play with him").

(3) *Conceptual differentiation*. The child begins to learn the boundary conditions of

a particular concept, e.g., "black person" — who can be included in the category and who can be excluded from it. This can be a difficult task. For example, the colour of a "black person" can vary considerably and is rarely actually black.

(4) *Recognition of the irrevocability of cues*. Although the world changes as the child matures, racial and similar cues remain stable.

(5) *Consolidation of group concepts*. This process, which begins at about five years of age, involves continued practice at correctly labelling and identifying members of particular groups. The end-product is an accurate concept of a group.

(6) *Perceptual elaboration*. Once concepts are consolidated there may be some "fine-tuning." Intergroup differences may be accentuated and intragroup differences down-played. This stage takes place while the child is still in elementary school.

(7) *Cognitive elaboration*. There is some question whether a child's early responses to members of outgroups can properly be called attitudes, mainly because they are not very complex. However, experience during the school years results in elaboration of the early orientation so that the term "attitude" may be properly applied.

(8) *Attitude crystallization*. The final stage in which the attitudes become a part of the child's "cognitive repertoire" and are not likely to be "rethought." These attitudes will be carried on into adolescence and adulthood.

A number of the steps in this sequence occur before the child's horizons have expanded much beyond the home. In these early years, the parents have sole control over the child's rewards and punishments. During the waking hours one or the other of them is in almost continuous contact with the child so that there are many opportunities for habits of thought and action to be acquired.

Social learning can occur in a number of ways and under a variety of conditions. Three types of learning which are usually distinguished are: instrumental conditioning, classical conditioning, and modelling. Each has different implications for the acquisition of prejudice.

Instrumental conditioning   One of the basic principles of instrumental (or operant) learning is that any behaviour or response which is followed by a reinforcement will be strengthened, that is, the probability that the response will occur again will be increased. Most of the reinforcements associated with the acquisition of prejudice are likely to be verbal or non-verbal indications of approval. For example, if a child says, "Those people are dirty," and the mother smiles and responds positively, then the child is likely to repeat this remark, make it part of his belief system and also generalize it to other similar-looking people.

Classical conditioning   Since Pavlov's first experiments with his salivating dogs, the classical conditioning paradigm has become part of almost everyone's psychological repertoire. In the original situation, an unconditioned stimulus (UCS), food, was used to elicit salivation in a dog. This UCS was then paired for a number of trials with the sound of a bell, the conditioned stimulus (CS). Subsequently, it was found that the CS, in the absence of the UCS, elicited salivation. This process is illustrated in Figure 7-1.

A similar process may account for at least some portion of the emotional or evaluative aspect of prejudice. For example, suppose a White child is playing with an East Indian child and the White child's mother, noticing this interaction, rushes out, yells at her child to stop, slaps her, and drags her into the house. This treatment is the

FIGURE 7–1
Classical conditioning

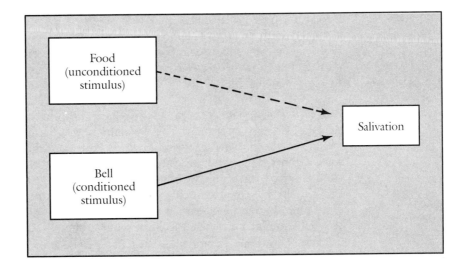

unconditioned stimulus which arouses hostility, fear, and anxiety in the child. The conditioned stimulus is the other, East Indian, child. If this situation is sufficiently traumatic and is repeated either with the same child or with other out-group children, ultimately the sight or presence of such a conditioned stimulus will be sufficient to elicit at least some portion of the negative feelings which were aroused in the original situation. This process is illustrated in Figure 7-2.

Modelling Not all learning involves the active intervention of a rewarding or punishing agent. Often a child will exhibit behaviour or express ideas which have not been deliberately taught but which have been observed being performed by others. Models, usually individuals with whom the child identifies, e.g., parents or teachers, have been shown to be highly effective in teaching attitudes and prejudice (Bandura, 1965). The process is both subtle and insidious because the child is not a direct participant in the event and the model may not be aware of the information that is

FIGURE 7–2
*Classical conditioning and
the development of prejudice*

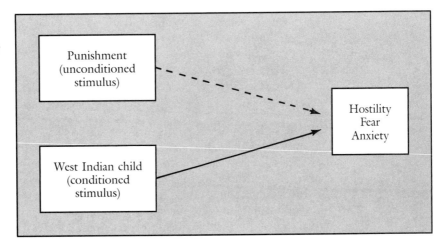

being transmitted or its effect. It also should be kept in mind that what the model *does not do* may be just as important as what the model does do. Thus, avoiding an Asian cashier in a supermarket or commenting that "you should always count your change after those people wait on you" may each communicate similar information to the observing child.

The prejudiced personality   Parents who have authoritarian traits teach their children that status is very important. These parents typically use harsh punishment, do not tolerate any hostility or aggression by the child toward them, act in a cold and impersonal manner, and withdraw love in order to maintain "proper" behaviour. Thus the child is forced to submit without question to his or her superiors and to suppress the hostility which is aroused naturally under these frustrating conditions. At the same time, by defining what is different as inferior, the parents give the child an acceptable outlet for pent-up feelings — out-groups.

These individuals, identified as having an *authoritarian personality*, also are likely to be prejudiced and ethnocentric. In this case, prejudice is incorporated in a belief and value system which forms a personality pattern first identified by Adorno, Frenkel-Brunswick, Levinson, and Sanford (1950). Adorno and his colleagues were initially interested in anti-Semitism but later broadened their perspective to include attitudes toward ethnic groups in general. As part of their study, they constructed a number of scales to measure anti-Semitic attitudes, ethnocentrism and authoritarianism. However, it was the concept of the "authoritarian personality" which attracted the most attention and which stimulated numerous subsequent research projects (e.g., Christie and Jahoda, 1954; Cherry and Byrne, 1977). It was found that individuals who can be characterized as authoritarian are likely to be highly prejudiced and to have a rigid personality in which the world is perceived in categorical black/white, superior/inferior, us/them terms. Moreover, these individuals are usually highly conventional and cynical. Designed to reveal such characteristics, one of the tests which emerged from the work of Adorno *et al.*, the F scale ("F" stands for fascism), includes the following items:

> Obedience and respect for authority are the most important virtues children should learn.
> Human nature being what it is, there will always be war and conflict.
> What the youth needs most is strict discipline, rugged determination and the will to work and fight for family and country.
> There is hardly anything lower than a person who does not feel a great love, gratitude and respect for his parents.
> The wild sex life of the old Greeks and Romans was tame compared to some of the goings-on in this country, even in places where people might least expect it.
> No sane, normal, decent person could ever think of hurting a close friend or relative.

People with authoritarian personalities may also have considerable pent-up hostility. One manifestation of this hostility is called *scapegoating*. Scapegoating may occur when individuals are frustrated by conditions or situations they cannot directly control or change, e.g., "the economic situation" or "the government." When the source of the frustration is vague and difficult to locate, tension and hostility may be aroused and *displaced* onto a convenient out-group. This out-group is then blamed for the discomfort and difficulties being experienced. Much of the treatment of the Jews during the Nazi regime in Germany may have been an example of scapegoating. Jews were blamed for all the economic woes that the Germans experienced after World War I and into the 1930s. A more recent example may be the frequently heard claim that immigrants are taking jobs away from Canadians.

The proportion of individuals who can be described as extreme authoritarians is not large but is often compensated by their vociferousness. Among them may be found individuals who belong to neo-Nazi movements, distribute hate literature, publish newsletters warning us that psychiatry is a Communist plot, insist that J.D. Salinger's *Catcher in the Rye* or Margaret Laurence's *The Diviners* be removed from school curricula and libraries, or (as happened in Manitoba) have teachers fired who suggest that their students read unconventional newspapers like the *Georgia Straight*. In some instances, the concerns of such individuals border on the ludicrous. For example, a womens' association in Texas demanded that *Robin Hood* be removed from the local library because it glorified Communism. (He took from the rich and gave to the poor.) In 1981, the trustees of a school district in Ontario removed John Steinbeck's *The Grapes of Wrath* from high school classrooms to review it for its "suitability." (The Nobel prize winner was in good company, however. Among other works removed during the purge were *The Apprenticeship of Duddy Kravitz* by Mordecai Richler, *Sons and Lovers* by D.H. Lawrence, and *Waiting for Godot* by Samuel Beckett.)

An additional serious social consequence of the authoritarian personality has been suggested by Bray and Noble (1978). They discovered, in a mock-jury experiment, that high authoritarians reached guilty verdicts more frequently and imposed more severe punishments than low authoritarians.

Parents, for better or worse, eventually give up their role as the major influence in children's lives. As children grow older their world increases in size. They begin to interact with peers, enter school, begin to read and spend some of each day watching TV. All of these situations may contribute to the formation or reinforcement of prejudice.

Teachers and schools

While parents are the child's first authority figures, other people — teachers, for instance — also exert considerable influence. Like everyone else, teachers have their prejudices and, although they may try to be as tolerant as possible, there are many opportunities in the classroom for less-than-desirable attitudes to be communicated to the pupils. For example, how will children in multiracial classrooms be treated? How will children who are either the butt or the source of racial slurs be handled? Certain courses, such as geography and history, give the teacher the opportunity to impart *correct* information about ethnic, racial, or other groups — but, there are dangers here as well. Does the teacher give equal time to both sides of an issue? Can attitudes toward Communism be held in check during a discussion about recent Russian or Chinese history? And, if not all topics can be covered in the time allotted, how is a decision made about what material should be omitted?

Until recently, when some of the worst examples started to be eliminated, many textbooks contained biased and inaccurate information about ethnic and other groups. For example, the Canadian Indian was frequently depicted as an alcohol-addicted, primitive savage with only a rudimentary social organization (conversely, the depiction was highly sentimental). Texts also typically relegated males and females to traditional roles. (In some cases, modifications of texts and other books designed to correct these biases have been overzealous, creating some backlash. Activist/journalist June Callwood recently castigated the Canadian publishing industry for producing "sanitized" books reflecting a "pious" history that never was.) Bias has also been evident in the *context* in which material is presented to the student. For instance, how is the student affected when his or her arithmetic problems involve only white collar business applications? Why is it that union officials or plumbers never do any calculations? The context within which problems are set can convey to students the attitudes and values of the instructor or text author.

The Media

Textbooks are only a step away from the mass media: magazines, newspapers, radio, television, and films. North American children spend a lot of time watching TV. In fact Lambert and Klineberg (1967) have reported that by the age of ten, children obtain most of their information from TV and school rather than from their parents. There are numerous ways in which attitudes can be influenced by the media—through selective or biased reporting in newspapers or by the repetition of stereotypes in television shows.

Visible minorities rarely appear in television commercials or magazine advertising in Canada. A survey conducted in Canada by Lateef and Bangash (1977) found that television commercials observed over a four-day period involved 2064 persons of whom only 48 were visible minority members. If the commercials of charitable organizations (e.g., CARE) and those from the United States are omitted, the percentage of visible minority members drops to .09 percent of the total commercials on television.

Six years later, in 1983, Moore and Cadeau (1985) analyzed the content of 1733 Canadian television commercials. They found that 88 percent of the voice-overs were done by men, fewer than 2 percent of the commercials included elderly people as central characters and, if elderly people were involved, they were most likely to be men. Visible minorities appeared in fewer than 4 percent of all commercials. Moreover, Aronoff (1974) has reported that when the elderly appear in television programs, they are portrayed more negatively than other age groups.

One television series, *All in the Family*, popular in the '70s, stimulated considerable discussion. Some people argued that by allowing the major character, Archie Bunker, to express his bigoted views, similar views held by audience members would be strengthened. A research study conducted by Vidmar and Rokeach (1974) provides a tentative response. They theorized that (1) viewers would get out of the program what they expect to get (*selective perception*); and (2) bigots and non-bigots would differ in the frequency with which they watch the show (*selective exposure*). The subjects in this experiment, Canadian adults and American adolescents, were first administered an attitude scale and then divided into two groups, "prejudiced" and "non-prejudiced." Next their reactions to *All in the Family* were compared. The major findings revealed that those in the prejudiced group liked bigoted Archie more than his liberal son-in-law, Mike, and that they admired Archie's values. However, the two groups did not differ in their overall enjoyment of the show. The experiment also indicated that those who watched the program more often also were likely to score higher on the measure of prejudice. It is important to note that the overall frequency of television viewing in general was not higher among the prejudiced than the non-prejudiced group, suggesting that the prejudiced were more attracted to this particular program. Pending further evidence, we can conclude that such programs may increase or strengthen prejudice depending on the predispositions of the viewers. That Canadians might not respond in the same way as Americans was found in another study (Surlin and Tate, 1976) which showed that Americans in Athens, Georgia, thought the *All in the Family* episodes were more humorous than did viewers in Saskatoon.

Peer groups

Peers exercise more influence over attitudes as the child matures. By adolescence, peers are likely to be more influential in many respects than a child's parents. In the early years, parents exercise considerable control over children's relationships and, since playmates are likely to come from similar socio-economic backgrounds, attitudes encountered in the home are likely to be reinforced and strengthened outside of it. But as children grow older, their contacts become more diverse and they are less apt to be influenced by parental standards. Like parents, the members of peer groups are effective in influencing attitudes and behaviour because they offer information, reward conformity, and punish non-conformity. This pressure to conform, which continues throughout a person's life, is powerful and hard to resist. Thus, expressing ideas and beliefs which the group considers to be correct is just as important as wearing clothes which the group considers to be appropriate. Indeed, Pettigrew (1961) argues that in the United States most prejudice is based on conformity. One welcome aspect of this theory is that unlike prejudice associated with deep-seated personality patterns, prejudice based on conformity may be more flexible. If the group norm changes or if individuals join new groups with different views, then their attitudes will likely shift in the same direction.

THE REDUCTION OF PREJUDICE

Although discrimination is a behaviour and can be controlled by laws, prejudice obviously cannot be dealt with in the same way. However, it is possible to make individuals more tolerant, sometimes deliberately through education or indirectly, through, for example, appropriate intergroup contact. In this section we consider some of the conditions which may lead to the reduction of prejudice.

Intergroup contact

It often is assumed that increased interaction between the members of various groups will enhance mutual understanding and good will. However, it is not only the frequency, but also the nature of the contact that is important. In order for prejudice to be decreased through *interethnic* contact, a number of conditions must be met (Amir, 1976):

(1) The members of each group must be of equal status (e.g., same income group or similar occupations) or the members of the minority group should be of a higher status than the majority group members.

(2) There must be a favourable climate for intergroup contact, and the contact must be of an intimate rather than a casual nature. Also, the contact must be rewarding and pleasant.

(3) The two groups should have a mutual goal which requires interdependent and cooperative action.

Rarely are all these conditions likely to be present in actual interethnic situations. Tourism, for example, has been advocated as a means of improving national as well as international understanding but experienced at its worst and most typical, from the windows of a bus, none of these conditions will be met. In this connection, Clément, Gardner and Smythe (1977) conducted a study which was designed to test the "contact hypothesis." Their subjects were 379 Anglophone grade eight students from London, Ontario. One hundred and eighty-one of these students went on an excursion to Québec City while the rest (198) constituted a control group and remained at home. All the students were administered a battery of tests before and after the trip. Those who visited Québec were subsequently divided into two groups on the basis of the amount of interaction they reported having with Francophones while in the city. It was found that the high contact group had more favourable attitudes than either the low contact or control groups towards French Canadians and learning French as a second language. In fact, the low contact group had a *less favourable* attitude toward learning French after the trip than before. Of some importance, however, is the observation that those students who reported more frequent contact had more favourable attitudes *before* the trip. Accordingly, Clément *et al.* have concluded that favourable attitudes following unstructured excursion programs might characterize only those individuals holding favourable attitudes *before* their participation in the program. A similar outcome was reported by Smith (1955) who administered a battery of tests including a measure of ethnocentrism, to individuals who were about to visit Europe. He warns that an extremely nationalistic and ethnocentric person who visits another culture for the purpose of enlarging his or her view of the world is likely to become more negative rather than positive.

Ideally, intergroup contact should disconfirm the negative stereotypes associated with the out-group. However, as Rothbart and John (1985) propose, this will not

Toronto's annual "Caribana" celebrates West Indian culture and always draws thousands of spectators. Can such events improve relations among ethnic groups?

FIGURE 7–3
Factors influencing the susceptibility of stereotypic traits to disconfirmation

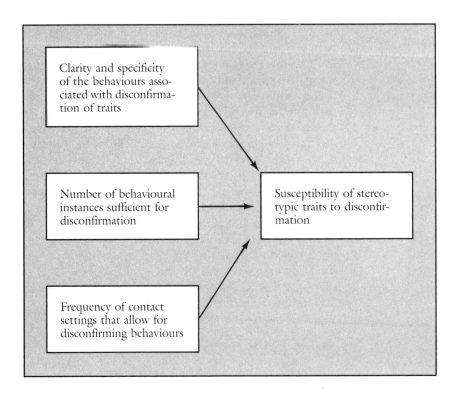

always happen because the susceptibility of a stereotype to disconfirmation (or confirmation) is a function of three factors, as illustrated in Figure 7-3. These are:

(1) *The clarity of the potentially disconfirming behaviours.* Some traits ascribed to outgroups such as "messy" or "talkative" are associated with clearly observable behaviours and can therefore be easily confirmed or disconfirmed. However, the behaviours that would confirm or disconfirm stereotypes such as "devious" and "untrustworthy" are more difficult to specify and to observe. These and similar stereotypes would be least likely to be modified by interethnic contact. Unfortunately, they also are the stereotypes with the most serious social implications.

(2) *The number of relevant observations.* Some ascribed characteristics are more susceptible to change than others. For example, Rothbart and John (1985) report that the more *un*favourable a trait, the *fewer* the number of instances required for confirmation, and the *greater* the number of instances required for disconfirmation. As they note, favourable stereotypes are difficult to acquire but easy to lose, but unfavourable stereotypes are easy to acquire and difficult to lose. This observation implies that if intergroup contact is infrequent, negative stereotypes are not likely to change.

(3) *The frequency of intergroup contact.* Obviously, there must be an occasion during which confirming or disconfirming actions can occur, but the situation will also determine what *type* of behaviour is likely to be expressed. In most social situations talkative or friendly behaviour is likely to be evident, but if the stereotype includes characteristics such as "heroic" or "cowardly," a situation may never arise in which these traits can be confirmed or disconfirmed.

If some modification of a stereotype does occur as a result of intergroup contact, how likely is it that the change will generalize to other members of the same group? Unfortunately, studies (e.g., Cook, 1984) indicate that the extent of generalization may be limited, and not extend beyond the situation or to other members of the group. This is so, Rothbart and John (1985) argue, because the individuals involved in the contact may not be perceived as "exemplars" of the larger category. The representative of the out-group is likely to be considered atypical. Thus a male could express positive views about the ability of a female friend and at the same time reveal traditional stereotypic beliefs about the incompetence of women. If confronted with this apparent contradiction, the reply would likely be, "Well, she isn't a typical woman!" Allport (1954) called this phenomenon "re-fencing." When categories conflict with the evidence, special cases are excluded and the category is kept intact.

It also is evident that even when the opportunity for contact exists, many people will not take advantage of it. Only 5 percent of the respondents in a study conducted by Henry (1978) in Toronto who reported that they had Black friends had met them in their own neighbourhood. Similarly, Henry cites a survey carried out in Britain which found that 25 percent of the respondents who had non-White neighbours had never talked to them. On the other hand, it appears that contact is not a necessary condition for tolerance. In Henry's study, almost 44 percent of the very tolerant had experienced no contact with minority group members. Her data, showing the relationship between contact and prejudice, can be seen in Table 7-4.

TABLE 7–4
Prejudice and social contact: How subjects described themselves

	None or little contact	Close or very close contact
Very prejudiced	82 *	18
Somewhat prejudiced	64.7	35.3
Somewhat tolerant	48.3	51.7
Very tolerant	43.5	56.4

*expressed as percentage of sample

Intergroup anxiety   One reason for the lack of contact between members of in and out-groups is *intergroup anxiety* (Stephan and Stephan, 1985). This anxiety arises from the anticipation that contact could result in one or more of four types of negative consequences. These are:

(1) *Negative psychological consequences for the self.* People often know very little about the values, norms, non-verbal behaviours, and expectations of the members of other groups. This ignorance about the "subjective culture" (Triandis, 1972) may lead to fear of embarrassment or of being made to appear incompetent in intergroup interactions. These fears can be quite realistic. For example, if an orthodox Hindu is present at a meal, can beef be served to the other guests? Or, should one bow and, if so, how low, when introduced to someone from Japan? Such concerns lead to anticipation of discomfort and awkwardness in these types of interactions. One resolution is not to get involved.

(2) *Negative behavioural consequences for the self.* In-group members also may believe that they will be taken advantage of or exploited, especially when they harbour stereotypes about the out-group as devious and dishonest. In extreme cases, they may fear that they will be physically abused.

(3) *Negative evaluations by in-group members*. Members of the in-group may be afraid that if they interact with the out-groups, they will be rejected by their own group.

(4) *Negative evaluations by out-group members*. Fear of rejection, of ridicule, or of disapproval by the out-group if contact is attempted is also a possibility.

Obviously there must be an opportunity for contact to occur. Such opportunities will be related to the number of members of a particular ethnic group who reside in a given location. This observation is confirmed by Kalin and Berry (1979a,b) who found that attitudes were more negative where the concentration of an ethnic group was low — where there was a very high concentration of a group, attitudes were more positive.

We do not know from these data to what extent tolerance results from the contact itself. It may be that individuals who are tolerant are more willing to interact with out-group members. However, since the prejudiced avoid associating with the members of other groups, opportunities for effective contact simply do not occur for them. This is a problem that interferes with any attempt, deliberate or otherwise, to modify the attitudes of people; we are often preaching only to the converted.

It is likely that if we could somehow, without using force, propel prejudiced individuals into the appropriate social milieu, some positive change might then occur. Cook (1970) has carried out extensive laboratory research in the United States which supports this contention. He employed a simulation game in which Black and White women interacted over a one-month period. All of the Black women and half of the White women were confederates of the experimenter. The real subjects, all White, initially had very negative attitudes towards Blacks. (Their attitudes had been measured in a different context so there would be no connection with the study.) The game required the participants to cooperate and to be in close contact in an equal-status situation. If they won, they shared the rewards. There were also breaks during each two-hour session so that the participants had the opportunity for more social

and personal contact "off the job" during which the Black confederate led the conversation to race-related issues. She also interjected personal comments which emphasized her individuality and distinguished her from the stereotype. In comparing the subjects' attitudes before and after this experience, it was found that about 40 percent of these White women, compared with only 12 percent of those in the control group, became more tolerant towards Blacks. Obviously, this sort of contact is effective — even though a majority of the White women didn't change and, inexplicably, a small number became more prejudiced.

While it would be expensive and difficult to mount a project of this sort to reduce prejudice among the general public, it would be quite feasible to create similar situations in schools where many opportunities exist for students to work together on cooperative educational projects. Weigel, Wiser and Cook (1975) and DeVries and Edwards (1974) tried this approach and found that those students who worked together in small, interdependent, inter-ethnic groups were more likely to later engage in cross-ethnic helping behaviour and to have greater respect for each other than those students from racially homogeneous groups.

Some support for this outcome emerges from a study conducted by Reich and Purbhoo (1975) in Toronto. They measured the attitudes of children attending an ethnically heterogeneous school and a more homogeneous school and found that the former were considerably more tolerant of ethnic diversity. Because they lived in the neighbourhood and had no choice about which school they attended, pre-selection bias is not likely to have seriously influenced this outcome.

We should be aware that competition often leads to interpersonal hostility and that teachers frequently use competition as a means of enhancing the motivation of their students. Maybe this is a dangerous tactic for, as will be discussed, Sherif and his colleagues (1961) were able to deliberately increase and decrease intergroup hostility and rivalry at a summer camp by manipulating the amount of competitive and cooperative interaction which took place (see Chapter 13).

Education Teachers, instruction, and the classroom milieu are part of the global process of education. There have been numerous studies which have examined the relationship between *level* of education and prejudice. The outcome of this research has been generally consistent in showing that as education increases, prejudice decreases. The data gathered by Henry (1978) in Toronto indicate this quite clearly (see Table 7-5). However, you will recall from our discussion of correlations in Chapter 2 that we cannot conclude from these data that education necessarily leads to tolerance. There are many factors associated with school attendance which might

TABLE 7–5
Level of education and prejudice: How subjects described themselves

| | Education attained | | |
	Primary	Secondary	University
Very prejudiced	17.4*	17.9	3.5
Somewhat prejudiced	53.7	33.6	19.8
Somewhat tolerant	23.6	36.4	37.9
Very tolerant	5.3	12.11	38.8

*expressed as percentage of sample

account for the relationship other than education *per se*. For example, individuals with more education are, on the average, more intelligent, know more facts, are more flexible thinkers, and come from the higher socio-economic levels of society than do persons with less education. Also, extra-curricular activities which offer the potential for social conformity — clubs, sports, discussions — may be the critical factor, rather than the formal education experience.

Research which could delineate clearly the variables in the educational process affecting prejudice is difficult to do and few, if any, experiments dealing with this question are completely satisfactory. For example, it is not sufficient to demonstrate, as some studies have done, that first-year university students are more prejudiced than those in their final year. Final year students are three years older, more highly selected, and have had three years more extra-curricular experience than new students. As a matter of fact, the effect may simply be due to a higher failure or drop-out rate among the less tolerant. Better investigations take a longitudinal approach and follow the same individuals from one point in their educational career to a later one. These studies also reveal an increase in tolerance over time but, again, are unable to specify the precise variables which may account for the change. It might be due to increased knowledge, improved analytical ability, more heterogeneous social contacts, and so on. Nevertheless, we can state in a general way that education, inside or out of the classroom, has a positive effect on the development of tolerance.

In Canada, the relationship of second language learning to attitudes has also received attention as an education issue. Much of the research has been carried out by Lambert and his associates at McGill (e.g., Lambert *et al.*, 1963; Gardner and Lambert, 1972). The social-psychological effects of bilingualism are discussed in detail in Chapter 11 on communication but it should be mentioned here that individuals who have acquired a second language seem to have more positive attitudes towards other cultural groups than monolinguals *if* their initial orientation was *integrative* rather than *instrumental*. Individuals who learn a language for instrumental reasons do so because they think it will be useful to them, while those with an integrative approach perceive the language as one part of a culture which interests them. It has also been shown that Anglophone parents with an integrative orientation have positive attitudes towards Francophones even though they may not know any representatives of that group (Gardner and Lambert, 1959).

The relationship of such attitudes and integrative motivation to competence in another language has been found to hold in locations as diverse as Maine, Louisiana and Connecticut in the United States as well as in the Philippines (Gardner, Gliksman and Smythe, 1978).

THE VICTIMS OF PREJUDICE

While much has been written on how prejudice develops and is maintained, as well as how the targets of prejudice and discrimination are selected, considerably less attention has been devoted to the reactions of the victims of prejudice and discrimination. How do minority group members respond and how do they defend themselves? Over 30 years ago Gordon Allport (1954) identified more than 15 possible consequences of being victimized. Among these are: withdrawal and passivity; clowning; militancy; aggression against own-group; and self-hate. Allport also suggested that these reactions could be encompassed within two general categories: *intropunitive* and *extra-*

punitive. Intropunitive defences are those which involve self-blame, while extrapunitive defences place the blame on others. Allport argues that minority group members who are intropunitive will be hostile to their own group, whereas those who are extrapunitive will be loyal to their own group and aggressive toward other groups.

Extending Allport's approach, Tajfel and Turner (1979) postulate three types of responses. The victimized can simply accept their situation with passivity and resignation (although not without resentment), they can try as individuals to break free and "make it" in society, or they can attempt collective action and improve the status of the group itself. Building on these alternatives, a five-stage model has been outlined showing how groups deal with prejudice and a disadvantaged position in society (Taylor and McKirnon, 1984). Notice that the model is attributional, and accounts for how the victimized may both interpret and respond to their situation:

(1) *Clearly stratified group relations*. This is a historical situation of deeply entrenched relationships of power and subordination between groups. The power difference is so clear and absolute as to be essentially unchallenged. In some cases, the subordinate group members react with self-hate (Allport, 1954), downgrading themselves as members of the "inferior" group and attributing their own inferior status to the fact of belonging to that group. Thus, in another era, Blacks may have attributed their poverty to inherent racial inferiority and French Canadians to their inability to speak English, and women may have attributed restrictions in their lives to their "inability" to compete with men.

(2) *Emergence of an individualistic ideology*. A society which has become an industrialized economy places great value on education, skills, and achievement. In this "meritocracy" it becomes increasingly awkward to discriminate against whole groups, and more focus is placed on the individual *per se*. How can such societies explain the persistence of status differences between groups? Attributions also shift from group membership in and of itself to the ability, effectiveness, and responsibility of individuals. Thus, if women do not gain their share of high-status jobs, it is not because of their inherent characteristics as women, but their lack of ability, motivation or training. Disadvantaged group members perceive their situation in a similar light.

(3) *Individual social mobility*. Certain group members try to "pass," to be accepted into the society of the dominant group. Where possible, they may change their names, language, culture, or religion in order to penetrate the dominant group. Or they may accommodate the dominant norms in every way possible, though unable to shed the recognizable characteristics of race or sex. Success or failure has now become almost entirely a matter of personal characteristics, particularly among the exceptional members of the disadvantaged group who have some chance of success. Notice that this situation implies an attributional conflict: a disadvantaged position is explained by group membership, yet an individual effort to succeed and "pass" provides an escape from the group.

(4) *Consciousness raising*. Of course, the dominant group "needs" a few successes from the out-group to support its ideology of individual responsibility and the myth of equal opportunity. Thus, some succeeed through tokenism, but many more fail and the disadvantaged status of the group remains unchanged. Over time, attributions within this group shift again, as the majority of those who cannot be accepted and successful in society realize that the fault lies neither in their inherent characteristics as group member nor as individuals. It now becomes apparent that their status in

society is an injustice, has been determined collectively, and can only change through collective action. Attribution for failure is attached to a group again, but now the in-group is blamed rather than the out-group.

(5) *Competitive intergroup relations*. Collective action by the disadvantaged group to improve their position can succeed only at a cost in power and privilege to the dominant group. Thus it will be resisted in some way, and a competitive relationship will endure until some sort of rough equality is obtained or until individuals in the group revert to individualistic striving. Notice an interesting divergence between attributions about the past and the future: "our" disadvantaged position was due primarily to "them" but "our" future success must depend on "us."

The theorists argue that groups proceed through these stages in sequence, coming ultimately to the point at which self-blame is futile but collective action is necessary. In terms of attributions, the implications of prejudice are particularly crucial. Recall the self-serving bias, in which individuals attribute their own successes to themselves and their failures to external factors. Because our identity as individuals is influenced so powerfully by our identity as members of groups — religious, ethnic, national, sexual — we can also conceive of a group-serving bias, in which we attribute successes to positive group characteristics and failures to external factors, such as discrimination. In this case, people might well blame themselves for failure in order to avoid blaming other members of the group.

Dion and his colleagues (1975, 1986) have demonstrated experimentally what can happen when minority group members perceive that they have been the target of prejudice. In these studies a situation was created in which members of an out-group (e.g., Jews, Chinese, and women) were asked to complete a task on which their success or failure depended on the action of in-group members (e.g., Christians and men). It was found that perceived prejudice led both Jews and women to *strengthen their positive stereotypes of themselves*. However, in the case of Chinese, perceived prejudice led to a *denial of the negative stereotypes* associated with that group. Dion (1986) suggests that the "visibility" of the minority group may account for these different reactions. The members of visible minorities focus on the negative stereotypes (*defensive self-presentation*). On the other hand, members of groups which are not so easily identified emphasize the positive stereotypes.

Other factors observed by Dion included self-esteem and amount of stress. Contrary to expectation, it was found that the experience of prejudice resulted in *enhanced* self-esteem for the members of the three groups — Jews, women and Chinese. It is not clear why this happened, but it may arise because discrimination increases awareness of group membership, and to be singled out in this way underscores the superiority of the minority.

Not surprisingly, the targets in these studies also experienced some degree of stress. For example, in the face of anti-Semitism, Jewish subjects reported feeling aggressive, sad, and anxious. Clearly, discrimination is perceived as threatening and under some circumstances those discriminated against may act overtly against the dominant group. For example, when prejudice and discrimination lead to deprivation and inequality in the distribution of employment or educational opportunities, riots may result. Caplan and Paige (1968) have reported that Blacks who took part in the U.S. race riots in the '60s were more sensitive to perceived discrimination, reported that they more frequently experienced discrimination, and were less willing to accept the stereotype of Black inferiority than Blacks who remained inactive.

Among the many groups experiencing prejudice and discrimination, the largest by

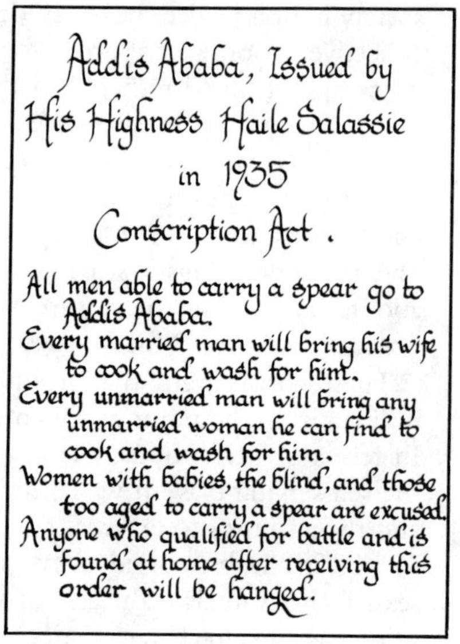

FIGURE 7–4
Ethiopian emperor Haile Salassie's edict of 1935 issued during the invasion of the Italians

> Addis Ababa, Issued by His Highness Haile Salassie in 1935 Conscription Act.
>
> All men able to carry a spear go to Addis Ababa.
>
> Every married man will bring his wife to cook and wash for him.
>
> Every unmarried man will bring any unmarried woman he can find to cook and wash for him.
>
> Women with babies, the blind, and those too aged to carry a spear are excused.
>
> Anyone who qualified for battle and is found at home after receiving this order will be hanged.

SOURCE: Espy, 1975

far is composed of women. In Canada, women have struggled long and hard to achieve the far from satisfactory status they have today. In many other parts of the world, progress has been minimal or non-existent and women continue to be relegated to the inferior roles they have occupied throughout history (see Figure 7-4). Prejudice and discrimination toward women are often subtle and rarely accompanied by the overt hostility that is often directed at other out-groups.

Sexism: Prejudice and discrimination without hostility

In a well-publicized study (Goldberg, 1968), identical essays were submitted to judges to be assigned a grade. In half the cases the "author" was identified as a female, in the other half, as male. Those essays ostensibly written by males received the highest grades, from *both* male and female judges. Apparently, simply being female means being perceived as less competent, a stereotype that continues to plague women in most societies in the world. As a former Mayor of Ottawa, Charlotte Whitton commented, "Whatever women do they must do twice as well as men to be thought half as good. Luckily, this is not difficult."

Among the many social stereotypes maintained about women (by both men and women) are those pertaining to *role-assignments*. Certain occupations — nursing, secretarial positions and truck-driving — are sex-typed. In addition, women who enter non-traditional occupations, such as engineering, may be viewed as aberrant. Similarly, levels within occupations are often available to men and women on an unequal basis. We find few women in positions of power in industry or commerce even though women may be equally or over-represented in the lower ranks (Kanter, 1975). For instance, 73 percent of Canadian bank employees are women. However, the number of executives with the rank of vice-president or higher at Canada's "big five" banks is 750, of which fewer than 12 are women — less than 2 percent (Olive, 1986).

Broverman and her colleagues (1972) define the sex-role stereotype of women as including the perception that women are less competent, less independent, less objective, and less logical than men. On the other hand, men are perceived as lacking interpersonal sensitivity, warmth, and expressiveness in comparison with women. They also point out that masculine traits are often perceived as more desirable than feminine traits. If these perceptions become incorporated into the self-image of women, it is not surprising that many women have a negative self-concept and low self-esteem, making them more vulnerable to "the self-fulfilling prophecy" syndrome. For instance, they may reduce their aspiration levels and remain satisfied with positions much below their real ability and competence. And even when women do well, they may not receive appropriate credit. For example, Deaux and Emswiller (1974) had subjects observe males and females successfully complete either a male or a female task. They then scored the performance on a scale indicating the extent to which the outcome was due to luck or ability. The observers did not discriminate between males and females on the feminine task but both male and female observers attributed male success on the male task to *ability* and female success on the same task to *luck*.

There is no doubt that the situation is changing, although more slowly than desirable. Some evidence that attitudes toward women — and out-groups in general — may not have changed as much as expected has been presented by Bechtold, Naccarato and Zanna (1986). They suggest that although overt discrimination has declined in Canada, it has not been accompanied by a parallel decline in underlying prejudice. Current social norms are such that tolerance and goodwill is expected but, under certain conditions, prejudicial attitudes may surface. To test this proposition Bechtold *et al.* (1986) asked male and female subjects to act as personnel officers and make hiring decisions based on the resumés of either male or female applicants for a marketing position. Some of the subjects were allowed ample time to arrive at a decision while the others were placed under considerable time pressure. It was found that those subjects under time pressure discriminated more against female applicants than did subjects who had no time constraints. In addition, the men discriminated against female applicants more than the women did. Another analysis showed that "traditional" female subjects, compared with "modern" female subjects, discriminated against the female applicants in the same way the male subjects had done.

The purpose of personnel selection is to select the best possible applicant for the job. Therefore, rigid stereotyping on the basis of sex (or age, or ethnic origin, or any other category) is not only an injustice to the job applicant who is victimized, but is detrimental to the interests of those who may not hire or promote the best available person. Research using the concepts and methods of social perception and cognition has shed light on the problem, which, it is hoped, will lead to better employment decisions.

Arvey (1979) argues that many jobs are sex-typed as being more appropriate to one sex than to the other, and that employment decisions are influenced by the congruency between the sex of the applicant and the sex-typing of the job. It is clear that there is still a distinct pattern of occupational segregation in Canada. Women make up the overwhelming majority of restaurant servers, telephone operators, secretaries, nurses, babysitters, dental hygienists, librarians, physiotherapists, and elementary and kindergarten teachers, while most of the lawyers, dentists, truck drivers, accountants, secondary school teachers, janitors, and industrial engineers are men (Greenglass, 1982).

Pharmacist at work: Is this occupation sex-typed?

Kalin and Hodgins (1984) note that sex-role congruence tends to be important only in the abstract situation where no other information is available. However in reality, the decision-maker has considerable information from interviews, letters, and the resumé, about the applicant's background and personal characteristics. They outline a social cognition model of occupational suitability judgments, in which the person begins with applicant-job schemata, including the following: (1) associations between social categories such as sex and occupation, e.g., "bank teller" is associated with a female, and "construction worker" with a male; (2) associations between social categories (sex, occupation) and personal characteristics. These are the stereotypes held by people about men, women, insurance agents, truck drivers, professors of psychology, and so forth; and (3) associations among various personal characteristics, e.g., "friendly" is associated with "trustworthy," (implicit personality theory). Thus, using information about social categories and personal characteristics, we base evaluations on patterns of associations among them. When we know only the categories, we may use a simple congruency rule between sex and occupation, e.g., "A suitable truck driver is male." However, when we have information about personal characteristics, we rely more on these impressions and we match them with occupational stereotypes. If the occupation is strongly sex-typed, then the occupational stereotype will include "masculine" or "feminine" characteristics. While far from ideal, occupational stereotyping is an improvement over simple sex-stereotyping and sex-job matching in that it does not exclude men or women *per se* from the job.

Hodgins and Kalin (1985) tested this model in two experiments in which the subjects (university students) were asked to play the role of guidance counsellors. They were given brief descriptions of three male and three female high school students, and were asked to rate their suitability for each of four male-typed occupations (commercial traveller, surveyor, engineering technician, sales manager) and four female-typed occupations (social worker, nurse, librarian, occupational therapist). In this minimal information situation, subjects showed a strong tendency to match sex of person with sex-type of the job. However, in a second experiment, subjects were also provided with brief descriptions of personality, consisting of traits previously rated by other subjects as "masculine" (self-confident, strong, assertive, opportunistic), "feminine" (affectionate, warm, sensitive, charming), or neutral (formal, calm, determined). In this case, subjects matched the sex-type of personality characteristics with the sex-type of the job, regardless of whether the actual client was male or female, in evaluating their suitability for various occupations. For example, a person was considered suitable for a "male" occupation if he or she was perceived as having "male" personality traits.

In this study, the occupations selected as female-typed and male-typed were those which previous research has shown to be equivalent in status. However, in the real world of contemporary Canada, although women have gained access to some of the high-status "male" occupations, most still work in "female" jobs which tend to be lower in status and lower in pay (Greenglass, 1982). Thus, in addition to removing barriers to occupational choice and abolishing inequities in pay for the same occupation, our society is becoming aware of inequities based on the sex-typing of occupations. Such an awareness is manifest in the slogan, "Equal pay for work of equal value."

It is also true that some studies do not completely support Goldberg's (1968) contention that females are generally perceived as less competent than males. For example, Pheterson, Kiesler and Goldberg (1971) asked women to evaluate works of art entered in a competition which had been produced either by a male or female. Some of these works had yet to be judged, while others had been awarded a prize. They found that if a decision had yet to be made about a work, the male artists received better evaluations than the female artists. However, when a work had already been judged, male and female artists then were evaluated as equally good. This outcome suggests that men are expected to be better than women until demonstrated otherwise. (The nature of the work being judged may also be important. Levenson, Burford, Bonno and Davis (1975) found that women did not rate articles on masculine, feminine, or neutral topics written by men higher such than articles written by women, but when women rated political science essays, they gave higher grades to essays written by women than to those written by men.)

Obviously there are many real differences between men and women. Some of these, such as the extent of cerebral lateralization, are biological. Other differences derive from wide-ranging child rearing practices. But it is important to understand that to be "different" is not to be inferior or superior.

SUMMARY

(1) Prejudice is a positive or negative attitude toward perceived differences of characteristics which is unjustly generalized to all the members of a group. Like other attitudes it has three components: cognitive, affective, and behavioural.

(2) Stereotypes are cognitions, or beliefs, about the members of other groups. They are usually overgeneralizations and are often inaccurate.

(3) Stereotypes can change depending on changes in social conditions and changes in the relationships between members of different groups.

(4) Those stereotypes which have some validity may arise from the operation of the "self-fulfilling prophecy" and the situational pressure which prejudice creates to make stereotypes come true.

(5) The behavioural component of prejudice is called discrimination and, in its more extreme form, racism. While laws have been enacted making discrimination illegal, many subtle forms, such as biased hiring practices, still exist.

(6) Sexism is usually directed at women and results, among other things, in differential treatment in employment.

(7) Innate fear of the unusual or the unfamiliar may be a primitive basis for prejudice. The acquisition of prejudice begins in the home when the child is about three years of age. Parents, teachers, peers, and the media all contribute at various times to this process.

(8) Some individuals who have been raised in a certain way are called authoritarian personalities. They are likely to be prejudiced and ethnocentric and may be hostile.

(9) One manifestation of pent-up hostility is called scapegoating and results in out-groups being blamed for the frustration the individual experiences.

(10) Under the appropriate circumstances, prejudice can be reduced by intergroup contact. Unfortunately, intergroup anxiety often prevents people from interacting with the members of other groups.

(11) A higher level of education is associated with increased tolerance.

(12) The victims of prejudice may react in a number of ways. These include aggression, changes in self-esteem, changes in group allegiance, or modification of the strength of positive or negative stereotypes held about one's own group.

FURTHER READING

ALLPORT, G.W. (1954). *The nature of prejudice*. Reading: Addison-Wesley.

AUSTIN, W.G. and WORCHEL, S. (Eds.) (1979). *Social psychology of intergroup relations*. Monterey: Brooks/Cole.

BERRY, J.W., KALIN, R. and TAYLOR, D.M. (1977) *Multiculturalism and ethnic attitudes in Canada*. Ottawa: Supply and Services, Canada.

GARDNER, R.C. and KALIN, R. (Eds.) (1981). *A Canadian social psychology of ethnic relations*. Toronto: Methuen.

GREENGLASS, E. (1982). *A world of difference. Gender roles in perspective*. Toronto: Wiley.

KATZ, P. (Ed.) (1976). *Towards the elimination of racism*. New York: Pergamon.

MILLER, A.C. (Ed.) (1982). *In the eye of the beholder: Contemporary issues in stereotyping*. New York: Praeger.

TAYLOR, D.M. and MOGHADDAM, F.M. (1987). *Theories of intergroup relations: International social psychological perspectives*. New York: Praeger.

C·H·A·P·T·E·R E·I·G·H·T

Interpersonal Attraction and Interpersonal Relationships

Marriage is popular because it combines
the maximum of temptation with the
maximum of opportunity.
George Bernard Shaw

There's more to marriage than four bare
legs in a blanket.
Robertson Davies

FOR REFLECTION

- Why do people want and need to be with others?
- How do we know whether we like or dislike someone?
- Do "opposites attract"?
- What is intimacy? Are men and women different in their perception of intimacy?
- Why do such problems as loneliness, jealousy, and divorce occur?

TO A GREAT extent, we all seek personal satisfaction and meaning in relation to other people. It is not surprising that artists, writers, philosophers, and religious leaders have long been interested in the factors responsible for attracting people to one another. However, it is only in recent years that scientific methods have been applied to study of relationships. Although the enterprise is not without its skeptics, those engaged in this research argue that human relationships are too important to be left outside the realm of scientific inquiry. While several other disciplines have provided important insights, this chapter concerns the contribution of social psychology.

The poet John Donne pointed out that "No man is an island, entire of itself." And so, this chapter begins with a brief discussion of the very human tendency to affiliate with other people. While human beings are not the only "social animals," their affiliative behaviour is characterized by the most complex patterns of communication and self-consciousness. Therefore, it is important to consider the selectivity of people, why they affiliate with some persons and not with others. This discussion considers attraction, a positive evaluation or attitude held by one person about another. Another feature of this selectivity is that we select different people as different types of affiliates—colleagues, casual friends, close friends, or lovers. Thus it is important to consider attraction in the context of various types of relationships.

While affiliation, attraction, and relationships are important to us all, the course of human relationships does not always run smoothly. In the latter part of this chapter, recent research on the dissolution of close relationships will be examined. The formation or continuation of relationships can also be disrupted by certain individual dispositions. Therefore, we also examine loneliness and jealousy from the perspective of social psychology.

ATTACHMENT AND AFFILIATION

Social attachment begins in early infancy and becomes particularly evident when the child learns to distinguish familiar persons, especially the mother, and to respond in a special way to them. The infant smiles and vocalizes to the attachment figure, shows distress when she leaves, and is obviously comforted by her. Later, the child forms other attachments to familiar caretakers such as the father, grandparents, regular babysitter, or close family friends. Bowlby (1969) argues that there is a biological basis for attachment, eliciting responses which are genetically "wired in" and which have great survival value for the infant. On the other hand, social learning theorists explain attachment behaviours in terms of the child associating the mother with rewards such as food, comfort, and physical closeness. It is generally accepted that the child is often vulnerable to later emotional problems after prolonged interference with the early attachment process, e.g., by serious early illness or premature birth, resulting in the infant being separated from the mother for a lengthy period.

Affiliation is profoundly important throughout the life span, a fact which has been demonstrated empirically. Subjects in one study (Csikszentmihalyi and Figurski, 1982) agreed to carry communication devices or "beepers" for several weeks. At random times during their waking hours, subjects were "beeped," a signal to fill out a brief questionnaire on what they were doing at that time. The study showed adults spent 71 percent of their time in situations involving other people (for adolescents, the

The love of cousins: Social attachment begins in infancy.

figure was 74 percent). Of course, work or school occupied the majority of these hours, but all involved affiliation.

Laboratory research also has identified some of the factors which tend to increase or decrease affiliation behaviour. An experiment by Schachter (1959) tested the hypothesis that under some conditions, people affiliate to reduce fear. Female subjects were informed by an experimenter, a gentleman dressed in a white lab coat with the rather ominous name of Dr. Gregor Zilstein, that they would be subjected to electric shocks which would be intense and painful (high fear condition) or which would resemble a tickle or a tingle (low fear condition). Then subjects were allowed to choose to spend a ten minute waiting period either alone or with other subjects. Those with high fear showed a strong preference to be with others. A subsequent experiment included high fear and low fear conditions and added a new one. Male subjects were told that they would be asked to perform a series of embarrassing tasks, such as sucking on rubber nipples and baby bottles. While subjects in the high fear condition wanted to be with others, subjects in the embarrassing condition preferred to be alone.

The key here seems to be the process of *social comparison*. In an unusual situation, when we are uncertain how to react, we turn to others as a source of information, to compare our feelings with people "in the same boat." To demonstrate this finding, another experiment (Schachter, 1959) used different groups of subjects who, after high fear arousal, were given three choices: to wait alone, to be with other experimental subjects, or to be with students waiting for interviews with faculty advisors. As social comparison theory predicts, fearful subjects preferred to be with others in the same situation (i.e., fearful), rather than people in a different situation. In reality, misery loves miserable company.

Affiliation can be vital to our well-being. Irving Janis (1951) found in a study of U.S. airmen in combat that those most able to endure this extreme form of stress were those who identified strongly with a cohesive combat unit. Those who lacked the closeness and support of their "buddies" in the unit were much more likely to suffer psychological breakdown under pressure. Of course, the existence of this external stress contributes to greater need for affiliation among those in combat situations, and thus to the closely-knit cohesive group.

INTERPERSONAL ATTRACTION

While we need to affiliate and to form close bonds with others, an obvious and important feature of virtually all types of relationships is their selectivity. That is, with rare exceptions, people will not share conversations, friendships, or love affairs with just anyone. Much of the research in this area has been devoted to *interpersonal attraction*, studying the reasons why one person will like another and evaluate him or her positively. It has been shown that — with certain qualifications — we tend to like people who are similar to us, who reward us, who like us, who are in close physical proximity, who are physically attractive, and who are pleasant, agreeable, competent, and otherwise good and desirable people. While these observations may seem straightforward, a few surprises and puzzles will be encountered.

Of course, there are many kinds of attraction. We may enjoy a casual conversation with the person beside us on an airplane and leave it at that. We may be attracted to a person as a friend but not a lover, as a tennis partner but not a close friend, as a colleague at work but not as a companion. What determines liking of a stranger will not necessarily be what determines attraction in an intimate relationship or what determines whether that relationship may persist. While the majority of research has emphasized attraction to a stranger, social psychologists have become more interested over time in the study of how long-term relationships begin, develop, and succeed or fail over time.

The model of Levinger and Snoek (1972) provides a useful frame of reference. They propose that interpersonal relationships can be described in terms of a series of identifiable stages. Figure 8-1 illustrates the stages or levels in terms of two circles, each of which represents one of the persons in the relationship. Briefly, the stages are:

(0) *Zero contact*. Two persons are unrelated and unaware of each other. Think of the thousands of instances in our lives in which we do not even notice or have contact with another person, although it may have been possible (a crowded stadium, a lecture theatre, an elevator, a grocery store, a bus, walking down St. Paul/Water/St. Denis/Yonge/Sparks/Portage/Jasper/Main Streets).

(1) *Awareness*. One person has formed an impression of the other. The awareness may or may not be reciprocated. As there is no interaction, attraction will depend upon what we can actually observe of physical characteristics or behaviour, what we can infer or attribute about the person, and what others may tell us about that person (accurate or otherwise).

(2) *Surface contact*. Awareness is bilateral and the two people are interacting. Interaction is superficial and may take the form of a first conversation with a casual acquaintance, or be restricted to communication between people in highly defined roles — a passenger and a regular bus driver, people at work, classmates, patient and physician, customer and salesperson.

(3) *Mutuality*. The lives of two people intersect to a greater extent as they share

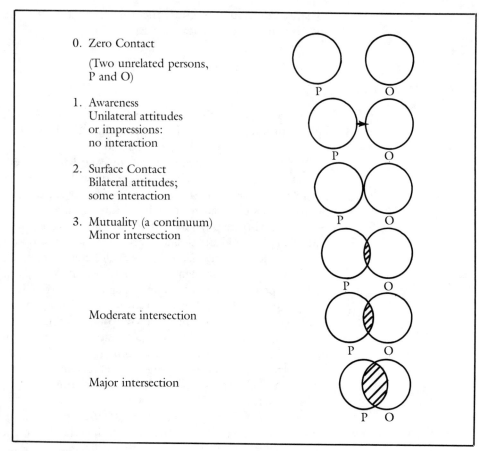

0. Zero Contact

(Two unrelated persons, P and O)

1. Awareness
Unilateral attitudes
or impressions:
no interaction

2. Surface Contact
Bilateral attitudes;
some interaction

3. Mutuality (a continuum)
Minor intersection

Moderate intersection

Major intersection

FIGURE 8–1
Levels of pair relatedness

SOURCE: Levinger, 1974

feelings, time, activities, and experiences. Mutuality represents a continuum of intimacy, a concern and empathy for the other, and a sense of "we-ness." Levinger (1977) further describes mutuality in terms of involvement (concern, interests, and experiences), commitment (feelings of obligation to each other and to the relationship), and symmetry (the extent to which the partners are equally involved and invested in the relationship).

A more complete understanding of these levels will be provided in the following discussion. At the outset, two fundamental points must be understood. First, a relationship may or may not become more intimate or intense. Of the thousands and thousands of persons who pass through our lives, we become aware of relatively few, have contact with fewer, form relationships with fewer still, and have intimate relationships with even fewer of those. Indeed, we are often quite content with many of our casual relationships — we enjoy the person at that level and have no desire to establish greater intimacy with that person. Second, we should remember that what is important as a determinant of attraction will change in different situations. The qualities we seek in a casual acquaintance or co-worker are not what we desire of a friend or lover. Let us now examine some of these variables.

AWARENESS

Much of the research described in Chapter 3 has relevance in this discussion. We form initial impressions and we observe and interpret what the person is doing in terms of various attributional processes. Certainly, in many cases, we become aware of someone through what others tell us of that person. At this stage, we decide whether we are sufficiently interested to get to know the person ourselves. Two variables have been shown to be particularly important: we are attracted to people who live, work, or are otherwise situated in close physical proximity to ourselves, and we are attracted to physically pleasing people.

While we are more likely to interact or at least want to interact with those who are attractive, there still has to be an opportunity for the first contact to take place. A factor which substantially increases the likelihood of people meeting and developing relationships is *geographic proximity* or *propinquity*. A study by Festinger, Schachter and Back (1950), more recently substantiated by Athanasiou and Yashioka (1973), provides a good example of this process. They selected graduate student apartments at Massachusetts Institute of Technology as the site for their investigation. A diagram of a typical apartment building can be seen in Figure 8-2.

Notice that the building contains two stories, has ten apartments, and a number of stairways. First, the experimenters asked all the residents to complete a "sociometric test" which identified their three closest friends in the apartment complex. Analyses of these patterns revealed systematic relationships between friendships and physical distance. Friends were most likely to be next-door neighbours, and the probability of friendship decreased as apartments became more distant. It also was found that people in the central apartments, numbers three and eight, were reported as friends more often than the residents of all the other apartments, probably because they had the advantage of being closest to the most apartments. These results were derived

FIGURE 8–2
Design of typical apartment building

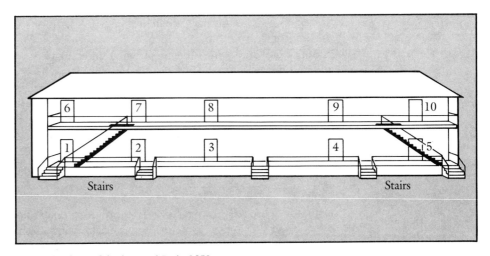

SOURCE: Festinger, Schachter and Back, 1950

from the horizontal choices. However, the vertical choices among people on different floors were also of interest. It was found that those in the end apartments, one and five, not only received the most friendship choices from the other floor but gave the most as well. The reason why is obvious if we refer, again, to the apartment illustration. The two stairs from the upper floor end in front of these two apartments, increasing the likelihood of those in the end apartments meeting the upper residents, and thus setting the stage for interaction and the development of liking.

It is also true that those in the middle apartment (three) were more often chosen as friends by people on other floors. This is probably because of a "snowball" effect — friends of friends are likely to become friends. (Remember that the middle people received the most choices of anyone on the same floor.)

Does this mean that deliberately selecting a middle apartment will automatically increase your number of friends? This is not necessarily the case. Keep in mind that in the study, all the participants were graduate students who shared many values, attitudes, and interests which would make interaction mutually rewarding. In most housing or apartment situations, residents are considerably more heterogeneous with respect to most personal characteristics, and the likelihood of becoming friends with a next-door neighbour would be considerably reduced.

Why are we so favourably disposed to those in close physical proximity? First, proximity increases opportunities for interaction, thus enabling people to notice their similarities, and discover that they like and are rewarding to each other. Proximity also increases the anticipation of interaction, and we generally tend to be pleasant to people whom we expect to see frequently. However, such explanations do not, in themselves, seem adequate to account for differences in attraction between neighbours in adjacent apartments and those at the other end of the hall. Moreover, those nearby also have greater capacity to irritate each other and even to become enemies. Yet, proximity promotes attraction more often than it leads to animosity.

The most important factor is probably the *mere exposure* effect. Contrary to the old saying, "Familiarity breeds contempt," an important body of research shows that familiarity with a novel stimulus usually leads to more positive ratings and greater attraction, (Zajonc, 1970), though there are situations in which excessive repetition has led to negative effects (Suedfeld *et al.*, 1975). In one experiment, subjects shown the photograph of the same person for four weeks showed greater liking for that person, compared with subjects shown a different photograph each week (Moreland and Zajonc, 1982). In another study, preschoolers who watched *Sesame Street* episodes involving Japanese Canadians and North American Indians were more likely to indicate a desire to play with such children than children not exposed to these episodes (Goldberg and Gorn, 1979). In general, we tend to prefer objects and people who are familiar to us, and proximity will obviously be related to a greater probability of increased exposure.

Physical attractiveness

Common sense tells us that "beauty is only skin deep" and "you can't judge a book by its cover." It seems somehow superficial, even undemocratic, to judge a person by his or her physical features. Yet, in affluent societies, a large amount of time and money is spent on physical appearance — hair, clothing, make-up, body fitness — suggesting that people really do understand the importance of being physically attractive and will do what they can to enhance what nature has endowed or inflicted upon

In affluent societies, a large amount of time and money is spent on physical appearance.

them. The research clearly shows that physical attractiveness is a powerful determinant of liking. It is not enough to say simply that "beauty is in the eye of the beholder." Within a given culture and age group, subjects who are asked to make independent ratings of the physical attractiveness of various target persons tend to show high levels of agreement in these ratings (Berscheid and Walster, 1974a). These average ratings by independent judges predict how much other subjects will like the target persons (Curran and Lippold, 1975).

Not unexpectedly, much of the research has concerned attraction between males and females. In these cases, it appears that males are somewhat more concerned about the physical attractiveness of females than females are about males (Miller and Rivenbark, 1970; Krebs and Adinolfi, 1975). However, these decade-old findings may not still apply today.

Physical attractiveness also increases the likelihood that two people will choose to have a first encounter. Therefore, it seems unusual that pairs of individuals, whether friends or lovers, tend to be similar in attractiveness (Cash and Derlega, 1978; Murstein, 1972). It has been suggested that this is the case because highly attractive people are perceived in both a positive and negative way. Their attractiveness increases the desire of others to interact with them but also increases other people's fear of rejection. Rather than risk the humiliation of being turned down, many people are satisfied to form relationships with others who are physically similar.

This matching process in heterosexual relationships is based on the development of a personal *level-of-aspiration*, or what we anticipate we can attain, based on our self-image and past experience. Thus, highly attractive individuals may find themselves "admired from a distance" (Berscheid and Walster, 1969; Shanteau and Nagy, 1979) while average looking people may seek out those more in line with their expectations. For example, Kiesler and Baral (1970) deliberately manipulated the self-esteem of male subjects and were able to show that those whose self-esteem had been lowered were more likely to make "advances" toward an unattractive female than toward an attractive female. The behaviour of those whose self-esteem had been enhanced was just the opposite.

It is important to understand that attractiveness is not an absolute. There is great variation in opinions as to what constitutes beauty among different cultures and sub-cultures, as well as within cultures at different times. The conditions under which the judgment is made can also be important. For instance, Kenrick and Gutierres (1980) found that males who had just watched an episode of the once popular TV program *Charlie's Angels* judged a female of average attractiveness lower than did other males who had not seen the program. Evidently, even an attractive person seems less so in comparison with a glamorous star, putting most of us at an unfair disadvantage.

B · O · X 8-1

BEAUTY IN THE BAR: FIELD RESEARCH ON PERCEIVED ATTRACTIVENESS

In the late '70s Pennebaker and a number of colleagues (1979) decided to test a hypothesis originally generated by country and western singer, Mickey Gilley: "The girls all get prettier at closing time, they all get to look like movie stars. . . ." The hypothesis was confirmed. These investigators asked 52 male and 61 female patrons of three bars to rate (on a scale from 1 to 10) the attractiveness of the other patrons at three different times (9:00 p.m., 10:30 p.m. and 12:00 midnight). Their results showed that as closing time approached, perceived attractiveness of the opposite sex significantly increased. The authors suggest the following explanation: "If the subjects were committed to going home with a person of the opposite sex, it would be dissonant to consider an unattractive partner. The most efficient way of reducing such dissonance could be to increase the perceived attractiveness of the prospective alternatives" (p. 124).

If we can assume that alcohol was not distorting the perception of beauty, the underlying hypothesis suggests that as the evening progressed, the motivation to meet members of the opposite sex increased. Another study asked bar patrons both to rate the attractiveness of opposite-sex patrons and to indicate their own interest in meeting someone (Sprecher *et al.*, 1984). They found that ratings of overall attractiveness declined as closing time approached, especially the ratings women gave to men. Although men generally expressed more interest than women in meeting someone of the opposite sex, the interest variable was related to ratings of attractiveness only among women. Of course, it is not possible to infer cause and effect from these data, and it is quite possible that subjects became interested in meeting someone after forming an impression that they were attractive.

Thus the dynamics of late-night bars are more complex than suggested in the song. Several other factors must also be considered. Perhaps the earlier and later patrons are not the same people, and more (or less) attractive people tend to wander in around closing time. Perhaps the number of people in the bar makes a difference, and patrons with only a few people to observe become more familiar and comfortable with them as a result. Finally, the type of bar may influence the results. Indeed, one study found that ratings of attractiveness increased near closing time in a country and western bar but not one at a university. Perhaps the patrons in the former bar were more likely to be familiar with the song, and the night became a musical self-fulfilling prophecy.

Similarly, situational factors (see Box 8-1) can also influence how we evaluate physical attractiveness.

While males and females are obviously attentive to each others' physical attractiveness, we should keep in mind that this variable also influences our attraction in other kinds of relationships. Even children as young as three years old prefer to look at pictures of other children who are attractive (Dion, 1972). Attractive fifth grade children are more popular among their same-sex peers (Cavior and Dorecki, 1969). In addition, adults treat attractive and unattractive children differently. For example, Clifford and Walster (1973) showed fifth grade teachers a report card about a hypothetical student which included a photograph of an attractive or unattractive boy or girl. Although the report cards were identical, the attractive child was assessed by the teachers as having a higher IQ and was expected to achieve more in the future.

Beautiful is good   Given that physical attractiveness does influence more than sexual attraction, how can we explain its pervasive importance? It seems—at least in Western societies — that people believe physical attractiveness indicates desirable personality characteristics. Recall, for example, that in most traditional children's stories, the hero or heroine is unusually handsome or beautiful, while the villain is often physically ugly. In one study (Dion, Berscheid and Walster, 1972), male and female students were presented with photographs of very attractive, average, and unattractive persons, and were asked to rate them on a number of personality characteristics. The attractive person was rated as having more desirable personality characteristics and a higher occupational status. Students also said they were more likely to be happily married and content in their social life and occupation. Females judged attractive males as more intelligent, moral, and adjusted. In another similar study, an attractive, middle-aged person was judged to be more outgoing, more pleasant, and of higher status (Adams and Huston, 1975). The age and sex of the person doing the judging did not matter in this case.

A medieval law stated that if two persons fell under suspicion of having committed a crime, the uglier one was to be regarded as more likely guilty. In a more subtle way, the "beautiful is good" assumption may influence judicial decisions today. For example, astute lawyers will usually advise their clients to clean up and dress well. In a mock jury study, subjects were given a description of a case involving cheating in college. The same facts were presented to all subjects, along with a photograph of the defendant. Physically attractive defendants were judged less guilty and received less severe punishment than less attractive defendants (Effran, 1974). However, in some situations, physical attractiveness may lead to more negative outcomes (Sigall and Ostrove, 1975; Izzett and Fishman, 1976). For example, it was found that female defendants who were particularly attractive were more likely to be convicted if they had apparently used their physical assets to accomplish the crime.

Physical attractiveness may also be important in politics, where the physical appearance of candidates is often vital. Effran and Patterson (1974) had judges rate the appearance of 79 candidates in the 1972 Canadian federal election. A comparison then revealed that the unattractive candidates averaged fewer votes (10 percent) than the attractive ones (32 percent). Moreover, of the 17 candidates studied who were not affiliated with one of the major parties (Liberals, Conservatives and the NDP) only one was above the median attractiveness rating. In other words, fringe groups such as the Libertarian or Marxist-Leninist parties do not seem to put forward attractive candidates. Why this happens is not yet known but one possible explanation

Physical attractiveness is also important in politics, where the physical appearance of candidates is vital.

derives from the concept of a *self-fulfilling prophecy*. If individuals are socially rejected and alienated by virtue of being perceived as unattractive, they may seek and find considerable satisfaction as members of organizations that advocate unpopular policies. (In other nations, different parties may attract the more "socially desirable" candidates.) It is also possible that those who belong to political movements which do not conform to the norms of the society are also less concerned with social norms regarding physical attractiveness.

In another study, (Dion and Dion, 1987) subjects were asked to fill out a Just World scale, a measure of their beliefs that people "get what they deserve" and "deserve what they get" in life (Lerner, 1974b; recall Chapter 3). They were then shown photographs of attractive and unattractive males and females, and asked to rate each stimulus person on a variety of characteristics. Believers in a just world rated physically attractive *males* as having more socially desirable characters than did those without strong just world beliefs. It seems that believers in a just world have a positive bias toward "winners" in life and perceive attractive males as belonging to that category. However, this bias was not found when the stimulus persons were females; believers in a just world did not perceive the personalities of attractive females as more socially desirable than unattractive ones. Evidently, the cue that they were female outweighed perceptions of attractiveness in making these stereotyped judgments.

Perfection is not always attractive   There also is some evidence that a person can be too attractive or "too perfect." Perhaps because they remind us of our own inadequacies, individuals who are extremely capable and competent, who have everything going for them, may be envied — but they may not be liked as much as someone who has at least some human failings. Public opinion polls, for example, revealed that the popularity of U.S. President John Kennedy increased after he ordered the invasion of Cuba which failed at the Bay of Pigs (Aronson, 1970), and that Pierre Trudeau's marital problems enhanced his public image.

This phenomenon is dramatically illustrated in an experiment by Aronson, Willerman and Floyd (1966). On audiotape, some subjects heard a student correctly answer 92 percent of a very difficult series of questions, while other subjects heard the same student correctly answer only 30 percent. For half of the subjects in each of these conditions the experiment ended at this point and, before leaving, they rated how much they liked the person whose voice they heard. The superior student received an average attractiveness rating of 20.8 and the less able student, a rating of 17.8. For the remaining subjects, the tape continued and they heard the student being given a cup of coffee, followed by "Oh, my goodness, I've spilled coffee all over my new suit." These subjects then completed the attractiveness rating which now resulted in mean evaluations of 30.2 for the superior student and −2.5 for the less able student. In other words the competent individual's rating increased after demonstrating at least some inadequacy.

This finding has to be qualified somewhat in view of the outcome of a subsequent study (Helmreich, Aronson and LeFan, 1970) which showed that the effect of the "blunder" depended on the self-esteem of the observers. The researchers felt that the results of the experiment conducted by Aronson *et al.* were applicable to observers who perceived themselves to be of average competence. They reasoned that others who thought of themselves as superior might react quite differently because they would identify with the very competent target person. Observers of low esteem would, it was predicted, also not increase their liking because they would look up to the target person as an ideal or model. The data clearly supported these possibilities, showing that high self-esteem observers decreased their liking for the target after the blunder as did those of low self-esteem, while average self-esteem observers reacted in the same way as the students in the previous study. In addition, when the target person was "incompetent," the self-esteem of the observers was unimportant and the effect of the blunder on attractiveness was negligible.

Thus far, the discussion has concerned processes by which we may become attracted to people without interacting with them. As we begin to interact, we become aware of new information about that person which assumes importance in determining whether we will like him or her. The following section explores this level of relationship.

SURFACE CONTACT

At the level of surface contact, the two people begin to interact directly, perhaps by personal conversation, by telephone, or by exchanging letters. The topics of conversation tend to be either restricted and technical (e.g., "shop-talk") or superficial — the weather, where you work or what you are studying, how the Roughriders, Stampeders, Blue Jays or Canadiens are doing this year, gossip about friends or acquaintances, politics (excepting emotionally charged issues, such as abortion). Activities and social contacts also tend to be superficial and predictable — dinner, a dance, a movie, a party, a class or meeting. At this level, two determinants of attraction tend to be crucial: we like people similar to ourselves and we like people who reward us. The interaction process allows for the discovery of similarities and rewards in the other person.

Similarity

Common sense tells us that "birds of a feather flock together" *and* that "opposites attract." Which is the case? While certain types of "opposites" may attract in certain relationships (the principle of *complementarity*, to be discussed later), more firmly established is the principle that we tend to like people similar to ourselves in attitudes, values, and interests. Indeed, in dating and mate selection, partners also tend to be similar in age, religion, education, physical attractiveness, and even height (Hill, Rubin and Peplau, 1976). In such situations the matching process discussed earlier is operating once again, and may represent the partners' levels of aspiration. That is, while most people would prefer an extremely attractive partner, only the most attractive person can realistically hope to attract such a partner unless they can offer some compensating attributes of value, such as fame, wealth, or power (Berscheid and Walster, 1978). In general, as mentioned earlier, people tend to select someone roughly equivalent in attractiveness to themselves, rather than risk rejection (Shanteau and Nagy, 1979).

In an early study, transfer students to a U.S. university were offered free housing in exchange for their participation in research (Newcomb, 1961). None of the students knew each other before arriving on campus. On arrival, and at intervals throughout the semester, they were asked to fill out a questionnaire which assessed: (1) their values and attitudes regarding religion, politics, and other matters; (2) their *perception* of each other's attitudes; and (3) how much they liked each other. The findings

"Frankly, what attracted me to Sylvia in the first place was the prospect of some really kinky sex. Of course, that was replaced with a deep and abiding mutual love."

showed a strong relationship between friendship and perceived similarity in attitudes and values. The timing of the formation of friendship is interesting. Friendships formed quite rapidly and friends tended to assume in the beginning that they were more similar than they really were. As they came to know each other better over time, friendships shifted so that *actual* attitude similarity was significantly related to attraction in the final weeks of the study. In other words, rather than change values and attitudes, the students changed friends (Newcomb, 1961).

In a series of well-controlled experiments, Byrne (1971) applied the similarity-attraction principle in the laboratory. The basic procedure involved the subject filling out a brief attitude questionnaire. Unknown to the subject, the experimenter then quickly filled out a blank questionnaire, responding with views which were similar or dissimilar, in varying degrees, to those of the subject. The subject was handed this questionnaire and told that it had been completed by another subject in the experiment. The subject was asked to look over the responses of this hypothetical stranger and indicate the degree of attraction or liking to this person. In this artificial, controlled situation, other factors relevant to liking, such as physical appearance, status or, personality were not relevant.

The findings of this study showed that attraction to the stranger increased as the proportion of similar attitudes increased. This has become known as Byrne's law: attraction to a stranger is a function of the *proportion* of similar attitudes. Consider a case in which we have assessed attitudes toward a nuclear freeze, rock music, unemployment insurance, abortion, and fine wines. Those who share all five attitudes will be more attracted to each other than those who share only four, who will be more attracted than those who share only three. Notice that the findings refer to the *proportion* of similar attitudes; whether four out of five or 536 out of 670 attitudes are measured as similar, the attraction will be the same.

Outside the laboratory, the effect holds up well. In one study, males and females were paired on the basis of similar or dissimilar responses to an attitude questionnaire (Byrne, Ervin and Lamberth, 1970). Each couple was introduced and sent away on a brief "coke date" nearby. (Note: "coke" referred to a popular soft drink of the time!) When they returned, couples with highly similar attitudes rated each other more favourably, indicated greater attraction, and even stood close to one another.

It should be pointed out that not all similarities are equally important. Kandel (1978) conducted an extensive longitudinal study of over 180 adolescents in New York, in which she compared the attitudes and values of each subject with those of the person named as his or her best friend. Best friends tended to be highly similar in attitudes toward drug use and in certain demographic characteristics such as age, grade in school, and ethnic group. However, best friends did not share similar attitudes towards teachers and parents. Finally, Hill and Stull (1981) found that among females who were roommates at university, similarity in values was very high among those who chose to room together and among those who wanted to stay together. However, sharing values was significantly less important to male roommates. As we will see, men and women seem to define or experience friendships differently.

Reasons for the similarity-attraction relationship Why are attitude similarity and attraction so strongly related? Several explanations are plausible. First, it is rewarding to have someone agree with our opinions, for it bolsters our confidence in our own ideas. Similar values and interests provide opportunities for doing something together with someone, such as playing tennis, working for a cause, or going to a movie (and agreeing on which movie to see). However, in certain circumstances, similarity may not be rewarding. In one variation of the Byrne "hypothetical stranger" study (Novak and Lerner, 1968) some subjects were led to believe that the other person had recently suffered a "nervous breakdown," had been hospitalized, and was still seeing a psychiatrist. In this case, similarity actually *decreased* liking. Somehow it seemed threatening to the subject that an emotionally disturbed person might be otherwise so similar to themselves.

Another explanation for the relationship between attitude similarity and attraction is derived from the principle that people strive to maintain consistency, harmony, or balance among their attitudes and orientations to others (Heider, 1958) (see Figure 8-3). To like someone while disagreeing with that person about something important is psychologically uncomfortable. Thus, as we saw in Newcomb's study, if you hold strong views about abortion, your feelings toward someone else will be influenced by his or her views on the subject. Of course, we rarely agree with our friends about *everything* and can often tolerate a good deal of inconsistency or imbalance. Indeed, agreement may not always signify liking and balance. If John and Brian agree about the many, unusually desirable attributes of Susan, the result may be bitter competition.

A third interpretation challenges the proposition that when we perceive someone as similar to us, we are then attracted to that person. If the similarity-attraction relationship is so pervasive, it must be part of our everyday common sense experience. Thus, we expect the people we like to be similar to ourselves. Indeed, recall that in his longitudinal study of a student rooming house, Newcomb (1961) found that attraction developed rapidly, before people had much information about who held

FIGURE 8-3
Striving for balance in attitude and orientation to others

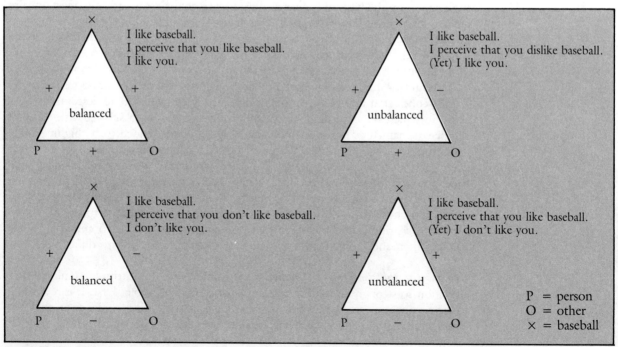

SOURCE: Heider, 1958

attitudes similar to their own. In another study (Murstein, 1972), engaged couples were each asked to fill out a set of personality scales for themselves, and then to predict how their partners would respond to the scales. Subjects tended to expect their partners' responses to bear more similarity to their own than they actually did. Thus the perception of attitude similarity is, to a considerable extent, an assumption which is influenced by how much we like that person. In fact, typically, people assume that others share their attitudes to a greater extent than may be the case, and thus tend to like other people in the absence of contrary information. (Byrne, Clore and Smeaton, 1986).

Another study shows that when we perceive someone as similar or dissimilar to ourselves, our actions toward that person are strongly influenced (Jellison and Oliver, 1982). Subjects completed an attitude questionnaire, and were then shown the similar or dissimilar responses of a hypothetical stranger. They were then asked to evaluate the person as a possible friend, roommate, or lover. Half of each group were instructed to evaluate the stranger in such a way as to induce the person to like them, while the others were instructed to try to create a negative impression of themselves. When trying to create a good impression of themselves, subjects followed the similarity-attraction rule, evaluating the similar person in a more favourable way than the dissimilar person. However, when trying to create a negative impression of themselves, subjects evaluated the similar person unfavourably, and the dissimilar person more favourably. That is, we seem to apply the similarity-attraction rule in such a way as to manage the impression that others will have of us. This explanation is consistent with the interpretation that within one culture, people share expectations or norms regarding similarity and attraction.

Reinforcement and attraction

We like people who reward us, who say nice things, and do good things for us. Indeed, as we have seen, some theorists believe that reinforcement underlies all attraction. We like someone with similar attitudes because it is rewarding to have someone agree with us. We like someone who is physically attractive because it is rewarding to be with and be seen with such a desirable person.

Byrne and Clore (1970) argue that we like a person with whom we associate reward, with feeling good — even if we do not attribute the reward and good feelings to that person. (This is known as the reinforcement-affect model of attraction; see Figure 8-4.) For example, subjects were given false feedback on a personality test which they had completed earlier. Half were informed that the test showed many strong, positive characteristics, while the other half were told that the test revealed many personal problems and inadequacies (of course, subjects were subsequently informed and reassured about the deception). Then the subject met a stranger in the waiting room. Those who received the positive feedback subsequently indicated greater attraction to this person.

Of course, we may become attracted to a person in unpleasant circumstances: people who survived the wartime bombardment of London recall the intense attraction which often developed during that time. As we have already seen, affiliation with others who share stressful circumstances can bring its own rewards (see also *excitation-transfer theory* in Chapter 9).

We certainly tend to like someone who likes us, or whom we believe likes us, a conviction which may develop at the "awareness" stage. In one classic study, Back-

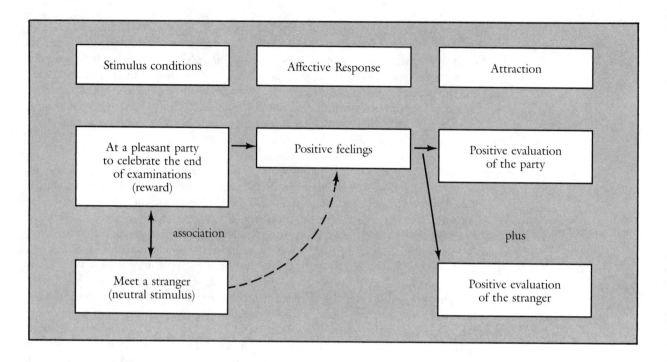

FIGURE 8–4
Reinforcement-affect model of attraction

man and Secord (1959) formed discussion groups composed of strangers. Before the first meeting, each subject was told privately that personality tests had revealed that certain members of the group would probably like that person very much. After the first session, subjects tended to prefer, as a team partner, someone who was expected to like them. At the end of later sessions, preferences no longer reflected these expectations. Subjects then knew how others reacted to them and responded accordingly.

Of course, we learn who likes us by their behaviour towards us. Those who praise us, even flatter us, will tend to be those who like us (unless we attribute ulterior motives to that person). We are not as concerned about accuracy or sincerity as we might wish to believe (Jones, 1964). In fact, the evidence suggests that we tend to believe the compliments given to us, especially if they concern characteristics which we might hope to have. Possibly, this effect may reflect the culture of the United States where most of the research was done, a culture in which people tend to have an unusually strong need for the approval and the liking of others. The emphasis on approval is most evident in television advertising, which repeatedly offers ways to increase popularity: use the right toothpaste or cosmetics, drive the right car, patronize the right restaurant or bar.

However, the mere *amount* of reinforcement may not be sufficient to predict attraction. Aronson and Linder (1965) show that a *gain or loss* of positive expression, or liking, from another is a more potent source of reward or punishment than is constant praise or criticism. In an experiment involving a complicated series of explanations and scenarios, subjects heard themselves being evaluated by a confederate on seven different occasions during the study. In one condition, the confederate was consistently positive about the subject while, in another, the confederate was consistently negative. In the third condition, the confederate was initially negative but gradually became more positive about the subject (the "gain" condition). A fourth group of subjects heard the confederate begin with a positive evaluation and gradually become negative about the subject ("loss" condition). Subsequently, the subjects were asked to indicate the degree to which they were attracted to the confederate.

Needless to say, subjects liked the person who liked them and disliked the person who evaluated them negatively. More importantly, the confederate was liked more in the gain condition than in the constant positive condition and disliked more in the loss condition than in the constant negative condition. Subsequent research suggests that the gain effect tends to be stronger than the loss effect (Clore, Wiggins and Itkin, 1975). In part, this outcome may be due to a contrast effect common in perception: the positive things said after negative things seem more positive. There may also have been an anxiety reduction in the gain condition which made the later, positive comments even more reinforcing. In any case, we obviously cannot assume that the more liking we receive, the better we feel.

Another limit to the reinforcement effect is represented by the principle of equity, or fairness, in our social relations (Walster, Walster and Berscheid, 1978). While we want rewarding relationships, we also want to feel that we are not exploited and that we are not taking unfair advantage of others. Thus situations in which we feel that we are being excessively rewarded by someone can be acutely uncomfortable. Indeed, people sometimes react quite negatively to generosity from others, particularly if they are unable to reciprocate or if it implies dependency or incompetence on their part. For example, in one study, subjects from Sweden, Japan, and the USA played a gambling game (Gergen, Ellsworth, Maslach and Seipel, 1975), which was rigged so that at a crucial moment, another player gave them ten chips which saved them from bankruptcy and, eventually, allowed them to win. While there were no cultural differences, the other player was better liked if he asked for his ten chips back than if he wanted no repayment or repayment with exorbitant interest. Findings such as these may explain in part why individuals who receive welfare and nations which receive aid may not always respond with gratitude and good feelings (see Chapter 10).

The role of interaction

We have already seen that when the initial impression of another person is reasonably positive, the likelihood increases that interaction will follow. During this subsequent interaction, additional information will be acquired which will enhance or detract from our rating of the individual's attractiveness. It is the case, however, that independent of any other facts which may be involved, interaction *by itself* can affect liking. An experiment by Insko and Wilson (1977) provides us with a good illustration of this process. These investigators brought subjects together in groups of three. By random selection, two of them were asked to "get to know one another" while the other observed. Then, after about ten minutes, they switched around and one of the interactors repeated the process with the observer. Identifying the three subjects as A, B, and C, we note that A interacts with B while C observes and B interacts with C while A observes. This creates a situation in which B has interacted with both of the others, A has only interacted with B, C has never interacted with A, and B has never been an observer. Given the simplicity of the situation, there are a surprising number of comparisons to be made but, for our purposes, let's stick to three categories: (1) interaction plus extra information (C to B and A to B); (2) interaction (B to C and B to A); and (3) no interaction (C to A and A to C). The "extra information" arises from the fact that in these two cases, C and A had also had the opportunity of observing B interacting with the other.

There were a number of estimates of attraction on the questionnaire but the major item consisted of a straightforward question: "To what extent do you like this person?" Subjects answered using a 7-point scale, ranging from "not at all" (1) to "very much" (7).

Analysis of these data revealed that there was no difference between the interaction-plus-information and interaction-only categories, but that both of these were statistically different from the no-interaction category. Since the no-interaction subjects heard and saw the same things as did the interaction subjects, the difference must be due to the interaction itself. Insko and Wilson (1977) offer a number of suggestions about what could be happening. They observe that when people come together this way, they deliberately seek out each other's common interests and similarities and, to the extent that they succeed, mutual liking will be enhanced. Since the subjects in this experiment were all students enrolled at the same university, the probability of having friends, interests, and other characteristics in common would be quite high. But why would the observer, who is drawn from the same population, not also feel some resonance with the discussion in progress? It seems that rapport between people does not develop on a second-hand basis; the process must be one of active *mutual* discovery of similarities.

Keep in mind that we are considering interpersonal contacts in which the parties are free to initiate or terminate the interaction at their discretion. There are many situations, however, over which the participants do not have control. Often we must interact with people — relatives, classmates, co-workers — whether we want to or not. Let us consider how we may come to like someone in this "constrained" situation.

No-choice relationships

What happens when we find ourselves in a situation with another person who is unpleasant, unattractive, or even repulsive, and we cannot escape? Do we simply put up with the situation? Do our feelings become even more intense? Or do they become less intense as time passes? Little research has been done in this area, but some information is available. Darley and Berscheid (1967) told subjects that at a future time, they either would or would not interact with another person. Those who anticipated meeting the other person also indicated that they liked the person more than did those in the other group, who had not been given this information. It has also been argued (Heider, 1958) that in order to maintain a balanced cognitive state, the anticipation of interaction will increase liking for neutral or negative others, but not for positive others. A study specifically designed to test this proposition (Mirels and Mills, 1964) showed that anticipated interaction with a person who had "many unpleasant characteristics" led to greater liking than anticipated interaction with a person who had "a few unpleasant characteristics."

A more complete approach to this problem was taken by Tyler and Sears (1977) who reported on two experiments. In one study, they led subjects to believe that they either would or would not interact with another person who was either "negative," "ambiguous," or "positive." The image of the other as negative, positive, or ambiguous was created by telling subjects that the stimulus person was pleasant and had the same opinions as they had on certain social issues (positive), was pleasant and disagreed on the issues or was unpleasant and agreed on the issues (two forms

Sometimes we have no choice but to associate with an obnoxious person.

of ambivalence), or was unpleasant and disagreed on the issues (negative). These manipulations generated more liking for the ambiguous and negative stimulus persons than for the positive stimulus persons. In fact, the effect was sufficiently strong to move even the most negatively evaluated persons above the neutral point on the liking scale.

In a second, more realistic study (Tyler and Sears, 1977), confederates of the experimenter were coached to act in a very obnoxious manner during an actual face-to-face discussion. They smoked without asking permission, rocked the discussion table, forgot names, snapped gum, avoided looking at the discussants while talking, told the discussants they were too young to have reasonable opinions, blew smoke in the discussants' faces, and remarked that the discussants were saying silly things. After 20 minutes, the discussion was interrupted and the participants were placed in separate rooms. Some of the real subjects then learned that they would continue the discussions with the same person for another 40 minutes and others were told they would change to another discussion group. As a control, other subjects interacted with other real subjects and they, too, were led to believe that they either would or would not continue the interaction with the same person. All subjects were asked to indicate how much they liked the other person at the end of the first session.

It was reported that those who anticipated interacting again with the obnoxious confederate rated the person more highly than did those who thought they would enter a different discussion group, and the liking of a real subject was not different in these two conditions.

This seems to be quite a powerful demonstration of the "no choice" effect but *why* it happens is not as clear. Tyler and Sears interpet it in terms of Heider's (1958) theory of *unit-sentiment balance*. This unit is formed when people feel that they "belong with" another person or object. One basis for creating a unit of this sort is *common fate* which, in this context, may be defined as the likelihood of future interaction. Since these interpersonal linkages must be cognitively balanced, feeling towards individuals with negative or mixed characteristics must then be adjusted in the positive direction. Obviously, no change has to occur for the evaluation to be positive in the case of persons who are already liked. As we have already noted, unbalanced cognitive states are psychologically unpleasant and individuals will be motivated to modify them.

So far, we have considered how we might come to like someone with whom we are interacting on a casual, superficial basis. Most of our encounters with people occur in this way, and we can accept and enjoy this interaction without expecting or wanting more. However, with some people, a more intimate relationship develops. The following section reviews some of the important variables which contribute to the development of *mutuality*.

MUTUALITY

Levinger and Snoek (1972) describe mutuality as a continuum representing degrees of intimacy in a relationship. The two persons are now interdependent to an extent, and assume some responsibility for the satisfaction and well-being of the other. To a considerable degree, the relationship becomes free of external, cultural norms and rules. The individuals have their own understanding, often unspoken, of the "rules" of the relationship. They have developed a sense of "we" and "us" vs. "you" and "I." Self-disclosure is fundamental to this kind of a relationship, and communication is enhanced.

Importance of self-disclosure

The development of a relationship involves "getting to know" the other person, which obviously depends on the willingness of the other person to allow this to happen. Although the processes of self-disclosure have been researched extensively, many questions remain to be answered. For example, do we reveal more to people we like, or do we come to like people to whom we have disclosed ourselves? Must self-disclosure be reciprocal, or can we accept situations in which A knows more about us than we know about A? Can we reveal too much, too soon? We do know that people in general and especially persons of different social classes and cultures vary in self-disclosure.

It is clear that people will reveal more about themselves to people they like than to people they dislike (Chaiken and Derlega, 1974). But what about the reverse? Will others increase their liking for us if we offer them some scintillating personal gossip? The evidence indicates that this may well be the case, but it depends on the stage the interaction has reached. Strangers may be repelled if we are overly intimate. In such cases, intermediate levels of disclosure create a more favourable impression (Cozby, 1973). The research also supports the notion that within certain limits, personal revelations are likely to be reciprocated. Studies by Rubin (1975, 1976) indicate, however, that if too much is revealed, the other person becomes suspicious and is likely to become less, rather than more, open. As we have already indicated (Chapter 6), the reciprocity norm is powerful in human affairs: we try to keep the "books balanced," whether it be Christmas cards or personal information. However, each of us has a threshold beyond which it would be too costly, painful, or anxiety-provoking to reciprocate (Altman, 1973; Chaiken and Darlega, 1974).

Self-disclosure is also influenced by gender roles (see Box 8-2). In one relevant study, male and female experimental assistants approached male and female travellers in an airport departure lounge (Rubin, 1974). Half requested travellers to participate in a study of handwriting analysis and the other half in a study of self-disclosure. Many refused, and their refusals were interesting. Regardless of what they believed the study

B · O · X   8-2

SEX DIFFERENCES IN INTIMATE COMMUNICATION

There are sex differences in styles of communication (see Chapter 11), at least in the United States, where most of the studies have been done. In her review of the research, Sharon Brehm (1985) summarizes the important differences in the context of relationships:

(1) Women tend to be more skillful at both sending and receiving non-verbal messages and in communicating warmth or comforting messages.

(2) Men tend to communicate more calmly, to compromise, and to act on feelings of empathy.

(3) Women tend to be more negative and emotional during conflict and to send "double messages" (e.g., to smile warmly while telling him how terrible he is).

(4) Men tend to communicate without appropriate emotional expressiveness.

It is necessary to be cautious about these findings.

First, like most sex differences, we are reporting *mean* differences between two overlapping distributions; there are many calm, even cold, women and many expressive, even, occasionally, hysterical men in the world and behaviour by an individual can vary considerably across situations. Second, the results may reflect the cultural stereotype of expressive women and practical men in two ways. People may perceive themselves and others as acting in these ways even if they do not. And, the self-fulfilling prophecy may cause men and women (and boys and girls) to act as they are expected to act. However, studies of early infant responses suggest the possibility of an inherent, biological basis for these differences (Haviland and Malatesta, 1981). All of these factors probably play a role, and it may never be possible to disentangle them.

was to be about, females were twice as likely to refuse a male than a female assistant. However, among males, the refusal rate was greater only when asked by a male to participate in a study of self-disclosure. The refusal rate for males in the handwriting analysis condition was equal to that of females who refused a female assistant.

Intimacy and communication

An interesting model of intimacy and communication is provided by Altman and Taylor (1973). They focus on the social penetration process by which we come to know someone well or intimately. According to the model, we can know many aspects of a person or only a few (breadth), and we can know any particular aspect of a person in a more or less personal way (depth). In other words, breadth refers to how many different attributes of a person we know, while depth refers to how intimate or personal the information is concerning a particular attribute.

For example, several people who work in the same office may take their coffee breaks together, and talk about many different topics (high in breadth) but never at an intensely personal level (low in depth). Teammates on a professional baseball team during a pennant-winning season may come to know everything that there is to know about one another as baseball players but rarely talk about anything else (depth without breadth). Typically, a relationship develops by first talking about a wide variety of topics and later, gradually becoming more personal or intimate about a few of the topics. Thus the process of "social penetration" is described in terms of a wedge —

broad at a superficial level, more narrow as the level of exchange becomes more intimate.

Later work by Altman and his colleagues revealed an interesting evolution in their thinking. Originally, they believed that if a relationship endured, it moved in one direction toward more intimacy. However, it became evident that relationships tended to fluctuate, rather than simply move or grow in one direction. Even in a successful marriage, the partners feel very close and intense at some times, relatively more distant and casual at others (Altman, Vincel and Brown, 1981). Altman (1975) suggests that people must satisfy two needs: to be close and intimate with someone and to maintain a sense of self and privacy. These needs for intimacy and privacy constitute an ongoing dialectical process, or process of reconciliation, in which we seek a balance. Such a balance does not consist simply of a compromise or middle-ground between the two states, but is a dynamic synthesis which is influenced by what is happening to us and our relationships with other people. At times, we feel the need for more intimacy; at other times, we crave more "space" or emotional distance. Hence, we may not reveal something important to our intimate partner, or we may suddenly choose to confide in a more casual acquaintance.

This model offers a rich and realistic conception of human relationships. Rather than simply describing or measuring the relationship in terms of the degree of intimacy present at one time, important relationships are shown to evolve and, to an extent, be inconsistent over time. Much work remains to be done to translate these ideas into testable hypotheses.

The picture is complicated by an important factor. Thus far, social penetration, including the regulation of privacy, has appeared to involve only verbal behaviour, especially self-disclosure. However, Altman and Taylor (1973) note that we can communicate to others in many non-verbal ways (see also Chapter 11). We may say something with or without certain vocal inflections or dynamics which reveal or conceal our feelings, even whether we are being truthful or open (consider the poker player who announces a substantial raise at a crucial time). Facial expressions, interpersonal distance, eye contact, and body orientation may all communicate or not communicate. The social context or the physical environment may also play a role. The same words may increase either the sense of intimacy or distance and privacy, whether spoken as a profession of love, a description of the weather, or a political opinion. Having a sip of wine may communicate a great deal of the sipper's feelings about the wine or the companion — depending on the quality and vintage (of the wine and the companion).

Argyle and Dean (1965) have proposed a model which takes into consideration the relationship between eye contact, amount of smiling, physical distance, and personal disclosure. They describe a compensatory system in which a change in one behaviour stimulates a change in another in order to maintain the stability of a given level of intimacy. For example, in a casual relationship, if distance between the parties decreases, eye contact should also decrease. The experimental evidence largely supports the Argyle and Dean proposal. It has been found that subjects looked less at an interviewer during an intimate interview than during a more neutral interview (Exline, Gray and Schuette, 1965). In addition, Jourard and Friedman (1970) observed that as distance between an experimenter and female subjects increased, the amount of disclosure increased. Goldberg, Kiesler and Collins (1969) noted that male subjects who sat two-and-a-half feet away from a male interviewer engaged in less eye contact than other subjects who sat six feet away. Similar results have also been recorded by Aiello (1972). Not only does this model emphasize the need to take a multi variable approach to social behaviour, but it also illustrates another application of the "balance principle" discussed earlier.

Equity and Social Exchange

Of course, equity is an important consideration in any relationship. Even when it entails sacrifice, we are motivated to maintain a sense of fairness between our friends and ourselves. The notion of social exchange, the principle of an interpersonal marketplace in which we try to maximize rewards and minimize costs, is most likely to be valid between strangers and casual acquaintances, and in the earliest stages of a relationship. However, as the bonds become more firmly established and mutuality develops, exchange — and even fairness — figure less and less. As intimate partners, we have more to gain and more to give, and we become increasingly concerned with giving.

Foa (1971) offers a useful framework for this discussion (Figure 8-5). He proposes six *interpersonal resources* which can be exchanged: love, status, information, money, goods, and services. These resources can be classified according to their particularism and their concreteness. *Particularism* refers to the extent to which a resource's value is influenced by the person who gives it. For example, money is valuable (subject to the rate of exchange) regardless of who gives it, a supper probably tastes better when cooked by a special person (service), and love's value depends almost entirely on who does the loving. *Concreteness* refers to the characteristic form of expression of the resources. Goods and services are tangible — things you can see, smell, taste or touch — while status (e.g., praise) and information (e.g., the shortest route from Nelson,

FIGURE 8–5
Rewards that people exchange

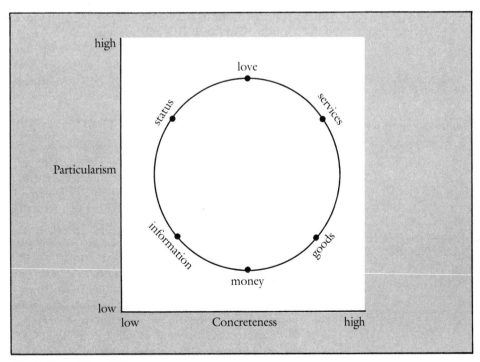

SOURCE: Foa and Foa, 1976

B.C. to Corner Brook, Nfld.) are verbal or symbolic, and love and money have both symbolic and concrete value. Generally speaking, we prefer exchanges within the same classes. She helps to repair his car (service) and he responds with flowers (goods), but we rarely exchange money for love. The books are balanced.

In intimate relationships the meaning of equitable exchange is transformed. Exchanges include particularistic and concrete resources: we give and receive affection, support and praise (status), we take the time to do more for each other (services), and to help each other with problems (information). In addition, intimate or "mutual" relationships have the benefit of time and variety of situations. For example, in our casual social lives, we may be very careful to reciprocate a dinner invitation within a reasonable period of time. Among close friends and lovers, however, we may reciprocate immediately with verbal praise and affection and not feel any further obligation. It is true that intimates spend much time "negotiating" the "terms" of their relationships, coming to know what they expect, hope, like and dislike of each other. But if they are secure in the sense that the relationship is mutually satisfying (i.e., equitable), they can forego immediate reciprocation, and will not need to "keep score" of rewards and costs. Indeed, such bookkeeping would violate the concept of mutuality.

Another problem which can arise in the exchange processes is an "egocentric bias." In short, we tend to overestimate the value of what we contribute to a relationship. In one study of married couples, spouses were asked to rate independently how they divided responsibility for twenty relevant activities, e.g., cleaning house, planning recreational activities, child care. On a 150-point scale, we might expect the self-rated responsibility by husband and wife to equal 150. For example, if he rated himself as 80/150 responsible for child care, she would rate her responsibility as 70/150. In fact, the average total for 73 percent of the couples came to *over* 150 (Ross and Sicoly, 1979). Generally, more satisfied couples tend to be in agreement about the contribution of each partner to the relationship (Christensen, Sullaway and King, 1983). The interesting issue is one of cause and effect. Perhaps agreement leads to satisfaction, or perhaps satisfaction leads the couples to greater agreement. Or perhaps a third factor, such as excellent communication, leads to both agreement and satisfaction.

Complementarity: Do opposites attract?

The strongest advocate of the idea that individuals can be attracted to each other on the basis of differences has been Winch (1954, 1958). His evidence is primarily concerned with the relationship between mate selection and personal needs, or motives. Winch argued that similarity of factors such as religion and socioeconomic status bring people together but it is the *complementarity* of needs that keeps them together. For example, a man with sadistic or aggressive needs is not likely to get along with a woman who also is aggressive, but if she were masochistic, each would find the relationship satisfying. Similarly, people who want to be "mothered" or "fathered" are likely to be happy with a partner who needs to take care of someone.

Winch (1958) described two types of complementarity, aptly labelled Type I and Type II. Type I describes a relationship in which one individual is high on a particular motive and the other is low on the same motive, e.g., high and low dominance. Type II describes a relationship in which one individual is high on one motive and the other is high on another complementary motive, e.g., high dominance complemented by high deference. Winch's research was severely criticized on methodological and statistical grounds but a little later, Kerckhoff and Davis (1962) reported a more convincing study of dating couples which led them to propose a *sequential filter theory*. This theory was derived from their observation that while the relationship between newly dating couples could be predicted over a six-month period on the basis of the extent to which they shared values, the relationship of couples who had been dating for a longer period was actually based on a complementarity of needs. According to Kerckhoff and Davis, individuals first compare themselves on social and demographic characteristics (religion, socioeconomic status). Then they look for what they have in common in attitudes and values. If the relationship survives, long-term commitment will be based on the extent to which their needs are complementary.

There continues to be considerable debate about the adequacy of this model (e.g., Levinger, Senn and Jorgensen, 1970). As Huston and Levinger note: "The idea of a sequentially ordered series of filters has continued to prove appealing" (1978, p. 137) and so, research continues (e.g., Murstein, 1976; Lewis, 1972). While any theory of development can involve a sequence of events or stages, it is too early in our understanding to assume a fixed, invariant sequence common to all couples.

How then can we describe an intimate relationship? Burgess and Huston (1979) suggest the following outline as a consensus of opinion on the subject of intimacy:

(1) The two people interact more often for a longer time and in more situations than do less intimate friends or acquaintances.
(2) When apart, they attempt to restore proximity.
(3) They "open up to each other," revealing secrets, feelings, praise, and criticism.
(4) They develop their own ways of communicating.
(5) Each develops the ability to anticipate how the other will behave and feel.
(6) Their behaviours and goals become "synchronized" — not identical, but they do not get in each other's way.
(7) Each becomes increasingly "invested" in the relationship.
(8) Increasingly, the self-interest of each depends on the well-being of the relationship.
(9) They see the relationship as virtually irreplaceable and unique.
(10) They tend to relate to others as a pair, or couple.
(11) They like, love, and trust each other.

Of course, this list represents a series of tendencies or directions in which relationships evolve, rather than absolute standards.

Intimacy can be found among family members and close friends as well as married couples and lovers. Since romantic love is a special form of intimacy, it has received special attention. Let us review some of this work.

LOVE

While philosophers, poets, songwriters, and artists have always been fascinated with the topic of love, it may be considered daring — perhaps presumptuous — for social psychologists to study it scientifically. Since love is a profound and personal experience, the reader must be warned that the present discussion cannot adequately represent its intense and unique qualities. Indeed, some have argued that science is misplaced in this area. Yet, the personal suffering and social turmoil accompanying the astronomical divorce rates provide ample evidence that we have much to learn about love. Perhaps the scientific method, which has proven to be so successful elsewhere, can be useful here as well.

To begin, it is important to understand the varieties of experience and relationships which incorporate love — love of parents for children, love of parents, grandparents, brothers and sisters, love of a friend, love of country or art, love of a spouse or sexual partner. In these various experiences of love, is there anything common to all? Sternberg (1986) has outlined a "triangular theory" in which he defines three fundamental components of all love relationships: (see Figure 8-6) intimacy, passion, and decision/commitment. *Intimacy* refers to the feeling of closeness or "connectedness," the experience of "warmth" in the relationship. *Passion* is the source of motivational arousal, experienced as physical attraction within a romantic relationship. In addition, love implies a *decision* to label our feelings as such, and a *commitment* to maintain the relationship in the future.

Of course, the relative strength or weighting of these three components will vary

FIGURE 8–6
Sternberg's triangular model of love

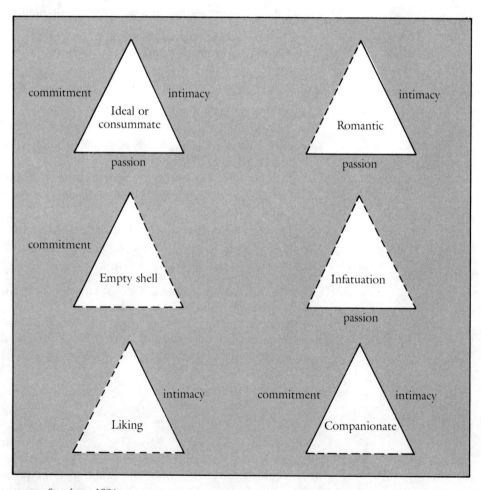

SOURCE: Sternberg, 1986

COHABITATION: AN ALTERNATIVE

For many or most people, a committed romantic relationship is an extremely valued part of their lives and an important source of life satisfaction. Marriage is the most usual form of such relationships, sanctioned by society and religion. Today, however, many people choose to delay entering into marriage. There are many reasons for this trend — the involvement of women in the workforce, the emphasis on personal identity and personal development, the desire of both sexes to work hard at careers and advance economically, and a reluctance to get into something which so often fails. Thus, many couples are living together without marriage in a social climate which accepts such arrangements as perfectly legitimate.

Newcomb (1986) reviews evidence that cohabitation offers a way to blend two opposing needs — for independence and relatedness. That is, while many people in this period of life are striving for independence, economic stability, and individual validation, they still want and need a relationship which is intimate and supportive.

It is interesting that most people who are living together now plan to marry in the future. In comparing married couples who had and had not lived together prior to marriage, the investigators found that those who had cohabited perceived themselves as more androgynous, more attractive, more objective about themselves, and less religious, and reported greater sexual experimentation. In most other personality and background characteristics, they are not particularly unique (Newcomb and Bentler, 1980).

When and why do they eventually get married? An obvious factor is the desire to have children, although there is no evidence of an unusually high birth rate in their first few years of marriage. Some may marry in response to pressure from the parents, or in the hope that the marriage contract will mend a troubled relationship (which often leads to disaster). For most couples, choosing to marry represents an additional step toward commitment, a stage beyond dating and living together. The research shows that cohabitors are not more or less likely to be satisfied with their marriage. In fact, their marriages are slightly more likely to end in divorce, probably because they are more accepting of divorce as a realistic alternative when the relationship founders. It is probably true that like any other couple, their success in negotiating solutions to common needs and problems, including the blend of relatedness and independence, will largely determine the outcome of their marriage.

in different relationships. Short-term relationships tend to be high on passion, lower on intimacy, and lower still on decision/commitment, while long-term relationships are characterized primarily by intimacy and commitment. Passion (i.e., intense emotional involvement) is specific to romantic relationships and generally absent from friendships and family relationships. Decision and commitment are usually high in relationships with our children and relatively low in the friendships which begin, flourish, and end for various reasons. However, intimacy seems to be at the core of most relationships which we describe as love, including love of parents, siblings, children, close friends and, of course, spouse or lover (see Box 8-3 for an example).

Romantic love always has been fascinating. In our culture, we tend to "fall in love" (a revealing expression!) and then marry. But there are many cultures (India, for example) in which the opposite is the rule. Marriages are arranged by the parents and the couple may not even have met until the time of the wedding. Love is not a motive for marriage, and is expected to develop with the passage of time. In the musical, *Fiddler on the Roof*, Tevye, a Jewish peasant living in a ghetto in Russia in the nineteenth century, asks his "arranged bride" of 25 years whether she loves him. After reminding him that she has, for 25 years, lived with him, cooked his meals, shared his bed, and borne his children, he repeats the question, "Do you love me?" Exasperated, she declares: "I'm your wife." Delighted, Tevye realizes that she has answered the question: "Then you *do* love me!" In other words love is an expected outcome of marriage in that culture.

There have been a number of attempts to describe the varied experiences of love. For different people, romantic love may represent a passionate emotional and physical involvement, an interpersonal "game" of manipulation without deep emotional

TABLE 8–1
Sample Items from Hendrick and Hendrick's Love Attitudes Scale

1. My lover and I have the right physical "chemistry" between us.
   strongly agree   agree   uncertain   disagree   strongly disagree

2. Our lovemaking is very intense and satisfying.
   strongly agree   agree   uncertain   disagree   strongly disagree

3. I enjoy playing the "game of love" with a number of different partners.
   strongly agree   agree   uncertain   disagree   strongly disagree

4. I try to keep my lover a little uncertain about my commitment to him/her.
   strongly agree   agree   uncertain   disagree   strongly disagree

5. The best kind of love grows out of a long friendship.
   strongly agree   agree   uncertain   disagree   strongly disagree

6. My most satisfying love relationships have developed from good friendships.
   strongly agree   agree   uncertain   disagree   strongly disagree

7. I consider what a person is going to become in life before I commit myself to him/her.
   strongly agree   agree   uncertain   disagree   strongly disagree

8. An important factor in choosing a partner is whether or not he/she will be a good parent.
   strongly agree   agree   uncertain   disagree   strongly disagree

9. When my lover doesn't pay attention to me, I feel sick all over.
   strongly agree   agree   uncertain   disagree   strongly disagree

10. When I am in love, I have trouble concentrating on anything else.
    strongly agree   agree   uncertain   disagree   strongly disagree

11. I cannot be happy unless I place my lover's happiness before my own.
    strongly agree   agree   uncertain   disagree   strongly disagree

12. I would rather suffer myself than let my lover suffer.
    strongly agree   agree   uncertain   disagree   strongly disagree

KEY: passionate (items 1 and 2)   game-playing (items 3 and 4)
       friendship (item 5 and 6)   pragmatic   (items 7 and 8)
       possessive (items 9 and 10)   selfless   (items 11 and 12)

SOURCE: Hendrick and Hendrick, 1986

involvement, or a relaxed, down-to-earth friendship. For others, romantic love may involve both passion and game-playing, and be desperately possessive, or it may simply define the process of choosing a suitable mate, rationally and deliberately. Scales have been developed for the various types of love (see Table 8-1), and several interesting findings have been reported. The research shows clearly that few people can be considered as "pure types," and most people experience romantic love as some combination of orientations, influenced by motives, previous experience, and what is happening at that time in their lives. Indeed, those who report that they are "in love now" scored higher than other respondents on all scales except that which measured a manipulative, game-playing approach. Thus it seems that being in love may cue a "flare-up of cognitions" involving various aspects of the state of romantic love.

Gender differences

Do males and females differ with respect to romantic love? At least in our culture, there do appear to be differences (Hendrick and Hendrick, 1986; Peplau and Gordon, 1985; Dion and Dion, 1985). Surprisingly, males tend to have a "romantic" view, believing that true romantic love comes once and lasts forever, conquers all barriers and social customs, is essentially strange and incomprehensible, and must be basic to marriage. On the other hand, females tend to be more pragmatic, i.e., they believe they can be in love many times, that it may not last, that it inevitably fades into some disillusionment when the honeymoon ends, and that economic security and friendship are more important as bases for marriage. These differences in beliefs may be related to greater emotional dependence by males and/or greater economic dependency by females, although the picture for women is obviously changing dramatically.

However, the actual experiences of females are not especially based on pragmatism. Males report that they tend to fall in love earlier than females in a relationship. However, females report that they have been in love more frequently and more intensely, and are more likely to have had both pleasant and unpleasant (e.g., unrequited love) experiences. They tend more to like and even idealize their partners (see Box 8-4), and they more often report emotional experiences and euphoric "symptoms" such as "floating on air," or having trouble concentrating (Brehm, 1985). Perhaps women are more pragmatic in their selection of a love partner and in defining what love means, and yet more able to experience love as an intense emotional experience. Or, perhaps women are simply more willing or able to report intimate, intense experiences and feelings. It is important to note that while these differences are statistically reliable, they represent "average" males and females from a given population, and that there is considerable variation within each sex in how romantic love is experienced.

Why have these differences developed in our society in what males and females believe about love and how they experience it? A functionalist interpretation considers how romantic love enables individuals to adapt to society and maintain social institutions such as marriage (Dion and Dion, 1985). Romantic love is seen as a bond keeping a couple together, which is particularly important in the absence of other types of limits such as social pressure, parental duties, or economic interdependence. Since women have traditionally contributed less than men to the family income, they would have more to gain by pragmatically linking love and marriage. On the other hand, men are traditionally trained to be economically independent; while the majority of wives now work, it is still considered unacceptable for husbands to be dependent

B · O · X   8-4

LIKING OR LOVING: DEFINITION AND MEASUREMENT

How can we go about doing research on the differences between *liking* and *loving*? In reviewing the research, Berscheid (1985) suggests several ways in which they differ:

(1) Liking is relatively stable over time, whereas romantic love tends to be more fragile and volatile.

(2) Liking is strongly influenced by the actual exchange of rewards, whereas romantic love is influenced more by what we anticipate in the future.

(3) Liking is influenced in a logical way by rewards (we like people more who reward us more), whereas romantic love is often unrelated or even intensified by frustration, rejection, and other suffering.

What seems clear is that loving is not simply an extreme form of liking; as emotions, they are qualitatively different.

Zick Rubin (1970, 1973), after reading an assortment of definitions and descriptions of love by novelists, poets, clinicians, and scientists, made up a series of statements and asked a number of judges to sort them into "liking" and "loving" categories. He found very high agreement on some items. Through several revisions, he ended up with two nine-item scales, one for liking and the other for loving. The following examples are drawn from both scales:

(1) *Liking Scale*
   a) evaluation:
      "Most people would react favourably to _____ after a brief acquaintance."
   b) judgment/respect:
      "I have great confidence in _____'s good judgment."
   c) adjustment:
      "In my opinion, _____ is an unusually mature person."

on the income of their wives. Thus they would be less concerned with the uses of romantic love as binding a marriage and would feel free to indulge in idealism or cynicism. It is interesting that men are more likely than women to endorse items such as "Marry whom you love, regardless of social position," while women are more likely to agree that "Economic security should be considered carefully before selecting a marriage partner." Research also suggests that men fall *into* love more readily and women fall *out of* love more readily; women evidently feel that they cannot waste too much time with the wrong partner (Hill, Rubin and Peplau, 1976).

One fascinating study revealing sex differences was conducted by Dion and Dion (1976). Couples were recruited in the Ontario Science Centre in Toronto. Each was asked to observe the other walking through an "Ames room," a perceptual distortion apparatus in which objects look unusually large at one end and unusually small at the other. For males, the distortion effect was evident in observing both their partners and a stranger in the Ames room. However, for females (particularly those who scored high on Rubin's measures of liking and loving, and a scale of interpersonal trust), the distortion of their partner's appearance was significantly reduced. Hence, love seemed to modify aspects of feminine perception with regard to a partner's physical appearance — in the direction of reality.

(2) *Loving Scale*
- a) attachment:
  "If I were lonely, my first thought would be to seek _____ out."
- b) caring:
  "I would do almost anything for _____."
- c) intimacy, absorption:
  "I feel very possessive about _____."

These scales were administered to 182 dating couples, each of whom filled them out about their partner and their best friend. The findings are noteworthy and seem to support the validity of these scales.

Scores on the two scales were correlated positively but only moderately so — .56 for males' liking and loving of their girlfriends and only .36 for females' liking and loving of their boyfriends. That is, the results suggest that while the two are related, people, especially males, can like someone very much without loving that person, and they can even love someone without liking him or her. The scores of both males and females on the love scale correlated highly with subjects' own reports of being "in love" and with estimates of how likely they estimated eventual marriage to their partners.

In a laboratory investigation, couples who scored highly on the love scale spent more time gazing into each other's eyes during a conversation. In a follow-up conducted six months later, Rubin found that those who had scored highly on the love scale reported that their relationship had become more intense.

In another study, Dermer and Pyszczynski (1978) asked one group of college males to read a "collegiate fantasy" which dealt, in explicit detail, with the sexual fantasies and actions of a college woman; the control group read a rather boring technical report on the mating behaviour of herring gulls. After the assigned reading was completed, they filled out Rubin's liking and loving scales. Results showed that those who had read the erotic passages had significantly higher love scores (for *their* partners), but not liking scores.

Love and cognition

Both males and females believe that a love relationship should be intrinsic, that is, it should exist on its own apart from external circumstances. In order to study this belief, Seligman, Fazio and Zanna (1980) recruited dating couples and then manipulated their cognitive set by having each subject complete open-ended sentences. Half were sentences containing the phrase "because I," while the others contained the phrase "in order to" (e.g., I date my boyfriend *because I* or *in order to* . . .). Previous research had shown that repeated exposure to the phrase *because I* induced an intrinsic cognitive set, while *in order to* led to an extrinsic set. Then, the set was reinforced by having the subject rank in order a group of reasons for dating their partner, either intrinsic reasons (inherent aspects of the relationship and the partner) or extrinsic ones (useful aspects of the relationship). Students given an extrinsic cognitive set then scored only about 50 on Rubin's love scale, while both those with the intrinsic set and a control group scored about 61. When the subjects became conscious of possible extrinsic reasons, their feelings of love actually waned. We are not supposed to have ulterior motives for love.

Note that the experiment does not suggest that thinking, in itself, diminishes love.

Tesser (1978) suggests that the more you think about an issue, the more polarized or extreme your attitude will be on that issue. Dating students were asked about their love for their partner and how often they thought about their partner (Tesser and Paulus, 1970). The data from two testing sessions two weeks apart showed that loving and thinking did influence each other: the more you love her, the more you think about her, and the more you think about her, the more you love her. Thus absence makes the heart grow fonder — unless you are too busy or distracted to think about your partner very much.

It is important to distinguish between passionate love and companionate love (Hatfield and Walster, 1978). Passionate love is an overwhelming, highly emotional, agonizing, and ecstatic condition, while companionate love is a low-key but deeply felt involvement, commitment, and friendship. It would seem reasonable to assume that passionate love characterizes the earlier stages of the relationship and that when the honeymoon ends, passion is inevitably replaced by companionate love. Yet, a study of women after an average of 33 years of marriage showed that they exhibited *both* companionate love and a considerable degree of passion for their mates (Traupmann and Hatfield, 1981). Evidently, these may not be different types of love but separate phases in a process which develops over a long-term relationship.

Can passionate love be a misattribution?

Berscheid and Walster (1974) propose that three conditions are necessary for someone to "fall in love" as we understand it. First, the person must be raised in a culture that believes in the idea of romantic love. As we noted earlier, many do not (although many popular East Indian movies today depict romantic couples who defy their parents). Second, the person feels a state of emotional arousal which is *interpreted* as love. The third condition is the presence of an appropriate love object, most often a physically attractive member of the opposite sex. Crucial to this model is how people interpret symptoms of their own physiological arousal, such as a faltering voice, faintness, erratic eye movements, inability to concentrate, blushing, heart palpitations, muscle tremors: An old song aptly advises that "you're not sick, you're just in love."

What is especially interesting is that arousal may be elicited by negative circumstances and then attributed to romantic sentiments. Many intense relationships occur during the tension and terror of wartime. Seriously ill patients often fall in love with their physicians, nurses, or therapists. While we may still be quite aware of the initial source of our state of arousal, we may still be vulnerable to romantic involvement because of the intense emotional state.

Both experimental and field studies have supported the model. For one study, unmarried and married couples were asked to report on aspects of their relationship at two different times, six to ten months apart (Driscoll, Davis and Lipetz, 1972). They found that those who reported more parental interference with their relationship also reported being more in love with their partners at that time. In looking at changes over time, the researchers noted that among the unmarried couples, romantic love increased (or decreased) as parental interference increased (or decreased). For obvious reasons, it was called the "Romeo and Juliet effect." In another study, males were instructed to walk across the shaky Capillano suspension bridge which crosses a deep gorge in Vancouver (Dutton and Aron, 1974). On the other side, they encountered an attractive female experimental assistant. By contrast with those who met the same young lady after crossing a solid, concrete bridge, subjects who met her in their aroused state included more sexual imagery in a projective test and were more likely to telephone her later. Somehow the arousal caused by fear while wobbling in space was subsequently misattributed to feelings of attraction to the woman.

Or was it? Kenrick and Cialdini (1977) criticize this interpretation of studies such as Dutton and Aron (1974) in terms of misattribution. They argue that when the subjects were meeting the attractive young lady, they were feeling relief at having reached solid ground, rather than arousal due to fear. Thus they associated the girl with the relief of escaping from the bridge (negative reinforcement). They do admit, however, that in other situations which involve a "highly ambiguous and diffuse state of arousal," and given the presence of the appropriate person, aroused feelings may be attributed to romantic love.

RELATIONSHIP PROBLEMS

To begin to understand the *process* of ending an intimate relationship, Hill, Rubin and Peplau (1976) compared 103 couples who had broken up with 117 who were still together. The majority of the break-ups were initiated unilaterally by women. Although satisfaction scores did not differ between males and females, dissatisfied women were more likely than men to make the decision to leave the relationship. Couples who broke up tended to be less similar in age, future educational plans, intelligence and physical attractiveness, although there were no differences between the two groups of couples in romanticism, sex-role attitudes, or religious beliefs. Whether or not the couples had engaged in sexual relations early or late in the relationship, or abstained from sexual involvement altogether, did not predict whether the couple stayed together or broke up. However, among those who broke up, typically one partner was less intensely involved than the other.

Levinger (1979) argues that in deciding to remain in or leave a marriage, people tend to consider both the rewards and costs of staying and the rewards and costs of leaving. Rewards such as an alternative relationship or the freedom of being single again will tend to lead the person to dissolve the relationship, while anything that makes separation more costly will tend to maintain the relationship. A person may stay in an unsatisfactory marriage because of a concern about the children, a fear that friendships and social networks will be disrupted, or a realization that a break-up will entail major financial sacrifices. Such an analysis explains the "empty shell marriage" in which the marriage itself is unsatisfactory or non-existent, but the barriers to leaving remain. Of course, social changes such as improved employment opportunities for women, less social stigma attached to divorce, and "no-fault" or less costly divorce procedures can attenuate these barriers. Ironically, by reducing the stress which accompanies divorce, we may also increase the rate of divorce.

Dissolution of relationships

There is abundant research evidence linking marital separation to a wide variety of stress-related disorders (Bloom, Asher and White, 1978). In comparison with both now-married and never-married persons, separated and divorced persons are more prone to automobile accidents, psychiatric disorders, alcoholism, suicide, and death from tuberculosis, cirrhosis of the liver, and certain forms of cancer and coronary diseases. More recent research has shown that people who are unhappily married tend to be less healthy than those who are no longer married. Obviously, stressful factors in divorce — financial difficulties, sexual problems, feelings of shame, guilt or failure, problems with children and sheer loneliness — play a role. Compounding these burdens may be a profound feeling of conflict or ambivalence, and each partner can have both intense negative and positive feelings toward the other. Weiss (1979) observes that a strong attachment often persists after love has disappeared.

Some evidence also suggests that men suffer more adverse effects of divorce than women (Chiriboga, Roberts and Stein, 1978). Perhaps a partial explanation may be found in evidence concerning gender differences in friendships. Wright (1980) describes friendships between females as "face-to-face" and those between males as "side-by-side." That is, female friendships are more characterized by reciprocal self-disclosure and emotional sharing, and male friendships, by companionship and common activities. In our culture, males are generally reluctant to be intimate with other males (Rand and Levinger, 1979).

It is not surprising that males tend to be more dependent on the marital romantic relationship than females. Fischer and Phillips (1982) found that when a man marries, he tends to give up friendships (often including non-physical friendships with women) but keeps in touch with casual acquaintances, including people at work. Women tend to do the opposite. Their circle of casual acquaintances diminishes but access to intimate friends is not affected. Thus, even with a greater social network, the male who loses the romantic relationship may be emotionally isolated. For example, divorced women report that the most stressful period was before the separation, while divorced men consider the period after the separation as the most difficult (Hagestad and Smyer, 1982).

Jealousy

Shakespeare's Othello is but one of many familiar characters destroyed by a tragic susceptibility to "the green-eyed monster." Salovey and Rodin (1984) argue that we can distinguish between *social relations jealousy*, the desire for exclusivity in a relationship, and *social comparison jealousy*, the desire to feel better than or at least as good as someone else. In a clever study conducted by these investigators, subjects working separately in pairs believed they were filling out a test of whether they had a "suitable personality" for various career choices. Then they were given bogus feedback in which they were told that their test score was either surprisingly high or surprisingly low on a dimension which was either relevant or irrelevant to their career choice (e.g., medical science aptitude, artistic sensitivity, business acumen). They then saw the bogus test results of their partner along with an essay ostensibly written by their partner about themselves (hobbies, interests, career plans, etc.). All subjects received the same essay but received different test results indicating success or failure by the partner.

Each subject was then asked to evaluate their partner on a questionnaire just before meeting that partner (who was always of the same sex). The group of interest consists of those who had just received negative relevant self-feedback, e.g., those who wanted medicine and scored poorly on that scale, and who believed that their partners had scored very well on their career relevant scale. These were the subjects in whom social

"Is he really working late tonight?"

comparison jealousy had been aroused. They tended to disparage their partners and rated them lower on a number of socially desirable characteristics but nevertheless expressed interest in a possible friendship. They also scored higher in measures of anxious and depressed mood states. Remember that these scores were obtained immediately prior to the point at which they expected to meet that person.

White (1981a) has outlined an interesting model of romantic jealousy. We begin, he says, with *primary appraisal*, perceiving a threat to our relationship that exceeds our tolerance level (e.g., you may react if someone smiles at your partner, dances with your partner, spends the whole evening with your partner, or leaves the party with your partner). A number of factors will influence this threshold of tolerance. We can tolerate more if we feel secure about the relationship, if we are not completely dependent on it, and if the partner is a casual friend rather than an exclusive lover or spouse. On the other hand, we would also react more strongly to a severe threat, e.g., a potential rival who is highly attractive, prestigious, wealthy, or socially adept. We may react differently to different types of threats — threats to sexual or emotional intimacy (which can be a same-sex friendship) or threats to the time spent with our partner (e.g., the Sunday "TV Football Widow" whose husband is obsessed with the game). Notice that the threat to the relationship may be another person or the other commitments or interests of the partner. All can arouse jealousy if threat is perceived.

The individual then proceeds to *secondary appraisal*, trying to understand the situation. The person may review evidence about the threat (e.g., was he or she really that interested in that person), alternative possibilities (e.g., he or she really was working late that night), and evidence that the relationship really isn't in danger (e.g., we're getting along so well together lately). While this can be a useful and rational introspective process, the arousal of feelings of threat may lead to "catastrophic thinking," e.g., she wasn't working that night, or other nights either, she's cheating on me, making a fool of me, everyone probably knows, she'll leave and I'll be alone and miserable for the rest of my life. . . . This train of thought involves the intense emotional reactions which constitute the jealousy experience and which accompany primary and secondary appraisal. The range is tremendous, from mild twinges to total obsession. One study found the fascinating mixture of negative and positive feelings: excitement, emotional and physical distress, feeling alive, anxiety, happiness, anger, confusion, victimization, embarrassment, passion (Pines and Aronson, 1983). In another study, jealousy in both males and females who were romantically involved at the time was found to be related to the expectations of exclusivity in the relationship and to feelings of personal inadequacy as a partner (White, 1981b). For males, jealousy was stronger among those with traditional beliefs about sex roles, low self-esteem, and those whose self-esteem depended upon their partner's favourable evaluation. Jealous females tended to feel more dependent on the relationship itself. Interestingly, neither the longevity of the relationship nor whether the couple reported themselves as dating casually or seriously, living together, engaged or married, was related to jealousy. Given a sufficient degree of investment in a romantic relationship, labels seem irrelevant.

What can be said about gender differences and stereotypes of clinging wives and insanely jealous husbands? There does not seem to be any global difference between males and females in self-reported levels of jealousy (White, 1981b), but there are differences in how jealousy seems to be experienced and expressed. Males tend to react to jealousy either by denial or in an angry, competitive way. Females tend to acknowledge their jealousy, blame themselves, become depressed, and exhibit increasingly dependent behaviour. Interestingly, males seem to be more concerned with the rival than with the partner; this competitive reaction has been called the "rooster effect" (Thompson and Richardson, 1983).

How can we best cope with jealousy? Brehm (1985) suggests that we must first "de-romanticize" jealousy. It is a sign of intense dependence and attachment but not of "true love." Indeed, over 300 years ago, LaRochefoucauld remarked, "In jealousy there is more self-love than love." Then we must distinguish between rational and irrational reactions to this threat. Rationally, we accept the fact that we may lose, we may suffer, and we can survive the pain. Irrationally, we tie our sense of self-worth completely to the relationship. Knowing that our self-esteem cannot depend on anyone else but ourselves will best enable us to cope with jealousy and to be a loving partner.

Loneliness

Most people have experienced or will experience situations in which they feel lonely — visiting a new country, moving to a new location, being temporarily separated from a loved one. However, some people suffer from chronic or dispositional loneliness, regardless of situations. In one longitudinal study of students during their first year of university, 75 percent experienced some degree of loneliness (Cutrona, 1982). By the end of the year, only 25 percent were still lonely. Those who overcame loneliness were not more likely than those who did not live on campus to join clubs, play intramural sports, or go to parties. However, those who overcame loneliness began with positive expectations and positive feelings about themselves.

Another study of how lonely students behave in conversation with a stranger revealed that they tend to be more self-focused, asking fewer questions and making fewer statements about the other person. Lonely persons also tend to be atypical in their style of self-disclosure (Solano, Batten and Parish, 1982). Either they pour their hearts out to a total stranger or they are unusually closed, revealing little of themselves, even to someone they know well. Moreover, chronically lonely persons tend to be less effective in non-verbal communication, such as expressing and judging emotions (Gerson and Perlman, 1979).

What is loneliness? Perlman and Peplau (1981) identify three characteristics.

(1) It results from perceived deficiencies in the person's relationships.
(2) It is distressing and unpleasant.
(3) It is subjective rather than objective — we can feel intensely lonely in a crowd and not at all lonely when alone. It is said, in order to portray loneliness, an artist must portray a person with others.

For example, Sadava and Matejcic (1987) report surprising evidence of significant levels of loneliness in a group of people who had been recently married. Loneliness was higher among husbands who felt less liking and less intimacy toward their wives, and had greater worries about communicating with them, and among wives who felt less liking and less love toward their husbands and manifested less self-disclosure to them. That is, loneliness reflected the *quality* of the relationship, rather than simply its presence or absence. Since the subjects were recently married, it may be that some of them were chronically lonely persons who chose mates unwisely or who lacked the social skills to make the marriages function more satisfactorily. In addition, married people in general are less lonely, particularly in comparison with the divorced or widowed (Perlman and Peplau, 1981). Among people who are separated, divorced, widowed, or who never have married, males tend to experience greater loneliness than women (Peplau, Bikwon, Rook and Goodchilds, 1982; Rubenstein and Shaver, 1982).

Loneliness can assume different forms. As noted earlier, loneliness may be transitory or situational, or may be a chronic disposition of the person. Weiss (1973) has distinguished between *social loneliness*, or a lack of a network of friends, acquaintances and colleagues, and *emotional loneliness*, which signifies a lack of intimate relationships. People may feel lonely because they lack romantic involvement, friendships, family bonds, or ties in the larger community (Sermat, 1978). The research suggests that individuals who feel a lack in one area will not necessarily perceive deficiencies in other kinds of social relationships, and that people usually cannot compensate for deficiencies in one area by involvement in another.

Notwithstanding these various types of loneliness, there also seems to be a generalized, underlying disposition or trait called loneliness, and several scales have been developed to measure it (see Table 8-2) (Rubenstein and Shaver, 1982; Russell, Peplau and Cutrona, 1980). People who score high on global measures of loneliness tend to manifest introversion, self-consciousness, a lack of assertiveness, low self-esteem, anxiety, depression, (Peplau and Perlman, 1982) and shyness. There is also some evidence that lonely persons, particularly males, are more likely to be hostile or aggressive, especially toward women (Check et al., 1983) and that lonely people who drink are more vulnerable to alcohol problems (Sadava and Thompson, 1986). Of course, any of these personal characteristics may be both a cause and a consequence of loneliness. For example, hostile or depressed people may experience failures in relationships, thereby increasing their loneliness, and their anger or depression.

Peplau, Russell and Heim (1979) outline an attributional model of loneliness, based upon Weiner's (1974) model of achievement attributions (see Chapter 3). Weiner observes that we explain our successes and failures in terms of internal or external causes, and stable or unstable causes. Thus, I may attribute a victory in a tennis match

TABLE 8–2
Sample items from loneliness scale

1. I feel in tune with people around me.
   never   rarely   sometimes   often
2. There is no one I can turn to.
   never   rarely   sometimes   often
3. I feel part of a group of friends.
   never   rarely   sometimes   often
4. I feel isolated from others.
   never   rarely   sometimes   often
5. There are people who really understand me.
   never   rarely   sometimes   often
6. People are around me but not with me.
   never   rarely   sometimes   often

SOURCE: Russell, Peplau and Cutrona, 1980

to my inherent talent (stable internal), my effort on this occasion (stable external), the lack of talent of my opponent (stable external), or sheer good luck (unstable external). Peplau *et al.* argue that the experience of loneliness depends on how we explain the time or circumstance in which we find ourselves alone or relatively isolated. Our response to loneliness may also depend on it.

Shyness

Given our need for satisfying social activities and relationships, and the distress of loneliness, it would seem surprising that so many people deliberately "hang back," withdraw, are unwilling to take risks. This is the problem of shyness, in which people excessively restrain their social interactions. Philip Zimbardo (1977), a social psychologist who has studied it extensively, describes shyness in terms of being afraid of people, particularly those who may be emotionally threatening, e.g., friends who may not like you, members of the opposite sex who may reject you, authorities who may disapprove of you, members of a seminar group who may disagree with you, strangers who are unpredictable, Many people are shy in some situations but not others. For example, a student may be terrified of speaking in class but totally comfortable at a party — or vice versa. Some people in the performing arts are at ease on stage but quite shy in one-to-one encounters. Other people are painfully shy in most types of social encounters, and suffer intensely because of it.

Zimbardo and his colleagues actually set up a shyness clinic at a U.S. university and developed a number of techniques to help people with this problem. One involves a cognitive "restructuring" of social encounters that arouse anxiety. For example, shy people may enter an interaction with their own "agenda," such as getting to know as much as possible about another person in a conversation. Concentrating on such a goal may distract them from their own anxiety and give them a sense of control in the situation.

Another technique involved assigning shy people to a particular social role, such as an interviewer in a survey (about shyness, perhaps!). Here their role is sanctioned by the situation and a script is provided — the participants are just doing what they are trained to do. Thus they need not fear personal rejection, and "their egos are completely off the hook" (p. 224). For each of about 100 interviews, the shy person was required to make the initial telephone contact, meet the stranger and carry out the interview for up to two hours. Often they invited the respondents for coffee afterwards.

Shyness can also be treated through social skills training, in which clients may observe models who interact comfortably, practice in role-playing situations in groups, observe videotape replays of their social behaviour, carry out "homework" assignments involving social situations. Thus they may learn how to speak comfortably on the telephone, carry on a conversation, give and receive compliments, express opinions. It may also involve learning how to interpret the reactions of others. Because they expect and fear rejection or disapproval, the shy person may tend to misinterpret how others respond to them — giving them more to fear and more reason to be shy.

Finally, it may be important to look at how shy people interpret themselves (Brodt and Zimbardo, 1981). Usually, the shy person experiences physiological symptoms in an encounter, e.g., increased heart rate, slight hand tremors (or knees), a dry mouth. According to attribution theory, we would notice these symptoms and attribute them to shyness, thus feeling more uncomfortable than ever ("There I go again. . . ."). Shy female students were told they were participants in an experiment on the effects of noise, and that they would likely feel effects such as increased heart rate, etc., which would persist for some time after the noise ended. Just after being bombarded with the unpleasant noise, the students met an attractive weak confederate of the experimenter. The shy females behaved in a more outgoing way to this person and, afterwards, reported having felt less shy. Because they were able to re-attribute their physical symptoms to the noise rather than their own shyness, they were able to overcome the problem in that situation.

A PERSPECTIVE

Research on the topic of interpersonal attraction has shifted dramatically in the past decade. The vast majority of the earlier studies consisted of laboratory experiments exploring initial attraction to a stranger. Such research has proven to be useful in establishing and refining our understanding of the importance of such variables as attitude similarity, physical proximity, physical attractiveness, reinforcement, reciprocated liking, communication patterns, and arousal. The study of real-life relationships, such as marriage and friendship, has been left largely to other social sciences and clinical disciplines.

However, contemporary research has focused more and more on the study of relationships, and how they are established, maintained, and terminated over time. Such research provides us with the necessary context within which the role of variables such as similarity or attractiveness becomes clear. For example, attitude similarity is critically important in the early stages of attraction, but becomes relatively less important later on, when it may be supplanted by communication leading to mutuality. The research activity in this area, influenced by other trends in social psychology, is also helping to form a theory of how interpersonal relationships evolve. The structure of this chapter has reflected this trend which promises to enhance our future understanding of this vital condition of human life.

SUMMARY

(1) The need to affiliate with others begins at the stage of infant attachment and persists throughout life. Certain factors, such as intense fear or stress, increase affiliative needs, while others, such as social anxiety, decrease affiliation.

(2) Why is someone attracted to a particular person? Such a question can be answered only in terms of the stage of relatedness: awareness, surface contact, or involvement at some level of mutuality.

(3) We tend to be attracted to people in close physical proximity and to those who are physically attractive. To an extent, we are influenced by a stereotype which equates attractiveness with "goodness," and we are motivated to choose others who are roughly equal to ourselves in attractiveness.

(4) When people are first getting to know each other (surface contact), attraction is related to the perception that people are similar and that the interaction is rewarding. We are attracted to people with similar attitudes because it is rewarding to be with

them, because we seek consistency in our attitudes and relationships, and because we expect people we like to be similar to us.

(5) If we have no choice about interacting in a situation, our liking of neutral or even negative persons may be enhanced.

(6) Mutuality involves the perception of interdependence and intimacy. Reciprocity in self-disclosure is crucial to intimacy. According to the social penetration model, self-disclosure increases in depth and breadth as intimacy increases, but is limited by a need to preserve privacy, and by the use of non-verbal as well as verbal communication.

(7) Equity is important to social relations, including exchange in love, status, information, money, goods, and services. In intimate relationships, exchange becomes more particularistic, more flexible, and less egocentric.

(8) In intimate relationships, the principle of complementarity becomes more important. The sequential filter model suggests that similar values are more important in the earlier stage of a relationship and that complementarity needs assume more prominence at a later stage.

(9) Romantic love consists of varying degrees of passion, decision, and intimacy. It is perceived as intrinsic, not dependent on extrinsic reasons. An attributional model suggests that if a culture propagates the notion of romantic love, a state of arousal and certain cognitive cues may lead the person to attribute their state to "being in love."

(10) The dissolution of a relationship may depend on the anticipated costs and rewards of leaving it, and on the anticipated costs and rewards of staying within it.

(11) Research distinguishes between social relation jealousy — the need for exclusivity in a relationship — and social comparison jealousy — the need to feel as good as somebody else.

(12) Loneliness arises from a perception of deficiencies in a person's relationships. It may be social or emotional in nature, and may have nothing to do with being alone.

FURTHER READING

BREHM, S. (1985). *Intimate relationships*. New York: Random House.

DUCK, S. and GILMOUR, R. (Eds.) (1981–84). *Personal relationships*. Vols. 1–5. New York: Academic Press.

HATFIELD, E. and WALSTER, G.W. (1985). *A new look at love*. Reading: Addison-Wesley.

HATFIELD, E. and SPRECHER, S. (1986). *Mirror, mirror . . . the importance of looks in everyday life*. New York: State University of New York.

HENDRICK, C. and HENDRICK, S. (1983). *Liking, loving, and relating*. Monterey, CA: Brooks Cole.

KELLEY, H.H. *Close relationships*. San Francisco: Freeman.

LEVINGER, G. and MOLES, O.C. (1979). *Divorce and separation: Context, causes and consequences*. New York: Basic Books.

PEPLAU, L.A. and PERLMAN, D. (Eds.) (1982). *Loneliness: A sourcebook of current theory, research and therapy*. New York: Wiley Interscience.

C·H·A·P·T·E·R N·I·N·E

Aggression and Violence

In Flanders Fields the poppies grow,
Between the crosses, row on row,
That mark our place. . . .

Lt. Col. John McCrae
First Canadian Contingent
Killed in Boulogne, France, 1918

FOR REFLECTION

- Is violence a problem of self-control or social control?
- Can aggressive tendencies be channelled safely into sports or watching television?
- To what extent do children learn aggression from their families?
- Does pornography lead to violence against women?

275

THE GREAT WAR of 1914–1918 (later referred to as World War I when it became necessary to number such wars) was so unprecedented in its destruction that Sigmund Freud could explain it only by postulating the existence of a *"death instinct."* He described this instinct as an innate drive towards self-destruction which, when thwarted by an opposing *"life instinct,"* was directed outward in the form of violence toward other people. Although that war was described by some politicians as "the war to end all wars," two decades after it had ended, the world was again immersed in mortal combat — this time, with new and deadlier weapons: dive-bombers, flame-throwers, rockets, and, finally, the atomic bomb. World War II cost over 50 million lives, including 9 percent of the total population of the U.S.S.R., 5 percent of the German population, and 1 percent of both the British and French populations (Livingstone, 1968).

Since the end of World War II, over 130 military conflicts in over 100 countries have led to the deaths of at least 35 million people. Over one-and-a-half million people, including 60 000 United States soldiers, died during the Vietnam war. The Iran-Iraq war, the armed conflicts in Central America, and terrorist bombings around the world are more recent examples of the continuing violence of human against human.

As violence has escalated, so has the power of weapons to annihilate the human species. Modern weapons, such as the intercontinental ballistic missile armed with

Wartime sentiments: Mothers issue their own statistics after WWI.

B·O·X   9-1

TORTURE AND PAIN

Whether practiced by secular or sacred institutions — for punishment, revenge, or the amusement of spectators (as in the days of the Roman empire) — torture has always been carried out with the secure knowledge that human beings universally fear pain. The deliberate infliction of pain is the torturer's *modus operandi*. For example, during the Inquisition carried out by the Church in the Middle Ages, the ecclesiastical judges insisted even on the torture of suspected witches who had confessed their crimes readily. In other words, victims were not to escape the painful treatment they "deserved" (Masters, 1966).

Centuries of social and technological evolution have replaced the rack with electric shock, and boiling oil with painful or nauseating drugs. Today's methods, used everywhere from Argentina to the U.S.S.R., are more sophisticated, more efficient in provoking suffering, and leave fewer visible traces.

But whatever the method, torture is always predicated on the notion that human beings want to avoid pain. In the words of Amnesty International:

> . . . [E]ven in an age of violence, torture stands out as a special horror for most people. Pain is a common human denominator, and while few people know what it is to be shot, to be burned by napalm, or even to starve, all know pain. Within every human being is the knowledge and fear of pain, the fear of helplessness before unrestrained cruelty. . . . It is significant that torture is the one form of violence that a state will always deny and never justify. The state may justify mass murder and glorify those who kill . . . but it never justifies torture nor glorifies those who torture. . . . And yet the use of torture has by all indications increased over the last few years (excerpted from *Amnesty International Report on Torture*, 1975, p. 21).

multiple nuclear warheads, are more destructive than anything used or contemplated during World War II, and tomorrow's arsenals — laser "death rays" and satellite-borne weapons systems (like the U.S. Strategic Defense Initiative, or "Star Wars") — will be more destructive still. In 1972, it was estimated that the world's nuclear arsenal included the explosive equivalent of over 50 billion tonnes of TNT, or about 12 tonnes for every man, woman and child on earth (Prosterman, 1972). In 1986, a year designated by the United Nations as the International Year of Peace, the various nations of the world spent an equivalent of $1.2 *trillion*, or approximately 6 percent of the world's gross national product, on weaponry. Even more ominous is the growing membership of the nuclear weapons club. Smaller nations, some with a history of political instability, are developing or seeking to acquire nuclear weapons, increasing the likelihood that such weapons will one day be used.

However, human beings do not just kill each other on a grand scale. History is brimming with accounts of torture and mutilation practiced by criminals and governments alike. According to Amnesty International (a worldwide group campaigning to abolish torture which was awarded the Nobel Prize for Peace in 1977), torture has been *officially* practiced in at least 98 countries around the world in the recent decade (Amnesty International, 1984; see Box 9-1). On an individual level, homicides and rapes are increasing and, in some parts of the world (e.g., Detroit and Miami), have reached epidemic proportions.

Why are some people motivated to murder or mutilate while other people, the vast majority, are not? Are we, as Freud suggested, innately violent, or are we more like Rousseau's "Noble Savage," born good and gentle but corrupted over time? Is aggressiveness "in our genes," or is it something, along with the ability to read the alphabet or ride a bicycle, that we acquire?

Social psychologists are interested in such questions because aggression by its very nature is *social* behaviour: the aggressor uses aggressive acts to harm, punish, or control others or to communicate feelings of anger. Therefore, social learning, social norms, and cultural values should all play a role in aggression as they do in any other social behaviour. (Recall that certain aspects of aggression were raised in the discussion of conformity in Chapter 6.) It is also important to remember that social psychology does not have a monopoly on the study of aggression; it is a multidisciplinary domain shared by biologists, neurologists, historians, and economists — among others.

WHAT IS AGGRESSION?

What is the *essence* of aggression? Is back alley fighting by a neighbourhood bully or brawling by hockey players "aggressive" in the same sense that a child is aggressive when he or she hits another child who has taken away a favourite toy? What about a mother who yells at her son? An infantryman who shoots at enemy soldiers? An air force bombardier who drops bombs on an unseen enemy? For something to be considered to be an act of aggression, is it necessary that someone be injured, or is the attempt to do harm sufficient? Must aggression be directed toward people, or is kicking the wall or the cat included as well? Must a person *intend* to injure another, or is accidental injury also included? Is the goal, or intent, important or is forcing a child to suffer a painful but life-saving injection also aggressive? Is emotional involvement ("anger") necessary? What about verbal attacks, poison pen letters, or giving someone the "cold shoulder?"

Aggression has been defined in two ways in the social psychological literature. Some researchers have considered it to be the *intentional* infliction of damage or harm on a target (e.g., Dollard, Doob, Miller, Mowrer and Sears, 1939), while others have tried to get around the difficulty of measuring intent by defining aggression as any response which results in noxious stimulation being applied to a target person (Buss, 1961). Although it is not without its difficulties, the first of these definitions is used in this chapter; that is, aggression is defined as *behaviour that is intended to harm or destroy*. Thus someone who fires a gun intending to hit another person would be considered aggressive even if the shot missed its mark.

The problem of determining intent (i.e., making attributions — see Chapter 3) must not be ignored, however. For example, perhaps the person with the gun intended only to scare the other person and hence deliberately missed. By our definition, this would not constitute aggression. It is often difficult to be sure one way or the other about someone's intentions and, indeed, misattributions are likely to be common since people usually attribute a harmful intent to a harmful action: "The man would have hurt the other man had the bullet hit him (harmful action); therefore, he must have shot at him because he wanted to hurt him (harmful intent)."

A further distinction can be made in our discussion of aggression. We all know that there seems to be a qualitative difference between the aggression of a bully who uses force to take someone's candy and the aggression of someone who is emotionally enraged towards another individual and wants to inflict harm. Because of this obvious distinction, psychologists distinguish between *instrumental* aggression, which is a means to some desired end, and *hostile* aggression, which is motivated by anger and which appears to have as its end the infliction of harm upon someone else (Berkowitz, 1984; Rule and Nesdale, 1974).

When studying aggression in the laboratory, investigators use an *operational* definition, describing it in terms of some directly and objectively observable measure. For example, an often-used technique (Buss, 1961) is the following: Two subjects, one a confederate, are assigned the roles of "teacher" and "learner" in a study ostensibly designed to examine the effects of punishment on learning. The "teacher" (always the real subject) is seated at a console with a series of buttons corresponding to different intensities of electric shock. The subject believes that the "learner" is seated in another room, hooked up to wires leading to a shock apparatus. The teacher must carry out a teaching task, while the learner must respond with correct answers. (In fact, the learner has been coached to make mistakes and insult the teacher from time to time.) Wrong answers are to be met with the administration of a shock by the teacher. Typically, the dependent variable (or observable behaviour) in such an experiment is the intensity and duration of the shock administered. In this way, the effect of such variables as insults or frustration level on the extent of the teacher's aggression toward the learner (i.e., how often the teacher shocks the learner) can be studied.

However, the narrowness of an operational definition of aggression may make it very difficult to generalize to other situations or to make comparisons with other studies using different operational definitions. Moreover, although intent is an aspect of aggression, it is so difficult to measure that most laboratory studies do not even try to ascertain the motives underlying subjects' "aggression" (Tedeschi, Smith, and Brown, 1974). In the Buss (1961) procedure described above, how can we be sure that the subject intends to harm the learner when shock is administered? After all, the subject is led to believe that punishment might increase the learner's learning rate, which should ultimately lead to less shock. Rule and Nesdale (1974) ran a study using such a method, but told some of the subjects that increasing the shock intensity would help the learner learn ("prosocial" condition), while other subjects were told that it would hinder the learner ("hostile" condition). In addition, half of the subjects in each group were insulted by the learner during the learning sequence. As Table 9-1 illustrates, when subjects were insulted in the prosocial condition, *less* intense shocks were given than when *no* insults were given. But more intense shocks were given in the hostile condition than when no insult had been made. Thus, if the subject believed the shock to be helpful and if he or she was not negatively disposed towards the other subject, more intense shock was given, not as an outburst of "aggression," but apparently, as an incentive to learn. Even though subjects believed that they were

TABLE 9-1

Mean intensities of shocks as a function of the confederate's insult and the value of the aggressive response

	Insult	No insult
Prosocial	52.07	90.39
Hostile	68.26	50.58

SOURCE: Rule and Nesdale, 1974

causing pain to another person, they believed that the person's own interests justified the pain. This kind of reasoning is used by parents and teachers who physically punish children: the line between what is benevolent and what is malevolent can be fuzzy.

CAUSES OF AGGRESSION

Consider an extreme but real-life example of antisocial, aggressive behaviour. Some years ago, in 1975, a teenage student who had no history of violence and no apparent provocation took his father's gun to his Brampton, Ontario, school and killed or wounded several classmates before killing himself. There appeared to be no sensible explanation for his behaviour; he did not give any indication of wanting to "settle a score" with anyone, and there was no obvious sign of mental or emotional disturbance beforehand. He did not single out specific targets, but shot his classmates at random.

How can such an outburst of violence be explained? If we had asked people at the time why they thought this incident had occurred, we might have obtained responses like these:

> *Sometimes the pressure builds up inside a person, and you just have to get it out of your system, so you end up kicking the cat or killing somebody.*
>
> *Could be he had a brain tumour, or something.*
>
> *He must have been brought up that way — to see violence as the way to deal with problems.*
>
> *It's our society — it encourages people to be violent.*
>
> *He's just a tough character who got carried away.*
>
> *What with all the violence on TV, it's a wonder that we don't have more of that.*

Each of these statements represents a partial explanation of aggressive behaviour; pinpointing such factors as the brain and nervous system, society, the family, and the media. These factors will be discussed in the sections to follow.

Because the Brampton boy's behaviour seemed to lack any purpose, it is tempting to view such aggression as the product of biological forces (i.e., some sort of uncontrollable outburst). The first two topics considered below, instinct/drive and physiology, expand on this viewpoint.

"You just have to get it out of your system": Aggression as instinct or drive

In the early days of social psychology, a great deal of social behaviour was explained in terms of *instincts*, so called inborn behavioural tendencies motivating individuals to act in certain ways. For example, it was said that women sought to marry and have a family on account of a "maternal" instinct, and that men were inclined to pursue hunting because of a "hunting" instinct. In one of the first social psychology textbooks ever published (MacDougall, 1908) many social behaviours were discussed in terms of instinct, sometimes reflecting the sexist attitudes of that era. The following example will suffice.

> The presence of the maternal element in the attitude of a woman towards her lover has been recognized by countless writers of romance. And that the tender protective element commonly enters into the sentiment of the man for the beloved woman is equally obvious. That sex love should thus combine the most purely altruistic with the most ruthlessly egoistic tendency of human nature seems sufficiently accounted for in the case of the woman by the great strength of the maternal impulse and the ease with which it is aroused in her in all personal relations; and in the man it is perhaps sufficiently accounted for by the fact that woman, especially at the age at which she is most strongly attractive to man, resembles in many respects, both mental and physical, the child, the normal object of the parental or protective impulse (MacDougall, 1908, pp. 394–395).

Although by the 1920s, as many as 10 000 different "instincts" had been identified, the instinct concept fell into disuse among experimental psychologists in the early 1930s. This happened for two reasons. First, it became clear that what had been labelled "instinctive behaviour" in animals depended very much on prenatal and postnatal environmental influences. Second, it was discovered that explanations based on instinct seemed to depend on circular reasoning. For example, how was it known that a maternal instinct existed? Because women wanted children and mothers devoted themselves to their children. Why did they devote themselves to their children? Because of their maternal instinct, of course. Thus the instinct designation began as a description of what was observed, and then was used to *explain* what was observed. However, if experimental psychologists found the instinct concept to be of little value, some personality theorists used it extensively. Sigmund Freud was one of these.

Freud's psychoanalytic approach to aggression   Freud believed that all behaviour is driven by two basic instincts: the life instinct, *Eros*, and the death instinct, *Thanatos*, whose goal it is to return the organism to its original inanimate state. When blocked by Eros, Thanatos "displaces" some of its accumulating energy outward onto other

"*Maurice has always been politically active.*"

human beings. Thus Freud believed that, ultimately, civilization and moral order must be based not on "love and charity" but on repression of this death instinct. He cautioned that if people were not allowed to give vent to their aggressive energy in a socially acceptable way (e.g., through sports) they would be forced to act in a destructive manner towards others in order to avoid their own self-destruction (Freud, 1933).

Could the Brampton boy have been the victim of Thanatos? Did he displace his own death wish, resulting in the deaths of his classmates? If so, the displacement was surely ineffective, or he would not have committed suicide immediately. In fact, although the psychoanalytic approach dominated personality theory and clinical psychology for much of the twentieth century, its influence has waned dramatically. There is no reason to believe in life instincts and death instincts and, as far as aggression is concerned, the psychoanalytic approach no longer predominates.

Lorenz's ethological approach While the Freudian approach has not proven to be useful in explaining aggression, the concept of instinctual aggressiveness has been given attention in recent years through the popular writings of ethologists such as Nobel prize winners Konrad Lorenz and Niko Tinbergen (ethology is the study of organisms in their natural habitat). Lorenz (1966) constructed a theory of aggression based on his study of aggressiveness in birds and animals. He argued that these creatures — and humans — possess an instinctive aggressive drive which is essential for survival and evolution: Infighting among members of a species forces them to spread out over a larger area and make more effective use of the food supply. Moreover, it permits selective breeding of the strongest and healthiest of the species.

Not unlike Freud, Lorenz argued that aggressive energy was constantly being generated within the nervous system and that sooner or later it must be "released" by an appropriate environmental stimulus (a *releasing stimulus*); otherwise, it would be displaced against a substitute stimulus or it might accumulate to the point that a sudden explosion of violence would occur without any stimulation from the environment being necessary at all (a *spontaneous discharge reaction*).

Lorenz's theory would be very important if it were true, since it suggests that we can only try to channel and control aggression, not eliminate it. This discharge of aggressive energy would occur through either actual aggression or displaced aggression (e.g., by kicking a football rather than an opponent), or even, to some extent, by witnessing aggression.

Could this explain the Brampton boy's behaviour? We could argue that aggressive energy had built up and was not being regularly discharged in a socially acceptable manner. In the absence of an appropriate releasing stimulus, this build-up of energy resulted in a spontaneous discharge reaction. (Indeed, outbursts of violence often seem to be associated with personalities which are otherwise very passive and unassertive. Perhaps there is no regular discharge of aggression.)

However, an explanation based on Lorenz's theory would be very unconvincing, for the theory — like Freud's — has not held up well to careful scrutiny, and it has many opponents (e.g., Bandura, 1973; Montague, 1973; Nelson, 1974). They argue that in generalizing from geese to mammals to humans, Lorenz ignored the powerful role that learning plays in human behaviour. Furthermore, there is no evidence of any accumulation of "aggressive energy" in the body or of any spontaneous motivation to fight others. In fact, energy is energy, and there is no energy in the body which is specifically "aggressive."

The frustration-aggression hypothesis While rejecting the idea of innate aggressive energy, some theorists have speculated that there may be an inborn tendency to aggress following frustration of some kind. This "frustration-aggression hypothesis" was originally proposed by Dollard *et al.* (1939) who suggested that every instance of frustration, defined as interference with behaviour directed toward a goal, produced some tendency towards aggression, and that every instance of aggression was preceded by some sort of frustration. It was assumed that both learning and environmental cues would determine the form that aggressiveness would take, and what its target would be. Unfortunately, research has shown that this view is also untenable, and that while frustration may lead to aggression, it may lead to other behaviours as well (e.g., passive withdrawal). Moreover, aggression is not always preceded by frustration.

Berkowitz (1962) suggested revising the hypothesis, arguing that frustration produced only a *readiness* for aggressive acts ("anger"). Then, depending on how an individual learned to deal with anger, the result would be aggression, withdrawal, or other non-aggressive behaviour. However, it is likely that the individual's social learning history would also influence whether or not a given situation was experienced as frustrating or challenging or something altogether different, and whether or not frustration produced anger. Therefore, while frustration may often lead to anger and aggression, it does not mean there exists a biological predisposition to aggress in the face of frustration.

Aversively stimulated aggression Most people know that when they are in pain, they are more irritable, and perhaps more ready to "lash out" at others with little provocation. Berkowitz (1983) has proposed that humans and some animals are biologically disposed to react with aggression when faced with pain or other unpleasantness. According to this view, frustration produces a state of unpleasantness which, in turn, elicits aggressive behaviour. He takes the position that unpleasant or aversive events of either a physical nature (e.g., pain) or a psychological nature (e.g., excessive heat, irritating cigarette smoke, frightening information) lead to both the motivation to escape *and* the motivation to attack. Drawing on both animal and human studies, he concludes that the connection between aversive stimulation and aggression is independent of how the individual interprets his or her sensations. Moreover, he says the evidence suggests that while there is a defensive component to this aggressiveness (i.e., in the attempt to remove the source of unpleasantness), there is also an active inclination to harm available targets. Such a process is subject to reinforcement, and social learning may lead either to a greater or lesser likelihood of aggression, as well as determine the target and the form of the aggression.

However, how might we then distinguish between heightened arousal (the "fight or flight response") conditioned by our environment, and spontaneous aggressive behaviour? Despite the limited evidence offered, we must hesitate to accept Berkowitz's argument at this time. Although their claims are disputed by Berkowitz, social learning theorists argue that aggressive behaviours (including hostile and instrumental aggression) are learned both directly and indirectly on account of their effectiveness.

Catharsis Instinct theories of aggression assume the build-up of aggressive energy held in check by various inhibiting forces, but which eventually must be discharged through activities which are aggressive or somehow related to aggression (e.g., contact sports). Freud referred to such discharge as "catharsis." According to this point of view, simply witnessing aggression will lead to some degree of catharsis. Even if the instinct approach is misguided, it could be true that aggressive impulses are reduced following some kind of cathartic release. The ancient philosopher Aristotle referred to catharsis in his writings. He believed, for example, that people's feelings of sorrow would diminish through watching dramatic tragedy and identifying with a hero. His predecessor, Plato, on the other hand, believed that witnessing emotional discharges *increased* emotional feelings. A difference of opinion regarding the effects of witnessing emotional outbursts continues to this day. As far as aggression is concerned, the question is, does watching or participating in aggressive activities decrease or increase aggressiveness?

Experimenters may assume that subjects have experienced catharsis if they are observed to be less aggressive following their own aggression. Yet there are often other explanations for such an outcome. For example, in a study by Doob and Wood (1972) subjects in one group were annoyed by a confederate, while subjects in a second group were left alone. One third of each of these groups then gave electric shocks to the confederate, another third observed the experimenter deliver the shocks to the confederate, and the final third neither witnessed nor gave any shock. If the original annoyance had increased the hostility of the subjects, then the opportunity to aggress against the object of annoyance should (if the catharsis hypothesis is correct) decrease the aggressiveness of the subjects and reduce their desire to shock the confederate in the future. When all subjects were given this opportunity, the following happened: while the experience of having witnessed or given shock to the confederate decreased the number of shocks administered on the second occasion by *annoyed* subjects, the same experience provoked *non-annoyed* subjects to give more shock on the second occasion (Table 9-2).

TABLE 9-2
Mean number of shocks delivered on the second occasion by subjects in Doob and Wood experiment

	Annoyed	Not Annoyed
Earlier shocked confederate	6.80	8.07
Earlier saw experimenter shock confederate	7.60	9.73
Neither witnessed nor gave shock	10.67	6.60

SOURCE: Doob and Wood, 1972

While some experimenters might have concluded that catharsis had occurred, either directly (i.e. when the subject shocked the confederate) or vicariously (i.e., when the subject watched the experimenter deliver the shocks), Doob and Wood were careful to point out that other explanations might apply. For instance, subjects who were annoyed and saw the confederate being hurt may have felt that "justice had been done" and that it was unnecessary to administer further punishment. It is also possible that following the administration of shock to the confederate, restraints against aggression may have increased. The subjects may have still felt hostile but after seeing the confederate suffer been reluctant to administer more shock — in order to avoid guilt, perhaps (Geen, Stonner and Shope, 1975).

In another similar experiment, a physiological correlate of arousal (blood pressure) was also measured (Geen *et al.*, 1975). Subjects were either shocked or not shocked by the confederate. It was observed that subjects who had been shocked and then had the opportunity to deliver shocks to the confederates gave shocks of *greater* intensity on the second occasion than did subjects in other control conditions. In addition, their blood pressure showed a greater reduction. Thus it appears that when care is taken to minimize restraints against aggression (by having the confederate attack first, thereby reducing guilt associated with shocking the confederate), the opposite of catharsis occurs: aggressiveness increases.

Doob and Kirshenbaum (1973a) studied the arousal effects of film violence by monitoring the blood pressure of university students who watched either a seven-minute clip in which 150 people were shot and killed or a neutral film. In addition, the subjects were either in a "frustrated" condition (having been interfered with by the experimenter during an earlier task) or were not frustrated. They found that the effects of frustration and of the violent film on arousal seemed to be additive. The most arousal was exhibited by subjects who had been both aroused and frustrated. This finding casts doubt on the idea that violent movies are tension reducing for either frustrated or non-frustrated people.

Other studies have also found that physiological changes follow aggressive behaviour. For example, angered subjects were found to experience a more rapid decrease in blood pressure to a normal level if they were allowed to counter-aggress against the person who had aggressed against them (Hokanson, 1970). In fact, all angered subjects in that study, whether or not they counter-aggressed, returned to a normal physiological level rather quickly — not what we would expect if catharsis occurred. One methodological problem with that study, however, is that subjects in the control group were left with nothing to do except to dwell on the insult they had experienced. This may have kept their physiological arousal at a high level ("self-arousal"), while the other subjects, engrossed in the activity of counter-aggression, may have experienced a normal decline in arousal as the result of being distracted from thoughts of having been victimized. A more appropriate experiment would compare the arousal levels of the counter-aggressing subjects with subjects allowed to engage in equally absorbing but non-aggressive activities (Bandura, 1973).

This self-arousal hypothesis has been supported in several experiments. In one study, it was found that blood pressure is more effectively maintained at a high level by exposing the subjects to their antagonist, rather than having them sit around and do nothing without the opportunity to counter-aggress (Vantress and Williams,

Anger may make you feel better, but will it make you feel less angry?

1972). In another study, subjects who were encouraged to verbalize their hostility towards another person who had annoyed them ended up disliking that person even more (Kahn, 1966). In addition, they took longer to calm down physiologically than other, equally annoyed, subjects who were left alone. This evidence contradicts the catharsis hypothesis.

The evidence against the catharsis hypothesis is rather compelling. Watching television or film violence, directing violence towards objects, or lashing out verbally at other people are *not* effective means of reducing aggressive behaviour. In fact, sometimes, such activity subsequently leads people to act *more* aggressively (Baron, 1983a). Participation in or witnessing aggressive sports generally produces *more* rather than less aggression (Quanty, 1976). Therefore, current evidence, at any rate, suggests that Plato was right and Aristotle was wrong.

"Could be he had a brain tumour, or something": Physiological influences on aggression

Even if aggression is not "instinctive," could it have a physiological basis, as do hunger and thirst? While there is a fine line between an "instinct" and a "physiological" theory, it could be that we have physiological systems which are specifically associated with aggression, and that our learned behaviour may either employ or override these systems.

There have been various attempts to demonstrate that aggressiveness is genetically transmitted, or that aggressiveness is best understood in terms of male sex hormones (see the section on gender and aggression later in this chapter). Others have approached the study of aggression by trying to find areas of the brain that either promote or inhibit aggressive behaviour (see Box 9-2). Of course, our behaviour is never completely free of the influence of physiology, and it is clear that there are many factors—neural, hormonal, genetic—which influence our behaviour. Based on current evidence, however, any effect of such factors on human aggressiveness is most likely indirect (Montague, 1973; Nelson, 1974, 1975; Valenstein, 1975). As a result of increased emotionality, pain, irritability, or frustration, aggressive behaviour may be elicited and we may strike out in some way. But the evidence does not support the view that "strike out we must." Although the biological approach to aggression is quite appropriate when dealing with animals, the powerful influence of learning upon human behaviour and the complexity of human social interaction almost compel a shift from a biological to a social-cultural perspective (Tedeschi, 1983). There is no doubt that our reaction, whether to fight or to withdraw, depends on how we have learned to react in similar situations in the past and on how our society encourages us to respond.

"He must have been brought up that way": Social-developmental influences

There are many factors that influence whether or not we learn "aggression" as a response. Although it is taken for granted that neurophysiological mechanisms exist,

B · O · X   9 - 2

BRAIN TUMOURS AND REPTILE BRAINS

On the morning of August 1, 1966, after having killed his wife and mother, Charles Whitman climbed a tower at the University of Texas, barricaded himself inside, and over the next hour shot indiscriminately with a high-power rifle at passersby. Before being fatally shot by police, he had killed 14 people and wounded 24 others. An investigation revealed that his murder spree had been well planned, and that he had complained of severe headaches and had spoken to a psychiatrist about occasional feelings of profound and almost uncontrollable hostility. An autopsy revealed a walnut-sized brain tumour which was described as being in the area of the amygdaloid nucleus (Sweet, Ervin and Mark, 1969), an area considered by some researchers to be an "aggression centre" in the brain. However, it was later revealed that not enough care had been taken during the autopsy to indicate exactly where the tumour had been (Valenstein, 1975).

In January 1985, 17-year-old Andrew Leyshon-Hughes went to visit his close friend, Nancy Eaton, a great great grand-daughter of the founder of Eaton's department store, in her Toronto home. She was a steady companion who had often helped him during difficult times in the past. Leyshon-Hughes had a history of periodic outbursts of explosive violence for which he had been treated in the past and for which he had sought treatment earlier that month. Nancy Eaton let Leyshon-Hughes spend the night on her living room sofa. The next morning, he took a kitchen knife, went to her bedroom and stabbed her

repeatedly. He left the apartment and returned several hours later to rape her corpse.

In the fall of 1986, Leyshon-Hughes was found not guilty of murder by reason of insanity, which was said to be the result of congenital brain damage. Testifying at the trial, psychiatrist Frank Ervin of McGill University stated that at the time of the murder, the boy was essentially a "crocodile man," using only that primitive part of the brain that humans have in common with reptiles.

Can a "crocodile brain" be responsible for such obviously acquired behaviour as stabbing with a knife? Leyshon-Hughes' behaviour did not reflect total loss of reasoning: he went to the kitchen, took a knife, walked to the bedroom, and stabbed the sleeping woman. His actions following the murder were carried out in a cool and deliberate manner.

Whitman's aggression was also well planned. While the legal defense of insanity might be justified in each case, is such insanity to be blamed on the brain? Or did a disorder in the personality or a history of unfortunate experiences produce feelings of hostility leading to fantasies of murder and destruction which, at a certain point, became so attractive, that each individual acted on them? Whitman's tumour and Leyshon-Hughes' brain disorder may have produced pain and frustration: these disorders may have increased their anger at life and the world. But the disorders were not necessarily responsible for the violence which ultimately involved the powers of reason.

allowing for the expression of aggressive behaviours, the use of these mechanisms is not automatic, but subject to cognitive control. In fact, attributions may be involved (recall our discussion of attributions in Chapter 3), even in the case of hostile aggression, which is often viewed as uncontrollable and irrational (Ferguson and Rule, 1983). For example, a comment which is interpreted as an insult will lead to activity in the hypothalamus, while a comment interpreted as an innocent remark will have no such effect (Bandura, 1983).

Our social environment can affect aggressiveness in several ways — we can be reinforced for aggression, or we can imitate others. Moreover, the physiological constitution of an individual interacts with the environment to produce a particular set of experiences which may help or hinder the learning of aggressiveness. The boy who is small for his age is not likely to be successful at "throwing his weight around," while a larger child may soon learn that aggression is useful in achieving certain goals. (One such goal may be simply the attention that aggression brings.) On the other hand, the small individual may tire of having "sand kicked in his face" and take measures to become more powerful, gradually adopting the role of bully, while the larger child may be "left alone," never developing the need to learn aggression-related physical skills.

Social learning theorists have studied the ways in which children learn various aggressive behaviours. They argue that children learn not only *how* to aggress, but also *when* to aggress, and against *whom* to aggress (Bandura, 1973). Most research has shown that the early period of life is a particularly critical time for learning about aggression (Olweus, 1972).

According to the social learning approach, both fear-withdrawal and rage-attack behaviours develop out of a single, undifferentiated response which corresponds to what is often called the "fight or flight" response. The learning process probably proceeds in the following manner (Sawrey and Telford, 1975).

The newborn infant responds to a limited range of stimuli — a loud noise, a sensation of falling, a cold draft, a hampering of body movement — with a single, diffuse emotional response pattern which might be labelled "excitement" or "fright." Through classical conditioning, other stimuli can come to evoke the same response. The "startle" reaction in infants is accompanied by internal physiological changes as well as behavioural changes. There is first a stiffening of the body, followed by tantrum-like behaviour involving squirming, uncoordinated thrashing about of the arms and legs, and crying. It is through the reduction of this discomfort that the infant learns to "aggress" or "withdraw" when frightened. If the child's outbursts are effective in removing the aversive stimulus, the diffuse outburst may be perpetuated. However, it is more likely that certain features of this reaction pattern are more effective than others in specific situations. Waving of the arms, for example, may stop the advances of an overly friendly cat, but crying may be totally ineffective!

Language eventually gains some control over behaviour. While pushing and hitting may reduce pain or frustration, the child may learn that in certain situations, aggression is met with counter-aggression. Overt aggression may then be displaced by verbal or symbolic aggression. It is presumed that this process persists in adult life, with modification.

Modelling   Although reinforcement is important in the development and maintenance of aggressive behaviour, children are capable of acquiring aggressive behaviour simply by "watching someone else do it." (Recall the discussion of social learning in Chapter 6.) If that person is rewarded, or not punished, children may be inclined to imitate such behaviour when they find themselves in a similar situation. Bandura and his colleagues have performed a series of classic experiments which demonstrate this thesis. For example, children were shown a television film of a boy playing with his toys who refused to share them with a second boy. The second child then began to beat the boy and throw darts at his toy cars. In one version of the film, the aggressor ended up with all the toys, and the film finished by showing him taking them all away. The second version of the film ended differently, with the aggressor being subjected to a punishing counter-attack by the first boy. While most of the children said they disapproved of the aggression, those who saw the unopposed-aggression ending were subsequently observed to behave more aggressively in a play situation than those who saw the other ending, or those who saw no film at all (Bandura, Ross and Ross, 1963a).

A model's aggression can elicit imitation through several different processes (Bandura, 1973):

(1) It is obvious that people can acquire new behaviours simply by observing them. Since children are likely to have been rewarded, or at least not punished, for imitating high-status models in the past, they are apt to continue imitating models who have high social status and/or power. Bandura, Ross and Ross (1963b) have found that children more readily imitate the aggressive behaviour of adults who have power than they do the behaviour of adults perceived as competing for power.

In another classic study (Bandura, Ross and Ross, 1963c), five groups of nursery school children matched for aggressiveness were observed in an experiment studying the effect of various aggressive models. One group saw a live adult model attack a large inflated "Bobo" doll by punching it in the face, hitting it with a hammer, sitting on it, and kicking it. The second group observed a filmed presentation of the same model's aggressive performance. A third group watched a model dressed up as a cartoon cat perform the same aggressive behaviour on a television screen. For the fourth group, the filmed models acted in a non-aggressive fashion, and the fifth group had no exposure at all to the modelling situation. The researchers wanted to examine the possibility that the less realistic the modelling situation is, the less likely it is that imitation will occur. After the observation phase, the children were deliberately frustrated in a mild way. Then each child was put in a room with the Bobo doll where his or her play behaviour could be observed. The results of the experiment showed that the imitative effect of the live and filmed models did not differ significantly. Not only did imitated aggression increase; non-imitated aggression also increased substantially and was unrelated to whether the model was live or on film. In fact, some studies have found filmed models to be even more effective than live models in eliciting aggressive modelling (e.g., Bandura, Ross and Ross, 1963c).

(2) A model's behaviour and the behaviour it elicits can strengthen or weaken already existing inhibitions about that behaviour. For instance, a child who has been punched for crossing the street against a red light will have an "inhibition" against such behaviour. Yet observing a high-status person (e.g., a teacher) behaving in this way may lift that inhibition. However, if the teacher is admonished by a police officer, the inhibition is likely to remain intact or even be strengthened. The model's outcome can help inform the observer about the reinforcement contingencies that are in effect, and reduce the probability that the behaviour will occur. For example, Bandura (1965) exposed children to an aggressive adult model who punched, kicked, hit with a mallet, and verbally abused an adult-size inflated Bobo doll. One group saw the model rewarded with praise and candy, a second group saw her punished, and a third group saw her neither rewarded nor punished. Later, in a play situation involving several toys, including a Bobo doll, those children who saw the model either rewarded or

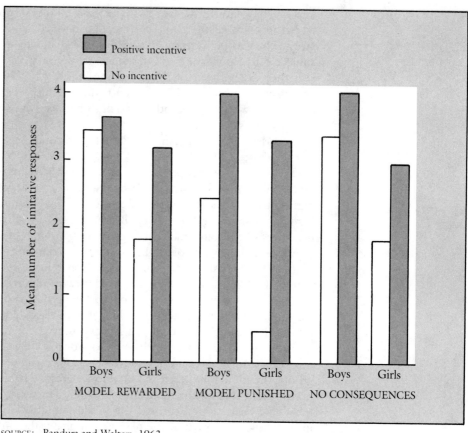

SOURCE: Bandura and Walters, 1963

unrewarded were much more imitatively aggressive than those who saw the punished model. However, when given incentives to reproduce the model's behaviour, all three groups were able to do so equally well (see Figure 9-1). Thus considerable imitative learning can occur without any reinforcement delivered either to the model or the observer.

(3) A model's behaviour may lead to *response facilitation*. In other words, behaviour that is already part of a person's repertoire and which is not affected by any inhibitions may be elicited by the observation of a model. If a spectator at a football game observes others throwing beer cans at the referee, that individual may be prompted to throw things as well.

(4) A model's behaviour may lead to *stimulus enhancement* in that observers may use specific objects used by the model. For example, in studies showing adult models abusing a Bobo doll, if the adult used a mallet to attack the doll, the children were much more likely to use a mallet in their attacks.

(5) A model's aggressive behaviour can heighten emotional arousal which, in turn, can facilitate an aggressive response, given the appropriate situational cues. For instance, watching an individual savagely fight against an opponent may increase emotional arousal: if one of the protagonists takes a swipe at you, you will react more vigorously as a result of that arousal.

The child-rearing process Since the social learning view is based on the idea that experience and reinforcement will determine whether or not a person grows up to be "aggressive," the behaviour of the parents, who largely control the child's world, will play a critical role. Attempts to verify this view empirically have been made, but such studies have methodological difficulties, since the researcher cannot manipulate independent variables or exclude extraneous variables. Since experimentation is inappropriate, the typical study examines the correlation between aspects of the parenting style and aspects of the child's behaviour or personality.

However, suppose, for example it were found that "aggressive" children had punitive parents, we could not be sure that the punitiveness caused the aggression; it could be that the children's aggressiveness produced the punishment. And, unless expensive and time-consuming longitudinal studies are done, we cannot be sure that a particular behaviour exhibited by a child will be exhibited in the future, or whether the behaviour is temporary. Neither can we detect whether there are certain periods ("critical periods") in the child's development in which the child is particularly sensitive or responsive to parental influence.

To be sure, some longitudinal studies have been done. One important finding is that the aggressive propensity of male children tends to remain stable from about age three into adulthood. However, because of greater social pressure on females to avoid aggression, we cannot predict which girls will be most aggressive as adults based on the amount of aggressiveness in early childhood (Kagan and Moss, 1962).

In a 22-year longitudinal study of intellectual competence and its relationship to aggression (Eron, Huesmann, Dubow, Romanoff and Yarmel, 1987), it was found that aggressiveness of most toddlers decreases as they grow and learn other coping strategies. However, the lower the child's IQ, the harder it may be to learn such skills. In fact, success at any endeavour may be more difficult for children with a low IQ, leading to increased frustration and more aggression. Aggression in turn interferes with the development of intellectual functioning. Aggressive children may be avoided by teachers and peers, so that learning opportunities are limited, and reinforcement may not be given for positive behaviours, owing to the generally negative attitude of the teacher toward the child.

Longitudinal research has also shown that aggression perpetuates itself within the family. Children from aggressive families are more likely to marry aggressive individuals, and their children are more likely to be aggressive (Huesmann, Eron, Lefkowitz and Walder, 1984). This effect has been observed across three generations (Huesmann, Eron and Yarmel, 1987).

Attempts have been made (Madden, 1976) to explain aggressiveness in terms of severe emotional thwarting during childhood. For example, it has been found that the parents of abused children were usually abused themselves as children. In effect, they are simply repeating the same child-rearing techniques they experienced (Sarles, 1960). However, we cannot satisfactorily explain the development of every hostile person by saying he or she was frustrated or mistreated as a child, since frustration and deprivation might just as often lead to apathetic withdrawal as to aggression.

Yet, it appears that no other variable is so strongly related to the development of aggressive behaviour as the use of *physical punishment* (Feshbach, 1970). It is likely that at least three factors are implicated in this development (Becker, 1964):

(1) Physical punishment, particularly in a rejecting context, is frustrating and leads directly to hostility and aggression.

Warm parents, regardless of their degree of permisiveness or restrictiveness, typically have non-agressive children.

(2) Parental use of physical punishment provides both a model and a partial sanctioning of aggressive responses.

(3) Hostile-punitive parents may reinforce the child's aggressive behaviour towards others.

Parents who frequently use power-assertive techniques (e.g., physical punishment or threat) tend to have highly aggressive sons (Becker, 1964). Moreover such parents are typically emotionally cold and rejecting. However, the children of parents who use love-oriented techniques such as praise, reasoning, and withdrawal of love usually have children whose incidence of aggression is low. It has also been shown (Becker, 1964) that cold or hostile but permissive parents raise highly aggressive children, while children of hostile and restrictive parents typically develop strong inner-aggressive tendencies and resentment, but little overt hostility. (Recall from the previous discussion in Chapter 7 that one way to express such hostility is through prejudice and discrimination). "Warm" parents, regardless of their degree of permissiveness or restrictiveness, typically have non-aggressive children.

A person's social conscience is developed by accepting the values and mores of the family and culture. If violence is used as a method of problem-solving in the family, the child will incorporate this value as a positive means of gaining approval (Sarles, 1976). The frequent use of power-assertive techniques has been found to produce a moral orientation based on fear of external detection and punishment, rather than on internalization of a moral code (Hoffman, 1984) This finding is supported by a study (McCord, McCord and Howard, 1963) of non-criminal and criminal men who had all been equally aggressive in childhood. Analysis of their family backgrounds suggested that a deviant-aggressive parent who practiced extreme punitiveness and neglect produced "anti-social" aggressiveness, while moderate punitiveness and neglect coupled with ineffective controls produced "socialized" aggression. Since there seems to be no independent relationship between the child's level of aggression and social class, it is unlikely that both the parents' and the child's behaviour are the results of a common social milieu.

While the nature of the relationship between parent and child and the kind of punishments employed by parents seem to have a direct effect on the development of aggressiveness, how parents react to aggression itself, whether parent-directed or peer-directed, appears to have little influence. Lambert (1971) studied the aggressiveness of children in several different cultures (United States, Mexico, India, Kenya, Japan, and the Netherlands). He argues that parental disciplinary practices relating to aggression should be viewed as symptoms, or effects, rather than the direct cause of physical aggression. The behaviour of the children he studied reflected the cultural value attached to aggression, rather than the particular effort made by parents to control or shape aggressive behaviour. Lambert has proposed a two-fold theory to support this claim. First, parental (especially maternal) care of babies provides the basis for the child's ability to interact with other children. Second, high social interactors are more influenced by peer responses to their aggression than low social interactors. Thus, according to this view, parents influence the degree of social confidence, while peers influence the degree of aggressiveness.

"It's our society": Cultural influences on aggression

Societies and cultures differ greatly in the value placed on aggression. Some encourage it, but there are many in which violence of any kind is actively discouraged. For example, the Pygmies, the Zuni Indians, the Lepchas, and, in Canada, the Blackfoot and Saulteaux Indians and the Inuit are all peace-loving groups. While the influence of Western culture is modifying the values of many societies, the fact that such groups can still be found who prefer and practice a non-aggressive existence illustrates that violence is not an inevitable aspect of social life.

Peaceful societies share several characteristics (Gorer, 1968):

(1) Such groups are generally small, technologically backward, and live in remote or inaccessible areas. In their isolation, they do not really need a warrior caste for defence. Their reaction to territorial encroachment is to retreat into an even more inaccessible region.

(2) While they all are hunting societies, they do not idealize bravery or aggressiveness as admirable traits which signify masculinity. In fact, they appear to make very little distinction between the ideal traits associated with masculinity and femininity.

(3) They appear to take great satisfaction in life and enjoy eating, drinking, and sex without guilt. A happy, productive life is thought to be within everyone's grasp.

(4) These societies lack aggressive religious deities. Gorer (1968) concludes:

> If our gods and heroes are killers — Lord of Hosts, warriors, successful revolutionaries — and if masculinity is demonstrated by the willingness to give and take punishment, then the joy of killing is always likely to re-emerge (p. 35).

Thus, while conflicts will always be present among individuals and groups, our culture plays a large role in determining how we deal with conflict, whether by negotiation, a flurry of fists, or a knife in the side.

However, people do not have to live in remote regions and possess gentle deities in order to live peaceful lives. Even within contemporary society, the Mennonites, the Amish, and the Hutterites renounce all kinds of force, and crime is practically unknown among them. In such cultures, aggressive behaviour goes unrewarded or discouraged, while pacifism is stressed as a lifestyle. And even though the children experience severe pressure in the course of being socialized (which should lead to frustration), they are virtually free of interpersonal aggression (Bandura and Walters, 1963).

We encourage aggression in many different ways, especially in males, who are taught that "winning" is important, and that aggression is often a means to that end. By contrast, children in Japan are actively discouraged from quarrelling through learning that yielding is more honourable and more desirable than being assertive in the quest for personal goals. Japanese mothers tell their children, when they start to argue or fight, *Makeru ga kachi*, which means, literally, "To lose is to win." The child who gives in, who contains his or her assertive drive in order to promote group peace and harmony, receives reinforcement from the mother and is viewed as more mature. Thus the unyielding child, while emerging the apparent victor, also bears a sense of loss since his or her behaviour does not receive approbation from adults (Azuma, 1984).

Since our culture has long associated masculinity with aggressiveness, to "back down" in the face of a threat is usually considered sissyish or "effeminate." Parents often openly encourage their sons to grow up to "be a man," while girls are traditionally encouraged to be non-aggressive, "weak," and dependent. The *Random House Dictionary of the English Language* defines "feminine" as "like a woman; weak; gentle," indicating how ingrained is the association between femininity and non-aggressiveness in Western society.

Canadians often like to believe that their history has proven them more peaceful and less aggressive than other nationalities, especially their neighbours to the south (see Chapter 7). There is no question that Canada is much less militaristic than many other countries. For example, three times as many American as Canadian citizens are members of the armed services and the U.S.A. allocates three times as much of its GNP to military expenditures as does Canada (Statistics Canada, 1980). Yet Canadian

TABLE 9-3
Violent crimes: A comparison of five countries in 1985

		(rates per 100 000 citizens)	
	Homicide	Assault	Rape
United Kingdom	1.0	243.0	43.0
Sweden	1.5	77.1	12.3
Australia	3.3	44.4	8.5
U.S.A.	7.9	302.9	36.6
Canada	2.9	127.0	10.0

SOURCES: Australian Bureau of Statistics
Central Office of Information, U.K.
Statistics Canada
U.S. Federal Bureau of Investigation

society may be more violent than we like to believe. Between 1976 and 1985 there was a 25.7 percent increase in the rate of violent crimes, and between 1974 and 1982 there was a 25 percent increase in police-reported rape (Statistics Canada, 1985). While Canada is lower in terms of violent crimes than some other countries (e.g., the United States), it certainly is not as low as many other advanced industrial states (see Table 9-3).

"He's just a tough character who got carried away": Aggression as a personality trait

A "trait" is a predisposition within a person to respond to a certain situation in a certain way. Is it possible that there is a trait of aggressiveness, that we can characterize people as being more or less aggressive? As we have already discussed, aggressive behaviour does seem to be a relatively stable part of a person's repertoire, at least in the case of males. The problem is that there is no single cluster of traits that describe the "aggressive" person. The same behaviour may be judged as aggressive or non-aggressive, depending on such variables as age or sex.

One way to approach aggression within the context of personality is to classify people into different character types. For example, Altmeyer (1981) suggests that "right-wing authoritarianism" (recall the discussion of the authoritarian personality in Chapter 7) may produce authoritarian aggression — that is, a general aggressiveness which is directed at various individuals and which is perceived as sanctioned by various authority figures. Megargee (1966) used the categories "overcontrolled," "undercontrolled," and "appropriate control" to describe three categories of people *vis-à-vis* aggressiveness. The "overcontrolled" person operates under rigid inhibitions. Even when frustrated or provoked, this person "keeps the lid" on anger. The undercontrolled person, by contrast, has not acquired the social controls necessary to inhibit antisocial motivations and behaviour. This type of person angers quickly and responds to frustration or provocation with physical aggression. The appropriately controlled person maintains a balance between assertiveness and inhibition, resorting to aggression only when it might be considered to be socially justified. Megargee (1966) reports that empirical studies of relatively mild aggression show that the overtly aggressive person has fewer controls and a greater "need" for aggression than does the overtly non-aggressive person. This evidence suggests that the way to discourage an aggressive person from acting aggressively is to help them develop internal controls. Prison programs are based on this general idea, giving rewards for non-aggression and punishment for aggression.

Often the extremely aggressive offender, particularly when the act can be characterized as impulsive, turns out to be a rather passive person with no previous history of aggression. The aggressive act is often completely uncharacteristic in a person who has always displayed extraordinarily high levels of control. (Keep this in mind the next time a "senseless" murder is reported by the press. Typically, the family and friends will describe the killer as having never been in trouble before, but having been passive, withdrawn, and a loner.)

Studies using the Minnesota Multiphasic Personality Inventory have found actively aggressive subjects to have more control and less hostility than non-aggressive criminals or normals (Johnson, 1972). The overcontrolled person buries resentment under rigid but brittle controls. Under certain circumstances, when resentment and anger escalate, the controls break down, the person lashes out in one violent impulsive act, and then he or she reverts to former passive (i.e., overcontrolled) behaviour. Thus, while the undercontrolled individual may commit numerous antisocial acts, it is the chronically overcontrolled individual who may pose the greater danger (Johnson, 1972).

Extreme aggression requires careful study and cannot be explained by extrapolation from studies of mild aggression. It is also clear that our methods of dealing with extreme aggression are imperfect. Prison for instance, a setting designed to promote self-control of aggression, does little to help the aggressive but overcontrolled individual. Such a person can easily appear to be a model prisoner. Training in how to express hostile feelings non-aggressively might prove more beneficial.

While personality factors undoubtedly play some role in aggressiveness, situational factors generally appear to be more important (Baron, 1977), often overriding the effects of personality. Nonetheless, we are all familiar with the perpetual bully who throws his or her weight around whenever circumstances make it clear that such behaviour will pay off. Such people may be insecure and actually trying to bolster their image by being tough. While insecurity seems to figure prominently in individuals with histories of aggression, other personality characteristics, such as selfishness, fear of being victimized by others (prompting the aggressive person to act first), and sadism may also play a role (Toch, 1969).

"What with all the violence on TV. . . . ": Media and aggression

Traditional members of the Cree community of Norway House on Lake Winnipeg refer to television by the Cree word *koosapachigan*, which means "shaking tent," a place where the shamans of the past conjured up spirits of the living and spirits of the dead. Some of these spirits were not very friendly.

Indeed, much of what is shown on television is not very "friendly." Yet children, adolescents and adults spend a considerable proportion of their leisure time in front of the television. Over 25 years ago, it was observed that the average child in the United States between ages three and 16 was spending more time watching television than in school (Schram, Lyle, and Parker, 1961). This situation has not improved. More recent U.S. research has shown that by the age of three or four, the typical child in the United States is already watching an average of four hours of television per day, a rate that increases as the child passes through school (Singer, 1983). Canadian children watch an average of about 20 hours of television per week; this figure is more or less stable from the age of two through adulthood (Statistics Canada, 1980).

As concern about crime and violence mounts, it is not surprising that people react with alarm both to violence on television and in the cinema. It was in response to such concern that the Ontario Government in 1975 appointed a Royal Commission to examine the extent to which media violence caused or influenced social violence. The Ontario Royal Commission on Violence in the Communications Industry reported that as much as 80 percent of U.S. prime time television programming contained the depiction of violence. Much of Canadian television drama originates in the United States, and the Commission found that around that time, the Canadian Television (CTV) network was broadcasting more crime drama than any other network in North America. In 1983, the United States-based National Coalition on Television Violence presented the results of its study of 30 television networks around the world to the United Nations Educational, Scientific, and Cultural Organization

(UNESCO). It concluded that CTV was the most violent of the 30, which included American, German, British, Japanese, and Australian networks. Sixty-five percent of CTV programming was found to be in the "high violence" category, with an average of 11.1 violent acts occurring per hour. Almost all this violent programming was imported from the United States.

An earlier American study reported that violence occurred in eight out of ten U.S. TV programs and in 93.5 percent of all TV cartoons directed at children, and that more than half the major characters depicted in prime time were violent (Baker and Ball, 1969). More recent research has reported that on the average, there are five to six violent incidents per hour of prime time American television, and 15 to 25 violent incidents for each hour of cartoons (Signorielli, Gross and Morgan, 1982). It has been estimated that based on 1968 programming, during the period between the ages of five and 15 the average child in the U.S. observes the violent destruction of more than 13 000 people on television (Waters and Malamud, 1975).

A study in St. Catharines, Ontario, reported by Gauthier (1977) found that between 4 and 11 p.m. on weekdays, about 44 percent of the available programs portrayed crime and violence. There were, on the average, six violent incidents per hour in the available programs between 8 a.m. and 11 p.m. on Saturdays and Sundays. What about news programs? Singer (1970) found that even after eliminating items about the Vietnam war, 40 percent of the CBS *Evening News* versus only 19 percent of the CBC's *National* was dedicated to aggression of some kind. Yet the Ontario Royal Commission, using a wider definition of aggression which included attacks on inanimate objects (e.g., arson), found that the Canadian radio and TV newscasts carried more reports of violence. However, conflict and property damage were emphasized in Canadian reports, while the U.S. newscasts seemed to be preoccupied with death. French-language television newscasts in Canada carry less violence than English newscasts, a fact which the Commission directly attributed to the lack of U.S. influence.

Films, music, magazines, newspapers, books, and even children's stories and nursery rhymes (see Boxes 9-3 and 9-4) often have violent themes.

B·O·X   9-3

A MODERN VERSION OF "JACK AND THE BEANSTALK"

Picture a poor boy and his poor, poor mother living in a small apartment. Upstairs, (two flights up by the fire-escape which passes the flat), lives an old man who, while being somewhat ill-tempered, never bothers anyone. He is relatively well-off financially. One day, the boy climbs up the fire-escape and steals a box containing a large sum of money. As he is about to leave, the old man comes in unexpectedly, begins threatening and cursing at the boy, and pursues him down the fire escape. The boy, money-box in hand, yells to his mother, who comes out with a large knife, and the moment her son is safely by her side, cuts the rope that holds the fire-escape ladder, throwing the old man screaming to his death. The boy gives his mother the money, she gives him a warm smile, and with her arm around his shoulder, they return inside (*Report of the Ontario Royal Commission on Violence in the Communications Industry*, 1977).

B · O · X   9 - 4

STORY-HOUR VIOLENCE

According to Geoffrey Handler-Taylor, who carried out an informal survey of nursery rhymes in 1952, "The average collection of 200 traditional nursery rhymes contains approximately 100 rhymes which personify all that is glorious and ideal for the child. Unfortunately, the remaining 100 rhymes harbour unsavoury elements. The incidents listed below occur in the average collection and may be accepted as a reasonably conservative estimate based on a general survey of this type of literature:

8 allusions to murder (unclassified)
2 cases of choking to death
1 case of death by devouring
1 case of cutting a human being in half
1 case of decapitation
1 case of death by squeezing
1 case of death by shrivelling
1 case of death by starvation
1 case of boiling to death
1 case of death by drowning
4 cases of killing domestic animals
1 case of body-snatching
21 cases of death (unclassified)
7 cases relating to the severing of limbs
1 allusion to a bleeding heart
1 case of devouring human flesh
5 threats of death
1 case of kidnapping

12 cases of torments and cruelty to human beings and animals
8 cases of whipping and lashing
3 allusions to blood
14 cases of stealing and general dishonesty
15 allusions to maimed human beings and animals
1 allusion to undertakers
2 allusions to graves
23 cases of physical violence (unclassified)
1 case of lunacy
16 allusions to misery and sorrow
1 case of drunkenness
4 cases of cursing
1 allusion to marriage as a form of death
1 case of scorning the blind
1 case of scorning prayer
9 cases of children being lost or abandoned
2 cases of house burning
9 allusions to poverty and want
5 allusions to quarrelling
2 cases of unlawful imprisonment
2 cases of racial discrimination

Expressions of fear, weeping, moans of anguish, biting, pain and evidence of supreme selfishness may be found in almost every other page" (*Report of the Ontario Royal Commission on Violence in the Communications Industry, 1977*).

In his report to the Ontario Royal Commission, Goddard (1977) expanded on the trend towards ugly violence in the contemporary rock music of that decade. The '70s saw the rise of Alice Cooper, who staged elaborate bits of macabre, including simulated guillotinings, the rock group Kiss, whose members dressed in chains and jack boots and who provided audiences with simulations of fire-breathing and vomiting of blood, and "heavy metal" bands, such as Iron Maiden (named after a notorious piece of torture apparatus used during the Spanish Inquisition). These and many other performers were noted for their emphasis on aggression, sexuality, and — not surprisingly — sexual aggression. Goddard recounted how the lead singer of a Toronto group had opened his show by butting a lighted cigarette on his arm, then asking if anyone would like to see him cut himself. In the '80s, rock videos have become popular, and many have incorporated violent and sexually aggressive themes.

In the '80s, rock videos — seen on 24-hour TV channels such as Canada's MuchMusic — have become popular, and some have incorporated violent or sexually aggressive themes.

Effects of television and film violence Defenders of violent programming sometimes argue that viewers become less aggressive as a result of watching violence because it has a cathartic effect. Setting aside the catharsis theory (which we have already examined and rejected), what *are* the effects of media violence? Does it lead to increased violence on an individual and societal level? What are the consequences for the developing child who is exposed to violent television fare every day for several years? What are the effects on adult viewers of films which portray typically weak and submissive individuals suddenly revolting against their own timidity and society, and using firearms to exact some kind of justice from an unfair world? Violent films like *Rambo* (to which U.S. President Reagan made favourable reference), in which a determined and armed individual rescues American POWs in Vietnam by decimating Vietnamese soldiers, may legitimize the notion of violent means to a desirable end.

Most studies of the effects of media violence have been carried out with children. One reason for this is that children are assumed to be more vulnerable than adults, since their beliefs and values and attitudes are actively developing. Aside from the issue of which population to study, conducting research in this area is very difficult, and there are many pitfalls to avoid. For example, we must be certain that any change in aggressiveness is not due simply to the excitement created by the film (rather than the aggressive content of the film) and we must also be careful to distinguish between a real decrement in aggressiveness and increased inhibition, for watching a weakling who attacks a powerful bully get beaten to a pulp hardly motivates a viewer to risk attacking a powerful bully (Howitt and Cumberbatch, 1975). Goranson (1970) cites a study he conducted in which a boxing scene ended with a boxer lying badly beaten on the mat. Subjects who were told that in the original film the fighter died shortly afterward were significantly less aggressive than subjects who were told there was a happy ending. In other words, people may become more inhibited when the consequences of violence are negative.

Social psychological studies of the effects of watching violent television have taken several forms, primarily (1) laboratory studies in which subjects are exposed to either a violent or a non-violent film and then observed when presented with the opportunity to aggress; (2) field studies in which children in natural (usually residential) settings are randomly assigned to a television diet either high or low in violence, then observed and measured for aggressiveness; and (3) correlational studies, in which measures of the amount of violent television watched are correlated with measures of aggressiveness. Some of these correlational studies have been of a longitudinal nature.

Laboratory studies have clearly demonstrated that the viewing of television or film violence in the laboratory leads to increased aggression in the laboratory, but we must hesitate to apply these results elsewhere (Freedman, 1984). It is not clear, for instance, that the measures of aggression in the laboratory (e.g., pushing a button to deliver shock to another person) have much to do with "real-life" aggression. More importantly, the demand characteristics of the laboratory situation would suggest that the experimenter approves of or permits the aggressive behaviours which the subject is subsequently given the choice to perform. It is also important to note that in reality, no one is exposed to a single violent film; television violence is likely viewed on a regular basis over a period of years. Furthermore, the violence will be interrupted with a good deal of non-violent programming; therefore, the net effect will probably be very different from what is found in a laboratory.

Many field studies have been carried out. One of the earliest and most influential studies of the effects of television violence was carried out by Feshbach and Singer (1971). In order to assess the effects of a steady diet of violent programs, they used as subjects nine to 15-year-old boys who resided in residential schools. Their TV viewing was closely regulated for six weeks, one group of boys watching only violent programs while the other group watched only non-violent programs. No evidence was found to support the notion that television violence generated aggression, and it was even argued that a catharsis effect had occurred, since highly aggressive boys who watched violent programs actually decreased in aggressiveness. However, this study has been subject to criticism because of methodological flaws, and is not generally viewed as providing firm support for the catharsis hypothesis.

A number of similar studies have been undertaken in the attempt to overcome the methodological shortcomings of the Feshbach and Singer study. In one longitudinal study, children's aggression and television viewing habits were measured in grade three, then again a decade later (Eron, Huesmann, Lefkowitz and Walder, 1972). The authors of the study concluded that the viewing of television violence over an extended period is a probable and longlasting cause of violence in children.

Another series of studies (Parke *et al.*, 1977) investigated the impact of movie violence on the behaviour of juvenile delinquents living in an institution. Initially, the behaviour of each of the boys was observed for a two-hour period on each of three successive days. During the following five days, all boys saw a film each evening. Boys in one group watched violent movies, while boys in the other group saw neutral, non-violent films. Records were kept of the boys' behaviour before, during, and after the films. On the day following the final film, the boys participated in a laboratory study, in which they were given the opportunity to shock a confederate. Some of the boys were "angered" and some "non-angered." Then, during a three-week follow-up period, the boys' behaviour was observed on three consecutive evenings each week. The study was carried out in both the United States and in Belgium. The results showed that exposure to film violence led to an increase in both physical and verbal aggression. There was evidence that boys who were initially more aggressive were most influenced by the violent films, suggesting that the effects of media violence may differ, depending on the aggressiveness of the viewer.

Yet children are exposed to both aggressive and non-aggressive models on television, and it is likely that the more the child identifies with and is similar to the television character, the more modelling will occur (Eron, 1980). It would also be expected that female characters would have more influence on girls, and male characters, more influence on boys.

Does a tendency towards aggressiveness lead aggressive people to *choose* violent television, thereby creating the impression of a positive correlation between the two variables when no causal relationship actually exists? In an attempt to examine this possibility, Eron *et al.* (1972) used what is called a "cross-lagged" procedure, and examined the relationship between the viewing of violence at age eight and aggression at age 18, *and* the relationship between aggression at age eight and violence viewing at age 18. It was found that violence viewing at age eight predicted aggression at 18 but that aggression at eight did not predict violence viewing at 18. A 22-year longitudinal study supports these observations. Subjects, first studied when they were eight, were contacted again at age 30. It was found that those who had watched more TV as children and had preferred violent programs were later more likely to have been convicted of serious criminal acts (Huesmann, 1986).

Life before and after television   A quasi-experimental study carried out in a small British Columbia logging town — one of the last communities in North America to get television — compared the aggressiveness of children before the introduction of TV and two years later when 90 percent of the homes had TV sets (Joy, Kimball and Zabrack, 1977, 1986). The behaviour of children in this town ("Notel") was compared with that of children in a similar town ("Unitel") which received only one TV channel (CBC), and that of children in another similar town ("Multitel") where CBC and three American channels were available. The children, all primary school students, were each observed at free play during 21 one-minute intervals over a period of seven to ten days. In addition, teacher and peer ratings of aggressiveness were noted. While there were no differences among the three samples of children at the time of the initial measurements, by the time the children were measured again, two years after the introduction of CBC-TV service to Notel, the Notel children were significantly more aggressive, both verbally and physically, than the children in the other two towns (see Figure 9-2). These results were not based simply on the fact that the children were two years older; the children were compared with children

FIGURE 9-2
Television and physical aggressiveness of children in three communities

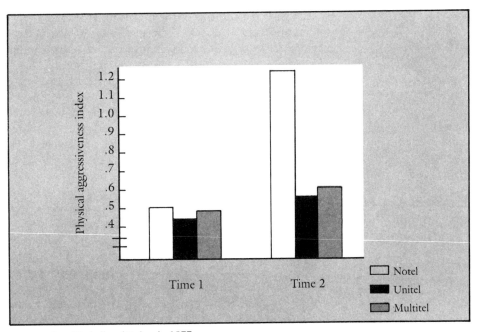

SOURCE: Joy, Kimball and Zabrack, 1977

who were two grades behind them and there were no differences in aggressiveness. It is important to note that this increase in aggressiveness occurred regardless of whether the children were initially low or high in aggressiveness. No changes in the *kinds* of aggressive acts were observed. The findings suggest a kind of ceiling effect; violence on television may lead to increased aggressiveness up to a certain point beyond which no change will occur.

On the other hand, another study (Hennigan *et al.*, 1982) examined the impact of the introduction of television in the United States on rates of violent crime, burglary, auto theft, and larceny. Only larceny was apparently influenced by the introduction of television, and the authors suggested that increased larceny might have been the result of advertising on television emphasizing upper- and middle-class lifestyles, perhaps fostering an uncontrollable desire for the consumer goods depicted. Another series of field experiments (Milgram and Shotland, 1973) also found no real-life effects of watching antisocial behaviour (e.g., theft) on television.

Inquiries into the effects of media violence   The research evidence is clearly mixed with regard to the effects of viewing violence, but because of the social importance of the issue, several inquiries have been carried out to assess the evidence. Such inquiries have generally concluded that viewing film or television violence leads to an increase in aggressive behaviour by the viewer (Goranson, 1977). The Royal Commission on Violence in the Communications Industry came to this conclusion in 1976, as did the U.S. Surgeon General's Report in 1972 and the U.S. National Institute of Mental Health report on television and behaviour (Pearl, Bouthilet and Lazar, 1982). The American Psychological Association (1985) also spoke out about the causal effect of media violence on childhood and adolescent aggression. Other researchers have noted that there appears to be a bidirectional effect — individuals with a higher propensity for violence may be more susceptible to and more interested in media portrayals of violence (Huesmann *et al.*, 1983).

However, in a review of the literature, Freedman (1984) takes issue with this viewpoint and concludes that there is very little convincing evidence that watching television violence in natural settings leads to an increase in subsequent aggressiveness. He argues, on the basis of social learning theory, that if violent acts on television were always rewarded, we could expect an increase in aggressiveness. Yet we cannot predict any such effect since we don't know the mix of rewarded and unrewarded violence seen by a given individual or how important television is to that person in comparison with other influences which might promote peacefulness and non-violence. Freedman's critique has itself been challenged (Friedrich-Cofer and Huston, 1986), although Freedman has held his ground (Freedman, 1986).

Indirect negative consequences of media aggression   Despite Freedman's critique, there are some good reasons to worry about the antisocial effects of television violence, and research into the impact of television violence is likely to continue. There are a number of *indirect* ways in which television violence can lead to negative social consequences: stimulus pairing, desensitization, imitation and contagion, changes in values, and increased apprehension about real-world violence. Each of these is discussed below.

(1) *Stimulus pairing and priming.* Berkowitz (1971) proposed that the constant pairing of weapons (e.g., guns) with aggression on television and in films may actually lead to the classical conditioning of impulsive ("emotional") aggression. His argument

was that covert (internal) aggressive reactions are pleasurable for many people because they have been associated with reward in the past (e.g., a child wants his brother's candy, hits him and takes it). This association accounts, he suggests, for the fascination that many people have with scenes of violence — whether they occur at the bull fights or in the hockey arena. Watching aggression elicits internal aggressive reactions which are pleasant to the extent that they have already been associated with pleasure.

Berkowitz suggests that people sometimes react violently in certain situations, not because they anticipate a positive outcome, nor because they are less inhibited about aggression, but because a situational stimulus (e.g., the presence of a gun) actually elicits an aggressive response. Thus, seeing a gun may always evoke aggressive feelings, although normally there is no "reason" to use the gun. However, when an individual is "frustrated" or "angered," the presence of the gun may elicit the behaviour it has so often been paired with on TV and film, i.e., shooting another person. Thus, says Berkowitz, people who, after shooting someone say that they don't understand why they did it, may be right.

The interpretation of aggression on the basis of conditioning has evolved into the "cognitive neo-associationism" model (Berkowitz, 1984) which emphasizes the processes of memory and recall, as well as communication's *meaning* to the viewer (See Chapter 3): When we are aware of a given thought, *priming* of semantically related thoughts occurs, making it easier for them to be activated later. Consequently, a violent film may elicit thoughts which prime semantically related thoughts and feelings, increasing the likelihood that the viewer will have other aggressive thoughts in the near future. This process can happen automatically, without the person's conscious attention. These ideas may eventually lead to aggressive behaviour. However, these effects would be tempered by other variables, such as whether an appropriate context for aggression is available, how the viewer interprets the witnessed actions (are they appropriate, morally justified, effective?), and whether the depicted incident is defined as fictional or real. This approach also stresses the importance of the meaning of observed aggression. If an individual watches another person act aggressively, the consequences of that aggression will strongly influence whether those behaviours will be imitated.

Huesmann *et al.* (1983) carried out a two-year longitudinal study of first and third grade children in which children in one group were given training sessions designed to teach them that the aggressive behaviours depicted by the people in television films do not represent the behaviours of most people — that the aggressive acts and unrealistic feats are the result of camera techniques and special effects. Children in the control group were not given such instruction. It was found that subjects in the experimental group not only were more aware of the possible harmful effects of viewing television violence, but that their propensity to behave aggressively was reduced, even though the amount of time spent viewing television violence was not reduced.

A final point about pairing and priming: During the '70s, aggression became more prevalent in sexually explicit films, books, and magazines (Malamuth, 1984), perhaps because milder fare had ceased to arouse the devotees of pornography. (The relationship between sexual arousal and aggression is examined later in this chapter.) It should be added here that there is a danger that the co-mixture of sex and aggression in film may lead to a conditioning process whereby aggressive acts come to elicit sexual arousal, or vice versa, not through misattribution, but as a result of a conditioned response (Malamuth, 1984).

(2) *Desensitization*. Media violence may lead to increased desensitization. Watching someone being beaten, it is argued, may be less upsetting if similar incidents have been seen on television. One study (Drabsman and Thomas, 1975) found that children aged eight to 11 who had just watched a violent television episode were markedly slower than those who had just watched a film of a baseball game to break up a squabble. The researchers concluded that the film had created a short-term increase in tolerance for aggression.

Other studies have also found evidence that repeated exposure to film violence leads to a decrease in emotional or physiological response. In one classic study (Lazarus *et al.*, 1962) subjects were shown a film of a primitive tribal ritual which involved "subincision," a bloody and agonizing operation performed on the genitalia of adolescent boys. Repeated exposure to the film led to decreased emotional reaction to it.

In another such study (Cline *et al.*, 1973) children with histories of high or low exposure to television were shown a moderately violent film; certain measures of autonomic arousal (blood volume, pulse amplitude, galvanic skin response) were taken before and after the presentation of the film. The high exposure subjects were found to be significantly less aroused autonomically than were the low exposure subjects, suggesting a possible generalization of desensitization to violence in many forms and under diverse conditions. Similar results have been achieved in other studies (e.g., Thomas, Horton, Lippincott and Drabsman, 1977). However, the decrease in arousal appears to occur primarily among those who are less apprehensive about becoming victims of violence (Rule and Ferguson, 1986). Berkowitz (1984) rejects the habituation explanation for desensitization, and argues that the desensitization to aggression following repeated exposure to aggression leads to increased acceptance of aggressive behaviour as proper or worthwhile.

(3) *Imitation and Contagion*. We have seen how children can learn to imitate aggressive models, even in a vicarious way. An equally important issue is the imitative repetition by adults of spectacular crimes of violence recounted in newspaper headlines. Such "contagion" is common; even in the nineteenth century the news of Jack the Ripper's exploits provoked a series of female mutilations in the English countryside (Berkowitz, 1971). Other examples of contagion abound. A flurry of assassination attempts around the world followed U.S. President Kennedy's assassination in 1963 (Weisz and Taylor, 1969), and both that assassination and other well-publicized murders have been followed by an unusual increase in violent crimes in the United States (Berkowitz and Macaulay, 1971). At least five murders seem to have been directly inspired by the "Texas Tower" shootings, when a student climbed a tower on the University of Texas campus and shot at pedestrians below (Berkowitz, 1971). Suicide rates, car, and airplane accident rates (which likely include some undetected suicides) have also been found to increase significantly following well-publicized suicides (Phillips, 1974, 1977, 1978, 1979, 1980, 1983). Homicides in the United States have been observed to increase by more than 12 percent, following championship prize fights in boxing (Phillips and Hensley, 1984). Overall, the data suggest that publicity about homicides or murder-suicides encourage further aggression of that kind; however, Phillips' research has been criticized on both theoretical and methodological grounds. His approach, while potentially useful, requires further elaboration and examination (Turner, Hesse and Peterson-Lewis, 1986).

Fictionalized accounts of disasters have also been known to provoke "copycat" behaviour. For instance, the film *The Doomsday Flight* is no longer aired on Canadian television precisely for this reason. The film's plot concerns an extortion attempt — a bomb is planted in a plane and set to explode when the plane descends to a certain altitude. Unless the airline company pays a ransom, the crew will not be told how to find and defuse the bomb. Station owners have acceded to the requests of airline pilots not to air this film since it often has spawned immediate imitations, usually in the form of hoax bomb threats. Within a few days of the film's debut in Montreal in 1970, BOAC received a series of hoax calls about one of its jets bound for London in which it was claimed that an altitude-sensitive bomb had been placed on the airplane. Many other hoax calls and extortion attempts have been made following the showing of the film in other cities. (See Box 9-5 for more examples of copycat violence.)

(4) *Effects on values and attitudes.* An analysis of the "message" of violent television

---

B · O · X   9 - 5

COPYCAT VIOLENCE

At a symposium on television violence in August 1975, Ted Kotcheff, a Canadian film director, described a TV drama that he directed in London, England. The play was set in the underground transit and involved a man contemplating suicide by throwing himself in front of a moving train. After seeing the script, London Transport authorities tried to persuade him to delete the suicide scene, fearing imitation. Kotcheff thought their fears were unfounded. However, the day after the broadcast, five people jumped in front of moving trains. Did they get the idea from watching his drama?

In 1975, a Brampton, Ontario, high school student went on a shooting spree in his school, killing a teacher, a fellow student, injuring several other students, and then killing himself. Six days after this incident, an 18-year-old boy in Iroquois Falls, Ontario, shot and wounded several people with a .22 rifle. In his court appearance, he said that he had often thought of shooting at people, but never had the nerve to do so until he read about the Brampton boy's behaviour in the newspaper (Stanley and Riera, 1977). In October of the same year, an Ottawa high school student went on a similar shooting spree in his school, wounding six students before killing himself. Were these two incidents related? The *Globe and Mail* had carried a follow-up story on the Brampton

shooting just two days before the Ottawa incident. Did the Ottawa boy read the *Globe and Mail* story? Psychiatrists who were consulted on the case concluded that a contagion effect was quite possibly involved (Stanley and Riera, 1977); however, there was no way of knowing it for certain.

Other examples of "copycat" violence have been cited in the report of the Ontario Royal Commission on Violence (1977): For example:

Born Innocent, a made-for-TV movie, was shown in September 1974. It included a scene in which a girl was raped with the end of a broomstick by her reformatory classmates. The very next day, four children raped a nine-year-old California girl in the identical manner.

A televised mock suicide caused a youth in Calgary to try the same technique on himself.

A movie scene involving a skid-row derelict being doused with gasoline and set on fire was followed by a rash of such crimes.

Two years after the film *The Deer Hunter* was released to television, 27 deaths had been recorded in the United States in which the film's Russian roulette scene was strongly implicated. Most of the deaths were accidental, but some were clearly suicide (*The Toronto Star*, February 2, 1983).

programming suggests that at least in the television world, violence is generally a successful means of obtaining personal goals, it is usually not punished, and that law enforcement agencies, whose job it is to reduce violence, often use violence to resolve conflicts (Gerbner, 1969). There is the obvious danger that violent acts against others may become unconsciously accepted as normal behaviour. The Ontario Royal Commission in its interim report (1977) was worried that

> television's traditional use of the violent solution for most human social problems sets up a value system that is drastically at variance with the ethical base of Canadian family life, where peaceful solutions reached with due respect to individual rights are recognized as the most desirable ends to any conflict (p. 4).

Other people have voiced concern that television and cinema may encourage the idea that women want to be victimized (see Malamuth and Briere, 1986).

(5) *Increased apprehension*. Television perpetuates stereotypes about criminals and their crimes that have little to do with reality. For example, while most murders in television dramas are committed by strangers to the victim, most murders in Canada are carried out by people who know the victim (Schloss and Giesbrecht, 1972; see also Table 9-4). Gerbner and his associates (e.g., Gerbner, Gross, Morgan, and Signorielli, 1980) argue that television violence cultivates a perception of the social world as a dangerous place where people must constantly be on guard. Gerbner (1975) has reported that people who watch a lot of TV dramatically overestimate the probability that they will sometime be the object of violence or a crime. The more people watch television, the more they appear to be fearful of violence. However, in a similar study carried out in Toronto (Doob and Macdonald, 1979) it was concluded that the correlation between fear of violence and amount of television viewing is illusory. In areas of that city where the crime rate is higher, people also watch television more often. In other words, people who live in high-density, run-down areas are really in more danger than the *average* Toronto resident, and they also happen to watch more television. Thus, their estimates of greater risk are not as exaggerated as they seem when compared with *average* crime rates across the city. This study provides an excellent lesson on the way in which reports such as Gerbner's can be misleading. When two factors, such as TV watching and perception of danger, vary together, it is always possible that — as in this case — the two are not causally connected, but are both dependent on a third variable.

In a survey of television viewers in Saskatoon (before American television channels could be received) it was found that viewers who regularly watched crime drama did not perceive it as reflecting real life. They watched it, they said, because it was both exciting and relaxing (Tate, 1977). When educational and occupational levels were controlled, there was no relationship between the number of hours spent watching television and the "fortress" mentality, (i.e., viewing the world outside as dangerous and hostile). However, viewers whose attitudes were generally authoritarian were more likely to have a fortress mentality to begin with. For them, television only reinforced what they already knew: the world was a dangerous place. These individuals believed that television had a great impact on viewers, and they wished to control and censor its contents.

(6) *"School for scandal."* Television and cinema may actually teach people how to commit crimes. In their report to the Ontario Royal Commission, Stanley and Riera (1977) cite several instances in which people have used knowledge gained from TV in committing a crime or eluding police! For example, in June 1976, *La Grande Casse*

TABLE 9-4
Relationship of murder suspects and victims in Canada*

	1964	1974
Domestic:		
Immediate family	28.6**	22.6
Kinship	4.0	5.6
Common-law family	7.5	9.0
Lover's quarrel and/or triangle	6.5	2.6
Domestic total	46.6	39.8
Social or business:		
Close acquaintance	12.6	8.2
Casual acquaintance	13.6	15.3
Business relationship	2.5	1.2
Social or business total	28.7	24.7
During commission of another criminal act	11.7	9.4
No known relationship	6.5	8.6
Unsolved	6.5	17.5
Total	100.0	100.0
TOTAL MURDER INCIDENTS	199	499

*Murder incidents counted here are based on the number of original charges of capital murder, non-capital murder, and murder — not specified. In murder incidents involving more than one suspect and/or victim, the incident is scored only once, according to the closest relationship of the accused to the victim(s).

**Expressed as percentage distribution by murder incidents.

SOURCE: Statistics Canada, 1977

had a long run in Montreal cinemas. It showed in detail how to steal cars, including how to start them without a key, etc. The car thieves were glorified and the police were portrayed as incompetent. The car theft rate in Montreal jumped almost immediately and a number of youths responsible for at least 45 car thefts were arrested. They admitted getting both the idea and technique from the film.

(7) *Notoriety*. Often, the media appear to provoke the imitation of social aggression by showering attention on perpetrators of violence — bombers, hijackers, murderers. As a result, some attention-seekers may try to emulate the violence described in order to acquire celebrity status. Lynette Fromme, one of Charles Manson's followers, became front-page news when she pointed a gun at U.S. President Ford in 1975; her picture was on the cover of both *Time* and *Newsweek*. Four weeks later, another woman made the front pages following a similar attack on President Ford (Stanley and Riera, 1977). The wave of FLQ bombings in Montreal during the '60s abated when the media, in response to a request from police and civic authorities, stopped giving front page coverage to every bomb incident, whether it was real or a false alarm.

Whether the prospect of being on TV actually affects the behaviour of violent activists also bears examination. While demonstrators may be moved to behave more aggressively in order to make a point with viewers, there is the risk of being identified as a dangerous person. On balance, the media probably deter rather than promote violence (Lang and Lang, 1972).

SPECIAL ISSUES

We have examined the physiological, developmental, social, personal, and media influences on aggression. It is clear that there is no one single explanation for aggressive behaviour; it has many dimensions and can arise from a wide variety of factors, probably acting in combination. Returning to our example of the Brampton boy's aggression — there is no simple answer. Perhaps over the years he developed an overcontrolled personality which prevented him from expressing hostility. He may have fantasized about how to get even with his classmates who, in his mind, were rejecting him or were better off than he was. He may have been influenced by media violence. Because he committed suicide, there was no way of exploring these questions. Obviously, it is important to find ways to head off such aggression before it begins. Before we turn to the subject of prevention of violence, however, let us conclude our discussion of influences on aggression by examining two related issues: the impact of violent pornography and the relationship of aggression to gender.

VIOLENT PORNOGRAPHY

The previous discussion of the effects of media violence pointed out the danger of becoming desensitized. The increasing availability of violent pornography raises the fear that a male's attitude towards females may be affected so that he becomes less sensitive to a female's cries of distress in a sexual encounter. Studies have shown that male viewers of violent pornography differ in their attitude to rape (Malamuth, 1984); compared to non-viewers, they view rape as less horrible and the victim as more desirous of being violated. This is not surprising, since most violent pornography implies that females secretly want to be assaulted and they will derive pleasure from the assault.

Sexual arousal and aggression

Sexual violence depicted in the media may elicit powerful sexual responses which can interact with aggressivity to produce behaviour which is of particular danger to females. Why is this so? The following section outlines several reasons.

The evolutionary concept of "survival of the fittest" suggests that those members of a species who are best suited to a given environment are most likely to reproduce successfully. As we have mentioned, Lorenz and many others have argued that aggression is an important part of the selection process, for if reproductive activity is won by the strongest of the males, then weaker, less adaptive males are unlikely to reproduce. In other words, there may be some link between sexual and aggressive motivation. However, if there is such a link in humans, its effect appears to be very weak and completely overshadowed by the effects of experience and socialization (Malamuth, Feshbach and Jaffe, 1977).

However, sexual arousal and aggressive arousal, along with other kinds of arousal, reflect the same underlying sympathetic nervous system arousal. On the basis of nervous system activity, the individual cannot differentiate excitation as "sexual" or "aggressive"; the excitation brought about by conflict or physical pain is no different from the excitation which underlies sexual desire and activity (Zillmann, 1984).

Excitation transfer theory   According to Zillmann's (1984) three-factor theory, emotion involves both a dispositional component, an excitatory component and an experiential component. The dispositional component refers to skeletal-motor behaviour which is largely under the control of stimuli and reinforcements (i.e., someone insults you and you raise your fist because you have learned to do so in such situations in the past). The excitatory component is a response-energizing mechanism which prepares the organism for vigorous action. It corresponds physiologically to heightened sympathetic nervous system arousal, and it may be unlearned, as in the case of a response to pain or to genital stimulation, or learned, as in the case of a response to stimuli which signal forthcoming pain or pleasure. The experiential component is the conscious experience of emotion, and it may operate to alter substantially the unfolding emotional behaviour. You experience the insult as anger-inducing, but you realize that it was made by a child, and you consciously work to reduce or change the emotional reaction.

According to this model, "excitation-transfer" can occur; it is assumed that the excitatory component does not disappear immediately when the stimuli that elicited it have disappeared. Residues of the excitation from one emotional reaction can add to and intensify a subsequent emotional state brought about by a changed stimulus situation. Thus, following sexual arousal, residues of this excitation can intensify subsequent emotional states such as those associated with aggression, just as residues following aggression can intensify subsequent sexual reactions.

In a demonstration of excitation-transfer involving sexual and aggressive arousal (Zillmann, 1971), subjects who had previously been provoked by a confederate of the experimenter watched either a sexually arousing film, an aggressive film, or a neutral film. Next, they were given the opportunity to administer electric shocks to

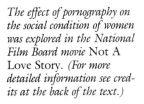

The effect of pornography on the social condition of women was explored in the National Film Board movie Not A Love Story. *(For more detailed information see credits at the back of the text.)*

the confederate; in addition, measures of physiological arousal were taken. Physiological arousal was greatest in the sexual film condition, followed by the aggressive film condition, and the neutral condition. Aggressive behaviour followed this same pattern: subjects who watched the sexual film were more aggressive than those who watched the aggressive film, who were in turn more aggressive than those who saw the neutral film. It would appear that the arousal, whatever its cause, was interpreted subsequently in terms of aggressiveness when the situational context made aggression relevant.

It is important to note that aggressive films can lead to physiological arousal because of high levels of fear-inducing stimuli and general "excitement," and that viewers may label this arousal as "aggressiveness" and therefore act aggressively because they *think* that they must be feeling aggressive if they have watched an aggressive film (Rule and Nesdale, 1976).

The consequences of repeated experiences of excitation transfer can be worrisome in that aggression-related stimuli can come to elicit sexual reactions. It has been reported that there is a high positive correlation among rapists between arousal from non-sexual aggression and arousal from rape (Abel, Barlow, Blanchard and Guild, 1977). Moreover, aggression may be sexually stimulating for a substantial minority of the general male population. In one study (Malamuth, Check and Briere, 1986), male subjects listened to one of four tape-recorded stories which reflected one of four orientations — sexual/aggressive, sexual/non-aggressive, non-sexual/aggressive, and non-sexual/non-aggressive. Sexual arousal was measured both by self-report and through penile tumescence monitored with a special strain gauge. Both self-reporting and measures of penile tumescence indicated that sexual arousal in about 70 percent of the subjects was inhibited by aggressive activity in the story. However, for the remaining 30 percent, sexual arousal was *enhanced* by the presence of aggression. The authors of that study speculate that the relationship between aggression and arousal is based in experience: During adolescence, those teenagers who believe that women need to be coerced into sexual behaviour may behave or fantasize in an aggressive way while experiencing actual sexual pleasure. Through classical conditioning, depictions of sexual aggression or actually behaving aggressively may elicit sexual arousal.

Inhibition of aggression   Sexual arousal does not always facilitate aggression. In some cases, it actually seems to reduce it. One important factor appears to be whether or not the individual labels the arousal as sexual or hostile. Subjects exposed to erotic materials prior to being angered by a confederate showed more aggression, and the greater the level of eroticism, the greater the aggression. Presumably, the arousal was misattributed to the anger-inducing incident. Yet when the erotic material was presented after the provocation, highly erotic material had no effect on aggression, presumably because the subject did not misattribute this arousal and, indeed, mild erotica actually reduced aggression, possibly because of its distracting features (Donnerstein *et al.*, 1975).

Outside the laboratory   There is evidence that sexual arousal from aggression is also related to aggression against women not only in the laboratory but also during dating (Malamuth, 1986). And it has been suggested that serial murderers — people who kill many times, sometimes over a period of years — often experience sexual arousal from aggressive activities (Darrach and Norris, 1984). Furthermore, there is evidence that some wife beaters (about 15 percent) experience sexual arousal from non-sexual assaults on their wives (Davidson, 1978). To summarize, the relationship between sexual arousal and aggression has serious implications for society, and should serve as a warning about the potential dangers of violent pornography. However, it is also important to note that most of those men who do experience sexual arousal as a result of aggression do not go out and rape, although they may be more aggressive during dating. A survey of a United States national sample of 6159 male and female post-secondary students is especially enlightening in this respect (Koss, Gidycz and Wisnieski, 1987). It was found that considerably more women and men (as perpetrators) in this *normal* sample reported incidents of rape, attempted rape, and sexual coercion than are represented by the usual crime statistics. The rape victimization rate among the females of this group was 10–15 times greater than the reported crime data, and the admission by men of committing rape, two to three times greater. The authors stress that most official surveys severely underestimate the full extent of sexual victimization. Several factors probably combine to produce rape, including attitudes towards women and personal values. Violent pornography may succeed in changing some of these attitudes for the worse. More importantly, for men who find aggression sexually arousing, the combination of erotic and aggressive stimulation may create an appetite for sexual violence which could be difficult to control in situations involving high sexual or aggressive emotion.

Gender and aggression

History is filled with accounts of men marching off to battle or men duelling to avenge wounded pride — or even men competing in boxing matches to see who can stand up the longest as each smashes away as savagely as possible at the other. These activities — soldiering, duelling, boxing — are male activities. Why is this so? Does this situation reflect a basic difference between the physiologies of males and females, or does it reflect differences in rearing?

Research has shown that within many species there are substantial sex differences in aggressiveness: the males fight readily while the females do not, except in defense of their young (Archer, 1976). Such differences do not seem to be the result of learning. For example, when infant monkeys are raised in isolation, males and females still show the usual differences in aggressiveness that are observed in monkeys given a more normal social environment: the males demonstrate more threatening and chasing behaviour and more rough-and-tumble play than the females (Harlow, 1958, 1959).

Sex hormones Such differences in aggressiveness have often been attributed to the so-called sex hormones — the "male" androgens and the "female" estrogens. Although both sexes actually produce both kinds of hormones, androgens predominate in males while estrogens predominate in females. The effect of sex hormones on animal aggression is seen in the longstanding practice of castrating male horses, bulls, and other animals to render them more docile. Such animals rarely fight. Since the major result of castration (apart from sterility) is the elimination of one of the androgens, testosterone, and since the administration of testosterone will restore "normal" aggressiveness, testosterone would appear to play an important role in animal aggression. Further support for the role of testosterone comes from the dramatic increase in male competitiveness that accompanies sexual maturity, precisely the time that the level of testosterone also increases dramatically. Hormones also seem to influence female aggressiveness which in many species parallels the sexual cycle, being at a low when the estrogen level is at its ebb (Johnson, 1972).

As in the animal domain, castration seems to reduce aggressivity of human males. Therapeutic castration has been legal voluntary treatment for sexual offenders in countries such as Scandinavia, Switzerland, and Germany for some time. Hundreds of individual case studies have shown that the operation leads to a "general pacification" and a relatively low rate of recidivism (Johnson, 1972). Males castrated to serve as harem attendants or opera singers (a practice which ended only when Pope Leo XIII abolished the custom of producing eunuchs for the papal choir in 1878) were typically described as being non-aggressive and feminine in their behaviour. Castration is still practiced in parts of India in order to produce eunuchs, who even have their own national association.

On the other hand, when testosterone is administered to normal adult human females, their physical activity and their general aggressiveness often increase to a level typical of males (Bardwick, 1971). Moreover, the propensity for hostility and aggression appears to increase significantly just prior to and during the menstrual period, that is, when the two major female sex hormones, estrogen and progesterone, are at their lowest level. Those women who take progesterone-based contraceptive pills which regulate the hormonal fluctuations do not seem to experience these symptoms to the same degree (Bardwick, 1971). It is evident that androgens are related to male aggression but it should not be assumed that the relationship is directly causal. For example, androgens enhance musculature and increases available energy, which makes the individual a more competent aggressor (Zillman, 1984).

Whether or not the research evidence supports the position that human sexual differences in aggression are partly due to biological differences is still a matter of some dispute. Some reviewers (e.g., Bleier, 1984) argue that the case is very weak, while others (e.g., Parke and Slaby, 1983) argue the opposite. Perhaps differences exist, but perhaps the effects of learning overwhelm whatever biological effects exist. Since sex differences in aggressiveness are greater in children than in adults, the influence of socialization and norms of conduct may become pivotal as the child matures (Eagly and Steffen, 1986).

There is no clear evidence that human males are predestined to be any more aggressive than females. Although hormones play a role, they do so by altering physique and affecting the energy available to the body. How that physique and energy are employed depends on socialization: in our society, the male role accepts, even demands, aggressiveness while the female role discourages it.

Gender roles   As with any other social behaviour, there are roles associated with aggressive behaviour, and norms associated with those roles (Eagly and Steffen, 1986; Lubek, 1979). In our society these roles differ for males and females. The male gender role actually encourages aggression. Indeed, when asked, people report that they *expect* males to be more aggressive (Cicone and Ruble, 1978). Other research has shown that males hold more favourable attitudes to aggressive behaviour than females across

Gender roles are learned at an early age.

a wide variety of social situations (Smith, 1984). However, social norms also impose limits upon male aggressiveness; men are expected to protect and defend the weak.

The female gender role has traditionally discouraged aggressiveness, but has also emphasized the avoidance of physical harm (Eagly and Steffen, 1986). Men may proudly wear the scars of warfare or water polo, but not women. It may be that women are sometimes unaggressive because they are expected to disapprove of aggressive behaviour. For example, in one study (Richardson, Bernstein and Taylor, 1979), women subjects responded to provocation in a more aggressive way when they were by themselves than when there was an audience. Furthermore, a supportive audience led to more aggression than did a silent audience. Other research indicates that women report greater guilt and anxiety about their aggressive behaviour than men do (Frodi, Macaulay and Thome, 1977) — as we would expect, if aggression involves norm transgression.

The association of aggressiveness with the masculine role is stronger in some cultures than in others — consider the *machismo* of Latin America, for example. In fact, the extent of sex-role differentiation within cultures seems to have some bearing on aggression. In a study of 17 cultures (McConahay and McConahay, 1977), a high positive correlation was found between sex-role rigidity (the degree to which various important tasks are assigned to only one sex or the other) and violence in the society. Among the unaggressive Arapesh of New Guinea, both men and women show "feminine" traits, and there is little emphasis on sex differences (Eysenck, 1953). However, as the !Kung hunters of Africa (a group which, until recently, had no contact with modern society) become more Westernized, their women are losing their egalitarian status and children are no longer being brought up to be non-aggressive (Kolata, 1974). Whether sex-role rigidity leads to violence or vice-versa, or whether both result from some third variable, e.g., social stratification, is not clear.

Are males really more aggressive?   People certainly think that males are more aggressive than females (Ruble, 1983). In childhood, this seems to be the case: studies of nursery school children have found boys to be twice as aggressive as girls, both physically and verbally (Hutt, 1974). Males are also likely to give indications of a greater propensity towards aggression. For example, when asked how they would have responded to hypothetical interpersonal conflict situations in adolescence, male university students selected physical aggression significantly more often than women did (Reinisch and Sanders, 1986).

However, considered as a body of evidence, the research literature offers only slight support for the belief in greater human male aggressiveness. A recent review of the empirical research literature (Eagly and Steffen, 1986) concluded that, while some studies have reported greater physical aggression by males, the differences between males and females are relatively small and are inconsistent across studies. Indeed, in some situations female subjects have been found to be *more* aggressive than male subjects (e.g., see Da Gloria and de Ridder, 1979). It seems that men and women tend to react differently to aggression-eliciting cues and provocation, so that what might be anger-inducing for men may be anxiety-inducing for women; however, when women see aggressive behaviour as justified or prosocial, they can be just as aggressive as men (Frodi, Macaulay and Thome, 1977).

While the research literature offers only weak support for sex differences in aggression, men continue to *appear* to be more aggressive than women. In real life, there is no doubt that males account for the great majority of violent crimes. In the United States, at age 18, ten times as many males as females are arrested for murder (Cairns and Cairns, 1985). Yet it is important to note that crime statistics can be very misleading, for men and women may be treated differently by the justice system. There is evidence that (at least in the past) a "chivalry factor" has protected women: women who did commit crimes were less likely than men to be reported to the police, less likely to be charged, and less likely to be found guilty (Reckless and Kay, 1967). Women who committed crimes were often viewed as "misguided creatures" who needed help, rather than dangerous criminals (Giallombardo, 1966). Still today, the woman who beats her husband is much less likely to be reported to the police than the man who beats his wife, undoubtedly because a man would be embarrassed to admit a need for protection from a woman. This situation may change as more and more women become active participants in law enforcement and jurisprudence.

We are left with some doubt, then, about the magnitude of sex differences in human aggression. Research studies suggest very little difference, but real-life experience points to men being much more aggressive. It may be that empirical research situations are not representative of real life; such research typically focuses on the behaviour of university students who are strangers to each other and who interact in one of a small number of situations over a short period of time (Krebs and Miller, 1985). On the other hand, sex differences which *do* appear in social psychological research could reflect the researchers' implicit assumption that aggression is the normal "male" reaction to provocation; women's aggressiveness (as in the case of child abuse, for example) has by and large been ignored by researchers (Macaulay, 1978). After carefully reviewing the literature, White (1983) concluded that females could be socialized to be as aggressive as males, but that traditional child-rearing techniques emphasizing sex-role stereotyping minimized the likelihood of female aggression.

THE REDUCTION AND CONTROL OF AGGRESSION

It is unlikely that aggression can be eliminated entirely from our society but certain steps could be taken to reduce aggression-associated problems considerably. Among these is *parent training*.

Most parents are unprepared for the extremely difficult task of training, educating, and socializing their children. It seems obvious that informing parents of the negative effects of viewing violent TV programs and advising them how to control children's viewing rights with a minimum of uproar would represent a substantial contribution. But the task is not easy. Singer and Singer (1981), for example, were quite discouraged when a course they ran for parents of preschoolers did not appear to affect television habits or reduce aggression. They advise that indirect methods — teaching parents how to interact with their children, using stimulating games — may be more effective than direct attempts to control the time spent watching TV.

As was discussed earlier, certain child-rearing practices in themselves are likely to increase aggressive patterns of behaviour. Among these are the excessive use of punishment and an emphasis on traditional masculine/feminine role behaviour. Thus, if boys were socialized more like girls, cooperation and sensitivity would likely be more evident than aggression (Eron, 1980).

Another problem which parents and, eventually, teachers and employers must face is the management of anger. One strategy involves the induction of responses incompatible with anger (Baron, 1983a, 1983b). Two of these are *empathy* and *humour*.

Empathy. When the aggressor is not extremely angry, signs of pain or suffering on the part of the victim may elicit empathy and reduce further aggression. However, if the anger is substantial, signs of pain may enhance the aggression.

Humour. Non-hostile humour and sexual humour have been shown to reduce anger and aggression. Hostile humour, because it includes hostile cues, may increase aggression.

Parents also differ in their "mediating styles" when reacting to the anger or aggression of their children. Most often the reaction is "Stop it!" Singer and Singer (1986) propose that a mediation involving discussion and explanation is more effective, especially over the long term.

Ignoring aggressive behaviour and reinforcing cooperative actions have also been shown to increase cooperation and decrease aggression in nursery school children (Brown and Elliot, 1965). Teaching children that the violent behaviour on television is not only faked, but that such behaviours rarely occur in real life is also important (Huesmann *et al.*, 1983).

No matter how desirable the reduction of aggression in a society may be, the likelihood of much success being achieved via parent education and appropriate socialization practices, except over the very long term, is minimal. As with the reduction of prejudice, the costs would be excessive and, more seriously, those who truly need the information are not likely to make themselves available.

Although we must be pessimistic about any substantial changes to the aggressive orientation and motivation of individuals, it does not mean that aggression cannot be reduced or controlled by *external or legal means*. In other words, no matter what personality characteristics people have which lead them to steal, if automobiles were

THE SCENE OF THE CRIME.

It's criminal what's happening to the game of hockey. What was once the scene of a great pastime, is becoming a spectacle that thrives on violence.

So who's to blame? It isn't just the players. Fans, coaches, the media — just about everyone has to take some responsibility. Because when something serious happens, just about everyone can suffer the pain. Including the game of hockey itself. How can we stop it? By promoting good sportsmanship. By cleaning up the game. Before it's no longer safe to go out on the ice.

LET'S GET BACK IN THE GAME.

FAIRPLAY

The Commission for Fair Play

Deglorifying hockey violence: In September 1987 the Commission for Fair Play and Federal Sport Minister Otto Jelinek launched a public campaign against violence in sport.

made impenetrable there would be no car thieves. There are, in fact, a number of ways in which aggression can be reduced or controlled. Among these are:

(1) *The deglorification of violence*. Reducing violence in the media (fictional violence and the extent to which news programs dwell on violent events in the world) would focus less attention on violent events in general. Similarly, the elimination or reduction of violence in sports, especially hockey, would decrease the number of players acting as aggressive role models for children.

(2) *Gun control*. The availability of guns increases the probability that they will be used. Forty-five percent of all murders in Canada are carried out with firearms. The government of Canada, through legislation in 1977, placed some controls on the purchase of firearms and people now are required to obtain a certificate which, among other things, cannot be issued to individuals with a history of violent behaviour. Nevertheless, guns are readily available, although not to the same extent as in the United States and many other countries.

A comparative distribution of homicide rates in a number of countries with different gun control laws can be seen in Table 9-3. The relationship between the two variables is clear but, since the data are correlational, it cannot be concluded that the availability of guns leads to violence. For example, those countries in which violence is commonplace may, because of the need for self-defense, be less prepared to pass gun control legislation. How, then, can such a vicious cycle be interrupted?

(3) *International diplomacy*. At the international level, the situation regarding violence is even more complicated, as will be seen in the chapter on conflict. Problems of terrorism, minor and major wars, and international "accidents" such as the Russian destruction of a Korean airliner have no simple solutions. However, in spite of numerous provocations, that the two major world powers — the U.S.S.R. and the U.S.A. — have not been involved in direct mutual aggression does offer some hope for the effective maintenance of peace.

If the only response to violence is better police protection or the reinstatement of capital punishment, violence will not disappear. What is required are changed values and better education. At the same time we should not be dissatisfied with "small effects" (Rosenthal, 1986). When considering the consequences of aggression and violence, the difference between social significance and statistical significance takes on special meaning. Intervention or training programs, for instance, may reduce the number of homicides by a statistically small percentage, but even a few lives saved have substantial social consequences.

SUMMARY

(1) Aggression is defined as behaviour that is intended to harm or destroy. It has numerous manifestations including verbal abuse, homicide, rape, and war.

(2) Aggression can be instrumental, used to achieve a desired goal, or hostile, instigated by anger and directed at harming another person.

(3) Aggressive behaviour has been explained on the basis of a) instinct or drive; b) physiological factors; c) social learning; and d) personality.

(4) The instinct or drive theories, psychoanalytic and ethological, have little empirical support. Some aggression may be due to frustration under certain circumstances. Sometimes aggression is a result of pain or other aversive states.

(5) Drive theories assume that aggressive energy held in check must eventually be released either directly or indirectly (catharsis). However, research evidence does not support catharsis as a means of reducing aggressive behaviour.

(6) While physiology must be implicated in all behaviour to some degree, attempts to isolate specific biological systems directly associated with aggression in humans have not been successful. Neural, hormonal, and genetic influences are indirect and are overlaid by learned behaviour.

(7) Social learning is concerned with the way children learn *how* to aggress, *when* to aggress, and against *whom* to aggress. Learning about aggression can occur by means of reinforcement and punishment or by observation of others.

(8) Certain child-rearing practices may enhance the aggressiveness of children. For instance, emotionally cold punitive parents often have highly aggressive children, especially sons. The socialization factor most strongly related to aggression is the use of physical punishment, especially within a rejecting atmosphere.

(9) The prevalence of aggressive behaviour varies considerably between cultures. In some, aggression is actively encouraged, while in others, violence of any sort is frowned upon and rarely occurs.

(10) Certain personality types are likely to be aggressive. These include "right-wing authoritarians" and individuals who are "undercontrolled." Although personality traits play some role in aggression, the effects are generally outweighed by situational factors.

(11) There has been considerable research on the effects, especially on children, of violence in the media. The emphasis has been on television and the general consensus, with some dissent, is that viewing violence and aggressive behaviour does increase the likelihood of violence in children and has long-lasting effects.

(12) Media aggression has other potentially harmful consequences. The pairing of stimuli, e.g., guns and aggression, may increase the likelihood of guns being used when an individual is angry. Certain stimuli may prime a series of aggressive, violent thoughts which may lead to aggressive behaviour. Media violence may also desensitize viewers or lead to similar real-life aggressive acts (the "copycat" syndrome).

(13) The depiction in the media of violence associated with sex may elicit both sexual and aggressive responses in males, posing special dangers to women. In addition, sexual arousal and aggressive arousal can confuse the individual, who may have difficulty distinguishing one from the other. In some cases, aggression-related stimuli may elicit sexual reactions that can lead to violent sex and rape.

(14) Androgen and estrogen balances account to some extent for differences in the amount of aggression exhibited by males and females. The relationship may not be causal but due to the effect of these hormones on physique and energy levels.

(15) Differences in aggressive behaviour between males and females are also related to learned gender roles. Aggression is encouraged in males, while passivity and the avoidance of physical encounters is encouraged in women.

(16) There is evidence that under appropriate conditions, e.g., if the aggression has a prosocial goal, women can be just as aggressive as men.

(17) Aggressive behaviour could be reduced by teaching parents how to socialize their children. This would include the appropriate use of punishment and a de-emphasis of traditional male/female role behaviour.

(18) Parents and others could also learn techniques of dealing with anger and aggression (e.g., effective mediation and the proper use of reinforcement).

(19) Aggressive behaviour could also be moderated by interventions such as the deglorification of violence in the media, the control of guns and, at the international level, effective diplomacy.

FURTHER READING

ALTEMEYER, B. (1981). *Rightwing authoritarianism*. Winnipeg: University of Manitoba Press.

BARON, R.A. (1977). *Human aggression*. New York: Plenum.

CROWELL, D.H., BLANCHARD, R.J., EVANS, I. and O'DONNELL, C.R. (Eds.) (1987). *Childhood aggression and violence: Sources of influence, prevention and control*. New York: Academic Press.

GEEN, R.G. and DONNERSTEIN, E.L. (Eds.) (1983). *Aggression: Theoretical and empirical reviews*. New York: Academic Press. Volumes 1 and 2.

HUESMANN, L.R. and MALAMUTH, N.M. (Eds.) (1986). Media violence and antisocial behaviour. *Journal of Social Issues*, *42* (3).

MALAMUTH, N.M. and DONNERSTEIN, E. (Eds.) (1984). *Pornography and sexual aggression*. New York: Academic Press.

OLWEUS, D., BLOCK, J. and RADKE-YARROW, M. (Eds.) (1985). *Development of anti-social and prosocial behaviour: Theories, research and issues*. New York: Academic Press.

C·H·A·P·T·E·R T·E·N

Altruism

PORTIA: The quality of mercy is not strain'd,
It droppeth as the gentle rain from heaven
Upon the place beneath. It is twice bless'd.
It blesseth him that gives and him that takes.

W. Shakespeare

FOR REFLECTION

- Is there such a thing as altruism — acting voluntarily to help others without expecting personal gain?
- Is there a "helpful personality" type?
- How can we explain incidents in which bystanders fail to help a victim in an emergency?
- What has been learned about heroism?

320

SOME PEOPLE DEVOTE their lives to selfless service to others. Jean Vanier, son of the late Governor-General Georges Vanier, has spent most of his life working with the handicapped, while urging others to share their lives with the disadvantaged. Mother Teresa, a Roman Catholic nun, has chosen to dedicate her life to the orphaned, the sick, and the poor in the slums of Calcutta. Norman Bethune (see Box 10-2) gave up a life of luxury to provide medical support for foreign armies fighting for causes which he believed to be in the best interests of humanity.

People like Norman Bethune, Mother Teresa, and Jean Vanier stand as testimony to the human willingness to sacrifice comfort, security, and prestige in order to help other less fortunate people. Sadly, the human story has its darker side: not only do most people *not* live up to these models of selflessness, but even worse, they often fail to assist people in urgent need of help, even when doing so might involve simply telephoning an ambulance or the police.

For example, in 1985, a man who tried to stop a group of teenagers who had stolen candy from a counter in the Toronto subway was savagely beaten while more than a hundred people looked on and did nothing; no one even called for help (*The Toronto Star*, January 19, 1985). In 1978, a dozen or more people refused to help a father rescue his seven-year-old son who had fallen into the Rivière des Prairies near Montreal. As they watched the boy drown, one person was heard to say "We're not going in there — the water's too dirty," referring to the fact that the boy had fallen in close to a sewage outlet (*The Globe and Mail*, January 6, 1978). In the same year in Edmonton, a 22-year-old woman stepped off a bus on her way home from work one night, unaware that a man on the bus had got off just behind her. A short distance from the bus stop, he assaulted her, beating her in the face, stripping off her clothing, and

People like Mother Teresa and Norman Bethune stand as testimony to the human willingness to sacrifice comfort and security in order to help less fortunate people.

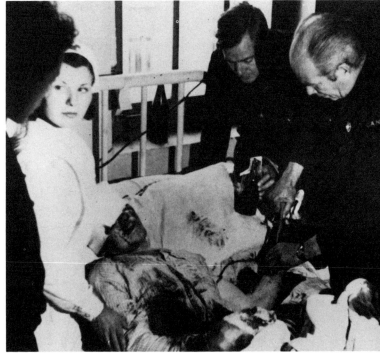

then raping her. Wearing only a coat, with blood flowing from her eyes, she sought help in a nearby apartment where she was told by a tenant to get out. She ran out to the street and asked two passersby for help, and was told to go to a nearby pay telephone. Finally, she found help at an all-night grocery where the staff called the police (*The Toronto Star*, November 1, 1978).

This chapter is concerned with the two types of behaviour discussed above. We will explore both the factors which influence individuals to donate time, money, and effort to help others, whether on a single occasion or across a lifetime, as well as the reasons why bystanders often fail to take action to help someone in distress, even in situations of minimal risk.

HELPING BEHAVIOUR

"Prosocial behaviour" and "altruism" are terms used to describe actions which are *voluntarily* carried out for the *sole purpose of helping others, without expectation of reward from external sources* (Bar-Tal, 1976). The term "prosocial behaviour" is a neologism invented by social psychologists to avoid some of the connotations historically associated with "altruism." Theologians and philosophers have traditionally defined altruism as behaviour which is intended to help others not only without anticipation of external reward but without anticipation of *self*-reward as well. Self-reward could be in the form of enhancement of self-esteem or avoidance of guilt or shame (possible effects of *not* helping). From a philosophical point of view, then, it could be argued that an act which brings pleasure, satisfaction, or relief (internal self-rewards) to the actor is no different in principle from one which brings praise or profit, or escape from punishment (external rewards). There have been debates across the centuries about whether any act can ever be "truly" altruistic in that sense.

B·O·X 10-1

HELPING PEOPLE TO HEALTH

According to a 1987 Gallup Poll (reported in the *Toronto Star* on March 16, 1987), 26 percent of Canadians have signed consent forms to donate their vital organs when they die. Another 34 percent are willing to make such donations but have not signed consent forms. These figures show a continuing increase in the number of people prepared for post-mortem altruism. The sharing of one's body need not await death, however. Many people regularly donate their blood so that other people can live. Blood is a renewable resource, of course, and its donation is not viewed as particularly noble. However, some people donate kidneys, possibly a more noble act, even though a person can survive quite nicely on one

kidney. Let us consider blood donation and kidney donation in turn.

The gift of blood
Every year about 900 000 Canadians donate blood to the Canadian Red Cross. Unlike in many countries, blood donors in Canada are not paid for their blood; nor are the recipients charged for it. While a similar system exists in Great Britain, almost 50 percent of all blood in both the United States and the Soviet Union is bought from donors and sold to recipients (in Japan, the commercial market accounts for 90 percent of the blood (Titmuss, 1971)). In Colombia, blood-selling rings have been active. During the '60s

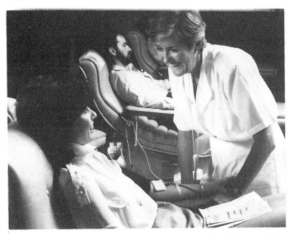

Every year about 900 000 Canadians donate blood to the Canadian Red Cross.

it was reported that young itinerants had been killed by these rings and their blood sold to hospitals! Titmuss (1971) points out that a non-commercial blood donor system is truly altruistic in that a person donates blood for the use of some anonymous stranger. Of course, it can also be argued that it is in the individual's interest to donate, since he or she might need blood at some future time. Yet, as we know from the study of collective dilemmas, many persons will not be motivated by such considerations since they know that whether they donate or not, they will be given blood should the need arise.

According to Titmuss, when blood collection is commercialized, fewer people give because they have no altruistic motive to do so. After all, if it is a commercial link that exists between the donor and the unknown recipient, why not "let someone else do it"? Most people are not going to be motivated by a few dollars recompense, but the recompense itself may destroy the feelings of altruism that the donor would otherwise have. In the long run, commercialization produces a greater shortage of blood. After surveying the blood collection systems of 27 countries, Titmuss (1971) also argues that commercialization leads to a lower quality of blood since those who are down and out and in need of money, as well as in poor health, are attracted to the blood clinics.

In Canada, private companies that collect blood for the manufacture of blood products have recently begun paying their donors for blood plasma. However, plasma donations take about one to one-and-a-half hours. Whether or not this move will

threaten the continued existence of the excellent non-commercial Canadian Red Cross blood services remains to be seen.

The gift of kidneys
A healthy individual can live as well with one kidney as with two. But how many people are willing to part with one of them so that someone else can live a normal life? Not many. There is a long list of kidney patients waiting for transplants, and most of those who are lucky enough to receive one will do so because someone had the foresight to specify that in the event of death, his or her kidneys should be immediately used for transplants.

What about the *living* organ donors, people who voluntarily give up a kidney while still young and healthy? While physicians' attitudes are slowly changing, and while in at least one Toronto hospital live donor kidney transplants are quite common, there is considerable evidence that members of the medical profession tend to be quite suspicious of the motivation of live donors (Fellner and Schwartz, 1971). If there is a family relationship between donor and recipient, family pressure is suspected; if there is no familial or emotional relationship, the person is considered to be mentally unbalanced and almost invariably will be excluded from donation. Yet it seems that a considerable number of people, especially among the well-educated youth, would be prepared to donate organs (Fellner and Schwartz, 1971) or bone marrow (Schwartz, 1970), even when the recipient is a stranger. Incidentally, in the Fellner and Schwartz study, it appeared that the decision to donate a kidney was not the result of a long, rational decision-making process, but rather the result of an immediate snap decision. More importantly, kidney donors have been found, even in follow-ups over a year after the donation, to have suffered no detrimental feelings or attitudes as a result of the decision. In fact, they typically report that the donation was a "peak experience of considerable positive impact on their overall life development" (Fellner and Marshall, 1970).

However, from the point of view of the social psychologists, it is difficult, if not impossible, to ascertain whether a given behaviour was carried out without any anticipation of self-reward. Moreover, as far as people who need help are concerned, perhaps even as far as society is concerned, it makes little difference whether people help because it makes them feel good or whether they help selflessly to benefit others. Therefore, in keeping with the norm of contemporary social psychology (Krebs and Miller, 1985), the terms "altruism" and "prosocial behaviour" are used interchangeably in this chapter to describe behaviour which was performed to help others without expectation of external reward.

Attributions play a major role in the evaluation of altruistic behaviour for we must decide what motivates an individual's actions. A politician campaigning for office who is seen helping an elderly person across a busy street may not be credited with altruism if observers attribute that behaviour to the desire to "look good" in order to win votes. A policewoman helping a lost child is unlikely to be viewed as altruistic since her action will be interpreted as motivated by duty: she is only doing her job.

The bases of altruism

Suppose we stopped people in the street and told them about Norman Bethune and Mother Teresa's devotion to helping others and asked them to explain why some people lead their lives in that fashion. Among the answers might be the following:

B · O · X   1 0 - 2

LIVING ONE'S LIFE IN SERVICE TO OTHERS

Norman Bethune (1890-1939), son of a Gravenhurst, Ontario, evangelical minister, became one of North America's leading thoracic surgeons, inventing some of his own surgical instruments while working in Montreal's Royal Victoria Hospital. However, he eschewed a life of fame and luxury in order to pursue causes which he thought were in the interests of the downtrodden masses. Having witnessed Franco's massacre of defenseless civilians on the streets of Madrid at the outbreak of the Spanish Civil War, a war supplied on Franco's side with tanks and planes — even back-up soldiers courtesy Hitler and Mussolini — Bethune went to work as a battlefield physician for the Loyalist forces who opposed Franco.

He founded the Canadian Blood Transfusion Service, the world's first mobile blood bank, which saved the lives of hundreds of Spaniards. After attempting unsuccessfully to rouse Canadian public opinion against the Nazi threat in Spain, his

disillusionment with democracy led him to become a Communist. When the Loyalist side was all but beaten in Spain, Bethune went to China to help in the fight against the Japanese invasion. He soon became chief medical officer to Mao Zedong's armies, training uneducated peasants to be field physicians and taking his mobile field hospital to wherever it was most needed. He died on November 12, 1949, after contracting an infection from a wound sustained during emergency surgery. Although recognition was slow to come in his native Canada because of his Communist affiliation, he is revered as a legendary hero — "Comrade Beth" — in China to this day. Mao Zedong's essay, *In memory of Norman Bethune*, which was one of three mandatory readings during the days of the Cultural Revolution, urges all Chinese to follow Bethune's example of social responsibility and devotion to others.

Some people just seem to be born saints — always putting other people first.

If you can put yourself in other people's shoes, if you can feel their suffering, then you've just got to help.

A good upbringing — they were obviously brought up to be helpful to others.

First you have to feel at peace with yourself — feel good about yourself — only then can a person take on other people's problems.

Physicians and nuns are supposed to act unselfishly — it's what's expected of them.

Each of these commonsense explanations touches on a body of social psychological theory and evidence bearing on the subject of altruistic behaviour. Each will be explored in turn.

"Born saints": Altruism as an innate predisposition

Some theorists argue that natural selection favours the genetic transmission of factors which predispose an organism to be altruistic towards other members of its species. Darwin himself suggested in his *Descent of Man* (1871):

> As man is a social animal it is almost certain that he would from an inherited tendency be willing to defend, in concert with others, his fellowmen; and be ready to aid them in any way which did not too greatly interfere with his own welfare or his own strong desires (cited in Latané and Rodin, 1969, p. 189).

Some studies have been interpreted to support the position that even animals are genetically programmed to act altruistically (Hebb, 1971; Hebb and Thompson, 1968). For example, it was found that rats would press a bar more often if the action lowered a struggling rat suspended in the air than if it lowered a styrofoam block (Rice and Gainer, 1962). However, such behaviour might be better interpreted in terms of arousal rather than altruism. In another study, it was found that rats would learn to make a response that terminated *either* a rat's squeals or loud noise (Lavery and Foley, 1963). Thus the "altruistic" rats were probably motivated to stop the noise made by their distressed brethren rather than by a desire to free them. This example emphasizes that it is very difficult to assess the motivation behind an animal's activity, even if it *appears* to be based on altruism. Reports that dolphins have been known to help other injured dolphins and even human swimmers in distress by lifting them to the surface do not necessarily indicate that the dolphins were trying to "help." After all, we have difficulty trying to decipher the motives of human beings, and we can talk to them!

Sociobiology An evolutionary approach to altruism is embodied in the controversial theory known as sociobiology. Sociobiology (Wilson, 1978) assumes that there are biological bases to at least some social behaviours and, consequently, these behaviours are subject to the same evolutionary processes that affect physical characteristics. According to this view, each organism is engaged in a struggle to send as many of its genes as possible into the next generation; any behaviour which promotes this end is itself likely to be "selected" and reproduced from generation to generation.

Sociobiology posits a "kin selection" principle. Since we share some of the same genes with our close relatives, by helping them to survive at least long enough to reproduce, we improve the chance that our own genes will be well-represented in the gene pool of the next generation. Therefore, a pattern of behaviour may be "selected" by the processes of evolution, even if it is not directly beneficial to the individual or to the individual's ability to reproduce, provided that it benefits other closely related individuals.

Besides predicting more altruism toward relatives than toward strangers, sociobiology has spawned a number of other ingenious hypotheses regarding altruism. For example, since males are much more capable of reproducing their genes than females (because a male can have many more children), mothers should be more protective and altruistic than fathers towards each child. The same reasoning would suggest that parents should be more altruistic toward male children than toward female children because males carry a greater potential for transporting each parent's genes into the next generation.

As fascinating as such hypotheses may be, they remain at the level of conjecture and are not taken seriously by most social psychologists. The kin selection principle in particular lacks supporting evidence and sociobiology in general does not take enough account of social learning. Actually, in opposition to sociobiology's claims, it can be argued that if behaviour of any sort were to be genetically transmitted, *selfish* behaviour might be a more likely candidate because it would be advantageous for both reproduction and survival, while altruism, particularly if it involved self-sacrifice, might be expected to *remove* an organism's genes from the gene pool (Campbell, 1975).

Research with humans Setting sociobiology aside, we might still wonder whether there is an inherited tendency towards altruism. Human studies of genetic bases of altruism are relatively few in number, since most current theorizing is based on social learning principles rather than genetic influences. Yet, in a recent study of altruism in monozygotic ("identical") and dizygotic ("fraternal") twins, it was concluded that the correspondence between the scores made by pairs of twins on a measure of altruism showed a strong genetic effect (Rushton, Fulker, Neale, Nias and Eysenck, 1986). Although such a finding would be important and remarkable if valid, it is not clear that altruism was actually being measured in that research, for it was assessed by the Self-Report Altruism Scale (Rushton, Chrisjohn and Fekken, 1981) which required subjects to indicate the frequency with which they had engaged in 20 specific behaviours, such as donating blood or giving directions to a stranger. However, subjects who reported a high level of such activities might have done so out of a greater need for approval rather than altruism, manifested either in the reporting of the behaviour (recall the discussion of social desirability in Chapter 2) or in the behaviour itself. Or perhaps they were acting prosocially, but only in order to avoid the guilt which might follow inaction.

At this point, the contention that altruism itself is genetically transmitted still lacks empirical verification. However, it may be that there are more general aspects of personality, such as anxiety-proneness, which might be influenced by heredity and which in turn might make prosocial behaviour more likely. It is not difficult to imagine that people who are more prone to anxiety might grow up to be particularly concerned about the reactions of others to their behaviours. Thus they may strive to do what is socially defined as "the right thing" in any situation. The right thing may often appear to be altruistic — giving blood, helping an elderly person across the street, and so on — but the behaviour may be performed to reduce anxiety rather than to extend help. In a society in which helpfulness is not viewed as socially desirable, such people might act in distinctly unhelpful ways.

"Other people's shoes": Altruism as an empathic response

We have learned (Box 10-2) that the Canadian humanitarian Norman Bethune was distressed at the sight of helpless civilians being massacred in the streets of Madrid during the Spanish Civil War. Is this why he later returned to Spain to help the Loyalist forces? No one knows for sure, but empathy with the suffering of others is a major factor in eliciting altruism (Krebs, 1975). Indeed, if there really is a biologically based altruistic influence in humans (other than the simple anxiety previously mentioned), it may be manifested primarily through empathy (Krebs and Miller, 1985). Empathic arousal appears to be a universal human response which is present to a degree even in one and two-day old infants, although it is modified by experience (Hoffman, 1981).

Yet the exact nature of empathy is uncertain, and it may well be that more than a single concept is involved when we speak of empathy. (Indeed, two of the most widely employed measures of empathy — the Hogan Empathy Scale and the Questionnaire Measure of Emotional Empathy — appear to measure *different* aspects of empathy (Chlopan, McCain, Carbonell, and Hagen, 1985)). Empathy is more than just sympathy. While sympathy refers to a heightened awareness of another person's suffering as something to be alleviated (Wispé, 1986), empathy is usually defined as a vicarious emotional response elicited by and congruent with the perceived emotional state of another person (Eisenberg and Miller, 1987; Wispé, 1986).

However, empathy has also been defined from a cognitive perspective, in terms of the capacity to "see things from the other person's point of view" (Goldstein, 1975). Probably *both* cognitive and affective processes are involved, with cognitive appraisal *preceding* emotional arousal: First, we must evaluate the distress produced by another

In deciding whether to help, we may put ourselves in the other person's situation.

person's plight by putting ourselves in the other person's situation. This leads to the empathic emotional response, which in turn generates the motivation to reduce the person's need (Coke, Batson, and McDavis, 1978). For example, if we see a legless man sitting on the sidewalk asking for money, we may sidestep him with some annoyance unless we ask ourselves how the man must feel being reduced to the status of beggar. Then we may feel an empathic response of distress which will lead us to make a donation. Helping those in distress may lead to a decrease in this vicarious discomfort (Hoffman, 1977). (It would be difficult to decide whether to call behaviour based on such a mechanism "self-rewarding" or "purely" altruistic since the helper's "reward" is based at once on the decreased distress of the other person and on a drop in his or her own vicariously experienced distress. It would not be easy to ascertain which decrease in distress was most reinforcing.)

Although various studies have found empathy to be involved in helping others who are in distress (Batson, O'Quin, Fultz, Vanderplas and Isen, 1983; Coke, Batson and McDavis, 1978; Krebs, 1975), there is, so far, no empirical basis for considering it to be a *necessary* condition of prosocial behaviour. Indeed, not all altruism is directed toward people in distress. For example, someone may decide to give a pair of football tickets to a visiting friend because the visitor has never seen a live football game. It would be unlikely that the donor is experiencing any sort of empathic distress.

"A good upbringing": Altruism as something that is acquired

Norman Bethune was the son of a clergyman, and undoubtedly grew up in an atmosphere which stressed caring for others. The socialization process — perhaps involving reinforcement for prosocial behaviour and the acquisition of parental values which encouraged selflessness — may have played a critical role in shaping his character.

Many studies have demonstrated that, at least in the context of North America and Western Europe, altruistic behaviour increases steadily with age up to about the age of ten (Bar-Tal, 1976). There are two major theoretical approaches regarding how the child acquires such behaviour. The cognitive-developmental or "personal morality" approach views altruistic behaviour as the consequence of attitudes and values shaped by the developing child's experience in the social environment. The social learning view, on the other hand, emphasizes the importance of reinforcement and modelling.

Cognitive-developmental theory   According to this view, people help other people because of a personal set of values and attitudes which obligate them to provide assistance in certain situations. Failure to do so brings about feelings of guilt which are aversive to the individual. This personal morality is said to develop gradually in the growing child. Piaget (1932) studied the acquisition of morality in children and tried to apply a structural approach to it, describing different levels of moral thinking acquired at different stages of maturity, each stage being qualitatively different from the preceding one, but the whole series being invariant for all human beings. For Piaget, the acquisition of morality involves moving from a view that adult rules are sacrosanct and unchangeable to a view that rules are made by human beings and are therefore somewhat relative to society.

Building on Piaget's work, Kohlberg (1964) described a six-stage typology of moral development (see Table 10-1) which, he also argued, represented an invariant and

TABLE 10-1
Stages of moral development according to Kohlberg (1981)

Stage	What is considered to be right
Stage 1: Obedience and punishment orientation	Obey in order to avoid breaking rules, which would lead to punishment. Avoid physical damage to persons and property.
Stage 2: Instrumental purpose and exchange	Comply with rules when it suits your own immediate interest. What is "right" is seen in terms of an equal exchange.
Stage 3: Interpersonal accord and conformity	Try to act according to the standards others set for you, or in the manner people generally expect of people in your role. Being "good" is important.
Stage 4: Social accord and system maintenance	Carry out the actual duties to which you have agreed; laws are always to be honoured, unless in extreme cases they are in conflict with other essential social duties. "Right" is enlarged to include making contributions to your group, institution, and society.
Stage 5: Social contract, utility, individual rights	Be aware of variety of values and opinions held by people. Most values and rules are arbitrary for your group but should usually be upheld because of your implicit social contract with the group. Social contract; belief that some values, such as life and liberty, are not arbitrary and must be upheld regardless of the opinion of the majority.
Stage 6: Universal ethical principles	Self-chosen ethical principles become the basis for behaviour, and particular laws or social norms are seen to be valid to the extent that they rest on these principles. These principles are viewed as universal principles of justice, for example, the equality of human rights and the inherent dignity of individual human beings. When social rules or laws conflict with these principles, it is the principles which guide behaviour. The reason for doing the "right thing" is the belief in the validity of universal principles and the personal sense of obligation to adhere to them.

SOURCE: Adapted from Snarey, 1985

universal developmental sequence, each stage occurring one after the other and always in the same order. In the first stage, the child is only concerned with the physical consequences of his actions, and behaves properly only to avoid punishment. Later, in the third and fourth stages, the child's conduct is governed by the desire to appear to be a good person in the eyes of other people through adherence to society's rules. Finally, in the sixth stage, not always attained, the individual's behaviour is guided by reference to self-chosen, abstract, ethical principles which encompass a sense of responsibility toward other persons. Thus a young child may help another child in order to avoid chastisement, and an older child may provide assistance to others in order to "look good," but the "mature" person will do so on the basis of personal principles.

SOCIALIZATION IN THE EAST AND IN THE WEST

Childrearing practices in Japan differ in many ways from those of Western societies. Japanese children are brought up to have a keen ability to participate vicariously in the experiences and feelings of their family members. Greater importance is attached to "skinship," i.e., prolonged body contact between family members through breastfeeding practices which encourage skin-to-skin contact well beyond the feeding itself, bathing in groups, and sharing the bed with the mother (and even other members of the family as the child grows older). Such activities, it is argued, push the child to develop a close alignment with persons other than him or herself. Japanese parents emphasize disciplinary methods which promote empathy, teaching the child how his or her behaviour will hurt other people's feelings.

Child training techniques in the United States focus on encouraging autonomy and individualism, goals reflected in Kohlberg's theory, which states that the ideal condition is one in which an individual relies on principles which have been personally constructed without reliance on others. In sharp contrast, moral development in Japan involves conformity to group norms. Cooperation and harmony are stressed (Weisz, Rothbaum and Blackburn, 1984).

There are many critics of Kohlberg's theory (e.g., Kurtines and Greif, 1974), and attempts to demonstrate that moral development is associated with altruistic behaviour have been disappointing (Rushton, 1976). Yet cross-cultural research carried out in 27 countries has provided support for Kohlberg's model (Snarey, 1985). Despite such cross-cultural evidence, however, a serious limitation of Kohlberg's theory, as well as his methodology — which involves confronting subjects with a number of moral dilemmas which make no sense to some nationalities (e.g., Chinese respondents) — is that it presupposes a Western conception of the individual as an autonomous being who is free to make choices and determine his or her future (Dien, 1982). Kohlberg's approach assumes that rules are needed to regulate conflicting claims, but such rules may compete with ethical principles, in which case the individual must choose a moral course of action. Morality develops as the individual takes on more and more responsibility for dealing with ethical dilemmas. However, in Eastern societies where group harmony and collective decision-making are stressed, morality may develop by a somewhat different process (see Box 10-3).

Even if Kohlberg were correct with regard to Western societies (and this question remains open), his theory still does not explain *how* a person comes to put other people's concerns ahead of personal ones. If the growing child comes to internalize society's values about obligation to others, what is the basis of this internalization? The social learning approach addresses this question.

Social learning approach   The social learning approach emphasizes the *acquisition* of altruistic behaviour, and takes for granted that prosocial behaviour is learned in the same way that any other behaviour is learned: through reinforcement, self-attributions, and modelling. We now examine the role of these factors, as well as the influence of parental disciplinary techniques, in the acquisition of altruism.

(1) *Reinforcement*. To a great degree, behaviour is controlled by its consequences. Thus it is not surprising to find that prosocial behaviour is acquired and maintained, at least in part, through positive consequences deriving from the behaviour. As you will recall from Chapters 6 and 9, social learning theorists have pointed out that a rigid view of reinforcement suggesting that humans are automatons responding on the basis of external reinforcement is misleading; in part, people regulate their actions by self-produced consequences (Bandura, 1974). Thus a child may learn to share toys or to help a sibling because he or she anticipates reward in the form of parental praise, praise which has been given for similar behaviour in the past. Both material and social reinforcement (such as praise) have been found to induce prosocial behaviour in children (Bar-Tal, 1976).

Prosocial behaviour may develop as the child is reinforced for such behaviour and gradually develops the capacity for internal self-reward (i.e., feeling good about oneself in some way). In other words, the child learns to help others because he or she anticipates either gain through self-reward or, if no action is taken, punishment through guilt.

(2) *Attributions*. Self-reward involves making attributions about ourselves: "I helped that man because I am a good person." Self-attributions may play an important role in the development of prosocial behaviour. Self-attributions are important because they help define a standard for our behaviour which we strive to maintain in order to avoid negative feelings about ourselves. If you see an elderly person who has just dropped a bag of groceries and is likely to have difficulty picking it up, it is hard to walk by without admitting to yourself that you are unhelpful and even callous. If such a statement contradicts your self-image as a helpful person, you will no doubt experience some discomfort. By fostering the development of positive self-attributions (i.e., helpfulness), prosocial behaviour can itself be encouraged.

Children are more likely to behave well if they attribute their behaviour to internal causes (their own personal morality) than to external causes, such as threats of punishment or hopes of reward (Walters and Grusec, 1977). For example, a child who is tempted to steal and who attributes feelings of anxiety to moral self-judgment is more likely to avoid antisocial behaviour than a child who interprets anxiety as fear of the teacher "coming back into the room." And a child who attributes his acts of charity to a personal concern with the welfare of others may be more likely to repeat such prosocial behaviour than the child who interprets her own generosity as the result of pressure from a parent.

There is some empirical support for the view that self-attributions are important. In one study, children who had donated to charity after watching a model do likewise were told either that they must have done so because they enjoy helping others or because they had been expected to do so. The children offered the first interpretation of their behaviour subsequently made greater donations and displayed greater altruism in another unrelated situation than the children offered the second explanation (Grusec, Kuczynski, Simutis and Rushton, 1978). In a study which compared the effects of verbal reinforcement with attributions (Grusec and Redler, 1980), children who had won some marbles in a game found themselves in a situation where they could share these marbles with a child who had none. Children in one condition were praised when they gave away some of their marbles, while children in another condition were helped to make positive self-attributions by being told that their donations reflected their inherent helpfulness. Children in a third condition were given neither praise nor help with their attributions when they made donations. Reinforcement (i.e., praise) and attribution were both about equally effective in producing donations well above the level of the control group. However, when the children were observed in a different context by different adults either a week or two weeks later, the children who had received the attributional statements were the most generous both in their efforts to be of help and in their willingness to make donations. Those children who had been in the reinforcement condition were the next most generous, while the children in the control condition showed considerably less generosity.

(3) *Modelling.* Whether or not models can influence children to act in a prosocial way has been the subject of a considerable amount of research. Prosocial models do in fact produce *imitative* prosocial behaviour in children (e.g., Grusec, 1972; Grusec and Skubiski, 1970; Staub, 1971; Rushton, 1980). However, it must be remembered that prosocial behaviour does not equal altruistic motivation. Before we can assume that there is an altruistic, or prosocial, motivation, it must be shown that the behavioural disposition endures through time, and can be generalized across situations (Krebs, 1970). (The problem of discriminating between behaviour and motivation is also important in the study of aggressive modelling, but with one important difference. Aggression can be externally reinforced, while prosocial or altruistic behaviour, by definition, cannot be. Therefore, in studying altruistic behaviour, the experimenter must ensure that the observed behaviour was not reinforced by her own approval of it or by the positive reaction of the recipient (Rushton, 1976).

Several studies have demonstrated that children's responses to charitable models are durable and can be generalized. For example, it was found in one study that the observation of an adult donating tokens to a charity positively influenced the children's own donations ten days later, even when the donations were elicited in a different setting by a different experimenter (Midlarsky and Bryan, 1972). In another study (Rushton, 1975) modelled behaviour, whether that of a generous or a selfish model, was still evident two months later despite changes in the situation between test and retest. Thus it seems that *internalization* does occur.

What is the explanation for this modelling? Why should the child be willing to do what an adult model did, especially if the behaviour is at some cost to him or herself? There is little evidence to support the notion that modelling occurs either because of identification, secondary reinforcement, or empathy (Krebs, 1970). It may be that the model is simply a pertinent source of information and that the child is striving to do the right thing (Bryan, 1972). The model provides cues for how a person should act in that specific situation, and the child may very well be reacting on this basis, rather than on the basis of some abstract value about helping others. This situation is reminiscent of experiments with adults who, above all, try to "look good" in front of the experimenter (the social desirability effect).

There are two major classes of socially responsible attitudes and behaviours which the child should master, and models can be helpful in each case (Kaufmann, 1970). The first consists of avoiding a wide range of forbidden acts (from picking one's nose in public to stealing another's person's possessions), while the second consists of acts which are socially desirable but not mandatory (such as helping someone who has tripped and fallen, or sharing toys with playmates). Behaviours of the first class are generally emphasized and acquired through the experience of punishment for performance. The child comes to experience fear when he or she is tempted to act in a in a prohibited way. It is not surprising, given the set-up of the traditional classroom, that children learn that any activity departing from the ordinary is probably forbidden!

The importance of "doing the right thing" was demonstrated by a study by Staub (1970a): seventh grade subjects heard a girl in the next room who seemed to be in considerable distress. They were more likely to go into the other room if they had been given permission to do so. In other words, they were very much concerned with rules, and with obeying the rules. In another study, it was found that the absence of explicit permission had the same effect as a prohibition (Staub, 1971).

Later in this chapter we will examine how, in general, an adult is more likely to help others in an emergency if he or she is alone than in a group. In a study of children from nursery to second grade level, it was found that they were generally unlikely to help in an emergency (Staub and Feagans, 1969). However, they were even less likely to help if they were alone — the opposite of what has been found with adults. Fourth and sixth grade children, on the other hand, were more like adults, helping more when alone. It may be that young children's fears were allayed by the presence of others, while older children viewed others as a potential source of negative evaluation should they do the wrong thing.

The emotion expressed by the model also appears to have some effect on imitation. For example, when a model demonstrates positive feeling after making a donation, imitative behaviour by children is increased (Midlarsky and Bryan, 1972), possibly because the model's positive affect makes the choice of appropriate behaviour even easier. Not only does the model indicate an appropriate behaviour, but also one which apparently brings personal pleasure.

a) *"Do as I say, not as I do."* If moral development has any effect on altruism, it should be most clearly demonstrated by the extent to which a child is affected by a model's behaviour *and* preaching (Rushton, 1976), for preaching should remind the child of his or her moral values. When models, like many parents, say one thing and do another, children's *actions* are influenced by the model's *actions*, while children's *words* are influenced by the model's *words* (Bryan and Walbeck, 1970). Hence the inconsistency of the model is imitated by the child. To elicit greater charity, then, a model who is actually charitable will have more effect than one who simply preaches charity. This observation has been confirmed empirically (Grusec and Skubiski, 1970): third and fifth grade children were more likely to make a donation after seeing a model donate than after simply hearing the model say that people should donate. Other studies have also found that preaching combined with actually doing what was preached promotes prosocial behaviour (e.g., Radke-Yarrow and Zahn-Waxler, 1984).

However, there is also some evidence (Midlarksy, Bryan, and Brickman, 1973) which suggests that children are also affected emotionally by the model's moral consistency, and that a "hypocrite's" extension of social approval for helping is aversive to the child. A model who practiced selfishness but who exhorted charity and who gave social approval to the children (eight and nine-year-olds) every time they made donations produced *less* charity on the part of the children than did a similar model who gave no such approval.

Moreover, it seems that the effect of preaching may be different for boys than for girls. Grusec (1972) studied the effects on subsequent imitation of observing a model either performing a particular behaviour (sharing) or merely saying that it was appropriate to act in that way. While seven-year-old girls shared in both the verbal and the

Media models: Superman in his TV, movie, and comic book reincarnations has provided a good example for thousands of youngsters.

performance conditions, the boys did so only in the performance condition. Grusec suggested that different rates of acquiring verbal and performance behaviour by boys could account for the differential effectiveness.

b) *Television models.* In the last chapter, considerable attention was given to the role that television models play in the development of aggression. Psychologists have naturally been interested in the extent to which altruistic models on TV elicit imitative altruism. In one study which examined this question (Sprafkin, Liebert and Poulos, 1975), 30 first-grade boys and girls watched one of three half-hour programs which were popular with children in the 1970s: an episode from the *Brady Bunch*—a situation comedy — an episode from *Lassie* in which a boy risked his life by hanging over the edge of a mining shaft to rescue a trapped puppy, and an episode from *Lassie* which did not portray altruism. The children then were placed in a game situation so arranged that each child at some point had to choose between continuing to play the game (which led to prizes for points accumulated) and helping a puppy in distress. Those who had seen the *Lassie* program with the helping scene helped significantly more than did the children from the other two groups.

Other studies have resulted in similar findings. Whether a five-minute film clip presented only once is used, or a series of one-hour programs spread over several weeks, the effect on children's free-play behaviour is the same: watching altruistic behaviour on television produces altruistic behaviour in children (Rushton, 1977). Whether adults are similarly influenced has not yet been established.

(4) *Parental discipline.* Aside from other factors, one of the most important determinants of the development of prosocial behaviour is the extent to which the parents expressly teach the child about the effects of his or her actions on others (Staub, 1975). Some support for this view comes from a study (Hoffman, 1975) of parent-child relationships in which it was found that altruistic children had at least one parent (usually same-sex) who communicated altruistic values, while the other parent typically used "victim-centred" discipline (i.e., drawing the child's attention to the feelings of the victims of the child's transgressions).

The degree to which the parent displays a nurturing, affectionate attitude toward the child also affects the development of altruism. By being guided and controlled through affectionate means, the child is likely to develop an internalized code of conduct involving a positive regard for others and the ability to delay immediate gratification of wants in order to examine other people's needs and feelings. (Recall the discussion of aggression in which it was stated that warm, love-oriented parents typically produce non-aggressive children).

Most discipline techniques involve both power-assertive features (e.g., a raised voice, slaps) and love-withdrawal features ("Get away from me — I don't want to talk to you — you've been a bad boy") (Hoffman, 1984). Moreover, most discipline techniques involve both an arousal component (often synonymous with power-assertion, e.g., raising one's voice) and an inductive component through which the child is alerted to the consequences of his or her behaviour (e.g., "How do you think mommy feels when she sees ink all over her new carpet?"). If there is too little arousal, the child may ignore the parent, but too much arousal can produce anxiety or anger which will interfere with the assimilation of the inductive message.

Research carried out on children between the ages of four and 12 years points to the following conclusions about the effects of different approaches to parental discipline (Hoffman, 1984):

a) The frequent use of induction leads to a moral orientation characterized by high guilt and independence from external sanctions. In other words, the individual has a strongly internalized moral code, and deviations from it lead to guilt.

b) The frequent use of power-assertive techniques tends to produce a moral orientation which is based on fear of external detection and punishment. The individual worries more about being caught than about whether or not a behaviour is morally correct.

c) The occasional use of power-assertive techniques to communicate to the child that the parent has particularly strong feelings about a particular behaviour or value, or to control an openly defiant child, contributes positively to moral internalization.

d) There is no apparent relationship between the use of love-withdrawal techniques and moral internalization.

"Feeling good about yourself": Altruism and mood

Do people like Norman Bethune and Mother Teresa help others because they already feel good? There *is* evidence that positive mood facilitates individual acts of charity or helping, while bad moods impede such behaviour (Rosenhan, Moore and Underwood, 1976). For example, when children in one study were asked to reminisce about happy experiences, they gave more to charity than did children asked to reminisce about sad experiences, or children who were not asked to reminisce at all (Rosenhan, 1972). In another study, a field experiment, subjects who found a dime in a pay telephone return slot (a condition intended to lead to a good mood) were more likely than control subjects to volunteer to help others, and subjects given free cookies (again, supposedly leading to a good mood) while studying in the library were subsequently more ready to provide help than those who were not given cookies (Isen and Levin, 1972). In another study, subjects who had just viewed sad movies donated less money to charity than other subjects who watched neutral movies (Underwood *et al.*, 1977). There is even evidence to suggest that people are more willing to help others during periods of sunshine than during cloudy periods (Cunningham, 1979)!

Possibly, being in a bad mood limits our ability to turn our attention to other people's difficulties or even to pay attention to the dictates of our conscience. On the other hand, being in a good mood may increase our *cognitive processing capacity* (Easterbrook, 1959; Rushton, 1980) — that is, increase our ability to notice what is going on around us and pay attention to our concerns. If this view is correct, then anything which leads to a decrease in cognitive capacity or, at least, a decrease in *available* capacity (for example, being preoccupied by some worry or some important problem), would decrease the tendency towards prosocial behaviour.

To examine this hypothesis, a study was conducted in which divinity students were required to pass by a groaning victim while on their way to give a talk on the parable of the Good Samaritan. Subjects in the experimental condition were led to believe that they were very late for their appointment and that the appointment was important, while no such preoccupation was induced in the control condition. Approximately two thirds of the control subjects offered help, while only 10 percent of those in the experimental condition did so (Darley and Batson, 1973). However, as will become more clear when rewards and costs of helping are taken into account, it could be that subjects in the experimental condition, rather than having failed to take cognizance of the fact that assistance was needed, simply evaluated the possibility of being delayed as too costly.

The warm glow of success   If success produces a good mood, then prosocial behaviour should be more evident following success than following failure. This was demonstrated in a study (Isen, 1970) in which subjects were given false feedback about their achievement in a series of tasks. Some subjects were told that they had scored well above the norm, while others were told that they had scored well below the norm. Control subjects were exposed to the same tasks but did not do them. Then, when the experimenter was out of the room, the subjects (who waited one at a time) were observed to see whether or not they would help another person. A confederate, laden down with books, passed in front of the subject and "accidentally" dropped a book. Subjects who had experienced success were more often helpful than subjects in either the failure or the control conditions. In a related study, it was found that "success" led to larger contributions to a charity than did failure. Isen (1970) interpreted these results in terms of a positive mood engendered by success — the "warm glow of success" which predisposes people toward events which will engender more good feelings.

Image repair   Although the "failure" subjects in Isen's study were not especially helpful, other studies have found that making a mistake or committing a *faux pas* in public actually influences people to help others. A person who is embarrassed by his or her behaviour may take advantage of a situation in which helping others may help to improve or *repair a damaged image*. A series of studies (Bégin, 1976) lends support to the image-repair hypothesis. In one study, subjects who experienced failure in a motor task subsequently helped the experimenter more than either subjects who had experienced success or subjects who were in a control condition. In a related study, it was found that whether or not the potential beneficiary knew about the subjects' previous success or failure was crucial. Failure subjects helped more when the beneficiary knew of their failure than when the beneficiary did not have that information. In a third study, subjects were assigned to either success or failure conditions on the basis of their *actual* scores obtained on a real exam. As they were leaving the teaching assistant's room after learning their score on the exam, subjects were asked individually to contribute to a worthy cause. The helpfulness of the "success" subjects, who had been informed that their grades were above the class mean, was not influenced by whether or not the canvasser knew their marks. Yet when the canvasser knew the marks of the "failure" subjects, those who had been told their grades were below the class mean, they contributed considerably more than "success" subjects. When the canvasser did not know their marks, they contributed significantly less than the "success" subjects.

These findings lend support to the image-repair hypothesis: when a request for help or charity comes from a person who is unaware of our failure, we will feel no urge to repair our image in his or her presence. However, if that person knows of our failure, we will take steps to mend the damage. Thus, while the warm glow of success leads successful people to act altruistically, those who have failed are likely to help only those who know of their failure.

Need for approval It has also been found that subjects who have more need for approval are more generous in their donations, particularly when the donations are made publicly (Satow, 1975). In another study, subjects with a high need for approval were more motivated to help someone who had dropped a load of books when they had previously experienced a social reward for helping the experimenter, while subjects without a strong need were unaffected by the prior experience (Deutsch and Lamberti, 1986). This makes intuitive sense, since by being publicly charitable, they can court the approval and admiration of others. Indeed, the image repair effect may simply reflect a momentarily increased need for approval.

Reparative altruism Experiments have shown that when a person has harmed or hindered another person, he or she often resorts to *reparative* altruism, in which efforts are made to compensate for the harm done, although these efforts are not always directed at the person who was harmed. For example, subjects who administered shocks in a Milgram-type obedience experiment (see Chapter 6) were more likely to volunteer to help in a humanitarian project than were those who did not give shocks (Carlsmith and Gross, 1969). Recall also from Chapter 6 the field experiment carried out in a shopping centre (Regan, Williams, and Sparling, 1972) in which women were asked by a male experimenter to take his picture for a project he was working on. The camera did not work, and he told subjects either that they had broken it (guilt condition) or that it was not their fault (control condition). Shortly afterward, a female confederate passed the subject, carrying a torn grocery sack trailing various items. While only 15 percent of the subjects in the control condition stopped the woman and told her about the broken bag, 55 percent of the subjects in the guilt condition did so. This phenomenon cannot be explained in terms of image repair since these subjects were being altruistic towards someone who did not know about their lapse. And unlike the situation in Bégin's studies, failure as such was not involved here. In fact, the *faux pas* occurred in the original act of helping. In this case, it can be argued that subjects are trying to expiate guilt by helping others, or at least to bolster their own self-esteem.

Putting the discussion into context, we should be aware that these studies have focused on temporary mood states. More importantly, people who repeatedly have good experiences and find success in life are more likely to develop a greater feeling of well-being than are people who experience repeated failure or rejection (Rushton, 1980). People whose experiences in life are generally positive may well become more happy and optimistic, and possibly more empathic and willing to help others as well.

"It's what's expected": Altruism as normative behaviour

As we saw in Chapter 6, social norms exert considerable and often unrecognized control over behaviour. Essentially, they refer to what acts are *not* to be done, and what acts *should* be done. We *should not* blow our noses on our sleeve; we should say "thank you" when someone serves us coffee. There are also more specific norms associated with particular roles, although behaviour carried out in the discharge of role responsibilities is not usually considered to be prosocial or altruistic. The crossing-guard is expected to show more helpfulness to children who wish to cross the street than to other pedestrians. Physicians and nuns are expected to help others, though only in a narrowly defined context.

We must be careful when trying to explain behaviour in terms of general norms. Although there are many shared beliefs about what behaviour is appropriate in a given situation, such norms are often both vague and conflicting (Latané and Darley, 1970). They are vague in that they do not generally specify what *specific* behaviour is required (e.g., "We should help those less fortunate than ourselves") and they are conflicting insofar as we are taught on the one hand to "keep our nose out of other people's affairs," and on the other, to help others when they need help. Thus social norms may appear useful after the fact for describing behaviour, but may actually mislead or confuse us when we must choose what to do.

Several norms are relevant to prosocial behaviour. The *norm of social responsibility* prescribes that people should help others who need help, whether or not there is a possibility of future reciprocation, and whether or not the people in need had provided help to the potential benefactor in the past (Berkowitz and Daniels, 1963). The *norm of reciprocity*, which Gouldner (1960) suggests is a universal norm, requires that people help, and not harm, those people who have helped them in the past. If everyone followed the norm, everyone would be helping everyone else and would be receiving help when needed.

It is difficult to separate the effects of these two norms in any given situation, that is, to determine whether a person helps because of the obligation to help others in need (social responsibility) or because of anticipated future helping or repayment for past help (reciprocity). Several studies have addressed this concern (e.g., Krishnan and Carment, 1979). In one such study (Greenglass, 1969) which allowed for both the possibilities of helping or harming another person, as well as a manipulation of the degree of similarity between a previous benefactor or harm-doer and the subject, it was found that subjects helped a similar benefactor, hindered a similar harm-doer, and helped a needy person when no similarity or dissimilarity was mentioned. This suggests the dual operation of reciprocity (in the first two instances) and social responsibility (in the third instance).

Another norm, the *norm of equity*, specifies that an individual should strive to keep a balance between the ratio of outcomes to inputs and the corresponding ratio for another person (Walster, Walster and Berscheid, 1978). Such a norm specifies a kind of "fairness" for all. (See the discussion of distributive justice in Chapter 13.)

The research literature indicates generally that people's behaviour often departs from what is prescribed by these norms and that a large number of situational variables influence whether normative behaviour will be performed (Krebs and Miller, 1985). Thus, while norms do play some role in altruistic behaviour, it is not a major one.

OTHER FACTORS WHICH INFLUENCE ALTRUISM

Cultural differences

There are great differences in when and how concern is shown for others among the many cultures of the world. Unfortunately, perhaps because of the inherent methodological difficulties, few psychological studies of altruism have been conducted cross-culturally. Anthropological research suggests that the emphasis put on altruism in Western societies is relatively rare in other parts of the world (Cohen, 1972) and appears to be the product of a love-oriented parent-child relationship and stable, monogamous marriages. The latter may be in the process of waning and, as the family becomes less and less effective as a socializer of children in North American society, we may be in danger of producing a generation of undersocialized children (Rushton, 1980).

Of the few studies that have been conducted, some have found Americans to be less willing to provide help; others have found the opposite. In research which compared the prosocial behaviour of children in India, Kenya, Mexico, the Philippines, Japan, and the United States, children in the United States were the *least* helpful in terms of offering assistance or advice to others in distress (Whiting and Whiting, 1975). The authors of that study concluded that prosocial behaviour is most evident among children who grow up in cultures where it is required of them — for example, in societies in which the typical family size is large and the child is required to share in the care and raising of other children and in managing the household.

Yet in another cross-cultural study (Feldman, 1968) Americans were more helpful than the French or Italians: people in Boston were found to be more likely to give directions to a foreigner or to mail a letter for a fellow citizen than were people in Paris or Athens. It is difficult to say whether that finding reflects general cultural differences in prosocial behaviour, or just differences specific to those three cities or to those two behaviours. On the other hand, a similar study was carried out in Taipei, Taiwan, and Albuquerque, New Mexico (Huang and Harris, 1974). Adults who were alone and presumably unoccupied (e.g., standing at a bus stop) were asked to mail a letter for another person. While there was no difference in the numbers of Chinese and Americans accepting the letter, significantly more of the letters given out in Taiwan were actually received. The authors suggest that this outcome likely reflects a true cultural difference in the willingness to keep a promise. (Yet, as they point out, poorer postal service in Albuquerque could account for the difference!)

In an experimental situation in which subjects could make donations at no cost to themselves (that is, they could allocate points or money without giving up any of their own) students in India were found to donate less than students in Canada (Carment, 1973) or the United States (L'Armand and Pepitone, 1975). It is possible that the norm of social responsibility, which L'Armand and Pepitone suggest is relatively weak in India, may be restricted to in-group (i.e., caste) members.

It is not clear how to put all these data together, for these studies involve comparisons among different types of tasks and different national groups. It may be that people in the United States are more helpful than some Europeans, but less helpful than many Asians; these data on the whole suggest this, but more research is required before anything substantive can be said in this regard.

Personality variables

As with any other behaviour, individuals differ in the degree to which they exhibit prosocial behaviour even though they have shared a common environment. Naturally, social psychologists have attempted to find personality correlates of altruism but the studies that have been done are not conclusive. For example, subjects who help have been found to be more socially oriented and more "internal" in terms of locus-of-control than subjects who do not help (Krebs, 1970; Ubbink and Sadava, 1974).

Although some researchers feel that it is futile to seek general personality predictors of helping behaviour (e.g., Gergen, Gergen and Meter, 1972), Rushton (1980, 1984) believes that the evidence is substantial enough to support the concept of a broadly-based altruistic trait. He argues that there is an "altruistic personality," which is associated with higher internalized standards of justice and responsibility, and with greater empathy, self-control, and integrity. However, much more evidence is required before the existence of such a personality pattern can be considered demonstrable.

Gender differences

As we have seen, empathy may play an important role in prosocial behaviour. There are, of course, individual differences in empathy, just as there are differences in the extent to which various situations elicit empathy (Archer *et al.*, 1981). There may also be differences in empathy resulting from gender roles. Since women have been found to experience more vicarious affective responses than men, perhaps because men have been trained traditionally to suppress emotional diplays (Hoffman, 1977), we might expect women to be more empathic. Yet, taking the evidence as a whole, it is not clear whether or not genuine gender differences in empathy exist; females *do* describe themselves as being more empathic than do males, but this may reflect more the image that is expected of them rather than some predisposition (Eisenberg and Lennon, 1983). Nor is there any clear evidence about gender differences in the willingness to help others, although adult women appear to be more willing to help highly dependent people, while men appear more helpful to those who are not so dependent (Schopler and Bateson, 1965). This could reflect the "caring" role which many females are brought up to assume.

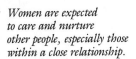

Women are expected to care and nurture other people, especially those within a close relationship.

The traditional norms which govern helping are quite different for males and females in our society (Eagly and Crowley, 1986). Males are expected both to rescue others who are in difficulty and to demonstrate courtesy and protectiveness towards subordinates. Such behaviour is expected both in close relationships and among strangers. Women, on the other hand, are expected to help through caring and nurturing other people, especially those within a close relationship. Women are actively discouraged from associating with strangers; this prohibition most likely discourages women from giving help to strangers as well.

In general, the research on helping behaviour suggests that men help more often than women, although there is a great deal of inconsistency in this regard from one study to another (Eagly and Crowley, 1986). It must also be remembered, however, that social psychological research has typically focused on short-term interactions with strangers and has therefore excluded by and large the very behaviours which are prescribed for the female gender role — behaviours which are manifest primarily in close, long-term relationships (Eagly and Crowley, 1986). Furthermore, since men and women still tend to occupy different social and occupational roles, the "masculine" roles and the skills that are acquired in them may better prepare men to assist others in distress. As women begin to assume traditional male roles, the differences in helping between the two sexes, even in the short-term interactions of the laboratory, may begin to disappear (see the discussion of gender stereotypes in Chapter 7).

Effects of religion

We naturally wonder about the effects of being religious on the propensity to be helpful. After all, Christianity, Judaism, Islam, Hinduism and Buddhism all promote altruistic behaviour to some degree, and view selflessness as a virtue. Yet various studies suggest that religious orientation does not correlate well with the demonstration of concern and compassion for those needing help; indeed, it may discourage it in some situations (Batson and Gray, 1981).

In one study, the effects of different religious orientations were examined insofar as they influenced the willingness of individuals to provide help to a lonely woman, either in a situation where she expressed a desire for such help or in a situation where she expressly indicated that she did not want help (Batson and Gray, 1981). The data indicated that intrinsically-oriented religious people for whom religion was seen as an end in itself (i.e., who viewed their whole duty as serving God) offered help whether or not the person in need desired it, while those for whom religion was viewed as an open-ended quest to find ultimate values offered help only when it was wanted. Intrinsically oriented religious people, then, may see providing help to others as a way of helping themselves achieve grace, or a place in Heaven.

Rural-urban differences

It often seems that the residents of big cities are less ready to help their fellow citizens than people in small towns and rural areas and there is some evidence to support this observation. For example, as will be discussed later, people from rural areas win a disproportionate number of Carnegie Medals for heroism, awarded for helping others

	Population Density							
	Low		Medium		High		High	
	Small Town		Toronto Suburbs		Toronto Inner City		New York City*	
Type of request	% Helping	N	% Helping	N	% Helping	N	% Helping	N
Time	97	92	95	150	91	272	85	92
Directions	97	85	90	150	88	276	85	90
Change	84	100	73	150	70	279	73	90
Name	51	65	39	150	26	246	29	277

*Based on data from Latané and Darley, 1970

SOURCE: Rushton, 1978

TABLE 10-2
Rural-urban differences in helping behaviour

under conditions of great personal risk (Lay *et al.*, 1974). In a field study directed at rural-urban differences in helping, requests for help (e.g., "I wonder if you could tell me what time it is?") were made in downtown Toronto, in a Toronto suburb, and in a small town just outside Toronto (Rushton, 1978); the response rates, along with comparable data collected in New York City (Latané and Darley, 1970) are shown in Table 10-2. For every type of request, the percentage of people giving help dropped, moving from the small town to the suburbs to downtown. There was little difference between the results in downtown Toronto and New York City.

However, even if people's behaviour in the city is less altruistic than that in the country, are the people themselves different, or is it the situation? Milgram (1970) argues that it is the latter, that people in the city, surrounded as they are by so many other people, of necessity limit their social relationships to a minority of the populace. He argues that the urban person cannot afford to help every person who is in need and must be selective to survive in the urban culture. In addition, while rural people are considerably affected by rare emergency situations such as fires, the city-dweller becomes blasé about them, assuming that there are authorities who will deal with the situation. Furthermore, the city dweller who witnesses an emergency is more likely to be in or to think him/herself in the company of other witnesses (Latané and Darley, 1969). Moreover, the city person must compete for service (taxis, etc.) and norms develop (privacy, aloofness, etc.) to protect people from the constant interaction with others. It has been suggested that the intensity of urban stimuli (noise, pollution) may also lead to less prosocial behaviour. People living in cities have been found to be less trusting and less willing to help than people living in towns (Merrens, 1973; Milgram, 1970).

An Australian study lends support to Milgram's contention. When correlated with rate of help-giving in a number of different locations, population size was found to be a strong and consistent predictor of helping rate, with the most help occurring when the population of an area was small (Amato, 1983). Yet the results of that study also suggest that urban lack of helpfulness was primarily limited to situations in which an individual was suddenly faced with the need to provide help to a stranger. This situation may be perceived as being more potentially dangerous by the city-dweller than by the rural inhabitant. This outcome points to the importance of considering the type of helping and the type of situation in any examination of rural-urban differences in prosocial behaviour.

While it seems that whatever rural-urban differences exist may be due to the exigencies of living in a rural or urban area, there is some evidence that the background (rural or urban) of a given individual continues to play a role, regardless of where he or she lives. In one field study, for example, it was people with a rural background who made up the majority of people who reported shoplifters (Gelfand, Hartmann, Walder and Page, 1973). It can be argued that children in rural areas are given more early training in responsibility for taking action. On the other hand, in a laboratory setting, rural subjects have been found to provide significantly less help than urban subjects (Weiner, 1976).

BYSTANDER INTERVENTION

Of all the forms of prosocial behaviour, certainly the most dramatic — by virtue of either its presence or its absence — is intervention behaviour, that is, the behaviour of an individual who voluntarily goes to the aid of someone needing emergency assistance despite the possible risk of personal danger. Emergency situations share several common elements that make them somewhat unique (Darley and Latané, 1970):

(1) They typically involve threat or harm to a victim. The person who intervenes can at best prevent further damage or possibly return the situation to the way it was before the emergency occurred.

(2) Since recipients of such aid are rarely better off following an emergency than before it, the rewards for positive action are often non-existent. Yet the possible costs, including possible legal action or even death or injury, are high.

(3) They are rare events, so that few people have experience in dealing with them.

(4) They are unpredictable, occurring suddenly and without warning, and immediate action is required. Thus people usually cannot plan for emergencies or consult with others about how to respond. The urgency of the situation is in itself stressful.

(5) They vary widely in their form and in terms of what response is appropriate, making it impossible to prepare everyone by teaching people a short list of rules for how to deal with emergencies.

Unfortunately, there are all too many real-life examples of emergency situations in which someone has been in physical danger and other people have stood by and observed the individual being victimized while doing nothing to provide help. This is the "bystander effect": people witness an emergency but stand by passively and do nothing, their willingness to act, as we shall see later, inhibited by the presence of others. Some recent examples of the bystander effect were given at the beginning of this chapter. A more important example is the Kitty Genovese murder (Box 10-4). It is important because it was the first well-researched example of bystander inaction in an emergency situation. When asked later why they had not called the police, most of the witnesses to that murder said that they had indeed been afraid to get involved, but they seemed unable to furnish a basis for this fear. Various social scientists proposed a variety of *ad hoc* explanations (Latané and Darley, 1970): alienation

B · O · X   1 0 - 4

THE BYSTANDER EFFECT

In March of 1964 in New York City, Catherine Genovese was attacked by a man with a knife as she was walking home at night. Her screams brought her neighbours to their windows, and the sudden glow of their bedroom lights and the sounds of their voices drove the attacker away temporarily. However, when he saw that no one responded to her cries for help, he attacked her again. She managed to get away from her attacker a second time, but again, despite her shouts for help, no one responded. The man returned to attack her yet again — this time killing her. A half hour had elapsed between the first attack and the time the killing took place, and even though at least 38 people watched from the windows of their apartments and houses as he attacked and repeatedly stabbed the young woman, no one even telephoned the police.

Before dismissing this as an example of New York incivility, consider this incident:

In September 1973, a man dragged a struggling, screaming 18-year-old girl 300 yards down a Scarborough, Ontario, street while cars swerved to avoid them but did not stop. She was taken to a grassy area opposite an apartment building, forced at knife-point to undress, and then raped. Despite the fact that several people were sitting on apartment balconies opposite her as she cried for assistance, no one even called the police. No one helped even though an anonymous phone call to the police would have posed no risk to any of them. (Ironically enough, at some later time the assailant was himself the victim of bystander inaction. He was beaten by three toughs on a busy thoroughfare while pleading in vain with the occupants of a stopped bus and taxi to call the police (Silverman, 1974)).

and apathy resulting from "depersonalization"; confusion of fantasy and reality brought about by a steady diet of television violence; even the vicarious gratification of sadistic impulses.

However, the witnesses were *not* apathetic. They did not turn away and ignore what was going on in the street below. Rather —

> Caught, fascinated, distressed, unwilling to act but unable to turn away, their behaviour was neither helpful nor heroic; but it was not indifferent or apathetic. . . . (Darley and Latané, 1970, p. 4).

Almost 15 years after the Genovese murder, a number of these witnesses were contacted. Again, they reported that they still felt responsible for Genovese's death (Walster, Walster and Berscheid, 1978).

The behaviour of these witnesses was very similar to that of any crowd that gathers around an accident victim, each waiting for someone else to take charge, to indicate what behaviour is appropriate. Sometimes people act; sometimes they do not. Yet, in any case, they are likely to experience distress. Several studies have found that when people witness another person being harmed, they show marked signs of emotional upheaval, such as gasping, running aimlessly around, sweating or trembling hands, chain-smoking, and an increase in galvanic skin response (Walster, Walster and Berscheid, 1978).

What accounts for the bystander effect? If people are not apathetic, if their behaviour is not callous, what is it that holds them back from helping a person in distress? There are several possible answers to these questions.

Norms and the bystander effect

The failure of people to help others is sometimes taken to suggest a breakdown in the power of social norms to regulate social behaviour, a rather alarming prospect. However, we saw earlier that while there are social norms which are involved in prosocial behaviour, their role is limited. Again, in the case of an emergency, norms are actually not very useful guides, partly because they are too vague to provide any useful information about what to do, and partly because they are conflicting (Darley and Latané, 1970). As an example of such conflict among norms, suppose that you are walking down Lovers' Lane on a wintry night and you see a couple sitting motionless in a parked car with the engine running. One norm tells you to try to help others who need your help: if they are dying of carbon monoxide, you should do something. Yet another norm teaches you to respect people's privacy. After all, they are in Lovers' Lane: if they are just necking or communing with nature, you should not butt in. Thus it is likely that norms have only a small role to play in intervention behaviour. The bystander effect does not reflect a breakdown of social norms, only their inadequacy.

The bystander effect is a social phenomenon; it occurs when a number of people mutually witness an emergency situation. A good way to begin understanding the bystander effect is by examining a series of laboratory experiments that were carried out to establish what happened in the Kitty Genovese situation. These are discussed next.

The presence of others: The lady in distress

It might seem reasonable to assume that if an individual is the sort of person who is likely to come to someone's assistance in an emergency, that person would be even more likely to do so if there were other people about, for these other people might be expected to lend at least moral support. Yet, before accepting that conclusion, it would be wise to recall the literature on social facilitation discussed in Chapter 6: the presence of others facilitates simple or well-learned tasks, but interferes with complex or novel tasks. Emergency situations probably involve the latter and so there may be some reason to suspect that the presence of others may not always have a positive effect on the readiness of an individual to render assistance.

In one of the earliest experimental studies of the bystander effect (Latané and Rodin, 1969), the influence of the presence of others was clearly evident. In that experiment, subjects who thought they were participating in a market research study heard a woman who had just left them to go into an adjoining room "climb up" on a chair to get something, and then "fall down" and cry for help. (In fact, both the climb and fall were produced by a high fidelity tape recording.) The experimenters wanted to see whether or not and how soon subjects would come to her assistance. Subjects could go directly into her office (the two rooms were separated only by a curtain), could go out into the hallway to seek help, or could call to her to find out what they could do to help.

In one condition, each subject was alone. In a second condition, each subject was with a confederate who had been instructed to be as passive as possible, responding to any queries from the real subject in as natural but neutral a way as possible. At the sound of the crash, the confederate looked up, stared for a moment at the curtain, then shrugged his shoulders and went back to work. In a third condition, two real subjects who were strangers to each other were tested together, while a fourth condition involved two subjects who were friends.

The results showed that when assistance was offered, it was always direct, either going into the room (75 percent of the intervening subjects) or calling out to the woman to see if she wanted help (24 percent). The most notable finding was that while 70 percent of the subjects in the alone condition offered help, the presence of another person strongly reduced the frequency of intervention (the bystander effect): only 7 percent of subjects paired with a passive confederate intervened, while only 40 percent of those in the "two strangers" condition offered help. The bystander effect was reduced when friends were paired together: in 70 percent of the pairs of friends there was at least one person who offered help. (However, it can be shown mathematically that if 70 percent of individuals who are alone are likely to intervene, then pairs of such individuals should contain at least one intervener 91 percent of the time. So, even with friends, the presence of another person is inhibitory.)

It seems strange at first that the presence of others inhibits rather than promotes helping. However, in post-experimental interviews, 59 percent of non-intervening subjects indicated that they were unsure about what had happened, while another 46 percent said they had thought that nothing serious had occurred. Perhaps people hesitate to help because the emergency situation seems ambiguous to them. Situational ambiguity merits a closer look; that subject is next.

Ambiguity of the situation: The smoke-filled room

Many emergency situations *are* ambiguous, and it is often surprisingly difficult to decide whether or not an emergency is occurring. If new neighbours in your apartment building seem to be having a squabble and you hear screams through the walls, do you intervene directly or call the police? It is difficult to decide whether or not someone is in trouble in such a situation, and usually a person does not want to look foolish by intervening if there is no emergency. Men are usually even more concerned than women are about the possibility of "doing the wrong thing" and looking foolish (Siem and Spence, 1986).

Although hearing a woman fall off a chair may not seem to present a particularly ambiguous situation, it must be remembered that the "accident" occurred out of sight of the subjects, and the sounds of climbing and falling and the calls for help were played over a tape recorder. It is possible that the reproduction did not sound totally real, thus producing some ambiguity. In fact, when the "Lady in Distress" study was repeated using live rather than taped noise, there was a high frequency of intervention (Staub, 1974). However, before concluding that the bystander effect simply reflects hesitation in the face of ambiguity, it must be remembered that the situation should have been equally ambiguous in all conditions. Nonetheless, the single subjects were much more willing to help, despite the ambiguity.

This outcome might suggest that the presence of others *contributes* to the ambiguity of the situation, that non-responding others lead an individual to wonder whether

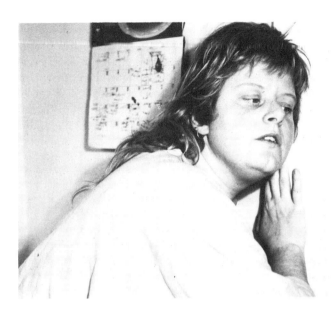

Is it an emergency? Many emergency situations are ambiguous.

or not his or her own feeling that intervention is required is in error. Of course, if all those present feel the same way, then all may hold back.

The experiment described next explored whether or not the presence of others could produce inhibition, even when there was little ambiguity about the situation and even when a person might be at risk by doing nothing. Imagine yourself writing an examination. The examiner leaves the room; a few minutes later the room begins to fill up with smoke. What would you do? Would you leave the room (particularly if other examinees are doing nothing)? We would not expect such a situation, which carries some potential for personal harm, to give rise to a bystander effect. Latané and Darley (1968) created such a situation: Subjects who were engaged in filling out a questionnaire worked either alone, with two "passive" confederates, or with two other naive subjects. Several minutes after the person in charge left the room, smoke was introduced into the room via a small wall vent. By the end of four minutes, the room was filled with acrid smoke to the extent that it obscured vision.

While you might imagine that no one would wait around that long, that was not the case. Only 75 percent of the subjects in the alone condition left the room to report the smoke to someone. The others toughed it out, working on their questionnaires despite the cloud of smoke! While that in itself is very surprising, when a subject was in the company of two passive confederates, only one of ten subjects reported the smoke. The others coughed, rubbed their eyes, and even opened the window, but did not leave the room. When three naive subjects worked together, in only 38 percent of the groups did someone intervene. In fact naive subjects working together did not intervene significantly more often than a single naive subject working with two passive confederates.

These results support the interpretation that the passivity of others contributes to the ambiguity of the situation. In other words, we use the reactions of others to help decide whether or not there is an emergency and what action is appropriate. However, it might also be that the hesitancy to act was due to a fear of looking foolish by possibly doing the wrong thing.

To differentiate between inhibition brought about on one hand by the ambiguity produced by the inaction of others, and on the other by the fear of looking foolish, Ross and Braband (1973) carried out a study that used either a blind or a sighted confederate in each of two emergency conditions. In the "internal" emergency condition, the subject and the blind confederate worked in a room which filled with odourless smoke; since the blind man could not see the smoke, he could not serve as a source of information about what reaction would be appropriate. In the "external" condition, the emergency was signalled by a scream from outside the room; in this case, the blind man would be aware of the emergency, and his reaction could serve as a guide to appropriate behaviour.

In fact, the subjects in the internal condition responded to the emergency just as quickly as did subjects in a control condition who worked alone. It could be argued, however, that these subjects were not concerned about acting inappropriately since the blind man could not see them. Yet this explanation is not tenable, for in the external condition, in which the blind man's reaction could be used as a guide, the subjects were inhibited to the same extent as when they were with a sighted confederate.

This experiment lends strong support to the notion that non-responding others inhibit a person's response because their inaction helps to define the situation as a non-emergency and thus makes intervention seem inappropriate. If non-intervention is largely caused by misinterpreting other people's reactions and believing that *they* know there is no cause for alarm, it follows that *not* knowing people's reactions should result in *not* being misled. Therefore, will people who know that others are aware of the possible emergency, but who cannot observe their reactions, be just as likely to intervene as people in an "alone" condition? This was the question addressed by the next experiment.

The epileptic seizure

Each subject in this study (Darley and Latané, 1968) sat in a separate room and was told that he or she would take part in a discussion of personal problems associated with college life. The discussion was to be conducted by means of an intercom system, ostensibly in order to protect the subjects' identities and spare them any embarrassment. Subjects had been told that the experimenter would not be listening to the initial discussion, and that a mechanical switching device would automatically give each subject in turn about two minutes to talk while all other microphones were switched off.

There was actually only one real subject at any one time. The other subjects, all confederates, had prerecorded their comments. From the point of view of the real subject, who believed that all the other speakers were actually present in the discussion, this is what occurred: The first person to speak discussed his adjustment difficulties and the fact that he was prone to epileptic seizures, especially when under stress. The next time it was his turn to speak, he became increasingly loud and incoherent and in a stuttering voice asked for help. Amid choking sounds, he stammered that he was going to die, called once more for help, and then was silent. When the seizure occurred, the real subject believed that all subjects could *hear* the seizure but that only the microphone of the seizure victim was switched on.

Group size	N	*% responding by end of seizure*	*% never responding*	*Time in seconds*
2 (subject and victim)	13	85	100	52
3 (subject, victim and one other)	26	62	85	93
6 (subject, victim and 4 others)	13	31	62	166

SOURCE: Latané and Darley, 1970

TABLE 10-3
Effects of group size on likelihood and speed of response

The major independent variable in this study was the apparent size of the group of participants, while the dependent variable was the time it took the subject to go and report the emergency to the experimenter. Comments made during the staged seizure and in later self-reports indicated that virtually all subjects believed the emergency was real. Yet the belief that other people were listening had a strong effect on both the rate and the speed of subjects' intervention (Table 10-3). Considerably more of the subjects in two-person (subject plus victim) groups reported the emergency than did people from the three-person groups, and people from the three-person groups responded more often than people from the six-person groups.

Thus it appears that a person is less likely to offer help if others are present or presumed to be present *even in the absence of ambiguity produced by the passivity of others.* Subjects in this study who did not report the emergency did not show signs of apathy or indifference. In fact, when the experimenter finally entered the room to end the study, they appeared to be considerably emotionally upset and concerned for the victim. They found themselves in a conflict situation, worried about the victim and about the guilt they would feel if he was not helped, yet concerned about looking foolish, overreacting, or ruining the experiment by leaving the room. When only the subject and the victim were involved, the victim's need could be met only by the subject, while when others seemed to be present (even in this case, via intercom), the subject had less responsibility in the matter. In other words, a *diffusion of responsibility* occurred: "Other people are listening, and so it is not up to me to take action; someone has probably already done something about it."

Three factors have emerged from the discussion so far. The bystander effect is the result of: (1) misperception of the emergency situation, based on the observation that others are not responding; (2) fear of doing the wrong thing and looking foolish; and (3) diffusion of responsibility. Many other studies and demonstrations have found results similar to those obtained by Latané and Darley. The bystander effect has been demonstrated on the streets of downtown Toronto, for instance (Ross, 1978): In one demonstration, which was filmed by a hidden camera, a confederate collapsed on busy Yonge Street. Many people walked by, stepping around the man, before someone finally stopped to offer help. In another demonstration, a confederate grabbed another confederate's purse in front of City Hall, in full view of a lunchtime crowd. The victim called for people to stop him, as she ran after him. No help was forthcoming. It had been expected that for each demonstration, several trials would have to be made before such blatant non-intervention could be observed and filmed.

B·O·X   1 0 - 5

ANOTHER VIEW OF BYSTANDER INTERVENTION

While the diffusion of responsibility hypothesis seems intuitively appealing, some researchers have had difficulty in demonstrating it. Silverman (1974) tried several situations before he finally found one in which speed of helping was hindered by group size: a person pretended to have lost a contact lens. (Hardly an emergency, though.)

Silverman (1974) presents a provocative thesis about the roots of bystander inactivity. Taking issue with the notion that people do things selflessly for others, he argues that people help because they want to maintain the self-image of being benevolent, because they enjoy other people's gratitude, because they want to feel powerful and capable, because they like adventure, or because they want to be heroic (see the discussion of heroism later in the chapter). What happens, then, in a situation where one witnesses an attack? Silverman speculates that, at least for males in our society, the model for heroism is direct effective intervention, and to simply call the police and wait around while they come is to admit to cowardice or incapability. If actual intervention is too fear-arousing, then in order to avoid the self-admission of cowardice, one must distort the situation, persuading oneself that it is a family quarrel, and not a rape which is occurring, and which does not require intervention.

In fact, in each case, only one trial was necessary. (The reader is invited to think about the ethical considerations inherent in carrying out such demonstrations.)

The social inhibition of helping is a remarkably consistent phenomenon and, in general, a victim stands a greater chance of being helped when only a single person witnesses the emergency (Latané and Nida, 1981). (Not all researchers agree; see Box 10-5.)

The Latané-Darley intervention model

Latané and Darley (1970) summarize the effects of ambiguity, fear of looking foolish and diffusion of responsibility in a five-step decision-making model of the intervention process (Table 10-4).

TABLE 10-4
The Latané-Darley model of bystander intervention

1. The bystander must notice that something is happening.
2. The bystander must interpret the situation as an emergency.
3. The bystander must decide whether or not he or she has a responsibility to intervene.
4. The bystander must decide in what way he or she can best be of assistance.
5. The bystander must choose how best to carry out this course of action.

First, we must notice that something is happening and then decide whether or not it is an emergency. If it is, the next step is to select an appropriate action: Do we personally try to do something? Do we call the police? After contemplating the alternatives, particularly if they involve personal risk, we might go back a step to the definition stage and decide that it really is not an emergency after all. The more ambiguous the situation, the greater the likelihood that this back-tracking will occur ("If they're really being gassed, I don't know what to do. I'll get them out of the car, I guess, but how do I give them artificial resuscitation? What if they die? Mind you, they're probably OK — just necking quietly. Boy, will I look stupid when I pound on their window and they turn out to be in no danger. Yeh, there's no problem here — after all this is Lovers' Lane."). So we might decide not to do anything, risking some guilt if it turns out there really *was* an emergency. (Obviously, however, we are not actually going to go through such a deliberate assessment of a possible emergency situation. These decision-making steps can occur quickly, almost without realization; recall the cognitive shortcuts that were discussed in Chapter 3.)

Rewards and costs of helping

A classic intervention carried out in New York has revealed yet another aspect of the bystander effect. This field experiment, taking place in a city with no outstanding reputation for altruism, found that no bystander effect occurred when a confederate of the experimenter collapsed on a moving subway car. The experiment examined the effects of certain characteristics of a victim (whether he appeared drunk or ill, whether he was Black or White) on the amount of help given. It was expected that the "drunk" confederate (who carried a bottle in a paper bag and who smelled of alcohol) would elicit less aid than an ill one (carrying a cane) since it was assumed people might anticipate the drunk becoming disgusting, embarrassing, or violent. The most surprising outcome was that there was a generally high rate of help-giving in all conditions. In fact, the "ill" person received help on 95 percent of the trials, and even the "drunk" was helped on half the trials. Moreover, when help was given, on 60 percent of those occasions more than one person helped. Since the ill person was thought to be not ill by choice while the drunk was clearly in need of help as a result of his own actions, people may have been less willing to help the drunk because he "deserved" his suffering (Piliavin, Rodin and Piliavin, 1969).

Why was so much inaction observed in the Darley and Latané laboratory research but not in the Piliavin field experiment? Why was there less diffusion of responsibility on the subway? There were important differences between the two sets of studies. First, the victim was in full view in the Piliavin study; thus the need for help was less ambiguous. Second, the natural groups were considerably larger than the laboratory groups. Thus any diffusion of responsibility that might have occurred may have been *more* than offset by the increased probability of *someone* actually helping in a large group. In other words, the larger number of bystanders in the subway study may have increased the probability of getting a prosocial response from someone (Piliavin *et al.*, 1972). Moreover, it was much more difficult for the subjects in the Piliavin study to leave the area than it was for participants in the Latané and Darley studies. This difference bears more examination.

Whether or not a person helps another may depend on how easily he or she can avoid the helping situation. In an experiment designed to examine this hypothesis (Staub, 1974), a confederate collapsed, holding either his chest or his knees (to vary the apparent seriousness of his condition) either in the pathway of a pedestrian (dif-

TABLE 10-5
Number of people refusing to help in the 1974 Staub study

	Bad knee		Bad heart	
	Help	*No help*	*Help*	*No help*
Easy escape	2	12	5	7
Difficult escape	9	7	14	2

SOURCE: Staub, 1974

ficult escape), or across the street (easy escape). As can be seen in Table 10-5, many more people helped when escape from the situation was difficult than when it was easy. In fact, the person with the apparent "heart attack" was almost always approached in the difficult escape condition. The results suggest that the perceived degree of need for help also influenced helping. More people approached the apparent coronary victim. Interestingly enough, a fat confederate who clutched his chest was more likely to receive aid than a non-obese confederate. It turned out that subjects more often considered the problem to be a coronary one when the victim was obese. Recall that in the Piliavin study, people could not easily escape; it was several minutes to next stop.

All that being said, it is sobering to learn that 30 or more passengers, including some hefty men, watched passively as three youths beat up a man in a moving subway car in Toronto in September 1973; no one even stood up or spoke. They watched in silence. While the New York subway riders had relatively little to lose by helping a sick person or a drunk, there is more to risk if we intervene in a fight. Thus, besides the factors already discussed — ambiguity, fear of looking foolish, diffusion of responsibility, difficulty of avoidance — it is clear that the readiness to help will be strongly affected by the potential costs to the helper. This subject is considered next.

The Piliavin intervention model

Emerging from the New York subway study discussed above is an "economic" model of helping (Piliavin, Davidio, Gaertner and Clark, 1981) which assumes that we experience negative, unpleasant arousal when we encounter someone in distress and that we are naturally motivated to reduce that arousal. We can choose among helping, fleeing (both of which will reduce anxiety), or doing nothing. The model predicts that (1) as arousal increases, the probability of one or more observers taking action of some kind increases; (2) for a given level of arousal, as cost for helping increases, the probability of helping directly *decreases* and the probability of giving help indirectly or of leaving *increases*; and (3) as cost for not helping increases for a given level of arousal, the probability of helping increases. Thus the potential helper faces an avoidance-avoidance conflict. The potential costs for both not helping (guilt, possible public criticism) and for helping (possible embarrassment, possible bungling of the effort, involvement with police if victim dies) are high.

The analysis of rewards and costs will be influenced by a number of factors: (1) The number of other people present — if we are alone we may face more guilt if we do nothing and also more potential harm if we intervene; (2) the reactions of other bystanders — the more they appear to be upset, the more aroused we become, but the more passive they are, the more our arousal is lessened; (3) the characteristics of the person in distress — we may be more upset to see a child in distress than we

TABLE 10-6
The Piliavin Intervention Model

Net costs for not helping	Net costs for helping	
	Low	*High*
High	Direct help	Indirect help
Low	Response a function of personality	Running away or apparently ignoring

Note: relatively high arousal is assumed.

SOURCE: Piliavin and Piliavin, 1972

would an adult, and we may be more upset to see someone collapse because of a heart attack than we would if they were simply drunk; (4) the degree of closeness in the relationship between the person in distress and ourselves. We are likely to experience more arousal when a friend or relative is in distress than when the victim is a stranger. Similarly, we may experience more arousal when the victim is from our group or subgroup than when the victim is from some other group.

Going back to the Piliavin *et al.* study (1969), the cost for helping the drunk was higher than for helping the ill man, while the cost for *not* helping the drunk was low, since little reproach was risked by ignoring him. However, the explanation could be simpler than that: perhaps people simply do not view a drunk's falling down as an emergency situation. For example, Piliavin *et al.* repeated their study in 1972, and instead of using an "ill" person and a drunk, they employed two "ill" persons, one of whom produced a small trickle of blood from his mouth after collapsing. It was assumed that this strategy would increase the perceived cost of helping, since the presence of blood should evoke feelings of fear and revulsion. At the same time, the cost for *not* helping would be thought to increase since the severity of the victim's condition would appear to be greater. On the basis of this cost matrix (Table 10-6) it was predicted that the "bloody" victim would receive more *indirect* help. The data confirmed this.

The two models of intervention discussed in this section are not antithetical. The Latané-Darley model seems most applicable in situations of some ambiguity, while the Piliavin model seems most applicable when ambiguity is less of a factor, e.g., when an individual collapses before the bystander's eyes. The first model suggests that when the emergency situation is ambiguous, people are more likely to be helped if there is only one passerby rather than many, while the Piliavin model suggests that in unambiguous situations, people are likely to be helped as long as the rewards for helping outweigh the costs associated with providing help.

ENCOURAGING BYSTANDER INTERVENTION

How might we encourage individuals to render assistance to others in emergencies — even in the presence of others? In other words, how can we prepare people to deal with the bystander effect? There are several courses of action which are likely to prove beneficial:

(1) *Combatting the bystander effect in the schools.* We teach children to obey and to

conform. We are much more careful to teach them what they are *not* to do than to teach them how to act prosocially. Children in emergency situations often experience a conflict between the wish to help and the desire to act appropriately; the absence of permission to intervene is often as powerful an inhibitor as a direct prohibition (Staub, 1974). This influence may endure into adulthood. It may be beneficial to teach children that it is all right to break rules in certain circumstances.

(2) *Combatting the bystander effect in the home.* By regularly assigning children the responsibility of caring for or helping others (a responsibility which is often automatic in large families), we may foster the development of a feeling of personal responsibility for the welfare of others. We might teach children that intervention behaviour is desirable — we could even have children rehearse such behaviour and then reward them for it. However, it must not be forgotten that emergencies are difficult to plan for, and that the problem of defining a situation as an emergency is bound to arise.

(3) *Increasing public awareness of the bystander effect.* Dissemination of information about the effects of group size on bystander intervention may help increase intervention as people realize "why" they are hesitating to help and as they pay less attention to the inaction of others around them. In a study of the effects of such knowledge (Rayko, 1977) half the subjects received information about diffusion of responsibility and about the ambiguity created by the inaction of others in emergency situations, while the other half received non-relevant information. Subjects waited either alone or with a confederate and, five minutes later, they heard a loud crash and a cry of pain from a workman they had seen go into the next room. The confederate reacted with a start to the sound of the crash, but then ignored it. The results showed a dual effect. Subjects who waited alone were faster and more likely to help than those who waited with the passive confederate, and subjects who had received information about emergency behaviour responded more rapidly than those who had not. However, the information about emergencies did not lead to a higher *proportion* of people helping

Some organizations help to encourage intervention by showing people exactly what to do in an emergency.

Would you know how to help?

We are all candidates for epilepsy. It can happen to anyone. At any age. Get to know the facts.

First aid for seizures:

1. Stay calm. Do not restrain movements.
2. Move sharp objects out of the way.
3. Do not place anything between the teeth.
4. Turn the person on one side. Place a jacket or soft object beneath the head.
5. Let the seizure run its course. Then, when the person regains consciousness, help in any way needed. But above all...
   Your reassurance and kindness are perhaps the best first aid of all.

For more information about epilepsy, call the

EPILEPSY ASSOCIATION OF METRO TORONTO *at* 363-4011

since, in fact, all subjects in the alone conditions helped sooner or later, compared with 70 percent of the relevant information group in the presence of a confederate, and 62 percent of the control group (these percentages do not differ significantly from each other).

(4) *Removing legal risks*. People sometimes believe that the person who provides emergency roadside first aid is liable for damages should he or she unintentionally harm the victim. Some physicians fear being held liable for damages if they give emergency medical care at the scene of an accident and the patient does not recover. This has led to pressure for the passage of Good Samaritan laws which exonerate from liability an individual who has assisted in good faith "unless it is established that the injuries or death were caused by gross negligence . . . " (*Emergency Medical Aid Act*, Revised Statutes of Alberta, 1970). In Canada, only three provinces — Alberta, Newfoundland, and Nova Scotia — have passed Good Samaritan laws. It is not known whether the absence of such laws *inhibits* emergency medical intervention but there has never been a case in North America in which anyone successfully sued a person who offered help in an emergency (Monaghan, 1975; Markus, 1975). There is obviously a need to educate people that their assistance will not result in damage suits.

Most people do not know about the bystander effect and most do not believe that it occurs frequently. It seems to contradict the proper etiquette of "responsible behaviour." By following some of the approaches just discussed, it would be possible to reduce the bystander effect. There is much work to be done toward that end.

THE BENEFICIARY

Who gets helped?

Not only are some rather than others likely to help, depending on the situation, but not all people in need are equally likely to be helped. You might be willing to assist a well-dressed senior citizen change a tire, but not if he or she appeared to be drunk. The degree to which a person is dependent on another also generally plays an important part in determining how much help will be given. Several studies have found a positive relationship between the potential beneficiary's level of dependence and the amount of help given, but this relationship may apply only when the cost for the helper is low (Krebs, 1970; Gruder, 1974).

When the cost of helping is great, we may resent the burden that the requester's needs places upon us (Berkowitz, 1973). The greater the person's dependency upon us, the greater our felt obligation to help, and the greater our "reactance," or desire to re-establish our independence and freedom (Brehm, 1966). We may gladly help a person in and out of a wheelchair unless we feel that we are obliged to do so. Perhaps a felt obligation robs us of the "good feelings" we would normally experience if we voluntarily helped the person.

Attributions may play an important role in determining who will or will not be helped. If another person's need appears to be controllable, that is, the person seems responsible for the plight he or she is in, we may be less willing to help than if we perceive the person's need as owing to circumstances beyond control (Weiner, 1980).

There has been some limited empirical support for this proposition (Reisenzein, 1986).

Other factors which affect the probability of receiving help are: physical attractiveness (West and Brown, 1975); degree of apparent need (Staub and Baer, 1974); and perceived similarity between the requester and the helper (Sole, Marton and Hornstein, 1975). Thus you are more likely to help someone who is physically attractive to you, who is in great need of help, and who is part of your in-group (race, social status). Even whether the potential helper and requester both need help can have an important effect. If you are in a very stressful situation and the potential recipient is in the same stressful situation, helping will be facilitated. However, a person will be less likely than usual to help if the requester is in a *less* stressful situation. (Dovidio and Morris, 1975). So, if you want directions to the post office, do not ask someone who is pushing her car to the gas station!

Reaction of the beneficiary

The act of providing help not only clearly distinguishes between helper and beneficiary, it also defines a power hierarchy (Worchel, 1984). If the person who is helped cannot repay the help in any way, then — at least in Western society — accepting help places the person in a position of inferiority. There may even be a perceived loss of face (Fisher, 1983). If you are desperately short of money and someone gives you money but refuses to accept repayment, you may feel some discomfort unless, of course, the benefactor is in a role which might justify munificence (e.g., your father or mother). In general, the greater the threat to self-esteem, the more likely it is that the recipient may feel negatively towards the helper (Fisher, Nadler and Whitcher-Alagna, 1982; Fisher, 1983).

Experimental studies carried out with subjects from the United States, Sweden, and Japan have found that subjects give more positive evaluations to "donors" who oblige them to repay the donation than those who ask nothing in return (Gergen, Ellsworth, Maslach and Seipel, 1975). Negative evaluation of donors who do not want reciprocation may occur at the international level as well. Developing nations may feel less gratitude for aid from developed nations if they have no way of reciprocating, for such aid underlines the beneficiary's position of dependency (Andreas, 1969). If receiving aid leads the recipient to feel inferior to the donor, there may be a strong need on the part of the recipient to repay the aid in order to regain independence. Such a reaction might be more expected when the donor is a close friend rather than a stranger (Nadler and Fisher, 1984), for it is more important to avoid feelings of inferiority with a friend. In fact, most people worry about "losing face" for nothing. There is actually little evidence to support the claim that donors perceive beneficiaries as inferior (Rosen, Tomarelli, Kidda and Medvin, 1986).

As we have seen, people do not automatically come to the assistance of others in need. They are often inhibited by feelings of ambiguity and fear. In the next section, a very special kind of intervention behaviour is discussed in which considerations of personal risk seem not to play a role.

HEROISM

• *In June 1944 Pilot Officer Andrew Charles Mynarski of Winnipeg was flying an RCAF Lancaster bomber in an attack on German positions when the airplane was hit and set afire. The crew parachuted to safety, except for the tail-gunner, Pat Brophy, who was trapped in his tiny rear compartment by a damaged door, and Mynarski, who lurched back through the flames to attempt to free him. Covered with blazing hydraulic fluid, he worked bare-handed to try to get the door open. Finally, driven back by the fire, he stood and saluted Brophy before bailing out. He had no chance of survival: his parachute was on fire. He was posthumously awarded the Victoria Cross on the evidence of the tail-gunner, who ironically survived the crash of the bomb-laden airplane when he was thrown free upon impact (Franklin, 1977).*

• *In May 1977, a Langley, B.C. man was awakened in the middle of the night by an eight-year-old neighbour girl who told him her home was on fire. After calling the fire department, he ran across the street and into the burning house. Groping around in the smoke he found one of the children and passed him through the window to the eight-year-old. Unfortunately, it was too late to save the rest of the family. When asked about his heroic deed later, he replied "I didn't think about anything. I was inside before I remembered I hadn't taken a deep breath before going in"* (The Globe and Mail, *August 15, 1973).*

These two examples of heroic action demonstrate the finest prosocial behaviour: individuals risking their own lives to try saving others. Such heroism is greatly admired in all societies. In 1972, three decorations were created by the Canadian government to honour those who perform such selfless acts of courage — the Cross of Valour, the Star of Courage, and the Medal of Bravery.

What is the stuff of heroism? While heroism is difficult to define because it is based on perception and attribution, most acts that are considered heroic involve altruistic intervention in the face of extraordinary personal risk.

Heroism and gender

We have seen that the male gender role is more conducive to helping in general. Indeed, almost all *recognized* acts of heroism have been carried out by men (Eagly and Crowley, 1986), acting alone in most cases. Given what is known about the bystander effect, that is not surprising. For example, consider the Carnegie Heroes. The Carnegie Hero Fund Commission was founded in the United States in 1904 to award medals for "outstanding acts of selfless heroism performed in the United States and Canada." An analysis of Carnegie Hero Medal recipients in the United States revealed that 96 of the 101 recipients in 1971 were male and that in the vast majority of cases, the hero acted alone (Lay, Allen and Kassirer, 1974). Since the inception of the award, only 8.9 percent of the 6955 medalists have been female (Eagly and Crowley, 1986).

In an analysis of recipients of Metropolitan Toronto Police Civilian Citations, which are awarded to people who have spontaneously come to the aid of the police either directly (e.g., chasing a suspect or helping defend a police officer) or indirectly (e.g., telephoning a police station when a police officer is under attack), it was also found that males were more likely than females to directly intervene (an action which is more likely to constitute heroism), while females were more likely to notify the police rather than take direct action (Lay, Allen and Kassirer, 1974). (However, since most of the aggressors were male, this outcome might be misleading). In about two thirds of the cases, the recipient acted alone. Only in the pursuit of an offender did it happen more frequently that more than one person was involved.

However, supporting the notion that heroism is implicitly defined in terms of the male gender role is the fact that the Carnegie Hero Commission excludes from consideration people who rescue family members, except if the rescuer dies or is severely injured. Thus women (who according to the female gender role should be particularly concerned with the welfare of their children) are not considered heroic if they risk their lives in saving their children. Heroism, therefore, appears to be a "male" concept, and we should not be surprised that women are less often viewed as heroic. As society becomes more egalitarian, and as male and female gender roles become less differentiated and less rigid, this perception will undoubtedly change.

The Scarlet Pimpernel phenomenon

The Scarlet Pimpernel is the name of a book and a fictional character created by Baroness Orczy. The book is set during the days of the French Revolution and concerns a British nobleman who could have followed the goings-on in the comfort and safety of his own homeland. Instead, he risked his life to smuggle French aristocrats out of Paris and out of the country, saving them from the certain fate of the guillotine.

This fictional tale of heroism was replayed again and again during the days of the Third Reich when a small number of individuals repeatedly risked their lives helping Jews escape from the Nazis. Later, during the trial of Adolph Eichmann on the charge of crimes against the Jewish people and against humanity arising from his role in the Nazi genocidal policy, reference was made to Christians who had rescued Jews from concentration camps. Subsequently, social psychologists tried to track down as many of these rescuers as possible to determine whether there were any common factors in their personalities or their family backgrounds (London, 1970). Although the project was prematurely terminated because of lack of funds, they did succeed in locating 27 rescuers and 42 rescued people. In a similar and ongoing study known as the Altruistic Personality Project, 220 of these same rescuers have been interviewed and there are plans to interview an additional 300 people in Canada, the United States, Europe, and Israel (Fogelman and Wiener, 1985).

No single motivation accounting for the behaviour of these rescuers has been identified. Some had deliberately chosen to rescue Jews, others got involved without thinking about it, or even by mistake: one person reluctantly agreed to let his secretary's Jewish husband stay in his office over the weekend to hide from the Nazis. Once involved, however, he was drawn in even deeper and developed considerable compassion for those he helped, eventually rescuing about 200 people at great personal risk and cost. Some of the rescuers were very religious, while others were atheist, and some were even anti-Semitic!

What did they have in common, if anything? London (1970), while cautioning us about the possible non-representativeness of his sample, found three characteristics that the rescuers shared. First, they showed a fondness for adventure and excitement, which was important in the initiation of the rescue work. Second, the rescuers tended to be socially deviant, and their social marginality provided the impetus and endurance necessary to carry out this rescue work. Third, and most important, the rescuers showed a strong identification with a parent who had definite opinions on moral questions and who provided a model for moral conduct.

Fogelman and Weiner (1985) reported that the rescuers seemed to fall into two groups — those whose motivation was of a moral nature, based on considerations of justice, and those whose motivation was primarily based on emotional attachment to the victim, which led to a sense of responsibility and care-giving. They discovered that morally motivated rescuers rescued people whether they liked them or disliked them, and whether or not they knew them previously. Again, they found that rescuers, regardless of the type of motivation, shared certain characteristics. Many reported that their parents had stressed — both in words and by behaviour — the importance of helping others and the importance of accepting that differences in group or race or culture do not make a person superior or inferior.

These studies recall our earlier discussion of the effects of models and upbringing on prosocial behaviour in general. Identification with an altruistic parent, a parent who both teaches and practices the importance of caring for and helping others, appears to be of outstanding importance in inculcating selflessness in individuals. This strong identification with a moralistic parent was also found to be an important characteristic of "fully committed" American civil rights workers in the late 1950s and early 1960s. These activists had been taught by their parents not only to believe in certain principles but to *act* upon them (Rosenhan, 1970).

SUMMARY

(1) Sociobiologists propose that altruism is genetically transmitted and is influenced by natural selection, a position which is not held by most psychologists.

(2) Empathy, a vicarious emotional response, is not a necessary condition for altruism, but may enhance the probability of such behaviour.

(3) Cognitive development theory proposes that moral thinking matures from a state of concern with pure self-interest, to responsiveness to the reactions of others, then to being guided by abstract principles.

(4) Social learning theory emphasizes the acquisition of altruism through processes of reinforcement, self-attribution, modelling, and parental discipline.

(5) Altruism may be influenced by various emotional states, and may involve attempts to repair our self-image.

(6) Norms of reciprocity and social responsibility can influence altruistic behaviour but their role is usually a minor one.

(7) The manifestation of altruism varies from one culture to another, between males and females, and between people in cities and rural areas.

(8) Emergency situations involve threat or harm to the victim, are rare and unpredictable, vary widely in form and appropriate response, and may involve risk or costs to the benefactor.

(9) People are less likely to help in an emergency when other bystanders are present (the "bystander effect").

(10) The bystander effect occurs when each bystander feels that he or she is less responsible for the victim's welfare because there are other people present who could take action ("diffusion of responsibility") and because the inaction of others makes the situation more ambiguous to each bystander with regard to whether help is needed and what response is appropriate.

(11) Bystander behaviour is also influenced by the anticipated rewards and costs of helping.

(12) Bystander intervention could be encouraged through increasing public awareness of the bystander effect, through teaching children to "break the rules" of social convention when necessary, by training children to take responsibility for helping others, and by removing the risk of legal liability.

(13) People are less likely to receive help if they are perceived as being overly dependent, or if their need for help appears to be controllable or brought on by their own actions.

(14) Recipients of help who cannot reciprocate sometimes react with resentment.

(15) People who repeatedly act heroically to assist others tend to be fond of adventure, to be socially marginal, and to identify with a parent who holds strong beliefs and acts on them.

FURTHER READING

FISHER, J.D., NADLER, A. and DEPAULO, B.M. (1983). *New directions in helping: Recipient reactions to aid*. New York: Academic Press.

PILIAVIN, J.A., DOVIDIO, J.F., GAERTNER, S.L. and CLARK, R.D. (1981). *Emergency intervention*. New York: Academic Press.

RUSHTON, J.P. (1980). *Altruism, socialization, and society*. Englewood Cliffs, NJ: Prentice-Hall.

RUSHTON, J.P. and SORRENTINO, R.M. (Eds.) (1981). *Altruism and helping behaviour*. New York: Academic Press.

STAUB, E., BAR-TAL, D., KARYLOWSKI, J. and REYKOWSKI, J. (Eds.) (1984). *Development and maintenance of pro-social behavior*. New York: Plenum Press.

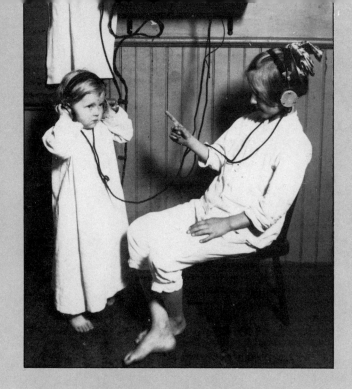

C·H·A·P·T·E·R E·L·E·V·E·N

Communication

If one knows his neighbour's tongue, he
possesses the key of his house.
Abbé Arthur Maheux

FOR REFLECTION

- How can we communicate without using words?
- What is involved in having a conversation?
- Is language uniquely human?
- Does the way we speak determine the way we think?
- Is there more to becoming bilingual than learning grammar and
  vocabulary?

362

COMMUNICATION IS THE essence of social interaction. Whether by words, facial expressions or gestures, whether through direct contact, telephone conversations or the printed page, humans inform each other of their thoughts and feelings, their wishes and ideals, their intentions and needs. They threaten, command, supplicate, reward, tease, and entertain each other. They teach, they exchange points of view, they coordinate their activities — the list goes on. Indeed, it is difficult to imagine being in the presence of another person without continually communicating in one way or another.

While non-verbal communication — communication by means of gestures, facial expressions, body position, or non-verbal speech, such as whistles, grunts, and groans — provides a powerful channel for conveying information, it is language which distinctly characterizes human communication. It is impossible to do justice to the study of human social activity without examining verbal activity, for virtually every utterance a person makes in the presence of others demands a response, and how the listener responds often reflects various aspects of the interaction itself, for example, the relative status levels of speaker and listener or the particular emotional relationship between them. These interactions in turn cannot be totally understood without taking into account the role that language plays in shaping them (Holtgraves, 1986). Not only does language play an important communicative role in social interactions between individuals, it also serves a function in relationships between groups of people in that it is used to mark group boundaries and to define group identities.

Given the importance of language in social interaction, it may come as a surprise to learn that until very recently, social psychologists have mostly neglected the study of language. Most social psychology textbooks do not even mention the subject (Clark, 1985). In Canada, of course, linguistic factors have always played an important role in our social and political lives. Thus we might expect social psychologists in this country to show particular interest in the subject. Moreover, Montreal is one of the world's natural living laboratories for the study of social psychological aspects of language and bilingualism, for it is the second largest French-speaking city in the world, and has an English-speaking population which is larger than all but a few other Canadian cities. Indeed, Canadian researchers are at the forefront in such research (Gardner and Desrochers, 1981).

This chapter begins with the examination of non-verbal methods of communication. Next, language is discussed, with a particular emphasis on its social aspects. Finally the role of language in intergroup relations is explored, as well as the social psychological aspects of bilingualism.

NON-VERBAL COMMUNICATION

A raise of the eyebrows, a pucker of the lips, or a clenching of the fist can often communicate more about how we feel than could a dozen words. Such non-verbal behaviours can serve a number of functions, including the following (Patterson, 1982, 1983): (1) They can provide information about feelings and intentions, e.g., when we wish to know whether or not an individual is interested in or attracted to us. (2) They can be used to regulate interactions, e.g., when we need to coordinate turn-taking in a conversational exchange. (3) They can be used to express intimacy, e.g., when two lovers gaze intently into each others' eyes. (4) They can promote social control, e.g., when we threaten others with non-verbal signals or ingratiate ourselves by smiling. (5) They can be used to facilitate goal attainment, e.g., when we draw another person's attention to something by pointing at it. These functions will be evident throughout the discussion that follows.

Within a given culture or society, virtually everyone understands the meaning of various facial expressions and gestures; otherwise, they would be of little use in communication. However, no formal training is ever given to show people how either to encode feelings or ideas into gestures or facial expressions or to decode (i.e., interpret) body language. We learn to use and to react to non-verbal communication through interaction with others just as we do initially in learning to use language. As children, we imitate the motions and gestures that older people make and, to one degree or another, we grow to be sensitive to various non-verbal cues even though we may not always know just what cue it was that gave us a particular impression about someone.

Not only are we usually unaware of the extent to which we are influenced by non-verbal cues from others, we often display them ourselves without much awareness of doing so. (An interesting example of non-verbal cueing without awareness is described in Box 11-1.) Consider pain, for example. Suppose you want to signal to someone by non-verbal means that you are in pain. What would you do? Perhaps you would grimace, or grit your teeth. Suppose, on the other hand, you *are* in pain but wish to conceal this fact from others; what cues would you try to *suppress*? Although most of us are rather unaware of which cues are important in such a context and which are not, research has shown that such movements as blinking, lowering the eyebrow, narrowing the eye aperture, and raising the upper lip serve as the most important indicators of pain to observers (Patrick, Craig, and Prkachin, 1986). We all display these signs when in pain, but we are unlikely to be aware of them.

As is the case with language, the use of non-verbal communication is governed by various social norms. For instance, you would hardly dare to roll your eyes towards the ceiling while listening to a professor criticize your essay plan. In our society, such an act would be disrespectful in context and would likely create tension between you and your professor. However, if the same professor asked you about how you were enjoying your part-time job, the same eyeroll could be employed quite appropriately and would probably convey your feelings about the job more succinctly than a verbal reply.

Women are somewhat better than men at both sending and picking up non-verbal cues across a wide range of situations (Brown, 1986; Hall, 1979), probably on account of child-rearing practices which encourage girls to be particularly emotionally expressive and attentive to others. Since we are rarely fully aware of information received non-verbally, it is easy to appreciate the persistent and popular belief in women's "intuition": women may pick up on non-verbal cues that men miss and, being unable to specify which cues led them to a certain inference, describe the inference in terms of a "feeling."

Non-verbal communication does more than simply send signals to other people. It can change considerably the meaning attributed to verbal signals. An utterance said with a smile will be interpreted quite differently than an utterance said with a frown. In fact, research has shown that non-verbal behaviour can impair memory for the specific meaning of utterances (Hertel and Navarez, 1986): subjects whose task it was to recall a dialogue they had heard in a videotaped conversation displayed confusion

LANGUAGE WITHOUT WORDS

In 1904 Wilhelm van Osten, a retired Berlin schoolteacher, claimed that he had found a way of teaching animals to think, "talk," and even do arithmetic. His only subject had been a horse, Clever Hans. By teaching Hans to associate a number with each letter of the alphabet (which he did by means of a blackboard!), the horse was able to tap out messages with his right front hoof. He also communicated by means of head movements, a nod indicating "yes," a side-to-side movement meaning "no." Hans could apparently combine letters into words and words into sentences, count up to 100, count objects or people, solve arithmetic questions, tell the time, and read German. He could select from a series of written words any word that someone spoke to him by pointing at it with his nose. He could answer questions such as "If the eighth day of the month comes on Tuesday, what is the date of the following Friday?" Indeed, the horse seemed to have telepathic abilities, for he could answer questions that someone was only thinking about.

Psychologist Oskar Pfungst (1911) set about systematically to study Hans' remarkable talent. He found that the presence of the horse's trainer was not necessary, thus ruling out the use of a secret cuing system. However, Pfungst discovered that Hans had to be able to see the questioner in order to respond correctly, and that if the questioner did not know the answer to his or her own question, Hans was unable to give a correct answer. After much perseverance, he determined that Hans had discovered regularities in human non-verbal behaviour: questioners were involuntarily giving cues to Hans which directed him to the correct answer. As Hans tapped out his answers, the questioner would make a slight and involuntary upward movement of the head when the correct number of taps was given, at which point Hans would stop. There were other involuntary cues as well, and Pfungst concluded that van Osten, unaware of the basis of Hans' "ability," had consistently and unwittingly reinforced the horse's responses to subtle cues while he was in the process of "educating" him. The horse was so sensitive to van Osten's movements that he was able to respond to movements of the trainer's head measuring only one fifth of a millimetre!

in their memories between what was said and how it was said. Thus, if someone says something negative, but in a friendly and jocular way, we may later remember their words as having been less negative than they actually were.

Three different sources of non-verbal signals are discussed below. The first of these involves *facial displays* and *eye contact*; the second is *body language*, which refers to information conveyed by the position or movements of the body and by physical contact and spatial behaviour; the third is *paralanguage* — aspects of speech, such as grunts, pauses or rhythm, which convey information apart from the actual language itself.

Facial expression and eye contact

In Shakespeare's *Macbeth* King Duncan remarks, "There's no art to find the mind's construction in the face" (Act I, scene 4). Unfortunately, the king had completely misjudged the character of MacBeth, not to mention his wife, and eventually pays for it with his life. Evidently, reading facial expressions is a little more complicated than King Duncan had realized. Facial expression plays a major role in communication, so major in fact that when there appears to be a contradiction between what is conveyed by words and what is conveyed by the face, the face is usually considered to be a more accurate guide to the *meaning* of what was said (Bugental, Kaswan and Love, 1970; Mehrabian, 1968).

Are facial displays of emotion universal? Charles Darwin suggested in 1872 that human emotional behaviour evolved from that of the lower animals. Thus, he said, we should expect that all human beings should be similar in their way of expressing emotion (Boucher, 1974). Darwin is proving to have been correct, for while other kinds of non-verbal signals vary from culture to culture, accumulating evidence points to basic similarities in facial expression of emotion in all cultures — in other words, the physical expression of emotion appears to be to some degree innate.

In one study which demonstrated the intercultural similarity of facial expressions of emotion (Ekman and Friesen, 1971), subjects in Japan, the United States, Borneo, New Guinea, and South America who were shown photographs of people from other cultures were generally able to correctly identify the emotions being displayed. Each photograph conveyed one of six "primary" emotions — fear, happiness, surprise, anger, sadness, and disgust. For example, when members of the Fore tribe, a Stone Age society living in a remote part of New Guinea, were shown photographs of American faces conveying specific emotions and then were read stories which described people in highly emotional circumstances, they were generally able to match the correct face to each story, despite the fact that most of them had never had any contact with Americans. When another group of New Guinea tribespeople were videotaped while demonstrating how they thought they would look if they were the people involved in the stories, American students subsequently had no difficulty in matching their facial expressions to the stories.

Other researchers have extended these findings by working with subjects from many other cultures. Even more impressive is the discovery that blind children develop the same facial displays of affect as do the sighted (Boucher, 1974).

Cultural variations in facial displays While it seems that there are universal patterns of facial display which accompany specific emotional reactions, these universalities are influenced by cultural norms. In our society, social norms dictate that we should suppress tears when we are very disappointed, but may show them at funerals; we may demonstrate happiness at parties but should suppress any sign of it if we have just humiliated an opponent on the squash court. People in Japan are taught to control their facial displays especially with regard to negative emotion, and to use laughter or smiling to conceal anger or grief (Argyle, 1975).

In a study of intercultural difficulty in reading other people's facial expressions, the emotions portrayed by English, Italian, and Japanese performers were observed by subjects from these three countries. The English and Italian subjects had equal success in judging the emotions of their own group and the other group. However, subjects from both groups had more difficulty in judging the Japanese than the Japanese did in judging them (Argyle, 1975) (see Table 11-1). Even the Japanese had difficulty in judging the emotional expression of fellow Japanese!

TABLE 11-1
Percentage of respondents who correctly judged facial expression of emotion

Judges	Performers		
	English	Italian	Japanese
English	63	58	38
Italian	53	62	28
Japanese	57	58	45

SOURCE: Argyle, 1975

Such cultural distinctiveness can lead to serious misperceptions. During World War II, Allied propaganda leaflets and posters showed a picture of a grinning Japanese soldier plunging his bayonet into an Allied soldier. While the expression on his face conveyed "sadistic glee" to Western eyes, to the Japanese, this same expression indicated grim determination rather than pleasure.

In the studies noted above, the emotions portrayed by various groups were *posed*, i.e., the individuals were deliberately attempting to convey a particular emotion. However, there are two separate pathways which carry signals from the brain to the facial muscles. One pathway corresponds with deliberate expression (i.e., under voluntary control) and the other with spontaneous (i.e., involuntary) expression. This branching is demonstrated by the existence of two separate neurological disorders: in one, a patient told a joke will produce a spontaneous smile but will not be able to smile when asked; in the other, the patient will smile when asked but will show no facial reaction when told the joke (Ekman, 1982). Recent research has studied *spontaneous* expressions of emotion by covertly photographing people's faces as they are exposed to some stimulus situation, and then showing these photographs to subjects and asking them to identify the emotion. It appears that although anger and disgust can be communicated at an above-chance rate, only "happiness" is easily communicated in this way (Wagner, MacDonald and Manstead, 1986).

Two smiles: The smile on the left is "posed," i.e., under voluntary control. The smile on the right is spontaneous — an involuntary expression of happiness.

An interesting example of the subtle role that facial expression can play in social interaction is provided by a study carried out in the United States (Mullen *et al.*, 1986). These researchers studied the facial expressions of network television newscasters when they referred either to Reagan or to Mondale during the 1984 presidential campaign. They discovered that one of the three newscasters exhibited significantly more positive facial expressions (e.g., smiling) when talking about Reagan than about Mondale, and that viewers who regularly watched that newscaster were significantly more likely to vote for Reagan. Although it could be that viewers partial to Reagan might have been more likely to watch that newscaster, the authors argued that it is more probable that a subtle kind of persuasion occurred as a result of the non-verbal communication.

Sometimes we deliberately *mimic* another person's facial expressions or produce facial expressions which are in line not with our emotional state but rather with the perceived state of the other individual. For example, it is common to wince when we see someone else being hurt, for instance, if we see someone cut himself. Is this reaction due to a vicarious emotional reaction? Does our wincing reflect our own discomfort in face of the pain suffered by the other person? The answer appears to be "no." Whether or not such motor mimicry occurs depends to a considerable degree upon whether or not the victim can see the mimicry (Bavelas, Black, Lemery and Mullett, 1986). Thus such mimicry appears to serve a communicative function, as if to tell the victim that "I feel *with* you."

Gaze   While facial expression can be captured by a photograph, a gaze (looking in the direction of another person's face and eyes) and eye contact ("mutual gaze") cannot. However, these too are very important channels of non-verbal behaviour. Indeed, think about what happens if your eyes come in contact with those of a stranger. Normally, you might be compelled to quickly look away, but if you do not do so quickly, and if the stranger maintains his or her gaze as well, you may experience the sensation of being almost unable to pull your eyes away — your eyes are momentarily "riveted" to those of the other person. Next, you might feel a sense of embarrassment, or you may even feel compelled to say something in order to explain yourself or reduce the anxiety produced by the situation. Thus eye contact can produce powerful emotional effects.

However, in many cultures people practice eye avoidance, for eye contact is considered disrespectful. Moreover, norms vary from culture to culture with regard to eye contact during conversations. This can sometimes lead to much misunderstanding in intercultural interactions. For example, recall (from Chapter 7) that studies carried out in the United States have found that while White Americans typically maintain eye contact with the speaker while listening, and while White *speakers* spend less time in eye contact with their listeners, the opposite is the case for Black Americans. The opportunity for misattribution in interracial communication is immense as a result, for white children are typically taught to "look a person in the eye if you have nothing to hide." Thus Whites speaking to Blacks detect, with or without awareness, that the Blacks shift their gaze more than White norms would dictate as desirable, and erroneous and prejudicial conclusions are drawn (LaFrance and Mayo, 1976).

Because of its importance in non-verbal communication, it is worthwhile to consider in some detail the various ways in which eye contact can be used. In fact, it can serve all the various functions of non-verbal behaviour listed earlier (Kleinke, 1986).

(1) *Providing information*. Eye contact can signal whether or not a person wishes to initiate or maintain a conversation with another person. When one person wants to initiate an interaction with another, he or she may look directly at the other's eyes. If the other person looks back, it means that he or she is also willing to engage in the interaction. However, by avoiding the gaze, by not letting someone "catch" his or her eye, an individual can avoid the obligation of interacting that accompanies having had one's eye "caught" (Argyle, 1971).

Information about degree of liking, credibility, and strength of emotion can also be signalled by eye contact. People who maintain considerable eye contact with each other are judged by observers to like each other more. Eye contact also seems to influence actual liking, although either too much or too little of it can lead to a negative reaction. We are judged to be more credible and more honest when we maintain eye contact when being questioned by others. Furthermore, there is a tendency to gaze more at another person when we are trying to communicate strong feelings, whether positive or negative (Kimble, Forte and Yoshikawa, 1981).

(2) *Regulating interaction*. In conversations, gazing is an important factor in controlling whose turn it is to talk, as will be discussed later.

(3) *Expressing intimacy*. Gazing increases as a function of positive attraction, although a high degree of eye contact does not *always* indicate affection (Patterson, 1972). The next time that you meet someone new at a party, think about how your eye contact (or deliberate avoidance of it) may signal to the other person whether you are interested even in pursuing a conversation. "Making eyes" at someone is a means of indicating sexual or affectional interest.

(4) *Social control*. Gazing can be used to signal displeasure with another's behaviour, even a threat. Suppose that someone seated nearby is making noise while you are trying to enjoy a play. Staring the person in the eye is one way to signal your displeasure.

Body language

One need only observe a mime artist to recognize the power of the eyes and face in communicating feelings and thoughts. But the mime communicates through the use of the whole body. Although less so than the face, the entire body is a source of non-verbal messages and in recent years a number of popular books have appeared which promise to teach readers how to understand and exploit "body language." For example, it might be claimed that a woman who sits with her arms crossed while talking to a particular man is unknowingly revealing a protective emotional stance. Such books rarely back up their claims with any empirical evidence and should be approached warily.

However, there is evidence that (accurate or not) certain postures are often *perceived* by others as reflecting specific feelings. For example, leaning toward another person or taking a position in close proximity is generally interpreted as a positive stance toward that person. Other examples appear in Figure 11-1.

FIGURE 11-1
*Body Language
Interpreted*

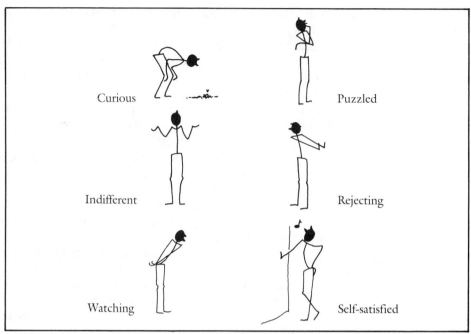

Curious   Puzzled

Indifferent   Rejecting

Watching   Self-satisfied

SOURCE: Argyle, 1975

Body contact is another form of "body language" and varies a great deal from culture to culture. In India, two men engaged in conversation often hold hands. To do that in Canada might lead to serious misunderstanding, for we have rather strict rules for men about touching members of the same sex. Non-verbal signals may differ in meaning depending upon the specific social situation. The significance of a man touching a woman differs according to whether that woman is his wife, a stranger, a patient, or a casual acquaintance (Argyle, 1975). A slap on the back can vary in meaning too. If a person has just scored a goal in a hockey game, it means only one thing, while if a person has just transgressed, it could mean something else.

Men have been observed to touch women more often than women touch men, and people are much more likely to touch members of the opposite sex than members of their own sex (Henley, 1973). The amount of touching behaviour also varies considerably from culture to culture. People in Latin America, Greece, Turkey, and the Arab countries tend to touch each other a great deal, while relatively little touching occurs among North Americans, Northern Europeans, and Orientals (Argyle, 1975). In a study of cross-cultural differences in touching, couples were observed while having coffee in cafes in different countries (Jourard, 1966). The observers recorded the number of times they touched each other during a one-hour period. In London, England, there was no touching, while in Gainesville, Florida, there were two touches on average, in Paris, 110 touches, and in San Juan, Puerto Rico, 180 touches. Therefore, touching someone in London would probably not have the same effect as touching someone in Paris. Obviously, the potential for misunderstanding is great when people from a "contact" culture visit a "non-contact" culture.

Within a given culture there are also differences with respect to *where* a person touches another person; the degree of bodily contact in North American society

The significance of a man touching a woman differs according to whether the woman is his wife, a stranger, a patient, or a casual acquaintance.

FIGURE 11-2
Areas of the body involved in bodily contact

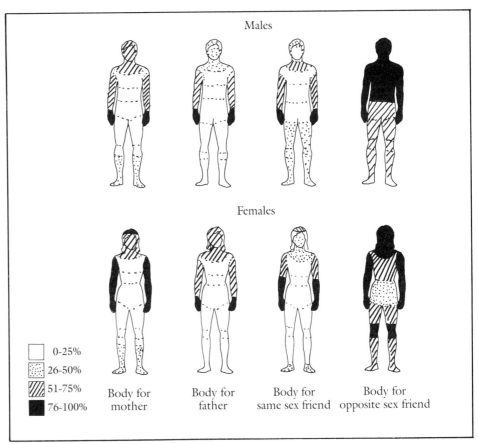

Males

Females

0-25%
26-50%
51-75%
76-100%

Body for mother

Body for father

Body for same sex friend

Body for opposite sex friend

SOURCE: Jourard, 1966

depends very much on the age and relationship of the individuals (Argyle, 1975). Jourard (1966) asked American students to indicate who had touched them where on their bodies; his results are summarized in Figure 11-2. As can be seen, parents confine their touching by and large to the hands and arms, while friends of the opposite sex demonstrate more contact. Although these data were collected over 20 years ago, it is unlikely that we would find much difference if we were to repeat the study today.

Gestures Gestures, yet another form of "body language," also vary from society to society and from culture to culture. Both Pierre Trudeau and René Levesque often communicate by means of a simple Gallic "shrug," which somehow might seem inappropriate if performed by an Anglophone. Is it true, as many people seem to think, that French Canadians speaking French typically make many more hand gestures than do English Canadians speaking English? In learning to speak French, some English Canadians find themselves picking up the practice of hand gesturing and using it when speaking in French! This question was studied by presenting both Anglophone and Francophone "judges" with videotapes of bilingual people (shown from the neck down) speaking at one time in French and at another time in English. While non-verbal behaviour did not vary as a function of the language being spoken, it varied substantially according to the native tongue of the speaker, i.e., whether the speaker's first language was French or English. In 71 percent of the cases, the judges successfully identified the speaker's mother tongues on the basis of non-verbal behaviour (Lacroix and Rioux, 1978). Francophone subjects, true to the stereotype, gestured more than Anglophones did, regardless of which language they spoke.

We have considerable difficulty in interpreting gestures which are specific to another culture or which we use but are used differently in another culture. For example, the Japanese are suprised when we point to our chest in referring to ourselves; they do so by putting a finger to the nose (DeVos and Hippler, 1969). A sidewise nod of the head means "no" in Canada but "yes" in much of India, while in Turkey, "no" is signalled by moving the head backwards and rolling the eyes upward (Rubin, 1976). Drawing one's finger across one's throat means "I've had it" in Canada; in Swaziland, it means "I love you." We invite people to approach us by beckoning with an upturned finger. Indians use all four downturned fingers to do the same thing. These cross-cultural differences in the meaning of some gestures can lead to serious communication difficulty, as when a missionary girl's attempt to shake hands with an African chieftain created problems when he interpreted the gesture as an attempt to throw him to the ground (Argyle, 1975)! As another example, Arabs and Latin Americans typically prefer a smaller distance between speaker and listener than other groups. This sometimes leads to situations in which they appear to be "chasing" a European or North American across the floor as the listener backs away.

Paralanguage

We can say exactly the same words in different ways and communicate different messages. *Paralanguage* refers to the "how" of speaking, the non-verbal aspects of speech; it includes such characteristics as volume, stress, pitch, speed, tone of voice, pauses, and even non-linguistic sounds such as throat-clearing, grunts, and sighs.

Timing, pitch, and loudness (the so-called the *prosodic* features of language in the terminology of linguists) (Argyle, 1975) are critically important in oral communication, for they can confer very different meanings on the same set of words. Saying "You pig!" to a friend dipping into a box of chocolates can communicate either friendly teasing or admonishment, depending on how it is said. Children acquire the ability to use these prosodic elements, e.g., raising the pitch at the end of a sentence to indicate a question, early in their language development. Prosodic features of speech are used to give emphasis to certain points, to indicate doubt, to suggest that we are thinking aloud, and in general to provide structure to the words that make up the verbal communication.

Studies of individuals and of cultures suggest that as with facial expressions, the role of prosodic elements in the expression of emotion is not a learned one, for there is very little evidence of variation in this behaviour either among individuals in a given culture of across cultures. Thus it seems that certain prosodic patterns may communicate specific emotions: aggression or dominance tends to be signalled by a low pitch, while happiness and lack of aggressiveness usually involves a higher pitch (Frick, 1985).

Coordination of non-verbal and verbal communication

One of the most important applications of prosodic cueing is in the regulation of verbal interactions. As everyone knows, language provides an efficient means of communication. We can communicate the same basic message in many different ways, using nuances to finely tune our verbal utterance to the thoughts or feelings being expressed. So why do we not use language for all communication? Why has non-verbal communication persisted as part of our cultural heritage when language has been available to supplant it? There are several possible reasons (Argyle, 1975):

(1) In some situations, non-verbal communication is easier to use, for instance, with regard to shapes. Apart from simple shapes, we have a limited vocabulary in this area and can more easily communicate by hand movements. Similarly, it is much easier to point to a flaw in a paint job than to try to describe the precise location verbally.

(2) Non-verbal signals are more powerful and more subtle than verbal signals in communicating emotion. While adults can teach children to correctly name objects and actions by actually using the label in the presence of the object or action, it is more difficult to teach children what labels to apply to emotional states. An adult can only infer whether a child feels "sad" or "happy" or remorseful" on the basis of the child's non-verbal behaviour and according to the context in which that behaviour occurred and, therefore, the adult can at best suggest a somewhat general label: "You're angry," "You're upset," "You're sad," and so on. Consequently, we do not grow up to be very competent at describing how we feel.

(3) Non-verbal signals are less easily controlled and therefore are more likely to convey genuine information. We can choose our words to project a certain emotional state, but our non-verbal behaviour may portray what we honestly feel.

(4) A second communication channel is valuable, especially when it can be used to regulate the exchange of information being conducted in the first channel.

Both non-verbal and verbal signals are involved in virtually any communication. Research suggests that often the total impact of a message is determined in only a small way by *what* is said; *how* it is said is more important and, as we have noted, facial expressions are often more important still, especially when emotion is involved. Perhaps this explains why foreign language films dubbed into English often seem rather "flat": the message communicated by the dubbing may not correspond to the message conveyed by the actors' faces (Vander Zanden, 1977). Normally, of course, we expect considerable consistency between verbal and non-verbal elements of communication. If someone is smiling when discussing his bad fortune, or if someone appears depressed while talking about how happy she feels, we become confused or start to worry about the speaker's emotional condition.

Spoken communications are themselves actually double-coded, in the sense that meaning is conferred both by the grammar and by the non-verbal structure imposed by prosodic elements (Fonagy, 1971). As a result, when spoken words are transcribed into print, punctuation must be added to convey the intended meaning but even then, some of the message may be lost (Argyle, 1975). People are capable of separating the two communications and interpreting each one individually when the two message elements are inconsistent. For example, in one study (Solomon and Yaeger, 1969), students listened to a teacher talking about a student's work. When the emotion communicated prosodically was at odds with the verbal content of the message, the students tended to interpret the verbal communication as indicative of how the teacher felt about the student's work, and the prosodic information as expressing how the teacher felt about the student.

Conversation control One area in which non-verbal and verbal communication clearly complement each other is in *conversation control*. While words make up the content of our conversation, non-verbal signals regulate the form of the conversation. Without such regulation — using rules which we have all learned but would have difficulty writing down — conversations would turn into verbal traffic jams. If we were going to explain the signals people use to indicate who is going to talk during a conversation, it would be a difficult task because the signals are subtle and not explicit. Yet the signals *are* there: intuitively, we seem to know when to speak and when to listen and we don't require a chairperson to monitor the flow of conversation. In every linguistic group, there are norms which cover not only who speaks next, but virtually every aspect of the verbal exchange from beginning to end. Other norms exist as well. For example, North Americans expect other people to respond to their statements right away, while in some cultures, people are taught to leave a gap between responses. As a result, North Americans tend to be uncomfortable if there are periods of silence during a conversation. On the other hand, people in cultures for whom scattered silences are normal may perceive North Americans as overly talkative, even thoughtless or disrespectful.

Some of the turn-yielding signals we use to indicate that we are ready to yield our turn are described in Box 11-2. What would happen if someone were to give one or more of these signals but instead of yielding, continued to speak? Considerable confusion would be created and would probably lead to constant interruption of the speaker by the listener, who would incorrectly assume that it was now time to speak (see Box 11-3 for an example).

B·O·X 1 1 - 2

TURN YIELDING SIGNALS

Argyle (1975) has described a number of signals people use to indicate that they are ending their utterance and giving the opportunity to the listener to respond:
(1) Coming to the end of a sentence.
(2) Prolonged intonation, for example, raising or lowering the voice as in "Do you like *this*?"
(3) Paralinguistic drawl — the final syllable is spoken in a slow, drawn-out fashion: "And when I came ho-m-m-me."
(4) Body motion — if hand gesturing was being employed, it now ceases; if the speaker's hands have appeared tense, they now relax. The speaker's eyes tend to open wider with the last note of a question, to indicate that the listener can begin to answer; if a question is being asked, the speaker tends to lift his or her head on the final syllable. In television interviews, it has been observed that people tend to look directly at the interviewer only when ready to finish making a point.
(5) Verbal cues, such as the end of phrases: "I was going to go to the movies tonight, but, uh . . . ."

We learn such signals without formal training and without awareness.

BREAKDOWN IN CONVERSATION CONTROL

British Prime Minister Margaret Thatcher, although capable of handling herself well in debate, has often been interrupted during television interviews. Careful analysis of her non-verbal behaviour during interviews has shown why this is so (Beattie, Cutler and Pearson, 1982). A videotape of one of her interviews was obtained, and different aspects of the interviews were presented to four groups of subjects. One group only listened to the audio portion of the interview; another group saw only the video portion with no audio; a third group both watched and listened to the interview; and the fourth group was only given a transcript to read. The subjects were then asked to identify situations in which she seemed to be yielding her turn in the conversation.

Those who only read the transcript were unable to identify any points in the interview when she seemed to be yielding her turn, but the other three groups were often mistaken in thinking that she had finished a point and yielded to the interviewer, even when she had not. Thatcher was unwittingly sending turn-yielding signals which invited interruption, even though she was not ready to be interrupted: She would pause at the wrong time, she would let her voice drop quickly from time to time, and she would look directly at the interviewer in the midst of her responses.

We are often unaware of the importance of non-verbal cues until, as in this case, problems arise in verbal communication.

Sometimes we try to butt in while someone else is speaking. In this case, the speaker who wants to continue puts out *attempt-suppressing* signals: the voice maintains the same pitch, the head remains straight, the eyes remain unchanged, the hands maintain the same gesture, the speaker may speak slightly louder or faster and may keep a hand in mid-gesture at the end of sentences (Argyle, 1975).

On the other hand, the listener regularly signals to the speaker that he or she is still listening, and not seeking to interrupt. This is done by means of what is called *back-channel communication*: the listener nods from time to time, or says "mm-hmm" or "OK." In Japan, back-channel communication on the telephone occurs at a higher rate than in Canada. Thus a Japanese person talking to a Canadian by telephone may frequently ask, "Are you still there?" because the Canadian emits back-channel signals at too slow a pace for the speaker.

How do we signal that we wish to terminate a conversation? When speaking face-

When signalling that we wish to terminate a conversation, we tend to move slightly away and to look away.

to-face, we tend to move slightly away and to look away. (Looking at our watch is also a powerful signal!) When using the telephone, we may allow for a longer interval before responding to the speaker who has stopped speaking.

In summary, facial expression, eye contact, gestures, posture, proximity, and paralanguage all serve as channels of non-verbal communication. Such communication is often a more accurate guide to an individual's feelings than is language, which is more easily bent to the expression of what an individual *wants* to communicate. Moreover, non-verbal communication is of critical importance in regulating the flow of information in verbal exchanges.

VERBAL COMMUNICATION

It is thought that language ability evolved in primitive humans because of the survival value conferred by the ability to communicate in a precise way. While non-verbal behaviour is often a better guide to the speaker's feelings and intentions, it does not go very far in helping two people coordinate their attempts to build a bridge or defend a village. This section begins with a discussion of how language has evolved and how its structure has developed over time.

The structure of language

All spoken language (as opposed to sign language) is based on a *phonetic* system in which short, meaningless sounds called "phonemes" are combined into units of meaning called "morphemes." By using a relatively small number of these sounds (up to 45, depending on the language) and by combining them two, three, or more at a time, different human languages have generated as many as 100 000 morphemes (Argyle, 1969). It was quite a step for our ancestors to go from speech to writing, and initially a different symbol was used for each word (e.g., a hieroglyphic). Such a system necessitated a very large number of symbols. (Indeed, the Chinese evolved a set of 10 000 characters, each one representing a different syllable in the language. These characters are still in use today, a situation which has posed problems with regard to literacy — in order to read a newspaper, it is necessary to know at least several thousand characters.) In most languages, a few letters reflecting the spoken phonetic code rather than syllables or words eventually came to be used in place of thousands of symbols.

Is language a uniquely human ability?

Humans have no doubt always wondered about whether animals "talk" to each other, and whether it is possible to learn to talk their language, if they have one, or teach them to use ours. Some researchers have even raised chimpanzees as part of their families in order to see whether they would acquire speech as children do. In one case (Kellogg and Kellogg, 1933) researchers raised an infant female chimp named Gua with their infant son. At the age of 16 months, Gua could understand about 100 different words, but could not speak any of them. In another case, a female chimp, Viki, was raised from infancy in the home of the researchers (Hayes and Hayes, 1952) and she actually learned to be able to whisper, or at least mouth, four words including "mama" and "papa" when food was used as a reinforcement, but she did so only with great difficulty.

Vocalization, however, is only one aspect of language. After all, deaf people learn to read and write and use sign language to communicate. Perhaps if apes were given the kind of linguistic training that is given to deaf people, they would be able to master language. This was the approach that Gardner and Gardner (1971) took. They decided to try to teach American Sign Language (the most common sign language used by deaf people in North America) to Washoe, a young female chimpanzee. To avoid the possible negative effects of being raised in a cage, Washoe was housed in a special house-trailer which was very much like a normal human home, complete with bathroom, kitchen, and bedroom. The Gardeners spent a great deal of time with Washoe and they minimized the use of speech, even communicating with each other by sign language. Through both direct imitation and through instrumental conditioning, Washoe was apparently forming phrases at the age of 24 months, and by the age of 36 months, could use a set of 245 combinations of three or more signs and had a vocabulary of 85 words. Even more impressive was her apparent ability to apply signs to novel stimuli, for example, applying "hat" to types of hats that she had never seen before.

Similarly, Koko, a seven-year-old gorilla, was apparently taught to communicate using the same technique that the Gardners used with Washoe (Patterson, 1978). After 36 months of training, Koko was reliably using 184 signs, and by the age of six-and-a-half, the gorilla had a regular working vocabulary of 375 signs but could reliably use a total of 645 different signs. Another female chimpanzee, Sarah, was taught to "read" using pieces of plastic in various colours and shapes. Each different colour-shape combination represented one word. Sarah developed a vocabulary of 130 items which she could apparently use with 75–80 percent reliability (Premack and Premack, 1972).

While some of the accounts in the popular media seem to suggest that as a result of these studies, we now know how to "talk with the animals," there is still controversy over just what these studies have shown about the language ability of chimpanzees and apes. Some critics argue that what the apes have produced is not really language, that in fact they are being conditioned to "speak" in much the same way that Clever Hans did at the turn of the century (Sebeok and Rosenthal, 1981).

Human language involves much more than just being able to assign names to things. For example, all human languages possess a hierarchical structure in which groups of words bear some special relationship to each other (Limber, 1977). The sentence "The person standing near the window with a crack in it was bitten by the dog" has a hierarchical arrangement in which the constituents, such as the "person standing near the window with a crack in it," can be broken down into even smaller groupings, such as "the window with a crack in it," which also exhibit specific structure. To try to say that human-like language is being produced when an animal can combine words and even generalize them to new instances is to underestimate the complexity of any human language. While young apes such as Washoe and Sarah seem capable of mastering as many words as young children are capable of mastering, the language structure of any normal three-year-old child has far surpassed even the most precocious ape (Limber, 1977), for practically every child has begun to use hierarchically-structured sentences by the end of the third year. Hence, we must treat the claims made for Washoe, Sarah, and others with extreme caution.

The acquisition of language

How is language *acquired*? How does a preschool child learn not only names for objects and actions, but how to combine words into hierarchically structured, grammatical sentences without formal instruction? This question generated a famous controversy between behaviourist B.F. Skinner and linguist Noam Chomsky. Skinner (1957) argued that speech behaviour is acquired through the same mechanism of reinforcement as other behaviour. Through classical conditioning, a child learns the names of objects by hearing the sound and seeing or feeling the object at the same time. However, because speech is a motor response, it is better understood in this view in terms of operant conditioning: behaviour is produced and then reinforced. However, this explanation says nothing about either the complex rules of grammar that a child acquires nor about the *meaning* of the words used.

According to Chomsky (1975), all human languages share fundamentally the same organization, or what he calls "linguistic universals." Since the young child receives very little information about the language as a result of listening to or interacting with older people, Chomsky argues, it is inconceivable that the child can discover and learn the basic structure needed both to make sense of language and to generate novel but understandable combinations of words. (In fact, bilingual children must acquire two sets of rules at the same time, all without formal instruction.) Yet, at an age when the child is not very capable of other kinds of complex intellectual achievement, the child manages to acquire grammar — a complex set of rules which very few adults are capable of even describing, despite using them all the time. The young child will, for instance, extend the grammatical "rules" to new situations in which they do not properly apply, e.g., saying "I goed to school this morning," using "goed" instead of "went" as the past tense of "go." Thus Chomsky believes that without innate guidelines, the child would arrive at various incorrect or incomplete grammars which might serve a purpose for a time but would prove inadequate later on. He argues that there must be some kind of innate predisposition to develop grammatical rules.

Learning theorists, however, have challenged Chomsky's argument that learning theory cannot account for language acquisition. They argue that the learning that occurs is much more than simple imitation or the result of direct reinforcement of specific utterances. Modelling is the process by which language is learned, according to this view (Bandura, 1977). Learning theorists also charge that similarities across languages need not be explained in terms of an "innate" skill, for every language uses nouns and verbs, just as all cultures sooner or later invent hammers and wheels. After all, all humans experience common environmental features involving agents, actions, and objects. Thus it should not be surprising that similar grammatical features develop, just as common experience should be expected to lead to the development of hammers and wheels.

The Piagetian school also challenges Chomsky's ideas about highly specific innate capacities, and argues that a child's acquisition of language "rules" is of a highly *general* order (Inhelder, 1978) and is linked to general cognitive development.

Since children learn language without formal instruction, it may be that the capacity to *learn* language is a specific ability which has evolved as part of our biological heritage (Limber, 1977). By contrast, apes are far more adept at learning visual-manual communication than they are the audio-vocal communication typical of humans. This fact in itself suggests inherent differences in the structure of the two brains.

Language and thought

While language is important for communicating with others, it is equally important in our personal cognitive functioning, for we constantly use language as a tool for cognitive tasks. It provides a means for "self-communication" in that we can reason, we can efficiently code complex behaviours in terms of words, we can rehearse behaviours by going over a verbal representation of the steps in a behaviour chain, and we can classify objects and feelings on the basis of words. In Piaget's (1966) view, language is a necessary condition (although not by itself sufficient) for the development of logical thought: language and thought are each necessarily dependent on the other, yet both depend on general intelligence which precedes language and is independent of it.

In the context of the interplay between language and thought, a question that has long tantalized psychologists and philosophers alike is this: Does the language we speak influence the way we perceive the world? If we spoke another language would we interpret the world differently? Does a particular language affect the process of thought so that, for instance, Aristotle's logic might have been very different had he been a Mexican rather than a Greek (Carroll, 1964)? Does a person whose language has only one word for "red" not notice visually the difference between "fuchsia" and "blood red"?

Linguistic relativity   The idea that our perception of the world has been influenced by the language we have learned is referred to as the *linguistic relativity hypothesis* (Whorf, 1956). For example, you will recall that in Chapter 3 it was pointed out that most of the research and theorizing on social cognition has been conducted in Western countries, and that we cannot be sure the results of such research are applicable to the cognitive processes of people in other cultures. Whorf went even further and proposed that language actually *determines* how we think about the world. For example, if a language provides a great many words which refer to slight variations in objects or conditions, then the language learner is forced to discriminate to an extent that persons of other languages do not. For example, the Inuit have many different words corresponding to different types of snow which non-Inuit people may not even be able to differentiate. However, we could argue that the need to distinguish different kinds of snow led to the creation of a variety of words in the language, and that if an English speaker needed to, he or she could use hyphenated words or invent new words to make the same distinctions. Skiers can also identify many types of snow.

More important, however, is Whorf's argument that our basic way of thinking is dependent on the language we have acquired. This might suggest, for example, that since the Hindi language does not have different words to indicate the past, present and future tense of a verb, Hindi-speaking people may be less concerned with time than speakers of European languages.

Cultural similarities in language   Although the linguistic relativity hypothesis garnered considerable interest in the 1950s and 1960s, by the 1970s, interest had declined as more attention was directed to cultural similarities, rather than differences, in language (Hoffman, Lau and Johnson, 1986). However, there has been renewed interest in the hypothesis in recent years. There are two general ways in which language influences our thought processes (Bloom, 1981). First, it has an effect on our classification system. For example, a child will learn to distinguish which animals do and which do not belong to the category "dog," not because there is a tremendous similarity among all dogs (for there is not) but rather, because the category exists and is referred to. The existence and use of the word "dog," then, is forced upon every member of the linguistic group, whether it is useful or not. Secondly, again according to Bloom (1981), those classifications which bear verbal labels, such as "dog," are more easily handled by our thought processes than are classifications which lack verbal labels.

However, if classification into categories is influenced by language, it should follow that since there are differences in the ways that various languages define such categories, this must influence the way the speaker categorizes things in general. For example, no language has names for all possible constellations of human traits, and no language is absolutely comparable to another in this regard (Hoffman, Lau and Johnson, 1986). While we cannot summarize in a single English expression a personality which is characterized by the adjectives "worldly," "experienced," "socially skillful," "devoted to his or her family," and "somewhat reserved," these traits are captured in a single Chinese term. Similarly, to say that a particular man is the "strong, silent type" implies much more than that the man has strength and does not talk much. You might also assume that he is reliable, reflective, and unflappable. In other words, the phrase "strong, silent type" evokes a schema which includes a number of characteristics not included in the phrase itself.

It should follow that a speaker of one language may more easily code verbally a constellation of traits for which a term already exists (i.e., there is a schema) than could a speaker of a language lacking a summarizing term for the collection of traits. However, once that coding is made, the person's recall and impression of the individual would most likely include all or most elements of the schema, whether or not they were present when the verbal classification was made. Thus you may code a man who is quiet, husky, and reserved as being the strong, silent type, even if he is a bit on the nervous side; later, you may recall the individual as being a calm person because calmness goes with the schema.

To examine this hypothesis, Hoffman, Lau and Johnson (1986) had subjects who were bilingual in Chinese and English each read four personality descriptions, two of which portrayed personalities which could be readily described by a word or phrase in Chinese, but not in English, and two which could also be readily described, but only in English. Half of the subjects were asked to make as much effort as possible to think and respond in Chinese, and the descriptions they received were in Chinese. The remaining subjects were asked to think and respond in English and received English language descriptions.

The subjects were instructed to read the four descriptions as often as they wished, until they felt that they had formed a strong impression of the four people being described and could remember their names. Then, five days later, they were interviewed about the four personalities and were also asked to assess the degree to which a number of new adjectives applied to each of them. As hypothesized, it was found that when the personality description evoked a schema in the language in which the subject was working, both the subject's memory and impressions were influenced significantly by that schema. Both recall and inferences about the individual, as reflected in their assessment of the applicability of new traits, reflected the introduction of other elements from the schema which did not appear in the original description.

Thus the availability of labelled categories (the "lexicon" of a language) influences the way in which people categorize and subsequently recall information. The above results are consistent with a watered-down version of the Whorfian hypothesis: certain ways of thinking are made easier or more difficult in a given language. However, it does not offer support for the original Whorfian view that a given language makes certain ways of thinking either compulsory or impossible (Hoffman, Lau and Johnson, 1986). Therefore, while language does influence thought and action to a degree, there is still no strong evidence that it can *determine* our cognitions in the way Whorf has suggested.

Linguistic relativity aside, how important is language for cognitive functioning? Could we "think" and solve problems if we didn't have language to help us? Of course, we could do simple kinds of things. We do not need language to pick up a sandwich from the table when we are hungry, but language becomes vitally important when more complex tasks are involved. You will recall that Piaget viewed language development and cognitive development as inextricably linked. Consider the example of deaf children: although they do not differ much from normal children in their cognitive development until approximately six, after that they are slower than normal children who are able to use language to help them carry out complex cognitive tasks, unless given special training.

We "think" using language. Try to keep your mind blank for a few moments. It is extremely difficult to prevent words from popping into mind. What would happen if we did *not* learn to use language in our cognitive tasks? Presumably, we would be like the deaf children described above. In fact, some disadvantaged groups may suffer

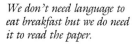

We don't need language to eat breakfast but we do need it to read the paper.

in school because of a failure to properly employ language "internally." For example, one study compared eight-year-old Indian and middle class White children in Alberta in terms of their ability to learn a task which involved choosing one of a stimulus pair in order to earn candies (Knowles and Boersma, 1971). For each pair of different stimuli presented, some common rule (such as "the smaller of the two" or "the darker of the two") governed which stimulus, if chosen, would be followed by rein-forcement. Subsequently, the rule was simply reversed. The Indian children were less successful than the middle class Whites in learning the reversal shift. Yet, in another condition in which some Indian children were *required* to verbalize (e.g., I want you to tell me which picture you are going to choose before you push the stick"), they learned the initial discrimination and made the reversal shift significantly more often than did the other Indian children in the non-verbal condition. The authors suggest that, barring the development of an educational system based on traditional Native skills and experience, Native students may be handicapped to the extent they are slower to use verbal mediation in problem solving. This characteristic affects their ability even within the scope of problem solving which does not involve linguistic comprehension or expression. A crucial ability of applying *words* to *non-verbal* tasks is something that most children acquire even before school age.

LANGUAGE AND GENDER

It is language which allows a social group to pass its knowledge, beliefs, and values from generation to generation. The words of Plato, Shakespeare, Hobbes, or Russell can inspire each new generation as much as they did when they were first uttered. Without language, modern culture as we know it could never have developed. Not only does language serve as a vehicle for transmission of ideas, but the form that language takes can itself reflect certain beliefs and values.

An important aspect of the transmission of values through language is the way that the English language has both reflected and reinforced the historical cultural view of masculine superiority and male domination (Smith, 1985). Until recently, we would say "his" instead of "his or hers," and we would speak of "mankind," "workmen's compensation boards," and so forth, as though women are not all that important. The great majority of agent nouns (e.g., author, professor, doctor, minister) evoke the image of a man more readily than a woman, while the addition of a diminutive suffix to obtain words such as "authoress" may reflect or lead to a diminution of the importance of the role. The usual order of words in which the male referent occurs first — husband and wife, son and daughter, host and hostess — also may imply relative importance. Indeed, our use of language has almost implied ownership of females by males: we speak of a woman whose husband died as "Bill's widow," but are less likely to describe Bill, should his wife predecease him, as "Eleanor's widower" (Smith, 1985). The Canadian Psychological Association and the American Psychological Asso-ciation now both insist on non-sexist language in any manuscripts submitted to their journals. This policy is becoming more common in other areas of Canadian society as a result of growing concern about human rights.

As society changes, so does language. In the case of sexist language, however, it is hoped by those who fight to eliminate it that changing women's position within the language will help change the image and position of women in society.

LANGUAGE AND SOCIAL INTERACTION

We have seen that language is a central feature in human social interaction and that verbal utterances are behaviours which are subject to reinforcement by the reactions of others, just as other behaviours are. According to "speech act theory" (Searle, 1969, 1975), a spoken sentence is more than just a set of symbols linked together; it is a collection of acts as well. By that we mean that there is not always a close correspondence between what is said and what the speaker wants to accomplish by saying it. (Recall how the expression "You pig" can have several different meanings depending on how it is said.) Speech act theory distinguishes between *direct* speech acts, in which the meaning of the sentence is consistent with the speaker's meaning, and *indirect* speech acts, which are lacking in consistency. The choice of direct or indirect speech acts is often influenced by perceived equality or difference in status between speaker and listener, and by the need to maintain "face" (a good public image), among other things.

Through the use of indirect acts, we can avoid direct challenges to authority or to "high-status" individuals which might cause difficulty. Suppose you are a student in conversation with a professor in a classroom. Should you wish to communicate your negative reaction to his or her pronouncements, you would probably choose to do so by means of indirect speech acts. You might say, "I am not quite sure if I follow you. I do not understand how, if the rise of capitalism is related to the rise of Protestantism, . . . " and so on. However, if you were the professor wishing to express an identical reaction to a student's pronouncement about Protestantism and the rise of capitalism, you might well use a direct speech act: "That explanation is untenable in that it does not accommodate the fact that . . . ." Status difference has a strong influence on the kinds of speech acts which are performed.

Indirect speech acts can usually spare any loss of face which might otherwise occur when dealing with threatening material (Holtgraves, 1986). For example, if Martha wears a dress to work which she worries may be viewed in a negative way by her co-workers, instead of asking, "Do you like my new dress?" she might say, "Have you noticed my new dress?" Instead of responding that the dress is ugly, which would be a threat to Martha's self-esteem, a co-worker could respond by saying, "Well, it certainly is different. Where did you get it?" Not only has face been spared by the indirect response, but the negative opinion has also been conveyed. Research has demonstrated that indirect speech acts are indeed more likely to be summoned than direct ones in face-threatening situations (e.g., Holtgraves, 1986).

Every verbal expression demands some degree of response, and the degree to which a response is required is actually encoded in the utterance itself (Holtgraves, 1986). When the co-worker asked Martha where she had bought her dress, there was a demand for a response to that question, but a clear indication that no response was required to the comment that the dress was "different." Thus Martha was not required to explore just exactly what that descriptor meant. By means of an indirect speech act, the co-worker conveyed that the dress was not worthy of praise, but also avoided any confrontation or loss of face for Martha. In our daily interactions with others, we continually try to help people save face, just as we strive to maintain our own self-esteem and face.

That the social interaction between two individuals, as well as considerations of their status, influences the choice of speech acts is all the more interesting if we realize that perception of status differences, especially in the absence of other information, is itself a consequence of speech style. Differences in speech style, accent, dialect, or mother tongue are used as markers of social status, as guidelines for forming impressions of others and for defining group boundaries. This subject is discussed next.

Speech style

Since most of our social interaction involves language, it is not surprising that our perception and evaluation of people is strongly influenced not just by what people say but also by the way they say it. By listening to a person talk, we can estimate his or her social class, amount of education and even, in some cases, the geographic locale of the person's growing years (Giles and Powesland, 1975). (There even are differences in the ways males and females use language; see Box 11-4). In Great Britain, some linguists can accurately determine the region of a person's origin by listening to his or her speech. (Recall the words from *My Fair Lady*: "An Englishman's way of speaking absolutely classifies him. The moment he talks he makes some other Englishmen despise him.") In the United States, distinctions are also possible: for example, the Brooklyn accent would never be confused with the upper class Boston accent or the Texas drawl!

Canadian English is a blend of American and British English. Geography and accent are much less related in Canada than in the United States or Europe, but even here, there are some distinctive regional variations. A Francophone from Québec City possesses an accent which is different from that of Montreal Francophones, for example (Vinay, Daviault and Alexander, 1962). Anglophones across the country speak in a more or less homogeneous way (Vinay *et al.*, 1962) but Newfoundland and Ottawa Valley accents are indicative of some regional variation. (Newfoundland even has some vocabulary of its own. The *Dictionary of Newfoundland English* (Story, Kirwin and Widdowson, 1982) lists many unique words and expressions, such as "figgy tit" — raisins wrapped in a thin cloth and given to older babies to suck — and "screedless," which means without a stitch of clothing.)

Regional variations aside, we often judge people by their command of their language. Speech style is so important socially that we make inferences about not only people's social class, ethnicity, or education on that basis, but even about their personality and intelligence. It is somewhat amazing that considering the thousands and thousands of words that we must learn, we often are surprised or even disappointed when educated persons mispronounce a word. It is enough to influence our evaluation of their intellect and "breeding"; yet we accept and even expect mispronunciation from people having little education, and it might strike us as odd if we heard a mechanic or a bus driver using "big" words. It is vocabulary more than grammar which is important in this context, for differences in the complexity of vocabulary — not differences in the complexity of the grammar — used by an individual have been found to affect the degree to which that person is perceived as competent (Bradac *et al.*, 1977).

The speech styles of students have been found to affect teachers' judgments of their intelligence as much or more than actual samples of their school work (Seligman, Tucker and Lambert, 1972). There is also evidence that speech style can even lead to bias in the marks assigned by a teacher to a student (Frender and Lambert, 1972).

B · O · X   1 1 - 4

DO MEN AND WOMEN TALK DIFFERENTLY?

Most people believe that men and women have typical and distinctive styles of speaking (Haas, 1979). Women are said to be more polite, more emotional, more positive and supportive in how they evaluate people, more tentative (It's cold, *isn't it?*"), less assertive, and more likely to talk about home and family. On the other hand, men are believed to use more slang and profanity, to argue, criticize, lecture and command more, and to be more likely to talk about business, politics, and sports. In addition, women are said to be *more* talkative than men.

Are these simply unflattering sex-role stereotypes? The research evidence suggests that there is some reality in this characterization. Men tend to use more "non-standard" forms of speech, such as new terminology (often technical), slang, profanity, and puns. Men *are* more likely to talk about sports, business, and politics, and women *are* more likely to talk about family and home. Men are more likely to use words and expressions about time, space and quantity, and about hostility and destructiveness, while women refer more to emotional states. Men tend to be more direct and assertive in making requests. On the other hand, while little girls tend to talk more than little boys, adult women tend to talk less, particularly in the presence of the opposite sex.

We must be cautious in interpreting this research, however. Almost all of it was conducted in the U.S.A. and may not apply to other societies. Some of the studies were done with children, and the findings

may not be applicable to other stages of life. Finally, much of the research was conducted years ago, some of it in the 1920s, and the findings may not be true today. Social norms change, and we might expect that men express feelings and women use profanity more frequently now than in the past.

Nonetheless, it is reasonable to expect that there are still gender differences in speech. It must be understood that while there are differences in the average or typical pattern, there are wide variations within each sex in how men and women speak. There are no discernible patterns of speaking which apply exclusively to one gender. The differences which exist reflect differences in actual experience as well as stereotypes. As sex-role stereotypes change, as more women have more involvement with finances and men with child rearing, these patterns can be expected to change.

Both sexes may speak differently depending on the sex of the listener, however. Subjects in one study (Hall and Braunwald, 1981) listened to audio clips of conversations taken from American television talk shows which had been electronically filtered to make it impossible to tell whether a man or a woman was speaking. When subjects were told that the person to whom the conversation was directed was a man, the speakers were rated as more dominant, business-like, condescending and unpleasant than when the listener was described as a woman.

In Great Britain, the opportunity for socioeconomic advancement can be seriously affected by accent, and educated people (for example, those with Cockney accents) sometimes take elocution lessons to "correct" their speech style. Even in the United States, it has been found that speech is an important source of information about social status: One study reported a strong correlation between a listener's judgment of a speaker's social status and the speaker's actual social status (see Giles and Powesland, 1975). The French are perhaps even more particular in this regard, with native Parisians generally viewing their speech style as superior to all others.

Standard and non-standard speech

Not all varieties of a particular language are treated as equal. Some speech styles are viewed as being "vulgar" or "low class" by those who speak in a more "refined" manner. How is it that one speech style comes to be the "standard" or prestige form against which others are judged? How is it, for example, that Parisian French is taken to be the paragon of that language?

Following the French Revolution in 1794, the Parisian bourgeoisie acted to impose unilingualism throughout France. Language laws were passed to enforce the linguistic and economic unity of France. The use of languages such as Breton in Brittany and Provençal in southern France was banned, and the French bourgeoisie chose their own "Ile de France" variety of French as the national "standard" of spoken French (Bourhis, 1982). (A more charitable view has been expressed that the revolutionary leaders wanted to ensure that all citizens of France would have the opportunity to rise to the top of society by learning the speech style of those who ruled the country and dominated the universities (Pagès, 1986.) All other varieties of French were vigorously excluded so that the use of non-standard accents and dialects of regional French was banned in schools. To this day, the "Ile de France" variety of French is considered the "standard" or "international" style of the French language (Bourhis, 1982).

The French-speaking population of Québec was not affected by the imposition of the Ile de France variety of French because for 200 years following the defeat of Montcalm's army on the Plains of Abraham in 1760, Québec was virtually cut off from France. During that time, Québec French and Ile de France French evolved quite independently. (It is worth noting that some other Francophone groups in Canada, for example, the Franco-Manitobans, trace their ancestry to *post*-Revolutionary France. It is at least possible that there are distinctive cultural differences between them and the Québécois as a result.) It is noteworthy that even today, the decision by the Parisian bourgeoisie to impose their speech style upon others still leads some people, both Anglophone and Francophone, to denigrate Québec French as "inferior." This judgment is without a good basis, as we shall see.

Is standard speech more aesthetically pleasing?   Could it be that a particular style of a language is accepted as the standard form because it is actually aesthetically more pleasing than other varieties of that language? Or do "standard" styles emerge because these are the styles of speech adopted by the most prestigious social group in the society who, by virtue of status, establish their own style as the "standard"? If Cockney English or Acadian French sounds less pleasant to some than Oxford English or Parisian French, is it because they *actually* are less pleasant? Or is it because the listener is reacting to the imposition of a particular accent as the prestige norm? These two possibilities were explored in a study conducted by Giles, Bourhis and Davies (1977), who articulated them in the form of two hypotheses:

(1) *The "inherent value" hypothesis.* The standard dialect became the prestige form of the language because it evolved as the aesthetically ideal form of that language.

(2) *The "imposed norm" hypothesis.* Standard and non-standard dialects are equally aesthetically pleasing, but the non-standard form is viewed negatively because of social norms which are biased against it.

To test these two hypotheses, researchers had Welsh students who knew no French listen to tape recordings of the same text voiced by the same person in three different French accents: European ("standard") French, educated Canadian French, and working-class Canadian French. Subjects then rated the speech in terms of pleasantness and aesthetic appeal and also rated the speaker in terms of status, intelligence, likeability, ambition, and toughness. While previous studies carried out in Québec had shown these French accents to be perceived as varying widely from each other on each of the ratings by Francophone listeners (d'Anglejan and Tucker, 1973), no significant differences were noted by the Welsh subjects, supporting the imposed norm hypothesis. The authors went on to suggest that people learning a second language usually learn the prestige form, and thus tend to view other forms as substandard. The imposed-norm hypothesis received further validation in a similar study in which British undergraduates who knew no Greek were exposed to both Cretan and the more prestigious Athenian dialects; again, they were unable to pick out the prestige form of the language (Giles, Bourhis, Trudgill and Lewis, 1974).

The prestige associated with the *arbitrarily* chosen standard dialect is so strong that studies conducted in the early 1970s showed French-speaking Québecois, both workers and students, to have strong preference for European French over their own Québec French (d'Anglejan and Tucker, 1973). Furthermore, in the 1960s, French-speaking Québec students rated a person speaking English more favourably than the same person speaking standard French, indicating a devaluation of French speakers by Francophones (Lambert, Frankel and Tucker, 1966). However, in 1970, a similar study found that standard French had replaced English in terms of highest status ratings (Rémillard, 1970). Nonetheless, Québec French came in third in both studies! In the future, Québec French may be viewed more positively by Québécois and others, given the renewed pride in Québécois culture which has been developing.

Language and group identity

Groups are differentiated by — among other characteristics — speech style, dialect, and even language. In-group speech can serve as a symbol of ethnic identity or cultural solidarity; language is often the major embodiment of this ethnicity (Bourhis, 1979). Language can be used to remind the group of its cultural heritage, transmit group feeling, exclude members of out-groups, and emphasize and signal in-group feelings under conditions of ethnic threat. In Canada, language of origin has served as the central force to unite immigrants into ethnic groups. Yet groups such as the Germans, Italians, and Ukrainians are no longer being replenished by large scale immigration and are not likely to survive as distinct linguistic entities, but will gradually be swallowed up by the process of assimilation (Berry, Kalin and Taylor, 1977). Without a unique language, ethnic survival is very difficult. Such concerns have led to efforts both to create or revive languages in order to foster group identity, and to invent a common language for all peoples in order to reduce the effects of group identification and foster world peace and understanding (see Box 11-5).

Interpersonal accommodation theory   Within one language, or even one dialect, there are different speech styles ("social registers") which people use for varying reasons (see Box 11-6). Why do people shift their speech styles in some instances and not in others? Interpersonal accommodation theory (Giles, Taylor and Bourhis, 1973) pro-

B·O·X 11-5

INVENTING LANGUAGE

Is it possible to implant a language in a society, or must language evolve as a society evolves? There have been attempts both to invent languages out of whole cloth and to revive and extend languages which have fallen into disuse. An example of an invented language is *esperanto*; Hebrew is an example of a revived language. Let us consider each of these.

Esperanto

During the middle ages, Latin was an international language in Europe, spoken by all educated people. French was not so long ago the international language of diplomacy. English is becoming the technical language of the electronic age. Yet, Latin, French, and English are all much too complicated to be easily mastered by most people.

Several hundred artificial languages have been constructed during the last three centuries in an attempt to provide an easy-to-learn language which could facilitate intergroup communication and understanding and reduce conflict. All of these have failed with the exception of one invented by Dr. Ludwig Zamenhof of Poland in 1887. He called his language *esperanto* (meaning the "hoping one," a pseudonym that he often employed).

Esperanto is based on common words from various European languages, but unlike a natural language, it is free of complicated grammatical rules and irregularities. There are only sixteen rules of grammar and there are no exceptions to them. Verbs have only one form for each tense, all nouns end in "o," all adjectives in "a," and all adverbs in "e." Because of its simplicity, people are able to learn the language relatively easily and quickly.

For a while, esperanto seemed destined to become a true international language. It has been used at some international conferences and meetings. However, the language has never really "caught on," but

neither has it died out. Societies for its promulgation continue to exist in a number of countries and it is taught as an elective in some Russian and Chinese universities. A score or more radio stations in various parts of the world (including Austria, Italy, Poland, and China) carry some programs in esperanto; the Bible, the Koran, and some of Shakespeare's works have been translated into the language as well.

Yet, there is a kind of vicious circle which limits its appeal: because so few people speak it (estimates vary between 1 million and 10 million), there is little incentive to learn it. But without an incentive to learn it, the number who speak it will not increase. Esperanto societies lobby for international governmental support but little has been forthcoming.

Modern Hebrew

While esperanto languishes, modern Hebrew demonstrates that a language can be created (or at least revived and extended) when it serves some important function, in this case, group identity.

The Academy of the Hebrew Language was founded by the Israeli Government in 1953 to foster the growth and development of the Hebrew language. The Academy grew out of the efforts of one man, Eliezer Ben-Yehuda, to revive the language which like Latin was all but "dead," being used only in religious ceremonies or by classical scholars. At a time when no one outside the world of scholars was familiar with Hebrew, Ben-Yehuda insisted that his family master the language and use it exclusively at home. He established a Hebrew newspaper, and used it to disseminate many new words of his own invention. He ran into considerable opposition from religious scholars who accused him of profanity as he tried to transform a sacred language into a language of everyday life.

When translating modern concepts into Hebrew,

the Academy first studies classical writings in the attempt to find an existing word which will meet the need. Often, however it is necessary to invent words; this the Academy does with an eye on the past. The Israeli Air Force wanted a Hebrew word for "helicopter"; the Academy invented the word *masok* which comes from the Biblical root *nasak*, which means "to go straight up."

While the English language comprises over half a million words, there are only 7238 different words in the Bible, and there were only about 6500 words in medieval Hebrew. Because of the efforts of Ben-Yehuda and those who followed in his footsteps, modern Hebrew is growing rapidly, both in usage and in the extent of its vocabulary, which currently includes more than 70 000 words.

B · O · X   1 1 - 6

SOCIAL REGISTERS

We all use various "registers" of speaking, depending on whom we are talking to and in what context. Baby talk ("BT") is one register that we are all familiar with. By BT, we are referring not to the talking done by babies, but to the talking by adults to babies. It is defined as the speech that adults address to two to five-year-olds, and it is recognizable by its high pitch and exaggerated intonations (Caporael, Lukaszewski and Culbertson, 1983). Baby talk appears to be a feature of all languages (Ferguson, 1977).

Perhaps of more interest to the social psychologist is what is called "secondary" baby talk, or the use of the BT register in contexts other than talking to babies. Most of us would resent being spoken to in such a manner, for we would find it belittling. However, such talk appears to be rather common in institutions for the elderly. Caporael (1981) conducted a field study in a private nursing home in California and found that 22 percent of the nurses aides' communications directed to elderly patients were in baby talk. While college students who subsequently listened to recordings of the nurses aides' speech judged the baby talk to be more positive (because of its "nurturant" quality) than

non-baby talk, only those people who actually had lower functional ability tended to prefer baby talk. Baby talk to the elderly residents of institutions may well promote helplessness and dependency.

Do we use a different speech register to speak to foreigners or to retarded adults? To answer this question, a study was conducted in which undergraduate women taught a block-design task either to a six-year-old child, a retarded adult, a peer who spoke English as a second language, or a peer who was an unimpaired native speaker of English (DePaulo and Coleman, 1986). It was found that the speech addressed to children was clearer, simpler, more attention-maintaining, and included longer pauses. While speech addressed to retarded adults was similar, in some ways (e.g., in its repetitiveness) it was even more babyish. On the other hand, speech addressed to foreigners, apart from being more repetitive, was not different from that spoken to native speakers.

The way we talk to people tells them a great deal about how we view them. Talking to retarded people as though they are children may well reinforce feelings of immaturity and helplessness, and discourage such individuals from developing to their fullest potential.

poses that because we generally want to be liked and approved of by other people, we may modify our speech style so that it is more like the other person's. This process is referred to as "convergence" (Giles, 1973). Even one-year-old children show convergence to the pitch patterns of their parents: they lower the basic frequency of their babbling in the presence of the father, and raise it in the presence of the mother (Giles and Smith, 1979). Convergence may be in an upward direction, e.g., if we try to speak in the style of a speaker from a more prestigious group, or it may be downward, e.g., if an employer from a high-status group tries to be "one of the boys" in interactions with workers. However, too much convergence may elicit a negative reaction since it may appear as an attempt at ingratiation. Furthermore, maximal convergence will not always be the most appropriate accommodative strategy. Imagine how British visitors would feel if we tried to mimic their British accent, speech rate, and verbal expressions all at once! In each interaction some optimal level of convergence is needed to gain favourable responses from the listener (Giles and Smith, 1979).

Interpersonal accommodation theory incorporates ideas from four different areas of social psychology: similarity-attraction; social exchange; causal attribution; and intergroup distinctiveness. Similarity-attraction theory suggests that the more similar we are to others in terms of attitudes and beliefs, the more likely it is that we will be attracted to them. Convergence is one way that we can increase our similarity to other people, or vice versa. According to how much we want to be liked or shown approval, our speech will show a degree of convergence (Giles, Taylor and Bourhis, 1973).

Social exchange theory reminds us that convergence may carry with it certain costs, as well as rewards. We must evaluate whether or not we will be perceived as having lost integrity or whether our group identity will be compromised. If the potential rewards exceed the costs, then social exchange theory would predict that convergence would occur (Giles and Smith, 1979).

According to causal attribution theory, we evaluate people and interpret their behaviour by reference to what we take (attribute) to be the intentions which underlie the behaviour. Thus, whether or not we react positively to another's convergence would depend upon what we took to be the motives behind it. In a study conducted by Simard, Taylor and Giles (1977), French Canadian listeners reacted positively to an Anglophone's convergence to French when they believed that he was motivated by a desire to break down cultural barriers, but were not so positive when they were led to believe that he had been forced by circumstances to converge. Conversely, when the Anglophone did *not* converge, the reaction was less negative when the non-convergence was attributed to social circumstances beyond the speaker's control than when it apparently reflected a lack of effort.

Regarding intergroup distinctiveness, a wealth of evidence is accumulating which demonstrates that when members of different groups interact, and when group membership is an important issue, divergence rather than convergence is likely to occur. Speech divergence is a dissociative strategy that can be used for distinguishing ourselves and our group from the members of a disliked out-group. Giles, Bourhis and Taylor (1977) have related strategies of convergence/divergence to Tajfel's (1970) theory of intergroup distinctiveness. They suggest that when members of a subordinate group view their low status as fair and just, they may try to merge themselves with the higher-status group. Thus they would be expected to converge to the speech style of the high-status group interlocutors. On the other hand, should members of the same group view their inferior status as unjust, they may very well attempt to redefine their group attributes in a more positive way. As a result, they might be expected to accentuate the distinctiveness of their group by means of speech divergence. From this point of view, English Canadians who view the apparently inferior status of Canada in Canada-United States relations as legitimate may imitate Americans, and in writing to Americans use American spellings (e.g., "color"). However, those who feel that Canada is in an illegitimately subordinate position *vis-à-vis* the United States may well attempt to accentuate the differences in our language by using British/Canadian spellings (e.g., "colour") in writing to Americans.

Bourhis and Giles (1977) conducted research to see whether or not accent divergence would occur in an interethnic context in which a member of the dominant group made derogatory remarks about certain attributes of the subject's own group. The study was done in Wales, a part of Britain with a long history of Welsh/English linguistic conflict. Welsh subjects who were studying the Welsh language (which was not their first language) were interviewed by an out-group Englishman speaking English with an upper class accent. When at one point he suggested that they were studying a "dying language with a dismal future," the subjects emphasized their verbal disapproval by significantly broadening their Welsh accent. In other words, they diverged linguistically to assert the difference between themselves (as a group) and the insulting member of the dominant out-group (the Englishman).

Bourhis, Giles, Leyens and Tajfel (1979) studied a similar situation occurring in Belgium, a country where linguistic conflicts between the Flemish and Francophone communities have toppled many governments. Even though the Flemish and French languages have, officially, equal status, French still enjoys more status than Flemish in the capital region of Brussels. Since language choice in encounters between Francophones and Flemish speakers has become so controversial, many such encounters are now conducted in a more neutral language — English. The study was conducted with Flemish undergraduate students who are trilingual in Flemish, French, and English. They were interviewed by a Francophone who spoke to them in English and who told them that he was also trilingual, that he would prefer it if they would respond in English, but that he would also accept French. When the subjects had been informed that the Francophone was unsympathetic to their ethnolinguistic background and when they were faced with his argument for downgrading the use of Flemish in the Belgian capital, half of the subjects voiced their disagreement in their own maternal language, Flemish. Divergent replies in Flemish reached 100 percent when the Francophone rephrased his anti-Flemish comments and actually diverted from English to French. In each case, Flemish subjects reported they diverged to Flemish because they wished to assert their group identity *vis-à-vis* an out-group Francophone from whom they wished to dissociate themselves. (Box 11-7 describes the way in which shifts in convergence reflect changes in intergroup attitudes).

Thus language serves not only to define group boundaries but to protect them, and can be used to widen or narrow the gap between individuals, depending upon the perceptions and motivations of the people involved. In the section that follows, we shall turn from the subject of how people from two different language groups interact to the subject of the social psychological issues involved when individuals acquire and use two languages.

A CASE STUDY OF TWO SOLITUDES

In 1977, the government of Québec passed Bill 101, a law which was intended once and for all to make French the language of the workplace and the sole official language of Québec. At least four factors prompted the Québec government to adopt the Bill 101 language law (d'Anglejan, 1984): (1) the decline of the French Canadian population outside Québec; (2) the decline of the French Canadian birth rate in Québec from the highest to the lowest of the ten Canadian provinces; (3) the tendency of immigrants to become integrated with Québec's English-speaking minority by sending their children to English schools; (4) the domination of English in Québec business.

By addressing each of these issues, Bill 101 reduced fears among Québec Francophones that they would one day be linguistically assimilated among the 240 million English speakers in Canada and the U.S.A. While Bill 101 received overwhelming support from Québec Francophones, it was viewed as a threat by the Anglophone minority which comprised about 20 percent of the Québec population (Bourhis, 1984a). The most symbolically threatening aspect of the law for Anglophones was the insistence that public signs be in French only, a measure which struck many citizens as extremely heavy-handed.

This bill, combined with the 1976 victory of the Parti Québécois government which passed it, catalysed the exodus of 15 percent of the Québec Anglophone population to other parts of Canada and to the U.S.A. (about 150 000 Anglophones left). Many large corporations also moved their headquarters from Montreal to Toronto. Many Anglophones were apprehensive about their future (Caldwell, 1984). By the mid-'80s, however, as more and more Québec Anglophones who stayed behind became proficient in French, and the heartbeat of Québec nationalism faded to a barely perceptible murmur, the Anglophones began to reassert themselves and their children began to stay at home rather than move to Ontario.

In the immediate post-Bill 101 period, a number of studies were conducted which examined linguistic convergence and divergence by Francophones and Anglophones in Québec. Right up until the mid-1970s, studies had shown that Francophones had traditionally converged towards Anglophones in cross-cultural interactions in Montreal (i.e., they switched to English), thus reflecting Francophones' long-time status as economic underdogs in Québec (d'Anglejan, 1984). Bourhis (1983) conducted a survey regarding cross-cultural communication in 1977, just two-and-a-half months after Bill 101 was passed, and subsequently conducted two field studies, one in 1977 and the other in 1979, in which Montreal pedestrians were accosted by a bilingual confederate who addressed them either in French or in English, and asked for directions to the Métro (Bourhis, 1984b).

While in the 1977 survey both Francophones and Anglophones reported using French more frequently "today" than "in the past" (Bourhis, 1983), the behavioural responses Bourhis (1984b) obtained in both the 1977 and 1979 studies appeared to reflect the more traditional pattern of language-switching to English. As a result, Bourhis warned of the discrepancies which can exist between self-reports and actual behaviour. Despite all that has been said about the plight of the Québec Anglophones, Bourhis found that Québec Anglophones are still more likely to be helped in English by Francophones than are Québec Francophones likely to be helped in French by Anglophones. In the 1979 study, Bourhis used Montreal downtown settings and university campus settings. The 1979 downtown study revealed a marginal increase in convergence by Anglophones when compared with the 1977 study.

But in the campus study, Bourhis found that the majority of Anglophone students accosted on the grounds of McGill University did converge to French when responding to someone questioning them in French; indeed, they were as likely to converge to French with the French-speaking confederate as the Université de Montréal Francophone students were to converge to English with an English-speaking questioner.

BILINGUALISM

According to the 1981 census, 60 percent of Canadians have English as their mother tongue, while 25 percent have French (Box 11-8). Since Canada has not followed the "melting pot" strategy of the United States, many descendants of immigrants have learned their parents' tongue as well as English or French. Not to be forgotten are the languages of the indigenous people of Canada, which are sadly ignored when linguistic policy is discussed. These languages have a long history and are fully adaptable to the complexities of our modern technological society (Darnell, 1971). Yet school children are almost never taught about the diversity of Native languages. There are six distinct languages indigenous to North America, and four of them — Algonquin, Athabascan, Iroquoian, and the language of the Inuit — are widely spoken among Native Canadians. These languages differ from each other more than French differs from English or English differs from Ukrainian (Darnell, 1971).

Despite a massive effort by the federal government following the passage of the *Official Languages Act* of 1969 to teach French to selected civil servants, it was generally conceded a decade later that the program had been a disappointment. One obvious problem is that a person who attains some degree of functional bilingualism will not be able to maintain it unless there is an opportunity to use the language on a regular basis. Unfortunately, opportunities to practice a second language are often scarce, and so bilingual skills can fade with time. However, opportunity for practice is by no means the only factor in language retention, as we shall see.

B · O · X   1 1 - 8

LINGUISTIC DIVERSITY IN CANADA

According to the 1981 census, while about 85 percent of Canadians are of English or French mother tongue (60 percent and 25 percent respectively), several other languages are also well represented. Approximately 2 percent of Canadians are of Italian mother tongue, another 2 percent of German mother tongue, and about 1 percent each are of Ukrainian and Chinese mother tongue. Native Indian and Inuit languages account for slightly more than one half of 1 percent.

The census reveals other interesting facts. For example:

- 33 percent of people whose mother tongue is French are bilingual, while only 8 percent of people whose mother tongue is English are bilingual;
- 82 percent of Québec residents and 34 percent of

the people of New Brunswick have French as their mother tongue;

- 50 percent of English-mother-tongue residents in Québec are bilingual versus only 7 percent in Ontario;
- Between 1971 and 1981 the number of Québec residents whose mother tongue is English declined from 13 percent to 11 percent of the population;
- Bilingualism is increasing. While the population of Canada grew 12 percent between 1971 and 1981, bilingualism increased by 27 percent;
- The most spectacular increase in bilingualism since 1971 was made by English outside Québec. Although only 5 percent of English people outside Québec are bilingual, their numbers have increased 78 percent in last decade, while bilingualism among the English in Québec has increased only 29 percent (Statistics Canada, 1985).

Myths about learning a second language

There are several popular beliefs which dissuade people from even attempting to learn a second language. It is commonly held that it is very difficult for an adult to learn a second language because the ability to acquire language is strongest in childhood and wanes in the pubertal years. It is also asserted that second-language acquisition is quite a different matter from first-language acquisition and that we must somehow absorb the second language by making it compatible with the structure of the first. This need supposedly results in considerable "interference" in that words which appear to be similar may have quite different meanings. For example, the French word "librairie" means "bookstore," not "library"; this sort of confusion can frustrate the Anglophone adult trying to learn French.

Let us consider in more detail the belief that children are more adept at learning languages than adults. Montreal neurosurgeon Wilder Penfield (Penfield and Roberts, 1959) argued that young children are better second-language learners than adults because of *neuropsychological plasticity*, that is, the child's brain is not yet "fixed" in terms of its organization (although, as we shall see, children's advantage really seems to apply only to accent). Penfield's argument seems logical enough, but the evidence suggests that neuroplasticity does not translate into ease of learning a language. We often underestimate the tremendous difficulty a child has in acquiring language, despite the fact that a child learning his or her first language enjoys a more comprehensive and profound exposure to it than an adult does learning a second language (McLaughlin, 1977). The child must expend a great deal of effort, and make many mistakes along the way. Although it is true that children of immigrant parents in Canada have done better learning English as a second language when they have begun at a younger age (Ramsey and Wright, 1974), the preponderance of research argues against the view that children have an advantage over adults in language acquisition; research has revealed that adults are almost always better at it than children, except with regard to pronunciation (McLaughlin, 1977).

There may also be a critical period for the development of accent, and once that point is reached, the neurophysiological mechanisms involved in the production of sounds may no longer be "plastic" enough to adapt to the requirements of a new accent. Apart from that, though, adults appear to have an advantage over children — if given the same exposure — in the acquisition of language, or at least they do no worse than children (MacNamara, 1973), and even older children usually learn more quickly than younger children (Ervin-Tripp, 1974).

The finding that adults can acquire a second language more readily than children may appear to be counter-intuitive at first. However, suppose you and your child were to move to Peking, and that you spent all your time among the common populace rather than working with people who speak English. Suppose that no one you encountered spoke any English, and furthermore, you had no inhibitions about making errors in Chinese. Given such a context — in which you learn the language "in the streets" during every moment that you are interacting with people outside the family — it is easier to see how you might be more successful than a child. Consider your adult intelligence and experience, your ability to organize your learning experience, your willingness to resort to a dictionary, your ability to see regularities in verbs: you actually have a considerable advantage over your child in acquiring the new language.

Does the person acquiring a second language do so in a way that is qualitatively different from the learning of the first language? Intuitively, we might expect the answer to be yes, since the person can translate from the new language to his or her own. Yet again there is no clear evidence to support this view, and a number of studies indicate that a child learning a second language follows the same process of acquisition of that language as a native speaker of that language (McLaughlin, 1977). In fact, very little interference seems to occur between the two languages, particularly when each language is used in a different context. Contrary to popular belief, bilingual children do not seem to have any advantage over unilingual children in the learning of a third language (Plastre, 1974). Thus it seems that by becoming bilingual, we do not automatically learn how to learn languages more efficiently.

Immersion programs in schools

Because of growing social and political recognition of both English and French as official languages in Canada, there is increasing interest across the country in fostering bilingualism among children. As a result, Canadian research is at the forefront in this domain. The most widely used approach is the enrollment of children in some form of immersion program in which the child learns the second language, not as a subject, but through being exposed to it as the language of instruction and interaction. There are various models of immersion; some involve total immersion from nursery school on, others involve only partial immersion, in which the student spends only a part of each school day or week in an immersion situation. This kind of variety often makes comparison of various studies of the consequences of immersion very difficult or impossible.

The "St. Lambert project," a bilingual education program run by the South Shore Protestant Regional School Board (Montreal) in response to demands by Anglophone and immigrant parents for a school immersion program, was a pioneer project in immersion (Lambert and Tucker, 1972). Bilingualism was a strong political issue at the time, and the idea of an immersion program emerged from considerations of politics and social life. The St. Lambert project was grounded in neuropsychological and social psychological theory (Genesee, 1984). The concept of "neuropsychological plasticity" was embraced while social psychological reasoning suggested that young children learning French would be much less affected than older children by ethnic stereotypes which might interfere with language acquisition. Furthermore, learning French at such an age was expected to produce more tolerant attitudes towards Francophones. The program began in 1965 with French immersion classes being introduced at the kindergarten level; immersion was subsequently extended to later grades year by year. At the kindergarten level, every effort was made to teach French as if the children were learning it as their native tongue. In grade one, all subjects were taught only in French. Children were not taught to read in English and their parents were urged not to teach them how at home. Starting in grade two, with a half-hour daily period of instruction in English language arts, the amount of English used increased so that by grade seven, a little over half of the curriculum was taught in English. The children were not in any way preselected, except that their parents desired their enrollment in the program. They were matched with two other groups of students, Francophone children instructed in French, and Anglophone children instructed in English (Lambert and Tucker, 1972).

While the children did not succeed in speaking French as well as native French speakers, they spoke at a level that Anglophone students in a French as a second language (FSL) program could never achieve. More importantly, however, they were able to speak, understand, and write English as well as the conventionally educated English students (Lambert, 1974a, 1974b). When tested in English on a subject taught in French, such as mathematics, the children did just as well as children in the control group. Thus the children suffered no apparent detrimental effects in terms of their English language competence or in terms of their general cognitive development. Not only did they attain a high proficiency in French, they also developed a positive attitude towards Francophones while maintaining a healthy attitude towards their own linguistic group.

Swain and Barik (1976) replicated this study in Ottawa to see whether or not the results were only relevant to bilingual Montreal. Their findings were virtually the same as those of the St. Lambert study. While both these studies involved children of middle class parents, the program has also proven suitable for children from working class families (Bruck, Tucker and Jakamik, 1973). Even late immersion programs begun in the seventh grade have proven to produce effects not unlike those of the early immersion program (Swain and Barik, 1976). However, more study is required before we can say anything about whether early or later immersion is most efficient. As we saw earlier, older children are, in fact, more adept at learning language than young children. All other things being equal, it is quite possible that considerations of accent aside, the "late" immersion programs may be more efficient. On the other hand, older students may have already formed negative impressions of second language learning that might impede their progress.

Immersion programs now exist across Canada, and systematic evaluation of these programs has confirmed the St. Lambert project findings: There are no long-term differences in English language proficiency or in academic proficiency in other subjects, e.g., maths and sciences, between students who have been in a regular English language program and those who have been in French immersion (Genesee, 1984). The same studies have also confirmed that although immersion students achieve very high levels of competence in French, their competence is still not quite that of a native speaker.

Social consequences of immersion schooling Acquiring competence in a second language might well be expected to have important social psychological consequences, such as engendering more positive attitudes toward the target language group. The results of the various studies surveyed by Genesee (1984) suggest that immersion students do initially show more positive attitudes towards the target group, but that later on, their attitudes come to resemble those of students in English schools. This may be because outside the school, they still operate in an English social milieu. Nonetheless, the positive attitudes towards the use of the French language and the immersion students' increased feelings of similarity to French Canadians offer hope in breaking down the barriers between Francophones and Anglophones in Canada (Genesee, 1984).

Sociolinguistic competence Becoming bilingual involves more than just learning a second language; it also requires mastering a new set of social norms. Furthermore, it is likely to influence an individual's attitudes about both the new linguistic group and his or her own group.

In acquiring the social norms of a new language, we must do several things. We must learn when to show deference, when to speak and when not to, and what subjects to speak about in a given context. Recall our earlier discussion of direct and indirect speech acts. We must learn to recognize when and how the intent of a communication in the second language is different from the meaning of the words spoken. Skill at using a language in a social context is referred to as *sociolinguistic competence* (Holmes and Brown, 1977), something which is difficult to teach formally since very often even the native speaker of the language cannot verbalize the rules. When we tell someone to "drop in anytime," how is someone just learning English to know that this is not in fact an invitation to *drop in anytime*? In French, particularly in France, "merci" spoken in response to being offered something usually means "no, thank you," not just "thank you." In English, "thanks" means in that context "yes, thank you."

Because of the necessity of acquiring sociolinguistic competence as well as language skill, the process of becoming bilingual is more of a *socialization* process than the student usually expects. Moreover, exposure to speakers of another language *in* their own language can often lead to difficulties with regard to group loyalty and group identity, as we shall see in the next section.

Bilingualism and identity

When a person acquires a second language, there are often some unexpected psychological consequences, not all of them positive. Imagine what would happen if you were part of a group that had misgivings about people who belonged to another linguistic group. Anglophones and Francophones in Canada have two separate and distinct identities, and it is their language more than their cultural heritage which is fundamental in determining this identity (Taylor, Simard and Aboud, 1972). An English speaker whose origins are in Scotland will most likely have more in common with another English speaker of German heritage than with a French speaker, even if by some quirk of history, the latter also has Scottish roots.

Once a person begins to achieve bilingual competence, the switching back and forth between languages has social psychological consequences, such as making the person aware of stereotypes held by members of each linguistic group about members of the other. These new insights can even assail a person's sense of identity — as, for example, when an individual becomes fluent enough to share jokes or criticisms with speakers of the new language about his or her maternal language group. If the person laughs at the jokes or does not oppose the criticism, he or she may feel uneasy or even guilty, while failure to laugh or responding defensively may lead to exclusion from the group. The same process can occur within the native group when criticisms of the other group are made by friends or relatives. Attempts to defend the other group may be met with negative reaction, leading to feelings of estrangement. The individual becomes a kind of "marginal person" — no longer a typical member of his or her own group but never fully "one of them" in the new group. (Recall the discussion of intergroup anxiety in Chapter 7). Immigrants, and especially children of immigrants, often must endure the position of the marginal person.

This estrangement process was observed in the changes that took place in the attitudes and feelings of students enrolled in a six-week intensive advanced course in French at McGill University's French Summer School (Lambert, 1967). When the students became so advanced that they began to think and even dream in French, and perceived themselves as thinking and feeling like a mature French speaker, the feelings of estrangement became so strong that they sought ways to reduce it. Reverting to English even though they had pledged to speak only French during the six-week period was one way to do this.

Thus, by becoming bilingual, the individual may be required to act in ways that are inconsistent with his or her ethnocentric attitude (i.e., the attitude of the native group which places that group first and others second). To avoid getting into this position of psychological inconsistency, some people may maintain a negative attitude toward second language learning, and they may support this attitude by clichés such as, "I'm too old to learn a new language," and by avoiding cross-cultural interaction which might remind the person of the need to acquire the second language (Lambert, 1981; Taylor and Simard, 1975).

The situation may be even more difficult for Canadian Francophones learning English. Because they are in the minority, learning the language of the majority is in some ways a threat to the continued existence of the minority's separate identity. Here, a distinction can be made between "additive" and "subtractive" bilingualism (Lambert, 1978; Lambert and Taylor, 1984): When Anglophones in South Africa learn Afrikaans, Israelis learn English, or Anglophone Canadians learn French, they are not threatening the continued existence of their sociolinguistic group. In this case, bilingualism is "additive" in that the individuals have acquired another socially useful skill. However, when minority groups are struggling to maintain their identity, learning the language of the majority can be considered to be "subtractive" in that it threatens the continued importance of the native language in that society. For example, Francophones who never learn English are unlikely to become assimilated into the English culture, while bilingualism may make Francophones vulnerable. Bilingualism is likely to be encouraged, or at worst ignored, when it is additive for a given group. It is likely to be actively discouraged when it is subtractive.

However, at least for some linguistic groups in Canada, linguistic association does not mean cultural assimilation. For example, Chinese students in Toronto who were most confident in English showed evidence of linguistic assimilation, but less evidence of cultural assimilation (Pak, Dion and Dion, 1985). Unlike the Québécois, who face losing their distinctive ethnic identity and being assimilated into the historically antagonistic Anglophone out-group, Chinese Canadians, as members of a visible racial minority, are most likely at less risk of losing their cultural identity by learning English. For them, bilingualism is additive.

Who succeeds in learning a second language?

Given the problems associated with language acquisition discussed above, why do some people persevere and manage to achieve linguistic competence in two languages, even when their social situation does not demand it? A series of experiments which examined the relationship between attitudinal and motivational variables and measures of linguistic aptitude on the one hand, and success in acquiring a second language in the classroom on the other, suggests that there are two distinct factors involved: intelligence/aptitude and motivation (Gardner and Lambert, 1972). The more intelligent the individual, and the greater aptitude the individual has for language learning, the more likely it is that he or she will master a second language if he or she so desires. In fact, this desire, or motivation, was found to be a crucial determinant of second language success. Students whose motivation was primarily "instrumental" (e.g., to get a good job, for example) did not do as well as those students who were "integratively" motivated (e.g., to be able to go to plays, see movies, talk to friends, meet members of the opposite sex) (Gardner and Lambert, 1959; Gardner, 1979, 1984). The relationship between attitude and achievement in mastering French as a second language has been replicated both in Canada (e.g., Smythe, Stennett and Feenstra, 1972) and the U.S.A. (Gardner and Lambert, 1972) as well as in cases of other second-language learning, e.g., Hebrew (Anisfeld and Lambert, 1961).

In another study, it was also shown that the success of Montreal Francophones learning English in high school also was influenced by whether or not they held a favourable attitude toward the English linguistic community (i.e., an integrative motivation) (Clément, Gardner and Smythe, 1977). However, while perseverance was dependent on this motivation, the student's actual competence in the second language seemed to be more closely related to the person's self-confidence based on prior experience with the language. Self-confidence, or lack of it appears to be an important factor in success or failure at second-language acquisition which is relatively independent of the integrative motivation (Gardner, Smythe, Clément and Gliksman,

1976). An individual may feel uncomfortable interacting with another person in the second language, particularly if not totally fluent.

As we have discussed earlier, anxiety can be generated in many social interactions. Sometimes when a second language is involved, a non-fluent speaker operating in that language may misattribute the source of his or her discomfort to the other person and, as a consequence, react negatively to the individual, or to the second language, or to speakers of it in general (Segalowitz, 1976). To test this hypothesis, Segalowitz had English-speaking students with medium ability in oral French either listen and speak to, or simply listen to, two ostensibly different interlocutors, one speaking in French, the other in English (actually, a tape recorded message of the same speaker speaking in the two languages was used). For one group (within each language condition) the interlocuter spoke in a formal style, while for a second, a casual style was used. The students then rated several factors of the situation, e.g., their own ease of understanding the speaker, and the personality of the speaker. In addition, the subjects who had been required to talk to the interlocuter answered questions about their feelings while speaking (e.g., "Were you relaxed or tense?"), their ease of presentation, and the impression that they thought they had conveyed about themselves to the other person.

The results showed that the subjects felt more relaxed, thought they were better understood, and said that they had expressed themselves better in the "formal" French condition than in the "casual" condition, just the opposite of what they felt when required to interact in English. Furthermore, subjects believed that they had appeared to be less self-confident and even less intelligent when they had to speak French in the casual condition, a style of speech that was not so familiar to them. Even more interesting, however, is the fact that when French was used, speaking subjects who spoke as well as listened rated the personality of the interlocuter as considerably more positive in the formal condition. When English was involved, the casual condition resulted in the most positive personality rating.

When subjects only had to listen, but were not required to talk, the casual style led to the highest personality ratings of both the French and English speakers, but it was even more pronounced in ratings of the French speakers. These results support the idea that the discomfort felt by the subjects was misattributed. They felt uncomfortable speaking to the interlocuter and therefore concluded that they didn't like him. This outcome is in line with Bem's (1972) self-perception theory (see Chapter 5): "I feel uncomfortable talking to him" becomes "He makes me feel uncomfortable," leading to the conclusion that "Because he makes me uncomfortable, I don't like him very much." Thus second-language interaction can be uncomfortable and unpleasant for the semi-fluent individual for reasons not related to skill in vocabulary, phonology or syntax. The result is that the speaker may shy away from second-language interaction.

SUMMARY

(1) Non-verbal communication is used to provide information about feelings and intentions, to regulate verbal and other interactions, to express intimacy, to promote social control, and to facilitate goal attainment.

(2) Facial displays of emotion share some universal features, although whatever biological basis there is for this similarity is modified by social conditioning.

(3) Eye contact, "body language," and gestures, along with facial displays, provide powerful non-verbal channels of communication.

(4) Paralanguage is the non-verbal component of speech; the prosodic features of paralanguage (timing, pitch, and loudness) appear to have a biological component in terms of their involvement in emotional reactions.

(5) All languages are based on a system of phonemes and morphemes. These elements are combined to form words and sentences. All languages involve hierarchical structures in that higher-order components can be broken down into smaller units, each of which carries its own meaning.

(6) The ability to learn language is probably inborn, although linguistic structures themselves must be acquired. It is doubtful that any animals have the ability to acquire the equivalent of human language.

(7) Research into the linguistic relativity hypothesis, while not demonstrating that language determines thought, has shown that certain ways of thinking are harder or easier depending on the constraints of a given language.

(8) Verbal utterances are essentially social acts which are subject to reinforcement. The utterance not only demands a response but carries with it an indication of what sort of response is required. Indirect speech acts are often used when face-saving, either by speaker or listener, is important.

(9) Differences in speech style are used as markers of social status, as guides for forming impressions of others, and as markers of group boundaries.

(10) The prestige or standard form of a language develops from the speech style of those who are in a position of power, rather than reflecting the aesthetically ideal form of the language.

(11) Interpersonal accommodation theory suggests that because people usually want to be liked and approved of by others, they modify their speech style to make it similar to the speech heard around them (convergence). However, if group identity is threatened, the opposite may occur, and individuals will accentuate the distinctiveness of their speech style (divergence) in the presence of members of another linguistic group associated with the threat.

(12) Becoming bilingual involves more than learning another language; we must also acquire relevant sociolinguistic skills.

(13) Learning a second language can lead to the perception of threat to our cultural identity, which can diminish the desire to become bilingual. Bilingualism is likely to be encouraged when it is additive, i.e., when it provides a socially useful skill without threatening the existence of the speaker's own language, but discouraged when it is subtractive, i.e., contributes to linguistic assimilation into the majority linguistic group.

(14) Those who do master a second language are likely to be more adept at language acquisition in general. They are also motivated by a positive regard for the culture and the people whose language they are learning. Self-confidence has also been shown to be an important contributor to perseverance in the learning of a second language.

FURTHER READING

ARGYLE, M. (1975). *Bodily communication*. London: Methuen.

BOURHIS, R.Y. (1984). *Conflict and language planning in Québec*. Clevedon, England: Multilingual Matters.

CUMMINGS, J. (Ed.) (1986). *Heritage language research in Canada*. Ottawa: Secretary of State (Multiculturalism). Ministry of Supply and Services.

EKMAN, P. (1982). *Emotion in the human face*. New York: Cambridge.

GARDNER, R.C. and KALIN, R. (Eds.) (1981). *A Canadian social psychology of ethnic relations*. Toronto: Methuen.

GILES, H. (Ed.) (1977). *Language, ethnicity and intergroup relations*. London: Academic Press.

HALL, J.A. (1979). Gender, gender roles, and nonverbal communication. In R. Rosenthal (Ed.) *Skill in nonverbal communication* (pp. 32–67), Cambridge, MA: Oelgeschlager, Gunn & Hain.

HESLIN, R. and PATTERSON, M.L. (1982). *Nonverbal behaviour and social psychology*. New York: Plenum.

LAFRANCE, M. and MAYO, C. (1978). *Moving bodies*. Monterey: Brooks/Cole.

RYAN, E.R. and GILES, H. (Eds.) (1982). *Attitudes towards language variation*. London: Edward Arnold.

SAMUDA, R. J., BERRY, J. W. and LAFERRIERE, M. (Eds.) (1984). *Multiculturalism in Canada*. Toronto: Allyn & Bacon.

SMITH, P.M. (1985). *Language, the sexes and society*. Oxford: Basil Blackwell.

WOLFGANG, A. (Ed.) (1984). *Nonverbal behaviour: Perspectives, applications, intercultural insights*. Toronto: C.J. Hogrefe.

Social Categorization, Groups, and Leadership

If there were one religion in England, its despotism would be terrible; if there were two, they would destroy each other; but there are thirty, and therefore they live in peace and happiness.

Voltaire

FOR REFLECTION

- When does a collection of people become a real group?
- How and why do we classify people as in-groups and out-groups?
- Is effective leadership the result of the leader's personality, the situation, or both?
- What is charisma?

403

EACH YEAR IN ancient Athens, the governing assembly cast ballots to determine whether or not to hold a special kind of vote, a vote of ostracism. When such a vote was held, each citizen marked the name of the individual that he wanted to see banished on a piece of broken pottery called an *ostrakon*. The person most often named in this way was then "ostracized" from the city for a period of ten years.

Social ostracism is as devastating to most people now as it was then. Being rejected by our group would be an emotionally traumatic experience for most of us. Even fear of rejection can motivate people to conform to the expectations of the group, as we learned in Chapter 6. We live our lives in groups and spend most of our waking hours in one group context or another — our families, our circles of friends, the people we work with or go to school with. We define ourselves in terms of groups: "I am a Canadian," "I am a McGill student," "I am Québécois." Many of the most important changes in our lives result from changing groups — leaving home, going to university, getting a job — and membership in new groups often leads to changes in our attitudes and values.

It is important to make a distinction between social categories and groups. For example, as you walk along the street, you can categorize people into "drivers" and "pedestrians," yet you would be unlikely to think of these categories as representing two distinct groups: there is little or no interaction among members of "the drivers" or "the pedestrians" and they probably do not know one another. A *group* is a special kind of category of people which is distinguished by much more than the mere similarities among them.

Each of us belongs to many different social categories: we are male, female, Canadian, American, Black, White, tinker, tailor, soldier, and so on. We all belong to many more categories than we probably even realize, categories based not only on gender, nationality, colour, and occupation, but also on religion, age group, ethnic group, geographical origin, or marital status. Although such categories may not always mean much to us, under certain circumstances they can become very important. This is the first subject discussed in this chapter. Next we examine small groups and, finally, the phenomenon of power within groups, and how such power manifests itself through leadership.

SOCIAL CATEGORIZATION

It would be difficult to interact with other people if we could not view them as part of some organized pattern. We tend to automatically put people whom we encounter into categories, or role schemata (see Chapter 3) that we already know something about, e.g., "male-teenager-school drop-out." This quick categorization allows us to act "appropriately" toward that person according to the social norms we have learned.

Although individuals interact directly with other individuals, they often do not deal with each other as individuals, but rather as members of particular social categories. At any given time, our interpersonal behaviour falls somewhere along a continuum. At one extreme is pure interpersonal behaviour in which all the interaction between two or more people is determined solely by their individual characteristics. For example, consider two lovers deeply infatuated with each other. Initially, they ignore social categories and focus on each other purely as individuals. At the other extreme is the pure intergroup behaviour of two or more people, which is determined by their membership in different social categories (Tajfel, 1978). For example, consider two armies confronting one another on the field of battle. Each soldier treats enemy soldiers as though they were all the same, without any individuality. Most of the time, however, behaviour in a social context depends both on our characteristics as individuals *and* the social categories describing ourselves and the people with whom we interact.

Since we each belong to many social categories, our behaviour at any given time will be influenced by whatever category is salient at that moment. If you are the only woman engineer at a meeting of engineers and someone starts telling jokes which denigrate women, the fact that you are a woman will suddenly become very important to you. It will also become important to the men at the meeting and will undoubtedly influence both your reaction and their behaviour. If you are the only engineer at a meeting of a women's rights group, and someone refers to engineers as "people who are too dumb to get through the science program," then it is likely that the engineering category will become very important in determining your reaction.

Often without being aware of it, we organize the social world in such a way that various social categories have some relationship to one another. Some people are viewed as superior, and others as relatively inferior. Thus we may act with deference toward someone we assume to be older and better-educated than we are, and with condescension toward someone younger. Perhaps the most important element of this "subjective" social order that we all construct for ourselves is the division of people into *in-groups* (categories to which we happen to belong) and *out-groups* (categories to which we do not belong), i.e., into "we" and "they" (Tajfel, 1970; recall the discussion of in-groups and out-groups as they relate to prejudice in Chapter 7).

The emphasis placed on teams and "team spirit," even in primary school, the in-group vs. out-group, we vs. they division in our society often produces a competitive relationship between the members of different social categories. We want "our" team, our age group, our sex, our neighbourhood, our province, our country to win, whether it is a spelling prize or an Olympic medal. If Calgary football fans watch a Western Conference final between Calgary and Vancouver, they will want Calgary to win and will view the Lions as the enemy. Yet, if Vancouver wins and goes to the Grey Cup game, those same Calgary fans will likely cheer for the Lions because they are "Westerners" and want the West to win.

Teams can become an extension of our own identity. Why did people care so much that Team Canada beat the Soviet hockey team in 1972? A victory or a defeat would have resulted in no personal consequences for the viewers of the game. The fact is that the competition focused attention on a "we-they" contest that went far beyond the hockey game. It was as though the hockey series involved the whole Canadian citizenry against all the population of the Soviet Union: "The Canadian team won; therefore, they are better than the Soviet team; therefore, Canadians should be proud because we excelled; therefore, I should feel good because we won." As player Paul Henderson reflected, "When I scored that final goal, I finally realized what democracy was all about." Thus, feelings of well-being and superiority were engendered among Canadians by a group of hockey players they had never met.

A generic norm

Repeated exposure to in-group/out-group categorizations, many of which involve some degree of resentment towards the out-group (e.g., "the Americans" are buying all our lakefront property; Ontario runs Canada for its own benefit and exploits the rest of us), leads to the development of a *generic norm* of behaviour towards out-groups (Tajfel, 1970). By "generic norm," Tajfel meant that we are prepared to act in a similarly discriminatory, competitive, or rejecting way toward all out-groups, regardless of the group and regardless of the context of the interaction. According to Tajfel, because of this generic norm: (1) discrimination against an out-group should be observable even when such discrimination in no way contributes to an individual's own self-interest; and (2) such discrimination may occur even in the absence of pre-existing hostility toward the out-group, and it may manifest itself in discriminatory behaviour even before any hostility or prejudice has formed.

To search for empirical support for the existence of such a generic norm, Tajfel and his colleagues carried out a series of studies on "assigned groups." The studies examined how arbitrary or even random assignments of individuals to artificial "minimal" groups (i.e., groups with no structure, no pre-existing norms, no history) lead to discrimination favouring the in-group.

In one such study (Tajfel, 1970) students were arbitrarily divided into artificial groups on the supposed basis of whether or not they had been "overestimators" or "underestimators" in a previously administered visual perception task. Each subject actually worked alone and did not know the identities of the other group members. Each subject participated in several trials in which it was necessary to select one of several different ways to assign a number of points to two people (neither of whom was the subject). These points were later to be exchanged for money, so something of real value was involved. On some trials, the subjects had to assign points to two members of their own group ("in-group choice"), while on other trials the assignment was to be made to two members of the other group ("out-group choice"). On still other trials, the subjects were to assign points to one member of the in-group and one member of the out-group ("intergroup choice"). Thus, by observing whom the subjects awarded points to, it was possible to determine if there was any bias toward the in-group or the out-group in the intergroup situation.

When a subject had the opportunity to assign points to two people who were members of the same group, either in-group or out-group, each person was given about an equal number of points. However, when points were assigned to a member of the in-group and a member of the out-group, a large majority of subjects awarded more points to members of their own group than to members of the other group. Thus, although they did not know who was in their group and who was in the other group, and even though the division into groups was based on a rather trivial criterion, and even though they would in no way benefit personally as a result of their choices, they discriminated in favour of their own group. This discrimination occurred in the absence of a conflict of interest or pre-existing antagonism, and even without any social interaction.

Why did the subjects act in this manner? It is possible that the subjects were acting in a discriminatory way because of social desirability: they simply wanted to look good in the experimenter's eyes. Yet even if that were the case, it would reveal much about the subjects' outlook, indicating they believed that it "looks good" to favour their own group and to show negative bias towards an out-group. Such an outlook would confirm the notion of a generic norm of discrimination toward the out-group (Tajfel and Turner, 1979; Lemyre and Smith, 1985).

It does appear, then, that people are prepared to discriminate more or less automatically towards out-groups and to favour their in-group. This tendency is the result of years of experience in which in-group/out-group discrimination has been subtly and not-so-subtly encouraged.

Social identity and social comparison

If someone were to ask, "Who are you?" — how would you respond? You might give your name, but if the interlocutor continued with "Yes, but who *are* you?" — what would you say? Depending on the circumstances, you might describe yourself as a student, a male or female student, a psychology student, a resident of Victoria or Fredericton, a Canadian, a North American, or even a member of a certain club. Not only do we categorize other people, but we also categorize ourselves. Indeed, our self-esteem, and how we perceive ourselves in relation to other people is tied up with group identification: "She wouldn't want to go out with me — I'm just in first year and she's in third."

The term *social identity* refers to those aspects of a person's self-image which depend upon the social categories and groups to which he or she belongs (Tajfel and Turner, 1979). *Social identification* is the process whereby individuals define themselves with respect to other people. Turner (1982, 1985) describes social identification as a three-part process. First, there is social categorization: individuals perceive themselves and

DAVID LEVINE

others in terms of membership in distinct categories or groups. Second, the typical norms, attitudes, and behaviours that distinguish the groups determine behaviour to a large degree. Third, individuals conform to what are perceived to be the stereotypes associated with the group. Tajfel and Turner (1979) predicted that when people's social identities are not satisfactory, they will either strive to improve their in-group relative to various out-groups or they will eventually leave the in-group and join some other group. Thus they hypothesized that social groups distinguish themselves from one another through members' striving to evaluate their own group positively relative to other groups. Since the aim of social differentiation is to provide a positive comparison with regard to some other relevant group, then such differentiation is basically competitive.

Categorical differentiation

In the psychology of perception and cognition, there is the well-known phenomenon of assimilation and contrast: We tend to exaggerate the similarities among objects from the same category and to exaggerate the differences among objects from different categories. The same phenomenon occurs in social differentiation. When we compare people from two different categories or social groups, we may see the members of each category as more similar than they in fact are and the differences between the two categories as greater than they really are. This tendency is referred to as *categorical differentiation* (Doise and Dann, 1976), or simply, *social differentiation* (Lemaine, Kastersztein and Personnaz, 1978). For example, if we know little about motorcycle clubs, all motorcyclists may seem very similar to us in terms of style of dress, attitudes, and so on. And if we were to compare three motorcycle club members with three members of the general public, we might perceive the two sets of people as being more different than they actually are.

To demonstrate social differentiation, Doise, Deschamps and Meyer (1978) conducted several experiments. In one of these, subjects were assigned to one of two conditions. Subjects in the "no anticipation" condition were told that they would be required to describe members of their own social category, but were not told that they would later also have to describe members of another category. Subjects in the "anticipation" condition were informed that they would be describing both members of their own category and members of another category.

School children served as subjects and an equal number of boys and girls were assigned to each condition. They were shown three photographs of girls and three photographs of boys, all of whom were unknown to them. They were required to indicate for each photograph which of 24 adjectives applied to the child. Subjects in the no anticipation group were first shown only the three photographs of children the same sex as themselves; the other three photographs were presented later. Subjects in the anticipation group were given all six photographs at once, although they were to begin with rating the three photos of the children the same sex as themselves. The results indicated that *inter*category (boy-girl) differences were greater, but that *intra*-category differences (i.e., differences within each gender group) were smaller when the subjects anticipated rating children of the opposite sex as well as children of their own sex than when there was no anticipation. The knowledge that they would be rating both girls and boys made the gender variable salient, leading the subjects to make a differentiation between the two categories. Similar results were obtained in an experiment using language rather than gender as the salient dimension. A feature (such as sex or language) that is used to create categories is said to have *diagnostic value* (Atkinson, 1986).

If being members of a category leads people to see members of another category as more different from themselves than they actually are, and more similar among themselves than they actually are, what happens when two people differ in one category but share a second category? This question is addressed next.

Cross-categorization

Depending on the context in which you meet someone, some social features of that person may be much more important to you than others. In fact the importance of each feature, or dimension, may change as the interaction continues. Suppose that you have a tendency to react negatively toward members of a particular category. Suppose that you are a young woman and a classical pianist, and that you believe that male football players are "macho jerks." Such a belief may be based on past experience, or it may not. If you meet a man at a party whom you discover is a fullback with the university football team, your prejudice toward football players may surface and lead you to experience a negative reaction toward him. Suppose, however, that he sits down at the piano and plays a touching rendition of Beethoven's *Moonlight Sonata*. How will you react after this? Now this man falls into two categories, one to which you respond negatively, and the other which you value.

This dilemma is applicable to any situation in which we encounter someone who shares one category with us but who is part of an out-group with regard to another. Since we all are simultaneously members of many overlapping groups, this is likely to occur very often. In such situation, the categories are said to be *crossed*.

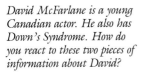

David McFarlane is a young Canadian actor. He also has Down's Syndrome. How do you react to these two pieces of information about David?

FIGURE 12-1
Design of categorization experiment

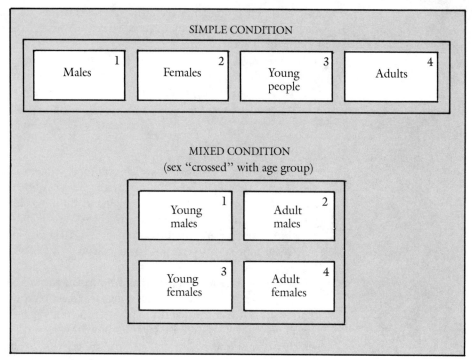

SOURCE: Deschamps and Doise, 1978

Deschamps and Doise (1978) conducted an experiment to examine what happens in this situation. The subjects were teenage students. Subjects in one condition ("simple" condition) were asked to describe, by means of an adjective check list, females, males, young people, and adults, while those in a second condition ("mixed" condition) were asked to describe young females, young males, female adults, and male adults. Thus in the second condition sex and age were "crossed." (Figure 12-1).

The crossing of the categories led to a decrease in the social differentiation. For example, subjects in the simple condition saw much more difference between males and females than subjects in the mixed condition saw between young males and young females. While each subject belonged to either the male or female category, all subjects belonged to the "young" category. When rating *adult* males and females, the perceived differences were also smaller than when rating males and females. These results indicate that when the subjects characterized groups of people similar to themselves with respect to one criterion, but different or opposite from themselves with respect to another, the perceived differences were smaller than when comparisons were made on the basis of a single feature which the subjects and targets did not share (e.g., male-female).

In another experiment (Deschamps and Doise, 1978), it was observed that while a simple division of people into in-group and out-group could produce a positive bias toward their own group, the introduction of a second, neutral category (i.e., producing no bias of itself) could eliminate the original discrimination in favour of the in-group. The subjects were nine- and ten-year-old boys and girls. Half of the subjects were in the simple category (male versus female) condition, and the rest were in the crossed category condition. In the crossed condition, half the boys and half the girls were assigned to a "red" category, and the remainder to a "blue" category. The children were required to work individually on a series of pencil and paper games similar to those found in children's magazines. Later, they were asked to estimate the number of games that each of the other children had correctly completed.

Subjects in the simple category condition rated the probable success of the other subjects of their sex as significantly higher than that of opposite-sex subjects, while no such distinction was made in the crossed category condition (even though the red-blue split did not by itself produce any difference). Thus, by adding an essentially meaningless variable and crossing it with the gender variable, discrimination on the basis of gender was eliminated.

Coser (1967) anticipated these findings when he wrote that conflict serves to bind the elements of society together. A society is composed of many categories and subcategories, and these groupings are often in conflict with each other. Yet, since individuals belong to many different categories, it is highly unlikely that a given set of people will be on the same side in every conflict. Thus a woman may oppose a man on the women's rights issue, but agree with him on a conservation issue, and so on. Hence, society is knit together (see Voltaire's words at the beginning of this chapter). It is easy to see how this binding process applies to the Canadian nation: As long as French Canadians and English Canadians are not divided on every major issue along linguistic and ethnic lines, but instead find these categories "crossed" with other categories (e.g., males versus females, capitalists versus socialists, environmentalists versus "exploiters"), the two groups will be bound together.

Redefinition of the social field

What do we do when, in comparison with people in another social category we seem to "come off" second best? A negative assessment can certainly be threatening to our self-esteem and our sense of identity. Canadians often feel a sense of inferiority when comparing themselves with Americans in areas such as technological and cultural achievement, or the cost of living. How do people deal with threats to identity and self-esteem? Members of the "inferior" group may attempt to be assimilated into the more favourable group when that is possible, or they may try to avoid such comparisons altogether. However, there is also another reaction that is commonly observed. Rather than trying to appear more similar to these others, the individual often tries to distinguish himself or herself from the comparison group in such a way that the dimension of comparison is no longer relevant or important (Lemaine, Kastersztein and Personnaz, 1978).

This process was demonstrated in a series of field studies carried out with children (Jamous and Lemaine, 1962; Lemaine, 1966; Lemaine and Kastersztein, 1972). One experimental situation (Lemaine, 1974) was set up as follows: two groups of boys — one group having an experimentally imposed disadvantage — competed for a prize, although they did not directly interact. Each group had to build a hut in the forest. By the toss of a coin, it was decided which group would be able to use string and which would not. It was found that the "handicapped" group was less efficient than the other group in terms of organizing and coordinating task-oriented activity; they were very much preoccupied with their disadvantage, and the possibility of actually withdrawing from the competition was seriously considered. They seemed to waste a lot of time watching the other group at work before they buckled down to work themselves, and then only after "closing their frontiers" and not allowing members of the advantaged group to observe what they were doing. They then set about to compensate for their handicap by doing things differently from the other group. While the goal was to build a hut, the disadvantaged group redefined the situation by arguing that building a hut also involved making a garden, a table, and a fireplace, items which they had built and the other group had not.

Similar findings were made in a study in which psychology students were asked to apply for a (fictitious) position as a psychologist in a market research bureau (Lemaine and Kastersztein, 1972). In the first instance, the students thought their letters were the only ones being "sent," but they were then asked to write a second letter after being informed that they were in competition with another applicant who was said to be either experienced in market research or was a graduate of a prestigious engineering school. It was found that in the second letter, subjects, now seeing themselves at a disadvantage, did not simply expand on personal competence for the position, but also made reference to new criteria, just as the disadvantaged children in the field studies had done. These new criteria demanded a new, more difficult evaluation of the candidates. Thus the subjects tried to make it harder for the other applicant to win by trying to redefine the basis for comparison.

These results identify a very important mechanism that people use to enhance or rescue their own self-esteem when they are being compared with others who have an advantage. When confronted with the fancy cars or elegant homes of people whose wealth has been inherited, how many of us tell ourselves that "money doesn't buy happiness," and that wealth only brings problems that we are fortunate enough to bypass? However, we are not likely to voice the same sentiments when we are comparing ourselves with those who are disadvantaged financially. We are unlikely to say, "My goodness, if only I could be as poor as that person, then I could be happy." When we are at a disadvantage, we tend to emphasize or create new criteria which allow us to minimize or avoid the disadvantage, and thereby distinguish ourselves from the advantaged group.

Social differentiation and aesthetics   Such differentiation can even be observed in the realm of aesthetic judgments. Personnaz, Kastersztein and Lemaine (1976–77) presented pairs of subjects with a slide of a painting which they were asked to describe according to 40 adjectives or expressions divided into four groups of ten: form, colour, description and "other." Subjects were required to choose exactly ten adjectives/ expressions to describe the painting.

One of the two subjects was always a confederate of the experimenter. In the experimental condition, and following the completion of the evaluation, the confederate let it be known that he had studied Fine Art for two years and had specialized in pictorial techniques. In the control condition, the confederate made no mention of any such expertise. The experimenter then told the subjects that he did not want first impressions, and that he would like each person to evaluate the painting a second time. He then crumpled up the sheets that the subjects had filled out and discarded them into a wastebasket.

The results of the study indicated that the real subject shifted his or her evaluation toward criteria unlikely to be chosen by the other, avoiding descriptions in the categories of form and colour. So, even though there was no overt competition involved and there were no "correct" or "incorrect" responses, subjects who appeared to be at a disadvantage in terms of aesthetic judgment chose to use criteria which made comparison with a more expert person more difficult.

Therefore, as people try to maintain their self-esteem in a situation which gives another party an advantage over themselves, they will look for some *new* point of comparison which will allow them to be compared more favourably with the other party. This happens in many different situations in the everyday world. For example, in a study conducted some years ago, it was found that while East Indians in South Africa considered themselves to be inferior to Whites in the context of science and the economy, they saw themselves as superior with regard to spiritual and social matters (Mann, 1963).

GROUPS

So far, the discussion has focused on general categories, or loosely defined groups of people. However, the most important social influences often occur not among members of categories — "males," "females," "drivers," "pedestrians" — but in the context of smaller groups of people who interact with and relate socially to one another in some important and ongoing manner.

A group is more than just a collection of people or a social category. When does a collection of people constitute a "group"? If you are part of a crowd milling about the baggage carousel at an airport while waiting for your luggage, it is unlikely you would think that you had just joined a group. What about spectators at a hockey game? Or a classroom of students? Where is the line to be drawn between "groups"

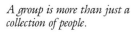

A group is more than just a collection of people.

of people and simple clusters of people who happen to be sharing the same physical space?

Several criteria need be met in order for there to be a group. First, there must be two or more people involved in an interaction in which they are aware of each other and mutually influence each other. Without mutual influence, there is no group. In a family, for example, each individual has some influence on every other individual. Mutual influence is not enough to define a group, however. Otherwise, a pedestrian who is splashed and the driver of the car that does the splashing would constitute a group, provided that each was aware of the other. The driver's actions certainly influence the pedestrian, and the pedestrian's reactions are likely to have some influence on the driver.

But lacking in the pedestrian-driver interaction is continuity within a stable framework. The driver and the pedestrian may never encounter each other again, or if they do, the situation might be quite different: both may be drivers or both may be pedestrians. When we think of groups, however, we think of enduring relationships that occur within a relatively stable framework. For example, a family, a poker club, and a local organization all involve continuing relationships among members, stability of the roles assumed by each member, and stability of the unwritten rules, or norms, that govern the members' interactions.

This developing description of what constitutes a group is still incomplete, however. To stop here would suggest that a prisoner and a guard in a penitentiary would constitute a group. They mutually influence each other and they may certainly have an enduring relationship within a very stable framework, but we would hardly view them as belonging to the same group. They stand in opposition to one another, while group members typically share a common goal — whether to accomplish something tangible or simply to have fun. Thus another characteristic of a group is that its members share a sense of purpose.

But still something is missing. Suppose that every morning, you share a bus shelter with the same set of people. There is likely to be at least some minimal mutual influence, and the relationship, minimal as it is, endures over time in a relatively stable way. Moreover, all of the individuals share a common goal — to get on the bus. Yet no one is likely to consider him or herself part of a "group." In the final analysis, a crucial characteristic of a group is the belief held by the individual members that they are part of a group (Tajfel, 1978, 1982), part of a specific entity.

The definition of a group must include all the points above, and can be summarized in this way: A group *involves two or more people*, who are *aware of each other*, who *both influence and are influenced by one another*, who *are engaged in an ongoing and relatively stable relationship*, who *share common goals*, and who *view themselves as belonging to a group*.

There are, of course, various kinds of groups. Some are formal, with a clearly specified structure, and providing clearly delineated roles for members. Others are informal, e.g., a group of friends who regularly get together for an evening of poker. Some groups begin in an informal way but gradually grow into more formal organizations, e.g., the Parti Québécois or the Cooperative Commonwealth Federation (see Chapter 13). Groups can also be differentiated on the basis of whether or not they are task-oriented or social-oriented. Task-oriented groups serve to accomplish some specific job, while social groups function to provide pleasure and social interaction.

Attraction to the group: cohesiveness

While children cannot decide what family to join, and while people called for jury duty cannot choose their fellow jurors, most groups involve voluntary membership. Why does an individual become involved in one group and not in another? There are two major reasons. First, sometimes we join groups because we wish to accomplish some specific goal and group membership is a means of moving toward that goal. An individual who wants to become knowledgeable about photography, or learn how to sail, or stop acid rain, may join a camera club, a sailing club, or an environmental group.

The second major reason for joining groups is for the company that being part of a group provides. This is most often the case with social groups, but can play a major role for some people motivated to join task-oriented groups. People vary in terms of the need for affiliation; those individuals high in this need may find almost any group membership rewarding, regardless of the nature of the group.

All the factors which contribute to group members' desire to belong to a particular group are referred to collectively as *cohesiveness*. The greater the number of factors keeping individuals in the group, and the smaller the number of factors tempting them to leave, the more cohesive the group. Some of the factors which contribute to cohesiveness are the degree to which members are personally attracted to each other, the extent to which the group goals are in line with individual goals, and the extent to which that group is unique in being able to satisfy individual needs. For example, if you belong to a poker group, and love playing poker, and know no other poker players outside the group, then leaving the group would involve considerable cost in that you would have to give up poker. On the other hand, if various groups of people were constantly trying to get you to play poker with them, then your allegiance to your present group would be based on other factors, such as your attraction to the individual members or the quality of the poker they play. Cohesiveness within groups usually increases when the group becomes more important to its members, for instance, when it is in competition with other groups or when there is some kind of external threat to the group.

Cohesiveness can have both positive and negative effects on the productivity of task-oriented groups. Members of highly cohesive groups are usually somewhat more influenced by group norms since group membership is very important to them (Berkowitz, 1954; Schachter, Ellertson, McBride and Gregory, 1951). Thus, if the group norm calls for high productivity, then cohesiveness will foster productivity, while if the norm calls for low productivity (as might be the case in some industrial settings where workers want to provide a minimum rather than a maximum of output), cohesiveness will promote lower output. Members of highly cohesive groups can also suffer in terms of productivity because of their mutual attraction for one another: they may spend more time in social interaction than members of less cohesive groups, and they may become so absorbed by the social interaction as to lose sight of the group goal.

Finally, cohesiveness typically leads to greater participation by each member in the group's activities, as well as more cooperation and greater communication (Lott and Lott, 1961). As a result, greater member satisfaction is experienced.

Differentiation within the group: roles and status

In most groups, and especially in task-oriented groups, different members have different duties to perform. Roles may be informal in that they have gradually evolved as a consequence of continued interaction, (such as "keeper of the chips," the person who looks after the poker chips between games in a poker club), or they may be organizational, in the sense that particular titles, such as "secretary" or "chairperson" are assigned. Two important informal roles which are found in most task-oriented groups are the "task specialist" and the "social-emotional specialist." The first role is generally filled by the person who is perceived as having the most competence for directing the group to its objective. However, such a person may not be suited to the task of guiding the group through all the emotional upsets which arise as the group is being pushed toward its goal. That task is left to the social-emotional specialist.

Within any group, there tends to be a kind of "pecking order" in that some members are of higher status than others. High-status members tend to dominate group discussions, play a more important part in decision-making, and have a greater influence on low-status members than vice versa. High-status members are naturally more likely to assume leadership roles, as will be discussed in a later section. High status can derive from a number of factors: helping the group achieve its goals, having personal characteristics which lead to popularity, or having a recognized role within the group (e.g., social convenor).

Regulation by the group: norms

As you recall, norms are shared beliefs about what behaviours are and are not acceptable for group members. They usually involve a certain amount of judgment on the part of group members. For example, if one of the norms of a poker club is that each member be available to play on a specified date once each month, no one may actually be able to specify how many times a player can miss each year before being considered to be letting down the group. A silent judgment is involved, since there is no explicit rule. Similarly, if you are part of a work group on the factory floor, there is unlikely to be any rule about productivity, but if you work too hard — if you produce too much — fellow workers will begin to become distressed because such behaviour may make other members of the group appear unproductive (see the discussion of conformity and social influence in Chapter 6). Sometimes, of course, groups try to codify their norms into a set of rules. However, it is impossible to anticipate all situations which group members will encounter, and rigid rules may prove detrimental by removing from group members the willingness to exercise judgment when it is most needed.

When norms are not observed, and if the transgression is considered serious, group members will usually take measures to draw the deviant member back into line. The ultimate threat, of course, is rejection from the group. To the extent that membership in a particular group is important, such a threat can push the member to conform to the norms. An example of group rejection occurs in Schachter's (1951) discussion groups (see Chapter 6). Recall that confederates took on the roles of "mode," adopting the group consensus as a personal opinion throughout the discussion, "slider," taking an extreme position at the outset but gradually shifting toward the consensus view during the interaction, or "deviate," initially taking an extreme position and not budging from it. Initially, group discussion was directed at trying to modify the views of the two extremists, the slider and the deviate, but as the slider gradually came in line with the group view and it became clear that the deviate was not going to change, the deviate was excluded from the group discussion. In the end, no further attention was directed either to the deviate's comments or to the deviate himself (ostracism).

Group decision-making

In addition to functioning smoothly from day to day, groups are often faced with making decisions. Some of these decisions involve choosing among actions that carry with them varying degrees of *risk*. Near the end of the '60s, studies of risk-taking in groups became a major research area in North American social psychology. However, the research did not examine actual risk-taking, but rather the willingness to make decisions implying varying degrees of risk in situations that were usually hypothetical in nature. Typically, a group of subjects (usually four) would begin by filling out questionnaires individually in which each item presented a decision-making situation involving risk: a person was described who was faced with making a decision between pursuing an attractive but risky outcome or a less attractive but more certain outcome (Table 12-1). The subject was required to indicate the *minimum* probability of success that would have to be associated with the attractive but risky alternative before he or she would recommend that the person make that choice. The lower this probability, the more risk the subject was assumed to be prepared to take personally. Following the completion of the questionnaire by each subject, the subjects discussed the situation as a group; the group was instructed to come to a unanimous decision. After this group decision (consensus) was achieved, subjects were then each given a new copy of the questionnaire and asked to state their individual preferences once again. The measures of interest were (1) the differences between individuals' initial choices and the consensus position of the group; and (2) the differences between individuals' initial and final choices.

Numerous experiments demonstrated that both the group decision and the average of the individuals' final decisions were more "risky" than the individuals' initial decisions. This *risky shift* effect was found not only with subjects in Canada and the United States, but also with subjects in several European countries and New Zealand. Even when the experimental situations involved *real* monetary gain or loss for the subjects (Bem, Wallach and Kogan, 1967), or when the subjects were risking painful shocks (Bem, Wallach and Kogan, 1965), the "risky shift" was still observed.

Both group discussion and the necessity to reach consensus play critical roles in the risky shift phenomenon: Kogan and Wallach (1964) found that groups which were required to reach consensus through discussion showed the typical risky shift, whereas groups which discussed the situation but were not required to reach consensus before restating their individual decision did not. Groups which had no discussion but were required to reach consensus by voting also showed no risky shift either. Initial divergence of opinion among group members is also an important factor, for without such divergence, no shift occurs (Moscovici and Zavolloni, 1969).

Various explanations have been offered for the risky shift. Diffusion of responsibility (recall the discussion of altruism) has been suggested: in a group, each member may feel less personally responsible for the decision (Kogan and Wallach, 1967). It has

---

Item 1:

Mr. E. is the president of a light metals corporation in the United States. The corporation is quite prosperous, and has strongly considered the possibilities of business expansion by building an additional plant in a new location. The choice is between building another plant in the U.S., where there would be a moderate return on initial investment, or building a plant in a foreign country. Lower labour costs and easy access to raw materials in that country would mean a much higher return on the initial investment. On the other hand, there is a history of political instability and revolution in the foreign country under consideration. In fact, the leader of a small minority party is committed to nationalizing, that is, taking over, all foreign investments.

Imagine that you are advising Mr. E. Listed below are several probabilities or odds of continued political stability in the foreign country under consideration.

Please check the *lowest* probability that you would consider acceptable for Mr. E's corporation to build a plant in that country.

_____ The chances are 1 in 10 that the foreign country will remain politically stable.

_____ The chances are 3 in 10 that the foreign country will remain politically stable.

_____ The chances are 5 in 10 that the foreign country will remain politically stable.

_____ The chances are 7 in 10 that the foreign country will remain politically stable.

_____ The chances are 9 in 10 that the foreign country will remain politically stable.

_____ Place a check here if you think Mr. E's corporation should *not* build a plant in the foreign country, no matter what the probabilities.

Item 2:

Mr. M is contemplating marriage to Miss T, a girl whom he has known for a little more than a year. Recently, however, a number of arguments have occurred between them, suggesting some sharp differences of opinion in the way each views certain matters. Indeed, they decide to seek professional advice from a marriage counselor as to whether it would be wise for them to marry. On the basis of these meetings with a marriage counselor, they realize that a happy marriage, while possible, would not be assured.

Imagine that you are advising Mr. M and Miss T. Listed below are several probabilities or odds that their marriage would prove to be a happy and successful one.

Please check the *lowest* probability that you would consider acceptable for Mr. M and Miss T to get married.

_____ Place a check here if you think Mr. M and Miss T should **not** marry, no matter what the probabilities.

_____ The chances are 9 in 10 that the marriage would be happy and successful.

_____ The chances are 7 in 10 that the marriage would be happy and successful.

_____ The chances are 5 in 10 that the marriage would be happy and successful.

_____ The chances are 3 in 10 that the marriage would be happy and successful.

_____ The chances are 1 in 10 that the marriage would be happy and successful.

SOURCE: Kogan and Wallach, 1964

also been suggested that risk-taking has a positive value in Western society and, consequently, a discussion will produce more argument favouring risk than favouring prudence. Group members will not want to look stodgy and conservative, so they will tend to opt for the riskier of the alternatives suggested by various groups members (Brown, 1965).

In a wide variety of situations group decisions have been found to be more extreme than the initial decisions of the individuals involved.

However, the shift toward risk is only a specific example of a much more general phenomenon: *group-induced attitude polarization*. In a wide variety of situations, group decisions are found to be more extreme than the initial decisions of the individuals involved and in the direction of the views of the majority, whether this is more risky or less risky. Thus, in some situations there may be a shift *away* from risk, if the initial positions of the group members lie in that direction. Majority opinion, not risk, is the important factor here — a shift can occur even when no risk is involved. For example, in one study (Moscovici and Zavalloni, 1969) discussions among French students about North Americans led to both a group consensus and individual post-consensus opinions which were more extreme than the initial attitudes.

Other studies have pointed out additional factors involved in this polarization. For example, subjects in the group must actively interact with one another for the effect to occur. When subjects were seated in a line there was less polarization than when they sat in a square, which facilitates interaction (Moscovici and Lecuyer, 1972).

Does the group polarization effect occur outside the laboratory? A number of studies have tried to demonstrate the effect in such diverse areas as business management and marketing, teacher evaluation by students, and jury deliberations. For example, the effect of a simulated jury's knowledge of a defendant's prior conviction record (one conviction) was minimal when jurors individually arrived at decisions regarding a burglary case, but the effect was considerably enhanced when the jurors reached a decision as a group (Hans and Doob, 1976). This outcome is in line with the group polarization effect: small inclinations on the part of individual group members are magnified by the group process. The group polarization effect is also evident in such situations as group aggression (in which individual tendencies toward aggressiveness are magnified by the group), and bystander intervention, when helping is inhibited in group situations because individuals want to avoid looking foolish.

The sources of polarization   What accounts for group-induced attitude polarization? Why does the group shift away from the *average* attitude in the group? Recent research has focused on three possible explanations. The first explanation is based on *social comparison processes*, the second on *persuasive argumentation*, and the third on *social identification*.

(1) *Social comparison*. The social comparison interpretation of the polarization effect (Sanders and Baron, 1977) assumes that individuals try to see themselves and present themselves to others in as favourable a light as possible. In order to know what will constitute ideas or behaviours which will be viewed positively by others, individuals must carefully observe how others act or express themselves. Then, if all or most individuals in a group shift in the direction in which the group is perceived to be leaning, the group decision will be more extreme but in the same direction as the original group average (i.e., the average of the initial judgments of members).

(2) *Persuasive argumentation*. The persuasive argumentation explanation (Burnstein and Vinokur, 1977) suggests that group discussion is responsible for the polarization effect insofar as individuals are exposed to arguments for and against a particular position. The quality and range of the arguments and the degree to which the individual can subsequently recall either pro or con arguments are important in determining the extent and the duration of change in the individual's position. Thus, according to the persuasive arguments view, a group shift will occur only if arguments which have a persuasive effect on the individual members are presented. If these arguments are already known by the individuals, they will lead to no shift; novelty is crucial. The direction of any group shift will depend upon the preponderance of persuasive and novel argumentation in one direction or the other. With this approach, if the type of argument presented is known, the direction and the extent of the group shift can be predicted (Isenberg, 1986).

(3) *Social identification*. Recall that social identification is a process whereby individuals define themselves with respect to other people, and conform to the norms and stereotypes associated with their group. Thus, in the group decision-making situation, social identification could produce this process: "I am a police officer, I am part of a group and I don't want to lose status in it or be rejected by departing too far from the others; the others will take a risky stance because police are brave and take many risks all the time." According to this explanation, individuals hold a stereotype of the group as more extreme than it actually is. As they are motivated to conform to this stereotype, a group polarization effect is achieved. Groups become more extreme because the members expect them to be more extreme. Unlike the social comparison or persuasive argumentation models, the social identification model of polarization is based on conformity to a perceived extreme group norm.

There has been empirical support for all three explanations (Isenberg, 1986; Mackie, 1986). Which explanation is most accurate is likely dependent on the particular situation and on the personalities of the individuals. For example, the persuasive argumentation view is suited to situations in which a rational evaluation of members' input is likely to occur. However, what if a group has to make a decision about an issue in which they are already emotionally involved? They may have already examined almost all possible arguments on the subject and would be unlikely to be persuaded by a group discussion. On the other hand, if no emotion was involved and the individuals had not yet examined all the angles of an issue, the effect of persuasive argumentation might provide the best explanation of the polarization effect.

As a demonstration of the applicability of the social identification model of polarization, consider two studies carried out by Mackie (1986): In the first, subjects were exposed to information attributed either to in-group members or to non-categorized individuals. The polarization occurred only when the source of information was perceived to be from within the in-group and was the result of subjects' conforming to the "extreme" group norm. In the next experiment, the subjects were asked to focus on individual or group performance. Focusing on individual performance led to no polarization, while a focus on group performance led to a perception of more extreme group norms, and a polarization effect.

As yet, no definitive statement can be made as to which of these three models is best. Until more evidence is in, it is wise to assume that all three processes operate to push a group toward more extreme attitudes, that is, to produce polarization.

POWER

Within any group, especially within task-oriented groups, there is a distribution of power; some members enjoy much more power than others. Similarly, within a collection of groups, some groups will have more power than others. Power refers to a person's or group's capacity to influence another person or group in a direction desired by the first (Pruitt, 1976). In its most primitive form, power derives from physical might. Power has always interested and intrigued social scientists and philosophers, and some of them have even argued that it should be the focus of the social sciences (Pollard and Mitchell, 1972). To quote the English philosopher Bertrand Russell (1962): "I shall be concerned to prove that the fundamental concept in social science is Power, in the same sense in which Energy is the fundamental concept in physics" (cited by Pollard *et al.*, 1972, p. 9).

While power has not so far attained such an important position in social psychological theory, various theories of social power have been developed.

Six major sources, or "types" of power have been discussed in the literature (Raven and Kruglanski, 1970):

(1) *Reward power*, through which one person can reward another (via money, approval, love, etc.) for complying. A mother can lead her son to clean up his room by promising him some chocolate cake as a reward. If the boy wants the cake and has no other way of obtaining it, he will likely do what his mother has asked.

(2) *Coercive power*, through which one can punish another for non-compliance. The same mother can threaten her child with a spanking if he does not clean up his room. Since she is bigger than he is, she can carry through the threat.

(3) *Legitimate power*, through which legitimate authorities (teachers, police) exercise their duties. Individuals comply with the demands of such people when they accept their authority. While such power is ultimately backed up by coercive power, if the individual has internalized the respect for designated authorities, no coercion is necessary. (Refer to the earlier discussion of roles in this chapter, and to role schemata described in Chapter 3.)

(4) *Expert power*, through which individuals having important and special knowledge offer guidance. We follow the orders of a physician, not because of coercion, but

because we believe that the physician knows more than we do about how to care for our bodies.

(5) *Informational power*, through which "people in the know" (newspaper editors, governmental press secretaries, university professors) provide or withhold information (Pruitt, 1976).

(6) *Referent power*, through which individuals exact obedience from followers who want to be like them. If you are a member of a political party and you admire and respect the party leader, you will most likely do as the leader says because you will assume it is the appropriate thing to do and because you will want to act in the way the leader would act.

These forms of power are not mutually exclusive; they can reside in the same individual. More research still needs to be done to substantiate this classification of sources of power (Podsakoff and Schriesheim, 1985), and the above is not necessarily an exhaustive list. For example, Pruitt (1976) adds *reciprocal power* to the above list. Reciprocal power refers to the influence one person has over another as a result of having helped the person in the past; there is often an obligation to return the favour (recall the norm of reciprocity). Various studies have shown that the strength of this norm varies not only from person to person, but as a function of the situation. For example, a politician may provide help to other politicians (possibly by supporting their cause in a debate) with the goal in mind of being able to call in the "political IOUs" when he or she needs support.

Despite the real power many of us wield in our relationships, only a few people rise to positions of power within an institution, e.g., a company or a government. Power in the institutional setting can be vast in scope. Henry Kissinger once referred to power as "the greatest aphrodisiac," while others have viewed power as having a corrupting influence: in the words of Lord Acton, "Power tends to corrupt, and absolute power corrupts absolutely." We often admire those who have such power while at the same time regarding them with some suspicion. It is sometimes disappointing to see the changes that power can bring to an individual's personality. A person with power is often surrounded by flatterers and sycophants, a situation which can easily lead the individual to magnify his or her own abilities. In addition, power often demands a changed perspective. While the individual employee may go out of his or her way to be considerate of others, if he or she becomes a manager, it may be necessary to step on some people's toes in order to carry out the job of managing the department. A prime minister who is unwilling to be firm and decisive in dealing with incompetent subordinates will be accused of weakness. It is also easier to influence others by maintaining a psychological distance from them and avoiding emotional involvement ("the loneliness of command"). This may lead to the perception by subordinates that the person who has assumed power has changed and lost interest in them. Moreover, the powerholder may begin to take more and more credit for the accomplishments of the "underlings," thereby devaluing their efforts and abilities. Gradually, harmonious interpersonal relationships become more and more difficult to maintain (Kipnis, 1972).

The effects of power on the relationship between the powerholder and those who are subject to that power were demonstrated in an experimental study carried out by Kipnis (1972). Subjects were individually given the role of a "manager" who was in charge of some "workers" said to be working on the same task as the manager, but in another room. In fact, there were no workers. The manager could speak to the "workers" but was told that the workers would not be able to respond. The manager's task was to maximize the workers "output." Every three minutes, preprogrammed "output records" were brought from the (non-existent) worker to the manager. In one condition, managers were given "power" in that they could make rewards (extra pay) or punishments (deduction from pay), or transfer the worker to a more boring job. In a second condition, no such power was available.

As predicted it was found that:

(1) Subjects with power made more attempts to influence the workers than those without it. Very few subjects (16 percent) relied solely on persuasion: most used the power at their disposal. The presence of power seemed to bring about its use.

(2) Subjects with power devalued the worth of their workers more than subjects without power, and they were more likely to attribute the workers' efforts to their desire to obtain pay. Only 28 percent of those with power, versus 72 percent of those without it, viewed the workers' performance as a self-motivated effort to do a good job.

(3) Psychological distance, as measured by the stated willingness to meet with the workers after the study, was greater among those with power. Seventy-nine percent of those without power, but only 35 percent of those with power, expressed a desire to meet socially with the workers.

These findings support the view that power over others, at least in an institutionalized setting, leads both to devaluation of the efforts of those who are subject to the power and to increased psychological distance from them. However, we must remember that in this study, there was no resistance by the "workers." Possibly, when the influence of the powerholder is actively resisted, devaluation may not occur so readily.

LEADERSHIP

Power and influence in a group are usually distributed across the membership—sometimes uniformly, especially in social groups. Yet there is often one person who is more influential than the others. This person, designated or not, is the leader. Thus the leader has the most influence, but the actual difference between leader and follower in terms of influence may only be one of degree. Indeed, a group may have more than one leader at the same time. Recall that one group member, having the most knowledge about how to achieve the group goal, may serve as the task leader, while another member may be more influential in getting members to cooperate and coordinate their efforts in pursuing the group goal. Another member may play the key role of helping sort out emotional problems that arise among members, thus maintaining group cohesiveness (Hamblin, 1958).

Moreover, the person chosen to be the formal "head" of a group may not be the actual leader. Heads are usually imposed from outside, while leaders emerge from within. If you are a soldier under the command of a weak sergeant who is laughed at by others in your unit, it may happen that someone else whose competence is more respected, a corporal, for example, becomes your real leader. The sergeant may have legitimate power, but the referent power of the corporal will be much more effective in managing the unit. Gradually, the sergeant may come to recognize this and actually yield to the implicit power of the corporal.

Exactly how a person comes to be a leader is a question that social psychologists have been studying for many years, and the question is still without a totally satisfying answer. A related question concerns whether a person who becomes a leader in one set of circumstances is likely to become a leader in another.

Characteristics of the leader

History, it has often been said, has been shaped by great leaders. Indeed, we often think of historical eras in terms of their leading figures — Genghis Khan, Charlemagne, Joan of Arc, Napoleon, Catherine the Great, Churchill, Mao, to name but a few. What is it that made such leaders so remarkable? Was it their character that led to their rise to greatness, or was it their situation — did they just happen to be in the right place at the right time? These possibilities, referred to in the literature as the *great person* (or *trait*) approach and the *situational* approach, have been explored in considerable detail by social psychologists. A more modern view, the interactionist approach, holds that both traits and situation are important. Each of these is examined below.

The great person approach   In the nineteenth century, Francis Galton investigated the hereditary background of "great men," and attempted to explain leadership on the basis of inherited capability (Stogdill, 1974). Good leaders, he assumed, were born and not made. Psychologists no longer accept the notion that leadership capability

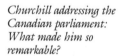

Churchill addressing the Canadian parliament: What made him so remarkable?

LEADERSHIP AND THE PERCEPTION OF HEIGHT

People tend to overestimate the height of people who are in high status positions (Keyes, 1980). During the Trudeau era in Canadian politics, for example, most people believed that Trudeau was rather tall, and certainly taller than then opposition leader Joe Clark. Students at the University of New Brunswick, when asked to estimate the heights of Trudeau and Clark, gave average estimates of 182.8 centimetres (six feet) for Trudeau and 172.7 centimetres (five feet eight inches) for Clark (Gillis, 1983). In reality, it is the opposite which is the case.

Napoleon, whom the British referred to as the "little corporal" was not so little for the times. In fact, he was the same height as Nelson, five feet eight, which was the average height of a Frenchman in those days. Calling him little was a British putdown.

is inborn. However, could it be that hereditary influence on personality and on personal characteristics is a determinant of leadership capability?

Although the question has been studied in detail, there has been little empirical evidence to support the great person view of leadership. There are some characteristics which are often associated with leadership, but the relationship between those traits and leadership is generally weak (Yukl, 1981). One characteristic that has a strong relationship to leadership is gender (see Box 12-2). There is also evidence of modest positive correlations between leadership and physical size, health, and physical attractiveness (Box 12-1). Whether these correlations are owing to the visual impact of such traits on followers or whether these traits have an early and indirect effect on personality by influencing the reactions of other people to the individual is an open question. A tall person, for example, may develop greater self-confidence as a result of being given more respect for physical prowess or being more successful in physical contests than a shorter person. Steadily maturing self-confidence, rather than height itself, might then be responsible for the leadership capacity. Indeed, leaders generally rate higher than followers in terms of self-confidence (Gibb, 1969).

Many studies have examined the relationship between intelligence and leadership and the large majority have found that leaders tend to be more intelligent than followers (Mann, 1959). Indeed, this trait seems to have the strongest relationship with leadership. This is not surprising since leadership is assumed at least partly on the basis of the leader's ability to provide followers with something they cannot provide for themselves. The relationship between intelligence and leadership is stronger in situations requiring problem-solving skills. Yet, if the gap in intelligence between the leader and followers is too great, the followers may become dissatisfied since they cannot identify with the leader and may have difficulty following his or her reasoning (Gibb, 1969)

Individuals who are high in dominance (i.e., have the need and willingness to dominate others) have been found to be more likely to emerge as leaders in small groups (Nyquist and Spence, 1986), and the ability to adapt to changing circumstances has also been found to promote leadership (Kenney and Zaccaro, 1983). Recall

GENDER AND LEADERSHIP

Traditionally, leadership has been the prerogative of males. Research indicates that even now, despite some advances in the quest for the elimination of sexual discrimination, males do predominate in leadership roles. Indeed, men and women alike are inclined to look toward males, rather than females, for leadership (Hollander, 1985). This is not surprising, given that children grow up in a patriarchal society where the father is traditionally invested with ultimate authority in the family.

Women continue to face a number of obstacles to becoming leaders in mixed-sex groups. There is, perhaps above all else, the expectation held by many men *and* women that women are not "suited" to leadership. Sexual stereotypes describe men as capable of being tough, assertive, brave, and commanding respect, while stereotypes of women emphasize not only their gentleness, but weakness, fickleness, and submissiveness. Not only is it more difficult for women to assume leadership positions in mixed-sex groups, but when they do, they are scrutinized more carefully. Ironically, female subordinates of female leaders in mixed-sex groups have been found to be more negative towards these leaders than male subordinates of the same leaders (Hollander, 1985). In other words, the successful woman has to struggle against the negative attitudes of both sexes.

These sexual stereotypes, combined with the socially inferior position of women, result in even more trouble for women leaders: they are not likely to receive the same treatment as male leaders from other people (both male and female) of equal or greater stature in the power hierarchy. Not only are women confronted with sexual harassment from male co-workers, but their viewpoints are less likely to be given attention in meetings and they are more likely to be interrupted when speaking, even by other women (Hollander, 1985).

Brown and Geis (1984) found that the evaluation of the quality of a leader's performance is significantly influenced by other people's affective reaction to that performance. Since such affective responding is likely to reflect cultural stereotypes, people may react with less enthusiasm to a woman leader than to a man. They then may interpret the lack of enthusiasm that they observe in others as owing to the ineffectiveness of the leader rather than a cultural stereotype. The results of the Brown and Geis study indicated that differences in the consensus of affective reactions surrounding a leader's performance produced discriminatory evaluations of equally competent women and men. Thus we might be inclined to judge a woman's leadership in a more negative light if those around us react negatively.

Since the leadership role has traditionally been defined in terms of the masculine stereotype (tough, decisive, aggressive), women who do succeed in leadership positions may experience a conflict between that role and their "femininity," a conflict not experienced by men; this, too, may add to the difficulties involved in female leadership.

As society becomes less discriminatory against women, and as the traditional sex roles become less sharply defined, women will undoubtedly move more steadily into leadership roles. Empirical studies of managers have found many of the assumptions about differences between male and female managers to be unfounded, whether with regard to ability, attitudes, or personality. Women managers do, however, show greater concern for relationships among people, but this trait should make for good leadership (Denmark, 1977; Hollander and Yoder, 1980). In the future, we shall no doubt see many more women leaders. It was only in 1957 that Ellen Fairclough became Canada's first woman Cabinet minister; now women in the Cabinet are relatively commonplace. How long will it be before a woman finally serves as Prime Minister?

from the discussion in Chapter 3 that cognitive complexity may be the key to understanding leadership longevity. Following a revolution, the situation faced by the leader is much more complex than either before or during the revolution, when the main task is leading a revolt.

The situational approach   The situational approach to leadership is based on the idea that different situations call for different kinds of leaders, and whoever happens to have those traits and abilities best suited to the leadership needs of the group at a particular time will emerge as leader. For example, Churchill was a great wartime leader, but lost the election following the war. Postwar Britain, it seems, wanted a different kind of leader to rebuild the country. Leaders have more influence when a group is facing a crisis; however, the group is likely to look for a new leader if the old one cannot deal with the crisis (Hamblin, 1958).

While the situational approach is superior to the trait approach since it does not assume that a person who is a good leader in one situation will be a good leader in all situations, it is also limited by excluding such variables as style of leadership (which may be related to personal traits), and the reactions of followers. Not only do leaders influence followers, but followers also influence leaders, and to be a successful leader, an individual must be in tune with the expectations and needs of the followers (Hollander, 1978; Sims and Manz, 1984). Thus successful leadership is a combination of "right leader" and "right situation," in other words, an interaction between the characteristics of the leader and the characteristics of the situation.

The interactionist approach: Leadership effectiveness   So far, we have assumed that it is possible to evaluate whether a leader is an *effective* leader. Yet, it is not clear just what makes a leader successful, or how this success should be measured. There is a problem of defining what "effectiveness means. Stogdill (1974) speaks of effectiveness in terms of the output of the group, the morale of the group, and the degree to which the members are satisfied. However, group output may be the most important of these (Fiedler, 1967), since in a task-oriented group, members may be more concerned with accomplishing the task.

Early studies of leadership effectiveness focused on democratic and autocratic leadership styles. Democratic leadership, which involves group members in decision-making rather than emphasizing clearcut orders, produces greater satisfaction among followers (Shaw, 1981). But does it lead to greater productivity? Some research has indicated that it does (e.g., Kahn and Katz, 1953); other researchers have reported that autocratic leadership is more effective in this regard (Hare, 1962). Further research has found that the situation itself is a key factor. Autocratic leadership leads to greater productivity in stressful situations, while democratic leadership produces greater productivity in non-stressful circumstances (Rosenbaum and Rosenbaum, 1971). Thus no one leadership style is likely to be effective in all situations.

Fiedler (1967, 1971, 1981) proposed a theory of leadership called "contingency theory," based on the ideas that there are two basic styles of leadership (the task-oriented leader and the socio-emotional leader) and that the leader's effectiveness is contingent upon appropriate matching of the particular leadership style to the group situation. The task-oriented leader, motivated by the need to gain satisfaction from the accomplishment of the task at hand, will not be overly concerned with the feelings

TABLE 12-2
Sample LPC items

Leaders are asked to select the person whom they least liked as a co-worker across their whole careers, and then to evaluate that person on a series of scales such as the following:

Friendly	<u>8</u> <u>7</u> <u>6</u> <u>5</u> <u>4</u> <u>3</u> <u>2</u> <u>1</u>	Unfriendly
Agreeable	<u>8</u> <u>7</u> <u>6</u> <u>5</u> <u>4</u> <u>3</u> <u>2</u> <u>1</u>	Disagreeable
Pleasant	<u>8</u> <u>7</u> <u>6</u> <u>5</u> <u>4</u> <u>3</u> <u>2</u> <u>1</u>	Unpleasant
Cooperative	<u>8</u> <u>7</u> <u>6</u> <u>5</u> <u>4</u> <u>3</u> <u>2</u> <u>1</u>	Uncooperative
Helpful	<u>8</u> <u>7</u> <u>6</u> <u>5</u> <u>4</u> <u>3</u> <u>2</u> <u>1</u>	Frustrating

By adding up the scale values, a total LPC score is derived. Rating the LPC in a negative way yields a low score; an individual producing such a rating is a *low-LPC leader* while an individual who produces a high score is referred to as a *high-LPC leader*.

and personal needs of the followers. The socio-emotional leader, being primarily oriented toward achieving good interpersonal relationships, will strive toward that end, even at the cost of lost efficiency in attaining group goals. Style of leadership, according to Fiedler, reflects the basic drive of the individual and is very resistant to modification.

Contingency theory proposes that the best way to measure leadership orientation is by assessing the leader's attitude towards the "least preferred coworker" (LPC) in the group. The LPC is determined by asking the leader to indicate who, out of all the people that he or she has ever encountered at work, was the most difficult to work with. Then the leader rates that person on a set of 18 pairs of bipolar adjectives (Table 12-2), such as "boring-interesting," using an eight-point scale. If the leader rates the LPC in a negative way, that leader is a low LPC leader, while a leader who rates the LPC in a positive manner is a high LPC leader. The high LPC leader is assumed to be more people-oriented, while the low LPC leader is assumed to be more task-oriented.

Fiedler's model assumes that the effectiveness of either of these leadership styles is contingent upon the requirements in a given leadership situation. Style of leadership interacts with *situational control*, which refers to the amount of control that the leader can exert over the members of the group. According to Fiedler, situational control depends on a combination of three factors. The three important aspects of the situation are: (1) the affective relationship between leader and followers; (2) the extent to which the task which the group is undertaking is structured or unstructured; and (3) the extent to which the leader is able to exercise power (i.e., is able to deliver positive outcomes or punishments) over the followers. Power is the least important of the three. The theory suggests that both the productivity of the group and the morale of the members will be increased when the leadership style matches the situational control (Chemers, 1983).

Task-oriented leadership should be most successful in the context of group performance in situations which are either very favourable or very unfavourable for the leader. Under unfavourable leadership conditions (ambiguous task, poor leader-follower relations, low leader power), the group may be more receptive to a leader who can get them moving towards their goal; a person-oriented leader may spend too much time on trying to promote greater interpersonal harmony and not enough time on the group goal. When conditions are highly favourable (structured task, good leader-follower relations, high leader power), the task-oriented leader, content that the group is moving toward its goal, may become more attentive to the "people" concerns. On the other hand, a people-oriented leader in a situation already characterized by interpersonal harmony may now try to demonstrate that he or she is *really* a leader by pursuing self-aggrandizing activities. In so doing, the leader may actually lose some esteem, while not being concerned enough with the task (Fiedler, 1971).

In intermediate conditions of favourableness, friction between group members may become more serious. In the highly unfavourable situation, members may be willing to overlook such problems in order to get on with the task. In this situation, the person-oriented leader can do more to cope with the group's needs (see Figure 12-2).

The contingency model has received support from a large number of different studies (e.g., Strube and Garcia, 1981) and has been viewed as the most useful approach for ascertaining the effectiveness of leadership, despite continuing controversy about it (Peters, Hartke and Pohlmann, 1985).

FIGURE 12-2
Contingency model of leadership and group performance

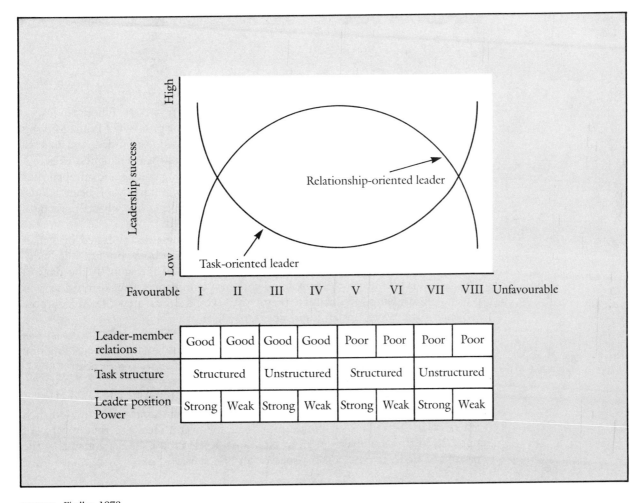

Leader-member relations	Good	Good	Good	Good	Poor	Poor	Poor	Poor
Task structure	Structured		Unstructured		Structured		Unstructured	
Leader position Power	Strong	Weak	Strong	Weak	Strong	Weak	Strong	Weak

SOURCE: Fiedler, 1978

The effect of Trudeau's charisma is evident in this photo taken at a Vancouver shopping centre.

The charismatic leader

In the 1960s, "Trudeaumania" swept a political neophyte — Pierre Elliott Trudeau — into leadership of the Liberal Party and eventually into the position of Prime Minister of Canada. For the next 16 years, Trudeau amazed, amused, astounded, and angered his fellow citizens, depending on their political views and their willingness to accept the idiosyncratic aspects of his behaviour. Whether wearing sandals and an open shirt into the House of Commons, "horsing around" in a swimming pool, being adored by the world press or asking farmers, "Why should we sell your wheat?", Trudeau had a powerful effect on everyone whom he encountered.

Pierre Trudeau had "charisma" and his political life was distinguished by "charismatic" leadership. People admired him or detested him or both, but few were indifferent. Many of those who jumped on the Trudeau bandwagon in the days of Trudeaumania later became disappointed with his performance. They had had a vision of a new leader who would uplift them, who would breath new life and purpose into their nation, perhaps an impossible task for any person.

The term *charismatic leader* was coined by Weber (1947). He described *charisma* (which is Greek for "divine gift") as an exceptional quality in a person enabling him or her to gather a large number of disciples as a result of appearing to possess supernatural, providential, or extraordinary powers.

History does not lack for other instances of such leaders — Churchill, Hitler, Gandhi, Martin Luther King, and Eva Peron are excellent examples. How do such leaders come to wield such power over their followers? How are they capable of appealing to their followers on a raw emotional level? House (1977) argues that the charismatic leader is typified by a specific set of characteristics:

(1) *An extremely high level of self-confidence.*

(2) *An extremely high level of dominance.* Such leaders seem to have a strong "need" to influence others; this very need drives them to acquire the necessary persuasive skills to be able to wield such influence.

(3) *An apparently strong conviction of the moral righteousness of their beliefs.* However, House suggests that it is at least possible that some charismatic leaders believe in neither themselves nor their beliefs, but are capable of acting as though they do in order to influence and control their followers. Certainly, there have been charismatic religious leaders who were later shown to be manipulators, using their charismatic abilities for their own ends (e.g., U.S. cult leader Jim Jones of the People's Temple, who led his followers to mass suicide in 1978, and evangelist Jim Bakker of the *PTL Club*, who left his TV ministry in 1987 following reports of sexual infidelity and financial exploitation).

To these can be added a fourth point:

(4) *Personal characteristics such as charm, originality, or even speech fluency.* These are essential attributes of the charismatic leader (Sashkin, 1977).

Charismatic leaders affect their followers in specific ways (House, 1977):

(1) They provide their followers with "transcendent" goals expressed in moral rhetoric. Consider Trudeau's speeches about a "Just Society"; Martin Luther King's civil rights utterances, "I have a dream . . ." and "We shall overcome . . ."; Churchill's depiction of the British as invincible, "We shall never surrender . . ."; Hitler's appeal to past and future German glory, "Germany awake!" and the "Thousand Year Reich"; Gandhi's vision of an India free of British Rule, "Quit India"; and John Kennedy's "Ask not what your country can do for you . . . ."

(2) Because the leader has high expectations of the followers as well as confidence in them, the self-esteem of the followers is enhanced and they are motivated toward achieving goals.

(3) The charismatic leader often provides a role model and a value system for the followers which are effective even after the leader's death. Even today, Gandhi is respected and admired and his teachings are followed by millions of Indians and non-Indians.

Shils (1965) argued that charisma is, in fact, much more common than we believe, that it is distributed here and there throughout society. Those who wield power are often viewed as being charismatic because of the awe in which we hold the power itself. However, there is more to it than that, since a great many powerful leaders are not "charismatic" in terms of their effect on their followers. More likely, the situation in which a charismatic leader flourishes is one in which any one of a number of people might flourish equally well, had they the opportunity. The charismatic leader often emerges in a time of stress, and he or she most often epitomizes the deeply held feelings of the followers. Yet, once the stress is lifted, the public can quickly throw off its fascination for the leader.

However, none of the sociological or political ideas about charismatic leadership have ever been empirically tested. We could begin to do so by first identifying charismatic leaders, then comparing their followers with followers of leaders chosen at random. Until this is done, our knowledge of charismatic leadership must remain at a somewhat speculative level.

A FINAL OBSERVATION

Originally, social psychologists pursued twin interests in the area of groups: group processes as they influenced the *individual* in the group (the "individualistic" approach) and group processes defined as how groups interrelate and mutually influence each other (the "systems" approach). However, beginning in the 1960s and continuing to the present, the dominant approach in North America, to the almost total exclusion of the systems approach, has been individualistic. In many ways this reflects the predominant ideology of the United States (Sampson, 1977) in which group relations are considered an extension of the psychology of interpersonal relations. Systems concerns, such as those associated with international conflict, have mainly been left to sociologists and political scientists (Brewer and Kramer, 1985). North American social psychologists, more so than Europeans, continue to be preoccupied with the reactions of individuals to some event that occurs in the group context (Smith and White, 1983; Stephan, 1985).

SUMMARY

(1) In any society, individuals define themselves largely in terms of groups and social categories.

(2) We construct our social world in terms of social categories, and govern our behaviour according to the salient category in a particular situation.

(3) One basic construct is the distinction we make between in-group and out-group. A "generic norm" of discrimination against an out-group leads to discrimination even in the absence of self-interest or pre-existing hostility toward the out-group.

(4) Individuals tend to see members of one category as more similar than they really are, and the differences between members of different categories as greater than they really are (social differentiation).

(5) Since individuals belong to different categories simultaneously, some being in-groups and others being out-groups, this leads to categories which reduce discrimination.

(6) When we are at a disadvantage relative to people of another category, we tend either to assimilate ourselves into that group or to differentiate ourselves from them in terms of other criteria in order to minimize that disadvantage.

(7) Mutual interaction and influence, ongoing and relatively stable relationships, shared goals, and the perception of belonging to a group are the defining characteristics of groups.

(8) People join groups to accomplish goals and to satisfy needs for affiliation. These factors contribute to group cohesiveness.

(9) Within a group, members may assume various roles, and norms regulate their behaviour.

(10) Group decisions tend to be more polarized than individual decisions. Three explanations have been suggested: social comparison, persuasive argumentation, and social identification.

(11) Leadership has been explained in terms of the traits of the leader, characteristics of the situation, and the interaction of leader and group characteristics

(12) Fiedler's contingency model of leadership effectiveness relates the characteristics of the group to task-oriented and interpersonal relationship-oriented leadership styles.

(13) Leaders described as "charismatic" tend to be self-confident and dominant, with strong convictions, who provide their followers with transcendent goals and a model for values.

FURTHER READING

AUSTIN, W.A. and WORCHEL, S. (Eds.) (1979). *Social psychology of intergroup relations*. Monterey: Brooks/Cole.

BILLIG, M. (1976). *Social psychology and intergroup relations*. London: Academic Press.

JANIS, I. (1983). *Groupthink: Psychological studies of policy decisions and fiascoes*. Third Edition. Boston: Houghton-Mifflin.

PAULUS, P.B. (1980) *The psychology of group influence*. Hillsdale, NJ: Erlbaum.

SHAW, M. (1981). *Group dynamics: The psychology of small group behavior*. Third Edition. New York: McGraw-Hill.

STOGDILL, R.M. (1984). *Handbook of leadership: A survey of theory and research*. New York: Free Press.

TAJFEL, H. (Ed.) (1978). *Differentiation between social groups: Studies in the social psychology of intergroup relations*. London: Academic Press.

TAYLOR, D.M. and MOGHADDAM, F.M. (1987). *Theories of intergroup relations: International social psychological perspectives*. New York: Praeger.

Conflict and its Resolution

The grim fact is that we prepare for war
like precocious giants and for peace like
retarded pygmies.
Lester B. Pearson

FOR REFLECTION

- Is conflict unavoidable, and is it always undesirable?
- Can we arrive at a definition of "justice"?
- When are people motivated to cooperate with each other? Compete with each other?
- What makes a threat successful?
- Can social psychology help to prevent war?

434

THE WORD "CONFLICT" is often used in common speech as a synonym for warfare or aggression, but there is an important distinction to be made between conflict and aggression. The term "conflict" properly refers to a situation of discord between two or more parties which can sometimes be peacefully resolved or which may, in some circumstances, lead to aggression. Conflict involves a divergence of interest, or the belief that the interests or aspirations of two or more parties cannot be achieved simultaneously (Pruitt and Rubin, 1986). For example, Bob wants Louise to stay at home and raise the children while Louise wants to put the children into a day nursery and pursue a career outside the home. Another example: Both Canada and the United States lay claim to the rich Georges Banks fishing grounds. In both of these examples, there is a set of goals which cannot be satisfied simultaneously. Bob and Louise cannot both achieve their desired goals; Canada and the United States cannot both possess the disputed territory.

In any dynamic society or relationship between groups or individuals, there will *always* be conflicts of one sort or another and, if viewed constructively and resolved or regulated peacefully, such conflicts allow people to react and accommodate to changing circumstances. Thus conflicts often lead to positive consequences. (Recall the discussion about how conflicts can serve to bind societies together, Chapter 12). In the example given above, the conflict between Louise and Bill may force them to examine their mutual and individual goals and their values concerning marriage and child-rearing. If they are successful in resolving their conflict in a peaceful and positive manner, their relationship is likely to be strengthened. The bond between them is likely to be stronger than if the conflict had not arisen, that is, if Louise, knowing that Bill wanted her to stay at home and raise the children, had simply ignored her own longings for a career.

Competition is a form of conflict, since each party wants to "win" and only one can do so. It is important to note that resolving conflicts does not necessarily mean giving up competition. Sometimes competition is desirable and people can agree to compete within a mutually accepted framework which establishes rules for the competition. For example, in a free enterprise system, competition among vendors is seen as advantageous for consumers. Thus, although Eaton's and Simpsons have an underlying conflict of interest — increases in sales by one company may be reflected in decreases in sales by the other — this particular "conflict," or competition, is not destructive because the companies compete according to certain established rules of fairness, much as two hockey teams compete.

The great Canadian department store face-off: A conflict of interest and a common understanding.

Unfortunately, far too many conflicts, rather than being regulated through negotiation and compromise, lead either to violence or avoidance. At the marital level, couples often endure in a warring relationship or separate rather than work to resolve their conflict, and thereby strengthen their relationship. In industry, both union and management too often lose through strikes and lockouts because they are unable to peacefully resolve some conflict about wages or working conditions. At the international level, nations all too often go to war over relatively minor conflicts (e.g., the battle between Great Britain and Argentina for the Falkland Islands), or break off diplomatic relations and refuse to deal with one another (e.g., the United States and Cuba).

Despite ever increasing scientific and technological progress, humans have advanced but little in their ability to prevent the destructive aspects of conflict. It is usually too appealing to try to force a solution to a conflict rather than to negotiate; often forcing the other side to back down becomes the most important goal. Two devastating world wars and countless smaller wars, thousands of labour disruptions, and spiralling divorce rates demonstrate that we are little better at dealing with conljflict in the twentieth century than were our forebearers in the centuries before (see Box 13-1).

CONFLICT: SOME BACKGROUND

Although the study of conflict was a popular subject for sociologists and political scientists in the latter part of the nineteenth and the early part of the twentieth centuries, by the middle of this century, very little development was taking place in

---

B · O · X   13 - 1

DESTRUCTIVE CONFLICT RESOLUTION

Although it has had neither the quantity nor intensity of the social strife of the United States, Canadian society has not entirely avoided the consequences of destructive conflict resolution. Yet Canadian violence has not generally involved loss of life, certainly not to the extent that is found in the United States and, apart from the terrorism practiced by the FLQ and the Sons of Freedom Doukhobors, most of the violence in Canada in this century has been labour-related.

Between 1910 and 1966, 227 strikes were attended by violence, with soldiers and the RCMP often being called in to put them down. Strikes such as the

Winnipeg General Strike and the Asbestos Québec strike are but a few examples. And, of course, there was the depression of the 1930s:

> The Depression saw some bloody strikes, a violent confrontation during the historical trek of unemployed people to Ottawa in 1935, and suspensions of civil liberties not seen at any time since. Workers protesting unfair management practices, unemployed people demanding work or assistance, people organizing to demand political change—all were harassed, often arrested, and sometimes killed by the police (especially the RCMP) . . . " (Jackson, Kelly and Mitchell, p. 177, 1977)

this area. As far as social psychology is concerned, the discipline not only ignored but often *avoided* the subject of conflict until the launching of Sputnik, the world's first space satellite, by the Soviets in 1958. The fear that Soviet science and technology had outstripped that of the U.S.A. suddenly made the need for advancement in the understanding of conflict, at least at the international level, seem much more pressing. New attempts were made to find ways of resolving conflicts on favourable terms without escalation to a dangerous level. Sputnik was a reminder that western powers could not count on military superiority to win conflicts.

Not everyone took the same approach to the study of conflict, however. While sociologists and political scientists downplayed the role of individuals in their theorizing, social psychologists tried to reduce groups and nations to the status of individuals to make their theorizing less complex. One social psychologist remarked on the trend, commenting that, "Such psychological concepts as 'perception,' 'intention,' 'value,' 'hostility,' 'trust' and 'suspicion' recur repeatedly in the discussions of war and peace. . . . I shall assume there is some merit in viewing nations like persons . . . and to conceive of international relations in terms analogous to those of interpersonal relations" (Deutsch, 1962).

In adopting such a perspective, social psychologists came to view conflict at the international level as amenable to study through the analysis of conflict at the interpersonal level. Consequently, the bulk of social psychological research into conflict has focused on the study of two or more individuals in conflict in the context of controlled laboratory studies.

Several sources of intergroup conflict have already been examined in earlier chapters. A number of factors at both the individual and the group level have been seen to contribute significantly both to discrimination and to the perception that out-groups pose some potential threat to us: (1) Stereotyping both reflects and encourages prejudice and discrimination towards members of other groups. (2) Authoritarianism is often accompanied by ethnocentrism, a trait which leads individuals to place their group above all others in value and to distrust and rigidly reject members of groups dissimilar to their own. (3) The mere process of social categorization (differentiation of groups) is enough to produce intergroup disharmony between groups who have had no contact with each other and who have no reason for conflict. Each of these factors actually represents a distinct line of research within social psychology, although each by itself goes only part way toward explaining intergroup conflict (Fisher, 1985). All of these factors represent sources of *unrealistic* conflict in that there is no basic reason for any conflict at all, apart from the fact that two or more groups differ from each other.

In this chapter we examine *realistic* conflicts, in which there is present some actual basis for disagreement, dispute, or hostility. Realistic conflicts between individuals or groups are *rational* in the sense that they reflect either competition for scarce resources, incompatible goals, or incompatible principles (e.g., "The environment must be protected at all costs" versus "Jobs are more important than lakes and rivers"). If a labour union demands higher salaries while management does not want to pay out more money, there is a realistic conflict. If Canada considers the Northwest Passage to be its territory and the United States wants to treat the passage as international waters (as has already occurred), there is a realistic conflict. If the provinces want more power in areas of jurisdiction that the federal government wishes to reserve for itself, there is a realistic conflict. Box 13-2 describes a realistic and enduring conflict.

THE LONG ROOTS OF CONFLICT

Individuals involved in intergroup conflict may not completely understand the historical process that has led to the confrontation. They may even be too young to remember the roots of the problem.

For instance, consider the "doctors' strike" which occurred in Saskatchewan in 1962: When the provincial government introduced North America's first Medicare legislation, providing for compulsory government medical insurance for every Saskatchewan resident, and stipulating that physicians' fees would be paid directly by the government, physicians across the province withdrew their services. Bitter feelings developed on both sides of the issue, with groups of citizens spontaneously organizing themselves in support of the doctors, and other voluntary groups springing up in defense of the government. Even families were sometimes seriously divided as people took different sides in the dispute.

Finally, three weeks after the withdrawal of services began, the physicians and the government managed to reach a compromise when the government agreed not to *force* the doctors to participate in the Medicare plan: physicians could bill patients directly, and these patients could then recover the cost from the government. The walkout was over, but bitter feelings continued for a long time. While it would be possible to analyze this dispute in terms of its dynamics and the characteristics of the principal negotiators involved, to stop there would be to miss the historical factors which were, perhaps, even more responsible for the doctors' protest than were the immediate conditions that led to it.

A sociological-historical analysis of the situation (Gouldner, 1968) suggests that the physician-government conflict had been building up slowly over the preceding 20 or 30 years. From the beginning the physicians had been a part of the Saskatchewan elite, while the farmers were a relatively powerless group, often struggling just to hold on to their land. As we shall see later, pressure from outside often leads people to band together to oppose a common threat. So did the desperate conditions brought about by the drought and depression of the '30s lead farmers to organize themselves, and through movements such as the Co-op, the Wheat Pool, the Credit Union, and the Cooperative Commonwealth Federation (CCF) party, they gradually won both economic and political strength. These movements, which led ultimately to the election of a CCF government, posed a threat to the physicians, for their social status and political power was eroded as their free market ideology was displaced by cooperative-socialist ideals. According to Gouldner's analysis, a latent conflict smoldered beneath the surface for years until the passage of the Medicare legislation, seen as a direct assault on the physicians' autonomy, pushed the physicians into action. When the strike ended, a new distribution of power had been accepted by both sides, although many individual physicians chose to leave the province. A few years later, the vast majority of physicians in the province described themselves as being quite content with Medicare (Thompson, 1965).

The doctors' strike, then, was the culmination of a long, latent conflict and the result of an ongoing process of redistribution of power. It transcended the individuals involved in that, without a doubt, few of the protagonists on either side had been around in the early days when the physicians enjoyed great power and status. However, the motivations and perceptions of the two groups survived, even as the membership of each group changed across the years (the contemporary fights over "opting out" and extra-billing are part of the legacy from this dispute). It is this transcendent reality of the group which is often neglected by the psychologist but which is taken very seriously by the sociologist.

Types of conflict

As with beauty, conflict may be in the eye of the beholder. Two individuals may have a conflict of interest, but if the conflict is not perceived, then it is unlikely to have much effect on their interaction. From the point of view of someone outside a conflict, conflicts can be categorized into various types, depending on the relationship between the actual conflict of interest and the manner in which the people involved interpret the conflict. For individuals, however, the conflict seems to be a real conflict. There are at least six different types of conflict which are distinguished from each other by the relationship between the perceived and the objective state of affairs (Deutsch, 1973):

(1) *Veridical conflict.* An objective conflict exists and is accurately perceived. For example, both husband and wife want to use the spare bedroom, he for an office, she for a darkroom. They have genuinely opposed interests in this case.

(2) *Contingent conflict.* In such conflicts, there are other resources available so that both parties can be satisfied, but they do not recognize this. The conflict is contingent upon this failure to recognize. For example, in the conflict concerning the spare bedroom if there is also an attic which can easily be converted to either an office or a darkroom, the conflict could be readily resolved. In contingent conflicts, a third party ("mediator") can often successfully resolve the conflict by pointing to a solution which will readily satisfy both.

(3) *Displaced conflict.* The dispute in this case is not about the real underlying issue. For example, a couple with sexual problems may be embarrassed about admitting their concerns and argue instead over converting the spare bedroom. Since the *actual* issue is not discussed, the *ostensible* issue, even if temporarily resolved, will not alleviate the basic conflict. A third party may be helpful by directing the protagonists to deal with the real issue.

(4) *Misattributed conflict.* The disputants in this kind of conflict wrongly blame each other for their difficulties. For example, suppose during a period of financial restraint, students criticize professors for not providing enough individual attention, while professors criticize students for demanding too much of their time. Both students and professors actually have *common* cause against the group (e.g., government) that controls the budget.

(5) *Latent conflict.* In this case, there is a conflict in the sense that the two parties have incompatible goals, but they are not yet aware of this incompatibility, or one party may be for the moment unwilling or unable to pursue goal satisfaction. Latent conflicts often involve a dominant-subordinate relationship. Slaves and masters may live in relative harmony because of the power of the latter over the former. However, the slaves would undoubtedly like freedom, while their masters would like to continue exploiting them. In some circumstances, both the oppressed and the ruling classes view their situation as fair and just, and each may be quite content with things as they are, despite the underlying conflict of interest and exploitation (Brickman, 1974). In such a case, no conflict is apparent unless and until some "consciousness raising" occurs which sensitizes the exploited to the inequity of their situation. Social reformers and revolutionaries alike attempt to accomplish just that. Whether considering the situation among French-speaking Québécois or American Blacks in the '60s, or among women and homosexuals in the '70s and '80s, a principal goal of "liberation"

B · O · X   13 - 3

A CONFLICT OVER FALSE PREMISES

During a smallpox epidemic in Montreal in 1885 (which killed at least 3 000 Montrealers that year), physicians successfully persuaded the city to pass a compulsory vaccination law. People who refused vaccinations were imprisoned. Superstition among the less well-educated, faced with a strange new medical procedure, led to strong resistance to the measure, and vaccinating teams were sometimes physically ejected from people's homes. One day, a protest mob rioted, smashing store windows and setting fires as they moved through the streets, and attacking the firemen who tried to extinguish the blazes. The Victoria Rifles were called in to quell the disturbance, and from then on, until the epidemic was over, the vaccination teams moved with armed escorts (Batten, 1977).

Both the physicians and the citizenry had the same goal; the good health of the citizenry. As we have already seen, it is the *perceptions* of the individuals involved which determine whether or not a conflict exists. Yet in a very real sense, it was not a conflict, since there was no *real* conflict of interest. Each side wanted exactly the same thing — the good health of the populace.

movements has been to persuade and convince those who are the objects of injustice that they are being treated inequitably by the larger society — in other words, to demonstrate that there is a conflict.

(6) *Conflict based on false premises.* This is a conflict over attributing the causes of a behaviour. There is no objective conflict of interest in this case. Such conflicts are amenable to resolution if information can be disseminated which will be accepted as truth, but that is often difficult to do. A simple example is that of a union which, acting upon the erroneous belief that management has much more money available than it does, goes out on strike. Its leaders attribute management's reluctance to make a better offer not to limited resources but to bad faith. If, indeed, the company is in serious financial difficulty, then the premise upon which the conflict is based — the availability of funds — is a false premise. Similarly, a man and a woman may argue because she forgot to buy him a birthday card. He may attribute this to a lack of love on her part, while she may attribute her oversight to fatigue (see Box 13-3).

As you can see, conflict can arise from various sources, and often an outsider is better able to see the real basis of conflict than are the disputants themselves. It is also important to understand that these six types of conflict are not mutually exclusive; for example, displaced or misattributed conflict is often associated with a latent conflict.

Social conflict as exchange

When two parties are in conflict, one simple form of resolution is to end the interaction altogether: sometimes nations break off diplomatic relations; sometimes factories are closed permanently; sometimes people divorce. This does not usually happen, however. For example, a man and a woman living together may endure a considerable level of conflict, even if its consequences are somewhat destructive, if there is no other relationship which can serve the needs this relationship continues to fulfill. In other words, even though there may be considerable bickering, each may bear with this in order to have company or share expenses. In such a situation, conflict can be approached from the point of view of social exchange. The two parties are exchanging all sorts of things: affection, finances, housework, babysitting. The exchange may be very good on some levels (e.g., economic) but very poor on others (e.g., affectionate). Conflict over affection may not be serious enough to break the union because of the importance of other mutual benefits. Similarly, labour and management usually continue to deal with each other, as does nation with nation.

Social exchange theory (Homans, 1958; Thibaut and Kelley, 1959) grew out of the philosophy of utilitarianism. According to this point of view, all social interaction can be viewed as a kind of economic interaction in which an individual or group obtains certain rewards but only at the expense of certain costs. The outcome, or "profit," is the difference between rewards and costs, and presumably an individual will be unhappy with a non-profitable interaction. Social exchange theory posits that people are very selective in their choice of interactions. For example, if you are at a cocktail party, you will likely wander around, joining in conversation with a person or group, perhaps finding that your rewards do not exceed the costs (i.e., you find the conversation boring and are straining to pretend politely that you are interested), so you sample other conversations until you find one in which the costs of participation are justified by the rewards. (Recall the discussion of social attraction in Chapter 4).

According to Thibaut and Kelley's analysis, an individual assesses the richness of the outcome in a given exchange situation not solely in terms of "rewards minus costs," but also in comparison with two other standards. The first is the *comparison level* (CL). A wife might compare her "outcome" in her marital situation with what she perceives to be the outcome of other wives, or with what her own outcome was earlier in the relationship, or even with her outcome in prior or other current relationships. While the CL is used to decide whether the person is receiving what he or she deserves or wants, a second standard, called *comparison level for alternatives* (CLalt) is used as a basis for deciding whether or not to stay in the relationship (i.e., the CLalt is used to decide whether the person can get a better deal anywhere else). If divorce or separation brings great stigma or economic ruin, the person may decide to stay in the relationship, unsatisfying though it is. CLalt, in other words, is the lowest level of outcome the person will accept, given the available alternatives to the relationship. Thus, only if the mutual outcomes are above *each* person's CLalt will the relationship continue.

Before most women were in a position to become well-educated and compete professionally with men, many of them accepted the role of mother/labourer/servant on the basis of such comparisons. When comparing their situation with those of relevant others (CL), they seemed to be doing well enough and if they chose to leave the relationship, their plight (CLalt) looked even worse. Now, however, the CL of many women is not that of the average housewife, but that of the "liberated" woman who enjoys a variety of options. Consequently, when married women experience severe discontent with their role, the possibility of leaving the relationship is not nearly so horrifying as it once was, for separation and divorce have become commonplace and widely accepted. In addition, alternative relationships offering higher rewards, at least in the short term, may be more readily available. Whether or not a conflict leads to rupture of a relationship depends not only upon the disputants themselves and the nature of the conflict, but also upon factors outside the conflict (Figure 13-1).

Of course, parties in a social interaction often try to influence the other side's perceptions of the profits being earned, the CL, and the negative aspects, or costs, of having the relationship. A weak partner may try to strengthen the relationship by actually increasing his or her dependence on the stronger party in order to make the costs associated with leaving the relationship higher (guilt or social conscience). The stronger partner may try to prevent the other from leaving by either offering more

FIGURE 13-1
Social exchange theory: The CL and the CLalt

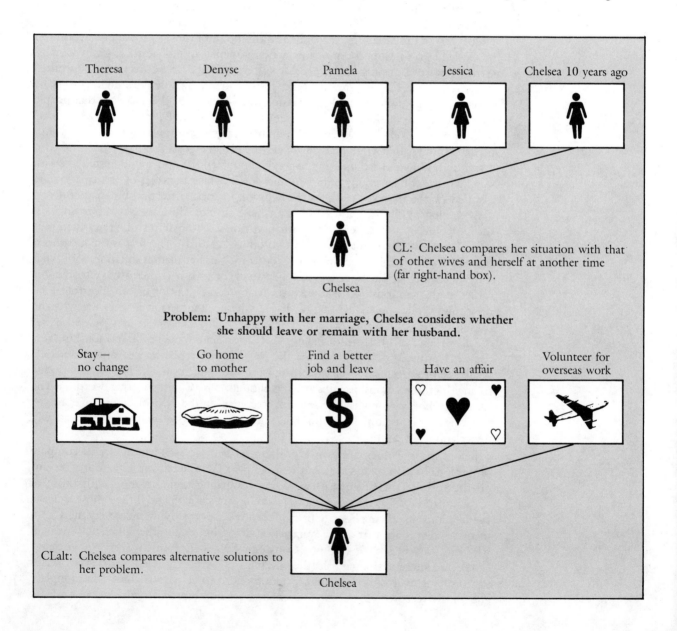

in the exchange, or by making alternative relationships less available to the other person, or by appealing to outside support (norms, rules) (Andreas, 1969). For example, an unhappy but dependent spouse could "manage" to be fired from work so that if the other person now "deserts," the deserter will feel greater guilt and be subject to greater social disapproval. Thus the CLalt is changed. Or the breadwinner in the family may try to prevent the partner from leaving the relationship by promising more money or affection, or by appealing indirectly to mutual friends for support, conveying the message that if the partner leaves the relationship, these friends may abandon the partner.

Social exchange theory is one model for viewing conflicts between individuals. It is based essentially on the concept of seeking a "fair deal" for both parties. It is only a short step from this theory to theories of justice, which are the object of much contemporary research. This topic is discussed next.

JUSTICE

The first social scientist to develop systematic postulates about fairness and justice in social behaviour was Homans (1961, 1974, 1982), although he acknowledges that the ancient philosopher Aristotle had similar ideas. Other theorists and researchers have since modified and refined Homans' formulations (e.g., Lerner, 1977; Walster, Walster and Berscheid, 1978). The central concerns of these theorists and researchers have been the conditions under which the allocation of a resource or the outcome of an event would be judged by the recipient, or by a third party, as just or unjust.

Distributive justice

We arrive at justice decisions on the basis of distribution rules, or norms, which are an integral part of our value system. It appears that these rules are universal, although how and why they are applied will vary from one culture to another. Three major rules of distributive justice have been identified, *merit* (or "equity"), *equality*, and *need* (Austin, 1979).

(1) *Merit (equity)*. Aristotle argued that distributive justice requires an "equality of proportions" which involves two aspects. First, the differences in merit and demerits between the parties need to be taken into account. Second, such differences must be considered relative to others in such a way that similar cases are treated in like fashion (Austin, 1979). In other words, we can measure our gains against what we view as our contributions and our worthiness, and we compare this ratio with the ratio for other people in similar or dissimilar situations. This concept translates into the social psychological notion of *equity*, formalized by Adams (1965) and Walster, Walster and Berscheid (1978). Equity theory is related to the theory of cognitive dissonance in the sense that fairness can be restored by changing behaviour or by changing perceptions. Equity theory proposes that a relationship between parties is a just one when the ratio of *perceived* outcomes to *perceived* inputs (those assets and

liabilities which lead to a deserved outcome) are equal (Austin, 1979). In a job situation, the inputs and corresponding outcomes might look like this (Table 13-1):

TABLE 13-1
*Inputs and outcomes in a
job situation*

Inputs	Outcomes
effort	salary
training	fringe benefits
experience	company car
seniority	interesting job
gender	opportunity for promotion

Gender may be considered an input by a "traditional" male who feels that he should be compensated at a better rate than women. The existence of the "equal pay for work of equal value" movement emphasizes that this problem has yet to be satisfactorily resolved. Other unexpected factors may also be considered inputs by some individuals who interpret their situation in a personal way. For example, at one time bank workers in Paris who were Parisian felt that they should receive more pay than their co-workers from the provinces (Homans, 1961).

All other things being equal, the individual who works hardest on a job (has the largest input) should reasonably expect to receive the most pay, otherwise the exchange will be perceived as being unfair, or "inequitable." It is important to remember that *perceptions* are crucial here. For example, the employee may feel that he or she is working too hard, while the employer may think that output is at an appropriate level. In such a case, the employer may view an exchange as equitable and the employee may view it as inequitable, leading to a conflict situation. The factors and conditions that lead to judgments of inequity in social exchanges have been developed by Walster *et al.* (1978), who base their theory on four principles:

a) People strive to get the most they can for themselves (maximize outcomes).
b) Societies and groups within societies have standards regarding what constitutes an equitable exchange.
c) Inequity gives rise to psychological discomfort. The more the inequity, the more the discomfort.
d) This discomfort will motivate individuals or groups to try to reduce the inequity.

Under some conditions individuals may feel that their outcomes are too low relative to their inputs. This situation will be associated with negative emotions, such as anger, hostility, and frustration. An attempt to correct the situation may follow, such as asking for a raise or filing a grievance. If not successful in rectifying the situation, the individual might put less effort into the work, take more days off "sick," seek other employment, or even resort to sabotage.

It also should be noted that an inequitable exchange can occur if the outcomes, are perceived as *excessive* relative to the inputs. As we might expect, it takes more to reach the threshold in this type of inequity than it does if the inequity is in the negative direction. In this case, associated feelings might include guilt and embarrassment. We seem better able to tolerate the situation when inequity is to our advantage. However, if extreme, some attempt to restore equity might occur. For example, if an individual feels "overpaid" she might donate some of her salary to charity.

(2) *Equality*. Sometimes resources are distributed equally rather than equitably, even though the participants have not made equal contributions. When group stability and *esprit de corps* are of primary concern, it may be disruptive to allocate outcomes differentially to group members (Sampson, 1975). Research has shown that allocations are likely to be equal if the participants expect to meet again, and that females have a preference for equality while males prefer equity (Major and Deaux, 1982). These different orientations based on gender have been shown to be present in children as young as seven years of age (Vinacke and Gullickson, 1964). It has been suggested (Benton, 1971; Weinstein *et al.*, 1969) that females are more concerned than males with the interpersonal aspects of the situation, exhibit less desire to create status differentials, and avoid actions that could disrupt the harmony of the group.

(3) *Need*. Another rule of distributive justice is that those who need the most should get the most. Need is closely associated with the norm of social responsibility and, not surprisingly, affects such activities as charitable donations (see Chapter 10): you perceive a need and your sense of social responsibility motivates you to respond to that need. Need also is taken into consideration at the interpersonal level in groups. For instance, an individual who has few resources may not be subjected to the norm of equality (Leventhal, Weiss and Long, 1969) and it has been shown that a person who lacks ability may be "overrewarded" in a work situation (Taynor and Deaux, 1973). It is important to note, however, that the manner in which the "deficit" is acquired is usually taken into consideration. If the individual is perceived as not being personally responsible (i.e., the deficit occurred because of low ability or lack of funds due to an earthquake), then need would be taken into consideration. But if the individual brought about his or her circumstances through stupid investments or excessive use of drugs, then others would be considerably less sensitive to his or her

Blaming the victim: Women who travel alone at night are often seen as partly responsible if they are attacked.

plight. (Recall the discussion of the just world hypothesis in Chapter 3.) People consider the world to be a just place and believe that "you get out of it what you deserve." The good prosper and the wicked suffer. One of the interesting consequences of this belief is the tendency of people to "derogate the victim." In other words, we often assume that a person who is being harmed deserves to suffer, even though he or she is perfectly innocent.

Do you recall how you felt when you discovered that a classmate who had not studied at all had obtained a higher mark than you, even though you pored over the books all night? Or perhaps you found out that you were being paid less than another person with the same seniority, same experience, and doing the same job. In both cases, distributive justice is at issue. Such issues also arise on a small scale; for example, you offer another person some advice which is accepted but for which nothing is received in return, not even a thank you. In each of these cases, the exchange is felt to be *unfair*, whether it is the exchange of effort for marks, work for pay, or help for gratitude. Foa (1971) complicated the issue by arguing that when we consider what is fair in a given distribution of resources, we have to consider the *type* of resource being exchanged. Thus the same principles apply whether the resource is tangible (e.g., money) or intangible (e.g., information). The resources that are exchanged in social interactions are many and varied, and can be divided into six categories (Foa, 1971): a) status; b) love; c) service; d) information; e) material goods; and f) money (see Figure 13-2). These resources vary in terms of two dimensions, *particularism* and *concreteness*. Particularism refers to the degree to which a resource is dependent on a particular individual and on the nature of the relationship. Love would be high on particularism and money would be low. Concreteness refers to the degree to which

FIGURE 13-2
The Foa circle

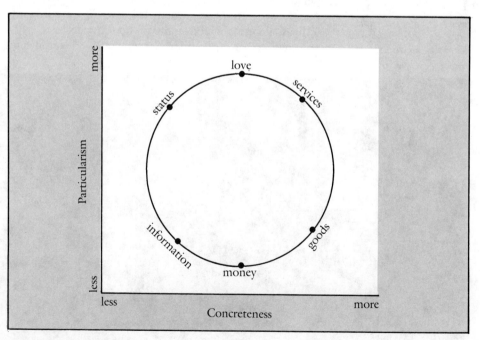

SOURCE: Foa and Foa, 1976

the resource is tangible. Thus status and information are more intangible than are service and material goods. These classifications also delimit the type of resource likely to be exchanged. For example, love is likely to be exchanged for love but not for money, while money is more likely to be exchanged for goods and services.

THE THEORY OF GAMES

In 1944, Von Neumann and Morgenstern published their classic *Theory of games and economic behaviour*, which provided a new model of conflict that influenced not only political science and economic theory but social psychology as well. This model treats all conflicts as though they involve exchanges of a variety of resources — material goods, services, affection. Each party to the conflict is viewed as *rational* in that each is capable of ordering preferences for various outcomes (e.g., prefers romantic love to friendship; prefers friendship to enmity) and each is capable of acting to minimize losses and maximize gains. In other words, it is assumed that in an exchange, people try to get the most for themselves. This is an important assumption which merits careful examination.

In the '60s and '70s, many social psychologists used "experimental games" to study the degree to which subjects did indeed act in a rational manner, as well as to study the influence of a wide range of psychological variables on the resolution of conflict. By the 1980s, the use of such games had declined substantially because it was thought that the games provided situations of questionable external validity (Apfelbaum and Lubek, 1976; Nemeth, 1970). Nonetheless, such experimental games can be used to study conflict resolution and to identify psychological processes, which are fundamental to all conflict, provided that reasonable care is taken to examine the degree to which findings made from such studies are applicable to real-world situations.

Given the difficulty of understanding conflict even in simple games, it would be unwise to generalize from game behaviour to much more complex real-life behaviour. For example, if we wish to study international conflict, we must remember that subjects in such experiments are not trained negotiators and do not have to worry about pressures from military-industrial sources or the possibility of nuclear war (Etzioni, 1969). Unfortunately, however, military strategists have found game theory very attractive. This preoccupation can lead to strategists actually making war *more* likely, as they analyze what actions are most likely to produce what effects, or how many citizens their side could "afford" to lose in an international atomic showdown (Rapoport, 1968). The war in Vietnam was " . . . the fullest gamed, fullest analyzed, and most intensively planned war in history" (Wilson, 1970). Henry Kissinger, the U.S. Secretary of State at that time, was by profession a political scientist who had worked with games, and there is evidence that he approached the Vietnam peace negotiations from the perspective of game theory (Walker, 1977).

A "game" in its broadest sense, is virtually any kind of situation in which two or more interdependent parties (or "players") make decisions which affect each other according to rules. The outcomes of these decisions depend on the joint actions of the players. There are two major classes of games, *zero-sum games* in which one party's gain is exactly matched by the opponent's loss — gains and losses always add up to zero and no cooperation is possible (e.g., a two-handed poker game) and *non-zero-sum* games, in which some of the outcomes are *mutually* preferable to some of the others. While the mathematical analysis of such games treats the players as rational (maximizing gains and minimizing losses), such rationality is not always — or even usually — present in real-life conflicts.

Sometimes it is difficult to assess the magnitude of gains and losses for the parties, for the same amount of money or other resources may have different value or importance for different people. A dollar means much more to a pauper than it does to a millionaire. Game theory requires that *utilities*, rather than objective measures of value, be used (Edwards 1954). Utility refers to the importance, or value, that a given outcome has for an individual. It is assumed that people can rank a number of different possible outcomes with regard to utility. For example, if you are in the desert, a glass of water might have much more utility than a new stereo, while if you are sitting comfortably in your living room, the opposite would be the case. Rational players act to maximize the utility that they can obtain in the conflict situation.

However, this fundamental assumption of rationality does not mean that people are always motivated by purely selfish ends; it is the *utility* and not the objective value of an outcome that is involved. If an adult plays a game of cards with a child and wants the child to win, then the maximum utility would be associated with a loss rather than a win for the adult.

The zero-sum game

In any game situation, the range of possible outcomes and the interdependence of the players is most simply represented in the form of a payoff matrix. In most experimental games, each of two players must choose between two possibilities in order to obtain one of four possible outcomes. As an example, consider the matrix in Figure 13-3. In this case, the matrix indicates that each of the players, **A** and **B**, has a choice to make. **A** can choose action a_1 or a_2, and **B** can choose b_1 or b_2. The joint outcome of their choices is indicated by the various cells of the matrix. It is a zero-sum game:

FIGURE 13-3
Payoff matrix for zero-sum game

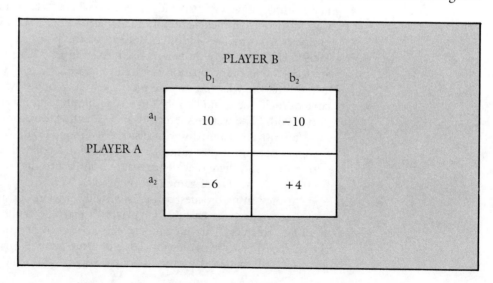

Player **A** receives the amount indicated, while **B** loses the same amount. Thus, if **A** chooses a₁ at the same time that **B** chooses b₁, then **A** will win 10 (points, dollars, etc.) and **B** will loose 10. However, if **A** chooses a₁ and **B** chooses b₂, **A** will lose 10 and **B** will gain 10. This situation represents pure competition. What one person wins the other must lose. No cooperation is possible and communication would not help in any way, since if players informed each other of their choices, their opponents could take advantage of the information.

The non-zero-sum game

Zero-sum games fail to capture the most important feature of most real-life conflict situations: even while two people may compete, they are also propelled by a certain element of cooperative motivation. For example, while the Allies and the Germans were engaged in life and death struggle in World War I, they still managed to cooperate by mutually banning the use of poison gas after it was used against Canadian soldiers at Ypres. The gas was never used in World War II because both sides considered it too dangerous to use. (Similarly, germ warfare has never been used.)

Non-zero-sum games are also called ''mixed-motive'' games because more than one motivation, pure competition, is involved. There is also a motivation to cooperate to a degree (see Box 13-4). Consider the example of the payoff matrix shown in Figure

---

B · O · X   13 - 4

NURSERY GAMES

In the late 1970s, more than 60 of the major Ontario flower growers formed a Co-op and began holding daily flower auctions, using a clock system that Dundas, Ontario grower Ben Veldhuis (the biggest cactus grower in North America) had observed in operation in the Netherlands, where it had been in use for more than a half-century. Each week day at 6:30 a.m., 100 or so buyers gathered in a large warehouse to *watch the clock*!

The clock was large — six feet in diameter. It was on one wall of the warehouse, and facing it were 91 seats arranged in tiers. Each seat was provided with a button. The numbers on the face of the clock began at 100 at the top and went around counterclockwise to 1. The single large hand could move around the whole face of the clock in just four seconds. The clock was the heart of the flower auction, where

wholesalers and florists came to buy. The grower brought his or her flowers to the auction and told the clock operator that he or she wanted the clock to start at some specific price — say \$1 (or even \$10 for an expensive plant). The operator would set the clock at 100 and switch it on. The first buyer to press the button got the flowers at the price the clock stopped at. (To ensure that the flowers would not go for nothing, each grower also had a button to press if he or she felt the price was going too low.) It is to the buyer's advantage to wait until the price is very low, but the longer the buyer waits, the more likely it is that someone else will purchase the flowers or the clock will be stopped by the seller.

Recently, the clock has been replaced by a solid state digital system, but the system continues as before.

FIGURE 13-4
Payoff matrix for non-zero-sum game

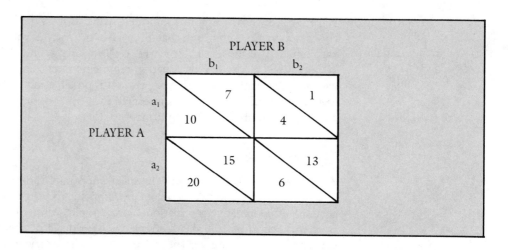

13-4. The number in the lower left half of each quadrant represents the payoff to player **A**, and the upper right-hand number, the payoff to player **B**, for each combination of actions. No longer is it the case (as it was in the zero-sum game) that one player's gains are always matched by the other's losses. Thus it is no longer a pure conflict situation; cooperation is also possible as players attempt to avoid mutually undesirable outcomes. In this particular matrix, **A** is clearly at an advantage, since for three of the possible outcomes, **A** will gain more than **B**. But what outcome is likely if the two players simultaneously choose one of their two possible responses? **A**, if rational, will recognize that a_2 is a better choice than a_1, since more will be gained (20 instead of 10, or 6 instead of 4), whether **B** chooses b_1 or b_2. Similarly, **B** stands to be better off, regardless of **A**'s choice, by choosing b_1 (7 instead of 1 if **A** chooses a_2, 15 instead of 13 if **A** chooses a_1). So we should expect that the players will choose the lower left-hand quadrant. Even if the game was repeated several times, there would be no reason for the players to change their choice, provided that they are only interested in their own gains. However, such individualistic motivation is not the only motive that affects real (as opposed to theoretically rational) players.

There exist at least three motivational orientations. *Individualistic* motivation leads to maximization of one's gains and minimization of one's losses without regard for the other party's outcomes. *Competitive* motivation in its pure form is directed at beating the other party, even at the expense of one's own loss, provided the other party loses more. *Cooperative* motivation leads one to seek the outcome that is the best for both parties collectively, even if one's own outcomes are low or even negative. Most people are motivated by a mixture of these three basic orientations.

In the matrix shown in Figure 13-5, for example, Player **B** may not like the fact that **A** gains 5 more points on each trial, so **B** may all of a sudden choose b_2, reducing his or her own gain slightly, but reducing **A**'s even more — in fact, beating **A**. Then we might expect that on the subsequent trial, **A** would choose a_1; if **B** continues with b_2, they would each receive even less. Thus such a game could be used simply as a means of determining whether or not such competitive motivation (the motivation to "beat" the other person) is present in a population of subjects. In fact, just such a matrix, referred to as a Maximizing Difference Game, or MDG, has been used by many researchers (e.g., McClintock and Nuttin, 1969; Carment, 1974a,b). Players in such a game should be quite content to choose a_1 and b_1 respectively if

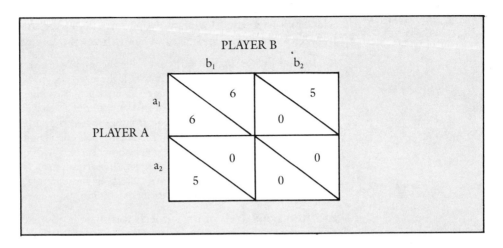

FIGURE 13-5
Payoff matrix for maximizing difference game

self-interest is the only motive operating. Yet they often do not. The only motive for making the competitive choice is to beat the other person.

For example, Carment (1974a) found a considerable degree of competitive responding in an MDG. Same-sex female dyads were most competitive (52 percent of trials) followed by same-sex male dyads (38 percent of trials). Males and females in mixed sex dyads were the least competitive and did not differ from each other (25 percent, 26 percent respectively). Obviously, the competitiveness was strongest when a subject was dealing with another subject of the same sex, but was reduced with a member of the opposite sex.

The variables that influence behaviour in a conflict situation can be grouped into three classes: (1) *structural* variables, which are directly related to the nature of the conflict situation (e.g., whether the situation is basically an MDG; whether communication is possible; whether the protagonists have equal power; (2) *strategic* variables (e.g., whether one or more of the protagonists adopts a conciliatory stance); and (3) *predispositional* variables, which refer to the characteristics of the protagonists themselves and to their prior history of interaction.

THE STRUCTURE OF CONFLICT

The nature of the conflict is often a powerful determinant of the course the conflict takes. For example, an individual who represents no one but him or herself in a negotiation will probably act somewhat differently from an individual who is the representative of a group. The latter person needs to be concerned not only with the course of the conflict process but also with how his or her actions are viewed by others in the group. There are many structural variables in a situation of conflict; only a few shall be examined here.

The dilemma game

Some conflicts are very difficult to resolve because the actions which are rational on an individual level can lead to collectively irrational or mutually destructive outcomes. The prototype of this problem is the so called Prisoner's Dilemma Game (PDG), which has been used for many laboratory studies of conflict. It is a special type of non-zero-sum game, and takes its name from the following "dilemma":

> Two suspects are apprehended following the murder of a wealthy man. The police are quite certain that the two are guilty, but lack the necessary evidence to convict them. A clever Crown Prosecutor decides to suggest a little plea-bargaining, and visits both suspects separately. She tells each suspect that she cannot hope to convict either of them on the murder charge without a confession, but promises that if the suspect confesses, she will agree to ask the court for clemency for him. The murder conviction of the other suspect will carry a sentence of 30 years while the confessor will get off with only a one-year sentence. However, if both confess, they will each get 20 years in prison, and if neither confesses she will see to it that they are charged with breaking and entering, which will lead to a two-year sentence. She then leaves each suspect to think about her offer by himself.

As it turns out, each of the suspects fortunately possesses some knowledge of game theory, and scratches out a matrix (Figure 13-6) on the wall of his police cell. A half hour later, each suspect confesses. The Crown Prosecutor has succeeded.

Why, you might ask, would the two prisoners choose to confess when by keeping silent each would have received only two years in prison? Was each prisoner so eager to get off with only a one-year sentence that friendship ceased to matter?

Before condemning the two as victims of their own selfishness, we must more carefully examine their choices. Since they could not communicate, each had to anticipate what the other would do. A may have said to himself, "Whatever he does, I am better off by confessing. If he confesses, by confessing, I'll get 20 years instead of 30. If he doesn't confess, I'll get one year instead of two. So, to confess is my best strategy. But it's also his best strategy for the same reason. Now even if I put my self-interest aside, and choose not to confess, how can I be sure that he will not confess? After all, for him not to confess, he must not only be prepared to accept two years instead of one, but he must also trust that I won't confess, or he will end up with 30 years." Thus, held *incommunicado*, each prisoner has little choice but to confess. Yet the product of their individually *rational* choices is collectively *ir*rational, since they each receive sentences of 20 years instead of two. That is the nature of the dilemma. Neither person, *regardless of what the other person does*, can improve his or her outcome by remaining silent. Yet, by both being "rational," they each end up with 20 years in prison.

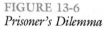

FIGURE 13-6
Prisoner's Dilemma

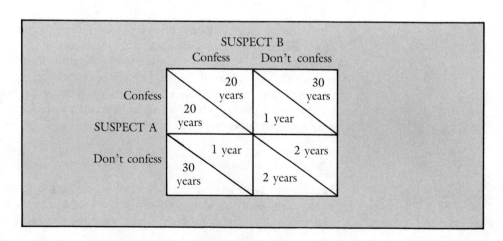

Because such factors as trust and suspicion are important in this game, the Prisoner's Dilemma captured the interest of experimental social psychologists. How would people behave in this kind of situation? Research using a matrix equivalent to the dilemma (where outcomes were points or money instead of prison terms) and which involved pairs of players playing the same game many times in succession demonstrated that real players do not play cooperatively at all. The percentage of mutually cooperative responses is typically quite low (around 30 to 40 percent) and tends to decrease as the game progresses. However, if enough trials are played, there is usually some increase in mutual cooperation, up to about 65 percent, (Rapoport 1963; Rapoport and Chammah, 1965; see Figure 13-7).

You may find the "normative" (i.e., theoretical) outcome (mutual confession) of the Prisoner's Dilemma Game a little unsatisfying. Surely, you might ask, two people would not act collectively in such an irrational way? This has bothered a great many researchers, even though laboratory studies using the PDG indicate that people do just that. However, one factor that has to be considered is the actual value of the outcomes to the players.

Consider the Prisoner's Dilemma story again, but this time, suppose that the suspects are a pair of lovers, Henry and Marie. For these two, the prospect of one going free after one year while the other languishes in jail for another 29 years is much more unpleasant than it would be for two ordinary criminals. Furthermore, each lover "knows" (i.e., trusts) that the other feels likewise. For these players, the only two outcomes worth thinking about are both confessing or both not confessing. Being free when the other is in prison has little utility for either one.

Furthermore, each no doubt strongly believes that the other will react the same way, and the only thing to do is to *not* confess. Neither confesses, and they go free after two years in prison.

Thus the utility of the possible outcomes for each person is not based solely on that person's preference. In addition, both Henry and Marie assume (or "trust")

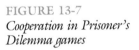

FIGURE 13-7
Cooperation in Prisoner's Dilemma games

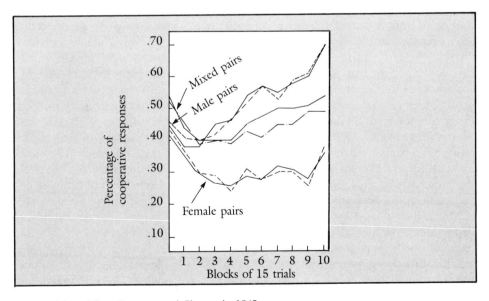

SOURCE: Adapted from Rapaport and Chammah, 1965.

that the other person has the same utility preferences as he or she. Judging the other person's ordering of utility is obviously crucial, since if one party misjudges (e.g., if Marie assumes that Henry values personal liberty above anything else), then that person's predictions of the other's behaviour will reflect that misjudgment. In negotiation situations people often try to misrepresent their real utility preferences, as well as modify the other person's utility (e.g., "I am really very attached to this car, so unless I get a very good offer, I won't sell it at all" or "This suit really makes you look very dashing").

Now, suppose the Crown Prosecutor has persuaded both Henry and Marie that the other is emotionally involved with a third person. In such a case, they would presumably modify their judgment of the other's utility structure and would also likely modify their own. However, if they really "trust" one another, they will not believe the allegations about the third party (see Box 13-5).

One constraint placed on the behaviour observed in the Prisoner's Dilemma Game is the absence of communication. Although communication channels by themselves do not always lead to more cooperation, in a situation as simple as the PDG, the opportunity to communicate would at least allow for the chance of parties informing each other of their real intentions. After all, the non-cooperative response in the PDG might be a defensive rather than an offensive move. In fact, when players in a PDG

B · O · X   13 - 5

TRUST

Trust is an essential part of human interaction (see Chapter 3). A general absence of trust is so uncommon that a person exhibiting this trait is considered to have a mental disorder (paranoia). We drive over a hill at 100 kilometres per hour, "trusting" that the people in the roads department have continued the road on the other side, even though we cannot see it. We put our money in a bank "trusting" that we will get it back, trusting that the laws of society will protect our interests.

Stephen Leacock (1959) gave a humorous example of what can happen when trust is misplaced: A magician became extremely annoyed with a heckler in the audience who tried to take away the wonder from each of his tricks by loudly whispered comments such as "He had it up his sleeve." At the end of the performance, the magician invited the heckler to the stage and, with his permission, demolished his gold watch with a sledge hammer, punched holes in his handkerchief, danced on his silk hat, burned his celluloid collar, and smashed his spectacles. The

heckler, of course, was fascinated by these latest "tricks," and while he was still wondering how the magician was so cleverly working the "deceptions," the magician announced that the performance was at an end. The heckler had *trusted* that the magician would not damage his property, even when the magician explicitly sought permission to do just that.

Trust involves a situation in which what is to be gained by trusting outweighs what could be lost (Deutsch, 1960). For example, parents who enage a babysitter stand to gain an evening's freedom, but stand to lose heavily should the babysitter prove to be irresponsible. The heckler stood to gain the excitement of being involved in a magic act. He stood to lose his spectacles, not to mention a fine gold watch. As you might well expect, in a problem-solving situation, trust leads to a more open exchange of ideas and views, while suspicion (distrust) often leads to distortion or concealment of information which, in turn, makes conflict resolution more difficult.

have been allowed to communicate, it has usually had a positive effect on the level of cooperation. However, as in real life, communication is sometimes used only to try to manipulate the other party, rather than to aid in the resolution of the dilemma.

There is no reason why this dilemma should be restricted to only two protagonists. Indeed, in an expanded form involving many participants, it more closely reflects many real-life conflict situations, as is described in the next section.

Collective dilemmas   A *collective dilemma* occurs whenever the individually rational actions of a number of interacting parties produce an outcome which is collectively undesirable. This is similar to the Prisoner's Dilemma situation, except that more than two players are involved. Collective dilemmas, also referred to as *social* dilemmas (Dawes, 1980), have been receiving more attention from researchers in the last few years (e.g., Brewer and Kramer, 1986; Komorita and Barth, 1985; Samuelson and Messick, 1986; Yamagishi and Sato, 1986).

Collective dilemmas occur repeatedly in every day life. For example, if the installation of pollution control devices on automobiles could lead to considerable improvement in the quality of the air, everyone should be willing to buy such equipment. However, closer analysis reveals that the "rational" choice, at least for the short term, is to adopt the selfish alternative, in other words, do nothing. If the majority of people install such devices, the air will be better even if you do nothing. If only a few people install such devices, your investment will be a waste of time, since the air quality will not improve anyway (see Figure 13-8). Population growth and resource depletion represent the same sort of dilemma. Why, even in the face of catastrophic overpopulation, should an Indian peasant limit his family to two children? He will receive no old age pension. He will need to depend on his children to support him. The more children he has, the better off he will be, even though his society may ultimately suffer. Even in an overpopulated world, he would be at a disadvantage in his old age if he had fewer children than his neighbours.

Collective dilemmas take two forms, the commons problem (or resource dilemma, as it is also called) and the provision of public goods problem (Brewer and Kramer, 1986). Each will be discussed in turn.

The *commons problem* involves individuals who have to decide how much of a public resource each should take for personal use, and takes its name from Hardin's (1968) description of the "tragedy of the commons": Historically, in England, public pas-

FIGURE 13-8

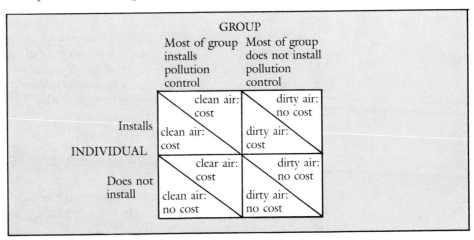

turage was set aside for common use by all farmers. However, as individual farmers expanded the sizes of their cattle herds, the "commons" were overgrazed to such an extent that an enclosure movement, which led to fencing off the commons into individual pastures, grew up in the 1800s. The heart of the problem was this: for each herdsman, the positive utility associated with enlarging his herd was much greater than the negative utility derived from the overgrazing. The short-term gains were more enticing than the possibility of losses in the long term. Thus everyone enlarged their herds to the point where everyone suffered.

While the commons dilemma involves people drawing individually from a common resource, the *public goods problem* is related to the contributions by individuals to the collective good, as with our example of pollution control. (There is sometimes difficulty in deciding just what is a public good; see Box 13-6). As long as most people act in line with the common good (reduce pollution, donate blood, do not spit on the sidewalk), the individual who does *not* contribute benefits as much from the efforts of the majority as it does from itself. This has also been referred to as the *free rider* problem (Frohlich and Oppenheimer, 1970). There would be no need to collect tickets on a train if everyone was honest about paying their fare. Such a system would most likely break down because free riders (literally!) would exploit the situation.

Both dilemmas are identical in terms of the decision facing the individual. He or she must decide whether to act according to individual self-interest, and risk suffering in the long run if most others do the same, or to act according to the collective interest at some cost to him or herself. The problem in each case really arises when each individual's behaviour has a relatively minor influence on the group outcome, while the overall group behaviour has a strong effect on each individual's outcome.

The resource dilemma has an additional, temporal component and is essentially a dilemma with delayed consequences (Messick and Brewer, 1983; Messick and McClelland, 1983). The English commons supported expanding herds up to a point where overgrazing threatened their continued existence. However, the collective dilemma evolved gradually, beginning long before there was any danger to the commons. Three separate motives are involved in the resource dilemma: self-interest, conformity to group norms, and the wish to act responsibly (Samuelson and Messick, 1986). In other words, each individual presumably wants to profit as much as possible while acting in a socially responsible manner and staying within the limits of group norms.

Sometimes, however, it is difficult to tell just what social responsibility involves, and sometimes no relevant norms exist. For example, is it or is it not socially responsible to use an aerosol spray? There are environmental reasons why you should not, yet such sprays are widely available and widely advertised. These sprays release fluorocarbons into the atmosphere where they slowly destroy the ozone layer which protects people from harmful ultraviolet radiation. Already, there has been an alarming decrease in the ozone layer. Like our predecessors who overused the commons in England, we damage our environment partly because we cannot easily foresee what is going to occur.

How should people deal with collective dilemmas? The philosopher Immanuel Kant suggested that behaviour should be guided by this precept: "Act only according to that maxim which you can at the same time will to be a universal law" (Joad, 1957, p. 393). Thus you should refrain from installing pollution control only if you would be content to have everyone do likewise. If everyone acted according to the

B · O · X   13 - 6

MULTICULTURALISM, REGIONALISM, AND THE PUBLIC GOOD

That we define Canada as a multicultural (pluralistic) society, or at least as a bilingual and bicultural (dualistic) one, leads to special problems. Unlike a *plural* society, in which two or more groups of different linguistic or ethnic or religious origins live side by side in one political unit without intermingling, a *pluralistic* society is one in which separate identities are maintained, while intermingling in many important spheres of social activity regularly takes place (Rabushka and Shepsle, 1972). In a plural society, politics are played along the same lines that divide the groups. To some extent, this is what is happening in Canada as the western regions lean away from the Liberal party, while French-speaking Canadians lean toward the Liberals.

Plural, as opposed to pluralistic societies, have a difficult time remaining united under a democratic system. Political conflicts are seen in ethnic or religious terms, and a majority is always tempted to use non-democratic means to impose its will on the minority. Conflict seems inevitable. In a homogeneous society, the erection of a cathedral or the purchase of a new submarine constitutes a "public good" in that everyone benefits directly or indirectly. However, in a plural society, a "public good" for one group may be a "public bad" for the other (Rabushka et al., 1972). The building of an atomic reactor in Ontario by the federal government might be viewed as a wasteful drain on the Québec taxpayer by separatists in Québec, while financial support for the Calgary Olympics might be viewed as a waste of taxpayers' money by people living outside Alberta. However, as mentioned earlier, Canada is not yet a plural society, although we may be moving in that direction.

Rabushka et al. (1972) studied 18 sovereign multiethnic societies around the world and found striking regularities in their political processes. They were drawn to the conclusion that the "resolution of intense but conflicting preferences in the plural society" is not manageable in a democratic framework. Unless Canada can avoid the drift towards a plural society, unless we can find a way to strengthen the basis we have for a bicultural or multicultural society, we are unlikely to survive the kind of conflict that has torn other plural societies apart.

Kantian imperative, collective dilemmas would vanish, although we might continue to damage our environment over disagreement or misunderstanding about the dangers of various actions. For example, the United States is reluctant to do very much about acid rain, which is destroying both American and Canadian lakes. They argue that there is not yet enough evidence to show that industrial pollution is the cause. In this case, their position may be politically based, but there are many situations in which ignorance of harmful consequences underlies resource depletion or environmental damage. In any case, people do not follow Kant's dictum. They do not for the simple reason that it is against their individual short-term interests to do so.

In real-world dilemmas, more than the tangible payoffs are important (Hardin, 1971). For example, the distribution of trust among the individuals may play a crucial role. Moreover, different people may see the situation in different ways. Some may see it as an opportunity to exploit others, while others may see it as an opportunity to solicit cooperation from their co-actors (e.g., Buckley, Burns and Meeker, 1974; Frohlich and Oppenheimer, 1970; Terhune, 1970). In some cases, people may hesitate to cooperate not because they do not want to contribute to the group goal, but because they suspect or misinterpret the motivation of others (Alcock and Mansell, 1977).

The effects of group size

Game theory predicts that individualism will predominate when a group is large enough that no individual's contribution makes a significant difference to the group as a whole; individuals will attempt to maximize their own payoffs. It may seem natural that more cooperation should exist in a small group than in a large group — after all, in a small group, an individual receives a larger proportion of the beneficial effects of his or her action, while at the same time, his or her action has a much more significant effect on the group outcome. But what would happen if we compared the behaviour of people in two groups, one a small group and the other a large group, but in which the reward magnitude was exactly the same? In other words, if only the size of the group, but not the actual reward varies, will people then still be more cooperative in smaller groups? This is indeed what has been observed in laboratory experiments. Hamburger, Guyer and Fox (1975) developed a game structure in which the size of the reward for an individual was the same whether a three-person or seven-person group was involved. Not only were the three-person groups more cooperative, but the probability of cooperative responses by persons from small groups being offered on a particular trial was independent of the actions of the other players on the previous trial. In the larger group there was a marked and systematic *decrease* in the probability of a player responding cooperatively as the number of people who cooperated on the previous trial increased. Thus cooperation did *not* foster cooperation.

Even when the temptation to be non-cooperative (i.e., the amount by which non-cooperation brings greater reward than cooperation) and the gain to the group brought about by one's cooperation are held constant, cooperation decreases with increasing group size (Bonacich, Shure, Kahan and Merker, 1976; Messick and McClelland, 1983). It is possible, of course, that this is due to the greater likelihood of having one or more "non-cooperators" in a larger group, but it is also suggested in the studies above that deindividuation may play a role: the larger the group, the more difficult it becomes to monitor the responses of each participant. Yet, in a study in which subjects in a five-person group either (1) were anonymous to each other, and were informed after each trial only of the total number of people who cooperated, or (2) were told how each of the people, identified by name, responded, no difference was found in the degree of cooperation (Mansell and Alcock, 1978). Deindividuation *per se* is not the explanation.

Rather, the explanation appears to lie with the size of the group itself. In 1833, Lloyd discussed this very point:

> Suppose the case of two persons agreeing to labour jointly, and that the result of their labour to be common property. Then, were either of them, at any time, to increase his exertions beyond the previous amount, only half of the resulting benefit would fall to his share; were he to relax them, he would bear only half the loss. If, therefore, we may estimate the motives of exertion by the magnitude of the personal consequences expected by each individual, these motives would in this case have only half the force which they would have were each labouring separately for his own individual benefit. Similarly, in the case of three partners, they would have only one-third of the force — in the case of four, only one-fourth — and in a multitude, no force whatsoever. For beyond a certain point of min-

uteness, the interest would be so small as to elude perception, and would obtain no hold whatever on the human mind (p. 8).

This brings us back to the same conclusion: when a group is large enough so that the actions of a given individual have little effect on the group, and when the immediate reward for non-cooperation is larger than the reward for cooperation, non-cooperation becomes the typical response.

One way to foster behaviour which is based on the collective good is to make the collective identity of the group more salient. For example, in one set of laboratory studies, individuals were found to be more likely to act in line with the collective good when the collective identity was emphasized than when emphasis was instead put on the identities of various subgroups within the larger group (Kramer and Brewer, 1984).

Another way to foster collectively oriented behaviour is through coercion. Indeed, Hardin (1968) suggested that mutual coercion, mutually agreed upon, is the only way out of the commons dilemma: we all agree to pay taxes and to punish those who do not. It may well be that only similar laws could regulate problems such as pollution or overpopulation. Sometimes, coercion in the form of normative pressure is enough to prevent individuals from acting only from self-interest and ignoring the common good (Samuelson, Messick, Rutte and Wilke, 1984; Allison and Messick, 1985). (See Box 13-7 for other examples of collective dilemmas.)

B · O · X   13 - 7

OTHER SOCIAL DILEMMAS

Even the electoral process poses a kind of collective dilemma. "If my party wins, it is unlikely that they would have lost if I didn't vote. If I go to vote (expend energy), and they lose, they would have lost anyway. If they win, they would have won anyway." Only very rarely does a candidate win or lose on the basis of one vote. Yet, if everyone pursued the same logic, no one, or almost no one, would vote, and the election results would be determined by a very small minority.

A related problem is that of the "missing hero" (Platt, 1973): everyone in a group suffers because no single person will take any action to eliminate the source of the suffering. As an example, consider the situation in which a long line of motorists are returning from the beach on a Sunday afternoon, and all are slowed down to a creeping pace because a mattress has fallen off the top of someone's station wagon and no one will get out and move it off the road (Schelling, 1971). After finally reaching the mattress, each motorist in turn views the problem as now being over. The effort of stopping to move the mattress would provide no personal advantage.

A slightly different but related situation is the "negative feedback loop" that Schelling (1971) illustrates by the example of the decay in railway passenger service: a few people decide not to travel by train since the service is declining. The railway makes less revenue, leading to further cuts in service, which leads to more people switching away from train travel. This kind of loop can destroy a transport system (e.g., passenger trains), despite a desire by a great many people to have such a service, but one of high quality. Another example: Anglophones in Québec fear becoming more and more ignored by the provincial government. This leads some to move out of the province, which reduces the power of the Anglophone group, which may lead to more neglect by the government, leading to a greater exodus, until the feared situation is finally brought about.

B · O · X   13 - 8

THE GAME OF "CHICKEN"

The prototypical dangerous game is the game of "chicken," which was played by teenagers in the 1950s. In the words of Bertrand Russell (1959):

> This sport is called chicken! It is played by choosing a long straight road with a white line down the middle and starting two very fast cars towards each other from opposite ends. As they approach each other mutual destruction becomes more and more imminent. If one of them swerves from the white line before the other, as he passes, he shouts chicken!, and the one who has swerved becomes an object of contempt.

In a later variation, teenagers would stand on airport runways at night, daring each other to remain in the path of an approaching airplane (Swingle, 1970). The game of chicken is not restricted to teenagers. In one way or another, many games of chicken are played out in politics, in labour-management negotiations, and in international disputes.

This game can be translated into a laboratory form by using a matrix such as that shown in Figure 13-9. If one "does not swerve" and the other does, one gains prestige (indicated by + 100) while the other loses face (− 100). If both decide not to swerve, they lose more than their faces (− 1000), while if both swerve, there is a "draw," with a slight loss of prestige (e.g., − 10). It is obviously a high-risk game,

each player being forced to risk substantial loss in order to threaten the other into yielding. It is a "pre-emption" game in that if one player can make it clear that he or she is committed to not swerving, the other must either back down or face almost certain heavy loss. As long as one person believes that the other will "back down," he or she will continue. Kahn (1962) suggests that getting into the car dead drunk, wearing very dark glasses, and throwing the steering wheel out of the window as soon as the car is travelling at maximum speed will put considerable pressure on your opponent to back down. You have reduced or eliminated *your* freedom to act: the opponent, who *can* act, is now in a weaker position and must back down or face suicide. You have *pre-empted* control of the game.

"Brinksmanship," pushing each other to the "brink" of war, describes the game of chicken as played at the international level. It is the "deliberate creation of a recognizable risk of war, a risk that one does not completely control" (Schelling, 1960, p. 200). The effectiveness of brinksmanship depends on how much the other nation believes you. If the Soviets believe that the Americans are committed to attack them if they invade some third country, they will hesitate. If they do not believe it, but it is in fact true, both sides will end up in a mutually destructive war.

FIGURE 13-9
Chicken

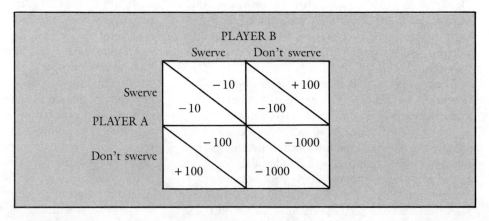

Dangerous games

In 1963, the Soviets were intent on shipping nuclear missiles to Cuba and the Americans were determined to stop them. The Americans put up a naval blockade around Cuba and threatened to sink any Russian ship carrying missiles to Cuba. Nevertheless, the Soviets sent ships carrying missiles toward Cuba, one of which was eventually spotted and appeared to be heading directly into the blockade. However, while the world held its breath, the Russian ship eventually stopped and turned back, ending the tense confrontation. American Secretary of State Dean Rusk was quoted as having told a reporter following this incident, "Remember when you report this . . . that eyeball to eyeball, they blinked first." Someone had to back down, or mutual disaster would result. Such a conflict is a *dangerous* conflict (or *dangerous game*, in the language of game theory) in that if neither side backs down, both may suffer catastrophic loss (e.g., nuclear war; see Box 13-8).

There are two important characteristics of the prototypical dangerous game: (1) It is non-negotiable. There can only be one winner; the other must lose, although both can lose disastrously. There is no way that cooperation can help, and any conciliatory move by one player will only encourage the other to press on. (2) The dangerous aspect is that the goal-directed behaviour and the threat behaviour are identical: the closer a person gets to the goal, the greater the likelihood of attaining it and the greater the probability of a mutual loss (Swingle, 1970).

Why do people or nations play such games? Insofar as nations are concerned, it is often appealing to force the opponent to back down by appearing to be more ready to accept mutual loss than they actually are (i.e., deceive the other about their utility structure). If the U.S.S.R. can convince the United States that its leaders are quite prepared to accept the loss of 60 percent of its people in all-out war, then the threat of nuclear war will put the U.S.A. at a disadvantage. If the leaders of a government can appear hardened or demented enough not to care about such losses, they can presumably "pre-empt" the "chicken" confrontation (see Box 13-8), forcing the other side to back down.

Analogues of these two game structures — the dilemma and the dangerous game — appear over and over in real life. However, real-life situations are much more complex than any matrix game, and they involve considerations such as threat and coercion, communication, and power. These factors are discussed in the next section.

Threat and coercion

When we promise to buy a toy for a child if the child cleans up the yard, we are saying that, "If you do action **A** (clean up the yard), I will do action **B** (buy you a toy)." If we have generally carried out our promises in the past, the child is likely to believe that **B** will be done if **A** is done. A *threat* is a kind of promise, except that the outcome, **B**, is undesirable. For example, "If you do action **A** (keep fooling around) then I will do action **B** (make you go to your room). Another example: "If the United States does not stop the development of the Star Wars program, the Soviet Union will restart its underground nuclear test program."

For the threat to be successful, it must first be credible. Credibility depends on several factors:

(1) If the party making the threat has in the past failed to carry out such threats, the credibility of the threat will be low. The credibility of the threat can be increased

if the person making the threat can show that he or she has little choice but to carry it out in the face of non-compliance. Union leaders who threaten illegal walkouts will have more credibility if they have told their followers that they would be failing them if they back down from their threats, and therefore should resign.

(2) The threatened action must have negative consequences for the person making the threat in order to assure the threatened party that the threat will not be carried out anyway, even if compliance is forthcoming. If a father tells his child who is hiding under the bed that he will spank him if he does not come out right away, the threat will be ineffective if the child believes that he will be spanked in any case.

(3) The threat must not carry too high a cost to either party or it is likely to suffer in terms of credibility (Mogy and Pruitt, 1974). A loving father who threatens to send his child to an orphanage if the child misbehaves is unlikely to be believed; both father and child would suffer too much if the threat were carried out.

Threats must be clearly communicated to the target if they are to have any effect. Schelling (1960) pointed out that kidnappers holding a hostage are effectively stymied if all communication with them is cut off. They cannot communicate the threat to harm the hostage or the demand for ransom. (Perhaps, Schelling pondered, a law should be passed which would require the immediate confinement of all relatives and friends of the hostage to make the likelihood of a ransom being paid very small!) Even children realize the strategic value of not allowing parents to communicate their threats. If they know their parents will be unlikely to rebuke them verbally in a certain social situation, they will often deliberately avoid their warning glances.

Threats serve the purpose for which they were intended only if they do not have to be carried out. A parent who threatens a child with a spanking does not *want* to give the spanking; otherwise, he or she would just get on with it rather than wasting words.

A classic study of threat was carried out by Deutsch and Krauss (1960). They devised a "trucking game" to study the effects of a number of variables, including threat and communication, on the outcome of a mixed-motive situation. Two subjects were each given the role of manager of a trucking company, and their task was to move their "trucks" from their factories to the markets. Several trials were run, and for each completed trip, the subject received 60 cents, less the "operating costs," calculated at the rate of one cent for each second taken to make the trip. The two players, labelled ACME and BOLT, operated electronic boxes to move the simulated trucks over the roadways shown in Figure 13-10.

As you see in the figure, part of the roadway for each player was a common single-lane road which meant that only one truck could pass through at a time. If the trucks met in this stretch of the road, either one had to back up while the other advanced, or both could back up, or they could both sit there facing each other. The clock kept moving, however. Thus the person whose truck backed up would lose more money than the person who passed directly through. Each subject also had an alternate route which was considerably longer than the main route, and subjects were told that they could expect to incur a net loss each time they used that route. Since each pair of players played several trials, the cooperative strategy would be for the players to alternate across trials in their use of the common section of road, that is, for one player to pass over the common roadway first on one trial, and for the other player to do so on the subsequent trial.

There were several experimental conditions. In one condition, no threat capability was present, but in another condition, one of the players was given a "gate"

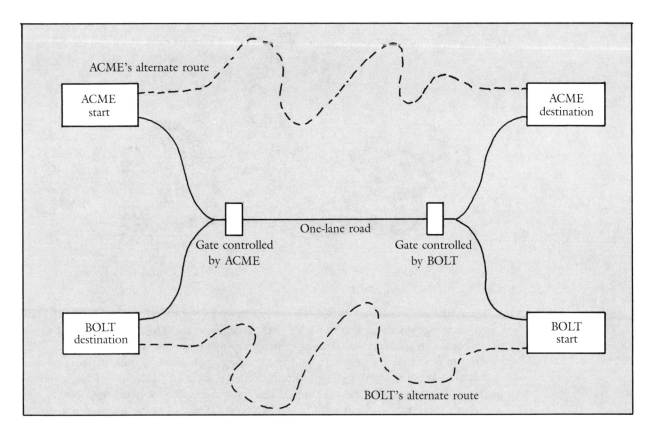

FIGURE 13-10
The Trucking Game

("unilateral threat"), and in a third condition, each player controlled a gate ("bilateral threat"). The gates were at the ends of the single lane road. By closing the gate, a player implicitly threatened that it would remain closed and each would have to use the non-profitable alternate routes.

The results of the study indicated that while subjects in the no-threat condition did learn to alternate cooperatively, the presence of either or both gates impeded such cooperation. While the player with the gate in the unilateral condition lost less money than the other player (but also lost *more* than either player in the no-threat condition), the presence of two gates led to even greater losses for both players. (This outcome suggests that if your opponent has a weapon, you may suffer more by having a similar weapon than if you cannot retaliate!) The effects of allowing the players in such a game to communicate will be discussed later in this chapter.

Why does threat often lead to increased conflict? It seems that the presence of a threat capability inevitably leads to its *use* as an individual tries to resolve the conflict. Once the threat is used, the nature of the conflict changes, and the material payoffs are no longer the only payoffs involved. In our culture, as in many others, yielding to threats or coercion is viewed negatively: it leads to a loss of "face" (Goffman, 1955), or self-esteem. Face-saving is important, not only in terms of self-esteem, but in terms of future interaction. Yielding now may encourage more threats in the future. For example, if a government gives in to terrorists' demands, the action may give encouragement to other terrorists.

Once a threat has been made, the preservation of face becomes a primary goal for each player, thus leading to increased determination to "hold one's ground" and to

"It started with one of their pigeons pecking one of ours."

respond with a counter-threat. A couple may have a conflict of interest with regard to some benign issue, such as where to go on an evening out. Once one of them makes a threat, however, the other may respond with a counter-threat. Now the dispute is not over where to spend the evening, but concerns who is going to win and who is going to back down. Often, there is a series of escalating threats, a *threat-counter-threat spiral* (or more simply, a *conflict spiral*); each disputant responds to the other's threats by more severe threats. Osgood (1962) suggests that such escalation is self-sustaining in that if it is successful, a person is likely to resort to it again, and if it fails (i.e., leads to counter-escalation), it is likely to result in a hardening of resolve and another round of escalation. Some conflicts are more vulnerable than others to the development of conflict spirals. Some conflicts are in states of "stable equilibrium" so that departures from that state lead to a series of adjustments which bring back the equilibrium (e.g., a manufacturer lowers his prices slightly, leading to a general lowering by competitors), while others are in a state of unstable equilibrium such that departure from the equilibrium leads to conflict spirals (e.g., a gasoline price war) (Pruitt and Rubin, 1986).

Conflict spirals appear to induce both a qualitative and a quantitative comparison (Gouldner, 1960). In terms of quality, bargainers or protagonists tend to respond to pressure tactics by using the same sort of pressure — responding to threats with threats and punishments with punishments (Youngs, 1986). In terms of quantity, retaliation is roughly of the same magnitude as the other response (tit-for-tat). However, there appears to be a tendency to overmatch low intensity threats or punishments, and undermatch high intensity ones. This overmatching at the low intensity level is the mechanism which leads to the conflict spiral, and the greater the overmatching, the more explosive the spiral.

The international arms race involves a threat-counter-threat spiral. One nation interprets another nation's actions as a threat to its security, and expands its armamentarium. This very action is, however, perceived as a threat by the other protagonist, who then adds to its arsenal, an act which will appear to the first nation as evidence that the second nation was indeed preparing for war. This is a positive feedback loop leading each side to interpret the other's reactions as threatening its security.

Communication

In real-life conflict situations, it is only rarely the case that there is no communication between protagonists. However, in the typical gaming study of conflict, subjects are not allowed to communicate with each other. After all, if there is any degree of trust between the players, the problem in the Prisoner's Dilemma immediately disappears, since each player can assure the other of the intention to choose the collectively beneficial outcome. Various studies have found that cooperative responding is facilitated in the PDG by allowing subjects to communicate (e.g., Swennson, 1967; Terhune, 1968; Voissem and Sistrunk, 1971).

Communication has been studied in a number of game situations. Deutsch (1958) found that cooperation in the trucking game was fostered by communication *only* when the instructions given the subject provided an "individualistic" orientation, that is, the subjects were instructed to try to make as many points for themselves as they could without being concerned about comparisons with the other person's gains or losses. The mere existence of channels of communication is no guarantee that communication will indeed take place, and the greater the competitive orientation of the parties vis-à-vis each other, the less likely are such channels to be used (Deutsch, 1973). Even when communication was made compulsory, subjects in the bilateral threat conditions of the trucking game were no more cooperative: they used the communication channel only to insult each other, not to coordinate their actions.

Why is communication found to be beneficial in some situations and of no value in others? It seems most likely that communication can help by improving each per-

---

B · O · X   13 - 9

WHY THE HOTLINE?

Herman Kahn (1960) has presented a scenario which illustrates the need for a hotline between the U.S.A. and the U.S.S.R. Why? To prevent the possibility of a third or fourth power country causing the U.S.A. and the U.S.S.R. to destroy one another in the following way: the country manages to obtain one nuclear missile and direct it at Washington, which is consequently destroyed. Russia learns immediately of the nuclear explosion via satellite. Even if both the Russians and the Americans know that it was not the Russians who destroyed the city, at NORAD headquarters in Colorado Springs, the thinking may go like this: whatever country gets its fleet of missiles away first stands the best chance of suffering the least, since it can destroy the enemy's missiles on the ground. "The Russians will think that we think that they destroyed Washington, and that we think that

more missiles are coming, so they will expect us to counter-attack. The only way the Russians can hope to save themselves, or at least to retaliate, is by getting their missiles off the ground first. Thus they *must* attack us, and thus, we must send *ours* off immediately."

Let's go one step further. Suppose the Soviets *know* that the Americans know they didn't bomb Washington. They don't know that the Americans know that *they* know this; hence, the same type of reasoning will lead both sides to send up their missiles. The only way out is through a hotline. If one leader (e.g., of the U.S.) can pick up the phone and say to the other "We know it wasn't you, relax," war can be averted. Considerations such as these led to the installation of the Washington-Moscow "hotline."

son's perception of the other's intentions (see Box 13-9). In situations like that posed by the trucking game, however, the presence of a threat option eliminated this advantage. Players attempted to shortcut the negotiation process by means of threat and coercion, thus changing the game into a situation in which not backing down became of greatest importance. If the only outcomes are now "win" or "lose," there can be no compromise, and communication cannot help. However, communication can be beneficial in a situation in which face-saving is probably not an important factor or in which no clear competitive motivation exists.

Even when communication does occur there is no guarantee that it will be understood. This can have serious implications, especially if the conflict is in the sphere of international relations. The "war" between Britain and Argentina over the Falkland Islands (Malvinas) is one example. Naturally, the two countries perceived the situation from their own perspective. As far as Argentina was concerned, the Malvinas were a natural part of their territory that had been occupied by a foreign power since 1833. Moreover, recent history had revealed that Britain was quite willing, even eager, to give up its colonies. There seemed little reason to believe that it would not release the Falklands as well. However, the British had quite a different point of view. They did not consider the Falklands to be a colony. It was populated by British citizens who wanted to remain part of Britain. Thus the Argentinian attack was not considered one of liberation but one of pure aggression. Argentina did not believe Britain would defend the Falklands but Britain thought no other course of action was possible, with tragic consequences for both sides (Jervis, Lebow and Stein, 1985).

Power

Power, the ability to influence what happens to another individual, has been discussed in some detail earlier (see Chapter 12). We now examine how different degrees of power among protagonists can influence the course of conflict. Of course, power is essential in carrying out a threat. A parent who threatens to spank a 17-year-old high school boxing champion probably lacks the power to carry out the threat.

There is evidence (Pruitt, 1976) that parties involved in a conflict may be more likely to use coercion when they have available moderate, rather than great or small, amounts of power. Little power is often viewed as ineffective, while great power risks mutual destruction. If you are guarding the cookie jar, and if you are *only* allowed to say "bad bad" when the child takes a cookie without permission, the measure will have no effect on the child if it is not backed up in any way, so why bother to use it? Similarly, if your only source of power is tied to your possession of a pistol, you are unlikely to use that power to protect the cookie jar from marauding toddlers. Likewise, the United States and the U.S.S.R. must give pause before risking nuclear war and, in fact, both nations are developing "limited nuclear options" which would allow for the use of small, "clean," nuclear weapons in response to provocation without necessarily provoking a full-scale retaliation.

What happens when someone thinks he or she has more power than is actually the case? Swingle (1968) says such people possess "illusory power." He studied illusory power using a "train game" in which each player electrically controlled a train with the object of getting the train through the tunnel. The subject who first entered the tunnel on a given trail received two points, the other, one point. However, if both trains were in any part of the tunnel at the same time, both subjects lost all the points they had accumulated up to and including that trial. Thus it was a "dangerous" game ("chicken"). The obvious cooperative strategy would have been to alternate going through the tunnel first across the trials.

Three conditions of power were created by simply varying the top speed of one of the trains: (1) "absolute" power, in which one of the players had complete control over goal attainment because that player's train was faster than the other and could get through the tunnel before the other reached it; (2) "illusory" power, in which the top speed of one train allowed it to reach the tunnel first but not pass through it before the other entered the tunnel, giving each player a large loss; and (3) "equal" power, in which both trains had the same range of speeds.

Swingle found, not surprisingly, that cooperation (alternation) was established most rapidly in the equal power condition. When one player had absolute power, there was typically no alteration; the powerful player went through the tunnel first 90 percent of the time. In the illusory power condition, the relationship between the players was in reality the same as in the equal power condition, except that it *seemed* that one player had an advantage. The result was that while the seemingly "stronger" player attempted to pass through the tunnel first, the "weaker" player submitted no more than did players in the equal power condition. Illusory power disrupts the development of cooperation because it makes the ultimatum process more salient without changing the distribution of power. The "stronger" player is capable of making "demands," but incapable of enforcing them.

Illusory power creates difficulties in many conflict situations. A spouse who assumes that he has power over his wife because she is more committed to the marriage than he is may be able to get his way by threatening a separation if she does not comply with his wishes. Suppose that his power is illusory, that indeed she is willing to risk separation. If he tries to force her to comply with his demands because he thinks she has little choice, both may ultimately lose (i.e., they separate). His use of illusory power will have led to a destructive, rather than a constructive, approach to the conflict.

STRATEGY

There are a number of important structural factors in addition to threats, communication, and power which influence the course of conflict and conflict resolution (e.g., Box 13-10). One of the most important of these is the strategy used. Whether at chess or at war, at the car dealer's or the bargaining table, many people try to work out a "strategy," or plan, in advance, a plan which anticipates various contingencies. A formal strategy is simply a plan which contains instructions about what to do in every imaginable contingency. In theory, any "game" can be reduced to a simple choice of strategies. For example, consider a game of X's and O's (tic-tac-toe): You could work out a strategy in detail such as, "If she chooses a corner on the first move, I'll choose the centre. If she chooses another corner on the second move, but not the corner directly opposite, I'll choose the middle position between the two corners. However, if she instead chooses . . . ." This interior monologue could continue until the game ends. There are many different possible strategies, but once a person has chosen a detailed strategy in advance, there is nothing left to decide. In a game of

B · O · X   13 - 10

SITTING DOWN TO NEGOTIATE

In real-life situations, even the physical setup for negotiations is important, or at least is believed by negotiators to be important. For example, even the seating order is often a matter of dispute, since where people sit may reflect either their status or their perceived relationship to each other (Lott and Sommer, 1967).

In 1848, it took six months of discussion before delegates to the Peace of Westphalia could agree on the order in which they should enter and be seated (Durant and Durant, 1961), and at the 1945 Potsdam conference, Truman, Churchill, and Stalin insisted on entering the room by emerging simultaneously from three separate doors (Kelman, 1965).

In the Paris peace talks dealing with the war in Vietnam, considerable debate raged prior to the talks about the seating plan and the table shape. North Vietnam wanted a seating plan and table shape that would suggest that the National Liberation Front had status as an independent political entity, while the United States and South Vietnam were opposed to this (Kitchens, 1974). Whether or not the seating plan *actually* influences the course of the negotiations is unimportant as long as the participants *believe* that it has an effect.

---

chess, there is such a large number of possible strategies available that one could never hope to specify them all. However, in a 2 × 2 matrix game, it is relatively easy to construct strategies because of the limited number of possible response patterns.

In experimental studies, the effects of a given strategy are examined either by having a confederate follow a preselected strategy or (in situations where subjects communicate via computer terminals) presenting a computer-generated response as the

Working on a strategy: A plan to deal with contingencies.

"other player." Many strategic factors can be studied. For example, does an opponent who cooperates 10 percent of the time (choosing these occasions at random) have more or less influence on the subject than one who cooperates 90 percent of the time? In fact, such fixed strategies have been found to have very little success in influencing subjects (Vinacke, 1969). Unconditionally cooperative or unconditionally "tough" strategies fail to produce cooperative responses from the opposition (Solomon, 1960).

However, dynamic strategies which are responsive to the other subject's behaviours have been found to be more effective. One of the most effective is the so called "tit-for-tat" (or "delayed matching") strategy whereby the confederate makes the same response on trial n + 1 as the subject made on trial n (Oskamp, 1971). (In other words, two people are in a repeated interaction, and each time that one person is cooperative, the other cooperates the *next* time, but when the other is non-cooperative, the other is non-cooperative the next time.) This strategy is effective because it responds in a positive way to the other person's cooperativeness, but does not reinforce hostile moves by the other player.

Strategy studies have also been done in a buyer-seller type game in which two players negotiate over the sale of some item. Generally, a tough strategy (extreme opening offer and infrequent concessions) has been the most successful in terms of obtaining the larger share of the joint payoff (Chertkoff and Conley, 1967). Pacifist strategies, on the other hand, typically result in exploitation.

In summary, the bulk of the evidence indicates that in a conflict or bargaining situation, neither an overly generous nor an overly tough position is effective in bringing about mutual cooperation. The most effective strategy is one of firm resistance to exploitation coupled with reciprocation of the other's cooperative behaviour.

PREDISPOSITIONAL VARIABLES

Would the course of World War II been different had Hitler, Churchill, Stalin, and Roosevelt been replaced by others? Would the Québec October Crisis of 1970 have been handled differently had Brian Mulroney been Prime Minister at the time? The study of predispositional variables focuses on the effects of personal characteristics of the individual protagonists — personality, age, gender, cultural variables — on the course of conflicts.

Cultural differences have been found in studies comparing the behaviour of subjects from various countries. For example, Carment (1973) compared the behaviour of students in Canada and India in a mixed-motive game in which one player (the "benefactor") could, by means of choosing one alternative, allow the other player (the "beneficiary") to choose an outcome that led either to equal point gain or to a large point gain for the benefactor. While Indians were more generous than Canadians at the outset, their response did not last long. More importantly, the Indian subjects, unlike the Canadians, avoided taking advantage of the other player's generosity. When the players later switched roles (something they did not anticipate) the new Indian beneficiary continued to be reluctant to accept the other's generosity, while the Canadians were even more eager to accept it. However, in another study involving a different game, when Indian subjects were led to believe that the opponent had an advantage over them, they became very submissive, while when they thought they were at an advantage, they became very competitive, exactly opposite of what was observed with Canadian males (Alcock, 1975). Many other similar cross-cultural comparisons have been made. Canadian Blackfoot Indian children have been found to be more cooperative in a game situation than urban Canadian children and, in fact, are even more predisposed towards cooperative behaviour than are children from the Israeli kibbutzim, where cooperation and sharing are explicitly encouraged (Miller and Thomas, 1972).

It seems that competitiveness increases with age (McClintock and Nuttin, 1969; Leventhal and Lane, 1970), especially among males. Vinacke and Gullickson (1964) compared subjects of ages seven and eight, 12–14, and university age and found that while females were similarly accommodating at all three age levels, males became steadily more exploitative with age. Yet such gender differences are not always found. In some studies males are more cooperative than females, in others the opposite is the case, and in still others, there is no difference at all. Some authors argue that females are less inclined toward risk-taking (e.g., Kogan and Wallach, 1964), others claim that they are less strategically oriented (Pilisuk, Skolnick and Overstreet, 1968), while still others argue that they are more compliant, and that when the demand characteristics appear to call for cooperation they will cooperate. In general, studies consistently indicate that females are more responsive to cues to cooperate than are males (Tedeschi, 1970). It is likely that while boys are traditionally raised to be independent and "aggressive," girls are trained to be sensitive to methods of reducing conflict. All this may change as parents strive to be less "sexist" in rearing their children.

It also seems that some people are more predisposed towards cooperation than others, quite apart from gender, cultural, or age considerations, but that such people are still likely to act competitively when dealing with other competitive people (Alcock and Mansell, 1977; Kelley and Stahelski, 1970). A "competitive" person, on the other hand, seems to act competitively regardless of the behaviour of others. For such a person, everyone else will seem to be competitive, since even "cooperators" will act competitively against such a person. Cooperators are more likely, as a result of their experience, to develop the view that some people are cooperative while some others are not, and to adjust their behaviour according to the behaviour of the other party.

As important as these predispositional effects may be, the evidence from game studies suggests that they are generally overridden by the effects of the structure of the situation. This overriding influence of structural variables may explain why correlations between personality variables and cooperative behaviour are repeatedly found to be very low.

RESOLUTION OF CONFLICT

Although most people are not very adept at solving serious conflicts, there are a number of ways in which conflicts can be lessened and destructiveness avoided. One way that people deal with some conflicts is through appeal to adjudication, that is, by recourse to the legal system. If one neighbour wants to play a stereo set at a high volume and the other does not like this, then the offended neighbour might call the police to complain. If there is a municipal ordinance against excessive noise, the neighbour with the stereo may be forced to turn it down. Some disputes end up in court, which brings us to the subject of justice. Earlier, distributive justice was discussed, but now we turn our attention to procedural justice, that is, the procedures through which justice decisions are made.

Procedural justice

The interest of social psychologists in procedural processes was first stimulated by the work of Thibaut and Walker (1975). Subsequent research has been focused on two contrasting models, the *adversary procedure* and the *inquisition procedure*. The adversary system is derived from the British model of legal justice, while the inquisitorial procedure is derived from the French legal system. In the adversary procedure the "case" is developed, argued, and defended by the parties to the dispute, or their agents. In the courts, lawyers for both sides argue their case before a judge. In the inquisitional procedure a "decision-maker" (in the courts, a judge) is assigned a similar role. This individual supervises the collection of evidence which bears upon the case, rather than simply listening to the two sides in the dispute.

Studies have shown that Americans prefer the adversary system and judge it to be more fair than the inquisitional system (Houlden, Latour, Walker and Thibaut, 1978; Lind, Kurtz, Musante, Walker and Thibaut, 1980). This should not be surprising, since people usually prefer something familiar to something strange. However, individuals from France, which has an inquisitional legal system, *also* prefer the adversary procedure (Lind, Erickson, Friedland and Dickenberger, 1978), a more interesting finding.

It has been argued that the critical distinction between the two procedures involves *process control* (Houlden *et al.*, 1978). In other words, in the adversary system the involved parties *control* the presentation of the case, whereas in the inquisitional system, the judge controls the presentation of evidence. Thibaut and Walker (1975) propose that any procedure that maximizes process control will be judged fair because the participants will feel more confident that all aspects of their case will be presented; under the inquisitional procedure, a "disinterested" person handles the case, so people may believe that some important evidence could be ignored or de-emphasized.

Of course, not all disputes or problems end up in the courts. At the more informal, interpersonal level the confrontational nature of the adversary process has the dangerous side effect of potentially disrupting or destroying positive group relationships. The inquisitional process, involving a mediator, has the added advantage of allowing concessions to be made with less loss of face since they occur in response to the mediator rather than to the direct pressures of the other person. The individual is not then perceived as "giving in" or "weak." Under this system neither person need feel a loser, whereas adjudication in an adversary process usually leads to an all-or-nothing outcome (Pruitt, 1981).

That the value systems of individuals affect procedural preferences has been demonstrated by a number of cross-cultural investigations. For example, it has been shown that mediation is preferred by Japanese (Peterson and Skimada, 1978), Chinese Americans (Doo, 1973), and Mexicans (Nader, 1969). Leung and Lind (1986) note that Chinese and Mexicans value collectivism; these are also societies in which inquisitorial or mediating procedures are preferred. They note that collectivism is associated with an emphasis on interpersonal harmony and group solidarity, while individualism stresses personal goals and interests and values self-sufficiency as considerably important. The procedural preferences clearly reflect these differing value orientations.

Dispelling misperceptions

Conflict behaviour is often attended by severe distortion, or misconception, of each party's motives and values, often resulting in even greater hostility. We tend to attribute to those we see as our opponents various characteristics which make it much more difficult for us to trust them.

When a mistaken perception can mean war and nuclear annihilation, it is vital for both people and their leaders on two sides of a conflict to view the situation and each other realistically and accurately. However, studies of conflict reveal the extent to which protagonists often misperceive. One common misperception is the belief that the people on the other side are really pro-us and that the real enemies are their leaders who mislead and manipulate them (White, 1969). This illusion serves to reinforce a party's "good intentions" toward the other side, and provides hope that the other side will someday see the light. It can also lead to disastrous errors in policy. For example, President Kennedy authorized limited support of the Bay of Pigs invasion of Cuba on the mistaken assumption that it would stimulate the Cuban people to overthrow the revolutionary government of Fidel Castro. Similar illusions have been apparent in U.S. policies in Vietnam and in Nicaragua.

Often, misperceptions tend to be shared by both sides of a conflict. Each party attributes the same virtues to itself and the same vices to the other side (a mirror-image). A U.S. psychologist who visited the U.S.S.R. and conversed with Soviet citizens observed that most of them said the same things about the United States that his own compatriots were saying about the U.S.S.R.: that they were militarily aggressive, that they could not be trusted, that they were deluded by their leaders (Bronfenbrenner, 1961). Other *mirror-image perceptions* have been observed in how the Soviets viewed the U.S. military involvement in Vietnam and how the U.S. viewed Soviet actions in Afghanistan (White, 1984). Such impressions only serve to intensify conflict.

Mediation

Obviously, any efforts which succeed in improving the accuracy of the perceptions of each protagonist will help to reduce the conflict. A husband who thinks that his wife is unhappy because he cannot satisfy her desire for a larger house will have a difficult time smoothing things out with a wife who is unhappy because she thinks her husband values his work more than he values her. A third party, a mediator, may be able to help the protagonists clear up the misperceptions and identify the basic conflict (Fisher, 1983).

Even with perfect perception of each other's motives and goals, conflicts over resources, status, and power still exist. As we have seen, once threats or coercion are employed, a conflict situation is changed to one in which saving face may be more important than the resolution of the original conflict. Obviously, then, if we wish to reduce such a conflict, we must try to find a way to allow the other party to agree to compromise without having them lose face in a big way. Such consideration applies as much to a marital fight as to an international "incident," something that marriage counsellors and labour mediators are keenly aware of.

Superordinate goals

Despite being opposed to each other with regard to certain issues, individuals can be brought together when their cooperation is required to achieve some mutually desired "superordinate" goal. This was clearly demonstrated in a classic study by Sherif (1958). He recruited 11-year-old boys, all strangers to one another, to go to a summer camp (at a place called "Robber's Cave") which was set up to serve as the basis for a field experiment. The boys were randomly divided into two groups, and these groups were isolated from each other for the first week. During the second week, the two groups interacted in athletic contests in which prizes could be won by either group. This produced friction between the two groups, and fighting developed as the members of each group began to describe the members of the other group as the "enemy" and to build up stereotypes about them. When asked about their friend-ships, over 90 percent chose members of their own group as the people with whom they wanted to be friends.

During the third and final week of camp, Sherif and his colleagues attempted to reduce the conflict their manipulation had generated. First, they tried simple inter-group contact: the two groups ate together, watched movies together, and shared common activities. This failed to reduce conflict. Then they set up common goals, in one instance by surreptitiously damaging the camp's water supply so that the boys had to work together to repair it. Other common goals, such as cooperating to raise money to buy a film to be shown at the camp, were also used. Working together toward these common, or "superordinate" goals led to a gradual reduction in hos-tility, and by the end of the third week, boys from each group were chumming around with each other.

The results of this study indicate that simple contact between hostile groups is not enough to reduce conflict, but that cooperative interaction brought about by the necessity of working together toward common goals can successfully reduce hostility. It must be remembered that the two groups of boys had no basic underlying conflict in the first place. Working together helped reduce incorrect perceptions and artificial differences. Superordinate goals have often caused groups to drop their grievances towards one another in order to work for the common good.

Conciliation

One method for reversing the buildup of both armaments and hostility was proposed by Osgood (1962). He argued that unilateral conciliatory action by one of the pro-tagonists is necessary in order to show the other that its perceptions are distorted. He suggested that one nation in a conflict announce its intention to gradually work towards tension reduction and eventual reversal of the arms race. To back up its words, he said, it must take a concrete step, such as stopping certain kinds of weapons testing, a step which, while showing good intent, does not make the nation imme-diately vulnerable or invite exploitative attack. The action should be accompanied by a call for the other side to reciprocate, but a few more such actions, each announced in advance, should be taken even if the other does not reciprocate, in order to dem-onstrate the sincerity of the moves. Should the other side reciprocate, then even larger conciliatory moves would be made. On the other hand, if the opponent tries to exploit the moves, the conciliatory approach is temporarily abandoned and retaliation is administered. Osgood called this approach "Graduated Reciprocated Initiative in

Tension-reduction," the words being chosen to spell the word GRIT (which he says will be a quality much in demand to carry out the program effectively (Stagner, 1967)). Although GRIT has been discussed a great deal, it has had little effect on the conduct of world affairs or on the U.S.A.-U.S.S.R. arms race. One major difficulty is that with the stakes being so high, and the history of suspicion so long, concessions are unlikely to be seen as anything other than attempts to either deceive the other side, to win points politically with non-aligned countries, or to seduce the other side into detente while the first side secretly builds up its arms.

PREVENTING THE WAR

Can social psychology contribute to the goal of preventing a nuclear war? Of course, decisions about war and peace are political decisions, influenced by public pressure and by historical events and ideologies. In terms of both power and level of knowledge, we have much to be modest about. Yet, some insights derived from psychological studies of conflict have been applied to the resolution of international negotiations.

There are two existing and contradictory schemata regarding conflict and how it can lead to war: the *deterrence* schema and the *conflict spiral* schema (Tetlock, 1983). Deterrence begins with the image of two protagonists, the "aggressor" and "status quo" powers. The aggressor power may doubt the ability of the status quo power to resist encroachment, even in issues or areas which are unimportant to its vital interests. If this doubt arises, the aggressor makes increasingly ambitious claims, with each concession from the other side leading to a greater demand. Finally, a situation occurs in which the status quo power must resist, but the aggressor cannot believe it and war results. Thus Hitler did not believe that Poland was the end of the line, despite clear and repeated warnings, because of an earlier appeasement policy which conceded the Rhineland, Austria, the Sudetenland, and the remainder of Czechoslovakia. Ironically, war can only be prevented by having a war-making capacity and a willingness to use it: a balance through mutual fear.

In the nuclear arms race, the nation that gets its missiles away first is most likely to come out best, (i.e., if it can successfully cripple the opponent's machinery for retaliation). Thus each side strives to protect its counter-strike capability in order to *deter* the other from the temptation of striking first. If each side can assure the other that it will always be able to destroy the other even if the other strikes first, then the other will not be tempted to strike. This is referred to by U.S. military strategists as MAD: Mutually Assured Destruction. The development of antimissile missiles, nuclear missile-carrying submarines, and the housing of missiles in underground concrete silos are all efforts made to deter the other from giving in to the temptation of "first strike." This situation is analogous to the gunfights which occurred during the opening up of the western United States. The person who shot first had the best chance of survival, so once the cowboys faced each other at opposite ends of the street, each had to try to shoot first. If being hit did not prevent the other person from firing also (suppose they were using blow darts, and the effect of the poison was only felt five minutes later), then even by getting away the first shot, a person's own chances of survival would not necessarily improve. In such a case, each person would be more likely to attempt to defuse the situation altogether (Schelling, 1960).

Decisions about war and peace are political, influenced by public pressure and historical events and ideologies.

When a threat, if carried out, will possibly eliminate the ability to execute a counter-threat, the situation is highly volatile.

The "conflict spiral" schema begins with the notion of competition between protagonists. In this schema, the defensive and deterrent actions of each side are interpreted as threatening by the other, who must respond with greater levels of counter-threat. Interests and goals are seen as incompatible, and the mutual fear itself causes an escalation (e.g., an arms race) and intensified competition at all levels. As we saw in Sherif's (1958) Robbers' Cave experiment, a relationship defined in purely competitive terms leads to out-group stereotyping and generalized mistrust. Many historians agree that World War I was caused by an unintended conflict spiral, not a failure of deterrence.

Both schemata may have elements of historical and contemporary validity, and it is important to understand that they underlie the decision-making process, particularly at an international level. Both are concerned with the possibility that misunderstanding and misperception can cause a war which is *not* intended. Deterrence types worry that "they" will *underestimate* "our" resolve to defend our interests, while conflict spiralists worry that "they" will *overestimate* our hostility (and vice versa). Perhaps by making the two schemata explicit and available for critical examination, an "unfreezing" in the thinking of international politicians and geopolitical strategists is possible.

Most of the research concerning the nuclear threat has been conducted in the United States, one of the two superpower protagonists in this crisis. While other nations, such as Canada, are allied to one side, they are mostly outsiders to the nuclear issue and will have very limited influence on its resolution. That is, although we will all suffer the same consequences from a nuclear war, we lack a sense of control over its outcome. Thus activism outside the U.S.A. and the U.S.S.R. may have a somewhat different meaning than activism within these nations.

The issue of nuclear war or peace seems to be massive, even overwhelming. The overwhelming nature of many of the great social issues of our times causes a state of high arousal which blocks innovative and creative thinking and produces feelings of helplessness, apathy, and avoidance. Weick (1984) argues for the utility of lowering our sights to smaller, explicit, and more manageable issues which we may solve with a much greater probability of success. Thus, rather than thinking in terms of ultimate solutions — "world government" or "complete nuclear disarmament" — we should aim for explicit and achievable goals: a nuclear freeze, a halt on major new technology, a ban or restriction on testing, limitations on weapons production or deployment. While none of these measures will remove the nuclear threat, we can expect several positive outcomes: providing hope and encouragement, attracting new allies who wish to migrate to a "winning side," deterring the hardline opposition, and avoiding un-realistic expectations or needlessly arousing opposition. Patience in accepting "small wins" may lead to better things and preserve a sense that there is a future.

SUMMARY

(1) Realistic conflict refers to situations in which there is a real basis for dis-pute, such as competition for scarce resources, incompatible goals, or incompatible principles.

(2) There are six types of conflict: veridical; contingent; displaced; misattributed; latent; and conflict based on false premises.

(3) Social exchange theory concerns the perception by each person of the relative value of rewards and costs in a relationship, evaluated in terms of the "comparison level"(CL) of others in that situation and the comparison level for alternatives to that relationship (CLalt).

(4) Distributive justice refers to fairness of outcome, which may be evaluated in terms of equity, equality, or need.

(5) Procedural justice refers to the fairness of the rules and methods for determining justice. There are two models, adversarial (British) and inquisitional (French), which differ in their presentation of evidence.

(6) A "game" refers to a situation in which two or more interdependent parties make decisions which affect each other according to rules. The two types of games are zero-sum, in which one party's gains match the opponent's losses, and non-zero-sum (mixed motive), in which some outcomes are mutually preferable to others.

(7) Games such as the Prisoner's Dilemma are based on the assumption that people act rationally to maximize utility. They may be motivated by individualistic, com-petitive, or cooperative concerns.

(8) A collective dilemma occurs when rational behaviour by individuals produces an outcome which is collectively undesirable, e.g., the commons problem and the provision of public goods problem.

(9) A game which is non-negotiable (only one winner), in which the goal-directed behaviour is threatening, and in which both players can lose disastrously is called a dangerous game.

(10) A threat is more credible when the threatener has behaved consistently in the past, the threatened action has negative consequences for the threatener as well as the party threatened, and the threatened consequences are not excessive in the situation.

(11) Threat often intensifies conflict because people need to "save face" and because of the possibility of a spiralling series of threats and counter-threats.

(12) Communication sometimes reduces conflict by clarifying the intentions of either side, but is unlikely to be helpful in a "win or lose" situation or when face-saving is important.

(13) The most effective strategy in bargaining combines firm resistance to exploitation with reciprocation of the other party's cooperative behaviour.

(14) "Cooperative" people tend to be female, young, from less competitive cultures, and they are more responsive to the cooperative actions of others.

(15) Conflict reduction may be accomplished through the graduated reciprocation of tension-reducing acts (GRIT) and the introduction of superordinate goals.

(16) "Deterrence" and "conflict spiral" models are two opposing schemata of conflict at the international level.

FURTHER READING

AUSTIN, W.G. and WORCHEL (Eds.) (1979). *The social psychology of intergroup relations*. Monterey, CA: Brooks/Cole.

BERCOVITCH, J. (1984). *Social conflicts and third parties: Strategies of conflict resolution*. Boulder, CO: Westview.

JERVIS, R., LEBOW, R.N. and STEIN, J.G. (1985). *Psychology and deterrence*. Baltimore, MD: Johns Hopkins University Press.

KELMAN, H.C. (Ed.) (1965). *International behavior: A social-psychological analysis*. New York: Holt, Rinehart and Winston.

LERNER, M.J. and LERNER, S. (Eds.) (1981). *The justice motive in social behavior*. New York: Plenum Press.

PRUITT, D.G. (1981). *Negotiation behavior*. New York: Academic Press.

PRUITT, D.G. and RUBIN, J.Z. (1986). *Social conflict*. New York: Random House.

RUBIN, J.Z. and BROWN, B.R. (1975). *The social psychology of bargaining and negotiation*. New York: Academic Press.

SWINGLE, P. (1970). *The structure of conflict*. New York: Academic Press.

TAYLOR, D.M. and MOGHADDAM, F.M. (1987). *Theories of intergroup relations: International social psychological perspectives*. New York: Praeger.

TEGER, A.I. (1980). *Too much invested to quit*. New York: Pergamon.

WHITE, H.C. (Ed.) (1986). *Psychology and the prevention of nuclear war*. New York: New York University Press.

Collective Behaviour

Only individuals think; gangs merely throb.

Robertson Davies

The scene during the last few minutes that the Empress remained on the surface of the water was one of utter, overwhelming despair and helplessness in the face of death.

The Globe, 1914

FOR REFLECTION

- Are crowds really "irrational" in their behaviour?
- How are rumours spread and why is the truth often distorted in the telling of a rumour?
- Why are we subject to fads and fashions?
- What causes people to panic?
- How do cults attract and retain their members?

- IN 1212, Etienne of Cloyes, a French shepherd boy, had a vision of Christ which instructed him to go to the Holy Land and recover the Holy Sepulchre. Thousands of children, some only eight years old, rushed to join him as he paraded through towns and villages on his way to Marseilles. Parents were powerless to keep their children from running away to join him. At Marseilles, the children expected the sea to part at Etienne's command. When it did not, they embarked on ships. Two ships sank and all aboard were lost, while the others sailed to Alexandria where the children were sold into slavery. A subsequent "Children's Crusade" occurred in 1237, and another in 1458.

- In 1968, many Canadians found themselves caught up in the excitement surrounding the emergence of a new political superstar, Pierre Elliott Trudeau, a balding, middle-aged man who was destined to become leader of the Liberal Party and Prime Minister of Canada. While not everyone was impressed, his "magnetism" was such that wherever he went, people crushed around him to shake his hand, to touch him or even to kiss him. Young women shrieked and swooned in a manner usually reserved for rock stars. Even the press was mesmerized by it all: it seemed that Trudeau could do no wrong. Rude gestures or clowning antics were interpreted as being "cute" or "refreshingly non-conformist."

- When crowds of curious people flocked to the scene of the crash of an Air Canada DC-8 near St. Thérèse in 1968 which had killed all aboard, reporters observed a number of individuals taking pieces of clothing and other personal objects belonging to the crash victims. In September of 1978, a Boeing 727 passenger plane and a small private plane collided over San Diego, California, killing 150 people. Police reported that several people were arrested for looting at the crash site, some trying to take money and rings from the bodies of victims.

- On October 7, 1968, about 30 000 people, some in wheelchairs, and some from as far away as New York and Ontario, waited in vain in the rain and the mud for the Virgin Mary to appear at a location near St. Bruno, Québec. She had apparently promised six young girls who had seen her two weeks earlier that she would reappear at that time.

Previous chapters have described the effects of mere presence of others on the behaviour of a person (social facilitation), as well as the pressures that individuals, groups, and organizations can exert (producing conformity, compliance, and obedience). The situations described above, however, cannot be readily understood in terms of these interpersonal or group processes. There was no leader or system demanding obedience — nor were there any pre-existing group norms which generated pressures to conform. Each of these examples involved collections of people who, for the most part, were strangers to one another. But in each case, the early actions of a few stimulated the later actions of a great many. Once the story spread that children were flocking in large numbers to join Etienne, once Trudeau was raised to "star" status, once one or two people began carting away souvenirs from the airplane crash, and once it became known that at least some people were taking the prediction of the Virgin's appearance seriously, the stage was set for similar behaviour by many others. Somehow, such behaviours depend on the presence of other people who are acting, or are prepared to act, similarly and who have a mutual influence on each other. It would have been more difficult and appeared less reasonable to have been the only one to run away from home, swoon in Trudeau's presence, loot the possessions of aircrash victims, or wait in the rain for the Blessed Virgin.

WHAT IS "COLLECTIVE BEHAVIOUR"?

The foregoing examples illustrate several characteristics which define collective behaviour: (1) It emerges spontaneously in a collectivity of people, e.g., a crowd or an entire society or culture; (2) it is relatively unorganized; (3) it is unplanned in its course of development and is therefore fairly unpredictable; and (4) it is the product of interstimulation among the participants, that is, individuals are influenced by the actions of others, and their reactions in turn influence the very people who have affected them (Milgram and Toch, 1969). These features reflect an absence of normal social convention; therefore, such behaviour is most likely to arise in situations where people are strangers, leaving them without the support and the normative framework of their usual groups. The interstimulation of members of the collectivity is reinforcing to some extent, or the behaviour would quickly die out. For example, if one spectator at a football game undresses and no applause or encouragement is forthcoming, others are unlikely to act similarly. If the crowd cheers, however, perhaps a second person will undress, and if this too is met with approval, others may do the same and the behaviour may spread throughout the audience.

Sometimes collective behaviour involves an intensification of reactions that were already anticipated. For example, while teenagers go to see their favourite rock groups expecting to be excited, the interaction which occurs among members of the audience (the "interstimulation" referred to above) can create a collective experience which is

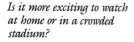

Is it more exciting to watch at home or in a crowded stadium?

more powerful than anticipated and more intense than anything the individual would experience either alone or in a small group. (Indeed, why is it more exciting to watch a football game in a crowded stadium than to watch it with only a small audience or at home on television, even though you might have a better view on TV?)

Collective behaviour is rather rare. Most groups of strangers, for example, people queuing for a bus or passengers standing in an elevator, do not exhibit such behaviour, although the potential may be there. Collective behaviour is *never* institutionalized behaviour, and so the label must not be applied to large-scale behaviour which is governed by appropriate social norms, such as the activities of a large group of strangers on New Year's Eve (Brown, 1965). People at a New Year's Eve party may appear to be out of control as they suddenly rush around kissing each other but, in fact, this activity is controlled by a norm which allows it to occur at midnight of that particular day and not at other times or on other days. However, even in this context, collective behaviour can occur: perhaps on one New Year's Eve, all the party participants rush out into the street and begin to dance wildly or smash store windows.

The study of collective behaviour is an important part of social psychology — not only for itself — but because there is hardly any aspect of social behaviour which does not occasionally find extreme expression in some type of collective behaviour episode (Milgram and Toch, 1969). Prejudice, aggression, and authoritarianism are readily apparent in the conduct of lynch mobs and provide the fuel for extreme public demonstrations, such as the Nuremberg Rallies of the Hitler era.

It is all but impossible to study most kinds of collective behaviour in the laboratory, both for practical and ethical reasons. We would have no idea how to generate something in the laboratory which is equivalent to a rock concert or a lynch mob, even if we wanted to. However, sporadic attempts have been made. In one such study, the creation of a mob was studied when subjects were successfully convinced that a terrible crime had been committed. The researchers' confederate then attempted to become the leader of the group and generate a mob to seek out the perpetrators. Only about 12 percent of the subjects were inclined to join the mob (Meier, Mennenga and Stoltz, 1941). In another study, French (1944) tried to simulate a panic by locking groups of subjects in a room, then sounding a fire alarm while forcing smoke under the door and into the room. However, ethics aside, the study was a failure: One group of subjects calmly discussed the possibility that they were being observed for their psychological reactions, while in a second group, the first person to notice the smoke kicked the door open, knocking over the smoke machine. There have been reports that Nazi researchers studied panic by using prisoners in real-life panic situations (Farago, 1942).

It also is difficult to study real-life collective behaviour because, in most instances, the behaviour is underway before we would have time to prepare studying it. Furthermore, it is difficult to isolate and measure the relevant variables; even the participants themselves are unlikely to be aware of all the important influences upon them. This no doubt explains why, despite the fact that the earliest social psychology texts gave considerable discussion to collective behaviour, relatively little has been done by psychologists to advance our understanding of the subject over the intervening years.

This chapter begins with a discussion of the nature of crowds and the phenomenon of rumours. Then, a number of different kinds of collective behaviour are explored: fads and fashions, contagions, social movements and cults.

CROWDS

It was the French sociologist Le Bon who stimulated modern interest in the study of collective behaviour through his book *The Crowd* (1895/1960). A *crowd* is a relatively large collection of people who are physically close enough to influence each other's behaviour, although there is no particular relationship among these individuals. A crowd is unorganized, anonymous, casual, and temporary (Milgram and Toch, 1969). Such a collectivity of people is ideal for the development of collective behaviour, given that such behaviour typically depends on a lack of group structure and appropriate norms.

Crowd behaviour can often appear bizarre or irrational, as we shall see when collective phenomena such as panics and riots are discussed. How can such behaviour be explained? Three approaches to understanding such apparent irrationality will be considered: contagion, deindividuation, and emergent norm formation.

Contagion and the irrationality of crowds

Contagion theory is based on the notion of the rapid spreading of emotionality, attitudes, and behaviour throughout a crowd or population. Its roots go back to Le Bon, who believed that in some situations, a crowd can develop a "collective mind" which is inherently irrational:

> Under certain given circumstances, and only under those circumstances, an agglomeration of men presents new characteristics very different from those of the individuals composing it. The sentiments and ideas of all the persons in the gathering take one and the same direction, and their conscious personality vanishes. A collective mind is formed, doubtless transitory but presenting clearly defined characteristics. The gathering has become what . . . I will call an organized crowd . . . or a psychological crowd (Le Bon 1895/1960, pp. 23–24).

According to Le Bon, several factors contribute to the development of this "collective mind." First, he argued, the sheer number of people in the collectivity produces a feeling of overwhelming power accompanied by a sense of anonymity and a reduction in individual responsibility (anticipating Darley and Latane's (1968) model of bystander non-intervention). This leads to the liberation of "savage, animalistic instincts" which are normally suppressed, he said. He saw suggestibility as the most important factor, which produces a vulnerability to *contagion*, a kind of hypnotic process which leads people to act in line with the actions of others, setting their own judgment aside.

While "instinct" is no longer an acceptable explanation for the behaviour of crowds, the metaphor of contagion is appealing in that crowd behaviour appears to involve the spreading out and acceptance of beliefs, fears, hopes, and actions. In the modern conception, contagion does not involve a hypnotic process, but rather the transmission of feelings, ideas, and behaviour through suggestions, rumour, imitation, or similar processes (see Box 14-1). A circular kind of interstimulation is said to occur in contagion in which one person copies the behaviour of a second person or at least acts in a similar way, and this second person, now seeing the first person react similarly, is reinforced in the belief that the reaction is appropriate. For example, consider a group of people alone in an old castle at night. There is a strange noise. One person becomes alarmed by this and he looks frightened. A second person is not scared until

B · O · X   14 - 1

MASS HYSTERIA

In 1931, a student of architecture attended a political speech delivered at the Institute of Technology of the University of Berlin. He describes how he and many others in the audience were "carried on a wave of enthusiasm which — one could almost feel this physically — bore the speaker along from sentence to sentence. It swept away any skepticism, any reservation" (Speer, 1970, p. 16). Knowing little of the speaker, the program or the ideology, and acting under what he describes as the "hypnotic impression" of the speaker, Adolf Hitler, the student, Albert Speer, joined the Nazi Party and eventually rose to a high position in that government.

The work of Charcot and others in the nineteenth century led to a general belief that the source of many of the phenomena which now make up social psychology could be found in the concept of suggestion (MacDougall, 1908). That is, experts believed that since what is understood to be the process by which people influence each other cannot be explained in terms of logic, there must be an element of influence without awareness, of people changing their minds without intending to do so. One such model of suggestion, or influence, seemed to be offered by hypnosis, an altered state of consciousness which was once called "mesmerism" or "animal magnetism." It perhaps is not coincidental

that until 1965, research in abnormal psychology and social psychology was published in the same journal. Even today, many people are inclined to think of social influence in terms of the "power of suggestion" and "mass hysteria."

In contemporary research, some argue that hypnosis is a unique state of consciousness, one in which people's awareness and thought processes depart significantly from their normal experience (Hilgard, 1978). However, other researchers have argued that hypnosis is *not* a unique state, and have demonstrated that subjects who are not hypnotized can be induced to perform unusual tasks if they are highly motivated and assured that they will be able to perform them (Barber, 1976; Spanos, 1982). It has been argued that hypnosis is an extreme example of role-playing, and that people who have been hypnotized are simply acting in accordance with a learned schema of how people under hypnosis are supposed to act.

Thus social psychology has come full circle. Whereas ordinary social influence used to be seen in terms of a mysterious, even magical hypnotic effect, hypnosis is now seen as one instance of social influence. In the presence of a "hypnotic" leader, and responding to strong behavioural cues by many convinced followers, it is not surprising that Albert Speer felt carried away, under the spell of the *Führer*.

she notices the first person's expression, and now she too becomes frightened. The first person sees the look of fear on his friend's face and interprets it to bolster the need to be fearful: "She's frightened too." The fear could thus spread through the group, even if most individuals had hardly noticed the noise or had discounted it as unimportant.

Even applause and laughter can be "contagious": In one study, visitors to the Ontario Science Centre watched a film, following which a confederate applauded (Freedman, Birsky and Cavoukian, 1980). They observed the number of people who joined in the applause, and found that when people were all seated closely together, the contagion of the applause was much greater than when the people were more spread out. The actual number of people also had an effect, but a smaller one: a large group of people experienced more contagion than a small group.

The contagion approach to collective behaviour continues to have its defenders, although there are several drawbacks to it (Turner, 1964). One problem is that it is extremely difficult to submit contagion theory to an empirical test. How could we measure how people stimulate emotional states in each other, for example? Another difficulty is that the theory tells us nothing about the development of leadership and other roles within the collectivity. Yet another problem is that those who defend the theory tend to cite rather uncommon and dramatic events which have not been observed directly by researchers but are dependent upon the notoriously unreliable eyewitness testimony of lay people. Further, such events are hardly typical of collective behaviour in general, and care must be taken not to generalize from those events to other more mundane forms of collective behaviour.

Deindividuation

Although the notion of animalistic instincts and collective mind appears naive and erroneous by contemporary standards, Le Bon's basic ideas have been honed and repackaged, without the concept of instincts, in the concept of *deindividuation*, a term coined by Festinger, Pepitone and Newcomb (1952). Zimbardo (1970) expanded on this concept, describing deindividuation as a complex process in which a series of antecedent social conditions leads to changes in self-perception (the person comes to see him or herself more as a member of a group than as an individual), leading in turn to a lowered threshold for normally restrained behaviour. When conditions are right, this can produce antisocial behaviour. Thus this approach does not view collective behaviour as the spreading of emotionality throughout a crowd, but as the flouting of social norms in a situation of relative anonymity, i.e., a crowd.

Deindividuation according to Zimbardo (1970) is the result of several factors:

(1) *Loss of identifiability*. This can occur when a person is standing in a crowd of strangers or wearing a mask.

(2) *Loss of responsibility*. If many people are engaging in violence, each person's share of the blame may seem to be smaller.

(3) *Presence of group physical activity which in itself is arousing and sustaining*. For example, when everyone is yelling and screaming at a rock concert, such stimulation may readily lead others to yell and scream.

(4) *Limited temporal perspective*. The person, "lives for the moment" and ignores past obligations and future accountings.

(5) *A novel or unstructured situation*. The absence of the cues which might otherwise restrain behaviour can lead to a lowering of inhibition (see Box 14-2).

Various studies of subjects' behaviour in conditions of anonymity have seemed to lend support to the deindividuation hypothesis. For example, when subjects were asked to discuss their parents in a group discussion, more negative comments were forthcoming when the subjects were dressed in gray laboratory coats and seated in a dimly lit room than when such anonymity was not present (Festinger *et al.*, 1952). In an attempt to demonstrate deindividuation, Zimbardo (1970) compared the "aggressive" behaviour (defined as the number and intensity of shocks given to a simulated victim) of college students in either of two situations. In the first situation, the subjects were dressed in shapeless overcoats, wore hoods over their faces, and sat in a darkened room. No subject could see how much shock the other two subjects

B · O · X   14 - 2

WHEN THE POLICE ARE ABSENT

Police are an important thread in the fabric of restraint against violence. People are afraid of arrest and punishment. What happens when the police are absent? In 1969 in Montreal, the police and fire departments went on strike. Once the formalized social controls the police represented were lifted, groups of people went on a rampage — smashing windows, looting, and setting fires. According to witnesses, while there was extreme tension, a sense of liberation — almost a "country fair" mood — seemed to characterize the demonstrators and those who watched them. The rampage continued until the return of the police, and the deployment of soldiers reinstituted the formal restraints against such activity.

Outbreaks of vandalism also occurred during police walkouts in Sydney, Nova Scotia, in 1971 and subsequently in Yarmouth. Even worse, during a massive power failure in New York City in July 1977 which caused the city administration to grind to a halt and greatly reduced the capacity of the police to carry out their duties, tens of thousands of people in ghetto areas all over the city engaged in an orgy of destruction and looting. The final bill for shop-keepers: $150 *million*. What seemed only too obvious was the almost carnival-like atmosphere and the lack of guilt displayed by the participants.

were administering to a "victim," in accordance with an experimental deception which permitted subjects to shock the victim as much or as little as they wished. In the second condition, subjects wore no hoods or overcoats, sat in a well-lit room, and even wore name tags. The subjects in the anonymous condition were much more "aggressive" than those in the other condition, in keeping with the deindividuation hypothesis.

In another study, conditions which reduced individual identity in a mock prison (see Box 14-3) led to brutalization of the "prisoners" by the "guards" even though all were, in reality, psychologically healthy college students (Zimbardo, Haney, Banks and Jaffee, 1982). It has even been reported that tribal societies whose warriors disguise themselves with masks or paint are more brutal in warfare than similar societies in which no such anonymity is provided (Watson, 1973).

However, there is some debate regarding whether deindividuation ever really occurs, that is, whether individuals' social inhibitions are actually temporarily dissolved, allowing them to be swept away by the group. Although many studies bear witness to the relationship between anonymity and antisocial behaviour, they do not by themselves demonstrate that deindividuation has occurred. Another possible explanation is simply that people, often tempted to behave antisocially, have learned to restrain this tendency out of fear of some form of punishment. Anonymity reduces the likelihood that the person can be identified and lowers the likelihood of punishment or social sanction (Freedman, 1982).

Thus, although the deindividuation concept is intriguing, perhaps articulating a collective fear of the "madness of crowds," more evidence is required to demonstrate its existence as a psychological state. Moreover, the concept of the "irrationality of crowds" is most likely wrong. Owing to its spontaneous formation, a crowd has little means by which to plan rational actions and no pre-existing norms for behaviour. Yet the behaviour of people in a crowd, which might be coupled in the heat of the

B · O · X   14 - 3

BRUTALITY IN THE CELLBLOCK: THE STANFORD PRISON STUDY

At times, the contrived situation of the psychological laboratory can become startlingly real. Researchers in one study (Zimbardo *et al.*, 1982) set out to simulate the deindividuating conditions of a real social institution by setting up a mock prison in the basement of the Stanford University psychology department. Voluntary subjects were randomly assigned the roles of guards and prisoners. Those designated as "guards" were given identical khaki uniforms, reflecting sunglasses, billy clubs, handcuffs, whistles, and sets of keys. The "prisoners" were picked up on the first day at their homes by police cars, taken to the police station where they were "processed," and then taken blindfolded to the "prison." They were assigned numbers as identification and wore identical hospital-type gowns and stocking caps. The guards were instructed to maintain "law and order," and events were allowed to unfold.

While subjects initially approached their role-playing in a light-hearted fashion, the situation soon began to deteriorate. The guards became increasingly abusive and punitive toward the prisoners, while the prisoners became passive, helpless, and showed symptoms of stress such as crying, agitation, confusion, and depression. Even the principal researcher, Zimbardo, found himself preoccupied with rumours of a "prison break," forgetting his responsibilities as a scientist. At this point, after six days, an experiment planned to last two weeks was terminated. The roles had become reality to the participants.

The experiment has been criticized on several grounds (Banuazizi and Movahedi, 1975; Thayer and Saarni, 1975). Subjects had signed consent forms in which they agreed to be paid to participate in a study in which some of their rights would be waived. Thus they might have felt a moral or legal obligation to continue, and might have exaggerated their symptoms of distress in order to get out of their obligation. The "guards" might have been acting as they did, as "good subjects," because it was expected of them in order to make the study more realistic. There were also some individual differences; some of the prisoners did not become apathetic or distressed and some of the guards were not abusive.

Nonetheless, the study shows the power of the situation, particularly in total institutions such as prisons. In a group of normal young people participating in a simulation experiment, loss of personal identity can cause dramatic changes in behaviour over a short period of time. We can readily extrapolate about the profound impact of long-term exposure in institutions such as prisons, hospitals, and the military.

moment with a spurious sense of belonging to — and identification with — a group, may be better described as *non*-rational rather than *ir*rational (Klapp, 1972), that is, people in a crowd may set aside their critical judgment. However, even in a crowd, norms may rapidly develop to govern behaviour.

Emergent norm theory

An alternative to contagion or deindividuation as an explanation for crowd behaviour is provided by *emergent norm theory* (Turner and Killiam, 1972). While contagion theory applies only to highly emotional interactions, emergent norm theory is as capable of describing very somber crowds as it is highly excited ones (Milgram and Toch, 1969). According to this view, individuals in a crowd act in a given way because they view that action as appropriate or necessary, and not because their personality and motivation is swallowed up into a collective will or because they are succumbing to some normally restrained motivations. From this viewpoint, crowds are considered to be initially heterogeneous with regard to goals, feelings, and behaviour. However, through rumour transmission and non-verbal communication, a shared perception of the situation develops, and individuals begin to perceive a consensus about what behaviour is appropriate (i.e., norms emerge). Even if they do not totally agree, crowd members then act according to the emergent norm because of actual or anticipated conformity pressure. Since such pressure is usually greater in conditions of non-anonymity, emergent norm theory would predict greater group conformity to norms which deviate from the norms of everyday life in situations in which the individuals are not anonymous. This outcome is just the opposite of what deindividuation theory predicts: it suggests that people are more likely to deviate from the norms of everyday life in situations of anonymity.

Thus deindividuation theory and emergent norm theory provide quite different perspectives on collective behaviour, antisocial behaviour in particular. According to deindividuation theory, antisocial collective behaviour occurs when anonymity brings about a sense of diminished responsibility and the lifting of internal restraints. In consequence, individuals are no longer responsive to the norms that usually constrain them. Emergent norm theory, on the other hand, predicts that antisocial behaviour will be manifested by a group if a norm which encourages such behaviour develops in the group. For conformity pressure to be effective, the members must be identifiable.

A laboratory study (Mann, Newton and Innes, 1982) pitted emergent norm theory against deindividuation theory in a study of aggressive behaviour. Groups of six to eight subjects listened to two people in a debate. In half of the groups there was anonymity among the members (each member sat at a separate table, and curtains among the tables prevented subjects from seeing one another), while the members of the remaining groups were identifiable to one another by name. The study was ostensibly a study of the effects of audience noise on the participants in a debate, and subjects were instructed to indicate their reactions to what the debaters were saying by varying the level of noise heard by the debaters, just as members of a real audience might react with spontaneous applauding or booing. Each subject sat at a separate control panel and could choose a noise level by pressing any one of a series of 11 buttons which they believed corresponded to several levels of noise from very soft to painfully loud. The subjects were told that the debaters actually heard a noise level which was the average of the choices of all the subjects in the group. The subjects themselves were given false feedback about that average level. Half of the subjects in each of the two conditions — anonymous and identifiable — were led to believe that the group "norm" was a lenient one, in other words, their feedback indicated that the noise being heard by the debaters was not aversive, while the other half was led to believe that the group norm was an aggressive one because the noise level apparently heard by the debaters was very high. The dependent variable was, of course, the noise level chosen by each subject. If deindividuation theory applied, anonymity should have produced the greatest "aggression." If emergent norm theory applied, then the greatest aggression should have been observed in the identifiable condition with the aggressive group norm. It was found, in line with deindividuation theory, that anonymity rather than a group norm of aggressiveness led to greater aggression (defined in terms of higher noise level chosen by the subject). Thus, no support was found for the emergent norm theory.

488 / Chapter Fourteen

At this point, then, although emergent norm theory provides a more general explanatory basis for collective behaviour, it still requires much more empirical support. Its appeal lies in the generalizing of a group process (norm formation) to the seemingly unorganized collective situation. However, even if norms do emerge in the collective situation, emergent norm theory does not tell us the basis on which they are formed, or why one norm (e.g., "Run for your lives") emerges in one situation but not in another similar situation.

Of course, it is unwise to try to explain a crowd's behaviour as though all individuals are reacting in a similar fashion or are affected by circumstances in a similar way. As was noted earlier, a single collectivity of people may manifest a variety of crowd forms; spectators at a soccer match may form a mob and attack the referee and then panic as squads of police arrive (Milgram and Toch, 1969). Indeed, empirical observations of crowds indicate that they are rarely homogeneous. Some members of a rioting crowd may be experiencing great hostility toward a target, while others may be simply enjoying the "ruckus" and excitement, and still others may be trying to get away from the crowd altogether.

Each of the three approaches discussed here — contagion, deindividuation, and emergent norm theory — has a certain "appeal of explanation" in that each can make sense of one collective event or another. Yet all three are problematic as explanations for collective behaviour. They are not well-defined theories to begin with, but this is hardly surprising, given the difficulty of capturing collective behaviour in order to study it. There are several other approaches to collective behaviour, none of which is without its own problems. Indeed, game theory (discussed in Chapter 13) has provided a basis for some forms of crowd behaviour (e.g., Berk, 1974), such as panic, a topic which will be discussed later in this chapter.

RUMOURS

Collective behaviour takes many forms, and some of these are driven by fear or apprehension. It is in such situations that rumour plays an especially important role. During times of crisis or of great social uncertainty, people thirst for information that will help them decide how to respond. However, it is during just such times that formal information channels often prove to be inadequate. Either information does not get through at all, or it is meager or untrustworthy. A news report that three convicted killers are loose in a neighbourhood will create a situation of uncertainty, but it will not satisfy the need for more information. (Recall the discussion of schematic information processing in Chapter 3.) In such situations, people try to make sense out of what is going on. They have to decide upon what action to take, if any, and to do so, they must anticipate what is likely to happen. This gives rise to *rumours*, which can spread rapidly through the populace.

When Mr. Jones tells his neighbour, Mr. Green, that he "thinks" some convicts might be hiding in the neighbourhood, Mr. Green, reacting no doubt with some alarm at the thought, may tell others that he has "heard" that they may be in the neighbourhood. As the story spreads gradually, it changes from one of clear speculation to one which seems to carry some important information. Even if people are not convinced that the contents of the rumour are correct, they often cannot afford to take a chance that the rumour is false. For example, during World War II, when an American psychology professor spent three months in a Canadian maritime fishing village without explaining the reasons for his presence, a rumour developed that he was a spy for the Germans (Doob, 1941). The rumour made "sense" of his behaviour and even if people doubted the truth of the rumour, they would have been foolhardy to ignore the *possibility* that it was indeed correct.

In the first epidemic of bubonic plague, the "Black Death" (1348–1350), fully a quarter of the European population perished; this proportion grew to more than a third during the next half-century (Langer, 1964). People were at a loss to know how to deal with the plague. Nothing they did seemed to help. While people accepted that it was God's punishment for their waywardness, rumours circulated which assigned the blame to various scapegoats, such as Jews (who were accused of poisoning the wells), witches (acting as agents of Satan), and even physicians, who were accused of encouraging the spread of the disease, perhaps to increase their business. The result was a wave of persecution of these people. Rumour in this case, as in general, served to relieve emotional tension. Not knowing the cause leaves people helpless to react, which only exacerbates the anxiety. If the cause of the plague is "known" (e.g., witches), direct action can be taken to fight it.

There is some parallel between the bubonic plague epidemic and the emerging epidemic of AIDS (Acquired Immune Deficiency Syndrome). Some airlines have had their hand forced by labour relations boards in the hiring of stewards; in one case, a Canadian airline had refused to do so because "most stewards are homosexual and the public fears catching AIDS." In the United States, some parents have kept their children home from schools because AIDS-infected children had been admitted to the school system. All such reaction occurs despite the fact that the AIDS virus is not spread except through the exchange of bodily fluids.

The study of rumours

How can rumours be studied? One approach has been to focus on the distortion that arises in serial transmissions of information. For example, Allport and Postman (1945) observed the development of such distortion of information when one subject described what he saw in a slide that had been projected on a screen to another subject who could not see the slide. The latter repeated the description to a third subject who, in turn, repeated it to a fourth subject, and so on. After five retellings, only 30 percent of the original detail was retained. (This recalls an old party game — "Telephone" — in which one person whispers a short description of some situation into another person's ear, and that person repeats it to the next person, and so on around the room, until the last person repeats aloud what was said, generally to the amusement of all. The end product is usually very different from what was initially said.)

Allport and Postman described the changes that took place in the "rumour" in terms of three processes: *levelling*, *sharpening*, and *assimilation*. Levelling refers to the finding that as rumour travels, it tends to grow shorter and to become more easily grasped and repeated. The greatest decline in the number of details occurs at the beginning. Sharpening refers to the selective emphasis and even exaggeration of some parts of the rumour. Assimilation refers to the way in which pre-existing interests, habits, expectations, and prejudices serve to distort the rumour. These three processes occur simultaneously and represent an effort to reduce the rumour to a simple form which will have adaptive meaning for the individual involved. The longer the time

As a rumour travels, it tends to grow shorter and become more easily grasped and repeated.

that passes between hearing the rumour and retelling it, the greater the influence this complex process will have.

However, we might argue that real-life rumour rarely takes place in the kind of situation used by Allport and Postman. Subjects in their study had no real emotional involvement, and the information they were receiving had no critical importance. In real life, subjects often have a strong need for relevant information. In such cases, it is not so much the process of verbal interchange that is of interest, but the collective belief and resulting action generated by the rumour (Shibutani, 1966).

Field studies of rumour among pre-existing groups have found, surprisingly, that little or no distortion occurs in the passage of the rumour from person to person. For example, one researcher (Caplow, 1947) reported that rumours in an army regiment were recirculated and subjected to repeated correction. In another study (Schachter and Burdeck, 1955) a rumour was planted in a girls' school and its evolution studied. First, the principal of the school went to each of four classrooms and did something very unprecedented: she pointed to one of the girls and instructed her to take her hat, coat, and books and accompany her out of the room. This was done to create *cognitive unclarity*, or *ambiguity*. Presumably, the students would try to find an explanation for the curious event. Then a rumour was planted in some of the classes by having a teacher say to each of two girls in the pertinent classes, "Do you know anything about some exams that were taken from the office?" Teachers were instructed to record all questions directed to them by the students, and this information, plus that gathered from individual interviews of all the students at the end of the day, provided the basic data. As it turned out, virtually every girl had heard the planted rumour. And it was in those classes in which the cognitive unclarity had been generated that the rumour had the greatest impact. The girls in these classes reported having spent twice as much time discussing the rumour as did girls from the class given the rumour without the unclarity manipulation. These girls also generated more *new* rumours (Figure 14-1). However, in no case was there any distortion of the planted rumour.

Why the difference between these results and those of Allport and Postman? First, the rumour was much less complex than the "rumour" used in the serial transmission

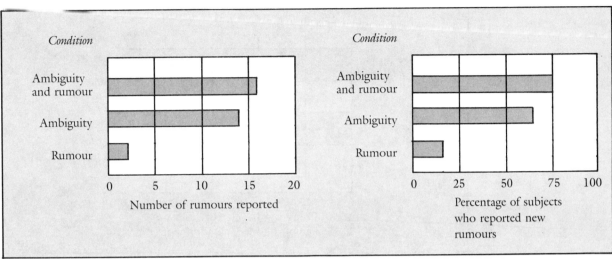

SOURCE: Rosnow and Fine, 1976

FIGURE 14-1

The number of different rumours and the percentage of students reporting new rumours in the Schachter and Burdick study

study. More importantly, the subjects in this study were emotionally involved — they were not just taking part in a laboratory study. They *wanted* information and perhaps were more careful with it as a result. Moreover, the rumour was undoubtedly recirculated, which may have led to an increase in its accuracy, for a person hearing a rumour a second time corrects the embellishments added in the interim, as we shall see below.

Set and anxiety level   Two factors, *set* and *anxiety level*, determine whether rumours will become progressively distorted or more and more accurate (Buckner, 1965). First, a person may approach the rumour with one of three orientations: a *critical set*, which is likely if the person has had some experience with similar situations; an *uncritical set*, which is likely if the person is in a crisis situation and/or the rumour satisfies certain needs; or a *transmission set* (only apt to occur in laboratory studies), which is likely if the person is only interested in passing on the rumour. According to this view, when people with a critical set are exposed to a rumour, the rumour will become more precise with each transmission as dubious elements are eliminated. However, multiple interaction in the absence of critical ability reduces accuracy through the creation of new variations of the information.

The second factor is *anxiety level*. While uncertainty about imminent events or about events already underway may well lead to anxiety, anxiety may in turn lead to a lessening of the ability to tolerate ambiguity in general (Rosnow and Fine, 1976). Cognitive dissonance theory suggests that when people are anxious but without good reason, they will strive to find a reason in order to reduce the dissonance between the cognitions "I am anxious" and "I have no reason to be anxious." Rumour may reduce this dissonance, e.g., "I am anxious because civil war is imminent." In a similar vein, hostility toward some group can be justified via rumour: "I don't like the neighbours because they may be communist spies."

Very little research has been carried out to examine the role of anxiety in rumour transmission. However, in one such study, students were assigned to either high or low chronic anxiety groups on the basis of their scores on a measure of anxiety (Anthony, 1973). A rumour was begun by telling a few students from each group that certain extracurricular activities were going to be reduced for budgetary reasons.

FIGURE 14-2
Percentages of students who heard the rumour that extracurricular activities were to be cut back

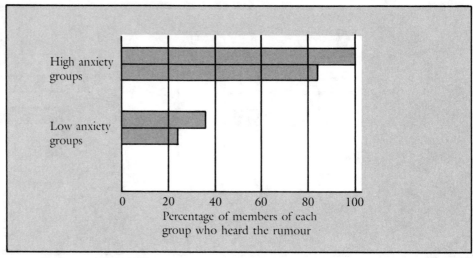

SOURCE: Rosnow and Fine, 1976

The results (Figure 14-2) showed that predictably, there was considerably more rumour transmission in the groups who scored high in chronic anxiety. If we assume that the anxiety itself is a rumour-motivation in that anxious people seek information to reduce their anxiety, then given that uncertainty in the environment is likely to increase anxiety even among those who are not chronically anxious, we can understand why rumours are more relevant in times of stress.

Rumour control Rumours, especially in wartime, can be very serious and demoralizing. Once begun, a rumour is very difficult to stop. Often, rumour-control programs have been necessary to provide people who have been exposed to rumours

Canadian wartime posters urge citizens to avoid "careless talk."

with accurate information or to halt the spread of confidential information (see photos).

Occasionally in the business world, rumours have been deliberately generated in an attempt to put a competitor into serious difficulty. For example, in 1934 the sale of Chesterfield cigarettes in the United States was adversely affected by the rumour that a person suffering from leprosy had been found working in the cigarette factory. Allegedly the rumour was started by a rival firm. Two-person teams would enter a crowded commuter train or subway car from opposite ends, move toward each other, and then have a conversation about the leper while other passengers stood between them (Shibutani, 1966). (See Box 14-4 for a more recent example of a rumour planted in an attempt to damage the reputation of a huge corporation.)

B · O · X   14 - 4

SATAN ON THE SOAP BOX

Even a large corporation can be the target of rumours. Around the beginning of 1980, malicious (and, it seems, deliberately inspired) rumours began to circulate in the United States and Canada that Procter & Gamble was linked to devil worship and that it regularly turned over some of its profits to Satanic cults. The basis for the rumour was the company's 135-year-old logo (see illustration) which portrays the Man in the Moon, a popular figure of the 1800s, and 13 stars (representing the original 13 colonies), which was claimed by the rumour-mongers to be a demonic symbol. Derivatory rumours claimed that Procter & Gamble was owned by the Unification Church (the "Moonies"), and that the head of Procter & Gamble had appeared on television and admitted the Satanist connections.

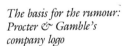
The basis for the rumour: Procter & Gamble's company logo

A leaflet campaign in English and in French which called for a boycott of Procter & Gamble products helped spread the rumours far and wide and, despite police investigations, the source of the leaflets was never uncovered. It seemed that many different individuals, alarmed by the charges, made photocopies of the leaflets and distributed them on their own.

Procter & Gamble took many steps to fight the rumours. The company obtained testaments of faith from prominent religious leaders, including high-ranking members of the Roman Catholic Church and several evangelical groups, which they disseminated to local clergy wherever the rumours were current. They set up telephone hotlines to deal with consumers' concerns about the subject and, by early 1982, were receiving about 15 000 calls per month from people wanting to find out if the rumours were true. Procter & Gamble's Canadian headquarters in Toronto received thousands of inquiries from concerned individuals and church groups across Canada requesting clarification of the company's position with regard to Satanism. The rumours died off for a while, following an extensive information campaign by the company, but then emerged again in 1985.

On April 24, 1985, the company announced that it would eliminate the Man in the Moon trademark from its packages, although the logo still appears on all corporate communication.

VARIETIES OF COLLECTIVE BEHAVIOUR

As we have seen, collective behaviour often occurs in crowds, but crowds are not needed for the exhibition of collective behaviour. It can occur as readily within a collectivity of people who are not in physical proximity. Indeed, some of the most dramatic instances of collective behaviour in terms of impact have occurred in the absence of crowds (e.g., rumour transmission, which creates a collective belief or apprehension).

The collective behaviours to be discussed next include fads, crazes and fashions, contagions of expression, contagions of enthusiasm, contagions of anxiety, contagions of hostility and rebellion. (The term "contagion" is used here to describe the process of beliefs and actions spreading throughout a crowd, and is not meant to suggest a preference for a contagion theory explanation rather than one based on deindividuation, the development of emergent norms, or other reasons.)

Fads and Fashions

Among the most common types of collective behaviour are fads and fashions. A fad is a short-lived, extreme, frivolous bit of behaviour that is "fun" because "everybody is doing it" (Klapp, 1972). Typically, fads develop quickly, enjoy wide-spread popularity for a time, and then vanish, usually never to appear again. Some fads, such as the "streaking" fad of the mid-'70s which led individuals to run naked through crowds of people, are actually the rebirth of fads which have come and gone decades before. (During the '70s, however, streaking was nourished by widespread media attention; television broadcasters scrambled to televise anyone who streaked at a sporting or entertainment event, and often sought to interview the individual afterwards (Anderson, 1977).) Others, such as flagpole sitting, goldfish swallowing, and telephone-booth stuffing have come and gone and, so far at least, have never returned.

Fad behaviour involves a great deal of anonymous interpersonal interaction. It is anonymous in that people do not directly communicate about whether or not they should buy a pet rock or run naked through the crowd, but each "knows" whether or not the behaviour is in keeping with the "times." They can anticipate how others will react to them. No one can predict when a fad will appear or what its nature will be.

Fads are often based upon the "ridiculous made trendy." One of the most unlikely economic success stories is that of the man who made himself a millionaire simply by packaging small pieces of rock and putting them up for sale as "pet rocks." The hula-hoop, invented by another now very rich man when he found himself unable to unload a great deal of plastic tubing which he bought on a speculative investment, had even more widespread acceptance, and unlike the pet rock, appeared to have some utility for exercise purposes.

Some fads are more serious. Diet fads ("the grapefruit diet," "the macrobiotic diet"), while not enjoying the same widespread popularity as some other more frivolous fads, can pose health risks for certain people. The use of recreational drugs also involves fad-like elements at the outset and may likewise jeopardize human health.

A *fashion* is more serious than a *fad* in that it begins with something perceived as necessary: we all need clothes, and most of us need cars. In 1986, Canadians spent more than $11 billion on clothing, so fashion in clothing is of some considerable

Cyclical fashions: This photo, taken in the '20s on Canadian Pacific's Trans Canada Limited, shows three young women in '80s-style gear. Note jewelry, bobbed hair, oversized coat.

consequence! Fashion is more likely than a fad to be cyclical, and bygone fashions may be brought into vogue again. New fashions are often "risky" in that they attack or violate existing social norms. When the brassière first made its appearance, women who wore them were considered to be "risquée" since the undergarment accentuated the bustline. Traditional society reacted somewhat negatively at such "shamelessness." Yet when some women in the 1960s began reverting to going without bras as their grandmothers and great-grandmothers had done, they were greeted with similar criticism. As for men, moustaches and vests, definitely "out" in the 1950s, were definitely "in" in the 1970s and 1980s. Long hair, the virtual symbol of counterculture in the 1960s and early 1970s, became acceptable, but then the fashion moved in the direction of shorter hair. Mini-skirts came and went (and have come again!), as did "punk" hairstyles.

Why do fashions continually change? Is it because the fashion industry thrives on change since clothing which does not wear out may become obsolete, thus leading to the purchase of new clothing? However, even the fashion industry is not omnipotent in deciding what people shall wear. People may *want* change, but not just *any* change, and not just at any time. The mini-skirt quickly gained wide acceptance, but longer skirts were much slower to catch on, despite the promotional campaigns of the fashion industry. Since fashion continues to change despite the drawbacks of spending money on a whole new wardrobe, it must serve some important function. While there is no good research which informs this concern, sociologists have suggested that fashion serves both to mark a person's status in the society, or at least status aspiration, and to relieve the banality of modern technological society (Klapp, 1972). Each of these factors merits a brief examination.

Status marking   Today, designer clothes and automobiles often serve to tell others of the status (real or coveted) of the owner. This is nothing new. Historically, clothing fashions have always distinguished people belonging to different social levels. It was easy to recognize an aristocrat or a peasant because each dressed in a distinctive way. However, for those who could afford it, there was always the temptation to emulate the dress of those a little higher in the hierarchy, which suggests a reason for the ever-changing fashions of the elite: they were constantly seeking to differentiate themselves

495

from those of lower status who imitated them. In fact, there have been occasions when the law itself has been used to prevent people from dressing themselves in attire inappropriate for their social level (Box 14-5).

Today, of course, fashion is not determined only by an elite, and almost any group may be the source of some new style. Consequently, fashion can serve to communicate more than social class; it can also tell others about a person's attitudes, values, and lifestyle. A professor who always wears a suit and tie is making a statement quite different from that of a professor who dresses in sweat-shirt and jeans. Even the believability of television newscasters has been found to be influenced by their style of dress (Solomon, 1986). For some people, it is important to be up-to-date. They see themselves as being "well-dressed," which can lead to slavish adherence to fashion trends. Such people derive attention and respect from their sartorial fastidiousness.

There seems to be a widely understood "language" of clothes which allows people to "read" other people or to tell others about themselves. For example, research has found that most people are in agreement about what certain types of clothes indicate. In a British study of teenage girls (Gibbins and Coney, 1981), it was reported that there was substantial agreement among them concerning the characteristics of girls who wore various types of clothes, including whether the girls smoked or drank and how many boyfriends they were likely to have. This "fashion sense" is acquired early: fourth and sixth grade children have been found to make differential personality infer- ences about others — including inferences about friendliness and popularity — on the basis of the brand of jeans worn (Calvin Klein, Levi Strauss, or Sears) (Solomon, 1986).

In the current climate emphasizing youth and individuality, many people try to dress in a manner that suggests they are youthful, even non-conformist. Here, fashion also serves as a status marker, although the status system is no longer a simple hier- archy. Cultural rebels may wear spiky hair only so long as the style does not become commonplace among members of the middle class. A successful and independent executive who wants to be differentiated from his peers may dress in tight jeans and pierce his ear(s) or nose. Yet for the vast majority who are financially or otherwise dependent on others for their livelihood, such deviations from regularity are not attractive. If technicians wear sports jackets and engineers wear suits, then the average engineer will opt for the suit and "dress for success," rather than risk being taken for a technician.

Women are faced with a special problem as they compete with men for positions in the world of business: to "dress for success" they must avoid styles which are traditionally feminine. In one study in which business executives were asked to eval- uate job applicants on the basis of personnel files which included photographs, it was reported that women who groomed themselves in a somewhat less feminine manner (plainly tailored clothes, little make-up, shorter hairstyles) were chosen over those who portrayed more traditionally feminine grooming styles (Solomon, 1986). A sur- vey of readers of a magazine for women executives found that although many of the respondents might have been fashion leaders (given their age, education, and income), they actually indicated little interest in fashion. On the other hand, they were highly conscious of the tactical importance of clothing and believed that dressing well is important to one's career (Solomon, 1986).

We might suspect that the greater the anxiety about social status, the more rapidly fashions may change (Klapp, 1972). If it is important to a rising executive to distin- guish himself or herself from those of "inferior" rank, then once junior players begin

B · O · X   14 - 5

SUMPTUARY LAWS

At various times throughout history, so-called "sumptuary laws" have been promulgated. The main goal of such laws has been to delineate clearly the distinctions among the various classes and to prevent people of lower class from dressing in the manner of a higher class, thereby encroaching on the position of supremacy enjoyed by the nobility:

> Sooner or later the rich, rising man ventures to assume the fine clothes [of those of higher social rank], and consternation, not to say panic, ensues among the upper classes. Hastily a sumptuary law is drafted and hastily passed (Laver, 1964, p. 5).

Such laws were intended to restore respect for the inequality of social ranks (Roach and Eicher, 1965). A secondary goal was to curb the extravagance of people who were risking bankruptcy in order to mimic the attire of the nobility.

Such laws were in force in ancient Greece and Rome, and existed in Japan until the mid-1800s. In Rome, colour of clothing served to denote rank, and laws were decreed which restricted the peasantry to one colour, officers to two colours, commanders to three colours, and members of royalty to seven colours (Roach and Eicher, 1965).

In Europe, sumptuary laws were common as well. Consider these examples:

- In 1301, the bride of Philip the Fair, who was king of France from 1285 to 1314, made her entry into Bruges, and the whole population turned out in their best attire to greet her. She is said to have announced with annoyance that "I thought I was the Queen, but I see that there are hundreds" (Roach and Eicher, 1965). Subsequently, Philip passed a number of sumptuary decrees, detailing precisely what sort of attire was allowed for people of various social ranks.
- During the reign of Charles IX in sixteenth-century France, silk dresses could be worn only by princesses and duchesses, and only ladies of high rank could carry fur muffs. Hoop skirts,

or "farthingales" could be no wider than one-and-a-half yards. These laws were still in effect at the time of the French Revolution, and one of the first acts of the General Assembly was to abolish all laws which concerned distinctions in dress (Roach and Eicher, 1965).

- In England, during the reign of Edward III, pearls and ermine could only be worn by members of royalty, while during the reign of Henry VIII, any woman below the rank of countess was not allowed to wear a train. Elizabeth I sternly enforced her own clothing laws, producing great discontent among her subjects. For example, she decreed that "no great ruff should be worn, nor any white colour, in doublet or hosen, nor any facing of velvet in gowns, but by such as were of the bench . . . . That no curled or long hair be worn, nor any gown but such as be made of sad colour" (Roach and Eicher, 1965).

On the other hand, some societies have tried to impose uniformity on the way that people dress in order to abolish any class distinctions. For example, when the Communists came to power in China in 1949, they followed the example of the Soviets and all citizens, men and women alike, were led to wear the "drab, baggy uniform" that we have come to associate with modern China (Horn, 1975).

Today, there are still distinctions of class associated with styles of dress, but there is nothing to stop people of one segment of society from donning the attire more typical of another segment. Bikers can dress in tuxedos if they wish, flower girls can wear ermine if they can afford it, and magistrates can spend their weekends in blue jeans. Moreover, the recent trend toward producing cheap, copycat versions of designer clothes and accessories — some so authentic in appearance that designers of the original items are truly alarmed — means that class distinctions in dress are even harder to enforce than they ever were.

to emulate the rising stars in their style of dress, the more senior people may seek new fashions in order to preserve the distinction between the two "classes." Klapp (1972) argues that the anonymity and rootlessness of the modern age produce anxiety about status, thus leading to greater pressure for fashion change.

Banality If you spent any amount of time in a country such as India, you would become used to seeing many different styles of clothing and grooming. Although there may be great regional and intracaste uniformity of dress, the multiplicity of subgroups leads to a wonderful diversity of dress. Returning to western society could be shocking because of the striking lack of variety in clothing.

Novelty appears to be a primary reinforcer of human behaviour (Berlyne, 1960); the same is true of many animals ("curiosity killed the cat"). That is, we seem to be predisposed to be curious and curiosity is encouraged by novel stimulation. Thus it should be expected that people living in a world in which there is so much uniformity would seek things which are different; this may lead to creations of new styles. If everyone wears a grey flannel suit and white shirt, one person may wear a blue shirt to be a "little different." If all cars were grey, many people would prefer a red one or a yellow one "just to be a bit different." Thus changing fashion, whether clothing or cars, may be an attempt to alleviate boredom and to assert our individuality. Klapp (1972) suggests that even the most frivolous fashions represent a search for uniqueness and individuality.

Sometimes, radical fashion may represent "style rebellion" aimed at the value system of the "establishment." Both "beatnik" and "punk" evolved separately in opposition to middle class neatness. This deviation from accepted style sometimes elicits a strong reaction from the dominant group, leading to forced haircuts, dress restrictions in restaurants, and so on. (The same principles apply to fashions other than clothing.)

How do fashions spread? While an element of contagion is involved, there is reason to believe that most people hesitate before adopting some new fashion. To be at the forefront of such change distinguishes people from their group and risks ridicule or even rejection. It seems that there is a "two-step flow of communication" where fashion is involved (Katz and Lazerfield, 1955; Rogers, 1962): "Local opinion leaders" who are most knowledgeable about fashion trends are the first to don the new garb, and their action seems an indication to others that such fashion is acceptable and "OK." (See also the discussion of acceptance of innovation in Chapter 6.)

In summary, fads and fashion do not necessarily involve behaviour that is very serious or consequential for an individual or a society. However, both may serve to provide relief from banality, and fashion likely serves the additional and important function of identifying the individual with regard to actual or aspired status. Fashion also plays an important role in self-definition and in interpersonal relationships, a role which is only now coming to be understood as social psychologists focus more research attention on it.

CONTAGIONS

There are several types of collective behaviour in which the development and spread of a strong emotional reaction is a central feature. These will be referred to as *contagions*. Contagions of enthusiasm, anxiety, fear, and aggression are discussed below.

While all collective behaviour involves contagion to some degree, sometimes the contagion carries with it such wild ideas and behaviours that the crowd or society almost appears trapped in a collective delusion (Klapp, 1972). For whatever reason, a crowd or a population finds itself at a given point in time *very* susceptible to ideas and rumours which would ordinarily carry little or no credence; consequently, such ideas and rumours can spread rapidly through a collectivity of people. While crowd behaviour involves mutual interpersonal stimulation, contagion is not limited to crowds and, indeed, direct person-to-person interaction is not required.

Unlike typical crowd behaviour, mass contagion often lasts for days or weeks, and sometimes even months and years. Contagions typically begin to build up slowly, and then as more and more people become involved, rise rapidly to a peak and then usually die down quickly, although some persist for much longer periods.

Contagions of expression

Expression contagions have no particular goal other than emotional release, whether they be motivated by joy, sorrow, frustration, or guilt (Klapp, 1972). Although such behaviour may infest an entire society, it is most often most apparent in crowd settings. An expressive crowd may gather to pay homage to a new Pope or cheer the return of a Stanley Cup champion hockey team. There is no external goal other than to see, touch, or applaud the object of admiration. The crowds that cheered Trudeau in his heyday fell into this category, as do the throngs of gasping teenagers that flock around rock stars wherever they make an appearance. Klapp (1972) views waves of religious revivals as contagions of expression which have as their prime motivating factor the expiation of guilt.

Contagions of enthusiasm

Tulips were introduced into Western Europe from Turkey in the middle of the sixteenth century. Over the next hundred years they became objects of such admiration, especially in Holland, that any man of substance without a decent collection of bulbs was held in some contempt. In the period 1634–1636, the Great Tulip Mania swept Holland, England, and France. The cost of bulbs soared so much that tracts of land and even small fortunes were sometimes traded for a single bulb. Special arrangements were made for the sale of rare tulip bulbs on the Amsterdam and Rotterdam stock exchanges. So frantic was the pursuit, so greedy were the speculators, so anxious were rich and poor alike to improve their lot by profiting from the rising market in bulbs, that normal industry in Holland fell into serious neglect: the nation had gone tulip-mad. Finally the market for bulbs, held artificially high by speculators, collapsed and many people suddenly realized that they had given up most of what they owned for a collection of tulip bulbs which no one wanted any more.

The Great Tulip Mania is an example of a contagion of enthusiasm. Such contagions embody an extraordinary hope or delusion, usually about becoming wealthy. Thus "Klondike Fever," spiked by rumours of massive deposits of readily obtainable gold, led tens of thousands of people, most of whom had never mined before nor knew anything about survival in the north, to the Yukon gold fields in 1898. While everyone dreamed of making a fortune, few were fortunate enough to do so. (See Pierre Berton's *Klondike* (1972) for an excellent description of this contagion.) As with other contagions, "the bubble bursts" sooner or later; in many cases, the costs can be enormous.

Contagions of anxiety

Contagions of anxiety (often referred to as "hysterical" contagions) involve the rapid dissemination of exaggerated fears, and often evoke unrestrained emotionalism. The fears are exaggerated in the sense that the response is hardly warranted by the initial cause.

Sometimes more than anxiety is involved; there may be symptoms of physical illness, and the terms "mass psychogenesis illness" or "mass hysteria" are sometimes used to describe such a phenomenon (Colligan, Pennebaker and Murphy, 1982). For example, in the fifteenth century, a nun in Germany developed a compulsion to bite other nuns, who in turn began compulsively to bite others. Gradually, this bizarre mania spread to convents throughout Italy, Holland, and Germany. In the eighteenth century there was an epidemic of nuns meowing like cats (Singer *et al.*, 1982), and between the tenth and fourteenth centuries, episodes of dancing mania periodically spread through parts of Europe. Victims would experience an uncontrollable impulse to dance in a most frenzied manner. In one such epidemic in Italy, entire populations of people danced convulsively in the belief that this behaviour was the result of having been bitten by a tarantula spider. The tunes to which they danced are still popular today, and the dance is known as the tarantella.

A pilot study carried out in Québec schools in 1973 estimated that there is one hysterical contagion for every 1000 school settings each year (Sirois, 1982). One factory in the United States experienced 20 outbreaks of mass psychogenic illness in 18 months, while in 1976, the American Footware Manufacturers' Association reported that half their member companies had experienced such incidents (Hopson, 1981). Thus it seems that contagions of hysteria occur with surprising frequency. Let us discuss two such contagions in some detail: (1) the great windshield pitting epidemic; and (2) the Yorkville hepatitis scare. Both examples illustrate how the build-up of tension found expression in hysterical contagion. The first example involved the transmission of fear alone, while the second also involved the spread of apparent physical symptoms.

The great windshield pitting epidemic   In the spring of 1954, Canadian newspapers were filled with reports of the American H-bomb tests at Eniwetok in the South Pacific. The power of the bomb seemed almost incomprehensible: a whole island disappeared as a result of one blast. One of the blasts was described as a "runaway," an out-of-control explosion which produced effects far beyond what was expected. In addition, the Russians were thought at that time to be very close to the development of their own H-bomb, and many newspaper stories dealt with politicians' and scientists' preoccupation with the imminent danger of nuclear war. Canadian cities were not at all protected against air raids, and concern about building bomb shelters spread.

Radioactivity had been detected in snow in Manitoba and Saskatchewan, presumably a result of the H-bomb tests. As well, paranoia was rampant on the international stage. Western countries feared communism as much as they feared war, and in the United States, the McCarthy Era, during which thousands of Americans were persecuted because of suspected disloyalty, was in full swing. It was claimed — out of fear — that there were 500 Communist organizations in the Toronto area alone.

It was in the context of this combined fear of atomic war and Communist subversion that the great windshield pitting epidemic began. It started in Seattle, Washington, where it was reported that hundreds of people had found small pockmarks

The Globe and Mail

Mostly Cloudy
High Here 65

32,559.   Final Edition   TORONTO, WEDNESDAY, APRIL 21, 1954.   5 Cents Per Copy   34 PAGES

Police Cycle Jumps Curb; Nine Injured

Problem for Ontario

Civil Defense Plan Change Forced by H-Bomb Potential

Old Pattern For A-Blast Outmoded

By WILLIAM KINMOND

Smith Urges Special Class Of Top Pupils

It Wasn't a Stone. Cracks Spread Across Windshield From Tiny Pit on Glass

Romanian Chief Quits Leadership In Party Shuffle

Puzzling Pitting Hits Toronto Windshields

Diplomat's Wife Thought Husband Was Dead: PM

By ROY L. CURTHOYS
New York Times Service

The great "pitting" story hit the Globe and Mail's *front page on April 21, 1954.*

in the windshields of their cars. The windshields also had small blobs of a metallic substance on them which, although not radioactive, were quickly assumed by some members of the public to be due to atomic fallout. While initial reports of damage were attributed to vandals using BB guns, the news emphasis gradually changed to one of mystery. Seattle's mayor finally declared that windshield damage was no longer a police matter, referred to the recent H-bomb test as a possible cause, and made an appeal to the Governor and President for emergency aid. The stage was set.

While physical scientists from the University of Washington had all emphasized road damage, hysteria, and air pollution as the causes, engineers from Boeing Aircraft suggested physical causes for the pitting, including supercharged particles from the H-bomb explosion, and a shifting in the earth's magnetic field. By April 19, 1954, the citizens of Vancouver were reporting the same kind of windshield damage, and even those who were initially skeptical, changed their tune when they found that their cars too had been affected. A Victoria used-car dealer discovered that the marks suddenly appeared in the windshields of the cars on his lot.

The reports quickly became front page news, and the incidents spread from B.C. to the prairies to Ontario. During the approximately two weeks that the "epidemic" lasted, the windshield-pitting delusion spread across Canada, although in the United States it was confined to the Seattle area. Newspapers reported that scientists and police officers were desperately searching for the cause. Some car dealers covered the windshields of their cars to protect them. Yet, a short time later, the interest suddenly vanished as quickly as it had materialized. While newspapers reported that scientists and police were desperately searching for the causes of the pittings, it was noted that although used car dealers were reporting that their cars had been damaged by the mysterious pittings, dealers of new cars could not find any damage to their windshields. The greater the car's mileage, the more likely was it that the windshield would be pitted. Once this began to sink in, it was realized that the pitting was the result of normal damage caused by pebbles thrown up from the roadway. People had not paid much attention to such pitting before. Once the publicity struck, however, people would take a good look at their windshields for the first time. This being said, the newspapers dropped their coverage and the epidemic died.

Two researchers (Medalia and Larsen, 1958) interviewed 1000 randomly selected Seattle residents. About 93 percent of the respondents knew of the windshield pitting: about half of those had learned of it from the newspapers, a quarter from radio and TV, about one fifth from talking to others, and the rest (6 percent) from direct experience. Fifty percent of the respondents accepted the "unusual physical agent" explanation while only 21 percent believed the "ordinary road damage" explanation.

The anxiety generated by the fear of after-effects of the H-bomb explosion apparently was relieved by focusing attention on automobile windshields. "Something is bound to happen to *us* as a result of the H-bomb tests — windshields became pitted — it's happened — now that threat is over" (Medalia and Larsen, 1958, p. 25). In other words, the waning of interest was not brought about simply by a more reasonable interpretation of the events and the subsequent lack of media interest, but by the diffusion of anxiety that was responsible for the original reports.

The Yorkville hepatitis epidemic In the summer of 1968, the Yorkville area of Toronto was the centre of the "hippie" counterculture in Toronto. Coffee houses, itinerant folk-singers, and street peddlers attracted throngs of young people to the area, and on most evenings Yorkville Avenue was filled with crowds of tourists and locals who came to mingle and gawk.

On August 3, 1968, the newspapers reported that there was an outbreak of hepatitis in Yorkville, and that 50 cases had already been reported by hospitals in the area. Youth workers were circulating handbills (see reproduction of the original flyer) warning the habitués of the dangers of hepatitis, and pointing out that untreated hepatitis could be fatal.

During the days that followed, physicians set up blood testing clinics in the area. Despite the statement of the Toronto medical officer of health that the incidence of hepatitis in the city was lower than it had been a year earlier, the media continued to report how an epidemic had broken out. Some physicians spoke out about the dangers of hepatitis, saying that it could kill within two or three weeks, and if left untreated, the symptoms could disappear but that the disease would continue to destroy the liver, resulting in death between six months and five years. It was sug-

```
DANGER!          DANGER!.          DANGER!


                   HEPATITIS
                  _____

INFECTIOUS HEPATITIS IS AN EXTREMELY DANGEROUS

DISEASE.  WHEN THERE IS NO TREATMENT FOR IT

50% OF THOSE CONTRACTING IT WILL DIE.  20% OF

TREATED FOR IT DIE, MAINLY BECAUSE TREATMENT
_____

IS BEGUN TOO LATE.  IF TREATMENT IS BEGUN

IMMEDIATELY, AN ALMOST TOTAL RECOVERY RATE

COULD BE OBTAINED.  THE EASIEST WAY OF FINDING

OUT WHETHER YOU HAVE HEPATITIS IS BY TAKING A

BLOOD TEST.  THE TEST IS FREE, PAINLESS AND FAST.


DOCTORS WILL BE TESTING IN THE TRAILER AND IN

FRONT OF THE GRAB BAG TONIGHT (AUGUST THE 5TH)
           _____

FROM 9 P.M. TILL 2 P.M.


                         HELP STOP AN EPIDEMIC.

                              _____THE TRAILER
```

Hepatitis handbill: The apparent number of victims continued to rise throughout the summer.

gested that one of every three people undergoing blood tests at the free clinics would have "possible" or "positive results."

Even the police who patrolled the area were found to be infected, it was reported. While the medical officer of health tried to impress upon people that a blood test could *not* be conclusive, the number of apparent victims continued to rise. Concern was raised about food handlers in the area's restaurants, and soon business, even in the posh ones, dropped to a small fraction of what it had been. Many were virtually empty. On August 8, the Ontario Department of Health took over the disease control program following an emergency meeting organized by the deputy minister of health. York Council voted 5 to 4 to ask the province to declare Yorkville off-limits to the general public, and to close all restaurants in the area until the epidemic was over. There was even concern about the safety of visitors to the huge Canadian National Exhibition, which was about to begin, even though it was held far from Yorkville.

By August 14, the epidemic had become daily front-page news. The Toronto medical officer of health was attacked for his restraint in dealing with the situation. Most of the youths in the Yorkville area who were interviewed by television reporters "knew" of someone who had come down with hepatitis. Local politicians concluded that stronger laws were needed to control hippies and two days before the planned opening of a transient centre for youth in another part of town, owners of businesses in the area demanded that it not be opened. "Hepatitis will follow the hippies," they declared.

Yet suddenly, the epidemic abruptly ended. The deputy minister of health stated on August 17 that the outbreak had stabilized. Despite the previous almost daily newspaper coverage, newspaper interest virtually ceased at this point and the epidemic withered away.

In the final analysis, *two* people had come down with "probable" infectious hepatitis, while 30 others had contracted serum hepatitis as the result of using infected syringes. The rest, with their headaches or fatigue or touch of fever, were responding to fear. There had been no more cases of infectious hepatitis than in other parts of the city and even fewer than in some areas. The real culprit was hysterical contagion.

Why such an "epidemic"? The Yorkville area was badly overcrowded during the summer of 1968, and tension was extremely high between the "hippies" and the members of the Yorkville business community. The hepatitis scare may have prevented violence in the area, not only because it cleared the area of its transient population, but also because it provided an alternative focus for the two sides of the long-term conflict (Kelner and Badgley, 1969). The precipitating event in this case seemed to be the decision by medical authorities to survey the extent of the needle-hepatitis problem.

The "phantom anaesthetist of Mattoon" is a classic case similar to the Yorkville contagion episode (Johnson, 1945). Some of the townspeople of Mattoon, in the U.S.A., fell "victim" to "someone" who apparently went around spraying something in their windows. Some smelled gas, and had coughing attacks or even partial paralysis. In fact, no evidence of any such anaesthetist or gas was ever found. A similar case (the "June Bug" incident) occurred in June of 1962 when women working in a southern U.S. textile factory came down with symptoms supposedly caused by a poisonous insect that it was believed came in with a shipment of imported material (Kerckhoff and Back, 1968). In 1983, a mysterious epidemic spread among teenaged Arab girls in the Israeli-occupied West Bank, and 943 cases were reported. Symptoms included headaches, blurred vision, dizziness, fainting, difficulty in breathing, and muscular pain. Initially Arab leaders charged that the malady was deliberately caused by Israelis spreading toxins, while Israeli leaders claimed that the symptoms were faked. It was finally concluded that the cause was mass psychogenic illness.

Such hysterical outbursts occur when generalized and diffuse anxiety builds up in a group of people and when some precipitating event allows the anxiety to be attached to some external threat. Psychological stress may produce discomfort, sweating, palpitations, terror, and even fainting. Without an apparent explanation, these symptoms may be more extreme and embarrassing than if people can point to a "logical" cause (a "foreign" insect or an anaesthetist). This is a case of misattributing the symptoms to some hypothetical cause. Personality factors may also play a role in susceptibility to such hysteria. Insecure people or those who are on the fringes of the social structure and thus less constrained by group norms may be more vulnerable. In the June Bug incident, Kerckhoff and Back (1968) found that the women in the textile mill who were under the most strain were the most susceptible to the effects of the imaginary bug.

Note that no mass psychogenic illness occurred following the Chernobyl nuclear disaster in 1986, or the earlier Three Mile Island disaster in the U.S. In these cases, facts about the actual risks were discussed in great detail by the media. People *knew* the risks, and had a reality-based fear. More importantly, however, these disasters did not occur in the context of a pre-existing, generalized, or poorly identified anxiety. Had they done so, this diffuse anxiety could have been transformed into mass psychogenic illness built around the theme of nuclear sickness.

Contagions of fear: Panic

While anxiety refers to a generalized feeling of unease which often cannot be attributed to any specific cause, fear always has some identifiable source and always involves the perception of danger. Sometimes fear of impending doom, provided that the threat is not immediate, leads to resignation (see Box 14-6). However, when a crowd is frightened and in danger, it is not surprising that people in the crowd will try to escape the danger. However, when a panic occurs in a building (as in the case of a fire), most people cannot even see the exit but assume that the movement of the crowd is directed towards one. Often, there is a "front-to-rear communications failure" (Janis *et al.*, 1964) with those at the back unaware that people at the front are unable to move more quickly, causing those at the front to be trampled. Consider this example:

On the afternoon of January 9, 1927, children flocked to the Laurier Palace theatre in Montreal's east end to see a comedy called, ironically, "Gets 'Em Young." Most of the children, contrary to the law of the time, were admitted to the theatre unaccompanied by adults. During the film, a child in the balcony dropped a lighted cigarette, starting a small fire. When someone in the balcony cried "fire," the theatre ushers were able to hush the resultant anxiety and begin an orderly evacuation. Smoke began to appear in larger and larger quantities. The ground floor spectators were evacuated without incident, while the children in the balcony moved quickly to two exit stairways and clamoured down stairs toward the sidewalk:

> Five steps from the sidewalk, five steps from safety the tragedy was born. Boys and girls in the van of the stampeding mob, pressed suddenly from the rear, stumbled and fell. Instant panic grasped those at the rear . . . a minute or two was enough for the stairway to be a solid, suffocating, groaning, shrieking and dying mass (*The Globe*, January 10, 1927).

Seventy-eight children died, 60 from asphyxiation, 11 from compression, and five from both asphyxiation and burns. No one need have died at all. The fire was a minor

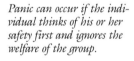

Panic can occur if the individual thinks of his or her safety first and ignores the welfare of the group.

REACTIONS TO A NEAR-DISASTER: THREE MILE ISLAND

On Wednesday, March 28, 1979, something went very wrong at the nuclear power plant at Three Mile Island, Pennsylvania. An air valve, opened to flush out a filter in the water system, was left open too long and the water needed to cool the nuclear reactor leaked. By some coincidence, a back-up cooling system had been closed for maintenance two days earlier. As a result, the fuelled rods in the nuclear reactor overheated, radioactive water leaked onto the floor of the enclosure for the nuclear reactor, and radioactive gas escaped from an adjoining vent.

For several days, the situation was highly uncertain and dramatic. While the corporate owners of the plant assured everyone that everything was under control, other experts argued that the fuel rods might get so hot that they would melt their containing structure, releasing extremely hazardous levels of radioactivity into the environment. This fear of a possible "meltdown" was intensified by yet another coincidence — the release of *The China Syndrome*, a movie starring Jane Fonda and Jack Lemmon which dealt with this very possibility and which portrayed management of that nuclear plant as deceitful and unconcerned with the public. Eventually, the technicians at Three Mile Island (TMI) managed to cool down the reactor and shut down the plant, although subsequent investigation by the U.S. Government regulatory agency revealed that it was a close call.

Baum and his colleagues (1983) set out to investigate the effects of this incident upon those who lived in the immediate area of danger. Of course, an ideal design for such a study would look for any changes *in these people* after the incident, but it is impossible to anticipate such events in advance in order to obtain data before the incident happens. Thus it was necessary to compare these residents with a proper control group, such as the people who lived further away from the area of danger. However, even this comparison would not eliminate the possibility that simply living near a nuclear power plant or a non-nuclear power plant generates stress *per se*. Therefore, the study compared TMI residents with three control groups: 1) those living near a nuclear power plant which functioned normally; 2) those living near a power plant which used coal-fired generators; and 3) those who lived outside the immediate area of any electrical power plant.

The study found that about 17 months after the accident, many TMI residents still showed signs of stress, including somatic complaints, anxiety, depression, and alienation. On tasks which involved proofreading for clerical errors and detecting embedded figures in pictures, TMI residents performed less well than the others, suggesting that they had difficulty in concentrating or were less motivated. Finally, significantly higher levels of urinary catecholamines (epinephrine, norepinephrine) were found in these subjects. While these levels were within what is considered the normal range, they do indicate that TMI residents experienced and continued to experience arousal of the sympathetic nervous system which is generally related to long-term chronic stress. Other studies had revealed that in the immediate period of time in which the crisis occurred, TMI residents showed evidence of stress reactions, including fear, demoralization, and anxiety. During the next couple of years, the plant was closed while the very severe damage was being repaired and continued concern about the plant and its reopening affected the residents.

The study revealed no significant effect on residents near another nuclear plant, despite the heavy publicity and the popularity of the movie. However, while nuclear power plants continue to function (e.g., Pickering, Ontario) and while proponents and governments continue to placate and reassure the public, the boom seems to be over as far as this source of energy is concerned.

one, and there was enough time for an orderly exit. They died, so it was said, because they panicked.

What is the nature of panic? The term is used very loosely in ordinary parlance: "I panicked when I realized I'd lost my wallet"; "When the lights went off, he got very panicky." Yet panic is more than anxiety or fear or terror, even though some earlier conceptualizations emphasized the covert emotional state of the individual (e.g., Cantril, 1940). In the context of collective behaviour, panic involves fear and flight and an avenue of escape (Quarantelli, 1954; Schultz, 1964). Yet, while flight is an essential element of panic, not *all* flight is panic. In a panic, flight is "non-social and non-rational" (Quarantelli, 1954): the individual thinks of his or her own physical survival, and pays no attention to how this action may be detrimental to the collective welfare of the group.

Panic usually occurs in crowds, where individuals mutually reinforce each other's concern about escape in the face of danger. However, panic can occur in the absence of a crowd. Consider this example (Cantril, 1940): In 1939, Orson Welles' Mercury Theatre radio program carried a dramatization of H.G. Wells' *The War of the Worlds*. Of an estimated 6 million listeners, about 1 million, many of whom had tuned in after the program had begun, unfortunately ignored cues which pointed to the fictional nature of the broadcast and reacted with panic, "heading for the hills" or looking for a place to hide. Police switchboards were jammed with calls, and traffic snarls occurred in some places as people tried to flee the "invasion." This was the first demonstration that mass panic can be triggered without the involvement of either rumours or crowds (Klapp, 1972). Most of those who were so affected had shown little critical ability and had made no attempt to check by switching to other radio stations or calling friends.

How could so many people react in this way to a radio drama? One reason is that they were faced with what appeared to be a genuine news report. Then, in telephoning the police — as many did — and being unable to get through because other people were making the same call, they were persuaded that the Martians had already knocked out telephone lines. Once begun, the panic reaction was hard to slow down. As people began to flee, it would have been easy to assume that other people who were going about their business in a normal way were just unaware of the emergency, while the sight of anyone else hurrying to get somewhere could easily be interpreted as a reflection of the need to escape.

When a truly catastrophic event occurs, one approaching incomprehensibility in its magnitude, its impact alone may be great enough to trigger panic flight (Foreman, 1953). This is what happened on the morning of December 6, 1917, at the height of World War I, when a Belgian ship collided with a French munitions carrier in Halifax harbour. Fifteen minutes later, the munitions ship exploded, producing the greatest human-made explosion in the history of the world until the atomic bombing of Hiroshima. Almost one third of the population of Halifax was killed and many thousands were seriously injured. Sixteen hundred buildings were totally destroyed. Just as occurred in the aftermath of the atomic bombings of Hiroshima and Nagasaki, people who were not killed outright or incapacitated fled in panic. The impact of such life-threatening events may be even greater psychologically if they have been defined in the past as unmanageable. People may run in terror simply from hearing a powerful term, such as the alarm "Gas!" in World War I. Yet, even in such cases the panic states do not usually last for more than a very short time, and non-adaptive behaviour can generally be dealt with if effective leadership and appropriate information is provided (Janis *et al.*, 1964).

Panic as a game   While it is both socially responsible and individually practical for you to await your turn during the orderly exit from a burning building, once there has been a departure from this orderliness, being cooperative is no longer individually profitable and the only "rational" solution is to push your way out as others push you. Once again, we encounter the collective dilemma; however, in this case it is like a collective game of chicken (see Chapter 13). Each individual is faced essentially with two choices of action: remain calm and proceed in turn, or run for the exit. If everyone exits in a calm and orderly manner, then perhaps all will escape. If you remain calm and others run, you may not escape. If everyone runs, then there is likely to be crowding at the door and many may die. Even smelling smoke in a crowded building may be enough to lead people to act non-cooperatively since they have been taught the danger of people panicking in a burning building! They expect others to run, so they do so first.

The classic simulation of panic is one provided by Mintz (1951), who observed subjects in groups of 15 to 20 persons whose task it was to remove aluminum cones from a narrow-necked bottle by means of a string attached to the cones (Figure 14-3). After the cones were placed in the bottle, each subject was given a piece of fishing line attached to only one of the cones. Then they were told that only one cone could pass through the neck of the bottle at a time. At the signal to start, water began flowing into the bottom of the bottle. Subjects were instructed to try to get their cones out without getting them wet. No "traffic jams" at the bottle's neck occurred when no rewards were given for success. However, in a second condition, subjects were told that 25 cents would be won by getting a cone out completely dry. If a third or less of the cone was wet, there would be no reward, and if more than

FIGURE 14-3
Mintz apparatus

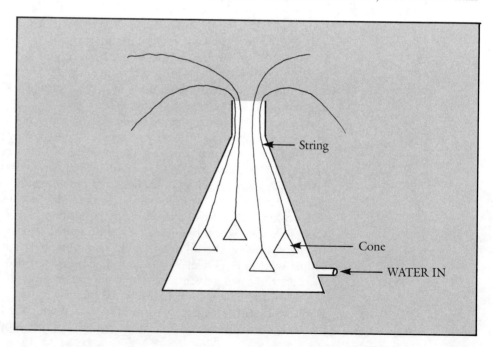

a third was wet, there would be a fine. In this case, "traffic jams" were experienced by more than half of the groups. This occurred whether or not the subjects were allowed to communicate. Mintz concluded that intense fear is not necessary to cause non-adaptive behaviour similar to panic behaviour.

In panic-producing situations, cooperation is rewarding as long as everyone cooperates. Once the cooperative pattern is disrupted, however, cooperation ceases to be rewarding. Pushing becomes advantageous in exiting a burning theatre if everyone else is pushing and appeals to order and calm are not working.

Organized groups, such as military units, are rarely subject to panic. Because of their training, the individuals are very responsive to the orders of the leader. Only when the leadership structure breaks down is there a danger of panic.

Social inhibition of escape behaviour Sometimes a crowd can actually inhibit escape from a dangerous situation by its refusal to become aroused. There have been several instances of fires in night clubs and theatres in which patrons warned of a fire have refused to leave. In the early 1960s, during the showing of a film entitled *Striptease* (a film which featured nude women, something which was still quite taboo in those days) at a Montreal cinema, a small fire broke out in the projection room. Despite pleas from firemen to evacuate, the largely male audience refused to leave and, once the fire was out, watched the rest of the film. In 1977, the Beverly Hills nightclub in Kentucky caught fire and, although a busboy ran to the stage and announced that there was a fire, the audience assumed he was part of the act and most people ignored his warning; 165 lives were lost. A fire broke out during a New Year's Eve party in a social club in Chapais, Québec, in the early hours of January 1, 1980. Most of the 44 people who died could have escaped. As in so many other similar circumstances, the victims apparently underestimated the danger. They carried on dancing or stood in a semi-circle, watching a pile of dry pine branches which had ignited blaze away. The euphoria of the crowd, the loud music, the alcohol, and the wish to avoid looking foolish or cowardly all combined to inhibit escape behaviour.

Rational behaviour in disasters The popular press and even some agencies whose job it is to deal with disasters typically describe people caught up in some disaster as acting in a highly disorganized, irrational, and hysterical way. Authorities sometimes hesitate to announce the possibility of an impending disaster for fear of causing unnecessary panic. (For example, the alarm bells on the *Andrea Doria*, sunk in a collision at sea in 1956, were not rung even though collision with an approaching ship was unavoidable, for fear of causing panic.) Yet, careful analysis of actual disasters in several different cultures shows that disorganized flight is seldom the case. Even when people are supposed to evacuate an area because of some oncoming disaster (flood, tornado, etc.), the majority of people do not leave (Quarantelli, 1960).

Most people manage to maintain a rational approach to situations of great danger. Researchers who have studied disastrous high-rise hotel fires report that most people do not panic, and that most of those who fail to escape when the opportunity presents itself do so because of errors in judgment rather than irrational behaviour (Keating and Loftus, 1981). However, it must be remembered that panic is a collective behaviour. Only if people are in a group and see other people running about is panic likely to break out. Most people in high-rise fires do not find themselves in circumstances that would promote collective behaviour.

When disaster does strike, another common myth suggests that once the immediate danger has passed, people sit around dazed and unable to cope. Yet in actual observations of disaster victims, this so called "disaster syndrome" (apathy, shock) has been seen to affect only a minority of people and only for a short time. In general, people react immediately and logically to their situation. Looting in such situations is actually very rare, also contrary to popular myth. The myth of the disaster syndrome may have arisen because people *seem* to run about aimlessly, while in fact they are desperately looking for missing friends and relatives (Killian, 1952). That is precisely what occurred on June 30, 1912, when the worst storm in the history of the West struck Regina, killing 36 people, toppling houses, and moving a grain elevator 50 feet. There was no panic, and once the storm abated, the populace rallied to locate survivors and care for the injured and homeless. (The same scene was played out 75 years later in Edmonton, when a tornado killed 25 people and injured at least 250 others.)

Nevertheless, panic *does* happen from time to time, and usually only in relatively small groups. It occurs in the presence of events considered to be acutely or uncontrollably dangerous, but only when being trapped is a *possibility* rather than an *actuality* (i.e., escape is still possible) (Foreman, 1953; Fritz and Marks, 1954), and when there is only one or a limited number of avenues of escape. Trapped coal miners do not panic (e.g., Lucas, 1968), for no way of escape is open to them. Consider the difference between the passengers of CP's *Empress of Ireland*, which sailed in 1914, and those of the *Noronic*, a cruise ship berthing in the Toronto harbour in 1949. In the former case, people had no avenue of escape. Bound for Liverpool with 1400 persons aboard, the *Empress* was rammed in heavy fog in the St. Lawrence River. Nearly 1000 people perished but, according to news accounts, "no panic prevailed." On the other hand, panic ensued immediately aboard the *Noronic* when the fire broke out, although help was close at hand and the fire department arrived quickly: one hundred and twenty-one lives were lost.

Panic can be viewed as the consequence of a process of attributional appraisal. First, something occurs which causes arousal. Then, this arousal must be interpreted in terms of the environmental context. If the context is perceived as dangerous, that arousal is labelled as fear. Whether a person engages in panic behaviour then depends on the behaviour of others in the vicinity whose actions serve as a model to increase or decrease the arousal level.

Contagions of hostility

We have seen how anxiety can sometimes lead to mass psychogenic illness. In other circumstances, people do not seek out a physical cause for a psychophysiological anxiety, but react with irrational hostility and violence toward scapegoats, individuals who provide safe and easy targets. In the Middle Ages, commonplace events — the drying up of crops, the stillbirth of an animal or child, the destruction of crops by hailstorms — were attributed to the actions of witches. Between 500 000 and 700 000 people were convicted of witchcraft and burned at the stake in Europe between the fifteenth and seventeenth centuries (Harris, 1974). In 1692, in Salem, Massachusetts, a witch mania occurred on a much smaller scale. Some young girls who had dabbled in Black magic developed hysterical illness which involved convulsive behaviour. They blamed witches for their problems and readily pointed out the "guilty adults." The mania spread beyond Salem to Boston. Twenty people, including a minister, as well as two dogs, were executed as witches. (The word *scapegoat* comes from the Biblical account of the Hebrews ridding themselves of evil by loading their sins onto a goat which was allowed to *escape* into the wilderness while a companion goat was sacrificed to God. Today, scapegoats do not escape; they are the objects of hostility and violence — see Chapter 7.)

Aggressive crowds provide localized and short-lived instances of contagions of hostility. Whether the aggressive crowd takes the form of a mob (the aggression is directed against a relatively powerless individual or a small group of individuals), or a riot (the aggression is expressed against another group having similar or greater power), the behaviour of the participants is still that of individuals for whom normal social restraints have been lifted.

It is impossible to predict with any certainty when an aggressive crowd is likely to form. In June of 1972, 2500 angry fans who could not get into a sold-out Rolling Stones concert in Vancouver rioted and hurled bottles, rocks, and even Molotov cocktails at the more than 200 police who fought to keep them out of the Pacific Coliseum, where the concert was being held. In Montreal in 1971, a riot broke out at Blue Bonnets Raceway after angry spectators reacted against what they thought was an exceptionally low quinella payoff. Soccer games have often been marred by rioting and, on a number of occasions in 1985, violence by British soccer fans spilled out into the streets, resulting in pitched battles with police. While some of these incidents appeared to reflect racial tensions, others did not. In 1984, rowdiness by British soccer fans during a game played by a British team against an Italian team in Belgium turned into violence and resulted in the deaths of 38 Italian spectators. Even hockey fans have rioted (Box 14-7).

B · O · X   14 - 7

THE AUDIENCE STRIKES BACK: VIOLENCE AT THE FORUM

On March 17, 1955, then National Hockey League President Clarence Campbell suspended Maurice "Rocket" Richard from the line-up of the Montreal Canadiens for the remaining three regular season games and all the play-off games. (Richard had twice punched an official in a game a few days earlier.) That night, as the Canadiens played the Detroit Red Wings at the Montreal Forum, the fans expressed their displeasure. When Campbell entered to take his seat after the game had begun, the audience stood up and booed him loudly. By the end of the first period, with Montreal trailing by 4 to 1, the crowd turned nasty. They pelted Campbell with tomatoes and eggs,

the game was called off, and then some spectators set off a tear gas bomb which sent thousands coughing and crying to the exits. Outside, thousands of other fans were milling about. The building was evacuated and the crowd began to smash windows and set fire to newspaper stands. Even at midnight, 15 000 people were besieging the Forum. Some of the crowd moved uptown, and 30 stores had their windows smashed and were looted along the way. The police were kept busy arresting people and hauling them away. An expressive crowd had become an aggressive crowd.

Spectator violence is not new. Thirty thousand Romans died in riots at the chariot races in 592 B.C., while the Roman Senate imposed a ten-year ban on gladiator contests in Pompeii following a rash of violence between fans of differing allegiances in 59 A.D. (Horn, 1985).

These various forms of contagions arise relatively quickly in crowds, and are generally short-lived. The discussion now turns to a form of collective behaviour which usually begins very slowly but then spreads and spreads, eventually producing a formal group oriented towards bringing about social change. Such groups can endure for years, decades, or longer.

SOCIAL MOVEMENTS

A social movement is "a spontaneous large group constituted in support of a set of purposes that are shared by the members" (Milgram and Toch, 1969). Although unlike any behaviour examined so far in this chapter, social movements are considered to be a type of collective behaviour since they are spontaneous and since large collections of people are involved. Generally, a social movement is aimed at either promoting or resisting change in society. It attracts people who feel that a problem exists, believe that something can be done about it, and *want* to do something about it (Toch, 1965).

Canada has given birth to many social movements, reflecting the high degree of social fragmentation and lack of consensus in the country (Grayson and Grayson, 1975). Various groups — farmers, women, French-speaking Canadians — have at one time or another felt estranged from the mainstream of society. As a result, movements such as the Farmers' Union, the Cooperative Commonwealth Federation, Social Credit, the National Action Committee for the Status of Women, and the Parti Québécois have evolved. Sometimes, however, such movements can take on an ugly form and express the dark side of human nature (see Box 14-8).

At its inception, a social movement often reflects no more than a dissatisfaction with contemporary society coupled with a dream about a new kind of society. As a social movement gathers impetus, it gradually takes on organizational form, with formal leaders, division of duties, and an agenda (Blumer, 1951). The suffragette movement, the women's liberation movement, and the gay liberation movement all began when various individuals expressed their dissatisfaction with their treatment and their desire to change society so that they would be admitted to the mainstream.

B · O · X   14 - 8

CANADIAN FASCISM

The depression of the '30s, coupled with the prairie drought, was a natural crucible for the birth of social movements. Communists appealed to the hungry unemployed to throw off their capitalist masters and assume control of their nation.

Fascism also made an ugly and not insignificant appearance. Adrien Arcand, a professional journalist in Montreal, started a movement in Québec based on racial nationalism in November 1929 (Betcherman, 1975). Called the "Ordre Patriotique des Goglus," and modelled after Italian fascism, by February 1930 it claimed 50 000 members, although this is probably a gross exaggeration. Even before Hitler came to power, Arcand was a publicist for him. He shared Hitler's anti-Semitism and organized boycotts of stores owned by Jews. Arcand edited a weekly newspaper which he used to promote his idea that the Jews should be expelled. He attacked communism and socialism, a move that won him support among some businessmen.

Once Hitler came to power, Arcand's group became even more virulent in its anti-Semitism. His followers wore blue shirts, aping the fascists of Europe. Other fascist groups, some competing with

Arcand's, sprang up as well. A brown-shirt gang, the Canadian Nationalist Party headed by William Whittaker, an ex-British soldier, was operating in Manitoba. It too published virulent anti-Semitic literature. In Ontario, "Swastika Clubs" sprang up, comprising gangs of youths who wore swastika insignia and who harassed Jews on public beaches or in parks. On July 4, 1939, a National Fascist convention was held in Massey Hall in Toronto, with about 2000 in attendance. Arcand, his group now called bilingually "Le Parti National Social Chrétien/ The National Social Christian Party of Canada," wanted to be known as the Canadian führer. Eventually, he far outdistanced his closest rivals — the black-shirted Canadian Union of Fascists — in the competition for dominance.

While this movement was continuing to gather momentum, the Nazis invaded Western Europe, Canadian troops were sent overseas, and Arcand and other fascists were arrested and imprisoned for the duration of the war. Following his release after the war, Arcand continued to produce anti-Semitic literature until his death in 1967.

B · O · X   14 - 9

A WOMEN'S SOCIAL MOVEMENT

Dr. Emily Stowe, Canada's first woman physician, had to study medicine in the United States because as a woman, she was unable to gain admission into a Canadian medical school. In 1876, she founded the Toronto Women's Literary Club, a reform organization whose name was changed in 1888 to the Toronto Women's Suffrage Association. This group was composed primarily of business and professional women and the wives of wealthy men. In other parts of Canada other women, most notably Thérèse Casgrain in Québec and Nellie McClung on the prairies, joined the quest for suffrage. They sought the right to vote not simply to obtain personal equality with men, but also to influence governments to work towards the elimination of serious social problems.

Canadian women working for suffrage preferred to be called "suffragists" rather than "suffragettes," as their British counterparts called themselves. This was because the Canadian women did not want to be seen as sharing the sometimes radical political views associated with the suffragette movement.

The vote for women was first won on the prairies, where women had received widespread support from various farmers' organizations. Manitoba extended suffrage to women in 1916, followed by Saskatchewan and Alberta in the same year. In 1917, British Columbia and Ontario did the same. Nova Scotia followed in 1918, New Brunswick in 1919, Prince Edward Island in 1922, Newfoundland (then not yet a part of Canada) in 1925, and Québec in 1940. Women were given the right to vote at the federal level in 1918, but it was only in 1929 that they legally became "people." In that year, the Supreme Court of Canada reversed an earlier ruling that women were not "persons" within the meaning of the *British North America Act*.

Social movements vary from being general in nature (e.g., they have the goal of obtaining equality for women across a wide range of situations — see Box 14-9), to being very specific, such as reform movements which accept the basic structure of society but seek to modify part of it (Blumer, 1969). Because they seek to overthrow the existing social order *revolutionary* movements are often driven underground, while reform movements appear respectable within society and attempt to gain support through discussion and persuasion. Reform movements try to win the support of the middle class, while revolutionary movements typically appeal to those in the oppressed or distressed group. The Front de Libération de Québec (FLQ), which never achieved the status of a social movement, was nevertheless typical of a revolutionary movement, trying to alter the social order radically by force. The Parti Québécois, on the other hand, provides a good example of a reform movement which began as an unorganized collectivity and grew into an institution. While the Parti Québécois spoke to the genuine injustices that have been suffered by French Canadians, the FLQ went far beyond that and advocated militant socialism, a stance not very likely to win support from the Québécois middle class.

While some social movements are nationalistic in nature, others are of a religious nature (Blumer, 1951). The Kingdom of Father Divine, which flourished in the U.S. during the 1930s, attracted many people, particularly Blacks who felt hopeless about their position in society, giving them a new life with the promise of a happy eternity. People turned over all their possessions to Father Divine who then provided them with the necessities of life and guaranteed eternal salvation. Jerry Falwell's "Moral Majority" is a more modern example of a religiously oriented social movement; in this case, there is a genuine attempt to win political power to change the social order. (Religious social movements are discussed in more detail in the section on cults.)

Some social movements evolve into mainline political forces. The Parti Québécois has already been mentioned in this context. The Social Credit Party and the CCF party, which evolved into the NDP, grew out of social unease on the prairies and the feeling that existing political parties did not serve prairie interests and needs. Their aim is to achieve political and social change.

The poverty and hunger of the 1930s formed a natural breeding ground for social movements as people struggled to change a system that seemed to be keeping them down. Communism and socialism had a natural appeal to the unemployed and to the drought-ridden farmers, since the blame for economic depression could be placed on the capitalistic system of ownership in the country. Communists organized workers and many demonstrations were held, demanding more help for the unemployed and changes in the economic order. The federal government tried to intimidate the communist organizers by arresting them under a provision of the Criminal Code, passed during the Winnipeg General Strike of 1919, which made it unlawful to belong to any party that advocated political change by means of force or violence. Agitators who were not Canadian citizens were deported. Between 1930 and 1934, 22 968 people suffered this fate!

Poverty and hunger in Canada in the 1930s gave rise to many social movements. The same phenomenon has happened and is continuing to happen in many Third World countries today. Some of these actually lead to the overthrow of governments. Castro's 26th of July Movement evolved from a social movement to the controlling political force in Cuba. There are many other examples.

The life of a social movement

A social movement often develops through a series of four stages (Blumer, 1969):

(1) *Social unrest stage*. A general discontentment with the status quo coupled with restlessness, but no definite goals, characterizes this stage. At this point, agitators are likely to play an important role as they try to make people aware of the shortcomings of contemporary society for them. The "consciousness raising" undertaken by Blacks and by women is typical of this stage.

(2) *Popular excitement stage*. More definite ideas about the causes of the problems and about the goals emerge.

(3) *Formalization stage*. At this point, a structure begins to develop. Policies and ideology are formalized and a leader, likely to be a kind of statesperson, is chosen. An ideology, or a collection of beliefs, myths, and doctrines, develops along with it. The ideology defines and defends the goals of the group, condemns the existing social order, outlines the policies and tactics, and contains the myths of the group. The intelligentsia of the group generally provide a highly respectable formal ideology which can be defended to certain of the intelligentsia outside the movement. But the ideology also takes on a popular form for the general masses, composed of emotional symbols, stereotypes, and so on.

(4) *Institutionalization*. The movement finally evolves into a fixed organization with a formal structure and specific division of duties.

Gay pride in Montreal: Social movements are more likely to arise in a society undergoing rapid social change than in a stable one.

The development of the Parti Québécois or the CCF are both good examples of this process. Note, for example, how the rabble-rousing of early spokespeople in the *séparatiste* movement gradually gave way to the statesman-like pronouncements of Réné Levesque and Marc Johnson.

Social movements are more likely to arise in a society undergoing rapid social change than in a stable one (Lang and Lang, 1961), a society in which changing aspirations and needs cannot be satisfied by the existing social norms. Following changes in the educational system in Québec during the "Quiet Revolution" brought about by the Lesage administration in the 1960s, the Church's influence was curtailed, and large numbers of French-speaking students pursued studies in areas previously left to the English — business administration, commerce, and marketing. But when these students graduated, they found that proficiency in English was a prerequisite for a good job in the business world. Social change was obviously needed.

As they gather momentum, social movements often lead the participants to assume that their continued survival depends on being acceptable to outsiders; thus they may gradually drop their most radical ideas (Milgram and Toch, 1969) (e.g., the Social Credit dropped its plan for radical changes to the banking system). This leads to an institutionalization of the movement whereby it becomes a part of regular society and ceases to appeal to those who are most discontented. These individuals are forced to look elsewhere and often to try to start another movement. Again, the Parti Québécois provides an excellent example. "Separatism" becomes "sovereignty-association," steps are taken to appease large industries which felt threatened by the party's policies and, by increasing its support among the public at large, the party alienates those members who want radical social change. Indeed, in 1987, the founding of a *new* separatist party was announced in Québec.

CULTS

During the 1960s and 1970s, while adherence to traditional, mainstream religion dropped, fundamentalist Christian sects and a wide variety of new religions and quasi-religions flourished. Some of these "new religions," most of which have been popularly labelled "cults" — the Church of Scientology, the Unification Church ("Moonies"), the Society for Krishna Consciousness — have become wealthy and influential.

Most of these cults are organized around a highly charismatic leader (almost always a man) who is responsible for enunciating the group doctrine, establishing rules and norms, and giving the adherents the promise of something akin to transcendence. Many such groups have been viewed with alarm because of their widespread appeal to teenagers and young adults, because it is believed that they use questionable means of recruitment and "brainwashing" tactics, and because, once a member, an individual may be constrained to stay through physical or psychological pressure.

On the other hand, there is the possibility that cults do provide emotional support to troubled recruits. Levine and Salter (1976) studied 109 members (they were volunteers and not a random selection) of a number of cult groups in southern Ontario. Levine found that the motivation to join such groups was almost exclusively tied to personal dissatisfaction with life and difficulty with coping. This vulnerability was countered by the ability of the group to fulfill needs which were not being met elsewhere, primarily through providing answers to essential questions regarding personal identity and the meaning of life. Levine and Salter pointed to the quasi-rational belief system of most of these groups as their major tool: members can turn their existential dilemma over to the new system of logic. Stringent rules and regulations give new structure to the lives of people who feel they have been drifting aimlessly through life, and the mysticism infusing the belief system of such groups provides a curious comfort. It is soothing to know that there are people who know, people who understand, people who will take care of the novices, and the sense of being part of an (enlightened) community may also contribute to a higher sense of self-worth.

The spreading cult phenomena produced a number of anti-cult groups — often set up by ex-cult members — to fight what they saw as the insidious threat of the cult movement. Often, cult members were considered to have been "programmed," and occasionally, professional "deprogrammers" were hired by distraught parents to kidnap their children who had joined cults and to restore their old belief system so they would come back home and assume their former lifestyle.

Authoritarianism

Many cults are built on authority and strict obedience. Such obedience can create a very dangerous situation (the Nazi movement, although it did not pretend to be a religious movement, is an example). The most chilling modern example of a religious cult becoming a "cult of the leader" is that of a group which was originally part of mainstream fundamentalist religion: The People's Temple, founded by the Reverend Jim Jones in the 1950s. Jones specialized in public faith-healing, as do many of today's television evangelists. In 1977, because of growing criticism in the media, Jones and 1000 of his followers moved his Temple from California to a remote location in the Guyanese jungle which came to be called Jonestown. Here he exercised even greater control over his followers than he had previously, and began to speak in a more and more violent and revolutionary fashion. He began to hold "white nights," which were rehearsals for mass suicide should the need arise.

In 1978, American congressman Leo Ryan went to Jonestown to investigate charges that some people were being held against their will. Later when Ryan and his party and two defectors from Jonestown tried to board a plane to leave, they were ambushed by Temple members. Ryan and four others were killed. That night, the last "white night" was held. Vats of poisoned fruit drink were brought out, and people lined up to take their final medicine. Those few who refused were forced.

Over 900 people died. Jones himself was unable to take the poison and, after almost everyone was dead, pleaded with a camp nurse to shoot him. She did, and then turned the gun on herself.

Osherow (1981) examined the Jonestown phenomenon in terms of three social psychological processes: (1) obedience; (2) persuasion; and (3) self-justification. Each is discussed below:

(1) *Obedience*. Jones' power was so pervasive that, whatever he decreed, people did, even when suicide was ordered. Obedience was deeply instilled in the followers; deviations were met with strict, sometimes sadistic, punishment. Defectors were hounded and threatened. Jones became more and more preoccupied with the "enemies" of his church, and less and less tolerant of any criticism from the faithful. Followers grew to live in fear of brutal punishment for perceived disobedience. He used informers to spy upon his flock. He strove to weaken family bonds by assigning many children to other members' custody, and even forcing parents to sign away their custody rights. He forced spouses into extramarital sexual relationships, often of a degrading nature, and he sometimes decreed that wives should become his sexual partners.

(2) *Persuasion*. If people complied with Jones' rules, and if they ultimately stayed because they were afraid to leave, why did they join the temple in the first place? Jones was an expert at impression management. His charismatic leadership, his careful choice of both the right audience and the most appealing message, his use of emotional and one-sided messages were all designed to put him and his movement in the most positive light.

Through the use of inoculation techniques, as well as control of information wherever possible, he prepared his followers to reject any information which countered his own pronouncements. By creating an external enemy, he was able to insure the cohesiveness of his own group.

(3) *Self-justification*. Once involved at the periphery of the People's Temple group, novices would find themselves being pressured to take on more and more work on behalf of the group, such as letter-writing to the press and to politicians, and going to several meetings each week. The newcomer was first expected to make donations, then subsequently to turn over a quantity of his or her income, and finally to turn over all personal assets (and social security cheques) to the temple. Hesitation was interpreted as lack of faith. Ultimately, the individuals were persuaded to live in Temple quarters in order to save on living costs.

Such extreme behaviour, through cognitive dissonance reduction, generated a self-justification process which led to attitude change favouring commitment to the Temple. A foot-in-the-door process was in operation for part of the self-justification schema. Jones began with small demands, and gradually increased them. What might have appeared to be an unreasonable demand in the first place seemed less unreasonable in comparison with earlier demands.

SUMMARY

(1) Collective behaviour emerges spontaneously in a group of people. It is relatively unorganized and unplanned, and is the product of interstimulation among participants.

(2) A crowd is unorganized, anonymous, casual, and temporary.

(3) Behavioural contagion refers to the rapid spreading of behaviour throughout a crowd by means of suggestion, rumour, and imitation.

(4) Deindividuation, the loss of a sense of personal identity, can lead to a lowering of normal restraints on behaviour. Conditions which contribute to deindividuation include a loss of identifiable characteristics (e.g., wearing a mask), loss of responsibility, an arousing group activity, loss of temporal perspective, and a novel situation without the usual restraining cues.

(5) In a crowd situation, new shared norms may emerge which may lead to apparently uncontrolled behaviour. This theory of emergent norms opposes the deindividuation hypothesis, which interprets crowd behaviour as being exhibited by individuals who are unresponsive to social norms.

(6) In the transmission of rumours, the message tends to become shorter and more simple (levelling); certain aspects are emphasized and often exaggerated (sharpening); and the message is assimilated into the framework of existing habits, expectations, and prejudices. Psychological sets and anxiety levels determine whether rumours become distorted.

(7) Collective behaviours may occur without interpersonal contact. These include fads and fashions, and contagions of enthusiasm, anxiety, hostility, and rebellion.

(8) Fads and fashions are related to status-marking, the desire of people to identify with certain groups and to differentiate themselves from other groups. They also provide relief from the banality of everyday life.

(9) A hysterical contagion refers to the spread of a strong emotional reaction. Ambiguity, the spreading of distorted rumours and the potentially serious consequences of some event or situation may contribute to these contagions.

(10) A social movement is a large group formed spontaneously in support of shared goals, such as nationalism, revolution, religion, or political change. Social movements often develop through stages of social unrest, popular excitement, formalization, and institutionalization.

(11) Cults tend to attract vulnerable people, providing emotional support along with a strong ideology and a demand for absolute commitment.

FURTHER READING

KAISER, B. (1985). *The social psychology of clothing*. New York: Macmillan.

KLAPP, O.E. (1972). *Currents of unrest*. New York: Holt, Rinehart and Winston.

MACKAY, C. (1841/1932). *Extraordinary popular delusions and the madness of crowds*. New York: Farrar, Straus and Giroux.

PAULUS, B.P. (Ed.) (1980). *Psychology of group influence*. Hillsdale, NJ: Erlbaum.

SOLOMON, M.R. (1985). *The psychology of fashion*. New York: Lexington Books.

TOCH, H. (1955). *The social psychology of social movements*. New York: Bobbs-Merrill.

C·H·A·P·T·E·R F·I·F·T·E·E·N

Social Psychology and Social Problems

Why do Western governments continue to worship at the temple of the Gross National Product? Shouldn't we . . . be replacing our reliance in the GNP with a more revealing figure — a new statistic which might be called Net Human Benefit?

Pierre E. Trudeau

FOR REFLECTION

- Can social psychology be applied in resolving social problems?
- Is eyewitness testimony reliable?
- Are there inherent biases in the jury system?
- How are people affected by crowding?
- How do people react to — and deal with — the threat of nuclear war?

FROM ITS INCEPTION, social psychology has always been vitally concerned with the problems of people and society. In its formative years, social psychologists worked to understand such phenomena as the economic depression, labour/management conflicts, racial prejudice and the rise of fascism in the 1930s (Fisher, 1984). In recent years, the range of real-life problems has broadened considerably (see Table 15-1 for examples).

Can all this research actually have practical benefits for people and societies? Public policy in Canada has been influenced significantly by work in a number of areas (Rule and Adair, 1984). As a result of pioneering research, most of it by Wallace Lambert's group in Montreal, an internationally recognized model of successful bilingual education has been developed which combines language training with cultural integration (Gardner and Desrochers, 1981). Research on the adaptation of northern Native peoples to cultural and economic changes, such as the James Bay hydroelectric project, has provided information which cannot be ignored by governments or by Native groups in future policy decisions (Berry, Wintrob, Sindell and Mawhinney, 1982). Other research has contributed to Canada's multiculturalism policy, which encourages various ethnic groups to maintain their cultural heritages while being integrated into the Canadian "mainstream" (Kalin and Berry, 1979). Recommendations for changes in our legal system by a parliamentary law reform commission were influenced by research concerning the reliability of eyewitness testimony, the unanimity rule in jury decisions, and the assessment of a defendant's "fitness" for trial. Research concerning the impact of TV advertising directed to young children led to a legislated ban on such "targeted" advertising in Québec and some voluntary restraints in the rest of Canada (Goldberg, 1982).

Social psychology can contribute to the betterment of society through evaluation research — the objective, data-based assessment of social programs or changes. Indeed, we might well deliberately adopt an experimental approach to social change, evaluating various attempts to solve social problems (Campbell, 1969b) (see Box 15-1).

TABLE 15-1
Some recent topics discussed in the Journal of Social Issues

Topic	Issues
Teenage parenting: Social determinants and consequences	1980, 36(1)
Old age: Environmental complexity and policy interventions	1980, 36(2)
Urban life	1980, 36(3)
Environmental stress	1981, 37(1)
Energy conservation	1981, 37(2)
Rape	1981, 37(4)
Women's use of drugs and alcohol	1982, 38(2)
Beyond nine to five: Sexual harassment on the job	1982, 38(4)
Images of nuclear war	1983, 39(1)
Reactions to victimization	1983, 39(2)
Criminal victimization	1984, 40(1)
The child witness	1984, 40(2)
Computing: Prophecy and experience	1984, 40(3)
Social support	1985, 41(1)
Intergroup contact	1985, 41(3)
Social issues and personal life	1986, 42(2)
Media violence and antisocial behaviour	1986, 42(3)

ON CHANGING THE MINIMUM DRINKING AGE: A QUASI-EXPERIMENT

In the early 1970s all ten provinces, as well as the majority of U.S. states, reduced the minimum drinking age from 21 to 18 or 19 to make it consistent with the "age of majority" for voting and other legal rights and responsibilities. However, this raised concerns based on the following: (1) the age group from 16 to 24 is at higher risk for automobile accidents. (2) Increased availability of alcohol tends to increase consumption. (3) Availability to 18-year-olds would increase availability and consumption in the 15 to 17-year-olds in the same high school. (4) Mid-adolescence is the time at which many, if not most, begin to drive. Is it really a good idea for inexperienced adolescent drivers to begin drinking at the same time? (5) Young people tend to do more night driving, compounding the effects of impaired perceptual-motor skills and attention. (6) Consistent with our present social norms, males tend to drink considerably more than females. Ironically, the same traditional but persistent norms dictate that the male should do the driving. For all of these reasons, it was important to monitor closely the results of this change, especially the incidence of teen driving under the influence of alcohol and the number of alcohol-related accidents.

The above has all the ingredients of a quasi-experiment, in which we assess the effects on behaviour (automobile collisions) of a change in a real-life independent variable (the minimum drinking

age). A change in the number of collisions — or even collisions involving alcohol — may be due to other factors, such as increased traffic, an unusually severe winter, changes in the price of gasoline, increased drinking in society as a whole, or simply random fluctuation: for no apparent reason, there are more accidents in some years than others. Therefore, the proper control groups must be included, such as people who are slightly older and who would be unaffected by the change in laws, or drivers in equivalent jurisdictions where the law has not changed. With this in mind, let us consider two studies.

Whitehead *et al.* (1975) examined the police records of all automobile collisions in London, Ontario, which involved a driver aged either 16–20 or 24, between January 1968 to June 1973 (the legal age for the purchase and consumption of alcohol was reduced in Ontario from 21 to 18 on July 1, 1971). They found that there was a significant increase in all age groups, both in the number of collisions and in the number of alcohol-related collisions. However, among the young people aged 19 or 20, those most affected by the law, there was a relatively higher increase in the number of drinking-related collisions. That is, even when accounting for the fact that there were more accidents generally in that group, and that there were more alcohol-related accidents involving those unaffected by the change (the 24-year-old

---

One example concerns welfare, particularly the problem of how some clients tend to become trapped in a cycle of dependency and hopelessness. As an alternative to welfare, some have suggested the strategy of a "negative income tax" to provide a minimum guaranteed income. In effect, people below a minimum income level would receive money from the government. Proponents have argued that this would reform the bureaucratic welfare system and avoid creating a separate social class of welfare recipients, while opponents have argued that it would eliminate the incentive to work. Experiments have been conducted in Canada (Manitoba's MINCOME Project) and in the U.S., in which matched groups of relatively poor people were assigned to various income maintenance conditions or to a control group within the conventional

group), a significant number of accidents clearly implicated the legal availability of alcohol for the 19–20 age group. The data from several U.S. states, some using as controls contiguous states where the law did not change, generally showed similar increases (Smart and Goodstadt, 1977).

As a consequence, several of these jurisdictions raised the age back to 20 or 21 (or 19 in Ontario). One study used both questionnaire survey data and fatal accident reports to see whether raising the age would reduce alcohol-related driving problems in the state of Massachussetts (Hingson *et al.*, 1983; Smith, Hingson *et al.*, 1984). Data were collected in the year prior to the change and in the three post-change years, and these data were compared with those from New York, where the age remained at 18. There were no changes in the proportion of adolescents who drank or in the volume of alcohol consumed, but there was a reduction in the frequency of driving after drinking. In both states, there was an equivalent reduction in both fatal and non-fatal automobile collisions. After the age was raised in Massachusetts, there was a relatively higher decline in the number of single-vehicle night-time fatal crashes involving people aged 18 or 19, but not aged 16 or 17. These and other data suggest that raising the legal age does have some beneficial effect, although not one that reverses the earlier effect produced by lowering the age. Perhaps the horse is gone and it is too late to close the barn door.

Careful research has revealed a profile of the typical driver involved in a serious, alcohol-related accident: he is young, male, drinks heavily and frequently (although he is not necessarily an alcoholic), has a high level of underlying hostility and anger, lacks the social skills to deal with frustration and to express anger appropriately, and drives to express anger and regain a sense of control (Donovan and Marlatt, 1982). Indeed, this profile of the angry, impulsive person with a low sense of personal control is typical of the high-risk driver who has frequent accidents and traffic violations. While alcohol clearly impairs performance of driving-related skills, it seems that the highest risk occurs among those who "act out" their anger behind the wheel.

Of course, various programs have been implemented to prevent the occurrence or recurrence of driving while intoxicated (DWI), e.g., information and advertising campaigns, treatment or education programs for offenders, increasing the legal penalties. But on the whole, *none* of these measures has been satisfactory, including more stringent penalties — indeed, license suspension has proven more effective than fines or jail sentences (Klajner, Sobell and Sobell, 1984). However, in recent years, public opinion has shifted, spurred by the vigorous efforts of visible law enforcement and by groups of the families of the victims of DWI. While their efforts have been directed primarily toward enacting tougher laws and more thorough enforcement, the important impact may well be in changing public opinion and social norms. Increased awareness on the part of hosts of their responsibility toward intoxicated guests, and the practice within convivial groups of establishing a "designated driver" who does not drink are indicative of this important change for the better.

welfare system. While the results in Manitoba have not been published, those in the U.S. showed quite clearly that income maintenance did *not* reduce participation in the labour force and that the increased income was spent largely on buying or renting better accommodations, and on food and clothing (Haveman and Watts, 1976).

Social psychology has evolved as a discipline in which there is constant feedback between laboratory-based research and real-life problems. In many cases, theories developed through "pure research" have been applied to social issues; for example, attribution theory has been applied in understanding the experience of being physically ill, marital conflicts, and addiction to cigarette smoking. On the other hand, some research begins at the level of a real-life problem (Fisher, 1982).

Lewin (1948) has described this work as *action research*, in which the researcher obtains data about a problem or organization, feeds these data into the relevant system in order to influence change, measures the changes, and then repeats the process. Note that this model implies that the social psychologist must become an agent of change, a skilled advocate of policies, as well as a theoretician and researcher.

PROBLEMS IN APPLYING SOCIAL PSYCHOLOGY

The early history of social psychology was marked by a euphoric optimism. For the first time, the methods of science were to be applied to human problems. Surely, it was believed, the same approach that had yielded spectacular advances in our understanding of medicine, atomic physics, chemistry, and geology would help us to understand and eventually solve the problem of violence, crime, poverty, and prejudice. Surely we could "conquer" war as we had "conquered" infectious diseases, and we could learn to live in harmony as we had learned to fly and to communicate over long distances.

While the discipline has advanced significantly in the succeeding decades, the serious social problems are still with us. Perhaps the fact that problems such as war, bigotry, and poverty are rooted in culture and in the political, moral, and economic realities of the times means that a purely psychological solution is unrealistic. It may also be true that social problems are more complex than biological or physical phenomena, and will not be solved so easily. We must also remember that social psychology is a rather young discipline.

There are also serious problems which limit the generality of research in social psychology. One problem is, of course, external validity, the extent to which the findings of controlled research in the laboratory can be applied to complex, real-life problems (see Chapter 2). Until research methods become more precise and specific, and the findings are replicated across different cultures, it is important to be aware of limitations.

In designing research, an attributional bias is evident in that problems tend to be interpreted in terms of "person blame" rather than "social system blame." Consider the term "psychological adjustment." In some cases, we may mean "if the shoe doesn't fit, there's something wrong with your foot," that is, that human problems are caused only by personal limitations, and not by society. It is argued that a social psychology which is exclusively psychological may actually deter social change. Gregg, Preston, Geist and Caplan (1979) reviewed 698 published research papers spanning 40 years, concerning the causes of delinquency, alcohol and other drug abuse, and rape. Each study was coded according to what causes had been investigated as follows: (1) the person, e.g., alcholism caused by abnormal dependency needs; (2) the milieu, e.g., alcoholism caused by the peer group or a broken home; and (3) the social system, e.g., alcoholism caused by high unemployment. Overall, the most common causal attribution for social problems was articulated in *person* terms; relatively few studies considered both the person and the environment.

Another important bias in the theories and concepts of social psychology is individualism. Characteristic of the culture of the United States, individualism expresses the "ideal" of a self-contained person who does not need other people, or a community and who exercises maximal individual freedom within a competitive society

(Sampson, 1977). This leads social psychologists to define certain problems and study certain phenomena, but to ignore others, e.g., to study excessive obedience to authority but not disobedience, conformity but not the lack of a sense of solidarity or community, "group-think" but not egocentric thinking, and ethnocentrism but not strong, affirmative group identity and pride. Clearly, the culture of the social psychologist will influence how problems are approached. As the discipline becomes more international, this problem will likely be self-corrected over time.

Discussion now turns to some important areas in which social psychology is concerned. The present chapter includes discussion of the social psychology of the law (particularly, the process of a trial in court), the physical environment (noise, heat, crowding, pollution, and the design of buildings), and how people are reacting to the nuclear threat. The next chapter will focus on how social psychology may be applied to health, both in improving health care and in promoting individual behaviour which enhances health.

SOCIAL PSYCHOLOGY AND THE LAW

Behaviour in relation to the legal system has proved to be a fertile field for research in social psychology. In particular, researchers have examined the judicial process, looking at social behaviour in the courtroom setting and the social behaviour during the trial process. While the courtroom would provide a concentrated real-life arena in which to study social psychological processes, it is obviously not possible or desirable for research to intrude. In spite of the difficulties in conducting research, social psychology offers a potentially powerful means of evaluating how well the system is working, and for recommending improvements. Insight has been gained into important questions which may lead to improvements and, possibly, greater justice. Among these questions examined are: When and how are witnesses accurate in their testimony? What determines whether jurors will believe the testimony of a witness? What factors influence the decisions of judges in imposing sentences or setting bail? Are there ways to select a jury that are unlikely to be biased? What dynamics occur within a jury which may influence its decision?

Eyewitness testimony

The evidence, as presented and interpreted by the lawyers, is the essential ingredient of a court case. While evidence may include such things as a fingerprint, a cancelled cheque, a weapon, or a document, the most convincing source of evidence is often the testimony of an eyewitness who can identify the perpetrator and describe what happened. Indeed, eyewitness testimony may be the most important reason why innocent people are convicted, even when the evidence has been discredited in court (Loftus, 1974).

Even if the eyewitness is honestly attempting to be truthful (see Box 15-2) there are two interrelated issues: (1) Is the testimony of an eyewitness usually accurate, and what factors contribute to error or bias? (2) What determines whether the testimony will be believed by jurors? Both questions are largely social psychological, and the research findings suggest that our legal system should re-examine them more carefully (Yarmey, 1979; Loftus, 1979).

B · O · X   15 - 2

LIE DETECTION AND THE POLYGRAPH

It is obvious that we cannot have "justice" in a criminal justice system unless we can determine the truth. We saw earlier (Chapter 3) that even the most well-trained among us are far from perfectly accurate in detecting deception. Thus many have argued that we should use other methods to enhance our chances of arriving at the truth.

According to Amnesty International, many nations on all continents routinely practice torture during interrogation. Apart from being morally repugnant, such methods often cause the victim to say what the interrogator wants to hear in order to end the ordeal. In medieval Britain, an accused was required to swallow a "trial slice" of bread and cheese. It was reasoned that an inability to swallow it would indicate a dry mouth, which might indicate lying. Today, in the civilized world of high-tech, we have the polygraph, which is being used not only in the legal system but by private corporations to screen employees.

The use of polygraphs is controversial. The research indicates accuracy from 70 to 90 percent of the time, which is impressive but not foolproof or "beyond a reasonable doubt" (Lykken, 1974; Yarmey, 1979; Horvath, 1977, 1984). There is evidence that certain types of people or those who have been coached beforehand can "beat the machine," such as by mentally distracting themselves during critical questions or biting their tongues during neutral questions (Honts, Hodes and Raskin, 1985). Other techniques, such as "truth drugs" or analysis of stress in voices, are equally fallible. There are also important ethical and legal issues in compelling people to submit to these procedures, such as invasion of privacy and self-incrimination. Perhaps, in the end, there is no substitute for competent and professional police work.

In one, reactions are compared while the person responds to critical, neutral, and control questions. It is reasoned that while the person may show increased arousal to any questions concerning the situation, a heightened level of arousal would be shown if upset is combined with lying. Thus reactions might be compared while the person responded to a general, control question ("Did *someone* murder your wife?") and then to a specific question ("Did *you* murder your wife?"). The other technique is to ask about details which only the perpetrator and police would know. For example, if the victim was wearing a green sweater, we would ask a series of yes/no questions: Was the victim wearing a green sweater? a white sweater? a blue ski jacket? a grey parka? a brown fur coat? If the accused shows arousal only to the true item while denying knowledge in all of them, then we may be on to something.

The use of polygraphs is controversial. The research indicates accuracy from 70 to 90 percent of the time, which is impressive but not foolproof or "beyond a reasonable doubt" (Lykken, 1974; Yarmey, 1979; Horvath, 1977, 1984). There is evidence that certain types of people or those who have been coached beforehand can "beat the machine," such as by mentally distracting themselves during critical questions or biting their tongues during neutral questions (Honts, Hodes and Raskin, 1985). Other techniques, such as "truth drugs" or analysis of stress in voices, are equally fallible. There are also important ethical and legal issues in compelling people to submit to these procedures, such as invasion of privacy and self-incrimination. Perhaps, in the end, there is no substitute for competent and professional police work.

One study has shown that while police officers and prosecuting lawyers agree that police are capable witnesses, defense lawyers and the public are more skeptical.

Eyewitnesses are often not accurate. For example, in a series of experiments in which a "crime" was staged, subjects later showed large variations in their estimates of height (average error of 20 centimetres), hair colour (83 percent in error), and age (average error of eight years) of the perpetrator (Loftus, 1979). In another experiment (Buckhout, 1980) television viewers in New York City were shown a 127-second tape of an incident in which a mugger stole a woman's purse and then ran directly toward the camera. Viewers were then shown a six-person lineup which included the actual criminal, and were invited to identify that person. Of the 2145 viewers who called the station, only 15.3 percent correctly identified the mugger, a figure close to what would be expected by pure chance. In fact, 33 percent identified the White assailant as being Black or Hispanic, and a few were even convinced that they had also been victimized by the same actor as appeared in the tape.

The U.S. Supreme Court in 1972 suggested five criteria for judging the reliability of eyewitness testimony: (1) the opportunity of the witness to view the criminal clearly at the time and place of the crime; (2) the extent to which the witness was paying attention to the incident; (3) the accuracy of the witness's description of the criminal *before* seeing the accused; (4) the extent to which the witness is certain in his or her own mind; and (5) the time elapsed between the crime and the identification. In spite of the experience of these eminent jurists, the research does not provide convincing empirical support for any of these criteria (Wells and Murray, 1983).

One study tested several of these criteria (Yarmey, 1986). Subjects were asked to imagine that they were in a park and were bystander witnesses to a crime in which a man assaulted and apparently raped a woman. They were shown a sequence of 60 colour slides depicting the crime in which the level of illumination was varied to simulate broad daylight, early or late twilight, or night. Subjects, as expected, recalled more and with greater accuracy in daylight or early twilight conditions, consistent with common sense and with the first criterion, the opportunity of the witness to view the criminal at the time of the crime. However, there was no significant relationship between the witnesses' accuracy in free recall conditions prior to seeing the accused and their later identification of the assailant in a line-up or through voice ID. In addition, subjects who expressed a high degree of certainty in their choice were no more accurate than those who were less certain (criterion four). The certainty issue has been explored in a number of studies which have suggested that police officers are not superior to other people in their skills of perception and memory (Yarmey, 1979). Another study has shown that while police officers themselves and prosecuting lawyers agree that police are capable and credible witnesses, defense lawyers and the general public are somewhat more skeptical (Yarmey, 1986). (See Box 15-3 for a real-life evaluation.)

The ability of someone to remember a criminal incident accurately can be influenced by a number of factors. For example, we are usually better able to identify people of our own race than those of other races (Brigham and Malpass, 1985). In one study, Black, White, and Asian students in the U.S. were all most accurate in identifying faces of their own race and differed widely in their capacity to recognize those of the other races (Luce, 1974). Similarly, Black Africans and White Europeans both were less accurate in identifying photographs of people of the other race than their own (Shepherd, Deregowski and Ellis, 1974). In general, people tend to perceive people of other races as more similar to each other than they really are: thus errors are more likely to occur (Barkowitz and Brigham, 1982).

Another factor, stress, can often influence and distort memory. For example, witnessing incidents which involve actual or threatened violence can cause stress and distress, even when the violence has not been directed at that witness (Yarmey and Jones, 1983). There is also research which shows that people tend to fixate their gaze on unusual or highly significant objects, such as a gun or other weapon (see Yarmey, 1979). Thus their attention may be distracted from the face and other characteristics of the person committing the crime. As witnesses are often not aware of how distracted they were at the time, their testimony may be well-intended but unreliable.

The police lineup Consider the police "lineup," in which the suspect stands among a group, usually of five to nine persons, and the witness attempts to identify the guilty party. The procedure was devised to overcome the effects of bias which would arise if the witness were asked directly whether a particular person "did it." However, this procedure is subject to its own biases, including police bias, witness bias, situ-

B · O · X   15 - 3

A CASE STUDY OF EYEWITNESS RECALL

On a spring afternoon in Burnaby, B.C., a thief entered a gun shop, tied up the proprietor and took some money and guns. After the thief left the store, the owner freed himself, grabbed a revolver, and rushed outside to record the license plate number of the thief. However, the thief had not yet entered his car. In a face-to-face encounter, separated by less than two metres, the two men engaged in a gunfight in which the thief was killed and the owner was seriously wounded. The incident occurred on a busy street, and was witnessed by people from adjacent buildings and passing automobiles. Twenty-one witnesses were interviewed by the police in the aftermath of the event.

Researchers contacted 20 of the witnesses, and 13 (not including the storeowner) were interviewed four to five months later (Yuille and Cutshall, 1986). In general, they found that the witnesses were remarkably accurate when their responses were compared with the composite report of the police. While witnesses varied in some detail, such as in describing the colour of clothing or in estimating people's

height, weight, and age, their memories of the sequence of events and the actions of various people were largely free of errors and not affected by attempts to mislead them through the use of biased or "leading" questions (e.g., asking whether they recalled seeing a broken headlight when there was no such broken headlight). Subjects who reported that they had experienced extreme anxiety at the time did not recall the accident with greater or less accuracy than did the other witnesses.

Of course, this study lacks the controls of a laboratory experiment. Some witnesses were directly involved in some way in the event while others were at a distance, and witnesses varied in what they had been able to see before, during, and after the shooting. However, the findings are not consistent with the essentially negative view of the eyewitness that emerges from laboratory research. More such field studies should provide us with a real-world data base from which the laboratory experiments can be interpreted.

---

ational bias, and response bias (Yarmey, 1979). Lineups are conducted by police officers to test their "hypothesis" regarding a suspect, and can be subject to "experimenter biases," such as leading questions to the witness ("How about the guy in the purple shirt on the right?"). Sometimes, the suspect is placed among a group of police officers — all of whom are out of uniform — who tend to turn their eyes slightly toward the accused (Gilligan, 1977). In other cases, the lineup consists entirely of suspects in the case, which tends to increase the probability of misidentification, perhaps because all of them show signs of nervousness (Wells and Turtle, 1986).

How can accuracy be increased in this kind of procedure? Wells and Turtle (1986) suggest that in cases of multiple suspects, a mixed lineup might include both the suspects and "foils" who are not suspected of having committed that crime. They also suggest that a "preceding blank lineup," consisting entirely of non-suspects, be used to identify eyewitnesses who are particularly prone to making false identifications (Wells, 1984). Yarmey (1979) argues that lineup identification procedures be standardized more carefully and that the lineup procedure should be conducted by an officer not involved in the case. Even better would be a "double-blind" procedure in which neither the individual conducting the inquiry nor the others in the lineup would know who is suspected.

Another study has shown how the structure of a lineup can seriously bias the outcome (Doob and Kirshenbaum, 1973b). The study was based on an actual case, *Regina vs. Shatford*, in which conviction of the defendant was a direct result of the testimony of an eyewitness. Shatford had allegedly taken part in a holdup in which the cashier could later recall only that the robbers were "very neatly dressed, and rather good looking and they looked enough alike to be brothers." In spite of this vague description, she was able to pick Shatford out of a 12-person lineup nine days later. What she had done was simply select the best looking person in the lineup. If the police had inserted other more attractive persons into the lineup, the probability is that one of them might have been identified instead. The critical feature of a lineup is not the absolute number but the "functional number" of participants from which the witness may identify the culprit. For example, if the suspect is fat, and there is only one other fat person in the lineup, the total number of people in that lineup may be nine but the functional number is only two — and there is a 50 percent probability of one being identified by pure chance.

Like experimental subjects, eyewitnesses generally want to be useful and may react to subtle demand characteristics. For example, they may feel compelled to identify *someone*, although none of the persons in the lineup may be guilty. Stereotypes regarding dress, race, age, hair style, and other physical features may reflect response biases, particularly if these stereotypes are shared by the officers conducting the inquiry. Even lighting and noise levels in the room may influence judgments, particularly if these conditions differ from those at the scene of the crime.

Giving testimony

In our Canadian system, trials proceed on the basis of an adversarial system in which lawyers are expected to be unreserved advocates for one side of the case. Witnesses are called to support one side, and can be cross-examined by the other side. As we have already noted in Chapter 13, this is not the only model for trials in a democracy. In most of Europe, the court assigns investigators to gather evidence concerning both sides of the case, and witnesses can be considered as neutral, and are summoned and questioned by the judge. The assumption in our system is that both sides are motivated by self-interest in a competitive situation to find and present all relevant evidence; thus truth will out and justice will prevail. This, of course, depends on the quality of the case prepared and presented by both sides, which may be affected by factors such as whether the defendant lacks financial resources. Further, the adversarial process of examination and cross-examination may lead to distortions in testimony.

A series of experiments shows how testimony can be influenced by the phrasing of questions (Loftus, 1979). In one, subjects were shown a film of an automobile accident in which a green car drove past. Immediately afterwards, they all were questioned about what they saw. Some were asked this question: "Did the blue car that drove past the accident have a ski rack on the roof?" Others were asked the same question without the word "blue." Later, subjects were asked to identify the colour of the car from a set of colour strips of various shades and hues. Most who were not asked about a "blue car" selected a shade of green which matched closely the actual colour of the car. However, those who were asked about a "blue car" selected a shade of blue or blue-green, consistant with what was suggested by the "leading question." The effect occurred after an interval of 20 minutes and persisted over one week.

Of course, the astute lawyer knows how to use this technique and to recognize it when used by the opponent. The very nature of the adversarial process may create subtle biases. In an experiment by Sheppard and Vidmar (1980), subjects were shown a filmed fight. They were told that they were to testify about what they had seen at a mock trial, and that they might be contacted by a lawyer before the trial. Other students, not shown the fight, were assigned roles as lawyers, some representing the plaintiff or defendant, and others in a neutral role representing the court. The "witness" subjects were interviewed by "lawyers," and then gave their testimony. A "judge" and two "observers" rated the accuracy and bias of the testimony.

Both the observers and the "judge" found little bias in the testimony of witnesses who had been interviewed by neutral or inquisitional "lawyers." However, those who had been interviewed by a "lawyer" representing one side gave testimony in a way which favoured that side, such as by offering testimony which favoured the defendant if interviewed by the defense lawyer. When interviewed after the experiment, none of the subjects were aware of having been influenced by the "lawyer's" style of questioning.

Research suggests that the procedures of giving testimony might be improved. In one study (Marquis, Marshall and Oskamp, 1972), subjects viewed a film in which two young men witnessed a female pedestrian being knocked down by a car. A fight ensues between her male companion and the driver, and the onlookers subsequently become involved in the argument. Trained observers had previously identified 884 distinct "facts" regarding the people and events in the film. All subjects were first asked to give a report of what happened in as much detail as possible. Then they were questioned in one of four formats: (1) broad, general questions; (2) specific questions equivalent to direct examination; (3) forced-choice "leading" questions equivalent to an aggressive cross-examination; or (4) multiple-choice questions of the type known and loved by most students. The results (Table 15-2) show that each technique has advantages and disadvantages. Free recall provides great accuracy, but relatively few details. Under more direct questioning, accuracy is somewhat reduced but the testimony becomes more complete. Perhaps witnesses should be allowed to narrate freely with as few interpretations as possible in the early stage of testimony. Then, subsequent questioning could elicit more detail.

TABLE 15-2
Percentage of facts identified and accuracy under different testimony conditions

	Completeness	Accuracy
Free recall narrative	28	96
Broad general questions	48	90
Specific direct examination	56	86
Forced-choice cross-examination	84	81
Multiple choice	83	82

SOURCE: Marquis, Marshall and Oskamp, 1972

Witness credibility Any competent lawyer knows that casting doubt on even one point of a witness's testimony can destroy the credibility of the entire testimony. A loss of confidence displayed by the witness will be noticed by jurors, and credibility may be lost as well. Thus witnesses are often rehearsed beforehand by lawyers who try to anticipate weaknesses in the testimony.

One factor in credibility may be the language of the eyewitness. In two studies conducted in the United States (Stephan and Stephan, 1986), simulated jurors read summaries of an assault case, and then heard the testimony of the defendant, who spoke English or another language (Spanish, Thai) which was translated into English by an interpreter. In both studies, subjects rated the defendant as more guilty when his testimony was not presented in English. However, it is encouraging to note that the language bias was offset among subjects who were instructed by the judge to ignore the fact that his testimony was translated. Perhaps in a bilingual, multicultural nation such as Canada, these instructions by judges to juries should be standard procedure.

B·O·X 15 - 4

ATTITUDES TOWARD CRIME AND PUNISHMENT

My object so sublime
I shall achieve in time
To make the punishment fit the crime
The punishment fit the crime

Gilbert and Sullivan
Mikado

Like the Mikado's Lord High Executioner, our views of crime and its punishment are central to our attitudes toward law and justice. Thus it is a serious matter if many people believe that the punishments handed down do not fit the crimes. In a national opinion poll conducted in 1983, fully 79.5 percent of Canadians believed that the sentences imposed by our courts were generally too lenient (Doob and Roberts, 1984). With some variations, this attitude is widely held across the regions of Canada and among the various linguistic and cultural groups.

Several studies show that this impression is not correct (Doob and Roberts, 1984). When subjects were presented with brief descriptions of cases involving convictions for criminal offenses and the sentences imposed by the court, large majorities rated the sentences as too lenient. However, when provided with additional information about the crime and criminal which were available to the court, many more were then satisfied with the sentence. One particular case had been given extensive newspaper coverage, including an editorial which criticized the "leniency" of the sentence. When presented only with the newspaper accounts, 63 percent rated the sentence as "too lenient," but when given a summary of the information actually presented in court, only 19 percent rated the sentence as "too lenient" and 52 percent as "too harsh." Obviously, the public is not provided with all the relevant information used in sentencing decisions. In addition, we probably are influenced by the "availability" heuristic, in which we use the few, sensationalized cases that we can remember to arrive at a generalized judgment about the courts.

Perhaps the most controversial and persistent issue is capital punishment. Vidmar (1974) points out that proponents of capital punishment support their position for both *retributive justice* and for *utilitarian* reasons. Many argue that for a crime such as murder,

The jury

Much of the research in the social psychology of law has concerned the deliberations of the jury. Of course, the jury is a natural focus because it is important and visible, and because the deliberations of a jury are so essentially a social psychological process involving leadership, influence, conformity, and other group dynamics — the fundamentals of social perception, cognition and memory, as well as prejudice and other relevant attitudes (see Box 15-4). Of course, it is not possible to intervene directly in a real trial in order to study it, and it is impossible to recapture the environment in the laboratory.

Hence, research uses jury simulations, in which summaries of the evidence and arguments are presented briefly to jurors in oral or written form. Many are studies of individual "jurors," in which influences on the decisions of individuals, but not the group decision, are examined. Others use the format of mock juries, in which subjects are presented with evidence, perhaps arguments by "lawyers," perhaps instructions by a "judge," and then must deliberate and reach a verdict.

the death penalty is the only punishment that "fits," and that justice is retribution in kind. They also argue that capital punishment can fulfill utilitarian functions for society, such as deterring others from committing such crimes, ensuring that the criminal will never do it again, or saving taxpayers' money from being used to support one more prisoner. In one study of 144 adults in Ontario, Vidmar (1974) found that retribution was, indeed, the most important reason cited by proponents, and that the majority of them would still favour the death penalty if provided with information showing that there was no deterrent effect (Sarat and Vidmar, 1976). Those who favoured capital punishment, particularly for retributive justice, also tended to score higher on measures of authoritarianism and dogmatism (see Chapter 8), and on a measure of prejudice towards French Canadians, Blacks, Indians, the poor, and individuals seen as part of the "counterculture"; similar findings are reported in U.S. studies. Proponents of capital punishment also indicated that they would obey the orders of an officer to shoot villagers suspected of aiding the enemy, an action similar to the My Lai massacre committed by U.S. soldiers in Vietnam. A U.S. study has confirmed that

proponents of retributive capital punishment tend to be authoritarian and accepting of military "crimes of obedience" (Hamilton, 1976). It may also be true that many jurors would be more reluctant to convict murderers if the death penalty is an outcome (*The Globe and Mail*, March 18, 1987).

The evidence, while never absolutely free of competing interpretations, does not support the hypothesis that capital punishment deters murder. In Canada, while 66.5 percent of Canadians believe that more murders have been committed in the years since the abolition of capital punishment in 1976, the facts show a *decrease* in that period (Doob and Roberts, 1984). A study conducted in the U.S. also shows that in this century, 343 people have been wrongfully convicted of murder and 25 have actually been executed (*The Globe and Mail*, November 15, 1985). In view of the evidence of bias and error in our judicial procedures, we can assume a similar injustice in Canada. After a study of how the death penalty is applied across the world, Amnesty International has adopted a position which opposes the practice for "all prisoners, without reservation." In 1987, the Canadian Parliament voted to continue abolition of capital punishment.

Do these simulations represent the reality of the courtroom? Recall from the discussion in Chapter 2 that there are several distinctive ways in which the validity of research can be evaluated: (1) in terms of how much we can generalize from our sample and procedures; and (2) in terms of how much the experimental situation represents the real-world environment of the courtroom. On both counts, the simulation studies leave much to be desired.

One problem is that jury studies often use only university students as subjects. A group made up entirely of university students is hardly representative of the typical heterogeneous groups drawn from a pool of eligible jurors. Indeed, there is some evidence that mock juries of students are more likely to acquit than are actual jury pool groups (Simon and Mahan, 1971). Further, some studies simply have people vote on a verdict without allowing them to deliberate to reach a unanimous decision. Such studies eliminate the crucial role of social influence on a group decision.

Real juries sit through an entire trial, while simulated juries read summaries or view videotaped excerpts. Thus real juries are exposed to a much richer array of information, including important non-verbal cues by lawyers, defendants, and witnesses. In addition, real juries make decisions that can have serious consequences for the defendants and perhaps for society. In one simulation study, some groups were told that their verdict in a case of a student accused of cheating would be accepted by the instructor, while others were told that the case was hypothetical. Jurors in an apparently "real" case were more likely to judge the defendant as guilty, and less likely to be influenced by characteristics of the defendant (Wilson and Donnerstein, 1976).

Nevertheless, the simulation studies should not be dismissed as irrelevant. It is possible to increase the complexity of details provided and expand sampling so as to more closely approximate the courtroom situation. As Zimbardo *et al.* (1982) showed so dramatically in their mock prison study (see Chapter 14), role-playing simulations can become startlingly real to the participants.

In spite of the limitations, important questions have been studied through simulations. For example, the choice of a jury leader can have significant effects upon the discussion and final decision. The research shows that the person most likely to be selected will be: (1) the person who is sitting at the head of the table at the first meeting: (2) one who has had previous experience as a juror; and (3) someone of a higher socioeconomic class (Strodtbeck and Lipinski, 1985). The selection process is generally very straightforward and uncontroversial, apparently influenced by the jurors' prototype of a leader. Let us examine research on other questions, including the characteristics of the individual juror, the influence of the judge, and the effect of jury size. Box 15-5 also considers the use of social psychology to select jurors.

The juror   The research shows that jurors who are older, less educated, and of lower socioeconomic levels are more likely to vote to convict (see Nemeth, 1981). Male and female jurors behave in a similar fashion except in rape trials. Under these circumstances, females are more likely to convict and to favour harsh sentences (Nemeth, 1981). Another predictor is the extent of similarity between jurors and the defendant: for example, a French-speaking female carpenter is more likely to receive a lenient judgment from jurors who also have one or more of these characteristics, an outcome consistent with the similarity-attraction rule (see Chapter 8).

B · O · X   15 - 5

STACKING THE JURY SOCIAL-PSYCHOLOGICALLY?

In our trial system, the attorneys representing both the Crown and the defense have a limited but important role in selecting the jury. Each side may "challenge for cause" any prospective juror when they can convince the judge of a probable bias in that juror. In addition, each side is permitted several "pre-emptory challenges" in which a juror is disqualified at the request of counsel. Thus, particularly in a case which is controversial or highly publicized, it becomes important to maximize each side's chances with a favourable jury. Recently, social psychologists have served as consultants in selecting juries for several well-publicized cases in the U.S., and concern has been expressed that we may be developing a technology to "stack" the jury.

Trying to select a more favourable jury is not a new idea *per se*. Lawyers always have had criteria which they have used to challenge certain individuals, and a study by Diamond and Zeisel (1974) indicates that their selections can affect the outcome of a trial. They compared the verdicts in ten cases involving groups of jurors selected in different ways. Some had been chosen randomly; others had been chosen by the defense or by the prosecution. The randomly selected jurors brought down a guilty verdict in all ten cases; the second group found five defendants guilty and five not guilty, and the third group found eight of the defendants guilty. Three judges who also heard the cases found only one defendant not guilty.

Can social psychologists help to select favourable juries and is it a good idea? Moran and Comfort (1982) examined the effect of 23 personality and demographic characteristics on the verdicts of a large sample of jurors. They concluded that with these data, verdicts could be predicted with 87 percent accuracy, a "batting average" which would impress the most talented trial lawyer. However, few people advocate that we administer a battery of personality tests to all potential jurors. Thus we must infer much about the juror from very limited information and data about people similar to that juror. For example, if we know that people in certain occupations or geographic locations tend to score high on the F scale (see Chapter 7) then we might infer or "bet" that a potential juror is authoritarian and less likely to be lenient or sympathetic to the defendant.

A number of studies show that people who favour the death penalty also tend to have a bias toward voting for conviction rather than acquittal (Haney, 1980). Prosecutors in murder trials in which the death penalty is involved usually try to exclude potential jurors who oppose capital punishment, reasoning that they would be unlikely to vote to send someone to death. However, defense lawyers argue that such a practice serves to stack the jury with people whose bias favours the prosecution, and contravenes the principle that the composition of a pool of jurors should be representative of their community.

From the perspective of a consultant psychologist, Christie (1976) argues that the social scientist and the lawyer are doing much the same thing. The lawyer relies on previous experience with other jury panel samples, while the social scientist relies on survey data to make predictions about the possible reactions of a potential juror. Nemeth (1981) notes that at best, the challenge during jury selection allows for the elimination of a juror with obvious biases, but not the selection of a favourable juror. As long as both sides have access to the same information, the system may even operate more effectively, and the evidence shows that the jury system, while imperfect, operates remarkably well (Hans and Vidmar, 1986).

One characteristic which has been studied extensively is authoritarianism, the syndrome in which individuals display rigid thinking, political conservatism and social conventionality, submissiveness to authority, and a hostile, punitive orientation towards those who deviate in any way from social norms (Adorno, Frenkel-Brunswick, Levinson and Sanford, 1950, see Chapter 7). Authoritarians are more apt to convict and to recommend severe sentences, particularly if the defendant is not similar to themselves (Mitchell and Byrne, 1973). However, authoritarians are *less* likely to convict if the defendant is perceived as representing authority, e.g., a police officer. For example, when mock-jury subjects were contacted one week after an experiment, high authoritarians recalled more about the defendant's character but less about the evidence (Berg and Vidmar, 1975). Apparently, authoritarians and non-authoritarians have different schemata and use different kinds of information in arriving at their judgments.

Admissibility of evidence   Section 12(1) of the *Canada Evidence Act* states: "A witness can be questioned as to whether he has been convicted of an offense and, upon being so questioned, if he either denies the fact or refuses to answer, the opposite party may prove such conviction." If the witness is the defendant, this is taken to mean that the jury is to use evidence of prior convictions in deciding how much to believe the person — although *not* in deciding whether the person is guilty or not of this particular charge.

Doob (1976) points out that there are two questionable assumptions here. First, it is assumed that a person with a criminal record is more likely to lie or otherwise be unreliable as a witness. Since the situational pressures on both sides are strong (e.g., perjury is a serious offense), it is less likely that a character trait such as honesty would be very useful as a predictor of witness reliability. The other assumption is that a jury will understand and follow the "limited use" instructions of the judge, considering the criminal record as relevant only to the reliability of that particular testimony but not to the person's guilt or innocence in the case.

The latter assumption was investigated in a simulation experiment (Doob, 1976). Subjects were presented with a case description of a break-and-enter robbery. Some subjects were given simply the written description of the robbery, some were also told that the accused had a previous record (seven previous convictions for related offenses), and others were told of the criminal record and instructed not to use that information to determine whether or not the accused was guilty. The results showed that individual jurors were likely to convict the person with the criminal record, regardless of how the judge instructed them to use this information.

This and other studies indicate why the tactics of lawyers in introducing questionable evidence or arguments are often effective. The judge has the authority and responsibility to rule on the legal admissibility of evidence or statements and can order jurors to "disregard" what is not admissible. However, these rulings may not have the intended influence on the jurors.

Jury size   It has been established through long history and custom that the jury consists of 12 persons and that a unanimous decision is required to convict a defendant. Recently, both of these rules have come under scrutiny — the 12 persons rule involves more public expense and personal sacrifices, while the "hung jury" requires the entire case to be retried. A number of states in the U.S. have experimented with six-person juries and with loosening the requirement of a unanimous decision. The U.S. Supreme Court ruled in 1978 that juries of six protected the constitutional rights of the defendant, citing social psychological research to support this conclusion.

It is difficult to evaluate the "quality" of actual jury decisions, as these decisions involve interpretation of evidence. However, reducing the size of the jury may adversely affect the *process* of decision-making, which would have adverse effects on the quality of the decision. In a review of the literature, Nemeth (1981) documents the following as the consequences of a smaller jury: (1) Because there are fewer people, less of the relevant evidence in a complex case may be remembered. (2) It is less likely that the biases of individual members will be overcome by others since there are fewer of them. (3) The opportunity for a meaningful representation of the community decreases — the "sample size" is smaller. (4) Smaller juries are more likely to convict, a crucial bias if the defendant is not guilty. (5) In studies of group decision-making, the decisions are more variable from one group to another when groups are smaller. Thus we could expect a degree of increased unpredictability, or unreliability, in the decisions of smaller juries.

In addition, the minority position is less likely to be represented adequately in smaller groups and there would be fewer "hung juries." (Kerr and MacCoun, 1985). Unanimity often occurs because the minority has abandoned its position, yielding to the pressure of the majority. Thus, if the majority favours conviction and the minority yields, an innocent person may be convicted. The larger jury should mean that there are more people on both the majority and minority sides, thus increasing the probability that a dissenting juror would have at least one supporter. You will recall from the study of conformity (Chapter 6) that the pressures to conform are dramatically reduced when the non-conformer has even one supporter. The dissenting opinion should be sustained more easily in a larger group, and a jury decision would represent the outcome of subtle influence and persuasion. In short, the 12-person jury may have more difficulty in arriving at a verdict, but the verdict is perhaps more likely to be just.

Finally, two biases have been uncovered which pertain to the jury decisions. First, most jury decisions tend to be those that were initially favoured by most of the jurors. That is, it is relatively rare for a minority to sway the decision of the majority, which bolsters the argument against weakening that minority by reducing the size of the jury. In addition, the tendency for the early majority to prevail is most pronounced when the verdict is to acquit. Apparently, jurors tend to be especially protective of the rights of the individual defendant (see Davis *et al.*, 1981).

THE PHYSICAL ENVIRONMENT

We have always known that our physical environment can influence how we think, feel, and act. We believe that our moods and our behaviour are influenced by the weather, whether we are in the city or country, perhaps even by the phases of the moon (see Box 15-6). We are also aware that our physical surroundings indoors — the design of classrooms, apartments, and theatres — can affect how we live and experience life.

Lately, we have become more concerned about our physical environment. Although in the past, we welcomed technology, industry, economic growth and expansion, today we are uneasy about "progress" (see Box 15-7). Familiar terms such as "the population bomb," acid rain, dioxins, waste disposal, "limits to growth," oil spills, the energy crisis, and well-known disasters (Three Mile Island, the Love Canal, Chernobyl, and Bhopal) all strengthen our growing concern about the physical environment. While we still may want economic growth and technology to provide jobs and maintain our standard of living, we are now compelled to consider the quality

B · O · X   15 - 6

SHEER LUNACY: THE PHASES OF THE MOON AND BEHAVIOUR

Since ancient times, a belief that the phases of the moon influence human behaviour has persisted in human cultures. The Bible (both Testaments), Plutarch, Hippocrates, and many others have written of the possible effects of the moon on sanity itself: From the Latin word "luna" (moon) comes lunatic and lunacy (Oliver, 1943). Of course, mystery writers and makers of horror movies take full advantage of the foreboding symbolism of full moon, new moon, or no moon. But the notion that there is a relationship between the phases of the moon and undesirable human behaviour is also a hypothesis which can be tested.

Rotton and Kelly (1985) have published a meta-analysis of 37 studies of the "Transylvania hypothesis" (Garzino, 1982). Behaviours examined in these studies include: homicide and other criminal behaviour; suicide and other self-harm; admissions to psychiatric treatment settings and disturbed behaviour within those settings; telephone calls to crisis centres; and miscellaneous behaviours such as helping, traffic accidents, voting behaviour and drug intoxication. While a few of the correlations reached statistical reliability, no clear or consistent pattern emerged to support the hypothesis in any of these cases. In addition, many of the studies did not use the appropriate statistical analyses or failed to control for other factors such as season, day of the week, or weather. There is also the "file drawer" problem to distort the picture: in many cases, scientists do not submit reports of non-significant results to journals,

and the journals do not publish null results.

Of course, as we already noted in Chapter 2, we must place the burden of proof where it belongs: "Just as we cannot prove that werewolves, unicorns and other creatures do not exist, we cannot prove that the moon does not influence behaviour" (Rotton and Kelly, 1985, p. 300). However, those who believe or suspect that this is true must provide evidence which is consistent across studies and convincing in terms of well-designed, controlled research.

Any hypothesis must also be grounded in theory or, at least a convincing and logical argument that it may be plausible. A number of explanations have been proposed as to *why* the phases of the moon might affect our behaviour: (1) The full moon provides more light, enabling us to do more at night — and the new moon provides the cover of darkness for evil and bizarre doings (but 75-90 percent of our time and behaviour at night are indoors). (2) Phases of the moon may affect levels of humidity and precipitation which could influence behaviour (but no such evidence has been uncovered). (3) The moon exerts a gravitational force which influences "biological tides" in electrolytes, hormones, and other body fluids (no such evidence has been found, and the gravitational pull of the earth is 5012 times as strong). (4) The lunar phase may influence geomagnetic forces or the balance of ions (electrically charged particles) in the air (no evidence).

of the air we breathe and the water we drink, the preservation of our agricultural land and energy resources, and the quality of life in our cities

Social psychologists have become concerned with the relationship between the

---

SOCIAL INDICATORS, OR THE QUALITY OF LIFE BEYOND A GROSS NATIONAL PRODUCT

Many of us are familiar with various statistical indicators of the state of the economy. Newspapers and broadcasts routinely discuss the latest gross national product (GNP) figures, the consumer price index (CPI), the rate of inflation, the rate of unemployment (seasonally adjusted), and the Bank of Canada weekly interest rate, knowing that most people will have some level of understanding of them. While a healthy economy is vital to all of us (consider that we refer to our "standard of living" in economic terms), it is clear that this is but one component of what we may refer to as our "quality of life." Thus, in the past decade, some work has been devoted to developing broad and detailed measures of the well-being and quality of life of individual groups, regions, and our society as a whole (Palys and Little, 1980; Campbell, Converse and Rodgers, 1976).

Various approaches have been used, including both "objective" and "subjective" indicators. There are the kinds of data which might be available from Statistics Canada or other sources, e.g., air pollution levels, percentage of people living below the "poverty line," unemployment rates, crime, or rates of various illnesses and life expectancies. Then there are the data obtained from surveys in which individuals rate their level of satisfaction with their lives in general, and with specific areas of life, e.g., marriage, job, housing and neighbourhood, income level, leisure time activities. While we have much to learn, several findings have emerged from the research so far. As we would expect, a general sense of well-being is associated with satisfaction in various domains of life. In one large-scale U.S. study, satisfaction with family life, leisure activities and income level were the

strongest predictors of general well-being. Life satisfaction was lower in certain groups — those who were poor, unemployed, Black, divorced, and living in the largest cities — and highest among retired senior citizens and people in small towns. There was no difference in the well-being of men and women. Interestingly, this and other studies show that there was far from a one-to-one correspondence between objective conditions and subjective satisfaction. For example, people who had unrealistically high aspirations and those who felt deprived and "hard done by" relative to most people were less satisfied with their lives, regardless of objective circumstances (Campbell, Converse and Rodgers, 1976).

What uses might this research serve? A number of possible uses are even now close to reality: (1) They can guide social policy and provide evidence as to whether certain policies are succeeding or failing to meet intended goals. (2) If we accumulate such data frequently and regularly, changes over time can help us to identify and anticipate problems. (3) Comparing different regions can help us to identify both problems and successes. Indeed, composite indices have been developed to help us compare the quality of life in various cities (e.g., cost of living, cultural and educational facilities, pollution levels, crime rates, leisure time amenities, public transportation). Such data can be useful in helping to guide individuals, institutions and industries in where to locate.

In general research can help us understand *how* people come to perceive their quality of life, and may serve as the basis for Campbell's ideal of an "experimenting society."

While economic growth and technology are still welcome, we are now moved to consider the quality of life, especially in large cities.

physical environment and human behaviour and experience. Research has been conducted on a number of environment-related issues, including the effects of noise, heat, and crowding, the development of certain attitudes and actions, such as conserving energy or littering, and the impact of the "built environment" — why certain architectural designs result in more efficient and pleasant environments for working, shopping, or living. This work is reviewed next.

The impact of environmental stressors

Interestingly, most of the research on environment focuses on negative conditions. Very little is known about what environmental conditions make people happy or comfortable (perhaps one exception is the effort to manipulate the environment of workers and shoppers to enhance productivity or profits). However, we are aware that our physical environment can generate stressful conditions, such as uncomfortable heat or noise, air pollution, or crowding. It is important to understand the concept of *stress*, a physiological and psychological response to threat or challenge (Lazarus and Cohen, 1977). There are at least three types of stressful conditions: (1) cataclysmic events such as war, a devastating earthquake or tornado; (2) more limited, powerful events such as illness, loss of a job, a crucial examination, death of a loved one; and (3) daily hassles such as coping with traffic, smog, noisy neighbours, and other features of normal, contemporary life.

It is the daily hassles which intrigue environmental psychologists, because they are so common and pervasive and because it is possible to control or ameliorate their effects. It is important to understand that environmental stressors are most intense when they are experienced as being unpredictable and uncontrollable, as the following research demonstrates.

Noise Noise is defined as an unwanted intensity or quality of sound. Traffic, construction and other types of machinery, and crowds of people, not to mention powerful stereo equipment, create constant levels of background noise which are often intense, especially in cities. The effects can be dramatic. For example, Cohen, Glass and Singer (1973) studied residents of an apartment building which was constructed over a freeway. While noise levels inside the entire building were high, they were most intense on the lower floors, which were closer to the freeway. Children who lived on the lower floors performed less well than those on the upper levels on both tests of their ability to discriminate between sounds and on tests of their reading achievement. Of course, the noise levels in a neighbourhood near an airport are not only intense but unpredictable and uncontrollable. Well-controlled studies show that residents in these neighbourhoods have higher rates of admission to mental hospitals, birth defects, and death from strokes (Dellinger, 1979).

The effects of predictability/controllability are shown in a series of ingenious experiments by Glass and Singer (1972). While performing various cognitive tasks, subjects were subjected to short intervals of loud or soft noise or no noise at all. In one study, noise bursts came at exactly one minute intervals or at randomly spaced intervals. While the subjects in both groups experienced equal overall amounts of noise, the effects were quite different. Performance *during* the noise was similar across subjects, regardless of how much or how predictable the noise was. However, after the period of noise, subjects who had experienced random noise performed more poorly, that is, they committed more errors than those subjected to regularly spaced, predictable noise, even though subjects in the random and regular noise conditions rated the noise as equally annoying.

In other experiments, some subjects were told that they could stop the noise at any time by pressing a button or by signaling a partner. Given this power to control the noise, their performance was not affected by it. It should be noted that subjects did not actually choose to stop the noise, yet the sense that they *could* control the noise attenuated the stressful effects. In a later study, groups of subjects were allowed to start the noise or stop it, or both, or neither. As in the previous research, a sense of control reduced the negative effect of noise on performance in a proofreading task. Those given control to do both were least affected by the noise (Sherrod, Hage, Halpern and Moore, 1977). Other research has shown that subjects who experienced noise were more likely to behave aggressively by delivering ostensible electric shocks to another person, particularly after being angered. However, when given a "button" which would stop the noise, they rarely used that button but their aggressive behaviour was no longer influenced by the occurrence of that noise (Donnerstein and Wilson, 1976). Thus awareness that the noise can be controlled reduces the propensity for aggression, probably by reducing the helpless frustration of being subjected to that noise.

Temperature Folk wisdom suggests that the heat of a "long, hot summer" also can influence social behaviour, e.g., affect aggression. Data from the U.S.A. on violent crime such as homicide, assault and battery, rape, and armed robbery show a linear relation, with aggression rates highest at the highest temperature (Anderson and Anderson, 1984). These data are consistent with findings from laboratory studies. In one experiment, subjects in a room heated to an uncomfortable 34°C behaved more aggressively than subjects in a more comfortable setting (Baron and Bell, 1975). However, studies of rioting in large U.S. cities suggest that in some cases, aggression levels may actually decline at very high levels of heat. Perhaps people feel too uncomfortable to do anything vigorous and may tend to attribute their negative emotional states to the heat rather than to annoyance at other people.

What of cold weather, one of the defining features of life in a nation such as Canada? Certainly, greater isolation and stress is characteristic of very cold climates (Fisher, Bell and Baum, 1984). With regard to aggression, the effects of cold appear to be analogous to those of heat: moderately cold temperatures increase aggression somewhat, while the discomfort of intense cold decreases aggression (Bell and Baron, 1977; Bennet, Rafferty, Canivez and Smith, 1983). Life in this climate may include reduced daylight, a frustrating and seemingly endless wait for spring, feelings of isolation and the "cabin fever" (feeling "cooped up" indoors), and disruption of normal patterns of living by winter storms. However, research has not yet been conducted on these factors.

Density, crowding, and behaviour

It will not be news to most people that the population of the world is rapidly increasing. Consider that it took several thousand years for the world population to reach half a billion but only 200 years for the population to double to one billion, 80 years to double again, 45 years to more than double again to the present five billion; it is estimated that it will double again in about 35 years, barring a nuclear war or other catastrophe, or dramatically greater success in birth control.

The overpopulation issue is not a simple one. While the population of the world is definitely increasing, the area in which these people live is not. Further, this population is not distributed evenly throughout the area, but is concentrated more and more in large urban regions. In much of the Third World, people are leaving the rural areas and small towns for urban centres and what they hope will be a better life: cities such as Nairobi, Mexico City, Sao Paulo, Calcutta, and Santiago have grown explosively. Even in the developed world, where the birthrate is around or below the replacement level, people are increasingly concentrated in urban areas. For example, the majority of Canadians live in three relatively small pockets of an immense nation: the region surrounding the St. Lawrence River from Montreal to Québec City, the "Golden Horseshoe" around Lake Ontario, from Niagara to Oshawa, and the southwest corner of British Columbia. Moreover, the populations in the affluent Western world place heavy demands on the food, water, energy, and other resources of the world.

It is important to understand that *population density* is not the same as *crowding*, the subjective experience of feeling uncomfortable because there are "too many people." For example, we might enjoy being in a high density situation at a rock concert or hockey game but may dislike it intensely in a library or on the subway at rush hour.

As we all know, there are situations in which "three is a crowd" even though there is, objectively, very low density.

Much of the earlier research equated sheer population density with high rates of crime and mental illness: the social-pathology hypothesis. Proponents of this hypothesis point to animal research such as Calhoun's (1962) "Behavioural Sink" study in which a colony of 48 rats was allowed to increase its population to 80 within the same space. Although they were provided with sufficient food and water, these rats exhibited many abnormal behaviours in nest-building, courtship, mating, behaviour with offspring, aggressiveness and, in general, social disorganization was apparent as density increased. Autopsies revealed signs of severe stress, such as enlarged adrenal glands. Clearly, these rats were reacting to crowding. Of course, in nature, the animals would expand their area and reduce density in order to obtain adequate food and water and satisfy territorial needs.

Cities have been blamed for many social ills. Indeed, controlled studies reveal a modest but significant correlation ($r = .35$) between crime and population density if only *those two variables* are considered (Freedman, Heshka and Levy, 1975). However, the most densely populated cities or neighbourhoods tend to be the poorest, and poverty is invariably related to crime and other social problems. When we control statistically for income levels, quality of housing and representation of disadvantaged minority groups, the relationship between density and social problems virtually disappears. This does not negate the possibility that poor people must live in crowded conditions and that crowding is one factor which causes crime. However, the problem does not seem to be intrinsic to cities *per se*. Indeed, the very large differences in crime rates between cities in the U.S. and Canada with similar population densities suggests that the density-social pathology hypothesis is not supportable. We must also remember that in Canada and elsewhere and throughout history, the cities have been and are the centres of activity and creativity in arts, science, commerce, politics, education, entertainment, and cultural diversity. Perhaps the high population density also contributes to advantages in the quality of life.

Theories of crowding   While density-social pathology has withered on the vine, other hypotheses have related crowding to stress. Three theoretical models have been proposed, each pertaining to somewhat different phenomena:

(1) *Sensory overload*. Milgram (1970) argued that when people are exposed to too much stimulation, sensory inputs are received at rates at which they cannot be processed. Crowding is one situation which involves too much actual or potential interaction, excessive physical proximity, and too many people doing too much to pay attention to all of it. People react to sensory overload by screening out much of the stimulation, such as by paying attention only to that which seems most important or unusual, interpreting what is noticed via various cognitive "short-cuts" (Chapter 3), and avoiding involvement, social contact or intimacy. Think of our behaviour on a crowded elevator. To compensate for the unaccustomed physical proximity on elevators, we stand silently with our arms clenched tightly to our sides, facing forward, watching the numbers light up in order to avoid eye contact. On a busy city street, we may not even notice the person who staggers and falls to her knees or we may assume that the person is drunk rather than ill.

The concept of overload is consistent with other work in psychology on the effects of adaptation level. A book entitled *The Lonely Crowd* described this sense of defensive

Some people enjoy studying in a noisy environment.

isolation in cities (Riesman, Glazer and Denny, 1961). However, we must also consider evidence of individual and cultural variation. Certainly, individuals differ in preferred levels of stimulation. Some enjoy studying in noisy rooms, watching TV while carrying on a conversation, and living with a constant background of high volume music. Others prefer to study in quiet surroundings, to watch TV or converse without distraction, and to listen to music undisturbed. To some people, high density situations may be pleasant or exciting while others feel crowded. People vary as to how they feel about city life and many of them live in cities by choice, not simply by necessity.

Milgram derived most of his analyses from observations made in New York City, a city with a very distinctive ambience. We have no evidence that the same symptoms of overload would be equally apparent in other cities in the U.S., in Canada, or in other nations or cultures. Recall that in Chapter 10 we saw evidence of considerable variation in bystander responses in different cultures. The experiences of travellers needing help suggests that we cannot simply consider Edmonton, Québec, Buenos Aires, Havana, London, Rome, Beijing, Tel Aviv, Baghdad, and Kinshasa as identical urban environments. Perhaps cultural habits and norms regarding social interaction, trust, and a sense of community are at least as important as stimulation levels in determining how people relate to each other, even in crowded cities.

(2) *Density intensity.* Freedman (1975) has observed that high density situations tend to be either extremely unpleasant or quite pleasant and exciting. It appears that high density magnifies our usual reactions to situations in the same way that turning up the volume of a stereo, within limits, magnifies our reaction to the music. We tend to enjoy a crowded situation more when it is a situation that we like and less if we dislike the situation to begin with. If we enjoy parties, we enjoy a party more with a lot of people. In fact, a few people in a huge room makes for a dull party and the guests will usually congregate in one corner of the room in order to increase density. If we dislike riding a bus, then a crowded bus is more unpleasant. The notion fits nicely with many of our experiences.

A number of laboratory experiments by Freedman and his colleagues support this hypothesis. In one, subjects worked together to solve complicated problems. The problems involved transforming one word into another by changing one letter at a time such that each change produced an acceptable English word: e.g., transform "gold" to "lead" by the sequence "gold-goad-load-lead." Groups of six to eight subjects worked in either a large room or a small room. Half of the groups in each density condition were given relatively easy problems and succeeded with most of them, while others were confronted with some extremely difficult problems, solving only five or six of the 15 within the time limit.

After the problem-solving sessions, all subjects were asked to rate their experience on a number of dimensions. Those who had a pleasant, successful experience in a small room rated it as being more interesting, lively and, generally, more positive than those who had experienced success in a large room. On the other hand, the groups who failed the task while working in the small room were more negative about their experience than were those in the large room. Thus increasing the density magnified the effects of both successes and failures. Interestingly, subjects in the crowded room were generally more positive about each other, tending to like each other more and perceiving the others as more friendly (Freedman, 1975).

(3) *Loss of control.* With many people in a small space, each person is less able to move around freely and to avoid unwanted social or physical contact. In short, we lose a sense of being in control in a high density situation; thus we experience stress and we feel "crowded" (Baron and Rodin, 1978). This loss of control can make us feel helpless and vulnerable and unable to maintain a degree of privacy (Altman, 1976). It can also lead to problems in coordinating activities and sharing resources; anyone who has lived in a small room or apartment with one or more persons can testify to problems such as eating, working, studying and sleeping schedules, use of the bathroom, TV and telephone, invited guests, and so on. One study (Fleming, Baum and Weiss, 1987) has shown that people in high-density neighbourhoods reported feeling more crowded and less able to control their social environment, and showed more psychological and physiological symptoms of stress.

We have already reviewed considerable evidence that noise is more stressful when it is experienced as unpredictable or uncontrollable. Similar research evidence shows that perceived control is related to the feeling of being crowded. For example, when subjects working in high density conditions were provided with a button to signal to the experimenter that they "wanted out," high density had considerably less effect on their performance or subjective experience (Sherrod, 1974). Just because they were aware that they were free to leave, the effects of high density were less stressful. Thus we don't feel crowded at a game or party because we expected to find a lot of people, we chose to be there, and we know that we are free to leave. On the other hand, people who must live or travel in high density situations may be there due to poverty, housing shortages, or the need to get to work on time. It is this absence of a sense of control over their environment which causes them to feel *crowded*.

Expectations regarding density may also vary between individuals with different experience in life. For example, people from Asian societies may be quite accustomed to living in situations which would seem to be crowded to people from Western societies. When suddenly thrust into the typical low-density living arrangements of North Americans, they might feel quite isolated and uncomfortable.

It is easy to see merit in each of the three models. Indeed, the overload reaction may be seen as a special case of the need to maintain or regain a sense of control, in this case, over the levels and variety of stimulation to which the person must be exposed. A complicating factor is evidence of differences in the way males and females handle overload. In an experiment, all-male and all-female "mock juries" were presented with cases and arrived at decisions in a large or small room. While males in a high-density situation recommended more severe sentences and liked each other less, women gave more lenient sentences in the high-density condition. Other studies have suggested that males tend to react more negatively to high density than females, perhaps because they prefer greater interpersonal distance when interacting with others (Paulus, 1980).

Can we derive any practical guidance from what has been described? Clearly, if perceived control is a problem, then informing people in advance of what to expect will lead to less stress in a high-density situation. Another approach is to change the environment in order to reduce the effects of overcrowding. For example, designing environments to provide for privacy might reduce stress, even in the event of high density. Above all, it is important to recognize that high density *can lead to problems* and to anticipate these problems accurately.

Environment-related attitudes and actions

Of course, nearly everyone is on the "right" side on most environmental issues. Nobody is in favour of the pollution of the air, water, or food supply and most favour, at least in principle, steps to clean up the environment. Most of us understand that our supplies of food and energy are finite and we favour, at least in principle, efforts to conserve agriculturally productive land and energy. While some environmental issues such as nuclear power plants or baby seals are controversial, nobody argues in favour of nuclear contamination, insufficient supplies of electricity, or causing species of seals or of fish to become extinct.

Yet our lifestyles continue to damage the environment by industrial and automobile pollution, wasteful use of energy, littering, and the generation of non-biodegradable waste. As noted in Chapter 4, general attitudes do not in themselves reliably predict actions. In part, this is probably due to the distance between perceived actions and observable consequences; while *you* may be conscientious in putting *your* garbage in the appropriate containers, the environment around you seems to be as littered as always. Unless cultural norms change to recognize these "social traps" and to produce the collective behavioural changes which can have an observable impact, isolated individual behaviours seem futile.

Actions which will benefit the environment may involve trade-offs, sacrifices in our affluent and consumerist lifestyle (recall the discussion of the "tragedy of the commons" in Chapter 14). Two studies illustrate the dilemma of the trade-off problem. Hummel *et al.* (1978) conducted surveys in the same U.S. town, one during and the other after a period in 1974 in which there was an acute shortage of gasoline in the U.S. While the majority of the people tended to blame oil companies and/or environmentalists during the crisis, afterward, more responsibility was attributed to individual consumers. Reflecting the strongly individualistic values of their culture, subjects strongly preferred to conserve energy by voluntary actions rather than mandatory controls. Yet any action on their part to reduce their driving — by walking or using a bus or bicycle — was unrelated to their attitudes regarding what caused the energy crisis. Only one variable was related to this form of energy conservation: the price of gasoline.

Making a point about pollution: But will individuals modify their own behaviour?

In another study, interviews were conducted with 181 adults living in residential areas adjacent to industries which emitted "malodorous gases" (Frenas, 1983). About 17 percent of the sample was employed in these industries and the region had long suffered from economic difficulties. Four general orientations to the trade-off problem were found: (1) a commercialist-expansionist orientation, stressing the absolute necessity for economic expansion and trusting the "conscience of industry" to deal with environmental problems; (2) a reformist orientation, seeing both the necessity and possibility of enhancing environmental quality; (3) a radical, pessimistic view of the possibility of enhancing environmental quality in the existing economic system, leading to reactions of apathetic withdrawal; and (4) sheer denial that there was an environmental problem. The least concern with pollution was expressed by those who felt most threatened by the economic situation, i.e., those employed by the industries and, for some reason, those who lived closest to the offending industry. Perhaps the reduction of cognitive dissonance best explains these findings.

Several conclusions can be drawn from research concerning attitudes and beliefs regarding energy conservation (see Olsen, 1981). First, most people are now convinced that the problem is genuine and serious, regardless of the manipulations of multinational corporations. While general attitudes on the issue are poor predictors of behaviour, beliefs about the specific consequences of personal energy consumption patterns, e.g., how it would affect their own personal comfort, predict behaviour quite well. Finally, increasing awareness on the part of people of how much energy they actually use, along with its cost, can increase conservation. In one study an experimental group of homeowners was provided with meters mounted outside their kitchen windows which displayed their daily consumption of electricity. Homeowners who were daily provided with this immediate feedback consumed an average of 10.5 percent less electricity than did a matched control group whose members were simply billed on a monthly basis (Seligman, Darley and Becker, 1978). In other words, constant monitoring seems necessary to alter wasteful habits.

Design and human factors

Our environment includes roads, houses, apartment buildings, universities, stadia, offices, factories, and shopping centres, that is, the "built environment." Of course, architects are concerned with making their design "work" for the user in addition to making it technically sound and aesthetically pleasing. Increasingly, social psychologists have become concerned with how these designs might be improved. Indeed, architects and interior designers often team up with psychologists, and many schools of architecture include psychologists and psychology courses in their programs.

Let us examine a few research studies which provide scientific foundation for this new collaboration. Baum and colleagues (Baum and Valins, 1977; Baum, Aiello and Calesnick, 1978) investigated the impact of various designs for university residences. Two basic types of dormitory designs were used: (1) single and/or double rooms along a single, long corridor with common social areas and bathrooms shared by all on that floor or wing; and (2) suites of several bedrooms located around a smaller common livingroom and bathroom. While the population density was more or less the same in both designs, the effects on the residents seemed to be quite different.

It was found that students in the suite arrangement tended to be more sociable and friendly. This is not too astonishing since it is much easier to come to know and interact with nine others in close proximity than with 39 others along a large corridor. However, this pattern of social behaviour was also observable in the psychology laboratory. The students, who had been recruited for another experiment, were taken to a waiting room in which another student, hired by the experimenter, was sitting. Suite residents tended to select a chair closer to the other person than did corridor residents and were much more likely to initiate a conversation.

However, it is not possible to conclude that the suite design *caused* these differences in social behaviour in this study. The suites may have been more desirable to many because they were newer units. There may have also been a problem of biased selection of subjects because friendly, sociable people may request suites and less sociable people may prefer corridor arrangements. To overcome these problems, Baum and Davis (1980) obtained permission from a university to institute the proper controls. In the same residence, some floors were converted into suites while others were maintained as long corridors (40 students) or short corridors (20 students). Density was the same in all three settings. Students were randomly assigned to rooms in one of the three living arrangements and were studied repeatedly over the year.

The findings confirmed the hypothesis of how design can influence behaviour. Suite residents perceived their situation as less crowded, although they had the same total living area as the others. They were more successful in making friends and interacted more, both in the residence and in the laboratory. Two factors seem to have been important. First, because of proximity and expectancies, the suite arrangement is more conducive to the development of individual friendship (see Chapter 8 on propinquity and attraction) and to the formation of groups. In addition, the smaller living unit increases the resident's sense of personal control. In the long corridor, residents are constantly required to interact with many people, regardless of personal preferences; thus they experience what we have called overload. The suite residents share their living space only with people whom they come to know quite well. With more control over the demands placed on them to interact and socialize, they are more comfortable and satisfied.

Consider the high-rise apartment building. While many such buildings are very luxurious and expensive, they are often viewed as a less desirable way to live. Of course, the experience can vary considerably and living in a luxurious apartment which is well-maintained, secure, and fashionably located cannot be equated with living in a poorly maintained, public housing building. The findings from research about high-rise living are inconsistent: while some studies have reported that high-rise residents felt socially isolated, more concerned with safety and more crowded, others have reported that they were quite satisfied with their living arrangements and social relations. Perhaps the expectations of people are crucial. High-rise residents may not value a friendly neighbourhood as much as others, which leaves them less vulnerable to disappointment and more likely to compensate for their situation in other ways (Wellman and Whitaker, 1974). While we still have much to learn, we cannot conclude at this point that high-rise living is hazardous to human health or happiness.

Finally, it is important to understand that design changes can be simple yet effective. In the 1950s, a new ward for female geriatric patients was constructed in a hospital in Saskatchewan. Although the common room was tastefully decorated, bright and cheerful, the patients seemed listless, depressed, and withdrawn. Psychological consultants noted that the chairs were lined up neatly, side by side, along the walls, facing in the same direction. When the chairs were rearranged in circles around coffee tables, the frequency of conversation doubled within a few short weeks (Sommer and Ross, 1958). Similarly, in another study pairs of subjects were instructed to listen to music and evaluate it (Mehrabian and Diamond, 1971). The chairs faced each other or were oriented at 90 degree or 180 degree angles, separated at distances of three to nine feet. Before the music began, conversation was more frequent and positive when the chairs faced each other directly. In another experiment, subjects were required to converse at a comfortable distance or at an uncomfortable distance of eleven feet. At a greater distance, subjects not only felt ill at ease but attributed their feelings to their partner rather than to the situation (Aiello and Thompson, 1980). The astute hostess or host will take note when trying to arrange a successful social occasion. Look at the cover of this book. What does it mean to you?

This principle has been applied to the design of "open concept" schools and offices in which there are few, if any, walls or physical barriers. While it has been reasoned that students or workers will interact and communicate more frequently and effectively, the research shows that employees consider "open concept" to be a mixed blessing. Job-related communication and contact is facilitated but privacy is lost (Sundstrom, Herbert and Brown, 1982). Often the lower level employees work in an open concept area, while executives have private offices. Several years ago, a new building at a Canadian university was designed as "open concept," where faculty would work in a communal area rather than in private offices. After almost unanimous and vociferous objections by the academics, private offices were added — to the detriment of the aesthetic design. Privacy and boundaries are felt to be essential to certain types of work.

THE NUCLEAR THREAT

The most important issue of our time is human survival. In our nuclear age, the age-old problem of war and peace has become transformed into a question of whether human life and civilization are to continue. Some theorists and strategists have argued that one side can wage a "limited" nuclear war with the other and win it. However, rarely in history has the side which was losing a war failed to use all of the power available to it and accepted its defeat gracefully. It has been argued that even in a nuclear exchange limited to about 1 percent of existing stockpiles, the smoke and particle pollution from the firestorms would be sufficient to block off a significant amount of sunlight, producing months of relative darkness and cold with a catastrophic effect on the vital oxygen-generating process of photosynthesis (Turco *et al.*, 1983).

Obviously, political, economic, and historical forces will have a decisive influence on our fate. How might psychology, particularly social psychology, be applied to the nuclear issue? Three major themes are considered: (1) the effects of a nuclear war on the behaviour of survivors; (2) the effects of the threat of nuclear war on attitudes and social behaviour; and (3) active responses to the threat. Let us examine some current research pertinent to each theme.

Psychosocial consequences of a nuclear war

How can the consequences of an event which is not only unprecedented but almost unimaginable be predicted? To some extent, it is possible to extrapolate from the only atomic precedents in history, Hiroshima and Nagasaki (Lifton, 1967), although these tragic events were miniscule relative to what we can expect from contemporary nuclear technology. We can also examine other massive historical tragedies such as the Nazi Holocaust inflicted on the European Jews, although a nuclear holocaust would not be so selective. For the most part, we can only use what is known from social psychological research to anticipate how people might react to what scientists can predict about the consequences of a nuclear war.

Let us briefly review several likely psychosocial consequences for the survivors of the blast (Allen, 1985):

(1) Even if the signs of intense international tension are unmistakable, most people tend to deny or ignore the possibility of such a devastating war. The war will be unexpected to most people, and few will evacuate target areas or take whatever protective action may be possible. Collective reactions of panic and paralyzing shock are likely.

(2) Consider that in an instant, your own familiar world will be transformed into unimaginable horror, trauma, and chaos. In a target area, many or most of your family, friends, and associates will be dead or dying. There will be none of the usual facilities such as electricity, running water, public transportation, telephone, or the

media. Services such as police, firefighting, and medical care will be decimated and overwhelmed. Thus physical sickness, depression and other mental illnesses, suicide and crime will be rampant.

(3) In the cold, dark "nuclear winter," food and fuel will be increasingly difficult to obtain. As the economic system will likely break down, bartering and looting will become the primary means of acquiring the necessities of life.

(4) The symptoms of radiation disease will be easily observable. In situations such as that experienced at Hiroshima (Lifton, 1967), "hysterical contagion" became common; many will believe they have the disease, regardless of the reality (see Chapter 14).

(5) People will live in conditions of semi-darkness and filth (because fresh water will be unavailable). They also will tend to join gangs to replace their lost family and other social ties. Such conditions for deindividuation will further reduce inhibitions against violence, looting, and other antisocial acts.

(6) Many people will be physically deformed from the effects of burns and radiation. Unless physical attractiveness becomes suddenly unimportant, stigmatization and rejection of these victims can be expected.

(7) In the complete breakdown of organization in society, democracy will become an early casualty. In such unfavourable conditions, authoritarian leadership will become almost inevitable: the choice will be between chaos and blind obedience to authority (Milgram, 1963).

As discussed earlier, people are compelled to understand, to make sense of their world, to have some sense of what to expect and how to control their fates. How will these survivors understand what happened to them and to their world? The schemata developed to enable people to function in society will be shattered and new ones will emerge in some form. A belief in a just world might lead people to blame each other and to blame themselves, rather than to see themselves as "victims." Or, as do the victims of traumas (Silver et al., 1983), they might search without success for an adequate understanding. The traumatic stress of the experience, and of waiting to die, would be expected to cause a reversion to a more simple-minded and rigid level of thinking. We might expect to see a strong reversion to stereotyping, scapegoating, authoritarianism, acceptance of dogmatic ideologies, and blind obedience — attitudes and behaviours that accompany this mode of cognition. From other historical traumas, we know that many will feel "survivor guilt," and be unable to explain or accept that they have survived and their loved ones have not. As some have suggested, the living may well envy the dead.

Reactions to the nuclear threat

Of course, nobody wants a nuclear war. However, the world has lived with this threat for over thirty years, and life goes on. Public interest in the issue waxes and wanes, with highest interest during periods of international crisis such as Hiroshima (1945), the first U.S.S.R. nuclear test (1953), the U.S. invasion of Cuba (1961), and the big-power confrontation of the 1980s (Klineberg, 1984; Kramer, Kalick and Milburn, 1983). Public concern has been manifested by strong stands taken by certain religious organizations and by peace groups within professions such as medicine, psychology, education, and science. In 1985 an international organization of concerned physicians was awarded the Nobel Peace Prize.

While attitudes toward the nuclear threat vary widely from person to person, five general orientations can be identified (deRivera, 1984):

(1) "It's not really a threat; we can deter them and pull ourselves together after a war."

(2) "It's too frightening to think about, and cannot happen."

(3) "It won't happen in my lifetime but will likely happen someday."

(4) "Why worry since we're helpless."

(5) "It is going to happen and we can't stop it."

Other research shows that people tend to respond in a consistent way about the threat of nuclear war and the dangers of nuclear power stations (Newcomb, 1986). That is, those concerned about nuclear weapons and the possibility of war also tend

TABLE 15-3

Nuclear Attitude Questionnaire Items and average responses

	Males	Females	Significant difference?
1. Nuclear power plants are a safe means of energy production.	+0.03	−0.48	yes
2. I am quite concerned about how many countries have nuclear weapons.	+1.07	+0.84	yes
3. I would feel frightened if I lived within ten miles of a nuclear power plant.	+0.17	+0.88	yes
4. It is essential for our protection that the United States produce as many nuclear weapons as possible.	−0.36	−0.38	no
5. Nuclear power plants are an efficient (cost effective) energy source.	+0.34	−0.02	yes
6. I imagine there will be a nuclear war in the next ten years.	−0.45	−0.08	yes
7. There is a strong link between nuclear power plants and nuclear weapons.	−0.11	+0.08	yes
8. It is a good idea for the United States to supply other countries with nuclear power plants.	−0.64	−0.86	yes
9. I feel frightened when I think of all the nuclear weapons in the world.	+0.53	+0.82	yes
10. I imagine I would survive a nuclear war.	−0.76	−0.75	no
11. I have never really worried about nuclear war.	−0.18	−0.36	no
12. Many people tend to overreact about the threat of nuclear war.	+0.10	−0.32	yes
13. There are times I have felt depressed thinking about the possibility of nuclear war.	−0.30	−0.06	yes
14. The world feels like a very dangerous place because of so many nuclear weapons.	+0.08	+0.27	yes
15. I have no hesitancy about raising a child with the threat of nuclear war.	+0.62	+0.18	yes

NOTE: Subjects respond on 5-point Likert scale; scores can range from −2 (strongly disagree) to +2 (strongly agree).

SOURCE: Newcomb, 1986

to be concerned about accidents at nuclear power stations, and analyses of their responses to the various items (see Table 15.3) reveal an underlying "nuclear anxiety." The data have shown relatively high levels of nuclear anxiety in a young California sample. Women exhibit somewhat higher levels of concern, perhaps because they tend to be more willing to express emotional states than men.

How does nuclear anxiety affect people's lives? Newcomb (1986) included measures of a number of relevant variables. In this study, subjects with high scores in nuclear anxiety also tended to see their own lives as unsatisfying and without purpose, reported having experienced more symptoms of depression, and were more likely to be heavy dieters and users of illicit drugs. Males and females reacted somewhat differently. Women with high nuclear anxiety tended more strongly to feel that their lives were unsatisfying and without purpose, while the link between nuclear anxiety and heavy drug involvement was stronger among males. Clearly, for many people, the threat of nuclear accidents and war significantly affects their emotional well-being.

Reactions of children Of particular interest are the attitudes of young people who have lived their entire lives in the nuclear age and must consider their future in relation to this threat. In one large-scale study in the U.S., most children were reported to be aware of the threat before the age of 12, and many of them felt that the issue influenced their daily thinking (Beardslee and Mack, 1982). When young people in Finland were asked to list their three greatest worries about the future, nuclear war headed the list. Interestingly, 12-year-olds expressed the most worry, and the possibility of nuclear war was mentioned less frequently in older groups.

Goldberg *et al.* (1985) conducted an intensive study of the attitudes of youth in grades seven to 12 in Ontario. In order to avoid the possibility that the interview itself might arouse anxiety about the nuclear threat, the questions were relatively open-ended and touched on "concerns about the future" with regard to employment and personal career goals, as well as the nuclear issue. Subjects were asked how much they talked, thought, and worried about each issue, how much information they had from various sources, and to what extent they felt capable of influencing the future course of events. The results indicated that while nuclear war was a frequent spontaneous worry, students were also preoccupied with unemployment and with their own career plans. Thus the nuclear threat did not overtly intrude in most subjects' future concerns.

A closer analysis of the data revealed that those who were *most* preoccupied with the nuclear threat also felt that there were *greater* opportunities to control and influence this threat. They did not react to their concern about war with helplessness and withdrawal from the future — in fact, those preoccupied with the nuclear threat were also the most involved with their own career plans. On the other hand, those who expressed little or no concern about the nuclear threat and felt helpless about it showed little interest in planning their own futures. In this group, the anxiety about the nuclear threat appears to have produced a defensive reaction in which subjects ignore the issue and feel that their future is beyond their control. Perhaps our culture of "instant gratification" (mass media entertainment, video games, fast food, "consumerism") reflects this sense of a lost future (Schwebel, 1982).

Attitudes and actions As we saw in Chapter 4, attitudes are not in themselves highly reliable predictors of behaviour. In the case of the nuclear threat, the sheer magnitude of the problem means that the individual has relatively little scope for effective action.

Indeed, the majority do not act at all. In this light, let us examine in some detail two innovative studies.

Among those who act in response to the nuclear threat are two groups: (1) anti-nuclear activists who choose political involvement in the hope of averting war or reducing risk; and (2) "survivalists," those who accept the inevitability of nuclear war, and act by stockpiling food, fuel, medicines and weapons, and arranging for shelter.

Intensive interviews were conducted in the U.S.A. with both types of activists and with a sample of people who were not affiliated with either type of group (Tyler and McGraw, 1983). All subjects were asked whether they believed a nuclear war to be (1) preventable and (2) survivable. The correlation between the two beliefs was − .51, indicating that those who believed in one did not believe in the other. As expected, anti-nuclear activists believed war to be preventable but believed that it was not survivable, while survivalists expected a war and hoped to survive. Activists tended in general to be politically liberal and to have internal locus of control beliefs ("What happens to me is a result of what I do"), while survivalists tended to be politically conservative and have external locus of control beliefs ("What happens to me is a result of chance, fate, and powerful other people").

Subjects were questioned in detail about their attributions about war and peace. That is, they were asked to what extent they perceived that war or peace would be caused by the general public, the government, or by chance — beyond the control of identifiable causes. They also were asked to indicate who they believed *ought* to control what happens. Again, a sharp contrast was apparent between the two groups. Anti-nuclear activists tended to see war as caused by both governments and citizens such as themselves. However, survivalists attributed causality to forces beyond their control or responsibility.

In a similar vein, Fiske, Pratto and Pavelchak (1983) asked the following of their subjects: "Almost everyone has thought of the possibility of a nuclear war and what it would be like. We are interested in what things come to mind when you think about a nuclear war. Please name off the top of your head the first few things that you think of when you imagine a nuclear war." Responses were analyzed in terms of their "images" of a nuclear war.

Several findings are of interest: Those who favoured a contained military escalation and opposed the peace movement tended not to respond directly to the question. Apart from referring to the familiar mushroom-shaped cloud and estimates of casualty figures, these subjects generally described such a war as limited in scope and one which could be survived. Some of their responses contained non-nuclear imagery, such as the possibility of the Soviet Union ruling the world. Among the others, images of nuclear war differed between those who were and those who were not politically active. Activists tended to express vivid, *concrete* images, such as the destruction of buildings, fire, illness, and deaths of specific people, as well as emotional reactions, such as terror or not knowing what to do. Non-activists tended to express more abstract images, such as the end of the civilized world, and offered explanations in terms of politics or religious doctrine, or numerical estimates of casualties. Other variables related to activist behaviour included favourable attitudes toward a nuclear freeze and other means of reducing tension with the U.S.S.R., a sense of personal involvement with the issue and, rather surprisingly, a belief that a nuclear war was *not* very probable. Other data show that activists tend to be politically involved in other ways, although it is not known whether this political involvement preceded their anti-nuclear activity (Watanabe and Milburn, 1986).

These findings are consistent with those of other studies discussed earlier. It seems that those who have more terrifying and concrete images of nuclear war see it as preventable if people *act*. In the end, they believe that war is not likely to happen *because* they are taking action to prevent it. Other research also shows that those who are active in the peace movement tend to be more hopeful and tend to be active on other political issues (Watanabe and Milburn, 1986).

Influencing reactions to the threat

The research reviewed thus far suggests that the attitudes of many people are frozen into helplessness, apathy, avoidance and non-involvement. This is arguably a rational reaction to an irrational reality. However, from the point of view of both individual mental health and the possibility of influencing history, it would seem desirable to induce a sense of involvement and action. Many attempts have been made to modify attitudes by means of direct persuasive communication, with varying results. Of greater interest are the studies of the effects on attitudes and behaviour of media presentations of nuclear war.

In one study, subjects were shown the film *Hiroshima-Nagasaki: 1945*, which contained actual vivid footage of the explosions and their effects (Granberg and Faye, 1972). A questionnaire was administered to some subjects before and after the film, to others only after the film, and to a control group before and after another, irrelevant film. The subjects were presented with ten scenarios which varied in the degree to which the U.S.A. was presented as having been provoked by the U.S.S.R. They were asked to indicate the degree of provocation which would be sufficient to justify the use of nuclear weapons by the U.S.A., and to indicate the highest level of casualties which would be tolerable if the U.S.A. were to become involved in a nuclear exchange. The effects of the film were to raise the threshold of provocation and to lower the tolerance level for casualties. That is, subjects were willing to accept greater provocation but fewer casualties before indicating that they would be willing (hypothetically) to approve a nuclear retaliation. Although subjects' *expectations* of surviving a nuclear war were not influenced, they were less certain that they would *want* to survive, and they reported greater anxiety about nuclear weapons. Thus, at least in the short run, viewing a graphic film of the only nuclear attacks in history seemed to sensitize subjects to the actual consequences of what had been to them an abstract issue, and to induce greater restraint.

On November 20, 1983, *The Day After*, a film depicting the aftermath of a nuclear attack on inhabitants of an American city, was shown on a U.S. television network in prime time on the Sunday evening preceding the U.S. Thanksgiving holiday. It was surrounded by publicity before and after, including headlines in major newspapers, cover stories in magazines, and condemnation by right-wing television evangelists. It attracted over 100 million viewers in the U.S. alone, plus millions of others in Canada, Europe, Japan, and elsewhere. While it was not generally considered an artistic triumph, it was a major public event at that time.

By means of public opinion polls and more intensive investigations (Schofield and Pavelchak, 1984, 1985; Oskamp *et al.*, 1985), a unique opportunity has been provided to gauge the effects of the film. First, it is striking to note that attitude change was equally likely among those who saw the film and those who had not. Obviously, the considerable public attention, discussion, and controversy increased the levels of salience and awareness of the nuclear issue. However, the effects were rather weak with regard to attitudes toward nuclear weapons and expectations surrounding war and the possibility of survival.

Several reasons have been suggested to account for the minimal impact of the film:

(1) As we discussed earlier (Chapter 5), persuasive communication based on the arousal of fear can be effective if the level of fear is moderate and if explicit recommendations are given about what to do and how to do it. The nuclear event is presented in the film as having somehow occurred, and nothing is said about why it happened or how it might have been prevented.

(2) Public opinion polls indicate that most people, when asked, see nuclear war as very possible. Thus we are accustomed to being aware at some level of the threat, and the film did not provide any new or surprising insights.

(3) Advance publicity warned of (or promised) an overwhelming emotional experience. However, the film was a rather restrained, even sanitized, portrayal of massive suffering and death (evidently, the network censors ruled that a maximum of three deaths could be shown for every seven buildings or other inanimate objects destroyed). The research showed that, to a public accustomed to the unrestrained violence and goriness of many contemporary U.S. movies, the film was "pretty tame stuff."

(4) While it did not have a happy or hopeful ending, the movie's plot was similar to the "disaster movie script" used so successfully and repeatedly to portray earthquakes, hurricanes, fires, sinking ships, or airplanes in trouble. In this familiar script, we come to know and identify with mostly likeable characters as they experience a disaster which is portrayed with impressive "special effects." One group of subjects rated the film as being more similar to other disaster movies than to what they thought would actually happen during a nuclear war.

Yet the data show that there were some observable effects which were apparent during the period in which the film was shown. Before the show, 58 percent indicated agreement with the statement that "Nuclear war is a real threat but I tend to put it out of my mind," while 26 percent indicated that they were actually "worried" about it. After the film, 88 percent indicated that they were worried and only 10 percent

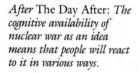

After The Day After: *The cognitive availability of nuclear war as an idea means that people will react to it in various ways.*

said that they could put it out of their mind. A post-movie panel discussion attracted a large audience, indicating a desire for more information, which is a common and effective way to reduce stress. For many, the movie evoked more "concrete images" of nuclear destruction (Fiske, Pratto and Pavelchak, 1983), despite the "disaster movie script." Moreover, more people indicated an intention to become involved in anti-nuclear activities, such as requesting to be on the mailing lists of relevant groups or writing to political leaders. Activist groups reported increased interest in the period following the movie. While no long-term data have been reported, it does appear the public involvement has remained relatively high during this decade.

A film and media event such as *The Day After* increased the *cognitive availability* of nuclear war as an idea and a set of images (Oskamp *et al.*, 1985). While the threat of nuclear war could thus become a schema used to interpret the world, individuals have differed in how these images of nuclear war would influence their thoughts and actions. Some have sought more information, some have become active in the peace movement, some have pressed for greater military strength, some have built fallout shelters, some have reacted with black humour. But for a period of time after the airing of the film, the issue could not be ignored.

A FINAL PERSPECTIVE

Lewin's vision of social psychology was of a science based on rigorous research which was directed to the solution of real-life problems. While the problems of an imperfect system of justice, a degraded environment, and the nuclear sword of Damocles are still with us, the research has become remarkably sophisticated, based on sound methodology and good theory. We have learned much about the reliability of eyewitness testimony, the effects of density and crowding, and the nature of life in the nuclear age.

Perhaps the "relevance" or "applicability" of social psychology must be seen in a different light. Research may indeed, in some cases, provide us with solutions, with a "psychotechnology" to design more livable environments, or a more just judicial system. The research may also give us new insights, new perspectives, or ways of looking at the issues which concern us. Indeed, we may arrive at a more realistic view of human nature and what is humanly possible or desirable (Miller, 1969). When we can better understand ourselves, we may begin to address our problems more successfully.

SUMMARY

(1) Social psychology has always been concerned with reciprocal, two-way influences of laboratory or real-life issues and vice-versa. It can also contribute to more realistic conceptions of human nature and to the development and evaluation of social policies.

(2) The reliability of eyewitness testimony is questionable, even if the witness seems confident. Important factors include: police lineup procedures; the nature of the incident; cross-racial identification; and the threat of violence.

(3) Testimony is influenced by techniques of questioning.

(4) Findings from simulated jury studies indicate bias in the selection of jurors and biases among jurors which are related to authoritarianism. Reducing jury size would create serious problems. Jurors often ignore judges' restrictions regarding the admissibility of evidence.

(5) Environmental stress is closely tied to a person's perceived ability to control his or her environment, regardless of intensity. The effects of noise, heat and cold, and pollution have been studied.

(6) Density is not equivalent to crowding, and a high density may or may not be related to social problems and individual discomfort. Important theories are: a) sensory overload, leading to "screening out" stimuli, and apparent apathy; b) density intensity — high-density situations magnify people's usual reactions in that situation; and c) loss of control, the key determinant of whether people feel crowded in a high-density situation.

(7) Environmentally relevant behaviour is often inconsistent with attitudes. The "trade-off" between personal cost and environmental benefit is often crucial.

(8) The design of residential and other buildings influences how people behave and feel. Privacy, opportunity to interact, and the perception of control are crucial.

(9) Concern over the nuclear threat persists among children and adults, as does the threat itself. Devastating psychosocial consequences of such a war are predicted. Reactions to the threat vary from intense anxiety to a defensive apathy or belligerence. Those most anxious about it tend to feel depressed and dissatisfied with life, and may become heavily involved with drugs. However, intense concern with the threat has also been related to activism, particularly when the individuals think of nuclear war in terms of concrete images rather than abstractions.

(10) Films and TV shows which portray nuclear war tend to heighten awareness and cognitive availability of the issue, but have minor effects on attitudes and behaviour.

FURTHER READING

BAUM, A. and VALINS, S. (1977). *Architecture and social behavior*. Hillsdale, NJ: Erlbaum.

FISHER, R.J. (1982). *Social psychology. An applied approach*. New York: St. Martin's Press.

FREEDMAN, J.L. (1975). *Crowding and behavior*. San Francisco: Jossey-Bass.

KONECNI, V.J. and EBBESEN, E.B. (1982). *The criminal justice system: A social psychological analysis*. San Francisco: Freeman.

SAKS, M.J. and HASTIE, R. (1978). *Social psychology in court*. New York: Van Nostrand.

SOMMER, R. (1969). *Personal space*. Englewood Cliffs: Prentice-Hall.

THOMPSON, J. (1985). *Psychological aspects of nuclear war*. Chichester: J. Wiley.

WELLS, G.L. and LOFTUS, E.A. (1984). *Eyewitness testimony: Psychological perspectives*. New York: Cambridge.

WHITE, R.E. (Ed.) (1986). *Psychology and the prevention of nuclear war*. New York: New York University Press.

YARMEY, D. (1979). *The psychology of eyewitness testimony*. New York: Free Press.

C·H·A·P·T·E·R S·I·X·T·E·E·N

Health and Illness

It is much more important to know what sort of patient has the disease than what sort of disease the patient has.
Sir William Osler

Trying to understand drug addiction by studying drugs makes about as much sense as trying to understand holy water by studying water.
Thomas Szasz

FOR REFLECTION

- Why do we sometimes ignore common sense advice about our health?
- Are some people more likely than others to develop problems with alcohol or drugs?
- Can stress or depression affect people's health?
- What is a "good patient"? Is being a good patient good for your health?
- What causes people to adopt a healthy lifestyle?

IN THE TWENTIETH century there has been a dramatic shift in the causes of death in industrialized nations from *infectious diseases* (typhoid, cholera, smallpox, poliomyelitis, tuberculosis) to accidents and the major *chronic diseases* (coronary and circulatory, respiratory, cancers). While medical technology has advanced and medical care has become more widely accessible, the most important contributions to the control of infectious diseases have been in the area of public health measures such as sanitation and immunization. A similar strategy of public health would be effective with respect to today's killer diseases, particularly by influencing people to adopt healthier lifestyles (Lalonde, 1974).

It is important to understand that these life-threatening illnesses are in part caused by voluntary behaviour. For example, the major risk factors in coronary heart disease

B·O·X   16-1

FEAR OF FATNESS AS A FEMALE DILEMMA

Clearly, obesity is a health risk. However, *being* obese is not the same as *feeling* "too fat." In our society, women in particular are prone to feeling that they are too fat. They may become "chronic dieters" (Herman and Polivy, 1975), although their concerns about dieting are not significantly related to their actual weight. More and more women are being diagnosed as suffering from eating disorders, including bulimia (episodes of severe binge eating) and anorexia nervosa (pursuit of excessive thinness, often to the point of self-starvation). It is important to understand that we are discussing an obsession with thinness which is related to social norms, not with health. It is a widespread concern, obvious in the huge proliferation of the diet book/diet food business. In one recent survey of a selected female population (readers of the American *Glamour* magazine), subjects were asked to choose which among four alternatives would make them happiest. Losing weight was selected by 42 percent, while 22 percent chose success at work, 21 percent dating a special man and 14 percent hearing from an old friend (Fallon and Rozin, 1984).

As we saw in Chapter 6, physical attractiveness is an important determinant of our impressions of people — "Beautiful is good" (Dion, Berscheid and Walster, 1972). Clearly, body weight is crucial to the impression of attractiveness, especially for women. Beginning in childhood, we have a negative stereotype regarding fat people. In one study (Staffieri, 1972) thin and fat children were shown silhouettes of children of various body types, and rated the endomorphic (i.e., relatively fat) child as "lazy, sloppy, mean, stupid, a cheater, dirty, argues a lot." While there were no differences between the thin and fat children in stereotyping, girls were more severe than boys. Canning and Mayer (1966) followed up a sample of graduating high school students in the U.S.A. Among the males, 53 percent of the non-obese and 50 percent of the obese graduates went on to university or college. However, among the females, significantly fewer obese (32 percent) than non-obese (52 percent) graduates continued their studies. Note that *no differences* were found between obese and non-obese in grades or measure of academic ability, and equal numbers actually applied. For some reason, there seems to have been discrimination against relatively obese women by those who made decisions on college admissions. These and many other studies show that in both

include cigarette smoking, stress, excessive alcohol use, lack of aerobic fitness, serum cholesterol (related in part to diet), and hypertension (stress-related and treatable by medication). Cancer risk is related to excessive exposure to tobacco smoke, alcohol, environmental and worksite pollutants, and certain foods. Thus our efforts to reduce illness and mortality should shift from medical treatment to *prevention*.

Perhaps in response to the new emphasis on health promotion, many changes in attitudes and behaviour have occurred over the past decade. For example, cigarette smoking has been drastically restricted, decaffeinated beverages have become popular, sales of many types of alcoholic beverages have declined, many people enroll in weight reduction programs and purchase diet books, and physical fitness has become a major popular concern. While concern may become an obsession for some (see Box 16-1),

obvious and non-obvious ways, our society is blatantly unfair to obese women.

It is also clear that our conception of what is "fat," "thin," and "normal" is unusual in that we prescribe a *very* thin ideal. Readers from families and cultural backgrounds outside of North America (e.g., most European cultures) will know this to be true: the ideal has actually become underweight. Contestants for the Miss America pageants and models in *Playboy* magazine centrefolds were actually thinner in 1979 than in 1959 (Garner, Garfinkel, Schwartz and Thompson, 1980). Ironically, during this period, actuarial data show that the typical woman had become heavier. It is unfortunate that as we discard sex role stereotypes in careers and relationships, we impose an extremely narrow one regarding physical beauty.

It is important to understand that the contemporary social norms for "fatness" and "thinness" are unrealistic in terms of biology (Rodin, Silberstein and Striegel-Moore, 1984). Some studies show that heredity is involved, that some people are genetically predisposed to be thinner or fatter than others. For example, identical twins, even when raised apart, tend to be more similar in weight than non-identical twins or siblings. This supports the hypothesis that most of us know by experience — that we differ in how we metabolize food and store fat (some can "pig out" and remain thin while others balloon at the sight of a pralines-and-cream ice cream cone!). Women tend to have lower rates of basal metabolism and a higher proportion of fat to lean tissues. There is also some evidence that the hormonal changes which accompany puberty, pregnancy, and menopause tend to induce increased fat storage. While women may blame themselves for the weight gain, it may be only a part of the natural course of biological development.

Thus cultural norms clash with biological reality to impose an unrealistic standard of "thinness" and attractiveness on women. And women respond with frantic attempts to diet. The "diet reaction" has been described by Susan Brownmiller (1984) as a form of self-mutilation equivalent to foot-binding or wearing an excruciatingly tight corset — all in the pursuit of "beauty." The final irony is that dieting tends not to be effective over time and most of the weight lost is regained — up to a point that is probably the person's genetically predisposed, natural weight. Indeed, evidence is accumulating that dieting is in itself harmful in that it disrupts the systems which metabolize food, leaving people more liable to gain weight when they eat. Polivy and Herman (1983) document a persuasive case for "breaking the diet habit." The roots of the habit are social and the habit itself may not be healthful.

and while good intentions are not always translated into action, more and more people are serious about following a healthier lifestyle.

During this same period social psychologists have also become interested in the problems of illness and health (Matarazzo, 1982). An understanding of why people choose to act in ways which enhance or undermine their health can lead to more effective public health measures. In addition, a better understanding of the social relationship between patients and physicians can contribute to a more effective practice of medicine and to better health and recovery from illness. Through the application of effective persuasion and through attitude change, people may be convinced to adopt healthier lifestyles.

This chapter reviews several areas of applied social psychological inquiry. First, several health-risk behaviours are discussed, such as excessive alcohol and tobacco use. Then the social implications of illness are explored, emphasizing in particular the patient-physician relationship. Finally, several contributions of social psychology to health promotion and the prevention of illness are presented.

HEALTH-RISK BEHAVIOUR

Among the major mysteries of human nature is why people persist in indulging in patterns of behaviour which they know to be hazardous to their lives or health. Excessive eating of junk foods, excessive gambling, driving recklessly and without seat belts, compulsive overworking, cigarette smoking, alcohol and drug abuse, and forgetting about exercise are among such behaviour patterns.

It must be understood that the relevant problem in this context is not necessarily an addiction but an excessive appetite for various pleasures which are not harmful in moderation (Orford, 1985). The evidence shows that repeated exposure to a drug and physiological dependence do not adequately explain why some users come to feel "dependent" on the drug or to use it excessively (Alexander and Hadaway, 1982). Even many addicts withdraw successfully from heroin, alcohol, or nicotine, and *then* relapse months or years later (Marlatt and Gordon, 1979). Many U.S. soldiers became addicted to high-quality heroin while participating in the Vietnam war, yet only 12 percent of them were still addicted three years after their return to the U.S.A. (Robins, 1978). In the U.K., cancer patients kept on a combination of heroin, cocaine, and alcohol (the Brompton Cocktail) to relieve pain tend to come off these narcotics easily if their cancer goes into remission (Twycross, 1974). In short, the causes of the excessive use of a drug are not found primarily in the drug itself but in the person who uses it and the circumstances in which it is used.

Problem behaviour theory

Much research has been devoted to finding the cause of excessive drug use in certain characteristics of the person or the environment. A more comprehensive and integrated approach is represented by Jessor's *problem behaviour theory* (Jessor and Jessor, 1977). In this approach, excessive alcohol or other drug use by adolescents is not viewed in isolation as the outcome of becoming "hooked" on the drug, but as a behaviour consistent with what the adolescent is like as a person (a "personality system"), how the adolescent is reacting to his or her home life and peer group (a

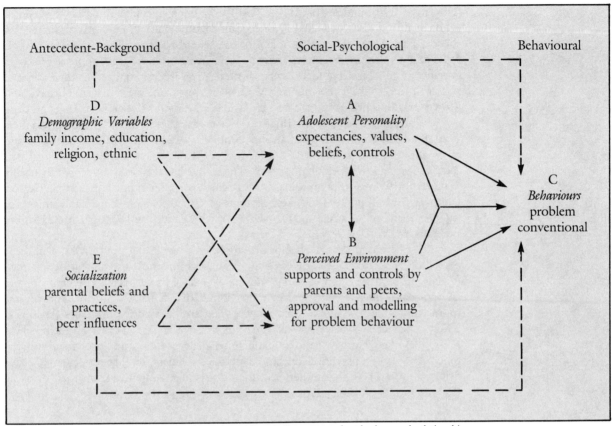

NOTE: Solid lines denote primary relationships; dotted lines indicate antecedent-background relationship.

SOURCE: Jessor and Jessor, 1977.

FIGURE 16-1
Problem behaviour theory

"perceived environment system"), and what the adolescent tends to be involved with apart from drugs (a "behaviour system"). (The model is presented in Figure 16-1). Several similar models, all based on the principle of interaction among person, environmental, and behavioural attributes, have generated extensive research in this area (see Sadava, 1987).

In problem behaviour theory, personality variables include low expectancies for success in school, high values for independence, and reduced constraints, represented by low religiosity and tolerant attitudes toward deviant behaviour. In the social environment, predispositions to problem behaviour include the perception that rewards for socially accepted behaviours are lacking, opportunities for problem behaviour are present, and that the influence of peer groups, particularly with respect to behaviours such as heavy drinking, is greater than that of the parents. Problem drinking also tends to be part of a more general pattern of *behaviour*, including marijuana and other drug use, deviant/delinquent acts such as lying and stealing, and precocious sexual involvement, along with less participation in conventional activities in school and church. The entire syndrome of personal, environmental, and behavioural characteristics is described as "non-conventional."

The problem behaviour model is being tested in a longitudinal study of high school and university students who are now being followed into their fourth decade of life

(Donovan, Jessor and Jessor, 1983). Results obtained thus far show that the level of problem drinking is correlated at one point in time with "non-conventional" psychosocial attributes. That is, problem drinkers tend to expect less success in school, value independence from their parents, are less involved in religion, approve or accept deviance in general, have friends who drink heavily, are less attached to their parents, and are more likely to be involved with illicit drugs and other deviant behaviours. Moreover, it has proven possible to predict, from early data, when drinking and drug use will begin. It is also interesting to observe that those who are problem drinkers as adults did not show unusual alcohol problems as adolescents but did show more marijuana use, had friends who engaged in problem behaviours, and expressed attitudes reflecting lower personal controls. The model has also been supported by results of several other major longitudinal studies which used a national U.S. sample (Jessor, Donovan and Widmer, 1980) and samples of Canadian high school and university students (Schlegel, Manske and D'Avernas, 1985; DiTecco and Schlegel, 1982; Sadava and Forsyth, 1977a, 1977b).

It must be noted that alcohol or drug problems, including health risks, cannot be predicted accurately by knowing *only* how much alcohol or drugs are consumed (Sadava, 1985). For example, while the rate of alcohol problems is considerably higher among males than females, research also shows that females who drink heavily are more vulnerable to adverse consequences than are heavy-drinking males (Wilsnack, 1982). The fact that heavy drinkers are more likely to engage in other problem behaviours, including excessive smoking and other drug use, also increases their vulnerability. And certain psychological states, such as loneliness, tend to render some heavy drinkers more likely than others to suffer adverse consequences from their drinking (Sadava and Thompson, 1986).

Modelling influences

In Chapter 6, it was shown that social influence may often be unintentional, and that our actions are often modelled after those observed in others (Bandura, 1977). Recall that there are three ways in which modelling may influence behaviour: in the *acquisition* or learning of a new behaviour, in the *inhibition or disinhibition* of a behaviour in certain situations, and in direct, immediate *imitation* at a given time (response facilitation). Thus the peer group may influence the adolescent to begin smoking, may influence where and when smoking occurs (for example, seeing a friend punished for smoking in school may inhibit smoking there), or may facilitate smoking at a given time (she lights up, then he lights up).

An important modelling influence is the behaviour of the parents. Several studies show that there is a high degree of consistency between parents and adolescents with regard to the use of drugs (Smart and Fejer, 1972). Parents who frequently use alcohol and tranquillizers and who smoke cigarettes are much more likely to have teenagers who drink, smoke cigarettes, use tranquillizers, and use marijuana and other illicit drugs. This is explained in terms of social modelling, in which the child learns to use psychoactive drugs as part of daily life or in reaction to emotional distress. It has also been demonstrated through longitudinal research that when adolescents have parents who drink heavily, they tend to seek out friends who drink heavily, and then begin to drink in the same manner as they do (Huba, Dent and Bentler, 1980).

An important modelling influence for children is the behaviour of their parents.

Modelling influences on drinking behaviour have also been shown in empirical studies in which the drinking behaviour of patrons in four Vancouver taverns was observed (Cutler and Storm, 1975). It was reported that patrons tended to drink at a relatively constant *rate* of almost three drinks per hour, regardless of the size of the group or the time spent in the tavern. However, larger groups tended to stay longer in the tavern (ordering rounds); thus individuals actually consumed more. Since this rate of drinking is above the rate at which alcohol can be metabolized, the blood alcohol levels of people in larger drinking groups eventually reached higher levels, and intoxication was therefore more frequent.

Do people who are drinking together actually influence the drinking of each other directly, or do they simply enjoy the social occasion for a longer time? In a laboratory experiment, subjects were asked to taste several wines, and to rate each on flavour, aroma, and other characteristics. The task involved allowing subjects to take any amount — from one small sip to an entire beaker — if they wished, of each wine. Another "subject" in the wine-tasting task, a "stooge" of the experimenter, drank either a lot or a little of each wine. Subjects who participated with a heavy-drinking model consumed significantly more than those with a light drinker or those without a partner (Caudill and Marlatt, 1975).

The experiment was repeated in a bar (Reid, 1978). Two observers, one male and one female, sat at a corner table, acting as an "affectionate couple" in order to avoid intrusion by waiters, waitresses, or other patrons. Other confederates of the experimenter, who were trained to behave in a friendly or cold way to single patrons at the bar, consumed either one or five drinks during a one-hour period. (Models were all selected for having a relatively high tolerance for alcohol). As you will recall (Chapter 6), models may inhibit or disinhibit behaviour, depending on factors such as whether the person likes or dislikes the model. When the model in this study behaved warmly to the subjects, the subjects' drinking was strongly influenced by the drinking of the model. However, the level of drinking by a cold, unlikable model did not affect consumption by the subjects. These studies emphasize that there are strong social influences on the actions that people take, including many which may have implications for health.

Thus far, we have seen that social psychological variables can influence the extent to which people act to protect or endanger their health. Apart from choices in behaviour, individuals also differ greatly in how vulnerable they are to certain illnesses. Let us examine some of the evidence.

Vulnerability to illness

Research has shown that people with certain personal characteristics and in certain stressful social circumstances (see Boxes 16-2 and 16-3) are more vulnerable to a range of diseases and disabilities, and are less likely to recover successfully. Let us look briefly at research pertaining to three important factors related to vulnerability: social support, perceived control, and the "coronary-prone personality."

Social support   In 1951, Janis conducted a study of how soldiers coped with the conditions of combat. He found that those who were able and willing to endure such severe stress belonged to a cohesive combat unit. Those who did not belong to

B · O · X   16 - 2

MAJOR STRESS AND MINOR HASSLES: WHAT REALLY AFFECTS US

We all know and accept that our physical health and well-being can be adversely affected by what happens to us. Holmes and Rahe (1967) proposed that it is the major changes in our lives that create stress and can cause problems. They developed a "social readjustment scale" which, based on research, measures the impact of such changes. The following are examples (the numbers refer to "life change units" or the relative amount of disruption or readjustment caused):

Death of spouse	100
Divorce	73
Jail term	63
Personal illness/injury	53
Marriage	50
Fired at work	47
Retirement	45
Pregnancy	40
Sexual difficulties	39
Mortgage or major loan	31
Trouble with boss	23
Change in social activities	18
Vacation	13

While the notion of life-change stress has been applied in much useful research, it has also been criticized. For example, the weightings for each event were derived from a particular sample and time and may differ considerably for other times, places, and people. In addition, the weightings do not account for the quality of the event. For example, they would predict that divorce (73) is more stressful if the person subsequently marries (50), while common sense would suggest otherwise.

Richard Lazarus and colleagues (Kanner, Coyne, Schaefer and Lazarus, 1981) argue that most of us can cope with most crises quite well, and that it is the minor, daily hassles of life that take their toll. The annoyances of commuting to work on a crowded bus or freeway, the delivery that does not show up, a missing and desperately needed book in the library, the repair job that must be done over, the car that won't start on a January morning, the "mouthy" teenager or whining child, minor arguments with friends — these are examples of daily hassles which infect our lives. Kanner *et al.* (1981) found the following to be the "top ten" of daily hassles:

Hassle	Percentage of respondents
Concern about weight	52.4
Health of family member	48.1
Increased price of common goods	43.7
Home maintenance	42.8
Too many things to do	38.6
Misplacing or losing things	38.1
Yard or outside home maintenance	38.1
Property investment, taxes	37.6
Crime	37.1
Physical appearance	35.9

They argue that the major life changes have their main effects by increasing the daily levels of hassles. These and several other studies suggest significant linkages with physical and emotional health (Stone and Neale, 1982; DeLongis *et al.*, 1982). It is also suggested that positive everyday experiences ("daily uplifts") may contribute to our health. Commonly endorsed examples of daily uplifts include relating well to spouse or lover (76.3 percent) and to friends (74.4 percent), completing a task (73.3 percent), getting enough sleep (69.7 percent), and eating out (68.4 percent), although surely the last example would be dependent on the restaurant.

THE LOSS EFFECT:
BEREAVEMENT, PSYCHOLOGY AND IMMUNOLOGY

Inevitably, we must all cope with the death of a family member, spouse or lover, or close friend. Beyond the painful period of mourning and the permanent sense of loss, there is evidence that such a death can threaten the health of the survivors. Careful analyses of data from Britain, Japan, the U.S.A., and West Germany show that in the year following the death of a spouse, the survivor is more likely to die than persons of the same age group who have not been widowed. When we control statistically for the possibility of suicide and of death from the same illness or accident, we still have a significantly higher mortality rate: the *loss effect* (Stroebe, Stroebe, Gergen and Gergen, 1982).

How can this be explained? Certainly, it is related to stress. The loss of a spouse is rated by most people as the most stressful of all conceivable life changes (Holmes and Rahe, 1967, see Box 16-2). Of course, the surviving spouse has lost the social and emotional support of intimacy (recall evidence of the devastating effects of loneliness presented in Chapter 6). In addition, he or she now must assume sole responsibility for matters which were formerly

shared — finances, running the home, parenting, to name a few. Interestingly, males seem to more adversely affected by the loss effect than are females. Perhaps women are more able to seek and obtain social support from family and friends.

While metaphors such as "broken-hearted" and the "loss of will to live" convey the devastating sense of loss, the most likely physical link to the loss effect is through the immune system. Clearly, physiological systems can be measurably affected by psychological factors; for example, brief exposure to erotic stimuli produces measurable physiological changes. Under certain stressful conditions, the manufacture and circulation of white blood cells tends to be somewhat diminished (Maier and Laudenslager, 1985). Reduced immunological defenses would leave the person more vulnerable to the effects of "foreign" elements such as bacteria, viruses, cancers. In the current period of intensive research in immunology, spurred in part by the AIDS epidemic, we can expect to learn much more about this process and, perhaps, how to compensate when people are most vulnerable.

such a closely-knit group often experienced psychological breakdown. People who lack supportive bonds with others are more likely to suffer illnesses and are less likely to recover quickly (Gottlieb, 1985). Some have not been able to establish intimate relationships, while others have experienced a disruption owing to marital separation or death of the spouse (Bloom, Asher and White, 1978; Stroebe and Stroebe, 1983).

Social support is clearly important to health. For example, many clinical and survey studies show relationships between an absence of social supports and heart disease (Lynch, 1977). A longitudinal study followed groups of teenage mothers through their pregnancies and after the birth of their babies. Social support from their families, friends, neighbours, and the fathers contributed to the adjustment and life satisfaction of these mothers, and to their effectiveness as parents. Social support was also correlated with the birth weight and the subsequent health and development of the child. As a result of these findings, programs were set up in which experienced, older women ("resource mothers") were able to be supportive to these women (Unger and Wandersman, 1985).

It is not entirely clear *how* social support contributes to health. Perhaps it "buffers" or protects the person against stress, or makes the person stronger and more resistant to illness. On the other hand, a lack of social support itself may be a stressor. That is, the person who is alienated from others or who loses support through death or separation may be at greater risk of disease (see Box 16-3). Finally, an individual with good support from others is more likely to comply with treatment, quit smoking, or do other things beneficial to his or her health. Supportive relationships may be found through involvement and participation with the community groups and institutions, regular interaction and support from specific persons, or in intimate relationships (Gottlieb, 1985).

However, social support may not always be beneficial. Family and friends, with the best of intentions, may reinforce maladaptive behaviours such as overeating, alcohol or other drug abuse, or even depression by protecting individuals from the consequences of their actions. Also, overprotection of elderly people, denying them the normal privileges of adults to care for themselves and make their own decisions, can be profoundly debilitating (Langer and Rodin, 1976).

Nevertheless, the research shows that in most cases, social support can protect the person from stress and provide the person with a sense of self-worth and stability in life (Cohen and McKay, 1984). However, in societies where people move frequently and divorce almost as frequently, social support can be difficult to obtain. In these circumstances, community support services, such as rape crisis centres, family services, hostels, or services for senior citizens, are vital (Pilisuk and Minkler, 1985).

Perceived control   As we saw earlier (Chapter 3), people need to feel that they are in control of their lives; otherwise, there can be adverse consequences for health. For example, institutionalized elderly persons live in a situation where all decisions are made for them, though for years, they may have enjoyed decision-making independence. In short they are often treated as children and even addressed in that way (see Chapter 11). Langer and Rodin (1976) investigated the consequences of such treatment in a residential nursing home in which residents and staff were divided into two groups. Residents of one floor were told that they would be well cared for and that all decisions and responsibilities would be assumed by staff, which is the usual situation in such institutions. The members of the other group were given messages that stressed that they were responsible. For example, *they* rather than the staff would select and care for the plants in the rooms, select movies, decide on activities and the arrangement of furniture.

Three weeks later, the group members for which personal control was stressed were found to be feeling happier and healthier and were rated by nurses as being more active and having a more positive outlook. Eighteen months later the differences were even more dramatic (Rodin and Langer, 1977). Nurses rated these residents as more active, sociable, and vigorous and physicians reported that they were in better health. In addition, 30 percent of the control group had died during this period, while only 15 percent of the personally responsible group had died.

This sense of control in life has other major impacts on our emotions, for example, depression. This was first observed in animals by Seligman (1975) who found that an animal exposed for a period to unavoidable shock was later unable to learn that the shock could be avoided and simply withdrew passively. The animal had learned to be *helpless*. Similarly, if a person has learned to attribute bad outcomes to uncontrollable external factors, that person will feel helpless. However, the research shows that if we attribute our failure to stable internal factors (e.g., lack of ability), this may affect our own self-esteem, and make depression even more likely (Abramson, Seligman and Teasdale, 1978). In addition to being in a prolonged state of sadness and

TABLE 16-1
Sample items from locus of control scale

This questionnaire is a measure of personal belief: obviously there are no right or wrong answers. Each item consists of a pair of alternatives lettered (A) or (B). Please select the one statement of each pair (and only one) which you more strongly believe as far as you are concerned. Be sure to select the one you actually believe to be more true rather than the one you think you should choose or the one you would like to be true.

Please answer these items carefully, but do not spend too much time on any one item. Be sure to find an answer for every choice. Circle the letter of the statement (A or B) which you choose.

In some cases you may discover that you believe both statements or neither one. In such cases, be sure to select the one you more strongly believe to be the case as far as you are concerned. Also try to respond to each item independently when making your choice: do not be influenced by your previous choices.

7. (A) For the average citizen becoming a success is a matter of hard work; luck has little or nothing to do with it.

   or (B) For the average guy getting a good job depends mainly on being in the right place at the right time.

15. (A) With fate the way it is, many times I feel that I have little influence over the things that happen to me.

   or (B) It is impossible for me to believe that chance or luck plays an important role in my life.

33. (A) People can and should do what they want to do both now and in the future.

   or (B) There is no point in people planning their lives too far in advance because other groups of people in our society will invariably upset their plans.

5. (A) There are institutions in our society that have considerable control over me.

   or (B) Little in this world controls me; I usually can do what I decide to do.

40. (A) When I make up my mind, I can always resist temptation and keep control of my behaviour.

   or (B) Even if I try not to submit, I often find I cannot control myself from some of the enticements of life such as overeating or drinking.

23. (A) Although sometimes it is difficult, I can always willfully restrain my immediate behaviour.

   or (B) Something I cannot do is have complete mastery over all my behavioural tendencies.

NOTE: *Items 7 and 15* refer to *fatalism*, or belief that people's behaviour controls their outcomes.
Items 33 and 5 refer to *social system control*, or the extent to which people in general can control the effects of society.
Items 40 and 23 refer to *self-control*, or the extent to which people can control their own impulses.

helplessness, depression can leave a person more vulnerable to disease and less likely to recover from it (Krantz and Glass, 1984).

Locus of control refers to the extent to which people believe that the events in their lives are caused by their own actions (internal) or by external factors such as fate, luck, bad powerful people or political institutions (Rotter, 1966) (see Table 16-1). People with internal orientations tend to know more about their illnesses and are more likely to take care of themselves (Strickland, 1978). When they become ill and if they are given appropriate information about their illness, "internals" tend to cope somewhat better. One particularly interesting study of coronary patients shows the importance of matching the treatment to the individual (Cromwell, Butterfield, Brayfield and Curry, 1977). Subjects were classified as either "internals" or "externals" and then some of them were given lots of information and discussion of their treatment and recovery (high participation), while others were provided with good care but no discussion (low participation). Of the 229 patients in the study, 12 were readmitted to hospital and five died within three months of discharge. All of these were in incongruent conditions: internals with low participation and externals with high participation. In general, all the externals showed more undesirable physical symptoms (such as higher sedimentation rates), while the internals were more cooperative in treatment and were discharged earlier from hospital.

Coronary-prone personality It has been known for many years that patients who suffer heart attacks are frequently competitive, achievement-oriented, rather impatient, and somewhat hostile. This profile has become known as the *Type A personality* (see Box 16-4). One large-scale longitudinal study showed that even after controlling for risk factors, such as family history, serum cholesterol levels, cigarette smoking and hypertension, Type A's were more likely than others to suffer from coronary disease and to die from it (Rosenman, Brand, Jenkins, Friedman, Straus and Wurm, 1975). It is ironic and tragic that the people most at risk are those who are rewarded with success in our competitive society. Perhaps for this reason, it is difficult for Type A people to modify this pattern of living (Burke and Weir, 1980).

Subsequent research has focused on the question of whether there is one specific factor within the Type A pattern which causes people to be at risk (Booth-Kewley and Friedman, 1987). Some suggest that underlying, unexpressed hostility is the specific predictor of coronary illness (Matthews, Glass, Rosenman and Bortner, 1977). In a laboratory experiment (Carver and Glass, 1978), subjects were put to work solving puzzles. In one condition, a confederate of the experimenter made derogatory remarks and wisecracks about the subjects while they worked, while in the control condition, the confederate made no such remarks. Then subjects were given the opportunity to administer what they believed to be electric shocks to the confederate (in the guise of a "teacher-learner" procedure often used in experiments on aggression). In the control condition, Type A's did not differ significantly from non-A's, but Type A's responded to the provocation with much higher levels of aggression. It also has been found that when Type A's express anger, angiographic measures show evidence of more stress on the heart than is found in other people (Krantz and Glass, 1984).

It has been argued that the risk factor is not anger but cynicism, a distrust of human nature and the motives of others. People who distrust others will experience more stress in interpersonal relations and are unable to obtain the support of others which

B · O · X   16 - 4

WHAT IS THE TYPE A?

Rosenman *et al.*'s (1975) structured interview is a commonly-used measure of the Type A pattern. In the interview, we must assess both the verbal responses of the subject and observed non-verbal reactions. Here are some of the observable behaviours exhibited by both personality types.

TYPE A	TYPE B
(1) Vigorous and confident	Relaxed, calm, quiet, attentive
(2) Firm handshake, walks briskly	Gentle handshake, moderate pace
(3) Loud and vigorous voice	Mellow voice
(4) Talks rapidly, especially near end	Talks slowly or moderately
(5) Emphatic one-word response ("Yes!"; "Never!")	No one-word responses
(6) Interrupts other speaker	Rarely interrupts
(7) "Explosive" speech (including expletives)	Explosive speech rare
(8) Hurries other speaker by nodding, saying "Yes," "Uh-huh"	Rarely hurries others
(9) Indicates upset at delay, wasted time	Not upset at delays
(10) Emphasis with clenched fist, pointing	No physical emphasis
(11) Hostility to interviewer or questions	Hostility rare
(12) Tense, abbreviated response	Lengthy, rambling response

Here are a few sample questions from Rosenman *et al.*'s structured interview:

(5) Would you describe yourself as a hard-driving, ambitious type of man/woman in accomplishing the things you want, getting things done as quickly as possible, or would you describe yourself as a relatively relaxed and easy-going person? (How would your husband/wife describe you?)

(6) When you get angry or upset, do people around you know about it? How do you show it?

(10) When playing games with people your own age, do you play for the fun of it or are you really in there to win?

(19) How do you feel about waiting in lines? Bank lines or supermarket lines? Post office lines?

(21) Do you have the feeling that time is passing too rapidly for you to accomplish all the things you'd like to get done?

can buffer them from the stresses of life. Consequently, they are at greater risk of stress-related illness, such as cardiovascular disease.

Type A's are nearly always impatient, always expressing urgency about time, checking their watches and feeling uncomfortable in lineups, elevators, and at red lights. Glass (1977) suggests that this reflects an attempt to maintain a sense of control over time, that precious, non-renewable resource in our lives. Perhaps their impatience represents a tendency to try harder initially, though also to give up more quickly and turn to something else (Nielson and Neufeld, 1986). In one study, subjects were placed in situations in which their opportunities to control the possibility of receiving electric shocks were varied (Pittner, Houston and Spiridi-Gliozzi, 1983). In the most stressful situations, where control was possible but quite difficult, blood pressure and

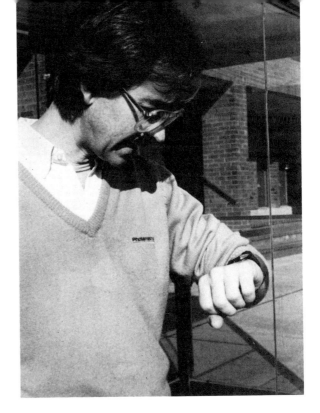

Type A's are especially time-conscious, uncomfortable when delayed.

heart rate increased in Type A's. Other research shows increases in free fatty acid levels when Type A's are trying to cope with stress (Matthews, 1982). On the other hand, programs have been devised to help Type A's cope with stress. However, although the Type A behaviours change as a result of such programming, corresponding changes in physiological reactions do not necessarily follow (Roskies *et al.*, 1986).

Kobasa (1979) approached this issue of control from the other direction by examining middle-level executives, all with relatively high stress levels. He found that the healthier executives did not necessarily take better care of themselves (e.g., in regular exercise). However, they responded differently to stress, interpreting it as a challenge rather than a threat. This *hardy personality* style also included a strong sense of self, beliefs in internal control, and a sense of life as being personally meaningful.

Illness and Treatment

We now turn to consider what is involved in being ill and seeking treatment. The characteristic actions of the person who is ill — how he or she communicates with family or physician, whether he or she follows the physician's orders — and the reactions of family, friends and physicians to that person constitute an interesting and important set of social psychological phenomena.

Sickness as a social role

When people are ill, they perceive themselves differently and others react to them in a different way. There are norms which govern the behaviour of the sick person, such as staying in bed, not working, not going out to play ball, and being a "good patient" (see Box 16-5). There also are norms which govern the actions of people responding to the sick person, such as offering sympathy, attention, and chicken soup. Thus, particularly in the case of long-term, disabling or life-threatening illnesses, sickness can be viewed as a social role and the people involved as behaving in accordance with a role schema for being sick (see Box 16-6).

Moos (1982) describes seven adaptive tasks faced by people with serious health problems. Some are related to the illness itself, and others concern their social relationship. The individual must: (1) deal with pain and incapacitation; (2) deal with stressful medical procedures (including being in the hospital); and (3) communicate with physicians, nurses, and health care personnel about symptoms, diagnosis, prognosis. In addition, the patient must: (4) preserve some degree of emotional balance, which may imply hope or acceptance; (5) maintain a sense of being a person worthy of respect and affection; (6) preserve relationships with family and friends; and (7) prepare for an uncertain future for him or herself and family. Being sick has social and physical implications which affect each other. In the health care system, as well as in our own relationships, we are becoming more aware of the social dimension of illness.

Consider the situation of a person who is suffering from a life-threatening condition such as cancer or AIDS. To a considerable extent, this person may be avoided — even stigmatized — by others. The behaviour of others toward the ill person is influenced

---

B · O · X   16 - 5

BEING A "GOOD PATIENT" MAY BE HAZARDOUS TO YOUR HEALTH

What is a good patient? Taylor (1979) points out that being a "good patient" may be good for the staff but not for the patient. Most people try to be cooperative, unquestioning of medical authority or hospital rules, passive and as cheerful (or at least uncomplaining) as they can manage in the circumstances. While they are well-liked by staff, they pay a price: (1) *Depersonalization*, a loss of personal identity; they now assume identity as a medical insurance number or become the "hernia repair in 214A"; (2) *Loss of control*, a sense that they must sacrifice the freedom normally expected by adults to a set of institutional rules and professional decisions; and (3) *Ignorance* of matters about which a normal adult would feel a right to know. In some cases, the patient may sink into a state of passive helplessness, which has been linked to depression and to a further erosion of health (Abramson, Seligman and Teasdale, 1978).

Is the "bad patient" in better shape? Taylor (1979) suggests that being a bad patient is a state of psychological reactance, acting in ways to counteract feelings of depersonalization, lost control, being uninformed, helpless. The patient may demand information, and treatment as an individual. Often, reactant behaviour becomes excessive, resulting in frequent complaints, demands, and attention-seeking ploys. It may also involve minor acts of mutiny, such as smoking where prohibited, making passes at nurses (or physicians), refusing to follow a prescribed diet. Of course, "bad patients" may also experience adverse effects on their health. With good reason, they will be disliked by patients and staff, which is inevitably distressing. Their complaints may not be taken seriously, and accurate diagnosis becomes more difficult.

B · O · X   16 - 6

BEING SICK AND BEING REJECTED

In some circumstances illness can become a stigma, a cause for rejection. For example, 94 adult epileptics in London, England, were interviewed (Scambler, 1964). When first diagnosed, most of them reacted with shock to the very word "epilepsy" and immediately recognized that this label could distance them from other people and cause them to be rejected. Therefore, they tended to conceal their condition and lived in a constant fear that their secret would become known.

Being mentally ill is also frequently a difficult and stigmatized role. This is shown clearly in an experiment (Fariña and Ring, 1965) in which voluntary subjects worked in pairs on a cooperative task. Before beginning the task, the subjects in separate booths were asked to write out and exchange brief descriptions of themselves to "get to know each other." Subjects actually received "self-descriptions" prepared by the experimenter. In one case, the person described herself as a relatively normal student, fairly popular, engaged, with no real problems. In the other, the person wrote that he experienced problems since high school, kept to himself with no close friends, and twice suffered a "nervous breakdown" in the past. Self-description was not related to performance in the cooperative task. After successful completion of the task, subjects who believed their partner to be mentally ill blamed that partner for an inadequate job (a false assertion), described him as less helpful, and said they would prefer to work alone in the future. In other words, when someone is perceived by others as mentally ill, whether now or in the past, even that person's successes are perceived as failures.

by feelings and beliefs about the illness itself. In the case of AIDS, research suggests that this reaction is based upon a fear of the unknown causes of the disease, coupled with a generalized prejudice against homosexuals (Triplet and Sugarman, 1987). The word "cancer" arouses strong feelings of anxiety and personal vulnerability. There may also be reactions of physical aversion if the physical appearance of the person has deteriorated as a result of the disease or treatment (Dunkel-Schetter and Wortmen, 1982).

More importantly, family, friends, and even medical personnel are uncertain about how to behave toward this person. Out of genuine concern for the person, they may feel obligated to be optimistic, cheerful, "positive" — a difficult task indeed in the situation. People may avoid the patient entirely and visits by friends, family, nurses, and physicians tend to become fewer and shorter. Their positive words may be discrepant with non-verbal cues such as fewer smiles, greater interpersonal distance, and the sadness or nervousness in their voice. In addition, they tend to avoid open communication about the important topic: cancer (or AIDS). Interviews with women who had radical mastectomies for breast cancer revealed that the vast majority had not discussed it with their husbands before or while in hospital, and only 50 percent had discussed it afterwards (Krantz and Johnson, 1978).

Terminal patients are in a terrible dilemma. Although they are understandably fearful, both about their health and their capacity to meet family responsibilities, and need to discuss these matters, they find it difficult to talk and others find it difficult to listen to them. Desperately, the patient may try various tactics to gain attention and support. For example, they may exaggerate their illness and discomfort, becoming "complaining patients." Another frequent tactic is to "tell them what they want to hear," being as "positive" as possible and becoming a player in the death-bed drama. A patient recalls, "I got congratulations for being so brave and cheerful. I liked that, so I got more brave and cheerful. And, the more brave and cheerful I was, the more everyone seemed to love me, so I kept it up. I became positively euphoric" (Rollins, 1976, p. 70).

Of course, few people have much experience in coping with serious illness in themselves or someone close to them. In a situation of intense uncertainty, we fall back on stereotyped roles and schematic reactions, or we avoid the issue as much as possible. The result is often isolation and a loss of intimacy at a time when it is most needed.

The physician-patient relationship

The practice of medicine is becoming increasingly technological and highly specialized. In an era in which patients must deal with a number of different specialized physicians, imposing machines, bureaucratic hospitals, and crowded waiting rooms, the relationship between physician and patient remains important. The reports of the patient can be a crucial source of information for the doctor, both in arriving at a correct diagnosis and in assessing the course of the illness and the effectiveness of treatment. In addition, the cooperation of the patient is often necessary in carrying out a treatment regimen. All of these are topics in which considerable research has been conducted.

Pain   Even with the new medical technologies, it is still important for the physician to determine what the patient is experiencing. Patients may *interpret* what they feel quite differently, and thus may report the same symptom differently or may not bother to report it. For example, individuals from various ethnic groups have been found to experience and report pain in distinctive ways. In a study of male patients (Zborowski, 1969), it was discovered that patients from the New England states tended to suffer quietly on the assumption that crying or complaining would not help. Irish patients also suppressed cries and complaints, but only to protect a masculine self-image. Italian patients, by contrast, were very expressive, in the expectation that they would gain sympathy and support from family and staff. Jewish patients were also very expressive, but for the purpose of communicating their symptoms (particularly to the physician), rather than gaining emotional support. With regard to the overall experience of pain, a later study (Lipton and Marbach, 1984) found that while ethnic groups tended to be rather similar, they were influenced by different factors. For example, the responses of Italians were related to how long the pain had lasted, of Jewish patients to their emotional distress, and of Irish patients to the extent to which they felt assimilated into the U.S. society (Lipton and Marbach, 1984). Thus the clinician must be alert to cultural differences in order to interpret the responses of patients.

The experience of pain itself is related to social psychological factors (Alcock, 1986). We have all learned to identify and label pain, particularly in accidents. The child falls down and cries, and the parent immediately asks, "Where does it hurt?" — although the child may be crying because of fear or surprise rather than pain itself. Once we learn how to identify pain, we must learn to express it appropriately (Craig,

1978). And we learn that while pain is unpleasant at best, it may also have its rewards. We need and want the sympathy and attention of others and to be excused from usual responsibilities. If we suffer from low back pain and complain about it, but walk and sit normally with little observable suffering, our complaints may not be taken seriously. Thus behaving in a disabled manner may become habitual.

These problems become magnified when the pain is chronic, and may become an issue in the relationship between patient and physician. Conflicting attributions may be made; the patient attributes this persisting condition to the inability of the physician to "cure" it, while the physician attributes it to malingering or neurotic exaggeration by the patient. Because of these conflicting attributions, there may be a breakdown in the patient-physician relationship, adding to the patient's stress.

Communication   Self-disclosure by a patient is dependent to a large degree on the nature of the relationship with the physician. Patients may be reluctant to disclose information which seems to be trivial; they want to be "good patients" and may feel intimidated by the prestige and power of the physician (Taylor, 1979). Patients may also be overly optimistic about their physician's skill and power.

As was discussed in Chapter 11, much of interpersonal communication is non-verbal. Friedman (1982) suggests that these non-verbal cues play a vital role, both in the diagnostic process and in communicating concern and empathy for the patient. For example, eye contact may be encouraging to a patient during a difficult time but excessive staring combined with the avoidance of eye contact may make the person feel like a "bad patient" or an object of curiosity. The "healing power" of touch also has a long history, and appropriate use by medical staff may be comforting.

In one study of 25 family practice physicians, a self-report measure of non-verbal expressiveness was administered. Over the subsequent six months, the more emotionally expressive physicians had more patients, and were more in demand (Friedman, Prince, Riggio and DiMatteo, 1980). Such physicians also may be more effective, for

"Yours is a sincere face, doctor. I'll bet you'd be very successful in advertising."

example, by helping the patient to believe in the treatment. The most obvious example of this is the well-known *placebo effect*, in which an inert or non-effective substance (e.g., a sugar pill) can have a powerful effect. If the physician and the patient expect the placebo to work, then it will tend to have a beneficial effect in at least some cases. That is, the physician is inadvertently communicating to the patient what to expect of the medication that is prescribed.

What to tell the patient   How much should the physician inform the patient, particularly about a life-threatening illness or a painful medical procedure? The question is troublesome from both sides of the relationship. On one hand, becoming a patient need not imply that a person sacrifices the right to decide about his or her body and health — or the right to receive the information needed to make such decisions. On the other hand, the physician bears the legal and ethical responsibility for the patient and may honestly believe that full disclosure would damage the health of the patient. Being human, physicians do not like to deliver bad news (Saul and Kass, 1969), and patients who are seriously ill may honestly prefer to cling to illusions and hopes (Miller and Mangan, 1983), even if most say that they want to be informed (Blumenfeld, Levy and Kaufman, 1979).

The reluctance of people to transmit bad news has been labelled the "MUM effect" (Tesser and Rosen, 1975). The communicator is motivated by a desire to please the recipient, perhaps by a concern that the recipient will evaluate him or her negatively. However, in the case of physicians, the primary concern must be the welfare of the patient.

Physicians may fear that bad news may upset their patients but pioneering field research by Janis (1958), which has been supported by other studies, indicates that such upset is not necessarily detrimental. When people must face major surgery, those who are moderately anxious about it actually fare best in post-operative recovery. Janis observed that these people tend to seek out information and to prepare themselves mentally for what is ahead — he calls this the "work of worrying." Low-anxiety patients do not think about it until they discover unexpectedly how terrible they feel, while highly anxious people avoid the topic. The key here is that accurate information allows the patient to prepare for and cope with the future event.

In a field experiment (Johnson and Leventhal, 1974) patients were given information about an upcoming endoscopic examination, an exceedingly unpleasant procedure in which a tube is slowly snaked down the patient's throat to view the gastrointestinal system from the inside. Two messages were given. One provided information about the uncomfortable sensory aspects of the experience, such as gagging and the feeling of fullness when air was pumped into the stomach. The other consisted of behavioural information, such as guidance in how to reduce gagging and ease insertion of the tube. Patients were divided into four groups — those who received both messages, one of the two messages, or very minimal information and instruction.

The results showed that gagging was significantly reduced and ease of insertion of the tube was significantly enhanced among those patients who received both messages. The sensory information was most effective in reducing signs of emotionality, while the behavioural instructions most effectively reduced fear. In short, the patient was more comfortable and less distressed, and the procedure was less difficult for the physician. This and other studies suggest that patients should be active participants in their own treatment (see Box 16-7).

B · O · X   16 - 7

HEALTH CARE OR — TAKE CARE OF YOURSELF

For each statement below decide whether you *agree* or *disagree* and circle the answer which *best* fits your opinion.

(2) Except for serious illness, it's generally better to take care of your own health than to seek professional help

AGREE   DISAGREE

(4) Instead of waiting for them to tell me, I usually ask the doctor or nurse immediately after an exam about my health

AGREE   DISAGREE

(6) Clinics and hospitals are good places to go for help since it's best for medical experts to take responsibility for health care

AGREE   DISAGREE

(7) Learning how to cure some of your illnesses without contacting a physician is a good idea

AGREE   DISAGREE

(16) I'd rather be given many choices about what's best for my health than to have the doctor make the decision for me

AGREE   DISAGREE

These items are taken from the Health Opinion Survey (HOS), a measure of the extent to which patients want to be *active participants* in caring for and making decisions about their own health, and whether they want an *informed role* in the process by having health professionals provide them with full and accurate information. This measure has proven useful in pinpointing whether people prefer to be "taken care of" or care for themselves: (1) Students who used a college infirmary (clinic) more frequently for routine treatment of minor illnesses score low on the HOS. (2) Students enrolled in a medical self-help course covering first aid, diet, etc., scored high on the HOS. (3) Patients who scored high on the HOS asked more questions and tried more often to diagnose themselves during a medical examination (as rated by nurses) (Krantz, Baum and Wideman, 1980).

Patient non-compliance

Typically, a visit to the office of a physician concludes with a recommendation: follow a restricted diet, have your child inoculated for polio or diphtheria, take a prescribed medication three times a day for two weeks, make another appointment, have some blood tests, X-rays, or an ultrasound examination. However, research shows that at least one third of all patients do not comply with the medical regimen prescribed for them (Stone, 1979). For instance, about 20 percent do not have their prescriptions filled (Boyd, Covington, Stanaszek and Coussons, 1974). In some cases, non-compliance levels are much higher, particularly when preventive health measures have been recommended. It is unfortunate that despite their best efforts, physicians are remarkably ineffectual in influencing patients to exercise more, drink less, smoke less, and eat more moderately.

Non-compliance is a common problem in the later stages of treatment, especially when the original symptoms are no longer evident. However, if a therapeutic measure continues to relieve severe pain or is seen as potentially life-saving (e.g., chemotherapy for cancer), the patient will usually comply. Thousands of patients quit smoking, lose weight, and exercise diligently — *after* their first heart attack. Antibiotic medications are often taken as prescribed for the first few days of acute illness — until the patient begins to feel better. Then compliance begins to wane and the illness often recurs.

One good example occurs in the treatment of hypertension (high blood pressure). Easily diagnosed and present in 17–25 percent of adults, it can lead to strokes, heart failure, renal failure, blindness, and coronary heart diseases (Herd and Weiss, 1984). The symptoms of hypertension are rarely detectable to the patient. However, many believe mistakenly that they can tell when their blood pressure is high, relying on unreliable cues such as an elevated pulse rate, warm hands and feet, or "stress" (Leventhal, Meyer and Nerenz, 1980). High blood pressure can be treated effectively, primarily by medication (beta-blockers and diuretics), weight control, a sodium-restricted diet, or using biofeedback techniques to train the patient in relaxation. Yet between 70 and 90 percent of patients diagnosed as hypertensive fail to take their medication regularly or to comply with other recommendations (Leventhal and Hirschman, 1982).

It is misleading to attribute non-compliance simply to the personality characteristics of patients. Rather, the tactics used by the health professional to elicit compliance and the relationship between physician and patient must be examined. For example, patients do not like assembly-line treatment of their afflicted organs by impersonal specialists, and are more likely to comply when they see the same physician over time. Research shows that patients comply when they perceive their physician as friendly, caring, and interested in them, as well as having sound knowledge and technical ability (DiNicola and DiMatteo, 1984). Warmth in an interpersonal relationship can be communicated non-verbally by eye contact, physical posture, and movement. Rodin and Janis (1979) also suggest that physicians can enhance the therapeutic relationship by encouraging self-disclosure by the patient, giving positive feedback of acceptance and understanding, asking whether the patient understands and accepts the recommendations, and implying that the patient has the ultimate control and responsibility in the situation.

Several other tactics also may be useful. For example, the health practitioner may first recommend the most beneficial regimen, and then "retreat" to a less demanding but still adequate regimen (see Chapter 6). Patients might be invited to write down their own health goals on the premise that behaviour discrepant with a public, self-selected commitment will arouse more cognitive dissonance (Sensenig and Cialdini, 1984). Ideally, of course, the new behaviour should become an *internalized* response, more than external compliance. In this context, the physician becomes a source of expertise, rather than an authority figure. Social support from significant others can be vital in this regard as well. For example, people with hypertension are more likely to continue taking their medication if encouraged by their spouses (Caplan, Robinson, French, Caldwell and Shinn, 1976).

A final observation

There is an implicit hypothesis that the physician/patient relationship must be independent of outside influence to be effective. Many physicians and medical organizations have attributed an apparent erosion of the physician-patient relationship to governmental control over the financial aspects of medical practice. As yet, no evidence has supported their arguments. Most of the research on physician-patient interaction has been conducted in the United States where the patient usually pays directly for services to the individual physician or to a private "health maintenance" corporation. In Canada, provincial governments administer "fee-for-services" health insurance, and in many Western European nations, physicians are paid a salary by the government. Given the importance of maintaining optimal relationships between physicians and their patients, it would be an important contribution to design and conduct comparative research in this area.

HEALTH PROMOTION

We now turn to a discussion of those factors which may assist individuals and society in preventing illness and preserving health. As we have already noted, much of the illness and mortality in our society can be attributed to unhealthy behaviours. In order to save lives, preserve health, and contain the escalating cost of medical care, health promotion and the prevention of disease are logical and necessary moves. Much research has been done in the areas of dietary selection, smoking, drinking, the use of seat belts in automobiles, exercise, and dental hygiene (Matarazzo, Weiss, Herd, Miller and Weiss, 1984). (See Table 16-2.)

In the field of public health, a distinction is drawn between primary and secondary prevention. Primary prevention refers to reducing the rate of occurrence of the disease or health problem, while secondary prevention refers to the earliest possible detection and treatment of the problem in order to minimize the risk to health. Examples of primary prevention include exercise, moderation in alcohol consumption, not driving after drinking, use of seat belts and child restraints in cars, not smoking, a moderate and balanced diet, inoculation against various infectious diseases, and proper care and precautions during pregnancy. Secondary prevention measures include the Pap smear for early detection of cervical cancer, early detection and intervention in problem drinking (e.g., employee assistance programs), dental check-ups, periodic stress-electrocardiograms in higher-risk persons, early diagnosis and treatment of hypertension, dietary restrictions to control diabetes, and self-examination for early signs of various cancers.

TABLE 16-2
A portrait of Canadian adult health practices

30% smoke cigarettes regularly
8% drink more than 15 alcoholic drinks per week
16% drink and drive
6% used cannabis in the past year
1% used cocaine in the past year
46% do not exercise three times per week
18% skip breakfast at least once per week
37% were overweight or obese (ratio of height to weight)
13% rarely or never use seatbelts

SOURCE: National Health Promotion Survey, Health and Welfare Canada, 1987

Ontario's RIDE (Reduce Impaired Driving Everywhere) program is one highly visible campaign against drunk driving.

A wide variety of approaches to prevention have been followed with varying degrees of success. One of these is the legislative route. For example, laws which mandate the use of seat belts and lower speed limits have generally reduced fatalities in automobile accidents (Robertson, 1984). While the long-term effect of laws against drunk driving has not been convincingly demonstrated, short-term, highly visible campaigns are relatively effective (Klajner, Sobell and Sobell, 1984).

With regard to alcohol use, some researchers have argued that accessibility to alcohol should be controlled or restricted by measures such as increasing the minimum drinking age, increasing prices, earlier closing times, and not allowing the purchase of beverages outside government outlets. This argument is based on the idea that increasing accessibility will increase the average per capita consumption of alcohol and increase the incidence of both social and health problems attributable to excessive drinking (Popham, Schmidt and DeLint, 1976). However, the evidence is based almost entirely on the number of mortalities from cirrhosis of the liver, and heavy drinkers may well be less affected than others by measures which restrict accessibility to alcohol.

Fear arousal and persuasion

In Chapter 5, the role of fear arousal in persuasion was discussed briefly. The use of this technique is quite common when discussing the health-related consequences of certain behaviours: smoking and cancer, lack of exercise and heart disease, and the use of seat belts in automobiles. Let us now examine the problem in more detail.

The *parallel response model* of fear-based persuasion (Leventhal, 1970) states that people respond to such messages in a way that accomplishes two purposes: to control or avert the danger mentioned in the message and to cope with the unpleasant feelings engendered by the message. Thus the obese person may respond to messages which stress the dangers of heart disease by following a sensible diet to lose weight (danger control) or by rationalizing about a 90-year-old obese aunt and ignoring such messages in the future. Thus messages which simply arouse fear will likely be ineffective. These tend to be effective only when accompanied by explicit recommendations about a course of action to avert the danger to health, such as an effective diet to lose weight, a strategy to stop smoking, or information about the location and hours of a clinic to receive tetanus shots (Sutton, 1982).

The *protection motivation model* (Rogers, 1975) explains when people will respond to fear-based messages in terms of danger control. It is suggested that motivation to protect oneself from a danger is based on four beliefs: the threat is severe; the person is vulnerable in some way; the person can perform the recommended action; and the recommended action will be effective. Thus, in a study of coronary disease prevention, a high fear arousal message resulted in better health practices when all four beliefs were held by individuals. Note that these beliefs seem to be independent of each other; a person may believe that smoking could cause an early death from a heart attack and that it could happen to him or her personally but not believe that he or she can quite smoking. It seems that the most effective message will persuade people of a real and personal danger, recommend a course of action *and* somehow persuade the people that they have the time, resources, and ability to do it. Unless action seems plausible and desirable, people tend to respond defensively and change is unlikely (Janis and Feshback, 1953).

Another study shows that the fear of adverse consequences may be virtually irrelevant in some cases (Best *et al.*, 1984). The subjects were sixth-graders, selected because this age group is at high risk for beginning to smoke. Indeed, most of these children had models who were smoking, such as parents, siblings or friends, and many of them were themselves smoking on occasion. One group attended sessions in which information was presented about the negative effects of smoking. In addition, they were encouraged to make public commitments not to smoke and were given role-playing training in how to resist social pressures to smoke. The control group attended sessions about health which did not deal specifically with smoking. A follow-up 30 months later showed that 43 percent of the experimental group had stopped smoking, compared with 25 percent of the control group. What is more interesting is that this and other studies (Evans, Raines and Hanselka, 1984) suggest that the most effective component of the anti-smoking program was its discussion of how to resist the social pressures to smoke. Indeed, it is likely that the decreasing social acceptability of public smoking has had significant benefits for the health of smokers and non-smokers alike. Many people who adopt healthier habits do so for reasons other than health, such as conformity, saving money, or looking better (Health and Welfare Canada, 1987).

Intervention programs

A technique such as fear arousal can be integrated into a larger framework. For instance, the Stanford Heart Disease Program (Meyer, Nash, McAlister, Maccoby and Farquhar, 1980) was a large-scale program of intervention in three California communities over a three-year period. There were three experimental conditions: media campaign plus face-to-face instruction, media campaign only, and a no-treatment control condition. Subjects in two communities were recipients of an intensive bilingual (English and Spanish) campaign on TV, radio, billboards, posters and direct mail, all designed to heighten awareness of risk factors in heart disease and to encourage specific behaviours such as losing weight, exercising more, and not smoking. In one community, participants also became involved in nine sessions of group instruction sessions based on principles of social learning. Subjects were taught specific behavioural skills related to health practices, such as techniques in self-control and how to cope with giving up smoking. The instructors themselves modelled appropriate behaviours, and social reinforcement was given by both instructors and the group to those who successfuly changed their own behaviour each week.

Each year, participants in all three communities were surveyed about their knowledge of health risks and how they had changed behaviour. In addition, their blood pressure and serum cholesterol levels were assessed. The findings were encouraging. People in both towns receiving the media campaign had greater knowledge of the risk factors in heart diseases. Further, there were some significant behaviour changes. For example, smoking was significantly reduced, particularly in the town where both the media and individualized instruction campaigns were received. Serum cholesterol levels and blood pressure reduced in both communities. In fact, blood pressure was reduced most dramatically among those whose blood pressure was highest before the study began. Of course, we do not know which components in the "package" really caused the changes, and there is no definitive evidence that heart disease was reduced. Still, the study clearly indicates that social psychology can be applied successfully to enhance health.

In health promotion it is important to be clear and specific about goals. For example, Jessor (1984) offers some interesting alternatives with regard to adolescents, beginning with the notion that most adolescents will sooner or later engage in some behaviours that constitute a potential risk to health. One such strategy, *minimization*, involves attempting to limit, if not prevent, risk behaviours, e.g., encouraging controlled or moderate drinking. Another is to *insulate* the risk behaviour from serious consequences, such as preventing the drunken teenager from driving, or protecting those who are sexually active from pregnancy or venereal diseases. A third is to *delay onset* of the behaviour, based on the premise that even one year's postponement of drinking or smoking can mean greater maturity and skills in dealing with the risks. All of these are precisely formulated goals, and the first two are clearly applicable to other age groups.

Decisions and actions about health

In Chapters 4 and 5, considerable discussion was devoted to the complexities in persuasive communication and attitude change and to the variables which influence the extent to which attitudes predict behaviour. In order to guide research and action in public health, a model has been developed which refers specifically to health-related attitudes and behaviours. This is the Health Beliefs Model (Becker, 1974) outlined in Figure 16-2. In order to work through the model, let us take the example of an individual whose physician has recommended some form of exercise (jogging, swimming, cycling, aerobics classes) to promote cardiovascular fitness and reduce the risk of heart attack.

The process begins with a person's readiness to act, to "do something" in order to become more physically fit (A). This readiness occurs because the person believes that he or she is susceptible to a serious illness: "A heart attack can be fatal" and "It could happen to me." This readiness to act (intent) becomes experienced as a real and personal threat (E). The sense of threat is influenced by other factors, such as demographic characteristics. For example, middle-aged people are usually more concerned with health risks and the finite nature of life, and members of certain ethnic groups tend to be more health conscious than are members of others.

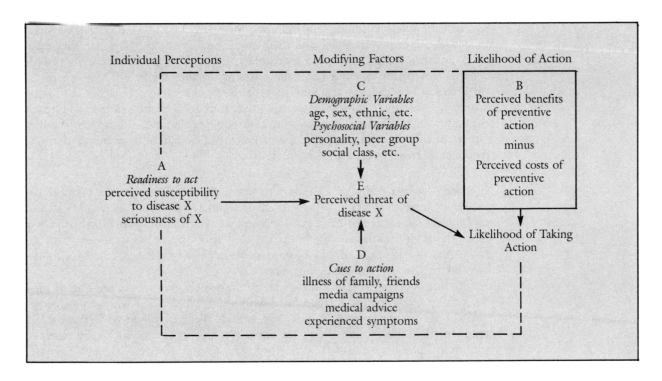

Individual Perceptions

Modifying Factors

Likelihood of Action

C
Demographic Variables
age, sex, ethnic, etc.
Psychosocial Variables
personality, peer group
social class, etc.

B
Perceived benefits
of preventive
action

minus

Perceived costs of
preventive
action

A
Readiness to act
perceived susceptibility
to disease X
seriousness of X

E
Perceived threat of
disease X

Likelihood of Taking
Action

D
Cues to action
illness of family, friends
media campaigns
medical advice
experienced symptoms

FIGURE 16-2
The Health Beliefs Model

If the perceived threat of possible illness is accompanied by cues to action (D), then behaviour change is likely to occur. These cues for action may include mass media campaigns for fitness, repeated urging by a physician, friends or family members who have suffered from the disease, or a personal experience of symptoms or illness. While the model at this point predicts that the individual is concerned about coronary disease and is eager to take action, the choice of action will depend upon the relative costs and benefits perceived for various alternatives. Aerobic exercise, for example, may be convincingly "sold" as an effective preventive action, and may also have more immediate benefits by reducing obesity, enhancing physical appearance and feelings of well-being. Costs or "perceived barriers" may include the time required on a regular basis, inconvenience, the cost of designer clothing and running shoes, health club membership fees, and problems such as "shin splints." In short, people are likely to begin — and continue — aerobic exercise if they believe that coronary disease is a real and personal threat, and if exercise is perceived as an effective way to reduce that threat without excessive personal sacrifice. Note, of course, that the benefits are in the long term while the costs are immediate and tangible.

Many studies, some of them longitudinal, have been generated by the model (see Janz and Becker, 1984). Programs have been designed and tested to influence people to be vaccinated against influenza, participate in genetic screening for Tay-Sachs disease, stop smoking, comply with therapy for hypertension or treatment for diabetes and end-state renal disease, and visit a physician for certain symptoms. In general, the model has been helpful in showing how beliefs about health become translated into action.

One interesting study of students (Weinstein, 1984) found that they have unrealistically optimistic beliefs about their own health. While they assume, often correctly, that factors such as family history might signify risk for an illness, they ignore the role of their own behaviour. For example, they perceived no relationship between their own risk of a heart attack and their own actions, such as how much they exercised, how much high cholesterol food they consumed, or how much they smoked. Indeed, most students tended to believe that while they might well develop colds, there was only a remote possibility of suffering a heart attack or having a drinking problem. While these students were not ignorant of good health practices and health risks, they did not believe that *they* were susceptible or that it could happen to them. Other research shows that people are often unaware of how their health practices reflect more basic values (Kristiansen, 1986).

Is decision-making rational? The Health Beliefs Model is based on the premise that people evaluate the risks and then weigh the benefits and costs of various actions consciously and rationally. Such rationality may be difficult to maintain when people face a threat to their health. Such a threat may be so stressful as to arouse defences, and people may be more affected by emotional reactions or habitual, schematic modes of thinking than by rational deliberation.

Janis and Mann (1977) conducted an impressive program of research based on a deceptively simple premise: when faced with a difficult decision with serious consequences (such as those involving own own health), the stress produced by this conflict tends to affect the quality of our decisions. We experience this conflict in terms of various symptoms, such as vacillation, hesitation, guilt, anxiety, shame. Then we select one of five coping strategies:

(1) *Unconflicted inertia.* We may simply decide not to bother obtaining the immunization shots, ignoring all warnings.

(2) *Unconflicted change.* We may accept and comply with whatever is recommended uncritically. This may not be adaptive; the expert may be wrong or the patient may not anticipate the suffering to be expected after surgery.

(3) *Defensive avoidance.* The individual may react by constructing "wishful rationalizations," such as denying the ominous symptoms of cancer or coronary disease or the ominous information regarding the health risks of smoking.

(4) *Hypervigilance.* In a state of conflict bordering on panic, the person may search desperately for a solution and then, suddenly and impulsively, act in a grossly inadequate way. Thus the cancer patient may suddenly check out of hospital and pass into the clutches of a faith healer or other quack.

(5) *Vigilance.* Here, decision-making is rational and effective, the outcome of a painstaking search for relevant information and a careful consideration among alternatives. The choice of a coping strategy will be influenced by awareness of risks, optimism about finding a satisfactory solution, and the time available to learn and think about it.

Maintenance or relapse

An important aspect of health-related behaviour is the strong tendency toward relapse well after the major effort to change behaviour has succeeded. While many people have begun exercise programs and have shown significant improvements in fitness, less than 30 percent of them continue to be active beyond a period of 3.5 years (Oldridge, 1982). While a calorie-restricted diet may help North Americans collectively lose metric tonnes of fat each year, few can keep it off beyond one year (Wilson,

1981). While many alcoholics, heroin addicts, and addicted cigarette smokers successfully complete treatment programs or quit by themselves, about two thirds relapse within three months *after* withdrawal from the addictive substance (Hunt, Barnett and Branch, 1971).

Almost inevitably, the individual will deviate from the prescribed pattern: a person forgets to take the antibiotic one night, the "weight-watcher" will give in to the lure of a Thanksgiving feast, the ex-smoker will accept an offered cigarette, the exerciser misses several sessions while busy at work, the abstinent alcoholic will have a drink at a party. Why does a "slip" become a relapse? The evidence shows that it is not some internal mechanism triggered by the slip which causes the person to lose control. For example, in an experimental situation in which subjects were asked to rate the taste and quality of various alcoholic beverages, even diagnosed alcoholics did not lose control over drinking (Marlatt, Demming and Reid, 1973).

To understand why people lose control after a lapse, it is important to understand how people *interpret* the slip (Marlatt and Gordon, 1980). Often there is an *abstinence violation effect*. In part, this effect involves the experience of cognitive dissonance between the slip as a behaviour and the individual's self-image as an ex-smoker, dieter, or recovering alcoholic. In part, the effect is due to a dispositional attribution — people explain the slip in terms of personal weakness and inadequacy, rather than blaming the situation or viewing it as a momentary lapse in judgment. Thus people see themselves differently and are emotionally upset about it. Understandably, the person is now in a poor state in which to regain self-control, and the slip becomes a full-blown relapse. Learning to have a "blow-out" once in a while and revert to good behaviour the next morning without drowning in self-recrimination is one of the keys.

In order to maintain healthier behaviour patterns, people must be equipped with the skills to cope with lapses into imperfection. In particular, they must develop expectations of self-efficacy (Bandura, 1977), the conviction that they can cope with high risk situations, even allowing for temporary transgression. It is important to note that most cigarette smokers who quit successfully usually do so after several attempts which had concluded in relapse (Schachter, 1982). It is also important to note the importance of social supports from others, both in bolstering the motivation to resist temptation and to buffer the impact of stressful situations. For example, one study found that those who quit smoking and did not relapse were those who felt that they had more support at work, both from co-workers and supervisors (Caplan, Cobb and French, 1975).

SOME FINAL OBSERVATIONS

This chapter began with the assumption that people want to be healthy and can be motivated to act accordingly. However, the research evidence does not show that people act in a consistent manner relevant to their health (Norman, 1985). For example, most researchers distinguish between *health behaviour*, that is acting to prevent illness, and *illness behaviour*, which means acting in response to symptoms. We cannot assume that people who live very healthy lifestyles (diet, exercise, and curtail drug use) will consult a physician when it is appropriate or will comply with her recommendations. Even within the category of preventive behaviours, we cannot assume consistency. The "health nut" who eats a healthy macrobiotic diet, runs ten kilometres per day, and avoids alcohol and tobacco may nevertheless not get enough sleep, drive insanely, or neglect inoculation "booster shots."

Clearly, different health-relevant behaviours may be influenced by different factors. For example, persons who think of health primarily in terms of medical treatment may be quite willing to accept *medical* procedures: they will show up faithfully for electrocardiograms but will not exercise or eat moderately. People may also do healthy things for reasons unrelated to health. For example, many who diet and faithfully attend strenuous exercise classes may be less concerned about health and fitness than they are about physical attractiveness. Conformity, social acceptance, pleasure, faith in the physician and in medicine are all powerful determinants of behaviour which influences health.

SUMMARY

(1) Behaviour is highly relevant to health, particularly in our society.

(2) Problem behaviour theory regards adolescent health-risk behaviour, such as drug abuse, as part of a syndrome of non-conventional personal characteristics (expectations, values, controls), social environment (peer groups, parent behaviour), and behaviours (sexuality, deviance, absence of school and church involvement).

(3) Social modelling influences health-risk behaviours by promoting the onset of the behaviour and eliciting it more frequently.

(4) Vulnerability to illness is increased by an absence of social support, a perception that life cannot be controlled, and by characteristics of the Type-A personality (coronary-prone syndrome).

(5) Being ill involves a social role in which we see ourselves differently and others treat us differently.

(6) Patients often fail to comply with medical recommendations. Patient compliance and accurate diagnosis are strongly influenced by the relationship and communication between patients and physicians.

(7) In general, conveying accurate information to patients contributes to their recovery, even when it provokes anxiety.

(8) Primary prevention refers to reducing the probability of the onset of a disease. Secondary prevention refers to early diagnosis and treatment.

(9) Persuasion, including fear arousal with recommended actions, can lead to behaviour change. Such techniques have been integrated into large-scale programs to reduce the risk of coronary disease.

(10) According to the Health Beliefs Model, people become "ready" to do something to promote health if they believe they are personally susceptible to a serious illness or problem. Their actions are determined by the perceived benefits and costs, and modified by characteristics of the person and by environmental cues. This model has been criticized as assuming that a purely rational, decision-making process underlies health-relevant behaviour.

(11) Relapse often occurs after behaviour change. The "abstinence violation effect," in which the person interprets a "slip" as dissonant and a sign of weakness, contributes to relapse.

FURTHER READING

BLANE, H.T. and LEONARD, K. (Eds.) (1986). *Psychological theories of drinking and alcoholism*. New York: Guilford.

DIMATTEO, M.R. and FRIEDMAN, H.S. (1982). *Social psychology and medicine*. Cambridge: Delgeschlager, Gunn & Haia.

EISER, J.R. (Ed.) (1982). *Social psychology and behavioral medicine*. New York: Wiley.

FRIEDMAN, H.S. and DIMATTEO, M.R. (1982). *Interpersonal issues in health care*. New York: Academic Press.

MATARAZZO, J.D., WEISS, S.M., HERD, J.A., MILLER, N.E. and WEISS, S.M. (Eds.) (1984). *Behavioral health: A handbook of health enhancement and disease prevention*. New York: Wiley.

SANDERS, G.S. and SULS, J. (Eds.) (1982). *Social psychology of health and illness*. Hillsdale: Erlbaum.

STONE, G.C., COHEN, F. and ADLER, N.E. (1979). *Health psychology — A handbook*. San Francisco: Jossey-Bass.

G·L·O·S·S·A·R·Y

abstinence violation effect *(16)* When recovering from substance abuse, people who experience a slip attribute it to themselves and experience the slip as dissonant; they are then likely to relapse.

action research *(15)* Studies in which the data are fed back into a system in order to influence change.

actor/observer bias *(3)* The tendency to attribute our own behaviour to situations and the behaviour of others to dispositions.

additive model *(3)* The hypothesis that our overall impression of someone is the sum of our evaluation of that person on various traits.

adjustive functions *(4)* Holding certain attitudes which serve to gain social approval for ourselves.

adversary procedure *(15)* A trial system in which both sides are responsible for gathering their own evidence and prersenting their own case to a neutral judge and/or jury.

aggression *(9)* Behaviour that is intended to harm.

altruism *(10)* Actions that are carried out voluntarily to help someone without expectations of reward from external sources.

androgens *(9)* Male sex hormones.

attachment *(8)* A state of intense emotional dependence on someone.

attempt-suppressing signals *(11)* Non-verbal cues used by a speaker in a conversation to prevent interruption.

attitude *(4)* A relatively stable pattern of beliefs, feelings and behavioural tendencies toward some object.

attribution *(3)* The inference of causality about a person's behaviour or an outcome of behaviour.

authoritarianism *(7)* A personality syndrome characterized by cognitive rigidity, prejudice, and an excessive concern with power.

autokinetic effect *(6)* An illusion in which a stationary spot of light in a dark environment appears to be moving.

availability heuristic *(3)* Strategy of making judgments in terms of information that is easily remembered and used.

averaging model *(3)* The hypothesis that our overall impression of someone is the sum of our evaluations of the person on various traits divided by the number of traits evaluated.

back channel communication *(11)* Non-verbal signals from listeners indicating attention and interest in a conversation.

behaviourism *(2)* A theoretical orientation that is based on the premise that all behaviour is governed by external reinforcement.

brainstorming *(6)* The uncritical and uninhibited expression of ideas, usually in a group setting.

bystander effect *(10)* A phenomenon in which the presence of others inhibits helping in an emergency.

catharsis *(9)* Reduction in arousal, e.g., anger as a result of acting out or observing the action of someone else.

central route persuasion *(5)* Attitude change which follows logical argumentaction and thought about the issue.

central trait *(3)* A characteristic of people that determines how we evaluate them on other characteristics.

charisma *(12)* Exceptional personal qualities in some leaders which enable them to attract many committed followers.

classical conditioning *(5)* Learning in which a neutral event which has been paired with another event elicits the response formerly elicited by that other event.

coaction *(6)* People behaving in a similar way at the same time and place but not interacting.

cognitive balance *(8)* A tendency for people to seek harmony or consistency among their attitudes and their relationships with other people.

cognitive dissonance *(5)* A state of uncomfortable arousal which occurs when one cognition is logically opposed to another.

cohesiveness *(12)* Extent to which members are attracted to the group.

collective behaviour *(14)* Relatively unorganized and unplanned actions which emerge spontaneously among a collectivity of people as a result of inter-stimulation among them.

collective contagion *(14)* The development and spreading of a strong emotional reaction among many people.

collective dilemma *(13)* A situation in which the individually rational actions of a number of people produce an outcome which is undesirable for all involved.

competition *(13)* A form of social exchange in which individuals act to maximize their gains in relation to others.

complementarity *(8)* A situation in which people are attracted because they satisfy each others' needs.

compliance *(6)* Acquiescent behaviour in response to a direct request.

conflict *(13)* A situation of discord between two or more parties.

conflict spiral *(13)* A series of escalating threats and counter-threats.

conformity *(6)* Behaviour that adheres to group norms and yields to perceived group pressures.

constructive reality *(6)* A view of the world, especially ambiguities, which is provided by the group.

contact hypothesis *(7)* The notion that if members of different groups can get together under certain circumstances, prejudice will be reduced.

contagion theory *(14)* The hypothesis which explains the rapid spreading of emotions, attitudes and behaviour throughout a crowd or population.

content analysis *(7)* The systematic study of verbal or written materials to determine underlying trends.

contingency theory *(12)* A theory attributing leadership effectiveness to a good match between leadership style and aspects of the group situation.

control *(15)* Perceived capacity to regulate or influence outcomes.

conversational control *(11)* Use of non-verbal communication to regulate the form and pace of a conversation.

cooperation *(13)* A form of social exchange in which two or more parties act together to achieve a shared goal.

correlation *(2)* Extent to which scores on one measure are predictable by the scores on another measure.

correspondent inference *(3)* Attribution of an act to a stable disposition.

covariation principle *(3)* A principle stating that if two events are perceived as occurring together and never separately, one will be interpreted as the cause of the other.

cross-cultural research *(2)* Studies in which subjects from more than one society or ethnic group are compared.

cross-lagged procedure *(9)* Method of comparing correlations between two variables over two points in time in order to infer which is more likely to be a cause of the other.

crowd *(14)* An unorganized and temporary large collectivity of people who are in close enough physical proximity to influence each other.

crowding *(15)* A subjective state of discomfort arising from the perception that there are too many people in that situation.

cult *(14)* A socially deviant, strongly ideological, and relatively closed group or social movement.

dangerous conflict *(13)* A conflict in which both sides may suffer unacceptable losses unless at least one side backs down.

debriefing *(2)* Informing subjects after they have been studied of any deceptions, and helping them to interpret and accept any self-relevant feedback.

dehumanization *(6)* Derogating intended or actual enemies or victims to make them appear less than human.

deindividuation *(14)* A state of relative anonymity in certain social conditions which leads to a lowered threshold for normally restrained behaviour.

density *(15)* The population in a given area.

density-intensity hypothesis *(15)* A proposition that high population density magnifies usual reactions in a social situation.

dependent variable *(2)* A measured outcome in an experiment.

deterrence *(13)* The assumption that a realistic threat can prevent war or other hostile acts.

diffusion of responsibility *(10)* When others are present, the individual feels less of a sense of personal duty to act in a prosocial manner.

discounting cue hypothesis *(5)* A hypothesis which states that when the source of a communication is not trusted, the message tends to be disregarded.

discounting principle *(3)* In attributions, the role of one factor is perceived as less important if other plausible causes are present.

discrepant behaviour *(5)* An action that is inconsistent with an attitude.

discrimination *(7)* Negative actions directed to members of a specific group.

distraction-conflict theory *(6)* This theory states that when people are in the presence of others, they may experience arousal caused by a conflict over whether to attend to the task or the audience.

distributive justice *(13)* Fairness of outcomes provided for various parties involved.

door-in-the face technique *(6)* A means of securing agreement to a moderate request by first making an unreasonable request.

double-blind *(2)* A control in research whereby neither the subject nor the experimenter who interacts with the subject knows which condition the subject has been assigned to.

ego-defensive functions *(4)* The holding of certain attitudes which protect or enhance self-esteem.

elaboration likelihood model *(5)* A theory that central and peripheral routes of attitude change are differentiated by the amount of cognitive activity involved.

emergent norm theory *(14)* The view that individuals in a crowd develop a shared perception of the situation and a consensus about what behaviours are appropriate.

empathy *(10)* A vicarious response elicited by the observed emotional reaction of someone else.

equality principle *(13)* Principle of distributive justice in which all parties receive the same outcomes.

equity principle *(13)* Principle of distributive justice in which the outcomes received by the parties are proportional to their contributions.

eros *(9)* The life instinct, according to Freud.

estrogens *(9)* Female sex hormones.

ethnocentrism *(7)* A generalized tendency to prefer one's own group and reject others.

ethology *(9)* The study of the behaviour of organisms in their natural habitat.

evaluation apprehension *(2)* A concern of subjects that they be perceived by the experimenter in a socially desirable light.

evaluation research *(15)* Empirical studies which are designed to assess social programs or policies.

excitation-transfer theory *(9)* A theory that residues of the arousal from one emotional reaction can increase a subsequent reaction in a different situation.

experimental realism *(2)* The extent to which the situation encountered in an experiment involves subjects so that they react in a natural way.

experimenter effects *(2)* Unintentional influence of the subject by the experimenter which biases the study in the direction of confirming the experimental hypothesis.

external validity *(2)* Degree to which findings from a laboratory can be generalized to predict how the subject would act in the outside world.

extraneous variable *(2)* A factor not included in the design of a study which influences the study's outcome.

facial display *(11)* A pattern of expressions which communicate information, particularly about the emotional state of the person.

fad *(14)* A short-lived, extreme and frivolous collective behaviour.

falsification *(2)* The empirical demonstration that an hypothesis is not correct.

fashion *(14)* A wide spread collective preference.

field study *(2)* Direct observation of people in a natural setting.

foot-in-the-door technique *(6)* A means of inducing compliance to a major request by first eliciting compliance to a small request.

frustration-aggression hypothesis *(9)* The hypothesis that aggression follows frustration and frustration precedes aggression.

fundamental attribution error *(3)* Tendency of people to exaggerate the importance of personal dispositions as the causes of behaviour.

gain/loss effect *(8)* People are most attracted to those who initially dislike them and eventually like them, and are least attracted to those who initially like them and eventually dislike them.

game theory *(13)* A model of social conflict in which people are assumed to act rationally in order to maximize their gains and minimize their losses.

generic norm *(12)* Disposition to reject or discriminate against members of all out-groups, regardless of the group or context.

GRIT (graduated and reciprocated initiatives in tension reduction) *(13)* A possible method of reversing a conflict spiral by making credible but non-damaging concessions.

group-think *(6)* Tendency of a highly cohesive and elitist group to achieve a rapid consensus without dissent or outside influences.

health behaviour *(16)* Actions taken to prevent illness.

health beliefs model *(16)* A theory which accounts for health-related behaviour in terms of recognizing a personally relevant/threat and a choice of actions.

health promotion *(16)* Actions taken to enhance and protect health and prevent illness, particularly through self-responsibility.

heroism *(10)* Altruistic act in the face of extraordinary risk.

hostile aggression *(9)* Aggression which expresses anger or some other negative emotion.

hypertension *(16)* High blood pressure.

hypothesis *(2)* A testable proposition derived from theory.

hypothetical construct *(2)* Variable which is presumed to exist and which is used to explain other variables or observations.

ideology *(4)* An integrated set of attitudes.

idiosyncrasy credits *(6)* A group tolerates more non-conformity from a high-status person who is perceived to have contributed much to the group.

illusion of control *(3)* A commonly held and exaggerated belief that people can determine their lives and the events around them.

illusory correlation *(3)* Tendency to have exaggerated expectancies of how events are related.

immersion program *(11)* A form of second-language education in which the second language is used for instruction and interaction rather than being treated as a separate subject.

implicit personality theory *(3)* The assumptions of people about which traits "go together" and about human nature.

independent variable *(2)* A condition in an experiment that is manipulated by the experimenter.

individualistic bias *(15)* A North American ideal of the self-contained person which has influenced the definition of concepts and problems in social psychology.

informational social influence *(6)* The matching of our own ideas to the group in order to determine whether they are "correct."

informed consent *(2)* Agreement of subjects to participate in an experiment after being told what will happen to them.

ingratiation *(3)* Strategies of enhancing our attractiveness to others in order to create a positive impression.

in-group *(12)* A social category to which a person belongs.

inoculation effect *(5)* Exposure to relatively weak arguments against our own position strengthens our later resistance to persuasion.

instinct *(9)* Inborn behavioural tendencies which motivate certain actions.

instrumental aggression *(9)* Behaviour intended to harm as a means to some desired end.

integrative complexity *(3)* Extent to which people can use several schemata and standards in a flexible way when processing information.

intergroup anxiety *(7)* Negative feelings regarding anticipated adverse consequences of contact between groups.

internal validity *(2)* Degree to which changes in behaviour were brought about by experimental manipulations rather than extraneous factors.

interpersonal accomodation theory *(11)* A theory that individuals modify their style of speech in order to be liked and approved by the people with whom they are interacting.

intimacy *(8)* A relationship characterized by emotional closeness and self-disclosure.

intropunitive reaction *(7)* Self-blame experienced by victims.

jealousy *(8)* An unpleasant reaction to a perceived rival arising out of social comparison or a desire for exclusivity.

just world hypothesis *(3)* A belief that people get what they deserve and that life is essentially fair.

kernel of truth hypothesis *(7)* The idea that social stereotypes are necessarily based on some supportable evidence.

language *(11)* A system of vocal sounds which constitute symbols that have meaning in communication.

leader *(12)* An individual in a group who has the greatest influence over other members.

learned helplessness *(16)* Repeated exposure to a negative and unavoidable stimulus whereby the organism is later unable to avoid it and exhibits passive withdrawal.

legitimate power *(12)* Our capacity to influence others based on their acceptance of our authority.

legitimized aggression *(6)* Violence authorized by social institutions and authorities.

levelling *(14)* A process through which a rumour tends to grow shorter, and is more easily grasped and repeated.

linguistic relativity hypothesis *(11)* The proposition that the way we organize our perceptions and cognitions about the world is largely determined by the language we speak.

linguistic universals hypothesis *(11)* The proposition that all human languages share the same fundamental organization, reflecting some innate predisposition to develop and use grammatical rules.

locus of control *(16)* The extent to which people believe that the events in their lives are caused by their own actions (internal), or by luck, higher forces, or powerful other people (external).

loneliness *(8)* Unpleasant emotional state arising out of perceived deficiencies in relationships.

longitudinal study *(2)* Research in which two or more variables are studied in the same sample at two more points in time.

low-ball technique *(6)* A means of inducing someone to carry out a requested act by first requesting him/her to carry out the act, and only then increasing the cost of fulfilling the request.

Machiavellianism *(3)* A philosophy stating that other people can and should be manipulated.

marginality *(11)* The experience of immigrants or people learning a new language of feeling estranged from their own group and not part of the new group.

matching hypothesis *(8)* Proposition that individuals with approximately equal social characteristics, such as physical attractiveness, tend to select each other as friends and lovers.

mere exposure effect *(6)* Repeated contact with some person or object tends to lead to more favourable evaluations of that object or person.

meta-analysis *(6)* A method of statistically combining the results of many different studies on the same topic in order to identify consistent patterns in these results.

mixed motive game *(13)* A conflict in which there are rewards for both competition and cooperation.

model *(2)* A mini-theory, or set of propositions and assumptions, about a specific phenomenon.

moral development *(10)* The process by which moral judgments are made throughout childhood.

morpheme *(11)* Unit of meaning in language.

multiculturalism hypothesis *(7)* Positive feelings toward members of other groups vary with how secure and comfortable people feel about their own cultural identity and background.

MUM effect *(16)* Reluctance of someone, e.g., a physician, to communicate bad news.

mundane realism *(2)* Extent to which a situation encountered in an experiment is perceived as naturalistic or corresponding to some real-life situation.

mutuality *(8)* A relationship characterized by some degree of involvement, commitment, and intimacy, between two people.

national character *(4)* Model patterns of attitudes and values which characterize the typical person of a society or culture.

negativity effect *(3)* Tendency for overall impressions of people to be more influenced by negative than by positive traits.

non-verbal communication *(11)* The sending of information to another person (or persons) without the use of words.

non-zero-sum game *(12)* A conflict situation in which some outcomes are mutually preferable — a mixed motive game.

norm *(12)* Shared beliefs about which behaviours are acceptable and not acceptable for group members.

norm of reciprocity *(10)* The generally shared belief that people should help those who have helped them.

norm of social responsibility *(10)* The generally shared belief that people should help those who need help.

nuclear anxiety *(15)* A state of objective discomfort concerning the threat of nuclear war and nuclear accident.

obedience *(6)* Acquiescent behaviour in response to a direct order.

observational learning *(6)* The experience of modelling influence through which a novel behaviour is acquired.

operational definition *(2)* A definition of a construct in terms of how it is measured.

opinion leaders *(6)* Highly influential people who transmit new attitudes to many others.

out-group *(12)* A social category to which an individual does not belong.

own-race bias *(15)* Tendency of people to recognize people of their own race better than those of another race.

panic *(14)* A collective contagion of intense fear, often uncontrolled and resulting in flight.

paralanguage *(11)* Non-verbal aspects of speech which convey information.

parallel response model *(16)* A model of fear-arousing communication which states that people respond by controlling the danger and dealing with unpleasant affect aroused by the message.

particularism *(8)* In social exchange, the extent to which the value of a resource is influenced by the person who provides it.

perceived norm *(4)* An expectation of how significant other people would react to a particular action by a person.

peripheral route persuasion *(5)* Attitude change not accompanying deliberate thought about the issue, usually occurring in association with distractors.

phonemes *(11)* The short, meaningless sounds which are combined into morphemes.

polarization effect *(12)* The tendency of group decisions to be more extreme than the decisions of individual members.

positivity bias *(3)* A tendency to perceive others in a favourable light.

post-decision dissonance *(5)* A state of psychological discomfort which occurs after a difficult choice has been made.

prejudice *(7)* Attitudes to members of a group which are illogical or distortions of fact and which are unjustifiable.

primacy effect *(5)* Tendency for information presented early in a sequence to have a greater impact than information presented later.

primary prevention *(16)* Measures taken to reduce the incidence of a disease or other health problems.

priming *(3)* The use of one event to make a subsequent cognitive process more rapid and efficient.

problem behaviour theory *(16)* A model of adolescent behaviour based on a syndrome of personal, environmental, and behavioural non-conventionality linked with consequences.

procedural justice *(13)* Fairness of rules involved in making decisions of justice.

propinquity rule *(8)* When people are in close physical proximity, the probability of interaction and attraction increases.

prosodic features of language *(11)* Non-verbal aspects of speech, such as timing, pitch, and loudness.

protection motivation model *(16)* A model of fear-arousing communication which states that people respond to danger if they believe the danger to be severe and personally relevant.

prototype *(3)* A typical example of a category.

proxemics *(15)* The study of the physical distance people maintain between each other.

quasi-experiment *(2)* A field study of the effects of some naturally occurring event or change.

randomization *(2)* Assignment of subjects by chance to various experimental conditions.

reactivity *(2)* Extent to which a measure influences the characteristic that it is measuring.

realistic conflict *(13)* A situation of disaccord between parties based on competition for scarce resources, incompatible goals, or incompatible principles.

reference group *(6)* A group an individual identifies with and would like to belong to.

reinforcement-affect model *(8)* Through a process of conditioning, people become attracted to others whom they associate with stimuli or events which arouse positive feelings.

reliability *(2)* The degree to which a measure yields the same results when used more than once to measure some unchanging object, trait, or behaviour.

reparative altruism *(10)* Helping or other prosocial acts performed by someone after having done something harmful in order to compensate for the harm done (not necessarily to the person harmed).

replication *(2)* Reproducing the results of a scientific study.

response facilitation *(6)* Increase in the likelihood that a behaviour will occur in a given situation as a result of modeling influence.

response set *(2)* A disposition of subjects in research to respond in a systematically biased manner.

reverse discrimination *(7)* Excessively positive actions toward members of specific group which may not reflect positive attitudes.

risky shift *(12)* Tendency for some group decisions to involve higher levels of risk than the average individual decision (see **polarization effect**).

rules of correspondence *(2)* The principles by which concepts are translated into terms that can be measured unambiguously.

rumour *(14)* Information, often distorted, which is transmitted through a collectivity.

sample *(2)* A relatively small group of subjects taken to be representative of a larger, defined population of interest.

sample mean *(2)* Average score in a group.

scapegoating *(7)* A response to frustration whereby the individual displaces aggression onto a socially disapproved out-group.

schema *(3)* An organized system of cognitions about something such as an event, a role, a type of person, or ourselves.

secondary prevention *(16)* Measures taken to detect and treat an illness at the earliest possible stage.

selective information-seeking *(5)* Deliberately attending to information that supports our position and avoiding contrary information.

self-fulfilling prophecy *(8)* A phenomenon whereby people's expectations lead them to behave in a way to cause the expectation to come true.

self-monitors *(3)* People who are unusually sensitive to the subtle responses of others in evaluating their own behaviour.

self-serving bias *(3)* Attributions which are motivated by a desire to protect or enhance our own self-esteem.

set *(14)* An expectation or predisposition to act in a certain way.

sexism *(7)* Prejudice based on the gender of a person.

sharpening *(14)* Selective emphasis of some parts of a rumour.

sick role behaviour *(16)* Actions in accordance with norms and a schema for how people are expected to behave when they are ill.

similarity effect *(8)* We tend to be attracted to people with attitudes and values that correspond to our own.

sleeper effect *(5)* Tendency for a communication to increase in persuasiveness over time when emanating from a low-credibility source.

social categorization *(12)* Labelling people in terms of their membership in various broad social groups, such as gender, ethnicity, and occupation.

social comparison *(8)* A tendency of people to evaluate themselves in relation to other people, especially when a situation is ambiguous or uncertain.

social deviance *(6)* Behaviour which departs sufficiently from norms to elicit negative responses.

social differentiation *(12)* Tendency to overestimate the similarities among members of the same category and to overestimate the differences among members of different categories.

social exchange *(13)* A view of social interaction which is based on the rewards and costs that people provide for each other.

social facilitation *(6)* An increment or decrement in behaviour resulting from the presence of one or more other individuals.

social identification *(12)* The process whereby individuals define themselves with respect to other people.

social loafing *(6)* A decrease in individual effort when coacting with others.

social modelling *(6)* Social influence experienced as a result of observing the behaviour of someone else.

social movement *(14)* A spontaneous, large collectivity constituted in support of a set of purposes shared by the members.

social penetration process *(8)* As a relationship develops over time, self-disclosure increases in both breadth (range of topics discussed) and depth (intimacy).

social psychology *(1)* The discipline which sets out to understand how the thoughts, feelings, and behaviours of individuals are influenced by the actual, imagined, or implied presence of others.

social support *(16)* Relationships with others that provide encouragement, acceptance and assistance for the person.

sociobiology *(10)* A discipline rooted in the premise of an evolutionary basis to behaviour.

speech act theory *(11)* The study of correspondence (or lack thereof) between what the speaker says and what is intended (i.e., direct versus indirect speech acts).

standard speech *(11)* A style of speaking defined socially as desirable or preferable.

statistical inferences *(2)* Procedures to determine whether, relative to chance, two variables vary in some systematic way with each other or two or more groups differ in terms of their scores on some variable.

status-marking *(14)* Actions taken by people to distinguish themselves from people in other groups.

stereotype *(7)* A rigid set of cognitions about a group that are applied indiscriminately to all members in the group.

stimulus overload *(15)* A situation, often high-density, in which people receive too much information to process it efficiently.

stress *(15)* A physiological or psychological response to threat or challenge.

superordinate goal *(13)* An outcome desired and shared by parties who must cooperate in order to achieve it.

survivalists *(15)* People who believe that a nuclear war is inevitable and act in order to maximize their chances of surviving it.

survivor guilt *(15)* Intense negative feelings experienced by people who did not die in a catastrophe, involving asking why they lived and others died.

testimony *(15)* Evidence presented in court under oath.

thanatos *(9)* According to Freud, a death instinct which promotes at an unconscious level a return to the original inanimate state.

theory *(2)* A set of statements and assumptions that link concepts and hypotheses to observations.

threat *(13)* A communication that the other person or group will suffer negative consequences unless they act as demanded.

trade-off reasoning *(4)* Cognitions which enable a person to resolve conflicting values or attitudes.

triangular model of love *(8)* A model which defines love in terms of intimacy, passion, and commitment.

type A personality *(16)* A pattern of competitiveness, impatience, and unexpressed anger, linked to a greater risk of coronary disease.

validity *(2)* Extent to which a measure corresponds to the characteristic that it is intended to measure.

value *(4)* Central, higher-order set of preferences for goals in life and ways of living which are felt to be ideal and important.

value-expressive functions *(4)* The holding of certain attitudes which represent an important principle for the person.

vicarious reinforcement *(6)* A positive feeling of reward in response to observing someone else being rewarded.

zero-sum game *(13)* A conflict situation in which one party's gains match exactly the losses of the other.

B·I·B·L·I·O·G·R·A·P·H·Y

ABEL, E. (1966). *The missile crisis*. New York: Lippincott.

ABEL, G.G., BARLOW, D.H., BLANCHARD, E. & GUILD, D. (1977). The components of rapists' sexual arousal. *Archives of General Psychiatry, 34,* 895–903.

ABELLA, I. & TROPER, H. (1983). *None is too many*. Toronto: Lester & Orpen Dennys.

ABELSON, R.P. (1968). Psychological implication. In R.P. Abelson, E. Aronson, W.J. McGuire, T.M. Newcomb, M.J. Rosenberg & P.H. Tannenbaum (Eds.), *Theories of cognitive consistency: A sourcebook*. Chicago: Rand McNally.

ABRAMSON, L.Y., SELIGMAN, M.E.P. & TEASDALE, J.D. (1978). Learned helplessness in humans: Critique and reformulation. *Journal of Abnormal and Social Psychology, 87,* 49–74.

ADACHI, K. (1976). *The enemy that never was: A history of the Japanese Canadians*. Toronto: McClelland and Stewart.

ADAIR, J.G. (1973). *The human subject*. Boston: Little, Brown.

ADAIR, J.G. (1980). Psychology at the turn of the century: Crises, challenges, promises. *Canadian Psychologist, 21,* 165–178.

ADAIR, J.G. (1984). The Hawthorne Effect: A reconsideration of the methodological artifact. *Journal of Applied Psychology, 69,* 334–345.

ADAIR, J.G. & SCHACHTER, B.S. (1972). To cooperate or to look good? The subjects' and experimenters' perceptions of each other. *Journal of Experimental Social Psychology, 8,* 74–85.

ADAIR, J.G. & SPINNER, B. (1983). Task perceptions and behavioural expectations: A process-oriented approach to subject behaviour in experiments. *Canadian Journal of Behavioural Science, 15,* 130–141.

ADAMS, G. & HUSTON, T. (1975). Social perception of middle-aged persons varying in physical attractiveness. *Developmental Psychology, 11,* 657–658.

ADAMS, J.L. (1980). *Conceptual blockbusting: A guide to better ideas*. Second edition. New York: Norton.

ADAMS, J.S. (1963). Toward an understanding of inequity. *Journal of Abnormal and Social Psychology, 67,* 422–436.

ADAMS, J.S. (1965). Inequity in social exchange. In L. Berkowitz (Ed.), *Advances in experimental social psychology* (Vol. 2). New York: Academic Press.

ADAMS, J.S. & FREEDMAN, S. (1976). Equity theory revisited: Comments and annotated bibliography. In L. Berkowitz & E. Walsten (Eds.), *Advances in Experimental Social Psychology* (Vol. 9). New York: Academic Press.

ADORNO, T.W., FRENKEL-BRUNSWICK, E., LEVINSON, D.J. & SANFORD, R.N. (1950). *The authoritarian personality*. New York: Harper.

AGNEW, N.M. & PYKE, S.W. (1969). *The science game.* Englewood Cliffs, NJ: Prentice-Hall.

AIELLO, J.R. (1972). A test of equilibrium theory: Visual interaction in relation to orientation, distance and sex of the interactants. *Psychonomic Science, 27,* 335–336.

AIELLO, J.R. & THOMPSON, D.E. (1980). Personal space, crowding and spatial behavior in a cultural context. In I. Altman, J.F. Wohlwill and A. Rapaport (Eds.), *Human behavior and environment: Vol. 4, Environment and culture.* New York: Plenum Press.

AJZEN, I. (1977). Intuitive theories of events and the effects of base-rate information on predictions. *Journal of Personality and Social Psychology, 35,* 303–314.

AJZEN, I. & FISHBEIN, M. (1973). Attitudinal and normative variables as predictors of specific behaviors. *Journal of Personality and Social Psychology, 27,* 41–57.

AJZEN, I. & FISHBEIN, M. (1977). Attitude-behavior relations: A theoretical analysis and review of empirical research. *Psychological Bulletin, 84,* 888–918.

AJZEN, I. & FISHBEIN, M. (1980). *Understanding attitudes and predicting social behavior.* Englewood Cliffs, NJ: Prentice-Hall.

ALCOCK, J.E. (1975). Motivation in an asymmetric bargaining situation: A cross-cultural study. *International Journal of Psychology, 10,* 69–81.

ALCOCK, J.E. (1981). *Parapsychology: Science or magic?* Oxford: Pergamon.

ALCOCK, J.E. (1986). Chronic pain and the injured worker. *Canadian Psychology, 27,* 196–203.

ALCOCK, J.E. & MANSELL, D. (1977). Predisposition and behaviour in a collective dilemma. *Journal of Conflict Resolution, 21,* 443–458.

ALEXANDER, B.K. & HADAWAY, P.F. (1982). Opiate addiction: The case for an adaptive orientation. *Psychological Bulletin, 92,* 367–381.

ALLEN, B.P. (1985). After the missiles. Sociopsychological effects of nuclear war. *American Psychologist, 40,* 927–937.

ALLEN, M.G. (1972). A cross-cultural study of aggression and crime. *Journal of Cross-cultural Psychology, 3,* 259–271.

ALLEN, V.L. & LEVINE, J.M. (1971). Social support and conformity: The role of independent assessment of reality. *Journal of Experimental and Social Psychology, 7,* 48–58.

ALLISON, S.T. & MESSICK, D.M. (1985). Effects of experience on performance in a replenishable resource trap. *Journal of Personality and Social Psychology, 49,* 943–948.

ALLPORT, F.H. (1924). *Social psychology.* Boston: Houghton-Mifflin.

ALLPORT, G.W. (1935). Attitudes. In C.M. Murchison (Ed.), *Handbook of Social Psychology* (798–844). Worchester, MA: Clark University Press.

ALLPORT, G.W. (1954). *The nature of prejudice.* Reading, MA: Addison Wesley

ALLPORT, G.W. & KRAMER, B.M. (1946). Some roots of prejudice. *Journal of Psychology, 22,* 9–39.

ALLPORT, G.W. & POSTMAN, L.J. (1945). Psychology of rumour. *Transactions of the New York Academy of Sciences, 8,* 61–81.

ALLPORT, G.W. & VERNON, P.E. (1931). *A study of values.* Boston: Houghton-Mifflin.

ALLPORT, G.W., VERNON, P.E. & LINDZEY, G. (1960). *A study of values* Third Edition. Boston: Houghton-Mifflin.

ALTEMEYER, B. (1981). *Right-wing authoritarianism.* Winnipeg: University of Manitoba Press.

ALTMAN, I. (1973). Reciprocity of interpersonal exchange. *Journal of the Theory of Social Behavior, 3,* 249–261.

ALTMAN, I. (1975). *The environment and social behavior: Privacy, personal space, territory, crowding.* Monterey, CA: Brooks/Cole.

ALTMAN, I. (1976). Privacy: A conceptual analysis. *Environment and Behavior, 8,* 7–29.

ALTMAN, I. & TAYLOR, D.A. (1973). *Social penetration: The development of interpersonal relationships.* New York: Holt, Rinehart & Winston.

AMATO, P.R. (1983). Helping behavior in urban and rural settings: Field studies based on a taxonomic organization of helping episodes. *Journal of Personality and Social Psychology, 45,* 571–586.

AMERICAN PSYCHOLOGICAL ASSOCIATION. (1985). *Violence on TV. A social issue release from the Board of Social and Ethical Responsibility for Psychology.* Washington, D.C: American Psychological Association.

AMIR, Y. (1976). The role of intergroup contact in change of prejudice and ethnic relations. In P.A. Katz (Ed.), *Towards the elimination of racism* (245–308). Elmsford, N.Y: Pergamon Press.

AMNESTY INTERNATIONAL (1975). *Report on torture.* New York: Farrar, Straus & Giroux.

AMNESTY INTERNATIONAL (1984). *Torture in the eighties: An Amnesty International report.* London, U.K.: Amnesty International Publications.

ANDERSON, C.A. & ANDERSON, D.C. (1984). Ambient temperature and violent crime: Tests of the linear and curvilinear hypotheses. *Journal of Personality and Social Psychology, 46,* 91–97.

ANDERSON, C.A., LEPPER, M.R. & ROSS, L. (1980). Perseverence of social theories: The role of explanation in the persistence of discredited information. *Journal of Personality and Social Psychology, 39,* 1037–1049.

ANDERSON, N.H. (1959). Test of a model of opinion change. *Journal of Abnormal and Social Psychology, 59,* 371–381.

ANDERSON, N.H. (1965). Adding versus averaging as a stimulus combination rule in impression formation. *Journal of Experimental Psychology, 70,* 394–400.

ANDERSON, N.H. (1978). Cognitive algebra: Integration theory applied to social attribution. In L. Berkowitz (Ed.) *Cognitive theories in social psychology*. New York: Academic Press.

ANDERSON, N.H. & HUBERT, S. (1963). Effects of concomitant verbal recall on order effects in personality impression formation. *Journal of Verbal Learning and Verbal Behavior, 2,* 379–391.

ANDERSON, W.A. (1977). The social organization and social control of a fad: Streaking on a college campus. *Urban Life, 6,* 221–239.

ANDREAS, C.R. (1969). "To receive from kings . . ." An examination of government-to-government aid and its unintended consequences. *Journal of Social Issues 25,* 167–180.

D'ANGLEJAN, A. (1984). Language planning in Québec: An historical overview and future trends. In R.Y. Bourhis (Ed.), *Conflict and language planning in Québec.* Clevedon, England: Multilingual Matters.

D'ANGLEJAN, A. & TUCKER, G.R. (1973). Sociolinguistic correlates of speech style in Québec. In. R.W.Shuy & R.W. Fasold (Eds.), *Language attitudes: Current trends and prospects* (1-27). Washington: Georgetown University Press.

ANISFELD, E. & LAMBERT, W.E. (1961). Social and psychological variables in learning Hebrew. *Journal of Abnormal and Social Psychology, 63,* 524–529.

ANTHONY, S. (1973). Anxiety and rumor. *Journal of Social Psychology, 89,* 91–98.

APFELBAUM, E. & LUBEK, I. (1976). Resolution vs. revolution? The theory of conflicts in question. In L. Strickland, F. Aboud & E. Gergen (Eds.), *Social psychology in transition* (71–94). New York: Plenum.

ARANOFF, C. (1974). Old age in prime time. *Journal of Communication, 24,* 86–87.

ARCHER, J. (1976). Biological explanations of psychological sex differences. In B. Lloyd & J. Archer (Eds.), *Exploring sex differences* (241–266). New York: Academic Press.

ARCHER, R.L., DIAZ-LOVING, R., GOLLWITZER, P.M., DAVIS, M.H. & FOUSHEE, H.C. (1981). The role of dispositional empathy and social evaluation in the empathic mediation of helping. *Journal of Personality and Social Psychology, 40,* 786–796.

ARGYLE, M. (1969). *Social interaction.* London: Tavistock.

ARGYLE, M. (1971). *The psychology of interpersonal behaviour.* Harmondsworth: Penguin Books.

ARGYLE, M. (1975). *Bodily communication.* London: Methuen & Co.

ARGYLE, M. & DEAN, J. (1965). Eye-contact, distance and affiliation. *Sociometry, 28,* 289–304.

ARONFREED, J. (1970). Socialization of behavior. In J. Macaulay and L. Berkowitz (Eds.), *Altruism and helping behavior.* New York: Academic Press.

ARONFREED, J. & PASKAL, V. (1965). Altruism, empathy, and the conditioning of positive affect. Unpublished manuscript, University of Pennsylvania. Cited by Aronfreed (1970).

ARONSON, E. (1968). Dissonance theory: Progress and problems. In R.P. Abelson, E. Aronson, W.J. McGuire, T.M. Newcomb, M.J. Rosenberg & P.H. Tannenbaum (Eds.), *Theories of cognitive consistency: A sourcebook* (5–27). Chicago: Rand-McNally.

ARONSON, E. (1970). Some antecedents of interpersonal attraction: In W.J. Arnold & D. Levine (Eds.), *Nebraska Symposium on Motivation, 1969* (143–173). Lincoln: University of Nebraska Press.

ARONSON, E. (1978). The theory of cognitive dissonance: A current perspective. In L. Berkowitz (Ed.), *Cognitive theories in social psychology* (215–220). New York: Academic Press.

ARONSON, E. (1980). Persuasion via self-justification: Large commitments for small rewards. In L. Festinger (Ed.), *Retrospections on Social Psychology.* New York: Oxford University Press.

ARONSON, E. (1984). *The social animal* Fourth Edition. New York: W.H. Freeman.

ARONSON, E. & CARLSMITH, J.M. (1963). Effect of the severity of threat on the devaluation of forbidden behavior. *Journal of Abnormal and Social Psychology, 66,* 584–588.

ARONSON, E. & CARLSMITH, J.M. (1968). Experimentation in social psychology. In G. Lindzey & E. Aronson (Eds.), *Handbook of social psychology* (Vol. 2) Second Edition. Reading, MA: Addison-Wesley.

ARONSON, E. & GOLDEN, B.W. (1962). The effect of relevant and irrelevant aspects of communicator credibility on attitude change. *Journal of Personality, 30,* 135–146.

ARONSON, E. & LINDER, D. (1965). Gain and loss of esteem as determinants of interpersonal attractiveness. *Journal of Experimental Social Psychology, 1,* 156–171.

ARONSON, E. & MILLS, J. (1959). The effect of severity of initiation on liking for a group. *Journal of Abnormal and Social Psychology, 59,* 177–181.

ARONSON, E., WILLERMAN, B. & FLOYD, J. (1966). The effect of a pratfall on increasing personal attractiveness. *Psychonomic Science, 4,* 157–158.

ARVEY, R.D. (1979). Unfair discrimination in the employment interview: Legal and psychological aspects. *Psychological Bulletin. 86,* 736–765.

ASCH, S.E. (1946). Forming impressions of personality. *Journal of Abnormal and Social Psychology, 41,* 258–290.

ASCH, S.E. (1951). Effects of group pressure upon the modification and distortion of judgements. In H. Guetzkow (Ed.), *Groups, leadership and men.* Pittsburgh: Carnegie Press.

ATHANASIÓU, R. & YASHIOKA, G. (1973). The spatial character of friendship formation. *Environmental Behavior, 5*, 43–65.

ATKINSON, M.L. (1986). The perception of social categories: Implications for social comparison process. In J.M. Olson, C.P. Herman & M.P. Zanna (Eds.), *Relative deprivation and social comparison: The Ontario Symposium* (Vol. 4). Hillsdale, N.J.: Erlbaum.

ATWOOD, M. (1972). *Survival.* Toronto: House of Anansi.

AUSTIN, W. (1979). Justice, freedom, and self-interest in intergroup conflict. In W.G. Austin & S. Worchel (Eds.), *The social psychology of intergroup relations* (121–144). Monterey, CA: Brooks/Cole.

AVIO, K.L. (1987). The Quality of Mercy: Exercise of the Royal Prerogative in Canada. Unpublished manuscript. Department of Economics, University of Victoria.

AZUMA, H. (1984). Secondary control as a heterogeneous category. *American Psychologist, 9*, 970–971.

BACKMAN, C.W. & SECORD, P.F. (1959). The effect of perceived liking on interpersonal attraction. *Human Relations, 12*, 379–384.

BAER, D.E. & CURTIS, J.E. (1984). French-Canadian English-Canadian differences in values: National survey findings. *Canadian Journal of Sociology, 9*, 405–427.

BAGOZZI, R.P. (1981). Attitudes, intentions, and behavior: A test of some key hypotheses. *Journal of Personality and Social Psychology, 41*, 607–627.

BAKAN, D., (1966). *The duality of human existence.* Chicago: Rand McNally.

BAKER, R.K. & BALL, S.J. (1969). *Mass media and violence* (Vol. 9). Washington, D.C.: United States Government Printing Office.

BALL-ROKEACH, S.J., ROKEACH, M. & GRUBE, J.W. (1984). *The great American values test. Influencing behavior and belief through television.* New York: The Free Press.

BANDURA, A. (1965). Influence of a model's reinforcement contingencies on the acquisition of imitative responses. *Journal of Personality and Social Psychology, 1*, 589–595.

BANDURA, A. (1973). *Aggression: A social learning analysis.* Englewood Cliffs, NJ: Prentice-Hall.

BANDURA, A. (1974). Behavior theories and the models of man. *American Psychologist, 29*, 859–869.

BANDURA, A. (1977). *Social learning theory.* Englewood Cliffs, NJ: Prentice-Hall.

BANDURA, A. (1983). Psychological mechanisms of aggression. In R.G. Geen & E.I. Donnerstein (Eds.), *Aggression: Theoretical and empirical reviews* (Vol. 1) (1–40). New York: Academic Press.

BANDURA, A., ROSS, D. & ROSS, S.A. (1963a). Vicarious reinforcement and imitative learning. *Journal of Abnormal and Social Psychology, 67*, 601–607.

BANDURA, A., ROSS, D. & ROSS, S.A. (1963b). A comparative test of the status envy, social power, and secondary reinforcement theories of identificatory learning. *Journal for Abnormal and Social Psychology, 67*, 527–534.

BANDURA, A., ROSS, D. & ROSS, S.A. (1963c). Imitation of film-mediated aggressive models. *Journal of Abnormal and Social Psychology, 66*, 3–11.

BANDURA, A. & WALTERS, R. (1963). *Social learning and personality development.* New York: Holt, Rinehart & Winston.

BANUAZIZI, A. & MOVAHEDI, S. (1975). Interpersonal dynamics in a simulated prison: A methodological analysis. *American Psychologist, 30*, 152–160.

BAR-TAL, D. (1976). *Prosocial behavior.* Washington, D.C.: Hemisphere.

BARBER, T.X. (1976). *Hypnosis: A scientific approach.* New York: Psychological Dimensions.

BARDWICK, J.M. (1971). *Psychology of women: A study of biocultural conflicts.* New York: Harper & Row.

BARGH, J.A. & CERNY, R. (1983). Automatic and conscious processes in impression formation. Unpublished manuscript. New York University.

BARKOWITZ, P.B. & BRIGHAM, J.C. (1982). Recognition of faces: Own-race bias, incentive and time delay. *Journal of Applied Social Psychology, 12*, 255–268.

BARON, R.A. (1977). *Human aggression.* New York: Plenum Press.

BARON, R.A. (1983a). The control of human aggression: An optimistic perspective. *Journal of Social and Clinical Psychology, 1*, 97–119.

BARON, R.A., (1983b). The control of human aggression: A strategy based on incompatible responses. In R.G. Geen and E.I. Donnerstein (Eds.), *Aggression: Theoretical and empirical reviews* (Vol. 2). New York: Academic Press.

BARON, R.A. & BELL, P.A. (1975). Aggression and heat: Mediating effects of prior provocation and exposure to an aggressive model. *Journal of Personality and Social Psychology, 31*, 825–832.

BARON, R.A. & RANSBERGER, V.M. (1978). Ambient temperature and the occurrence of collective violence: The "long hot summer" revisited. *Journal of Personality and Social Psychology, 36*, 351–360.

BARON, R.M. & RODIN, J. (1978). Perceived control and crowding stress: Processes mediating the impact of spatial and social density. In A. Baum & Y. Epstein (Eds.), *Human response to crowding.* Hillsdale, NJ: Erlbaum Associates.

BARON, R.S. (1986). Distraction-conflict theory: Progress and problems. In L. Berkowitz (Ed.), *Advances in experimental social psychology* (Vol. 20). New York. Academic Press.

BARON, R.S., MOORE, D. & SANDERS, G.S. (1978). Distraction as a source of drive in social facilitation research. *Journal of Personality and Social Psychology, 36,* 816–824.

BARRON, F. (1969). *Creative person and creative process.* New York: Holt, Rinehart & Winston.

BATSON, C.D., BOLEN, M.H., CROSS, J.A. & NEURINGER-BENEFIEL, H.E. (1986). Where is the altruism in the altruistic personality? *Journal of Personality and Social Psychology, 50,* 212–220.

BATSON, C.D. & GRAY, R.A. (1981). Religious orientation and helping behavior: Responding to one's own or the victim's needs? *Journal of Personality and Social Psychology, 40,* 511–520.

BATSON, C.D., O'QUIN, K., FULTZ, J., VANDERPLAS, M. & ISEN, A. (1983). Self-reported distress and empathy and egoistic versus altruistic motivation to help. *Journal of Personality and Social Psychology, 45,* 706–718.

BATTEN, J. (1977). *Canada moves westward 1880–1890.* Toronto: National Science Library of Canada.

BAUM, A., AIELLO, J.R. & CALESNICK, L.E. (1978). Crowding and personal control: Social density and the development of learned helplessness. *Journal of Personality and Social Psychology, 36,* 1000–1011.

BAUM, A. & DAVIS, G.E. (1980). Reducing the stress of high-density living: An architectural intervention. *Journal of Personality and Social Psychology, 38,* 417–481.

BAUM, A., GATCHEL, R.J. & SCHAEFFER, M.A. (1983). Emotional, behavioral and physiological effects of chronic stress at Three Mile Island. *Journal of Consulting and Clinical Psychology, 51,* 565–572.

BAUM, A. & VALINS, S. (1977). *Architecture and social behavior. Psychological studies and social density.* Hillsdale, NJ: Erlbaum.

BAUMRIND, D. (1964). Some thoughts on ethics of research: After reading Milgram's "Behavioral study of obedience." *American Psychologist, 19,* 421–423.

BAVELAS, J.B., BLACK, A., LEMERY, C.R. & MULLETT, J. (1986). "I *show* how you feel": Motor mimicry as a communicative act. *Journal of Personality and Social Psychology, 50,* 322–329.

BEARDSLEE, W. & MACK, J. (1982). The impact on children and adolescents of nuclear developments. In *American Psychiatric Association Task Force Report No. 20: Psychosocial Aspects of Nuclear Developments* (64–93). Washington, D.C.: American Psychiatric Association.

BEATTIE, G.W., CUTLER, A. & PEARSON, M. (1982). Why is Mrs. Thatcher interrupted so often? *Nature, 300,* 744–747.

BECHTOLD, A., NACCARATO, M.E. & ZANNA, M.P. (1986). Need for structure and the prejudice-discrimination link. Paper presented at the Annual Meeting of the Canadian Psychological Association, Toronto, June 19.

BECKER, M.H. (Ed.) (1974). The health belief model and personal health behavior. *Health Education Monographs. 2.* (Whole No. 4).

BECKER, M.H. & MAIMAN, L.A. (1975). Socio-behavioral determinants of compliance with health and medical care recommendations. *Medical Care, 13,* 10–24.

BECKER, W.C. (1964). Consequences of different kinds of parental discipline. In M.L. Hoffman & L.W. Hoffman (Eds.), *Review of child development research* (Vol. 1). New York: Russell Sage.

BÉGIN, G. (1976). The effects of success and failure on helping behaviour. Unpublished doctoral thesis. McMaster University, Hamilton, Ontario.

BELL, P.A. & BARON, R.A. (1977). Aggression and ambient temperature: The facilitating and inhibiting effects of hot and cold environments. *Bulletin of the Psychonomic Society, 9,* 443–445.

BEM, D.J. (1967). Self-perception: An alternative interpretation of cognitive dissonance. *Psychological Review, 74,* 183–200.

BEM, D.J. (1970). *Beliefs, attitudes and human affairs.* Belmont, CA: Brooks/Cole.

BEM, D.J. (1972). Self-perception theory. In L. Berkowitz (Ed.), *Advances in experimental social psychology.* Vol. 6. New York: Academic Press.

BEM, D.J., WALLACH, M.A. & KOGAN, N. (1965). Group decision making under risk of aversive consequences. *Journal of Personality and Social Psychology, 1,* 453–560.

BEM, S.L. (1974). The measure of psychological androgyny. *Journal of Consulting and Clinical Psychology, 42,* 155–162.

BEM, S.L. (1975). Sex role adaptibility: One consequence of psychological androgyny. *Journal of Personality and Social Psychology, 31,* 634–643.

BEM, S.L. (1985). Androgyny and gender role scheme theory: A conceptual and empirical integration. *Nebraska Symposium on Motivation 1984* (179–226). Lincoln: University of Nebraska Press.

BENNET, R., RAFFERTY, J.M., CANIVEZ, G.L. & SMITH, J.M. (May, 1983). The effects of cold temperature on altruism and aggression. Paper presented at the Midwestern Psychological Association, Chicago.

BENTLER, P.M. & SPECKART, G. (1981). Attitudes "cause" behavior: A structural equation analysis. *Journal of Personality and Social Psychology, 40,* 226–238.

BENTON, A.A. (1971). Productivity, distributive justice, and bargaining among children. *Journal of Personality and Social Psychology, 18,* 68–78.

BERCUSON, D. & WERTHEIMER, D. (1985). *A trust betrayed. The Keegstra affair.* Toronto: Doubleday.

BERG, K.O. & VIDMAR, N. (1975). Authoritarianism and recall of evidence about criminal behavior. *Journal of Research in Personality, 9*, 147–157.

BERGER, S.M., CARLI, L.C., GARCIA, R. & BRODY, J.J. Jr. (1982). Audience effects in anticipating learning: A comparison of drive and proactive-inhibition analyses. *Journal of Personality and Social Psychology, 42*, 378–386.

BERGLAS, S. (1987). The self-handicapping model of alcohol abuse. In H.T. Blane & K.E. Leonard (Eds.), *Psychological theories of drinking and alcoholism* (305–345). New York: Guilford Press.

BERK, R.A. (1974). A gaming approach to crowd behavior. *American Sociological Review, 39*, 355–373.

BERKOWITZ, L. (1954). Group standards, cohesiveness, and productivity. *Human Relations, 7*, 509–519.

BERKOWITZ, L. (1962). *Aggression: A social psychological analysis.* New York: McGraw-Hill.

BERKOWITZ, L. (1971). The contagion of violence: An S-R mediational analysis of some effects of observed aggression. *Nebraska Symposium on Motivation 1970.* Lincoln: University of Nebraska Press.

BERKOWITZ, L. (Ed.) (1972). Social norms, feelings, and other factors affecting helping and altruism. In L. Berkowitz (Ed.), *Advances in Experimental Social Psychology* (Vol. 6). New York: Academic Press.

BERKOWITZ, L. (1973). Reactance and the unwillingness to help others. *Psychological Bulletin, 79*, 310–317.

BERKOWITZ, L. (1983). Aversively stimulated aggression: Some parallels and differences in research with animals and humans. *American Psychologist, 38*, 1135–1144.

BERKOWITZ, L. (1984). Some effects of thoughts of anti- and prosocial influences of media events: A cognitive-neoassociation analysis. *Psychological Bulletin, 95*, 410–427.

BERKOWITZ, L. (1986). Situational influences on reactions to observed violence. *Journal of Social Issues, 42*, 93–106.

BERKOWITZ, L. & DANIELS, L.R. (1963). Responsibility and dependency. *Journal of Abnormal and Social Psychology, 66*, 664–669.

BERKOWITZ, L. & DONNERSTEIN, E. (1982). External validity is more than skin deep: Some answers to criticism of laboratory experiments. *American Psychologist, 37*, 245–257.

BERKOWITZ, L. & LUTTERMAN, K. (1968). The traditionally socially responsible person. *Public Opinion Quarterly, 32*, 169–185.

BERKOWITZ, L. & MACAULAY, J. (1971). The contagion of criminal violence. *Sociometry, 34*, 238–260.

BERLYNE, D.E. (1960). *Conflict, arousal, and curiosity.* New York: McGraw-Hill.

BERNSTEIN, W.M., STEPHAN, W.G. & DAVIS, M.H. (1979). Explaining attributions for achievement: A path analytic approach. *Journal of Personality and Social Psychology, 37*, 1810–1821.

BERRY, J.W. (1978). Social psychology: Comparative, societal and universal. *Canadian Psychological Review, 19*, 93–104.

BERRY, J.W., KALIN, R. & TAYLOR, D. (1977). *Multiculturalism and ethnic attitudes in Canada.* Ottawa: Supply and Services Canada.

BERRY, J.W., WINTRES, R.M., SINDELL, P.S. & MAWHINNEY, T.A. (1982). Psychological adaptations to cultural change among the James Bay Cree. *Naturaliste Canadien, 109*, 965–975.

BERSCHEID, E. (1985). Interpersonal attraction. In G. Lindzey & E. Aronson (Eds.), *The handbook of social psychology.* Third Edition. New York: Random House.

BERSCHEID, E. & WALSTER, E. (1969). *Interpersonal Attraction.* Reading, MA: Addison-Wesley.

BERSCHEID, E. & WALSTER, E. (1974a). Physical attractiveness. In L. Berkowitz (Ed.), *Advances in experimental social psychology* (Vol. 7). New York: Academic Press.

BERSCHEID, E. & WALSTER, E. (1974b). A little bit about love. In T.L. Huston (Ed.), *Foundations of interpersonal attraction.* New York: Academic Press.

BERSCHEID, E. & WALSTER, E. (1978). *Interpersonal attraction.* Second Edition. Reading, MA: Addison-Wesley.

BETCHERMAN, L-R. (1975). *The swastika and the maple leaf.* Toronto: Fitzhenry & Whiteside.

BERTON, P. (1972). *Klondike: The last great gold rush, 1896–1899.* Toronto: McClelland & Stewart.

BERTON, P. (1976). It's the cops. *Quest, 5,* (2).

BEST, J.A., FLAG, B.R., TOWSON, S.M.J., RYAN, K.B., PERRY, C.L., BROWN, K.S., KERSELL, K.W. & D'AVERNAS, J.R. (1984). Smoking prevention and the concept of risk. *Journal of Applied Social Psychology, 14*, 257–273.

BICKMAN, L. (1972). Environmental attitudes and actions. *Journal of Social Psychology, 87*, 323–324.

BICKMAN, L. (1983). The evaluation of prevention programs. *Journal of Social Issues, 39*, 181–194.

BILLIG, M. & TAJFEL, H. (1973). Social categorization and similarity in intergroup behavior. *European Journal of Social Psychology, 3*, 27–52.

BISHOP, G.F. (1975). Resolution and tolerance of cognitive inconsistency in a field situation: Change in attitude and beliefs following the Watergate affair. *Psychological Reports, 36*, 747–753.

BLEIER, R. (1984). *Science and gender. A critique on biology and its theories on women.* New York: Pergamon Press.

BLOOM, A.H. (1981). *The linguistic shaping of thought: A study of the impact of language on thinking in China and the West.* Hillsdale, NJ: Erlbaum.

BLOOM, B., ASHER, S.J. & WHITE, S.W. (1978). Marital disruption as a stressor: A review and analysis. *Psychological Bulletin, 85*, 867–894.

BLUMENFELD, M., LEVY, N.B. & KAUFMAN, D. (1979). The wish to be informed of a fatal illness. *Omega, 9*, 323–326.

BLUMENTHAL, M.D., KAHN, R.L., ANDREWS, F.M. & HEAD, K.B. (1972). *Justifying violence: Attitudes of American men.* Ann Arbor, MI: Survey Research Center, Institute for Social Research, University of Michigan.

BLUMER, H. (1951). Social movements. In A.M. Lee (Ed.), *New outline of the principles of sociology.* Second Edition (199–220). New York: Barnes & Noble.

BLUMER, H. (1969). *Symbolic interactionism.* Englewood Cliffs, NJ: Prentice-Hall.

BOGARDUS, E.S. (1925). Measuring social distance. *Journal of Applied Psychology, 9*, 299–308.

BOLLEN, K.A. & PHILLIPS, D.P. 1982). Imitative suicides: A national study of the effects of television news stories. *American Sociological Review, 47*, 802–809.

BONACICH, P. SHURE, G.H., KAHAN, J.P. & MERKER, R.J. (1976). Cooperation and group size in the N-person Prisoner's Dilemma. *Journal of Conflict Resolution, 20*, 687–706.

BOND, C.F., Jr. & TITUS, L.J. (1983). Social facilitation: A meta-analysis of 241 studies. *Psychological Bulletin, 94*, 265–292.

BOND, S. (1981). *A hundred and one uses for a dead cat.* London: Eyre Methuen Ltd.

BOOTH-KEWLEY, S. & FRIEDMAN, H.S. (1987). Psychological predictors of heart disease: A quantitative review. *Psychological Bulletin, 101*, 343–362.

BOOTZIN, R.R., HERMAN, C.P. & NICASSIO, P. (1976). The power of suggestion: Another examination of misattribution and insomnia. *Journal of Personality and Social Psychology, 34*, 673–679.

BOUCHER, J.D. (1974). Display rules and facial affective behavior: A theoretical discussion and suggestions for research. *Topics in Culture Learning, 2*, 87–102.

BOULDING, K.E. (1980). Science: Our common heritage. *Science, 207*, 831–836.

BOURHIS, R.Y. (1979). Language in ethnic interaction: A social psychological approach. In H. Giles & B. Saint-Jacques (Eds.), *Language and ethnic relations.* Oxford: Pergamon.

BOURHIS, R.Y. (1982) Language policies and language attitudes: Le monde de la francophonie. In E.R. Ryan and H. Giles (Eds.), *Attitudes towards language variation* (34–62) London: Edward Arnold.

BOURHIS, R.Y. (1983). Language attitudes and self reports of French-English language usage in Québec. *Journal of Multilingual and Multicultural Development, 4*, 163–180.

BOURHIS, R.Y. (1984a). The charter of French language and cross-cultural communication in Montréal. In R.Y. Bourhis (Ed.), *Conflict and language planning in Québec.* Clevedon, England: Multilingual Matters.

BOURHIS, R.Y. (1984b). Cross-cultural communication in Montréal: Two field studies since Bill 101. *International Journal of the Sociology of Language, 46*, 33–47.

BOURHIS, R.Y. & GILES, H. (1977). The language of intergroup distinctiveness. In H. Giles (Ed.), *Language, ethnicity and intergroup relations.* London: Academic Press.

BOURHIS, R.Y., GILES, H. & LAMBERT, W.E. (1975). Social consequences of accommodating one's style of speech: a cross-national investigation. *International Journal of the Sociology of Language, 6*, 55–72.

BOURHIS, R.Y., GILES, H., LEYENS, J.P. & TAJFEL, H. (1979). Psycholinguistic distinctiveness: Language divergence in Belgium. In H. Giles & R. St. Clair (Eds.), *Language and social psychology.* Oxford: Blackwell.

BOWERS, K.S. (1973) Situationism in psychology: An analysis and critique. *Psychological Review, 80*, 307–336.

BOWLBY, J. (1969). *Attachment and loss.* (Vol. 1) *Attachment.* New York: Basic Books.

BOYD, J.R., COVINGTON, T.R., STANASZEK, W.F. & COUSSONS, R.T. (1974). Drug defaulting: II Analysis of noncompliance patterns. *American Journal of Hospital Pharmacy, 31*, 485–491.

BRADAC, J.J., DAVIES, R.A., COURTRIGHT, J.A., DESMOND, R.J. & MURDOCK, J.I. (1977). Richness of vocabulary: An attributional analysis. *Psychological Reports. 41*, 1131–1134.

BRAGINSKY, D. (1970). Machiavellianism and manipulative interpersonal behaviour in children. *Journal of Experimental Social Psychology, 6*, 77–99.

BRAY, R.M. & NOBLE, A.M. (1978). Authoritarianism and decisions of mock juries: Evidence of jury bias and group polarization. *Journal of Personality and Social Psychology, 36*, 1424–1430.

BRECKLER, S.J. (1984). Empirical validation of affect, behavior and cognition as distinct components of attitude. *Journal of Personality and Social Psychology, 47*, 1191–1205.

BREHM, J.W. (1966). *A theory of psychological reactance.* New York: Academic Press.

BREHM, J.W. & COHEN A.R. (1962). *Explorations in cognitive dissonance.* New York: Wiley.

BREHM, S.S. (1985). *Intimate relationships.* New York: Random House.

BREWER, M.B., DULL, V. & LUI, L. (1981). Perception of the elderly: Stereotypes as prototypes. *Journal of Personality and Social Psychology, 41*, 656–670.

BREWER, M.B. & KRAMER, R.M. (1985). The psychology of intergroup attitudes and behavior. *Annual Review of Psychology, 36*, 219–243.

BREWER, M.B. & KRAMER, R.M. (1986). Choice behavior in social dilemmas: Effects of social identity, group size, and decision framing. *Journal of Personality and Social Psychology, 50,* 543–549.

BRICKMAN, P. (1974). Rule structures and conflict relationships. In P. Brickman (Ed.), *Social conflict* (1–33). Lexington, MA: D.C. Heath.

BRIGHAM, J.C. (1971). Ethnic stereotypes. *Psychological Bulletin, 76,* 15–38.

BRIGHAM, J.C. (1973). Ethnic stereotypes and attitudes: A different mode of analysis. *Journal of Personality, 41,* 206–233.

BRIGHAM, J.C. & BARKOWITZ, P.B. (1978). Do "they all look alike?" The effect of race, sex, experience and attitudes on the ability to recognize faces. *Journal of Applied Social Psychology, 8,* 306–318.

BRIGHAM, J.C. & GIESBRECHT, L.W. (1976). The effects of viewed bigotry: Racial attitudes and "All in the Family." *Journal of Communications, 26,* 69–74.

BRIGHAM, J.C. & MALPASS, R.S. (1985). The role of experience and contact in the recognition of faces of own- and other-race persons. *Journal of Social Issues, 41,* 139–156.

BROADFOOT, B. (1977). *Years of sorrow, years of shame.* Toronto: Doubleday Canada.

BRODT, S.E. & ZIMBARDO, P.G. (1983). Modifying shyness-related social behavior through symptom misattribution. *Journal of Personality and Social Psychology, 41,* 437–449.

BRONFENBRENNER, U. (1961). The mirror image in Soviet-American relations: A social psychologist's report. *Journal of Social Issues, 17,* 45–56.

BROVERMAN., I.K., VOGEL, S.R., BROVERMAN, D.M., CLARKSON, F.E. & ROSENKRANTZ, P.S. (1972). Sexual stereotypes: A current appraisal. *Journal of Social Issues, 28,* 59–78.

BROWN, J.A.C. (1963). *Techniques of persuasion: From propaganda to brainwashing.* London, Penguin Books.

BROWN, P. & ELLIOT, R. (1965). Control of aggression in a nursery school class. *Journal of Experimental Child Psychology, 2,* 103–107.

BROWN, R. (1965). *Social psychology.* New York: Free Press.

BROWN, R. (1986). *Social Psychology, the second edition.* London: Collier MacMillan.

BROWN, V. & GEIS, F.L. (1984). Turning lead into gold: Evaluations of men and women leaders and the alchemy of social consensus. *Journal of Personality and Social Psychology, 46,* 811–824.

BROWNMILLER, S. (1984). *Femininity.* New York: Simon & Schuster.

BRUCK, M., TUCKER, G.R. & JAKAMIK, J. (1975). Are French immersion programs suitable for working class children? In W. Von Raffler Engle (Ed.), *Prospects in child language.* The Hague: Mouton.

BRUNER, J.S. & TAGIURI, R. (1954). The perception of people. In G. Lindzey (Ed.), *Handbook of Social Psychology* (634–654). Reading, MA: Addison-Wesley.

BRYAN, J.H. (1972) Why children help: a review. *Journal of Social Issues, 28,* 87–104.

BRYAN, J.H. & WALBECK, N. (1970). The impact of words and deeds concerning altruism upon children. *Child Development, 41,* 747–757.

BRYSON, J.B. (1977). Situational determinants of the expression of jealousy. In H. Sigall (Chair), Sexual jealousy. Symposium presented at the Annual Meeting of the American Psychological Association, San Francisco, U.S.A.

BUCKHOUT, R. (1980). Nearly 2000 witnesses can be wrong. *Bulletin of the Psychonomic Society, 16,* 307–310.

BUCKLEY, W., BURNS, T. & MEEKER, L.D. (1974). Structural resolutions of collective action problems. *Behavioral Science, 19,* 277–297.

BUCKNER, H.T. (1965). A theory of rumor transmission. *Pubic Opinion Quarterly, 29,* 54–70.

BUGENTAL, D.E., KASWAN, J.E. & LOVE, L.R. (1970). Perception of contradictory meanings conveyed by verbal and nonverbal channels. *Journal of Personality and Social Psychology, 16,* 647–655.

BULMAN, R.J. & WORTMAN, C.B. (1977). Attributions of blame and coping in the "real world": Severe accident victims react to their lot. *Journal of Personality and Social Psychology, 35,* 351–363.

BURGER, J.M. (1981). Motivational biases in the attribution of responsibility for an accident: A meta-analysis of the defensive attribution hypothesis. *Psychological Bulletin, 90,* 496–513.

BURGER, J.M. (1986). Increasing compliance by improving the deal: The that's-not-all technique. *Journal of Personality and Social Psychology, 51,* 277–283.

BURGER, J.M. & PETTY, R.E. (1981). The low-ball compliance technique: Task or person commitment? *Journal of Personality and Social Psychology, 40,* 492–500.

BURGESS, E.W. & HUSTON, T.L. (Eds.), (1979). *Social exchange in developing relationships.* New York: Academic Press.

BURKE, R.J. & WEIR, T. (1980). The Type A experience: Occupational and life demands, satisfaction and well-being. *Journal of Human Stress, 6,* 28–38.

BURNKRANT, R.E. & PAGE, T.J., Jr. (1982). An examination of the convergent, discriminant, and predictive validity of Fishbein's behavioral intention model. *Journal of Marketing Research, 19,* 550–561.

BURNSTEIN, E. & VINOKUR, A. (1977). Persuasive argumentation and social comparison as determinants of attitude polarization. *Journal of Experimental Social Psychology, 13,* 315–322.

BUSS, A.H. (1961). *The psychology of aggression.* New York: Wiley.

BYRNE, D. (1969). Attitudes and attraction. In L. Berkowitz (Ed.), *Advances in experimental social psychology* (Vol. 4) (36–89).

BYRNE, D. (1971). *The attraction paradigm*. New York: Academic Press.

BYRNE, D. & CLORE, G.L. (1970). A reinforcement model of evaluative responses. *Personality: An International Journal, 1*, 103–128.

BYRNE, D., CLORE, G.L. & SMEATON, G. (1986). The attraction hypothesis. Do similar attitudes affect anything? *Journal of Personality and Social Psychology, 51*, 1167–1170.

BYRNE, D., CLORE, G.L. & WORCHEL, P. (1966). Effect of economic similarity-dissimilarity on interpersonal attraction. *Journal of Personality and Social Psychology, 4*, 220–224.

BYRNE, D., ERVIN, C. & LAMBERTH, J. (1970). Continuity between the experimental study of attraction and real-life computer dating. *Journal of Personality and Social Psychology, 51*, 157–165.

BYRNE, D., GRIFFIT, W. & STEFONIAK, D. (1967). Attraction and similarity of personality characteristics. *Journal of Personality and Social Psychology, 5*, 82–90.

BYRNE, D., LONDON, O. & REEVES, K. (1968). The effects of physical attractiveness, sex, and attitude similarity on interpersonal attraction. *Journal of Personality, 36*, 259–271.

CAIRNS, R. & CAIRNS, B. (1985). The developmental-interactional view of social behavior: Four issues in adolescent aggression. In D. Olweus, J. Block & M. Radke-Yarrow (Eds.), *Development of anti-social and prosocial behavior: Theories, research and issues* (315–342). New York: Academic Press.

CALDWELL, G. (1984). Anglo-Québec: Demographic realities and options for the future. In R.Y. Bourhis (Ed.), *Conflict and language planning in Québec*. Clevedon, England: Multilingual Matters.

CALHOUN, J.B. (1962). Population density and social pathology. *Scientific American, 206*, 139–148.

CALLWOOD, J. (1987). Sanitized textbooks reflect a pious paradise that never was. *The Globe and Mail*, March 18, 1987.

CAMPBELL, D.T. (1969a) Prospective: Artifact and control. In R. Rosenthal and R.L. Rosnow (Eds.), *Artifact in behavioral research* (351–382). New York: Academic Press.

CAMPBELL, D.T. (1969b). Reforms as experiments. *American Psychologist, 24*, 409–429.

CAMPBELL, D.T. (1975). On the conflicts between biological and social evolution and between psychology and moral tradition. *American Psychologist, 30*, 1103–1126.

CAMPBELL, D.T., CONVERSE, P.E. & RODGERS, W.L. (1976). *The quality of American life*. New York: Russell Sage Foundation.

CAMPBELL, D.T., SIEGMAN, C.R. & REES, M.B. (1967). Direction-of-wording effects in the relationships between scales. *Psychological Bulletin, 68*, 293–303.

CAMPBELL, D.T. & STANLEY, J.C. (1963). *Experimental and quasi-experimental designs for researchers*. Chicago: Rand-McNally.

CANNING, H. & MAYER, J. (1966). Obesity: Its possible effect on college acceptance. *New England Journal of Medicine, 275*, 1172–1174.

CANTOR, N. & MISCHEL, W. (1979). Prototypes in person perception. In L. Berkowitz (Ed.), *Advances in experimental social psychology* (Vol. 12). New York: Academic Press.

CANTRIL, H. (1940). *The invasion from Mars*. Princeton, NJ: Princeton University Press.

CAPLAN, N.S. & PAIGE, J.M. (1968). A study of ghetto rioters. *Scientific American, 219*, 15–21.

CAPLAN, R.D., COBB, S. & FRENCH, J.R.P. (1975). Relation of cessation of smoking with job stress, personality and social support. *Journal of Applied Psychology, 60*, 211–219.

CAPLAN, R.D., ROBINSON, E., FRENCH, J.R.P., Jr., CALDWELL, J.R. & SHINN, M. (1976). *Adherence to medical regimens*. Ann Arbor: Institute for Social Research.

CAPLOW, T. (1947). Rumors in war. *Social Forces, 25*, 298–302.

CAPORAEL, L.R. (1981). The paralanguage of care-giving: Baby talk to the institutionalized aged. *Journal of Personality and Social Psychology, 40*, 876–884.

CAPORAEL, L.R., LUKASZEWSKI, M.P. & CULBERTSON, G.H. (1983). Secondary baby talk: Judgments by institutionalized elderly and their caregivers. *Journal of Personality and Social Psychology, 44*, 746–754.

CARLSMITH, J.M., COLLINS, B.E. & HELMREICH, R.L. (1966). Studies on forced compliance: I. The effect of pressure for compliance on attitude change produced by face-to-face role-playing and anonymous essay writing. *Journal of Personality and Social Psychology, 4*, 1–13.

CARLSMITH, J.M., ELLSWORTH, R.C. & ARONSON, E. (1976). *Methods of research in social psychology*. Reading, MA: Addison-Wesley.

CARLSMITH, J.M. & GROSS, A.E. (1969). Some effects of guilt on compliance. *Journal of Personality and Social Psychology, 11*, 232–239.

CARMENT, D.W. (1970). Rate of simple motor responding as a function of coaction, competition, and sex of the participants. *Psychonomic Science, 19*, 342–343.

CARMENT, D.W. (1973). Giving and receiving in Canada and India. McMaster University Technical Report #53.

CARMENT, D.W. (1974a). Indian and Canadian behavior in a maximizing difference game and in a game of chicken. *International Journal of Psychology, 9*, 213–221.

CARMENT, D.W. (1974b). Indian and Canadian choice behavior in a mixed-motive game. *International Journal of Psychology, 11,* 57–64.

CARMENT, D.W. & HODKIN, B. (1973). Coaction and competition in India and Canada. *Journal of Cross-Cultural Psychology, 4,* 459–469.

CARMENT, D.W. & LATCHFORD, M. (1970). Rate of simple motor responding as a function of coaction, sex of the participants and the presence or absence of the experimenter. *Psychonomic Science, 20,* 253–254.

CARROLL, J.B. (1964). *Language and thought.* Englewood Cliffs, NJ: Prentice-Hall.

CARROLL, J.S. (1978). The effect of imagining an event on expectations for the event: An interpretation in terms of the availability heuristic. *Journal of Experimental Social Psychology, 14,* 88–96.

CARVER, G.S. & GLASS, D.C. (1978). Coronary-prone behavior pattern and interpersonal aggression. *Journal of Personality and Social Psychology, 36,* 361–366.

CASH, T.F. & DERLEGA, V.J. (1978). The matching hypothesis: Physical attractiveness among same-sexed friends. *Personality and Social Psychology Bulletin, 4,* 240–243.

CASSEL, J. (1976). The contribution of the social environment to host resistance. *American Journal of Epidemiology, 102,* 107–123.

CAUDILL, B.D. & MARLATT, G.A. (1975). Modeling influences in social drinking: An experimental analogue. *Journal of Consulting and Clinical Psychology, 43,* 405–415.

CAVIOR, N. & DORECKI, P.R. (1969). Physical attractiveness and popularity among fifth grade boys. Paper presented at the Meetings of the Southwestern Psychology Association. Austin, TX. (April).

CHAIKEN, A.L. & DERLEGA, V.J. (1974). *Self-disclosure.* Morristown, NJ: General Learning.

CHAIKEN, S. & BALDWIN, M.W. (1981). Affective-cognitive consistency and the effect of salient behavioral information on the self presentation of attitudes. *Journal of Personality and Social Psychology, 41,* 1–12.

CHAIKEN, S. & EAGLY, A.H. (1976). Communication modality as a determinant of message persuasiveness and message comprehensibility. *Journal of Personality and Social Psychology, 34,* 605–614.

CHAIKEN, S. & EAGLY, A.H. (1983). Communication modality as a determinant of persuasion: The role of communicator salience. *Journal of Personality and Social Psychology, 45,* 241–256.

CHANDLER, T.A., SHAMA, D.D., WOLF, F.M. & PLANCHARD, S.K. (1981). Misattributional causality: A five cross-national samples study. *Journal of Cross-Cultural Psychology, 12,* 207–221.

CHAPANIS, N.P. & CHAPANIS, A.C. (1964). Cognitive dissonance: Five years later. *Psychological Bulletin, 61,* 1–22.

CHAPMAN, L.J. & CHAPMAN, J.P. (1969). Illusory correlations as an obstacle to the use of valid psychodiagnostic signs. *Journal of Abnormal and Social Psychology, 74,* 271–280.

CHECK, J.V.P., PERLMAN, D. & MALAMUTH, N.M. (1983). Loneliness and aggressive behavior. Paper presented at the Annual Meeting of the American Psychological Association, Anaheim, CA. (August).

CHEMERS, M.M. (1983). Leadership theory and research: A systems-process integration. In P.B. Paulus (Ed.), *Basic group processes.* New York: Springer-Verlag.

CHERRY, F. & BYRNE, D. (1977). Authoritarianism. In T. Blass (Ed.), *Personality variables in social behavior.* Hillsdale, NJ: Erlbaum.

CHERTKOFF, J.M. & CONLEY, M. (1967). Opening offer and frequency of concession as bargaining strategies. *Journal of Personality and Social Psychology, 7,* 181–185.

CHERTKOFF, J.M. & ESSER, J.K. (1977). A test of three theories of coalition formation when agreements can be short-term or long-term. *Journal of Personality and Social Psychology, 35,* 237–249.

CHLOPAN, B.E., McCAIN, M.L., CARBONELL, J.L. & HAGEN, R.L. (1985). Empathy: Review of available measures. *Journal of Personality and Social Psychology, 48,* 635–653.

CHOMSKY, N. (1975). *Reflections on language.* New York: Pantheon.

CHOMSKY, N. (1986). *Turning the tide: The U.S. and Latin America.* Montreal: Black Rose Books.

CHRISTIANSEN, A., SULLAWAY, M. & KING, C. (1983). Systematic error in behavioral reports of dyadic interaction: Egocentric bias and contrast effects. *Behavioral Assessment, 5,* 131–142.

CHRISTIE, R. (1976). Probability vs. precedence: The social psychology of jury selection. In G. Berman, C. Nemeth & N. Vidmar (Eds.), *Psychology and the Law* (265–282). Lexington, MA: Heath.

CHRISTIE, R. & GEIS, F. (1968). Some consequences of taking Machiavelli seriously. In E.F. Borgatta and W.W. Lambert (Eds.), *Handbook of personality theory and research.* Chicago: Rand McNally.

CHRISTIE, R. & GEIS, F. (1970) (Eds.). *Studies in Machiavellianism.* New York: Academic Press.

CHRISTIE, R., HAVEL, J. & SEIDENBERG, B. (1958). Is the F scale irreversible? *Journal of Abnormal and Social Psychology, 56,* 143–159.

CHRISTIE, R. & JAHODA, M. (1954) (Eds.). *Studies in the scope and method of "The Authoritarian Personality."* New York: Free Press.

CIALDINI, R.B., BUCKMAN, L. & CACIOPPO, J.T. (1979). An example of consumeristic social psychology: Bargaining tough in the new car showroom. *Journal of Applied Social Psychology, 9,* 115–126.

CIALDINI, R.B., CACIOPPO, J.T., BASSETT, R. & MILLER, J.A. (1978). Low-ball procedure for producing compliance: Commitment then cost. *Journal of Personality and Social Psychology, 36,* 463–476.

CIALDINI, R.B, DARBY, B.L. & VINCENT, J.E. (1973). Transgression and altruism: A case for hedonism. *Journal of Experimental Social Psychology, 9,* 502–516.

CIALDINI, R.B., VINCENT, J.E., LEWIS, S.K., CATALON, J., WHEELER, D. & DARBY, B.L. (1975). Reciprocal concessions procedure for inducing compliance: The door-in-the-face technique. *Journal of Personality and Social Psychology, 31,* 206–215.

CICONE, M.V. & RUBIE, D.N. (1978). Beliefs about males. *Journal of Social Issues, 34,* 5–16.

CLARK, H.H. (1985). Language use and language users. In G. Lindzey & E. Aronson (Eds.), *Handbook of social psychology* Third Edition. (Vol. 2) (179–232). New York: Random House.

CLARK, R.D. & WORD, L.E. (1972). Why don't bystanders help? Because of ambiguity? *Journal of Personality and Social Psychology, 24,* 392–400.

CLARK, R.D. & WORD, L.E. (1974). Where is the apathetic bystander? Situational characteristics of the emergency. *Journal of Personality and Social Psychology, 29,* 279–287.

CLÉMENT, R., GARDNER, R.C. & SMYTHE, P.C. (1977). Interethnic contact: Attitudinal consequences. *Canadian Journal of Behavioural Science, 9,* 205–215.

CLIFFORD, M. & WALSTER, E. (1973). The effects of physical attraction on teacher expectation. *Sociology of Education, 46,* 248.

CLINE, V.B., CROFT, R.G. & COURRIER, S. (1973). Desensitization of children to television violence. *Journal of Personality and Social Psychology, 27,* 360–365.

CLORE, G.L., WIGGINS, N.H. & ITKIN, G. (1975). Gain and loss in attraction: Attributions from non-verbal behavior. *Journal of Personality and Social Psychology, 31,* 706–712.

COHEN, A.R. (1962). An experiment on small rewards for discrepant compliance and attitude change. In J.W. Brehm & A.R. Cohen, (Eds.), *Explorations in cognitive dissonance* (97–104). New York: Wiley.

COHEN, R. (1972). Altruism: Human, cultural, or what? *Journal of Social Issues, 28,* 39–58.

COHEN, S., GLASS, D.C. & SINGER, J.E. (1973). Apartment noise, auditory discrimination and reading ability in children. *Journal of Experimental Social Psychology, 9,* 407–422.

COHEN, S. & McKAY, G. (1984). Social support, stress and the buffering hypothesis: A theoretical analysis. In A. Baum, J.E. Singer & S.E. Taylor (Eds.), *Handbook of psychology and health,* (Vol. 4) (253–267). Hillsdale, NJ: Erlbaum.

COKE, J.S., BATSON, C.D. & McDAVIS, K. (1978). Empathic mediation of helping: A two-stage model. *Journal of Personality and Social Psychology, 36,* 752–766.

COLLIER, J. (1947). *Indians of the Americas.* New York: Mentor.

COLLIGAN, M.J., PENNEBAKER, J.W. & MURPHY, L.R. (1982). *Mass psychogenic illness.* Hillsdale, NJ: Erlbaum.

COLLINS, B.E. & HOYT, M.F. (1972). Personal responsibility-for-consequences: An integration and extension of the forced compliance literature. *Journal of Experimental Social Psychology, 8,* 558–593.

COLLINS, R.L. & MARLATT, G.A. (1981). Social modeling as a determinant of drinking behavior: Implications for prevention and treatment. *Addictive Behaviors, 6,* 233–239.

CONN, L.K. & CROWNE, D.P. (1964). Instigation to aggression, emotional arousal, and defensive emulation. *Journal of Personality, 32,* 163–179.

CONROY, W.S., KAPKIN, E.S. & BARNETTE, N.L. (1973). Modification of cigarette smoking by the use of a self-confrontational technique. Proceedings of the South Eastern Division, American Psychological Association.

CONWAY, M. & ROSS, M. (1984). Getting what you want by revising what you had. *Journal of Personality and Social Psychology, 47,* 738–748.

COOK, S.W. (1970). Motives in a conceptual analysis of attitude-related behavior. In W.J. Arnold & D. Levine (Eds.), *Nebraska symposium on motivation,* 1969. Lincoln, NE: University of Nebraska Press.

COOK, S.W. (1984). Experimenting on social issues: The case of school desegregation. Paper presented at the 92nd Annual Convention of the American Psychological Association, Toronto.

COOK, S.W. & SELLTIZ (1964). A multiple-indicator approach to attitude measurement. *Psychological Bulletin, 62,* 36–55.

COOK, T.D., GRUDER, G.L., HENNIGAN, K.M. & FLAY, B.R. (1979). History of the sleeper effect: Some logical pitfalls in accepting the null hypothesis. *Psychological Bulletin, 35,* 140–158.

COOK, T.D., KENDZIERSKY, D.A. & THOMAS, S.V. (1983). The implicit assumptions of television: An analysis of the 1982 NIMH Report on Television and Behavior. *Public Opinion Quarterly, 47,* 161–201.

COOPER, H.M. (1979). Sex differences in conformity research. *Journal of Personality and Social Psychology, 37,* 131–146.

COOPER, J. & CROYLE, R.T. (1984). Attitudes and attitude change. *Annual Review of Psychology, 35,* (395–423).

COOPER, J. & FAZIO, R.H. (1984). A new look at dissonance theory. In L. Berkowitz (Ed.), *Advances in experimental social psychology* (Vol. 17) (229–266). New York: Academic Press.

COOPER, J. & WORCHEL, S. (1970). Role of undesired consequences in arousing cognitive dissonance. *Journal of Personality and Social Psychology, 16,* 199–206.

COOPER, J., ZANNA, M.P. & GOETHALS, G.R. (1971). Mistreatment of an esteemed other as a consequence affecting dissonance reduction. *Journal of Experimental Social Psychology, 10,* 224–233.

COOPER, J., ZANNA, M.P. & TAVES, P.A. (1978). Arousal as a necessary condition for attitude change following induced compliance. *Journal of Personality and Social Psychology, 36,* 1101–1106.

COSER, L.A.(1967). *Continuities in the study of social conflict.* New York: Free Press.

COTTRELL, N.B. (1972). Social facilitation. In C.G. McClintock (Ed.), *Experimental social psychology.* New York: Holt, Rinehart & Winston.

COTTRELL, N.B., WACK, D.L., SEKERAK, G.J. & RITTLE, R.H. (1968). Social facilitation of dominant responses by the presence of an audience and the mere presence of others. *Journal of Personality and Social Psychology, 9,* 245–250.

COZBY, P.C. (1973). Self-disclosure: A literature review. *Psychological Bulletin, 79,* 73–91.

CRAIG, K.D. (1978). Social modeling influences on pain. In R.A. Sternbach (Ed.), *The psychology of pain* (73–110. New York: Raven Press.

CRAIG, K.D. & PRKACHIN, K.M. (1980). Social influences on public and private components of pain. In I.G. Sarason & C. Spielberg (Eds.), *Stress and anxiety.* (Vol. 7) New York: Hemisphere Books.

CRANO, W.D. & BREWER, M.B. (1973). *Principles of research in social psychology.* New York: McGraw-Hill.

CRAWFORD, C. (1979). George Washington, Abraham Lincoln, and Arthur Jensen. Are they compatible? *American Psychologist, 34,* 664–672.

CRAWFORD, M.P. (1939). The social psychology of the vertebrates. *Psychological Bulletin, 36,* 407–466.

CRITCHLOW, B. (1985). The blame in the bottle: Attributions about drunken behavior. *Personality and Social Psychology Bulletin, 11,* 258–274.

CROCKER, J. (1981). Judgement of covariation by social perceivers. *Psychological Bulletin, 90,* 272–292.

CROMWELL, R.L. BUTTERFIELD, E.C., BRAYFIELD, F.M. & CURRY, J.L. (1977). *Acute myocardial infarction: Reaction and recovery.* St. Louis: Mosby.

CRONBACH, L.J. (1957). The two disciplines of scientific psychology. *American Psychologist, 12,* 671–684.

CROWNE, D.P. & MARLOWE, D. (1960). New scale of social desirability independent of pathology. *Journal of Consulting Psychology, 24,* 349–354.

CRUTCHFIELD, R.A. (1955). Conformity and character. *American Psychologist, 10,* 191–198.

CSIKSZENTMIHALYI, M. & FIGURSKI T.J. (1982). Self-awareness and overside experience in everyday life. *Journal of Personality, 50,* 15–28.

CULBERTSON, G.H. & CAPORAEL. L.R.(1983). Baby talk speech to the elderly: Complexity and content of messages. *Personality and Social Psychology Bulletin, 9,* 305–312.

CUNNINGHAM, M.R. (1979). Weather, mood and helping behavior: Quasi-experiments with the Sunshine Samaritan. *Journal of Personality and Social Psychology, 37,* 1947–1956.

CURRAN, J.P. (1977). Skills training as an approach to the treatment of heterosexual social anxiety: A review. *Psychological Bulletin, 84,* 140–157.

CURRAN, J.P. & LIPPOLD, S. (1975). The effects of physical attraction and attitude similarity on attraction in dating dyads. *Journal of Personality, 43,* 528–538.

CUTLER, R.E. & STORM, T. (1975). Observational study of alcohol consumption in natural settings. *Journal of Studies on Alcohol, 36,* 1173–1183.

CUTRONA, C.E. (1982). Transition to college: Loneliness and the process of social adjustment. In L.A. Peplau & D. Perlman (Eds.), *Loneliness: A sourcebook of current theory, research and therapy.* New York: Wiley.

DA GLORIA, J. & DE RIDDER, R. (1979). Sex differences in aggression: Are current notions misleading? *European Journal of Social Psychology, 9,* 49–66.

DARLEY, J.M. & BATSON, C.D. (1973). "From Jerusalem to Jericho": A study of situational and dispositional variables in helping behavior. *Journal of Personality and Social Psychology, 27,* 100–108.

DARLEY, J.M. & BERSCHEID, E. (1967). Increased liking as a result of anticipation of personal contact. *Human Relations, 20,* 29–39.

DARLEY, J.M. & GROSS, P. (1983). A hypothesis-confirming bias in labeling effects. *Journal of Personality and Social Psychology, 44,* 20–33.

DARLEY, J.M. & LATANÉ, B. (1968). Bystander intervention in emergencies: Diffusion of responsibility. *Journal of Personality and Social Psychology, 8,* 377–383.

DARLEY, J.M. & LATANÉ, B. (1970). Norms and normative behavior: Field studies of social interdependence. In J. Macaulay & L. Berkowitz (Eds.), *Altruism and helping behavior* (83–101). New York: Academic Press.

DARLINGTON, R.B. & MACKER, D.F. (1966). Displacement of guilt-produced altruistic behavior. *Journal of Personality and Social Psychology, 4,* 442–443.

DARNELL, R. (1971). Sociolinguistic perspectives on linguistic diversity. In R. Darnell (Ed.), *Linguistic diversity in Canadian society.* Edmonton: Linguistic Research.

DARRACH, B. & NORRIS, J. (1984). An American tragedy. *Life, 7,* 58–84.

DARWIN, C. (1871). *The descent of men and selection in relation to sex.* New York: Appleton.

DASHIELL, J.F. (1935). Experimental studies of the influence of social situations on the behavior of individual human adults. In C. Murchison (Ed.), *Handbook of social psychology* (1097–1158). Worcester, MA: Clark University.

DAVIDOWICZ, L.C. (1975). *The war against the Jews, 1933–1945.* Holt, Rinehart & Winston: New York.

DAVIDSON, A.R. & MORRISON, D.M. (1983). Predicting contraceptive behavior from attitudes: A comparison of within- versus across-subjects procedures. *Journal of Personality and Social Psychology, 45,* 997–1009.

DAVIDSON, T. (1978). *Conjugal crime.* New York: Ballantine Books.

DAVIS, J.H., HOLT, R.W., SPITZER, C.E. & STASSER, G. (1981). The effects of consensus requirements and multiple decisions on mock juror verdict preferences. *Journal of Experimental Social Psychology, 17,* 1–15.

DAVIS, D., RAINEY, H. & BROCK, T. (1976). Interpersonal physical pleasuring: Effects of sex combinations, recipient attributes, and anticipated future interaction. *Journal of Personality and Social Psychology, 33,* 89–106.

DAWES, R.M. (1972). *Fundamentals of attitude measurement.* New York: John Wiley & Sons.

DAWES, R.M. (1980). Social dilemmas. *Annual Review of Psychology, 31,* 169–193.

DEAUX, K. (1972). To err is humanizing, but sex makes a difference. *Representative Research in Social Psychology, 3,* 20–28.

DEAUX, K. (1976). *The behavior of women and men.* Monterey, CA: Brooks/Cole.

DEAUX, K. (1984). From individual differences to social categories. *American Psychologist, 39,* 105–116.

DEAUX, K. & EMSWILLER, T. (1974). Explanations of successful performance on sex-linked tasks: What is skill for the male is luck for the female. *Journal of Personality and Social Psychology, 29,* 80–85.

DECI, E.L. (1971). Effects of externally mediated rewards on intrinsic motivation. *Journal of Personality and Social Psychology, 15,* 105–115.

DECI, E.L., NEZLEK J. & SHEINMAN, L. (1981). Characteristics of the rewarder and intrinsics of the motivation of the rewardee. *Journal of Personality and Social Psychology, 40,* 1–10.

DECI, E.L. & RYAN, R.M. (1985). *Intrinsic motivation and self-determination on human behavior.* New York: Plenum.

DEIGHTON, L. (1979). *Blitzkrieg: From the rise of Hitler to the fall of Dunkirk.* London: Jonathon Cape.

DELLINGER, R.W. (1979). Jet roar: Health problems take off near airports. *Human Behavior, 8,* 50–51.

DEJONG, W. (1979). An examination of self-perception mediation of the foot-in-the-door effect. *Journal of Personality and Social Psychology, 37,* 2221–2239.

DELONGIS, A., COYNE, J.C., KAKOF, G., FOLKMAN, S. & LAZARUS, R.S. (1982). Relationship of daily hassles, uplifts and major life events to health status. *Health Psychology, 1,* 119–136.

DENMARK, F.L. (1977). Styles of leadership. *Psychology of Women Quarterly, 2,* 99–113.

DEPAULO, B.M. & COLEMAN, L.M. (1986). Talking to children, foreigners, and retarded adults. *Journal of Personality and Social Psychology, 51,* 945–959.

DEPAULO, B.M. & ROSENTHAL, R. (1979). Telling lies. *Journal of Personality and Social Psychology, 37,* 1713–1722.

DERIVERA, J. (1984). Facing nuclear weapons. *American Behavioral Scientist, 27,* 739–758.

DERMER, M. & PYSZCZYNSKI, T.A. (1978). Effects of erotica upon men's loving and liking responses for women they love. *Journal of Personality and Social Psychology, 36,* 1302–1309.

DERMER, M.L. & JACOBSEN, E. (1986). Some potential negative social consequences of cigarette smoking: Marketing research in reverse. *Journal of Applied Social Psychology, 16,* 702–725.

DESCHAMPS, J-C. & DOISE, W. (1978). Crossed category memberships in intergroup relations. In H. Tajfel (Ed.), *Differentiation between social groups: Studies in the social psychology of inter-group relations* (141–158). London: Academic Press.

DEUTSCH, F.M. & LAMBERTI, D.M. (1986). Does social approval improve helping? *Personality and Social Psychology Bulletin, 12,* 149–158.

DEUTSCH, M. (1958). Trust and suspicion. *Journal of Conflict Resolution, 2,* 265–279.

DEUTSCH, M. (1960). The effect of motivational orientation on trust and suspicion. *Human Relations, 13,* 123–139.

DEUTSCH, M. (1962). Cooperation and trust: Some theoretical notes. In M. Jones (Ed.), *Nebraska symposium on motivation.* Lincoln: University of Nebraska Press.

DEUTSCH, M. (1973). *The resolution of conflict: Constructive and destructive processes.* New Haven: Yale University Press.

DEUTSCH, M. & KRAUSS, R.M. (1960). The effect of threat on interpersonal bargaining. *Journal of Abnormal and Social Psychology, 61,* 181–189.

DEVOS, G.A. & HIPPLER, A.E. (1969). Cultural psychology: Comparative studies of human behavior. In G. Lindzey & E. Aronson (Eds.), *The handbook of social psychology.* Second Edition (Vol. 4) (322–417). Reading, MA: Addison-Wesley.

DEVRIES, D.L. & EDWARDS, K.J. (1974). Student teams and learning games: Their effects on cross-race and cross-sex interaction. *Journal of Educational Psychology, 66,* 741–749.

DIAMOND S. & ZEISEL, H. (1974). A courtroom experiment on juror selection and decision-making. *Personality and Social Psychology Bulletin, 1,* 276–277.

DIEN, D. (1982). A Chinese perspective on Kohlberg's theory of moral development. *Developmental Review, 2,* 331–341.

DIMOND, S.J. (1970). *The social behaviour of animals,* London: Batsford.

DINICOLA, D.D. & DIMATTEO, M.R. (1984). Practitioners, patients and compliance with medical regimes: A social psychological perspective. In A. Baum, S.E. Taylor & J.E. Singer (Eds.), *Handbook of psychology and health,* (Vol. 4) (55–64). Hillsdale: Erlbaum.

DION, K.K. (1972). Physical attractiveness and evaluations of children's transgressions. *Journal of Personality and Social Psychology, 24,* 207–213.

DION, K.K., BERSCHEID, E. & WALSTER, E. (1972). What is beautiful is good. *Journal of Personality and Social Psychology, 24,* 285–290.

DION, K.L. (1973). Cohesiveness as a determinant of ingroup-outgroup bias. *Journal of Personality and Social Psychology, 28,* 163–171.

DION, K.L. (1975). Women's reactions to discrimination from members of the same or opposite sex. *Journal of Research in Personality, 9,* 294–306.

DION, K.L. & DION, K.K. (1976). The Ames phenomenon revisited: Factors underlying the resistance to perceptual distortion of one's partner. *Journal of Personality and Social Psychology, 33,* 170–177.

DION, K.K. & DION, K.L. (1985). Personality, gender and the phenomenology of romantic love. *Review of Personality and Social Psychology, 6,* 209–20.

DION, K.L. & DION, K.K. (1987). Belief in a just world and physical attractiveness stereotyping. *Journal of Personality and Social Psychology, 52,* 775–780.

DION, K.L. & EARN, B.M. (1975). The phenomenology of being a target of prejudice. *Journal of Personality and Social Psychology, 32,* 944–940.

DION, K.L., EARN, B.M. & YEE, P.H.N. (1986). The experience of being a victim of prejudice: An experimental approach. In B. Earn and S. Towson (Eds.), *Readings in social psychology: Classic and Canadian contributions.* Peterborough: Broadview Press.

DITECCO, D. & SCHLEGEL, R.P. (1982). Alcohol use among young males: An application of problem-behavior theory. In J.R. Eiser (Ed.), *Social psychology and behavioral medicine.* Chichester, U.K.: J.R. Wiley.

DOISE, W. & DANN, H-D. (1976). New theoretical perspectives in the study of intergroup relations. *Italian Journal of Psychology, 3,* 285–304.

DOISE, W., DESCHAMPS, J-C. & MEYER, G. (1978). The accentuation of intra-category similarities. In H. Tajfel (Ed.), *Differentiation between social groups: Studies in the social psychology of intergroup relations* (159–168). London: Academic Press.

DOLLARD, J., DOOB, L.W., MILLER, N.E., MOWRER, O.H. & SEARS, R.R. (1939). *Frustration and aggression.* New Haven: Yale University Press.

DONNERSTEIN, E.I. (1983). Erotica and human aggression. In R.G. Geen & E.I. Donnerstein (Eds.), *Aggression: Theoretical and empirical reviews* (Vol. 2) (127–154). New York: Academic Press.

DONNERSTEIN, E., DONNERSTEIN, M. & EVANS, R. (1975). Erotic stimuli and aggression: Facilitation or inhibition. *Journal of Personality and Social Psychology, 32,* 237–244.

DONNERSTEIN, E. & WILSON, D.W. (1976). The effects of noise and perceived control upon ongoing and subsequent aggressive behavior. *Journal of Personality and Social Psychology, 34,* 774–781.

DONOVAN, D.M. & MARLATT, G.A. (1982). Personality subtypes among driving-while-intoxicated offenders: Relationship to driving behavior, driving risk and treatment implications. *Journal of Consulting and Clinical Psychology, 50,* 241–249.

DONOVAN, J.E., JESSOR, R. & JESSOR, L. (1983). Problem drinking in adolescence and young adulthood. A follow-up study. *Journal of Studies on Alcohol, 44,* 109–137.

DOO, L. (1973). Dispute settlement in Chinese-American communities. *American Journal of Comparative Law, 21,* 627–663.

DOOB, A.N. (1976). Evidence, procedure and psychological research. In G. Bermant, C. Nemeth & N. Vidmar (Eds.), *Psychology and the law* (135–148). Lexington, MA: Lexington Books.

DOOB, A.N. & GROSS, A.E. (1968). States of frustration as an inhibitor of horn-honking responses. *Journal of Social Psychology, 76,* 213–218.

DOOB, A.N. & KIRSHENBAUM, H.M. (1972). Some empirical evidence on the effect of S. 12 of the Canada Evidence Act on an accused. *Criminal Law Quarterly, 15,* 88–96.

DOOB, A.N. & KIRSHENBAUM, H.M. (1973a). The effects on arousal of frustration and aggression films. *Journal of Experimental Social Psychology, 9,* 57–64.

DOOB, A.N. & KIRSHENBAUM, H.M. (1973b). Bias in police lineups — partial remembering. *Journal of Police Science and Administration, 1,* 287–293.

DOOB, A.N. & MacDONALD, G.E. (1977). The news media and perceptions of violence. In *Report of the Royal Commission on Violence in the Communications Industry* (Vol. 5) (171–226). Toronto: Publication Centre, Government of Ontario.

DOOB, A.N. & MacDONALD, G.E. (1979). Television viewing and fear of victimization: Is the effect causal? *Journal of Personality and Social Psychology, 37,* 170–179.

DOOB, A.N. & ROBERTS, J.V. (1984). Social psychology, social attitudes and attitudes toward sentencing. *Canadian Journal of Behavioural Science, 16,* 269–280.

DOOB, A.N. & WOOD, L.E. (1972). Catharsis and aggression: Effects of annoyance on aggressive behavior. *Journal of Personality and Social Psychology, 22,* 156–162.

DOOB, L.W. (1941). War reactions of a rural Canadian community. *Journal of Abnormal Psychology, 36,* 200–223.

DOVIDIO, J.F. & MORRIS, W.N. (1975). Effects of stress and commonality of fate on helping behavior. *Journal of Personality and Social Psychology, 31,* 145–149.

DRABSMAN, R.S. & THOMAS, M.H. (1975). Does TV violence breed indifference? *Journal of Communications, 25,* 86–89.

DRISCOLL, R., DAVIS, K.W. & LIPETZ, M.E. (1972). Parental interference and romantic love. *Journal of Personality and Social Psychology, 24,* 1–10.

DUNKEL-SCHETTER, C. & WORTMAN, C.B. (1982). The interpersonal dynamics of cancer: Problems in social relationships and their impact on the patient. In H.S. Friedman & M.R. DiMatteo (Eds.), *Interpersonal issues in health care* (69–100). New York: Academic.

DURANT, W. & DURANT, A. (1961). *The story of civilization: Part VII. The age of reason begins.* New York: Simon and Schuster.

DUTTON, D.G. (1971). Reactions of restauranteurs to blacks and whites violating restaurant dress requirements. *Canadian Journal of Behavioural Science, 3,* 298–331.

DUTTON, D.G. (1973). The relationship of amount of perceived discrimination toward a minority group on behaviour of majority group members. *Canadian Journal of Behavioural Science, 5,* 34–45.

DUTTON, D.G. & ARON, A.P. (1974). Some evidence for heightened sexual attraction under conditions of high anxiety. *Journal of Personality and Social Psychology, 30,* 510–517.

DUTTON, D.G. & LAKE, R. (1973). Threat of own prejudice and reverse discrimination in interracial situations. *Journal of Personality and Social Psychology, 28,* 94–100.

DUTTON, D.G. & LENNARC, V.I. (1974). The effect of prior "token" compliance on subsequent interracial behaviour. *Journal of Personality and Social Psychology, 29,* 65–71.

EAGLY, A.H. (1967). Involvement as a determinant of response to favorable and unfavorable information. *Journal of Personality and Social Psychology, 7,* 1–15 (Whole No. 643).

EAGLY, A.H. (1974). Comprehensibility of persuasive arguments as a determinant of opinion change. *Journal of Personality and Social Psychology, 29,* 758–773.

EAGLY, A.H. (1978). Sex differences in influenceability. *Psychological Bulletin, 85,* 85–116.

EAGLY, A.H. & CARLI, L.L. (1981). Sex of researcher and sex-typed communications as determinants of sex differences in influenceability: A meta-analysis of social influence studies. *Psychological Bulletin, 90,* 1–20.

EAGLY, A.H. & CHAIKEN, S. (1978). Causal inferences about communicators and their effect on opinion change. *Journal of Personality and Social Psychology, 36,* 424–435.

EAGLY, A.H. & CROWLEY, M. (1986). Gender and helping behavior: A meta-analytic review of the social psychological literature. *Psychological Bulletin, 100,* 283–308.

EAGLY, A.H. & STEFFEN, V.J. (1986). Gender and aggressive behavior: A meta-analytic review of the social psychological literature. *Psychological Bulletin, 100,* 309–330.

EAGLY, A.H. & TELAAK, K. (1972). Width of the latitude of acceptance as a determinant of attitude change. *Journal of Personality and Social Psychology, 23,* 388–397.

EAGLY, A.H. & WOOD, W. (1982). Inferred sex differences in status as a determinant of gender stereotypes about social influence. *Journal of Personality and Social Psychology, 43,* 915–928.

EAGLY, A.H. & WOOD, W. (1985). Gender and influenceability: Stereotype versus behavior. In V.E. O'Leary, R.K. Unger & B.S. Wallston (Eds.), *Women, gender and social psychology* (225–256). Hillsdale, NJ: Erlbaum.

EAGLY, A., WOOD, W. & FISHBAUGH, L. (1981). Sex differences in conformity: Surveillance by the group as a determinant of male non-conformity. *Journal of Personality and Social Psychology, 40,* 384–394.

EASTERBROOK, J.A. (1959). The effect of emotion on cue utilization and the organization of behavior. *Psychological Review, 66,* 183–201.

EBBESON, E.B., KJOS, G.L. & KONECNI, V.J. (1976). Spatial ecology: Its effects on the choice of friends and enemies. *Journal of Experimental Social Psychology, 12,* 505–518.

EDWARDS, A.L. (1957). Social desirability and probability of endorsement of items in the interpersonal check list. *Journal of Abnormal and Social Psychology, 55,* 394–395.

EDWARDS, W. (1954). The theory of decision-making. *Psychological Bulletin, 51,* 380–417.

EFFRAN, M.G. (1974). The effect of physical appearance on the judgment of guilt, interpersonal attraction, and severity of recommended punishment in a simulated jury task. *Journal of Research in Personality, 8,* 45–54.

EFFRAN, M.G. & PATTERSON, E.W.J. (1974). Voters vote beautiful: The effect of physical appearance on a national election. *Canadian Journal of Behavioural Science, 6,* 352–356.

EHRLICH, D., GUTTMAN, I., SCHONBACH, P. & MILLS, J. (1957). Post-decision exposure to relevant information. *Journal of Personality and Social Psychology, 54,* 98–102.

EHRLICH, H.J. (1969). Attitudes, behavior and the intervening variables. *American Sociologist, 4,* 29–34.

EHRLICH, H.J. (1973). *The social psychology of prejudice.* New York: Wiley.

EINHORN, H.S. & HOGARTH, R.M. (1978). Confidence in judgement: Persistence in the illusion of validity. *Psychological Review, 85,* 395–416.

EISENBERG, N. & LENNON, R. (1983). Sex differences in empathy and related capacities. *Psychological Bulletin, 94,* 100–131.

EISENBERG, N. & MILLER, P.A. (1987). The relation of empathy to pro-social and related behaviors. *Psychological Bulletin, 101,* 91–119.

EISER, J.R. (1982). Addiction and attribution: Cognitive processes in giving up smoking. In J.R. Eiser (Ed.), *Social psychology and behavioral medicine.* New York: Wiley.

EISER, J.R. & VAN DER PLIGT, J. (1982). Accentuation and perspective in attitudinal judgments. *Journal of Personality and Social Psychology, 42,* 224–238.

EKMAN, P. (1982). *Emotion in the human face.* New York: Cambridge.

EKMAN, P. & FRIESEN, W.V. (1969). Nonverbal leakage and clues to deception. *Psychiatry, 32,* 88–106.

EKMAN, P. & FRIESEN, W.V. (1971). Constants across cultures in the face and emotion. *Journal of Personality and Social Psychology, 17,* 124–129.

EKMAN, P. & FRIESEN, W. (1974). Detecting deception from the body or face. *Journal of personality and Social Psychology, 29,* 188–198.

ELMS, A.C. (1982). Keeping deception honest: Justifying conditions for social scientific research strategies. In T.L. Beauchamp & R. Faden (Eds.), *Ethical issues in social science research.* Baltimore: Johns Hopkins University Press.

ELMS, A.C. & JANIS, I.L. (1965). Counter-norm attitudes induced by consonant versus dissonant conditions of role-playing. *Journal of Experimental Research in Personality, 1,* 50–60.

ENDLER, N.S. (1976). Grand illusions: Traits or interaction. *Canadian Psychological Review, 17,* 174–181.

ENDLER, N.S. & MAGNUSSEN, D. (1976). Toward an interactional psychology of personality. *Psychological Bulletin, 83,* 956–974.

ERON, L.D. (1980). Prescription for reduction of aggression. *American Psychologist, 35,* 244–252.

ERON, L.D., HUESMANN, L.R., DUBOW, E., ROMANOFF, R. & YARMEL, P.W. (1987). Aggression and its correlates over 22 years. In N.H. Crowell, R.J. Blanchard, I. Evans & C.R. O'Donnel (Eds.), *Childhood aggression and violence: Sources of influence, prevention and control.* New York: Academic Press.

ERON, L.D., HUESMANN, L.R., LEFKOWITZ, M.M. & WALDER, L.O. (1972). Does television violence cause aggression? *American Psychologist, 27,* 253–263.

ERVIN-TRIPP, S.M. (1974). Is second language learning really like the first? *TESOL Quarterly, 8,* 111–127.

ESPY, W.R., (1975). *An almanac of words at play.* New York: Clarkson N. Potter.

ETZIONI, A. (1969). Social-psychological aspects of international relations. In G. Lindzey & E. Aronson (Eds.), *Handbook of social psychology* Second Edition (Vol. 5) (538–601). Reading: MA.: Addison-Wesley.

EVANS, R.I. (1984). A social inoculation strategy to defer smoking in adolescents. In V.D. Matarazzo, S.M.

Weiss, J.A. Herd, N.E. Miller & S.M. Weiss (Eds.), *Behavioral health. A handbook of health enhancement and disease prevention* (765–774). New York: Wiley.

EVANS, R.I., RAINES, B.E. & HANSELKA, L. (1984). Developing data-based communication in social psychological research: Adolescent smoking prevention. *Journal of Applied Social Psychology, 14,* 289–295.

EXLINE, R., GRAY, D. & SCHUETTE, D. (1965). Visual behavior in a dyad as affected by interview content and sex of the respondent. *Journal of Personality and Social Psychology, 1,* 201–209.

EXLINE, R.V., THIBAUT, J., HICKEY, C.B. & GUMPERT, P. (1970). Visual interaction in relation to Machiavellianism and an unethical act. In. R. Christie & F. Geis (Eds.), *Studies in Machiavellianism* (53–75). New York: Academic Press.

EYSENCK, H.J. (1953). *Uses and abuses of psychology.* Harmondsworth, England: Penguin.

FALLON, A.E. & ROZIN, P. (1984). Sex differences in perceptions of body weight. Unpublished manuscript.

FARAGO, L. (1942). *German psychological warfare.* New York: G.P. Putnam's Sons.

FARINA, A. & RING, K. (1965). The influence of perceived mental illness on interpersonal relations. *Journal of Abnormal Psychology, 70,* 47–51.

FAZIO, R.H., CHEN, J., McDONEL, E.C. & SHERMAN, S.J. (1982). Attitude accessibility, attitude-behavior consistency and the strength of the object-evaluation association. *Journal of Experimental Social Psychology, 18,* 339–357.

FAZIO, R.H., SANBONMATSU, D.M., POWELL, M.C. & KARDES, F.R. (1986). On the automatic activation of attitudes. *Journal of Personality and Social Psychology, 50,* 229–238.

FAZIO, R.H., ZANNA, M.P. & COOPER, V. (1977). Dissonance and self-perception. An integrative view of each theory's proper domain of application. *Journal of Experimental Social Psychology, 13,* 464–479.

FEARN, G.F.N. (1973). *Canadian social organization.* Toronto: Holt, Rinehart & Winston.

FELDMAN, R.E. (1968). Response to compatriot and foreigner who seek assistance. *Journal of Personality and Social Psychology, 10,* 202–214.

FELDMAN, S. & WILSON, K. (1981). The value of interpersonal skills in lawyering. *Law and Human Behavior, 5,* 311–324.

FELLNER, C.H. & MARSHALL, J.R. (1970). Kidney donors. In J. Macaulay & L. Berkowitz (Eds.), *Altruism and helping behavior.* New York: Academic Press.

FELLNER, C.H. & SCHWARTZ, S.H. (1971). Altruism in disrepute: Medical vs. public attitudes towards the living organ donor. *New England Journal of Medicine, 184,* 582–585.

FERGUSON, C.A. (1977). Baby talk as a simplified register. In C.E. Snow & C.A. Ferguson (Eds.), *Talking to children: Language input and acquisition.* New York: Cambridge University Press.

FERGUSON, T.J. & RULE, B.G. (1983). An attributional perspective on anger and aggression. In R.G. Geen & E.I. Donnerstein (Eds.), *Aggression: Theoretical and empirical reviews.* (Vol. 1) (41–74). New York: Academic Press.

FESHBACH, S. (1961). The stimulating versus cathartic effects of a vicarious aggressive activity. *Journal of Applied Social Psychology, 63,* 381–385.

FESHBACH, S. (1970). Aggression. In P.H. Mussen (Ed.), *Carmichael manual of child psychology,* Revised Edition. New York: Wiley.

FESHBACH, S. & SINGER, R. (1971). *Television and aggression.* San Francisco: Jossey-Bass.

FESTINGER, L. (1954). A theory of social comparison processes. *Human Relations, 7,* 117–140.

FESTINGER, L. (1957). *A theory of cognitive dissonance.* Stanford, CA: Stanford University Press.

FESTINGER, L. (1964). *Conflict, decision and dissonance.* Stanford CA: Stanford University Press.

FESTINGER, L. & CARLSMITH, J.M. (1959). Cognitive consequences of forced compliance. *Journal of Abnormal and Social Psychology, 58,* 203–210.

FESTINGER, L., PEPITONE, A. & NEWCOMB, T. (1952). Some consequences of deindividuation in a group. *Journal of Personality and Social Psychology, 47,* 382–389.

FESTINGER, L., RIECKEN, H.W. & SCHACHTER, S. (1956). *When prophecy fails: A social and psychological study of a modern group that predicted the destruction of the world.* New York: Harper.

FESTINGER, L., SCHACHTER, S. & BACK, K.W. (1950). *Social pressures in informal groups. A study of human factors in housing.* New York: Harper & Brothers.

FIEDLER, F.E. (1967). *A theory of leadership effectiveness.* New York: McGraw-Hill.

FIEDLER, F.E. (1971). *Leadership.* Morristown, NJ: General Learning Press.

FIEDLER, F.E. (1978). The contingency model and the dynamics of the leadership process. In L. Berkowitz (Ed.), *Advances in experimental social psychology* (Vol. 11). New York: Academic Press.

FIEDLER, F.E. (1981). Leadership effectiveness. *American Behavioral Scientist, 24,* 619–632.

FISCHHOFF, B., PIDGEON, N. & FISKE, S.T. (1983). Social science and the politics of the arms race. *Journal of Social Issues, 39,* 161–180.

FISHBEIN, M. (Ed.) (1967). *Attitude and the mediation of behavior. Readings in attitude theory and measurement.* New York: Wiley.

FISHBEIN, M. & AJZEN, I. (1972). Attitudes and opinions. *Annual Review of Psychology, 23,* 487–544.

FISHBEIN, M. & AJZEN, I. (1974). Attitudes toward objects as predictors of single and multiple behavioral criteria. *Psychological Review, 81,* 59–74.

FISHBEIN, M. & AJZEN, I. (1975). *Belief, attitude, intention and behavior: An introduction to theory and research.* Reading, MA: Addison-Wesley.

FISHER, J.D., BELL, P.A. & BAUM, A. (1984). *Environmental psychology.* Second Edition. New York: Holt, Rinehart & Winston.

FISHER, J.D., NADLER, A & DePAULO, B.M. (1983). *New directions in helping* (Vol. 1). New York: Academic Press.

FISHER, J.D., NADLER, A. & WHITCHER-ALAGNA, S. (1982). Recipient reactions to aid. *Psychological Bulletin, 91,* 27–54.

FISHER, R.J. (1982). *Social psychology: An applied approach.* New York: St. Martin's Press.

FISHER, R.J. (1983). Third Party Consultation as a method of intergroup conflict resolution. *Journal of Conflict Resolution, 27,* 301–334.

FISHER, R.J. (1985). The social psychology of intergroup conflict: Toward eclectic theory. Paper presented at the Annual Meeting for the Canadian Psychological Association, Halifax.

FISHER, R.J. & WHITE, J.H. (1976). Reducing tensions between neighbourhood housing groups: A pilot study in third-party consultation. *International Journal of Group Tensions, 6,* 46–52.

FISKE, S.T. (1980). Attention and weight on person perception. *Journal of Personality and Social Psychology, 38,* 889–906.

FISKE, S.T., PRATTO, F. & PAVELCHAK, M.A. (1983). Citizens' images of nuclear war: Contents and consequences. *Journal of Social Issues, 39,* 41–66.

FISKE, S.T. & TAYLOR, S.E. (1984). *Social cognition.* Don Mills, Ontario: Addison-Wesley.

FLAMENT, C. (1958). Influence sociale et perception. *Anneé psychologique, 58,* 378–400.

FLEMING, I., BAUM, A. & WEISS, L. (1987). Social density and perceived control as mediators of crowding stress in a high-density residential neighbourhood. *Journal of Personality and Social Psychology, 52,* 899–906.

FLOWERS, M.L. (1977). A laboratory test of some implications of Janis's groupthink hypothesis. *Journal of Personality and Social Psychology, 35,* 888–896.

FOA, U.G. (1971). Interpersonal and economic resources. *Science, 171,* 345–351.

FOA, U.G. & FOA, E.B. (1975). *Resource theory of social exchange.* Morristown, NJ: General Learning Press.

FOGELMAN, E. & WIENER, V.L. (1985). The few, the brave, the noble. *Psychology Today, 19,* 61–65.

FONAGY, I. (1971). Double coding in speech. *Semiotica, 3,* 189–222.

FOREMAN, P.B. (1953). Panic theory. *Sociology and Social Research, 37,* 295–304.

FRABLE, D.E.S. & BEM, S.L. (1985). If you are gender schematic, all members of the opposite sex look alike. *Journal of Personality and Social Psychology, 49,* 459–468.

FRANKL, V. (1963). *Man's search for meaning*. New York: Washington Square Press.

FRANKLIN, S. (1977). *A time of heroes 1940/1950*. Toronto: Natural Science of Canada Limited.

FREEDMAN, J.L. (1965). Long-term behavioral effects of cognitive dissonance. *Journal of Experimental Social Psychology, 1,* 145–155.

FREEDMAN, J.L. (1975). *Crowding and behavior*. New York: Viking Press.

FREEDMAN, J.L. (1982). Theories of contagion as they relate to mass psychogenic illness. In M.J. Colligan, J.W. Pennebaker & L.R. Murphy (Eds.), *Mass psychogenic illness*, (171–182). Hillsdale, NJ: Erlbaum.

FREEDMAN, J.L. (1984). Effects of television violence on aggressiveness. *Psychological Bulletin, 96,* 227–246.

FREEDMAN, J.L. (1986). Television violence and aggression: A rejoinder. *Psychological Bulletin, 100,* 372–378.

FREEDMAN, J.L., BIRSKY, J. & CAVOUKIAN, A. (1980). Environmental determinants of behavioral contagion: Density and number. *Basic and Applied Social Psychology, 1,* 155–161.

FREEDMAN, J.L. & FRASER, S.C. (1966). Compliance without pressure: The foot-in-the-door technique. *Journal of Personality and Social Psychology, 4,* 195–202.

FREEDMAN, J.L., HESHKA, S. & LEVY, A. (1975). Population density and pathology: Is there a relationship? *Journal of Experimental Social Psychology, 11,* 539–552.

FREEDMAN, J.L., WALLINGTON, S.A. & BLESS, E. (1967). Compliance without pressure: The effect of guilt. *Journal of Personality and Social Psychology, 7,* 117–124.

FRENAS, R.S. (1983). Attitudes toward industrial pollution, strategies to protect the environment, and environment-economic tradeoffs. *Journal of Applied Social Psychology, 13,* 310–327.

FRENCH, J.R.P. (1944). Organized and unorganized groups under fear and frustration. *University of Iowa Studies of Child Welfare, 20,* 231–308.

FRENDER, R & LAMBERT, W.E. (1972). The influence of pupils' speech styles on teacher evaluations. 23rd Annual Round Table Meeting, Georgetown University, Washington, D.C. Cited by Bourhis, Giles & Lambert (1975).

FRENKEL, O.J. & DOOB, A.N. (1976). Post-decision dissonance at the polling booth. *Canadian Journal of Behavioural Science, 8,* 347–350.

FREUD, S. (1933). Why war? In J. Rickman (Ed.) (1968), *Civilization, war and death: Selections from five works by Sigmund Freud* (82–97). London: Hogarth.

FREY, D. (1986). Recent research on selective exposure to information. In L. Berkowitz (Ed.), *Advances in experimental social psychology* (Vol. 19) (41–80). New York: Academic Press.

FRICK, R.W. (1985). Communicating emotion: The role of prosodic features. *Psychological Bulletin, 97,* 412–429.

FRIEDMAN, H.S. (1982). Nonverbal communication in medical interaction. In H.S. Friedman & M.R. DiMatteo (Eds.), *Interpersonal issues in health care*. New York: Academic Press.

FRIEDMAN, H.S., PRINCE, L., RIGGIO, R. & DiMATTEO, M. (1980). Understanding and assessing nonverbal expressiveness. *Journal of Personality and Social Psychology, 14,* 351–364.

FRIEDMAN, M. & ROSENMAN, R.H. (1959). Association of a specific behavior pattern with blood and cardiovascular findings: Blood cholesterol levels, blood clotting time, incidence of arcus senilis and clinical coronary artery disease. *Journal of American Medical Association, 169,* 1286–1296.

FRIEDRICH-COFER, L. & HUSTON, A.C. (1986). Television violence and aggression: The debate continues. *Psychological Bulletin, 100,* 364–371.

FRIEZE, I. & WEINER, B. (1971). Cue utilization and attributional judgments for success and failure. *Journal of Personality, 39,* 591–605.

FRITZ, C.E. & MARKS, E.F. (1954). The NORC studies of human behavior in disaster. *Journal of Social Issues, 10,* 26–41.

FRODI, A., MACAULAY, J. & THOME, P.R. (1977). Are women always less aggressive than men? A review of the experimental literature. *Psychological Bulletin, 84,* 634–660.

FROLICH, N. & OPPENHEIMER, J. (1970). I get by with a little help from my friends. *World Politics, 23,* 104–120.

FROMKIN, H.L. (1972). Feelings of interpersonal undistinctiveness: An unpleasant affective state. *Journal of Experimental Research in Personality, 6,* 178–185.

FUGITA, S.S., HOGREBE, M.C. & WEXLEY, K.N. (1980). Perception of deception: Perceived expertise in detecting deception, successfulness of deception and nonverbal cues. *Personality and Social Psychology Bulletin, 6,* 637–643.

FURNHAM, A. (1985). Just world beliefs in an unjust society: A cross-cultural comparison. *European Journal of Social Psychology, 15,* 363–366.

GAMSON, W.A. (1961). A theory of coalition formation. *American Sociological Review, 26,* 373–382.

GAMSON, W.A. (1964). Experimental studies of coalition formation. In L. Berkowitz (Ed.), *Advances in experimental social psychology* (Vol. 1) (82–110). New York: Academic Press.

GAMSON, W.A. & MODIGLIANI, A. (1974). *Conceptions of social life*. Boston: Little, Brown.

GARCIA, L.T. & GRIFFIT, W. (1978). Impact of testimonial evidence as a function of witness characteristics. *Bulletin of the Psychonomic Society, 11,* 37–40.

GARDNER, D.S. (1933). The perception and memory of witnesses. *Cornell Law Quarterly, 18,* 391–409.

GARDNER, R.A. & GARDNER, B.T.(1971). Teaching sign language to a chimpanzee. *Science, 165,* 664–672.

GARDNER, R.C. (1979). Social psychological aspects of second language acquisition. In H. Giles & R. St. Clair (Eds.), *Language and psychology.* Oxford: Basil Blackwell.

GARDNER, R.C. (1984). *Social psychological aspects of second language learning.* London: Edward Arnold.

GARDNER, R.C. & DESROCHERS, A. (1981). Second language acquisition and bilingualism: Research in Canada (1970–1980). *Canadian Psychology, 22,* 146–162.

GARDNER, R.C., GLIKSMAN, L. & SMYTHE, P.C. (1978). Attitude and behaviour in second language acquisition: A social psychological interpretation. *Canadian Psychological Review, 19,* 173–186.

GARDNER, R.C., KIRBY, D.M., SMYTHE, P.C., DUMAS, G., ZELMAN, M. & BROMWELL, J.R. (1974). Bicultural excursion programme: Their effects on students' stereotypes, attitudes and motivation. *Alberta Journal of Educational Research, 20,* 270–277.

GARDNER, R.C. & LAMBERT, W.E. (1959). Motivational variables in second language acquisition. *Canadian Journal of Psychology, 13,* 266–272.

GARDNER, R.C. & LAMBERT, W.E. (1972). *Attitudes and motivation in second-language learning.* Rowley, MA: Newbury House.

GARDNER, R.C., SMYTHE, P.C., CLÉMENT, R. & GLIKSMAN, L. (1976). Second language acquisition: A social psychological perspective. *Canadian Modern Language Review, 32,* 198–213.

GARNER, D.M., GARFINKEL, P.E., SCHWARTZ, D. & THOMPSON, M. (1980). Cultural expectations of thinness in women. *Psychological Reports, 47,* 483–491.

GARZINO, S. (1982). Lunar effects on behavior: A defence of the empirical research. *Environment and Behavior, 14,* 395–417.

GAUTHIER, J. (1977). Brief. *Report of the Royal Commission on Violence in the Communications Industry* (Vol. 1) (336–345). Toronto: Publication Centre, Government of Ontario.

GEEN, R.G. AND GANGE, J.J. (1977). Drive theory of social facilitation: Twelve years of theory and research. *Psychological Bulletin, 84,* 1267–1288.

GEEN, R.G., STONNER, D. & SHOPE, G.L. (1975). The facilitation of aggression by aggression: Evidence against the catharsis hypothesis. *Journal of Personality and Social Psychology, 31,* 721–726.

GELFAND, D.M., HARTMANN, D.P., WALDER, P. & PAGE, B. (1973). Who reports shoplifters? A field-experimental study. *Journal of Personality and Social Psychology, 25,* 276–285.

GENESEE, F. (1984). Beyond bilingualism: Social psychological studies of French immersion programs in Canada. *Canadian Journal of Behavioural Science, 16,* 338–352.

GERARD, H. (1967). Choice difficulty, dissonance, and the decision sequence. *Journal of Personality, 35,* 91–108.

GERBASI, K.C., ZUCKERMAN, M. & REIS, H.T. (1977). Justice needs a new blindfold: A review of mock jury research. *Psychological Bulletin, 84,* 323–345.

GERBNER, G. (1969). The television world of violence. In R.K. Baker & S.J. Ball (Eds.), *Mass media and violence: A staff report to the National Commission on the causes and prevention of violence.* Washington, D.C: U.S. Government Printing Office.

GERBNER, G. (1975). Scenario for violence. *Human Behavior, 4,* 64–69.

GERBNER, G. & GROSS, L. (1976). The scary world of TV's heavy viewer. *Psychology Today, 9* (11), 41–42, 44–45, 89.

GERBNER, G., GROSS, L., MORGAN, M. & SIGNORIELLI, N. (1980). The "mainstreaming" of America: Violence profile No. 11. *Journal of Communication, 30,* 10–29.

GERGEN, K.J., ELLSWORTH, P., MASLACH, P. & SEIPEL, M. (1975). Obligation, donor resources, and the reactions to aid in three nations.*Journal of Personality and Social Psychology, 31,* 390–400.

GERGEN, K.J., GERGEN, M.M. & METER, K. (1972). Individual orientations to prosocial behavior. *Journal of Social Issues, 28,* 105–130.

GERSON, A.C. & PERLMAN, D. (1979). Loneliness and expressive communication. *Journal of Abnormal Psychology, 88,* 258–261.

GIALLOMBARDO, R. (1966). *Society of women: A study of a women's prison.* New York: Wiley.

GIBB, C.A. (1969). Leadership. In G. Lindzey & E. Aronson (Eds.), *Handbook of social psychology* (Vol. 4). Second Edition. Reading, MA: Addison-Wesley.

GIBBINS, K. & CONEY, J.R. (1981). Meaning of physical dimensions of women's clothes. *Perceptual and Motor Skills, 53,* 720–722.

GILBERT, G.M. (1951). Stereotype persistence and change among college students. *Journal of Abnormal and Social Psychology, 46,* 245–254.

GILES, H. (1973). Accent mobility: A model and some data. *Anthropological Linguistics, 15,* 87–105.

GILES, H., BOURHIS, R.Y. & DAVIES, A. (1977). Prestige speech styles: The imposed norm and inherent value hypotheses. In W.C. McCormack & S. Wurm (Eds.), *Language and society: Anthropological issues.* The Hague: Mouton.

GILES, H., BOURHIS, R.Y. & TAYLOR, D.M. (1977). Towards a theory of language in ethnic group relations. In H. Giles (Ed.), *Language, ethnicity and intergroup relations* (307–348). London: Academic Press.

GILES, H., BOURHIS, R., TRUDGILL, P. & LEWIS, A. (1974). The imposed norm hypothesis: A validation. *The Quarterly Journal of Speech, 60,* 405–410.

GILES, H. & POWESLAND, P. (1975). *Speech style and social evaluation.* London: Academic Press.

GILES, H. & SMITH, P.M. (1979). Accommodation theory: Optimal levels of convergence. In H. Giles & R. St. Clair (Eds.), *Language and social psychology.* Oxford: Basil Blackwell.

GILES, H., TAYLOR, D.M. & BOURHIS, R.Y. (1973). Toward a theory of interpersonal accommodation through speech: Some Canadian data. *Language in Society, 2,* 177–192.

GILLIG, P.M. & GREENWALD, A.G. (1974). Is it time to lay the sleeper effect to rest? *Journal of Personality and Social Psychology, 29,* 132–139.

GILLIGAN, F. (1977). Comments: Eyewitness identification. *Military Law Review, 58,* 183–207.

GILLIS, J.S. (1983). *Too tall too small.* Montreal: Book Centre.

GLASS, D.C. (1977). *Behavior patterns, stress and coronary disease.* Hillsdale, NJ: Erlbaum.

GLASS, D.C. & SINGER, J.E. (1972). *Urban stress.* New York: Academic Press.

GODDARD, P. (1977). Violence and popular music. In *Report of the Royal Commission on Violence in the Communications Industry* (Vol. 4) (223–236). Toronto: Publication Centre, Government of Ontario.

GOFFMAN, E. (1955). On face-work: An analysis of ritual elements in social interaction. *Psychiatry, 18,* 213–231.

GOLDBERG, G.N., KIESLER, C.A. & COLLINS, B.E. (1969). Visual behavior and face-to face distance during interaction. *Sociometry, 32,* 43–53.

GOLDBERG, M.E. (1982). TV advertising directed at children: Inherently unfair or simply in need of regulation? In S.J. Shapiro & L. Heslop (Eds.), *Marketplace Canada: Some controversial dimensions.* Toronto: McGraw-Hill Ryerson.

GOLDBERG, M.E. & GORN, G.J. (1979). Television's impact on preferences for non-white playmates: Canadian *Sesame Street* inserts. *Journal of Broadcasting, 23,* 27–32.

GOLDBERG, P. (1968). Are some women prejudiced against women? *Trans-Action, 5,* 28–30.

GOLDBERG, S., LaCOMB, S., LEVINSON, D., PARKER, R., ROSS, C. & SOMMERS, F. (1985). Thinking about the threat of nuclear war: Relevance to mental health. *American Journal of Orthopsychiatry, 55,* 503–512.

GOLDSTEIN, J.H. (1975). *Aggression and crimes of violence.* New York: Oxford.

GOLDSTEIN, J.H., DAVIS, R.W. & HERMON, D. (1975). Escalation of aggression: Experimental studies. *Journal of Personality and Social Psychology, 35,* 162–170.

GOODMAN, M. (1964). *Race awareness in young children.* Second Edition. New York. Crowell-Collier.

GORANSON, R.E. (1970). Media violence and aggressive behavior: A review of experimental research. In L. Berkowitz (Ed.), *Advances in experimental social psychology* (Vol. 5) (1–30). New York: Academic Press.

GORANSON, R.E. (1977). Television violence effects: Issues and evidence. In *Report of the Royal Commission on Violence in the Communications Industry* (Vol. 5) (1–31). Toronto: Publication Centre, Government of Ontario.

GORDON, W.J.J. (1961). *Synectics: The development of creative capacity.* New York: Harper & Row.

GORER, G. (1968). Man has no "killer" instinct. In M.F.A. Montagu (Ed.), *Man and aggression.* (27–36). New York: Oxford University Press.

GORER, G. (1980) The pornography of death. In E.S. Shneidman (Ed.), *Death: Current perspectives.* Second Edition (47–55). Palo Alto, CA: Mayfield.

GOTTLIEB, B.H. (1985). Social networks and social support: An overview of research, practice and policy implications. *Health Education Quarterly, 12,* 221–238.

GOULDNER, A.W. (1960). The norm of reciprocity: A preliminary statement. *American Sociological Review, 25,* 161–179.

GOULDNER, J.W. (1968). The doctors' strike: Change and resistance to change in Saskatchewan. In S.M. Lipset (Ed.), *Agrarian socialism.* Toronto: Doubleday.

GRANBERG, D. & FAYE, N. (1972). Sensitizing people by making the abstract concrete. Study of the effect of "Hiroshima-Nagasaki." *American Journal of Orthopsychiatry, 42,* 811–815.

GRANT, P.R. (1978). *Attribution of an ethnic stereotype.* Unpublished Masters Thesis, University of Waterloo.

GRAYSON, J.P. & GRAYSON, L. (1975). Social movements and social change in contemporary Canada. *Quarterly of Canadian Studies, 4,* 50–57.

GREENGLASS, E.R. (1969). Effects of prior help and hindrance on willingness to help another: Reciprocity or social responsibility? *Journal of Personality and Social Psychology, 11,* 224–231.

GREENGLASS, E.R. (1982). *A world of difference: Gender roles in perspective.* Toronto: Wiley.

GREENWALD, A.G. & RONIS, D.L. (1978). Twenty years of cognitive dissonance: A case study of the evaluation of a theory. *Psychological Review, 85,* 53–57.

GREGG, G., PRESTON, T., GEIST, A. & CAPLAN, N. (1979). The caravan rolls on: Forty years of social problem research. *Knowledge: Creation, Diffusion, Utilization, 1,* 31–61.

GROFF, B.D., BARON, R.S. & MOORE, D.L. (1983). Distraction, attentional conflict, and drivelike behavior. *Journal of Experimental Social Psychology, 19,* 359–380.

GROSS, A.E. & FLEMING, J. (1982). Twenty years of deception in social psychology. *Personality and Social Psychology Bulletin, 8,* 402–408.

GRUDER, C.L. (1974). Cost and dependency as determinants of helping and exploitation. *Journal of Conflict Resolution, 18,* 473–485.

GRUDER, C.L., COOK, T.D., HENNIGAN, K.M., FLAY, B.R. & HALAMAJ, J. (1978). Empirical tests of the absolute sleeper effect predicted from the discounting cue hypothesis. *Journal of Personality and Social Psychology, 36,* 1061–1074.

GRUSEC, J.E. (1972). Demand characteristics of the modelling experiment: Altruism as a function of age and aggression. *Journal of Personality and Social Psychology, 22,* 139–148.

GRUSEC, J.E., KUCZYNSKI, L., SIMUTIS, Z. & RUSHTON, J.P. (1978). Modeling, direct instruction, and attributions: Effects on altruism. *Developmental Psychology, 14,* 51–57.

GRUSEC, J.E. & REDLER, E. (1980). Attribution, reinforcement and altruism: A developmental analysis. *Developmental Psychology, 16,* 525–534.

GRUSEC, J.E. & SKUBISKI, S.L. (1970). Model nurturance, demand characteristics of the modelling experiment, and altruism. *Journal of Personality and Social Psychology, 14,* 352–359.

GUTTMAN, L. (1944). A basis for scaling qualitative data. *American Sociological Review, 9,* 139–150.

HAAS, A. (1979). Male and female spoken language differences: Stereotypes and evidence. *Psychological Bulletin, 86,* 616–626.

HAGERSTRAND, T. (1965). Quantitative techniques for analysis of the spread of information and technology. In C.A. Anderson & M.J. Bowman (Eds.), *Education and economic development.* Chicago: University of Chicago Press.

HAIRE, M., & GRUNE, W.F. (1950). Perceptual defenses: Processes protecting an organized perception of another personality. *Human Relations, 3,* 403–412.

HALL, J.A. (1979). Gender, gender roles, and nonverbal communication. In R. Rosenthal (Ed.), *Skill in nonverbal communication* (32–67). Cambridge, MA: Oelgeschlager, Gunn & Hain.

HALL, J.A. & BRAUNWALD, K.G. (1981). Gender cues in conversations. *Journal of Personality and Social Psychology, 40,* 99–110.

HALLOWELL, A.I. (1940). Aggression in Saulteaux society. *Psychiatry, 3,* 395–407.

HAMBLIN, R.L. (1958). Leadership and crises. *Sociometry, 21,* 322–335.

HAMBURGER, H., GUYER, M. & FOX, J. (1975). Group size and cooperation. *Journal of Conflict Resolution, 19,* 503–531.

HAMILL, R., WILSON, T.D. & NISBETT, R.E. (1980). Insensitivity to sample bias: Generalizing from atypical cases. *Journal of Personality and Social Psychology, 39,* 578–589.

HAMILTON, D.L. (1976). Individual differences in ascriptions of responsibility, guilt and appropriate judgement. In G. Berman, C. Nemeth & N. Vidmar (Eds.), *Psychology and the law* (239–264). Lexington, MA: Heath.

HAMILTON, D.L. (1979). A cognitive-attributional analysis of stereotyping. In L. Berkowitz (Ed.), *Advances in experimental social psychology* (Vol. 12). New York: Academic press.

HAMILTON, D.L. (1981). Illusory correlation as a basis for stereotyping. In D.L. Hamilton (Ed.), *Cognitive processes in stereotyping and intergroup behavior.* Hillsdale, NJ: Erlbaum.

HAMILTON, D.L. & GIFFORD, R.K. (1976). Illusory correlation in interpersonal perception: A cognitive basis of stereotypic judgements. *Journal of Experimental Social Psychology, 12,* 392–407.

HAMILTON, D.L. & ROSE, T.L. (1980). Illusory correlation and the maintenance of stereotypes. *Journal of Personality and Social Psychology, 39,* 832–845.

HAMILTON, D.L. & ZANNA, M.P. (1972). Differential weighting of favorable and unfavorable attributes in impressions of personality. *Journal of Experimental Research in Personality, 6,* 204–212.

HAMMOND, K.R. (1948). Measuring attitudes by error-choice: An indirect method. *Journal of Abnormal and Social Psychology, 43,* 38–48.

HANEY, C. (1980). Juries and the death penalty: Readdressing the Witherspoon question. *Crime and Delinquency, 12,* 512–527.

HANEY, C. & MANZOLATTI, J. (1981). Television criminology: Network illusions of criminal justice reality. In E. Aronson (Ed.), *Readings about the social animal.* Third Edition (125–136). San Francisco: W.H. Freeman.

HANS, V. & DOOB, A.N. (1976). Section 12 of the Canada Evidence Act and the deliberations of simulated jurors. *Criminal Law Quarterly, 11,* 235–253.

HANS, V.P. & VIDMAR, N. (1986). *Judging the jury.* Toronto: Carswell.

HARDIN, G. (1968). The tragedy of the commons. *Science, 162,* 1243–1248.

HARDIN, G. & BADEN, J. (1977). *Managing the commons.* San Francisco: W.H. Freeman.

HARDIN, R. (1971). Collective action as an agreeable N-Prisoner's Dilemma. *Behavioral Science, 16,* 472–481.

HARDYCK, J.A. & BRADEN, M. (1962). When prophecy fails again: A report of a failure to replicate. *Journal of Abnormal and Social Psychology, 65,* 136–141.

HARE, A.P. (1962). *Handbook of small group research.* Glencoe, NY: Free Press.

HARLOW, H. (1958). The nature of love. *American Psychologist, 13,* 673–685.

HARLOW, H. (1959). Love in infant monkeys. *Scientific American, 200,* 68–74.

HARLOW, H.F. (1965). Sexual behavior in the rhesus monkey. In F.A. Beach (Ed.), *Sex and behavior.* New York: Wiley.

HARRIS, E.E. (1970). *Hypothesis and perception.* London: George Allen & Unwin.

HARRIS, M. (1974). *Cows, pigs, wars and witches: The riddles of cultures.* New York: Random House.

HARRISON, A.A. (1977). Mere exposure. In L. Berkowitz (Ed.), *Advances in experimental social psychology* (Vol. 1) (39–83). New York: Academic Press.

HARRISON, M. & PEPITONE, A. (1972). Contrast effect in the use of punishment. *Journal of Personality and Social Psychology, 23,* 398–404.

HASS, R.G. & GRADY, K. (1975). Temporal delay, type of forewarning, and resistance to influence. *Journal of Experimental Social Psychology, 11,* 459–469.

HASTIE, R. (1984). Causes and effects of causal attribution. *Journal of Personality and Social Psychology, 46,* 44–56.

HASTIE, R. & KUMAR, P.A. (1979). Personal memory: Personality traits as organizing principles in memory for behavior. *Journal of Personality and Social Psychology, 37,* 25–38.

HATFIELD, E. & WALSTER, G.W. (1978). *A new look at love.* Reading, MA: Addison-Wesley.

HAVEMAN, R.H. & WATTS, H.W. (1976). Social experimentation and policy research. In C.V. Glass (Ed.), *Evaluation studies review annual* (Vol. 1) (172–197). Beverly Hills, CA: Sage.

HAVILAND, J.M. & MALATESTA, C.M. (1981). The development of sex differences in nonverbal signals: Fallacies, facts and fantasies. In C. Mayo & N.M. Henley (Eds.), *Gender and non-verbal behavior.* New York: Springer-Verlag.

HAYES, K. & HAYES, C. (1952). Imitation in a home-raised chimpanzee. *Journal of Comparative and Physiological Psychology, 45,* 450–459.

HEALTH AND WELFARE CANADA (1987). *The Active Health Report: Perspectives on Canada's Health Promotion Survey, 1985.* Catalogue No. H-39–106/1987E. Ottawa: Supply and Services Canada.

HEBB, D.O. (1971). Comment on altruism: The comparative evidence. *Psychological Bulletin, 76,* 409–410.

HEBB, D.O. & THOMPSON, W.R. (1968). The social significance of animal studies. In G. Lindzey & E. Aronson (Eds.), *The handbook of social psychology.* Second Edition (Vol. 1). Reading, MA: Addison-Wesley.

HEIDER, F. (1958). *The psychology of interpersonal relations.* New York: Wiley.

HELMREICH, R., ARONSON, E. & LeFAN, J. (1970). To err is humanizing sometimes: Effects of self-esteem, competence, and a pratfall on interpersonal attraction. *Journal of Personality and Social Psychology, 16,* 259–264.

HELMUTH, H. (1973). Human behavior: Aggression. In A. Montagu (Ed.), *Man and aggression,* Second Edition. London: Oxford University Press.

HENDRICK, C. & HENDRICK, S. (1983). *Liking, loving and relating.* Monterey, CA: Brooks/Cole.

HENDRICK, C. & HENDRICK, S. (1986). A theory and a method of love. *Journal of Personality and Social Psychology, 50,* 392–402.

HENLEY, M. (1973). Status and sex: some touching observations. *Bulletin of the Psychonomic Society, 2,* 21–27.

HENNIGAN, K.M., DelROSARIO, M.L., HEATH, L., COOK, T.D., WHARTON, J.D. & CALDER, B.J. (1982). Impact of the introduction of television on crime in the United States: Empirical findings and theoretical implications. *Journal of Personality and Social Psychology, 42,* 461–477.

HENRY, F. (1978). The dynamics of racism in Toronto. Unpublished research report. York University.

HENRY F. & GINZBERG, E. (1985). *Who gets the work: A test of racial discrimination in employment in Toronto.* Toronto: The Urban Alliance on Race Relations and the Social Planning Council of Metropolitan Toronto.

HERD, J.A. & WEISS, S.M. (1984). Overview of hypertension: Its treatment and prevention. In J.D. Matarazzo, S.M. Weiss, J.A. Herd, N.E. Miller & S.M. Weiss (Eds.), *Behavioral health* (789–804). New York: Wiley.

HERMAN, C.P. & POLIVY, J. (1975). Anxiety, restraint and eating behavior. *Journal of Abnormal Psychology, 84,* 666–672.

HERTEL, P.T. & NAVAREZ, A. (1986). Confusing memories for verbal and nonverbal communication. *Journal of Personality and Social Psychology, 50,* 474–481.

HEWSTONE, M. & BROWN, R. (1986). *Contact and conflict in intergroup relations.* Oxford: Blackwell.

HIGBEE, K.L. (1969). Fifteen years of fear arousal: Research on threat appeals: 1953–1968. *Psychological Bulletin, 72,* 426–444.

HIGGINS, E.T. & BRYANT, S.L. (1982). Consensus information and the fundamental attribution error: The role of development and in-group versus out-group knowledge. *Journal of Personality and Social Psychology, 43,* 889–900.

HILGARD, E.R. (1978). Hypnosis and consciousness. *Human Nature, 1,* 2–49.

HILL, C.T., RUBIN, Z. & PEPLAU, L.A. (1976). Breakups before marriage: The end of 103 affairs. *Journal of Social Issues, 32,* 147–168.

HILL, C.T. & STULL, D.E. (1981). Sex differences in the effects of social and value similarity in same-sex friendships. *Journal of Personality and Social Psychology, 41,* 488–502.

HILL, W.F. (1978). Effects of mere exposure on preferences in nonhuman animals. *Psychological Bulletin, 85,* 1177–1198.

HINGSON, R.W., SCOTCH, N., MANGIANE, T., MEYERS, A., GLANTZ, L., HEZREN, T., LIN, N., MUCATEL, M. & PIERCE, G. (1983). Impact of legislation raising the legal drinking age in Massachusetts from 18 to 20. *American Journal of Public Health, 73,* 163–170.

HODGINS, D.C. & KALIN, R. (1985). Reducing sex bias in judgements of occupational suitability by provision of sex-typed personality information. *Canadian Journal of Behavioural Science, 17,* 346–358.

HOFFMAN, C., LAU, I. & JOHNSON, D.R. (1986). The linguistic relativity of person cognition: An English-Chinese comparison. *Journal of Personality and Social Psychology, 51,* 1097–1105.

HOFFMAN, M.L. (1975). Altruistic behavior and the parent-child relationship. *Journal of Personality and Social Psychology, 31,* 937–943.

HOFFMANN, M.L. (1977). Sex differences in empathy and related behaviors. *Psychological Bulletin, 84,* 712–722.

HOFFMANN, M.L. (1981). Is altruism a part of human nature? *Journal of Personality and Social Psychology, 40,* 121–137.

HOFFMAN, M.L. (1984). Parent discipline, moral internalization, and development of prosocial motivation. In E. Staub, D. Bar-Tal, J. Karylowski & J. Reykowski (Eds.), *Development and maintenance of prosocial behavior* (117–137). New York: Plenum.

HOFLING, C.K., BRODZSMAN, E., DALRYMPLE, S., GRAVES, N. & PIERCE, C.M. (1966). An experimental study in nurse physician relationships. *The Journal of Nervous and Mental Disease, 143,* 171–180.

HOFSTEDE, G. (1983). Dimensions of national cultures in fifty countries and three regions. In J.B. Deregowaki, S. Dziurawiec, & R.C. Annis (Eds.), *Expiscations in cross-cultural psychology* (335–355). Lisse, The Netherlands: Swets & Zeitlinger B.V.

HOKANSON, J.E. (1970). Psychophysical evaluation of the catharsis hypothesis. In E.I. Megargee & J.E. Hokanson (Eds.), *The dynamics of aggression: Individual, group, and international analyses.* New York: Harper & Row.

HOLLANDER, E.P. (1958). Conformity, status, and idiosyncrasy credit. *Psychological Review, 65,* 117–127.

HOLLANDER, E.P. (1978). *Leadership dynamics: A practical guide to effective relationships.* New York: Free Press.

HOLLANDER, E.P. (1985). Leadership and power. In G. Lindzey & E. Aronson (Eds.), *The Handbook of Social Psychology.* Third Edition. New York: Random House.

HOLLANDER, E.P. & YODER, J. (1980). Some issues in comparing women and men as leaders. *Basic and Applied Social Psychology, 1,* 267–280.

HOLMES, D.S. (1976). Debriefing after psychological experiments: II. Effectiveness of post-experimental desensitizing. *American Psychologist, 31,* 868–876.

HOLMES, J. & BROWN, D.F. (1977). Sociolinguistic competence and second language learning. In *Topics in culture learning, Volume 5.* Honolulu: East-West Culture Learning Institute.

HOLMES, T.H. & RAHE, R.H. (1967). The social readjustment rating scale. *Journal of Psychosomatic Research, 11,* 213–218.

HOLTGRAVES, T. (1986). Language structure in social interaction: Perceptions of direct and indirect speech acts and interactants who use them. *Journal of Personality and Social Psychology, 51,* 305–314.

HOLTZWORTH-MUNROE, A. & JACOBSON, N.S. (1985). Causal attributions of married couples: When do they search for causes? What do they conclude when they do? *Journal of Personality and Social Psychology, 48,* 1398–1412.

HOMANS, G.C. (1958). Social behavior and exchange. *American Journal of Sociology, 63,* 597–606.

HOMANS, G.C. (1961). *Social behavior: Its elementary forms.* New York: Harcourt, Brace and World.

HOMANS G.C. (1974). *Social behavior: Its elementary forms.* Revised Edition. New York: Harcourt Brace Jovanovich.

HOMANS, G.C. (1982). The present state of sociological theory. *Sociological Quarterly, 23,* 285–299.

HONTS, C.R., HODES, R.L. & RASKIN, D.C. (1985). Effects of physical counter measures on the physiological detection of deception. *Journal of Applied Psychology, 70,* 177–187.

HOPSON, J. (1981). Evil spirits in the factory. *Science Digest,* October, 58, 114.

HORN, J.C. (1985). Fan violence: Fighting the injustice of it all. *Psychology Today, 19 (10),* 30–31.

HORN, M.J. (1975). *The second skin: An interdisciplinary study of clothing.* Boston: Houghton-Mifflin.

HORTON, R.W. & SANTAGROSSI, D.A. (1978). The effects of adult commentary on reducing the influence of televised violence. *Personality and Social Psychology Bulletin, 4,* 337–340.

HORVATH, F. (1977). Effect of selected variables on interpretation of polygraph records. *Journal of Applied Psychology, 62,* 127–136.

HORVATH, F. (1984). Detecting deception in eyewitness cases: Problems and prospects in the use of the polygraph. In G.L. Wells & E.F. Loftus (Eds.), *Eyewitness testimony: Psychological perspectives* (214–255). Cambridge, U.K.: Cambridge University Press.

HOULDEN, P., LATOUR, S., WALKER, L. & THIBAUT, J. (1978). Preference for modes of dispute resolution as a function of process and decision control. *Journal of Experimental Social Psychology, 14,* 13–30.

HOUSE, R. (1977). A 1976 theory of charismatic leadership. In J.G. Hunt and L. Larson (Eds.), *Leadership: The cutting edge* (189–207). Carbondale: Southern Illinois University Press.

HOVLAND, C.I., HARVEY, O.J. & SHERIF, M. (1957). Assimilation and contrast effects in reactions to communications and attitude change. *Journal of Abnormal and Social Psychology, 55,* 244–252.

HOVLAND, C.I., JANIS, I. & KELLEY, H.H. (1953). *Communication and persuasion.* New Haven: Yale University Press.

HOVLAND, C.I., LUMSDAINE, A.A. & SHEFFIELD, F.D. (1949). *Experiments on mass communication.* Princeton, NJ: Princeton University Press.

HOVLAND, C.I., MANDELL, W., CAMPBELL, E.H., BROCK, T., LUCHINO, A.S., COHEN, A.E., McGUIRE, W.J., JANIS, I.L., FEIERABEND, R.L. & ANDERSON, N.H. (1957). *The order of presentation in persuasion.* New Haven: Yale University Press.

HOVLAND, C.I. & SHERIF, M. (1952). Judgmental phenomena and scales of attitude measurement: Item displacement in Thurstone scales. *Journal of Abnormal and Social Psychology, 47,* 822–832.

HOWITT, D. & CUMBERBATCH, G. (1975). *Mass media violence and society.* London: Paul Elek.

HUANG, L.C. & HARRIS, M.B. (1974). Altruism and imitation in Chinese and Americans: A cross-cultural experiment. *Journal of Social Psychology, 93,* 193–195.

HUBA, G.J., DENT, C. & BENTLER, P.M. (1980). Causal models of peer-adult support and youthful alcohol use. Paper presented to the American Psychological Association, Montréal (September).

HUESMANN, L.R. (1986). Psychological processes promoting the relation between exposure to media violence and aggressive behavior by the receiver. *Journal of Social Issues, 42,* 125–139.

HUESMANN, L.R., ERON, L.D., KLEIN, R., BRICE, P. & FISCHER, P. (1983). Mitigating the imitation of aggressive behaviors by changing children's attitudes about media violence. *Journal of Personality and Social Psychology, 44,* 899–910.

HUESMANN, L.R., ERON, L.D., LEFKOWITZ, M.M., & WALDER, L.O. (1984). Stability of aggression over time and generations. *Developmental Psychology, 20,* 1120–1134.

HUESMANN, L.R., ERON, L.D. & YARMEL, P.W. (1987). Intellectual functioning and aggression. *Journal of Personality and Social Psychology, 52,* 232–240.

HUGHES, C.C., TREMBLAY, M.A., RAPOPORT, R.N. & LEIGHTON, A.H. (1960). *People of cove and woodlot.* New York: Basic Books.

HUMMEL, C.F., LEVITT, L. & LOOMIS, S.J. (1978). Perceptions of the energy crisis: Who is blamed and how do citizens react to environmental-lifestyle trade-offs. *Environment and Behavior, 10,* 37–88.

HUNT, W.A., BARNETT, L.W. & BRANCH, L.G. (1971). Relapse rate in addiction programs. *Journal of Clinical Psychology, 27,* 455–456.

HUNTER, I. (1987). Human rights: Liberty can't be legislated. In R. Jackson, D. Jackson & N. Baxter-Moore (Eds.), *Contemporary Canadian politics: Readings and notes* (61–64). Scarborough: Prentice-Hall.

HUSTON, T.L., & LEVINGER, G. (1978). Interpersonal attraction and relationships. *Annual Review of Psychology, 29,* 115–156.

HUTT, C. (1974). Sex: What's the difference? *New Scientist, 62,* 405–407.

INGHAM, A.G., LEVINGER, G., GRAVES, J. & PECKHORN, V. (1974). The Ringelmann effect: Studies of group size and group performance. *Journal of Experimental Social Psychology, 10,* 371–384.

INHELDER, B. (1978). Language and thought: Some remarks on Chomsky and Piaget. *Journal of Psycholinguistic Research, 7,* 263–268.

INKELES, A. & SMITH, D.H. (1974). *Becoming modern: Individual change in six developing countries.* Cambridge, MA: Harvard University Press.

INNES, J.M. (1972). The effect of presence of co-workers and evaluative feedback on performance of a simple reaction time task. *European Journal of Social Psychology, 2,* 466–470.

INSKO, C.A. (1964). Primacy versus recency in persuasion as a function of the timing of arguments and measures. *Journal of Abnormal and Social Psychology, 69,* 381–391.

INSKO, C.A. & WILSON, M. (1977). Interpersonal attraction as a function of social interaction. *Journal of Personality and Social Psychology, 35,* 903–911.

ISEN, A.M. (1970). Success, failure, attention and reaction to others. *Journal of Personality and Social Psychology, 15,* 294–301.

ISEN, A.M. & LEVIN, P.F. (1972). Effect of feeling good on helping: Cookies and kindness. *Journal of Personality and Social Psychology, 21,* 384–388.

ISENBERG, D.J. (1986). Group polarization: A critical review and meta-analysis. *Journal of Personality and Social Psychology, 50,* 1141–1151.

IZZETT, R. & FISHMAN, L. (1976). Defendant sentences as a function of attractiveness and justification for actions. *Journal of Social Psychology, 100,* 285–290.

JACKSON, J.M. & PADGETT, V.R. (1982). With a little help from my friend: Social loafing and the Lennon-McCartney songs. *Personality and Social Psychology Bulletin, 8,* 672–677.

JACKSON, R.J., KELLY, M.J. & MITCHELL, T.H. (1977). Collective conflict, violence and the media. In *Report of the Royal Commission on Violence in the Communications Industry* (Vol. 5) (227–314). Toronto: Publication Centre, Government of Ontario.

JACOBS, L., BERSCHEID, E. & WALSTER, E. (1971). Self-esteem and attraction. *Journal of Personality and Social Psychology, 17,* 84–91.

JAIN, H.C., NORMAND, J. & KANUNGO, R.N. (1979). Job motivation of Canadian Anglophone and Francophone hospital employees. *Canadian Journal of Behavioural Science, 11,* 160–163.

JAKES, J. (1980). Causal attributions and sex-role stereotypes in the perceptions of women managers. *Canadian Journal of Behavioural Science, 12,* 52–63.

JAMOUS, H. & LEMAINE, W. (1962). Compétition entre groupes d'inégales resources. Expérience dans un cadre naturel. *Psychologie française, 7,* 216–222.

JANIS, I.L. (1951). *Air war and emotional stress. Psychological studies of bombing and civilian defense.* New York: McGraw-Hill.

JANIS, I.L. (1958). *Psychological stress.* New York: Wiley.

JANIS, I.L. (1972). *Victims of groupthink.* Boston: Houghton Mifflin.

JANIS, I.L. (1984). Improving adherence to medical recommendations: Prescriptive hypotheses derived from recent research in social psychology. In A. Baum, S.E. Taylor & J.E. Singer (Eds.), *Handbook of psychology and health* (Vol. 4) (113–148). Hillsdale, NJ: Erlbaum.

JANIS, I.L., CHAPMAN, D.W., GILLIN, J.P. & SPIEGEL, J.P. (1964). The problem of panic. In D.P. Schultz (Ed.), *Panic behavior* (118–127). New York: Random House.

JANIS, I.L. & FESHBACH, S. (1953). Effects of fear-arousing communications. *Journal of Abnormal and Social Psychology, 48,* 78–92.

JANIS, I.L. & FIELD, P.B. (1959). Sex differences and personality factors related to persuasibility. In I.L. Janis, C.I. Hovland *et al.*, *Personality and persuasibility* (55–68). New Haven: Yale University Press.

JANIS, I.L. & GILMORE, J.B. (1965). The influence of incentive conditions on the sources of role playing in modifying attitudes. *Journal of Personality and Social Psychology, 1,* 17–27.

JANIS, I.L. & HOFFMAN, D. (1970). Facilitating effects of daily contact between partners who make a decision to cut down on smoking. *Journal of Personality and Social Psychology, 17,* 25–35.

JANIS, I.L. & HOVLAND, C.I. (1959). An overview of persuasibility research. In C.I. Hovland & I.L. Janis (Eds.), *Personality and persuasibility* (1–28). New Haven, CT: Yale University Press.

JANIS, I.L. & MANN, L. (1977). *Decision making.* New York: Free Press.

JANZ, N.K. & BECKER, M.H. (1984). The Health Belief Model: A decade later: *Health Education Quarterly, 11,* 1–47.

JELLISON, J.M. & OLIVER, D.F. (1983). Attitude similarity and attraction: An impression management approach. *Personality and Social Psychology Bulletin, 9,* 111–115.

JENNERS, D. (1977). *The Indians of Canada.* Seventh Edition. Toronto: University of Toronto Press.

JENSEN, A.R. (1969). How much can we boost IQ and scholastic achievement? *Harvard Educational Review, 39,* 1–123.

JENSEN, A.R. (1973). *Educability and group differences.* New York: Harper & Row.

JERVIS, R., LEBOW, R.N. & STEIN, J.G. (1985). *Psychology and deterrence.* Baltimore, MD: Johns Hopkins Press.

JESSOR, R. (1984). Adolescent development and behavioral health. In J.D. Matarazzo, S.M. Weiss, J.A. Herd, N.E. Miller & S.M. Weiss (Eds.), *Behavioral health* (89–90). Toronto: Wiley.

JESSOR, R., DONOVAN, J.E. & WIDMER, K. (1980). *Psychosocial Factors in Adolescent Alcohol & Drug Use: The 1978 National Sample Study and the 1974–78 Panel Study.* Boulder, CO: Institute of Behavioral Science, University of Colorado. 1–161.

JESSOR, R. & JESSOR, S.L. (1977). *Problem behavior and psychosocial development: A longitudinal study of youth.* New York: Academic Press.

JOAD, C.E.M. (1957). *Guide to philosophy.* New York: Dover.

JOHNSON, J.E. & LEVENTHAL, H. (1974). Effects of accurate expectations and behavioral instructions on reactions during a noxious medical examination. *Journal of Personality and Social Psychology, 29,* 710–718.

JOHNSON, D.M. (1945). The "phantom anesthetist of Mattoon": A field study of mass hysteria. *Journal of Abnormal and Social Psychology, 40,* 175–186.

JOHNSON, R.N. (1972). *Aggression in man and animals.* Philadelphia: Saunders.

JONES, E.E. (1964). *Ingratiation: A social psychological analysis.* New York: Appleton-Century-Crofts.

JONES, E.E. & DAVIS, K.E. (1965). From acts to dispositions: The attribution process in person perception. In L. Berkowitz (Ed.), *Advances in experimental social psychology* (Vol. 2). New York: Academic Press.

JONES, E.E., DAVIS, K.E. & GERGEN, K. (1961). Role playing variations and their informational value for person perception. *Journal of Abnormal and Social Psychology, 63,* 302–310.

JONES, E.E., GERGEN, K.J. & DAVIS, K.E. (1962). Some determinants of reactions to being approved or disapproved as a person. *Psychological Monographs, 76,* (Whole no. 521).

JONES, E.E., GERGEN, K.J., GUMPERT, P. & THIBAUT, J.W. (1965). Some conditions affecting the use of ingratiation to influence performance evaluation. *Journal of Personality and Social Psychology, 1,* 613–625.

JONES, E.E. & HARRIS, V.A. (1976). The attribution of attitude. *Journal of Experimental Psychology, 3,* 1–24.

JONES, E.E., JONES, R.G. & GERGEN, K.J. (1963). Tactics of ingratiation among leaders and subordinates in a status hierarchy. *Psychological Monographs, 77,* (Whole No. 566).

JONES, E.E. & McGILLIS, D. (1976). Correspondent inferences and the attribution cube: A comparative reappraisal. In H.H. Harvey, W.J. Ickes, & R.F. Kidd (Eds.), *New directions in attribution research* (Vol. 1). Hillsdale, NJ: Erlbaum.

JONES, E.E. & NISBETT, R.E. (1971). The actor and the observer: Divergent perceptions of the causes of behavior. In E.E. Jones, D.E. Kanouse, H.H. Kelley, R.E. Nisbett, S. Valins, & B. Weiner, *Attribution: Perceiving the causes of behavior* (79–94). Morristown, NJ: General Learning Press.

JONES, E.E. & PITTMAN, T.S. (1982). Toward a general theory of strategic self-presentation. In J. Suls (Ed.), *Psychological perspectives on the self.* Hillsdale, NJ: Erlbaum.

JONES, E.E. & SIGALL, H. (1971). The bogus pipeline: A new paradigm for measuring affect and attitude. *Psychological Bulletin, 76,* 349–364.

JONES, E.E. & WORTMAN, C. (1973). *Ingratiation: An attributional approach.* Morristown, NJ: General Learning Press.

JONES, R.A., LINDER, D.E., KRESLER, C.A., ZANNA, M. & BREHM, J.W. (1968). Internal states or external stimuli: Observers' attitude judgements and the dissonance theory – self-persuasion controversy. *Journal of Experimental Social Psychology, 4,* 247–249.

JOURARD, S.M. (1966). An exploratory study of body-accessibility. *British Journal of Social and Clinical Psychology, 5,* 221–231.

JOURARD, S.M. & FRIEDMAN, R. (1970). Experimenter-subject "distance" and self-disclosure. *Journal of Personality and Social Psychology, 15,* 278–282.

JOY, L.A., KIMBALL, M.M. & ZABRACK, M.L. (1977) Television exposure and children's aggressive behaviours. Paper presented at the Canadian Psychological Association Annual Conference, Vancouver, B.C.

JOY, L.A., KIMBALL, M.M. & ZABRACK, M.L. (1986). Television and aggressive behaviour. In T.M. Williams (Ed.), *The impact of television: A natural experiment involving three towns* (303–360). New York: Academic Press.

KAGAN, J. & MOSS, H.A. (1962). *Birth to maturity: A study in psychological development.* New York: Wiley.

KAHN, A.S., HOTTES, J. & DAVIS, W.L. (1971). Cooperation and optional responding in the Prisoner's Dilemma game: Effects of sex and physical attractiveness. *Journal of Personality and Social Psychology, 17,* 267–279.

KAHN, A.S. & KOHLS, J.W. (1972). Determinants of toughness in dyadic bargaining. *Sociometry, 35,* 305–315.

KAHN, G.R. & KATZ, D. (1953). Leadership practices in relation to productivity and morale. In D. Cartwright & A. Zander (Eds), *Group dynamics: Research and theory.* Evanston, IL: Row, Peterson.

KAHN, H. (1960). *On thermonuclear war.* Princeton, NJ: Princeton University Press.

KAHN, H. (1962). *Thinking about the unthinkable.* New York: Avon.

KAHN, M. (1966). The physiology of catharsis. *Journal of Personality and Social Psychology, 3,* 278–286.

KAHNEMAN, D. & TVERSKY, A. (1982). The simulation heuristic. In D. Kahneman, P. Slovic & A. Tversky (Eds.), *Judgements under uncertainty: Heuristics and biases.* New York: Cambridge University Press.

KALIN, R. & BERRY, J.W. (1979). *Ethnic attitudes and identity in the context of national unity.* Final report to Multiculturalism Directorate, Secretary of State, Government of Canada.

KALIN, R. & HODGINS, D.C. (1984). Sex bias in judgements of occupational suitability. *Canadian Journal of Behavioural Science, 16,* 311–325.

KAMIN, L.J. (1974). *The science and politics of IQ.* New York: Holsted Press.

KAMIN, L.J. (1978). Comment on Munsinger's review of adoption studies. *Psychological Bulletin, 85,* 194–201.

KANDEL, D.B. (1978a). Convergences in prospective longitudinal surveys of drug use in normal populations. In D.B. Kandel (Ed.), *Longitudinal research on drug use. Empirical findings and methodological issues.* Washington, D.C.: Hemisphere.

KANDEL, D.B. (1978b). Similarity in real-life adolescent friendship pairs. *Journal of Personality and Social Psychology, 36,* 306–312.

KANDEL, D.B., KESLER, R.C. & MARGULIES, J. (1978). Antecedents of adolescent initiation into stages of drug use: A developmental analysis. In D.B. Kandel (Ed.), *Longitudinal research on drug use. Empirical findings and methodological issues* (73–100). Washington: Hemisphere Publications.

KANNER, A.D., COYNE, J.C., SCHAEFER, C. & LAZARUS, R.S. (1981). Comparison of two models of stress measurement: Daily hassles and uplifts versus major life events. *Journal of Behavioral Medicine, 4,* 1–29.

KANTER, R.M. (1975). Women and the structure of organizations: Explorations in theory and behavior. In M. Millman, & R.M. Kanter (Eds.), *Another voice: Feminist perspectives on social life and social science.* New York: Doubleday.

KANUNGO, R.N., GORN, G.J. & DAUDERIS, H.J. (1976). Motivational orientation of Canadian Anglophone and Francophone managers. *Canadian Journal of Behavioural Science, 8,* 107–121.

KARLINS, M. & ABELSON, H.I. (1970). *How opinions and attitudes are changed.* Second Edition. New York: Springer.

KARLINS, M., COFFMAN, T.L. & WALTERS, G. (1969). On the fading of social stereotypes: Studies in three generations of college students. *Journal of Personality and Social Psychology, 13,* 1–16.

KASTERBAUM, R. (Ed.) (1977). *Between life and death.* New York: Springer.

KATZ, D. (1960). The functional approach to the study of attitudes. *Public Opinion Quarterly, 24,* 163–204.

KATZ, D. & BRALY, K. (1933). Racial stereotypes of one hundred college students. *Journal of Abnormal and Social Psychology, 28,* 280–290.

KATZ, E. (1957). The two-step flow of communication: An up-to-date report on a hypothesis. *Public Opinion Quarterly, 21,* 61–78.

KATZ, E. & LAZERFIELD, P.F. (1955). *Personal influence: The part played by people in the flow of mass communication.* Glencoe, IL: Free Press.

KATZ, P.A. (1976). The acquisition of racial attitudes in children. In P.A. Katz (Ed.), *Towards the elimination of racism.* New York: Pergamon.

KATZMAN, R. & CARASU, T.B. (1975). Differential diagnosis of dementia. In W.S. Fields (Ed.), *Neurological and sensory disorders in the aged* (103–104). Miami: Symposia Specialist Medical Books.

KAUFMANN, H. (1970). *Aggression and altruism.* New York: Holt, Rinehart and Winston.

KEATING, J.P. & LOFTUS, E.F. (1981). The logic of fire escape. *Psychology Today, 15* (6) (June), 14–18.

KELLEY, H.H. (1950). The warm-cold variable in first impressions of persons. *Journal of Personality, 18,* 431–439.

KELLEY, H.H. (1972a). Attribution in social interaction. In E.E. Jones, D.E. Kanouse, H.H. Kelley, R.E. Nisbett, S. Valins & B. Weiner (Eds.), *Attribution: Perceiving the causes of behavior.* Morristown, NJ: General Learning Press.

KELLEY, H.H. (1972b). Causal schemata and the attribution process. In E.E. Jones, D.E. Kanouse, H.H. Kelley, R.E. Nisbett, S. Valins & B. Weiner (Eds.), *Attributions: Perceiving the causes of behavior.* Morristown, NJ: General Learning Press.

KELLEY, H.H., BERSCHEID, E., CHRISTENSEN, A., HARVEY, J., HUSTON, T., LEVINGER, G., McCLINTOCK, E., PEPLAU, A. & PETERSON, D.R. (Eds.) (1983). *Close relationships.* San Francisco: Freeman.

KELLEY, H.H., HOVLAND, C.I., SCHWARTZ, M. & ABELSON, R.P. (1955). The influence of judges' attitudes in three methods of scaling. *Journal of Sociological Psychology, 42,* 147–158.

KELLEY, H.H. & STAHELSKI, A.J. (1970). The social interaction basis of cooperators' and competitors' beliefs about others. *Journal of Personality and Social Psychology, 16,* 66–91.

KELLOGG, W.N. & KELLOGG, L.A. (1933). Another film of the ape and child. *Psychological Bulletin, 30,* 581–582.

KELLY, G.A. (1955). *The psychology of personal constructs.* New York: Norton.

KELMAN, H.C. (1958). Compliance, identification, and internalization: Three processes of attitude change. *Journal of Conflict Resolution, 2,* 51–60.

KELMAN, H.C. (1961). Processes of opinion change. *Public Opinion Quarterly, 25,* 57–78.

KELMAN, H.C. (1965). Social-psychological approaches to the study of international relations: The question of relevance. In H.C. Kelman (Ed.), *International behavior: A social-psychological analysis.* New York: Holt, Rinehart and Winston.

KELMAN, H.C. (1967). Human use of human subjects: The problem of deception in social psychological experiments. *Psychological Bulletin, 67,* 1–11.

KELMAN, H.C. (1973). Violence without moral restraint: Reflections on the dehumanization of victims and victimisers. *Journal of Social Issues, 29,* 25–62.

KELNER, M. & BADGLEY, R.F. (1969). Sociological aspects. In *Hepatitis in Yorkville 1968. Report of the Coordinating Committee established by the Ontario Department of Health.* Toronto: Ontario Department of Health.

KENDON, A. (1967). Some functions of gaze-direction in social interaction. *Acta Psychologica, 26,* 22–63.

KENNEY, D.A. & ZACCARO, S.J. (1983). An estimate of variance due to traits in leadership. *Journal of Applied Psychology, 68,* 678–685.

KENRICK, D.T. & CIALDINI, R.B. (1977). Romantic attraction: Misattribution versus reinforcement explanations. *Journal of Personality and Social Psychology, 35,* 381–391.

KENRICK, D.T., CIALDINI, R.B. & LINDER, D.E. (1979). Misattribution under fear-producing circumstances: Four failures to replicate. *Journal of Personality and Social Psychology, 5,* 329–334.

KENRICK, D.T. & GUTIERRES, S.E. (1980). Contrast effects and judgements of physical attractiveness: When beauty becomes a social problem. *Journal of Personality and Social Psychology, 38,* 131–140.

KERCKHOFF, A.C. & BACK, K.W. (1968). *The June Bug: A study of hysterical contagion.* New York: Appleton-Century-Crofts.

KERCKHOFF, A.C. & DAVIS, K.E. (1962). Value consensus and need complementarity in mate selection. *American Sociological Review, 27,* 295–303.

KERR, N.L. (1978). Beautiful and blameless: Effects of victim attractiveness and responsibility on mock jurors' verdicts. *Journal of Personality and Social Psychology, 4,* 479–482.

KERR, N.L. & MacCOUN, R.J. (1985). The effects of jury size and polling method on the process and product of jury deliberation. *Journal of Personality and Social Psychology, 48,* 349–363.

KEYES, R. (1980). *The height of your life.* Boston: Little, Brown.

KIESLER, C.A. (1968). Commitment. In R.P. Abelson, E. Aronson, W.J. McGuire, T.H. Newcomb, M.J. Rosenberg & P.H. Tannenbaum (Eds.), *Theories of cognitive consistency: A sourcebook.* Skokie, IL: Rand-McNally.

KIESLER, C.A. (1971). *The psychology of commitment*. New York. Academic Press.

KIESLER, C.A. & MUNSON, P.A. (1975). Attitudes and opinions. *Annual Review of Psychology, 26*, 415–456.

KIESLER, C.A. & PALLAK, M.S. (1976). Arousal properties of dissonance manipulations. *Psychological Bulletin, 83*, 1014–1025.

KIESLER, S. & BARAL, R. (1970) The search for a romantic partner: The effects of self-esteem and physical attractiveness on romantic behavior. In K.J. Gergen and D. Marlowe (Eds.), *Personality and social behavior*, Reading, MA: Addison-Wesley.

KILLIAN, L.M. (1952). The significance of multiple-group membership in a disaster. *American Journal of Sociology, 57*, 309–314.

KIMBLE, C.E., FORTE, R.A. & YOSHIKAWA, J.C. (1981). Nonverbal concomitants of enacted emotional intensity and positivity: Visual and vocal behavior. *Journal of Research in Personality, 49*, 271–283.

KING, A.K., ROBERTSON, A.S. & WARREN, W.K. (1985). *Summary Report. Canada Health Attitudes and Behaviours Survey – 9, 12 and 15-year olds*. Ottawa: Health and Welfare Canada.

KIPNIS, D. (1972). Does power corrupt? *Journal of Personality and Social Psychology, 24*, 33–41.

KISKER, G.W. (1964). *The disorganized personality*. New York: McGraw-Hill.

KITCHENS, A. (1974). Shape-of-the-table negotiations at the Paris peace talks on Vietnam. In C.M. Loo (Ed.), *Crowding and behavior* (224–245). New York: MFS Information Company.

KLAJNER, F., SOBELL, L.C. & SOBELL, M.B. (1984). Prevention of drunk driving. In P.M. Miller & T.D. Nirenberg (Eds.), *Prevention of alcohol abuse* (441–468). New York: Plenum.

KLAPP, O.E. (1972). *Currents of unrest*. New York: Holt, Rinehart & Winston.

KLEINKE, C.L. (1986). Gaze and eye contact: A research review. *Psychological Bulletin, 100*, 78–100.

KLINEBERG, O. (1984). Public opinion and nuclear war. *American Psychologist, 39*, 1245–1253.

KLINGER, E. (1964). Feedback effects and social facilitation of vigilance performance: Mere coaction versus potential evaluation. *Psychonomic Science, 14*, 161–162.

KNOWLES, D.W. & BOERSMA, F.J. (1971). A comparison of optimal shift performance and language skills in middle-class and Canadian Indian children. *Canadian Journal of Behavioural Science, 3*, 246–258.

KNOX, R.E. & INKSTER, J.A. (1968). Post-decision dissonance at post-time. *Journal of Personality and Social Psychology, 8*, 319–323.

KOBASA, S.C. (1979). Stressful life events, personality and health: An inquiry into hardiness. *Journal of Personality and Social Psychology, 37*, 1–11.

KOGAN, N. & WALLACH, M.A. (1964). *Risk taking*. New York: Holt, Rinehart and Winston

KOGAN, N. & WALLACH, M.A. (1967). Risk taking as a function of the situation, the person, and the group. In G. Mandler, P. Mussen, N. Kogan & M.A. Wallach (Eds.), *New directions in psychology III*. New York: Holt, Rinehart and Winston.

KOHEN, J. (1975). Liking and self-disclosure in opposite-sex dyads. *Psychological Reports, 36*, 695–698.

KOHLBERG, L. (1964). Development of moral character and moral ideology. In M. Hoffman & L. Hoffman (Eds.), *Review of child development research*. New York: Russell Sage Foundation.

KOHLBERG, L. (1981). *The philosophy of moral development: Essays in moral development* (Vol. 1). New York: Harper & Row.

KOLATA, G.B. (1974). !Kung hunter-gatherers. *Science, 185*, 932.

KOMORITA, S.S (1979). On equal excess model of coalition formation. *Behavioral Science, 24*, 369–381.

KOMORITA, S.S. & BARTH, J.M. (1985). Components of reward in social dilemmas. *Journal of Personality and Social Psychology, 48*, 364–373.

KOMORITA, S.S. & CHERTKOFF, J.M. (1973). A bargaining theory of coalition formation. *Psychological Review, 80*, 149–162.

KOMORITA, S.S. & TUMONIS, T.M. (1980). Extensions and tests of some descriptive theories of coalition formation. *Journal of Personality and Social Psychology, 39*, 256–269.

KOSS, M.P., GIDYCZ, C.A. & WISNIESKI, N. (1987). The scope of rape: Incidence and prevalence of sexual aggression and victimization in a national sample of higher education students. *Journal of Consulting and Clinical Psychology, 55*, 162–170.

KOTHANDAPONI, V. (1971). Validation of feeling, belief, and intention to act as three components of attitude and their contribution to prediction of contraceptive behavior. *Journal of Personality and Social Psychology, 19*, 321–333.

KRAMER, R.M. & BREWER, M.B. (1984). Effects of group identity on resource use in a simulated commons dilemma. *Journal of Personality and Social Psychology, 46*, 1044–1057.

KRAMER, B.M., KALICK, S.M. & MILBURN, M.A. (1983). Attitudes toward nuclear weapons and nuclear war: 1945-1982. *Journal of Social Issues, 39*, 7–24.

KRANTZ, D., BAUM, A. & WIDEMAN, M.V. (1980). Assessment of preferences for self-treatment and information in healthcare. *Journal of Personality and Social Psychology, 39*, 977–990.

KRANTZ, D.S. & GLASS, D.C. (1984). Personality behavior patterns and physical illness: Conceptual and methodological issues. In W.D. Gentry (Ed.), *Handbook of behavioral medicine* (38–86). New York: Guilford Press.

KRANTZ, M.J. & JOHNSON, L. (1978). Family members' perceptions of communications in late stage cancer. *International Journal of Psychiatry in Medicine, 8,* 203–216.

KRAUT, R.E. (1978). Verbal and non-verbal cues in the detection of lying. *Journal of Personality and Social Psychology, 36,* 380–391.

KRAUT, R.E. & POE, D. (1980). Behavioral roots of person perceptions: The deception judgements of the customs inspectors and laymen. *Journal of Personality and Social Psychology, 39,* 784–798.

KRAVITZ, D.A. & MARTIN B. (1986). Ringelmann rediscovered: The original article. *Journal of Personality and Social Psychology, 50,* 936–941.

KREBS, D. (1970). Altruism — an examination of the concept and a review of the literature. *Psychological Bulletin, 73,* 258–302.

KREBS, D. (1975). Empathy and altruism. *Journal of Personality and Social Psychology, 32,* 1134–1146.

KREBS, D. & ADINOLFI, A.H. (1975). Physical attractiveness, social relations and personality style. *Journal of Personality and Social Psychology, 31,* 245–253.

KREBS, D.L. & MILLER, D.T. (1985). Altruism and aggression. In G. Lindzey & E. Aronson (Eds.), *Handbook of social psychology.* Third Edition (Vol. 2) (1–71). New York: Random House.

KRECH, D., CRUTCHFIELD, R.S., & BALLACHEY, E.L. (1962). *Individual in society.* New York: McGraw-Hill.

KRISHNAN, L. & CARMENT, D.W. (1979). Reactions to help: Reciprocity, responsibility and reactance. *European Journal of Social Psychology, 9,* 435–439.

KRISTIANSEN, C.M. (1985). Value correlates of preventive health behavior. *Journal of Personality and Social Psychology, 49,* 748–758.

KRISTIANSEN, C.M. (1986). A two-value model of preventive health behavior. *Basic and Applied Social Psychology, 7,* 173–183.

KRISTIANSEN, C.M. & ZANNA, M.P. (1986). When do attitudes express values? Paper presented at the Annual Meeting of the Canadian Psychological Association, Toronto (June).

KRUGLANSKI, A.W. & FREUND, T. (1983). The freezing and unfreezing of lay-inferences: Effects on impressional primacy, ethnic stereotyping and numerical anchoring. *Journal of Experimental Social Psychology, 19,* 448–468.

KUHN, T. (1959). *The Copernican revolution.* New York: Vintage Books.

KURTINES, W. & GREIF, E.B. (1974). The development of moral thought: Review and evaluation of Kohlberg's approach. *Psychological Bulletin, 81,* 453–470.

KUTNER, B., WILKINS, C. & YARROW, P.R. (1952). Verbal attitudes and overt behavior involving social prejudice. *Journal of Abnormal and Social Psychology, 47,* 649–652.

L'ARMAND, K. & PEPITONE, A. (1975). Helping to reward another: A cross-cultural analysis. *Journal of Personality and Social Psychology, 31,* 189–198.

LACROIX, J.M. & RIOUX, Y. (1978). La communication non-verbale chez les bilingues. *Canadian Journal of Behavioural Science, 10,* 130–140.

LaFRANCE, M. & MAYO, C. (1976). Racial differences in gaze behavior during conversation: Two systematic observational studies. *Journal of Personality and Social Psychology, 33,* 547–552.

LALONDE, M. (1974). *A new perspective on the health of Canadians.* Ottawa: Ministry of Supply and Services Canada, Catalogue No. H31–1374.

LAMBERT, W.E. (1967). A social psychology of bilingualism. *Journal of Social Issues, 23,* 91–109.

LAMBERT, W.E. (1974a). The St. Lambert project. In S.T. Carey (Ed.), *Bilingualism, biculturalism and education* (231–247). Edmonton: University of Alberta.

LAMBERT, W.E. (1974b). Culture and language as factors in learning and education. In F.E. Aboud & R.D. Meade (Eds.), *The fifth western symposium on learning and education.* Washington: Bellingham.

LAMBERT, W.E. (1978). Some cognitive and sociocultural aspects of being bilingual. In J.P. Alatis (Ed.), *International dimensions of bilingual education.* Washington, DC: Georgetown University Press.

LAMBERT, W.E. (1981). Bilingualism and language acquisition. *Annals of the New York Academy of Sciences, 379,* 9–22.

LAMBERT, W.E., FRANKEL, H. & TUCKER, G.R. (1966). Judging personality through speech: A French-Canadian example. *Journal of Communication, 16,* 305–321.

LAMBERT, W.E., GARDNER, R.C., BARIK, H.C. & TUNSTALL, K. (1963). Attitudinal and cognitive aspects of intensive study of a second language. *Journal of Abnormal and Social Psychology, 66,* 358–368.

LAMBERT, W.E. & KLINEBERG, O. (1967). *Children's views of foreign people: A cross-national study.* New York: Appleton.

LAMBERT, W.E., MERMIGIS, L. & TAYLOR, D.M. (1986). Greek Canadians' attitudes toward own group and other Canadian ethnic groups: A test of the multiculturalism hypothesis. *Canadian Journal of Behavioural Science, 18,* 35–51.

LAMBERT, W.E. & TAYLOR, D. (1984). Language and the education of ethnic minority children in Canada. In R.J. Samuda, J.W. Berry & M. Laferriere (Eds.), *Multiculturalism in Canada.* Toronto: Allyn & Bacon.

LAMBERT, W.E. & TUCKER, G.R. (1972). *Bilingual education in children: The St. Lambert experiment.* Rowley, MA: Newbury House.

LAMBERT, W.E., YACKLEY, A. & HEIN, R.N. (1971). Child training values of English Canadian and French Canadian parents. *Canadian Journal of Behavioural Science, 3,* 217–236.

LAMBERT, W.W. (1971). Cross-cultural backgrounds to personality development and the socialization of aggression: Findings from the six-culture study. In W.W. Lambert & R. Weisbrod (Eds.), *Comparative perspectives on social psychology*. Boston: Little, Brown.

LAMM, H. & TROMMSDORFF, G. (1971). Group versus individual performance on tasks requiring ideational proficiency (brainstorming): A review. *European Journal of Social Psychology, 3,* 361–388.

LANA, R.E. (1964). Three theoretical interpretations of order effects in persuasive communications. *Psychological Bulletin, 61,* 314–320.

LANDY, D. & ARONSON, E. (1969). The influence of the character of the criminal and his victim on the decisions of simulated jurors. *Journal of Experimental Social Psychology, 5,* 141–152.

LANG, G.L. & LANG, K. (1972). Some pertinent questions on collective violence and the news media. *Journal of Social Issues, 28,* 93–110.

LANG, K. & LANG, G. (1961). *Collective dynamics*. New York: Crowell.

LANGER, E.J. (1975). The illusion of control. *Journal of Personality and Social Psychology, 32,* 311–328.

LANGER, E.J., BLANK, A. & CHANOWITZ, B. (1978). The mindlessness of ostensibly thoughtful action: The role of "placebic" information in interpersonal interaction. *Journal of Personality and Social Psychology, 36,* 635–642.

LANGER, E.J. & RODIN, J. (1976). The effects of choice and enhanced personal responsibility for the aged: A field experiment in an institutional setting. *Journal of Personality and Social Psychology, 34,* 191–198.

LANGER, W.L. (1964). The black death. *Scientific American, 210,* 114–121.

LaPIERE, R.T. (1934). Attitudes vs. actions. *Social Forces, 13,* 230–237.

LARSEN, K. (1974). Conformity in the Asch experiment. *Journal of Social Psychology, 94,* 303–304.

LARSEN, K.S. (1985). Attitudes toward nuclear disarmament and their correlates. *Journal of Social Psychology, 125,* 17–21.

LATANÉ, B. & DARLEY, J.M. (1968). Group inhibition of bystander intervention. *Journal of Personality and Social Psychology, 10,* 215–221.

LATANÉ, B. & DARLEY, J.M. (1969). Bystander "apathy." *American Scientist, 57,* 244–268.

LATANÉ, B. & DARLEY, J.M. (1970). *The unresponsive bystander: Why doesn't he help?* New York: Appleton-Century-Crofts.

LATANÉ, B. & HOTHERSALL, D. (1972). Social attraction in animals. In P.C. Dodwell (Ed.), *New horizons in psychology II*. Harmondsworth, England: Penguin.

LATANÉ, B., MELTZER, J., JAY, V., LUBELL, B. & CAPPELL, H. (1972). Stimulus determinants of social attraction in rats. *Journal of Comparative and Physiological Psychology, 79,* 12–21.

LATANÉ, B. & NIDA, S. (1981). Ten years of research on group size and helping. *Psychological Bulletin, 89,* 308–324.

LATANÉ, B. & RODIN, J. (1969). A lady in distress: Inhibiting effects of friends and strangers on bystander intervention. *Journal of Experimental Social Psychology, 5,* 187–202.

LATANÉ, B., WILLIAMS, K., & HARKINS, S. (1979). Many hands make light the work: The causes and consequences of social loafing. *Journal of Personality and Social Psychology, 37,* 822–832.

LATEEF, O. & BANGASH, Z. (1977). *Visible minorities in mass media advertising*. Ottawa: Canadian Consultative Council on Multiculturalism.

LAU, R.R., HARTMAN, K.A. & WARE, J.E. (1986). Health as a value: Methodological and theoretical considerations. *Health Psychology, 5,* 25–43.

LAU, R.R. & RUSSELL, D. (1980). Attribution in sports pages. *Journal of Personality and Social Psychology, 39,* 28–38.

LAVER, J. (1964). Laver's law. *Women's Wear Daily,* 13 July, 1964. Cited by Horn (1975).

LAVERY, J.J. & FOLEY, P.J. (1963). Altruism or arousal in the rat? *Science, 140,* 172–173.

LAVOIE, M., GRENIER, G. & COULOMBE, S. (1986). Discrimination and performance differentials in the National Hockey League. Research Paper #8604. Department of Economics, University of Ottawa.

LAWSON, H. & TROMMSDORFF, G. (1973). Group versus individual performance on tasks requiring ideational proficiency (brainstorming): A review. *European Journal of Social Psychology, 3,* 361–388.

LAY, C., ALLEN, M. & KASSIRER, A. (1974). The responsive bystander in emergencies: Some preliminary data. *Canadian Psychologist, 15,* 220–227.

LAZARUS, R., & COHEN, J.B. (1977). Environmental stress. In I. Altman & J.F. Wohlwill (Eds.), *Human behavior and environment* (Vol. 1). New York: Plenum Press.

LAZARUS, R., SPEISMAN, J., MORDKOFF, A. & DAVIDSON, R. (1962). A laboratory study of the psychological stress produced by a motion-picture film. *Psychological Monographs, 76,* (Whole No. 553).

LEACOCK, S. (1959). The conjurer's revenge. In *Literary lapses*. Toronto: McClelland & Stewart.

LeBON, G. (1895/1960). *The crowd: A study of the popular mind*. London: Ernest Benn.

LEEDS, R. (1963). Altruism and the norm of giving. *Merrill-Palmer Quarterly, 9,* 229–240.

LEMAINE, G. (1966). Inégalité, comparaison et incomparabilité: Esquisse d'une théorie de l'originalité sociale. *Bulletin de Psychologie, 20,* 24–32.

LEMAINE, G. (1974). Social differentiation and social originality. *European Journal of Social Psychology, 4,* 17–52.

LEMAINE, G., KASTERSZTEIN, J. (1972). Recherches sur l'originalité sociale, la différentiation et l'incomparabilité. *Bulletin de Psychologie, 25,* 673–693.

LEMAINE, G., KASTERSZTEIN, J. & PERSONNAZ, B. (1978). Social differentiation. In H. Tajfel (Ed.), *Differentiation between social groups: Studies in the social psychology of intergroup relations* (269–300). London: Academic Press.

LEMYRE, L. & SMITH, P.B. (1985). Intergroup discrimination and self-esteem in the minimal group paradigm. *Journal of Personality and Social Psychology, 49,* 660–670.

LEPPER, M.R., GREENE, D. & NISBETT, R.E. (1973). Undermining children's intrinsic interest with extrinsic reward: A test for the over-justification hypothesis. *Journal of Personality and Social Psychology, 28,* 129–137.

LEPPER, M.R., ZANNA, M.P. & ABELSON, R.P. (1970). Cognitive irreversibility in a dissonance reduction situation. *Journal of Personality and Social Psychology, 16,* 191–198.

LERNER, M.J. (1974a). The justice motive: "Equity" and "parity" among children. *Journal of Personality and Social Psychology, 29,* 539–550.

LERNER, M.J. (1974b). Social psychology of justice and interpersonal attraction. In T. Huston (Ed.), *Foundations of interpersonal attraction.* New York: Academic Press.

LERNER, M.J. (1977). The justice motive: Some hypotheses as to its origins and forms. *Journal of Personality, 45,* 1–52.

LERNER, M.J. (1982). The justice motive in human relations and the economic model of man: A radical analysis of facts and fictions. In V.J. Derlega & J. Grzelak (Eds.), *Cooperation and helping behavior. Theories and research* (249–278). New York: Academic Press.

LERNER, M.J. & MATHEWS, G. (1967). Reactions to suffering of others under conditions of indirect responsibility. *Journal of Personality and Social Psychology, 5,* 319–325.

LERNER, M.J. & MILLER, D.T. (1978). Just world research and the attribution process: Looking back and ahead. *Psychological Bulletin, 85,* 1030–1051.

LERNER, M.J. & SIMMONS, C.H. (1966). Observer's reactions to the "innocent victim": Comparison or rejection? *Journal of Personality and Social Psychology, 4,* 203–210.

LEUNG, K. & LIND, E.A. (1986). Procedural justice and culture: Effects of culture, gender, and investigator status on procedural preference. *Journal of Personality and Social Psychology, 50,* 1134–1140.

LEVENSON, H., BURFORD, B., BONNO, B. & DAVIS, L. (1975). Are women still prejudiced against women? A replication and extension of Goldberg's study. *Journal of Psychology, 89,* 67–71.

LEVENTHAL, G.S. (1970). Findings and theory in the study of fear communications. In L. Berkowitz (Ed.), *Advances in experimental social psychology* (Vol. 5) (119–186). New York: Academic Press.

LEVENTHAL, G.S. (1976). Fairness in social relationships. In J. Thibaut, J. Spence & R. Carson (Eds.), *Contemporary topics in social psychology.* Morrestown, NJ: General Learning.

LEVENTHAL, G.S. & LANE, D.W. (1970). Sex, age, and equity behavior. *Journal of Personality and Social Psychology, 15,* 312–316.

LEVENTHAL, G.S., WEISS, T. & LONG, G. (1969). Equity, reciprocity, and reallocating the rewards in the dyad. *Journal of Personality and Social Psychology, 13,* 300–315.

LEVENTHAL, H. & HIRSCHMAN, R.S. (1982). Social psychology and prevention. In G.S. Sanders & J. Suls (Eds.), *Social psychology of health and illness* (387–401). Hillsdale, NJ: Erlbaum.

LEVENTHAL, H., MEYER, D.C. & NERENZ, D. (1980). The common sense representation of illness danger. In S. Rachman (Ed.), *Medical psychology* (Vol. 2) 184–211). New York: Pergamon.

LEVENTHAL, H. & SHARP, E. (1965). Facial expressions as indicators of distress. In S.S. Tomkins & C.E. Izard (Eds.), *Affect, cognition and personality: Empirical studies.* New York: Springer.

LEVINE, R.A. (1967). The internalization of political values in state-less societies. In R. Hunt (Ed.), *Personalities and cultures.* Garden City, NY: Natural History Press.

LEVINE, R.A. & CAMPBELL, D.T. (1972). *Ethnocentrism.* New York: Wiley.

LEVINE, S. & SALTER, N.E. (1976). Youth and contemporary religious movements: Psychosocial findings. *Canadian Psychiatric Association Journal, 21,* 411–420.

LEVINGER, G.A. (1977). Re-viewing the close relationship. In G. Levinger & H.L. Raush (Eds.), *Close relationships: Perspectives on the meaning of intimacy.* Amherst: University of Massachusetts Press.

LEVINGER, G.A. (1979). A social psychological perspective on marital dissolution. In G.A. Levinger & O.C. Moles (Eds.), *Divorce and separation,* New York: Basic Books.

LEVINGER, G.A., SENN, D.J. & JORGENSEN, B.W. (1970). Progress toward permanence in courtship: A test of the Kerckhoff-Varies hypotheses. *Sociometry, 33,* 427–443.

LEVINGER, G.A. & SNOEK, J.D. (1972). *Attraction in relationships: A new look at interpersonal attraction.* Morristown, NJ: General Learning.

LEWIN, K. (1951). *Field theory in social science.* New York: Harper.

LEWIN, K. (1948). *Resolving social conflicts.* New York: Harper & Row.

LEWIS, R.A. (1972). A developmental framework for the analysis of premarital dyadic formation. *Family Proceedings, 11,* 17–48.

LIFTON, R. (1967). *Death in life: Survivors of Hiroshima.* New York: Random House.

LIKERT, R. (1932). A technique for the measurement of attitudes. *Archives of Psychology, 22,* no. 140.

LIMBER, J. (1977). Language in child and chimp? *American Psychologist, 32,* 280–295.

LIND, E.A., ERICKSON, B.E., FRIEDLAND, N. & DICKENBERGER, M. (1978). Reactions to procedural models for adjudicative conflict resolution. *Journal of Conflict Resolution, 22,* 318–341.

LIND, E.A., KURTZ, S., MUSANTE, L., WALKER, L. & THIBAUT, J. (1980). Procedure and outcome effects on reactions to adjudicated resolution of conflicts of interest. *Journal of Personality and Social Psychology, 39,* 643–653.

LINDER, D.E., COOPER, J. & JONES, E.E. (1967). Decision freedom as a determinant of the role of incentive magnitude in attitude change. *Journal of Personality and Social Psychology, 6,* 245–254.

LINDSKOLD, S. (1978). Trust development, the GRIT proposal, and the effects of conciliatory acts on conflict and cooperation. *Psychological Bulletin, 85,* 772–793.

LINDSKOLD, S., HAN, G. & BETZ, B. (1986). The essential elements of communication in the GRIT strategy. *Personality and Social Psychology Bulletin, 12,* 179–186.

LINDSKOLD, S., McELWAIN, D.C. & WAYNER, M. (1977). Cooperation and the use of coercion by groups and individuals. *Journal of Conflict Resolution, 21,* 531–550.

LIPPMAN, W. (1922). *Public opinion.* New York: Harcourt, Brace & World.

LIPSET, S.M. (1968). *Revolution and counterrevolution: Change and persistence in social structures.* New York: Basic Books.

LIPTON, J.A. & MARBACH, J.J. (1984). Ethnicity and the pain experience. *Social Science & Medicine, 19,* 1279–1288.

LISKA, A.E. (1984). A critical examination of the causal structure of the Fishbein/Ajzen attitude-behavior model. *Social Psychology Quarterly, 47,* 61–74.

LITTLEPAGE, G.E. & PINEAULT, M.A. (1979). Detection of deceptive factual statements from the body and the face. *Personality and Social Psychology Bulletin, 5,* 325–328.

LIVINGSTONE, F.B. (1968). The effects of warfare on the biology of the human species. In M. Fried, M. Harris & R. Murphy (Eds.), *War: The anthropology of armed conflict and aggression.* Garden City, NY: Natural History Press.

LLOYD, W.F. (1833/1976). On checks to the population. Reprinted in G. Hardin & J. Baden (Eds.) (1976), *Managing the commons* (8–15). San Francisco: W.H. Freeman.

LOFTUS, E.F. (1974). Reconstructing memory: The incredible eyewitness. *Psychology Today, 8,* 116–119.

LOFTUS, E.G. (1979). *Eyewitness testimony.* Cambridge, MA: Harvard University Press.

LOFTUS, E.F. (1983). Silence is not golden. *American Psychologist, 38,* 504–572.

LOH, W.D. (1975). Nationalistic attitudes in Québec and Belgium. *Journal of Conflict Resolution, 29,* 217–249.

LOKEN, B. (1982). Heavy smokers', light smokers', and non-smokers' beliefs about cigarette smoking. *Journal of Applied Psychology, 67,* 616–622.

LONDON, P. (1970). The rescuers: Motivational hypotheses about Christians who saved Jews from the Nazis. In J. Macaulay & L. Berkowitz (Eds.), *Altruism and helping behavior.* New York: Academic Press.

LORENZ, K. (1966). *On aggression.* London: Methuen.

LOTT, A.J. & LOTT, B.E. (1961). Group cohesiveness, communication level, and conformity. *Journal of Abnormal and Social Psychology, 62,* 408–412.

LOTT, D.F. & SOMMER, R. (1967). Seating arrangements and status. *Journal of Personality and Social Psychology, 7,* 90–94.

LOWE, J.B., WINDSOR, R.A., ADAMS, B., MORRIS, J. & REESE, Y. (1986). Use of a bogus pipeline method to increase accuracy of self-reported alcohol consumption among pregnant women. *Journal of Studies on Alcohol, 47,* 173–175.

LOWERY, C.R., DENNEY, D.R. & STORMS, M.D. (1979). Insomnia: A comparison of the effects of pill attribution and non-pejorative self-attributions. *Cognitive Therapy Research, 3,* 161–164.

LUBEK, I. (1979). A brief social psychological analysis of research on aggression in social psychology. In A.R. Buss (Ed.), *Psychology in social context* (259–306). New York: Irvington.

LUCAS, R.A. (1968). Social implications of the immediacy of death. *The Canadian Review of Sociology and Anthropology, 5,* 1–16.

LUCE, T.S. (1974). The role of experience in inter-racial recognition. Paper presented at the annual meeting of the American Psychological Association, New Orleans.

LUCHINS, A.S. (1957). Experimental attempts to minimize the impact of first impressions. In C.I. Hovland *et al.* (Eds.), *The order of presentation in persuasion* (62–75). New Haven: Yale University Press.

LUND, F.H. (1925). The psychology of belief: IV. The law of primacy in persuasion. *Journal of Abnormal and Social Psychology, 20,* 183–191.

LUSSIER, Y. & ALAIN, M. (1986). Attribution et vécu émotionnel post-divorce. *Canadian Journal of Behavioural Science, 18,* 248–256.

LYKKEN, D. (1974). Psychology and the lie detector industry. *American Psychologist, 29,* 725–739.

LYNCH, J. (1977). *The broken heart. The medical consequences of loneliness.* New York: Basic Books.

MAASS, A. & CLARK, R.D. III. (1984). Hidden impact of minorities: Fifteen years of minority influence research. *Psychological Bulletin, 95,* 428–450.

MacANDREW, C. & EGERTON, R.B. (1969). *Drunken comportment: A social explanation.* Chicago: Aldine.

MACAULAY, J. (1978). Cultural limits on understanding aggression. *Society for the Advancement of Social Psychology Newsletter, 4,* 3–4.

MacDONALD, D., Jr. & MAJUNDER, R.K. (1973). On the resolution and tolerance of cognitive inconsistency in another naturally occurring event: Attitudes and beliefs following the Senator Eagleton incident. *Journal of Applied Social Psychology, 3,* 132–143.

MacDOUGALL, W. (1908). *An introduction to social psychology.* London: Methuen & Co.

MACKIE, D.M. (1986). Social identification effects in group polarization. *Journal of Personality and Social Psychology, 50,* 720–728.

MacNAMARA, J. (1973). Nurseries, streets and classrooms. *Modern Language Journal, 57,* 250–254.

MADDEN, D.J. (1976) Psychological approaches to violence. In D.J. Madden & J.R. Lion (Eds.), *Rage, hate, assault and other forms of violence* (135–152). New York: Spectrum.

MAIER, S. & LAUDENSLAGER, M. (1985). Stress and health: Exploring the links. *Psychology Today, 19,* 44–50.

MAJOR, B. & DEAUX, K. (1982). Individual differences in justice behavior. In J. Greenberg & R. Cohen (Eds.), *Equity and justice in social behavior* (43–76). New York: Academic Press.

MALAMUTH, N.M. (1984). Aggression against women: Cultural and individual causes. In N.M. Malamuth & E. Donnerstein (Eds.), *Pornography and sexual aggression.* Orlando, FL: Academic Press.

MALAMUTH, N.M. (1986). Predictors of naturalistic sexual aggression. *Journal of Personality and Social Psychology, 50,* 953–962.

MALAMUTH, N.M. & BRIERE, J. (1986). Sexual violence in the media: Indirect effects on aggression against women. *Journal of Social Issues, 42,* (3), 75–92.

MALAMUTH, N.M., CHECK, J.V.P. & BRIERE, J. (1986). Sexual arousal in response to aggression: Ideological, aggressive, and sexual correlates. *Journal of Personality and Social Psychology, 50,* 330–340.

MALAMUTH, N.M., FESHBACH, S. & JAFFE, Y. (1977). Sexual arousal and aggression: Recent experiments and theoretical issues. *Journal of Social Issues, 33,* 110–133.

MANN, J.W. (1963). Rivals of different rank. *Journal of Social Psychology, 61,* 11–27.

MANN, L. (1970). The social psychology of waiting lines. *Scientific American, 58,* 390–398.

MANN, L. (1981). The baiting crowd in episodes of threatened suicide. *Journal of Personality and Social Psychology, 41,* 703–709.

MANN, L., NEWTON, J.W. & INNES, J.M. (1982). A test between deindividuation and emergent norm theories of crowd aggression. *Journal of Personality and Social Psychology, 42,* 260–272.

MANN, L. & TAYLOR, K.R. (1969). Queue counting: The effects of motives upon estimates of numbers in waiting lines. *Journal of Personality and Social Psychology, 12,* 95–103.

MANN, R. (1959). A review of the relationship between personality and performance in small groups. *Psychological Bulletin, 56,* 241–270.

MANSELL, D. & ALCOCK, J.E. (1978). Communication and deindividuation in a collective dilemma. Paper presented at the Annual Meeting of the Canadian Psychological Association, Ottawa.

MARKUS, H. (1977). Self-schemata and processing information about the self. *Journal of Personality and Social Psychology, 35,* 63–78.

MARKUS, R.M. (1975). Good Samaritan laws: An American lawyer's point of view. *La revue juridique themis, 10,* 28–32.

MARLATT, G.A., DEMMING, B. & REID, J.B. (1973). Loss of control of drinking in alcoholics: An experimental analogue. *Journal of Abnormal Psychology, 81,* 233–241.

MARLATT, G.A. & GORDON, J.R. (1979). Determinants of relapse: Implications for the maintenance of behavior change. In P. Davidson (Ed.), *Behavioral medicines: Changing health lifestyles.* New York: Brunner/Mazel.

MARLATT, G.A. & ROHSENOW, D. (1980). Cognitive processes in alcohol use: Expectancy and the balanced placebo design. In N. Mello (Ed.), *Advances in substance abuse: Behavioral and biological research.* Greenwich, CT: JAI Press.

MARQUIS, K.H., MARSHALL, J. & OSKAMP, S. (1972). Testimony validity as a function of question form, atmosphere and item difficulty. *Journal of Applied Social Psychology, 2,* 167–186.

MARTENS, R., & LANDERS, D.M. (1972). Evaluation potential as a determinant of coaction effect. *Journal of Experimental Social Psychology, 8,* 347–359.

MASSELLI, M.D. & ATTROCCHI, J. (1969). Attribution of intent. *Psychological Bulletin, 71,* 445–454.

MASTERS, R.E.L. (1966). *Eros and evil.* New York: Matrix.

MATARAZZO, J.D. (1982). Behavioral health's challenge to academic, scientific and professional psychology. *American Psychologist, 37,* 1–14.

MATARAZZO, J.D., WEISS, S.M., HERD, J.A., MILLER, N.E. & WEISS, S.M. (Eds.) (1984). *Behavioral health: A handbook of health enhancement and disease prevention.* Toronto: Wiley.

MATLIN, M. & STANG, D. (1978). *The Pollyanna principle: Selectivity of language, memory and thought.* Cambridge, MA: Schenkman.

MATTHEWS, K.A. (1982). Psychological perspectives on Type A behavior pattern. *Psychological Bulletin, 91,* 293–323.

MATTHEWS, K.A., GLASS, D.C., ROSENMAN, R.H. & BORTNER, R.W. (1977). Competitive drive, Pattern A and coronary heart disease: A further analysis of some data from the Western Collaborative Study. *Journal of Chronic Disease, 30,* 489–498.

MAUSS, M. (1967). *The gift.* New York: Norton.

MAYO, E. (1933). *The human problems of an industrial civilization.* New York: Macmillan.

McARTHUR, L.A. (1972). The how and what of why: Some determinants of consequences of causal attributions. *Journal of Personality and Social Psychology, 22,* 171–193.

McCAULEY, C. & STITT, C.L. (1978). An individual and quantitative measure of stereotypes. *Journal of Personality and Social Psychology, 36,* 929–940.

McCAULEY, C., STITT, C.L. & SEGAL, M. (1980). Stereotyping: From prejudice to prediction. *Psychological Bulletin, 87,* 195–208.

McCLELLAND, D.C. (1961). *The achieving society.* Princeton, NJ: D. Van Nostrand Co.

McCLINTOCK, C.G. (1958). Personality syndromes and attitude change. *Journal of Personality, 26,* 479–493.

McCLINTOCK, C.G. & HUNT, R.G. (1975). Nonverbal indicators of affect and deception in an interview setting. *Journal of Applied Social Psychology, 5,* 54–67.

McCLINTOCK, C.G. & NUTTIN, J.M., Jr. (1969). Development of competitive game behavior in children across two cultures. *Journal of Experimental Social Psychology, 5,* 203–218.

McCONAHAY, S.A. & McCONAHAY, J.B. (1977). Sexual permissiveness, role rigidity, and violence across cultures. *Journal of Social Issues, 33,* 134–143.

McCORD, J., McCORD, W. & HOWARD, A. (1963). Family interaction as antecedent to the direction of male aggressiveness. *Journal of Abnormal and Social Psychology, 66,* 239–342.

McCORMACK, L.H. (1920). *Characterology: An exact science.* Chicago: Rand-McNally.

McGRATH, J. (1984). *Groups: Interaction and performance.* Englewood Cliffs, NJ: Prentice-Hall.

McGRATH, J.E., MARTIN, J. & KULKA, R.A. (1982). *Judgement calls in research.* Beverly Hills, CA: Sage.

McGUIRE, W.J. (1968). Personality and susceptibility to social influence. In E.F. Borgatta & W.W. Lambert (Eds.), *Handbook of personality: Theory and research.* (1130–1187). Chicago: Rand-McNally.

McGUIRE, W.J. (1969). The nature of attitudes and attitude change. In G. Lindzey and E. Aronson (Eds.), *The handbook of social psychology,* Second Edition. (Vol. 3). (136–314). New York: Addison Wesley

McGUIRE, W.J. & PAPAGEORGIS, D. (1961). The relative efficacy of various types of prior belief-defense in producing immunity against persuasion. *Journal of Abnormal & Social Psychology, 62,* 327–337.

McGUIRE, W.J. AND PAPAGEORGIS, D. (1962). Effectiveness of forewarning in developing resistance to persuasion. *Public Opinion Quarterly, 26,* 24–32.

McLAUGHLIN, B. (1977). Second-language learning in children. *Psychological Bulletin, 84,* 438–459.

MEAD, M. (1935). *Sex and temperament in three primitive societies.* New York: Morrow.

MEADE, R.D. (1972). Future time perspectives of Americans and subcultures in India. *Journal of Cross-Cultural Psychology, 1,* 93–99.

MEDALIA, N.Z. & LARSEN, D.N. (1958). Diffusion and belief in a collective dilemma: The Seattle windshield pitting epidemic. *American Sociological Review, 23,* 222–232.

MEEUS, W., & RAAIJSMAKERS, Q. (1986). Administrative obedience as a social phenomenon. In W. Doise & S. Moscovici (Eds.), *Current issues in European social psychology* (Vol. 2). Cambridge: Cambridge University Press.

MEGARGEE, E.I. (1966). Undercontrolled and overcontrolled personality types in extreme antisocial aggression. *Psychological Monographs, 80,* whole issue.

MEHRABIAN, A. (1968). Communication without words. *Psychology Today, 2* (September), 53–55.

MEHRABIAN, A. (1971). Nonverbal betrayal of feeling. *Journal of Experimental Research in Personality, 5,* 64–73.

MEHRABIAN, A. & DIAMOND, S. (1971). Seating arrangement and conversation. *Sociometry, 34,* 281–289.

MEIER, N.C., MENNENGA, G.H. & STOLTZ, H.J. (1941). An experimental approach to the study of mob behavior. *Journal of Abnormal Psychology, 36,* 506–524.

MELTON, A.W. (1936). Distribution of attention in galleries in a museum of science and industry. *Museum News, 13,* 5–8.

MENTZER, S.J. & SNYDER, M.L. (1982). The doctor and the patient: A psychological perspective. In G.S. Sanders & J. Suls (Eds.), *Social psychology of health and illness* (161–181). Hillsdale, NJ: Erlbaum.

MERRENS, M.R. (1973). Nonemergency helping behavior in various sized communities. *Journal of Social Psychology, 90,* 327–328.

MERTON, R.K. (1957). *Social theory and social structure.* Revised Edition. Glencoe, IL: Free Press.

MESSICK, D.M. & BREWER, M.B. (1983). Solving social dilemmas: A review. *Review of Personality and Social Psychology, 4,* 11–44.

MESSICK, D.M. & McCLELLAND, C.L. (1983). Social traps and temporal traps. *Personality and Social Psychology Bulletin, 9,* 105–110.

MEUMANN, E. (1904). Haus-und schularbeit: Experimente an kindern der volksschule. *Die Deutsche Schule, 8,* 278–303, 337–359, 416–431.

MEYER, A.J., NASH, J.D., McALISTER, A.L., MACCOBY, N. & FARQUHAR, J.W. (1980). Skills training in a cardiovascular education campaign. *Journal of Consulting and Clinical Psychology, 35,* 331–342.

MIDDLEBROOK, P.N. (1974). *Social psychology and modern life.* New York: Alfred A. Knopf.

MIDLARSKY, E. & BRYAN, J.H. (1967). Training charity in children. *Journal of Personality and Social Psychology, 5,* 408–415.

MIDLARSKY, E. & BRYAN, J.H. (1972). Affect expressions and children's imitative altruism. *Journal of Experimental Research in Personality, 6,* 195–203.

MIDLARSKY, E., BRYAN, J.H. & BRICKMAN, P. (1973). Aversive approval: Interactive effects of modeling and reinforcement on altruistic behavior. *Child Development, 44,* 321–328.

MILGRAM, S. (1963). Behavioral study of obedience. *Journal of Applied Social Psychology, 67,* 371–378.

MILGRAM, S. (1964). Issues in the study of obedience: A reply to Baumrind. *American Psychologist, 19,* 848–852.

MILGRAM, S. (1965). Some conditions of obedience and disobedience to authority. *Human Relations, 18,* 57–76.

MILGRAM, S. (1969). The lost letter technique. *Psychology Today, 2,* 30–33.

MILGRAM, S. (1970). The experience of living in cities. *Science, 167,* 1461–1468.

MILGRAM, S. (1974). *Obedience to authority.* New York: Harper & Row.

MILGRAM, S., MANN, L. & HARTER, S. (1965). The lost-letter technique: A tool of social research. *Public Opinion Quarterly, 29,* 437–438.

MILGRAM, S., LIBERTY, H.J., TOLEDO, R. & WACKENHUT, J. (1986). Response to intrusion into waiting lines. *Journal of Personality and Social Psychology, 51,* 683–689.

MILGRAM, S. & SHOTLAND, R.L. (1973). *Television and anti-social behavior.* New York: Academic Press.

MILGRAM, S. & TOCH, H. (1969). Collective behavior: Crowds and social movements. In G. Lindzey & E. Aronson (Eds.), *The handbook of social psychology.* Second Edition. (Vol. 4) (507–610). Reading, MA: Addison-Wesley.

MILL, J.S. (1973/1843). A system of logic ratiocinative and inductive. In J.M. Robson (Ed.), *Collected works of John Stuart Mill* (Vol. 7). Toronto: University of Toronto Press.

MILLER, A.G. & THOMAS, R. (1972). Cooperation and competition among Blackfoot Indian and rural Canadian children. *Child Development, 34,* 1104–1110.

MILLER, D.T. & PORTER, C.A. (1983). Self blame in victims of violence. *Journal of Social Issues, 39,* 139–152.

MILLER, G.A. (1969). Psychology as a means of promoting human welfare. *American Psychologist, 34,* 1063–1075.

MILLER, G.R. & BURGOON, J.K. (1982). Factors affecting assessments of witness credibility. In N. Kerr & R. Bray (Eds.), *The psychology of the courtroom.* New York: Academic Press.

MILLER, J.G. (1984). Culture and the development of everyday social explanation. *Journal of Personality and Social Psychology, 46,* 961–978.

MILLER, N. & CAMPBELL, D.T. (1959). Recency and primacy in persuasion as a function of the timing of speeches and measurement. *Journal of Abnormal and Social Psychology, 59,* 1–9.

MILLER, R.M. & RIVENBARK, W. (1970). Sexual differences in physical attractiveness as a determinant of heterosexual liking. *Psychological Reports, 27,* 701–702.

MILLER, S.M. & MANGAN, C.E. (1983). Interacting effects of information and coping style in adapting to gynecologic stress. Should the doctor tell all? *Journal of Personality and Social Psychology, 45,* 223–236.

MILLS, J. & HARVEY, J. (1972). Opinion change as a function of when information about the communicator is received and whether he is attractive or expert. *Journal of Personality and Social Psychology, 21,* 52–55.

MINTZ, A. (1951). Non-adaptive group behavior. *Journal of Abnormal and Social Psychology, 46,* 150–159.

MIRELS, H. & MILLS, J. (1964). Perception of the pleasantness and competence of a partner. *Journal of Applied Social Psychology, 68,* 456–459.

MITA, T.H., DERMER, M. & KNIGHT, J. (1977). Reversed facial images and the mere-exposure hypothesis. *Journal of Personality and Social Psychology, 35,* 597–601.

MITCHELL, H.E. (1979). Informational and affective determinants of juror decision making. Unpublished doctoral dissertion. Purdue University.

MITCHELL, H.E. & BYRNE, D. (1973). The defendant's dilemma: Effects of juror's attitudes and authoritarianism on judicial decisions. *Journal of Personality and Social Psychology, 25,* 123–129.

MOGY, R.B. & PRUITT, D.G. (1974). Effects of threatener's enforcement costs on threat credibility and compliance. *Journal of Personality and Social Psychology, 29,* 173–180.

MONAGHAN, E.D. (1975). Emergency services and Good Samaritans. *La revue juridique themis, 10,* 20–23.

MONSON, T.C. & HESLEY, J.W. (1982). Causal attributions for behaviors consistent or inconsistent with an actor's personality traits: Differences between those offered by actors and observers. *Journal of Personality and Social Psychology, 18,* 416–432.

MONTAGUE, A. (1973). *Man and aggression*. Second Edition. London: Oxford University Press.

MOORE, T.E. & CADEAU, L. (1985). The representation of women, the elderly and minorities in Canadian television commercials. *Canadian Journal of Behavioural Science, 17,* 215–225.

MOOS, R.H. (1982). Coping with acute health crises. In T. Millon, C. Green & R. Meagher (Eds.), Handbook of clinical health psychology. New York: Plenum.

MORAN, G. & COMFORT, J.C. (1982). Scientific juror selection. Sex as a moderator of demographic and personality predictors of impanelled felony juror behavior. *Journal of Personality and Social psychology, 43,* 1052–1063.

MORELAND, R.L. & ZAJONC, R.B. (1982). Exposure effects in person perception: Familiarity, similarity and attraction. *Journal of Experimental Social Psychology, 18,* 395–415.

MORLAND, K. (1969). Race awareness among American and Hong Kong Chinese children. *American Journal of Sociology, 75,* 360–374.

MORRIS, C. (1956). *Varieties of human value*. Chicago: University of Chicago Press.

MORRIS, W.N. & MILLER, R.S. (1975). The effects of consensus-breaking and consensus preempting partners on reduction of conformity. *Journal of Experimental Social Psychology, 11,* 215–223.

MOSCOVICI, S. (1980). Toward a theory of conversion behavior. In L. Berkowitz (Ed.), *Advances in experimental social psychology* (Vol. 13) (202–239). New York: Academic Press.

MOSCOVICI, S., LAGE, E. & NAFFRECHOUX, M. (1969). Influence of a consistent minority on the responses of a majority in color perception task. *Sociometry, 32,* 365–380.

MOSCOVICI, S. & LECUYER, R. (1972). Studies in group decision I: Social space, patterns of communication and group consensus. *European Journal of Social Psychology, 2,* 221–244.

MOSCOVICI, S. & NEMETH, C. (1974). Social Influence II: Minority influence. In C. Nemeth (Ed.), *Social psychology: Classic and contemporary integrations*. Chicago: Rand McNally College Publishing.

MOSCOVICI, S. & ZAVOLLONI, M. (1969). The group as a polarizer of attitudes. *Journal of Personality and Social Psychology, 12,* 125–135.

MOULIK, T.K. & LOKHANDE, M.R. (1969). Value orientation of North Indian farmers and its relation to adoption of farm practices. *Rural Sociology, 34,* 375–382.

MULLEN, B., FUTRELL, D., STAIRS, D., TICE, D.M., BAUMEISTER, R.F., DAWSON, K.E., RIORDAN, C.A., RADLOFF, C.E., GOETHALS, G.R., KENNEDY, J.G. & ROSENFELD, P. (1986). Newscasters' facial expressions and voting behavior of viewers: Can a smile elect a president? *Journal of Personality and Social Psychology, 51,* 291–295.

MUNSTERBERG, H. (1908). *On the witness stand*. New York: Doubleday.

MURSTEIN, B.I. (1972). Physical attractiveness and marital choice. *Journal of Personality and Social Psychology, 22,* 8–12.

MURSTEIN, B.I. (1976). *Who will marry whom?* New York: Springer.

MUSSINGER, H. (1978). Reply to Kamin. *Psychological Bulletin, 85,* 202–206.

MYERS, D.G. (1982). Polarizing effects of social interaction. In H. Brandstatter, J.H. Davies & G. Stocher-Kreichgauer (Eds.), *Contemporary problems in decision-making* (125–161). New York: Academic Press.

NADER, L. (1969). Styles of court procedure: To make the balance. In L. Nader (Ed.), *Law in Culture and Society* (69–91). Chicago: Aldine.

NADLER, A. (1986). Help seeking as a cultural phenomenon: Differences between city and kibbutz dwellers. *Journal of Personality and Social Psychology, 51,* 976–982.

NADLER, A. & FISHER, J.D. (1984). Effects of donor-recipient relationship on recipient's reactions to aid. In E. Staub, D. Bar-Tal, J. Karylowski & J. Reykowski (Eds.), *Development and maintenance of prosocial behavior* (397–418). New York: Plenum Press.

NASAR, J.L. & GREENBERG, M.L. (1984). The preparedness and reactions of cities to warnings and crisis relocation for nuclear attack. *Journal of Applied Social Psychology, 14,* 487–506.

NEL, E., HELMREICH, R. & ARONSON, E. (1969). Opinion change in the advocate as a function of the persuasibility of his audience. *Journal of Personality and Social Psychology, 12,* 117–124.

NELSON, A. (1985). Psychological equivalence. Awareness and response-ability in our nuclear age. *American Psychologist, 40,* 549–560.

NELSON, S.D. (1974). Nature/nurture revisited I: A review of the biological bases of conflict. *Journal of Conflict Resolution, 18,* 285–335.

NELSON, S.D. (1975). Nature/nurture revisited II: Social, political, and technological implications of biological approaches to human conflict. *Journal of Conflict resolution, 19,* 734–761.

NEMETH, C. (1970). Bargaining and reciprocity. *Psychological Bulletin, 74,* 297–308.

NEMETH, C. (1981). Jury trials: Psychology and law: *Advances in experimental social psychology, 14,* 309–367.

NEMETH C. (1985). Dissent, group process and creativity: The contribution of the minority influence. In E. Lawlor (Ed.), *Advances in group processes* (Vol. 2) (57–75). Greenwood, CT: JAI Press.

NEMETH, C. (1986). Differential contributions of majority and minority influence. *Psychological Review, 93,* 23–32.

NEWBORN, C.R. & ROGERS, R.W. (1979). Effects of threatening and reassuring components of fear appeals on physiological and verbal measures of emotions and attitudes. *Journal of Experimental Social Psychology, 15,* 242–253.

NEWCOMB, M.D. (1986). Nuclear attitudes and reactions: Associations with depression, drug use and quality of life. *Journal of Personality and Social Psychology, 50,* 906–920.

NEWCOMB, M.D. & BENTLER, E.M. (1980). Cohabitation before marriage: A comparison of married couples who did and did not cohabit. *Alternative Life Styles, 3,* 65–85.

NEWCOMB, T.M. (1961). *The acquaintance process.* New York: Holt, Rinehart & Winston.

NIELSON, W.R. & NEUFELD, R.W.J. (1986) Utility of the uncontrollability construct in relation to the Type A behaviour pattern: A multidimensional investigation. *Canadian Journal of Behavioural Science, 18,* 224–237.

NISBETT, R.E. & BORGIDA, E. (1975). Attribution and the psychology of prediction. *Journal of Personality and Social Psychology, 32,* 932–943.

NISBETT, R.E., CAPUTO, C., LEGANT, P. & MARACEK, J. (1973). Behavior as seen by the actor and as seen by the observer. *Journal of Personality and Social Psychology, 27,* 154–164.

NISBETT, R.E. & GORDON, A. (1967). Self-esteem and susceptibility to social influence. *Journal of Personality and Social Psychology, 5,* 268–276.

NISBETT, R.E. & WILSON, T.D. (1977). Telling more than we can know: Verbal reports on mental processes. *Psychological Review, 84,* 231–259.

NOSSITER, B.D. (1970). *The soft state.* New York: Harper & Row.

NORMAN, R.N.G. (1985). The nature and correlates of health behaviour. Ottawa: Health Promotion Directorate.

NOVACO, R.W. (1975). *Anger control: The development and evaluation of an experimental treatment.* Lexington, MA: Lexington Books.

NOVAK, D. & LERNER, M.J. (1968). Rejection as a consequence of perceived similarity. *Journal of Personality and Social Psychology, 9,* 147–152.

NYQUIST, L.V. & SPENCE, J.T. (1986). Effects of dispositional dominance and sex role expectations on leadership behaviors. *Journal of Personality and Social Psychology, 50,* 87–93.

O'BARR, W.M. & CONLEY, J.M. (1976). When a juror watches a lawyer. *Barrister, 3,* 8–11.

OLDRIDGE, N.B. (1982). Compliance and exercise in primary and secondary prevention of coronary heart disease: A review. *Preventive Medicine, 11,* 56–70.

OLIVER, J.F. (1943). Moonlight and nervous disorders: A historical study. *Journal of Psychiatry, 99,* 579–584.

OLSEN, M.E. (1981). Consumers' attitudes toward energy conservation. *Journal of Social Issues, 37,* 108–131.

OLWEUS, D. (1972). Personality and aggression. *Nebraska symposium on motivation, 1972* (261–323). Lincoln, NB: University of Nebraska Press.

ONTARIO ROYAL COMMISSION ON VIOLENCE IN THE COMMUNICATIONS INDUSTRY (1976). *Interim Report.* Toronto: Government of Ontario.

ONTARIO ROYAL COMMISSION ON VIOLENCE IN THE COMMUNICATIONS INDUSTRY (1977). *Report* (Vols. 1–7). Toronto: Government of Ontario.

OPTON, E.M. (1971). Lessons of My Lai. In R. Buckhout (Ed.), *Toward social change.* New York: Harper & Row.

ORFORD, J. (1985). *Excessive appetites: A psychological view of addictions.* Toronto: Wiley.

ORNE, M.T. (1962). On the social psychology of the psychology experiment: With particular reference to demand characteristics and their implications. *American Psychologist, 17,* 776–783.

OSGOOD, C.E. (1962). *An alternative to war or surrender.* Urbana: University of Illinois Press.

OSGOOD, C.E., SUCI, D.J. & TANNENBAUM, P.H. (1957). *The measurement of meaning.* Urbana: University of Illinois Press.

OSGOOD, C.E. & TANNENBAUM, P.H. (1955). The principle of congruity in the prediction of attitude change. *Psychological Review, 62,* 42–55.

OSHEROW, N. (1981). Making sense of the nonsensical: An analysis of Jonestown. In E. Aronson (Ed.), *Readings about the social animal.* Third Edition. San Francisco: W.H. Freeman.

OSKAMP, S. (1971). Effects of programmed strategies on cooperation in the prisoner's dilemma and other mixed-motive games. *Journal of Conflict Resolution, 15,* 225–229.

OSKAMP, S. (1977). *Attitudes and opinions.* Englewood Cliffs, NJ: Prentice-Hall.

OSKAMP, S., KING, J.C., BURN, S.M., KONRAD, A.M., POLLARD, J.A. & WHITE, M.A. (1985). The media and nuclear war: Fallout from TV's "The Day After." In S. Oskamp (Ed.), *International conflict and national public policy issues.* Applied Social Psychology Annual 6 (127– 158). Beverly Hills, CA: Sage Publications.

OSLER, W. (1892). *Lectures on angina pectoris and allied states.* New York: Appleton-Century-Crofts.

OSTROM, T.M. (1973). The bogus pipeline: A new ignis fatuus? *Psychological Bulletin, 79,* 252–259.

PAGÈS, R. (1986). Personal communication.

PAK, A. W-P., DION, K.L. & DION, K.K. (1985). Correlates of self-confidence with English among Chinese students in Toronto. *Canadian Journal of Behavioural Science, 17,* 369–378.

PALYS, T.S. & LITTLE, B.R. (1980). Social indicators and the quality of life. *Canadian Psychology, 21,* 67–74.

PARKE, R.D., BERKOWITZ, L., LEYENS, J.P., WEST, S.G. & SEBAS-TIAN, R.J. (1977). Some effects of violent and non-violent movies on the behavior of juvenile delinquents. In L. Berkowitz (Ed.), *Advances in experimental social psychology* (Vol. 10) (135–172). New York: Academic Press.

PARKE, R.D. & SLABY, R.G. (1983). The development of aggression. In P.H. Mussen (Ed.), *Handbook of child psychology* (Vol. 4) (547–641). New York: Wiley.

PATRICK, C.J., CRAIG, K.D. & PRKACHIN, K.M. (1986) Observer judgements of acute pain: Facial action determinants. *Journal of Personality and Social Psychology, 50,* 1291–1298.

PATTERSON, F. (1978). Conversations with a gorilla. *National Geographic,* 154 (4), 438–465.

PATTERSON, M.L. (1982). A sequential functional model of nonverbal exchange. *Psychological Review, 89,* 231–249.

PATTERSON, M.L. (1983). *Nonverbal behaviour: A functional perspective.* New York: Springer.

PAULUS, P.B. (1980). *The psychology of group influence.* Hillsdale, NJ: Erlbaum.

PAULUS, P.B. & MURDOCK, P. (1971). Anticipated evaluation and audience presence in the enhancement of dominant responses. *Journal of Experimental Social Psychology, 7,* 280–291.

PEARL, D., BOUTHILET, L. & LAZAR, J.B. (Eds.) (1982). *Television and Behavior: Ten years of scientific progress and implications for the 80's* (Vols. 1 and 2). Washington, D.C.: U.S. Government Printing Office.

PENDLETON, M.G. & BATSON, C.D. (1979). Self-presentation and the door-in-the-face technique for inducing compliance. *Journal of Personality and Social Psychology, 5,* 77–81.

PENFIELD, W. & ROBERTS, L. (1959). *Speech and brain mechanisms.* Princeton, NJ: Princeton University Press.

PENNEBAKER, J.W., DYER, M.A., CAULKINS, R.S., LITOWITZ, D.L., ACKERMAN, P.L., ANDERSON, D.B. & McGRAW, K.M. (1979). Don't the girls get prettier at closing time: A country and western application to psychology. *Personality and Social Psychology Bulletin, 5,* 122–125.

PENNINGTON, N. & HASTIE, R. (1981). Juror decision-making models: The generalization gap. *Psychological Bulletin, 89,* 246–287.

PEPLAU, L.A., BIKSON, F.K., ROOK, K.S., & GOODCHILDS, J.D. (1982). Being old and living alone. In L.A. Peplau & D. Perlman (Eds.), *Loneliness: A sourcebook of current theory, research, and therapy* (327–349). New York: Wiley Interscience.

PEPLAU, L.A. & GORDON, S.L. (1985) Women and men in love: Gender differences in close heterosexual relationships. In V.E. O'Leary, R.K. Unger & B.S. Walloton (Eds.), *Women, gender, and social psychology.* Hillsdale, NJ: Erlbaum.

PEPLAU, L.A. & PERLMAN, D. (1982). Perspectives on loneliness. In L.A. Peplau & D. Perlman (Eds.), *Loneliness: A sourcebook of current theory, research and therapy.* New York: Wiley.

PEPLAU, L.A., RUSSELL, D. & HEIM, M. (1979). The experience of loneliness. In I.H. Frieze, D. Bar-Tal & J.S. Carroll (Eds.), *New approaches to social problems: Applications of attribution theory.* San Francisco: Jossey-Bass.

PERLMAN, D. & OSKAMP, S. (1971). The effects of picture content and exposure frequency on evaluations of Negroes and Whites. *Journal of Experimental Social Psychology, 7,* 503–514.

PERLMAN, D. & PEPLAU, L.A. (1981). Toward a social psychology of loneliness. In S. Duck & R. Gilmour (Eds.), *Personal relationships 3: Personal relationships in disorder.* London: Academic Press.

PERRIN, S. & SPENCER, C. (1981). Independence or conformity in the Asch experiment as a reflection of cultural and situational factors. *British Journal of Social Psychology, 20,* 205–209.

PERSONNAZ, B., KASTERSZTEIN, J. & LEMAINE, G. (1976–77). L'originalité sociale: Etude de la différenciation sociale dans un système semi-fermé. *Bulletin de Psychologie, 30,* 451–454.

PERVIN, L. (1976). The representative design of person-situation research. In D. Magnussen & N.S. Endler (Eds.), *Personality at the crossroads: Current issues in interactional psychology.* Hillside, NJ: Erlbaum.

PESSIN, J. (1933). The comparative effects of social and mechanical stimulation on memorizing. *American Journal of Psychology, 45,* 263–270.

PETERS, L.H., HARTKE, D.D. & POHLMAN, J.T. (1985). Fiedler's contingency theory of leadership: An application of the meta-analytic procedure of Schmidt and Hunter. *Psychological Bulletin, 97,* 274–285.

PETERSON, R.B. & SKIMADA, J.Y. (1978). Sources of management problems in Japanese-American joint ventures. *Academy of Management Review, 3,* 796–804.

PETTIGREW, T.F. (1961). Social psychology and desegregation research. *American Psychologist, 16,* 105–112.

PETTY, R.E. & CACIOPPO, J.T. (1977). Forewarning, cognitive responding, and resistance to persuasion. *Journal of Personality and Social Psychology, 35,* 645–655.

PETTY, R.E. & CACIOPPO, J.T. (1981). *Attitude and persuasion: Classic and contemporary approaches.* Dubuque, IO: W.C. Brown.

PETTY, R.E. & CACIOPPO, J.T. (1986). The elaboration likelihood model of persuasion. In L. Berkowitz (Ed.), *Advances in experimental social psychology* (Vol. 19) (123–205). New York: Academic Press.

PETTY, R.E., OSTROM, T.M. & BROCK, T.C. (1981). *Cognitive responses in persuasive communication: A text in attitude change.* Hillsdale, NJ: Erlbaum.

PFUNGST, O. (1911). *Clever Hans (the horse of Mr. von Osten): A contribution to experimental, animal and human psychology* (translated by C. Rahn). New York: Holt.

PHETERSON, G.I., KIESLER, S.B. & GOLDBERG, P.A. (1971). Evaluation of the performance of women as a function of their success, achievements, and personal history. *Journal of Personality and Social Psychology, 19,* 114–118.

PHILLIPS, D.P. (1974). The influence of suggestion on suicide: Substantive and theoretical implications of the Werther effect. *American Sociological Review, 39,* 340–349.

PHILLIPS, D.P. (1977). Motor vehicle fatalities increase just after publicized suicide stories. *Science, 196,* 1464–1465.

PHILLIPS, D.P. (1978). Airplane accident fatalities increase just after newspaper stories about murder and suicide. *Science, 201,* 748–749.

PHILLIPS, D.P. (1979). Suicide, motor vehicle fatalities and the mass media. Evidence toward a theory of suggestion. *American Journal of Sociology, 84,* 1150–1174.

PHILLIPS, D.P. (1980). Airplane accidents, murder and the mass media: Towards a theory of imitation and suggestion. *Social Forces, 58,* 1001–1024.

PHILLIPS, D.P. (1983). The impact of mass media violence on U.S. homicides. *American Sociological Review, 48,* 560–568.

PHILLIPS, D.P. & HENSLEY, J.E. (1984). When violence is rewarded or punished: The impact of mass media stories on homicide. *Journal of Communication, 34,* 101–116.

PIAGET, J. (1932). *The moral development of the child.* London: Routledge & Kegan Paul.

PIAGET, J. (1966). Le langage et la pensée du point de vue génétique. In Piaget, J., *Six études de psychologie.* Genève: Gonthier.

PILIAVIN, I.M. & PILIAVIN, J.A. (1972). The effect of blood on reactions to a victim. *Journal of Personality and Social Psychology, 23,* 253–261.

PILIAVIN, I.M., RODIN, J. & PILIAVIN, J.A. (1969). Good Samaritanism: An underground phenomenon? *Journal of Personality and Social Psychology, 13,* 289–299.

PILIAVIN, J.A., DAVIDIO, J.F., GAERTNER, S.L. & CLARK, R.D. (1981). *Emergency intervention.* New York: Academic Press.

PILISUK. M. & MINKLER, M. (1985). Supportive ties: A political economy perspective. *Health Education Quarterly, 12,* 93–106.

PILISUK, M., SKOLNICK, P. & OVERSTREET, E. (1968). Predicting cooperation from the two sexes in a conflict simulation. *Journal of Personality and Social Psychology, 10,* 35–43.

PINES, A. & ARONSON, E. (1983). Antecedents, correlates and consequences of romantic jealousy. *Journal of Personality, 51,* 108–136.

PITTMAN, W. (1977). *Now is not too late.* Toronto: Metropolitan Council Task Force.

PITTNER, M.G., HOUSTON, B.K. & SPIRIDI-GLIOZZI, G. (1983). Control over stress, Type A behavior pattern and response to stress. *Journal of Personality and Social Psychology, 44,* 627–637.

PLASTRE, G. (1974). Bilinguisme d'enfance et apprentissage ultérieur d'une langue vivante. In S.T. Carey (Ed.), *Bilingualism, biculturalism and education* (59–74). Edmonton: University of Alberta.

PLATT, J. (1973). Social traps. *American Psychologist, 28,* 641–651.

PODSAKOFF, R.M. & SCHRIESHEIM, C.A. (1985). Field studies of French and Raven's bases of power: Critique, reanalysis and suggestions for future research. *Psychological Bulletin, 97,* 387–411.

POLIVY, J., HACKETT, R. & BYCIO, P. (1979). The effect of perceived smoking status on attractiveness. *Personality and Social Psychology Bulletin, 5,* 401–404.

POLIVY, J. & HERMAN, P. (1983). *Breaking the diet habit.* New York: Basic Books.

POLLARD, W.E. & MITCHELL, T.R. (1972). Decision theory analysis of social power. *Psychological Bulletin, 78,* 433–446.

POPHAM, R.E., SCHMIDT, W. & DELINT, J. (1976). The effects of legal restraint on drinking. In B. Kissin & H. Begleiter (Eds.), *The biology of alcoholism* (Vol. 4) (234–278). New York: Plenum.

POPPER, K.R. (1959). *The logic of scientific discovery.* New York: Basic Books.

POPPER, K.R. (1972). *Objective knowledge.* Oxford: Oxford University Press.

PORIER, G.W. & LOTT, A.J. (1967). Galvanic skin responses and prejudice. *Journal of Personality and Social Psychology, 5,* 253–259.

PREMACK, A.J. & PREMACK, D. (1972). Teaching language to an ape. *Scientific American, 227,* 92–99.

PRICE, K.H. & GARLAND, H. (1981). Compliance with a leader's suggestions as a function of perceived leader/member's competence and potential reciprocity. *Journal of Applied Psychology, 66,* 329–336.

PROSTERMAN, R.L. (1972). *Surviving to 3000.* Belmont, CA: Wadsworth.

PRUITT, D.G. (1976). Power and bargaining. In B. Seidenberg & A. Snadowsky (Eds.), *Social psychology: An introduction* (343–376). New York: Free Press.

PRUITT, D.G. (1981). *Negotiating Behavior.* New York: Academic Press.

PRUITT, D.G. & RUBIN, J.Z. (1986). *Social conflict: Escalation, stalemate and settlement.* New York: Random House.

PYSZCZYNSKI, T., GREENBERG, J., MACK, D. & WRIGHTSMAN, L. (1981). Opening statements in a jury trial: The effects of promising more than the evidence can show. *Journal of Applied Social Psychology, 11,* 434–444.

PYSZCZYNSKI, T. & WRIGHTSMAN, L. (1981). The effects of opening statements on mock jurors' verdicts in a simulated criminal trial. *Journal of Applied Social Psychology, 11,* 301–313.

QUANTY, M.B. (1976). Aggression catharsis: Experimental investigations and implications. In R.C. Geen & E.C. O'Neal (Eds.), *Perspectives on aggression.* New York: Academic Press.

QUARANTELLI, E.L. (1960). Images of withdrawal behavior in disasters: Some basic misconceptions. *Social Problems, 8,* 1968–1978.

QUIGLEY-FERNANDEZ, B. & TEDESCHI, J.T. (1978). The bogus pipeline as lie detector: Two validity studies. *Journal of Personality and Social Psychology, 36,* 247–256.

RABUSHKA, A. & SHEPSLE, K.A. (1972). *Pitfall in plural societies: A theory of democratic instability.* Columbus, OH: Merrill.

RADKE-YARROW, M. & ZAHN-WAXLER, C. (1984). Roots, motives, and patterns in children's prosocial behavior. In E. Staub, D. Bar-Tal, J. Karylowski & J. Reykowski (Eds.), *Development and maintenance of prosocial behavior* (81–99). New York: Plenum Press.

RAMSEY, C.A. & WRIGHT, E.N. (1974). Age and second language learning. *Journal of Social Psychology, 94,* 115–121.

RANK, S.G. & JACOBSON, C.K. (1977). Hospital nurses' compliance with medication overdose orders: A failure to replicate. *Journal of Health and Social Behavior, 18,* 1888–1993.

RAPOPORT, A. (1963). Mathematical models of social interaction. In R.D. Luce, R.R. Bush & E. Galanter (Eds.), *Handbook of mathematical psychology* (493–579). New York: Wiley.

RAPOPORT, A. (1968). Prospects for experimental games. *Journal of Conflict Resolution, 12,* 461–470.

RAPOPORT, A. (1974). *Conflict in man-made environment.* Harmondsworth: Penguin.

RAPOPORT, A. & CHAMMAH, A.M. (1965). *Prisoner's dilemma: A study in conflict and cooperation.* Ann Arbor: University of Michigan Press.

RAVEN, B.H. & KRUGLANSKI, A.W. (1970). Conflict and power. In P.G. Swingle (Ed.), *The structure of conflict* (69–110). New York: Academic Press.

RAYKO, D.S. (1977). Does knowledge matter? Psychological information and bystander helping. *Canadian Journal of Behavioural Science, 9,* 295–304.

RECKLESS W.C. & KAY, B.A. (1967). *The female offenders.* President's Commission on Law Enforcement and the Administration of Justice 1967. Cited by Simon, R.J. (1975). *Women and crime.* Lexington, MA: Heath.

REGAN, D.T., WILLIAMS, M. & SPARLING, S. (1972). Voluntary expiation of guilt: A field experiment. *Journal of Personality and Social Psychology, 24,* 42–45.

REGAN, D.T. & TOTTEN, J. (1975). Empathy and attribution: Turning observers into actors. *Journal of Personality and Social Psychology, 32,* 850–856.

REICH, C. & PURBHOO, M. (1975). The effect of cross-cultural contact. *Canadian Journal of Behavioural Science, 7,* 313–327.

REID, J.B. (1978). Study of drinking in natural settings. In G.A. Marlatt & P. Nathan (Eds.), *Behavioral approaches to alcoholism* (58–75). New Brunswick, NJ: Rutgers Center of Alcohol Studies.

REINISCH, J.M. & SANDERS, S.A. (1986). A test of sex differences in aggressive response to hypothetical conflict situations. *Journal of Personality and Social Psychology, 50,* 1045–1049.

REISENZEIN, R. (1986). A structural equation analysis of Weiner's attribution-affect model of helping behavior. *Journal of Personality and Social Psychology, 50,* 1123–1133.

RÉMILLARD, L. (1970). Evaluation of personality through speech by French-Canadian students in northeastern Montréal. Unpublished manuscript. Department of Psychology and Linguistics, Université de Montréal.

REMPEL, J.F., HOLMES, J.G. & ZANNA, M.P. (1985). Trust in close relationships. *Journal of Personality and Social Psychology, 49,* 95–112.

RICE, B. (1982). The Hawthorne defect: Persistence of a flawed theory. *Psychology Today, 16* (February), 70–74.

RICE, G.E. & GAINER, P. (1962). "Altruism" in the albino rat. *Journal of Comparative and Physiological Psychology, 55,* 123–125.

RICE, R.W. & KASTENBAUM, D.R. (1983). The contingency model of leadership: Some current issues. *Basic and Applied Social Psychology, 4,* 373–392.

RICHARDSON, D.C., BERNSTEIN, S. & TAYLOR, S.P. (1979). The effect of situational contingencies on female retaliative behavior. *Journal of Personality and Social Psychology, 37,* 2044–2048.

RIESMAN, D., GLAZER, N. & DENNY, R. (1961). *The lonely crowd: A study of the changing American character.* New Haven: Yale University Press.

RIESS, M., ROSENFELD, R., MELBURG, V. & TEDESCHI, J.T. (1981). Self-serving attributions: Biased private perceptions and distorted public descriptions. *Journal of Personality and Social Psychology, 41,* 224–231.

RINGELMANN, M. (1913). Recherches sur les moteurs animés: Travail de l'homme. *Annales de l'Institut National Agronomique,* 2e Série-tome XII, 1–40.

ROACH, M.E. & EICHER, J.B. (1965). *Dress, adornment, and the social order.* New York: Wiley.

ROBERTSON, L.S. (1984). Behavior and injury prevention: Whose behavior? In J.D. Matarazzo, S.M. Weiss, J.A. Herd, N.E. Miller & S.M. Weiss (Eds.), *Behavioral health* (980–989). Toronto: Wiley.

ROBINS, L. (1978). Interaction of setting and predisposition in explaining novel behavior: Drug initiations before, in, and after Vietnam. In D.B. Kandel (Ed.), *Longitudinal research in drug use. Empirical findings and methodological issues* (179–195). Washington: Hemisphere.

ROBINSON, J.P. & SHAVER, P.R. (1973). *Measures of social psychological attitudes*. Revised Edition. Survey Research Center, Institute for Social Research, Ann Arbor, Michigan.

RODIN, J. & JANIS, I.L. (1979). The social power of health care practitioners as agents of change. *Journal of Social Issues, 35*, 60–81.

RODIN, J. & LANGER, E. (1977). Long-term effect of a control-relevant intervention with the institutionalized aged. *Journal of Personality and Social Psychology, 35*, 897–902.

RODIN, J. & LANGER, E. (1980). Aging labels: The decline of control and the fall of self-esteem. *Journal of Social Issues, 36*, 12–29.

RODIN, J., SILBERSTEIN, L. & STRIEGEL-MOORE, R. (1985). Women and weight: A normative discontent. In T.B. Sanderegger (Ed.), *Psychology and gender.* Nebraska Symposium on Motivation, 1984. Lincoln: University of Nebraska Press.

RODRIGUES, A. (1981). Latin-American social psychology: A review. *Spanish-Language Psychology, 1*, 39–60.

RODRIGUES, A. (1983). Replication: A neglected type of research in social psychology. *Interamerican Journal of Psychology, 16*, 91–109.

ROGERS, E.M. (1962). *The diffusion of innovations*. New York: Free Press.

ROGERS, E.M. (1969). *Modernization among peasants: The impact of communication*. New York: Holt, Rinehart & Winston.

ROGERS, E. & SHOEMAKER, F. (1971). *Communication of innovations: A cross-cultural approach*. New York: Free Press.

ROGERS, R.W. (1975). A protection motivation theory of fear appeals and attitude change. *Journal of Psychology, 91*, 93–114.

ROGERS, R.W. (1984). Changing health-related attitudes and behavior: The role of preventive health psychology. In J.H. Harvey, J.E. Maddox, R.P. McGlynn & C.D. Stoltenberg (Eds.), *Social perception in clinical and counseling psychology* (Vol. 2) (91–112). Lubbock: Texas Technical University.

ROKEACH, M. (1960). *The open and closed mind*. New York: Basic Books.

ROKEACH, M. (1968). *Beliefs, attitudes, and values*. San Francisco: Jossey-Bass.

ROKEACH, M. (1973). *The nature of human values*. New York: Free Press.

ROKEACH, M. (1979). *Understanding human values: Individual and societal*. New York: Free Press.

ROKEACH, M. & KLIEJUNAS, P. (1972). Behavior as a function of attitude-toward-object and attitude-toward-situation. *Journal of Personality and Social Psychology, 22*, 194–201.

ROKEACH, M. & MEZEI, L. (1966). Race and shared belief as factors in social choice. *Science, 151*, 167–172.

ROLLINS, B. (1976). *First you cry*. Philadelphia: Lippincott.

ROOK, K.S. & PEPLAU, L.A. (1982). Perspectives on helping the lonely. In L.A. Peplau & D. Perlman (Eds.), *Loneliness: A sourcebook of current theory, research and therapy*. New York: Wiley Inter-science.

ROOTMAN, I. (1985). Afterword: Psychosocial research on alcohol problems from an international perspective. In M.A. Schuckit (Ed.), *Alcohol patterns and problems* (267–272). New Brunswick, NJ: Rutgers University Press.

RORER, L. (1965). The great response-style myth. *Psychological Bulletin, 63*, 129–156.

ROSEN, S., TOMARELLI, M.M., KIDDA, M.L., Jr. & MEDVIN, N. (1986). Effects of motive for helping recipient's inability to reciprocate, and sex on devaluation of the recipient's competence. *Journal of Personality and Social Psychology, 50*, 729–736.

ROSENBAUM, L.L. & ROSENBAUM, W.B. (1971). Morale and productivity consequences of group leadership style, stress and type of task. *Journal of Applied Psychology, 55*, 343–348.

ROSENBERG, M.J. (1965). When dissonance fails: On eliminating evaluation apprehension from attitude measurement. *Journal of Personality and Social Psychology, 1*, 28–42.

ROSENBERG, M.J. (1969). The conditions and consequences of evaluation apprehension. In R. Rosenthal & R.L. Rosnow (Eds.), *Artifact in behavioral research*. New York: Academic Press.

ROSENBERG, M.J. & HOVLAND, C.I. (1960). Cognitive, affective and behavioral components of attitudes. In M.J. Rosenberg (Ed.), *Attitude organization and change* (1–14). New Haven, CT: Yale University Press.

ROSENBERG, S. & SEDLAK, A. (1972). Structural representations of implicit personality theory. In L. Berkowitz (Ed.), *Advances in experimental social psychology* (Vol. 6) (235–297). New York: Academic.

ROSENHAN, D. (1970). The natural socialization of altruistic autonomy. In J. Macaulay & L. Berkowitz (Eds.), *Altruism and helping behavior*. New York: Academic Press.

ROSENHAN, D. (1972). Learning theory and prosocial behavior. *Journal of Social Issues, 28*, 151–164.

ROSENHAN, D.L., MOORE, B.S. & UNDERWOOD, B. (1976). The social psychology of moral behavior. In T. Likona (Ed.), *Moral development and behavior*. New York: Holt, Rinehart and Winston.

ROSENMAN, R.H., BRAND, R.J., JENKINS, C.D., FRIEDMAN, M., STRAUS, R. & WURM, M. (1975). Coronary heart disease in the Western Collaborative Group Study: Final follow-up experience of 8½ years. *Journal of the American Medical Association, 233,* 872–877.

ROSENSTEIN, M.P. & CHECK, J.V.P. (1985). Sex and violence in rock videos. Paper presented at the Annual Meeting of the Canadian Psychological Association, Halifax, June 1985.

ROSENTHAL, R, (1966). *Experimenter effects in behavioral research.* New York: Appleton-Century-Crofts.

ROSENTHAL, R. (1986). Media violence, antisocial behavior, and the social consequences of small effects. *Journal of Social Issues, 42,* 141–15.

ROSKIES, E., SERAGANIAN, P., OSEASOHN, R., HANLEY, J.A., CALLU, R., MARTIN, N. & SMILGA, C. (1986). The Montreal Type A Intervention Project: Major Findings. *Health Psychology, 5,* 45–70.

ROSNOW, R.L. (1981). *Paradigms in transition: The methodology of social inquiry.* New York: Oxford University Press.

ROSNOW, R.L. & FINE, G.A. (1976). *Rumor and gossip: The social psychology of hearsay.* New York: Elsevier.

ROSS, A. (1977). *The booming fifties.* 1950/1960. Toronto: Natural Science of Canada Limited.

ROSS, A.S. (1970). The effect of observing a helpful model on helping behavior. *Journal of Social Psychology, 81,* 131–132.

ROSS, A.S. (1971). Effect of increased responsibility on bystander intervention: The presence of children. *Journal of Personality and Social Psychology, 19,* 306–310.

ROSS, A.S. (1978). *It's shorter in a crowd.* (Film by W. Troyer). Toronto: TAAW Productions.

ROSS, A.S. & BRABAND, J. (1973). Effect of increased responsibility on bystander intervention II: The cue value of a blind person. *Journal of Personality and Social Psychology, 25,* 254–258.

ROSS, E.A. (1908). *Social psychology.* New York: MacMillan.

ROSS, L. (1977). The intuitive psychologist and his shortcomings: Distortions in the attribution process. In L. Berkowitz (Ed.), *Advances in experimental social psychology* (Vol. 10). New York: Academic Press.

ROSS, M. & SICOLY, F. (1979). Egocentric biases in availability and attribution. *Journal of Personality and Social Psychology, 37,* 322–336.

ROSS, M., McFARLAND, C., CONWAY, M. & ZANNA, M.P. (1983). Reciprocal relation between attitude and behavior recall: Committing people to newly formed attitudes. *Journal of Personality and Social Psychology, 45,* 257–267.

ROTHBART, M., EVANS, M. & FULERO, S. (1979). Recall for confirming events: Memory processes and the maintenance of social stereotypes. *Journal of Experimental Social Psychology, 15,* 343–355.

ROTHBART, M., FULERO, S., JENSEN, C., HOWARD, J. & BIRRELL, B. (1978). From individual to group impressions: Availability heuristics in stereotype formation. *Journal of Experimental Social Psychology, 14,* 237–255.

ROTHBART, M. & JOHN, O.P. (1985). Social categorization and behavioral episodes: A cognitive analysis of intergroup contact. *Journal of Social Issues, 41,* 81–104.

ROTTER, J.B. (1966). Generalized expectancies for internal versus external control of reinforcement. *Psychological Monographs, 80,* (1, Whole No., 609).

ROTTER, J.B. (1967). A new scale for the measurement of interpersonal trust. *Journal of Personality, 35,* 651–665.

ROTTER, J.B. (1971). Generalized expectancies for interpersonal trust. *American Psychologist, 26,* 443–452.

ROTTER, J.B. (1980). Interpersonal trust, trustworthiness, and gullibility. *American Psychologist, 35,* 1–7.

ROTTON, J. & KELLY, I.W. (1985). Much ado about the full moon: A meta-analysis of lunar-lunacy research. *Psychological Bulletin, 97,* 286–306.

RUBENSTEIN, C.M. & SHAVER, P. (1982). The experience of loneliness. In L. Peplau & D. Perlman (Eds.), *Loneliness: A sourcebook of current theory, research and therapy.* New York: Wiley.

RUBIN, J. (1976). How to tell when someone is saying no. *Topics in Culture Learning, 4,* 61–65.

RUBIN, Z. (1970a). Measurement of romantic love. *Journal of Personality and Social Psychology, 16,* 265–273.

RUBIN, Z. (1970b). *Liking and loving.* New York: Holt, Rinehart & Winston.

RUBIN, Z. (1973). *Liking and loving: An invitation to social psychology.* New York: Holt, Rinehart and Winston.

RUBIN, Z. (1974). Lovers and other strangers. The development of intimacy in encounters and relationships. *American Scientist, 62,* 182–190.

RUBIN, Z. (1975). Disclosing oneself to a stranger: Reciprocity and its limits. *Journal of Experimental Social Psychology, 11,* 233–260.

RUBIN, Z. (1976). Naturalistic studies of self-disclosure. *Personality and Social Psychology Bulletin, 2,* 260–263.

RUBIN, Z. & PEPLAU, L.A. (1975). Who believes in a just world? *Journal of Social Issues, 31,* 65–89.

RUBIN, Z. & SHENKER, S. (1978). Friendship, proximity and self-disclosure. *Journal of Personality, 46,* 1–23.

RUBLE, T.L. (1983). Sex stereotypes: Issues of change in the 1970s. *Sex Roles, 9,* 397–402.

RUCH, F.L. & ZIMBARDO, P.G. (1971). *Psychology and life.* Eighth Edition. Glenview, IL.: Scott, Foresman.

RULE, B.G. & ADAIR, J. (1984). Contributions of psychology as a social science to Canadian society. *Canadian Psychology, 25,* 52–58.

RULE, B.G., BISANZ, G.L. & KOHN, M. (1985). Anatomy of a persuasion schema: Targets, goals and strategies. *Journal of Personality and Social Psychology, 48,* 1127–1140.

RULE, B.G. & FERGUSON, T.J. (1986). The effects of media violence on attitudes, emotions and cognitions. *Journal of Social Issues, 2,* 29–50.

RULE, B.G. & NESDALE. A.R. (1974). Differing functions of aggression. *Journal of Personality, 42,* 467–481.

RULE, B.G. & NESDALE, A.R. (1976). Emotional arousal and aggressive behavior. *Psychological Bulletin, 83,* 851–863.

RUSHTON, J.P. (1975). Generosity in children: Immediate and long-term effects of modeling, preaching, and moral judgement. *Journal of Personality and Social Psychology, 31,* 459–466.

RUSHTON, J.P. (1976). Socialization and the altruistic behavior of children. *Psychological Bulletin, 83,* 898–913.

RUSHTON, J.P. (1977). Television and prosocial behaviour. *Report of the Royal Commission on Violence in the Communications Industry* (Vol. 5.) (31–56). Toronto: Government of Ontario.

RUSHTON, J.P. (1978). Urban density: Helping strangers in a Canadian city, suburb, and small town. *Psychological Reports, 43,* 987–990.

RUSHTON, J.P. (1980). *Altruism, socialization, and society.* Englewood Cliffs, NJ: Prentice-Hall.

RUSHTON, J.P. (1984). The altruistic personality. In E. Staub, D. Bar-Tal, J. Karylowski & J. Reykowski (Eds.), *Development and maintenance of prosocial behavior* (271–290). New York: Plenum Press.

RUSHTON, J.P., CHRISJOHN, R.D. & FEKKEN, G.C. (1981). The altruistic personality and the self-report altruism scale. *Personality and Individual Differences, 2,* 292–302.

RUSHTON, J.P., FULKER, D.W., NEALE, M.C., NIAS, D.K.B. & EYSENCK, H.J. (1986). Altruism and aggression: The heritability of individual differences. *Journal of Personality and Social Psychology, 50,* 1192–1198.

RUSSELL, B. (1959). *Common sense and nuclear warfare.* London: Unwin Brothers.

RUSSELL, B. (1962). *Power.* New York: Barnes & Noble.

RUSSELL, D., PEPLAU, L.A. & CUTRONA, C.E. (1980). The revised UCLA loneliness scale: Concurrent and discriminant validity evidence. *Journal of Personality and Social Psychology, 39,* 472–480.

RUSSO, N.F. & BRACKBILL, Y. (1973). Population and youth. In J.T. Fawcett (Ed.), *Psychological perspectives on population.* New York: Basic Books.

SABINI, J. & SILVER, M. (1982). *Moralities of everyday life.* Oxford; Oxford University Press.

SADAVA, S.W. (1972). Stages of college student drug use: A methodological contribution to cross-sectional study. *Journal of Consulting and Clinical Psychology, 38,* 298.

SADAVA, S.W. (1985). Problem behavior theory and consumption and consequences of alcohol use. *Journal of Studies on Alcohol, 46,* 392–397.

SADAVA, S.W. (1987). Interactional theories. In H.T. Blane & K.E. Leonard (Eds.), *Psychological theories of drinking and alcoholism* (90–130). New York: Guilford.

SADAVA, S.W., ANGUS, L. & FORSYTH, R. (1980). Perceived mental illness and diminished responsibility: A study of attributions. *Social Behavior and Personality, 8,* 129–136.

SADAVA, S.W. & FORSYTH, R. (1977a). Person-environment interaction and college student drug use: A multivariate longitudinal study. *Genetic Psychology Monographs, 96,* 211–245.

SADAVA, S.W. & FORSYTH, R. (1977b). Turning on, turning off and relapse: Social psychological determinants of status change in cannabis use. *International Journal of the Addictions, 12,* 509–528.

SADAVA, S.W. & MATEJCIC, C. (1987). Generalized and specific loneliness in early marriage. *Canadian Journal of Behavioural Science, 19,* 56–66.

SADAVA, S.W. & THOMPSON, M.M. (1986). Loneliness, social drinking and vulnerability to alcohol problems. *Canadian Journal of Behavioural Science, 18,* 133–139.

SADAVA, S.W. & WIETHE, H. (1985). Maintenance and attributions about smoking among smokers, non-smokers and ex-smokers. *International Journal of the Addictions, 20,* 1522–1544.

SAFER, M.A. (1980). Attributing evil to the subject, not the situation: Student reaction to Milgram's film on obedience. *Personality and Social Psychology Bulletin, 6,* 205–209.

SAKS, M.J. (1977). *Jury verdicts.* Lexington, MA: Lexington Books.

SAKS, M.J. & HASTIE, R. (1978). *Social psychology in court.* New York: Van Nostrand Reinhold.

SALOVEY, P. & RODIN, J. (1984). Some antecedents and consequences of social comparison jealousy. *Journal of Personality and Social Psychology, 47,* 780–792.

SAMPSON, E.E. (1975). On justice as equality. *Journal of Social Issues, 31,* 45–64.

SAMPSON, E.E. (1977). Psychology and the American ideal. *Journal of Personality and Social Psychology, 35,* 767–782.

SAMUELSON, C.D. & MESSICK, D.M. (1986). Inequities in access to and use of shared resources in social dilemmas. *Journal of Personality and Social Psychology, 51,* 960–967.

SAMUELSON, C.D., MESSICK, D.M., RUTTE, C.G. & WILKE, H. (1984). Individual and structural solutions to resource dilemmas in two cultures. *Journal of Personality and Social Psychology, 47,* 94–104.

SANDERS, G.S. (1983). An attentional process model of social facilitation. In A. Hare, H. Blumberg, V. Kent, and M. Davies (Eds.), *Small Groups*. London: Wiley.

SANDERS, G.S. & BARON, R.S. (1977). Is social comparison irrelevant for producing choice shifts? *Journal of Experimental Social Psychology, 13*, 303–314.

SANDERS, G.S., BARON, R.S. & MOORE, D.L. (1978). Distraction and social comparison as mediators of social facilitation effects. *Journal of Experimental Social Psychology, 14*, 291–303.

SARAT, A. & VIDMAR, N. (1976). Public opinion, the death penalty and the eighth amendment. Testing the Marshall hypothesis. *Wisconsin Law Review, 27*, 171–206.

SARBIN, T.R. & COE, W.C. (1972). *Hypnosis: A social psychological analysis of influential communications*. New York: Holt, Rinehart & Winston.

SARLES, R.M. (1976). Child abuse. In D.S. Madden & J.R. Lion (Eds.), *Rage, hate, assault and other forms of violence* (1–16). New York: Spectrum.

SASFY, J. & OKUM, M. (1974). Form of evaluation and audience expertness as joint determinants of audience effects. *Journal of Experimental Social Psychology, 10*, 461–467.

SASHKIN, M. (1977). The structure of charismatic leadership. In J.G. Hunt & L.L. Larson (Eds.), *Leadership: The cutting edge* (212–218). Carbondale: Southern Illinois University Press.

SATOW, K.L. (1975). Social approval and helping. *Journal of Experimental Social Psychology, 11*, 501–509.

SAUL, E.V. & KASS, T.S. (1969). Study of anticipated anxiety in a medical school setting. *Journal of Medical Education, 44*, 526.

SAULNIER, K. & PERLMAN, D. (1981). The actor-observer bias is alive and well in prison: A sequel to Wells. *Personality and Social Psychology Bulletin, 7*, 559–564.

SAWHNEY, M.M. (1967). Farm practice adoption and the use of information sources and media in a rural community in India. *Rural Sociology, 32*, 310–323.

SAWREY, J.M. & TELFORD, C.W. (1975). *Adjustment and personality*. Fifth Edition. Boston: Allyn & Bacon.

SCAMBLER, G. (1984). Perceiving and coping with stigmatizing illness. In R. Fitzpatrick, J. Hinton, S. Newman, G. Scambler & J. Thompson. *The experience of illness* (203–226). London: Tavistock Publications.

SCARR, S. (1978). From evolution to Larry P. What should we do about IQ tests? *Intelligence, 2*, 325–342.

SCHACHTER, S. (1951). Deviation, rejection and communication. *Journal of Abnormal Social Psychology, 46*, 190–207.

SCHACHTER, S. (1959). *The psychology of affiliation*. Stanford, CA: Stanford University Press.

SCHACHTER, S. (1964). The interaction of cognitive and physiological determinants of emotional state. In Leonard Berkowitz (Ed.), *Advances in experimental social psychology* (Vol. 1) (49–80). New York: Academic Press.

SCHACHTER, S. (1982). Recidivism and self-cure of smoking and obesity. *American Psychologist, 37*, 436–444.

SCHACHTER, S. & BURDECK, H. (1955). A field experiment on rumour transmission and distortion. *Journal of Abnormal and Social Psychology, 50*, 363–371.

SCHACHTER, S., DeMONCHAUX, C., MANCORPS, P., OSMER, D., DUJBER, H., ROMMETVEIT, R. & ISRAEL, J. (1954). Cross-cultural experiments on threat and rejection. *Human Relations, 7*, 403–439.

SCHACHTER, S., ELLERTSON, N., McBRIDE, D. & GREGORY, D. (1951). An experimental study of cohesiveness and productivity. *Human Relations, 4*, 229–238.

SCHACHTER, S. & SINGER, J. (1962). Cognitive, social and physiological determinants of emotional state. *Psychological Review, 69*, 379–399.

SCHELLING, T.C. (1960). *The strategy of conflict*. Cambridge: Harvard University Press.

SCHELLING, T.C. (1971). On the ecology of micromotives. *Public Interest, 25*, 61–98.

SCHERER, K.R., ABELES, R.P. & FISCHER, C.S. (1975). *Human aggression and conflict*. Englewood Cliffs, NJ: Prentice-Hall.

SCHLEGEL, R.F., MANSKE, S.R. & d'AVERNAS, J.R. (1985). Alcohol and drug use in young adults. Selected findings in a longitudinal study. *Bulletin of the Society of Psychologists in Addictive Behavior, 4*, 213–225.

SCHLEGEL, R.P. & DITECCO, D. (1982). Attitudinal resources and the attitude-behavior relation. In M.P. Zanna, E.T. Higgins & C.P. Herman (Eds.), *Consistency in social behavior: The Ontario symposium* (Vol. 2). Hillsdale, NJ: Erlbaum.

SCHLOSS, B. & GIESBRECHT, N.A. (1972). *Murder in Canada: A report on capital and non-capital murder statistics 1961–1970*. Toronto: Centre of Criminology, University of Toronto.

SCHMIDTT, B.H., GILOVICH, T., GOORE, N., & JOSEPH, L. (1986). Mere presence and socio-facilitation: One more time. *Journal of Experimental Social Psychology, 22*, 242–248.

SCHNEIDER, A.M. & TARSHIS, B. (1975). *Physiological psychology*. New York: Random House.

SCHNEIDER, D.J. (1973). Implicit personality theory: A review. *Psychological Bulletin, 79*, 294–309.

SCHNEIDMAN, E.S. (Ed.) (1980). *Death: Current Perspectives*. Second Edition. Palo Alto, CA: Mayfield.

SCHOENRADE, P.A., BATSON, D.C., BRANDT, J.R. & LOUD, R.E., Jr. (1986). Attachment, accountability, and motivation to benefit another not in distress. *Journal of Personality and Social Psychology, 51*, 557–563.

SCHOFIELD, J., & PAVELCHAK, M.A. (1984). Origins of anti-nuclear behavior: Cognitive and affective determinants. Presented at 23rd International Congress of Psychology, Acapulco, Mexico.

SCHOFIELD, J. & PAVELCHAK, M. (1985). The day after. Impact of a media event. *American Psychologist, 40,* 542–548.

SCHOPLER, J. & BATESON, N. (1965). The power of dependence. *Journal of Personality and Social Psychology, 2,* 247–254.

SCHRAM, W., LYLE, J. & PARKER, E.B. (1961). *Television in the lives of our children.* Stanford, CA: Stanford University Press.

SCHULTZ, D.P. (1964). *Panic behavior.* New York: Random House.

SCHWARTZ, S.H. (1970). Elicitation of moral obligation and self-sacrificing behavior: An experimental study of volunteering to be a bone marrow donor. *Journal of Personality and Social Psychology, 15,* 283–293.

SCHWARTZ, S.H. (1977). Normative influences on altruism. In L. Berkowitz (Ed.), *Advances in experimental social psychology (Vol. 10)* (221–279).

SCHWARTZ, S.H. & CLAUSEN, G. (1970). Responsibility, norms, and helping in an emergency. *Journal of Personality and Social Psychology, 16,* 299–310.

SCHWARTZ, S.H. & TESSLER, R.C. (1972). A test of a model for reducing measured attitude-behavior discrepancies. *Journal of Personality and Social Psychology, 24,* 225–236.

SCHWEBEL, M. (1982). Effects of the nuclear war threat on children and teenagers: Implications for professionals. *American Journal of Orthopsychiatry, 52,* 608–618.

SEARLE, J.R. (1969). *Speech acts.* Cambridge: Cambridge University Press.

SEARLE, J.R. (1975). Indirect speech acts. In P. Cole & J.L. Morgan (Eds.), *Syntax and semantics 3: Speech acts* (283–298). Hillsdale, NJ: Erlbaum.

SEARS, D.O. (1983). The person-positivity bias. *Journal of Personality and Social Psychology, 44,* 233–250.

SEARS, D.O. (1986). College sophomores in the laboratory: Influences of a narrow data base on social psychology's view of human nature. *Journal of Personality and Social Psychology, 51,* 515–530.

SEARS, D.O. & ABELES, R.P. (1969). Attitudes and opinions. *Annual Review of Psychology, 20,* 253–288.

SEBEOK, T.A. & ROSENTHAL, R. (1981). *The Clever Hans phenomenon: Communication with horses, whales, apes and people.* New York: New York Academy of Sciences.

SEGALOWITZ, N. (1976). Communicative incompetence and the non-fluent bilingual. *Canadian Journal of Behavioural Science, 8,* 122–131.

SELIGMAN, C., DARLEY, J.M. & BECKER, L.J. (1978). Behavioral approaches to residential energy conservation. *Energy and Buildings, 1,* 325–337.

SELIGMAN, C., FAZIO, R.H. & ZANNA, M.P. (1980). Effects of salience of extrinsic rewards on liking and loving. *Journal of Personality and Social Psychology, 38,* 453–460.

SELIGMAN, C.R., TUCKER, G.R. & LAMBERT, W.E. (1972). The effects of speech style and other attributes on teachers' attitudes towards pupils. *Language in Society, 1,* 131–142.

SELIGMAN, M.E.P. (1975). *Helplessness: On depression, development and death.* San Francisco: W.H. Freeman.

SENSENIG, P.E. & CIALDINI, R.B. (1984). Social psychological influences on the compliance process: Implications for behavioral health. In J.D. Matarazzo, S.M. Weiss, J.A. Herd, N.E. Miller & S.M. Weiss (Eds.), *Behavioral health* (384–392). Toronto: Wiley.

SERMAT, V. (1978). Sources of loneliness. *Essence, 2,* 271–276.

SERMAT, V. & SMYTH, M. (1973). Content analysis in the development of a relationship. *Journal of Personality and Social Psychology, 25,* 332–346.

SHANTEAU, J. & NAGY, G.F. (1979). Probability of acceptance in dating choice. *Journal of Personality and Social Psychology, 37,* 522–533.

SHAVER, K.G. (1970). Defensive attribution: Effects of severity and relevance on the responsibility assigned for an accident. *Journal of Personality and Social Psychology, 14,* 101–113.

SHAW, M.E. (1981). *Group dynamics: The psychology of small group behavior.* Third Edition. New York: McGraw-Hill.

SHEPHERD, J.W., DEREGOWSKI, J.B. & ELLIS, H.D. (1974). A cross-cultural study of recognition memory for faces. *International Journal of Psychology, 9,* 205–211.

SHEPPARD, A. (1981). Responses to cartoons and attitudes toward aging. *Journal of Gerontology, 36,* 122–126.

SHEPPARD, B.H. & VIDMAR, N. (1980). Adversary pretrial procedure and testimonial evidence: Effects of lawyer's role and Machiavellianism. *Journal of Personality and Social Psychology, 39,* 320–332.

SHERIF, M. (1935). A study of some social factors in perception. *Archives of Psychology, 27,* No. 187.

SHERIF, M. (1936). *The psychology of social norms.* New York: Harper & Row.

SHERIF, M. (1937). An experimental approach to the study of attitudes. *Sociometry, 1,* 90–98.

SHERIF, M. (1958). Superordinate goals in the reduction of intergroup conflict. *American Journal of Sociology,* 349–356.

SHERIF, M., HARVEY, O.J., WHITE, B.J., HOOD, W.R. & SHERIF, C. (1961). *Intergroup conflict and cooperation: The Robber's Cave experiment.* Norman: University of Oklahoma Press.

SHERIF, M. & SHERIF, C. (1953). Groups in harmony and tension: An integration of studies in intergroup behavior. New York: Harper & Row.

SHERIF, M. & SHERIF, C.W. (1969). *Social Psychology.* New York: Harper & Row.

SHERIF, C.W., SHERIF, M. & NEBERGALL, R.E. (1965). *Attitude and attitude change: The social judgement-involvement approach.* Philadelphia: W.B. Saunders.

SHERIFF, M. & HOVLAND, C.I. (1961). *Social Judgement: Assimilation and contrast effects in communication and attitude change.* New Haven: Yale University Press.

SHERROD, D.R. (1974). Crowding, perceived control and behavioral aftereffects. *Journal of Applied Social Psychology, 4,* 171–186.

SHERROD, D.A., HAGE, J.N., HALPERN, P.L. & MOORE, B.S. (1977). Effects of personal causation and perceived control on responses to an aversive environment. The more control, the better. *Journal of Experimental Social Psychology, 13,* 14–27.

SHETZ, J.N. (1974). An investigation of relationships among evaluative beliefs, affect, behavioral intentions, and behavior. In J.V. Farley, J.A. Howard, & L.W. Ring (Eds.), *Consumer behavior: Theory and applications* (89–114). Boston: Allyn & Bacon.

SHIBUTANI, T. (1966). *Improvised news: A sociological study of rumor.* Indianapolis: Bobbs-Merrill.

SHILS, E.A. (1965). Charisma, order and status. *American Sociological Review, 30,* 199–213.

SHOCKLEY, W. (1971). Models, mathematics and moral obligation to diagnose the origin of Negro IQ deficits. *Review of Educational Research, 41,* 369–377.

SIEGEL, A.E. & SIEGEL, S. (1957). Reference groups, membership groups, and attitude change. *Journal of Abnormal and Social Psychology, 55,* 360–364.

SIEM, F.M. & SPENCE, J.T. (1986). Gender-related traits and helping behaviors. *Journal of Personality and Social Psychology, 51,* 615–621.

SIGALL, H. & LANDY, D. (1973). Radiating beauty: The effects of having a physically attractive partner on person perception. *Journal of Personality and Social Psychology, 28,* 218–224.

SIGALL, H. & OSTROVE, N. (1975). Beautiful but dangerous: Effects of offender attractiveness and nature of the crime on juridic judgement. *Journal of Personality and Social Psychology, 31,* 410–414.

SIGALL, H. & PAGE, R. (1971). Current stereotypes: A little fading, a little faking. *Journal of Personality and Social Psychology, 18,* 247–255.

SIGALL, H. & PAGE, R. (1972). Reducing attenuation in the expression of interpersonal affect via the bogus pipeline. *Sociometry, 35,* 629–642.

SIGNORIELLI, N., GROSS, L. & MORGAN, M. (1982). Violence in television programs: Ten years later. In D. Pearl, L. Bouthilet & J. Lazar (Eds.), *Television and behav-* *ior: Ten years of scientific progress and implications for the eighties: Vol. 2, Technical reviews* (158–173). Washington: United States Government Printing Office.

SILVER, R.L., BOON, C. & STONES, M.H. (1983). Searching for meaning in misfortune: Making sense of incest. *Journal of Social Issues, 39,* 81–100.

SILVERMAN, I. (1971). On the resolution and tolerance of cognitive consistency in a natural occurring event: Attitudes and beliefs following the Senator Edward M. Kennedy incident. *Journal of Personality and Social Psychology, 17,* 171–178.

SILVERMAN, I. (1974). Some hedonistic considerations regarding altruistic behavior. Paper presented at the Southeastern Psychological Association Annual Meeting, Miami.

SILVERMAN, I. (1977). *The human subject in the psychological experiment.* Elmsford, NY: Pergamon Press.

SIMARD, L., TAYLOR, D.M. & GILES, H. (1977). Attribution processes and interpersonal accommodation in a bilingual setting. *Language and Speech, 19,* 374–387.

SIMON, R.J. & MAHAN, L. (1971). Quantifying burdens of proof: A view from the bench, the jury and the classroom. *Law and Society Review, 5,* 319–330.

SIMON, T.R. & HARDYK, C.D. (1953). Contributions to role-taking theory: Role perception on the basis of postural cues. Unpublished manuscript. Cited by Argyle (1975).

SIMS, H.P. & MANZ, C.C. (1984). Observing leader verbal behavior: Toward reciprocal determinism in leadership theory. *Journal of Applied Psychology, 69,* 222–232.

SINGER, B.D. (1970). Violence, protest and war in television news. The U.S. and Canada compared. *Public Opinion Quarterly, 34,* 611–619.

SINGER, D.G. (1983). A time to reexamine the role of television in our lives. *American Psychologist, 38,* 815–816.

SINGER, J.E. (1964). The use of manipulative strategies: Machiavellianism and attractiveness. *Sociometry, 27,* 128–150.

SINGER, J.E., BAUM, C.S., BAUM, A. & THEW, B.D. (1982). Mass psychogenic illness: The case for social comparison. In M.J. Colligan, J.W. Pennebaker & L.R. Murphy (Eds.), *Mass psychogenic illness* (155–170). Hillsdale, NJ: Erlbaum.

SINGER, J.L. & SINGER, D.G. (1981). *Television, imagination, and aggression: A study of pre-schoolers.* Hillsdale, NJ: Erlbaum.

SINGER, J.L. & SINGER, D.G. (1986). Family experiences and television viewing as predictors of children's imagination, restlessness and aggression. *Journal of Social Issues, 42,* 107–124.

SINGH, V.P. & PAREEK, U. (1970). Discriminant function in a profile pattern of key communicators in an Indian village. *International Journal of Psychology, 5,* 99–107.

SIROIS, F. (1982). Perspectives on epidemic hysteria. In M.J. Colligan, J.W. Pennebaker & L.R. Murphy (Eds.), *Mass psychogenic illness: A social psychological analysis* (217–236). Hillsdale, NJ: Erlbaum.

SISTRUNK, F. & McDAVID, V.W. (1971). Sex variable in conformity behavior. *Journal of Personality and Social Psychology, 17,* 200–207.

SIVACEK, J. & CRANO, W.D. (1982). Vested interest as a moderator of attitude-behavior consistency. *Journal of Personality and Social Psychology, 43,* 210–221.

SKINNER, B.F. (1957). *Verbal Behavior.* New York: Appleton-Century-Crofts.

SMART, R.G. & FEJER, D. (1972). Drug use among adolescents and their parents: Closing the generation gap in mood modification. *Journal of Abnormal Psychology, 79,* 153–160.

SMART, R.G. & GOODSTADT, M.S. (1977). Effects of reducing the legal alcohol-purchasing age on drinking and drinking problems. *Journal of Studies on Alcohol, 38,* 1313–1323.

SMITH, H.P. (1955). Do intercultural experiences affect attitudes? *Journal of Abnormal and Social Psychology, 51,* 469–477.

SMITH, K.K. & WHITE, G.L. (1983). Some alternatives to traditional social psychology of groups. *Personality and Social Psychology Bulletin, 9,* 65–73.

SMITH, P.M. (1985). *Language, the sexes and society.* Oxford: Basil Blackwell.

SMITH, R.A., HINGSON, R.W., MORELOCK, S., HEEREN, T., MUCATEL., M., MONGRONE, T. & SCOTCH, N. (1984). Legislation raising the drinking age in Massachusetts from 18 to 20: Effect on 16 and 17 year-olds. *Journal of Studies on Alcohol, 45,* 534–539.

SMITH, T.W. (1984). The polls: Gender and attitudes toward violence. *Public Opinion Quarterly, 48,* 384–396.

SMYTHE, P.C., STENNETT, R.G & FEENSTRA, H.J. (1972). Attitude, aptitude, and type of instructional programme in second-language acquisition. *Canadian Journal of Behavioural Science, 4,* 307–321.

SNAREY, J.R. (1985). Cross-cultural universality of social-moral development: A critical review of Kohlbergian research. *Psychological Bulletin, 97,* 202–232.

SNOW, C.P. (1961). Either-or. *Progressive,* February 24.

SNYDER, M. (1979). Self-monitoring processes. In L. Berkowitz (Ed.), *Advances in experimental social psychology* (Vol. 12). New York: Academic Press.

SNYDER, M. & DeBONO, K.G. (1985). Appeals to image and claims about quality: Understanding the psychology of advertising. *Journal of Personality and Social Psychology, 49,* 586–597.

SOLANO, C.H., BATTEN, P.G. & PARISH, E.A. (1982). Loneliness and patterns of self-disclosure. *Journal of Personality and Social Psychology, 43,* 524–531.

SOLANTAUS, T., RIMPELA, M. & TAIPALE, V. (1984). The threat of war in the minds of 12–18 year olds in Finland. *The Lancet, 8380,* 784–785.

SOLE, K., MARTON, J. & HORNSTEIN, H.A. (1975). Opinion similarity and helping: Three field experiments investigating the bases of promotive tension. *Journal of Experimental Social Psychology, 11,* 1–13.

SOLOMON, D. & YAEGER, J. (1969). Effect of content and intonation on perceptions of verbal reinforcers. *Perceptual and Motor Skills, 28,* 319–327.

SOLOMON, L. (1960). The influence of some types of power relationships and game strategies upon the development of interpersonal trust. *Journal of Abnormal and Social Psychology, 61,* 223–230.

SOLOMON, M.R. (1986). Dress for effect. *Psychology Today, 20 (4),* 20–28.

SOMMER, R. & ROSS, H. (1958). Social interaction on a geriatric ward. *International Journal of Social Psychiatry. 4,* 128–133.

SPANOS, N.P. (1982). Hypnotic behavior: A cognitive, social psychological perspective. *Research Communications in Psychology, Psychiatry and Behavior, 3,* 199–213.

SPEARS, R., VAN DER PLIGT, J. & EISER, J.R. (1985). Illusory correlation in the perception of group attitudes. *Journal of Personality and Social Psychology, 48,* 863–875.

SPECHER, S., DeLAMATER, J., NEUMAN, N., NEUMAN, M., KAHN, P., ORBUCH, D. & McKINNEY, K. (1984). Asking questions in bars. *Personality and Social Psychology Bulletin, 110,* 482–488.

SPEER, ALBERT (1970). *Inside the Third Reich.* Toronto: MacMillan.

SPENCE, J.T. & HELMREICH, R.L. (1978). *Masculinity and femininity: Their psychological dimensions, correlates and antecedents.* Austin: University of Texas Press.

SPENCE, J.T. & HELMREICH, R.L. (1981). Androgyny versus gender scheme: A comment on Bem's gender scheme theory. *Psychological Review, 88,* 365–368.

SPINNER, B., ADAIR, J.G. & BARNES, G.E. (1977). A reexamination of the faithful subject role. *Journal of Experimental Social Psychology, 13,* 543–551.

SPRAFKIN, J.N., LIEBERT, R.M. & POULOS, R.W. (1975). Effects of a prosocial televised example on children's helping. *Journal of Experimental Child Psychology, 20,* 119–126.

SRULL, T.K. & WYER, R.S., Jr. (1979). Role of category accessibility in the interpretation of information about persons: Some determinants and implications. *Journal of Personality and Social Psychology, 37,* 1660–1672.

SRULL, T.K. & WYER, R.S., Jr. (1980). Category accessibility and social perception: Some implications for the study of personal memory and interpersonal judgements. *Journal of Personality and Social Psychology, 38,* 841–856.

STAATS, A.W. & STAATS, C.K. (1958). Attitudes established by classical conditioning. *Journal of Applied Social Psychology, 57,* 37–40.

STAFFIERI, J.R. (1972). Body build and behavioural expectancies in young females. *Developmental Psychology, 6,* 125–127.

STAGNER, R. (1967). *Psychological aspects of international conflict.* Belmont, CA: Brooks/Cole.

STANG, D.J. (1972). Conformity, ability, and self-esteem. *Representative Research in Social Psychology, 3,* 97–103.

STANLEY, P.R. & RIERA, B. (1977). Replications of media violence. In *Report of the Royal Commission on Violence in the Communications Industry* (Vol. 5) (89–170). Toronto: Publication Centre, Government of Ontario.

STATISTICS CANADA (1977). *Perspectives Canada II.* Ottawa: Ministry of Supply and Services Canada.

STATISTICS CANADA (1980). *Perspectives Canada III.* Ottawa: Ministry of Supply and Services Canada.

STATISTICS CANADA (1985). *Language in Canada.* Ottawa: Ministry of Supply and Services Canada.

STAUB, E. (1970a). A child in distress: The effects of focusing responsibility on children on their attempts to help. *Developmental Psychology, 2,* 152–153.

STAUB, E. (1970b). A child in distress: The influence of age and the number of witnesses on children's attempts to help. *Journal of Personality and Social Psychology, 14,* 130–141.

STAUB, E. (1971). A child in distress: The influence of nurturance and modeling on children's attempts to help. *Developmental Psychology, 5,* 124–132.

STAUB, E. (1974). Helping a distressed person: Social, personality and stimulus determinants. In L. Berkowitz (Ed.), *Advances in experimental social psychology* (Vol. 7). New York: Academic Press.

STAUB, E. (1975). *The development of prosocial behavior in children.* Morristown, NJ: Silver Burdett/General Learning Press.

STAUB, E. & BAER, R.S. (1974). Stimulus characteristics of a sufferer and difficulty of escape as determinants of helping. *Journal of Personality and Social Psychology, 30,* 279–285.

STAUB, E. & FEAGANS, L. (1969). Effects of age and number of witnesses on children's attempt to help another child in distress. Paper presented at the Eastern Psychological Association Annual Meeting, Philadelphia.

STEELE, C.M. & LIU, T.J. (1983). Dissonance process as self-affirmation. *Journal of Personality and Social Psychology, 45,* 5–19.

STEELE, C.M., SOUTHWICK, L.C. & CRITCHLOW, B. (1981). Dissonance and alcohol: Drinking your troubles away. *Journal of Personality and Social Psychology, 41,* 831–846.

STEINER, I.D. (1972). *Group process and productivity.* New York: Academic press.

STEPHAN, C.W. & STEPHAN, W.G. (1986). Habla ingles? The effects of language translation on simulated juror decisions. *Journal of Applied Social Psychology, 16,* 577–589.

STEPHAN, W.G. (1985). Intergroup relations. In G. Lindzey & E. Aronson (Eds.), *Handbook of social psychology.* Third Edition. (599–698). New York: Random House.

STEPHAN, W.G., BERSCHEID, E. & WALSTER, E. (1971). Sexual arousal and heterosexual perception. *Journal of Personality and Social Psychology, 20,* 93–101.

STEPHAN, W.G. & STEPHAN, C.W. (1985). Intergroup anxiety. *Journal of Social Issues, 41,* 157–175.

STERNBERG, R.J. (1986). A triangular theory of love. *Psychological Review, 93,* 119–135.

STERNBERG, R.J., CONWAY, B.E., KETRON, J.L. & BERNSTEIN, M. (1981). People's conceptions of intelligence. *Journal of Personality and Social Psychology, 41,* 37–55.

STEWART, R. (1965). Effects of continuous responding on the order effect in personality impression formation. *Journal of Personality and Social Psychology, 1,* 161–165.

STOGDILL, R. (1974). *Handbook of leadership.* New York: Free Press.

STONE, A. & NEALE, J.M. (1982). Development of a methodology for assessing daily experiences. In A. Baum & J.E. Singer (Eds.), *Advances in environmental psychology* (Vol. 4). Hillsdale: Erlbaum.

STONE, G.C. (1979). Patient compliance and the role of the expert. *Journal of Social Issues, 35,* 34–59.

STORMS, M.D. (1973). Videotape and the attribution process: Reversing actor's and observer's points of view. *Journal of Personality and Social Psychology, 27,* 165–175.

STORMS, M.D. & NISBETT, R.E. (1970). Insomnia and the attribution process. *Journal of Personality and Social Psychology, 16,* 319–328.

STORY, G.M., KIRWIN, W.J. & WIDDOWSON, J.D.A. (1982). *Dictionary of Newfoundland English.* Toronto: University of Toronto Press.

STOVER, E. & NIGHTINGALE, E.O. (1985). *The breaking of bodies and minds. Torture, psychiatric abuse, and the health professions.* New York: W.H. Freeman.

STREETER, L.A., KRAUSS, R.M., GELLER, V., OLSON, C. & APPLE, W. (1977). Pitch changes during attempted deception. *Journal of Personality and Social Psychology, 35,* 345–350.

STRICKER, L.J., MESSICK, S. & JACKSON, D.N. (1970). Conformity, anticonformity and independence: Their dimensionality and generality. *Journal of Experimental Social Psychology, 16,* 494–507.

STRICKLAND, B.R. (1978). Internal-external expectancies and health-related behaviors. *Journal of Consulting and Clinical Psychology, 46,* 1192–1211.

STRODTBECK, F.L. & LIPINSKI, R.M. (1985). Becoming first among equals: Moral considerations in jury foreman selection. *Journal of Personality and Social Psychology*, *49*, 927–936.

STROEBE, M.S. & STROEBE, W. (1983). Who suffers more? Sex differences in health risks of the widowed. *Psychological Bulletin*, *93*, 279–301.

STROEBE, W.H., STROEBE, M., GERGEN, K.J. & GERGEN, M.M. (1982). The effects of bereavement on mortality: A social psychological analysis. In J.R. Eisere (Ed.), *Social psychology and behavioral medicine*. London: Wiley.

STRUBE, M.J. & GARCIA, J.E. (1981). A meta-analytic investigation of Fiedler's contingency model of leadership effectiveness. *Psychological Bulletin*, *90*, 307–321.

SUEDFELD, P. & PIEDRAHITA, L.E. (1984). Intimations of mortality: Integrative simplification as a precursor of death. *Journal of Personality and Social Psychology*, *47*, 848–852.

SUEDFELD, P. & RANK, A.D. (1976). Revolutionary leaders: Long-term success as a function of changes in conceptual complexity. *Journal of Personality and Social Psychology*, *34*, 169–176.

SUEDFELD, P., RANK, D. & BORRIE, R. (1975). Frequency of exposure and evaluation of candidates and campaign speeches. *Journal of Applied Psychology*, *5*, 118–126.

SUMNER, W.G., KELLER, A.G. & DAVIE, M.R. (1927). *The science of society* (Vol. 4). Oxford: Oxford University Press.

SUNDSTROM, E., HERBERT, R.K. & BROWN, D. (1982). Privacy and communication in an open office plan. *Environment and Behavior*, *14*, 379–392.

SURLIN, F.H. & TATE, E.D. (1977). "All in the family": Is Archie funny? *Journal of Communications*, *27*, 61–68.

SUTTON, S.R. (1982). Fear-arousing communications: A critical examination of theory and research. In J.R. Eiser (Ed.), *Social psychology and behavioral medicine* (303–338). New York: Wiley.

SWACEK, J. & CRONO, W.D. (1982). Vested interest as a moderator of attitude-behavior consistency. *Journal of Personality and Social Psychology*, *43*, 210–221.

SWAIN, M. AND BARIK, H.C. (1976). Bilingual education for the English-Canadian: Recent developments. In A. Simoes, Jr. (Ed.), *The bilingual child* (91–112). New York: Academic Press.

SWANN, W.B. & READ, S.J. (1981). Acquiring self-knowledge: The search for feedback that fits. *Journal of Personality and Social Psychology*, *41*, 1119–1128.

SWEET, W.H., ERVIN, F. & MARK, V.H. (1969). The relationship of violent behaviour to focal cerebral disease. In S. Garattini & E.B. Sigg (Eds.), *Aggressive behaviour* (336–352). New York: Wiley.

SWENNSON, R.G. (1967). Cooperation in the Prisoner's Dilemma game I: the effect of asymmetric payoff information and explicit communication. *Behavioral Science*, *12*, 314–322.

SWINGLE, P.G. (1968). Illusory power in a dangerous game. *Canadian Journal of Psychology*, *22*, 176–185.

SWINGLE, P.G. (1970). Dangerous games. In P.G. Swingle (Ed.), *The structure of conflict* (235–276). New York: Academic Press.

TAJFEL, H. (1970). Experiments in intergroup discrimination. *Scientific American*, *223*, 5, 96–102.

TAJFEL, H. (Ed.) (1978). *Differentiation between social groups: Studies in the social psychology of inter-group relations*. London: Academic Press.

TAJFEL, H. (1982). Social psychology of intergroup relations. *Annual Review of Psychology*, *33*, 1–39.

TAJFEL, H. & BILLIG, M. (1974). Familiarity and categorization in intergroup behavior. *Journal of Experimental Social Psychology*, *10*, 159–170.

TAJFEL, H., BILLIG, M., BUNDY, R. & FILAMENT, C. (1971). Social categorization and intergroup behavior. *European Journal of Social Psychology*, *1*, 149–178.

TAJFEL, H. & TURNER, J.C., (1979). An integrative theory of intergroup conflict. In W.G. Austin & S. Worchel (Eds.), *The social psychology of intergroup relations*. (33–47). Monterey, CA: Brooks/Cole.

TANFORD, S., & PENROD, S. (1984). Social influence model: A formal integration of research on majority and minority influence processes. *Psychological Bulletin*, *95*, 189–225.

TANNENBAUM, P.H. (1967). The congruity principle revisited: Studies in the reduction, induction, and generalization of persuasion. In L. Berkowitz (Ed.), *Advances in experimental social psychology* (Vol. 3) (270–320). New York: Academic Press.

TAPP, J.L. (1970). Psychology and the law: An overture. In M.R. Rosenzweig & L.W. Porter (Eds.), *Annual review of psychology* (Vol. 27). Palo Alto, CA: Annual Reviews.

TAPP, J.L. (1980). Psychological and policy perspectives on the law: Reflections on a decade. *Journal of Social Issues*, *36*, 165–192.

TATE, E.D. (1977). Viewers' perceptions of selected television programs. In *Report of the Royal Commission on Violence in the Communications Industry* (Vol. 6) (283–401). Toronto: Publication Centre, Government of Ontario.

TATE, E.D. & SURLIN, H.F. (1976). Agreement with opinionated television characters: A cross-cultural comparison. *Journal Quarterly*, *53*, 199–203.

TAYLOR, D.M. (1981). Stereotypes and intergroup relations. In R.C. Gardner & R. Kalin (Eds.), *A Canadian social psychology of ethnic relations* (151–171). Toronto: Methuen.

TAYLOR, D.M. & GARDNER, R.C. (1969). Ethnic stereotypes: Their effects on the perception of communicators of varying credibility. *Canadian Journal of Psychology, 23,* 161–173.

TAYLOR, D.M. & McKIRNAN, D.J. (1984). A five-stage model of intergroup relations. *British Journal of Social Psychology, 23,* 291–300.

TAYLOR, D.M. & SIMARD, L. (1975). Social interaction in a bilingual setting. *Canadian Psychological Review, 16,* 240–254.

TAYLOR, D.M., SIMARD, L.M. & ABOUD, F.E. (1972). Ethnic identification in Canada: A cross-cultural investigation. *Canadian Journal of Behavioural Science, 4,* 13–20.

TAYLOR, M.C. & HALL, J.A. (1980). Psychological androgyny: Theories, methods and conclusions. *Psychological Bulletin, 92,* 347–366.

TAYLOR, S.E. (1975). On inferring one's attitudes from one's behavior: Some delimiting conditions. *Journal of Personality and Social Psychology, 31,* 126–131.

TAYLOR, S.E. (1979). Hospital patient behavior: Reactance, helplessness or control? *Journal of Social Issues, 35,* 156–184.

TAYNOR, J. & DEAUX, K. (1973). Equity and perceived sex differences: Role behavior as defined by the task, the mode, and the actor. *Journal of Personality and Social Psychology, 32,* 381–390.

TEDESCHI, J.T. (1970). Threats and promises. In P.G. Swingle (Ed.), *The structure of conflict* (155–193). New York: Academic Press.

TEDESCHI, J.T. (1983). Social influence theory and aggression. In R.G. Geen & E.I. Donnerstein (Eds.), *Aggression: Theoretical and empirical reviews* (Vol. 1) (135–162). New York: Academic Press.

TEDESCHI, J.T., SMITH, R.B. & BROWN, R.C. (1974). A reinterpretation of research on aggression. *Psychological Bulletin, 81,* 540–562.

TEPPERMAN, L. (1977). *Crime control.* Toronto: McGraw-Hill Ryerson.

TERHUNE, K.W. (1968). Motives, situation, and interpersonal conflict within the Prisoner's Dilemma. *Journal of Personality and Social Psychology, 8,* Monograph Supplement, Part 2.

TERHUNE, K.W. (1970). The effects of personality in cooperation and conflict. In P.G. Swingle (Ed.), *The structure of conflict* (193–234). New York: Academic Press.

TESSER, A. (1978). Self-generated attitude change. In L. Berkowitz (Ed.), *Advances in experimental social psychology* (Vol. 11). New York: Academic Press.

TESSER, A. & PAULHUS, D.L. (1976). Toward a causal model of love. *Journal of Personality and Social Psychology, 34,* 1095–1105.

TESSER, A. & ROSEN, S. (1975). Why subjects say they would or would not communicate affectively-toned messages. Paper presented at the annual meeting of Southeastern Psychological Association, Atlanta, GA.

TETLOCK, P.E. (1979). Identifying victims of groupthink from public statements of decision makers. *Journal of Personality and Social Psychology, 37,* 1314–1324.

TETLOCK, P.E. (1983). Policymakers' images of international conflict. *Journal of Social Issues, 39,* 67–86.

TETLOCK, P.E. (1984). Cognitive style and political belief systems in the British House of Commons. *Journal of Personality and Social Psychology, 46,* 365–375.

TETLOCK, P.E. (1986). A value pluralism model of ideological reasoning. *Journal of Personality and Social Psychology, 50,* 819–827.

THAYER, S. & SAARNI, C. (1975). Demand characteristics are everywhere (anyway): A comment on the Stanford prison experiment. *American Psychologist, 30,* 1015–1016.

THIBAUT, J.W. & KELLEY, H.H. (1959). *The social psychology of groups.* New York: Wiley.

THIBAUT, J. & WALKER, L. (1975). *Procedural justice: A psychological analysis.* Hillsdale, NJ: Erlbaum.

THISTLETHWAITE, D.L. (1950). Attitude and structure as factors in the distortion of reasoning. *Journal of Abnormal and Social Psychology, 45,* 442–458.

THOMAS, M.H., HORTON, R.W., LIPPINCOTT, E.C. & DRABSMAN, R.S. (1977). Desensitization to portrayals of real-life aggression as a function of exposure to television violence. *Journal of Personality and Social Psychology, 35,* 450–458.

THOMPSON, H.L. & RICHARDSON, D.R. (1983). The rooster effect: Same-sex rivalry and inequity as factors in retaliatory aggression. *Personality and Social Psychology Bulletin, 9,* 415–525.

THOMPSON, K.S. & OSKAMP, S. (1974). Difficulties in replicating the proselytizing effect in doomsday groups. *Psychological Reports, 35,* 971–978.

THOMPSON, W.P. (1965). Saskatchewan doctors' opinions of "Medicare": A questionnaire survey. *Canadian Medical Association Journal, 93,* 971–976.

THORNTON, B. (1977). Effect of rape victim's attractiveness in a jury simulation. *Personality and Social Psychology Bulletin, 3,* 666–669.

THURSTONE, L.L. (1931). The measurement of attitudes. *Journal of Abnormal and Social Psychology, 26,* 249–269.

THURSTONE, L.L. & CHAVE, E.J. (1929). *The measurement of attitude.* Chicago: University of Chicago Press.

TITMUSS, R.M. (1971). *The gift relationship: From human blood to social policy.* New York: Random House.

TOCH, H. (1965). *The social psychology of social movements.* Indianapolis: Bobbs-Merrill.

TOCH, H. (1969). *Violent men.* Chicago: Aldine.

TRAUPMANN, J. & HATFIELD, E. (1981). Love and its effect on mental and physical health. In R. Fogel, E. Hatfield, S. Kiesler & E. Shanas (Eds.), *Aging: Stability and change in the family* (253–274). New York: Academic Press.

TRAVIS, L.E. (1925). The effect of a small audience upon eye-hand coordination. *Journal of Abnormal and Social Psychology, 20,* 142–146.

TREMBLAY, M. (1953). Orientations de la pensée sociale. In J.C. Falardeau (Ed.), *Essais sur le Québec contemporain.* Québec: Les Presses Universitaires Laval.

TRIANDIS, H.C. (1967). Toward an analysis of the components of interpersonal attitudes. In C. Sherif and M. Sherif (Eds.), *Attitudes, ego-involvement, and change.* New York: Wiley.

TRIANDIS, H.C. (1971). *Attitude and attitude change.* New York: Wiley.

TRIANDIS, H.C. (1972). *The analysis of subjective culture.* New York: John Wiley & Sons.

TRIANDIS, H.C. & BRISLIN, R.W. (Eds.) (1980). *Handbook of cross-cultural psychology: Social psychology* (Vol. 5). Boston: Allyn & Bacon.

TRIPLET, R.G. & SUGARMAN, D.B. (1987). Reactions to AIDS victims: Ambiguity breeds contempt. *Personality and Social Psychology Bulletin, 13,* 265–274.

TRIPLETT, N. (1897). The dynamogenic factors in pace-making and competition. *American Journal of Psychology, 9,* 507–533.

TURCO, R.P., TOON, O.B., ACKERMAN, T.P., POLLACK, J.B. & SAGAN, C. (1983). Nuclear winter: Global consequences of multiple nuclear explosions. *Science, 222,* 1283–1292.

TURNER, C.W., HESSE, B.W. & PETERSON-LEWIS, S. (1986). Naturalistic studies of the long-term effects of television violence. *Journal of Social Issues, 42,* 51–73.

TURNER, J.C. (1982). Toward a cognitive redefinition of the social group. In H. Tajfel (Ed.), *Social identity and intergroup relations* (15–40). Cambridge: Cambridge University Press.

TURNER, J.C. (1985). Social categorization and the self-concept: A social-cognitive theory of group behaviour. In J.E. Lawler (Ed.), *Advances in group processes* (Vol. 2) (77–122). Greenwich: JAI Press.

TURNER, R.H. (1964). Collective behaviour. In R.E.L. Faris (Ed.), *Handbook of modern sociology* (382–425). Chicago: Rand McNally.

TURNER, R.H. & KILLIAM, L.M. (1972). *Collective behavior.* Second Edition. Englewood Cliffs, NJ: Prentice-Hall.

TVERSKY, A. & KAHNEMAN, D. (1974). Judgement under uncertainty: heuristics and biases. *Science, 185,* 1124–1131.

TWYCROSS, R.G. (1974). Clinical experience with diamorphine in advanced malignant disease. *International Journal of Clinical Pharmacology, Therapy and Toxicology, 9,* 184–198.

TYLER, T.R. & McGRAW, K.M. (1983). The threat of nuclear war: Risk interpretation and behavioral response. *Journal of Social Issues, 39,* 25–40.

TYLER, T.R. & SEARS, D.O. (1977). Coming to like obnoxious people when we must live with them. *Journal of Personality and Social Psychology, 35,* 200–211.

UBBINK, E.M. & SADAVA, S.W. (1974). Rotter's generalized expectancies as predictors of helping behavior. *Psychological Reports, 35,* 865–866.

UNDERWOOD, B., FROMING, W.J. & MOORE, B.S. (1977). Mood, attention, and altruism: A search for mediating variables. *Developmental Psychology, 13,* 541–542.

UNGER, D.G. & WANDERSMAN, L.P. (1985). Social support and adolescent mothers: Action research contributions to theory and applications. *Journal of Social Issues, 41,* 29–46.

UPSHAW, H.S. (1965). The effects of variable perspectives on judgements of opinion statements for Thurstone scales: Equal appearing intervals. *Journal of Personality and Social Psychology, 2,* 60–69.

VALENSTEIN, E.S. (1975). Brain stimulation and behavior control. *Nebraska Symposium on Motivation, 22,* 251–292.

VALLERAND, R.J. & REID, G. (1984). On the causal effects of perceived competence on intrinsic motivation: A test of cognitive evaluation theory. *Journal of Sports Psychology, 6,* 94–102.

VANDER ZANDEN, J.W. (1977). *Social psychology.* New York: Random House.

VANTRESS, F.E. & WILLIAMS, C.B. (1972). The effect of the presence of the provocator and the opportunity to counteraggress on systolic blood pressure. *Journal of General Psychology, 86,* 63–68.

VEEVERS, J.E. (1971). Drinking attitudes and drinking behavior: An exploratory study. *Journal of Social Psychology, 85,* 103–109.

VIDMAR, N. (1974). Retributive and utilitarian motives of Canadian attitudes toward the death penalty. *Canadian Psychologist, 15,* 337–356.

VIDMAR, N. & ROKEACH, M. (1974). Archie Bunker's bigotry: A study in selective perception and experience. *Journal of Communication, 24,* 36–47.

VINACKE, W.E. (1969). Variables in experimental games: Toward a field theory. *Psychological Bulletin, 71,* 293–318.

VINACKE, W.E. & GULLICKSON, G.R. (1964). Age and sex differences in the formation of coalitions. *Child Development, 35,* 1217–1231.

VINAY, J.P., DAVIAULT, P. & ALEXANDER, H. (1962). *The Canadian Dictionary.* Toronto: McClelland & Stewart.

VOISSEM, N.H. & SISTRUNK, F. (1971). Communication schedules and cooperative game behavior. *Journal of Personality and Social Psychology, 19,* 160–167.

VON NEUMANN, J. & MORGENSTERN, O. (1944). *Theory of games and economic behavior.* Princeton, NJ: Princeton University Press.

WAGNER, H.L., MacDONALD, C.J. & MANSTEAD, A.S.R. (1986). Communication of individual emotions by spontaneous facial expression. *Journal of Personality and Social Psychology, 50,* 737–743.

WAGNER, R.V. (1985). Psychology and the threat of nuclear war. *American Psychologist, 40,* 534–535.

WALKER, S.G. (1977). The interface between beliefs and behavior. *Journal of Conflict Resolution, 21,* 121–168.

WALLACH, M.A., KOGAN, N. & BEM, D.J. (1964). Diffusion of responsibility and level of risk taking in groups. *Journal of Abnormal and Social Psychology, 68,* 263–274.

WALLINGTON, S.A. (1973). Consequences of transgression: Self-punishment and depression. *Journal of Personality and Social Psychology, 28,* 1–7.

WALSTER, E. (1964). The temporal sequence of post-decision processes. In L. Festinger (Ed.), *Conflict, decision and dissonance* (112–128). Stanford, CA: Stanford University Press.

WALSTER, E. (1966). Assignment of responsibility for an accident. *Journal of Personality and Social Psychology, 3,* 73–79.

WALSTER, E. & BERSCHEID, E. (1971). Adrenalin makes the heart grow fonder. *Psychology Today, 5,* 47–62.

WALSTER, E., WALSTER, G.W. & BERSCHEID, E. (1978). *Equity theory and research.* Boston: Allyn & Bacon.

WALSTER, E., WALSTER, G.W., PILIAVIN, J. & SCHMIDT, L. (1976). "Playing hard to get": Understanding an elusive phenomenon. *Journal of Personality and Social Psychology, 26,* 113–121.

WALTERS, G.C. & GRUSEC, J.E. (1977). *Punishment.* San Francisco: W.H. Freeman.

WALTERS, R. (1970). Implications of laboratory studies of aggression for the control and regulation of violence. In E.I. Megargee & J.E. Hokanson (Eds.), *The dynamics of aggression* (124–131). New York: Harper & Row.

WARE, J.E. & YOUNG, J. (1979). Issues in the conceptualization and measurements of the value placed on health. In S.J. Mushkin & D.W. Dunlop (Eds.), *Health: What is it worth?* (141–156). New York: Pergamon.

WASMAN, G. & FLYNN, J.P. (1962). Direct attack elicited from hypothalamus. *Archives of Neurology, 6,* 220–227.

WATANABE, P.Y. & MILBURN, M.A. (1986). Activism against Armageddon: Determinants of nuclear-related political behavior. Paper presented at the Ninth Annual Meeting of the International Society of Political Psychology, Amsterdam.

WATERS, H.F. & MALAMUD, P. (1975). Drop that gun, Captain Video! *Newsweek, 85* (10), 81–82.

WATSON, D. (1982). The actor and the observer: How are the perceptions of causality divergent? *Psychological Bulletin, 92,* 682–700.

WATSON, R.I. (1973). Investigation into deindividuation using a cross-cultural survey technique. *Journal of Personality and Social Psychology, 25,* 342–345.

WEBB, E.J., CAMPBELL, D.T., SCHWARTZ, R.D. & SECHREST, L. (1966). *Unobtrusive measures: Nonreactive research in the social sciences.* Chicago: Rand McNally, 1966.

WEBB, E.J., CAMPBELL, D.T., SCHWARTZ, R.D., SECHREST, L. & GROVE, J.B. (1981). *Nonreactive measures in the social sciences.* Boston: Houghton-Mifflin.

WEBER, M. (1947). *The theory of social and economic organization.* Glencoe, IL: Free Press.

WEBER, S.J. & COOK, T.D. (1972). Subject effects in laboratory research: An examination of subject roles, demand characteristics and valid inference. *Psychological Bulletin, 77,* 273–295.

WEICK, K.E. (1984). Small wins: Refining the scale of social problems. *American Psychologist, 39,* 40–49.

WEIGEL, R.H. & NEWMAN, L.S. (1976). Increasing attitude-behavior correspondence by broadening the scope of the behavioral measure. *Journal of Personality and Social Psychology, 33,* 793–802.

WEIGEL, R.H., WISER, P.L. & COOK, S.W. (1975). The impact of cooperative learning experience on cross-ethnic relations and attitudes. *Journal of Social Issues, 31,* 219–244.

WEIMANN, G. & WINN, C. (1986). *Hate on trial: The Zundel affair, the media, and public opinion in Canada.* Oakville: Mosaic Press.

WEINER, B. (1974). *Achievement motivation and attribution theory.* Morristown, NJ: General Learning Press.

WEINER, B. (1979). A theory of motivation for some classroom experiences. *Journal of Educational Psychology, 71,* 3–25.

WEINER, B. (1980). A cognitive (attribution)-emotion-action model of motivated behavior: An analysis of judgements of help giving. *Journal of Personality and Social Psychology, 39,* 186–200.

WEINER, B. (1985). "Spontaneous" causal thinking. *Psychological Bulletin, 97,* 74–84.

WEINER, B., FRIEZE, I., KUKLA, A., REED, L., REST, S. & ROSENBAUM, R.M. (1972). Perceiving the causes of success and failure. In E.E. Jones, D.E. Kanouse, H.H. Kelley, R.E. Nisbett, S. Valins & B. Weiner (Eds.), *Attribution: Perceiving the causes of success and failure.* Morristown, NJ: General Learning Press.

WEINER, B. & KUKLA, A. (1970). An attributional analysis of achievement motivation. *Journal of Personality and Social Psychology, 15,* 144–151.

WEINER, F.H. (1976). Altruism, ambiance and action: The effects of rural and urban rearing on helping behavior. *Journal of Personality and Social Psychology, 34,* 112–124.

WEINSTEIN, E.A., DeVAUGHAN, W.L. & WILEY, M.G. (1969). Obligation and the flow of deference. *Sociometry, 32,* 1–12.

WEINSTEIN, N.D. (1984). Why it won't happen to me: Perceptions of risk factors and susceptibility. *Health Psychology, 3,* 431–457.

WEISS, R. (1973). *Loneliness: The experiences of emotional and social isolation.* Cambridge, MA: MIT Press.

WEISS, R.S. (1975). *Marital separation.* New York: Basic Books.

WEISS, W. (1971). Mass communication. *Annual Review of Psychology, 22,* 309–336.

WEISZ, A.E. & TAYLOR, R.L. (1969). American Presidential assassinations. *Diseases of the Nervous System, 30,* 659–668.

WEISZ, J.R., ROTHBAUM, F.M. & BLACKBURN, T.C. (1984). Swapping recipes for control. *American Psychologist, 39,* 974–975.

WELLMAN, B. & WHITAKER, M. (1974). *High-rise, low-rise: The effects of high-density living.* Ottawa: Ministry of State for Urban Affairs (B.74.29).

WELLS, G.L. (1984). The psychology of lineup identifications. *Journal of Applied Psychology, 14,* 89–103.

WELLS, G.L., LINDSAY, R.C.L. & FERGUSON, T.J. (1979). Accuracy, confidence and juror perceptions in eyewitness testimony. *Journal of Applied Psychology, 64,* 440–448.

WELLS, G.L., LINDSAY, R.C.L., & TOUSIGNANT, J.P. (1980). Effects of expert psychological advice on human performance in judging the validity of eyewitness testimony. *Law and Human Behavior, 4,* 275–285.

WELLS, G.L. & MURRAY, B.M. (1983). What can psychology say about the Neil vs. Biggers criteria for judging eyewitness accuracy? *Journal of Applied Psychology, 68,* 347–362.

WELLS, G.L. & TURTLE, J.W. (1986). Eye-witness identification: The importance of lineup models. *Psychological Bulletin, 29,* 320–329.

WELLS, G.L., WRIGHTSMAN, L.S. & MIENE, P.K. (1985). The timing of the defence opening statement: Don't wait until the evidence is in. *Journal of Applied Social Psychology, 15,* 758–772.

WERNER, C.O. & LATANÉ, B. (1974). Interaction motivates attraction: Rats are fond of fondling. *Journal of Personality and Social Psychology, 29,* 328–334.

WEST, S.G. & BROWN, T.J. (1975). Physical attractiveness, the severity of the emergency and helping: A field experiment and interpersonal simulation. *Journal of Experimental Social Psychology, 11,* 531–538.

WHITE, G.L. (1981a). A model of romantic jealousy. *Motivation and Emotion, 5,* 295–310.

WHITE, G.L. (1981b). Some correlates of romantic jealousy. *Journal of Personality, 49,* 129–147.

WHITE, J.W. (1983). Sex and gender issues in aggression research. In R.G. Geen & E.I. Donnerstein (Eds.), *Aggression: Theoretical and empirical reviews* (Vol. 2) (1–26). New York: Academic Press.

WHITE, R.K. (1969). Three not-so-obvious contributions of psychology to peace. *Journal of Social Issues, 25,* 23–39.

WHITE, R.K. (1984). *Fearful warriors: A psychological profile of U.S.-Soviet relationships.* New York: Free Press.

WHITEHEAD, P.C., CRAIG, J., LANGFORD, N., MacARTHUR, C., STANTON, B. & FERRENCE, R.G. (1975). Collision behavior of young drivers. Impact of the change in the age of majority. *Journal of Studies on Alcohol, 36,* 1208–1223.

WHITING, B.B. & WHITING, J.W.M. (1975). *Children of six cultures: A psychocultural analysis.* Cambridge, MA: Harvard University Press.

WHORF, B.L. (1956). *Language, thought and reality: Selected writings of Benjamin Lee Whorf.* T.B. Carroll (Ed.). New York: Wiley.

WICKER, A.W. (1969). Attitudes versus actions: The relationship of verbal and overt behavioral responses to attitude objects. *Journal of Social Issues, 25,* 41–78.

WICKLUND, R.A. & BREHM, J.W. (1976). *Perspectives on cognitive dissonance.* New York: Wiley.

WIEGMAN, O. (1985). Two politicians in a realistic experiment: Attraction, discrepancy, intensity of delivery, and attitude change. *Journal of Applied Social Psychology, 15,* 673–686.

WIENER, M., CARPENTER, J.T. & CARPENTER, B. (1957). Some determinants of conformity behavior. *Journal of Social Psychology, 45,* 289–297.

WIGGINS, J.S., RENNER, E.K., CLORE, G.L. & ROSE, R.J. (1971). *The psychology of personality.* Reading, MA: Addison-Wesley.

WILDER, D.A. (1977). Perception of group size of opposition and social influence. *Journal of Experimental Social Psychology, 13,* 253–268.

WILDER, D.A. (1978). Reduction of intergroup discrimination through individuation of the out-group. *Journal of Personality and Social Psychology, 36,* 1361–1374.

WILLIAMS, E. (1975). Medium or message: Communications medium as a determinant of interpersonal evaluations. *Sociometry, 38,* 119–130.

WILLIAMS, T.M. (Ed.) (1986). *The impact of television: A natural experiment in three communities.* Orlando: Academic Press.

WILLIS, R.H. (1965). Conformity, independence and anticonformity. *Human Relations, 18,* 373–388.

WILSNACK, S. (1982). Prevention of alcohol problems in women. In N.I.A.A.A. *Alcohol and health Monograph #4. Special population issues* (77–110). D.H.H.S. Publication No. (ADM) 82–1193. Washington: US Government Printing Office.

WILSON, A. (1970). *War gaming.* Harmondsworth, England: Penguin.

WILSON, D.W. & DONNERSTEIN, E. (1976). Legal and ethical aspects of nonreactive social research: An excursion into the public mind. *American Psychologist, 36,* 765–773.

WILSON, E.O. (1978). The genetic evolution of altruism. In L. Wispé (Ed.), *Altruism, sympathy and helping.* New York: Academic Press.

WILSON, G.T. (1984). Weight control treatments. In J.D. Mattarazzo, S.M. Weiss, J.A. Herd, N.E. Miller & S.M. Weiss (Eds.), *Behavioral health* (657–670). New York: Wiley.

WILSON, W. & MILLER, H. (1968). Repetition, order of presentation, and timing of arguments and measures as determinants of opinion change. *Journal of Personality and Social Psychology, 9,* 184–188.

WINCH, R.F. (1954). The theory of complementary needs in mate selection: An analytic and descriptive study. *Annual Social Review, 19,* 241–249.

WINCH, R.F. (1958). *Mate selection: A study of complementary needs.* New York: Harper & Row.

WISHNER, J. (1960). Reanalysis of "impressions of personality." *Psychological Review, 67,* 96–112.

WISPÉ, L. (1972). Positive forms of social behavior: An overview. *Journal of Social Issues, 28,* 1–20.

WISPÉ, L. (1986). The distinction between sympathy and empathy: To call forth a concept, a word is needed. *Journal of Personality and Social Psychology, 50,* 314–321.

WITHEY, S.B. (1954). *Fourth survey of public knowledge and attitudes concerning civil defence.* Ann Arbor, MI: Survey Research Center, Institute for Social Research, University of Michigan.

WORCHEL, S. (1984). The darker side of helping. In E. Staub, D. Bar-Tal, J. Karylowski & J. Reykowski (Eds.), *Development and maintenance of prosocial behavior* (375–395). New York: Plenum Press.

WORCHEL, S., ANDREOLI, V. & EASON, J. (1975). Is the medium the message? A study of the effects of media, communicator and message characteristics on attitude change. *Journal of Applied Social Psychology, 5,* 157–172.

WORTMAN, C.B. (1975). Some determinants of perceived control. *Journal of Personality and Social Psychology, 31,* 282–294.

WORTMAN, C.B. & DUNKEL-SCHETTER, C. (1979). Interpersonal relationships and cancer: A theoretical analysis. *Journal of Social Issues, 35,* 120–154.

WRIGHT, P.L. (1974). Analyzing media effects on advertising responses. *Public Opinion Quarterly, 38,* 192–205.

WRIGHT, R.A. & CONTRADA, R.J. (1983). Dating selectivity and interpersonal attractiveness: Support for a "common sense" analysis. Unpublished manuscript. University of Texas, Austin.

WRIGHTSMAN, L.S. (1964). Measurement of philosophies of human nature. *Psychological Reports, 14,* 743–751.

WRIGHTSMAN, L.S. (1972). *Social psychology in the seventies.* Monterey, CA: Brooks/Cole.

WU, C. & SHAFFER, D.R. (1987). Susceptibility to persuasive appeals as a function of source credibility and prior experience with the attitude object. *Journal of Personality and Social Psychology, 52,* 677–688.

YAMAGISHI, T. & SATO, K. (1986). Motivational bases of the public goods problem. *Journal of Personality and Social Psychology, 50,* 67–73.

YARMEY, A.D. (1979). *The psychology of eyewitness testimony.* New York: Free Press.

YARMEY, A.D. (1986). Verbal, visual and voice identification of a rape suspect under different levels of illumination. *Journal of Applied Social Psychology, 71,* 363–370.

YARMEY, A.D. & JONES, H.P.T. (1983). Is eyewitness identification a matter of common sense? In S. Lloyd-Bostock & B.R. Clifford (Eds.), *Evaluating eyewitness evidence.* London: Wiley.

YOUNGER, J.C., WALKER, L. & ARROWOOD, A.J. (1977). Post decision dissonance at the fair. *Personality and Social Psychology Bulletin, 3,* 284–287.

YOUNGS, G.A., Jr. (1986). Patterns of threat and punishment reciprocity in a conflict setting. *Journal of Personality and Social Psychology, 51,* 541–546.

YUILLE, J.C. & CUTSHALL, J.L. (1986). A case study of eyewitness memory of a crime. *Journal of Applied Psychology, 71,* 291–301.

YUKL, G. (1981). *Leadership in organizations.* Englewood Cliffs, NJ: Prentice-Hall.

ZAJONC, R.B. (1965). Social facilitation. *Science, 149,* 269–274.

ZAJONC, R.B. (1968a). Attitudinal effects of mere exposure. *Journal of Personality and Social Psychology,* Monograph Supplement, 9, 1–27.

ZAJONC, R.B. (1968b). Cognitive theories in social psychology. In G. Lindzey & E. Aronson (Eds.), *The handbook of social psychology.* Second Edition (Vol. 1) (320–411). Reading, MA: Addison-Wesley.

ZAJONC, R.B. (1969). *Animal social psychology.* New York: Wiley.

ZAJONC, R.B. (1970). Brainwashing: Familiarity breeds comfort. *Psychology Today* (February), 32–35, 60–62.

ZANDER, A. & HAVELIN, A. (1960). Social comparison and interpersonal attraction. *Human Relations, 13,* 21–32.

ZANNA, M.P. & COOPER, J. (1974). Dissonance and the pill: An attributional approach to studying the arousal properties of dissonance. *Journal of Personality and Social Psychology, 29,* 703–709.

ZANNA, M.P. & FAZIO, R.H. (1982). The attitude-behavior relation. Moving toward a third generation of research. In M.P. Zanna, E.T. Higgins & C.P. Herman (Eds.), *Consistency in social behavior: The Ontario symposium* (Vol. 2) (283–301). Hillsdale: NJ: Erlbaum.

ZANNA, M.P., KIESLER, C.A. & PILKONIS, P.A. (1970). Positive and negative attitudinal affect established by classical conditioning. *Journal of Personality and Social Psychology, 14,* 321–328.

ZANNA, M.P. & KRISTIANSEN, C.M. (1986). The justification of attitudes by selective appeals to values. Paper presented at the Annual Meeting of the Canadian Psychological Association, Toronto (June).

ZBOROWSKI, M. (1969). *People in pain.* San Francisco: Jossey-Bass.

ZILLMANN, D. (1971). Excitation transfer in communication-mediated aggressive behavior. *Journal of Experimental Social Psychology, 7,* 419–434.

ZILLMANN, D. (1984). Transfer of excitation in emotional behavior. In J.T. Cacioppo & R.E. Petty (Eds.), *Social psychophysiology: A sourcebook* (215–240). New York: Guilford Press.

ZILLMANN, D., KATCHER, A.H. & MILAVSKY, B. (1972). Excitation transfer from physical exercise to subsequent aggressive behavior. *Journal of Experimental Social Psychology, 8,* 247–259.

ZIMBARDO, P.G. (1970). The human choice: Individuation, reason, and order versus deindividuation, impulse, and chaos. In W.J. Arnold, & D. Levine (Eds.), *Nebraska symposium on motivation* (Vol. 17). Lincoln: University of Nebraska Press.

ZIMBARDO, P.G. (1977). *Shyness: What it is and what to do about it.* Reading, MA: Addison-Wesley.

ZIMBARDO, P.G., EBBESEN, E.B. & MASLACH, C. (1977). *Influencing attitudes and changing behavior.* Second Edition. Reading, MA: Addison-Wesley.

ZIMBARDO, P.G., HANEY, C., BANKS, W.C. & JAFFE, D. (1982). The psychology of imprisonment. In J.C. Brigham & L. Wrightsman (Eds.), *Contemporary issues in social psychology.* Fourth Edition. (230–35). Monterey, CA: Brooks/Cole.

ZUBEK, J.P. & SOLBERG, P.A. (1952). *Doukhobors at war.* Toronto: The Ryerson Press.

P·R·O·P·E·R   N·A·M·E   I·N·D·E·X

Radke-Yarrow, M., 333
Rafferty, J.M., 542
Rahe, R.H., 567, 568
Ramsay, C.A., 394
Rand, 268
Rank, A.D., 92
Rank, S.G., 180
Rapoport, A., 447, 453
Raskin, D.C., 526
Raven, B.H., 421
Rayko, D.S., 354
Read, S.J., 84
Reagan, Ronald, 6, 113, 299, 368
Reckless, W.C., 314
Redler, E., 331
Reese, Y., 98
Regan, D.T., 72, 177, 337
Reich, C., 224
Reid, J.B., 566
Reinisch, J.M., 314
Reisenzein, R., 356
Remillard, L., 387
Rice, B., 34
Rice, G.E., 325
Richard, Maurice, 511
Richardson, D.C., 313
Richardson, D.R., 270
Richler, Mordecai, 217
Riecken, H.W., 125
Riel, Louis, 185, 195
Riera, B., 305, 306, 307
Riesman, D., 544
Riess, M., 73
Riggio, R., 577
Ring, K., 575
Ringelmann, M., 160
Rioux, Y., 372
Rivenbark, W., 241
Roach, M.E., 497
Roberts, J.V., 532, 533
Roberts, L., 394
Robertson, L.S., 582
Robins, L., 562
Robinson, E., 580
Robinson, J.P., 96
Rodgers, W.L., 539
Rodin, J., 268, 325, 345, 351, 545, 561, 569, 580
Rodrigues, A., 37, 77, 132
Rogers, E., 190
Rogers, E.M., 498
Rohsenow, D., 79
Rokeach, M., 101, 102, 103, 104, 106, 110, 111, 188, 189, 218
Rollins, Betty, 576
Romanoff, R., 291
Ronis, D.L., 131
Rook, K.S., 271

Roosevelt, Franklin D., 469
Rose, T.L., 204
Rosen, S., 357, 578
Rosenbaum, L.L., 427
Rosenbaum, W.B., 427
Rosenberg, M.J., 35, 126, 127
Rosenberg, S., 53
Rosenfeld, R., 73
Rosenhan, D., 335, 359
Rosenman, R.H., 571, 572
Rosenstein, M.P., 28
Rosenthal, R., 34, 60, 317, 377
Roskies, E., 573
Rosnow, R.L., 45, 491, 492
Ross, A.S., 348, 349
Ross, D., 289
Ross, E.A., 7
Ross, H., 549
Ross, L., 54, 71
Ross, M., 85, 86, 258
Ross, S.A., 289
Rothbart, M., 85, 89, 220, 221, 222
Rothbart, F.M., 330
Rotter, J.B., 571
Rotton, J., 538
Rousseau, Jean-Jacques, 278
Rozin, 560
Rubenstein, C.M., 271
Rubin, J., 372
Rubin, J.Z., 435, 464
Rubin, Z., 246, 254, 264, 265, 267, 372
Ruble, D.N., 312
Ruble, T.L., 314
Rule, B.G., 137, 279, 287, 310, 304, 521
Rushton, J.P., 326, 330, 331, 332, 333, 334, 335, 337, 339, 340, 342
Rusk, Dean, 461
Russell, B., 382, 421, 460
Russell, D., 70, 271
Rutte, C.G., 459
Ryan, Leo, 517
Ryan, R.M., 63

Saarni, C., 486
Sadava, S.W., 72, 75, 116, 270, 271, 339, 563, 564
Safer, M.A., 180
Salinger, J.D., 217
Salovey, P., 268
Salter, N.E., 517
Sampson, E.E., 38, 77, 432, 445, 525
Samuelson, C.D., 455, 456, 459
Sanbonmatsu, D.M., 109
Sanders, G.S., 158, 420
Sanders, S.A., 314
Sanford, R.N., 7, 216, 536
Sarat, A., 532
Sarles, R.M., 291, 292

S·U·B·J·E·C·T   I·N·D·E·X

670

C·R·E·D·I·T·S

Service; p. 167 Photo by Liza McCoy; p. 186 Courtesy Chrysler Canada Limited.

Chapter 7: p. 192 Ku Klux Klan in Kingston, Ontario on July 31, 1927 — © Miller Services Ltd; p. 194 CANAPRESS Photo Service; p. 196 By permission of the *Penticton Herald*; p. 211 Courtesy Metropolitan Toronto Convention and Visitors Association; p. 220 Courtesy Metropolitan Toronto Convention and Visitors Association; p. 228 Calligraphy by Sandra Brown; p. 230 Photo by Liza McCoy.

Chapter 8: p. 234 Archives of Ontario /ACC-9508 8330; p. 236 Photo by S.W. Sadava; p. 241 Photo by Marina Santin; p. 244 Photo by Carl Bigras of Iona Campagnolo during the Liberal Party's 1982 national convention — courtesy the Liberal Party of Canada; p. 253 Photo by Melissa McClellan; p. 269 Photo by Melissa McClellan.

Chapter 9: p. 275 Photo by Nikki Abraham; p. 276 National Archives of Canada /PA 60562; p. 205 Photo by Melissa McClellan; p. 292 Photo by Melissa McClellan; p. 299 Photo by Melissa McClellan; p. 309 (left to right) Bonnie Klein, Linda Lee Tracey, Suze Randall — courtesy the National Film Board of Canada; p. 313 Photo by Nikki Abraham; p. 316 Lowe Goodgoll, Toronto; Art direction by Jeff Katz, writing by T.J. Harrison — courtesy Sportcom International Inc.

Chapter 10: p. 320 Photo by Melissa McClellan; p. 321 (left) Photo of Mother Teresa in Toronto by Mike Mastromatteo courtesy *The Catholic Register*; (right) National Archives of Canada /C-67451; p. 323 Courtesy the Canadian Red Cross Society; p. 327 Photo by Melissa McClellan; p. 334 Photo by Nikki Abraham; p. 340 Photo by Patrick Gallagher; p. 347 Photo by Melissa McClellan; p. 354 Courtesy the Epilepsy Association of Metro Toronto.

Chapter 11: p. 362 Toronto City Hall Photo Archives /8054; p. 367 Photos by Melissa McClellan; p. 370 Photo by Nikki Abraham; p. 375 Photo by Nikki Abraham; p. 381 Photo by Patrick Gallagher.

Chapter 12: p. 403 Photo by Melissa McClellan; p. 409 Photo of David McFarlane by Michael Jackson courtesy *the Human*; p. 413 Photo by Marina Santin; p. 419 Photo by David Smiley; p. 424 Sir Winston Churchill's visit to Ottawa, December 1941, National Archives /C-22140; p. 430 CANAPRESS Photo Service.

Chapter 13: p. 434 Photo by David Smiley; p. 435 Photos by Melissa McClellan; p. 445 Photo by David Smiley; p. 468 Courtesy Metropolitan Toronto Convention and Visitors Association; p. 475 Photo by David Smiley.

Chapter 14: p. 478 Photo by David Smiley; p. 480 Photo by Melissa McClellan; p. 490 Photo by Melissa McClellan; p. 492 Courtesy the Baldwin Collection, Department of Canadian History, Metropolitan Toronto Reference Library (left) Espionage item #5, (right) Espionage item #1; p. 493 Procter and Gamble logo reproduced by permission of the Procter & Gamble Company, Public Affairs Division, Cincinnati, Ohio; p. 495 Archives of CP Rail; p. 501 By permission of *The Globe and Mail*; p. 503 Original document courtesy the authors; p. 505 Courtesy the Toronto Fire Department; p. 516 By permission of *Body Politic*.

Chapter 15: p. 520 Photo by Nikki Abraham; p. 527 Courtesy *the Human*; p. 540 Ministry of Industry and Tourism; p. 544 Photo by Melissa McClellan; p. 547 Photo by David Smiley; p. 556 Photo by Melissa McClellan.

Chapter 16: p. 559 Photo by Liza McCoy; p. 565 Courtesy Health and Welfare Canada, Health Promotion Directorate; p. 573 Photo by Melissa McClellan; p. 582 Courtesy RIDE and the Metropolitan Toronto Police.

Textual Credits

Chapter 2: p. 32 Box 2-5 Excerpted from *Medical World News*, September 1, 1972. Reprinted by permission.

Chapter 4: p. 107 Box 4-3 Excerpted from "It's the cops" by Pierre Berton, originally published in *Quest*, 5, no. 2. Reprinted by permission of the author.

Chapter 6: p. 187 Box 6-5 Excerpted from *Synectics* by W.J. Gordon, published by the SES Association, Cambridge, MA. Reprinted by permission of the author.

Chapter 7: p. 206 Box 7-4 "Store rebuffs Indian given Canada award" reprinted by permission of Canadian Press; p. 207 Quotation taken from *Years of Sorrow, Years of Shame* by B. Broadfoot. Reprinted by permission of Doubleday and Company, Inc; p. 209 Box 7-6 "Blacks died in U.S. syphilis experiment" reprinted by permission of Associated Press.

Chapter 9: p. 277 Box 9-1 Quotation reprinted by permission of Amnesty International.

Chapter 13: p. 460 Box 13-8 Quotation taken from *Common Sense and Nuclear Warfare* by Bertrand Russell. Reprinted by permission of Unwin Hyman Limited, London, England.

Chapter 14: p. 482 Quotation taken from *The Crowd* by G. Lebon. Reprinted by permission of Larlin Corporation; p. 505 Quotation reprinted by permission of Canadian Press.